GIVE ME LIBERTY!

An American History

AP* Third Edition

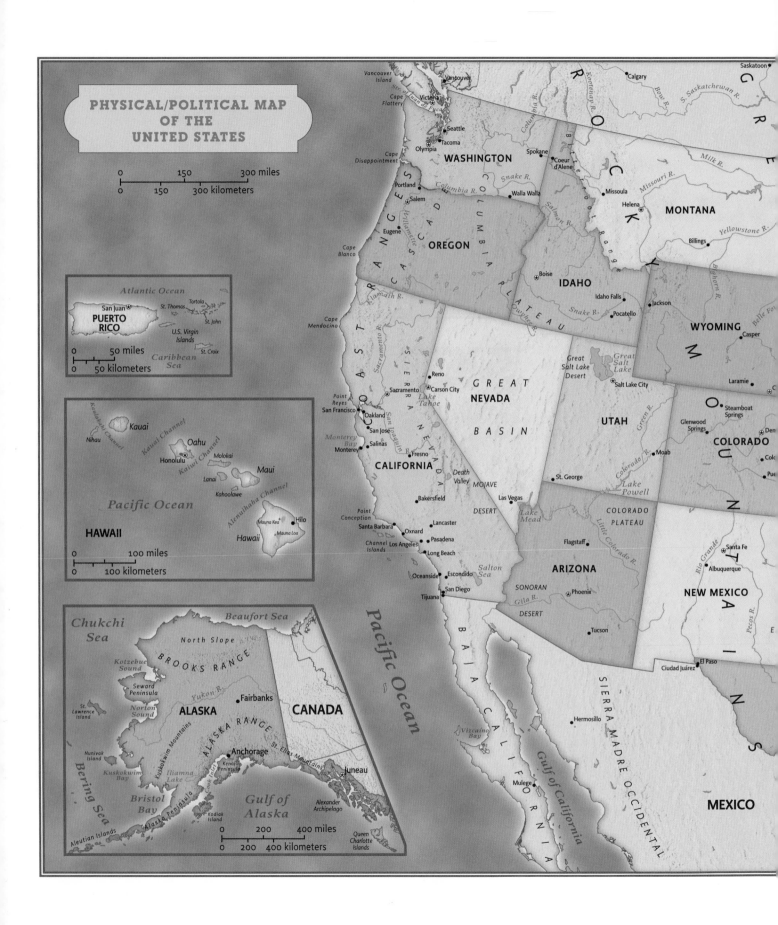

PHYSICAL/POLITICAL MAP OF THE UNITED STATES

0   150   300 miles
0   150   300 kilometers

PUERTO RICO

Atlantic Ocean

San Juan ⊛   St. Thomas   Tortola
Tortola
U.S. Virgin Islands   St. John
St. Croix

Caribbean Sea

0   50 miles
0   50 kilometers

HAWAII

Pacific Ocean

Nihau   Kauai
Kauaikahi Channel
Oahu
Honolulu   Kaiwi Channel   Molokai
Lanai   Maui
Kahoolawe
Alenuihaha Channel
Mauna Kea   Hilo
Mauna Loa
Hawaii

0   100 miles
0   100 kilometers

ALASKA

Chukchi Sea   *Beaufort Sea*
North Slope
Kotzebue Sound   BROOKS RANGE
Seward Peninsula   Yukon R.
St. Lawrence Island   Norton Sound   Fairbanks
Nunivak Island   ALASKA   CANADA
Kuskokwim Mountains   ALASKA RANGE   St. Elias Mountains
Kuskokwim Bay   Iliamna Lake   Anchorage   Juneau
Bristol Bay   Kenai Peninsula   Alexander Archipelago
Kodiak Island   Gulf of Alaska
Aleutian Islands   Queen Charlotte Islands
Bering Sea

0   200   400 miles
0   200   400 kilometers

Vancouver Island   Vancouver
Cape Flattery   Victoria
Str. of Juan de Fuca   Seattle
Tacoma
Olympia   **WASHINGTON**
Cape Disappointment   Spokane
Coeur d'Alene
Portland   Columbia R.   Walla Walla   Missoula   Helena   **MONTANA**
Salem   Snake R.   Billings
Eugene   **OREGON**   Boise   **IDAHO**
Cape Blanco   Idaho Falls   Jackson
Cape Mendocino   Klamath R.   Snake R.   Pocatello   **WYOMING**   Casper
Great Salt Lake Desert   Great Salt Lake   Laramie
Reno   **GREAT**   Salt Lake City   Steamboat Springs
Sacramento   Carson City   **NEVADA**   **UTAH**   Glenwood Springs   **COLORADO**   Den
Lake Tahoe   **BASIN**   Green R.   Moab   Col
San Francisco   Oakland   San Jose   Salinas   Fresno   Colorado R.   Lake Powell   Pue
Monterey Bay   Death Valley   St. George   **COLORADO PLATEAU**
Monterey   **CALIFORNIA**   MOJAVE   Little Colorado R.
Point Conception   Bakersfield   Las Vegas   **DESERT**   Flagstaff   Santa Fe
Santa Barbara   Lancaster   Lake Mead   Albuquerque
Oxnard   Pasadena   **ARIZONA**   **NEW MEXICO**
Channel Islands   Los Angeles   Long Beach   Salton Sea   Phoenix   Pecos R.
Oceanside   Escondido   **SONORAN**   Tucson
San Diego   **DESERT**   El Paso
Tijuana   Gila R.   Ciudad Juárez

Calgary   Saskatoon
Bow R.   S. Saskatchewan R.
Kootenay R.   Milk R.
Columbia R.
Missouri R.
Yellowstone R.
Bighorn R.   Belle Fou

ROCKY   **G R E**
M
O
U
N
T
A
I
N
S

SIERRA MADRE OCCIDENTAL
Hermosillo

Pacific Ocean

BAJA CALIFORNIA
Vizcaino Bay
Gulf of California
Mulege

MEXICO

POLITICAL MAP of the WORLD

Scale at equator

0 — 750 — 1,500 miles
0 — 750 — 1,500 kilometers

Arctic Ocean

Ellesmere Island

Queen Elizabeth Islands

Greenland (Denmark)

Banks Island

Beaufort Sea

Amundsen Gulf

Victoria Island

Baffin Bay

Baffin Island

Denmark Strait

ICELAND

Reykjavík

Chukchi Sea

RUSSIA

Bering Sea

Alaska (U.S.)

Gulf of Alaska

Aleutian Islands

Foxe Basin

Hudson Strait

Hudson Bay

CANADA

Labrador Sea

North Atlantic Ocean

IRELAND

Celtic Sea

English

North Pacific Ocean

Ottawa   Montréal
Toronto
Chicago

San Francisco

UNITED STATES

New York
Washington, D.C.

Los Angeles

Dallas

Bermuda (U.K.)

PORTUGAL

Azores (Por.)

Lisbon

Madeira Islands (Por.)

Rabat

MOROC

Hawaii (U.S.)

Gulf of Mexico

MEXICO

Mexico City

Nassau
Havana

BAHAMAS

CUBA   HAITI

JAMAICA

BELIZE

DOMINICAN REPUBLIC
Puerto Rico (U.S.)
ST. KITTS AND NEVIS
DOMINICA
ST. LUCIA
ST. VINCENT AND THE GRENADINES
BARBADOS
TRINIDAD AND TOBAGO

Canary Islands (Sp.)

Western Sahara (Mor.)

Nouakchott

MAURITANIA

CAPE VERDE

SENEGAL

GAMBIA

GUINEA-BISSAU   GUINEA

GUATEMALA
EL SALVADOR
HONDURAS
NICARAGUA
COSTA RICA
PANAMA

Caribbean Sea

VENEZUELA

Caracas

GUYANA

SIERRA LEONE

LIBERIA

CÔTE D'IV

Kiritimati (Kiribati)

Galapagos Islands (Ecuador)

Bogotá

COLOMBIA

Quito

ECUADOR

French Guiana (Fr.)

SURINAME

Phoenix Islands

KIRIBATI

Marquesas Islands (Fr.)

PERU

Lima

BRAZIL

Brasília

Ascension (L

SÃO

SAMOA

Apia   Pago Pago

South Pacific Ocean

Papeete

La Paz

BOLIVIA

Sucre

FIJI

Nuku'alofa

TONGA

Cook Islands

French Polynesia (Fr.)

Pitcairn Islands (U.K.)

Adamstown

Easter Island (Chile)

Rio de Janeiro

PARAGUAY

Asunción

Santiago

Juan Fernandez Archipelago (Chile)

Buenos Aires

URUGUAY

Montevideo

South Atlan Ocean

Tristan D Group (U

ARGENTINA

CHILE

Falkland Islands (U.K.)

South Georgia

South Sandwich Islands

Southern

THE POLES

Atlantic Ocean

60°S

Southern Ocean

Pacific Ocean

180°

60°W

180°

60°E

Pacific Ocean

60°N

75°N

ASIA

SOUTH AMERICA

75°S

ANTARCTICA

NORTH AMERICA

Arctic Ocean

Pacific Ocean

Southern Ocean

Indian Ocean

Atlantic Ocean

EUROPE

0 — 1,500 miles
0 — 1,500 kilometers

Scotia Sea

South Shetland Islands

South Orkney Islands

W · W · NORTON & COMPANY · NEW YORK · LONDON

GIVE ME LIBERTY!

AN AMERICAN HISTORY

AP* Third Edition

by ERIC FONER

W. W. Norton & Company has been independent since its founding in 1923, when William Warder Norton and Mary D. Herter Norton first published lectures delivered at the People's Institute, the adult education division of New York City's Cooper Union. The firm soon expanded its program beyond the Institute, publishing books by celebrated academics from America and abroad. By midcentury, the two major pillars of Norton's publishing program—trade books and college texts—were firmly established. In the 1950s, the Norton family transferred control of the company to its employees, and today—with a staff of 400 and a comparable number of trade, college, and professional titles published each year—W. W. Norton & Company stands as the largest and oldest publishing house owned wholly by its employees.

Editor: Steve Forman
Editorial Assistant: Rebecca Charney and Justin Cahill
Managing Editor, College: Marian Johnson
Associate Managing Editor, College: Kim Yi
Copy Editor: JoAnn Simony
Marketing Manager: Tamara McNeill
Media Editor: Steve Hoge
Production Manager: Eric Pier-Hocking
Art Director: Rubina Yeh
Designers: Antonina Krass and Joan Greenfield
Photo Researchers: Patricia Marx and Stephanie Romeo
Composition and layout: TexTech and Carole Desnoes
Manufacturing: Transcontinental

Library of Congress Cataloging-in-Publication Data
Foner, Eric.
    Give me liberty!: an American history / Eric Foner. — AP 3rd ed.
        p. cm.
    Includes index.
    ISBN 978-0-393-91955-4 (hardcover)
1. United States—History.   2. United States—Politics and government.
3. Democracy—United States—History.   4. Liberty—History.   I. Title.

E178.F66 2013
973—dc23   2012018532

W. W. Norton & Company, Inc., 500 Fifth Avenue, New York, NY 10110
www.wwnorton.com

W. W. Norton & Company Ltd., Castle House, 75/76 Wells Street, London W1T 3QT
1 2 3 4 5 15 14 13 12

For my mother, Liza Foner (1909–2005), an accomplished artist who lived through most of the twentieth century and into the twenty-first

This registration code provides access to certain documents available at the *Give Me Liberty!*, Third Edition, StudySpace site: wwnorton.com/foner.

SIIX–XEKP

Brief Contents for the AP* Edition

Contents

Part 1 American Colonies to 1763

Part 2 A New Nation, 1763–1840

Part 3 Slavery, Freedom, and the Crisis of the Union, 1840–1877

12. AN AGE OF REFORM, 1820–1840 • 452

Part 4 Toward a Global Presence, 1870–1920

Part 5 Depression and Wars, 1920–1953

AMERICA UNDER COMMUNISM!

Part 6 What Kind of Nation? 1953–2010

28. SEPTEMBER 11 AND THE NEXT AMERICAN CENTURY • 1168

Appendix

DOCUMENTS

TABLES AND FIGURES

AP* Skills Handbooks

LIST OF MAPS, TABLES, AND FIGURES

Introduction to the AP* Edition

This edition of *Give Me Liberty!* is designed to expand and strengthen your understanding of American history in preparation for the AP* United States History exam. Dr. Foner's text, along with the AP*-specific support materials in the front and back of this edition, will provide you with a comprehensive treatment of United States history and a strong foundation in the skills you will need to succeed in your AP* endeavors. This AP* Edition contains important information about the exam, invaluable test-taking strategies, and useful explanations of the scoring of the test. In addition, it correlates the textbook with the AP* United States History course framework developed by the College Board. Most important, it emphasizes and develops writing, thinking, and primary-source skills that will enrich your classroom experience and maximize your achievement on the AP* examination. Mastery of the materials between the covers of this book will not only improve your performance in AP* United States History but will also set a strong foundation of success for the rest of your high school career and beyond.

ABOUT THE EXAM

COLLEGES AND THE AP* EXAM

Advanced Placement* courses are the gold standard of American education today. Colleges and universities in the United States view these rigorous courses, taught at the secondary school level, as the finest academic preparation available to high school students. The AP* program is recognized as a national measure of intellectual excellence. Furthermore, college admission officers are very impressed with student transcripts replete with AP* courses. A high school senior with a strong record of AP* classes has a decided advantage in the competition for entrance into the college of their choice.

Advanced Placement* programs are well established in American high schools, with over 18,000 schools giving examinations in 2011. Moreover, the AP* program has grown exponentially since its inception in 1954, when 532 students took the first series of exams. In May 2011, nearly 2 million students took AP* tests, with over 406,000 students taking the AP* United States History exam alone.

AP* courses offer many advantages to high school students. Most fundamental, a student experiences a college-level course while attending his or her local secondary school. In these classes, students are exposed to in-depth content that far surpasses the level of detail found in regular classes. AP* students also develop advanced writing and thinking skills that stay with them throughout their college careers and beyond. Moreover, with AP* credit, students often avoid redundant survey courses in their freshman year of college, which can allow them to pursue a double major, participate in off-campus study, try courses outside their majors, or graduate early.

More than 3,600 colleges and universities have AP* placement and credit policies, with most institutions offering credit for AP* classes based on the scores on the national examination given each May. When a student scores a 3 or better on a 5-point scale in a specific subject area, the College Board certifies that the test taker is qualified to receive credit and/or placement in that subject. Although each college ultimately decides the amount of credit to grant, qualifying scores on several AP* tests can advance a student's academic career and offer many financial and intellectual advantages.

> **To determine specific credit/placement policies for a college or university, students should consult www.collegeboard.com/AP/creditpolicy.**

CONTENT AND FORMAT OF THE AP* U.S. HISTORY EXAM

The AP* United States History exam is three hours and five minutes in length. It is divided into two major areas: an eighty-item multiple-choice section (55 minutes) and a free-response section (130 minutes), which is further divided into parts A, B, and C. Part A of the essay portion of the test consists of a mandatory Document-Based Question (DBQ). In Part B, you must select one essay question from a choice of two prompts, usually pertaining to events from 1492 to the late 1800s. Finally, in Part C, you must choose from two standard essay questions on twentieth-century American history. We recommend that you spend 60 minutes planning and writing your DBQ and 35 minutes on each of the essays in Parts B and C.

The test deals with events and concepts ranging from the age of European exploration to the present, but the majority of the multiple-choice items will ask about nineteenth- and twentieth-century American history. The following chart offers a proportional breakdown of the multiple-choice portion of the test by historical time period:

Pre-Columbian to 1789	20%
1790 to 1914	45%
1915 to Present	35%

In terms of topical areas, themes, and approaches, the multiple-choice items deal with:

Political Issues	35%
Social/Cultural Intellectual Issues	40%
Diplomatic/International Relations	15%
Economic Issues	10%

In addition to mastering the factual content of United States history, you must also write well-developed essays containing strong arguments supported by substantial historical information. Your final grade is a function of your combined score on the multiple-choice and the various essay components. The multiple-choice section of the exam accounts for 50 percent of your overall grade on the test. The three essays account for the remaining 50 percent of the grade, with the DBQ essay weighted at 22.5 percent of the overall grade and each of the free-response essays in Parts B and C counting as 13.75 percent of the final grade.

STRATEGIES FOR TAKING THE AP* EXAM

Whether or not you have taken another Advanced Placement* course before this one, you should familiarize yourself with the format and structure of the AP* United States History exam. This section provides you with vital information about the individual components of the exam, as well as strategies to help you succeed. Don't wait until the weeks before the exam to learn these details and techniques. By learning them now, you can prepare more efficiently and increase your chances of earning a high score.

THE MULTIPLE-CHOICE SECTION

As you prepare for the multiple-choice section of the AP* test, you should be aware that the questions do not ask you simply to recall facts. Memorizing lists of key terms, dates, names, or battles is unlikely to enhance your performance on this section of the test. Instead, you should be prepared for questions that deal with themes and concepts. The following list illustrates the types of questions you will encounter on the exam:

- Beliefs of individuals
- Motivation of individuals
- Political principles
- Definitions of concepts
- Cause and effect relationships
- Significance of concepts and ideas
- Consequences of events
- Social and economic conditions
- Functions of beliefs and organizations

Keep in mind that military history is *not* emphasized on the test. You should know the *significance* of battles and strategies rather than, say, specific troop movements.

Of the eighty multiple-choice questions on the exam, a small percentage will require you to analyze primary historical documents. You should be prepared to analyze short excerpts from textual documents, including letters, speeches, court rulings, state and national laws, and government documents, as well as visual materials such as cartoons, charts, and photographs. These types of questions generally ask you to identify the speaker, the point of view, or the significance of the source.

The strategies provided here will help you master the multiple-choice portion of the exam:

1. Answer *every* question in the section, even if you are only able to guess. Unlike in previous versions of the AP* United States History exam, there is no longer a penalty for guessing, so you will maximize your score by answering as many questions as possible.

2. Watch the clock and pace yourself! Remember that you have been allotted only 55 minutes for this portion of the exam. Be sure to leave enough time to complete all eighty multiple-choice questions.

3. Before looking at the answer choices, formulate your own answer to the question. Say to yourself, "I'm looking for . . ."

4. For each question, read *all* of the answer choices before making a selection. The first answer choice may not always be the best option. The directions for the multiple-choice section tell you to choose the *best* answer, which means that more than one answer choice may *seem* correct.

5. Eliminate as many answer choices as possible—narrowing the options from five to two or three can increase your performance on the multiple-choice section.

6. In the answer choices, watch for absolute terms such as *all, one, always, never*—these words often indicate an incorrect choice.

7. Once you've made your selection, change your answer only for a *strong* reason.

THE DOCUMENT-BASED QUESTION

The DBQ is a required essay on the exam. Unlike in Parts B and C, you will not have a choice of essay prompts in this section. Your answer for the DBQ must address the eight to ten primary documents provided, as well as *outside information*. This means that, in addition to addressing the eight to ten primary source excerpts provided, you will also need to introduce historical evidence to contextualize your response and demonstrate your knowledge of United States history.

Remember that the DBQ is worth nearly a quarter of your overall score on the exam. The strategies provided below will help you excel at the DBQ portion of the exam:

1. Read the question five times, and then restate the prompt into a clarifying question—what are you being asked to do?

2. Before you look at the documents, jot down a list of main facts and events of the *time period*, not just the topic of the question. From this list will come the vital outside information for your essay.

3. Analyze the documents. You should begin by summarizing each document. Keep in mind that a summary is just a starting point for

building an analysis; simply summarizing a document in your final essay will not be sufficient.

4. Put the documents into categories such as political, social, economic, or cultural.
5. Sort the documents and outside information into a pro/con chart to help you identify support or opposition to your thesis.
6. Construct a thesis from *both* the documents *and* the outside information.
7. Write an answer using *both* the documents *and* the outside information.
8. Use the documents as evidence to prove your thesis; avoid starting a sentence with "Document A says . . ."
9. Use as many documents as possible. Most high-scoring essays address all of the documents, though it is not a firm requirement.
10. Be prepared to write a "concession paragraph" just before the conclusion. A concession paragraph acknowledges challenges and conflicts to the thesis. Although this paragraph should never *repudiate* the thesis, its inclusion demonstrates that you are attuned to the complexity and controversy that may surround the issues in your answer.

THE FREE-RESPONSE QUESTIONS

The free-response questions, also sometimes referred to as the standard essays, will be judged by the strength of your thesis, the significance of your argument, and the quality of the evidence that you use to support your argument. The strategies below will help you prepare for the standard essay questions in Part B and Part C of the exam:

1. Choose wisely between the two essays in each part. After reading each question several times, you should draw up a list of facts and ideas about each of the prompts that would possibly become part of your response. The question with the longer, more detailed list is likely to be the better choice for you to answer.
2. Create a short outline based on your initial list of facts and ideas.
3. Spend no more than 35 minutes writing the first essay. Remember that Part C carries the same credit as Part B, so you must address it carefully and completely.
4. Answer *all* parts of the question and cover the entire time period mentioned in the prompt.
5. Create a strong thesis and state it early in the essay.
6. Use the facts and concepts from your original list; avoid using opinions or broad generalities to support your thesis.
7. Tell the "why" as well as the "what" in your answer. Analyze the topic by drawing warranted inferences and conclusions based on your facts.
8. Try to leave time to write a conclusion.
9. Proofread your answer.

HOW TO ANSWER THE *PRECISE* QUESTION ASKED

In some classes you may have had great freedom in answering essay questions. For example, if an essay prompt asked you to "explain why the Americans defeated the British in the American Revolution," you might have been able to describe the American effort in a general way without specifically addressing the defeat of the British. Moreover, if you used good grammar, a strong vocabulary, and a well-defined essay structure, you may have received an "A" grade. This approach will *not* work with AP* free-response questions.

AP* essay prompts ask a specific question that needs to be addressed completely and with substantial relevant information. For example, consider the following essay question:

> Analyze the political, economic, and social factors that affected slavery in the United States from the 1780s through the 1830s.

To write a successful response, you must first identify the three categories (political, economic, social), and then establish what people, events, and laws you will cite as evidence for each category. In addition, *ensure that everything you discuss falls within the time period that the question addresses.* A common mistake that students make is to consider factors or events that lie outside the time period.

For this type of prompt, you might organize your essay using the three categories outlined in the question. An effective response would likely have at least three paragraphs, one for each category. Students who establish the relative importance of each category will earn the highest scores. Specifically, the best essays will say, for example, that the economic factors are more significant than the political and the social factors.

Finally, and most importantly, your essay must have a clear thesis. *The importance of a strong, clear, sophisticated thesis cannot be overemphasized.* Your thesis will be graded on its clarity and how well it is supported by historical evidence. Consider the verb used in the essay prompt above: "analyze." In general, no two people will analyze history in the same exact way. Therefore, your thesis will not be graded as "right" or "wrong," but rather on whether you have stated a clear, concise argument. For example, the thesis statement "*Powerful political, economic, and social factors had an impact on slavery from the 1780s through the 1830s*" is not as effective as "*Economic factors were more influential than political and social factors in their effect on slavery from the 1780s to the 1830s.*" Another student might interpret history in such a way that social factors are more important, which would be equally valid, provided that the student could support this thesis with appropriate and abundant historical evidence.

In summary, a high-scoring essay has a clear, well-developed thesis that addresses exactly what the question is asking and is confined to the time period of the question. Moreover, high-scoring essays should also be well organized. It is helpful, but not essential, that all your spelling and punctuation be correct. Don't spend valuable time fretting over the exact usage and spelling of certain words. On a similar note, if you do not remember the exact date of a specific event, place it into a general time period. In the final evaluation, it is your thesis and the sophistication of your analysis that matter most.

DEVELOPING WRITING, THINKING, AND DOCUMENT SKILLS IN AN AP* COURSE

An AP* United States History course is likely to be among your most rigorous academic experiences in high school. The course moves very quickly through a lot of content, covering United States history from 1491 to the 1980s. In addition, the curriculum develops high-level skills that prepare you not only for the national examination but also for your collegiate experience and beyond. AP* United States History is a rewarding challenge, but it can also be very demanding of your time and energy.

One of the most important skills you will develop in the course is the ability to write analytical essays under strict time constraints. Because essays are worth 50 percent of the overall credit on the AP* test, you will be expected to write a series of in-class essays throughout the school year. Your AP* teacher realizes the importance of writing for your success and will closely monitor your progress with frequent writing assignments. By exam time in May, you will have a strong foundation in essay writing—undoubtedly one of the building blocks for success on the national test and at all levels of education.

Along with proficiency in college-level writing, you will also develop enhanced critical-thinking abilities. Among other skills, you will learn how to establish cause-and-effect relationships, weigh evidence, categorize information, and evaluate diverse points of view. By working on these types of procedures, you will begin to see historical topics in new and unique ways. The development of writing, thinking, and document competencies are the foundation of a strong AP* United States History class.

UNDERSTANDING HISTORICAL DOCUMENTS

The AP* United States History curriculum leans heavily on the analysis and application of primary-source documents. These materials are one of the cornerstones of instruction in the course, appearing regularly on the annual examination in any of several forms. In the multiple-choice section, primary sources are often used as prompts that students must read, analyze, and interpret. And perhaps most importantly, primary sources make up the essential component of the Document-Based Question. Mastery of this essay question is critical for maximum achievement on the AP* test. Unless you have a consistent strategy of document analysis, you will find these passages confusing and daunting. Your chances for success in the AP* United States History class, and ultimately on the test in May, depends on your ability to work with primary sources. Your teacher knows this and will inundate you with documents throughout the year. Your teacher will expect you to decode primary sources and incorporate them into written historical arguments.

In preparation for answering the DBQs, you must become adept at analyzing primary-source materials such as letters, diaries, public documents, and court rulings. You must be able to summarize the meaning of a source, interpret it, assess its importance, and use it to support a thesis. In many ways, this type of document analysis replicates the work that professional historians do as they ply their craft.

You can manage this process easily if you adopt a strategy for unlocking information from a source and utilizing it in a written argument. In the Skills Handbooks found in the back of this book, we have provided easy-to-remember strategies for each type of primary-source document that you will encounter throughout this course and on the exam, including images, documents, maps, and political cartoons.

UNDERSTANDING VISUAL MATERIALS

Photographs and other images are an important, but at times overlooked, source of historical information. They may seem to be nothing more than illustrations intended to enliven the pages of a textbook, yet they can offer rich insights into history. They often appear on the AP* United States History test as sources in both the multiple-choice questions and DBQ sections of the exam. Photographs and art are more than academic window dressing; they should enhance your understanding of America's past. Students who take the AP* course, in particular, should carefully examine all photographs and pictures beyond the mere descriptive level.

Indeed, photographs and other images are important historical artifacts. They mirror the social, economic, or political realities of a time period, as seen through the lens or brushes of the photographer or artist. The artist or photographer had a specific purpose in making the representation. You *must* consider this motive in analyzing the object. Furthermore, a basic tenet of all visual arts analysis is the idea that all photographic images convey a certain point of view that reflects the motivation or bias of the photographer. Every photograph in your textbook offers a message—sometimes hidden—to be uncovered.

Photographs and pictures require you to observe, analyze, and contextualize the topic being depicted. In some cases, you may be able to compare one era with another or draw warranted judgments about how the image reflects trends or ideas in a specific time period. You should not take these images at face value as reflections of the past. More than just glimpses into a specific moment in time, these images can indicate deeper trends or themes.

WORKING WITH MAPS

Maps are a powerful tool for analyzing historical events. Study them carefully. Passing over them quickly with only a cursory look shortchanges your understanding of the information presented in that section or chapter.

In some cases, maps enhance and expand an author's presentation of facts and concepts, supporting and reinforcing historical ideas. In other cases, maps broaden perspectives on events. For example, you can answer the Focus Question that opens each chapter in this book more completely when you address it through the prism of the chapter's textual sources and its visuals, including maps. Maps add insights to historical development, and at minimum, should be studied carefully along with their labels/captions as you read through the chapter.

Maps also play a substantial role in your preparation for the AP* United States History exam. Maps commonly appear on the multiple-choice section of the test. These types of questions will ask you to interpret the meaning and significance of a map as part of an explanation of economic, social, and/or political trends and developments. In addition, the DBQ is likely to contain a map as one of the sources to be analyzed, interpreted, and incorporated into your essay answer. Mastering map skills and strategies is a vital part of the AP* United States History course.

ANALYZING CARTOONS

Another important type of visual source that play a substantial role in United States history are cartoons. These visuals usually offer one-sided commentaries on historical events. They present pointed critiques of events, cultural assumptions, and prevailing attitudes of an era. And although cartoons sometimes exaggerate a particular point of view, they are no less significant as historical resources.

Be aware that you will likely face certain challenges in dealing with cartoons. Almost certainly the greatest hurdle will be viewing the image out of context. You must *always* place cartoons within the context of the time period and location in which they were created. Without an understanding of the historical background, setting, and intended audience of a cartoon, you cannot grasp the symbolism and point of view being expressed, nor will you be able to grasp its broader historical implications.

Another problem with analyzing cartoons is that they lack a structure to facilitate their dissection. You may feel flooded with information when studying a cartoon, which will make it difficult to know where to start your analysis. Cartoons have no topic sentences or paragraphs to help unlock their meaning. Accordingly, you must develop your own plan of attack for interpreting a cartoon. A detailed strategy for cartoon analysis has been provided in the "Cartoon Skills Workbook" in the back of this book to aid you in this challenging task.

HOW THE AP* U.S. HISTORY EXAM IS SCORED

Once you complete your examination in early May, the papers are packed up and shipped to Princeton, New Jersey, where they are sorted and eventually assessed. The multiple-choice section is quickly graded by a machine. First, the machine records the number of correct responses out of eighty possible. This raw score is then multiplied by a coefficient of 1.125 for a possible score of 90 (see the chart below).

The essay portions of the exam are separated into groups according to the combination of essays that you chose during the exam. Every test taker must complete the DBQ, but various combinations are possible for Parts B and C. Each essay option, including both the DBQ and the free-response questions, is given a number. The DBQ is labeled as question 1, the first essay in Part B as question 2, the second question in Part B as question 3, the first question in Part C as question 4, and the second question in Part C as question 5. Thus, exams by students who choose questions 2 and 4 are grouped together; those who choose 2 and 5 become another group; and so on.

Once the papers are sorted, the Educational Testing Service (ETS) sends them to various sites around the United States for assessment. The *readers* of the United States History exam are experienced AP* teachers and college instructors. The readers work in groups of seven or eight, with a table leader assigned to each group to ensure productivity and accuracy during the grading process. Each of your three essays is read by a different reader at a different table. Thus, three separate teachers will grade your writing. Your answers are read only once, but the readers are constantly monitored to assure that they are providing fair and consistent evaluations. The exam readings last a total of seven days, with three days spent on the free-response essays and four days devoted to the DBQ.

The DBQ is scored on a 0-to-9 scale, and that score is multiplied by a coefficient of 4.5 (see the chart on the next page) to determine your final grade. The free-response questions are also evaluated on a 9-point scale, but with each multiplied by a coefficient of 2.75. As you can see below, the possible score on the three essays is 90 points, equal to the total for the multiple-choice portion of the test. A perfect score on the test is 180 points. Candidates' scores are tabulated and arranged on a continuum from 0 to 180.

AP* United States Worksheet for Determining Grades

Multiple–Choice Section:

$$\underline{\hspace{5cm}} \quad \times \ 1.125 \ = \qquad \underline{\hspace{5cm}}$$

Number Correct (0–80)   *Total Score on MC*
                                                      (0–90)

Essay Section:

$$\underline{\hspace{5cm}} \quad \times \ 4.5 \ = \quad \underline{\hspace{5cm}}$$

DBQ Score (0–9)

$$\underline{\hspace{5cm}} \quad \times \ 2.75 \ = \quad \underline{\hspace{5cm}}$$

Part B FRQ Score (0–9)

$$\underline{\hspace{5cm}} \quad \times \ 2.75 \ = \quad \underline{\hspace{5cm}}$$

Part C FRQ Score (0–9)

                                                   Total Score on Essays
                                                            (0–90)

Total Score for Essays and Multiple–Choice: $\underline{\hspace{4cm}}$
                                                                  (0–180)

The Chief Faculty Consultant (that is, the chief reader) and the Educational Testing Service staff establish the specific number of points a candidate must accumulate in order to achieve a particular grade on the test. These scores range from 1 (the lowest possible score) to 5 (the highest possible score). This is the score that you will receive in early July and that colleges and universities will use to determine whether you are qualified to receive placement and/or credit.

CORRELATION WITH THE CURRENT AP* UNITED STATES HISTORY COURSE FRAMEWORK

Give Me Liberty! is a valuable tool and a perfect fit for an AP* U.S. History course. Because it takes students from the 1490s to the recent past, its scope coincides very nicely with the demands of the AP* curriculum. In addition, it includes a clear explanation of the major political, social, economic, and cultural concepts outlined in the AP* U.S. History course. Its most outstanding feature, however, is that it does all this by developing the over-arching theme of the changing contours of American freedom. This special focus links the key AP* concepts in a web of connections that gives this textbook a depth and cohesion often lacking in other textbooks.

The correlation chart provided here will help you connect the key concepts of the AP* U.S. History course to the wealth of content you will find in *Give Me Liberty!*

Key Concept	Chapters	Illustrative Examples
Key Concept 1.1 Before the arrival of Europeans, native populations in North America developed a wide variety of social, political and economic structures based in part on interactions with the environment and each other.	Chapter 1	The First Americans, pp.1–49
Key Concept 1.2 European overseas expansion resulted in the Columbian Exchange, a series of interactions and adaptations between societies across the Atlantic.	Chapter 1	The First Americans, pp.1–49
Key Concept 1.3 Contacts among American Indians, Africans, and Europeans challenged the worldview of each group.	Chapter 1	A New World, pp. 4–51
	Chapter 2	Beginnings of English America, pp. 52–91
	Chapter 3	Creating Anglo America, pp. 92–133
	Chapter 4	Slavery, Freedom, and the Struggle for Empire to 1763, pp. 134–81
Key Concept 2.1 Differences in imperial goals, cultures, and the environments they confronted led Europeans to develop diverse patterns of colonization.	Chapter 1	A New World, pp. 4–51
	Chapter 2	Beginnings of English America, pp. 52–91
Key Concept 2.2 European colonization efforts in North America stimulated intercultural contact and intensified conflict between the various groups of colonizers and native peoples.	Chapter 1	A New World, pp. 4–51
	Chapter 2	Beginnings of English America, pp. 52–91
	Chapter 3	Creating Anglo America, pp. 92–133
Key Concept 2.3 The increasing political, economic, and cultural exchanges within the Atlantic World had a profound impact on the development of colonial societies in North America.	Chapter 2	Beginnings of English America, pp. 52–91
Key Concept 3.1 Britain's victory over France in the imperial struggle for North America led to new conflicts among the British government, the North American colonists, and the American Indians, culminating in the creation of a new nation, the United States.	Chapter 4	Slavery, Freedom, and the Struggle for Empire to 1763, pp. 166–75
	Chapter 5	The American Revolution, 1763–1783, pp. 184–217

Key Concept 8.3 Significant economic, demographic, and technological changes had far-reaching impacts on American society, politics, and the environment.	Chapter 25	The Sixties, 1960–1968, pp. 1034–79
Key Concept 9.1 A new conservatism grew to prominence in U.S. culture and politics, defending traditional social values and rejecting liberal views about the role of government.	Chapter 26	The Triumph of Conservatism, 1969–1988, pp. 1080–1121
Key Concept 9.2 The end of the Cold War and new challenges to U.S. leadership in the world forced the nation to redefine its foreign policy and global role.	Chapter 27	Globalization and Its Discontents, 1989–2000, pp. 1126–36
Key Concept 9.3 Moving into the twenty-first century, the nation continued to experience challenges stemming from social, economic, and demographic changes.	Chapter 28	The Sixties, 1960–1968, pp. 1068–1211

CORRELATION WITH PEOPLES EDUCATION'S *U.S. HISTORY SKILLBOOK*, SECOND EDITION

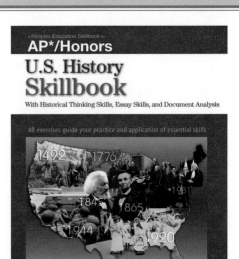

To augment your AP* U.S. History exam preparation, we recommend Peoples Education's *U.S. History Skillbook*, Second Edition, by Michael Henry, Ph.D. This supplement provides several types of instructional enhancements. Each chapter of the skillbook begins with a concise review of the major topics that you have studied in your primary text. These two- or three-pages summaries, along with the review questions and a discussion of the most significant people and ideas of the era, will help you recall important content and refresh your memory about specific historical developments. In addition, each chapter of the skillbook develops historical thinking, writing, and document skills based on the content from the chapters in both the skillbook and in this textbook. These skills are vital for your success on the AP* exam. As you work through them you will not only develop critical proficiencies for the exam preparation but you will also have another chance to work with the content presented earlier in this textbook. The table below shows how the chapters in the skillbook correspond with those in your textbook.

Give Me Liberty!	*U.S. History Skillbook*
Chapter 1	Chapter 1
Chapters 2–4	Chapter 2
Chapters 5–6	Chapter 3
Chapter 7	Chapter 4
Chapters 8–10	Chapter 5, 6
Chapter 12	Chapter 7
Chapter 13	Chapter 8
Chapters 14–15	Chapter 9
Chapters 16–17	Chapter 10
Chapter 18	Chapter 12
Chapter 19	Chapter 11
Chapters 20–22	Chapter 13
Chapters 23–25	Chapter 14
Chapter 26	Chapters 15, 16

ACKNOWLEDGMENTS

Content for the AP* Edition by Michael Henry, Ph.D.

Dr. Michael Henry taught AP* U.S. History for twenty-one years in Prince Georges County, Maryland, and is currently an adjunct professor of history at Prince Georges Community College in Largo, Maryland. He earned his Ph.D. and two master's degrees from the University of Maryland, College Park. He regularly serves as a consultant for the College Board and as an exam leader at the annual AP* reading in Louisville, Kentucky. Dr. Henry has written two books on AP* U.S. History, numerous teacher's guides, and eighteen articles on the teaching of history and social studies at the high school and college levels. Dr. Henry is also a member of the Organization of American Historians.

Supporting Writers:

Robert Naeher: History and Social Sciences Chair, Emma Willard School, Troy, NY

Robert Rodey: AP* U.S. History Teacher, Marian Catholic High School, Chicago Heights, IL

David Rodgers: AP* U.S. History Teacher, Zionsville Community High School, Zionsville, IN

Mike Smith: Social Studies Chair/Advanced Placement Coordinator/AP* U.S. History Teacher, San Bernardino City Unified School District, San Bernardino, CA

Beverly Vaillancourt: Educational Consultant, Author, Online Educator, La Valle, WI

Advisory Panel:

Robert O'Dell: Social Studies Coordinator, Nutley Public Schools, Nutley, NJ

Robert Rodey: AP* U.S. History Teacher, Marian Catholic High School, Chicago Heights, IL

Kathleen Walter: AP* U.S. History Teacher, Glen Rock High School, Glen Rock, NJ

Reviewers:

Tom Antonucci: History Instructor/Director of the Taft Summer School, The Taft School, Watertown, CT

Matt Ellington: AP* U.S. History Teacher, Chino Valley Unified School District, Chino Hills, CA

Geraldine Hastings: Social Studies Department Chairman, Catonsville High School, Baltimore County Public Schools, MD

Paul Magoni: IB U.S. History Teacher, Zionsville Community High School, Zionsville, IN

Robert Naeher: History and Social Sciences Chair, Emma Willard School, Troy, NY

William Shelton: History Teacher, Trinity Valley School, Fort Worth, TX

Jose Vas: U.S. History Teacher, Danbury High School, Danbury, CT

Joseph Villano: Adjunct Professor, Barry University, Miami Shores, FL

Adam Wright: Supervisor of Social Studies, Montgomery Township Schools, NJ

ERIC FONER is DeWitt Clinton Professor of History at Columbia University, where he earned his B.A. and Ph.D. In his teaching and scholarship, he focuses on the Civil War and Reconstruction, slavery, and nineteenth-century America. Professor Foner's publications include *Free Soil, Free Labor, Free Men: The Ideology of the Republican Party before the Civil War; Tom Paine and Revolutionary America; Nothing but Freedom: Emancipation and Its Legacy; Reconstruction: America's Unfinished Revolution, 1863–1877; The Story of American Freedom;* and *Forever Free: The Story of Emancipation and Reconstruction.* His history of Reconstruction won the *Los Angeles Times* Book Award for History, the Bancroft Prize, and the Parkman Prize. He has served as president of the Organization of American Historians and the American Historical Association. In 2006 he received the Presidential Award for Outstanding Teaching from Columbia University. His most recent book is *The Fiery Trial: Abraham Lincoln and American Slavery.*

Author's Preface

Give Me Liberty! An American History is a survey of American history from the earliest days of European exploration and conquest of the New World to the first years of the twenty-first century. It offers students a clear, concise narrative whose central theme is the changing contours of American freedom.

I am extremely gratified by the response to the first two editions of *Give Me Liberty!*, which have been used in survey courses at many hundreds of two- and four-year colleges and universities throughout the country. The comments I have received from instructors and students encourage me to think that *Give Me Liberty!* has worked well in their classrooms. Their comments have also included many valuable suggestions for revisions, which I greatly appreciate. These have ranged from corrections of typographical and factual errors to thoughts about subjects that needed more extensive treatment. In making revisions for this Third Edition, I have tried to take these suggestions into account. I have also incorporated the findings and insights of new scholarship that has appeared since the original edition was written.

The most significant changes in this Third Edition reflect my desire to place American history more fully in a global context. The book remains, of course, a survey of American, not world, history. But in the past few years, scholars writing about the American past have sought to delineate the connections and influences of the United States on the rest of the world as well as the global developments that have helped to shape the course of events here at home. They have also devoted greater attention to transnational processes—the expansion of empires, international labor migrations, the rise and fall of slavery, the globalization of economic enterprise—that cannot be understood solely within the confines of one country's national boundaries. Without in any way seeking to homogenize the history of individual nations or neglect the domestic forces that have shaped American development, the Third Edition reflects this recent emphasis in American historical writing. Small changes relating to this theme may be found throughout the book. The major additions seeking to illuminate the global context of American history are as follows:

Chapter 4 includes a brief discussion of how the Great Awakening in the American colonies took place at a time of growing religious fundamentalism in many parts of the world. Chapter 5 now devotes attention to the global impact of the American Declaration of Independence, including how both colonial peoples seeking national independence and groups who felt themselves deprived of equal rights seized upon the Declaration's language to promote their own causes. Chapter 8 discusses how the slave revolution in Saint Domingue, which established the black republic of Haiti, affected the thinking of both black and white Americans in the early 1800s. The chapter also contains a new section on the Barbary Wars, the first armed encounter between the United States and Islamic states.

In Chapter 10, I have added a new section discussing the response in the United States to the Latin American wars of independence of the early nineteenth century, and the similarities and differences between these struggles and our own War of Independence. Chapter 11 contains a new section discussing the abolition of slavery elsewhere in the Western Hemisphere and how the aftermath of emancipation in other areas affected the debate over slavery in the United States. Chapter 13 compares the California gold rush with the consequences of the discovery of gold in Australia at the same time, and also adds a discussion of the "opening" of Japan to American commerce in the 1850s. And in Chapter 14, I added to the discussion of the Civil War a comparison of its destructiveness with that of other conflicts of the era, and also an examination of how the consolidation of national power in the United States reflected a worldwide process underway at the same time in other countries. In that chapter, too, reflecting the findings of recent scholarship, there are new discussions of the war's impact on American religion and on Native Americans. Chapter 15, dealing with the era of Reconstruction, now compares the aftermath of slavery in the United States with the outcome in other places where the institution was abolished.

In Chapter 16, a new section places the westward movement in the United States in the context of the settlement of frontier regions of other countries, ranging from Argentina to Australia and South Africa, and discusses the consequences for native populations in these societies. Chapter 17 expands on the acquisition by the United States of an overseas empire as a result of the Spanish-American War, and includes a new section on the Global Color Line—the worldwide development of national policies intended to guarantee white supremacy. I have strengthened, in Chapter 19, the discussion of the aftermath of World War I by examining the impact around the world of President Woodrow Wilson's rhetoric concerning national self-determination, and the disappointment felt when the principle was not applied to the Asian and African colonies of European empires. Chapter 22 now includes a section on black internationalism— how World War II led many black Americans to identify their campaign for equal rights with the struggle for national independence of colonial peoples in other parts of the world. In Chapter 23, I have expanded the discussion of the idea of human rights to indicate some of the ambiguities of the concept as it emerged as a major theme of international debate after World War II. There is a new section in Chapter 24 on the global reaction to American racial segregation and to the stirrings in the 1950s of the civil rights movement. I have strengthened the treatment of the 1960s by adding a discussion of the global 1968—how events in the United States in that volatile year occurred at the same time as uprisings of young people in many other parts of the world.

And in Chapter 28, the book's final chapter, I have significantly expanded coverage of the last few years of American history, including the election of Barack Obama, the nation's first African-American president, the continuing controversy over the relationship between liberty and security in the context of a global war on terror, and the global economic crisis that began in 2008.

As in the Second Edition, the Voices of Freedom sections in each chapter now include two documents; I have changed a number of them to reflect the new emphasis on the global context of American history. I have also revised the end-of-chapter bibliographies to reflect current scholarship. And I now include references to websites that contain digital images and documents relating to the chapter themes.

This Third Edition also introduces some new features. Visions of Freedom, a parallel to the Voices of Freedom document excerpts that have proven useful to instructors and students, highlights in each chapter an image that illuminates an understanding of freedom. I believe that examining this theme through visual as well as written evidence helps students to appreciate how our concepts of freedom have changed over the course of American history. The Visions of Freedom feature includes a headnote and questions that encourage students to think critically about the images.

The pedagogy in the book has been revised and enhanced to give students more guidance as they move through chapters. The end-of-chapter review pages have been expanded with additional review questions, many more key terms with page references, and a new set of questions on the freedom theme. The aim of the pedagogy, as always, is to offer students guidance through the material without getting in the way of the presentation.

I have also added new images in each chapter to expand the visual representation of key ideas and personalities in the text. Taken together, I believe these changes enhance the purpose of *Give Me Liberty!*: to offer students a clear, concise, and thematically enriched introduction to American history.

Americans have always had a divided attitude toward history. On the one hand, they tend to be remarkably future-oriented, dismissing events of even the recent past as "ancient history" and sometimes seeing history as a burden to be overcome, a prison from which to escape. On the other hand, like many other peoples, Americans have always looked to history for a sense of personal or group identity and of national cohesiveness. This is why so many Americans devote time and energy to tracing their family trees and why they visit historical museums and National Park Service historical sites in ever-increasing numbers. My hope is that this book will convince readers with all degrees of interest that history does matter to them.

The novelist and essayist James Baldwin once observed that history "does not refer merely, or even principally, to the past. On the contrary, the great force of history comes from the fact that we carry it within us, . . . [that] history is literally present in all that we do." As Baldwin recognized, the force of history is evident in our own world. Especially in a political democracy like the United States, whose government is designed to rest on the consent of informed citizens, knowledge of the past is essential—not only for those of us whose profession is the teaching and writing of history, but for everyone. History, to be sure, does not offer simple lessons or immediate answers to current questions. Knowing the history of immigration to the United States, and all of the tensions, turmoil, and aspirations associated with it, for example, does not tell us what current immigration policy ought to be. But without that knowledge, we have no way of understanding which approaches have worked and which have not—essential information for the formulation of future public policy.

History, it has been said, is what the present chooses to remember about the past. Rather than a fixed collection of facts, or a group of interpretations that cannot be challenged, our understanding of history is constantly changing. There is nothing unusual in the fact that each generation rewrites history to meet its own needs, or that scholars disagree among themselves on basic questions like the causes of the Civil War or the reasons for the Great Depression. Precisely because each generation asks different questions of the past, each generation formulates different answers. The past thirty years have witnessed a remarkable expansion of the scope of historical study. The experiences of groups neglected by earlier scholars, including women, African-Americans, working people, and others, have received unprecedented attention from historians. New subfields—social history, cultural history, and family history among them—have taken their place alongside traditional political and diplomatic history.

Give Me Liberty! draws on this voluminous historical literature to present an up-to-date and inclusive account of the American past, paying due attention to the experience of diverse groups of Americans while in no way neglecting the events and processes Americans have experienced in common. It devotes serious attention to political, social, cultural, and economic history, and to their interconnections. The narrative brings together major events and prominent leaders with the many groups of ordinary people who make up American society. *Give Me Liberty!* has a rich cast of characters, from Thomas Jefferson to campaigners for woman suffrage, from Franklin D. Roosevelt to former slaves seeking to breathe meaning into emancipation during and after the Civil War.

Aimed at an audience of undergraduate students with little or no detailed knowledge of American history, *Give Me Liberty!* guides readers through the complexities of the subject without overwhelming them with excessive detail. The unifying theme of freedom that runs through the text gives shape to the narrative and integrates the numerous strands that make up the American experience. This approach builds on that of my earlier book, *The Story of American Freedom* (1998), although *Give Me Liberty!* places events and personalities in the foreground and is more geared to the structure of the introductory survey course.

Freedom, and the battles to define its meaning, has long been central to my own scholarship and undergraduate teaching, which focuses on the nineteenth century and especially the era of the Civil War and Reconstruction (1850–1877). This was a time when the future of slavery tore the nation apart and emancipation produced a national debate over what rights the former slaves, and all Americans, should enjoy as free citizens. I have found that attention to clashing definitions of freedom and the struggles of different groups to achieve freedom as they understood it offers a way of making sense of the bitter battles and vast transformations of that pivotal era. I believe that the same is true for American history as a whole.

No idea is more fundamental to Americans' sense of themselves as individuals and as a nation than freedom. The central term in our political language, freedom—or liberty, with which it is almost always used interchangeably—is deeply embedded in the record of our history and the language of everyday life. The Declaration of Independence lists liberty among mankind's inalienable rights; the Constitution announces its purpose as securing liberty's blessings. The United States fought the Civil War to bring about a new birth of freedom, World War II for the Four Freedoms, and the Cold War to defend the Free World. Americans' love of liberty has been represented by liberty poles, liberty caps, and statues of liberty, and acted out by burning stamps and burning draft cards, by running away from slavery, and by demonstrating for the right to vote. "Every man in the street, white, black, red, or yellow," wrote the educator and statesman Ralph Bunche in 1940, "knows that this is 'the land of the free' . . . 'the cradle of liberty.'"

The very universality of the idea of freedom, however, can be misleading. Freedom is not a fixed, timeless category with a single unchanging definition. Indeed, the history of the United States is, in part, a story of debates, disagreements, and struggles over freedom. Crises like the American Revolution, the Civil War, and the Cold War have permanently transformed the idea of freedom. So too have demands by various groups of Americans to enjoy greater freedom. The meaning of freedom has been constructed not only in congressional debates and political treatises, but on plantations and picket lines, in parlors and even bedrooms.

Over the course of our history, American freedom has been both a reality and a mythic ideal—a living truth for millions of Americans, a cruel mockery for others. For some, freedom has been what some scholars call a "habit of the heart," an ideal so taken for granted that it is lived out but rarely analyzed. For others, freedom is not a birthright but a distant goal that has inspired great sacrifice.

Give Me Liberty! draws attention to three dimensions of freedom that have been critical in American history: (1) the *meanings* of freedom; (2) the *social conditions* that make freedom possible; and (3) the *boundaries* of freedom that determine who is entitled to enjoy freedom and who is not. All have changed over time.

In the era of the American Revolution, for example, freedom was primarily a set of rights enjoyed in public activity—the right of a community to be governed by laws to which its representatives had consented and of individuals to engage in religious worship without governmental interference. In the nineteenth century, freedom came to be closely identified with each person's opportunity to develop to the fullest his or her innate talents. In the twentieth, the "ability to choose," in both public and private life, became perhaps the dominant understanding of freedom. This development was encouraged by the explosive growth of the consumer marketplace (a development that receives considerable attention in *Give Me Liberty!*), which offered Americans an unprecedented array of goods with which to satisfy their needs and desires. During the 1960s, a crucial chapter in the history of American freedom, the idea of personal freedom was extended into virtually every realm, from attire and "lifestyle" to relations between the sexes. Thus, over time, more and more areas of life have been drawn into Americans' debates about the meaning of freedom.

A second important dimension of freedom focuses on the social conditions necessary to allow freedom to flourish. What kinds of economic institutions and relationships best encourage individual freedom? In the colonial era and for more than a century after independence, the answer centered on economic autonomy, enshrined in the glorification of the independent small producer—the farmer, skilled craftsman, or shopkeeper—who did not have to depend on another person for his livelihood. As the industrial economy matured, new conceptions of economic freedom came to the fore: "liberty of contract" in the Gilded Age, "industrial freedom" (a say in corporate decision-making) in the Progressive era, economic security during the New Deal, and, more recently, the ability to enjoy mass consumption within a market economy.

The boundaries of freedom, the third dimension of this theme, have inspired some of the most intense struggles in American history. Although founded on the premise that liberty is an entitlement of all humanity, the United States for much of its history deprived many of its own people of freedom. Non-whites have rarely enjoyed the same access to freedom as white Americans. The belief in equal opportunity as the birthright of all Americans has coexisted with persistent efforts to limit freedom by race, gender, class, and in other ways.

Less obvious, perhaps, is the fact that one person's freedom has frequently been linked to another's servitude. In the colonial era and nineteenth century, expanding freedom for many Americans rested on the lack of freedom—slavery, indentured servitude, the subordinate position of women—for others. By the same token, it has been through battles at the boundaries—the efforts of racial minorities, women, and others to secure greater freedom—that the meaning and experience of freedom have been deepened and the concept extended into new realms.

Time and again in American history, freedom has been transformed by the demands of excluded groups for inclusion. The idea of freedom as a universal birthright owes much both to abolitionists who sought to extend the blessings of liberty to blacks and to immigrant groups who insisted on full recognition as American citizens. The principle of equal protection of the law without regard to race, which became a central element of American freedom, arose from the antislavery struggle and the Civil War and was reinvigorated by the civil rights revolution of the 1960s, which called itself the "freedom movement." The battle for the right of free speech by labor radicals and birth control advocates in the first part of the twentieth century helped to make civil liberties an essential element of freedom for all Americans.

Although concentrating on events within the United States, *Give Me Liberty!* also, as indicated above, situates American history in the context of developments in other parts of the world. Many of the forces that shaped American history, including the international migration of peoples, the development of slavery, the spread of democracy, and the expansion of capitalism, were worldwide processes not confined to the United States. Today, American ideas, culture, and economic and military power exert unprecedented influence throughout the world. But beginning with the earliest days of settlement, when European empires competed to colonize North America and enrich themselves from its trade, American history cannot be understood in isolation from its global setting.

Freedom is the oldest of clichés and the most modern of aspirations. At various times in our history, it has served as the rallying cry of the powerless and as a justification of the status quo. Freedom helps to bind our culture together and exposes the contradictions between what America claims to be and what it sometimes has been. American history is not a narrative of continual progress toward greater and greater freedom. As the abolitionist Thomas Wentworth Higginson noted after the Civil War, "revolutions may go backward." Though freedom can be achieved, it may also be taken away. This happened, for example, when the equal rights granted to former slaves immediately after the Civil War were essentially nullified during the era of segregation. As was said in the eighteenth century, the price of freedom is eternal vigilance.

In the early twenty-first century, freedom continues to play a central role in American political and social life and thought. It is invoked by individuals and groups of all kinds, from critics of economic globalization to those who seek to secure American freedom at home and export it abroad. I hope that *Give Me Liberty!* will offer beginning students a clear account of the course of American history, and of its central theme, freedom, which today remains as varied, contentious, and ever-changing as America itself.

ACKNOWLEDGMENTS

All works of history are, to a considerable extent, collaborative books, in that every writer builds on the research and writing of previous scholars. This is especially true of a textbook that covers the entire American experience, over more than five centuries. My greatest debt is to the innumerable historians on whose work I have drawn in preparing this volume. The Suggested Reading list at the end of each chapter offers only a brief introduction to the vast body of historical scholarship that has influenced and informed this book. More specifically, however, I wish to thank the following scholars, who generously read portions of this work and offered valuable comments, criticisms, and suggestions:

For the First Edition:
    Valerie Adams, Embry-Riddle Aeronautical University
    Terry Alford, Northern Virginia Community College
    Tyler Anbinder, George Washington University
    Eric Arnesen, University of Illinois, Chicago
    Ira Berlin, University of Maryland
    Nikki Brown, Kent State University
    Jon Butler, Yale University
    Diane S. Clemens, University of California, Berkeley
    Paul G. E. Clemens, Rutgers University
    Jane Dailey, Johns Hopkins University
    Douglas Deal, State University of New York, Oswego
    Ricky Dobbs, Texas A&M University, Commerce
    Thomas Dublin, State University of New York, Binghamton
    Joel Franks, San Jose State University
    Kirsten Gardner, University of Texas at San Antonio

Lawrence B. Glickman, University of South Carolina
Colin Gordon, University of Iowa
Sam Haynes, University of Texas at Arlington
Rebecca Hill, Borough of Manhattan Community College
Jesse Hingson, Manatee Community College
Wallace Hutcheon, Northern Virginia Community College
Kevin Kenny, Boston College
Peter Kolchin, University of Delaware
Bruce Laurie, University of Massachusetts, Amherst
Daniel Letwin, Pennsylvania State University
Peter Mancall, University of Southern California
Louis Masur, City College, City University of New York
Alan McPherson, Howard University
Don Palm, Sacramento City College
Larry Peterson, North Dakota State University
John Recchiuti, Mount Union College
Scott Sandage, Carnegie-Mellon University
Bryant Simon, University of Georgia
Brooks Simpson, Arizona State University
Judith Stein, City College, City University of New York
George Stevens, Dutchess Community College
Thomas Sugrue, University of Pennsylvania
Alan Taylor, University of California, Davis
Daniel B. Thorp, Virginia Polytechnic Institute
Helena Wall, Pomona College
Jon Wiener, University of California, Irvine

For the Second Edition:
Marsha Ackermann, Eastern Michigan University
Valerie Adams, Embry-Riddle Aeronautical University
Omar Ali, Towson University
Ellen Baker, Columbia University
Ruth Bloch, University of California, Los Angeles
Roger Bromert, Southern Oklahoma State University
Charlotte Brooks, University at Albany, State University of New York
Barbara Calluori, Montclair State University
Robert Cassanello, University of Central Florida
Thomas Clarkin, San Antonio College
Gerard Clock, Pace University
Ronald Dufour, Rhode Island College
Mike Green, Community College of Southern Nevada
Maurine Greenwald, University of Pittsburgh
Evan Haefeli, Columbia University
Sharon A. Roger Hepburn, Radford College
Tam Hoskisson, Northern Arizona University
David Hsiung, Juniata College
Jeanette Keith, Bloomsburg University of Pennsylvania
Daniel Kotzin, Kutztown University
Robert M. S. McDonald, U.S. Military Academy
Stephen L. McIntyre, Missouri State University
Cynthia Northrup, University of Texas at Arlington
Kathleen Banks Nutter, Stony Brook University, State University of New York
John Paden, Rappahannock Community College
Sarah Phillips, Columbia University
Charles K. Piehl, Minnesota State University, Mankato

Ann Plane, University of California, Santa Barbara
Charles Postel, California State University, Sacramento
John Recchiuti, Mount Union College
Rob Risko, Trinity Valley Community College, Athens
Wade Shaffer, West Texas A&M University
Silvana R. Siddali, Saint Louis University
Judith Stein, The City College of the City University of New York
George Stevens, Dutchess Community College
Matthew A. Sutton, Oakland University
Timothy Thurber, Virginia Commonwealth University
David Voelker, University of Wisconson—Green Bay
Peter Way, Bowling Green State University
Richard Weiner, Indiana University—Purdue University Fort Wayne
Barbara Welke, University of Minnesota

For the Third Edition:
Vicki Arnold, Northern Virginia Community College
James Barrett, University of Illinois
Stephen Branch, College of the Canyons
Cynthia Clark, University of Texas at Arlington
Sylvie Coulibaly, Kenyon College
Ashley Cruseturner, McLennan Community College
Kevin Davis, Central Texas College
Jennifer Duffy, Western Connecticut State University
Melody Flowers, McLennan Community College
Lawrence Foster, Georgia Institute of Technology
Monica Gisolfi, University of North Carolina, Wilmington
Adam Goudsouzian, University of Memphis
Katie Graham, Diablo Valley College
Mike Green, Southern Nevada Community College
Dan Greene, Baylor University
Jennifer Gross, Jacksonville State University
Sandra Harvey, Lone Star College–CyFair
Toby Higbie, University of California, Los Angeles
Ernest Ialongo, Hostos Community College
Justin Jackson, Columbia University
Norman Love, El Paso Community College
James M. McCaffrey, University of Houston
John McCusker, Trinity University, San Antonio
Gil Montemayor, McLennan Community College
David Orique, University of Oregon
Michael Pebworth, Cabrillo College
Ray Raphael, Humboldt State University
Andrew Reiser, Dutchess Community College
Esther Robinson, Lone Star College–CyFair
Jerry Rodnitzky, University of Texas at Arlington
Diane Sager, Maple Woods Community College
Claudio Saunt, University of Georgia
James Seymour, Lone Star College–CyFair
Adam Simmons, Fayetteville State University
Andrew Slap, East Tennessee State University
Tim Solie, Minnesota State University
David Stebenne, Ohio State University
George Stevens, Dutchess Community College
Robert Tinkler, California State University, Chico

Kathleen Thomas, University of Wisconsin, Stout
Elaine Thompson, Louisiana Tech University
Doris Wagner, University of Louisville
Greg Wilson, University of Akron
William Young, Maple Woods Community College

I am particularly grateful to my colleagues in the Columbia University Department of History: Pablo Piccato, for his advice on Latin American history; Evan Haefeli and Ellen Baker, who read and made many suggestions for improvements in their areas of expertise (colonial America and the history of the West, respectively); and Sarah Phillips, who offered advice on treating the history of the environment.

I am also deeply indebted to the graduate students at Columbia University's Department of History who helped with this project. Theresa Ventura offered invaluable assistance in gathering material for the new sections placing American history in a global context. James Delbourgo conducted research for the chapters on the colonial era. Beverly Gage did the same for the twentieth century. Daniel Freund provided all-round research assistance. Victoria Cain did a superb job of locating visual images. I also want to thank my colleagues Elizabeth Blackmar and Alan Brinkley for offering advice and encouragement throughout the writing of this book.

Many thanks to Joshua Brown, director of the American Social History Project, whose website, History Matters, lists innumerable online resources for the study of American history. Bill Young at Maple Woods Community College did a superb job revising and enhancing the in-book pedagogy. Monica Gisolfi (University of North Carolina, Wilmington) and Robert Tinkler (California State University, Chico) did excellent work on the Instructor's Manual and Test Bank. Kathleen Thomas (University of Wisconsin, Stout) helped greatly in the revisions of the companion media packages.

At W. W. Norton & Company, Steve Forman was an ideal editor—patient, encouraging, always ready to offer sage advice, and quick to point out lapses in grammar and logic. I would also like to thank Steve's assistant, Rebecca Charney, for her indispensable and always cheerful help on all aspects of the project; JoAnn Simony for her careful work as manuscript editor; Stephanie Romeo and Patricia Marx for their resourceful attention to the illustrations program; Rubina Yeh and the irreplaceable Antonina Krass for their refinements of the book design; Debra Morton-Hoyt for splendid work on the covers for the Third Edition; Kim Yi for keeping the many threads of the project aligned and then tying them together; Christine D'Antonio and Chris Granville for their efficiency and care in book production; Steve Hoge for orchestrating the rich media package that accompanies the textbook; Nicole Netherton, Tamara McNeill, Steve Dunn, and Mike Wright for their alert reads of the U.S. survey market and their hard work in helping establish *Give Me Liberty!* within it; and Drake McFeely, Roby Harrington, and Julia Reidhead for maintaining Norton as an independent, employee-owned publisher dedicated to excellence in its work.

 Many students may have heard stories of how publishing companies alter the language and content of textbooks in an attempt to maximize sales and avoid alienating any potential reader. In this case, I can honestly say that W. W. Norton allowed me a free hand in writing the book and, apart from the usual editorial corrections, did not try to influence its content at all. For this I thank them, while I accept full responsibility for the interpretations presented and for any errors the book may contain. Since no book of this length can be entirely free of mistakes, I welcome readers to send me corrections at ef17@columbia.edu.

My greatest debt, as always, is to my family—my wife, Lynn Garafola, for her good-natured support while I was preoccupied by a project that consumed more than its fair share of my time and energy, and my daughter, Daria, who while a ninth and tenth grader read every chapter as it was written and offered invaluable suggestions about improving the book's clarity, logic, and grammar.

Eric Foner
New York City
July 2010

GIVE ME LIBERTY!

An American History

AP* Third Edition

Part 1

AMERICAN COLONIES TO 1763

The colonial period of American history was a time of enormous change, as the people of four continents—North America, South America, Europe, and Africa—were suddenly and unexpectedly thrown into contact with one another. The period also initiated a new era in the history of freedom. It was not, however, a desire for freedom that drove early European explorations of North and South America. Contact between Europe and the Americas began as a byproduct of the quest for a sea route for trade with Asia. But it quickly became a contest for power between rival empires, who moved to conquer, colonize, and exploit the resources of the New World.

At the time of European contact, the Western Hemisphere was home to tens of millions of people. Within the present border of the United States there existed Indian societies based on agriculture, hunting, or fishing, with their own languages, religious practices, and forms of government. All experienced wrenching changes after Europeans arrived, including incorporation into the world market and epidemics of disease that devastated many native groups.

The colonies that eventually came to form the United States originated in very different ways. Virginia, the first permanent colony to be established, was created by a private company that sought to earn profits through exploration for gold and the development of transatlantic trade. Individual proprietors—well-connected Englishmen given large grants of land by the king—established Maryland and Pennsylvania. New York, which had been founded by the Dutch, came into British hands as the result of a war. Religious groups seeking escape from persecution in England and hoping to establish communities rooted in their understanding of the principles of the Bible founded colonies in New England.

In the seventeenth century, all the British colonies experienced wrenching social conflicts as groups within them battled for control. Relations with Indians remained tense and sometimes violent. Religious and political divisions in England, which experienced a civil war in the 1640s and the ouster of the king in 1688, reverberated in the colonies. So did wars between European powers, which spilled over into North America. Nonetheless, after difficult beginnings, Britain's mainland colonies experienced years of remarkable growth in population and economic activity. By the eighteenth century, the non-Indian population of Britain's North American colonies had far outstripped that of the colonies of France and Spain.

In every colony in British America, well-to-do landowners and merchants dominated economic and political life. Nonetheless, emigration to the colonies offered numerous settlers opportunities they had not enjoyed at home, including access to land, the freedom to worship as they pleased, and the right to vote. Every British colony had an elected assembly that shared power with a governor, who was usually appointed from London. Even this limited degree of self-government contrasted sharply with the lack of representative institutions in the Spanish and French empires. All these circumstances drew thousands of English emigrants to North America in the seventeenth century, and thousands more from Ireland, Scotland, and the European continent in the eighteenth century.

Yet the conditions that allowed colonists to enjoy such freedoms were made possible by lack of freedom for millions of others. For the native inhabitants of the Western Hemisphere, European colonization brought the spread of devastating epidemics and either dispossession from the land or forced labor for the colonizers. Millions of Africans were uprooted from their homes and transported to the New World to labor on the plantations of Brazil, the Caribbean, and England's North American colonies. Even among European immigrants, the majority arrived not as completely free individuals but as indentured servants who owed a prearranged number of years of labor to those who paid their passage.

In colonial America, many modern ideas of freedom did not exist, or existed in very different forms than today. Equality before the law was unknown—women, non-whites, and propertyless men enjoyed far fewer rights than landowning white male citizens. Economic freedom, today widely identified with participation in an unregulated market, meant independence—owning land or a shop and not relying on another person for a livelihood. Most colonies had official churches, and many colonists who sought religious liberty for themselves refused to extend it to others. Speaking or writing critically of public authorities could land a person in jail.

Nonetheless, ideas about freedom played a major role in justifying European colonization. The Spanish and French claimed to be liberating Native Americans by bringing them advanced civilization and Roman Catholicism. England insisted that true freedom for Indians meant adopting English ways, including Protestantism. Moreover, the expansion of England's empire occurred at a time when freedom came to be seen as the defining characteristic of the English nation. Slavery existed in every New World colony. In many, it became the basis of economic life. Yet most Britons, including colonists, prided themselves on enjoying "British liberty," a common set of rights that included protection from the arbitrary exercise of governmental power.

Thus, freedom and lack of freedom expanded together in the colonies of British North America that would eventually form the United States.

CHAPTER 1

Their greene corne.

Corne newly sprong.

A New World

The Village of Secoton, by John White, an English artist who spent a year on the Outer Banks of North Carolina in 1585–1586 as part of an expedition sponsored by Sir Walter Raleigh. A central street links houses surrounded by fields of corn. In the lower part, dancing Indians take part in a religious ceremony.

• What were the major patterns of Native American life in North America before Europeans arrived?

• How did Indian and European ideas of freedom differ on the eve of contact?

• What impelled European explorers to look west across the Atlantic?

• What happened when the peoples of the Americas came in contact with Europeans?

• What were the chief features of the Spanish empire in America?

• What were the chief features of the French and Dutch empires in North America?

"The discovery of America," the British writer Adam Smith announced in his celebrated work *The Wealth of Nations* (1776), was one of "the two greatest and most important events recorded in the history of mankind." Historians no longer use the word "discovery" to describe the European exploration, conquest, and colonization of a hemisphere already home to millions of people. But there can be no doubt that when Christopher Columbus made landfall in the West Indian islands in 1492, he set in motion some of the most pivotal developments in human history. Immense changes soon followed in both the Old and New Worlds; the consequences of these changes are still with us today.

The peoples of the American continents and Europe, previously unaware of each other's existence, were thrown into continuous interaction. Crops new to each hemisphere crossed the Atlantic, reshaping diets and transforming the natural environment. Because of their long isolation, the inhabitants of North and South America had developed no immunity to the germs that also accompanied the colonizers. As a result, they suffered a series of devastating epidemics, the greatest population catastrophe in human history. Within a decade of Columbus's voyage, a fourth continent—Africa—found itself drawn into the new Atlantic system of trade and population movement. In Africa, Europeans found a supply of unfree labor that enabled them to exploit the fertile lands of the Western Hemisphere. Indeed, of approximately 10 million men, women, and children who crossed from the Old World to the New between 1492 and 1820, the vast majority, about 7.7 million, were African slaves.

From the vantage point of 1776, the year the United States declared itself an independent nation, it seemed to Adam Smith that the "discovery" of America had produced both great "benefits" and great "misfortunes." To the nations of western Europe, the development of American colonies brought an era of "splendor and glory." The emergence of the Atlantic as the world's major avenue for trade and population movement, Smith noted, enabled millions of Europeans to increase the "enjoyments" of life. To the "natives" of the Americas, however, Smith went on, the years since 1492 had been ones of "dreadful misfortunes" and "every sort of injustice." And for millions of Africans, the settlement of America meant a descent into the abyss of slavery.

Long before Columbus sailed, Europeans had dreamed of a land of abundance, riches, and ease beyond the western horizon. Once the "discovery" of this New World had taken place, they invented an America of the imagination, projecting onto it their hopes for a better life. Here, many believed, would arise unparalleled opportunities for riches, or at least liberation from poverty. Europeans envisioned America as a religious refuge, a society of equals, a source of power

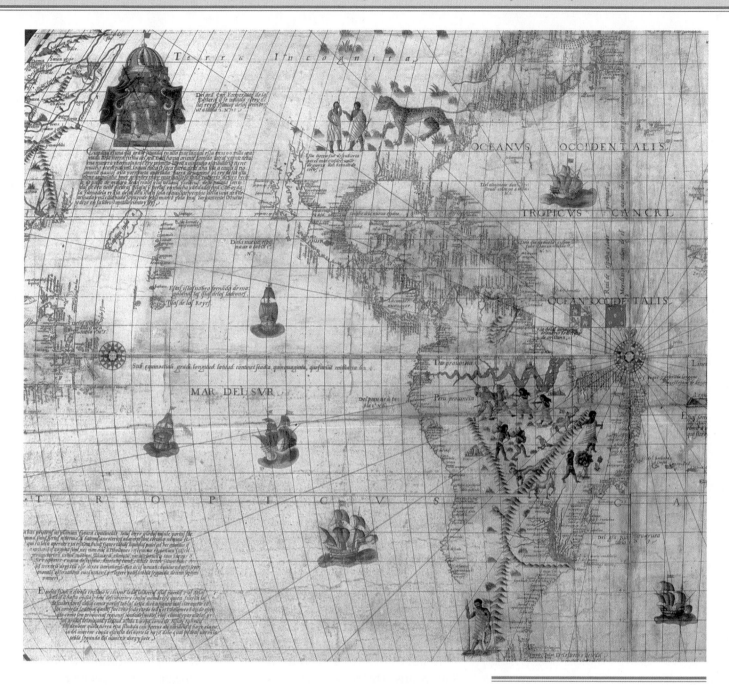

and glory. They searched the New World for golden cities and fountains of eternal youth. Some sought to establish ideal communities based on the lives of the early Christian saints or other blueprints for social justice.

Some of these dreams of riches and opportunity would indeed be fulfilled. To many European settlers, America offered a far greater chance to own land and worship as they pleased than existed in Europe, with its rigid, unequal social order and official churches. Yet the conditions that enabled millions of settlers to take control of their own destinies were made possible by the debasement of millions of others. The New World

A 1544 engraving of the Western Hemisphere by Sebastian Cabot, the son of the Italian-born explorer John Cabot and, like his father, an accomplished mariner. In the early sixteenth century, sailing for England and then Spain, Sebastian Cabot led several expeditions to the New World. The ships depicted are caravels, the first European vessels capable of long-distance travel, and the map also shows stylized scenes of Native Americans, including a battle with Spanish conquistadores.

became the site of many forms of unfree labor, including indentured servitude, forced labor, and one of the most brutal and unjust systems ever devised by man, plantation slavery. The conquest and settlement of the Western Hemisphere opened new chapters in the long histories of both freedom and slavery.

There was a vast human diversity among the peoples thrown into contact with one another in the New World. Exploration and settlement took place in an era of almost constant warfare among European nations, each racked by internal religious, political, and regional conflicts. Native Americans and Africans consisted of numerous groups with their own languages and cultures. They were as likely to fight one another as to unite against the European newcomers. All these peoples were changed by their integration into the new Atlantic economy. The complex interactions of Europeans, American Indians, and Africans would shape American history during the colonial era.

THE FIRST AMERICANS

THE SETTLING OF THE AMERICAS

The residents of the Americas were no more a single group than Europeans or Africans. They spoke hundreds of different languages and lived in numerous kinds of societies. Most, however, were descended from bands of hunters and fishers who had crossed the Bering Strait via a land bridge at various times between 15,000 and 60,000 years ago—the exact dates are hotly debated by archaeologists. Others may have arrived by sea from Asia or Pacific islands. Around 14,000 years ago, when glaciers began to melt at the end of the last Ice Age, the land link became submerged under water, once again separating the Western Hemisphere from Asia.

History in North and South America did not begin with the coming of Europeans. The New World was new to Europeans but an ancient homeland to those who already lived there. The hemisphere had witnessed many changes during its human history. First, the early inhabitants and their descendants spread across the two continents, reaching the tip of South America perhaps 11,000 years ago. As the climate warmed, they faced a food crisis as the immense animals they hunted, including woolly mammoths and giant bison, became extinct. Around 9,000 years ago, at the same time that agriculture was being developed in the Near East, it also emerged in modern-day Mexico and the Andes, and then spread to other parts of the Americas, making settled civilizations possible. Throughout the hemisphere, maize (corn), squash, and beans formed the basis of agriculture. The absence of livestock in the Western Hemisphere, however, limited farming by preventing the plowing of fields and the application of natural fertilizer.

THE FIRST AMERICANS

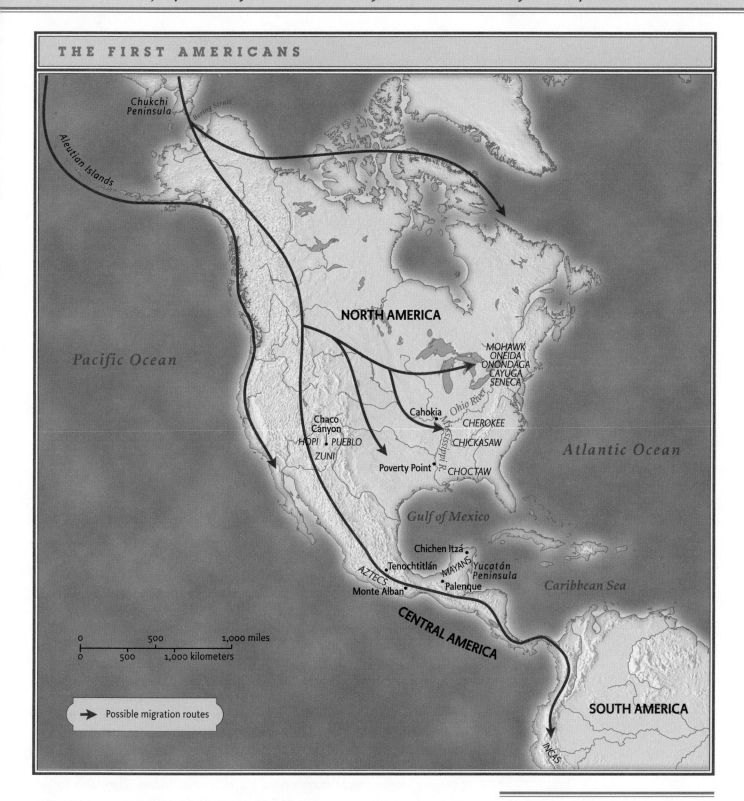

A map illustrating the probable routes by which the first Americans settled the Western Hemisphere at various times between 15,000 and 60,000 years ago.

INDIAN SOCIETIES OF THE AMERICAS

North and South America were hardly an empty wilderness when Europeans arrived. The hemisphere contained cities, roads, irrigation systems, extensive trade networks, and large structures such as the pyramid-temples whose beauty still inspires wonder. With a population close to

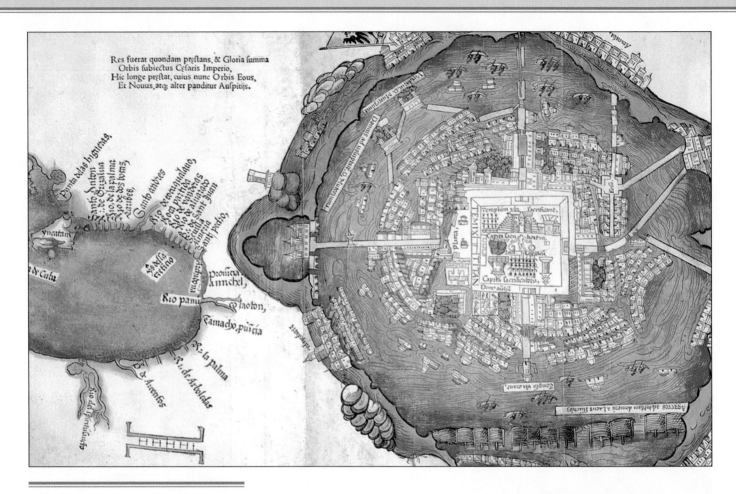

Map of the Aztec capital Tenochtitlán and the Gulf of Mexico, probably produced by a Spanish conquistador and published in 1524 in an edition of the letters of Hernán Cortés. The map shows the city's complex system of canals, bridges, and dams, with the Great Temple at the center. Gardens and a zoo are also visible.

250,000, Tenochtitlán, the capital of the Aztec empire in what is now Mexico, was one of the world's largest cities. Its great temple, splendid royal palace, and a central market comparable to that of European capitals made the city seem "like an enchanted vision," according to one of the first Europeans to encounter it. Further south lay the Inca kingdom, centered in modern-day Peru. Its population of perhaps 12 million was linked by a complex system of roads and bridges that extended 2,000 miles along the Andes mountain chain.

When Europeans arrived, a wide variety of native peoples lived within the present borders of the United States. Indian civilizations in North America had not developed the scale, grandeur, or centralized organization of the Aztec and Inca societies to their south. North American Indians lacked the technologies Europeans had mastered, such as metal tools and machines, gunpowder, and the scientific knowledge necessary for long-distance navigation. No society north of Mexico had achieved literacy (although some made maps on bark and animal hides). They also lacked wheeled vehicles, since they had no domestic animals like horses or oxen to pull them. Their "backwardness" became a central justification for European conquest. But, over time, Indian societies had perfected techniques of farming, hunting, and fishing, developed structures of political power and religious belief, and engaged in far-reaching networks of trade and communication.

MOUND BUILDERS OF THE MISSISSIPPI RIVER VALLEY

Remarkable physical remains still exist from some of the early civilizations in North America. Around 3,500 years ago, Native Americans constructed a large community centered on a series of giant semicircular mounds on a bluff overlooking the Mississippi River in present-day Louisiana. Known today as Poverty Point, it was a commercial and governmental center whose residents established trade routes throughout the Mississippi and Ohio River valleys. Archaeologists have found there copper from present-day Minnesota and Canada, and flint mined in Indiana.

More than a thousand years before Columbus sailed, Indians of the Ohio River valley, called "mound builders" by eighteenth-century settlers who encountered the large earthen burial mounds they created, had traded across half the continent. After their decline, another culture flourished in the Mississippi River valley, centered on the city of Cahokia near present-day St. Louis, a fortified community with between 10,000 and 30,000 inhabitants in the year 1200. Its residents, too, built giant mounds, the largest of which stood 100 feet high and was topped by a temple. Little is known of Cahokia's political and economic structure. But it stood as the largest settled community in what is now the United States until surpassed in population by New York and Philadelphia around 1800.

A modern aerial photograph of the ruins of Pueblo Bonita, in Chaco Canyon in present-day New Mexico. The rectangular structures are the foundations of dwellings, and the circular ones are kivas, or places of religious worship.

WESTERN INDIANS

In the arid northeastern area of present-day Arizona, the Hopi and Zuni and their ancestors engaged in settled village life for over 3,000 years. During the peak of the region's culture, between the years 900 and 1200, these peoples built great planned towns with large multiple-family dwellings in local canyons, constructed dams and canals to gather and distribute water, and conducted trade with groups as far away as central Mexico and the Mississippi River valley. The largest of their structures, Pueblo Bonita, in Chaco Canyon, New Mexico, stood five stories high and had over 600 rooms. Not until the 1880s was a dwelling of comparable size constructed in the United States.

After the decline of these communities, probably because of drought, survivors moved to the south and east, where they established villages and perfected the techniques of desert farming, complete with irrigation systems to provide water for crops of corn, beans, and cotton. These were the people Spanish explorers called the Pueblo Indians (because they lived in small villages, or *pueblos*, when the Spanish first encountered them in the sixteenth century).

Cliff dwellings in Cañon de Chelly, in the area of modern-day Arizona, built sometime between 300 and 1300 and photographed in 1873.

Another drawing by the artist John White shows ten male and seven female Native Americans dancing around a circle of posts in a religious ritual. White was a careful observer of their clothing, body markings, and objects used in the ceremony.

On the Pacific coast, another densely populated region, hundreds of distinct groups resided in independent villages and lived primarily by fishing, hunting sea mammals, and gathering wild plants and nuts. As many as 25 million salmon swam up the Columbia River each year, providing Indians with abundant food. On the Great Plains, with its herds of buffalo—descendants of the prehistoric giant bison—many Indians were hunters (who tracked animals on foot before the arrival of horses with the Spanish), but others lived in agricultural communities.

INDIANS OF EASTERN NORTH AMERICA

In eastern North America, hundreds of tribes inhabited towns and villages scattered from the Gulf of Mexico to present-day Canada. They lived on corn, squash, and beans, supplemented by fishing and hunting deer, turkeys, and other animals. Indian trade routes crisscrossed the eastern part of the continent. Tribes frequently warred with one another to obtain goods, seize captives, or take revenge for the killing of relatives. They conducted diplomacy and made peace. Little in the way of centralized authority existed until, in the fifteenth century, various leagues or confederations emerged in an effort to bring order to local regions. In the Southeast, the Choctaw, Cherokee, and Chickasaw each united dozens of towns in loose alliances. In present-day New York and Pennsylvania, five Iroquois peoples—the Mohawk, Oneida, Cayuga, Seneca, and Onondaga—formed a Great League of Peace, bringing a period of stability to the area. Each year a Great Council, with representatives from the five groupings, met to coordinate behavior toward outsiders.

The most striking feature of Native American society at the time Europeans arrived was its sheer diversity. Each group had its own political system and set of religious beliefs, and North America was home to literally hundreds of mutually unintelligible languages. Indians had no sense of

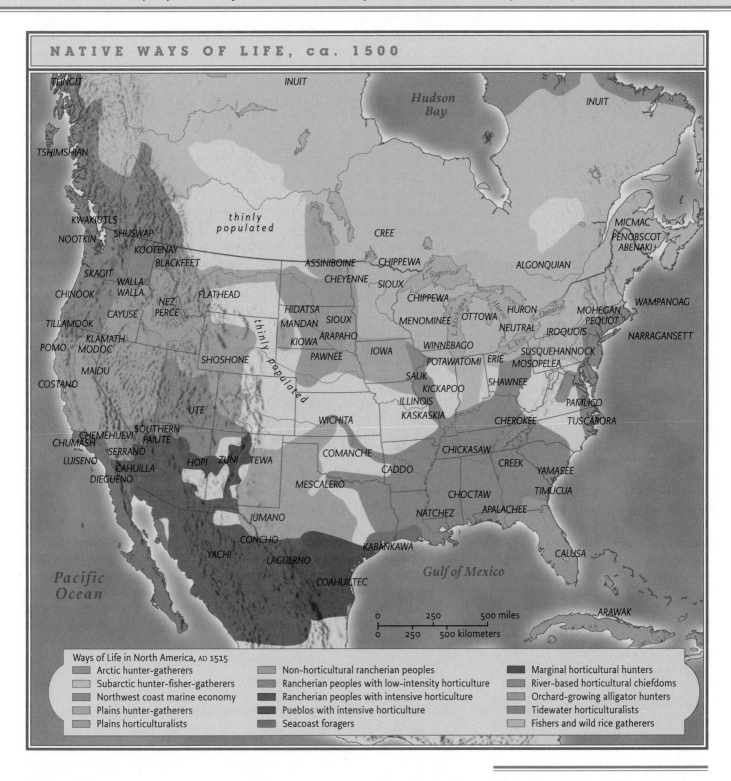

NATIVE WAYS OF LIFE, ca. 1500

Ways of Life in North America, AD 1515
- Arctic hunter-gatherers
- Subarctic hunter-fisher-gatherers
- Northwest coast marine economy
- Plains hunter-gatherers
- Plains horticulturalists
- Non-horticultural rancherian peoples
- Rancherian peoples with low-intensity horticulture
- Rancherian peoples with intensive horticulture
- Pueblos with intensive horticulture
- Seacoast foragers
- Marginal horticultural hunters
- River-based horticultural chiefdoms
- Orchard-growing alligator hunters
- Tidewater horticulturalists
- Fishers and wild rice gatherers

The native population of North America at the time of first contact with Europeans consisted of numerous tribes with their own languages, religious beliefs, and economic and social structures. This map suggests the numerous ways of life existing at the time.

"America" as a continent or hemisphere. They did not think of themselves as a single unified people, an idea invented by Europeans and only many years later adopted by Indians themselves. Indian identity centered on the immediate social group—a tribe, village, chiefdom, or confederacy. When Europeans first arrived, many Indians saw them as simply one group among many. Their first thought was how to use the newcomers to enhance their standing in relation to other native peoples, rather than to unite against them. The sharp dichotomy between Indians and "white" persons did not emerge until later in the colonial era.

NATIVE AMERICAN RELIGION

Nonetheless, the diverse Indian societies of North America did share certain common characteristics. Their lives were steeped in religious ceremonies often directly related to farming and hunting. Spiritual power, they believed, suffused the world, and sacred spirits could be found in all kinds of living and inanimate things—animals, plants, trees, water, and wind. Through religious ceremonies, they aimed to harness the aid of powerful supernatural forces to serve the interests of man. In some tribes, hunters performed rituals to placate the spirits of animals they had killed. Other religious ceremonies sought to engage the spiritual power of nature to secure abundant crops or fend off evil spirits. Indian villages also held elaborate religious rites, participation in which helped to define the boundaries of community membership. In all Indian societies, those who seemed to possess special abilities to invoke supernatural powers—shamans, medicine men, and other religious leaders—held positions of respect and authority.

Indian religion did not pose a sharp distinction between the natural and the supernatural, or secular and religious activities. In some respects, however, Indian religion was not that different from popular spiritual beliefs in Europe. Most Indians held that a single Creator stood atop the spiritual hierarchy. Nonetheless, nearly all Europeans arriving in the New World quickly concluded that Indians were in dire need of being converted to a true, Christian faith.

LAND AND PROPERTY

Equally alien in European eyes were Indian attitudes toward property. Numerous land systems existed among Native Americans. Generally, however, village leaders assigned plots of land to individual families to use for a season or more, and tribes claimed specific areas for hunting. Unclaimed land remained free for anyone to use. Families "owned" the right to use land, but they did not own the land itself. Indians saw land, the basis of economic life for both hunting and farming societies, as a common resource, not an economic commodity. In the nineteenth century, the Indian leader Black Hawk would explain why, in his view, land could not be bought and sold: "The Great Spirit gave it to his children to live upon, and cultivate as far as necessary for their subsistence; and so long as they occupy and cultivate it, they have a right to the soil." Few if any Indian societies were familiar with the idea of a fenced-off piece of land belonging forever to a single individual or family. There was no market in real estate before the coming of Europeans.

Nor were Indians devoted to the accumulation of wealth and material goods. Especially east of the Mississippi River, where villages moved every few years when soil or game became depleted, acquiring numerous possessions made little sense. However, status certainly mattered in Indian societies. Tribal leaders tended to come from a small number of families, and chiefs lived more splendidly than average members of society. But their

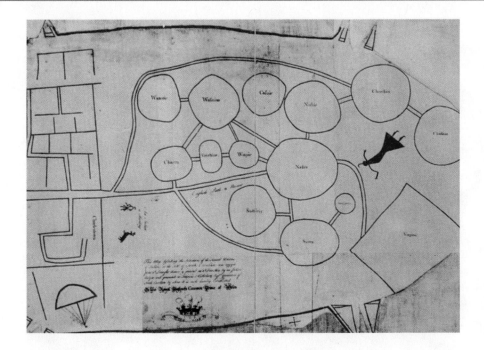

A Catawba map illustrates the differences between Indian and European conceptions of landed property. The map depicts not possession of a specific territory, but trade and diplomatic connections between various native groups and with the colony of Virginia, represented by the rectangle on the lower right.

reputation often rested on their willingness to share goods with others rather than hoarding them for themselves.

A few Indian societies had rigid social distinctions. Among the Natchez, descendants of the mound-building Mississippian culture, a chief, or "Great Sun," occupied the top of the social order, with nobles, or "lesser suns," below him, and below them, the common people. In general, however, wealth mattered far less in Indian society than in European society at the time. Generosity was among the most valued social qualities, and gift giving was essential to Indian society. Trade, for example, meant more than a commercial transaction—it was accompanied by elaborate ceremonies of gift exchange. A central part of Indian economies, gift giving bound different groups in webs of mutual obligation. Although Indians had no experience of the wealth enjoyed at the top of European society, under normal circumstances no one in Indian societies went hungry or experienced the extreme inequalities of Europe. "There are no beggars among them," reported the English colonial leader Roger Williams of New England's Indians.

GENDER RELATIONS

The system of gender relations in most Indian societies also differed markedly from that of Europe. Membership in a family defined women's lives, but they openly engaged in premarital sexual relations and could even choose to divorce their husbands. Most, although not all, Indian societies were matrilineal—that is, centered on clans or kinship groups in which children became members of the mother's family, not the father's. Tribal leaders were almost always men, but women played an important role in certain religious ceremonies, and female elders often helped to select male village leaders and took part in tribal meetings. Under English law, a married man controlled the family's property and a wife had no independent

Indians fishing, in a 1585 drawing by John White. The canoe is filled with fish, while two men harpoon others in the background. Among the wildlife illustrated are hammerhead sharks and catfish.

legal identity. In contrast, Indian women owned dwellings and tools, and a husband generally moved to live with the family of his wife. In Indian societies, men contributed to the community's well-being and demonstrated their masculinity by success in hunting or, in the Pacific Northwest, by catching fish with nets and harpoons. Because men were frequently away on the hunt, women took responsibility not only for household duties but for most agricultural work as well. Among the Pueblo of the Southwest, however, where there was less hunting than in the East, men were the primary cultivators.

EUROPEAN VIEWS OF THE INDIANS

Europeans tended to view Indians in extreme terms. They were regarded either as "noble savages," gentle, friendly, and superior in some ways to Europeans, or as uncivilized and brutal savages. Giovanni da Verrazano, a Florentine navigator who sailed up and down the eastern coast of North America in 1524, described Indians he encountered as "beautiful of stature and build." (For their part, many Indians, whose diet was probably more nutritious than that of most Europeans, initially found the newcomers weak and ugly.)

Over time, however, negative images of Indians came to overshadow positive ones. Early European descriptions of North American Indians as barbaric centered on three areas—religion, land use, and gender relations. Whatever their country of origin, European newcomers concluded that Indians lacked genuine religion, or in fact worshiped the devil. Their shamans and herb healers were called "witch doctors," their numerous ceremonies and rituals at best a form of superstition, their belief in a world alive with spiritual power a worship of "false gods." Christianity presented no obstacle to the commercial use of the land, and indeed in some ways encouraged it, since true religion was thought to promote the progress of civilization. Whereas the Indians saw nature as a world of spirits and souls, the Europeans viewed it as a collection of potential commodities, a source of economic opportunity.

Europeans invoked the Indians' distinctive pattern of land use and ideas about property to answer the awkward question raised by a British minister at an early stage of England's colonization: "By what right or warrant can we enter into the land of these Savages, take away their rightful inheritance from them, and plant ourselves in their places?" While the Spanish claimed title to land in America by right of conquest and papal authority, the English, French, and Dutch came to rely on the idea that Indians had not actually "used" the land and thus had no claim to it. Despite the Indians' highly developed agriculture and well-established towns, Europeans frequently described them as nomads without settled communities. The land was thus deemed to be a vacant wilderness ready to be claimed by newcomers who would cultivate and improve it. European settlers believed that mixing one's labor with the earth, which Indians supposedly had failed to do, gave one title to the soil.

In the Indians' gender division of labor and matrilineal family structures, Europeans saw weak men and mistreated women. Hunting and fishing, the primary occupations of Indian men, were considered leisure activities in much of Europe, not "real" work. Because Indian women worked in the fields, Europeans often described them as lacking freedom. They were "not much better than slaves," in the words of one English commentator. Europeans considered Indian men "unmanly"— too weak to exercise authority within their families and restrain their wives' open sexuality, and so lazy that they forced their wives to do most of the productive labor. Throughout North America, Europeans promoted the ideas that women should confine themselves to household work and that men ought to exercise greater authority within their families. Europeans insisted that by subduing the Indians, they were actually bringing them freedom—the freedom of true religion, private property, and the liberation of both men and women from uncivilized and unchristian gender roles.

INDIAN FREEDOM, EUROPEAN FREEDOM

INDIAN FREEDOM

And what of liberty as the native inhabitants of the New World understood it? Many Europeans saw Indians as embodying freedom. The Iroquois, wrote one colonial official, held "such absolute notions of liberty that they allow of no kind of superiority of one over another, and banish all servitude from their territories." But most colonizers quickly concluded that the notion of "freedom" was alien to Indian societies. Early English and French dictionaries of Indian languages contained no entry for "freedom" or *liberté*. Nor, wrote one early trader, did Indians have "words to express despotic power, arbitrary kings, oppressed or obedient subjects."

Indeed, Europeans considered Indians barbaric in part because they did not appear to live under established governments or fixed laws, and had no

Indian women planting crops while men break the sod. An engraving by Theodor de Bry, based on a painting by Jacques Le Moyne de Morgues. Morgues was part of an expedition of French Huguenots to Florida in 1564; he escaped when the Spanish destroyed the outpost in the following year.

A seventeenth-century engraving by a French Jesuit priest illustrates many Europeans' view of Indian religion. A demon hovers over an Iroquois longhouse, suggesting that Indians worship the devil.

respect for authority. "They are born, live, and die in a liberty without restraint," wrote one religious missionary. In a sense, they were *too* free, lacking the order and discipline that Europeans considered the hallmarks of civilization. Even slavery, wrote Richard Eden, an English writer of the mid-sixteenth century, was preferable to the Indians' condition before European contact, which he described as "rather a horrible licentiousness than a liberty." When Giovanni da Verrazano described the Indians as living in "absolute freedom," he did not intend this as a compliment.

The familiar modern understanding of freedom as personal independence, often based on ownership of private property, had little meaning in most Indian societies. But Indians certainly had their own ideas of freedom. While the buying and selling of slaves was unknown, small-scale slavery existed in some Indian societies. So too did the idea of personal liberty as the opposite of being held as a slave. Indians would bitterly resent the efforts of some Europeans to reduce them to slavery.

Although individuals were expected to think for themselves and did not always have to go along with collective decision making, Indian men and women judged one another according to their ability to live up to widely understood ideas of appropriate behavior. Far more important than individual autonomy were kinship ties, the ability to follow one's spiritual values, and the well-being and security of one's community. In Indian culture, group autonomy and self-determination, and the mutual obligations that came with a sense of belonging and connectedness, took precedence over individual freedom. Ironically, the coming of Europeans, armed with their own language of liberty, would make freedom a preoccupation of American Indians, as part and parcel of the very process by which they were reduced to dependence on the colonizers.

CHRISTIAN LIBERTY

On the eve of colonization, Europeans held numerous ideas of freedom. Some were as old as the city-states of ancient Greece, others arose during the political struggles of the early modern era. Some laid the foundations for modern conceptions of freedom, others are quite unfamiliar today. Freedom was not a single idea but a collection of distinct rights and privileges, many enjoyed by only a small portion of the population.

One conception common throughout Europe understood freedom less as a political or social status than as a moral or spiritual condition. Freedom meant abandoning the life of sin to embrace the teachings of Christ. "Where the Spirit of the Lord is," declares the New Testament, "there is liberty." In this definition, servitude and freedom were mutually reinforcing, not contradictory states, since those who accepted the teachings of Christ simultaneously became "free from sin" and "servants to God."

"Christian liberty" had no connection to later ideas of religious toleration, a notion that scarcely existed anywhere on the eve of colonization. Every nation in Europe had an established church that decreed what forms of religious worship and belief were acceptable. Dissenters faced persecution by the state as well as condemnation by church authorities. Religious uniformity was thought to be essential to public order; the modern idea that a person's religious beliefs and practices are a matter of private choice, not legal obligation, was almost unknown. The religious wars that racked

Europe in the sixteenth and seventeenth centuries centered on which religion would predominate in a kingdom or region, not the right of individuals to choose which church in which to worship.

FREEDOM AND AUTHORITY

In its secular form, the equating of liberty with obedience to a higher authority suggested that freedom meant not anarchy but obedience to law. Aristotle had described the law as liberty's "salvation," not its enemy. The identification of freedom with the rule of law did not, however, mean that all subjects of the crown enjoyed the same degree of freedom. Early modern European societies were extremely hierarchical, with marked gradations of social status ranging from the king and hereditary aristocracy down to the urban and rural poor. Inequality was built into virtually every social relationship. The king claimed to rule by the authority of God. Persons of high rank demanded deference from those below them. Less than 5 percent of the population monopolized English economic wealth and political power.

Within families, men exercised authority over their wives and children. According to the widespread legal doctrine known as "coverture," when a woman married she surrendered her legal identity, which became "covered" by that of her husband. She could not own property or sign contracts in her own name, control her wages if she worked, write a separate will, or, except in the rarest of circumstances, go to court seeking a divorce. The husband conducted business and testified in court for the entire family. He had the exclusive right to his wife's "company," including domestic labor and sexual relations.

Everywhere in Europe, family life depended on male dominance and female submission. Indeed, political writers of the sixteenth century explicitly compared the king's authority over his subjects with the husband's over his family. Both were ordained by God. To justify this argument, they referred to a passage in the New Testament: "As the man is the head of the woman, so is Christ the head of the Church." Neither kind of authority could be challenged without threatening the fabric of social order.

LIBERTY AND LIBERTIES

In this hierarchical society, liberty came from knowing one's social place and fulfilling the duties appropriate to one's rank. Most men lacked the freedom that came with economic independence. Property qualifications and other restrictions limited the electorate to a minuscule part of the adult male population. The law required strict obedience of employees, and breaches of labor contracts carried criminal penalties.

European ideas of freedom still bore the imprint of the Middle Ages, when "liberties" meant formal, specific privileges such as self-government, exemption from taxation, or the right to practice a particular trade, granted to individuals or groups by contract, royal decree, or purchase. One legal dictionary defined a liberty as "a privilege . . . by which men may enjoy some benefit beyond the ordinary subject." Only those who enjoyed the "freedom of the city," for example, could engage in certain economic activities.

Numerous modern civil liberties did not exist. The law decreed acceptable forms of religious worship. The government regularly suppressed publications it did not like, and criticism of authority could lead to imprisonment. In England, members of the House of Commons enjoyed freedom of speech during parliamentary sessions, but the right did not extend to ordinary citizens. Personal independence was reserved for a small part of the population, and this was one reason why authorities found "masterless men"—those without regular jobs or otherwise outside the control of their social superiors—so threatening. Nonetheless, every European country that colonized the New World claimed to be spreading freedom—for its own population and for Native Americans.

THE EXPANSION OF EUROPE

It is fitting that the second epochal event that Adam Smith linked to Columbus's voyage of 1492 was the discovery by Portuguese navigators of a sea route from Europe to Asia around the southern tip of Africa. The European conquest of America began as an offshoot of the quest for a sea route to India, China, and the islands of the East Indies, the source of the silk, tea, spices, porcelain, and other luxury goods on which international trade in the early modern era centered. For centuries, this commerce had been conducted across land, from China and South Asia to the Middle East and the Mediterranean region. Profit and piety—the desire to eliminate Islamic middlemen and win control of the lucrative trade for Christian western Europe—combined to inspire the quest for a direct route to Asia.

CHINESE AND PORTUGUESE NAVIGATION

At the beginning of the fifteenth century, one might have predicted that China would establish the world's first global empire. Between 1405 and 1433, Admiral Zheng He led seven large naval expeditions in the Indian Ocean. The first convoy consisted of 62 ships that were larger than those of any European nation, along with 225 support vessels and more than 25,000 men. On his sixth voyage, Zheng explored the coast of East Africa. China was already the world's most important trading economy, with trade routes dotting the Indian Ocean. Zheng's purpose was not discovery, but to impress other peoples with China's might. Had his ships continued westward, they could easily have reached North and South America. But as a wealthy land-based empire, China did not feel the need for overseas expansion, and after 1433 the government ended support for long-distance maritime expeditions. It fell to Portugal, situated on the western corner of the Iberian Peninsula, far removed from the overland route to Asia, to take advantage of new techniques of sailing and navigation to begin exploring the Atlantic.

The development of the caravel, a ship capable of long-distance travel, and of the compass and quadrant, devices that enabled sailors to determine their location and direction with greater accuracy than in the past, made it possible to sail down the coast of Africa and return to Portugal. Portuguese seafarers initially hoped to locate the source of gold that for centuries had been transported in caravans across the Sahara Desert to North Africa and

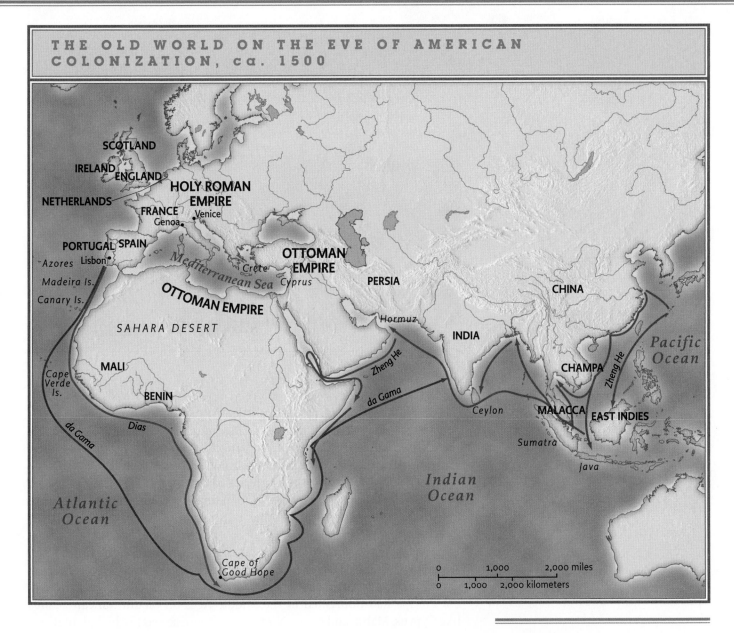

THE OLD WORLD ON THE EVE OF AMERICAN COLONIZATION, ca. 1500

Europe. This commerce, which passed through the African kingdom of Mali on the southern edge of the Sahara, provided Europe with most of its gold. Around 1400, it rivaled trade with the East in economic importance. And like trade with Asia, it was controlled by Muslim merchants.

PORTUGAL AND WEST AFRICA

Today, Africa is the world's poorest continent. In the fifteenth century, it was known for its wealth. Mansa Mūsā, the ruler of Mali, had literally put his realm on the map in 1324 when he led a great pilgrimage to Mecca, distributing so much gold along the way that its price was depressed for a decade. Until 1434, however, no European sailor had seen the coast of Africa below the Sahara, or the forest kingdoms south of Mali that contained the actual gold fields. But in that year, a Portuguese ship brought a sprig of rosemary from West Africa, proof that one could sail beyond

In the fifteenth century, the world known to Europeans was limited to Europe, parts of Africa, and Asia. Explorers from Portugal sought to find a sea route to the East in order to circumvent the Italian city-states and Middle Eastern rulers who controlled the overland trade.

An engraving, published in 1668, of a procession of the oba (king) outside Benin on the western coast of Africa. The image suggests the extent of the city, a center of government, trade, and the arts.

the desert and return. Little by little, Portuguese ships moved farther down the coast. In 1485, they reached Benin, an imposing city whose crafts-men produced bronze sculptures that still inspire admiration for their artistic beauty and superb casting techniques. The Portuguese established fortified trading posts on the western coast of Africa. The profits reaped by these Portuguese "factories"—so named because merchants were known as "factors"—inspired other European powers to follow in their footsteps.

Portugal also began to colonize Madeira, the Azores, and the Canary and Cape Verde Islands, which lie in the Atlantic off the African coast. Sugar plantations worked by Muslim captives and slaves from Slavic areas of east-ern Europe had flourished in the Middle Ages on Mediterranean islands like Cyprus, Malta, and Crete. Now, the Portuguese established plantations on the Atlantic islands, eventually replacing the native populations with thousands of slaves shipped from Africa—an ominous precedent for the New World. Soon, the center of sugar production would shift again, to the Western Hemisphere.

FREEDOM AND SLAVERY IN AFRICA

Slavery in Africa long predated the coming of Europeans. Traditionally, African slaves tended to be criminals, debtors, and captives in war. They worked within the households of their owners and had well-defined rights, such as possessing property and marrying free persons. It was not uncom-mon for African slaves to acquire their freedom. Slavery was one of several forms of labor, not the basis of the economy as it would become in large parts of the New World. The coming of the Portuguese, soon followed by traders from other European nations, accelerated the buying and selling of slaves within Africa. At least 100,000 African slaves were transported to

Spain and Portugal between 1450 and 1500. In 1502, the first African slaves were transported to islands in the Caribbean. The transatlantic slave trade, and its impact on Africa, will be discussed in Chapter 4.

Having reached West Africa, Portuguese mariners pushed their explorations ever southward along the coast. Bartholomeu Dias reached the Cape of Good Hope at the continent's southern tip in 1487. In 1498, Vasco da Gama sailed around it to India, demonstrating the feasibility of a sea route to the East. With a population of under 1 million, Portugal established a vast trading empire, with bases in India, southern China, and Indonesia. It replaced the Italian city-states as the major European commercial partner of the East. But six years before da Gama's voyage, Christopher Columbus had, he believed, discovered a new route to China and India by sailing west.

THE VOYAGES OF COLUMBUS

A seasoned mariner and fearless explorer from Genoa, a major port in northern Italy, Columbus had for years sailed the Mediterranean and North Atlantic, studying ocean currents and wind patterns. Like nearly all navigators of the time, Columbus knew the earth was round. But he drastically underestimated its size. He believed that by sailing westward he could relatively quickly cross the Atlantic and reach Asia. No one in Europe knew that two giant continents lay 3,000 miles to the west. The Vikings, to be sure, had sailed from Greenland to Newfoundland around the year 1000 and established a settlement, Vinland, at a site now known as L'Anse aux Meadows. But this outpost was abandoned after a few years and had been forgotten, except in Norse legends.

Columbus sought financial support throughout Europe for the planned voyage. His brother Bartholomew even visited Henry VII of England to ask for assistance. Most of Columbus's contemporaries, however, knew that he considerably underestimated the earth's size, which helps to explain why he had trouble gaining backers for his expedition. Eventually, King Ferdinand and Queen Isabella of Spain agreed to become sponsors. Their marriage in 1469 had united the warring kingdoms of Aragon and Castile. In 1492, they completed the *reconquista*—the "reconquest" of Spain from the Moors, African Muslims who had occupied part of the Iberian Peninsula for centuries. The capture of Grenada, the Moors' last stronghold, accomplished Spain's territorial unification. To ensure its religious unification, Ferdinand and Isabella ordered all Muslims and Jews to convert to Catholicism or leave the country. Along with the crown, much of Columbus's financing came from bankers and merchants of Spain and the Italian city-states, who desperately desired to circumvent the Muslim stranglehold on eastern trade. Columbus set sail with royal letters of introduction to Asian rulers, authorizing him to negotiate trade agreements.

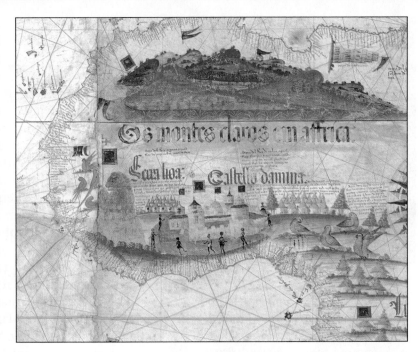

A detail from the Cantino World Map *depicting the western coast of Africa at the beginning of the Atlantic slave trade. Created by an anonymous Portuguese mapmaker in 1502, the map included Europe, Africa, and a small part of the Western Hemisphere, described as "the islands lately discovered in the parts of India." It was smuggled out of Portugal by Alberto Cantino, a diplomat representing an Italian city-state.*

Columbus's Landfall, *an engraving from*
La lettera dell'isole *(Letter from the
Islands). This 1493 pamphlet reproduced,
in the form of a poem, Columbus's first
letter describing his voyage of the previous
year. Under the watchful eye of King
Ferdinand of Spain, Columbus and his
men land on a Caribbean island, while
local Indians flee.*

CONTACT

COLUMBUS IN THE NEW WORLD

On October 12, 1492, after only thirty-three days of sailing from the
Canary Islands, where he had stopped to resupply his three ships,
Columbus and his expedition arrived at the Bahamas. His exact landing
site remains in dispute, but it was probably San Salvador, a tiny spot of
land known today as Watling Island. Soon afterward, he encountered the
far larger islands of Hispaniola (today the site of Haiti and the Dominican
Republic) and Cuba. When one of his ships ran aground, he abandoned it
and left thirty-eight men behind on Hispaniola. But he found room to
bring ten inhabitants of the island back to Spain for conversion to
Christianity.

In the following year, 1493, European colonization of the New World
began. Columbus returned with seventeen ships and more than 1,000 men
to explore the area and establish a Spanish outpost. Columbus's settlement
on the island of Hispaniola, which he named La Isabella, failed, but in 1502
another Spanish explorer, Nicolás de Ovando, arrived with 2,500 men and
established a permanent base, the first center of the Spanish empire in
America. Before he died in 1506, Columbus made two more voyages to the
New World, in 1498 and 1502. He went to his grave believing that he had
discovered a westward route to Asia. The explorations of another Italian,
Amerigo Vespucci, along the coast of South America between 1499 and
1502 made plain that a continent entirely unknown to Europeans had been
encountered. The New World would come to bear not Columbus's name
but one based on Vespucci's—America. Vespucci also realized that the
native inhabitants were distinct peoples, not residents of the East Indies as
Columbus had believed, although the name "Indians," applied to them by
Columbus, has endured to this day.

EXPLORATION AND CONQUEST

The speed with which European exploration proceeded in the aftermath
of Columbus's first voyage is remarkable. The technique of printing
with movable type, invented in the 1430s by the German craftsman
Johannes Gutenberg, had made possible the rapid spread of information
in Europe, at least among the educated minority. News of Columbus's
achievement traveled quickly. One writer hailed him as "a hero such as
the ancients made gods of." Others were inspired to follow in his wake.
John Cabot, a Genoese merchant who had settled in England, reached
Newfoundland in 1497. Soon, scores of fishing boats from France, Spain,
and England were active in the region. Pedro Cabral claimed Brazil for
Portugal in 1500.

But the Spanish took the lead in exploration and conquest. Inspired by a
search for wealth, national glory, and the desire to spread Catholicism,
Spanish conquistadores, often accompanied by religious missionaries and
carrying flags emblazoned with the sign of the cross, radiated outward
from Hispaniola. In 1513, Vasco Núñez de Balboa trekked across the isthmus of Panama and became the first European to gaze upon the Pacific
Ocean. Between 1519 and 1522, Ferdinand Magellan led the first expedition

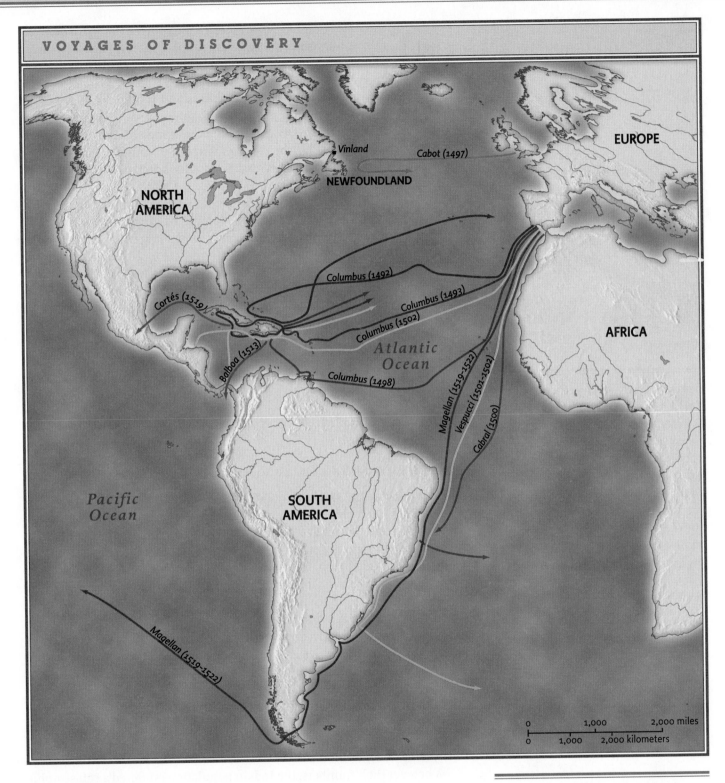

VOYAGES OF DISCOVERY

EUROPE

Vinland

Cabot (1497)

NEWFOUNDLAND

NORTH AMERICA

AFRICA

Cortés (1519)

Columbus (1492)

Columbus (1493)

Columbus (1502)

Balboa (1513)

Columbus (1498)

Atlantic Ocean

Magellan (1519–1522)

Vespucci (1501–1502)

Cabral (1500)

Pacific Ocean

SOUTH AMERICA

Magellan (1519–1522)

| 0 | 1,000 | 2,000 miles |
| 0 | 1,000 | 2,000 kilometers |

to sail around the world, encountering Pacific islands and peoples previously unknown to Europe. Magellan was killed in the Philippines, but his fleet completed the journey, correcting once and for all Columbus's erroneous assessment of the earth's size.

The first explorer to encounter a major American civilization was Hernán Cortés, who in 1519 arrived at Tenochtitlán, the nerve center of

Christopher Columbus's first Atlantic crossing, in 1492, was soon followed by voyages of discovery by English, Portuguese, Spanish, and Italian explorers.

Engravings, from the Florentine Codex, *of the forces of Cortés marching on Tenochtitlán and assaulting the city with cannon fire. The difference in military technology between the Spanish and Aztecs is evident. Indians who allied with Cortés had helped him build vessels and carry them in pieces over mountains to the city. The codex (a volume formed by stitching together manuscript pages) was prepared under the supervision of a Spanish missionary in sixteenth-century Mexico.*

the Aztec empire, whose wealth and power rested on domination of numerous subordinate peoples nearby. The Aztecs were violent warriors who engaged in the ritual sacrifice of captives and others, sometimes thousands at a time. This practice thoroughly alienated their neighbors and reinforced the Spanish view of America's native inhabitants as barbarians, even though in Europe at this time thousands of men and women were burned at the stake as witches or religious heretics, and criminals were executed in public spectacles that attracted throngs of onlookers.

With only a few hundred European men, the daring Cortés conquered the Aztec city, relying on superior military technology such as iron weapons and gunpowder, as well as shrewdness in enlisting the aid of some of the Aztecs' subject peoples, who supplied him with thousands of warriors. His most powerful ally, however, was disease—a smallpox epidemic that devastated Aztec society. A few years later, Francisco Pizarro conquered the great Inca kingdom centered in modern-day Peru. Pizarro's tactics were typical of the conquistadores. He captured the Incan king, demanded and received a ransom, and then killed the king anyway. Soon, treasure fleets carrying cargoes of gold and silver from the mines of Mexico and Peru were traversing the Atlantic to enrich the Spanish crown.

THE DEMOGRAPHIC DISASTER

The transatlantic flow of goods and people, sometimes called the Columbian Exchange, altered millions of years of evolution. Plants, animals, and cultures that had evolved independently on separate continents were now thrown together. Products introduced to Europe from the Americas included corn, tomatoes, potatoes, peanuts, tobacco, and cotton, while people from the Old World brought wheat, rice, sugarcane, horses, cattle, pigs, and sheep to the New. But Europeans also carried germs previously unknown in the Americas.

No one knows exactly how many people lived in the Americas at the time of Columbus's voyages—current estimates range between 50 and 90 million. The European population in 1492 (including Russia) was around 90 million, the African population was around 40 million, and about 210 million lived in China and modern-day India. Most inhabitants of the New World lived in Central and South America. In 1492, the Indian population within what are now the borders of the United States was between 2 and 5 million.

Whatever their numbers, the Indian populations suffered a catastrophic decline because of contact with Europeans and their wars, enslavement, and especially diseases like smallpox, influenza, and measles. Never having encountered these diseases, Indians had not developed antibodies to fight them. The result was devastating. Many West Indian islands were all but depopulated. On Hispaniola, the native population, estimated at between 300,000 and 1 million in 1492, had nearly disappeared fifty years later. The population of Mexico would fall by more than 90 percent in the sixteenth century, from perhaps 20 million to under 2 million. As for the area that now forms the United States, its Native American population fell continuously. It reached its lowest point around 1900, at only 250,000.

Overall, the death of perhaps 80 million people—close to one-fifth of humankind—in the first century and a half after contact with Europeans represents the greatest loss of life in human history. It was disease as much as military prowess and more advanced technology that enabled Europeans to conquer the Americas.

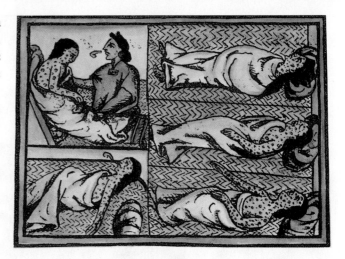

Another scene from the Florentine Codex *depicts the smallpox epidemic that ravaged the Aztec capital after the arrival of Cortés.*

THE SPANISH EMPIRE

By the middle of the sixteenth century, Spain had established an immense empire that reached from Europe to the Americas and Asia. The Atlantic and Pacific oceans, once barriers separating different parts of the world, now became highways for the exchange of goods and the movement of people. Spanish galleons carried gold and silver from Mexico and Peru eastward to Spain and westward to Manila in the Philippines and on to China.

The Spanish empire included the most populous parts of the New World and the regions richest in natural resources. Stretching from the Andes Mountains of South America through present-day Mexico and the Caribbean and eventually into Florida and the southwestern United States, Spain's empire exceeded in size the Roman empire of the ancient world. Its center in North America was Mexico City, a magnificent capital built on the ruins of the Aztec city of Tenochtitlán that boasted churches, hospitals, monasteries, government buildings, and the New World's first university. Unlike the English and French New World empires, Spanish America was essentially an urban civilization, an "empire of towns." For centuries, its great cities, notably Mexico City, Quito, and Lima, far outshone any urban centers in North America and most of those in Europe.

GOVERNING SPANISH AMERICA

Spain's system of colonial government rivaled that of ancient Rome. Alarmed by the destructiveness of the conquistadores, the Spanish crown replaced them with a more stable system of government headed by lawyers and bureaucrats. At least in theory, the government of Spanish America reflected the absolutism of the newly unified nation at home. Authority originated with the king and flowed downward through the Council of the Indies—the main body in Spain for colonial administration—and then to viceroys in Mexico and Peru and other local officials in America. The Catholic Church also played a significant role in the administration of Spanish colonies, frequently exerting its authority on matters of faith, morals, and treatment of the Indians.

Successive kings kept elected assemblies out of Spain's New World empire. Royal officials were generally appointees from Spain, rather than

An eighteenth-century view of the marketplace in Havana, Cuba, a major center of the Spanish empire in America.

criollos, as persons born in the colonies of European ancestry were called. The imperial state was a real and continuous presence in Spanish America. But as its power declined in Europe beginning in the seventeenth century, the local elite came to enjoy more and more effective authority over colonial affairs. Given the vastness of the empire, local municipal councils, universities, merchant organizations, and craft guilds enjoyed considerable independence.

COLONISTS IN SPANISH AMERICA

Despite the decline in the native population, Spanish America remained populous enough that, with the exception of the West Indies and a few cities, large-scale importations of African slaves were unnecessary. Instead, the Spanish forced tens of thousands of Indians to work in gold and silver mines, which supplied the empire's wealth, and on large-scale farms, or *haciendas*, controlled by Spanish landlords. In Spanish America, unlike other New World empires, Indians performed most of the labor, and although the Spanish introduced livestock, wheat, and sugar, the main agricultural crops were the same ones grown before colonization—corn, beans, and squash.

"The maxim of the conqueror must be to settle," said one Spanish official. The government barred non-Spaniards from emigrating to its American domains, as well as non-Christian Spaniards, including Jews and Moors. But the opportunity for social advancement drew numerous colonists from Spain—225,000 in the sixteenth century and a total of 750,000 in the three centuries of Spain's colonial rule. Eventually, a significant number came in families, but at first the large majority were young, single men, many of them laborers, craftsmen, and soldiers. Many also came as government officials, priests, professionals, and minor aristocrats, all ready to direct the manual work of Indians, since living without having to labor was a sign of noble status. The most successful of these colonists enjoyed lives of luxury similar to those of the upper classes at home.

COLONISTS AND INDIANS

Although persons of European birth, called *peninsulares*, stood atop the social hierarchy, they never constituted more than a tiny proportion of the population of Spanish America. Unlike in the later British empire, Indian inhabitants always outnumbered European colonists and their descendants in Spanish America, and large areas remained effectively under Indian control for many years. Like the later French empire and unlike the English, Spanish authorities granted Indians certain rights within colonial society and looked forward to their eventual assimilation. Indeed, the success of the Spanish empire depended on the nature of the native societies on which it could build. In Florida, the Amazon, and Caribbean islands like Jamaica, which lacked major Indian cities and large native populations, Spanish rule remained tenuous.

The Spanish crown ordered wives of colonists to join them in America and demanded that single men marry. But with the population of Spanish women remaining low, the intermixing of the colonial and Indian peoples soon began. As early as 1514, the Spanish government formally approved of such marriages, partly as a way of bringing Christianity to the native population. By 1600, *mestizos* (persons of mixed origin) made up a large part of the urban population of Spanish America. In the century that followed, *mestizos* repopulated the Valley of Mexico, where disease had decimated the original inhabitants. Over time, Spanish America evolved into a hybrid culture, part Spanish, part Indian, and in some areas part African, but with a single official faith, language, and governmental system. In

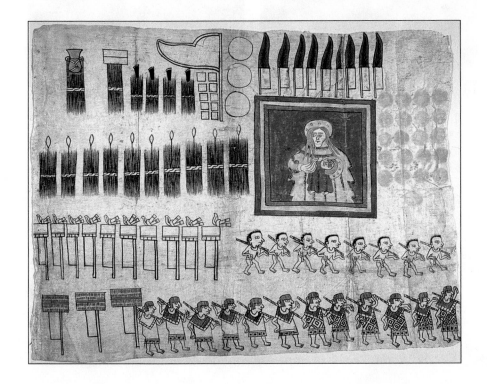

An illustration from the Huexotzinco Codex *(1531) depicts Mexicans providing products and services as taxes to the Spanish conquerors. The banner of the Virgin Mary and baby Jesus reflects the early spread of Christianity. The people of Huexotzinco, a town near Mexico City, had aided Hernán Cortés in his conquest of the Aztec empire. The codex was part of a successful lawsuit, endorsed by Cortés, in which the Indians challenged excessive taxation by colonial officials.*

Four Racial Groups, *taken from a series of paintings by the eighteenth-century Mexican artist Andrés de Islas, illustrates the racial mixing that took place in the Spanish empire and some of the new vocabulary invented to describe it. Top left: The offspring of a Spaniard and Indian is a* mestizo. *Right: A Spaniard and a* mestiza *produce a* castizo. *Bottom left: The child of an Indian and a* mestiza *is a* coyote. *Right: And the child of an Indian man and African woman is a* chino.

1531, a poor Indian, Juan Diego, reported seeing a vision of the Virgin Mary, looking very much like a dark-skinned Indian, near a Mexican village. Miracles began to be reported, and a shrine was built in her honor. The Virgin of Guadalupe would come to be revered by millions as a symbol of the mixing of Indian and Spanish cultures, and later of the modern nation of Mexico.

JUSTIFICATIONS FOR CONQUEST

What allowed one nation, the seventeenth-century Dutch legal thinker Hugo Grotius wondered, to claim possession of lands that "belonged to someone else"? This question rarely occurred to most of the Europeans who crossed the Atlantic in the wake of Columbus's voyage, or to rulers in the Old World. They had immense confidence in the superiority of their own cultures to those they encountered in America. They expected these societies to abandon their own beliefs and traditions and embrace those of the newcomers. Failure to do so reinforced the conviction that these people were uncivilized "heathens" (non-Christians).

Europeans brought with them not only a long history of using violence to subdue their internal and external foes but also missionary zeal to spread the benefits of their own civilization to others, while reaping the rewards of empire. Spain was no exception. The establishment of its empire in America took place in the wake of Spain's own territorial unification, the rise of a powerful royal government, and the enforcement of religious orthodoxy by the expulsion of Muslims and Jews in 1492. To further legitimize Spain's claim to rule the New World, a year after Columbus's first voyage Pope Alexander VI divided the non-Christian world between Spain and Portugal. The line was subsequently adjusted to give Portugal control of Brazil, with the remainder of the Western Hemisphere falling under Spanish authority.

A banner carried by the forces of Cortés, conqueror of the Aztec kingdom, features an image of the Virgin Mary, illustrating how the desire to spread the Roman Catholic faith provided a justification for conquest.

SPREADING THE FAITH

Not surprisingly, the pope justified this pronouncement by requiring Spain and Portugal to spread Catholicism among the native inhabitants of the Americas. The missionary element of colonization, already familiar because of the long holy war against Islam within Spain itself, was powerfully reinforced in the sixteenth century, when the Protestant Reformation divided the Catholic Church. In 1517, Martin Luther, a German priest, posted his Ninety-Five Theses, which accused the Church of worldliness and corruption. Luther wanted to cleanse the Church of abuses such as the sale of indulgences (official dispensations forgiving sins). He insisted that all believers should read the Bible for themselves, rather than relying on priests to interpret it for them. His call for reform led to the rise of new Protestant churches independent of Rome and plunged Europe into more than a century of religious and political strife.

Spain, the most powerful bastion of orthodox Catholicism, redoubled its efforts to convert the Indians to the "true faith." National glory and religious mission went hand in hand. Convinced of the superiority of Catholicism to all other religions, Spain insisted that the primary goal of colonization was to save the Indians from heathenism and prevent them from falling under the sway of Protestantism. The aim was neither to exterminate nor to remove the Indians, but to transform them into obedient, Christian subjects of the crown. Indeed, lacking the later concept of "race" as an unchanging, inborn set of qualities and abilities, many Spanish writers insisted that Indians could in time be "brought up" to the level of European civilization. Of course, this meant not only the destruction of existing Indian political structures but also a transformation of their economic and spiritual lives.

PIETY AND PROFIT

To the Spanish colonizers, the large native populations of the Americas were not only souls to be saved but also a labor force to be organized to extract gold and silver that would enrich the mother country. The tension

A benign view of Spanish colonization. This engraving from a 1621 book depicts Spanish missionaries bringing Christianity to New World natives while priests do construction work. A fortified colonial town is visible in the background.

between these two outlooks would mark Spanish rule in America for three centuries. On the one hand, Spanish rulers proclaimed the goal of bringing true "freedom" to the Indians by instructing them in Christianity. Even enslaving the natives was justified as a means of liberating them from their own backwardness and savagery and enabling them to become part of Christian civilization. Religious orders established missions throughout the empire, and over time millions of Indians were converted to Catholicism.

On the other hand, Spanish rule, especially in its initial period, witnessed a disastrous fall in Indian population, not only because of epidemics but also because of the brutal conditions of labor to which Indians were subjected. The conquistadores and subsequent governors, who required conquered peoples to acknowledge the Catholic Church and provide gold and silver, saw no contradiction between serving God and enriching themselves. Others, however, did.

LAS CASAS'S COMPLAINT

As early as 1537, Pope Paul III, who hoped to see Indians become devout subjects of Catholic monarchs, outlawed their enslavement (an edict never extended to apply to Africans). His decree declared Indians to be "truly men," who must not be "treated as dumb beasts." Fifteen years later, the Dominican priest Bartolomé de Las Casas published an account of the decimation of the Indian population with the compelling title *A Very Brief Account of the Destruction of the Indies*. Las Casas's father had sailed on Columbus's second voyage, and he himself had participated in the conquest of Cuba. But in 1514 Las Casas freed his own Indian slaves and began to preach against the injustices of Spanish rule.

Las Casas's writings denounced Spain for causing the death of millions of innocent people. "It has been Spain's practice," he reported, "in every land they have discovered to stage a massacre" in order to make the inhabitants "tremble with fear." He narrated in shocking detail the "strange cruelties" carried out by "the Christians," including the burning alive of men, women, and children and the imposition of forced labor. The Indians, he wrote, had been "totally deprived of their freedom and were put in the harshest, fiercest, most terrible servitude and captivity." Long before the idea was common, Las Casas insisted that Indians were rational beings, not barbarians, and that Spain had no grounds on which to deprive them of their lands and liberty. "The entire human race is one," he proclaimed, and while he continued to believe that Spain had a right to rule in America, largely on religious grounds, he called for Indians to enjoy "all guarantees of liberty and justice" from the moment they became subjects of Spain. "Nothing is certainly more precious in human affairs, nothing more esteemed," he wrote, "than freedom." Yet Las Casas also suggested that importing slaves from Africa would help to protect the Indians from exploitation.

Spanish conquistadores murdering Indians at Cuzco, in what is now known as Peru. The Dutch-born engraver Theodor de Bry and his sons illustrated ten volumes about New World exploration published between 1590 and 1618. A Protestant, de Bry created vivid images that helped to spread the Black Legend of Spain as a uniquely cruel colonizer.

REFORMING THE EMPIRE

Like other Spaniards, Las Casas believed that the main justification for empire was converting the Indians to Christianity. Spanish cruelty, he feared, undermined this effort. Largely because of Las Casas's efforts, Spain in 1542 promulgated the New Laws, commanding that Indians no longer be enslaved. Not everyone welcomed the change. Gonzalo Pizarro, brother of the conqueror of Peru, organized an unsuccessful rebellion in protest. In 1550, Spain abolished the *encomienda* system, under which the first settlers had been granted authority over conquered Indian lands with the right to extract forced labor from the native inhabitants. In its place, the government established the *repartimiento* system, whereby residents of Indian villages remained legally free and entitled to wages, but were still required to perform a fixed amount of labor each year. The Indians were not slaves—they had access to land, were paid wages, and could not be bought and sold. But since the requirement that they work for the Spanish remained the essence of the system, it still allowed for many abuses by Spanish landlords and by priests who required Indians to toil on mission lands as part of the conversion process. Indeed, a long struggle ensued among settlers, missionaries, and colonial authorities for control of Indian labor. Each party proclaimed itself a humane overlord and denounced the others for exploiting the native population.

By the end of the sixteenth century, work in the Spanish empire consisted largely of forced wage labor by native inhabitants and slave labor by Africans on the West Indian islands and a few parts of the mainland. Like all empires, Spain's always remained highly exploitative. Over time, the initial brutal treatment of Indians improved somewhat. But Las Casas's writings, translated almost immediately into several European languages, contributed to the spread of the Black Legend—the image of Spain as a uniquely brutal and exploitative colonizer. This would provide a potent justification for other European powers to challenge Spain's predominance in the New World.

A 1791 view of Mission San Carlos in what is now California depicts the Indian community and a corral in the background, while missionaries and Spanish explorers greet each other in the foreground.

EXPLORING NORTH AMERICA

While the Spanish empire centered on Mexico, Peru, and the West Indies, the hope of finding a new kingdom of gold soon led Spanish explorers into territory that now forms part of the United States. Juan Ponce de León, who had conquered Puerto Rico, entered Florida in 1513 in search of slaves, wealth, and a fabled fountain of youth, only to be repelled by local Indians. In 1528, another expedition seeking plunder in Florida embarked from Spain, but after a series of storms only a handful of men reached the Gulf Coast. For seven years they traversed the Southwest until a few survivors arrived in Mexico in 1536. One, Álvar Núñez Cabeza de Vaca, wrote an account of his adventures, including tales told by native inhabitants (possibly to persuade the newcomers to move on) of the seven golden cities of Cibola, somewhere over the horizon.

In the late 1530s and 1540s, Juan Rodriguez Cabrillo explored the Pacific coast as far north as present-day Oregon, and expeditions led by Hernando de Soto, Cabeza de Vaca, Francisco Vásquez de Coronado, and others marched through the Gulf region and the Southwest, fruitlessly searching for another Mexico or Peru. Coronado explored much of the interior of the continent, reaching as far north as the Great Plains, and became the first European to encounter the immense herds of buffalo that roamed the West. These expeditions, really mobile communities with hundreds of adventurers, priests, potential settlers, slaves, and livestock, spread disease and devastation among Indian communities. De Soto's was particularly brutal. His men tortured, raped, and enslaved countless Indians and transmitted deadly diseases. When Europeans in the seventeenth century returned to colonize the area traversed by de Soto's party, little remained of the societies he had encountered. Where large towns had existed, explorers found only herds of grazing bison.

SPANISH FLORIDA

Nonetheless, these explorations established Spain's claim to a large part of what is now the American South and Southwest. The first region to be colonized within the present-day United States was Florida. Spain hoped to establish a military base there to combat pirates who threatened the treasure fleet that each year sailed from Havana for Europe loaded with gold and silver from Mexico and Peru. Spain also wanted to forestall French incursions in the area. In 1565, Philip II of Spain authorized the nobleman Pedro Menéndez de Avilés to lead a colonizing expedition to Florida. Menéndez destroyed a small outpost at Fort Caroline, which a group of Huguenots (French Protestants) had established in 1562 near present-day Jacksonville. Menéndez and his men massacred the 500 colonists and went on to establish Spanish forts on St. Simons Island, Georgia, and at St. Augustine, Florida. The latter remains the oldest site in the United States continuously inhabited by European settlers and their descendants.

Spanish expeditions soon established forts from present-day Miami into South Carolina, and Spanish religious missionaries set up outposts in Florida and on the Sea Islands, hoping to convert the local Indians to Christianity. Most of the forts fell into disuse, and many of the missions were destroyed by local Guale Indians in an uprising that began in 1597. The Indians explained their revolt by noting that the missionaries had sought to eliminate "our dances, banquets, feasts, celebrations, and wars. . . . They persecute our old people by calling them witches." The missions were soon rebuilt, only to be devastated again a century later, this time by English and Indian forces from South Carolina. In general, Florida failed to attract settlers, remaining an isolated military settlement, in effect a fortified outpost of Cuba. As late as 1763, Spanish Florida had only 4,000 inhabitants of European descent.

SPAIN IN THE SOUTHWEST

Spain took even longer to begin the colonization of the American Southwest. Although de Soto and others made incursions into the area in the sixteenth century, their explorations were widely considered failures, since they had discovered neither gold nor advanced civilizations whose populations could be put to work for the Spanish empire. Spain then neglected the area for another half-century. It was not until 1598 that Juan de Oñate led a group of 400 soldiers, colonists, and missionaries north from Mexico to establish a permanent settlement. While searching for fabled deposits of precious metals, Oñate's nephew and fourteen soldiers were killed by inhabitants of Acoma, the "sky city" located on a high bluff in present-day New Mexico.

Oñate decided to teach the local Indians a lesson. After a two-day siege, his forces scaled the seemingly impregnable heights and destroyed Acoma, killing more than 800 of its 1,500 or so inhabitants, including 300 women. Of the 600 Indians captured, the women and children were consigned to servitude in Spanish families, while adult men were punished by the cutting off of one foot. Not until the 1640s was Acoma, which had been

Table 1.1 ESTIMATED REGIONAL POPULATIONS: THE AMERICAS, ca. 1500	
North America	3,800,000
Mexico	17,200,000
Central America	5,625,000
Hispaniola	1,000,000
The Caribbean	3,000,000
The Andes	15,700,000
South America	8,620,000
Total	54,945,000

Table 1.2 ESTIMATED REGIONAL POPULATIONS: THE WORLD, ca. 1500	
India	110,000,000
China	103,000,000
Other Asia	55,400,000
Western Europe	57,200,000
The Americas	54,000,000
Russia and Eastern Europe	34,000,000
Sub-Saharan Africa	38,300,000
Japan	15,400,000
World Total	467,300,000

By around 1600, New Spain had become a vast empire stretching from the modern-day American Southwest through Mexico, Central America, and into the former Inca kingdom in South America. This map shows early Spanish exploration in the present-day United States.

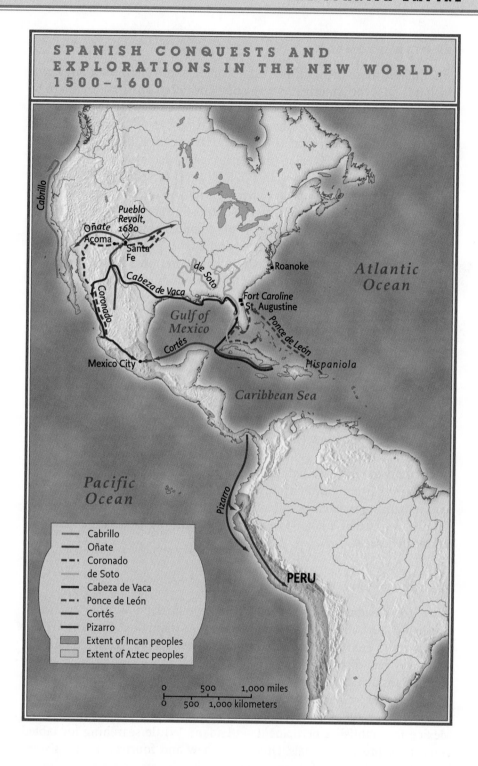

SPANISH CONQUESTS AND EXPLORATIONS IN THE NEW WORLD, 1500–1600

Cabrillo
Oñate
Pueblo Revolt, 1680
Acoma
Santa Fe
de Soto
Roanoke
Atlantic Ocean
Cabeza de Vaca
Coronado
Fort Caroline
St. Augustine
Ponce de León
Gulf of Mexico
Cortés
Hispaniola
Mexico City
Caribbean Sea
Pacific Ocean
Pizarro
PERU

Cabrillo
Oñate
Coronado
de Soto
Cabeza de Vaca
Ponce de León
Cortés
Pizarro
Extent of Incan peoples
Extent of Aztec peoples

0   500   1,000 miles
0   500   1,000 kilometers

inhabited since the thirteenth century, rebuilt. Oñate's message was plain—any Indians who resisted Spanish authority would be crushed. But his method of rule, coupled with his failure to locate gold, alarmed authorities in Mexico City. In 1606, Oñate was ordered home and punished for his treatment of New Mexico's Indians. In 1610, Spain established the capital of New Mexico at Santa Fe, the first permanent European settlement in the Southwest.

THE PUEBLO REVOLT

In 1680, New Mexico's small and vulnerable colonist population numbered less than 3,000. Most were *mestizos* (persons of mixed Spanish and Indian origin), since few European settlers came to the region. Relations between the Pueblo Indians and colonial authorities had deteriorated throughout the seventeenth century, as governors, settlers, and missionaries sought to exploit the labor of an Indian population that declined from about 60,000 in 1600 to some 17,000 eighty years later. Franciscan friars worked relentlessly to convert Indians to Catholicism, often using intimidation and violence. Their spiritual dedication and personal courage impressed many Indians, however, as did the European goods and technologies they introduced. Some natives welcomed them as a counterbalance to the depredations of soldiers and settlers and accepted baptism, even as they continued to practice their old religion, adding Jesus, Mary, and the Catholic saints to their already rich spiritual pantheon. But as the Inquisition—the persecution of non-Catholics—became more and more intense in Spain, so did the friars' efforts to stamp out traditional religious ceremonies in New Mexico. By burning Indian idols, masks, and other sacred objects, the missionaries alienated far more Indians than they converted. A prolonged drought that began around 1660 and the authorities' inability to protect the villages and missions from attacks by marauding Navajo and Apache Indians added to local discontent.

The Pueblo peoples had long been divided among themselves. The Spanish assumed that the Indians could never unite against the colonizers. In August 1680, they were proven wrong.

Little is known about the life of Popé, who became the main organizer of an uprising that aimed to drive the Spanish from the colony and restore the Indians' traditional autonomy. A religious leader born around 1630 in San Juan Pueblo in present-day New Mexico, Popé first appears in the historical record in 1675, when he was one of forty-seven Pueblo Indians arrested for "sorcery"—that is, practicing their traditional religion. Four of the prisoners were hanged, and the rest, including Popé, were brought to Santa Fe to be publicly whipped. After this humiliation, Popé returned home and began holding secret meetings in Pueblo communities.

Under Popé's leadership, New Mexico's Indians joined in a coordinated uprising. Ironically, because the Pueblos spoke six different languages, Spanish became the revolt's "lingua franca" (a common means of communication among persons of different linguistic backgrounds). Some 2,000 warriors destroyed isolated farms and missions, killing 400 colonists, including 21 Franciscan missionaries. They then surrounded Santa Fe. The Spanish resisted fiercely but eventually had no choice but to abandon the town. Most of the Spanish survivors, accompanied by several hundred Christian Indians, made their way south out of New Mexico. Within a few weeks, a century of colonization

Acoma, the "sky city," as it appeared in 1904.

VOICES OF FREEDOM

FROM BARTOLOMÉ DE LAS CASAS, *History of the Indies* (1528)

Las Casas was the Dominican priest who condemned the treatment of Indians in the Spanish empire. His widely disseminated *History of the Indies* helped to establish the Black Legend of Spanish cruelty.

The Indians [of Hispaniola] were totally deprived of their freedom and were put in the harshest, fiercest, most horrible servitude and captivity which no one who has not seen it can understand. Even beasts enjoy more freedom when they are allowed to graze in the fields. But our Spaniards gave no such opportunity to Indians and truly considered them perpetual slaves, since the Indians had not the free will to dispose of their persons but instead were disposed of according to Spanish greed and cruelty, not as men in captivity but as beasts tied to a rope to prevent free movement. When they were allowed to go home, they often found it deserted and had no other recourse than to go out into the woods to find food and to die. When they fell ill, which was very frequently because they are a delicate people unaccustomed to such work, the Spaniards did not believe them and pitilessly called them lazy dogs and kicked and beat them; and when illness was apparent they sent them home as useless. . . . They would go then, falling into the first stream and dying there in desperation; others would hold on longer but very few ever made it home. I sometimes came upon dead bodies on my way, and upon others who were gasping and moaning in their death agony, repeating "Hungry, hungry." And this was the freedom, the good treatment and the Christianity the Indians received.

About eight years passed under [Spanish rule] and this disorder had time to grow; no one gave it a thought and the multitude of people who originally lived on the island . . . was consumed at such a rate that in these eight years 90 per cent had perished. From here this sweeping plague went to San Juan, Jamaica, Cuba and the continent, spreading destruction over the whole hemisphere.

FROM "DECLARATION OF JOSEPHE" (DECEMBER 19, 1681)

Josephe was a Spanish-speaking Indian questioned by a royal attorney in Mexico City investigating the Pueblo Revolt. The revolt of the Indian population, in 1680, temporarily drove Spanish settlers from present-day New Mexico.

Asked what causes or motives the said Indian rebels had for renouncing the law of God and obedience to his Majesty, and for committing so many of crimes, [he answered] the causes they have were alleged ill treatment and injuries received from [Spanish authorities], because they beat them, took away what they had, and made them work without pay. Thus he replies.

Asked if he has learned if it has come to his notice during the time that he has been here the reason why the apostates burned the images, churches, and things pertaining to divine worship, making a mockery and a trophy of them, killing the priests and doing the other things they did, he said that he knows and had heard it generally stated that while they were besieging the villa the rebellious traitors burned the church and shouted in loud voices, "Now the God of the Spaniards, who was their father, is dead, and Santa Maria, who was their mother, and the saints, who were pieces of rotten wood," saying that only their own god lived. Thus they ordered all the temples and images, crosses and rosaries burned, and their function being over, they all went to bathe in the rivers, saying that they thereby washed away the water of baptism. For their churches, they placed on the four sides and in the center of the plaza some small circular enclosures of stone where they went to offer flour, feathers, and the seed of maguey [a local plant], maize, and tobacco, and performed other superstitious rites, giving the children to understand that they must all do this in the future. The captains and the chiefs ordered that the names of Jesus and Mary should nowhere be uttered. . . . He has seen many houses of idolatry which they have built, dancing the dance of the cachina [part of a traditional Indian religious ceremony], which this declarant has also danced. Thus he replies to the question.

QUESTIONS

1. Why does Las Casas, after describing the ill treatment of Indians, write, "And this was the freedom, the good treatment and the Christianity the Indians received"?

2. What role did religion play in the Pueblo Revolt?

3. What ideas of freedom are apparent in the two documents?

St. Anthony and the Infant Jesus, *painted on a tanned buffalo hide by a Franciscan priest in New Mexico in the early eighteenth century. This was not long after the Spanish reconquered the area, from which they had been driven by the Pueblo Revolt.*

in the area had been destroyed. From their own point of view, the Pueblo Indians had triumphantly reestablished the freedom lost through Spanish conquest.

The Pueblo Revolt was the most complete victory for Native Americans over Europeans and the only wholesale expulsion of settlers in the history of North America. According to a royal attorney who interviewed the Spanish survivors in Mexico City, the revolt arose from the "many oppressions" the Indians had suffered. The victorious Pueblos turned with a vengeance on all symbols of European culture, uprooting fruit trees, destroying cattle, burning churches and images of Christ and the Virgin Mary, and wading into rivers to wash away their Catholic baptisms. They rebuilt their places of worship, called "kivas," and resumed sacred dances the friars had banned. "The God of the Spaniards," they shouted, "is dead."

Cooperation among the Pueblo peoples, however, soon evaporated. By the end of the 1680s, warfare had broken out among several villages, even as Apache and Navajo raids continued. Popé died around 1690. In 1692, the Spanish launched an invasion that reconquered New Mexico. Some communities welcomed them back as a source of military protection. But Spain had learned a lesson. In the eighteenth century, colonial authorities adopted a more tolerant attitude toward traditional religious practices and made fewer demands on Indian labor.

THE FRENCH AND DUTCH EMPIRES

If the Black Legend inspired a sense of superiority among Spain's European rivals, the precious metals that poured from the New World into the Spanish treasury aroused the desire to try to match Spain's success. The establishment of Spain's American empire transformed the balance of power in the world economy. The Atlantic replaced the overland route to Asia as the major axis of global trade. During the seventeenth century, the French, Dutch, and English established colonies in North America. England's mainland colonies, to be discussed in the next chapter, consisted of agricultural settlements with growing populations whose hunger for land produced incessant conflict with native peoples. New France and New Netherland were primarily commercial ventures that never attracted large numbers of colonists. More dependent on Indians as trading partners and military allies, these French and Dutch settlements allowed Native Americans greater freedom than the English.

FRENCH COLONIZATION

The first of Spain's major European rivals to embark on New World explorations was France. The French initially aimed to find gold and to locate a Northwest Passage—a sea route connecting the Atlantic to the Pacific. But the hopes of the early French explorers were soon disappointed, and North America came to seem little more than a barrier to be crossed, not a promising site for settlement or exploitation. For most of the sixteenth century, only explorers, fishermen, pirates preying on Spanish shipping farther south, and, as time went on, fur traders visited the eastern coast of North

America. French efforts to establish settlements in Newfoundland and Nova Scotia failed, beset by native resistance and inadequate planning and financing. Not until the seventeenth century would France, as well as England and the Netherlands, establish permanent settlements in North America.

The explorer Samuel de Champlain, sponsored by a French fur-trading company, founded Quebec in 1608. In 1673, the Jesuit priest Jacques Marquette and the fur trader Louis Joliet located the Mississippi River, and by 1681 René-Robert Cavelier, Sieur de La Salle, had descended to the Gulf of Mexico, claiming the entire Mississippi River valley for France. New France eventually formed a giant arc along the St. Lawrence, Mississippi, and Ohio rivers.

Until 1663, when the population of European origin was fewer than 3,000, French Canada was ruled by the Company of New France through a governor-general appointed in Paris. There was no representative assembly. In that year, the French government established a new company. It granted land along the St. Lawrence River in *seigneuries* to well-connected nobles and army officers who would transport colonists to take their place in a feudal society. But most of the *engagés*, or indentured servants, returned home after their contracts expired. More than 80 percent of the migrants were men. Apart from nuns, fewer than 1,800 women (compared with more than 12,000 men) emigrated to French Canada in the seventeenth century. And during the entire colonial period, only about 250 complete families did so.

By 1700, the number of white inhabitants of New France had risen to only 19,000. With a far larger population than England, France sent many fewer emigrants to the Western Hemisphere. The government at home feared that significant emigration would undermine France's role as a European great power and might compromise its effort to establish trade and good relations with the Indians. Unfavorable reports about America circulated widely in France. Canada was widely depicted as an icebox, a land of savage Indians, a dumping ground for criminals. Most French who left their homes during these years preferred to settle in the Netherlands, Spain, or the West Indies. The revocation in 1685 of the Edict of Nantes, which had extended religious toleration to French Protestants, led well over 100,000 Huguenots to flee their country. But they were not welcome in New France, which the crown desired to remain an outpost of Catholicism.

NEW FRANCE AND THE INDIANS

With its small white population and emphasis on the fur trade rather than agricultural settlement, the viability of New France depended on friendly relations with local Indians. The French prided themselves on adopting a more humane policy than their imperial rivals. "Only our nation," declared one French writer, "knows the secret of winning the Indians' affection." Lacking the voracious appetite for land of the English colonies and relying on Indians to supply furs to trading posts, the French worked out a complex series of military, commercial, and diplomatic connections, the most enduring alliances between Indians and settlers in colonial North America. They neither appropriated substantial amounts

A Native American in present-day Nova Scotia carved this image of a European ship on a rock. Long before explorers and colonists descended on the area, its residents were familiar with Europeans. One chief, Membertou, acquired a French ship and traded with fishermen out at sea.

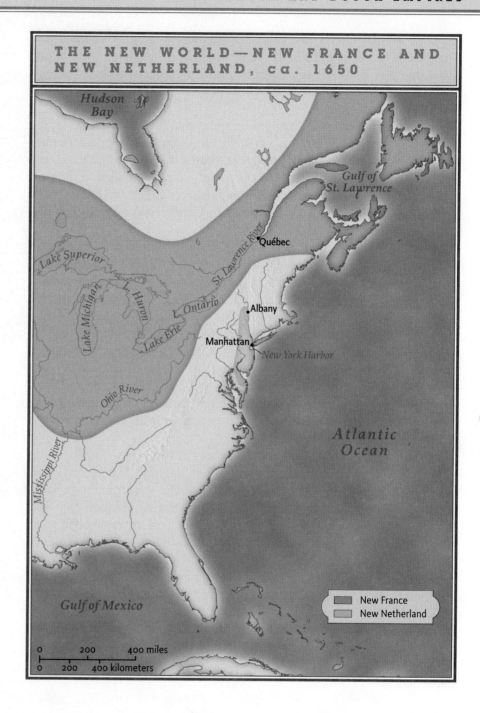

THE NEW WORLD—NEW FRANCE AND NEW NETHERLAND, ca. 1650

New France and New Netherland.

of Indian land, like the English, nor conquered native inhabitants militarily and set them to forced labor, like the Spanish. Samuel de Champlain, the intrepid explorer who dominated the early history of New France, insisted on religious toleration for all Christians and denied that Native Americans were intellectually or culturally inferior to Europeans—two positions that were unusual for his time. Although he occasionally engaged in wars with local Indians, he dreamed of creating a colony based on mutual respect between diverse peoples. The Jesuits, a missionary religious order, did seek, with some success, to convert Indians to Catholicism. But unlike Spanish missionaries in early New Mexico, they

VISIONS OF FREEDOM

France Bringing the Faith to the Indians of New France. *European nations justified colonization, in part, with the argument that they were bringing Christianity—without which true freedom was impossible—to Native Americans. In this painting from the 1670s, attributed to a Franciscan missionary, an Indian kneels before a female representation of France. Both hold a painting of the Trinity. The figure of France points skyward, where God hands the earth to Christ.*

QUESTIONS

1. In what ways does the painting suggest that Indians freely accepted Catholicism and French rule?

2. How do the houses, ship, and dress of the Indian reinforce the painting's message?

This engraving, which appears in Samuel de Champlain's 1613 account of his voyages, is the only likeness of the explorer from his own time. Champlain, wearing European armor and brandishing an arquebus (an advanced weapon of the period), stands at the center of this pitched battle between his Indian allies and hostile Iroquois.

allowed Christian Indians to retain a high degree of independence and much of their traditional social structure, and they did not seek to suppress all traditional religious practices.

Like other colonists throughout North America, however, the French brought striking changes in Indian life. Contact with Europeans was inevitably followed by the spread of disease. Participation in the fur trade drew natives into the burgeoning Atlantic economy, introducing new goods and transforming hunting from a search for food into a quest for marketable commodities. Indians were soon swept into the rivalries among European empires, and Europeans into conflicts among Indians. As early as 1615, the Huron of present-day southern Ontario and upper New York State forged a trading alliance with the French and many converted to Catholicism. In the 1640s, however, after being severely weakened by a smallpox epidemic, the tribe was virtually destroyed in a series of attacks by Iroquois armed by the Dutch.

As in the Spanish empire, New France witnessed considerable cultural exchange and intermixing between colonial and native populations. On the "middle ground" of the upper Great Lakes region in French America, Indians and whites encountered each other for many years on a basis of relative equality. And *métis*, or children of marriages between Indian women and French traders and officials, became guides, traders, and interpreters. Like the Spanish, the French seemed willing to accept Indians as part of colonial society. They encouraged Indians to adopt the European division of labor between men and women, and to speak French. Indians who converted to Catholicism were promised full citizenship. In fact, however, it was far rarer for natives to adopt French ways than for French settlers to become attracted to the "free" life of the Indians. "It happens more commonly," one official complained, "that a Frenchman becomes savage than a savage becomes a Frenchman."

THE DUTCH EMPIRE

In 1609, Henry Hudson, an Englishman employed by the Dutch East India Company, sailed into New York Harbor searching for a Northwest Passage to Asia. Hudson and his crew became the first Europeans to sail up the river that now bears his name. Hudson did not find a route to Asia, but he did encounter abundant fur-bearing animals and Native Americans more than willing to trade furs for European goods. He claimed the area for the Netherlands, and his voyage planted the seeds for what would eventually become a great metropolis, New York City. By 1614, Dutch traders had established an outpost at Fort Orange, near present-day Albany. Ten years later, the Dutch West India Company, which had been awarded a monopoly of Dutch trade with America, settled colonists on Manhattan Island.

These ventures formed one small part in the rise of the Dutch overseas empire. In the early seventeenth century, the Netherlands dominated international commerce, and Amsterdam was Europe's foremost shipping and banking center. The small nation had entered a golden age of rapidly accumulating wealth and stunning achievements in painting, philosophy, and the sciences. The Dutch invented the joint stock company, a way of pooling financial resources and sharing the risk of maritime voyages, which proved central to the development of modern capitalism. With a population of only 2 million, the Netherlands established a far-flung empire that reached from Indonesia to South Africa and the Caribbean and temporarily wrested control of Brazil from Portugal.

DUTCH FREEDOM

The Dutch prided themselves on their devotion to liberty. Indeed, in the early seventeenth century they enjoyed two freedoms not recognized elsewhere in Europe—freedom of the press and broad religious toleration. Even though there was an established church, the Dutch Reformed, individuals could hold whatever religious beliefs they wished. Amsterdam had become a haven for persecuted Protestants from all over Europe, including French Huguenots, German Calvinists, and those, like the Pilgrims, who desired to separate from the Church of England. Jews, especially those fleeing from Spain, also found refuge there. Other emigrants came to the Netherlands in the hope of sharing in the country's prosperity. During the seventeenth century, the nation attracted about half a million migrants from elsewhere in Europe. Many of these newcomers helped to populate the Dutch overseas empire.

FREEDOM IN NEW NETHERLAND

Despite the Dutch reputation for cherishing freedom, New Netherland was hardly governed democratically. New Amsterdam, the main population center, was essentially a fortified military outpost controlled by appointees of the West India Company. Although the governor called on prominent citizens for advice from time to time, neither an elected assembly nor a town council, the basic unit of government at home, was established.

t' Fort nieuw Amsterdam op de Manhatans

A view of New Amsterdam from 1651 illustrates both the tiny size of the outpost but also its status as a center of international trade between Europeans and Native Americans.

In other ways, however, the colonists enjoyed more liberty, especially in religious matters, than their counterparts elsewhere in North America. Even their slaves possessed rights. The Dutch dominated the Atlantic slave trade in the early seventeenth century, and they introduced slaves into New Netherland as a matter of course. By 1650, the colony's 500 slaves outnumbered those in the Chesapeake. Some enjoyed "half-freedom"—they were required to pay an annual fee to the company and work for it when called upon, but they were given land to support their families. Settlers employed slaves on family farms or for household or craft labor, not on large plantations as in the West Indies.

Women in the Dutch settlement enjoyed far more independence than in other colonies. According to Dutch law, married women retained their separate legal identity. They could go to court, borrow money, and own property. Men were used to sharing property with their wives. Their wills generally left their possessions to their widows and daughters as well as sons. Margaret Hardenbroeck, the widow of a New Amsterdam merchant, expanded her husband's business and became one of the town's richest residents after his death in 1661.

Most striking was the religious toleration that attracted to New Netherland a remarkably diverse population. As early as the 1630s, at least eighteen languages were said to be spoken in New Amsterdam, whose residents included not only Dutch settlers but also Africans, Belgians, English, French, Germans, Irish, and Scandinavians. Meanwhile, Puritan emigrants from New England established towns on Long Island. Religious toleration extended not only to Protestants but also to Catholics and, grudgingly, to Jews. Twenty-three Jews arrived in New Amsterdam in 1654 from Brazil and the Caribbean. Referring to them as "members of a deceitful race," Governor Peter Stuyvesant ordered the newcomers to leave. But the compa-

ny overruled him, noting that Jews at home had invested "a large amount of capital" in its shares.

SETTLING NEW NETHERLAND

In an attempt to attract settlers to North America, the Dutch West India Company promised colonists not only religious toleration but also cheap livestock and free land after six years of labor. Eventually, it even surrendered its monopoly of the fur trade, opening this profitable commerce to all comers. Many settlers, Stuyvesant complained, had been lured by "an imaginary liberty" and did not display much respect for the company's authority.

In 1629, the company adopted a plan of "Freedoms and Exemptions," offering large estates to *patroons*—shareholders who agreed to transport tenants for agricultural labor. The patroon was required to purchase title to the land from Indians, but otherwise his "freedoms" were like those of a medieval lord, including the right to 10 percent of his tenants' annual income and complete authority over law enforcement within his domain. Only one patroonship became a going concern, that of Kiliaen van Rensselaer, who acquired some 700,000 acres in the Hudson Valley. His family's autocratic rule over the tenants, as well as its efforts to extend its domain to include lands settled by New Englanders who claimed that they owned their farms, would inspire sporadic uprisings into the mid-nineteenth century.

During the seventeenth century, the Netherlands sent 1 million people overseas (many of them recent immigrants who were not in fact Dutch) to populate and govern their far-flung colonies. Very few, however, made North America their destination. By the mid-1660s, the European population of New Netherland numbered only 9,000. New Netherland remained a tiny backwater in the Dutch empire. So did an even smaller outpost near present-day Wilmington, Delaware, established in 1638 by a group of Dutch merchants. To circumvent the West India Company's trade monopoly, they claimed to be operating under the Swedish flag and called their settlement New Sweden. Only 300 settlers were living there when New Netherland seized the colony in 1655.

NEW NETHERLAND AND THE INDIANS

The Dutch came to North America to trade, not to conquer. They were less interested in settling the land than in exacting profits from it. Mindful of the Black Legend of Spanish cruelty, the Dutch determined to treat the native inhabitants more humanely than the Spanish. Having won their own independence from Spain after the longest and bloodiest war of sixteenth-century Europe, many Dutch identified with American Indians as fellow victims of Spanish oppression. They justified their imperial ambitions, in part, as an effort to liberate the New World from the tyranny of Spain and the Catholic Church. Initially, however, they aimed less to convert the Indian population than to employ it in the profitable fur trade.

From the beginning, Dutch authorities recognized Indian sovereignty over the land and forbade settlement in any area until it had been purchased. But they also required tribes to make payments to colonial authorities.

The seal of New Netherland, adopted by the Dutch West India Company in 1630, suggests the centrality of the fur trade to the colony's prospects. Surrounding the beaver is wampum, a string of beads used by Indians in religious rituals and as currency.

Near the coast, where most newcomers settled, New Netherland was hardly free of conflict with the Indians. The expansionist ambitions of Governor William Kieft, who in the 1640s began seizing fertile farmland from the nearby Algonquian Indians, sparked a three-year war that resulted in the death of 1,000 Indians and more than 200 colonists. With the powerful Iroquois Confederacy of the upper Hudson Valley, however, the Dutch established friendly commercial and diplomatic relations.

Thus, before the planting of English colonies in North America, other European nations had established various kinds of settlements in the New World. Despite their differences, the Spanish, French, and Dutch empires shared certain features. All brought Christianity, new forms of technology and learning, new legal systems and family relations, and new forms of economic enterprise and wealth creation. They also brought savage warfare and widespread disease. These empires were aware of one another's existence. They studied and borrowed from one another, each lauding itself as superior to the others.

From the outset, dreams of freedom—for Indians, for settlers, for the entire world through the spread of Christianity—inspired and justified colonization. It would be no different when, at the beginning of the seventeenth century, England entered the struggle for empire in North America.

A map of the Western Hemisphere, published in 1592 in Antwerp, then ruled by Spain and now part of Belgium. It shows North America divided between New France and New Spain before the coming of the English.

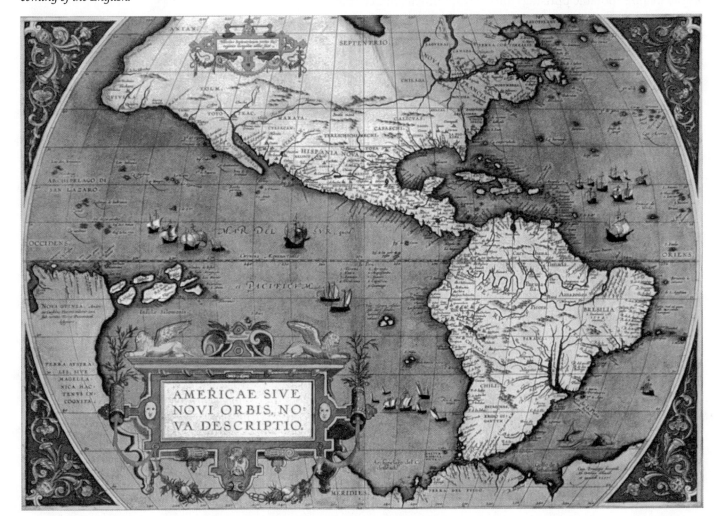

SUGGESTED READING

BOOKS

Bailyn, Bernard. *Atlantic History: Concept and Contours* (2005). Argues for writing the history of the entire Atlantic region, rather than any particular nation or empire.

Bender, Thomas. *A Nation among Nations: America's Place in World History* (2006). Attempts to place American history in an international context; the opening chapters offer a global portrait of the age of exploration and conquest.

Calloway, Colin G. *One Vast Winter Count: The American West before Lewis and Clark* (2003). A comprehensive portrait of Indian life in one key region of North America.

Crosby, Alfred J. *The Columbian Exchange: Biological and Cultural Consequences of 1492* (1972). Examines the flow of goods and diseases across the Atlantic and their consequences.

Elliott, J. H. *Empires of the Atlantic World: Britain and Spain in America 1492–1830* (2006). A fascinating comparison of the development of two New World empires.

Fernández-Armesto, Felipe. *Pathfinders: A Global History of Exploration* (2006). A history of explorations throughout the centuries, including those of the fifteenth and sixteenth centuries.

Fischer, David H. *Champlain's Dream* (2008). A lively account of Samuel de Champlain's effort to built a French colony in North America based on toleration and mutual respect between settlers and Native Americans.

Gibson, Charles. *Spain in America* (1966). Surveys the history of Spain's American empire.

Gutiérrez, Ramón A. *When Jesus Came, the Corn Mothers Went Away: Marriage, Sexuality, and Power in New Mexico, 1500–1846* (1991). Discusses the changes in Indian life in New Mexico as a result of Spanish colonization.

Knaut, Andrew L. *The Pueblo Revolt of 1680: Conquest and Resistance in Seventeenth-Century New Mexico* (1997). A recent account of the largest revolt of native peoples.

Mann, Charles C. *1491: New Revelations of the Americas before Columbus* (2005). A comprehensive portrait of life in the Western Hemisphere before the arrival of Europeans.

Parry, J. H. *The Age of Reconnaissance* (1981). A global history of the era of European exploration and colonization.

Richter, Daniel K. *Facing East from Indian Country* (2001). Examines the era of exploration and settlement as viewed through the experience of Native Americans.

———. *The Ordeal of the Longhouse: The Peoples of the Iroquois League in the Era of European Colonization* (1992). Describes life among one of the most important Indian groups before and after the arrival of Europeans.

WEBSITES

Archive of Early American Images: www.brown.edu/Facilities/John_Carter_Brown_Library/pages/ea_hmpg.html

Exploring the Early Americas: www.loc.gov/exhibits/earlyamericas/

France in America: http://international.loc.gov/intldl/fiahtml/fiahome.html

Jamestown, Québec, Santa Fe: Three North American Beginnings: http://americanhistory.si.edu/exhibitions/small_exhibition.cfm?key=1267&exkey=244

REVIEW QUESTIONS

1. Describe why the "discovery" of America was one of the "most important events recorded in the history of mankind," according to Adam Smith.

2. Using what you read in this chapter about the movement of peoples, explain how North America became the location where East and West came together.

3. One of the most striking features of the Native American society at the time of European discovery was its sheer diversity. Support this statement.

4. Compare and contrast European values and ways of life to that of the Indians. Be sure to look at religion, views on property ownership, gender relations, and views of freedom.

5. What were the main factors fueling the European age of expansion?

6. Describe the political, religious, and economic motivations for Spanish conquest.

7. Compare the political, economic, and religious motivations behind the French and Dutch empires with those of New Spain.

8. Describe how the attitudes and actions of the French and Dutch differed from those of Spain.

9. How would European settlers explain their superiority to Native Americans and justify both the conquest of Native lands and terminating their freedom?

FREEDOM QUESTIONS

1. Although some European observers believed Native Americans embodied freedom, most reached the conclusion that Native Americans did not know what freedom was because they were "too free." On what basis did they make this claim?

2. On the eve of colonization, European concepts of freedom bore little resemblance to our modern concepts of personal liberties. Explain how the ideals of "Christian liberty," obedience to authority, and adhering to one's social rank shaped the fifteenth-century idea of freedom.

3. Spanish and French settlers both claimed to be freeing Native Americans by bringing them advanced civilization and Catholicism. Justify this claim with specific examples as either of these European powers would have at the time.

4. How did Popé's revolt in 1680 immediately restore freedom to the Pueblo Indians, and what happened once the Spanish returned?

5. Both at home and in the New World, the Dutch enjoyed greater freedoms than other European citizens. Explore this comparison using specific examples.

KEY TERMS

maize (p. 8)

Tenochtitlán (p. 10)

Cahokia (p. 11)

Iroquois (p. 12)

"Christian liberty" (p. 18)

Zheng He (p. 20)

caravel (p. 20)

factories (p. 22)

reconquista (p. 23)

Columbian Exchange (p. 26)

peninsulares (p. 29)

mestizos (p. 29)

encomienda system (p. 33)

Black Legend (p. 33)

Pueblo Revolt (p. 37)

Popé (p. 37)

Huguenots (p. 41)

métis (p. 44)

patroons (p. 47)

wampum (p. 47)

REVIEW TABLE

Early Explorers of the New World

Explorer	Dates	Area Explored
Christopher Columbus	1492	Caribbean and Central America
John Cabot	1497	Newfoundland
Amerigo Vespucci	1499–1502	Coast of Brazil, Gulf of Mexico
Pedro Cabral	1500	South America (Brazil)
Juan Ponce de León	1513	Florida
Ferdinand Magellan	1519–1522	Sailed around the world
Hernando de Soto	1539–1541	American Southwest
Francisco Vásquez de Coronado	1540–1541	American Southwest
Juan Oñate	1598	American Southwest
Nicolás de Ovando	1502	Hispaniola
Vasco Núñez de Balboa	1513	Panama Isthmus
Francisco Pizarro	1530s	Peru
Samuel de Champlain	1608	Canada and Quebec
Henry Hudson	1609	Hudson River and New York
Jacques Marquette and Louis Joliet	1673	Mississippi River

CHAPTER 2

Beginnings of English America, 1607–1660

The Armada Portrait *of Queen Elizabeth I, by the artist George Gower, commemorates the defeat of the Spanish Armada in 1588 and appears to link it with English colonization of the New World. England's victorious navy is visible through the window, while the queen's hand rests on a globe, with her fingers pointing to the coast of North America.*

FOCUS QUESTIONS

• What were the main contours of English colonization in the seventeenth century?

• What obstacles did the English settlers in the Chesapeake overcome?

• How did Virginia and Maryland develop in their early years?

• What made the English settlement of New England distinctive?

• What were the main sources of discord in early New England?

• How did the English Civil War affect the colonies in America?

On April 26, 1607, three small ships carrying colonists from England sailed out of the morning mist at what is now called Cape Henry into the mouth of Chesapeake Bay. After exploring the area for a little over two weeks, they chose a site sixty miles inland on the James River for their settlement, hoping to protect themselves from marauding Spanish warships. Here they established Jamestown (named for the king of England) as the capital of the colony of Virginia (named for his predecessor, Elizabeth I, the "virgin queen"). But despite these bows to royal authority, the voyage was sponsored not by the English government, which in 1607 was hard-pressed for funds, but by the Virginia Company, a private business organization whose shareholders included merchants, aristocrats, and members of Parliament, and to which the queen had given her blessing before her death in 1603.

When the three ships returned home, 104 settlers remained in Virginia. All were men, for the Virginia Company had more interest in searching for gold and in other ways exploiting the area's natural resources than in establishing a functioning society. Nevertheless, Jamestown became the first permanent English settlement in the area that is now the United States. The settlers were the first of tens of thousands of Europeans who crossed the Atlantic during the seventeenth century to live and work in North America. They led the way for new empires that mobilized labor and economic resources, reshaped societies throughout the Atlantic world, and shifted the balance of power at home from Spain and Portugal to the nations of northwestern Europe.

The founding of Jamestown took place at a time of heightened European involvement in North America. Interest in colonization was spurred by national and religious rivalries and the growth of a merchant class eager to invest in overseas expansion and to seize for itself a greater share of world trade. As noted in Chapter 1, it was quickly followed by the founding of Quebec by France in 1608, and Henry Hudson's exploration in 1609 of the river that today bears his name, leading to the founding of the Dutch colony of New Netherland. In 1610, the Spanish established Santa Fe as the capital of New Mexico. More than a century after the voyages of Columbus, the European penetration of North America had finally begun in earnest. It occurred from many directions at once—from east to west at the Atlantic coast, north to south along the St. Lawrence and Mississippi rivers, and south to north in what is now the American Southwest.

English North America in the seventeenth century was a place where entrepreneurs sought to make fortunes, religious minorities hoped to worship without governmental interference and to create societies based on biblical teachings, and aristocrats dreamed of re-creating a vanished world of feudalism. Those who drew up blueprints for settlement expected to reproduce the social structure with which they were familiar, with all its hierarchy and inequality. The lower orders would occupy the

same less-than-fully-free status as in England, subject to laws regulating their labor and depriving them of a role in politics. But for ordinary men and women, emigration offered an escape from lives of deprivation and inequality. "No man," wrote John Smith, an early leader of Jamestown, "will go from [England] to have less freedom" in America. The charter of the Virginia Company, granted by James I in 1606, promised that colonists would enjoy "all liberties" of those residing in "our realm of England." The settlers of English America came to enjoy greater rights than colonists of other empires, including the power to choose members of elected assemblies, protections of the common law such as the right to trial by jury, and access to land, the key to economic independence.

Many degrees of freedom coexisted in seventeenth-century North America, from the slave, stripped completely of liberty, to the independent landowner, who enjoyed a full range of rights. During a lifetime, a person might well occupy more than one place on this spectrum. The settlers' success, however, rested on depriving Native Americans of their land and, in some colonies, on importing large numbers of African slaves as laborers. Freedom and lack of freedom expanded together in seventeenth-century America.

ENGLAND AND THE NEW WORLD

UNIFYING THE ENGLISH NATION

Although John Cabot, sailing from England in 1497, had been the first European since the Vikings to encounter the North American continent, English exploration and colonization would wait for many years. As the case of Spain suggests, early empire building was, in large part, an extension of the consolidation of national power in Europe. But during the sixteenth century, England was a second-rate power racked by internal disunity. Henry VII, who assumed the throne in 1485, had to unify the kingdom after a long period of civil war. His son and successor, Henry VIII, launched the Reformation in England. When the Pope refused to annul his marriage to Catherine of Aragon, Henry severed the nation from the Catholic Church. In its place he established the Church of England, or Anglican Church, with himself at the head. Decades of religious strife followed. Under Henry's son Edward VI, who became king at the age of ten in 1547, the regents who governed the country persecuted Catholics. When Edward died in 1553, his half sister Mary became queen. Mary temporarily restored Catholicism as the state religion and executed a number of Protestants. Her rule was so unpopular that reconciliation with Rome became impossible. Mary's successor, Elizabeth I (reigned 1558–1603), restored the Anglican ascendancy and executed more than 100 Catholic priests.

Mary Tudor, the queen who tried to restore Catholicism in England, as painted in 1554 by Antonio Moro, who made numerous portraits of European royalty. He depicts her as a woman of firm determination.

ENGLAND AND IRELAND

England's long struggle to conquer and pacify Ireland, which lasted well into the seventeenth century, absorbed money and energy that might have been directed toward the New World. In subduing Ireland, whose Catholic population was deemed a threat to the stability of Protestant rule in England, the government employed a variety of approaches, including military conquest, the slaughter of civilians, the seizure of land and introduction of English economic practices, and the dispatch of large numbers of settlers. Rather than seeking to absorb the Irish into English society, the English excluded the native population from a territory of settlement known as the Pale, where the colonists created their own social order.

Just as the "reconquest" of Spain from the Moors established patterns that would be repeated in Spanish New World colonization, the methods used in Ireland anticipated policies England would undertake in America. Some sixteenth-century English writers directly compared the allegedly barbaric "wild Irish" with American Indians. Like the Indians, the Irish supposedly confused liberty and license. They refused to respect English authority and resisted conversion to English Protestantism. The early English colonies in North America and the West Indies were known as "plantations" (that is, communities "planted" from abroad among an alien population); the same term was originally used to describe Protestant settlements in Ireland.

ENGLAND AND NORTH AMERICA

Not until the reign of Elizabeth I did the English turn their attention to North America, although sailors and adventurers still showed more interest in raiding Spanish cities and treasure fleets in the Caribbean than establishing settlements. The government granted charters (grants of exclusive rights and privileges) to Sir Humphrey Gilbert and Sir Walter Raleigh, authorizing them to establish colonies in North America at their own expense.

With little or no support from the crown, both ventures failed. Gilbert, who had earned a reputation for brutality in the Irish wars by murdering civilians and burning their crops, established a short-lived settlement on Newfoundland in 1582. Three years later, Raleigh dispatched a fleet of five ships with some 100 colonists (many of them his personal servants) to set up a base on Roanoke Island, off the North Carolina coast, partly to facilitate continuing raids on Spanish shipping. But the colonists, mostly young men under military leadership, abandoned the venture in 1586 and returned to England. A second group of 100 settlers, composed of families who hoped to establish a permanent colony, was dispatched that year. Their fate remains a mystery. When a ship bearing supplies arrived in 1590, the sailors found the colony abandoned, with the inhabitants evidently having moved to live among the Indians. The word "Croaton," the Indian name for a nearby island or tribe, had been carved on a tree. Raleigh, by now nearly bankrupt, lost his enthusiasm for colonization. To establish a successful colony, it seemed clear, would require more planning and economic resources than any individual could provide.

SPREADING PROTESTANTISM

As in the case of Spain, national glory, profit, and religious mission merged in early English thinking about the New World. The Reformation heightened the English government's sense of Catholic Spain as its mortal enemy (a belief reinforced in 1588 when a Spanish naval armada unsuccessfully attempted to invade the British Isles). Just as Spain justified its empire in part by claiming to convert Indians to Catholicism, England expressed its imperial ambitions in terms of an obligation to liberate the New World from the tyranny of the Pope. By the late sixteenth century, anti-Catholicism had become deeply ingrained in English popular culture. Reports of the atrocities of Spanish rule were widely circulated. English translations of Bartolomé de Las Casas's writings appeared during Elizabeth's reign. One, using a common Protestant term for the Catholic Church, bore the title, "Popery Truly Displayed."

Although atrocities were hardly confined to any one nation—as England's own conduct in Ireland demonstrated—the idea that the empire of Catholic Spain was uniquely murderous and tyrannical enabled the English to describe their own imperial ambitions in the language of freedom. In *A Discourse Concerning Western Planting*, written in 1584 at the request of Sir Walter Raleigh, the Protestant minister and scholar Richard Hakluyt listed twenty-three reasons why Queen Elizabeth I should support the establishment of colonies. Among them was the idea that English settlements would strike a blow against Spain's empire and therefore form part of a divine mission to rescue the New World and its inhabitants from the influence of Catholicism and tyranny. "Tied as slaves" under Spanish rule, he wrote, the Indians of the New World were "crying out to us ... to come and help." They would welcome English settlers and "revolt clean from the Spaniard," crying "with one voice, Liberta, Liberta, as desirous of liberty and freedom." England would repeat much of Spain's behavior in the New World. But the English always believed that they were unique. In their case, empire and freedom would go hand in hand.

An engraving by Theodor de Bry depicts colonists hunting and fishing in Virginia. Promotional images such as this emphasized the abundance of the New World and suggested that colonists could live familiar lives there.

MOTIVES FOR COLONIZATION

But bringing freedom to Indians was hardly the only argument Hakluyt marshaled as England prepared to step onto the world stage. National power and glory were never far from the minds of the era's propagandists of empire. Through colonization, Hakluyt and other writers argued, England, a relatively minor power in Europe at the end of the sixteenth century, could come to rival the wealth and standing of great nations like Spain and France.

Other considerations also weighed heavily in their arguments. Spanish claims to the south and French explorations in the area of present-day Canada left to England the middle part of North America, a region deemed worthless by other powers because it lacked

precious metals and was unsuitable for sugar cultivation, the two paths to riches in early American empires. This did not, however, prevent promoters of colonization from painting a portrait of a fertile land of "great plenty." Its animals were supposedly so abundant and its climate and soil so favorable that colonists could enrich the mother country and themselves by providing English consumers with goods now supplied by foreigners and opening a new market for English products. Unlike early adventurers such as Raleigh, who thought of wealth in terms of deposits of gold, Hakluyt insisted that trade would be the basis of England's empire.

THE SOCIAL CRISIS

Equally important, America could be a refuge for England's "surplus" population, benefiting mother country and emigrants alike. The late sixteenth century was a time of social crisis in England, with economic growth unable to keep pace with the needs of a population that grew from 3 million in 1550 to about 4 million in 1600. For many years, English peasants had enjoyed a secure hold on their plots of land. But in the sixteenth and seventeenth centuries, landlords sought profits by raising sheep for the expanding trade in wool and introducing more modern farming practices such as crop rotation. They evicted small farmers and fenced in "commons" previously open to all.

While many landlords, farmers, and town merchants benefited from the "enclosure" movement, as this process was called, thousands of persons were uprooted from the land. Many flooded into England's cities, where wages fell dramatically. Others, denounced by authorities as rogues, vagabonds, and vagrants, wandered the roads in search of work. Their situation grew worse as prices throughout Europe rose, buoyed by the influx of gold and silver from the mines of Latin America into Spain. A pioneering study of English society conducted at the end of the seventeenth century estimated that half the population lived at or below the poverty line. The cost of poor relief fell mainly on local communities. "All our towns," wrote the Puritan leader John Winthrop in 1629, shortly before leaving England for Massachusetts, "complain of the burden of poor people and strive by all means to rid any such as they have." England, he added somberly, "grows weary of her inhabitants."

The government struggled to deal with this social crisis. Under Henry VIII, those without jobs could be whipped, branded, forced into the army, or hanged. During Elizabeth's reign, a law authorized justices of the peace to regulate hours and wages and put the unemployed to work. "Vagrants" were required to accept any job offered to them and could be punished if they sought to change employment. Another solution was to encourage the unruly poor to leave for the New World. Richard Hakluyt wrote of the advantages of settling in America "such needy people of our country who now

William Hogarth's well-known engraving Gin Lane *(1751) offers a satiric glimpse of lower-class life in London. Hogarth was particularly concerned about the abuse of alcohol. A drunken woman allows her baby to fall from her arms while, on the left, a man and his wife pawn their coats, tools, and cooking utensils for money for liquor.*

trouble the commonwealth and ... commit outrageous offenses." As colonists, they could become productive citizens, contributing to the nation's wealth.

MASTERLESS MEN

As early as 1516, when Thomas More published *Utopia*, a novel set on an imaginary island in the Western Hemisphere, the image of America as a place where settlers could escape from the economic inequalities of Europe had been circulating in England. This ideal coincided with the goals of ordinary Englishmen. Although authorities saw wandering or unemployed "masterless men" as a danger to society and tried to force them to accept jobs, popular attitudes viewed economic dependence as itself a form of servitude. Working for wages was widely associated with servility and loss of liberty. Only those who controlled their own labor could be regarded as truly free. Indeed, popular tales and ballads romanticized the very vagabonds, highwaymen, and even beggars denounced by the propertied and powerful, since despite their poverty they at least enjoyed freedom from wage work.

The image of the New World as a unique place of opportunity, where the English laboring classes could regain economic independence by acquiring land and where even criminals would enjoy a second chance, was deeply rooted from the earliest days of settlement. John Smith had scarcely landed in Virginia in 1607 when he wrote that in America "every man may be the master and owner of his own labor and land." In 1623, the royal letter approving the recruitment of emigrants to New England promised that any settler could easily become "lord of 200 acres of land"—an amount far beyond the reach of most Englishmen. The main lure for emigrants from England to the New World was not so much riches in gold and silver as the promise of independence that followed from owning land. Economic freedom and the possibility of passing it on to one's children attracted the largest number of English colonists.

THE COMING OF THE ENGLISH

ENGLISH EMIGRANTS

Seventeenth-century North America was an unstable and dangerous environment. Diseases decimated Indian and settler populations alike. Colonies were racked by religious, political, and economic tensions and drawn into imperial wars and conflict with Indians. They remained dependent on the mother country for protection and economic assistance. Without sustained immigration, most settlements would have collapsed. With a population of between 4 million and 5 million, about half that of Spain and a quarter of that of France, England produced a far larger number of men, women, and children willing to brave the dangers of emigration to the New World. In large part, this was because economic conditions in England were so bad.

Between 1607 and 1700, more than half a million people left England.

A pamphlet published in 1609 promoting emigration to Virginia.

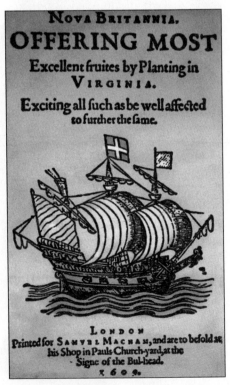

North America was not the destination of the majority of these emigrants. Approximately 180,000 settled in Ireland, and about the same number migrated to the West Indies, where the introduction of sugar cultivation promised riches for those who could obtain land. Nonetheless, the population of England's mainland colonies quickly outstripped that of their rivals. The Chesapeake area, where the tobacco-producing colonies of Virginia and Maryland developed a constant demand for cheap labor, received about 120,000 settlers, most of whom landed before 1660. New England attracted 21,000 emigrants, nearly all of them arriving before 1640. In the second part of the seventeenth century, the Middle Colonies (New York, New Jersey, and Pennsylvania) attracted about 23,000 settlers. Although the arrivals to New England and the Middle Colonies included many families, the majority of newcomers were young, single men from the bottom rungs of English society, who had little to lose by emigrating. Many had already moved from place to place in England. Colonial settlement was in many ways an extension of the migration at home of an increasingly mobile English population.

INDENTURED SERVANTS

Settlers who could pay for their own passage—government officials, clergymen, merchants, artisans, landowning farmers, and members of the lesser nobility—arrived in America as free persons. Most quickly acquired land. In the seventeenth century, however, nearly two-thirds of English settlers came as indentured servants, who voluntarily surrendered their freedom for a specified time (usually five to seven years) in exchange for passage to America.

Like slaves, servants could be bought and sold, could not marry without the permission of their owner, were subject to physical punishment, and saw their obligation to labor enforced by the courts. To ensure uninterrupted work by female servants, the law lengthened the term of their indenture if they became pregnant. "Many Negroes are better used," complained Elizabeth Sprigs, an indentured servant in Maryland who described being forced to work "day and night . . . then tied up and whipped." But, unlike slaves, servants could look forward to a release from bondage. Assuming they survived their period of labor, servants would receive a payment known as "freedom dues" and become free members of society.

For most of the seventeenth century, however, indentured servitude was not a guaranteed route to economic autonomy. Given the high death rate, many servants did not live to the end of their terms. Freedom dues were sometimes so meager that they did not enable recipients to acquire land. Many servants found the reality of life in the New World less appealing than they had anticipated. Employers constantly complained of servants running away, not working diligently, or being unruly, all manifestations of what one commentator called their "fondness for freedom."

LAND AND LIBERTY

Access to land played many roles in seventeenth-century America. Land, English settlers believed, was the basis of liberty. Owning land gave men

An indenture (a contract for labor for a period of years) signed by James Mahoney, who emigrated from Ireland to North America in 1723.

control over their own labor and, in most colonies, the right to vote. The promise of immediate access to land lured free settlers, and freedom dues that included land persuaded potential immigrants to sign contracts as indentured servants. Land in America also became a way for the king to reward relatives and allies. Each colony was launched with a huge grant of land from the crown, either to a company or to a private individual known as a proprietor. Some grants, if taken literally, stretched from the Atlantic Ocean to the Pacific.

Land was a source of wealth and power for colonial officials and their favorites, who acquired enormous estates. Without labor, however, land would have little value. Since emigrants did not come to America intending to work the land of others (except temporarily in the case of indentured servants), the very abundance of "free" land eventually led many property owners to turn to slaves as a workforce.

ENGLISHMEN AND INDIANS

Land in North America, of course, was already occupied. And the arrival of English settlers presented the native inhabitants of eastern North America with the greatest crisis in their history. Unlike the Spanish, English colonists did not call themselves "conquerors." They wanted land, not dominion over the existing population. They were chiefly interested in displacing the Indians and settling on their land, not intermarrying with them, organizing their labor, or making them subjects of the crown. The marriage between John Rolfe and Pocahontas, the daughter of Virginia's leading chief, discussed below, is well known but almost unique. No such mixed marriage took place in seventeenth-century Massachusetts and only two more in Virginia before the legislature outlawed the practice in 1691. The English exchanged goods with the native population, and Indians often traveled through colonial settlements. Fur traders on the frontiers of settlement sometimes married Indian women, partly as a way of gaining access to native societies and the kin networks essential to economic relationships. Most English settlers, however, remained obstinately separate from their Indian neighbors.

Despite their insistence that Indians had no real claim to the land since they did not cultivate or improve it, most colonial authorities in practice recognized Indians' title based on occupancy. They acquired land by purchase, often in treaties forced upon Indians after they had suffered military defeat. Colonial courts recorded numerous sales of Indian land to governments or individual settlers. To keep the peace, some colonial governments tried to prevent the private seizure or purchase of Indian lands, or they declared certain areas off-limits to settlers. But these measures were rarely enforced and ultimately proved ineffective.

An engraving by John White of an Indian village surrounded by a stockade.

New settlers and freed servants sought land for themselves, and those who established families in America needed land for their children.

The seventeenth century was marked by recurrent warfare between colonists and Indians. These conflicts generated a strong feeling of superiority among the colonists and left them intent on maintaining the real and imagined boundaries separating the two peoples. In the initial stages of settlement, English colonists often established towns on sites Indians had cleared, planted Indian crops, and adopted Indian technology such as snowshoes and canoes, which were valuable for travel in the American wilderness. But over time the English displaced the original inhabitants more thoroughly than any other European empire.

THE TRANSFORMATION OF INDIAN LIFE

Many eastern Indians initially welcomed the newcomers, or at least their goods, which they appreciated for their practical advantages. Items like woven cloth, metal kettles, iron axes, fishhooks, hoes, and guns were quickly integrated into Indian life. Indians also displayed a great desire for goods like colorful glass beads and copper ornaments that could be incorporated into their religious ceremonies.

As Indians became integrated into the Atlantic economy, subtle changes took place in Indian life. European metal goods changed their farming, hunting, and cooking practices. Men devoted more time to hunting beaver for fur trading. Older skills deteriorated as the use of European products expanded, and alcohol became increasingly common and disruptive. Indians learned to bargain effectively and to supply items that Europeans desired. Later observers would describe this trade as one in which Indians exchanged valuable commodities like furs and animal skins for worthless European trinkets. In fact, both Europeans and Indians gave up goods they had in abundance in exchange for items in short supply in their own society. But as the colonists achieved military superiority over the Indians, the profits of trade mostly flowed to colonial and European merchants. Growing connections with Europeans stimulated warfare among Indian tribes, and the overhunting of beaver and deer forced some groups to encroach on territory claimed by others. And newcomers from Europe brought epidemics that decimated Indian populations.

CHANGES IN THE LAND

Traders, religious missionaries, and colonial authorities all sought to reshape Indian society and culture. But as settlers spread over the land, they threatened Indians' ways of life more completely than any company of soldiers or group of bureaucrats. As settlers fenced in more and more land and introduced new crops and livestock, the natural environment changed in ways that undermined traditional Indian agriculture and hunting. Pigs and cattle roamed freely, trampling Indian cornfields and gardens. The need for wood to build

The only known contemporary portrait of a New England Indian, this 1681 painting by an unnamed artist was long thought to represent Ninigret II, a leader of the Narragansetts of Rhode Island. It has been more recently identified as David, an Indian who saved the life of John Winthrop II, a governor of colonial Connecticut. Apart from the wampum beads around his neck, everything the Indian wears is of English manufacture.

and heat homes and export to England depleted forests on which Indians relied for hunting. The rapid expansion of the fur trade diminished the population of beaver and other animals. "Since you are here strangers, and come into our country," one group of Indians told early settlers in the Chesapeake, "you should rather conform yourselves to the customs of our country, than impose yours on us." But it was the Indians whose lives were most powerfully altered by the changes set in motion in 1607 when English colonists landed at Jamestown.

SETTLING THE CHESAPEAKE

THE JAMESTOWN COLONY

The early history of Jamestown was, to say the least, not promising. The colony's leadership changed repeatedly, its inhabitants suffered an extraordinarily high death rate, and, with the company seeking a quick profit, supplies from England proved inadequate. The hopes of locating riches such as the Spanish had found in Mexico were quickly dashed. "Silver and gold they have none," one Spanish observer commented, their local resources were "not much to be regarded," and they had "no commerce with any nation." The first settlers were "a quarrelsome band of gentlemen and servants." They included few farmers and laborers and numerous sons of English gentry and high-status craftsmen (jewelers, stonecutters, and the like), who preferred to prospect for gold rather than farm. They "would rather starve than work," declared John Smith, one of the colony's first leaders.

Jamestown lay beside a swamp containing malaria-carrying mosquitoes, and the garbage settlers dumped into the local river bred germs that caused dysentery and typhoid fever. Disease and lack of food took a heavy toll. By the end of the first year, the original population of 104 had fallen by half. New arrivals (including the first two women, who landed in 1608) brought the numbers up to 400 in 1609, but by 1610, after a winter long remembered as the "starving time," only 65 settlers remained alive. At one point, the survivors abandoned Jamestown and sailed for England, only to be intercepted and persuaded to return to Virginia by ships carrying a new governor, 250 colonists, and supplies. By 1616, about 80 percent of the immigrants who had arrived in the first decade were dead.

Only rigorous military discipline held the colony together. John Smith was a forceful man whose career before coming to America included a period fighting the Turks in Hungary, where he was captured and for a time enslaved. He imposed a regime of forced labor on company lands. "He that will not work, shall not eat," Smith declared. Smith's autocratic mode of governing alienated many of

By 1650, English settlement in the Chesapeake had spread well beyond the initial colony at Jamestown, as tobacco planters sought fertile land near navigable waterways.

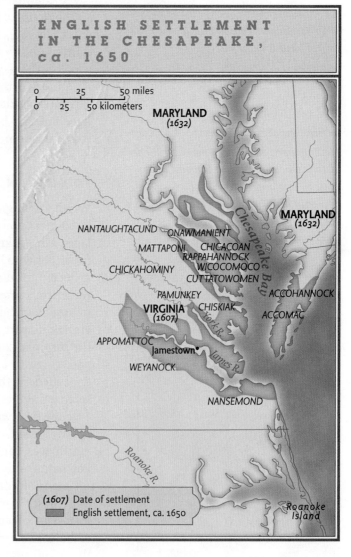

ENGLISH SETTLEMENT
IN THE CHESAPEAKE,
ca. 1650

MARYLAND
(1632)

MARYLAND
(1632)

NANTAUGHTACUND ONAWMANIENT

MATTAPONI CHICACOAN
RAPPAHANNOCK
CHICKAHOMINY WICOCOMOCO
CUTTATOWOMEN

PAMUNKEY ACCOHANNOCK

VIRGINIA CHISKIAK
(1607) ACCOMAC

APPOMATTOC
Jamestown•

WEYANOCK

NANSEMOND

Chesapeake Bay

York R.
James R.
Roanoke R.

(1607) Date of settlement
English settlement, ca. 1650

Roanoke
Island

0 25 50 miles
0 25 50 kilometers

A portrait of John Smith, the leader of the early Virginia colony, engraved on a 1624 map of New England.

The only portrait of Pocahontas during her lifetime was engraved by Simon van de Passe in England in 1616. After converting to Christianity, Pocahontas took the name Rebecca.

the colonists. After being injured in an accidental gunpowder explosion in 1609, he was forced to return to England. But his immediate successors continued his iron rule.

FROM COMPANY TO SOCIETY

The Virginia Company slowly realized that for the colony to survive it would have to abandon the search for gold, grow its own food, and find a marketable commodity. It would also have to attract more settlers. With this end in view, it announced new policies in 1618 that powerfully shaped Virginia's development as a functioning society rather than an outpost of London-based investors. Instead of retaining all the land for itself, the company introduced the headright system, awarding fifty acres of land to any colonist who paid for his own or another's passage. Thus, anyone who brought in a sizable number of servants would immediately acquire a large estate. In place of the governor's militaristic regime, a "charter of grants and liberties" was issued, including the establishment of a House of Burgesses. When it convened in 1619, this became the first elected assembly in colonial America.

The House of Burgesses was hardly a model of democracy—only landowners could vote, and the company and its appointed governor retained the right to nullify any measure the body adopted. But its creation established a political precedent that all English colonies would eventually follow. Also in 1619, the first twenty blacks arrived in Virginia on a Dutch vessel. The full significance of these two events would not be apparent until years later. But they laid the foundation for a society that would one day be dominated economically and politically by slaveowning planters.

POWHATAN AND POCAHONTAS

When the English arrived at Jamestown, they landed in an area inhabited by some 15,000 to 25,000 Indians living in numerous small agricultural villages. Most acknowledged the rule of Wahunsonacock, a shrewd and forceful leader who had recently consolidated his authority over the region and collected tribute from some thirty subordinate tribes. Called Powhatan by the settlers after the Indian word for both his tribe and his title of paramount chief, he quickly realized the advantages of trade with the newcomers. For its part, mindful of Las Casas's condemnation of Spanish behavior, the Virginia Company instructed its colonists to treat local Indians kindly and to try to convert them to Christianity. Realizing that the colonists depended on the Indians for food, John Smith tried to stop settlers from seizing produce from nearby villages, lest the Indians cut off all trade.

In the first two years of Jamestown's existence, relations with Indians were mostly peaceful and based on a fairly equal give-and-take. At one point, Smith was captured by the Indians and threatened with execution by Powhatan, only to be rescued by Pocahontas, reputedly the favorite among his many children by dozens of wives. The incident has come down in legend (most recently a popular animated film) as an example of a rebellious, love-struck teenager defying her father. In fact, it was probably part of an elaborate ceremony designed by Powhatan to demonstrate his power over the colonists and incorporate them into his realm. Pocahontas subsequently became an intermediary between the two peoples, bringing food and messages to Jamestown.

John Smith's return to England raised tensions between the two groups and a period of sporadic conflict began in 1610, with the English massacring villagers indiscriminately and destroying Indian crops. Pocahontas herself was captured and held as a hostage by the settlers in 1613. While confined to Jamestown, she converted to Christianity. As part of the restoration of peace in 1614, she married the English colonist John Rolfe. Two years later, she accompanied her husband to England, where she caused a sensation in the court of James I as a symbol of Anglo-Indian harmony and missionary success. But she succumbed to disease in 1617. Her father died the following year.

THE UPRISING OF 1622

Once it became clear that the English were interested in establishing a permanent and constantly expanding colony, not a trading post, conflict with local Indians was inevitable. The peace that began in 1614 ended abruptly in 1622 when Powhatan's brother and successor, Opechancanough, led a brilliantly planned surprise attack that in a single day wiped out one-quarter of Virginia's settler population of 1,200. The surviving 900 colonists organized themselves into military bands, which then massacred scores of Indians and devastated their villages. A spokesman for the Virginia Company explained the reason behind the Indian assault: "The daily fear that . . . in time we by our growing continually upon them would dispossess them of this country." But by going to war, declared Governor Francis Wyatt, the Indians had forfeited any claim to the land. Virginia's policy, he continued, must now be nothing less than the "expulsion of the savages to gain the free range of the country."

Indians remained a significant presence in Virginia, and trade continued throughout the century. But the unsuccessful uprising of 1622 fundamentally shifted the balance of power in the colony. The settlers' supremacy was reinforced in 1644 when a last desperate rebellion led by Opechancanough, now said to be 100 years old, was crushed after causing the deaths of some 500 colonists. Virginia forced a treaty on the surviving coastal Indians, who now numbered less than 2,000, that acknowledged their subordination to the government at Jamestown and required them to move to tribal reservations to the west and not enter areas of European settlement without permission. This policy of separation followed the precedent already established in Ireland. Settlers spreading inland into the Virginia countryside continued to seize Indian lands.

The destruction caused by the uprising of 1622 was the last in a series of blows suffered by the Virginia Company. Two years later, it surrendered its charter and Virginia became the first royal colony, its governor now appointed by the crown. Virginia had failed to accomplish any of its goals for either the company or the settlers. Investors had not turned a profit, and although the company had sent 6,000 settlers to Virginia, its white population numbered only 1,200 when the king assumed control. Preoccupied with affairs at home, the government in London for years paid little attention to Virginia. Henceforth, the local elite, not a faraway company, controlled the colony's development. And that elite was growing rapidly in

POWHATAN
In solcher Maiestät hat sich der
Konig für dem gefangenen Capitain
Schmidt erzeigt und sehen lafsen.

Powhatan, the most prominent Indian leader in the original area of English settlement in Virginia. This image, showing Powhatan and his court, was engraved on John Smith's map of Virginia and included in Smith's General History of Virginia, *published in 1624.*

Theodor de Bry's engraving of the 1622 Indian uprising in Virginia depicts the Indians massacring defenseless colonists (who are shown unarmed although many in fact owned guns).

An advertisement for tobacco includes images of slaves with agricultural implements.

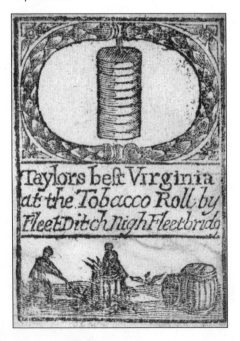

wealth and power thanks to the cultivation of a crop introduced from the West Indies by John Rolfe—tobacco.

A TOBACCO COLONY

King James I considered tobacco "harmful to the brain and dangerous to the lungs" and issued a spirited warning against its use. But increasing numbers of Europeans enjoyed smoking and believed the tobacco plant had medicinal benefits. As a commodity with an ever-expanding mass market in Europe, tobacco became Virginia's substitute for gold. It enriched an emerging class of tobacco planters, as well as members of the colonial government who assigned good land to themselves. The crown profited from customs duties (taxes on tobacco that entered or left the kingdom). By 1624, more than 200,000 pounds were being grown, producing startling profits for landowners. Forty years later, the crop totaled 15 million pounds, and it doubled again by the 1680s. The spread of tobacco farming produced a dispersed society with few towns and little social unity. It inspired a get-rich-quick attitude and a frenzied scramble for land and labor. By the middle of the seventeenth century, a new influx of immigrants with ample financial resources—sons of merchants and English gentlemen—had taken advantage of the headright system and governmental connections to acquire large estates along navigable rivers. They established themselves as the colony's social and political elite.

The expansion of tobacco cultivation also led to an increased demand for field labor, met for most of the seventeenth century by young, male indentured servants. Despite harsh conditions of work in the tobacco fields, a persistently high death rate, and laws mandating punishments from whipping to an extension of service for those who ran away or were unruly, the abundance of land continued to attract migrants. Of the 120,000 English immigrants who entered the Chesapeake region during the seventeenth century, three-quarters came as servants. Virginia's white society increasingly came to resemble that of England, with a wealthy landed gentry at the top; a group of small farmers, mostly former indentured servants who had managed to acquire land, in the middle; and an army of poor laborers—servants and landless former indentured servants—at the bottom. By 1700, the region's white population had grown to nearly 90,000.

WOMEN AND THE FAMILY

Virginia, however, lacked one essential element of English society—stable family life. The colony avidly promoted the immigration of women, including several dozen "tobacco brides" who arrived in 1620 and 1621 for arranged marriages. But given the demand for male servants to work in the tobacco fields, men in the Chesapeake outnumbered women for most of the seventeenth century by four or five to one. The vast majority of women who emigrated to the region came as indentured servants. Since they usually had to complete their terms of service before marrying, they did not begin to form families until their mid-twenties. The high death rate, unequal ratio between the sexes, and late age of marriage for those who found partners retarded population growth and produced a society with large numbers of single men, widows, and orphans. Although patriarchal ideals remained intact in Virginia, in practice the traditional authority of husbands and fathers was weakened. Because of their own low life expectancy, fathers found it difficult to supervise the careers and marriages of their children.

In the colonies as in England, a married woman possessed certain rights before the law, including a claim to "dower rights" of one-third of her husband's property in the event that he died before she did. When the widow

Processing tobacco was as labor-intensive as caring for the plant in the fields. Here scantily clad slaves and female indentured servants work with the crop after it has been harvested.

died, however, the property passed to the husband's male heirs. (English law was far less generous than in Spain, where a woman could hold independently any property inherited from her parents, and a man and wife owned jointly all the wealth accumulated during a marriage.)

Social conditions in the colonies, however, opened the door to roles women rarely assumed in England. Widows and the few women who never married took advantage of their legal status as femme sole (a woman alone, who enjoyed an independent legal identity denied to married women) to make contracts and conduct business. Margaret Brent, who emigrated to the Chesapeake in 1638, acquired land, managed her own plantation, and acted as a lawyer in court. Some widows were chosen to administer their husbands' estates or were willed their husbands' property outright, rather than receiving only the one-third "dower rights." But because most women came to Virginia as indentured servants, they could look forward only to a life of hard labor in the tobacco fields and early death. Servants were frequently subjected to sexual abuse by their masters. Those who married often found themselves in poverty when their husbands died.

THE MARYLAND EXPERIMENT

Although it began under very different sponsorship and remained much smaller than Virginia during the seventeenth century, the second Chesapeake colony, Maryland, followed a similar course of development. As in Virginia, tobacco came to dominate the economy and tobacco planters the society. But in other ways, Maryland's history was strikingly different.

Maryland was established in 1632 as a proprietary colony, that is, a grant of land and governmental authority to a single individual. This was Cecilius Calvert, the son of a recently deceased favorite of King Charles I. The charter made Calvert proprietor of the colony and granted him "full, free, and absolute power," including control of trade and the right to initiate all legislation, with an elected assembly confined to approving or disapproving his proposals. Calvert imagined Maryland as a feudal domain. Land would be laid out in manors with the owners paying "quitrents" to the proprietor. Calvert disliked representative institutions and believed ordinary people should not meddle in governmental affairs. On the other hand, the charter also guaranteed to colonists "all privileges, franchises, and liberties" of Englishmen. While these were not spelled out, they undoubtedly included the idea of a government limited by the law. Here was a recipe for conflict, and Maryland had more than its share during the seventeenth century.

RELIGION IN MARYLAND

Further aggravating instability in the colony was the fact that Calvert, a Catholic, envisioned Maryland as a refuge for his persecuted coreligionists in England, especially the younger sons of Catholic gentry who had few economic or political prospects in England. In Maryland, he hoped, Protestants and Catholics could live in a harmony unknown in Europe. The first group of 130 colonists included a number of Catholic gentlemen and two priests. Most appointed officials were also Catholic, including relatives of the proprietor, as were those to whom he awarded the choicest land grants. But Protestants always formed a majority of the settlers. Most, as in Virginia, came as indentured servants, but others took advantage of Maryland's generous headright system to acquire land by transporting workers to the colony.

As in Virginia, the death rate remained very high. In one county, half the marriages during the seventeenth century lasted fewer than eight years before one partner died. Almost 70 percent of male settlers in Maryland died before reaching the age of fifty, and half the children born in the colony did not live to adulthood. But at least initially, Maryland seems to have offered servants greater opportunity for landownership than Virginia. Unlike in the older colony, freedom dues in Maryland included fifty acres of land. As tobacco planters engrossed the best land later in the century, however, the prospects for landless men diminished.

THE NEW ENGLAND WAY

THE RISE OF PURITANISM

As Virginia and Maryland evolved toward societies dominated by a small aristocracy ruling over numerous bound laborers, a very different social order emerged in seventeenth-century New England. The early history of that region is intimately connected to the religious movement known as "Puritanism," which arose in England late in the sixteenth century. The term was initially coined by opponents to ridicule those not satisfied with the progress of the Protestant Reformation in England, who called themselves not Puritans but "godly" or "true Protestants." Puritanism came to define a set of religious principles and a view of how society should be organized. Puritans differed among themselves on many issues. But all shared the conviction that the Church of England retained too many elements of Catholicism in its religious rituals and doctrines. Puritans saw elaborate church ceremonies, the rule that priests could not marry, and ornate church decorations as vestiges of "popery." Many rejected the Catholic structure of religious authority descending from a pope or king to archbishops, bishops, and priests. Only independent local congregations, they believed, should choose clergymen and determine modes of worship. These Puritans were called "Congregationalists." All Puritans shared many of the beliefs of the Church of England and the society as a whole, including a hatred of Catholicism and a pride in England's greatness as a champion of liberty. But they believed that neither the Church nor the nation was living up to its ideals.

Puritans considered religious belief a complex and demanding matter and urged believers to seek the truth by reading the Bible and listening to sermons by educated ministers, rather than devoting themselves to sacraments administered by priests and to what Puritans considered formulaic prayers. The sermon was the central rite of Puritan practice. In the course of a lifetime, according to one estimate, the average Puritan listened to some 7,000 sermons. In their religious beliefs, Puritans followed the ideas of the French-born Swiss theologian John Calvin. The world, Calvin taught, was divided between the elect and the damned. All persons sought salvation, but whether one was among the elect destined to be saved had already been determined by God. His will, ultimately, was unknowable, and nothing one did on earth—including prayers, good works, and offerings—would make

The first book printed in the English mainland colonies, The Whole Book of Psalmes Faithfully Translated into English Metre *was published in Cambridge, Massachusetts, in 1640. Worshipers used it to sing psalms (religious songs from the Bible, sung in Massachusetts unaccompanied by music, which Puritan churches banned).*

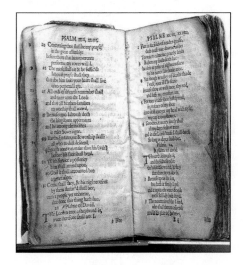

A portrait of John Winthrop, first governor of the Massachusetts Bay Colony, painted in the 1640s.

any difference. But while there were no guarantees of salvation, worldly success—leading a good life, prospering economically—might well be indications of God's grace. Idleness and immoral behavior were sure signs of damnation.

MORAL LIBERTY

Puritanism, however, was not simply a set of ideas but a state of mind, a zealousness in pursuing the true faith that alienated many who held differing religious views. A minority of Puritans (such as those who settled in Plymouth Colony) became separatists, abandoning the Church of England entirely to form their own independent churches. Most, however, hoped to purify the Church from within. But in the 1620s and 1630s, as Charles I seemed to be moving toward a restoration of Catholic ceremonies and the Church of England dismissed Puritan ministers and censored their writings, many Puritans decided to emigrate. They departed England not so much due to persecution, but because they feared that "Popish" practices had grown to such "an intolerable height," as one minister complained, that "the consciences of God's saints . . . could no longer bear them." By the same token, Puritans blamed many of England's social problems on the wandering poor, whom they considered indolent and ungodly. When Puritans emigrated to New England, they hoped to escape what they believed to be the religious and worldly corruptions of English society. They would establish a "city set upon a hill," a Bible Commonwealth whose influence would flow back across the Atlantic and rescue England from godlessness and social decay.

Like so many other emigrants to America, Puritans came in search of liberty, especially the right to worship and govern themselves in what they deemed a truly Christian manner. Freedom for Puritans was primarily a spiritual affair. It implied the opportunity and the responsibility to obey God's will through self-government and self-denial. It certainly did not mean unrestrained action, improper religious practices, or sinful behavior, of which, Puritans thought, there were far too many examples in England. In a 1645 speech to the Massachusetts legislature explaining the Puritan conception of freedom, John Winthrop, the colony's governor, distinguished sharply between two kinds of liberty. "Natural" liberty, or acting without restraint, suggested "a liberty to do evil." This was the false idea of freedom supposedly adopted by the Irish, Indians, and bad Christians generally. Genuine "moral" liberty—the Christian liberty described in Chapter 1— meant "a liberty to that only which is good." It was quite compatible with severe restraints on speech, religion, and personal behavior. True freedom, Winthrop insisted, depended on "subjection to authority," both religious and secular; otherwise, anarchy was sure to follow. To Puritans, liberty meant that the elect had a right to establish churches and govern society, not that others could challenge their beliefs or authority.

THE PILGRIMS AT PLYMOUTH

The first Puritans to emigrate to America were a group of separatists known as the Pilgrims. They had already fled to the Netherlands in 1608, believing that Satan had begun "to sow errors, heresies and discords" in England. A decade later, fearing that their children were being corrupted by being drawn into the surrounding culture, they decided to emigrate to Virginia. The expedition was financed by a group of English investors who hoped to establish a base for profitable trade. In September 1620, the *Mayflower*, carrying 150 settlers and crew (among them many non-Puritans), embarked from England. Blown off course, they landed not in Virginia but hundreds of miles to the north, on Cape Cod. Here the 102 who survived the journey established the colony of Plymouth. Before landing, the Pilgrim leaders drew up the Mayflower Compact, in which the adult men going ashore agreed to obey "just and equal laws" enacted by representatives of their own choosing. This was the first written frame of government in what is now the United States.

An early seventeenth-century engraving shows the English explorer Bartholomew Gosnold encountering Native Americans. Gosnold landed at Cape Cod in 1602 and then established a small outpost on nearby Cuttyhunk Island. The region's Indians had much experience with Europeans before Pilgrims settled there.

A century earlier, when Giovanni da Verrazano explored the Atlantic coast of North America, he encountered thickly settled villages and saw the smoke of innumerable Indian bonfires. By the time the Pilgrims landed, hundreds of European fishing vessels had operated off New England, landing to trade with Indians and bringing, as elsewhere, epidemics. The Pilgrims arrived in an area whose native population had recently been decimated by smallpox. They established Plymouth on the site of an abandoned Indian village whose fields had been cleared before the epidemic and were ready for cultivation. Nonetheless, the settlers arrived six weeks before winter without food or farm animals. Half died during the first winter. The colonists only survived through the help of local Indians, notably Squanto, who with twenty other Indians had been kidnapped and brought to Spain in 1614 by the English explorer Thomas Hunt, who planned to sell them as slaves. Rescued by a local priest, Squanto somehow made his way to London, where he learned English. He returned to Massachusetts in 1619 only to find that his people, the Patuxet, had succumbed to disease. He served as interpreter for the Pilgrims, taught them where to fish and how to plant corn, and helped in the forging of an alliance with Massasoit, a local chief. In the autumn of 1621, the Pilgrims invited their Indian allies to a harvest feast celebrating their survival, the first Thanksgiving.

The Pilgrims hoped to establish a society based on the lives of the early Christian saints. Their government rested on the principle of consent, and voting was not restricted to church members. All land was held in common until 1627, when it was divided among the settlers. Plymouth survived as an independent colony until 1691, but it was soon overshadowed by Massachusetts Bay to its north.

THE GREAT MIGRATION

Chartered in 1629, the Massachusetts Bay Company was founded by a group of London merchants who hoped to further the Puritan cause and

VISIONS OF FREEDOM

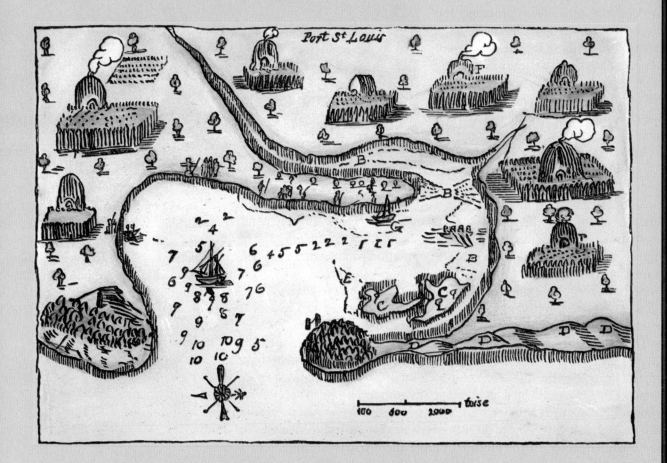

Samuel de Champlain's 1605 sketch of Plymouth Harbor, made when he was exploring the coast of modern-day New England in search of a site for a French settlement, shows the area dotted with wigwams and fields of corn, squash, and beans. By the time the Pilgrims arrived in 1620, epidemics had destroyed this thriving Indian community.

QUESTIONS

1. What does Champlain's sketch tell us about Native American life in New England before the advent of English settlement?

2. Why do you think many Europeans claimed that Indians did not live in settled communites?

turn a profit through trade with the Indians. The first five ships sailed from England in 1629, and by 1642 some 21,000 Puritans had emigrated to Massachusetts. Long remembered as the Great Migration, this flow of population represented less than one-third of English emigration in the 1630s. Far more English settlers arrived in Ireland, the Chesapeake, and the Caribbean. After 1640, migration to New England virtually ceased, and in some years more colonists left the region than arrived. Nonetheless, the Great Migration established the basis for a stable and thriving society.

In many ways, the settling of New England was unique. Although servants represented about one-quarter of the Great Migration, most settlers arrived in Massachusetts in families. They came for many reasons, including the desire to escape religious persecution, anxiety about the future of England, and the prospect of economic betterment. Compared with colonists in Virginia and Maryland, they were older and more prosperous, and the number of men and women more equally balanced. Because of the even sex ratio and New England's healthier climate, the population grew rapidly, doubling every twenty-seven years. Although the region received only a small fraction of the century's migration, by 1700 New England's white population of 91,000 outnumbered that of both the Chesapeake and the West Indies. Nearly all were descendants of those who crossed the Atlantic during the Great Migration.

THE PURITAN FAMILY

While the imbalance between male and female migrants made it difficult for patriarchal family patterns fully to take root in the Chesapeake until the end of the seventeenth century, they emerged very quickly in New England. Whatever their differences with other Englishmen on religious matters, Puritans shared with the larger society a belief in male authority within the household as well as an adherence to the common-law tradition that severely limited married women's legal and economic rights. Puritans in America carefully emulated the family structure of England, insisting that the obedience of women, children, and servants to men's will was the foundation of social stability. The father's authority was all the more vital because in a farming society without large numbers of slaves or servants, control over the labor of one's family was essential to a man's economic success.

To be sure, Puritans deemed women to be the spiritual equals of men, and women were allowed to become full church members. Although all ministers were men, the Puritan belief in the ability of believers to interpret the Bible opened the door for some women to claim positions of religious leadership. The ideal Puritan marriage was based on reciprocal affection and companionship, and divorce was legal. Yet within the household, the husband's authority was virtually absolute. Indeed, a man's position as head of his family was thought to replicate God's authority in spiritual matters and the authority of the government in the secular realm. Magistrates sometimes intervened to protect wives from physical abuse, but they also enforced the power of fathers over their children and husbands over their wives. Moderate "correction" was considered appropriate for women who violated their husbands' sense of proper behavior.

Seal of the Massachusetts Bay Colony. The Indian's scanty attire suggests a lack of civilization. His statement "Come Over and Help Us," based on an incident in the Bible, illustrates the English conviction that they were liberating the native population, rather than exploiting them as other empires had.

Their responsibilities as wives and mothers defined women's lives. In his 1645 speech on liberty quoted above, John Winthrop noted that woman achieved genuine freedom by fulfilling her prescribed social role and embracing "subjection to her husband's authority." The family was the foundation of strong communities, and unmarried adults seemed a danger to the social fabric. An early law of Plymouth declared that "no single person be suffered to live of himself." The typical New England woman married at twenty-two, a younger age than her English counterpart, and gave birth seven times. Because New England was a far healthier environment than the Chesapeake, more children survived infancy. Thus, much of a woman's adult life was devoted to bearing and rearing children.

GOVERNMENT AND SOCIETY IN MASSACHUSETTS

In a sermon aboard the *Arabella*, on which he sailed for Massachusetts in 1630, John Winthrop spoke of the settlers binding themselves together "in the bond of brotherly affection" in order to promote the glory of God and their own "common good." Puritans feared excessive individualism and lack of social unity. Unlike the dispersed plantation-centered society of the Chesapeake, the leaders of Massachusetts organized the colony in self-governing towns. Groups of settlers received a land grant from the colony's government and then subdivided it, with residents awarded house lots in a central area and land on the outskirts for farming. Much land remained in commons, either for collective use or to be divided among later settlers or the sons of the town's founders. Each town had its own Congregational Church. Each, according to a law of 1647, was required to establish a school, since the ability to read the Bible was central to Puritan belief. To train an educated ministry, Harvard College was established in 1636 (nearly a century after the Royal University of Mexico, founded in 1551), and two years later the first printing press in English America was established in Cambridge.

The Savage Family, *a 1779 painting by the New England artist Edward Savage, depicts several generations of a typically numerous Puritan family.*

The government of Massachusetts reflected the Puritans' religious and social vision. Wishing to rule the colony without outside interference and to prevent non-Puritans from influencing decision making, the shareholders of the Massachusetts Bay Company emigrated to America, taking the charter with them and transforming a commercial document into a form of government. At first, the eight shareholders chose the men who ruled the colony. In 1634, a group of deputies elected by freemen (landowning church members) was added to form a single ruling body, the General Court. Ten years later, company officers and elected deputies were divided into two legislative houses. Unlike Virginia, whose governors were appointed first by a faraway company and, after 1624, by the crown, or Maryland, where authority rested with a single proprietor, the freemen of Massachusetts elected their governor.

The principle of consent was central to Puritanism. Church government was decentralized—each congregation, as one minister put it, had "complete liberty to stand alone." Churches were formed by voluntary agreement among members, who elected the minister. No important church decision was made without the agreement of the male members. Towns governed themselves, and local officials, delegates to the General Court, and the colonial governor were all elected. Puritans, however, were hardly believers in equality. Church membership, a status that carried great prestige and power, was a restrictive category. Anyone could worship at a church, or, as the Puritans preferred to call it, meeting house, but to be a full member required demonstrating that one had experienced divine grace and could be considered a "visible saint," usually by testifying about a conversion experience. Although male property holders generally chose local officials, voting in colony-wide elections was limited to men who had been accepted as full church members. This requirement at first made for a broad electorate, especially compared with England. But as time went on, it meant that a smaller and smaller percentage of the population controlled the government. Puritan democracy was for those within the circle of church membership; those outside the boundary occupied a secondary place in the Bible Commonwealth.

An embroidered banner depicting the main building at Harvard, the first college established in the English colonies. It was probably made by a Massachusetts woman for a husband or son who attended Harvard.

PURITAN LIBERTIES

Seventeenth-century New England was a hierarchical society in which socially prominent families were assigned the best land and the most desirable seats in church. "Some must be rich and some poor, some high and eminent in power and dignity; others mean and in subjection" declared John Winthrop. This was part of God's plan, reinforced by man-made law and custom. The General Court forbade ordinary men and women from wearing "the garb of gentlemen." Ordinary settlers were addressed as "goodman" and "goodwife," while the better sort were called "gentleman" and "lady" or "master" and "mistress." When the General Court in 1641 issued a Body of Liberties outlining the rights and responsibilities of Massachusetts colonists, it adopted the traditional understanding of liberties as privileges that derived from one's place in the social order. Inequality was considered an expression of God's will, and while some liberties applied to all inhabitants, there were separate lists of rights for freemen, women, children, and servants. The Body of Liberties also allowed for slavery. The first African slave appears in the records of Massachusetts Bay in 1640.

Massachusetts forbade ministers from holding office so as not to interfere with their spiritual responsibilities. But church and state were closely interconnected. The law required each town to establish a church and to levy a tax to support the minister. There were no separate church courts, but the state enforced religious devotion. The Body of Liberties affirmed the rights of free speech and assembly and equal protection of the law for all within the colony, but the laws of Massachusetts prescribed the death penalty for, among other things, worshiping "any god, but the lord god," practicing witchcraft, or committing blasphemy.

NEW ENGLANDERS DIVIDED

The Puritans exalted individual judgment—hence their insistence on reading the Bible. The very first item printed in English America was a broadside, *The Oath of a Freeman* (1638), explaining the rights and duties of the citizens of Massachusetts and emphasizing that men should vote according to their "own conscience . . . without respect of persons, or favor of any men." Yet modern ideas of individualism, privacy, and personal freedom would have struck Puritans as quite strange. They considered too much emphasis on the "self" dangerous to social harmony and community stability. In the closely knit towns of New England, residents carefully monitored one another's behavior and chastised or expelled those who violated communal norms. In the Puritan view, as one colonist put it, the main freedom possessed by dissenters was the "liberty to keep away from us." Towns banished individuals for such offenses as criticizing the church or government, complaining about the colony in letters home to England, or, in the case of one individual, Abigail Gifford, for being "a very burdensome woman." Tolerance of difference was not high on the list of Puritan values.

ROGER WILLIAMS

Differences of opinion about how to organize a Bible Commonwealth, however, emerged almost from the founding of Massachusetts. With its emphasis on individual interpretation of the Bible, Puritanism contained the seeds of its own fragmentation. The first sustained criticism of the existing order came from the young minister Roger Williams, who arrived in Massachusetts in 1631 and soon began to insist that its congregations withdraw from the Church of England and that church and state be separated. "Soul liberty," Williams believed, required that individuals be allowed to follow their consciences wherever they led. To most Puritans, the social fabric was held together by certain religious truths, which could not be questioned. To Williams, any law-abiding citizen should be allowed to practice whatever form of religion he chose. For the government to "molest any person, Jew or Gentile, for either professing doctrine or practicing worship" violated the principle that genuine religious faith is voluntary.

Williams aimed to strengthen religion, not weaken it. The embrace of government, he insisted, corrupted the purity of Christian faith and drew believers into endless religious wars like those that racked Europe. To leaders like John Winthrop, the outspoken minister's attack on the religious-political establishment of Massachusetts was bad enough, but Williams compounded the offense by rejecting the conviction that Puritans were an elect people on a divine mission to spread the true faith. Williams denied that God had singled out any group as special favorites.

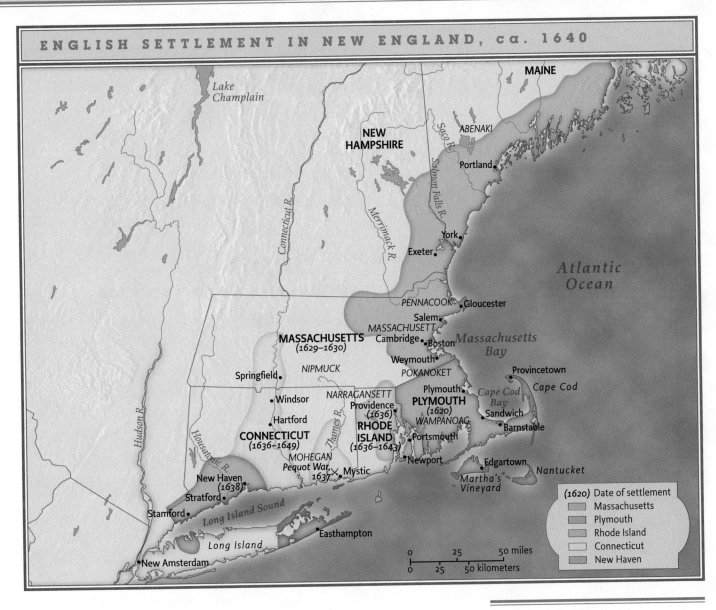

ENGLISH SETTLEMENT IN NEW ENGLAND, ca. 1640

By the mid-seventeenth century, English settlement in New England had spread well inland and up and down the Atlantic coast.

RHODE ISLAND AND CONNECTICUT

Banished from Massachusetts in 1636, Williams and his followers moved south, where they established the colony of Rhode Island, which eventually received a charter from London. In a world in which the right of individuals to participate in religious activities without governmental interference barely existed, Rhode Island became a beacon of religious freedom. It had no established church, no religious qualifications for voting until the eighteenth century, and no requirement that citizens attend church. It became a haven for Dissenters (Protestants who belonged to denominations other than the established church) and Jews persecuted in other colonies. Rhode Island's frame of government was also more democratic. The assembly was elected twice a year, the governor annually, and town meetings were held more frequently than elsewhere in New England.

Religious disagreements in Massachusetts generated other colonies as well. In 1636, the minister Thomas Hooker established a settlement at

VOICES OF FREEDOM

FROM JOHN WINTHROP,
Speech to the Massachusetts General Court
(July 3, 1645)

John Winthrop, governor of the Massachusetts Bay Colony, describes two very different definitions of liberty in this speech.

The great questions that have troubled the country, are about the authority of the magistrates and the liberty of the people. . . . Concerning liberty, I observe a great mistake in the country about that. There is a twofold liberty, natural (I mean as our nature is now corrupt) and civil or federal. The first is common to man with beasts and other creatures. By this, man, as he stands in relation to man simply, hath liberty to do what he lists; it is a liberty to do evil as well as to [do] good. This liberty is incompatible and inconsistent with authority, and cannot endure the least restraint of the most just authority. The exercise and maintaining of this liberty makes men grow more evil, and in time to be

worse than brute beasts. . . . This is that great enemy of truth and peace, that wild beast, which all the ordinances of God are bent against, to restrain and subdue it.

The other kind of liberty I call civil or federal, it may also be termed moral. . . . This liberty is the proper end and object of authority, and cannot subsist without it; and it is a liberty to that only which is good, just, and honest. . . . This liberty is maintained and exercised in a way of subjection to authority; it is of the same kind of liberty wherewith Christ hath made us free. The woman's own choice makes . . . a man her husband; yet being so chosen, he is her lord, and she is to be subject to him, yet in a way of liberty, not of bondage; and a true wife accounts her subjection her honor and freedom, and would not think her condition safe and free, but in her subjection to her husband's authority. Such is the liberty of the church under the authority of Christ.

FROM ROGER WILLIAMS,
Letter to the Town of
Providence (1655)

A pioneer of the idea of religious toleration in the colonies, Roger Williams left Massachusetts to found Rhode Island, where, unlike in Puritan Massachusetts, he established separation of church and state. Believing his views had been misunderstood by some of the settlers of Providence, he wrote this letter to explain his understanding of liberty and its extent and limits.

That ever I should speak or write a tittle, that tends to ... an infinite liberty of conscience, is a mistake, and which I have ever disclaimed and abhorred. To prevent such mistakes, I shall at present only propose this case: There goes many a ship to sea, with many hundred souls in one ship, whose weal or woe is common, and is a true picture of a commonwealth, or a human combination or society. It hath fallen out sometimes, that both papists and protestants, Jews and Turks [Muslims], may be embarked in one ship; upon which supposal I affirm, that all the liberty of conscience, that ever I pleaded for, turns upon these two hinges—that none of the papists, protestants, Jews, or Turks, be forced to come to the ship's prayers or worship, nor compelled from their own particular prayers or worship, if they practice any. I further add, that I never denied, that notwithstanding this liberty, the commander of this ship ought to command the ship's course, yea, and also command that justice, peace and sobriety, be kept and practiced, both among the seamen and all the passengers. If any of the seamen refuse to perform their services, or passengers to pay their freight; if any refuse to help, in person or purse, towards the common charges or defense; if any refuse to obey the common laws and orders of the ship, concerning their common peace or preservation; if any shall mutiny and rise up against their commanders and officers, because all are not equal in Christ, therefore no masters nor officers, no laws nor orders, nor corrections nor punishments;—I say, I never denied, but in such cases, whatever is pretended, the commander or commanders may judge, resist, compel and punish such transgressors.

QUESTIONS

1. Why does Winthrop consider "natural" liberty dangerous?

2. In what ways does Williams place limits on liberty?

3. How do the views of Winthrop and Williams differ, and in what ways are they similar?

Hartford. Its system of government, embodied in the Fundamental Orders of 1639, was modeled on that of Massachusetts—with the significant exception that men did not have to be church members to vote. Quite different was the colony of New Haven, founded in 1638 by emigrants who wanted an even closer connection between church and state. In 1662, Hartford and New Haven received a royal charter that united them as the colony of Connecticut.

THE TRIALS OF ANNE HUTCHINSON

More threatening to the Puritan establishment both because of her gender and because she attracted a large and influential following was Anne Hutchinson. A midwife and the daughter of a clergyman, Hutchinson, wrote John Winthrop, was "a woman of a ready wit and bold spirit." She arrived in Massachusetts with her husband in 1634 to join their minister, John Cotton, who had been expelled from his pulpit in England by church authorities. Hutchinson began holding meetings in her home, where she led discussions of religious issues among men and women, including a number of prominent merchants and public officials. In Hutchinson's view, salvation was God's direct gift to the elect and could not be earned by good works, devotional practices, or other human effort. Most Puritans shared this belief. What set Hutchinson apart was her charge that nearly all the ministers in Massachusetts were guilty of faulty preaching for distinguishing "saints" from the damned on the basis of activities such as church attendance and moral behavior rather than an inner state of grace.

In Massachusetts, where church and state reinforced each other, both ministers and magistrates were intent on suppressing any views that challenged their own leadership. Their critics denounced Cotton and Hutchinson for Antinomianism (a term for putting one's own judgment or faith above both human law and the teachings of the church). In 1637, she was placed on trial before a civil court for sedition (expressing opinions dangerous to authority). Her position as a "public woman" made her defiance seem even more outrageous. Her meetings, said Governor Winthrop, were neither "comely in the sight of God nor fitting to your sex." A combative and articulate woman, Hutchinson ably debated interpretation of the Bible with her university-educated accusers. She more than held her own during her trial. But when she spoke of divine revelations, of God speaking to her directly rather than through ministers or the Bible, she violated Puritan doctrine and sealed her own fate. Such a claim, the colony's leaders felt, posed a threat to the very existence of organized churches—and, indeed, to all authority. Hutchinson and a number of her followers were banished. Her family made its way to Rhode Island and then to Westchester, north of what is now New York City, where Hutchinson and most of her relatives perished during an Indian war.

Anne Hutchinson lived in New England for only eight years, but she left her mark on the region's religious culture. As in the case of Roger Williams, her career showed how the Puritan belief in each individual's ability to interpret the Bible could easily lead to criticism of the religious and political establishment. It would take many years before religious toleration—which violated the Puritans' understanding of "moral liberty" and social harmony—came to Massachusetts.

PURITANS AND INDIANS

Along with disruptive religious controversies, New England, like other colonies, had to deal with the difficult problem of relations with Indians. The native population of New England numbered perhaps 100,000 when the Puritans arrived. But because of recent epidemics, the migrants encountered fewer Indians near the coast than in other parts of eastern North America. In areas of European settlement, colonists quickly outnumbered the native population. Some settlers, notably Roger Williams, sought to treat the Indians with justice. Williams learned complex Indian languages, and he insisted that the king had no right to grant land already belonging to someone else. No town, said Williams, should be established before its site had been purchased. While John Winthrop believed uncultivated land could legitimately be taken by the colonists, he recognized the benefits of buying land rather than simply seizing it. But he insisted that such purchases (usually completed after towns had already been settled) must carry with them Indian agreement to submit to English authority and pay tribute to the colonists.

To New England's leaders, the Indians represented both savagery and temptation. In Puritan eyes, they resembled Catholics, with their false gods and deceptive rituals. They enjoyed freedom, but of the wrong kind—what Winthrop condemned as undisciplined "natural liberty" rather than the "moral liberty" of the civilized Christian. Always concerned that sinful persons might prefer a life of ease to hard work, Puritans feared that Indian society might prove attractive to colonists who lacked the proper moral fiber. In 1642, the Connecticut General Court set a penalty of three years at hard labor for any colonist who abandoned "godly society" to live with the Indians. To counteract the attraction of Indian life, the leaders of New England also encouraged the publication of "captivity" narratives by those captured by Indians. The most popular was *The Sovereignty and Goodness of God* by Mary Rowlandson, who had emigrated with her parents as a child in 1639 and was seized along with a group of other settlers and held for three months until ransomed during an Indian war in the 1670s. Rowlandson acknowledged that she had been well treated and suffered "not the least abuse or unchastity," but her book's overriding theme was her determination to return to Christian society.

Puritans announced that they intended to bring Christian faith to the Indians, but they did nothing in the first two decades of settlement to accomplish this. They generally saw Indians as an obstacle to be pushed aside, rather than as potential converts.

THE PEQUOT WAR

Indians in New England lacked a paramount chief like Powhatan in Virginia. Coastal Indian tribes, their numbers severely reduced by disease, initially sought to forge alliances with the newcomers to enhance their own position against inland rivals. But as the white population expanded and new towns proliferated, conflict with the region's Indians became unavoidable. The turning point came in 1637 when a fur trader was killed by Pequots— a powerful tribe who controlled southern New England's fur trade and exacted tribute from other Indians. A force of Connecticut and Massachusetts soldiers, augmented by Narragansett allies, surrounded the main Pequot

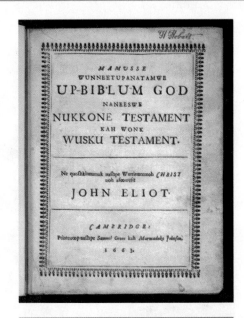

The title page of a translation of the Bible into the Massachusett language, published by John Eliot in 1663.

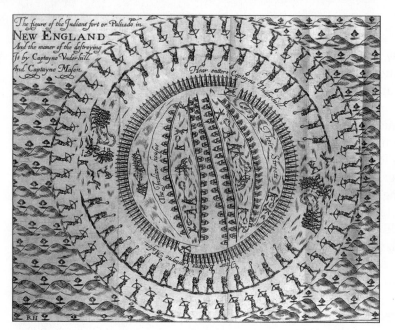

An engraving from John Underhill's News from America, *published in London in 1638, shows the destruction of the Pequot village on the Mystic River in 1637. The colonial forces, firing guns, are aided by Indian allies with bows and arrows.*

fortified village at Mystic and set it ablaze, killing those who tried to escape. Over 500 men, women, and children lost their lives in the massacre. By the end of the war a few months later, most of the Pequot had been exterminated or sold into Caribbean slavery. The treaty that restored peace decreed that their name be wiped from the historical record.

The destruction of one of the region's most powerful Indian groups not only opened the Connecticut River valley to rapid white settlement but also persuaded other Indians that the newcomers possessed a power that could not be resisted. The colonists' ferocity shocked their Indian allies, who considered European military practices barbaric. A few Puritans agreed. "It was a fearful sight to see them frying in the fire," the Pilgrim leader William Bradford wrote of the raid on Mystic. But to most Puritans, including Bradford, the defeat of a "barbarous nation" by "the sword of the Lord" offered further proof that they were on a sacred mission and that Indians were unworthy of sharing New England with the visible saints of the church.

THE NEW ENGLAND ECONOMY

The leaders of the New England colonies prided themselves on the idea that religion was the primary motivation for emigration. "We all came into these parts of America," proclaimed an official document of the 1640s, "with one and the same end and aim, namely, to advance the kingdom of our Lord Jesus Christ and to enjoy the liberties of the Gospel in purity with peace." But economic motives were hardly unimportant. One promotional pamphlet of the 1620s spoke of New England as a place "where religion and profit jump together."

Most Puritans came to America from East Anglia, an internationally renowned cloth-producing region. One of the most economically advanced areas of England, East Anglia in the 1620s and 1630s was suffering from a series of poor harvests and the dislocations caused by a decline in the cloth trade. A majority of the emigrants from this area were weavers, tailors, or farmers. But while they were leaving a depressed region, they were relatively well-off. Most came from the middle ranks of society and paid for their family's passage rather than indenturing themselves to labor. They sought in New England not only religious liberty but also economic advancement—if not riches, then at least a "competency," the economic independence that came with secure landownership or craft status. When one preacher proclaimed that the "main end" of settlement was to honor God, a man in the congregation cried out, "Sir, you are mistaken . . . our main end was to catch fish." But to Puritans no contradiction existed between piety and profit so long as one did not forget the needs of the larger community. Success in one's calling might be taken as a sign of divine grace.

Lacking a marketable staple like sugar or tobacco, New Englanders turned to fishing and timber for exports. But the economy centered on family farms producing food for their own use and a small marketable surplus. Although the Body of Liberties of 1641, as noted above, made provision for slavery in the Bible Commonwealth, there were very few slaves in seventeenth-century New England. Nor were indentured servants as central to the economy as in the Chesapeake. Most households relied on the labor of their own members, including women in the home and children in the fields. Sons remained unmarried into their mid-twenties, when they could expect to receive land from their fathers, from local authorities, or by moving to a new town. Indeed, while religious divisions spawned new settlements, the desire for land among younger families and newcomers was the major motive for New England's expansion. In Sudbury, Massachusetts, for example, one resident proposed in 1651 that every adult man be awarded an equal parcel of land. When a town meeting rejected the idea, a group of young men received a grant from the General Court to establish their own town farther west.

THE MERCHANT ELITE

Per capita wealth in New England lagged far behind that of the Chesapeake, but it was much more equally distributed. A majority of New England families achieved the goal of owning their own land, the foundation for a comfortable independence. Nonetheless, as in the Chesapeake, economic development produced a measure of social inequality. On completing their terms, indentured servants rarely achieved full church membership or received grants of land. Most became disenfranchised wage earners.

New England gradually assumed a growing role within the British empire based on trade. As early as the 1640s, New England merchants shipped and marketed the staples of other colonies to markets in Europe and Africa. They engaged in a particularly profitable trade with the West Indies, whose growing slave plantations they supplied with fish, timber, and agricultural produce gathered at home. Especially in Boston, a powerful class of merchants arose who challenged some key Puritan policies, including the subordination of economic activity to the common good. As early as the 1630s, when the General Court established limits on prices and wages—measures common in England—and gave a small group of merchants a monopoly on imports from Europe, others protested. Indeed, merchants were among the most prominent backers of Anne Hutchinson's challenge to colonial authority. Some left Boston to establish a new town at Portsmouth, in the region eventually chartered as the royal colony of New Hampshire. Others remained to fight, with increasing success, for the right to conduct business as they pleased. By the 1640s, Massachusetts had repealed many of its early economic regulations.

Although the Puritans never abandoned the idea that economic activity should serve the general welfare, Boston merchants soon came to exercise a decisive influence in public affairs. The government of Massachusetts Bay Colony actively promoted economic development by building roads and bridges, offering bounties to economic enterprises, and abandoning laws limiting prices. Eventually, the Puritan experiment would evolve into a merchant-dominated colonial government.

A self-portrait from around 1680, painted by Thomas Smith. A sailor who came to New England from Bermuda around 1650, Smith acquired considerable wealth, as evidenced by his fashionable clothing. The background depicts a naval battle involving Dutch and English ships (possibly a reference to their joint attack on a North African port in 1670). In the foreground is a poem with Smith's initials. This is the earliest-known American self-portrait.

Mrs. Elizabeth Freake and Baby Mary. *Painted by an anonymous artist in the 1670s, this portrait depicts the wife and daughter of John Freake, a prominent Boston merchant and lawyer. To illustrate the family's wealth, Mrs. Freake wears a triple strand of pearls, a garnet bracelet, and a gold ring, and her child wears a yellow silk dress.*

THE HALF-WAY COVENANT

In the mid-seventeenth century, some Puritan leaders began to worry about their society's growing commercialization and declining piety, or "declension." By 1650, less than half the population of Boston had been admitted to full church membership. Massachusetts churches were forced to deal with a growing problem—the religious status of the third generation. Children of the elect could be baptized, but many never became full church members because they were unable to demonstrate the necessary religious commitment or testify to a conversion experience. What was the status of their children? New Englanders faced a difficult choice. They could uphold rigorous standards of church admission, which would limit the size and social influence of the Congregational Church. Or they could make admission easier, which would keep the church connected to a larger part of the population but would raise fears about a loss of religious purity.

The Half-Way Covenant of 1662 tried to address this problem by allowing for the baptism and a kind of subordinate, or "half-way," membership for grandchildren of those who emigrated during the Great Migration. In a significant compromise of early Puritan beliefs, ancestry, not religious conversion, became the pathway to inclusion among the elect. But church membership continued to stagnate.

By the 1660s and 1670s, ministers were regularly castigating the people for selfishness, manifestations of pride, violations of the Sabbath, and a "great backsliding" from the colony's original purposes. These warnings, called "jeremiads" after the ancient Hebrew prophet Jeremiah, interpreted crop failures and disease as signs of divine disapproval and warned of further punishment to come if New Englanders did not mend their ways. Yet hard work and commercial success in one's chosen calling had always been central Puritan values. In this sense, the commercialization of New England was as much a fulfillment of the Puritan mission in America as a betrayal.

RELIGION, POLITICS, AND FREEDOM

THE RIGHTS OF ENGLISHMEN

Even as English emigrants began the settlement of colonies in North America, England itself became enmeshed in political and religious conflict, in which ideas of liberty played a central role. The struggle over English liberty in the first half of the seventeenth century expanded the definition of freedom at home and spilled over into early English North America.

By 1600, the traditional definition of "liberties" as a set of privileges confined to one or another social group still persisted, but alongside it had arisen the idea that certain "rights of Englishmen" applied to all within the kingdom. This tradition rested on the Magna Carta (or Great Charter) of 1215. An agreement between King John and a group of barons—local lords whose private armies frequently fought against each other and the crown—the Magna Carta attempted to put an end to a chronic state of civil unrest. It listed a series of "liberties" granted by the king to "all the free men of our realm." This was a restricted group at the time, since a large part of the English population still lived as serfs—peasants working land owned by feudal lords and legally bound to provide labor and other services. The liberties mentioned in the Magna Carta included protection against arbitrary imprisonment and the seizure of one's property without due process of law.

The principal beneficiaries of the Magna Carta were the barons, who obtained the right to oversee the king's conduct and even revolt if he violated their privileges. But over time, the document came to be seen as embodying the idea of "English freedom"—that the king was subject to the rule of law, and that all persons should enjoy security of person and property. These rights were embodied in the common law, whose provisions, such as habeas corpus (a protection against being imprisoned without a legal charge), the right to face one's accuser, and trial by jury came to apply to all free subjects of the English crown. And as serfdom slowly disappeared, the number of Englishmen considered "freeborn," and therefore entitled to these rights, expanded enormously.

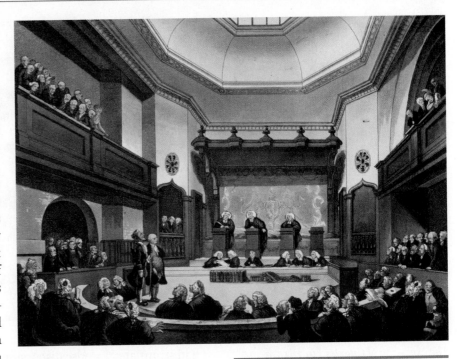

The Court of Common Pleas. *Trial by jury was a central element in the definition of "English liberty." This watercolor appeared in a three-volume series,* The Microcosm of London *(1808–1810).*

THE ENGLISH CIVIL WAR

At the beginning of the seventeenth century, when English emigrants began arriving in the New World, "freedom" still played only a minor role in England's political debates. But the political upheavals of that century elevated the notion of "English freedom" to a central place. The struggle for political supremacy between Parliament and the Stuart monarchs James I and Charles I culminated in the English Civil War of the 1640s. This long-running battle arose from religious disputes about how fully the Church of England should distance its doctrines and forms of worship from Catholicism. Conflict also developed over the respective powers of the king and Parliament, a debate that produced numerous invocations of the idea of the "freeborn Englishman" and led to a great expansion of the concept of English freedom.

The leaders of the House of Commons (the elective body that, along with the hereditary aristocrats of the House of Lords, makes up the English Parliament) accused the Stuart kings of endangering liberty by imposing taxes without parliamentary consent, imprisoning political foes, and leading the nation back toward Catholicism. Civil war broke out in 1642, resulting in a victory for the forces of Parliament. In 1649, Charles I was beheaded, the monarchy abolished, and England declared "a Commonwealth and Free State"—a nation governed by the will of the people. Oliver Cromwell, the head of the victorious Parliamentary army, ruled for almost a decade after the execution of the king. In 1660, the monarchy was restored and Charles II assumed the throne. But by then, the breakdown of authority

The execution of Charles I in 1649, a central event of the English Civil War.

A 1629 portrait by John Aubrey depicts John Milton, the philosopher of liberty, when he attended Cambridge University.

had stimulated intense discussions of liberty, authority, and what it meant to be a "freeborn Englishman."

ENGLAND'S DEBATE OVER FREEDOM

The idea of freedom suddenly took on new and expanded meanings between 1640 and 1660. The writer John Milton, who in 1649 called London "the mansion-house of liberty," called for freedom of speech and of the press. New religious sects sprang up, demanding the end of public financing and special privileges for the Anglican Church and religious toleration for all Protestants. The Levellers, history's first democratic political movement, proposed a written constitution, the Agreement of the People, which began by proclaiming "at how high a rate we value our just freedom." At a time when "democracy" was still widely seen as the equivalent of anarchy and disorder, the document proposed to abolish the monarchy and House of Lords and to greatly expand the right to vote. "The poorest he that lives in England hath a life to live as the greatest he," declared the Leveller Thomas Rainsborough, and therefore "any man that is born in England . . . ought to have his voice in election." Rainsborough even condemned African slavery.

The Levellers offered a glimpse of the modern definition of freedom as a universal entitlement in a society based on equal rights, not a function of social class. Another new group, the Diggers, went even further, hoping to give freedom an economic underpinning through the common ownership of land. Previous discussion of freedom, declared Gerard Winstanley, the Diggers' leader, had been misguided: "You are like men in a mist, seeking for freedom and know not what it is." True freedom applied equally "to the poor as well as the rich"; all were entitled to "a comfortable livelihood in this their own land." Even before the restoration of the monarchy, the Levellers, Diggers, and other radical movements spawned by the English Civil War had been crushed or driven underground. But some of the ideas of liberty that flourished during the 1640s and 1650s would be carried to America by English emigrants.

ENGLISH LIBERTY

These struggles elevated the notion of "English liberty" to a central place in Anglo-American political culture. It became a major building block in the assertive sense of nationhood then being consolidated in England. The medieval idea of liberties as a collection of limited entitlements enjoyed by specific groups did not suddenly disappear. But it was increasingly overshadowed by a more general definition of freedom grounded in the common rights of all individuals within the English realm. By self-definition, England was a community of free individuals and its past a "history of liberty." All Englishmen were governed by a king, but "he rules over free men," according to the law, unlike the autocratic monarchs of France, Spain, Russia, and other countries.

By 1680, in his book *English Liberties, or, The Free-Born Subject's Inheritance*, the writer Henry Care described the English system of government as a "qualified Monarchy," which he considered the best political structure in the world because, even though the "nobility" enjoyed privileges not available to others, all citizens were "guarded in their persons and properties by the fence of law, [which] renders them Freemen, not Slaves." The belief in freedom as the common heritage of all Englishmen and the conception of the British empire as the world's guardian of liberty helped to legitimize English colonization in the Western Hemisphere and to cast its imperial wars against Catholic France and Spain as struggles between freedom and tyranny.

Meeting of the General Council of the Army at Putney, *scene of the debate in 1647 over liberty and democracy between Levellers and more conservative army officers.*

THE CIVIL WAR AND ENGLISH AMERICA

These struggles, accompanied by vigorous discussions of the rights of free-born Englishmen, inevitably reverberated in England's colonies, dividing them from one another and internally. Most New Englanders sided with Parliament in the Civil War of the 1640s. Some returned to England to join the Parliamentary army or take up pulpits to help create a godly commonwealth at home. But Puritan leaders were increasingly uncomfortable as the idea of religious toleration for Protestants gained favor in England. It was the revolutionary Parliament that in 1644 granted Roger Williams his charter for the Rhode Island colony he had founded after being banished from Massachusetts.

Meanwhile, a number of followers of Anne Hutchinson became Quakers, one of the sects that sprang up in England during the Civil War. Quakers held that the spirit of God dwelled within every individual, not just the elect, and that this "inner light," rather than the Bible or teachings of the clergy, offered the surest guidance in spiritual matters. When Quakers appeared in Massachusetts, colonial officials had them whipped, fined, and banished. In 1659 and 1660, four Quakers who returned from exile were hanged, including Mary Dyer, a former disciple of Hutchinson. The treatment of Quakers gave Massachusetts a reputation in England as a hotbed of religious persecution. When Charles II, after the restoration of the monarchy in 1660, reaffirmed the Massachusetts charter, he ordered the colony to recognize the "liberty of conscience" of all Protestants. But while hangings ceased, efforts to suppress the Quakers continued, as did attacks on Baptists, whose disdain for a learned ministry also seemed to threaten Puritan beliefs.

A portrait of Oliver Cromwell, who ruled England after the execution of Charles I, by the artist Sir Peter Lely.

THE CRISIS IN MARYLAND

Unlike the New England colonies, Virginia sided with Charles I. Its leaders even proclaimed Charles II king after his father's execution in 1649, although Oliver Cromwell's government in London soon brought the rebellious colony under control. In Maryland, the combination of the religious and political battles of the Civil War, homegrown conflict between Catholic and Protestant settlers, and anti-proprietary feeling produced a violent civil war within the colony, later recalled as the "plundering time." Indeed, Maryland in the 1640s verged on total anarchy, with a pro-Parliament force assaulting those loyal to Charles I. The emerging Protestant planter class longed to seize power from the Catholic elite created by Cecelius Calvert. The assembly's Protestant majority rejected laws proposed by the proprietor and claimed the same power to legislate and levy taxes enjoyed by the House of Commons in England.

To stabilize the colony and attract more settlers, Calvert appointed a Protestant governor and offered refuge to Protestant Dissenters being persecuted in Virginia, where Anglicanism was the established religion and laws restricted the religious and political rights of others. In 1649, Maryland adopted an Act Concerning Religion, which institutionalized the principle of toleration that had prevailed from the colony's beginning. All Christians were guaranteed the "free exercise" of religion. The Act did not establish religious liberty in a modern sense, since it punished those who denied the divinity of Jesus Christ or the doctrine of the Holy Trinity. Indeed, a Jewish physician was soon arrested under its provisions. Nonetheless, the law was a milestone in the history of religious freedom in colonial America.

Turmoil, however, continued. During the 1650s, the Commonwealth government in London placed Maryland under the control of a Protestant council, which repealed the Toleration Act and forbade Catholics from openly practicing their religion. In 1657, however, Calvert's authority was restored and with it Maryland's experiment in religious freedom.

CROMWELL AND THE EMPIRE

Oliver Cromwell, who ruled England from 1649 until his death in 1658, undertook an aggressive policy of colonial expansion, the promotion of Protestantism, and commercial empowerment in the British Isles and the Western Hemisphere. His army forcibly extended English control over Ireland, massacring civilians, banning the public practice of Catholicism, and seizing land owned by Catholics. In the Caribbean, England seized Jamaica, a valuable sugar island, from Spain. In 1651, as will be related in Chapter 3, Parliament passed the first Navigation Act, which sought to challenge the Dutch hold on international commerce by confining colonial trade to English ships and ports.

Thus, by the middle of the seventeenth century, several English colonies existed along the Atlantic coast of North America. Established as part of an ad hoc process rather than arising under any coherent national plan, they differed enormously in economic, political, and social structure. The seeds had been planted, in the Chesapeake, for the development of plantation societies based on unfree labor, and in New England, for settlements centered on small towns and family farms. Throughout the colonies, many residents enjoyed freedoms they had not possessed at home, especially access to land and the right to worship as they desired. Others found themselves confined to unfree labor for many years or an entire lifetime.

The next century would be a time of crisis and consolidation as the population expanded, social conflicts intensified, and Britain moved to exert greater control over its flourishing North American colonies.

SUGGESTED READING

BOOKS

Anderson, Victoria D. *New England's Generation: The Great Migration and the Formation of Society and Culture in the Seventeenth Century* (1991). A careful study of emigration from England to New England.

Banner, Stuart. *How the Indians Lost Their Land: Law and Power on the Frontier* (2005). Argues that most Indian land came into settlers' hands by legal processes rather than conquest.

Bonomi, Patricia. *Under the Cope of Heaven: Religion, Society, and Politics in Colonial America* (1986). Traces the interrelationship of religion and politics and the rise of religious diversity in the colonies.

Brown, Kathleen. *Good Wives, Nasty Wenches, and Anxious Patriarchs: Gender, Race, and Power in Colonial Virginia* (1996). A pioneering study of gender relations and their impact on Virginia society.

Cronon, William. *Changes in the Land: Colonists and the Ecology of New England* (1983). A path-breaking examination of how English colonization affected the natural environment in New England.

Gleach, Frederic W. *Powhatan's World and Colonial Virginia: A Conflict of Cultures* (1997). A study of Indian culture and the impact of European colonization upon it.

Hill, Christopher. *The Century of Revolution* (1961). A survey stressing the causes and consequences of the English Civil War.

Horn, James. *Adapting to a New World: English Society in the Seventeenth-Century Chesapeake* (1994). A detailed examination of the lives of early settlers in England and later in Virginia.

Morgan, Edmund S. *The Puritan Family* (1944). An early examination of family life and gender relations in colonial America.

Pestana, Carla G. *The English Atlantic in an Age of Revolution, 1640–1661* (2001). Analyzes how the English Civil War reverberated in the American colonies.

Philbrick Nathaniel. *Mayflower* (2006). An account of one of the most celebrated voyages of the colonial era, and the early history of the Plymouth colony.

Price, David A. *Love and Hate in Jamestown: John Smith, Pocahontas, and the Start of a New Nation* (2003). Presents the legend and reality of John Smith, Pocahontas, and early Virginia.

Taylor, Alan. *American Colonies* (2001). A comprehensive survey of the history of North American colonies from their beginnings to 1763.

Winship, Michael. *Making Heretics: Militant Protestantism and Free Grace in Massachusetts, 1636–1641* (2002). The most recent account of Anne Hutchinson and the Antinomian controversy.

WEBSITES

Plymouth Colony Archive Project: www.histarch.uiuc.edu/plymouth/index.html

Virtual Jamestown: www.virtualjamestown.org

REVIEW QUESTIONS

1. Compare and contrast England's settlement history in the Americas to Spain's. Consider the treatment of Indians, the role of the Church, the significance of women, and economic development.

2. For the English, land was the basis of liberty. Explain the reasoning behind that concept and how it was markedly different from the Indians' conception of land.

3. Many Puritans claimed they came to North America seeking religious freedom, but they were extremely intolerant of other beliefs. In fact, there was greater liberty of conscience back in their native England. How do you explain this?

4. Describe who chose to emigrate to North America from England in the seventeenth century and explain their reasons.

5. In what ways did the New England economy and government differ from those in the Chesapeake colonies?

6. The English believed that, unlike the Spanish, their motives for colonization were pure, and that the growth of empire and freedom would always go hand-in-hand. How did the expansion of the British empire affect the freedoms of Native Americans, the Irish, and even many English citizens?

7. Considering politics, social tensions, and debates over the meaning of liberty, how do the events and aftermath of the English Civil War demonstrate that the English colonies in North America were part of a larger Atlantic community?

8. How did the tobacco economy draw the Chesapeake colonies into the greater Atlantic world?

FREEDOM QUESTIONS

1. With many degrees of freedom coexisting in seventeenth-century North America, a person might go from having no rights to possessing many in a lifetime. Use examples to demonstrate this fact.

2. To provide full freedoms for the higher social orders in both England and English North America, lower social orders had to do without. Explain how and why this was so.

3. How did the concepts and goals of "freedom" differ for the following settlers: newcomers to John Smith's Jamestown; a Puritan family in 1630s Massachusetts; and a Catholic landowner in 1640s Maryland?

4. Explain how the Puritans used their concept of moral liberty to justify their actions against others in the New World. Then discuss why some Puritans, other English settlers in the New World, and those remaining in England might see these justifications as hypocritical.

5. Review the debates over the true meaning of freedom and "English liberty" following the English Civil War. What would you say was the lasting significance of these debates?

KEY TERMS

Virginia Company (p. 54)

Roanoke colony (p. 56)

plantation (p. 56)

A Discourse Concerning Western Planting (p. 57)

enclosure movement (p. 58)

indentured servant (p. 60)

John Smith (p. 63)

headright system (p. 64)

House of Burgesses (p. 64)

Uprising of 1622 (p. 65)

tobacco colony (p. 66)

dower rights (p. 67)

Puritans (p. 69)

moral liberty (p. 70)

John Winthrop (p. 70)

Pilgrims (p. 70)

Mayflower Compact (p. 71)

Great Migration (p. 71)

captivity narratives (p. 81)

The Sovereignty and Goodness of God (p. 81)

Pequot War (p. 81)

Half-Way Covenant (p. 84)

English liberty (p. 84)

Act Concerning Religion (p. 88)

REVIEW TABLE

Early Colonial British Settlements

Colony	Date Established	Sponsor	Founder/ Governor	Major Religion
Virginia	1607	Virginia Company	John Smith	Anglican
Plymouth	1620	English investors	William Bradford	Pilgrims (Puritan Separatists)
Massachusetts	1630	Massachusetts Bay Company	John Winthrop	Puritan/ Congregationalists
Maryland	1632	Proprietary colony	Cecilius Calvert	Protestant and Catholic
Rhode Island	1636	Royal charter	Roger Williams	Haven for all religions
Connecticut	1636	Royal charter	Thomas Hooker	Puritan/ Congregationalists

Chapter 3

Creating Anglo-America, 1660–1750

Charles Town Harbor, *a watercolor painted around 1740 by the artist Bishop Roberts, depicts the flourishing major port city of South Carolina. The ships all fly British flags, since the Navigation Acts prevented foreign vessels from carrying the colony's main export, rice. South Carolina was home to the wealthiest elite in Britain's mainland colonies, and ships carried imported luxury goods for them from Great Britain.*

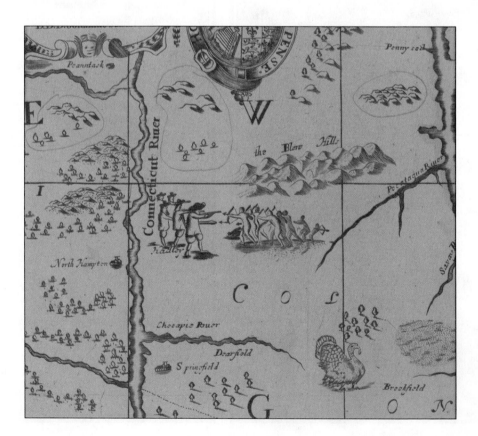

FOCUS QUESTIONS

- How did the English empire in America expand in the mid-seventeenth century?

- How was slavery established in the Western Atlantic world?

- What major social and political crises rocked the colonies in the late seventeenth century?

- What were the directions of social and economic change in the eighteenth-century colonies?

- How did patterns of class and gender roles change in eighteenth-century America?

On the last quarter of the seventeenth century, a series of crises rocked the European colonies of North America. Social and political tensions boiled over in sometimes ruthless conflicts between rich and poor, free and slave, settler and Indian, and members of different religious groups. At the same time, struggles within and between European empires echoed in the colonies. Aggrieved groups seized upon the language of freedom to advance their goals. Although each conflict had its own local causes, taken together they added up to a general crisis of colonial society in the area that would become the United States.

The bloodiest and most bitter conflict occurred in southern New England, where in 1675 an Indian alliance launched attacks on farms and settlements that were encroaching on Indian lands. It was the most dramatic and violent warfare in the region in the entire seventeenth century.

New Englanders described the Wampanoag leader Metacom (known to the colonists as King Philip) as the uprising's mastermind, although in fact most tribes fought under their own leaders. By this time, the white population considerably outnumbered the Indians. But the fate of the New England colonies hung in the balance for several months. By 1676, Indian forces had attacked nearly half of New England's ninety towns. Twelve in Massachusetts were destroyed. As refugees fled eastward, the line of settlement was pushed back almost to the Atlantic coast. Some

A scene from King Philip's War, included on a 1675 map of New England.

1,000 settlers, out of a population of 52,000, and 3,000 of New England's 20,000 Indians, perished in the fighting.

In mid-1676, the tide of battle turned and a ferocious counterattack broke the Indians' power once and for all. Although the uprising united numerous tribes, others remained loyal to the colonists. The role of the Iroquois in providing essential military aid to the colonists helped to solidify their developing alliance with the government of New York. Together, colonial and Indian forces inflicted devastating punishment on the rebels. Metacom was captured and executed, Indian villages destroyed, and captives, including men, women, and children, killed or sold into slavery in the West Indies. Most of the survivors fled to Canada or New York. Even the "praying Indians"—about 2,000 Indians who had converted to Christianity and lived in autonomous communities under Puritan supervision—suffered. Removed from their towns to Deer Island in Boston Harbor, supposedly for their own protection, many perished from disease and lack of food. Both sides committed atrocities in this merciless conflict, but in its aftermath the image of Indians as bloodthirsty savages became firmly entrenched in the New England mind.

In the long run, King Philip's war produced a broadening of freedom for white New Englanders by expanding their access to land. But this freedom rested on the final dispossession of the region's Indians.

GLOBAL COMPETITION AND THE EXPANSION OF ENGLAND'S EMPIRE

THE MERCANTILIST SYSTEM

As the New World became a battleground in European nations' endless contests for wealth and power, England moved to seize control of Atlantic trade, solidify its hold on North America's eastern coast, and exert greater control over its empire. By the middle of the seventeenth century, it was apparent that the colonies could be an important source of wealth for the mother country. According to the prevailing theory known as "mercantilism," the government should regulate economic activity so as to promote national power. It should encourage manufacturing and commerce by special bounties, monopolies, and other measures. Above all, trade should be controlled so that more gold and silver flowed into the country than left it. That is, exports of goods, which generated revenue from abroad, should exceed imports, which required paying foreigners for their products. In the mercantilist outlook, the role of colonies was to serve the interests of the mother country by producing marketable raw materials and importing manufactured goods from home. "Foreign trade," declared an influential work written in 1664 by a London merchant, formed the basis of "England's treasure." Commerce, not territorial plunder, was the foundation of empire.

Under Oliver Cromwell, as noted in Chapter 2, Parliament passed in 1651

EASTERN NORTH AMERICA IN THE SEVENTEENTH AND EARLY EIGHTEENTH CENTURIES

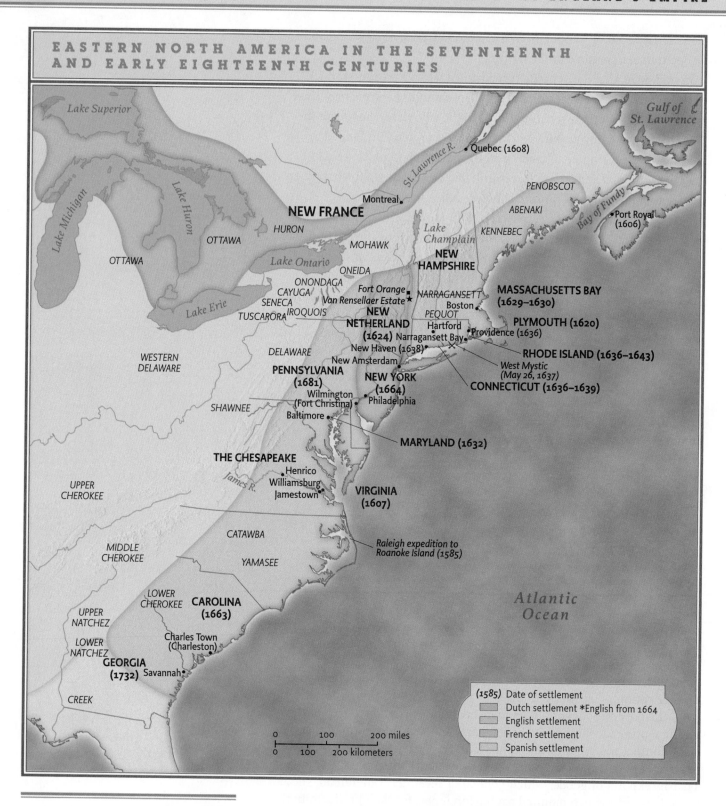

By the early eighteenth century, numerous English colonies populated eastern North America, while the French had established their own presence to the north and west.

the first Navigation Act, which aimed to wrest control of world trade from the Dutch, whose merchants profited from free trade with all parts of the world and all existing empires. Additional measures followed in 1660 and 1663. England's new economic policy, mercantilism, rested on the idea that England should enjoy the profits arising from the English empire.

According to the Navigation laws, certain "enumerated" goods—essentially the most valuable colonial products, such as tobacco and sugar—had to be transported in English ships and sold initially in English ports, although they could then be re-exported to foreign markets. Similarly, most European goods imported into the colonies had to be shipped through England, where customs duties were paid. This enabled English merchants, manufacturers, shipbuilders, and sailors to reap the benefits of colonial trade, and the government to enjoy added income from taxes. As members of the empire, American colonies would profit as well, since their ships were considered English. Indeed, the Navigation Acts stimulated the rise of New England's shipbuilding industry.

THE CONQUEST OF NEW NETHERLAND

The restoration of the English monarchy when Charles II assumed the throne in 1660 sparked a new period of colonial expansion. The government chartered new trading ventures, notably the Royal African Company, which was given a monopoly of the slave trade. Within a generation, the number of English colonies in North America doubled. First to come under English control was New Netherland, seized in 1664 during an Anglo-Dutch war that also saw England gain control of Dutch trading posts in Africa. King Charles II awarded the colony to his younger brother James, the duke of York, with "full and absolute power" to govern as he pleased. (Hence the colony's name became New York.)

New Netherland always remained peripheral to the far-flung Dutch empire. The Dutch fought to retain their holdings in Africa, Asia, and South America, but they surrendered New Netherland in 1664 without a fight. English rule transformed this minor military base into an important imperial outpost, a seaport trading with the Caribbean and Europe, and a launching pad for military operations against the French. New York's European population, around 9,000 when the English assumed control, rose to 20,000 by 1685.

NEW YORK AND THE RIGHTS OF ENGLISHMEN AND ENGLISHWOMEN

English rule expanded the freedom of some New Yorkers, while reducing that of others. The terms of surrender guaranteed that the English would respect the religious toleration and property holdings of the colony's many ethnic communities. But English law ended the Dutch tradition by which married women conducted business in their own name and inherited some of the property acquired during marriage. As colonists of Dutch origin adapted to English rule, their wills directed more attention to advancing the fortunes of their sons than providing for their wives and daughters. There had been many female traders in New Amsterdam (often widows who had inherited a deceased husband's property), but few remained by the end of the seventeenth century.

The English also introduced more restrictive attitudes toward blacks. In colonial New York City, as in New Amsterdam, those residents who enjoyed the status of "freeman," obtained by birth in the city or by an act of local authorities, enjoyed special privileges compared to others, including the right to work in various trades. But the English, in a reversal of Dutch practice, expelled free blacks from many skilled jobs.

An engraving representing the Grand Council of the Iroquois Nations of the area of present-day upstate New York. From a book about American Indians published in Paris by a Jesuit missionary, who depicts the Indians in the attire of ancient Romans. Note the prevalence of wampum belts in the image, in the foreground and in the hand and at the feet of the central figure. Wampum was used to certify treaties and other transactions.

Others benefited enormously from English rule. The duke of York and his appointed governors continued the Dutch practice of awarding immense land grants to favorites, including 160,000 acres to Robert Livingston and 90,000 to Frederick Philipse. By 1700, nearly 2 million acres of land were owned by only five New York families who intermarried regularly, exerted considerable political influence, and formed one of colonial America's most tightly knit landed elites.

NEW YORK AND THE INDIANS

Initially, English rule also strengthened the position of the Iroquois Confederacy of upstate New York. After a complex series of negotiations in the mid-1670s, Sir Edmund Andros, who had been appointed governor of New York after fighting the French in the Caribbean, formed an alliance known as the Covenant Chain, in which the imperial ambitions of the English and Indians reinforced one another. The Five (later Six) Iroquois Nations assisted Andros in clearing parts of New York of rival tribes and helped the British in attacks on the French and their Indian allies. Andros, for his part, recognized the Iroquois claim to authority over Indian communities in the vast area stretching to the Ohio River. But beginning in the 1680s, Indians around the Great Lakes and Ohio Valley regrouped and with French aid attacked the Iroquois, pushing them to the east. By the end of the century, the Iroquois Nations adopted a policy of careful neutrality, seeking to play the European empires off one another while continuing to profit from the fur trade.

THE CHARTER OF LIBERTIES

Many colonists, meanwhile, began to complain that they were being denied the "liberties of Englishmen," especially the right to consent to taxation.

There had been no representative assembly under the Dutch, and the governors appointed by the duke of York at first ruled without one. Discontent was especially strong on Long Island, which had been largely settled by New Englanders used to self-government.

In 1683, the duke agreed to call an elected assembly, whose first act was to draft a Charter of Liberties and Privileges. The Charter required that elections be held every three years among male property owners and the freemen of New York City; it also reaffirmed traditional English rights such as trial by jury and security of property, as well as religious toleration for all Protestants. In part, the Charter reflected an effort by newer English colonists to assert dominance over older Dutch settlers by establishing the principle that the "liberties" to which New Yorkers were entitled were those enjoyed by Englishmen at home.

THE FOUNDING OF CAROLINA

For more than three decades after the establishment of Maryland in 1634, no new English settlement was planted in North America. Then, in 1663, Charles II awarded to eight proprietors the right to establish a colony to the north of Florida, as a barrier to Spanish expansion. Not until 1670 did the first settlers arrive to found Carolina. In its early years, Carolina was the "colony of a colony." It began as an offshoot of the tiny island of Barbados. In the mid-seventeenth century, Barbados was the Caribbean's richest plantation economy, but a shortage of available land led wealthy planters to seek opportunities in Carolina for their sons. At first, Carolinians armed friendly Indians, employing them on raids into Spanish Florida, and enslaved others, shipping them to other mainland colonies and the West Indies. Indeed, between 1670 and 1720, the number of Indian slaves exported from Charleston was larger than the number of African slaves imported. In 1715, the Yamasee and Creek, alarmed by the enormous debts they had incurred in trade with the settlers and by slave traders' raids into their territory, rebelled. The uprising was crushed, and most of the remaining Indians were enslaved or driven out of the colony into Spanish Florida, from where they occasionally launched raids against English settlements.

The Fundamental Constitutions of Carolina, issued by the proprietors in 1669, proposed to establish a feudal society with a hereditary nobility (with strange titles like landgraves and caciques), serfs, and slaves. Needing to attract settlers quickly, however, the proprietors also provided for an elected assembly and religious toleration—by now recognized as essential to enticing migrants to North America. They also instituted a generous headright system, offering 150 acres for each member of an arriving family (in the case of indentured servants, of course, the land went to the employer) and 100 acres to male servants who completed their terms.

None of the baronies envisioned in the Fundamental Constitutions was actually established. Slavery, not feudalism, made Carolina an extremely hierarchical society. The proprietors instituted a rigorous legal code that promised slaveowners "absolute power and authority" over their human property and included imported slaves in the headright system. This allowed any persons who settled in Carolina and brought with them slaves, including planters from Barbados who resettled in the colony, instantly to acquire large new landholdings. In its early days, however, the economy centered on cattle raising and trade with local Indians, not agriculture. Carolina grew slowly until planters discovered the staple—rice—that would make them the wealthiest elite in English North America and their colony an epicenter of mainland slavery.

THE HOLY EXPERIMENT

The last English colony to be established in the seventeenth century was Pennsylvania. The proprietor, William Penn, envisioned it as a place where those facing religious persecution in Europe could enjoy spiritual freedom, and colonists and Indians would coexist in harmony. Penn's late father had been a supporter and creditor of Charles II. To cancel his debt to the Penn family and bolster the English presence in North America, the king in 1681 granted Penn a vast tract of land south and west of New York, as well as the old Swedish-Dutch colony that became Delaware.

A devout member of the Society of Friends, or Quakers, Penn was particularly concerned with establishing a refuge for his coreligionists, who faced increasing persecution in England. He had already assisted a group of English Quakers in purchasing half of what became the colony of New Jersey from Lord John Berkeley, who had received a land grant from the duke of York. Penn was largely responsible for the frame of government announced in 1677, the West Jersey Concessions, one of the most liberal of the era. Based on Quaker ideals, it created an elected assembly with a broad suffrage and established religious liberty. Penn hoped that West Jersey would become a society of small farmers, not large landowners.

An early eighteenth-century engraving depicts William Penn welcoming a German immigrant on the dock in Philadelphia. Penn sought to make migrants from all over Europe feel at home in Pennsylvania.

QUAKER LIBERTY

Like the Puritans, Penn considered his colony a "holy experiment," but of a different kind—"a free colony for all mankind that should go hither." He hoped that Pennsylvania could be governed according to Quaker principles, among them the equality of all persons (including women, blacks, and Indians) before God and the primacy of the individual conscience. To Quakers, liberty was a universal entitlement, not the possession of any single people—a position that would eventually make them the first group of whites to repudiate slavery. Penn also treated Indians with a consideration almost unique in the colonial experience, arranging to purchase land before reselling it to colonists and offering refuge to tribes driven out of other colonies by warfare. Sometimes, he even purchased the same land twice, when more than one Indian tribe claimed it. Since Quakers were pacifists who came to America unarmed and did not even organize a militia until the 1740s, peace with the native population was essential. Penn's Chain of Friendship appealed to the local Indians, promising protection from rival tribes who claimed domination over them.

Religious freedom was Penn's most fundamental principle. He condemned attempts to enforce "religious Uniformity" for depriving thousands of "free inhabitants" of England of the right to worship as they desired. His Charter of Liberty, approved by the assembly in 1682, offered "Christian liberty" to all who affirmed a belief in God and did not use their freedom to promote "licentiousness." There was no established church in Pennsylvania, and attendance at religious services was entirely voluntary, although Jews were barred from office by a required oath affirming belief in the divinity of Jesus Christ. At the same time, the Quakers upheld a strict code of personal morality. Penn's Frame of Government prohibited swearing, drunkenness, and adultery, as well as popular entertainments of the era such as "revels, bull-baiting, and cock-fighting." Private religious belief may not have been enforced by the government, but moral public behavior certainly was. Not religious uniformity but a virtuous citizenry would be the foundation of Penn's social order.

A Quaker Meeting, *a painting by an unidentified British artist, dating from the late eighteenth or early nineteenth century. It illustrates the prominent place of women in Quaker gatherings.*

LAND IN PENNSYLVANIA

Given the power to determine the colony's form of government, Penn established an appointed council to originate legislation and an assembly elected by male taxpayers and "freemen" (owners of 100 acres of land for free immigrants and 50 acres for former indentured servants). These rules made a majority of the male population eligible to vote. Penn owned all the colony's land and sold it to settlers at low prices rather than granting it outright. Like other proprietors, he expected to turn a profit, and like most of them, he never really did. But if Penn did not prosper, Pennsylvania did. A majority of the early settlers were Quakers from the British Isles. But Pennsylvania's religious toleration, healthy climate, and inexpensive land, along with Penn's aggressive efforts to publicize the colony's advantages, soon attracted immigrants from all over western Europe.

Ironically, the freedoms Pennsylvania offered to European immigrants contributed to the deterioration of freedom for others. The colony's successful efforts to attract settlers would eventually come into conflict with Penn's benevolent Indian policy. And the opening of Pennsylvania led to an immediate decline in the number of indentured servants choosing to sail for Virginia and Maryland, a development that did much to shift those colonies toward reliance on slave labor.

ORIGINS OF AMERICAN SLAVERY

No European nation, including England, embarked on the colonization of the New World with the intention of relying on African slaves for the bulk of its labor force. But the incessant demand for workers spurred by the spread of tobacco cultivation eventually led Chesapeake planters to turn to the transatlantic trade in slaves. Compared with indentured servants, slaves offered planters many advantages. As Africans, they could not claim the protections of English common law. Slaves' terms of service never expired, and they therefore did not become a population of unruly landless men. Their children were slaves, and their skin color made it more difficult for them to escape into the surrounding society. African men, moreover, unlike their Native American counterparts, were accustomed to intensive agricultural labor, and they had encountered many diseases known in Europe and developed resistance to them, so were less likely to succumb to epidemics.

ENGLISHMEN AND AFRICANS

The English had long viewed alien peoples with disdain, including the Irish, Native Americans, and Africans. They described these strangers in remarkably similar language as savage, pagan, and uncivilized, often comparing them to animals. "Race"—the idea that humanity is divided into well-defined groups associated with skin color—is a modern concept that had not fully developed in the seventeenth century. Nor had "racism"—an ideology based on the belief that some races are inherently superior to others and entitled to rule over them. The main lines of division within humanity were thought to be civilization versus barbarism or Christianity versus heathenism, not color or race.

Nonetheless, anti-black stereotypes flourished in seventeenth-century England. Africans were seen as so alien—in color, religion, and social practices—that they were "enslavable" in a way that poor Englishmen were not. Most English also deemed Indians to be uncivilized. But the Indian population declined so rapidly, and it was so easy for Indians, familiar with the countryside, to run away, that Indian slavery never became viable. Some Indians were sold into slavery in the Caribbean. But it is difficult to enslave a people on their native soil. Slaves are almost always outsiders, transported from elsewhere to their place of labor.

SLAVERY IN HISTORY

Slavery has existed for nearly the entire span of human history. It was central to the societies of ancient Greece and Rome. Slavery survived for centuries in northern Europe after the collapse of the Roman Empire. Germans, Vikings, and Anglo-Saxons all held slaves. Slavery persisted even longer in the Mediterranean world, where a slave trade in Slavic peoples survived into the fifteenth century. (The English word "slavery" derives from "Slav.") Pirates from the Barbary Coast of North Africa regularly seized Christians from ships and enslaved them. In West Africa, as noted in Chapter 1, slavery and a slave trade predated the coming of Europeans, and small-scale slavery existed among Native Americans. But slavery in nearly all these instances differed greatly from the institution that developed in the New World.

In the Americas, slavery was based on the plantation, an agricultural enterprise that brought together large numbers of workers under the control of a single owner. This imbalance magnified the possibility of slave resistance and made it necessary to police the system rigidly. It encouraged the creation of a sharp boundary between slavery and freedom. Labor on slave plantations was far more demanding than in the household slavery common in Africa, and the death rate among slaves much higher. In the New World, slavery would come to be associated with race, a concept that drew a permanent line between whites and blacks. Unlike in Africa, slaves who became free always carried with them in their skin color the mark of

Cutting Sugar Cane *an engraving from* Ten Views in Antigua, *published in 1823. Male and female slaves harvest and load the sugar crop while an overseer on horseback addresses a slave. During the eighteenth century, sugar was the chief crop produced by Western Hemisphere slaves.*

bondage—a visible sign of being considered unworthy of incorporation as equals into free society.

SLAVERY IN THE WEST INDIES

A sense of Africans as alien and inferior made their enslavement by the English possible. But prejudice by itself did not create North American slavery. For this institution to take root, planters and government authorities had to be convinced that importing African slaves was the best way to solve their persistent shortage of labor. During the seventeenth century, the shipping of slaves from Africa to the New World became a major international business. But only a relative handful were brought to England's mainland colonies. By the time plantation slavery became a major feature of life in English North America, it was already well entrenched elsewhere in the Western Hemisphere. By 1600, huge sugar plantations worked by slaves from Africa had made their appearance in Brazil, a colony of Portugal. In the seventeenth century, England, Holland, Denmark, and France joined Spain as owners of West Indian islands. English emigrants to the West Indies outnumbered those to North America in the first part of the seventeenth century. In 1650, the English population of the West Indies exceeded that in all of North America. Generally, the first settlers established mixed economies with small farms worked by white indentured servants. But as sugar planters engrossed the best land, they forced white farmers off island after island. White indentured servants proved as discontented as elsewhere. In 1629, when a Spanish expedition attacked the British island of Nevis, servants in the local militia joined them shouting, "Liberty, joyful liberty!"

With the Indian population having been wiped out by disease, and with the white indentured servants unwilling to do the back-breaking, monotonous work of sugar cultivation, the massive importation of slaves

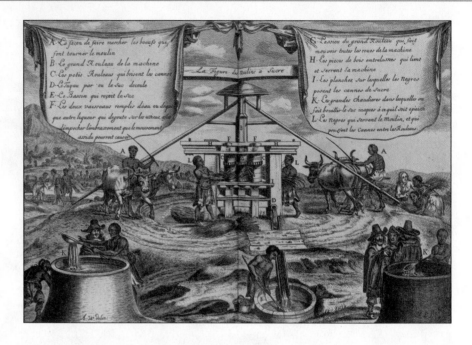

An engraving from Charles de Rochefort's Histoire Naturelle et Morale des Îles Antilles de l'Amerique *(1665), depicts a sugar mill powered by cattle, with slaves feeding the cane into rollers, which grind it to crush out the juice. The text describes how the various parts of the machinery work.*

from Africa began. In 1645, for example, Barbados, a tiny island owned by England, was home to around 11,000 white farmers and indentured servants and 5,000 slaves. As sugar cultivation intensified, planters turned increasingly to slave labor. By 1660, the island's population had grown to 40,000, half European and half African. Ten years later, the slave population had risen to 82,000, concentrated on some 750 sugar plantations. Meanwhile, the white population stagnated. By the end of the seventeenth century, huge sugar plantations manned by hundreds of slaves dominated the West Indian economy, and on most of the islands the African population far outnumbered that of European origin.

Sugar was the first crop to be mass-marketed to consumers in Europe. Before its emergence, international trade consisted largely of precious metals like gold and silver, and luxury goods aimed at an elite market, like the spices and silks imported from Asia. Sugar was by far the most important product of the British, French, and Portugese empires, and New World sugar plantations produced immense profits for planters, merchants, and imperial governments. Saint Domingue, today's Haiti, was the jewel of the French empire. In 1660, Barbados generated more trade than all the other English colonies combined.

Compared to its rapid introduction in Brazil and the West Indies, slavery developed slowly in North America. Slaves cost more than indentured servants, and the high death rate among tobacco workers made it economically unappealing to pay for a lifetime of labor. For decades, servants from England formed the backbone of the Chesapeake labor force, and the number of Africans remained small. As late as 1680, there were only 4,500 blacks in the Chesapeake, a little over 5 percent of the region's population. The most important social distinction in the seventeenth-century Chesapeake was not between black and white but between the white plantation owners who dominated politics and society and everybody else— small farmers, indentured servants, and slaves.

SLAVERY AND THE LAW

Centuries before the voyages of Columbus, Spain had enacted *Las Siete Partidas*, a series of laws granting slaves certain rights relating to marriage, the holding of property, and access to freedom. These laws were transferred to Spain's American empire. They were often violated, but nonetheless gave slaves opportunities to claim rights under the law. Moreover, the Catholic Church often encouraged masters to free individual slaves. The law of slavery in English North America would become far more repressive than in the Spanish empire, especially on the all-important question of whether avenues existed by which slaves could obtain freedom.

For much of the seventeenth century, however, the legal status of Chesapeake blacks remained ambiguous and the line between slavery and freedom more permeable than it would later become. The first Africans, twenty in all, arrived in Virginia in 1619. British pirates sailing under the Dutch flag had seized them from a Portuguese ship carrying slaves from Angola, on the southwestern coast of Africa, to modern-day Mexico. Small numbers followed in subsequent years. Although the first black arrivals were almost certainly treated as slaves, it appears that at least some managed to become free after serving a term of years. To be sure, racial distinctions were enacted into law from the outset. As early as the 1620s, the law barred blacks from serving in the Virginia militia. The government punished sexual relations outside of marriage between Africans and Europeans more severely than the same acts involving two white persons. In 1643, a poll tax (a tax levied on individuals) was imposed on African but not white women. In both Virginia and Maryland, however, free blacks could sue and testify in court, and some even managed to acquire land and purchase white servants or African slaves. It is not known exactly how Anthony Johnson, who apparently arrived in Virginia as a slave during the 1620s, obtained his freedom. But by the 1640s, he was the owner of slaves and of several hundred acres of land on Virginia's eastern shore. Blacks and whites labored side by side in the tobacco fields, sometimes ran away together, and established intimate relationships.

THE RISE OF CHESAPEAKE SLAVERY

Evidence of blacks being held as slaves for life appears in the historical record of the 1640s. In registers of property, for example, white servants are listed by the number of years of labor, while blacks, with higher valuations, have no terms of service associated with their names. Not until the 1660s, however, did the laws of Virginia and Maryland refer explicitly to slavery. As tobacco planting spread and the demand for labor increased, the condition of black and white servants diverged sharply. Authorities sought to

In this scene depicted on an English handkerchief, male and female slaves work in the tobacco fields alongside a white indentured servant (right).

improve the status of white servants, hoping to counteract the widespread impression in England that Virginia was a death trap. At the same time, access to freedom for blacks receded.

A Virginia law of 1662 provided that in the case of a child one of whose parents was free and one slave, the status of the offspring followed that of the mother. (This provision not only reversed the European practice of defining a child's status through the father but also made the sexual abuse of slave women profitable for slaveholders, since any children that resulted remained the owner's property.) In 1667, the Virginia House of Burgesses decreed that religious conversion did not release a slave from bondage. Thus, Christians could own other Christians as slaves. Moreover, authorities sought to prevent the growth of the free black population by defining all offspring of interracial relationships as illegitimate, severely punishing white women who begat children with black men, and prohibiting the freeing of any slave unless he or she were transported out of the colony. By 1680, even though the black population was still small, notions of racial difference were well entrenched in the law. In England's American empire, wrote one contemporary, "these two words, Negro and Slave [have] by custom grown homogenous and convertible." In British North America, unlike the Spanish empire, no distinctive mulatto, or mixed-race, class existed; the law treated everyone with African ancestry as black.

BACON'S REBELLION: LAND AND LABOR IN VIRGINIA

Virginia's shift from white indentured servants to African slaves as the main plantation labor force was accelerated by one of the most dramatic confrontations of this era, Bacon's Rebellion of 1676. Governor William Berkeley had for thirty years run a corrupt regime in alliance with an inner circle of the colony's wealthiest tobacco planters. He rewarded his followers with land grants and lucrative offices. At first, Virginia's tobacco boom had benefited not only planters but also smaller farmers, some of them former servants who managed to acquire farms. But as tobacco farming spread inland, planters connected with the governor engrossed the best lands, leaving freed servants (a growing population, since Virginia's death rate was finally falling) with no options but to work as tenants or to move to the frontier. At the same time, heavy taxes on tobacco and falling prices because of overproduction reduced the prospects of small farmers. By the 1670s, poverty among whites had reached levels reminiscent of England. In addition, the right to vote, previously enjoyed by all adult men, was confined to landowners in 1670. Governor Berkeley maintained peaceful relations with Virginia's remaining native population. His refusal to allow white settlement in areas reserved for Indians angered many land-hungry colonists.

As early as 1661, a Virginia indentured servant was accused of planning an uprising among those "who would be for liberty and free from bondage." Fifteen years later, long-simmering social tensions coupled with widespread resentment against the injustices of the Berkeley regime erupted in Bacon's Rebellion. The spark was a minor confrontation between Indians and colonists on Virginia's western frontier. Settlers now demanded that the governor authorize the extermination or removal of the colony's Indians, to open more land for whites. Fearing all-out warfare and continuing to profit from the trade with Indians in deerskins, Berkeley refused. An uprising followed that soon careened out of control. Beginning with a series of Indian massacres, it quickly grew into a full-fledged rebellion against Berkeley and his system of rule.

To some extent, Bacon's Rebellion was a conflict within the Virginia elite. The leader, Nathaniel Bacon, a wealthy and ambitious planter who had arrived in Virginia in 1673, disdained Berkeley's coterie as men of "mean education and employments." His backers included men of wealth outside the governor's circle of cronies. But Bacon's call for the removal of all Indians from the colony, a reduction of taxes at a time of economic recession, and an end to rule by "grandees" rapidly gained support from small farmers, landless men, indentured servants, and even some Africans. The bulk of his army consisted of discontented men who had recently been servants.

THE END OF THE REBELLION, AND ITS CONSEQUENCES

Bacon promised freedom (including access to Indian lands) to all who joined his ranks. His supporters invoked the tradition of "English liberties" and spoke of the poor being "robbed" and "cheated" by their social superiors. In 1676, Bacon gathered an armed force for an unauthorized and indiscriminate campaign against those he called the governor's "protected and darling Indians." He refused Berkeley's order to disband and marched on Jamestown, burning it to the ground. The governor fled, and Bacon became the ruler of Virginia. His forces plundered the estates of Berkeley's supporters. Only the arrival of a squadron of warships from England restored order. Bacon's Rebellion was over. Twenty-three of his supporters were hanged (Bacon himself had taken ill and died shortly after Berkeley's departure).

The specter of a civil war among whites greatly frightened Virginia's ruling elite, who took dramatic steps to consolidate their power and improve their image. They restored property qualifications for voting, which Bacon had rescinded. At the same time, planters developed a new political style in which they cultivated the support of poorer neighbors. Meanwhile, the authorities reduced taxes and adopted a more aggressive Indian policy, opening western areas to small farmers, many of whom prospered from a rise in tobacco prices after 1680. To avert the further rise of a rebellious population of landless former indentured servants, Virginia's authorities accelerated the shift to slaves (who would never become free) on the tobacco plantations. As Virginia reduced the number of indentured servants, it redefined their freedom dues to include fifty acres of land.

A SLAVE SOCIETY

Between 1680 and 1700, slave labor began to supplant indentured servitude on Chesapeake plantations. Bacon's Rebellion was only one among several factors that contributed to this development. As the death rate finally began to fall, it became more economical to purchase a laborer for life. Improving conditions in England reduced the number of transatlantic migrants, and the

Sir William Berkeley, governor of colonial Virginia, 1641–1652 and 1660–1677, in a portrait by Sir Peter Lely. Berkeley's authoritarian rule helped to spark Bacon's Rebellion.

opening of Pennsylvania, where land was readily available, attracted those who still chose to leave for America. Finally, the ending of a monopoly on the English slave trade previously enjoyed by the Royal Africa Company opened the door to other traders and reduced the price of imported African slaves.

By 1700, blacks constituted more than 10 percent of Virginia's population. Fifty years later, they made up nearly half. Recognizing the growing importance of slavery, the House of Burgesses in 1705 enacted a new slave code, bringing together the scattered legislation of the previous century and adding new provisions that embedded the principle of white supremacy in the law. Slaves were property, completely subject to the will of their masters and, more generally, of the white community. They could be bought and sold, leased, fought over in court, and passed on to one's descendants. Henceforth, blacks and whites were tried in separate courts. No black, free or slave, could own arms, strike a white man, or employ a white servant. Any white person could apprehend any black to demand a certificate of freedom or a pass from the owner giving permission to be off the plantation. Virginia had changed from a "society with slaves," in which slavery was one system of labor among others, to a "slave society," where slavery stood at the center of the economic process.

NOTIONS OF FREEDOM

One sentiment shared by Europeans, Native Americans, and Africans was fear of enslavement. Throughout history, slaves have run away and in other ways resisted bondage. They did the same in the colonial Chesapeake. Colonial newspapers were filled with advertisements for runaway slaves. These notices described the appearance and skills of the fugitive and included such comments as "ran away without any cause" or "he has great notions of freedom." Some of the blacks brought to the region during the seventeenth century were the offspring of encounters between European traders and Africans on the western coast of Africa or the Caribbean. Familiar with European culture and fluent in English, they turned to the colonial legal system in their quest for freedom. Throughout the seventeenth century, blacks appeared in court claiming their liberty, at first on the basis of conversion to Christianity or having a white father. This was one reason Virginia in the 1660s closed these pathways to freedom. But although legal avenues to liberty receded, the desire for freedom did not. After the suppression of a slave conspiracy in 1709, Alexander Spotswood, the governor of Virginia, warned planters to be vigilant. The desire for freedom, he reminded them, can "call together all those who long to shake off the fetters of slavery."

COLONIES IN CRISIS

King Philip's War of 1675 and Bacon's Rebellion the following year coincided with disturbances in other colonies. In Maryland, where the proprietor, Lord Baltimore, in 1670 had suddenly restricted the right to vote to owners of fifty acres of land or a certain amount of personal property, a Protestant uprising unsuccessfully sought to oust his government and restore the suffrage for all freemen. In several colonies, increasing settlement on the frontier led to resistance by alarmed Indians. A rebellion by Westo Indians was suppressed in Carolina in 1680. The Pueblo Revolt of the same year (discussed in Chapter 1) indicated that the crisis of colonial authority was not confined to the British empire.

THE GLORIOUS REVOLUTION

Turmoil in England also reverberated in the colonies. In 1688, the long struggle for domination of English government between Parliament and the crown reached its culmination in the Glorious Revolution, which established parliamentary supremacy once and for all and secured the Protestant succession to the throne. Under Charles II, Parliament had asserted its authority in the formation of national policy. It expanded its control of finance, influenced foreign affairs, and excluded from political and religious power Catholics and Dissenters (Protestants who belonged to a denomination other than the official Anglican Church).

When Charles died in 1685, he was succeeded by his brother James II (formerly the duke of York), a practicing Catholic and a believer that kings ruled by divine right. In 1687, James decreed religious toleration for both Protestant Dissenters and Catholics. The following year, the birth of James's son raised the prospect of a Catholic succession, alarming those who equated "popery" with tyranny. A group of English aristocrats invited the Dutch nobleman William of Orange, the husband of James's Protestant daughter Mary, to assume the throne in the name of English liberties. William arrived in England in November 1688 with an army of 21,000 men, two-thirds of them Dutch. As the landed elite and leaders of the Anglican Church rallied to William's cause, James II fled and the revolution was complete.

Unlike the broad social upheaval that marked the English Civil War of the 1640s, the Glorious Revolution was in effect a coup engineered by a small group of aristocrats in alliance with an ambitious Dutch prince. They had no intention of challenging the institution of the monarchy. But the overthrow of James II entrenched more firmly than ever the notion that liberty was the birthright of all Englishmen and that the king was subject to the rule of law. To justify the ouster of James II, Parliament in 1689 enacted a Bill of Rights, which listed parliamentary powers such as control over taxation as well as rights of individuals, including trial by jury. These were the "ancient" and "undoubted . . . rights and liberties" of all Englishmen. In the following year, the Toleration Act allowed Protestant Dissenters (but not Catholics) to worship freely, although only Anglicans could hold public office.

As always, British politics were mirrored in the American colonies. The period from the 1660s to the 1680s had been one of growing religious toleration in both regions, succeeded by a tightening of religious control once William of Orange, a Protestant, became king. Indeed, after the Glorious Revolution, Protestant domination was secured in most of the colonies, with the established churches of England (Anglican) and Scotland (Presbyterian) growing the fastest, while Catholics and Dissenters suffered various forms of discrimination. Despite the new regime's language of liberty, however, religious freedom was far more advanced in some American colonies, such as Rhode Island, Pennsylvania, and Carolina, than in England. Nonetheless, throughout English America the Glorious Revolution powerfully reinforced among the colonists the sense of sharing a proud legacy of freedom and Protestantism with the mother country.

King William III, a portrait by an unknown artist, painted around 1697. William, who came to power in England as a result of the Glorious Revolution, wears an ermine cape.

THE GLORIOUS REVOLUTION IN AMERICA

The Glorious Revolution exposed fault lines in colonial society and offered local elites an opportunity to regain authority that had recently been challenged. Until the mid-1670s, the North American colonies had essentially governed themselves, with little interference from England. Governor Berkeley ran Virginia as he saw fit; proprietors in New York, Maryland, and Carolina governed in any fashion they could persuade colonists to accept; and New England colonies elected their own officials and openly flouted trade regulations. In 1675, England established the Lords of Trade to oversee colonial affairs. Three years later, the Lords questioned the Massachusetts government about its compliance with the Navigation Acts. They received the surprising reply that since the colony had no representatives in Parliament, the Acts did not apply to it unless the Massachusetts General Court approved.

In the 1680s, England moved to reduce colonial autonomy. Shortly before his death, Charles II revoked the Massachusetts charter, citing wholesale violations of the Navigation Acts. Hoping to raise more money from America in order to reduce his dependence on Parliament, James II between 1686 and 1688 combined Connecticut, Plymouth, Massachusetts, New Hampshire, Rhode Island, New York, and East and West Jersey into a single super-colony, the Dominion of New England. It was ruled by the former New York governor Sir Edmund Andros, who did not have to answer to an elected assembly. These events reinforced the impression that James II was an enemy of freedom. In New England, Andros's actions alienated nearly everyone not dependent on his administration for favors. He appointed local officials in place of elected ones, imposed taxes without the approval of elected representatives, declared earlier land grants void unless approved by him, and enforced religious toleration for all Protestants. His rule threatened both English liberties and the church-state relationship at the heart of the Puritan order.

THE MARYLAND UPRISING

In 1689, news of the overthrow of James II triggered rebellions in several American colonies. In April, the Boston militia seized and jailed Edmund Andros and other officials, whereupon the New England colonies reestablished the governments abolished when the Dominion of New England was created. In May, a rebel militia headed by Captain Jacob Leisler established a Committee of Safety and took control of New York. Two months later, Maryland's Protestant Association overthrew the government of the colony's Catholic proprietor, Lord Baltimore.

All of these new regimes claimed to have acted in the name of English liberties and looked to London for approval. But the degrees of success of these coups varied markedly. Most triumphant were the Maryland rebels. Concluding that Lord Baltimore had mismanaged the colony, William revoked his charter (although the proprietor retained his land and rents) and established a new, Protestant-dominated government. Catholics retained the right to practice their religion but were barred from voting and holding office. In 1715, after the Baltimore family had converted to Anglicanism, proprietary power was restored. But the events of 1689 transformed the ruling group in Maryland and put an end to the colony's unique history of religious toleration.

LEISLER'S REBELLION

The outcome in New York was far different. The German-born Leisler, one of the wealthiest merchants in the city, was a fervent Calvinist who feared that James II intended to reduce England and its empire to "popery and slavery." Although it was not his intention, Leisler's regime divided the colony along ethnic and economic lines. Members of the Dutch majority seized the opportunity to reclaim local power after more than two decades of English rule, while bands of rebels ransacked the homes of wealthy New Yorkers. Prominent English colonists, joined by some wealthy Dutch merchants and fur traders, protested to London that Leisler was a tyrant. William refused to recognize Leisler's authority and dispatched a new governor, backed by troops. Many of Leisler's followers were imprisoned, and he himself was condemned to be executed. The grisly manner of his death—Leisler was hanged and then had his head cut off and body cut into four parts—reflected the depths of hatred the rebellion had inspired. For generations, the rivalry between Leisler and anti-Leisler parties polarized New York politics.

CHANGES IN NEW ENGLAND

After deposing Edmund Andros, the New England colonies lobbied hard in London for the restoration of their original charters. Most were successful, but Massachusetts was not. In 1691, the crown issued a new charter that absorbed Plymouth into Massachusetts and transformed the political structure of the Bible Commonwealth. Town government remained intact, but henceforth property ownership, not church membership, would be the requirement to vote in elections for the General Court. The governor was now appointed in London rather than elected. Thus, Massachusetts became a royal colony, the majority of whose voters were no longer Puritan "saints." Moreover, it was required to abide by the English Toleration Act of 1690—that is, to allow all Protestants to worship freely. The demise of the "New England way" greatly benefited non-Puritan merchants and large landowners, who came to dominate the new government.

These events produced an atmosphere of considerable tension in Massachusetts, exacerbated by raids by French troops and their Indian allies on the northern New England frontier. The advent of religious toleration heightened anxieties among the Puritan clergy, who considered other Protestant denominations a form of heresy. "I would not have a hand in setting up their Devil worship," one minister declared of the Quakers. Indeed, not a few Puritans thought they saw the hand of Satan in the events of 1690 and 1691.

THE PROSECUTION OF WITCHES

Belief in magic, astrology, and witchcraft was widespread in seventeenth-century Europe and America, existing alongside the religion of the clergy and churches. Many Puritans believed in supernatural interventions in the affairs of the world. They interpreted as expressions of God's will such events as lightning that struck one house but spared another, and epidemics that reduced the population of their Indian enemies. Evil forces could also affect daily life. Witches were individuals, usually women, who were accused of having entered into a pact with the devil to obtain supernatural powers, which they used to harm others or to interfere with natural processes. When a child was stillborn or crops failed, many believed that witchcraft was at work.

In Europe and the colonies, witchcraft was punishable by execution. It is estimated that between the years 1400 and 1800, more than 50,000 people were executed in Europe after being convicted of witchcraft. Witches were, from time to time, hanged in seventeenth-century New England. Most were women beyond childbearing age who were outspoken, economically independent, or estranged from their husbands, or who in other ways violated traditional gender norms. The witch's alleged power challenged both God's will and the standing of men as heads of family and rulers of society.

THE SALEM WITCH TRIALS

Until 1692, the prosecution of witches had been local and sporadic. But in the heightened anxiety of that year, a series of trials and executions took place in the town of Salem that made its name to this day a byword for fanaticism and persecution. The crisis began late in 1691 when several young girls began to suffer fits and nightmares, attributed by their elders to witchcraft. Soon, three witches had been named, including Tituba, an Indian from the Caribbean who was a slave in the home of one of the girls. Since the only way to avoid prosecution was to confess and name others, accusations of witchcraft began to snowball. By the middle of 1692, hundreds of residents of Salem had come forward to accuse their neighbors. Some, it appears, used the occasion to settle old scores within the Salem community. Local authorities took legal action against nearly 150 persons, the large majority of them women. Many confessed to save their lives, but fourteen women and five men were hanged, protesting their innocence to the end. One man was pressed to death (crushed under a weight of stones) for refusing to enter a plea.

An illustration from Cotton Mather's 1692 account of witchcraft depicts a witch on her broomstick, accompanied by Satan.

In Salem, accusations of witchcraft spread far beyond the usual profile of middle-aged women to include persons of all ages (one was a child of four) and those with no previous history of assertiveness or marital discord. As accusations and executions multiplied, it became clear that something was seriously wrong with the colony's system of justice. Toward the end of 1692, the governor of Massachusetts dissolved the Salem court and ordered the remaining prisoners released. At the same time, the prominent clergyman Increase Mather published an influential treatise, *Cases of Conscience Concerning Evil Spirits*, warning that juries should not take seriously either the testimony of those who claimed to be possessed or the confessions and accusations of persons facing execution. The events in Salem discredited the tradition of prosecuting witches and accelerated a commitment among prominent colonists to finding scientific explanations for natural events like comets and illnesses, rather than attributing them to magic. In future years, only two accused witches would be brought to trial in Massachusetts, and both were found not guilty.

THE GROWTH OF COLONIAL AMERICA

The Salem witch trials took place precisely two centuries after Columbus's initial voyage. The Western Hemisphere was dramatically different from the world he had encountered. Powerful states had been destroyed and the native population decimated by disease and in some areas deprived of its land. In North America, three new and very different empires had arisen, competing for wealth and power. The urban-based Spanish empire, with a small settler elite and growing mestizo population directing the labor of a large Indian population, still relied for wealth primarily on the gold and silver mines of Mexico and South America. The French empire centered on Saint Domingue, Martinique, and Guadeloupe, plantation islands of the West Indies. On the mainland, it consisted of a thinly settled string of farms and trading posts in the St. Lawrence Valley. In North America north of the Rio Grande, the English colonies had far outstripped their rivals in population and trade.

As stability returned after the crises of the late seventeenth century, English North America experienced an era of remarkable growth. Between 1700 and 1770, crude backwoods settlements became bustling provincial capitals. Even as epidemics continued in Indian country, the hazards of disease among colonists diminished, agricultural settlement pressed westward, and hundreds of thousands of newcomers arrived from the Old World. Thanks to a high birthrate and continuing immigration, the population of England's mainland colonies, 265,000 in 1700, grew nearly tenfold, to over 2.3 million seventy years later. (It is worth noting, however, that because of the decline suffered by the Indians, the North American population was considerably lower in 1770 than it had been in 1492.)

A DIVERSE POPULATION

Probably the most striking characteristic of colonial American society in the eighteenth century was its sheer diversity. In 1700, the colonies were essentially English outposts. Relatively few Africans had yet been brought to the mainland, and the overwhelming majority of the white population—close to 90 percent—was of English origin. In the eighteenth century, African and non-English European arrivals skyrocketed, while the number emigrating from England declined (see Table 3.1).

As economic conditions in England improved, the government began to rethink the policy of encouraging emigration. No longer concerned with an excess population of vagabonds and "masterless men," authorities began to worry that large-scale emigration was draining labor from the mother country. About 40 percent of European immigrants to the colonies during the eighteenth century continued to arrive as bound laborers who had temporarily sacrificed their freedom to make the voyage

Table 3.1 ORIGINS AND STATUS OF MIGRANTS TO BRITISH NORTH AMERICAN COLONIES, 1700–1775

	Total	Slaves	Indentured Servants	Convicts	Free
Africa	278,400	278,400	—	—	—
Ireland	108,600	—	39,000	17,500	52,100
Germany	84,500	—	30,000	—	54,500
England/Wales	73,100	—	27,200	32,500	13,400
Scotland	35,300	—	7,400	2,200	25,700
Other	5,900	—	—	—	5,900
Total	585,800	278,400	103,600	52,200	151,600

to the New World. But as the colonial economy prospered, poor indentured migrants were increasingly joined by professionals and skilled craftsmen—teachers, ministers, weavers, carpenters—whom England could ill afford to lose. This brought to an end official efforts to promote English emigration.

ATTRACTING SETTLERS

Yet while worrying about losing desirable members of its population, the government in London remained convinced that colonial development enhanced the nation's power and wealth. To bolster the Chesapeake labor force, nearly 50,000 convicts (a group not desired in Britain) were sent to work in the tobacco fields. Officials also actively encouraged Protestant immigration from the non-English (and less prosperous) parts of the British Isles and from the European continent, promising newcomers easy access to land and the right to worship freely. A law of 1740 even offered European immigrants British citizenship after seven years of residence, something that in the mother country could only be obtained by a special act of Parliament. The widely publicized image of America as an asylum for those "whom bigots chase from foreign lands," in the words of a 1735 poem, was in many ways a byproduct of Britain's efforts to attract settlers from non-English areas to its colonies.

Among eighteenth-century migrants from the British Isles, the 80,000 English newcomers (a majority of them convicted criminals) were consider-

Among the most striking features of eighteenth-century colonial society was the racial and ethnic diversity of the population (except in New England). This resulted from increased immigration from the non-English parts of the British Isles and from mainland Europe, as well as the rapid expansion of the slave trade from Africa.

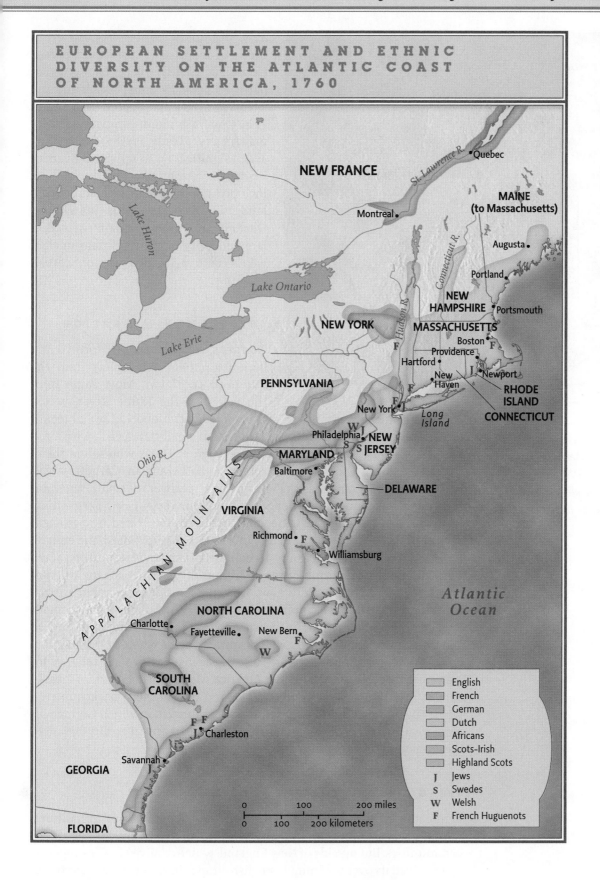

EUROPEAN SETTLEMENT AND ETHNIC DIVERSITY ON THE ATLANTIC COAST OF NORTH AMERICA, 1760

NEW FRANCE

Quebec

Montreal

MAINE
(to Massachusetts)

Augusta

Portland

NEW HAMPSHIRE   Portsmouth

MASSACHUSETTS

Boston

Providence

Hartford

New Haven   Newport

NEW YORK

PENNSYLVANIA

New York

Long Island

RHODE ISLAND

CONNECTICUT

Philadelphia   NEW JERSEY

MARYLAND

Baltimore

DELAWARE

VIRGINIA

Richmond

Williamsburg

Atlantic Ocean

NORTH CAROLINA

Charlotte

Fayetteville   New Bern

SOUTH CAROLINA

Charleston

GEORGIA   Savannah

FLORIDA

Lake Huron

Lake Ontario

Lake Erie

St. Lawrence R.

Connecticut R.

Hudson R.

Ohio R.

APPALACHIAN MOUNTAINS

0   100   200 miles
0   100   200 kilometers

English
French
German
Dutch
Africans
Scots-Irish
Highland Scots
J   Jews
S   Swedes
W   Welsh
F   French Huguenots

A German-language illustrated family record from late seventeenth-century Pennsylvania. Numerous Germans settled in the colony, attracted by William Penn's generous policies about acquiring land and his promise of religious freedom.

ably outnumbered by 145,000 from Scotland and Ulster, the northern part of Ireland, where many Scots had settled as part of England's effort to subdue the island. Scottish and Scotch-Irish immigrants had a profound impact on colonial society. Mostly Presbyterians, they added significantly to religious diversity in North America. Their numbers included not only poor farmers seeking land but also numerous merchants, teachers, and professionals (indeed, a large majority of the physicians in eighteenth-century America were of Scottish origin).

THE GERMAN MIGRATION

Germans, 110,000 in all, formed the largest group of newcomers from the European continent. Most came from the valley of the Rhine River, which stretches through present-day Germany into Switzerland. In the eighteenth century, Germany was divided into numerous small states, each with a ruling prince who determined the official religion. Those who found themselves worshiping the "wrong" religion—Lutherans in Catholic areas, Catholics in Lutheran areas, and everywhere, followers of small Protestant sects such as Mennonites, Moravians, and Dunkers—faced persecution. Many decided to emigrate. Other migrants were motivated by persistent agricultural crises and the difficulty of acquiring land. Indeed, the emigration to America represented only a small part of a massive reshuffling of the German population within Europe. Millions of Germans left their homes during the eighteenth century, most of them migrating eastward to Austria-Hungary and the Russian empire, which made land available to newcomers.

Wherever they moved, Germans tended to travel in entire families. English and Dutch merchants created a well-organized system whereby "redemptioners" (as indentured families were called) received passage in exchange for a promise to work off their debt in America. Most settled in frontier areas—rural New York, western Pennsylvania, and the southern backcountry—where they formed tightly knit farming communities in which German for many years remained the dominant language. Their arrival greatly enhanced the ethnic and religious diversity of Britain's colonies.

RELIGIOUS DIVERSITY

Eighteenth-century British America was not a "melting pot" of cultures. Ethnic groups tended to live and worship in relatively homogeneous communities. But outside of New England, which received few immigrants and retained its overwhelmingly English ethnic character, American society had a far more diverse population than Britain. Nowhere was this more evident than in the practice of religion. In 1700, nearly all the churches in the colonies were either Congregational (in New England) or Anglican. In the eighteenth century, the Anglican presence expanded considerably. New churches were built and new ministers arrived from England. But the number of Dissenting congregations also multiplied.

Apart from New Jersey (formed from East and West Jersey in 1702), Rhode Island, and Pennsylvania, the colonies did not adhere to a modern separation of church and state. Nearly every colony levied taxes to pay the salaries of ministers of an established church, and most barred Catholics and Jews from voting and holding public office. But increasingly, de facto toleration among Protestant denominations flourished, fueled by the establishment of new churches by immigrants, as well as new Baptist, Methodist, and other congregations created as a result of the Great Awakening, a religious revival that will be discussed in Chapter 4. By the mid-eighteenth century, dissenting Protestants in most colonies had gained the right to worship as they pleased and own their churches, although many places still barred them from holding public office and taxed them to support the official church. A visitor to Pennsylvania in 1750 described the colony's religious diversity: "We find there Lutherans, Reformed, Catholics, Quakers, Menonists or Anabaptists, Herrnhuters or Moravian Brethren, Pietists, Seventh Day Baptists, Dunkers, Presbyterians, . . . Jews, Mohammedans, Pagans."

"Liberty of conscience," wrote a German newcomer in 1739, was the "chief virtue" of British North America, "and on this score I do not repent my immigration." Equally important to eighteenth-century immigrants, however, were other elements of freedom, especially the availability of land, the lack of a military draft, and the absence of restraints on economic opportunity common in Europe. Skilled workers were in great demand. "They earn what they want," one emigrant wrote to his brother in Switzerland in 1733. Letters home by immigrants spoke of low taxes, the right to enter trades and professions without paying exorbitant fees, and freedom of movement. "In this country," one wrote, "there are abundant liberties in just about all matters."

Baptists were among the numerous religious denominations in the eigthteenth-century colonies. In this engraving, from a history of American Baptists published in 1770, a minister baptizes a new member in the Schuylkill River in Pennsylvania, while members of the congregation look on.

SCHUYLKILL

VOICES OF FREEDOM

From Letter by a Female Indentured Servant
(September 22, 1756)

Only a minority of emigrants from Europe to British North America were fully free. Indentured servants were men and women who surrendered their freedom for a specified period of time in exchange for passage to America. This letter by Elizabeth Sprigs of Maryland to her father in England expresses complaints voiced by many indentured servants.

Honored Father,

My being forever banished from your sight, will I hope pardon the boldness I now take of troubling you with these. My long silence has been purely owing to my undutifulness to you, and well knowing I had offended in the highest degree, put a tie on my tongue and pen, for fear I should be extinct from your good graces and add a further trouble to you. . . .

O Dear Father, believe what I am going to relate the words of truth and sincerity and balance my former bad conduct [to] my sufferings here, and then I am sure you'll pity your distressed daughter. What we unfortunate English people suffer here is beyond the probability of you in England to conceive. Let it suffice that I am one of the unhappy number, am toiling almost day and night, and very often in the horse's drudgery, with only this comfort that you bitch you do not do half enough, and then tied up and whipped to that degree that you now serve an animal. Scarce any thing but Indian corn and salt to eat and that even begrudged nay many Negroes are better used, almost naked no shoes nor stockings to wear, and the comfort after slaving during master's pleasure, what rest we can get is to wrap ourselves up in a blanket and lie upon the ground. This is the deplorable condition your poor Betty endures, and now I beg if you have any bowels of compassion left show it by sending me some relief. Clothing is the principal thing wanting, which if you should condescend to, may easily send them to me by any of the ships bound to Baltimore town, Patapsco River, Maryland. And give me leave to conclude in duty to you and uncles and aunts, and respect to all friends. . . .

Elizabeth Sprigs

FROM Letter by a Swiss-German Immigrant to Pennsylvania (August 23, 1769)

Germans were among the most numerous immigrants to the eighteenth-century colonies. Many wrote letters to family members at home, relating their experiences and impressions.

Dearest Father, Brother, and Sister and Brother-in-law,

I have told you quite fully about the trip, and I will tell you what will not surprise you—that we have a free country. Of the sundry craftsmen, one may do whatever one wants. Nor does the land require payment of tithes [taxes to support a local landlord, typical in Europe]. . . . The land is very big from Canada to the east of us to Carolina in the south and to the Spanish border in the west. . . . One can settle wherever one wants without asking anyone when he buys or leases something. . . .

I have always enough to do and we have no shortage of food. Bread is plentiful. If I work for two days I earn more bread than in eight days [at home]. . . . Also I can buy many things so reasonably [for example] a pair of shoes for [roughly] seven Pennsylvania shillings. . . . I think that with God's help I will obtain land. I am not pushing for it until I am in a better position.

I would like for my brother to come . . . and it will then be even nicer in the country. . . . I assume that the land has been described to you sufficiently by various people and it is not surprising that the immigrant agents [demand payment]. For the journey is long and it costs much to stay away for one year. . . .

Johannes Hänner

QUESTIONS

1. Why does Elizabeth Sprigs compare her condition unfavorably to that of blacks?

2. What does Johannes Hänner have in mind when he calls America a "free country"?

3. What factors might explain the different experiences of these two emigrants to British North America?

INDIAN LIFE IN TRANSITION

The tide of newcomers, who equated liberty with secure possession of land, threatened to engulf the surviving Indian populations. By the eighteenth century, Indian communities were well integrated into the British imperial system. Indian warriors did much of the fighting in the century's imperial wars. Their cultures were now quite different from what they had been at the time of first contact. Indian societies that had existed for centuries had disappeared, the victims of disease and warfare. New tribes, like the Catawba of South Carolina and the Creek Confederacy, which united dozens of Indian towns in South Carolina and Georgia, had been created from their remnants. Few Indians chose to live among whites rather than in their own communities. But they had become well accustomed to using European products like knives, hatchets, needles, kettles, and firearms. Alcohol introduced by traders created social chaos in many Indian communities. One Cherokee told the governor of South Carolina in 1753, "The clothes we wear, we cannot make ourselves, they are made to us. We use their ammunition with which we kill deer. . . . Every necessary thing we must have from the white people."

While traders saw in Indian villages potential profits and British officials saw allies against France and Spain, farmers and planters viewed Indians as little more than an obstruction to their desire for land. They expected Indians to give way to white settlers. The native population of the Virginia and South Carolina frontier had already been displaced when large numbers of settlers arrived. In Pennsylvania, however, the flood of German and Scotch-Irish settlers into the backcountry upset the relatively peaceful Indian-white relations constructed by William Penn. At a 1721 conference, a group of colonial and Indian leaders reaffirmed Penn's Chain of Friendship. But conflicts over land soon multiplied. The infamous Walking Purchase of 1737 brought the fraudulent dealing so common in other colonies to Pennsylvania. The Lenni Lanape Indians agreed to an arrangement to cede a tract of land bounded by the distance a man could walk in thirty-six hours. To their amazement, Governor James Logan hired a team of swift runners, who marked out an area far in excess of what the Indians had anticipated.

By 1760, when Pennsylvania's population, a mere 20,000 in 1700, had grown to 220,000, Indian-colonist relations, initially the most harmonious in British North America, had become poisoned by suspicion and hostility. One group of Susquehanna Indians declared "that the white people had abused them and taken their lands from them, and therefore they had no reason to think that they were now concerned for their happiness." They longed for the days when "old William Penn" treated them with fairness and respect.

REGIONAL DIVERSITY

By the mid-eighteenth century, the different regions of the British colonies had developed distinct economic and social orders. Small farms tilled by family labor and geared primarily to production for local consumption predominated in New England and the new settlements of the backcountry (the area stretching from central Pennsylvania southward through the

William Penn's Treaty with the Indians. *Penn's grandson, Thomas, the proprietor of Pennsylvania, commissioned this romanticized painting from the artist Benjamin West in 1771, by which time harmony between Indians and colonists had long since turned to hostility. In the nineteenth century, many reproductions of this image circulated, reminding Americans that Indians had once been central figures in their history.*

Shenandoah Valley of Virginia and into upland North and South Carolina). The backcountry was the most rapidly growing region in North America. In 1730, the only white residents in what was then called "Indian country" were the occasional hunter and trader. By the eve of the American Revolution, the region contained one-quarter of Virginia's population and half of South Carolina's. Most were farm families raising grain and livestock, but slaveowning planters, seeking fertile soil for tobacco farming, also entered the area.

In the older portions of the Middle Colonies of New York, New Jersey, and Pennsylvania, farmers were more oriented to commerce than on the frontier, growing grain both for their own use and for sale abroad and supplementing the work of family members by employing wage laborers, tenants, and in some instances slaves. Because large landlords had engrossed so much desirable land, New York's growth lagged behind that of neighboring colonies. "What man will be such a fool as to become a base tenant," wondered Richard Coote, New York's governor at the beginning of the eighteenth century, "when by crossing the Hudson river that man can for a song purchase a good freehold?" With its fertile soil, favorable climate, initially peaceful Indian relations, generous governmental land distribution policy, and rivers that facilitated long-distance trading, Pennsylvania came to be known as "the best poor man's country." Ordinary colonists there enjoyed a standard of living unimaginable in Europe.

THE CONSUMER REVOLUTION

During the eighteenth century, Great Britain eclipsed the Dutch as the leading producer and trader of inexpensive consumer goods, including colonial

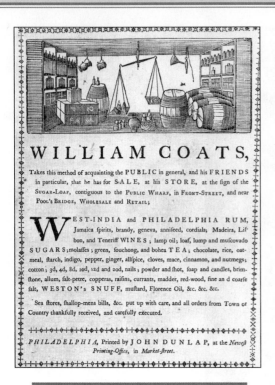

This 1772 broadside offers a rare view of the interior of a Philadelphia shop and lists some of the many European and West Indian goods on sale, including rum, tea, spices, and gun powder—a sign of the ongoing consumer revolution linked to international trade.

products like coffee and tea, and such manufactured goods as linen, metalware, pins, ribbons, glassware, ceramics, and clothing. Trade integrated the British empire. As the American colonies were drawn more and more fully into the system of Atlantic commerce, they shared in the era's consumer revolution. In port cities and small inland towns, shops proliferated and American newspapers were filled with advertisements for British goods. British merchants supplied American traders with loans to enable them to import these products, and traveling peddlers carried them into remote frontier areas.

Consumerism in a modern sense—the mass production, advertising, and sale of consumer goods—did not exist in colonial America. Nonetheless, eighteenth-century estate inventories—records of people's possessions at the time of death—revealed the wide dispersal in American homes of English and even Asian products. In the seventeenth century, most colonists had lived in a pioneer world of homespun clothing and homemade goods. Now, even modest farmers and artisans owned books, ceramic plates, metal cutlery, and items made of imported silk and cotton. Tea, once a luxury enjoyed only by the wealthy, became virtually a necessity of life. "People that are least able to go to the expense," one New Yorker noted, "must have their tea though their families want bread."

COLONIAL CITIES

Britain's mainland colonies were overwhelmingly agricultural. Nine-tenths of the population resided in rural areas and made their livelihood from farming. Colonial cities like Boston, New York, Philadelphia, and Charleston were quite small by the standards of Europe or Spanish America. In 1700, when the population of Mexico City stood at 100,000, Boston had 6,000 residents and New York 4,500. As late as 1750, eight cities in Spanish America exceeded in size any in English North America.

English American cities served mainly as gathering places for agricultural goods and for imported items to be distributed to the countryside. Nonetheless, the expansion of trade encouraged the rise of port cities, home to a growing population of colonial merchants and artisans (skilled craftsmen) as well as an increasing number of poor. In 1770, with some 30,000 inhabitants, Philadelphia was "the capital of the New World," at least its British component, and, after London and Liverpool, the empire's third busiest port. The financial, commercial, and cultural center of British America, its growth rested on economic integration with the rich agricultural region nearby. Philadelphia merchants organized the collection of farm goods, supplied rural storekeepers, and extended credit to consumers. They exported flour, bread, and meat to the West Indies and Europe.

COLONIAL ARTISANS

The city was also home to a large population of furniture makers, jewelers, and silversmiths serving wealthier citizens, and hundreds of lesser artisans like weavers, blacksmiths, coopers, and construction workers. The typical artisan owned his own tools and labored in a small workshop, often his home, assisted by family members and young journeymen and apprentices learning the trade. The artisan's skill, which set him apart from the common laborers below him in the social scale, was the key to his existence, and it gave him a far greater degree of economic freedom than those dependent on others for a livelihood. "He that hath a trade, hath an estate," wrote Benjamin Franklin, who had worked as a printer before achieving renown as a scientist and statesman.

Despite the influx of British goods, American craftsmen benefited from the expanding consumer market. Most journeymen enjoyed a reasonable chance of rising to the status of master and establishing a workshop of their own. Some achieved remarkable success. Born in New York City in 1723, Myer Myers, a Jewish silversmith of Dutch ancestry, became one of the city's most prominent artisans. Myers produced jewelry, candlesticks, coffeepots, tableware, and other gold and silver objects for the colony's elite, as well as religious ornaments for both synagogues and Protestant churches in New York and nearby colonies. He used some of his profits to acquire land in New Hampshire and Connecticut. Myers's career reflected the opportunities colonial cities offered to skilled men of diverse ethnic and religious backgrounds.

This piece of china made in England and exported to New England celebrates the coronation of James II in 1685. It is an example of the growing colonial demand for English consumer goods.

AN ATLANTIC WORLD

People, ideas, and goods flowed back and forth across the Atlantic, knitting together the empire and its diverse populations—British merchants and consumers, American colonists, African slaves, and surviving Indians—and creating webs of interdependence among the European empires. Sugar, tobacco, and other products of the Western Hemisphere were marketed as far away as eastern Europe. London bankers financed the slave trade between Africa and Portugese Brazil. Spain spent its gold and silver importing goods from other countries. As trade expanded, the North American and West Indian colonies became the major overseas market for British manufactured goods. Although most colonial output was consumed at

As Atlantic trade expanded, shipbuilding became a major enterprise in the colonies. This painting from around 1750 by an unknown artist depicts vessels under construction at the Grey's Inn Creek Shipyard in Maryland.

home, North Americans shipped farm products to Britain, the West Indies, and with the exception of goods like tobacco "enumerated" under the Navigation Acts, outside the empire. Virtually the entire Chesapeake tobacco crop was marketed in Britain, with most of it then re-exported to Europe by British merchants. Most of the bread and flour exported from the colonies was destined for the West Indies. African slaves there grew sugar that could be distilled into rum, a product increasingly popular among both North American colonists and Indians, who obtained it by trading furs and deerskins that were then shipped to Europe. The mainland colonies carried on a flourishing trade in fish and grains with southern Europe. Ships built in New England made up one-third of the British empire's trading fleet.

Membership in the empire had many advantages for the colonists. Most Americans did not complain about British regulation of their trade because commerce enriched the colonies as well as the mother country and lax enforcement of the Navigation Acts allowed smuggling to flourish. In a dangerous world, moreover, the Royal Navy protected American shipping. And despite the many differences between life in England and its colonies, eighteenth-century English America drew closer and closer to, and in some ways became more and more similar to, the mother country across the Atlantic.

SOCIAL CLASSES IN THE COLONIES

THE COLONIAL ELITE

Most free Americans benefited from economic growth, but as colonial society matured an elite emerged that, while neither as powerful or wealthy as the aristocracy of England, increasingly dominated politics and society. Indeed, the gap between rich and poor probably grew more rapidly in the eighteenth century than in any other period of American history. In New England and the Middle Colonies, expanding trade made possible the emergence of a powerful upper class of merchants, often linked by family or commercial ties to great trading firms in London. There were no banks in colonial America. Credit and money were in short supply, and mercantile success depended on personal connections as much as business talent. By 1750, the colonies of the Chesapeake and Lower South were dominated by slave plantations producing staple crops, especially tobacco and rice, for the world market. Here great planters accumulated enormous wealth. The colonial elite also included the rulers of proprietary colonies like Pennsylvania and Maryland.

A 1732 portrait of Daniel, Peter, and Andrew Oliver, sons of a wealthy Boston merchant. The prominent display of their delicate hands tells the viewer that they have never had to do manual labor.

America had no titled aristocracy as in Britain. It had no system of legally established social ranks or family pedigrees stretching back to medieval times. Apart from the De Lanceys, Livingstons, and Van Rensselaers of New York, the Penn family in Pennsylvania, and a few southern planters, it had no one whose landholdings, in monetary value, rivaled those of the British aristocracy. But throughout British America, men of prominence controlled colonial government. In Virginia, the upper class was so tight-knit and intermarried so often that the colony was said to be governed by a "cousinocracy." Members of the gentry controlled the vestries, or local governing bodies, of the established Anglican Church, dominated the county courts (political as well as judicial institutions that levied taxes and enacted local ordinances), and were prominent in Virginia's legislature. In the 1750s, seven members of the same generation of the Lee family sat in the House of Burgesses.

Eighteenth-century Virginia was a far healthier environment than in the early days of settlement. Planters could expect to pass their wealth down to the next generation, providing estates for their sons and establishing family dynasties. Nearly every Virginian of note achieved prominence through family connections. The days when self-made men could rise into the Virginia gentry were long gone; by 1770, nearly all upper-class Virginians had inherited their wealth. Thomas Jefferson's grandfather was a justice of the peace (an important local official), militia captain, and sheriff, and his father was a member of the House of Burgesses. George Washington's father, grandfather, and great-grandfather had been justices of the peace. The Virginia gentry used its control of provincial government to gain possession of large tracts of land as western areas opened for settlement. Grants of 20,000 to 40,000 acres were not uncommon. Robert "King" Carter, a speaker of the House of Burgesses, acquired 300,000 acres of land and 1,000 slaves by the time of his death in 1732.

ANGLICIZATION

For much of the eighteenth century, the American colonies had more regular trade and communications with Britain than among themselves. Elites in different regions slowly developed a common lifestyle and sense of common interests. But rather than thinking of themselves as distinctively American, they became more and more English—a process historians call "Anglicization."

Wealthy Americans tried to model their lives on British etiquette and behavior. Somewhat resentful at living in provincial isolation—"at the end of the world," as one Virginia aristocrat put it—they sought to demonstrate their status and legitimacy by importing the latest London fashions and literature, sending their sons to Britain for education, and building homes equipped with fashionable furnishings modeled on the country estates and town houses of the English gentry. Their residences included large rooms for entertainment, display cases for imported luxury goods, and elaborate formal gardens. Some members of the colonial elite, like George Washington, even had coats of arms designed for their families, in imitation of English upper-class practice.

Desperate to follow an aristocratic lifestyle, many planters fell into debt. William Byrd III lived so extravagantly that by 1770 he had accumulated

A portrait of Elijah Boardman, a merchant in New Milford, Connecticut. Boardman wears the attire of a gentleman and rests his arm on his counting desk. In the rear, bolts of cloth are visible. But Boardman chose to emphasize his learning, not his wealth, by posing with books, including two plays of Shakespeare, John Milton's Paradise Lost, *and the* London Magazine.

Built in the 1750s by Carter Burwell, grandson of the original Robert "King" Carter, Carter's Grove, near Williamsburg, Virginia, was a grand plantation mansion with large formal gardens, in imitation of English landscape design.

a debt of £100,000, an amount almost unheard of in England or America. But so long as the world market for tobacco thrived, so did Virginia's gentry.

THE SOUTH CAROLINA ARISTOCRACY

The richest group of mainland colonists were South Carolina planters (although planters in Jamaica far outstripped them in wealth). Elite South Carolinians often traveled north to enjoy summer vacations in the cooler climate of Newport, Rhode Island, and they spent much of the remainder of their time in Charleston, the only real urban center south of Philadelphia and the richest city in British North America. Here aristocratic social life flourished, centered on theaters, literary societies, and social events. Like their Virginia counterparts, South Carolina grandees lived a lavish lifestyle amid imported furniture, fine wines, silk clothing, and other items from England. They surrounded themselves with house slaves dressed in specially designed uniforms. In 1774, the per capita wealth in the Charleston District was £2,300, more than four times that of tobacco areas in Virginia and eight times the figure for Philadelphia or Boston. But wealth in South Carolina was highly concentrated. The richest 10 percent of the colony owned half the wealth in 1770, the poorest quarter less than 2 percent.

Throughout the colonies, elites emulated what they saw as England's balanced, stable social order. Liberty, in their eyes, meant, in part, the power to rule—the right of those blessed with wealth and prominence to dominate over others. They viewed society as a hierarchical structure in which some men were endowed with greater talents than others and destined to rule. The social order, they believed, was held together by webs of influence that linked patrons and those dependent on them. Each place in the hierarchy carried with it different responsibilities, and one's status was revealed in dress, manners, and the splendor of one's home. "Superiority" and "dependence," as one colonial newspaper put it, were natural elements of any society. An image of refinement served to legitimate wealth and political power. Colonial elites prided themselves on developing aristocratic manners, cultivating the arts, and making productive use of leisure. Indeed, on both sides of the Atlantic, elites viewed work as something reserved for common folk and slaves. Freedom from labor was the mark of the gentleman.

POVERTY IN THE COLONIES

At the other end of the social scale, poverty emerged as a visible feature of eighteenth-century colonial life. Although not considered by most colonists part of their society, the growing number of slaves lived in impoverished conditions. Among free Americans, poverty was hardly as widespread as in Britain, where in the early part of the century between one-quarter and one-half of the people regularly required public assistance. But as the colonial population expanded, access to land diminished rapidly, especially in long-settled areas. In New England, which received few immigrants, the high birthrate fueled population growth. With the supply of land limited, sons who could not hope to inherit farms were forced to move to other colonies or to try their hand at a trade in the region's towns. By mid-century, tenants and wage laborers were a growing presence on farms in the Middle Colonies.

In colonial cities, the number of propertyless wage earners subsisting at the poverty line steadily increased. In Boston, one-third of the population in 1771 owned no property at all. In rural Augusta County, carved out of Virginia's Shenandoah River valley in 1738, land was quickly engrossed by planters and speculators. By the 1760s, two-thirds of the county's white men owned no land and had little prospect of obtaining it unless they migrated further west. Taking the colonies as a whole, half of the wealth at mid-century was concentrated in the hands of the richest 10 percent of the population.

Attitudes and policies toward poverty in colonial America mirrored British precedents. The better-off colonists generally viewed the poor as lazy, shiftless, and responsible for their own plight. Both rural communities and cities did accept responsibility for assisting their own. But to minimize the burden on taxpayers, poor persons were frequently set to labor in workhouses, where they produced goods that reimbursed authorities for part of their upkeep. Their children were sent to work as apprentices in local homes or workshops. And most communities adopted stringent measures to "warn out" unemployed and propertyless newcomers who might become dependent on local poor relief. This involved town authorities either expelling the unwanted poor from an area or formally declaring certain persons ineligible for assistance. In Essex County, Massachusetts, the number of poor persons warned out each year rose from 200 in the 1730s to 1,700 in the 1760s. Many were members of families headed by widowed or abandoned women.

THE MIDDLE RANKS

The large majority of free Americans lived between the extremes of wealth and poverty. Along with racial and ethnic diversity, what distinguished the mainland colonies from Europe was the wide distribution of land and the economic autonomy of most ordinary free families. The anonymous author of the book *American Husbandry*, published in 1775, reported that "little freeholders who live upon their own property" made up "the most considerable part" of the people, especially in the northern colonies and the nonplantation parts of the South. Altogether, perhaps two-thirds of the free male population were farmers who owned their own land. England, to be sure, had no class of laborers as exploited as American slaves, but three-fifths of its people owned no property at all.

By the eighteenth century, colonial farm families viewed landownership almost as a right, the social precondition of freedom. They strongly resented efforts, whether by Native Americans, great landlords, or colonial governments, to limit their access to land. A dislike of personal dependence and an understanding of freedom as not relying on others for a livelihood sank deep roots in British North America. These beliefs, after all, accorded with social reality—a wide distribution of property that made economic independence part of the lived experience of large numbers of white colonists.

WOMEN AND THE HOUSEHOLD ECONOMY

In the household economy of eighteenth-century America, the family was the center of economic life. Most work revolved around the home, and all members—men, women, and children—contributed to the family's livelihood. The independence of the small farmer depended in considerable measure on the labor of dependent women and children. "He that hath an industrious family shall soon be rich," declared one colonial saying, and the high birthrate in part reflected the need for as many hands as possible on colonial farms. Most farmers concentrated first on growing food for their own consumption and acquiring enough land to pass it along to their sons. But the consumer revolution and expanding networks of Atlantic trade drew increasing numbers of farmers into production for the market as well.

As the population grew and the death rate declined, family life stabilized and more marriages became lifetime commitments. Free women were expected to devote their lives to being good wives and mothers. Already enshrined in law and property relations, male domination took on greater and greater social reality. In several colonies, the law mandated primogeniture— meaning that estates must be passed intact to the oldest son. As colonial society became more structured, opportunities that had existed for women in the early period receded. In Connecticut, for example, the courts were informal and unorganized in the seventeenth century, and women often represented themselves. In the eighteenth century, it became necessary to hire a lawyer as one's spokesman in court. Women, barred from practicing as attorneys, disappeared from judicial proceedings. Because of the desperate need for labor, men and women in the seventeenth century both did various kinds of work. In the eighteenth century, the division of labor

VISIONS OF FREEDOM

The Van Bergen Overmantel. *The opportunity to achieve economic independence was central to American colonists' idea of freedom. This section is part of a seven-foot-long painting by John Heaten from around 1773, probably designed to hang above a wide fireplace in the home of Marten Van Bergen, a Dutch farmer in colonial New York. The house and farm buildings are in Dutch style. The painting offers a rare contemporary view of a prosperous colonial farm, with its full granary and livestock. Native Americans and African-American slaves, as well as workers who probably were indentured servants, are among the individuals depicted by the artist.*

QUESTIONS

1. What does the painting suggest about gradations of freedom at the time it was created?

2. What indications of prosperity are evident in the painting?

This portrait of the Cheney family by an unknown late eighteenth-century artist illustrates the high birthrate in colonial America, and suggests how many years of a woman's life were spent bearing and raising children.

along gender lines solidified. Women's work was clearly defined, including cooking, cleaning, sewing, making butter, and assisting with agricultural chores. The work of farmers' wives and daughters often spelled the difference between a family's self-sufficiency and poverty.

"Women's work is never done." This popular adage was literally true. Even as the consumer revolution reduced the demands on many women by making available store-bought goods previously produced at home, women's work seemed to increase. Lower infant mortality meant more time spent in child care and domestic chores. The demand for new goods increased the need for all family members to contribute to family income. For most women, work was incessant and exhausting. "I am dirty and distressed, almost wearied to death," wrote Mary Cooper, a Long Island woman, in her diary in 1769. "This day," she continued, "is forty years since I left my father's house and come here, and here have I seen little else but hard labor and sorrow."

NORTH AMERICA AT MID-CENTURY

By the mid-eighteenth century, the area that would become the United States was home to a remarkable diversity of peoples and different kinds of social organization, from Pueblo villages of the Southwest to tobacco plantations of the Chesapeake, towns and small farms of New England, landholdings in the Hudson Valley that resembled feudal estates, and fur trading outposts of the northern and western frontier. Elites tied to imperial centers of power dominated the political and economic life of nearly every colony. But large numbers of colonists enjoyed far greater opportunities for freedom—access to the vote, prospects of acquiring land, the right to worship as they pleased, and an escape from oppressive government—than existed in Europe. Free colonists probably enjoyed the highest per capita income in the world. The colonies' economic growth contributed to a high birthrate, long life expectancy, and expanding demand for consumer goods.

In the British colonies, writes one historian, lived "thousands of the freest individuals the Western world has ever known." Yet many others found themselves confined to the partial freedom of indentured servitude or to the complete absence of freedom in slavery. Both timeless longings for freedom and new and unprecedented forms of unfreedom had been essential to the North American colonies' remarkable development.

SUGGESTED READING

BOOKS

Bailyn, Bernard. *The Peopling of British North America* (1986). A brief survey of the movement of peoples across the Atlantic.

Berlin, Ira. *Many Thousands Gone: The First Two Centuries of Slavery in North America* (1998). The most extensive study of the origins and development of colonial slavery.

Bushman, Richard. *The Refinement of America: Persons, Houses, Cities* (1992). A study of how a more "refined" lifestyle emerged in the eighteenth-century colonies.

Dayton, Cornelia H. *Women before the Bar: Gender, Law, and Society in Connecticut, 1639–1789* (1995). Examines the changing legal status of women in one American colony.

Jordan, Winthrop D. *White over Black: American Attitudes toward the Negro, 1550–1812* (1968). A detailed look at how ideas about race developed over time in England and the American colonies.

Kidd, Thomas S. *The Great Awakening* (2007). An account of the religious movement that swept the American colonies in the eighteenth century.

Kulikoff, Allan. *Tobacco and Slaves: The Development of Southern Cultures in the Chesapeake, 1680–1800* (1986). Explores how the rise of slave-grown tobacco affected society in the Chesapeake.

Lemon, James T. *The Best Poor Man's Country: A Geographical Study of Early Southeastern Pennsylvania* (1972). A study of agriculture and the environment in one of the most successful farming areas of colonial America.

Lepore, Jill. *The Name of War: King Philip's War and the Origin of American Identity* (1998). An examination not only of the war itself but also of its long-term consequences for Indian-white relations.

Lovejoy, David S. *The Glorious Revolution in America* (1972). Explores how the revolution in England in 1689 affected the American colonies.

Mintz, Sidney. *Sweetness and Power: The Place of Sugar in Modern History* (1985). A global history of the significance of sugar in the making of the modern world.

Morgan, Edmund S. *American Slavery, American Freedom: The Ordeal of Colonial Virginia* (1975). An influential study of the slow development of slavery in seventeenth-century Virginia.

Norton, Mary Beth. *In the Devil's Snare: The Salem Witchcraft Crisis of 1692* (2002). A study of the witch trials that places them in the context of anxieties over Indian warfare on the Massachusetts frontier.

Saxton, Martha. *Being Good: Women's Moral Values in Early America* (2003). Examines social standards for women's behavior and how women tried to live up to them.

WEBSITES

The Atlantic Slave Trade and Slave Life in the Americas: http://hitchcock.itc.virginia.edu/Slavery/index.php

Afro-Louisiana History and Genealogy: www.ibiblio.org/laslave/

REVIEW QUESTIONS

1. Both the Puritans and William Penn viewed their colonies as "holy experiments." How did they differ?

2. The textbook states, "Prejudice by itself did not create American slavery." Examine the forces and events that led to slavery in North America, and the role that racial prejudice played.

3. How were the actions of King James II toward New England perceived as threats to colonial liberty?

4. How did King Philip's War, Bacon's Rebellion, and the Salem witch trials illustrate a widespread crisis in British North America in the late seventeenth century?

5. The social structure of the eighteenth-century colonies was growing more open for some but not for others. For whom was there more opportunity, and for whom not?

6. By the end of the seventeenth century, commerce was the foundation of empire and the leading cause of competition between European empires. Explain how the North American colonies were directly linked to Atlantic commerce by laws and trade.

7. If you traveled outside of eighteenth-century New England, you might agree with fellow travelers that the colonies were demonstrating greater diversity in many ways. How would you support this claim?

8. Despite their lack of rights, hard-working women and children were often the key to the success of independent family farmers. Demonstrate the truth of this statement.

FREEDOM QUESTIONS

1. English settlers insisted that true freedom for Native Americans meant they must abandon their traditions and accept English ways. Examine the changes to Native American life by the mid-eighteenth century, and discuss whether Native American freedom increased by any standards.

2. Freedom and lack of freedom existed side-by-side in the English colonies. Using examples from Pennsylvania and elsewhere, demonstrate how greater freedom for some colonists in one area meant less freedom for others.

3. British citizens connected freedom and liberty to land ownership and not having to work for wages. Why did they make these connections and what were the consequences for the social structure?

4. Some historians have argued that the freedoms and prosperity of the British empire were all based on slavery. Examine this statement using specific examples.

5. Many British settlers in North America believed it was the "best poor man's country," and that they were the freest people in the world. What factors would lead to such a claim?

REVIEW TABLE

Colonial Crises in the Late Seventeenth Century

Crisis	Dates	Origins of Conflict	Action	Resolution
King Philip's War	1675–1676	White settlers' encroachment on Indian land	Philip's forces attack forty-five New England towns	Settlers counter-attack, breaking Indians' power
Bacon's Rebellion	1676	Corruption of Virginia's government	Bacon burns Jamestown and takes power	Virginia's ruling elite undertake reforms
Glorious Revolution	1688	James II threatens to restore Catholicism to England	A bloodless coup to overthrow James II; colonists overthrow Dominion of New England	Protestants William and Mary of Orange are crowned
Salem Witch Trials	1691–1692	Amidst political and social tensions, young girls begin to experiment with magic	Hundreds accused of witchcraft and nineteen people are hanged	Governor dissolves the Salem court

Chapter 4

Slavery, Freedom, and the Struggle for Empire to 1763

The Old Plantation, *a late-eighteenth-century watercolor by an unknown artist, depicts slaves dancing in a plantation's slave quarters, perhaps at a wedding. The scene may take place in South Carolina, where the painting was found. The musical instruments and pottery are African in origin while much of the clothing is of European manufacture, indicating the mixing of African and white cultures among the era's slaves.*

☞ FOCUS QUESTIONS

- How did African slavery differ regionally in eighteenth-century North America?

- What factors led to distinct African-American cultures in the eighteenth century?

- What were the meanings of British liberty in the eighteenth century?

- What concepts and institutions dominated colonial politics in the eighteenth century?

- How did the Great Awakening challenge the religious and social structure of British North America?

- How did the Spanish and French empires in America develop in the eighteenth century?

- What was the impact of the Seven Years' War on imperial and Indian–white relations?

Sometime in the mid-1750s, Olaudah Equiano, the eleven-year-old son of a West African village chief, was kidnapped by slave traders. He soon found himself on a ship headed for Barbados. After a short stay on that Caribbean island, Equiano was sold to a plantation owner in Virginia and then purchased by a British sea captain, who renamed him Gustavus Vassa. He accompanied his owner on numerous voyages on Atlantic trading vessels. While still a slave, he enrolled in a school in England where he learned to read and write, and then enlisted in the Royal Navy. He fought in Canada under General James Wolfe in 1758 during the Seven Years' War. In 1763, however, Equiano was sold once again and returned to the Caribbean. Three years later, he was able to purchase his freedom. Equiano went on to live through shipwrecks, took part in an English colonizing venture in Central America, and even participated in an expedition to the Arctic Circle.

Equiano eventually settled in London, and in 1789 he published *The Interesting Narrative of the Life of Olaudah Equiano, or Gustavus Vassa, the African,* which he described as a "history of neither a saint, a hero, nor a tyrant," but of a victim of slavery who through luck or fate ended up more fortunate than most of his people. He condemned the idea that Africans were inferior to Europeans and therefore deserved to be slaves. He urged the European reader to recall that "his ancestors were once, like the Africans, uncivilized" and asked, "did nature make them inferior . . . and should they too have been made slaves?" Persons of all races, he insisted, were capable of intellectual improvement. The book became the era's most widely read account by a slave of his own experiences. Equiano died in 1797.

Recent scholars have suggested that Equiano may actually have been born in the New World rather than Africa. In either case, while his rich variety of experience was no doubt unusual, his life illuminates broad patterns of eighteenth-century American history. As noted in the previous chapter, this was a period of sustained development for British North America. Compared to England and Scotland—united to create Great Britain by the Act of Union of 1707—the colonies were growing much more rapidly. Some contemporaries spoke of British America as a "rising empire" that would one day eclipse the mother country in population and wealth.

It would be wrong, however, to see the first three-quarters of the eighteenth century simply as a prelude to American independence. As Equiano's life illustrates, the Atlantic was more a bridge than a barrier between the Old and New Worlds. Ideas, people, and goods flowed back and forth across the ocean. Even as the colonies' populations became more diverse, they were increasingly integrated into the British empire. Their laws and political institutions were extensions of those of Britain, their ideas about society and culture reflected British values, their economies were geared to serving the empire's needs. As European powers jockeyed for advantage in North America, colonists were drawn into an almost continuous series of wars with France and its Indian allies, which reinforced their sense of identification with and dependence on Great Britain.

Equiano's life also underscores the greatest irony or contradiction in the history of the eighteenth century—the simultaneous expansion of freedom and slavery. This was the era when the idea of the "freeborn Englishman" became powerfully entrenched in the outlook of both colonists and Britons. More than any other principle, liberty was seen as what made the British empire distinct. Yet the eighteenth century was also the height of the Atlantic slave trade, a commerce increasingly dominated by British merchants and ships. One of the most popular songs of the period included the refrain, "Britons never, never, never will be slaves." But during the eighteenth century, more than half the Africans shipped to the New World as slaves were carried on British vessels. Most were destined for the plantations of the West Indies and Brazil, but slaves also made up around 280,000 of the 585,000 persons who arrived in Britain's mainland colonies between 1700 and 1775. Although concentrated in the Chesapeake and areas farther south, slavery existed in every colony of British North America. And unlike Equiano, very few slaves were fortunate enough to gain their freedom.

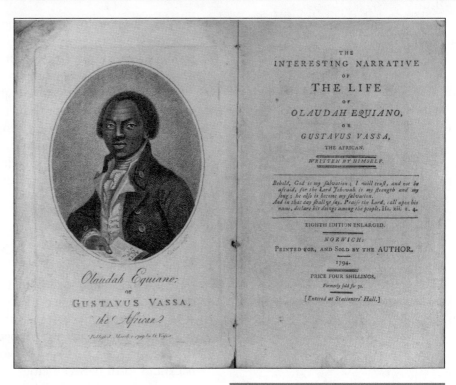

The title page of Olaudah Equiano's account of his life, the best-known narrative by an eighteenth-century slave. The portrait of Equiano in European dress and holding a Bible challenges stereotypes of blacks as "savages" incapable of becoming civilized.

SLAVERY AND EMPIRE

Of the estimated 7.7 million Africans transported to the New World between 1492 and 1820, more than half arrived between 1700 and 1800. The Atlantic slave trade would later be condemned by statesmen and general opinion as a crime against humanity. But in the eighteenth century, it was a regularized business in which European merchants, African traders, and American planters engaged in complex bargaining over human lives, all with the expectation of securing a profit. The slave trade was a vital part of world commerce. Every European empire in the New World utilized slave labor and battled for control of this lucrative trade. The *asiento*—an agreement whereby Spain subcontracted to a foreign power the right to provide slaves to Spanish America—was an important diplomatic prize. Britain's acquisition of the *asiento* from the Dutch in the Treaty of Utrecht of 1713 was a major step in its rise to commercial supremacy.

In the British empire of the eighteenth century, free laborers working for wages were atypical and slavery was the norm. Slave plantations contributed mightily to English economic development. The first mass consumer goods in international trade were produced by slaves—sugar, rice, coffee, and tobacco. The rising demand for these products fueled the rapid growth of the Atlantic slave trade.

ATLANTIC TRADE

In the eighteenth century, the Caribbean remained the commercial focus of the British empire and the major producer of revenue for the crown. But slave-grown products from the mainland occupied a larger and larger part of Atlantic commerce. A series of triangular trading routes crisscrossed the Atlantic, carrying British manufactured goods to Africa and the colonies, colonial products including tobacco, indigo, sugar, and rice to Europe, and slaves from Africa to the New World. Most colonial vessels, however, went back and forth between cities like New York, Charleston, and Savannah, and to ports in the Caribbean. Areas where slavery was only a minor institution also profited from slave labor. Merchants in New York, Massachusetts, and Rhode Island participated actively in the slave trade, shipping slaves from Africa to the Caribbean or southern colonies. The slave economies of the West Indies were the largest market for fish, grain, livestock, and lumber exported from New England and the Middle Colonies. In 1720, half the ships entering or leaving New York Harbor were engaged in trade with the Caribbean. Indeed, one historian writes, "The growth and prosperity of the emerging society of free colonial British

A mid-eighteenth-century image of a woman going to church in Lima, Peru, accompanied by two slaves. Slavery existed throughout the Western Hemisphere.

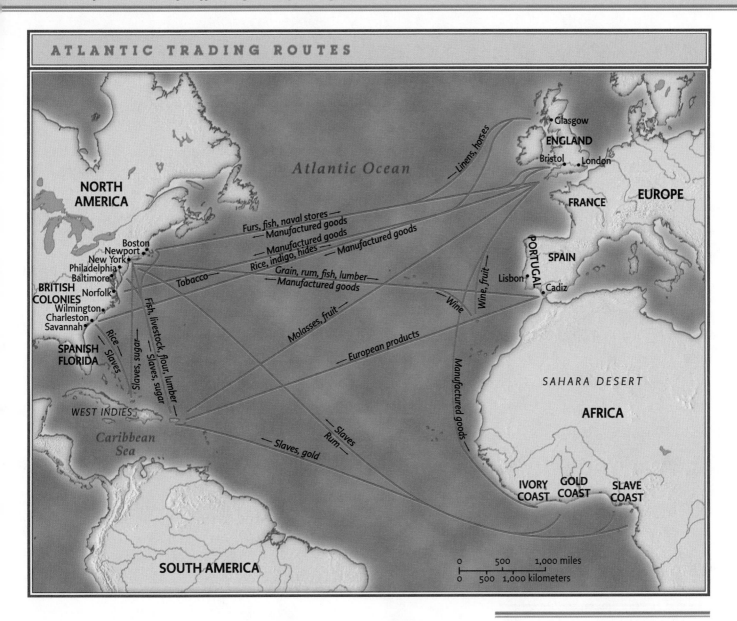

ATLANTIC TRADING ROUTES

A series of trading routes crisscrossed the Atlantic, bringing manufactured goods to Africa and Britain's American colonies, slaves to the New World, and colonial products to Europe.

America . . . were achieved as a result of slave labor." In Britain itself, the profits from slavery and the slave trade stimulated the rise of ports like Liverpool and Bristol and the growth of banking, shipbuilding, and insurance. They also helped to finance the early industrial revolution.

Overall, in the eighteenth century, Atlantic commerce consisted primarily of slaves, crops produced by slaves, and goods destined for slave societies. It should not be surprising that for large numbers of free colonists and Europeans, freedom meant in part the power and right to enslave others. And as slavery became more and more entrenched, so too, as the Quaker abolitionist John Woolman commented in 1762, did "the idea of slavery being connected with the black color, and liberty with the white."

AFRICA AND THE SLAVE TRADE

A few African societies, like Benin for a time, opted out of the Atlantic slave trade, hoping to avoid the disruptions it inevitably caused. But most African

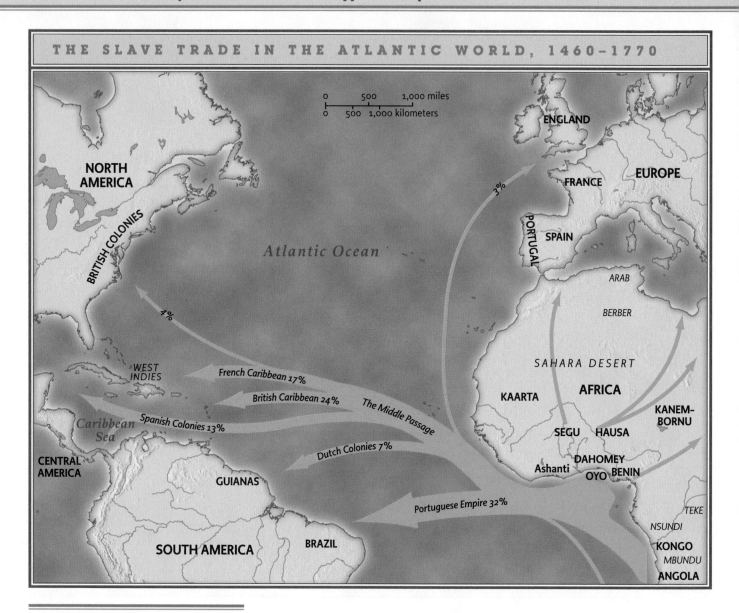

THE SLAVE TRADE IN THE ATLANTIC WORLD, 1460–1770

The Atlantic slave trade expanded rapidly in the eighteenth century. The mainland colonies received only a tiny proportion of the Africans brought to the New World, most of whom were transported to Brazil and the West Indies.

rulers took part, and they proved quite adept at playing the Europeans off against one another, collecting taxes from foreign merchants, and keeping the capture and sale of slaves under their own control. Few Europeans ventured inland from the coast. Traders remained in their "factories" and purchased slaves brought to them by African rulers and dealers.

The transatlantic slave trade made Africa a major market for European goods, especially textiles and guns. Both disrupted relationships within and among African societies. Cheap imported textiles undermined traditional craft production, while guns encouraged the further growth of slavery, since the only way to obtain European weapons was to supply slaves. By the eighteenth century, militarized states like Ashanti and Dahomey would arise in West Africa, with large armies using European firearms to prey on their neighbors in order to capture slaves. From a minor institution, slavery grew to become more and more central to West African society, a source of wealth for African merchants and of power for newly emerging African kingdoms. The loss every year of tens of thousands of men and women in the prime of their lives to the slave trade weakened and distorted West Africa's society and economy.

THE MIDDLE PASSAGE

For slaves, the voyage across the Atlantic—known as the Middle Passage because it was the second, or middle, leg in the triangular trading routes linking Europe, Africa, and America—was a harrowing experience. Since a slave could be sold in America for twenty to thirty times the price in Africa, men, women, and children were crammed aboard vessels as tightly as possible to maximize profits. "The height, sometimes, between decks," wrote one slave trader, "was only eighteen inches, so that the unfortunate human beings could not turn around, or even on their sides . . . and here they are usually chained to the decks by their necks and legs." Equiano, who later described "the shrieks of the women and the groans of the dying," survived the Middle Passage, but many Africans did not. Diseases like measles and smallpox spread rapidly, and about one slave in five perished before reaching the New World. Ship captains were known to throw the sick overboard in order to prevent the spread of epidemics. The crews on slave ships also suffered a high death rate.

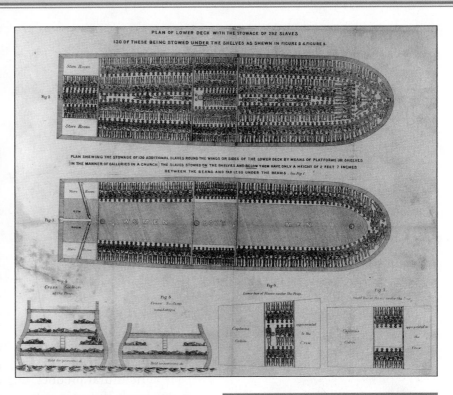

An architect's plan for a slave ship. These drawings illustrate the conditions under which slaves endured the Middle Passage across the Atlantic.

Only a small proportion (less than 5 percent) of slaves carried to the New World were destined for mainland North America. The vast majority landed in Brazil or the West Indies, where the high death rate on the sugar plantations led to a constant demand for new slave imports. As late as 1700, only about 20,000 Africans had been landed in Britain's colonies in North America. In the eighteenth century, however, their numbers increased steadily. Overall, the area that was to become the United States imported between 400,000 and 600,000 slaves. By 1770, due to the natural reproduction of the slave population, around one-fifth of the estimated 2.3 million persons (not including Indians) living in the English colonies of North America were Africans and their descendants.

CHESAPEAKE SLAVERY

By the mid-eighteenth century, three distinct slave systems were well entrenched in Britain's mainland colonies: tobacco-based plantation slavery in the Chesapeake, rice-based plantation slavery in South Carolina and Georgia, and nonplantation slavery in New England and the Middle Colonies. The largest and oldest of these was the tobacco plantation system of the Chesapeake, where more than 270,000 slaves resided in 1770, nearly half of the region's population. On the eve of the Revolution, Virginia and Maryland were as closely tied to Britain as any other

Benjamin Latrobe's watercolor, An Overseer Doing His Duty, *was sketched near Fredericksburg, Virginia, in 1798. The title is meant to be ironic: the well-dressed overseer relaxes while two female slaves work in the fields.*

colonies and their economies were models of mercantilist policy (described in Chapter 3). They supplied the mother country with a valuable agricultural product, imported large amounts of British goods, and were closely linked in culture and political values to London. As we have seen, the period after 1680 witnessed a rapid shift from indentured servitude to slavery on the region's tobacco plantations. In the eighteenth century, the growing world demand for tobacco encouraged continued slave imports. When tobacco prices fell in the early part of the century, some planters shifted to grain production. But tobacco remained their primary source of wealth.

As Virginia expanded westward, so did slavery. By the eve of the American Revolution, the center of gravity of slavery in the colony had shifted from the Tidewater (the region along the coast) to the Piedmont farther inland. Most Chesapeake slaves, male and female, worked in the fields, but thousands labored as teamsters, as boatmen, and in skilled crafts. Numerous slave women became cooks, seamstresses, dairy maids, and personal servants. The son of George Mason, one of Virginia's leading planters and statesmen, recorded that his father's slaves included "coopers, sawyers, blacksmiths, tanners, shoemakers, spinners, weavers, knitters, and even a distiller." Slavery was common on small farms as well as plantations; nearly half of Virginia's white families owned at least one slave in 1770. Because there is little "economy of scale" in tobacco growing—that is, enlarging the size of the producing unit does not lower costs and maximize productivity—Chesapeake plantations tended to be smaller than in the Caribbean, and daily interactions between masters and slaves were more extensive.

Slavery laid the foundation for the consolida-

A detail from a 1768 map of Virginia and Maryland illustrates a tobacco wharf. A planter negotiates with a merchant or sea captain, while slaves go about their work.

tion of the Chesapeake elite, a landed gentry that, in conjunction with merchants who handled the tobacco trade and lawyers who defended the interests of slaveholders, dominated the region's society and politics. Meanwhile, even as the consumer revolution improved the standard of living of lesser whites, their long-term economic prospects diminished. As slavery expanded, planters engrossed the best lands and wealth among the white population became more and more concentrated. Slavery transformed Chesapeake society into an elaborate hierarchy of degrees of freedom. At the top stood large planters, below them numerous lesser planters and landowning yeomen, and at the bottom a large population of convicts, indentured servants, tenant farmers (who made up half the white households in 1770), and, of course, the slaves.

FREEDOM AND SLAVERY IN THE CHESAPEAKE

With the consolidation of a slave society in the Chesapeake, planters filled the law books with measures enhancing the master's power over his human property and restricting blacks' access to freedom. Violence lay at the heart of the slave system. Even a planter like Landon Carter, who prided himself on his concern for the well-being of his slaves, noted casually in his diary, "they have been severely whipped day by day."

Race took on more and more importance as a line of social division. Whites increasingly considered free blacks dangerous and undesirable. Free blacks lost the right to employ white servants and to bear arms, were subjected to special taxes, and could be punished for striking a white person, regardless of the cause. In 1723, Virginia revoked the voting privileges of property-owning free blacks. When the Lords of Trade in London asked Virginia's governor to justify discriminating among "freemen, merely upon account of their complexion," he responded that "a distinction ought to be made between their offspring and the descendants of an Englishman, with whom they never were to be accounted equal." Because Virginia law required that freed slaves be sent out of the colony, free blacks remained only a tiny part of the population—less than 4 percent in 1750. "Free" and "white" had become virtually identical.

INDIAN SLAVERY IN EARLY CAROLINA

Farther south, a different slave system, based on rice production, emerged in South Carolina and Georgia. The Barbadians who initially settled South Carolina in the 1670s were quite familiar with African slavery, but their first victims were members of the area's native population. The early Carolina economy focused on the export to the Caribbean of Indian slaves and to England of deerskins and furs obtained from Indians. The local Creek Indians initially welcomed the settlers and began selling them slaves, generally war captives and their families, most of whom were sold to the West Indies. They even launched wars against neighboring tribes specifically for the purpose of capturing and selling slaves. As the plantation system expanded, however, the Creeks became more and more concerned, not only because it led to encroachments on their land but also because they feared enslavement themselves. They were aware that only a handful of slaves worked in nearby Spanish Florida. The Creeks, one leader

Henry Darnall III, painted around 1710 by Justus Engelhardt Kühn, who produced numerous portraits of prominent Marylanders in the early eighteenth century. The boy, clearly the son of a member of the colony's wealthy gentry, stands next to a young slave, a symbol of his family's wealth. The background is an idealized European palace and formal garden.

remarked in 1738, preferred to deal with the Spanish, who "enslave no one as the English do."

THE RICE KINGDOM

As in early Virginia, frontier conditions allowed leeway to South Carolina's small population of African-born slaves, who farmed, tended livestock, and were initially allowed to serve in the militia to fight the Spanish and Indians. And as in Virginia, the introduction of a marketable staple crop, in this case rice, led directly to economic development, the large-scale importation of slaves, and a growing divide between white and black. South Carolina was the first mainland colony to achieve a black majority. By the 1730s (by which time North Carolina had become a separate colony), two-thirds of its population was black. In the 1740s, another staple, indigo (a crop used in producing blue dye), was developed. Like rice, indigo required large-scale cultivation and was grown by slaves.

Ironically, it was Africans, familiar with the crop at home, who taught English settlers how to cultivate rice, which then became the foundation of South Carolina slavery and of the wealthiest slaveowning class on the North American mainland. Since rice production requires considerable capital investment to drain swamps and create irrigation systems, it is economically advantageous for rice plantations to be as large as possible. Thus, South Carolina planters owned far more land and slaves than their counterparts in Virginia. Moreover, since mosquitoes bearing malaria (a disease to which Africans had developed partial immunity) flourished in the watery rice fields, planters tended to leave plantations under the control of overseers and the slaves themselves.

In the Chesapeake, field slaves worked in groups under constant supervision. Under the "task" system that developed in eighteenth-century South Carolina, individual slaves were assigned daily jobs, the completion of which allowed them time for leisure or to cultivate crops of their own. In 1762, one rice district had a population of only 76 white males among 1,000 slaves. Fearful of the ever-increasing black population majority, South Carolina's legislature took steps to encourage the immigration of "poor Protestants," offering each newcomer a cash bounty and occasionally levying taxes on slave imports, only to see such restrictions overturned in London. By 1770, the number of South Carolina slaves had reached 100,000, well over half the colony's population.

THE GEORGIA EXPERIMENT

Rice cultivation also spread into Georgia in the mid-eighteenth century. The colony was founded in 1733 by a group of philanthropists led by James Oglethorpe, a wealthy reformer whose causes included improved conditions for imprisoned debtors and the abolition of slavery. Oglethorpe hoped to establish a haven where the "worthy poor" of England could enjoy economic opportunity. The government in London supported the creation of Georgia to protect South Carolina against the Spanish and their Indian allies in Florida.

Initially, the proprietors banned the introduction of both liquor and slaves, leading to continual battles with settlers, who desired both. By the

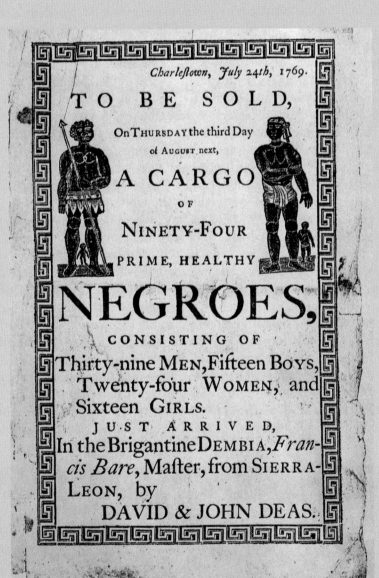

Slave Sale Broadside. *This 1769 broadside advertises the sale of ninety-four slaves who had just arrived in Charleston from West Africa. Broadsides like this one were displayed prominently by slave traders to drum up business.*

QUESTIONS

1. What was the artist who created the broadside trying to convey by the way he depicted the slaves?

2. How do you think colonists, who at this very time were defending their liberty against British policies, justified importing and selling slaves?

1740s, Georgia offered the spectacle of colonists pleading for the "English liberty" of self-government so that they could enact laws introducing slavery. In 1751, the proprietors surrendered the colony to the crown. The colonists quickly won the right to an elected assembly, which met in Savannah, Georgia's main settlement. It repealed the ban on slavery (and liquor), as well as an early measure that had limited land holdings to 500 acres. Georgia became a miniature version of South Carolina. By 1770, as many as 15,000 slaves labored on its coastal rice plantations.

SLAVERY IN THE NORTH

Compared to the plantation regions, slavery was far less central to the economies of New England and the Middle Colonies, where small farms predominated. Slaves made up only a small percentage of these colonies' populations, and it was unusual for even rich families to own more than one slave. Sections of Rhode Island and Connecticut did develop large tobacco and livestock farms employing slave labor, but northern slaves were far more dispersed than in the South. Nonetheless, slavery was not entirely marginal to northern colonial life. Slaves worked as farm hands, in artisan shops, as stevedores loading and unloading ships, and as personal servants. In the early eighteenth century, about three-quarters of the urban elite owned at least one slave. But with slaves so small a part of the population that they seemed to pose no threat to the white majority, laws were less harsh than in the South. In New England, where in 1770 the 17,000 slaves represented less than 3 percent of the region's population, slave marriages were recognized in law, the severe physical punishment of slaves was prohibited, and slaves could bring suits in court, testify against whites, and own property and pass it on to their children—rights unknown in the South.

Slavery had been present in New York from the earliest days of Dutch settlement. With white immigration lagging behind that of Pennsylvania, the colony's Hudson Valley landlords, small farmers, and craftsmen continued to employ considerable amounts of slave labor in the eighteenth century. As New York City's role in the slave trade expanded, so did slavery in the city. In 1746, its 2,440 slaves amounted to one-fifth of New York City's total population. Some 30 percent of its laborers were slaves, a proportion second only to Charleston among American cities. Most were domestic work-

Slavery existed in the eighteenth century in all the colonies. In this 1741 painting of the Potter family of Matunuck, Rhode Island, a young African-American boy serves tea.

ers, but slaves worked in all sectors of the economy. In 1770, about 27,000 slaves lived in New York and New Jersey, 10 percent of their total population. Slavery was also a significant presence in Philadelphia, although the institution stagnated after 1750 as artisans and merchants relied increasingly on wage laborers, whose numbers were augmented by population growth and the completion of the terms of indentured servants. In an urban economy that expanded and contracted according to the ups and downs of international trade, many employers concluded that relying on wage labor, which could be hired and fired at will, made more economic sense than a long-term investment in slaves.

SLAVE CULTURES AND SLAVE RESISTANCE

BECOMING AFRICAN-AMERICAN

The nearly 300,000 Africans brought to the mainland colonies during the eighteenth century were not a single people. They came from different cultures, spoke different languages, and practiced many religions. Eventually, an African-American people would emerge from the diverse peoples transported to the British colonies in the Middle Passage. Slavery threw together individuals who would never otherwise have encountered one another and who had never considered their color or residence on a single continent a source of identity or unity. Their bond was not kinship, language, or even "race," but slavery itself. The process of creating a cohesive culture and community took many years, and it proceeded at different rates in different regions. But by the nineteenth century, slaves no longer identified themselves as Ibo, Ashanti, Yoruba, and so on, but as African-Americans. In music, art, folklore, language, and religion, their cultural expressions emerged as a synthesis of African traditions, European elements, and new conditions in America.

For most of the eighteenth century, the majority of American slaves were African by birth. For many years, they spoke African languages and practiced African religions. Advertisements seeking information about runaways often described them by African origin ("young Gambia Negro," "new Banbara Negro fellow") and spoke of their bearing on their bodies "country marks"—visible signs of ethnic identity in Africa. Indeed, during the eighteenth century, black life in the colonies was "re-Africanized" as the earlier Creoles (slaves born in the New World) came to be outnumbered by large-scale importations from Africa. Compared with the earliest generation of slaves, the newcomers worked harder, died earlier, and had less access to freedom. Charles Hansford, a white Virginia blacksmith, noted in a 1753 poem that he had frequently heard slaves speak of their desire to "reenjoy" life in Africa:

> I oft with pleasure have observ'd how they
> Their sultry country's worth strive to display
> In broken language, how they praise their case
> And happiness when in their native place . . .
> How would they dangers court and pains endure
> If to their country they could get secure!

Table 4.1 SLAVE POPULATION AS PERCENTAGE OF TOTAL POPULATION OF ORIGINAL THIRTEEN COLONIES, 1770

Colony	Slave Population	Percentage
New Hampshire	654	1%
Massachusetts	4,754	2
Connecticut	5,698	3
Rhode Island	3,761	6
New York	19,062	12
New Jersey	8,220	7
Pennsylvania	5,561	2
Delaware	1,836	5
Maryland	63,818	32
Virginia	187,600	42
North Carolina	69,600	35
South Carolina	75,168	61
Georgia	15,000	45

AFRICAN-AMERICAN CULTURES

By the mid-eighteenth century, the three slave systems in British North America had produced distinct African-American cultures. In the Chesapeake, because of a more healthful climate, the slave population began to reproduce itself by 1740, creating a more balanced sex ratio than in the seventeenth century and making possible the creation of family-centered slave communities. Because of the small size of most plantations and the large number of white yeoman farmers, slaves here were continuously exposed to white culture. They soon learned English, and many were swept up in the religious revivals known as the Great Awakening, discussed later in this chapter.

In South Carolina and Georgia, two very different black societies emerged. On the rice plantations, slaves lived in extremely harsh conditions and had a low birthrate throughout the eighteenth century, making rice production dependent on continued slave imports from Africa. The slaves seldom came into contact with whites and enjoyed far more autonomy than elsewhere in the colonies. The larger structures of their lives were established by slavery, but they were able to create an African-based culture. They constructed African-style houses, chose African names for their children, and spoke Gullah, a language that mixed various African roots and was unintelligible to most whites. Despite a continuing slave trade in which young, single males predominated, slaves slowly created families and communities that bridged generations. The experience of slaves who labored in Charleston and Savannah as servants and skilled workers was quite different. These assimilated more quickly into Euro-American culture, and sexual liaisons between white owners and slave women produced the beginnings of a class of free mulattos.

In the northern colonies, where slaves represented a smaller part of the population, dispersed in small holdings among the white population, a distinctive African-American culture developed more slowly. Living in close proximity to whites, they enjoyed more mobility and access to the mainstream of life than their counterparts farther south. Slaves in cities like Philadelphia and New York gathered on holidays to perform African dances. But they had fewer opportunities to create stable family life or a cohesive community.

RESISTANCE TO SLAVERY

The common threads that linked these regional African-American cultures were the experience of slavery and the desire for freedom. Throughout the eighteenth century, blacks risked their lives in efforts to resist enslavement. Colonial newspapers, especially in the southern colonies, were filled with advertisements for runaway slaves. Most fugitives were young African men who had arrived recently. In South Carolina and Georgia, they fled to Florida, to uninhabited coastal and river swamps, or to Charleston and Savannah, where they could pass for free. In the Chesapeake and Middle Colonies, fugitive slaves tended to be familiar with white culture and therefore, as one advertisement put it, could "pretend to be free."

What Edward Trelawny, the colonial governor of Jamaica, called "a dangerous spirit of liberty" was widespread among the New World's slaves. The eighteenth century's first slave uprising occurred in New York City in 1712, when a group of slaves set fire to houses on the outskirts of the city and killed the first nine whites who arrived on the scene. Subsequently, eighteen conspirators were executed; some were tortured and burned alive in a public spectacle meant to intimidate the slave population. During the 1730s and 1740s, continuous warfare involving European empires and Indians opened the door to slave resistance. In 1731, a slave rebellion in Louisiana, where the French and Natchez Indians were at war, temporarily halted efforts to introduce the plantation system in that region. There were uprisings throughout the West Indies, including in the Virgin Islands, owned by Denmark, and on the French island of Guadeloupe. On Jamaica, a major British center of sugar production, communities of fugitive slaves known as "maroons" waged outright warfare against British authorities until a treaty of 1739 recognized their freedom, in exchange for which they agreed to return future escapees.

THE CRISIS OF 1739–1741

On the mainland, slaves seized the opportunity for rebellion offered by the War of Jenkins' Ear, which pitted England against Spain. In September 1739, a group of South Carolina slaves, most of them recently arrived from Kongo where some, it appears, had been soldiers, seized a store containing numerous weapons at the town of Stono. Beating drums to attract followers, the armed band marched southward toward Florida, burning houses and barns, killing whites they encountered, and shouting "Liberty." (Florida's Spanish rulers offered "Liberty and Protection" to fugitives from the British colonies.) The group eventually swelled to some 100 slaves. After a pitched battle with the colony's militia, the rebels were dispersed. The rebellion took the lives of more than two dozen whites and as many as 200 slaves. Some slaves managed to reach Florida, where in 1740 they were armed by the Spanish to help repel an attack on St. Augustine by a force from Georgia. The Stono Rebellion led to a severe tightening of the South Carolina slave code and the temporary imposition of a prohibitive tax on imported slaves.

In 1741, a panic (which some observers compared to the fear of witches in Salem in the 1690s) swept New York City. After a series of fires broke out, rumors spread that slaves, with some white allies, planned to burn part of the city, seize weapons, and either turn New York over to Spain or murder the white population. More than 150 blacks and 20 whites were arrested, and 34 alleged conspirators, including 4 white persons, were executed. Historians still disagree as to how extensive the plot was or whether it existed at all. But dramatic events like revolts, along with the constant stream of runaways, disproved the idea, voiced by the governor of South Carolina, that slaves had "no notion of liberty." In eighteenth-century America, dreams of freedom knew no racial boundary. When white colonists rose in rebellion against British rule, tens of thousands of slaves would seize the opportunity to strike for their own liberty.

An advertisement seeking the return of a runaway slave from Port Royal, in the Sea Islands of South Carolina. "Mustee" was a term for a person of mixed European and African ancestry. From the South Carolina Gazette, June 11, 1747.

Run away on the 13th of *March* laſt, a Muſtee Fellow named *Cyrus*, who lately belonged to Meſſrs. *Mulryne* and *Williams* of *Port-Royal.* Whoever ſecures, or brings the ſaid Fellow to me, or to Mr. *David Brown* of *Charles-Town* Shipwright, ſhall have TWENTY POUNDS Reward, and the Charges allow'd by Law. And whoever gives me Information of his being employed by any Perſon, ſo that he may be convicted thereof, ſhall, upon ſuch Conviction, have THIRTY POUNDS current Money paid him, by   *David Linn.*
A bay ſtray Horſe, about 13 Hands and an half

AN EMPIRE OF FREEDOM

BRITISH PATRIOTISM

Despite the centrality of slavery to its empire, eighteenth-century Great Britain prided itself on being the world's most advanced and freest nation. It was not only the era's greatest naval and commercial power but also the home of a complex governmental system with a powerful Parliament representing the interests of a self-confident landed aristocracy and merchant class. In London, the largest city in Europe with a population approaching 1 million by the end of the eighteenth century, Britain possessed a single political-cultural-economic capital. It enjoyed a common law, common language, and, with the exception of a small number of Jews, Catholics, and Africans, common devotion to Protestantism. For much of the eighteenth century, Britain found itself at war with France, which had replaced Spain as its major continental rival. This situation led to the development of a large military establishment, high taxes, and the creation of the Bank of England to help finance European and imperial conflicts. For both Britons and colonists, war helped to sharpen a sense of national identity against foreign foes.

British patriotic sentiment became more and more assertive as the eighteenth century progressed. Symbols of British identity proliferated: the songs "God Save the King" and "Rule Britannia," and even the modern rules of cricket, the national sport. The rapidly expanding British economy formed another point of pride uniting Britons and colonists. Continental peoples, according to a popular saying, wore "wooden shoes"—that is, their standard of living was far below that of Britons. Writers hailed commerce as a progressive, civilizing force, a way for different peoples to interact for mutual benefit without domination or military conflict. Especially in contrast to France, Britain saw itself as a realm of widespread prosperity, individual liberty, the rule of law, and the Protestant faith. Wealth, religion, and freedom went together. "There is no Popish nation," wrote the Massachusetts theologian Cotton Mather in 1710, "but what by embracing the Protestant Religion would . . . not only assert themselves into a glorious liberty, but also double their wealth immediately."

THE BRITISH CONSTITUTION

Central to this sense of British identity was the concept of liberty. The fierce political struggles of the English Civil War and the Glorious Revolution bequeathed to eighteenth-century Britons an abiding conviction that liberty was their unique possession. They believed power and liberty to be natural antagonists. To mediate between them, advocates of British freedom celebrated the rule of law, the right to live under legislation to which one's representatives had consented, restraints on the arbitrary exercise of political authority, and rights like trial by jury enshrined in the common law. On both sides of the Atlantic, every political cause, it seemed, wrapped itself in the language of liberty and claimed to be defending the "rights of Englishmen." Continental writers dissatisfied with the lack of liberty in their own countries looked to Britain as a model. The House of Commons, House of Lords, and king each checked the power of the others. This structure, wrote the

French political philosopher Baron Montesquieu, made Britain "the one nation in the world whose constitution has political liberty for its purpose." In its "balanced constitution" and the principle that no man, even the king, is above the law, Britons claimed to have devised the best means of preventing political tyranny. Until the 1770s, most colonists believed themselves to be part of the freest political system mankind had ever known.

As the coexistence of slavery and liberty within the empire demonstrated, British freedom was anything but universal. It was closely identified with the Protestant religion and was invoked to contrast Britons with the "servile" subjects of Catholic countries, especially France, Britain's main rival in eighteenth-century Europe. It viewed nearly every other nation on earth as "enslaved"—to popery, tyranny, or barbarism. One German military officer commented in 1743 on the British "contempt" of foreigners: "They [pride] themselves not only upon their being free themselves, but being the bulwarks of liberty all over Europe; and they vilify most of the Nations on the continent . . . for being slaves, as they call us." British liberty was fully compatible with wide gradations in personal rights. Yet in the minds of the free residents of Great Britain and its North American colonies, liberty was the bond of empire.

THE LANGUAGE OF LIBERTY

These ideas sank deep roots not only within the "political nation"—those who voted, held office, and engaged in structured political debate—but also far more broadly in British and colonial society. Laborers, sailors, and artisans spoke the language of British freedom as insistently as pamphleteers and parliamentarians. Increasingly, the idea of liberty lost its traditional association with privileges derived from membership in a distinct social class and became more and more identified with a general right to resist arbitrary government.

Even though less than 5 percent of the British population enjoyed the right to vote, representative government was central to the eighteenth-century idea of British liberty. In this painting from 1793, Prime Minister William Pitt addresses the House of Commons.

A 1770 engraving from the Boston Gazette *by Paul Revere illustrates the association of British patriotism and liberty. Britannia sits with a liberty cap and her national shield, and releases a bird from a cage.*

On both sides of the Atlantic, liberty emerged as the battle cry of the rebellious. Frequent crowd actions protesting violations of traditional rights gave concrete expression to popular belief in the right to oppose tyranny. Ordinary persons thought nothing of taking to the streets to protest efforts by merchants to raise the cost of bread above the traditional "just price," or the Royal Navy's practice of "impressment"—kidnapping poor men on the streets for maritime service.

REPUBLICAN LIBERTY

Liberty was central to two sets of political ideas that flourished in the Anglo-American world. One is termed by scholars "republicanism" (although few in eighteenth-century England used the word, which literally meant a government without a king and conjured up memories of the beheading of Charles I). Republicanism celebrated active participation in public life by economically independent citizens as the essence of liberty. Republicans assumed that only property-owning citizens possessed "virtue"—defined in the eighteenth century not simply as a personal moral quality but as the willingness to subordinate self-interest to the pursuit of the public good. "Only a virtuous people are capable of freedom," wrote Benjamin Franklin.

In eighteenth-century Britain, this body of thought about freedom was most closely associated with a group of critics of the established political order known as the "Country Party" because much of their support arose from the landed gentry. They condemned what they considered the corruption of British politics, evidenced by the growing number of government appointees who sat in the House of Commons. They called for the election of men of "independence" who could not be controlled by the ministry, and they criticized the expansion of the national debt and the growing wealth of financial speculators in a commercializing economy. Britain, they claimed, was succumbing to luxury and political manipulation—in a word, a loss of virtue—thereby endangering the careful balance of its system of government and, indeed, liberty itself. In Britain, Country Party publicists like John Trenchard and Thomas Gordon, authors of *Cato's Letters*, published in the 1720s, had little impact. But their writings were eagerly devoured in the American colonies, whose elites were attracted to Trenchard and Gordon's emphasis on the political role of the independent landowner and their warnings against the constant tendency of political power to infringe upon liberty.

LIBERAL FREEDOM

The second set of eighteenth-century political ideas celebrating freedom came to be known as "liberalism" (although its meaning was quite different from what the word suggests today). Whereas republican liberty had a public and social quality, liberalism was essentially individual and private. The leading philosopher of liberty was John Locke, whose *Two Treatises of*

Government, written around 1680, had limited influence in his own lifetime but became extremely well known in the next century. Many previous writers had compared government to the family, assuming that in both, inequality was natural and power always emanated from the top. Locke held that the principles that governed the family were inappropriate for organizing public life. Government, he wrote, was formed by a mutual agreement among equals (the parties being male heads of households, not all persons). In this "social contract," men surrendered a part of their right to govern themselves in order to enjoy the benefits of the rule of law. They retained, however, their natural rights, whose existence predated the establishment of political authority. Protecting the security of life, liberty, and property required shielding a realm of private life and personal concerns—including family relations, religious preferences, and economic activity—from interference by the state. During the eighteenth century, Lockean ideas—individual rights, the consent of the governed, the right of rebellion against unjust or oppressive government—would become familiar on both sides of the Atlantic.

Like other Britons, Locke spoke of liberty as a universal right yet seemed to exclude many persons from its full benefits. Since the protection of property was one of government's main purposes, liberalism was compatible with substantial inequalities in wealth and well-being. Moreover, while Locke was one of the first theorists to defend the property rights of women and even their access to divorce, and condemned slavery as a "vile and miserable estate of man," the free individual in liberal thought was essentially the propertied white man. Locke himself had helped to draft the Fundamental Constitutions of Carolina, discussed in Chapter 3, which provided for slavery, and he was an investor in the Royal African Company, the

The Polling, by the renowned eighteenth-century British artist William Hogarth, satirizes the idea that British elections are decided by the reasoned deliberations of upstanding property owners. Inspired by a corrupt election of 1754, Hogarth depicts an election scene in which the maimed and dying are brought to the polls to cast ballots. At the center, lawyers argue over whether a man who has a hook for a hand can swear on the Bible.

slave-trading monopoly. Slaves, he wrote, "cannot be considered as any part of civil society." Nonetheless, by proclaiming that all individuals possess natural rights that no government may violate, Lockean liberalism opened the door to the poor, women, and even slaves to challenge limitations on their own freedom.

Republicanism and liberalism would eventually come to be seen as alternative understandings of freedom. In the eighteenth century, however, these systems of thought overlapped and often reinforced each other. Both political outlooks could inspire a commitment to constitutional government and restraints on despotic power. Both emphasized the security of property as a foundation of freedom. Both traditions were transported to eighteenth-century America. Ideas about liberty imported from Britain to the colonies would eventually help to divide the empire.

THE PUBLIC SPHERE

Colonial politics for most of the eighteenth century was considerably less tempestuous than in the seventeenth, with its bitter struggles for power and frequent armed uprisings. Political stability in Britain coupled with the maturation of local elites in America made for more tranquil government. New York stood apart from this development. With its diverse population and bitter memories of Leisler's rebellion (see Chapter 3, p. 111), New York continued to experience intense political strife among its many economic interests and ethnic groups. By the 1750s, semipermanent political parties competed vigorously for popular support in New York elections. But in most other colonies, although differences over policies of one kind or another were hardly absent, they rarely produced the civil disorder or political passions of the previous century.

THE RIGHT TO VOTE

In many respects, politics in eighteenth-century America had a more democratic quality than in Great Britain. Suffrage requirements varied from colony to colony, but as in Britain the linchpin of voting laws was the property qualification. Its purpose was to ensure that men who possessed an economic stake in society and the independence of judgment that went with it determined the policies of the government. The "foundation of liberty," the parliamentary leader Henry Ireton had declared during the English Civil War of the 1640s, "is that those who shall choose the lawmakers shall be men freed from dependence upon others." Slaves, servants, tenants, adult sons living in the homes of their parents, the poor, and women all lacked a "will of their own" and were therefore ineligible to vote. The wide distribution of property in the colonies, however, meant that a far higher percentage of the population enjoyed voting rights than in the Old World. It is estimated that between 50 and 80 percent of adult white men could vote in eighteenth-century colonial America, as opposed to fewer than 5 percent in Britain at the time.

Colonial politics, however, was hardly democratic in a modern sense. In a few instances—some towns in Massachusetts and on Long Island—propertied women, generally widows, cast ballots. But voting was almost

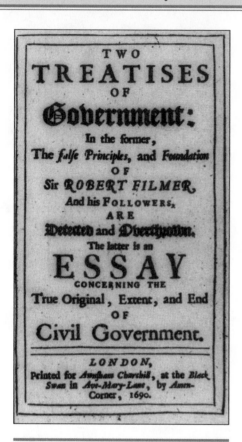

The title page of John Locke's Two Treatises of Government, *which traced the origins of government to an original state of nature and insisted that political authorities must not abridge mankind's natural rights.*

The British political philosopher John Locke, painted by Michael Dahl around 1696.

everywhere considered a male prerogative. In some colonies, Jews, Catholics, and Protestant Dissenters like Baptists and Quakers could not vote. Propertied free blacks, who enjoyed the franchise in Virginia, North Carolina, South Carolina, and Georgia in the early days of settlement, lost that right during the eighteenth century (although North Carolina restored it in the 1730s). In the northern colonies, while the law did not bar blacks from voting, local custom did. Native Americans were generally prohibited from voting.

POLITICAL CULTURES

Despite the broad electorate among white men, "the people" existed only on election day. Between elections, members of colonial assemblies remained out of touch with their constituents. Strongly competitive elections were the norm only in the Middle Colonies. Elsewhere, many elections went uncontested, either because only one candidate presented himself or because the local culture stressed community harmony, as in many New England towns. Considerable power in colonial politics rested with those who held appointive, not elective, office. Governors and councils were appointed by the crown in the nine royal colonies and by the proprietors of Pennsylvania and Maryland. Only in Rhode Island and Connecticut were these offices elective. Moreover, laws passed by colonial assemblies could be vetoed by governors or in London. In New England, most town officers were elected, but local officials in other colonies were appointed by the governor or by powerful officials in London. The duke of Newcastle alone could appoint eighty-three colonial officials.

Property qualifications for officeholding were far higher than for voting. In South Carolina, for example, nearly every adult male could meet the voting qualification of fifty acres of land or payment of twenty shillings in taxes, but to sit in the assembly one had to own 500 acres of land and ten slaves or town property worth £1,000. As a result, throughout the eighteenth century nearly all of South Carolina's legislators were planters or wealthy merchants. Despite its boisterous and competitive politics, New York's diminutive assembly, with fewer than thirty members, was dominated by relatives and allies of the great landed families, especially the Livingstons and DeLanceys. Of seventy-two men who sat in the New York Assembly between 1750 and 1776, fifty-two were related to the families who owned the great Hudson River estates.

In some colonies, a majority of free men possessed the right to vote, but an ingrained tradition of "deference"—the assumption among ordinary people that wealth, education, and social prominence carried a right to public office—sharply limited effective choice in elections. Virginia politics, for example, combined political

This anonymous engraving depicting a 1764 Pennsylvania election suggests the intensity of political debate in the Middle Colonies.

democracy for white men with the tradition that voters should choose among candidates from the gentry. Aspirants for public office actively sought to ingratiate themselves with ordinary voters, distributing food and liquor freely at the courthouse where balloting took place. In Thomas Jefferson's first campaign for the House of Burgesses in 1768, his expenses included hiring two men "for bringing up rum" to the polling place. Even in New England, with its larger number of elective positions, town leaders were generally the largest property holders and offices frequently passed down from generation to generation of the same family. Few Americans vigorously pursued elective office or took an active role in public affairs. By the mid-eighteenth century, the typical officeholder was considerably richer than the norm when the century began.

COLONIAL GOVERNMENT

Preoccupied with events in Europe and imperial rivalries, successive British governments during the first half of the eighteenth century adopted a policy of "salutary neglect" toward the colonies, leaving them largely to govern themselves. With imperial authority so weak, the large landowners, merchants, and lawyers who dominated colonial assemblies increasingly claimed the right to control local politics.

Convinced that they represented the will of the people, elected colonial assemblies used their control of finance to exert influence over appointed governors and councils. Although governors desired secure incomes for themselves and permanent revenue for their administrations (some, like Robert Hunter of New York, demanded a life salary), assemblies often authorized salaries only one year at a time and refused to levy taxes except in exchange for concessions on appointments, land policy, and other issues. Typically, members of the British gentry who had suffered financial reversals and hoped to recoup their fortunes in America, governors learned that to rule effectively they would have to cooperate with the colonial elite.

THE RISE OF THE ASSEMBLIES

In the seventeenth century, the governor was the focal point of political authority, and colonial assemblies were weak bodies that met infrequently. But in the eighteenth, as economic development enhanced the power of American elites, the assemblies they dominated became more and more assertive. Their leaders insisted that assemblies possessed the same rights and powers in local affairs as the House of Commons enjoyed in Britain. The most successful governors were those who accommodated the rising power of the assemblies and used their appointive powers and control of land grants to win allies among assembly members.

The most powerful assembly was Pennsylvania's, where a new charter, adopted in 1701, eliminated the governor's council, establishing the only unicameral (one-house) legislature in the colonies. Controlled until mid-century by an elite of Quaker merchants, the assembly wrested control of finance, appointments, and the militia from a series of governors representing the Penn family. Close behind in terms of power and legislative independence were the assemblies of New York, Virginia, South Carolina, and, especially, Massachusetts, which successfully resisted governors' demands for permanent salaries for appointed officials. Many of the conflicts between governors and elected assemblies stemmed from the colonies' economic growth. To deal with the scarcity of gold and silver coins, the only legal form of currency, some colonies printed paper money, although this was strongly opposed by the governors, authorities in London, and British merchants who did not wish to be paid in what they considered worthless paper. Numerous battles also took place over land policy (sometimes involving divergent attitudes toward the remaining Indian population) and the level of rents charged to farmers on land owned by the crown or proprietors.

In their negotiations and conflicts with royal governors, leaders of the assemblies drew on the writings of the English Country Party, whose emphasis on the constant tension between liberty and political power and the dangers of executive influence over the legislature made sense of their own experience. Of the European settlements in North America, only the British colonies possessed any considerable degree of popular participation in government. This fact reinforced the assemblies' claim to embody the rights of Englishmen and the principle of popular consent to government. They were defenders of "the people's liberty," in the words of one New York legislator.

POLITICS IN PUBLIC

This language reverberated outside the relatively narrow world of elective and legislative politics. The "political nation" was dominated by the American gentry, whose members addressed each other in letters, speeches, newspaper articles, and pamphlets filled with Latin expressions and references to classical learning. But especially in colonial towns and cities, the eighteenth century witnessed a considerable expansion of the "public sphere"—the world of political organization and debate independent of the government, where an informed citizenry openly discussed questions that had previously been the preserve of officials.

In Boston, New York, and Philadelphia, clubs proliferated where literary, philosophical, scientific, and political issues were debated. Among the best known was the Junto, a "club for mutual improvement" founded by Benjamin Franklin in Philadelphia in 1727 for weekly discussion of political and economic questions. Beginning with only a dozen members, it eventually evolved into the much larger American Philosophical Society. Such groups were generally composed of men of property and commerce, but some drew ordinary citizens into discussions of public affairs. Colonial taverns and coffeehouses also became important sites not only for social conviviality but also for political debates. Philadelphia had a larger number of drinking establishments per capita than Paris. In Philadelphia, one clergyman commented, "the poorest laborer thinks himself entitled to deliver his sentiments in matters of religion or politics with as much freedom as the gentleman or scholar."

THE COLONIAL PRESS

Neither the Spanish possessions of Florida and New Mexico nor New France possessed a printing press, although missionaries had established one in Mexico City in the 1530s. In British North America, however, the

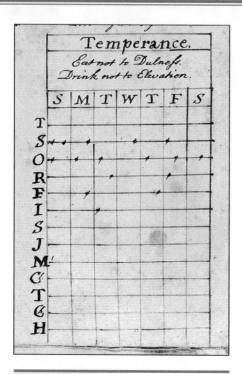

Benjamin Franklin's quest for self-improvement, or, as he put it in his autobiography, "moral perfection," is illustrated in this "Temperance diagram," which charts his behavior each day of the week with regard to thirteen virtues. They are listed on the left by their first letters: temperance, silence, order, resolution, frugality, industry, sincerity, justice, moderation, cleanliness, tranquility, chastity, and humility. Franklin did not always adhere to these virtues.

press expanded rapidly during the eighteenth century. So did the number of political broadsides and pamphlets published, especially at election time. Widespread literacy created an expanding market for printed materials. By the eve of the American Revolution, some three-quarters of the free adult male population in the colonies (and more than one-third of the women) could read and write, and a majority of American families owned at least one book. Philadelphia boasted no fewer than seventy-seven bookshops in the 1770s.

Circulating libraries appeared in many colonial cities and towns, making possible a wider dissemination of knowledge at a time when books were still expensive. The first, the Library Company of Philadelphia, was established by Benjamin Franklin in 1731. "So few were the readers at that time, and the majority of us so poor," Franklin recalled in his *Autobiography* (1791), that he could find only fifty persons, mostly "young tradesmen," anxious for self-improvement and willing to pay for the privilege of borrowing books. But reading, he added, soon "became fashionable." Libraries sprang up in other towns, and ordinary Americans came to be "better instructed and more intelligent than people of the same rank" abroad.

The first continuously published colonial newspaper, the *Boston News-Letter*, appeared in 1704 (a predecessor, *Publick Occurrences, Both Foreign and Domestick*, established in Boston in 1690, had been suppressed by authorities after a single issue for criticizing military cooperation with the Iroquois). There were thirteen colonial newspapers by 1740 and twenty-five in 1765, mostly weeklies with small circulations—an average of 600 sales per issue. Probably the best-edited newspaper was the *Pennsylvania Gazette*, established in 1728 in Philadelphia and purchased the following year by Benjamin Franklin, who had earlier worked as an apprentice printer on his brother's Boston periodical, the *New England Courant*. At its peak, the *Gazette* attracted 2,000 subscribers. Newspapers initially devoted most of their space to advertisements, religious affairs, and reports on British society and government. But by the 1730s, political commentary was widespread in the American press.

FREEDOM OF EXPRESSION AND ITS LIMITS

The public sphere thrived on the free exchange of ideas. But free expression was not generally considered one of the ancient rights of Englishmen. The phrase "freedom of speech" originated in Britain during the sixteenth century in Parliament's struggle to achieve the privilege of unrestrained debate. A right of legislators, not ordinary citizens, it referred to the ability of members of Parliament to express their views without fear of reprisal, on the grounds that only in this way could they effectively represent the people. Outside of Parliament, free speech had no legal protection. A subject could be beheaded for accusing the king of failing to hold "true" religious beliefs, and language from swearing to criticism of the government exposed a person to criminal penalties.

As for freedom of the press, governments on both sides of the Atlantic viewed this as extremely dangerous, partly because they considered ordinary citizens prone to be misled by inflammatory printed materials. During the English Civil War of the 1640s, the Levelers had called for the adoption of a written constitution, an Agreement of the People, containing guarantees of religious liberty and freedom of the press. But until 1695, when a British law requiring the licensing of printed works before publication lapsed, no newspaper, book, or pamphlet could legally be printed without a government license. The instructions of colonial governors included a warning about the "great inconveniences that may arise by the liberty of printing." After 1695, the government could not censor newspapers, books, and pamphlets before they appeared in print, although it continued to try to manage the press by direct payments to publishers and individual journalists. Authors and publishers could still be prosecuted for "seditious libel"—a crime that included defaming government officials—or punished for contempt.

Elected assemblies, not governors, most frequently discouraged freedom of the press in colonial America. Dozens of publishers were hauled before assemblies and forced to apologize for comments regarding one or another member. If they refused, they were jailed. James Franklin, Benjamin's older brother, spent a month in prison in 1722 after publishing a piece satirizing public authorities in Massachusetts. Colonial newspapers vigorously defended freedom of the press as a central component of liberty, insisting that the citizenry had a right to monitor the workings of government and subject public officials to criticism. Many newspapers reprinted passages from *Cato's Letters* in which Trenchard and Gordon strongly opposed prosecutions for libel. "Without freedom of thought," they declared, "there can be no such thing as wisdom, and no such thing as public liberty, without freedom of speech." But since government printing contracts were crucial for economic success, few newspapers attacked colonial governments unless financially supported by an opposition faction.

A portrait of Benjamin Franklin in fur hat and spectacles, dated 1777, depicts him as a symbol of America.

THE TRIAL OF ZENGER

The most famous colonial court case involving freedom of the press demonstrated that popular sentiment opposed prosecutions for criticism of public officials. This was the 1735 trial of John Peter Zenger, a German-born printer who had emigrated to New York as a youth. Financed by wealthy opponents of Governor William Cosby, Zenger's newspaper, the *Weekly Journal*, lambasted the governor for corruption, influence peddling, and "tyranny." New York's council ordered four issues burned and had Zenger himself arrested and tried for seditious libel. The judge instructed the jurors to consider only whether Zenger had actually published the offending words, not whether they were accurate. But Zenger's attorney, Andrew Hamilton, urged the jury to judge not the publisher but the governor. If they decided that Zenger's charges were correct, they must acquit him, and, Hamilton proclaimed, "every man who prefers freedom to a life of slavery will bless you."

Zenger was found not guilty. The case sent a warning to prosecutors that libel cases might be very difficult to win, especially in the superheated atmosphere of New York partisan politics. To be sure, had Zenger lambasted the assembly rather than the governor, he would in all likelihood have been lodged in jail without the benefit of a trial. The law of libel remained on the books. But the outcome helped to promote the idea that the publication of truth should always be permitted, and it demonstrated that the idea of free expression was becoming ingrained in the popular imagination.

The first page of the New York Weekly Journal, *edited by John Peter Zenger, one of four issues ordered to be burned by local authorities.*

THE AMERICAN ENLIGHTENMENT

During the eighteenth century, many educated Americans began to be influenced by the outlook of the European Enlightenment. This philosophical movement, which originated among French thinkers and soon spread to Britain, sought to apply to political and social life the scientific method of careful investigation based on research and experiment. Enlightenment ideas crisscrossed the Atlantic along with goods and people. Enlightenment thinkers insisted that every human institution, authority, and tradition be judged before the bar of reason. The self-educated Benjamin Franklin's wide range of activities—establishing a newspaper, debating club, and library; publishing the widely circulated *Poor Richard's Almanack*; and conducting experiments to demonstrate that lightning is a form of electricity—exemplified the Enlightenment spirit and made him probably the best-known American in the eighteenth-century world.

One inspiration for the Enlightenment was a reaction against the bloody religious wars that racked Europe in the seventeenth century. Enlightenment thinkers hoped that "reason," not religious enthusiasm, could govern human life. The criticism of social and political institutions based on tradition and hereditary privilege rather than the dictates of reason could also be applied to established churches. John Locke himself had published *The Reasonableness of Christianity* in 1695, which insisted that religious belief should rest on scientific evidence. During the eighteenth century, many prominent Americans moved toward the position called Arminianism, which taught that reason alone was capable of establishing the essentials of religion. Others adopted Deism, a belief that God essentially withdrew after creating the world, leaving it to function according to scientific laws without divine intervention. Belief in miracles, in the revealed truth of the Bible, and in the innate sinfulness of mankind were viewed by Arminians, Deists, and others as outdated superstitions that should be abandoned in the modern age.

In the seventeenth century, the English scientist Isaac Newton had revealed the natural laws that governed the physical universe. Here, Deists believed, was the purest evidence of God's handiwork. Many Protestants of all denominations could accept Newton's findings while remaining devout churchgoers (as Newton himself had). But Deists concluded that the best form of religious devotion was to study the workings of nature, rather than to worship in organized churches or appeal to divine grace for salvation. By the late colonial era, a small but influential group of leading Americans, including Benjamin Franklin and Thomas Jefferson, could be classified as Deists.

THE GREAT AWAKENING

Like freedom of the press, religion was another realm where the actual experience of liberty outstripped its legal recognition. Religion remained central to eighteenth-century American life. Sermons, theological treatises, and copies of the Bible were by far the largest category of material produced by colonial printers. Religious disputes often generated more public attention than political issues. Yet many church leaders worried about lax religious observance as colonial economic growth led people to be more and more preoccupied with worldly affairs.

RELIGIOUS REVIVALS

Many ministers were concerned that westward expansion, commercial development, the growth of Enlightenment rationalism, and lack of individual engagement in church services were undermining religious devotion. These fears helped to inspire the revivals that swept through the colonies beginning in the 1730s. Known as the Great Awakening, the revivals were less a coordinated movement than a series of local events united by a commitment to a "religion of the heart," a more emotional and personal Christianity than that offered by existing churches. The revivals redrew the religious landscape of the colonies.

Jonathan Edwards, one of the most prominent preachers of the Great Awakening.

The eighteenth century witnessed a revival of religious fundamentalism in many parts of the world, in part a response to the rationalism of the Enlightenment and a desire for greater religious purity. In the Middle East and Central Asia, where Islam was widespread, followers of a form of the religion known as Wahhabism called for a return to the practices of the religion's early days. In Eastern Europe, Hasidic Jews emphasized the importance of faith and religious joy as opposed to what they considered the overly academic study of Jewish learning and history in conventional Judaism. Methodism and other forms of enthusiastic religion were flourishing in Europe. Like other intellectual currents of the time, the Great Awakening was a transatlantic movement.

During the 1720s and 1730s, the New Jersey Dutch Reformed clergyman Theodore Frelinghuysen, his Presbyterian neighbors William and Gilbert Tennent, and the Massachusetts Congregationalist minister Jonathan Edwards pioneered an intensely emotional style of preaching. Edwards's famous sermon *Sinners in the Hands of an Angry God* portrayed sinful man as a "loathsome insect" suspended over a bottomless pit of eternal fire by a slender thread that might break at any moment. Edwards's preaching, declared a member of his congregation, inspired worshipers to cry out, "What shall I do to be saved—oh, I am going to hell!" Only a "new birth"— immediately acknowledging one's sins and pleading for divine grace— could save men from eternal damnation. "It is the new birth that makes [sinners] free," declared the Reverend Joshua Tufts.

THE PREACHING OF WHITEFIELD

Religious emotionalism was not confined to the American colonies—it spread through much of mid-eighteenth-century Europe as well. More than any other individual, the English minister George Whitefield, who declared "the whole world his parish," sparked the Great Awakening. For two years after his arrival in America in 1739, Whitefield brought his highly emotional brand of preaching to colonies from Georgia to New England. God, Whitefield proclaimed, was merciful. Rather than being predestined

George Whitefield, the English evangelist who helped to spark the Great Awakening in the colonies. Painted around 1742 by John Wollaston, who had emigrated from England to the colonies, the work depicts Whitefield's powerful effect on male and female listeners. It also illustrates Whitefield's eye problem, which led critics to dub him "Dr. Squintum."

for damnation, men and women could save themselves by repenting of their sins. Whitefield appealed to the passions of his listeners, powerfully sketching the boundless joy of salvation and the horrors of damnation. In every sermon, he asked his listeners to look into their own hearts and answer the question, "Are you saved?" If not, they must change their sinful ways and surrender their lives to Christ.

Tens of thousands of colonists flocked to Whitefield's sermons, which were widely reported in the American press, making him a celebrity and helping to establish the revivals as the first major intercolonial event in North American history. Although a Deist, Benjamin Franklin helped to publicize Whitefield's tour (and made a tidy profit) by publishing his sermons and journals. In Whitefield's footsteps, a host of traveling preachers or "evangelists" (meaning, literally, bearers of good news) held revivalist meetings, often to the alarm of established ministers.

Critics of the Great Awakening produced sermons, pamphlets, and newspaper articles condemning the revivalist preachers for lacking theological training, encouraging disrespect for "the established church and her ministers," and filling churches with "general disorder." Connecticut sought to stem the revivalist tide through laws punishing disruptive traveling preachers. By the time they subsided in the 1760s, the revivals had changed the religious configuration of the colonies and enlarged the boundaries of liberty. Whitefield had inspired the emergence of numerous Dissenting churches. Congregations split into factions headed by Old Lights (traditionalists) and New Lights (revivalists), and new churches proliferated—Baptist, Methodist, Presbyterian, and others. Many of these new churches began to criticize the colonial practice of levying taxes to support an established church; they defended religious freedom as one of the natural rights government must not restrict.

THE AWAKENING'S IMPACT

Although the revivals were primarily a spiritual matter, the Great Awakening reflected existing social tensions, threw into question many forms of authority, and inspired criticism of aspects of colonial society. They attracted primarily men and women of modest means—"rude, ignorant, void of manners, education or good breeding," one Anglican minister complained. Revivalist preachers frequently criticized commercial society, insisting that believers should make salvation, not profit, "the one business of their lives." In New England, they condemned merchants who ensnared the unwary in debt as greedy and unchristian. Preaching to the small farmers of the southern backcountry, Baptist and Methodist revivalists criticized the worldliness of wealthy planters and attacked as sinful activities such as gambling, horse racing, and lavish entertainments on the Sabbath.

A few preachers explicitly condemned slavery. And a few converts, such as Robert Carter III, the grandson of the wealthy planter Robert "King" Carter, emancipated their slaves after concluding that black and white were brothers in Christ. Most masters managed to reconcile Christianity and slaveholding. But especially in the Chesapeake, the revivals brought numerous slaves into the Christian fold, an important step in their acculturation as African-Americans. And a few blacks, touched by the word of God, took up preaching themselves. The revivals also spawned a group of female exhorters, who for a time shattered the male monopoly on preaching.

The revivals broadened the range of religious alternatives available to Americans, thereby leaving them more divided than before and at the same time more fully integrated into transatlantic religious developments. But the impact of the Great Awakening spread beyond purely spiritual matters. The newspaper and pamphlet wars it inspired greatly expanded the circulation of printed material in the colonies. The revivals encouraged many colonists to trust their own views rather than those of established elites. In listening to the sermons of self-educated preachers, forming Bible study groups, and engaging in intense religious discussions, ordinary colonists asserted the right to independent judgment. "The common people," proclaimed Baptist minister Isaac Backus, "claim as good a right to judge and act for themselves in matters of religion as civil rulers or the learned clergy." The revivalists' aim was spiritual salvation, not social or political revolution. But the independent frame of mind they encouraged would have significant political consequences.

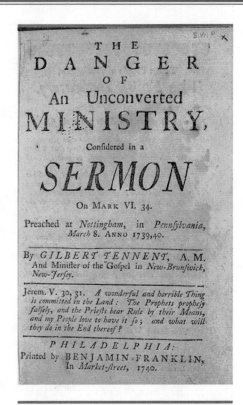

This 1740 pamphlet by Gilbert Tennent, a Presbyterian minister in Philadelphia, defended the Great Awakening by comparing anti-revival ministers to the false prophets described in the Bible.

IMPERIAL RIVALRIES

SPANISH NORTH AMERICA

The rapid growth of Britain's North American colonies took place at a time of increased jockeying for power among European empires, involving much of the area today included in the United States. But the colonies of England's rivals, although covering immense territories, remained thinly populated and far weaker economically. The Spanish empire encompassed an area that stretched from the Pacific coast and New Mexico into the Great Plains and eastward through Texas and Florida. After 1763, it also included Louisiana, which Spain obtained from France. On paper a vast territorial empire, Spanish North America actually consisted of a few small and isolated urban clusters, most prominently St. Augustine in Florida, San Antonio in Texas, and Santa Fe and Albuquerque in New Mexico.

In the second half of the century, the Spanish government made a concerted effort to reinvigorate its empire north of the Rio Grande. It stabilized relations with Indians, especially the nomadic Comanches and Apaches who had wreaked havoc in New Mexico. But although ranching expanded in New Mexico and Texas, the economy of the Spanish colonies essentially rested on trading with and extracting labor from the surviving Indian population. New Mexico's population in 1765 was only 20,000, equally divided between Spanish settlers and Pueblo Indians. Spain began the colonization of Texas at the beginning of the eighteenth century, partly as a buffer to prevent French commercial influence, then spreading in the Mississippi Valley, from intruding into New Mexico. The Spanish established complexes consisting of religious missions and *presidios* (military outposts) at Los Adaes, La Bahía, and San Antonio. But the region attracted few settlers. Texas had only 1,200 Spanish colonists in 1760. Florida stagnated as well, remaining an impoverished military outpost. Around 1770, its population consisted of about 2,000 Spanish, 1,000 black slaves, and a few hundred Indians, survivors of many decades of war and disease.

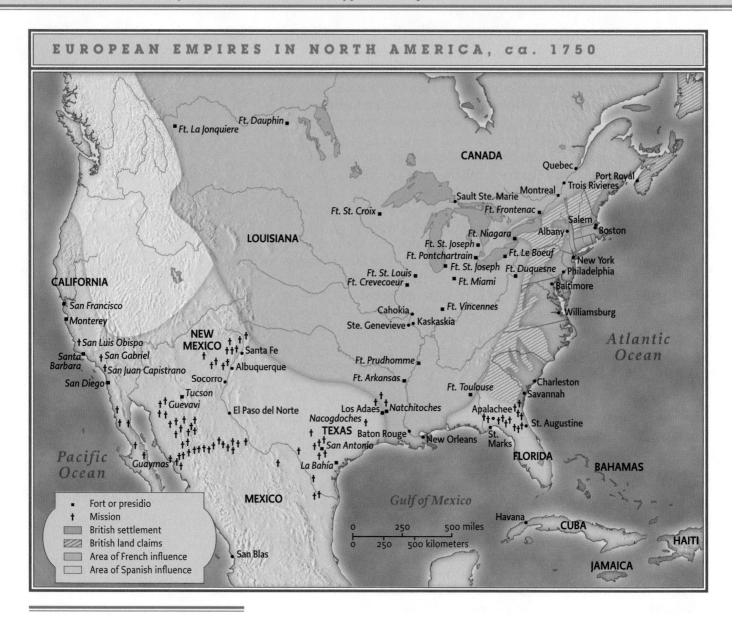

EUROPEAN EMPIRES IN NORTH AMERICA, ca. 1750

Three great empires—the British, French, and Spanish—competed for influence in North America for much of the eighteenth century.

THE SPANISH IN CALIFORNIA

On the Pacific coast, Russian fur traders in the eighteenth century established a series of forts and trading posts in Alaska. Although only a handful of Russian colonists lived in the region, Spain, alarmed by what it saw as a danger to its American empire, ordered the colonization of California. A string of Spanish missions and *presidios* soon dotted the California coastline, from San Diego to Los Angeles, Santa Barbara, Monterey, San Francisco, and Sonoma. Born on the Spanish Mediterranean island of Mallorca, Father Junípero Serra became one of the most controversial figures in California's early history. He founded the first California mission, in San Diego, in 1769 and administered the mission network until his death in 1784. Serra was widely praised in Spain for converting thousands of Indians to Christianity, teaching them Spanish, and working to transform their hunting-and-gathering economies by introducing settled agriculture and skilled crafts. Today, he is being considered by the Catholic Church for elevation to sainthood. But forced labor and disease took a heavy toll among Indians who lived at the missions Serra directed.

In this lithograph from 1816, Indians perform a dance at Mission San Francisco in California. Priests watch from the front of the mission church.

Present-day California was a densely populated area, with a native population of perhaps 250,000 when Spanish settlement began. But as in other regions, the coming of soldiers and missionaries proved a disaster for the Indians. More than any other Spanish colony, California was a mission frontier. These outposts served simultaneously as religious institutions and centers of government and labor. Their aim was to transform the culture of the local population and eventually assimilate it into Spanish civilization. Father Serra and other missionaries hoped to convert the natives to Christianity and settled farming. The missions also relied on forced Indian labor to grow grain, work in orchards and vineyards, and tend cattle. The combination of new diseases and the resettlement of thousands of Indians in villages around the missions devastated Indian society. By 1821, when Mexico won its independence from Spain, California's native population had declined by more than one-third. But the area had not attracted Spanish settlers. In 1800, Los Angeles, with a population of 300, was the largest town. When Spanish rule came to an end in 1821, *Californios* (California residents of Spanish descent) numbered only 3,200.

THE FRENCH EMPIRE

Spain's North American colonies remained peripheral parts of its empire when compared with its possessions in Central and South America and the Caribbean. A greater rival to British power in North America—as well as in Europe and the Caribbean—was France. During the eighteenth century, the population and economy of Canada expanded. At the same time, French traders pushed into the Mississippi River valley southward from the Great Lakes and northward from Mobile, founded in 1702, and New Orleans, established in 1718. In the St. Lawrence River valley of French Canada, prosperous farming communities developed. By 1750, the area had a population of about 55,000 colonists. Another 10,000 (about half Europeans, half African-American slaves) resided in Louisiana, mostly concentrated on the lower Mississippi River and along the Gulf Coast. By mid-century, sugar plantations had sprung up in the area between New Orleans and Baton

A sketch of New Orleans as it appeared in 1720.

Rouge. New Orleans already had a vibrant social life as well as an established community with churches, schools, and governmental buildings.

Nonetheless, the population of French North America continued to be dwarfed by the British colonies. Prejudice against emigration to North America remained widespread in France. A French novel written in 1731, known today as the basis for the nineteenth-century opera *Manon*, told the story of a prostitute punished by being transported to Louisiana and of her noble lover who followed her there. It expressed the popular view of the colony as a place of cruel exile for criminals and social outcasts. Nonetheless, by claiming control of a large arc of territory and by establishing close trading and military relations with many Indian tribes, the French empire posed a real challenge to the British. French forts and trading posts ringed the British colonies. In present-day Mississippi and Alabama and in the western regions of Georgia and the Carolinas, French and British traders competed to form alliances with local Indians and control the trade in deerskins. The French were a presence on the New England and New York frontiers and in western Pennsylvania.

BATTLE FOR THE CONTINENT

THE MIDDLE GROUND

For much of the eighteenth century, the western frontier of British North America was the flashpoint of imperial rivalries. The Ohio Valley became caught up in a complex struggle for power involving the French, British, rival Indian communities, and settlers and land companies pursuing their own interests. Here by mid-century resided numerous Indians, including Shawnees and Delawares who had been pushed out of Pennsylvania by advancing white settlement, Cherokees and Chickasaws from the southern colonies who looked to the region for new hunting grounds, and Iroquois seeking to exert control over the area's fur trade. On this "middle ground" between European empires and Indian sovereignty, villages sprang up where members of numerous tribes lived side by side, along with European traders and the occasional missionary.

By the mid-eighteenth century, Indians had learned that direct military confrontation with Europeans meant suicide, and that an alliance with a

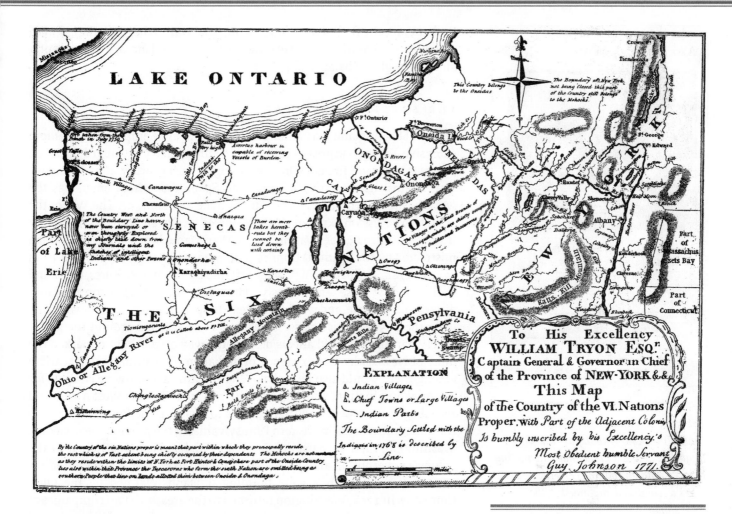

A map of upstate New York by Governor William Tryon of colonial New York demonstrates that the area was considered the realm of the Six Iroquois Nations, whose domain also stretched into the Ohio Valley.

single European power exposed them to danger from others. The Indians of the Ohio Valley recognized that the imperial rivalry of Britain and France posed both threat and opportunity. As one Delaware spokesman remarked, it was impossible to know "where the Indians' land lay, for the French claimed all the land on one side of the Ohio River and the English on the other side." On the other hand, Indians sought (with some success) to play European empires off one another and to control the lucrative commerce with whites. The Iroquois were masters of balance-of-power diplomacy. The British accepted their sovereignty in the Ohio Valley, but it was challenged by the French and their Indian allies.

In 1750, few white settlers inhabited the Ohio Valley. But already, Scotch-Irish and German immigrants, Virginia planters, and land speculators were eyeing the region's fertile soil. In 1749, the government of Virginia awarded an immense land grant—half a million acres—to the Ohio Company, an example of the huge domains being parceled out to those with political connections. The company's members included the colony's royal governor, Robert Dinwiddie, and the cream of Virginia society—Lees, Carters, and the young George Washington. The land grant threatened the region's Indians as well as Pennsylvania land speculators, who also had claims in the area. It sparked the French to bolster their presence in the region. It was the Ohio Company's demand for French recognition of its land claims that inaugurated the Seven Years' War (known in the colonies as the French and

The cover of a magazine published in Pennsylvania in 1758 depicts an Englishman and a Frenchman attempting to trade with an Indian. The Frenchman offers a tomahawk and musket, the Englishman a Bible and cloth. Of course, the depictions of the two Europeans reflect pro-British stereotypes.

Indian War), the first of the century's imperial wars to begin in the colonies and the first to result in a decisive victory for one combatant. It permanently altered the global balance of power.

THE SEVEN YEARS' WAR

Before 1688, England was a marginal power. Spain's empire was far more extensive, France had greater influence in Europe, and the Dutch dominated overseas trade and finance. Only in the eighteenth century, after numerous wars against its great rivals France and Spain, did Britain emerge as the world's leading empire and its center of trade and banking. The War of the Spanish Succession (known in the colonies as Queen Anne's War) lasted from 1702 to 1713; the War of Jenkins' Ear (named after a British seaman mistreated by the Spanish) from 1739 to 1742; and King George's War from 1740 to 1748. To finance these wars, Britain's public expenditures, taxes, and national debt rose enormously. The high rate of taxation inspired discontent at home, and would later help to spark the American Revolution.

By the 1750s, British possessions and trade reached around the globe. "Every part of the world affects us, in some way or another," remarked the duke of Newcastle. The existence of global empires implied that warfare among them would also be global. What became a worldwide struggle for imperial domination, which eventually spread to Europe, West Africa, and Asia, began in 1754 with British efforts to dislodge the French from forts they had constructed in western Pennsylvania. In the previous year, George Washington, then only twenty-one years old, had been dispatched by the colony's governor on an unsuccessful mission to persuade French soldiers to abandon a fort they were building on lands claimed by the Ohio Company. In 1754, Washington returned to the area with two companies of soldiers. He hastily constructed Fort Necessity. After an ill-considered attempt to defend it against a larger French and Indian force, resulting in the loss of one-third of his men, Washington was forced to surrender. Soon afterward, an expedition led by General Edward Braddock against Fort Duquesne (today's Pittsburgh) was ambushed by French and Indian forces, leaving Braddock and two-thirds of his 3,000 soldiers dead or wounded.

For two years, the war went against the British. French and Indian forces captured British forts in northern New York. The southern backcountry was ablaze with fighting among British forces, colonists, and Indians. Inhumanity flourished on all sides. Indians killed hundreds of colonists in western Pennsylvania and pushed the line of settlement all the way back to Carlisle, only 100 miles west of Philadelphia. In Nova Scotia, the British rounded up around 5,000 local French residents, called Acadians, confiscated their land, and expelled them from the region, selling their farms to settlers from New England. Some of those expelled eventually returned to France; others ended up as far away as Louisiana, where their descendants came to be known as Cajuns.

As the British government under Prime Minister William Pitt, who took office in 1757, raised huge sums of money and poured men and naval forces into the war, the tide of battle turned. Pitt's strategy was to provide funds to Prussia and Austria to enable them to hold the line against France and its ally Spain in Europe, while the British struck at the French weak point, its colonies. By 1759, Britain—with colonial and Indian soldiers playing a major role—had captured the pivotal French outposts of Forts Duquesne, Ticonderoga (north of Albany), and Louisbourg on Cape Breton Island, which guarded the mouth of the St. Lawrence River. In September of that year, a French army was defeated on the Plains of Abraham near Quebec. In 1760, Montreal, the last outpost of New France, surrendered. British forces also seized nearly all the islands in the French Caribbean and established control of India. In Europe, meanwhile, Prussia and Austria managed to fend off the coalition of France, Russia, and Spain.

A WORLD TRANSFORMED

"As long as the world has stood there has not been such a war," declared a British emissary to the Delaware Indians. Britain's victory fundamentally reshaped the world balance of power. In the Peace of Paris in 1763, France ceded Canada to Britain, receiving back in return the sugar islands of Guadeloupe and Martinique (far more lucrative colonies from the point of view of French authorities). As part of the reshuffling of imperial possessions, Spain ceded Florida to Britain in exchange for the return of the Philippines and Cuba (seized by the British during the war). Spain also acquired from France the vast Louisiana colony. France's 200-year-old North American empire had come to an end. With the exception of two tiny islands retained by France off the coast of Newfoundland, the entire continent east of the Mississippi River was now in British hands.

"Peace," remarked Prime Minister Pitt, "will be as hard to make as war." Eighteenth-century warfare, conducted on land and sea across the globe, was enormously expensive. The Seven Years' War put strains on all the participants. The war's cost produced a financial crisis in France that almost three decades later would help to spark the French Revolution. The British would try to recoup part of the cost of war by increasing taxes on their American colonies. "We no sooner leave fighting our neighbors, the French," commented the British writer Dr. Samuel Johnson, "but we must fall to quarreling among ourselves." In fact, the Peace of Paris was soon followed by open warfare in North America between the British and Native Americans.

PONTIAC'S REBELLION

Throughout eastern North America, the abrupt departure of the French in the aftermath of the Seven Years' War eliminated the balance-of-power diplomacy that had enabled groups like the Iroquois to maintain a significant degree of autonomy. Even as England and its colonies celebrated their victory as a triumph of liberty, Indians saw it as a threat to their own freedom. Indians had fought on both sides in the war, although mainly as allies of the French. Their primary aim, however, was to maintain their independence from both empires. Domination by any outside power, Indians feared, meant the loss of freedom. Without consulting them, the French had ceded land Indians claimed as their own, to British control. The Treaty of Paris left Indians more dependent than ever on the British and ushered in a period of confusion over land claims, control of the fur trade, and tribal relations in general. To Indians, it was clear that continued expansion of the British colonies posed a dire threat. One British army officer reported that Native Americans "say we mean to make slaves of them," by taking their land.

In 1763, in the wake of the French defeat, Indians of the Ohio Valley and Great Lakes launched a revolt against British rule. Although known as Pontiac's Rebellion after an Ottawa war leader, the rebellion owed at least as much to the teachings of Neolin, a Delaware religious prophet. During a religious vision, the Master of Life instructed Neolin that his people must reject European technology, free themselves from commercial ties with whites and dependence on alcohol, clothe themselves in the garb of their ancestors, and drive the British from their territory (although friendly French inhabitants could remain). Neolin combined this message with the relatively new idea of pan-Indian identity. All Indians, he preached, were a single people, and only through cooperation could they regain their lost independence. The common experience of dispossession, the intertribal communities that had developed in the Ohio country, and the mixing of Indian warriors in French armies had helped to inspire this sense of identity as Indians rather than members of individual tribes.

THE PROCLAMATION LINE

In the spring and summer of 1763, Ottawas, Hurons, and other Indians besieged Detroit, then a major British military outpost, seized nine other forts, and killed hundreds of white settlers who had intruded onto Indian lands. British forces soon launched a counterattack, and over the next few years the tribes one by one made peace. But the uprising inspired the government in London to issue the Proclamation of 1763, prohibiting further colonial settlement west of the Appalachian Mountains. These lands were reserved exclusively for Indians. Moreover, the Proclamation banned the sale of Indian lands to private individuals. Henceforth, only colonial governments could arrange such purchases.

The British aim was less to protect the Indians than to stabilize the situation on the colonial frontier and to avoid being dragged into an endless series of border conflicts. But the Proclamation enraged both settlers and speculators hoping to take advantage of the expulsion of the French to consolidate their claims to western lands. They ignored the new policy. George Washington himself ordered his agents to buy up as much Indian land as possible, while keeping the transactions "a profound secret" because of their illegality. Failing to offer a viable solution to the question of westward expansion, the Proclamation of 1763 ended up further exacerbating settler-Indian relations.

PENNSYLVANIA AND THE INDIANS

The Seven Years' War not only redrew the map of the world but produced dramatic changes within the American colonies as well. Nowhere was this more evident than in Pennsylvania, where the conflict shattered the decades-old rule of the Quaker elite and dealt the final blow to the colony's policy of accommodation with the Indians. During the war, with the frontier ablaze with battles between settlers and French and Indian warriors, western Pennsylvanians demanded that colonial authorities adopt a more aggressive stance. When the governor declared war on hostile Delawares, raised a militia, and offered a bounty for Indian scalps, many of the assembly's pacifist Quakers resigned their seats, effectively ending their control

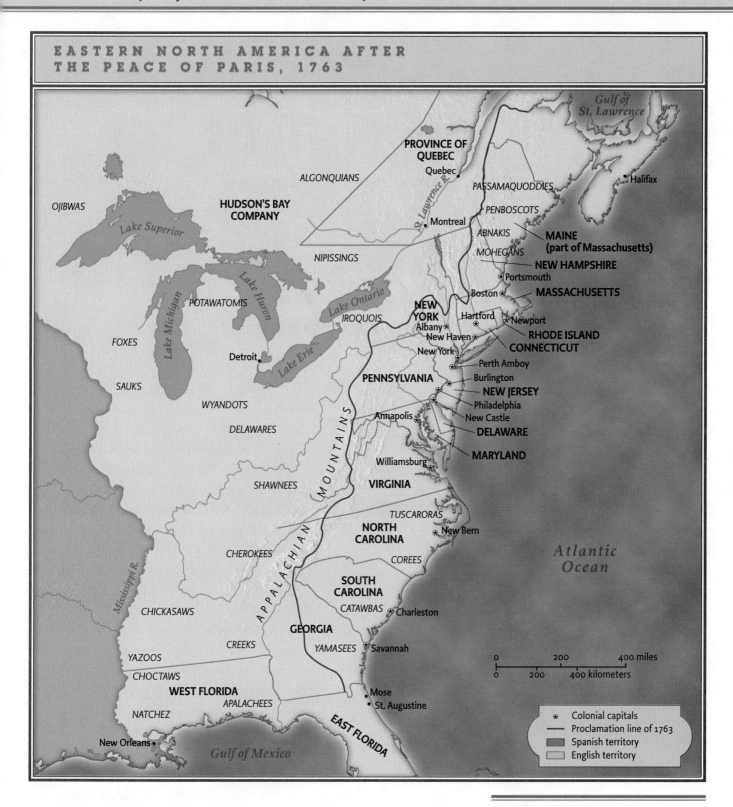

EASTERN NORTH AMERICA AFTER THE PEACE OF PARIS, 1763

Legend:
- ⊛ Colonial capitals
- — Proclamation line of 1763
- ▓ Spanish territory
- ░ English territory

of Pennsylvania politics. The war deepened the antagonism of western farmers toward Indians and witnessed numerous indiscriminate assaults on Indian communities, both allies and enemies.

In December 1763, while Pontiac's Rebellion still raged, a party of fifty armed men, mostly Scotch-Irish farmers from the vicinity of the Pennsylvania town of Paxton, destroyed the Indian village of Conestoga, massacring half

The Peace of Paris, which ended the Seven Years' War, left all of North America east of the Mississippi in British hands, ending the French presence on the continent.

VOICES OF FREEDOM

FROM *The Interesting Narrative of the Life of Olaudah Equiano, or Gustavus Vassa, the African* (1789)

Olaudah Equiano's autobiography, published in London, was the most prominent account of the slave experience written in the eighteenth century. In this passage, which comes after Equiano's description of a slave auction in the Caribbean, he calls on white persons to live up to their professed belief in liberty.

We were not many days in the merchant's custody before we were sold after their usual manner, which is this:—On a signal given (as the beat of a drum), the buyers rush in at once into the yard where the slaves are confined, and make choice of that parcel they like best. . . . In this manner, without scruple, are relations and friends separated, most of them never to see each other again. I remember in the vessel in which I was brought over, . . . there were several brothers, who, in the sale, were sold in different lots; and it was very moving on this occasion to see and hear their cries at parting.

O, ye nominal Christians! Might not an African ask you, learned you this from your God? Who says unto you, Do unto all men as you would men should do unto you? Is it not enough that we are torn from our country and friends to toil for your luxury and lust of gain? Must every tender feeling be sacrificed to your avarice? Are the dearest friends and relations, now rendered more dear by their separation from their kindred, still to be parted from each other, and thus prevented from cheering the gloom of slavery with the small comfort of being together and mingling their sufferings and sorrows? Why are parents to lose their children, brothers their sisters, or husbands their wives? Surely this is a new refinement in cruelty.

FROM PONTIAC, Speeches
(1762 and 1763)

Pontiac was a leader of the pan-Indian resistance to English rule known as Pontiac's Rebellion, which followed the end of the Seven Years' War. Neolin was a Delaware religious prophet who helped to inspire the rebellion.

———————————

Englishmen, although you have conquered the French, you have not yet conquered us! We are not your slaves. These lakes, these woods, and mountains were left to us by our ancestors. They are our inheritance; and we will part with them to none. Your nation supposes that we, like the white people, cannot live without bread and pork and beef! But you ought to know that He, the Great Spirit and Master of Life, has provided food for us in these spacious lakes, and on these woody mountains.

[The Master of Life has said to Neolin:]

I am the Maker of heaven and earth, the trees, lakes, rivers, and all else. I am the Maker of all mankind; and because I love you, you must do my will. The land on which you live I have made for you and not for others. Why do you suffer the white man to dwell among you? My children, you have forgotten the customs and traditions of your forefathers.

Why do you not clothe yourselves in skins, as they did, use bows and arrows and the stone-pointed lances, which they used? You have bought guns, knives, kettles and blankets from the white man until you can no longer do without them; and what is worse, you have drunk the poison firewater, which turns you into fools. Fling all these things away; live as your wise forefathers did before you. And as for these English,—these dogs dressed in red, who have come to rob you of your hunting-grounds, and drive away the game,—you must lift the hatchet against them. Wipe them from the face of the earth, and then you will win my favor back again, and once more be happy and prosperous.

═══════════

QUESTIONS

1. What aspect of slavery does Equiano emphasize in his account, and why do you think he does so?

2. What elements of Indian life does Neolin criticize most strongly?

3. How do Equiano and Pontiac differ in the ways they address white audiences?

Benjamin Franklin produced this famous cartoon in 1754, calling on Britain's North American colonies to unite against the French.

a dozen men, women, and children who lived there under the protection of Pennsylvania's governor. They then marched on Lancaster, where they killed fourteen additional Indians. Like participants in Bacon's Rebellion nearly a century earlier, they accused colonial authorities of treating Indians too leniently. They petitioned the legislature to remove all Indians from the colony. The Indians' "claim to freedom and independency," they insisted, threatened Pennsylvania's stability. When the Paxton Boys marched on Philadelphia in February 1764, intending to attack Moravian Indians who resided near the city, the governor ordered the expulsion of much of the Indian population. By the 1760s, Pennsylvania's Holy Experiment was at an end and with it William Penn's promise of "true friendship and amity" between colonists and the native population. No other large colony had a smaller Indian population or a more remorseless determination on the part of settlers to eliminate those who remained.

COLONIAL IDENTITIES

Like the Indians, colonists emerged from the Seven Years' War with a heightened sense of collective identity. Before the war, the colonies had been largely isolated from one another. Outside of New England, more Americans probably traveled to England than from one colony to another. In 1751, Governor George Clinton of New York had called for a general conference on Indian relations, but only three colonies bothered to send delegates. The Albany Plan of Union of 1754, drafted by Benjamin Franklin at the outbreak of the Seven Years' War, envisioned the creation of a Grand Council composed of delegates from each colony, with the power to levy taxes and deal with Indian relations and the common defense. Rejected by the colonial assemblies, whose powers Franklin's proposal would curtail, the plan was never sent to London for approval.

Participation in the Seven Years' War created greater bonds among the colonies. But the war also strengthened colonists' pride in being members of the British empire. It has been said that Americans were never more British than in 1763. Colonial militiamen and British regulars fought alongside each other against the French. Tensions developed between the professional British military and the often undisciplined American citizen-soldiers, but the common experience of battle and victory also forged bonds between them. For much of the century, New Englanders had called for the conquest of Canada as a blow for "Protestant freedom" against "popish slavery." Now that this had been accomplished, British victory in the Seven Years' War seemed a triumph of liberty over tyranny. The defeat of the Catholic French reinforced the equation of British nationality, Protestantism, and freedom.

In fact, however, after 1763 Britain's global empire was not predominantly Protestant or British or free. It now included tens of thousands of French Catholics and millions of persons in India governed as subjects rather than as citizens. The English statesman Edmund Burke wondered whether British liberty could be reconciled with rule over this "vast, heterogeneous, intricate mass of interests." Burke was almost alone in seeing the newly expanded empire as a challenge to the principles of British freedom. But soon, the American colonists would come to believe that membership in the empire jeopardized their liberty. When they did, they set out on a road that led to independence.

SUGGESTED READING

BOOKS

Anderson, Fred. *Crucible of War: The Seven Years' War and the Fate of Empire in British North America, 1754–1766* (2000). A general history of the Seven Years' War and its consequences.

Beeman, Richard R. *Varieties of Political Experience in Eighteenth-Century America* (2004). Explores how political life differed from colony to colony, and what characteristics they had in common.

Blackburn, Robin. *The Making of New World Slavery: From the Baroque to the Modern, 1492–1800* (1997). A comprehensive history of the rise of slavery in the Western Hemisphere and its centrality to European empires.

Calloway, Colin G. *The Scratch of a Pen: 1763 and the Transformation of North America* (2006). Examines the impact of the Peace of Paris on North America, especially the Native American population.

Clark, Charles E. *The Public Prints: The Newspaper in Anglo-American Culture, 1665–1740* (1994). Presents the early history of newspapers in colonial America.

Colley, Linda. *Britons: Forging the Nation, 1707–1837* (1992). An influential study of the rise of a sense of national identity in Great Britain, relevant also for the American colonies.

Gomez, Michael A. *Exchanging Our Country Marks: The Transformation of African Identities in the Colonial and Antebellum South* (1998). The most detailed study of the process by which Africans became African-Americans.

Greene, Jack P. *The Quest for Power: The Lower Houses of Assembly in the Southern Royal Colonies, 1689–1776* (1963). A careful examination of how elected assemblies expanded their authority in the eighteenth-century South.

Morgan, Philip D. *Slave Counterpoint: Black Culture in the Eighteenth-Century Chesapeake and Lowcountry* (1998). A detailed comparison of the nature of slave life in the two key slave systems of British North America.

Noll, Mark. *The Rise of Evangelicalism: The Age of Edwards, Whitefield, and the Wesleys* (2004). Explores the Great Awakening on both sides of the Atlantic and its impact on religious life.

Rediker, Marcus. *The Slave Ship: A Human History* (2007). A fascinating and disturbing account of the Atlantic slave trade that focuses on the captains, sailors, and slaves aboard the slave ships.

Weber, David J. *The Spanish Frontier in North America* (1992). The most comprehensive account of Spanish settlement in what is now the United States.

White, Richard. *The Middle Ground: Indians, Empires, and Republics in the Great Lakes Region, 1650–1815* (1991). The book that developed the idea of a middle ground where Europeans and Indians both exercised authority.

Wood, Peter H. *Black Majority: Negroes in Colonial South Carolina from 1670 through the Stono Rebellion* (1974). Examines how the expansion of rice production affected the slave system and the lives of slaves in South Carolina.

WEBSITES

Africans in America: www.: www.pbs.org/wgbh/aia/
Web de Anza: http://anza.uoregon.edu

REVIEW QUESTIONS

1. Why was Father Junípero Serra such a controversial and significant figure?

2. How did the ideas of republicanism and liberalism differ in eighteenth century British North America?

3. Three distinct slave systems were well entrenched in Britain's mainland colonies. Describe the main characteristics of each system.

4. What were the bases of the colonists' sense of a collective British identity in the eighteenth century?

5. What ideas generated by the American Enlightenment and the Great Awakening prompted challenges to religious, social, and political authorities in the British colonies?

6. How involved were colonial merchants in the Atlantic trading system, and what was the role of the slave trade in their commerce?

7. We often consider the impact of the slave trade only on the United States, but its impact extended much further. How did it affect West African nations and society, other regions of the New World, and the nations of Europe?

8. Using eighteenth-century concepts, explain who had the right to vote in the British colonies and why the restrictions were justified.

FREEDOM QUESTIONS

1. Although many British colonists claimed theirs was an "empire of freedom," most African-Americans disagreed. Why would African-Americans instead have viewed Spain as a beacon of freedom, and what events in the eighteenth century demonstrated this?

2. The eighteenth century saw the simultaneous expansion of both freedom and slavery in the North American colonies. Explain the connection between these two contradictory forces.

3. Explain how the ideals of republican liberty and liberal freedoms became the widespread rallying cries of people from all social classes in the British empire.

4. Today we treasure freedom of expression in all its forms, and codify these rights in the First Amendment. Why were these freedoms considered dangerous in the eighteenth century and thus not guaranteed to everyone in the British empire?

KEY TERMS

REVIEW TABLE

Major Labor Systems of Eighteenth-Century North America

Region	Major Economy	Dominant Labor Force
Chesapeake and North Carolina	Tobacco	Smaller plantations with substantial master-slave contact
South Carolina and Georgia	Rice and indigo	Large plantations with intensive slave labor
Middle Colonies	Large-scale farms Family farms Urban trade and commerce	Indentured servants on large farms Urban laborers and artisans
New England	Family farms Urban trade and commerce	Family members on farms Urban laborers and artisans
New Spain	Large-scale agriculture Cattle raising	Native Americans attached to lands

Part 2

A NEW NATION, 1763–1840

During the 1760s and 1770s, a dispute over taxation within the British empire escalated into a conflict that gave birth to a new nation, the United States of America. The American Revolution inaugurated an era of political upheaval throughout the Western world, known to historians ever since as the Age of Revolution. It helped to inspire popular uprisings in Europe, the Caribbean, and Latin America and forever changed the course of American development. Liberty emerged as the era's foremost rallying cry. The revolutionary generation insisted that the meaning of their struggle lay not only in political independence but also in the establishment of what the writer Thomas Paine called an asylum of liberty for all mankind.

The American Revolution not only broke the political bond with Great Britain but also inspired groups within American society to claim greater rights for themselves. Propertyless men demanded the right to vote. Women began to challenge their subordination to men. Indentured servants ran away from their masters. And slaves seized the opportunity to gain their freedom by fighting in the Continental army or by escaping to the British side.

By the time it had run its course, the Revolution had greatly expanded some realms of American freedom. It severed the connection between church and state, promoted the emergence of a lively public sphere in which ordinary men and, sometimes, women participated in political debate, and it challenged the monopoly on political power by colonial elites. It set in motion the abolition of slavery in the northern states. On the other hand, for some Americans independence meant a loss of liberty. Many of those who had remained loyal to England were persecuted and

forced to leave the country. The end of the British presence removed the last barrier to the westward expansion of the American population, making inevitable the dispossession of the remaining Indian population east of the Mississippi River. And the formation of a national government in which slaveowners occupied the presidency for most of the half-century after independence, helped to consolidate the institution of slavery in the South.

Three processes set in motion by the Revolution gained strength in the early decades of the nineteenth century and profoundly affected Americans' ideas about freedom. The first was the democratization of politics. Most members of the convention that drafted the nation's Constitution in 1787 assumed that men of property and education would dominate the new American government. But the democratic upsurge inspired by the Revolution, coupled with the swift emergence of political parties offering radically different programs for national development, encouraged a broad popular participation in politics. By the 1830s, a flourishing democratic system was firmly in place. Property qualifications for voting had been eliminated in nearly every state, two parties competed throughout the country, and voter turnout stood at record levels. Political democracy had become a defining element of American freedom.

Second, the development of steamboats, canals, and railroads brought rapid improvements in transportation and communication and created a broad market for farm products and manufactured goods. The "market revolution" opened up vast areas of the American interior to commercial farming, and it stimulated the early development of factory production. It offered new opportunities for personal advancement to many Americans while reducing others to what seemed an "unfree" situation—working for wages under the constant supervision of an employer. The market revolution also made possible the third major development of this era, the population's westward movement and the rise of the West as a distinct social and political region. The market revolution and westward shift of population also helped to reshape the idea of freedom, identifying it more and more closely with economic opportunity, physical mobility, and individual self-definition and fulfillment.

Many of the founding fathers had feared that economic growth, rapid territorial expansion, and the development of political parties would endanger the unity of the new republic. And between the coming of independence and 1840, the new nation faced a series of crises, as Americans divided according to political and regional loyalties and battled for advantage in the expanding economy. Political conflict often revolved around the relationship between government and the economy. Should the

national government seek to promote economic development and direct its course by enacting a system of tariffs, internal improvements, and a national bank? Or should it stand aside and allow Americans to pursue economic self-interest without governmental interference? In the 1790s, the former view was represented by the Federalist Party, the latter by the Jeffersonian Republicans. In the 1830s, a similar division emerged between Whigs and Democrats. Advocates of both visions of the role of the national government insisted that theirs was the best program to promote American liberty.

American freedom also continued to be shaped by the presence of slavery. Rather than dying out, as some of the founders had hoped, slavery expanded rapidly in territorial extent and economic importance. Slavery helped to define the boundaries of American freedom. The privileges of voting, officeholding, and access to economic opportunity were increasingly restricted to whites. Women, too, were barred from these elements of freedom. Their role, according to the prevailing social values, was to remain in the "private sphere" of the home.

The contradiction embedded in American life from the earliest days of settlement—expanding freedom for some coexisting with and, indeed, depending on lack of freedom for others—continued to bedevil the new nation.

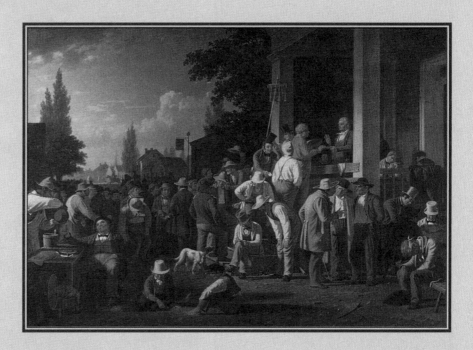

CHAPTER 5

The American Revolution, 1763–1783

The Apotheosis of Benjamin Franklin and George Washington, *a cotton fabric printed in Great Britain soon after the end of the American War of Independence and used as a bedcover. Franklin, accompanied by a goddess of liberty with her liberty cap, carries a banner reading "where liberty dwells there is my country," while angels display a map of the United States.*

FOCUS QUESTIONS

- What were the roots and significance of the Stamp Act controversy?

- What key events sharpened the divisions between Britain and the colonists in the late 1760s and early 1770s?

- What key events marked the move toward American independence?

- How were American forces able to prevail in the Revolutionary War?

On the night of August 26, 1765, a violent crowd of Bostonians assaulted the elegant home of Thomas Hutchinson, chief justice and lieutenant governor of Massachusetts. Hutchinson and his family were eating dinner when the rioters arrived. They barely had time to escape before the crowd broke down the front door and proceeded to destroy or carry off most of their possessions, including paintings, furniture, silverware, and notes for a history of Massachusetts Hutchinson was writing. By the time they departed, only the outer walls of the home remained standing.

The immediate cause of the riot was the Stamp Act, a recently enacted British tax that many colonists felt violated their liberty. Critics of the measure had spread a rumor that Hutchinson had written to London encouraging its passage (in fact, he privately opposed it). Only a few days earlier, Hutchinson had helped to disperse a crowd attacking a building owned by his relative Andrew Oliver, a merchant who had been appointed to help administer the new law. Both crowds were led by Ebenezer Mackintosh, a shoemaker who had fought against the French during the Seven Years' War and enjoyed a wide following among Boston's working people. Arrested after the destruction of Hutchinson's home, Mackintosh was released after the intervention of the Loyal Nine, a group of merchants and craftsmen who had taken the lead in opposing the Stamp Act. The violence had gone far beyond what the Loyal Nine intended, and they promised authorities that resistance to the Stamp Act would henceforth be peaceful. The riot, nonetheless, convinced Hutchinson that for Britain to rule America effectively, "there must be an abridgement of what are called English liberties." Whether colonists would accept such an abridgement, however, was very much in doubt.

The riot of August 26 was one small episode in a series of events that launched a half-century of popular protest and political upheaval throughout the Western world. The momentous era that came to be called the Age of Revolution began in British North America, spread to Europe and the Caribbean, and culminated in the Latin American wars for independence. In all these struggles, liberty emerged as the foremost rallying cry for popular discontent. Rarely has the idea played so central a role in political debate and social upheaval.

If the attack on Hutchinson's home demonstrated the depths of feeling aroused by Britain's efforts to impose greater control over its empire, it also revealed that revolution is a dynamic process whose consequences no one can anticipate. The crowd's fury expressed resentments against the rich and powerful quite different from colonial leaders' objections to Parliament's attempt to tax the colonies. The Stamp Act crisis inaugurated not only a struggle for colonial liberty in relation to Great Britain but also a multi-sided battle to define and extend liberty within America.

THE CRISIS BEGINS

When George III assumed the throne of Great Britain in 1760, no one on either side of the Atlantic imagined that within two decades Britain's American colonies would separate from the empire. But the Seven Years' War, which left Britain with an enormous debt and vastly enlarged overseas possessions to defend, led successive governments in London to seek ways to make the colonies share the cost of empire. Having studied the writings of British opposition thinkers who insisted that power inevitably seeks to encroach upon liberty, colonial leaders came to see these measures as part of a British design to undermine their freedom. Having only recently gloried in their enjoyment of "British liberty," they came to conclude that membership in the empire was a threat to freedom, rather than its foundation. This conviction set the colonies on the road to independence.

CONSOLIDATING THE EMPIRE

The Seven Years' War, to which the colonists contributed soldiers and economic resources, underscored for rulers in London how important the empire was to Britain's well-being and its status as a great power. Now, they believed, new regulations were needed to help guarantee the empire's continued strength and prosperity. Before 1763, Parliament had occasionally acted to forbid the issuance of paper money in America and to restrict colonial economic activities that competed with businesses at home. The Wool Act of 1699, Hat Act of 1732, and Iron Act of 1750 forbade colonial manufacture of these items. The Molasses Act of 1733 sought to curtail trade between New England and the French Caribbean by imposing a prohibitive tax on French-produced molasses used to make rum in American distilleries. And the Navigation Acts, discussed in Chapter 3, sought to channel key American exports like tobacco through British ports. The colonists frequently ignored all these measures.

As to internal affairs within the colonies, the British government frequently seemed uninterested. There was no point, one official said, in worrying about the behavior of colonists who "plant tobacco and Puritanism only, like fools." Beginning in the late 1740s, the Board of Trade, which was responsible for overseeing colonial affairs, attempted to strengthen imperial authority. It demanded that colonial laws conform to royal instructions and encouraged colonial assemblies to grant permanent salaries to royal governors. But the outbreak of the Seven Years' War suspended this initiative.

Having treated the colonists as allies during the war, Britain reverted in the mid-1760s to seeing them as subordinates whose main role was to enrich the mother country. During this period, the government in London concerned itself with the colonies in unprecedented ways, hoping to make British rule more efficient and systematic and to raise funds to help pay for the war and to finance the empire. Nearly all British political leaders supported the new laws that so enraged the colonists. Americans, Britons felt, should be grateful to the empire. To fight the Seven Years' War, Britain had borrowed from banks and individual investors more than £150 million (the equivalent of tens of trillions of dollars in today's money).

An engraving from a Massachusetts almanac published in 1774 depicts Lieutenant Governor Thomas Hutchinson, whose house had been destroyed by a mob nine years earlier. The devil carries a list of Hutchinson's "crimes." It was common in this period to use religious symbols to demonize political opponents.

According to the doctrine of "virtual representation," the House of Commons represented all residents of the British empire, whether or not they could vote for members. In this 1775 cartoon criticizing the idea, a blinded Britannia, on the far right, stumbles into a pit. Next to her, two colonists complain of being robbed by British taxation. In the background, according to an accompanying explanation of the cartoon, stand the "Catholic" city of Quebec and the "Protestant town of Boston," the latter in flames.

Interest on the debt absorbed half the government's annual revenue. The tax burden in Britain had reached unprecedented heights. It seemed only reasonable that the colonies should help pay this national debt, foot part of the bill for continued British protection, and stop cheating the Treasury by violating the Navigation Acts.

Nearly all Britons, moreover, believed that Parliament represented the entire empire and had a right to legislate for it. Millions of Britons, including the residents of major cities like Manchester and Birmingham, had no representatives in Parliament. But according to the widely accepted theory of "virtual representation"—which held that each member represented the entire empire, not just his own district—the interests of all who lived under the British crown were supposedly taken into account. When Americans began to insist that because they were unrepresented in Parliament, the British government could not tax the colonies, they won little support in the mother country. To their surprise, however, British governments found that the effective working of the empire required the cooperation of local populations. Time and again, British officials backed down in the face of colonial resistance, only to return with new measures to centralize control of the empire that only stiffened colonial resolve.

The British government had already alarmed many colonists by issuing writs of assistance to combat smuggling. These were general search warrants that allowed customs officials to search anywhere they chose for smuggled goods. In a celebrated court case in Boston in 1761, the lawyer James Otis insisted that the writs were "an instrument of arbitrary power, destructive to English liberty, and the fundamental principles of the Constitution," and that Parliament therefore had no right to authorize them. ("American independence was then and there born," John Adams later remarked—a considerable exaggeration.) Many colonists were also outraged by the Proclamation of 1763 (mentioned in the previous chapter) barring further settlement on lands west of the Appalachian Mountains.

TAXING THE COLONIES

In 1764, the Sugar Act, introduced by Prime Minister George Grenville, reduced the existing tax on molasses imported into North America from the French West Indies from six pence to three pence per gallon. But the act also established a new machinery to end widespread smuggling by colonial merchants. And to counteract the tendency of colonial juries to acquit merchants charged with violating trade regulations, it strengthened the admiralty courts, where accused smugglers could be judged without benefit of a jury trial. Thus, colonists saw the measure not as a welcome reduction in taxation but as an attempt to get them to pay a levy they would otherwise have evaded.

At the same time, a Revenue Act placed goods such as wool and hides, which had previously been traded freely with Holland, France, and southern

Europe, on the enumerated list, meaning they had to be shipped through England. Together, these measures threatened the profits of colonial merchants and seemed certain to aggravate an already serious economic recession resulting from the end of the Seven Years' War. They were accompanied by the Currency Act, which reaffirmed the earlier ban on colonial assemblies issuing paper as "legal tender"—that is, money that individuals are required to accept in payment of debts.

THE STAMP ACT CRISIS

The Sugar Act was an effort to strengthen the long-established (and long-evaded) Navigation Acts. The Stamp Act of 1765 represented a new departure in imperial policy. For the first time, Parliament attempted to raise money from direct taxes in the colonies rather than through the regulation of trade. The act required that all sorts of printed material produced in the colonies—newspapers, books, court documents, commercial papers, land deeds, almanacs, etc.—carry a stamp purchased from authorities. Its purpose was to help finance the operations of the empire, including the cost of stationing British troops in North America, without seeking revenue from colonial assemblies.

Whereas the Sugar Act had mainly affected residents of colonial ports, the Stamp Act managed to offend virtually every free colonist—rich and poor, farmers, artisans, and merchants. It was especially resented by members of the public sphere who wrote, published, and read books and newspapers and followed political affairs. The prospect of a British army permanently stationed on American soil also alarmed many colonists. And by imposing the stamp tax without colonial consent, Parliament directly challenged the authority of local elites who, through the assemblies they controlled, had established their power over the raising and spending of money. They were ready to defend this authority in the name of liberty.

Opposition to the Stamp Act was the first great drama of the revolutionary era and the first major split between colonists and Great Britain over the meaning of freedom. Nearly all colonial political leaders opposed the act. In voicing their grievances, they invoked the rights of the freeborn Englishman, which, they insisted, colonists should also enjoy. Opponents of the act occasionally referred to the natural rights of all mankind. More frequently, however, they drew on time-honored British principles such as a community's right not to be taxed except by its elected representatives. Liberty, they insisted, could not be secure where property was "taken away without consent."

TAXATION AND REPRESENTATION

At stake were clashing ideas of the British empire itself. American leaders viewed the empire as an association of equals in which free settlers overseas enjoyed the same rights as Britons at home. Colonists in other outposts of the empire, such as India, the West Indies, and Canada, echoed this outlook. All, in the name of liberty, claimed the right to govern their own affairs. British residents of Calcutta, India, demanded the "rights inherent in Englishmen." British merchants in Quebec said that to allow French

An engraving of James Otis graces the cover of the Boston Almanack *for 1770. He is flanked by the ancient gods Hercules and Minerva (carrying a liberty cap).*

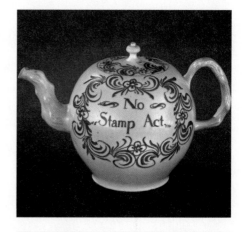

This teapot protesting the Stamp Act was produced in England and marketed in colonial America, illustrating the close political and economic connections between the two.

A woodcut depicting a crowd attempting to intimidate a New Hampshire official charged with carrying out the Stamp Act. They throw stones at his effigy, while, to the left, a mock funeral begins.

laws to remain in force would reduce them to "slavery." The British government and its appointed representatives in America, by contrast, saw the empire as a system of unequal parts in which different principles governed different areas, and all were subject to the authority of Parliament. To surrender the right to tax the colonies would set a dangerous precedent for the empire as a whole. "In an empire, extended and diversified as that of Great Britain," declared Governor Francis Bernard of Massachusetts in 1765, "there must be a supreme legislature, to which all other powers must be subordinate." Parliament, Bernard continued, was the "sanctuary of liberty"—a description with which many Americans were beginning to disagree.

Some opponents of the Stamp Act distinguished between "internal" taxes like the stamp duty, which they claimed Parliament had no right to impose, and revenue legitimately raised through the regulation of trade. But more and more colonists insisted that Britain had no right to tax them at all, since Americans were unrepresented in the House of Commons. "No taxation without representation" became their rallying cry. Virginia's House of Burgesses approved four resolutions offered by the fiery orator Patrick Henry. They insisted that the colonists enjoyed the same "liberties, privileges, franchises, and immunities" as residents of the mother country and that the right to consent to taxation was a cornerstone of "British freedom." (The House of Burgesses rejected as too radical three other resolutions, including Henry's call for outright resistance to unlawful taxation, but these were also reprinted in colonial newspapers.)

In October 1765, the Stamp Act Congress, with twenty-seven delegates from nine colonies, including some of the most prominent men in America, met in New York and endorsed Virginia's position. Its resolutions began by affirming the "allegiance" of all colonists to the "Crown of Great Britain" and their "due subordination" to Parliament. But they went on to insist that the right to consent to taxation was "essential to the freedom of a people." Soon, merchants throughout the colonies agreed to boycott British goods until Parliament repealed the Stamp Act. This was the first major cooperative action among Britain's mainland colonies. In a sense, by seeking to impose uniformity on the colonies rather than dealing with them individually as in the past, Parliament had inadvertently united America.

LIBERTY AND RESISTANCE

No word was more frequently invoked by critics of the Stamp Act than "liberty." Throughout the colonies, opponents of the new tax staged mock funerals in which liberty's coffin was carried to a burial ground only to have the occupant miraculously revived at the last moment, whereupon the assembled crowd repaired to a tavern to celebrate. As the crisis continued, symbols of liberty proliferated. The large elm tree in Boston on which protesters had hanged an effigy of the stamp distributor Andrew Oliver to persuade him to resign his post came to be known as the Liberty Tree. Its image soon began to appear in prints and pamphlets throughout the colonies. Open-air meetings were held beneath the tree, and as a result the space came to be called Liberty Hall. In New York City, a pine mast erected in 1766 as a meeting place for opponents of the Stamp Act was called the Liberty Pole.

Colonial leaders resolved to prevent the new law's implementation, and by and large they succeeded. Even before the passage of the Stamp Act, a Committee of Correspondence in Boston communicated with other colonies to encourage opposition to the Sugar and Currency Acts. Now, such committees sprang up in other colonies, exchanging ideas and information about resistance. Initiated by colonial elites, the movement against the Stamp Act quickly drew in a far broader range of Americans. The act, wrote John Adams, a Boston lawyer who drafted a set of widely reprinted resolutions against the measure, had inspired "the people, even to the lowest ranks," to become "more attentive to their liberties, more inquisitive about them, and more determined to defend them, than they were ever before known." Political debate, Adams added, pervaded the colonies—"our presses have groaned, our pulpits have thundered, our legislatures have resolved, our towns have voted."

POLITICS IN THE STREETS

Opponents of the Stamp Act, however, did not rely solely on debate. Even before the law went into effect, crowds forced those chosen to administer it to resign and destroyed shipments of stamps. In New York City, processions involving hundreds of residents shouting "liberty" paraded through the streets nearly every night in late 1765. They were organized by the newly created Sons of Liberty, a body led by talented and ambitious lesser merchants like Alexander McDougall, Isaac Sears, and John Lamb. Fluent in Dutch, French, and German, Lamb became the Sons' liaison to the city's numerous ethnic groups. These self-made men had earned fortunes as privateers plundering French shipping during the Seven Years' War and, complained New York's lieutenant governor, opposed "every limitation of trade and duty on it." While they enjoyed no standing among the colony's wealthy elite and carried little weight in municipal affairs, they enjoyed a broad following among the city's craftsmen, laborers, and sailors.

The Sons posted notices reading "Liberty, Property, and No Stamps" and took the lead in enforcing the boycott of British imports. Their actions were viewed with increasing alarm by the aristocratic Livingston and De Lancey families, who dominated New York politics. As the assault on Thomas Hutchinson's house in Boston demonstrated, crowds could easily get out of hand. In November 1765, a New York crowd reportedly

A warning by the Sons of Liberty against using the stamps required by the Stamp Act, which are shown on the left.

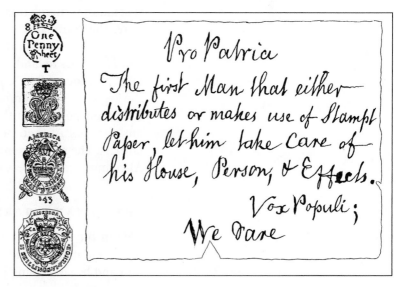

composed of sailors, blacks, laborers, and youths hurled stones at Fort George at the tip of Manhattan Island. They then proceeded to destroy the home of Major Thomas James, a British officer who was said to have boasted that he would force the stamps down New Yorkers' throats.

Stunned by the ferocity of American resistance and pressured by London merchants and manufacturers who did not wish to lose their American markets, the British government retreated. In 1766, Parliament repealed the Stamp Act. But this concession was accompanied by the Declaratory Act, which rejected Americans' claims that only their elected representatives could levy taxes. Parliament, proclaimed this measure, possessed the power to pass laws for "the colonies and people of America . . . in all cases whatever." Since the debt-ridden British government continued to need money raised in the colonies, passage of the Declaratory Act promised further conflict.

THE REGULATORS

The Stamp Act crisis was not the only example of violent social turmoil during the 1760s. Many colonies experienced contentious internal divisions as well. As population moved westward, the conflicting land claims of settlers, speculators, colonial governments, and Indians sparked fierce disputes. Rural areas had a long tradition of resistance by settlers and small farmers against the claims of land speculators and large proprietors. As in the Stamp Act crisis, "liberty" was their rallying cry, but in this case liberty had less to do with imperial policy than secure possession of land.

Beginning in the mid-1760s, a group of wealthy residents of the South Carolina backcountry calling themselves Regulators protested the under-representation of western settlements in the colony's assembly and the legislators' failure to establish local governments that could regularize land titles and suppress bands of outlaws. The lack of courts in the area, they claimed, had led to a breakdown of law and order, allowing "an infernal gang of villains" to commit "shocking outrages" on persons and property. They added: "We are *Free-men*—British subjects—Not Born Slaves."

A parallel movement in North Carolina mobilized small farmers, who refused to pay taxes, kidnapped local officials, assaulted the homes of land speculators, merchants, and lawyers, and disrupted court proceedings. Here, the complaint was not a lack of government, but corrupt county authorities. These local officials, the Regulators claimed, threatened inexpensive access to land and the prosperity of ordinary settlers through high taxes and court fees. Demanding the democratization of local government, the Regulators condemned the "rich and powerful" (the colony's elite) who used their political authority to prosper at the expense of "poor industrious" farmers. At their peak, the Regulators numbered around 8,000 armed farmers. The region remained in turmoil until 1771, when, in the "battle of Alamance," the farmers were suppressed by the colony's militia.

THE TENANT UPRISING

Also in the mid-1760s, tenants on the Livingston, Philipse, and Cortland manors along the Hudson River north of New York City stopped paying rent and began seizing land. Like opponents of the Stamp Act, they called themselves the Sons of Liberty. The original Sons, however, opposed their uprising, and it was soon suppressed by British and colonial troops. Meanwhile, small farmers in the Green Mountains took up arms to protect their holdings against intrusions by New York landlords. The legal situation there was complex. The area was part of New York, but during the 1750s the governor of New Hampshire had issued land grants to New England families, pocketing a fortune in fees. When New Yorkers tried to enforce their own title to the area, the settlers' leader, Ethan Allen, insisted that land should belong to the person who worked it. Outsiders, he claimed, were trying to "enslave a free people." In the mid-1770s, Allen and his Green Mountain Boys gained control of the region, which later became the state of Vermont.

The emerging rift between Britain and America eventually superimposed itself on conflicts within the colonies. But the social divisions revealed in the Stamp Act riots and backcountry uprisings made some members of the colonial elite fear that opposition to British measures might unleash turmoil at home. As a result, they were more reluctant to challenge British authority when the next imperial crisis arose.

THE ROAD TO REVOLUTION

THE TOWNSHEND CRISIS

In 1767, the government in London decided to impose a new set of taxes on Americans. They were devised by the chancellor of the Exchequer (the cabinet's chief financial minister), Charles Townshend. In opposing the Stamp Act, some colonists, including Benjamin Franklin (then representing the Pennsylvania assembly in London), had seemed to suggest that they would not object if Britain raised revenue by regulating trade. Taking them at their word, Townshend persuaded Parliament to impose new taxes on goods imported into the colonies and to create a new board of customs commissioners to collect them and suppress smuggling. He intended to use the new revenues to pay the salaries of American governors and judges, thus freeing them from dependence on colonial assemblies. Although many merchants objected to the new enforcement procedures, opposition to the Townshend duties developed more slowly than in the case of the Stamp Act. Leaders in several colonies nonetheless decided in 1768 to reimpose the ban on importing British goods.

HOMESPUN VIRTUE

The boycott began in Boston and soon spread to the southern colonies. Reliance on American rather than British goods, on homespun clothing rather than imported finery, became a symbol of American resistance. It also reflected, as the colonists saw it, a virtuous spirit of self-sacrifice as compared with the self-indulgence and luxury many Americans were coming to associate with Britain. Women who spun and wove at home so as not to purchase British goods were hailed as Daughters of Liberty.

The idea of using homemade rather than imported goods especially appealed to Chesapeake planters, who found themselves owing increasing amounts of money to British merchants. Nonimportation, wrote George Washington, reflecting Virginia planters' concern about their growing burden of debt, gave "the extravagant man" an opportunity to "retrench his expenses" by reducing the purchase of British luxuries, without having to advertise to his neighbors that he might be in financial distress. In this way, Washington continued, Virginians could "maintain the liberty which we have derived from our ancestors," while reducing their "considerable" debts. Virginia's leaders also announced a temporary ban on the importation of slaves, but smaller planters in the Piedmont region away from the coast, where the institution was expanding, ignored this restriction.

Urban artisans, who welcomed an end to competition from imported British manufactured goods, strongly supported the boycott. Philadelphia and New York merchants at first were reluctant to take part, although they eventually agreed to go along. Nonimportation threatened their livelihoods and raised the prospect of unleashing further lower-class turmoil. As had happened during the Stamp Act crisis, the streets of American cities filled with popular protests against the new duties. Extralegal local committees attempted to enforce the boycott of British goods.

THE BOSTON MASSACRE

Boston once again became the focal point of conflict. Royal troops had been stationed in the city in 1768 after rioting that followed the British seizure of the ship *Liberty* for violating trade regulations. The sloop belonged to John Hancock, one of the city's most prominent merchants. The soldiers, who competed for jobs on Boston's waterfront with the city's laborers, became more and more unpopular. On March 5, 1770, a fight between a snowball-throwing crowd of Bostonians and British troops escalated into an armed confrontation that left five Bostonians dead. One of those who fell in what came to be called the Boston Massacre was Crispus Attucks, a sailor of mixed Indian-African-white ancestry. Attucks would later be remembered as the "first martyr of the American Revolution." The commanding officer and eight soldiers were put on trial in Massachusetts. Ably defended by John Adams, who viewed lower-class crowd actions as a dangerous method of opposing British policies, seven were found not guilty, while two were convicted of manslaughter. But Paul Revere, a member of the Boston Sons of Liberty and a silversmith and engraver, helped to stir up indignation against the British army by producing a widely circulated (and quite inaccurate) print of the Boston Massacre depicting a line of British soldiers firing into an unarmed crowd.

By 1770, as merchants' profits shriveled and many members of the colonial elite found they could not do without British goods, the nonimportation movement was collapsing. The value of British imports to the colonies declined by about one-third during 1769, but then rebounded to its former level. British merchants, who wished to remove a possible source of future interruption of trade, pressed for repeal of the Townshend duties. When the British ministry agreed, leaving in place only a tax on tea, and agreed to remove troops from Boston, American merchants quickly abandoned the boycott.

VISIONS OF FREEDOM

Engrav'd Printed & Sold by PAUL REVERE BOSTON

The Boston Massacre. *Less than a month after the Boston Massacre of 1770, in which five colonists died, Paul Revere produced this engraving of the event. Although it inaccurately depicts what was actually a disorganized brawl between residents of Boston and British soldiers, this image became one of the most influential pieces of political propaganda of the revolutionary era.*

QUESTIONS

1. How does Revere depict the British and colonists in this encounter, and who does he blame for the five colonists' deaths?

2. What attitude toward British authorities is Revere attempting to promote through this engraving?

William Hogarth's depiction of John Wilkes holding a liberty cap. Wilkes's publication, North Briton, *bitterly attacked the king and prime minister, for which Wilkes was arrested, tried, and acquitted by a London jury. He became a popular symbol of freedom on both sides of the Atlantic.*

The Bostonians Paying the Excise-Man, *a 1774 engraving, shows colonists pouring tea down the throat of a tax collector, who has been covered with tar and feathers. A noose hangs menacingly from the Liberty Tree. In the background is the Boston Tea Party.*

WILKES AND LIBERTY

Once again, an immediate crisis had been resolved. Nonetheless, many Americans concluded that Britain was succumbing to the same pattern of political corruption and decline of liberty that afflicted other countries. The overlap of the Townshend crisis with a controversy in Britain over the treatment of John Wilkes reinforced this sentiment. A radical journalist known for scandalous writings about the king and ministry, Wilkes had been elected to Parliament from London but was expelled from his seat. "Wilkes and Liberty" became a popular rallying cry on both sides of the Atlantic. In addition, rumors circulated in the colonies that the Anglican Church in England planned to send bishops to America. Among members of other Protestant denominations, the rumors—strongly denied in London— sparked fears that bishops would establish religious courts like those that had once persecuted Dissenters. The conviction that the British government had set itself on a course dangerous to liberty underpinned colonial resistance when the next crisis arose.

THE TEA ACT

The next crisis underscored how powerfully events in other parts of Britain's global empire affected the American colonies. The East India Company, a giant trading monopoly, effectively governed recently acquired British possessions in India. Numerous British merchants, bankers, and other individuals had invested heavily in its stock. A classic speculative bubble ensued, with the price of stock in the company rising sharply and then collapsing. To rescue the company and its investors, the British government decided to help it market its enormous holdings of Chinese tea in North America.

Tea, once a preserve of the wealthy, had by now become a drink consumed by all social classes in England and the colonies. To further stimulate its sales and bail out the East India Company, the British government, now headed by Frederick Lord North, offered the company a series of rebates and tax exemptions. These enabled it to dump low-priced tea on the American market, undercutting both established merchants and smugglers. Money raised through the taxation of imported tea would be used to help defray the costs of colonial government, thus threatening, once again, the assemblies' control over finance.

The tax on tea was not new. But many colonists insisted that to pay it on this large new body of imports would acknowledge Britain's right to tax the colonies. As tea shipments arrived, resistance developed in the major ports. On December 16, 1773, a group of colonists disguised as Indians boarded three ships at anchor in Boston Harbor and threw more than 300 chests of tea into the water. The event became known as the Boston Tea Party. The loss to the East India Company was around £10,000 (the equivalent of more than $4 million today).

THE INTOLERABLE ACTS

The British government, declared Lord North, must now demonstrate "whether we have, or have not, any authority in that country." Its response to the Boston Tea Party was swift and decisive. Parliament closed the port of

Boston to all trade until the tea was paid for. It radically altered the Massachusetts Charter of 1691 by curtailing town meetings and authorizing the governor to appoint members to the council—positions previously filled by election. Parliament also empowered military commanders to lodge soldiers in private homes. These measures, called the Coercive or Intolerable Acts by Americans, united the colonies in opposition to what was widely seen as a direct threat to their political freedom.

At almost the same time, Parliament passed the Quebec Act. This extended the southern boundary of that Canadian province to the Ohio River and granted legal toleration to the Roman Catholic Church in Canada. With an eye to the growing tensions in colonies to the south, the act sought to secure the allegiance of Quebec's Catholics by offering rights denied to their coreligionists in Britain, including practicing their faith freely and holding positions in the civil service. The act not only threw into question land claims in the Ohio country but persuaded many colonists that the government in London was conspiring to strengthen Catholicism—dreaded by most Protestants—in its American empire. Fears of religious and political tyranny mingled in the minds of many colonists. Especially in New England, the cause of liberty became the cause of God. A gathering of 1,000 residents of Farmington, Connecticut, in May 1774 adopted resolutions proclaiming that, as "the sons of freedom," they would resist every attempt "to take away our liberties and properties and to enslave us forever." They accused the British ministry of being "instigated by the devil."

The Mitred Minuet, *a British cartoon from 1774, shows four Roman Catholic bishops dancing around a copy of the Quebec Act. On the left, British officials Lord Bute, Lord North, and Lord Mansfield look on, while the devil oversees the proceedings.*

THE COMING OF INDEPENDENCE

THE CONTINENTAL CONGRESS

British actions had destroyed the legitimacy of the imperial government in the eyes of many colonists. Opposition to the Intolerable Acts now spread to small towns and rural areas that had not participated actively in previous resistance. In September 1774, in the town of Worcester, Massachusetts, 4,600 militiamen from thirty-seven towns (half the adult male population of the entire county) lined both sides of Main Street as the British-appointed officials walked the gauntlet between them. In the same month, a convention of delegates from Massachusetts towns approved a series of resolutions (called the Suffolk Resolves for the county in which Boston is located) that urged Americans to refuse obedience to the new laws, withhold taxes, and prepare for war.

To coordinate resistance to the Intolerable Acts, a Continental Congress convened in Philadelphia that month, bringing together the most prominent political leaders of twelve mainland colonies (Georgia did not take part). From Massachusetts came the "brace of Adamses"—John and his more radical cousin Samuel. Virginia's seven delegates included George Washington, Richard Henry Lee, and the renowned orator Patrick Henry. Henry's power as a speaker came from a unique style that combined moral appeals with blunt directness. His manner, one contemporary observed, "was vehement, without transporting him beyond the power of self-command. . . . His lightning consisted in quick successive flashes." "The distinctions between Virginians, Pennsylvanians, New Yorkers, and New Englanders," Henry declared, "are no more. I am not a Virginian, but an American." In March 1775, Henry concluded a speech urging a Virginia convention to begin military preparations with a legendary credo: "Give me liberty, or give me death!"

THE CONTINENTAL ASSOCIATION

Before it adjourned at the end of October 1774 with an agreement to reconvene the following May if colonial demands had not been met, the Congress endorsed the Suffolk Resolves and adopted the Continental Association, which called for an almost complete halt to trade with Great Britain and the West Indies (at South Carolina's insistence, exports of rice to Europe were exempted). The Association also encouraged domestic manufacturing and denounced "every species of extravagance and dissipation." Congress authorized local Committees of Safety to oversee its mandates and to take action against "enemies of American liberty," including businessmen who tried to profit from the sudden scarcity of goods.

The Committees of Safety began the process of transferring effective political power from established governments whose authority derived from Great Britain to extralegal grassroots bodies reflecting the will of the people. By early 1775, some 7,000 men were serving on local committees throughout the colonies, a vast expansion of the "political nation." The committees became training grounds where small farmers, city artisans, propertyless laborers, and others who had heretofore had little role in government discussed political issues and exercised political power. In Philadelphia, the extralegal committees of the 1760s that oversaw the boycott of British goods had been composed almost entirely of prominent lawyers and merchants. But younger merchants, shopkeepers, and artisans dominated the committee elected in November 1774 to enforce the Continental Association. They were determined that resistance to British measures not be dropped as it had been in 1770. When the New York assembly refused to endorse the Association, local committees continued to enforce it anyway.

THE SWEETS OF LIBERTY

By 1775, talk of liberty pervaded the colonies. The past few years had witnessed an endless parade of pamphlets with titles like *A Chariot of Liberty* and *Oration on the Beauties of Liberty* (the latter, a sermon delivered in Boston by Joseph Allen in 1772, became the most popular public address of the years before independence). Sober men spoke longingly of the "sweets of liberty." While sleeping, Americans dreamed of liberty. One anonymous essayist reported a "night vision" of the word written in the sun's rays. Commented a British emigrant who arrived in Maryland early in 1775: "They are all liberty mad."

The right to resist oppressive authority and the identification of liberty with the cause of God, so deeply ingrained by the imperial struggles of the eighteenth century, were now invoked against Britain itself, by colonists of all backgrounds. The first mass meeting in the history of Northampton County, Pennsylvania, whose population was overwhelmingly of German ancestry, gathered in 1774. By the following year, a majority of the county's adult population had joined militia associations. Many German settlers, whose close-knit communities had earlier viewed with some suspicion "the famous English liberty" as a byword for selfish individualism, now claimed all the "rights and privileges of natural-born subjects of his majesty."

As the crisis deepened, Americans increasingly based their claims not simply on the historical rights of Englishmen but on the more abstract language of natural rights and universal freedom. The First Continental Congress defended its actions by appealing to the "principles of the English constitution," the "liberties of free and natural-born subjects within the realm of England," and the "immutable law of nature." John Locke's theory of natural rights that existed prior to the establishment of government offered a powerful justification for colonial resistance. Americans, declared Thomas Jefferson in *A Summary View of the Rights of British America* (written in 1774 to instruct Virginia's delegates to the Continental Congress), were "a free people claiming their rights, as derived from the laws of nature, and not as the gift of their chief magistrate." Americans, Jefferson insisted, still revered the king. But he demanded that empire henceforth be seen as a collection of equal parts held together by loyalty to a constitutional monarch, not a system in which one part ruled over the others.

THE OUTBREAK OF WAR

By the time the Second Continental Congress convened in May 1775, war had broken out between British soldiers and armed citizens of Massachusetts. On April 19, a force of British soldiers marched from Boston toward the nearby town of Concord seeking to seize arms being stockpiled there. Riders from Boston, among them Paul Revere, warned local leaders of the troops' approach. Militiamen took up arms and tried to resist the British advance. Skirmishes between Americans and British soldiers took place at Lexington and again at Concord. By the time the British retreated to the safety of Boston, some forty-nine Americans and seventy-three members of the Royal Army lay dead.

What the philosopher Ralph Waldo Emerson would later call "the shot heard 'round the world" began the American War of Independence. It reverberated throughout the colonies. When news of the skirmish reached Lemuel Roberts, a poor New York farmer, he felt his "bosom glow" with the "call of liberty." Roberts set off for Massachusetts to enlist in the army. In May 1775, Ethan Allen and the Green Mountain Boys, together with militiamen from Connecticut led by Benedict Arnold, surrounded

The Battle of Concord, as depicted in a 1775 engraving by Amos Doolittle, a New Haven silversmith. Under musket fire from colonials, the British retreat across Concord's North Bridge. In his poem "Concorde Hymn" (1837), Ralph Waldo Emerson immortalized the moment:
By the rude bridge that arched the flood,
Their flag to April's breeze unfurled,
Here once the embattled farmers stood,
And fired the shot heard 'round the world.

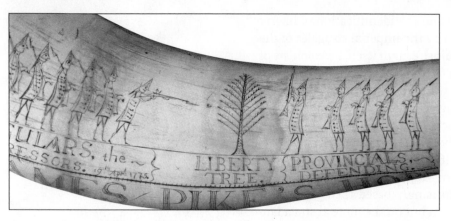

In March 1776, James Pike, a soldier in the Massachusetts militia, carved this scene on his powder horn to commemorate the battles of Lexington and Concord. At the center stands the Liberty Tree.

Fort Ticonderoga in New York and forced it to surrender. The following winter, Henry Knox, George Washington's commander of artillery, arranged for some of the Ticonderoga cannon to be dragged hundreds of miles to the east to reinforce the siege of Boston, where British forces were ensconced. On June 17, 1775, two months after Lexington and Concord, the British had dislodged colonial militiamen from Breed's Hill, although only at a heavy cost in casualties. (The battle came to be named after the nearby Bunker Hill.)

But the arrival of American cannon in March 1776 and their entrenchment above the city made the British position in Boston untenable. The British army under the command of Sir William Howe was forced to abandon the city. Before leaving, Howe's forces cut down the original Liberty Tree.

Meanwhile, the Second Continental Congress authorized the raising of an army, printed money to pay for it, and appointed George Washington its commander. Washington, who had gained considerable fighting experience during the Seven Years' War, was not only the colonies' best-known military officer but also a prominent Virginian. John Adams, who proposed his name, recognized that having a southerner lead American forces would reinforce colonial unity. In response, Britain declared the colonies in a state of rebellion, dispatched thousands of troops, and ordered the closing of all colonial ports.

INDEPENDENCE?

By the end of 1775, the breach with Britain seemed irreparable. But many colonists shied away from the idea of independence. Pride in membership in the British empire was still strong, and many political leaders, especially in colonies that had experienced internal turmoil, feared that a complete break with the mother country might unleash further conflict. Anarchy from below, in their view, was as much a danger as tyranny from above. Many advocates of independence, one opponent warned, would find it "very agreeable" to divide the property of the rich among the poor.

Such fears affected how colonial leaders responded to the idea of independence. The elites of Massachusetts and Virginia, who felt supremely confident of their ability to retain authority at home, tended to support a break with Britain. Massachusetts had borne the brunt of the Intolerable Acts. Southern leaders not only were highly protective of their political liberty but also were outraged by a proclamation issued in November 1775 by the earl of Dunmore, the British governor and military commander in Virginia, offering freedom to any slave who escaped to his lines and bore arms for the king.

In New York and Pennsylvania, however, the diversity of the population made it difficult to work out a consensus on how far to go in resisting British measures. Here opposition to previous British laws had unleashed demands by small farmers and urban artisans for a greater voice in political affairs. As a result, many established leaders drew back from further resistance. Joseph Galloway, a Pennsylvania leader and delegate to the Second Continental Congress who worked to devise a compromise between British and colonial positions, warned that independence would be accompanied by constant disputes within America. He even predicted a war between the northern and southern colonies. Americans, Galloway declared, could only enjoy "true liberty"—self-government and security for their persons and property—by remaining within the empire.

COMMON SENSE

As 1776 dawned, America presented the unusual spectacle of colonists at war against the British empire but still pleading for their rights within it. Even as fighting raged, Congress in July 1775 had addressed the Olive Branch Petition to George III, reaffirming Americans' loyalty to the crown and hoping for a "permanent reconciliation." Ironically, it was a recent emigrant from England, not a colonist from a family long-established on American soil, who grasped the inner logic of the situation and offered a vision of the broad significance of American independence. An English craftsman and minor government official, Thomas Paine had emigrated to Philadelphia late in 1774. He quickly became associated with a group of advocates of the American cause, including John Adams and Dr. Benjamin Rush, a leading Philadelphia physician. It was Rush who suggested to Paine that he write a pamphlet supporting American independence.

Its author listed only as "an Englishman," *Common Sense* appeared in January 1776. The pamphlet began not with a recital of colonial grievances but with an attack on the "so much boasted Constitution of England" and the principles of hereditary rule and monarchical government. Rather than being the most perfect system of government in the world, Paine wrote, the English monarchy was headed by "the royal brute of England," and the English constitution was composed in large part of "the base remains of two ancient tyrannies . . . monarchical tyranny in the person of the king [and] aristocratical tyranny in the persons of the peers." "Of more worth is one honest man to society, and in the sight of God," he continued, "than all the crowned ruffians that ever lived." Far preferable than monarchy would be a democratic system based on frequent elections, with citizens' rights protected by a written constitution.

Turning to independence, Paine drew on the colonists' experiences to make his case. "There is something absurd," he wrote, "in supposing a Continent to be perpetually governed by an island." Within the British empire, America's prospects were limited; liberated from the Navigation Acts and trading freely with the entire world, its "material eminence" was certain. Paine tied the economic hopes of the new nation to the idea of commercial freedom. With independence, moreover, the colonies could for the first time insulate themselves from involvement in the endless imperial wars of Europe. Britain had "dragged" its American colonies into conflicts with countries like Spain and France, which "never were . . . our enemies as *Americans*, but as our being the subjects of Great Britain." Membership in the British empire, Paine insisted, was a burden to the colonies, not a benefit.

Toward the close of the pamphlet, Paine moved beyond practical considerations to outline a breathtaking vision of the historical importance of the

Thomas Paine, advocate of American independence, in a 1791 portrait.

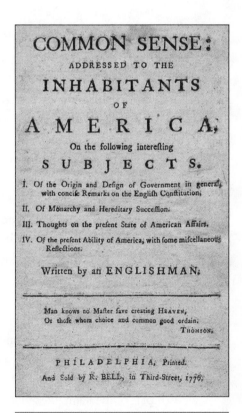

The cover of Common Sense, *Thomas Paine's influential pamphlet denouncing the idea of hereditary rule and calling for American independence.*

VOICES OF FREEDOM

From Thomas Paine,
Common Sense (1776)

A recent emigrant from England, Thomas Paine in January 1776 published *Common Sense*, a highly influential pamphlet that in stirring language made the case for American independence.

In the following pages I offer nothing more than simple facts, plain arguments, and common sense....

Male and female are the distinctions of nature, good and bad the distinctions of heaven; but how a race of men came into the world so exalted above the rest, and distinguished like some new species, is worth enquiring into, and whether they are the means of happiness or of misery to mankind.... One of the strongest *natural* proofs of the folly of hereditary right in kings, is, that nature disapproves it, otherwise she would not so frequently turn it into ridicule, by giving mankind an *ass for a lion*....

The sun never shined on a cause of greater worth. 'Tis not the affair of a city, a country, a province, or a kingdom, but of a continent—of at least one eighth part of the habitable globe. 'Tis not the concern of a

day, a year, or an age; posterity are virtually involved in the context, and will be more or less affected, even to the end of time, by the proceedings now. Now is the seed time of continental union, faith and honor....

I challenge the warmest advocate for reconciliation to show a single advantage that this continent can reap by being connected with Great Britain.... But the injuries and disadvantages which we sustain by that connection, are without number.... Any submission to, or dependence on, Great Britain, tends directly to involve this Continent in European wars and quarrels, and set us at variance with nations who would otherwise seek our friendship, and against whom we have neither anger nor complaint.

O ye that love mankind! Ye that dare oppose, not only the tyranny, but the tyrant, stand forth! Every spot of the old world is overrun with oppression. Freedom hath been hunted round the globe. Asia, and Africa, have long expelled her. Europe regards her like a stranger, and England hath given her warning to depart. O! Receive the fugitive, and prepare in time an asylum for mankind.

FROM JAMES CHALMERS,
Plain Truth, Addressed to the Inhabitants
of America (1776)

Common Sense inspired a wide-ranging debate about whether American freedom would be more secure inside or outside the British empire. James Chalmers, a Maryland plantation owner, made the case for the Loyalists, as those who opposed American independence were called.

If indignant at the doctrine contained in the pamphlet entitled Common Sense I have expressed myself in the following observations with some ardor . . . [it is because] I adore my country. Passionately devoted to true liberty, I glow with the purest flame of patriotism [and have an] abhorrence of Independency, which if effected, would inevitably plunge our once preeminently envied country into ruin, horror, and desolation. . . .

Can a reasonable being for a moment believe that Great Britain, whose political existence depends on our constitutional obedience, who but yesterday made such prodigious efforts to save us from France, will not exert herself as powerfully to preserve us from our frantic schemes of Independency? . . . We remember with unfeigned gratitude, the many benefits derived through our connections with Great Britain, by whom but yesterday we were emancipated from slavery and death. . . . We venerate the constitution, which with all its imperfections (too often exaggerated) we apprehend almost approaches as near to perfection as human kind can bear. . . .

His scheme of independency would soon, very soon give way to a government imposed on us, by some Cromwell of our armies. . . . A failure of commerce [would] preclude the numerous tribe of planters, farmers and others, from paying their debts. . . . A war will ensue between the creditors and their debtors, which will eventually end in a general abolition of debts.

Volumes were insufficient to describe the horror, misery and desolation, awaiting the people at large in the form of American independence. In short, I affirm that it would be most excellent policy in those who wish for True Liberty to submit by an advantageous reconciliation to the authority of Great Britain. . . . Independence and Slavery are synonymous terms.

QUESTIONS

1. What does Paine see as the global significance of the American struggle for independence?

2. Why does Chalmers equate independence with slavery?

3. How does the language used by the two writers differ, and what does this tell us about their views of politics?

American Revolution. "The cause of America," he proclaimed in stirring language, "is in great measure, the cause of all mankind." The new nation would become the home of freedom, "an asylum for mankind."

PAINE'S IMPACT

Most of Paine's ideas were not original. What made *Common Sense* unique was his mode of expressing them and the audience he addressed. Previous political writings had generally been directed toward the educated elite. "When I mention the public," declared John Randolph of Virginia in 1774, "I mean to include the rational part of it. The ignorant vulgar are unfit . . . to manage the reins of government." Just as evangelical ministers had shattered the trained clergy's monopoly on religious preaching, Paine pioneered a new style of political writing, one designed to expand dramatically the public sphere where political discussion took place. He wrote clearly and directly, and he avoided the complex language and Latin phrases common in pamphlets aimed at educated readers. *Common Sense* quickly became one of the most successful and influential pamphlets in the history of political writing, selling, by Paine's estimate, some 150,000 copies. Paine directed that his share of the profits be used to buy supplies for the Continental army.

In February 1776, the Massachusetts political leader Joseph Hawley read *Common Sense* and remarked, "Every sentiment has sunk into my well prepared heart." The hearts of Hawley and thousands of other Americans had been prepared for Paine's arguments by the extended conflict over Britain's right to tax the colonies, the outbreak of war in 1775, and the growing conviction that Britain was a corrupt society where liberty was diminishing. The intensification of fighting in the winter of 1775–1776, when Americans unsuccessfully invaded Canada while the British burned Falmouth (now Portland), Maine, and bombarded Norfolk, Virginia, gave added weight to the movement for independence. In the spring of 1776, scores of American communities adopted resolutions calling for a separation from Britain. Only six months elapsed between the appearance of *Common Sense* and the decision by the Second Continental Congress to sever the colonies' ties with Great Britain.

THE DECLARATION OF INDEPENDENCE

On July 2, 1776, the Congress formally declared the United States an independent nation. Two days later, it approved the Declaration of Independence, written by Thomas Jefferson and revised by the Congress before approval. (See the Appendix for the full text.) Most of the Declaration consists of a lengthy list of grievances directed against King George III, ranging from quartering troops in colonial homes to imposing taxes without the colonists' consent. Britain's aim, it declared, was to establish "absolute tyranny" over the colonies. One clause in Jefferson's draft, which condemned the inhumanity of the slave trade and criticized the king for overturning colonial laws that sought to restrict the importation of slaves, was deleted by the Congress at the insistence of Georgia and South Carolina.

The Declaration's enduring impact came not from the complaints against

An early draft, with corrections, of the Declaration of Independence, in Thomas Jefferson's handwriting. Note how the elimination of unnecessary words added to the document's power—"all men are created equal and independent" became "all men are created equal," and "inherent and inalienable" rights became "inalienable" (in the final version, this would be changed to "unalienable").

George III but from Jefferson's preamble, especially the second paragraph, which begins, "We hold these truths to be self-evident, that all men are created equal, that they are endowed by their Creator with certain unalienable Rights, that among these are Life, Liberty, and the pursuit of Happiness." By "unalienable rights," Jefferson meant rights so basic, so rooted in human nature itself (or in what John Locke had called the state of nature), that no government could take them away.

Jefferson then went on to justify the breach with Britain. Government, he wrote, derives its powers from "the consent of the governed." When a government threatens its subjects' natural rights, the people have the authority "to alter or to abolish it." The Declaration of Independence is ultimately an assertion of the right of revolution.

THE DECLARATION AND AMERICAN FREEDOM

The Declaration of Independence changed forever the meaning of American freedom. It completed the shift from the rights of Englishmen to the rights of mankind as the object of American independence. In Jefferson's language, "the Laws of Nature and of Nature's God," not the British constitution or the heritage of the freeborn Englishman, justified independence. No longer a set of specific rights, no longer a privilege to be enjoyed by a corporate body or people in certain social circumstances, liberty had become a universal entitlement.

Jefferson's argument—natural rights, the right to resist arbitrary authority, etc.—drew on the writings of John Locke, who, as explained in the previous chapter, saw government as resting on a "social contract," viola-

America as a symbol of liberty, a 1775 engraving from the cover of the Pennsylvania Magazine, *edited by Thomas Paine soon after his arrival in America. The shield displays the colony's coat of arms. The female figure holding a liberty cap is surrounded by weaponry of the patriotic struggle, including a cartridge box marked "liberty," hanging from a tree (right).*

tion of which destroyed the legitimacy of authority. But when Jefferson substituted the "pursuit of happiness" for property in the familiar Lockean triad that opens the Declaration, he tied the new nation's star to an open-ended, democratic process whereby individuals develop their own potential and seek to realize their own life goals. Individual self-fulfillment, unimpeded by government, would become a central element of American freedom. Tradition would no longer rule the present, and Americans could shape their society as they saw fit.

AN ASYLUM FOR MANKIND

A distinctive definition of nationality resting on American freedom was born in the Revolution. From the beginning, the idea of "American exceptionalism"—the belief that the United States has a special mission to serve as a refuge from tyranny, a symbol of freedom, and a model for the rest of the world—has occupied a central place in American nationalism. The new nation declared itself, in the words of Virginia leader James Madison, the "workshop of liberty to the Civilized World." Paine's remark in *Common Sense*, "we have it in our power to begin the world over again," and his description of the new nation as an "asylum for mankind," expressed a sense that the Revolution was an event of global historical importance. Countless sermons, political tracts, and newspaper articles of the time repeated this idea. Unburdened by the institutions— monarchy, aristocracy, hereditary privilege—that oppressed the peoples of the Old World, America and America alone was the place where the principle of universal freedom could take root. This was why Jefferson addressed the Declaration to "the opinions of mankind," not just the colonists themselves or Great Britain.

First to add his name to the Declaration of Independence was the Massachusetts merchant John Hancock, president of the Second Continental Congress, with a signature so large, he declared, according to legend, that King George III could read it without his spectacles.

THE GLOBAL DECLARATION OF INDEPENDENCE

The American colonists were less concerned with securing human rights for all mankind than with winning international recognition in their struggle for independence from Britain. But Jefferson hoped that this rebellion would become "the signal of arousing men to burst the chains . . . and to assume the blessings and security of self-government." And for more than two centuries, the Declaration has remained an inspiration not only to generations of Americans denied the enjoyment of their natural rights, but to colonial peoples around the world seeking independence. The

Declaration quickly appeared in French and German translations, although not, at first, in Spanish, since the government feared it would inspire dangerous ideas among the peoples of Spain's American empire.

In the years since 1776, numerous anti-colonial movements have modeled their own declarations of independence on America's. The first came in Flanders (part of today's Belgium, then part of the Austrian empire), where rebels in 1790 echoed Jefferson's words by declaring that their province "is and of rights ought to be, a Free and Independent State." By 1826, the year of Jefferson's death, some twenty other declarations of independence had been issued in Europe, the Caribbean, and Spanish America. Today, more than half the countries in the world, in places as far-flung as China (issued after the revolution of 1911) and Vietnam (1945), have such declarations. Many of these documents, like Jefferson's, listed grievances against an imperial power to justify revolution. Few of these documents, however, have affirmed the natural rights—life, liberty, and the pursuit of happiness—Jefferson invoked. Over time, the Declaration in a global context has become an assertion of the right of various groups to form independent states, rather than a list of the rights of citizens that their governments could not abridge.

But even more than the specific language of the Declaration, the principle that legitimate political authority rests on the will of "the people" has been adopted around the world. In 1776, the Declaration inspired critics of the British system of government to demand political reform. In 1780, even as the American War of Independence raged, a Jesuit-educated Indian of Peru took the name of the last Inca ruler, Túpac Amaru, and led an uprising against Spanish rule. By the time it was suppressed in 1783, some 10,000 Spanish and 100,000 Indians had perished. In the Dutch, French, and Spanish empires, where European governments had been trying to tighten their control much as the British had done in North America, local elites demanded greater autonomy, often drawing on the constitutional arguments of American patriots. The idea that "the people" possess rights was quickly internationalized. Slaves in the Caribbean, colonial subjects in India, and indigenous inhabitants of Latin America could all speak this language, to the dismay of those who exercised power over them.

SECURING INDEPENDENCE

THE BALANCE OF POWER

Declaring Americans independent was one thing; winning independence another. The newly created American army confronted the greatest military power on earth. Viewing the Americans as traitors, Britain resolved to crush the rebellion. On the surface, the balance of power seemed heavily weighted in Britain's favor. It had a well-trained army (supplemented by hired soldiers from

Inspired by the American Revolution, the British reformer John Cartwright published an appeal for the annual election of Parliament as essential to liberty in Britain. He included an engraving contrasting the principles of reform, on the left, with despotism, on the right.

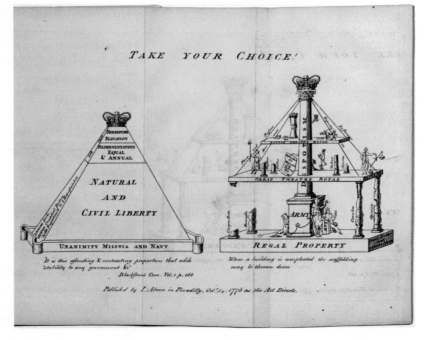

A French engraving depicts New Yorkers tearing down the statue of King George III in July 1776, after the approval of the Declaration of Independence. The statue was later melted down to make bullets for the Continental army.

German states like Hesse), the world's most powerful navy, and experienced military commanders. The Americans had to rely on local militias and an inadequately equipped Continental army. Washington himself felt that militiamen were too "accustomed to unbounded freedom" to accept the "proper degree of subordination" necessary in soldiers. Moreover, many Americans were not enthusiastic about independence, and some actively supported the British.

On the other hand, many American soldiers did not lack military experience, having fought in the Seven Years' War or undergone intensive militia training in the early 1770s. They were fighting on their own soil for a cause that inspired devotion and sacrifice. During the eight years of war from 1775 to 1783, some 200,000 men bore arms in the American army (whose soldiers were volunteers) and militias (where service was required of every able-bodied man unless he provided a substitute). As the war progressed, enlistment waned among propertied Americans and the Continental army increasingly drew on young men with limited economic prospects—landless sons of farmers, indentured servants, laborers, and African-Americans. The patriots suffered dearly for the cause. Of the colonies' free white male population aged sixteen to forty-five, one in twenty died in the War of Independence, the equivalent of nearly 3 million deaths in today's population. But so long as the Americans maintained an army in the field, the idea of independence remained alive no matter how much territory the British occupied.

Despite British power, to conquer the thirteen colonies would be an enormous and expensive task, and it was not at all certain that the public at home wished to pay the additional taxes that a lengthy war would require. The British, moreover, made a string of serious mistakes. From the outset the British misjudged the degree of support for independence among the American population, as well as the capacity of American citizen-soldiers. "These people," admitted the British general Thomas Gage, "show a spirit and conduct against us that they never showed against the French [in the Seven Years' War], and everybody has judged them from their former appearance and behavior, which has led many into great mistakes." Moreover, European rivals, notably France, welcomed the prospect of a British defeat. If the Americans could forge an alliance with France, a world power second only to Britain, it would go a long way toward equalizing the balance of forces.

BLACKS IN THE REVOLUTION

At the war's outset, George Washington refused to accept black recruits. But he changed his mind after Lord Dunmore's 1775 proclamation, mentioned above, which offered freedom to slaves who joined the British cause. Some 5,000 blacks enlisted in state militias and the Continental army and navy. Since individuals drafted into the militia were allowed to provide a substitute, slaves suddenly gained considerable bargaining power. Not a few acquired their freedom by agreeing to serve in place of an owner or his son. In 1778, Rhode Island, with a higher proportion of slaves in its population than any other New England state, formed a black regiment and promised freedom to slaves who enlisted, while compensating the owners for their loss of property. Blacks who fought under George Washington and in other state militias did so in racially integrated companies (although invariably under white officers). They were the last black American soldiers to do so officially until the Korean War (except for the few black and white soldiers who fought alongside each other in irregular units at the end of World War II).

Except for South Carolina and Georgia, the southern colonies also enrolled free blacks and slaves to fight. They were not explicitly promised freedom, but many received it individually after the war ended. And in 1783, the Virginia legislature emancipated slaves who had "contributed towards the establishment of American liberty and independence" by serving in the army.

Fighting on the side of the British also offered opportunities for freedom. Before his forces were expelled from Virginia, 800 or more slaves had escaped from their owners to join Lord Dunmore's Ethiopian Regiment, wearing uniforms that bore the motto "Liberty to Slaves." During the war, blacks fought with the British in campaigns in New York, New Jersey, and South Carolina. Other escaped slaves served the Royal Army as spies, guided their troops through swamps, and worked as military cooks, laundresses, and construction workers. George Washington himself saw seventeen of his slaves flee to the British, some of whom signed up to fight the colonists. "There is not a man of them, but would leave us, if they believed they could make their escape," his cousin Lund Washington reported. "Liberty is sweet."

American Foot Soldiers, Yorktown Campaign, *a 1781 watercolor by a French officer, includes a black soldier from the First Rhode Island Regiment, an all-black unit of 250 men.*

Triumphant Entry of the Royal Troops into New York, *an engraving showing the army of Sir William Howe occupying the city in 1776. New York City would remain in British hands for the duration of the War of Independence.*

THE FIRST YEARS OF THE WAR

Had the British commander, Sir William Howe, prosecuted the war more vigorously at the outset, he might have nipped the rebellion in the bud by destroying Washington's army. But while he suffered numerous defeats in the first years of the war, Washington generally avoided direct confrontations with the British and managed to keep his army intact. Having abandoned Boston, Howe attacked New York City in the summer of 1776. Washington's army had likewise moved from Massachusetts to Brooklyn to defend the city. Howe pushed American forces back and almost cut off Washington's retreat across the East River. Washington managed to escape to Manhattan and then north to Peekskill, where he crossed the Hudson River to New Jersey. But the 3,000 men he had left behind at Fort Washington on Manhattan Island were captured by Howe.

Howe pursued the American army but never managed to inflict a decisive defeat. Demoralized by successive failures, however, many American soldiers simply went home. Once 28,000 men, Washington's army dwindled to fewer than 3,000. Indeed, Washington feared that without a decisive victory, it would melt away entirely. To restore morale and regain the initiative, he launched successful surprise attacks on Hessian soldiers at Trenton, New Jersey, on December 26, 1776, and on a British force at Princeton on January 3, 1777. Shortly before crossing the Delaware River to attack the Hessians, Washington had Thomas Paine's inspiring essay *The American Crisis* read to his troops. "These are the times that try men's souls," Paine wrote. "The summer soldier and the sunshine patriot will, in this crisis,

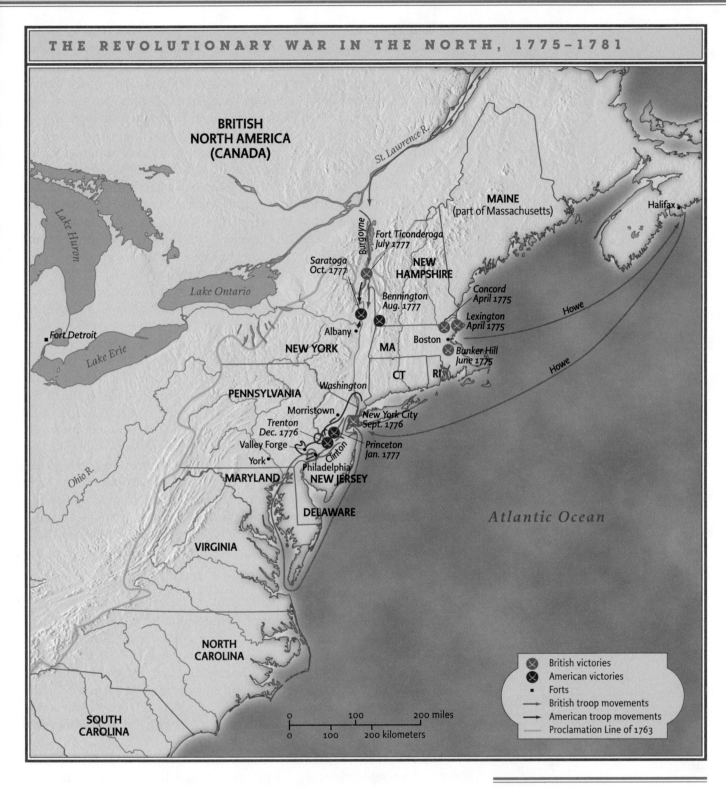

THE REVOLUTIONARY WAR IN THE NORTH, 1775–1781

BRITISH NORTH AMERICA (CANADA)

Lake Huron

Lake Ontario

Fort Detroit

Lake Erie

Ohio R.

St. Lawrence R.

MAINE (part of Massachusetts)

Halifax

Burgoyne

Fort Ticonderoga July 1777

NEW HAMPSHIRE

Saratoga Oct. 1777

Bennington Aug. 1777

Concord April 1775

Lexington April 1775

Howe

Albany

NEW YORK

MA

CT

RI

Boston

Bunker Hill June 1775

Howe

Washington

PENNSYLVANIA

Morristown

Trenton Dec. 1776

Valley Forge

York

Clinton

Philadelphia

NEW JERSEY

New York City Sept. 1776

Princeton Jan. 1777

MARYLAND

DELAWARE

VIRGINIA

Atlantic Ocean

NORTH CAROLINA

SOUTH CAROLINA

	British victories
	American victories
	Forts
	British troop movements
	American troop movements
	Proclamation Line of 1763

0   100   200 miles
0   100   200 kilometers

shrink from the service of their country; but he that stands it *now*, deserves the love and thanks of man and woman."

THE BATTLE OF SARATOGA

In the summer of 1777, a second British army, led by General John Burgoyne, advanced south from Canada hoping to link up with Howe and isolate New

Key battles in the North during the War of Independence included Lexington and Concord, which began the armed conflict; the campaign in New York and New Jersey; and Saratoga, sometimes called the turning point of the war.

England. But in July, Howe instead moved his forces from New York City to attack Philadelphia. In September, the Continental Congress fled to Lancaster, in central Pennsylvania, and Howe occupied the City of Brotherly Love. Not having been informed of Burgoyne's plans, Howe had unintentionally abandoned him. American forces blocked Burgoyne's way, surrounded his army, and on October 17, 1777, forced him to surrender at Saratoga. The victory provided a significant boost to American morale.

During the winter of 1777–1778, the British army, now commanded by Sir Henry Clinton, was quartered in Philadelphia. (In the Revolution, as in most eighteenth-century wars, fighting came to a halt during the winter.) British officers took part in an elegant social life complete with balls and parties. Most notable was the great *Meschianza*, an extravaganza that included a regatta, a procession of medieval knights, and a jousting tournament. Meanwhile, Washington's army remained encamped at Valley Forge, where they suffered terribly from the frigid weather.

But Saratoga helped to persuade the French that American victory was possible. In 1778, American diplomats led by Benjamin Franklin concluded a Treaty of Amity and Commerce in which France recognized the United States and agreed to supply military assistance. Still smarting from their defeat in the Seven Years' War, the French hoped to weaken Britain, their main European rival, and perhaps regain some of their lost influence and territory in the Western Hemisphere. Soon afterward, Spain also joined the war on the American side. French assistance would play a decisive part in the war's end. At the outset, however, the French fleet showed more interest in attacking British outposts in the West Indies than directly aiding the Americans. And the Spanish confined themselves to regaining control of Florida, which they had lost to the British in the Seven Years' War. Nonetheless, French and Spanish entry transformed the War of Independence into a global conflict. By putting the British on the defensive in places ranging from Gibraltar to the West Indies, it greatly complicated their military prospects.

THE WAR IN THE SOUTH

In 1778, the focus of the war shifted to the South. Here the British hoped to exploit the social tensions between backcountry farmers and wealthy planters that had surfaced in the Regulator movements, to enlist the support of the numerous colonists in the region who remained loyal to the crown, and to disrupt the economy by encouraging slaves to escape. In December 1778, British forces occupied Savannah, Georgia. In May 1780, Clinton captured Charleston, South Carolina, and with it an American army of 5,000 men.

The year 1780 was arguably the low point of the struggle for independence. Congress was essentially bankrupt, and the army went months without being paid. The British seemed successful in playing upon social conflicts within the colonies, as thousands of southern Loyalists joined up with British forces (fourteen regiments from Savannah alone) and tens of thousands of slaves sought freedom by fleeing to British lines. In August, Lord Charles Cornwallis routed an American army at Camden, South Carolina. The following month one of Washington's ablest commanders, Benedict Arnold, defected and almost succeeded in turning over to the

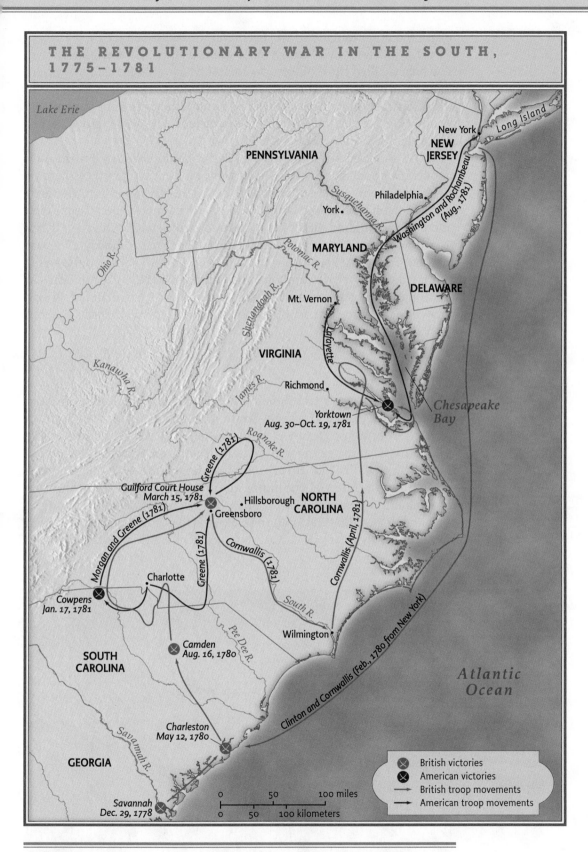

THE REVOLUTIONARY WAR IN THE SOUTH, 1775–1781

Lake Erie

PENNSYLVANIA

New York

NEW JERSEY

Long Island

Susquehanna R.

Philadelphia

York

Washington and Rochambeau (Aug., 1781)

MARYLAND

Potomac R.

DELAWARE

Ohio R.

Shenandoah R.

Mt. Vernon

Lafayette

Kanawha R.

VIRGINIA

James R.

Richmond

Chesapeake Bay

Yorktown
Aug. 30–Oct. 19, 1781

Roanoke R.

Greene (1781)

Guilford Court House
March 15, 1781

Hillsborough

NORTH CAROLINA

Greensboro

Cornwallis (April, 1781)

Morgan and Greene (1781)

Greene (1781)

Cornwallis (1781)

Charlotte

Cowpens
Jan. 17, 1781

South R.

Pee Dee R.

Wilmington

Camden
Aug. 16, 1780

SOUTH CAROLINA

Clinton and Cornwallis (Feb., 1780 from New York)

Atlantic Ocean

Savannah R.

Charleston
May 12, 1780

GEORGIA

Savannah
Dec. 29, 1778

| 0 | 50 | 100 miles |
| 0 | 50 | 100 kilometers |

⊗ British victories
⊗ American victories
→ British troop movements
→ American troop movements

After 1777, the focus of the War of Independence shifted to the South, where it culminated in 1781 with the British defeat at Yorktown.

British the important fort at West Point on the Hudson River. On January 1, 1781, 1,500 disgruntled Pennsylvania soldiers stationed near Morristown, New Jersey, killed three officers and marched toward Philadelphia, where Congress was meeting. Their mutiny ended when the soldiers were promised discharges or bounties for reenlistment. Harsher treatment awaited a group of New Jersey soldiers who also mutinied. On Washington's orders, two of their leaders were executed.

But the British failed to turn these advantages into victory. British commanders were unable to consolidate their hold on the South. Wherever their forces went, American militias harassed them. Hit-and-run attacks by militiamen under Francis Marion, called the "swamp fox" because his men emerged from hiding places in swamps to strike swiftly and then disappear, eroded the British position in South Carolina. A bloody civil war engulfed North and South Carolina and Georgia, with patriot and Loyalist militias inflicting retribution on each other and plundering the farms of their opponents' supporters. The brutal treatment of civilians by British forces under Colonel Banastre Tarleton persuaded many Americans to join the patriot cause.

VICTORY AT LAST

In January 1781, American forces under Daniel Morgan dealt a crushing defeat to Tarleton at Cowpens, South Carolina. Two months later, at Guilford Courthouse, North Carolina, General Nathanael Greene, while conducting a campaign of strategic retreats, inflicted heavy losses on Lord Charles Cornwallis, the British commander in the South. Cornwallis moved into Virginia and encamped at Yorktown, located on a peninsula that juts into Chesapeake Bay. Brilliantly recognizing the opportunity to surround Cornwallis, Washington rushed his forces, augmented by French troops under the Marquis de Lafayette, to block a British escape by land.

A 1781 French engraving showing the surrender of Lord Charles Cornwallis's army at Yorktown, ending the War of Independence. The French fleet sits just offshore.

NORTH AMERICA, 1783

The newly independent United States occupied only a small part of the North American continent in 1783.

Meanwhile, a French fleet controlled the mouth of the Chesapeake, preventing supplies and reinforcements from reaching Cornwallis's army.

Imperial rivalries had helped to create the American colonies. Now, the rivalry of European empires helped to secure American independence. Taking land and sea forces together, more Frenchmen than Americans participated in the decisive Yorktown campaign. On October 19, 1781,

A satirical cartoon depicts America, represented by an Indian holding a flag and liberty cap, celebrating her independence, while her allies—the King of France, a Dutchman, and a Spaniard—complain that they have not been reimbursed for their support. On the left, King George III recognizes American independence, while Ireland (above) demands its own freedom.

Cornwallis surrendered his army of 8,000 men. When the news reached London, public support for the war evaporated and peace negotiations soon began. Given its immense military prowess, Britain abandoned the struggle rather quickly. Many in Britain felt the West Indies were more valuable economically than the mainland colonies. In any event, British merchants expected to continue to dominate trade with the United States, and did so for many years.

Two years later, in September 1783, American and British negotiators concluded the Treaty of Paris. The American delegation—John Adams, Benjamin Franklin, and John Jay—achieved one of the greatest diplomatic triumphs in the country's history. They not only won recognition of American independence but also gained control of the entire region between Canada and Florida east of the Mississippi River, and the right of Americans to fish in Atlantic waters off of Canada (a matter of considerable importance to New Englanders). At British insistence, the Americans agreed that colonists who had remained loyal to the mother country would not suffer persecution and that Loyalists' property that had been seized by local and state governments would be restored.

Until independence, the thirteen colonies had formed part of Britain's American empire, along with Canada and the West Indies. But Canada rebuffed repeated calls to join the War of Independence, and leaders of the West Indies, fearful of slave uprisings, also remained loyal to the crown. With the Treaty of Paris, the United States of America became the Western Hemisphere's first independent nation. Its boundaries reflected not so much the long-standing unity of a geographical region, but the circumstances of its birth.

SUGGESTED READING

BOOKS

Armitage, David. *The Declaration of Independence: A Global History* (2007). Traces the international impact of the Declaration of Independence in the years since it was written.

Bailyn, Bernard. *The Ideological Origins of the American Revolution* (1967). A classic study of the ideas that shaped the movement for independence.

Bloch, Ruth. *Visionary Republic: Millennial Themes in American Thought, 1756–1800* (1988). Explores how the religious vision of a more perfect society contributed to the coming of the Revolution.

Breen, T. H. *Marketplace of Revolution: How Consumer Politics Shaped American Independence* (2004). An examination of how the colonists' very dependence on British consumer goods led them to resent interference with trade.

Countryman, Edward. *The American Revolution* (rev. ed., 2002). A brief summary of the Revolution's causes, conduct, and consequences.

Foner, Eric. *Tom Paine and Revolutionary America* (1976). Examines the ideas of the era's greatest pamphleteer of revolution and how they contributed to the struggle for independence.

Gross, Robert. *The Minutemen and Their World* (1976). A social history of the militia of Concord, Massachusetts, where the War of Independence began.

Maier, Pauline. *American Scripture: Making the Declaration of Independence* (1997). The most detailed study of the writing of the Declaration and of previous calls for independence within the colonies.

Middlekauff, Robert. *The Glorious Cause: The American Revolution, 1763–1789* (1982). A comprehensive history of the Revolution.

Morgan, Edmund S., and Helen M. Morgan. *The Stamp Act Crisis: Prologue to Revolution* (1953). An influential study of the first crisis over British taxation of the colonies.

Nash, Gary. *The Urban Crucible: Social Change, Political Consciousness, and the Origins of the American Revolution* (1979). Explores how the social history of American cities contributed to the coming of the Revolution.

Raphael, Ray. *The First American Revolution: Before Lexington and Concord* (2002). A study of grassroots resistance to British measures before the outbreak of war.

Royster, Charles. *A Revolutionary People at War: The Continental Army and American Character* (1979). A social history of the army and the impact of military service on American soldiers.

Withington, Anne. *Toward a More Perfect Union: Virtue and the Formation of American Republics* (1991). Considers how the boycotts of British goods promoted the idea of America's superior virtue, contributing to the movement for independence.

WEBSITES

Declaring Independence: www.loc.gov/exhibits/declara/declara1.html

The American Revolution and Its Era: Maps and Charts of North America and the West Indies: http://memory.loc.gov/ammem/gmdhtml/armhtml/armhome.html

The Coming of the American Revolution: www.masshist.org/revolution/

REVIEW QUESTIONS

1. Explain what "homespun virtue" meant and how it set the colonists apart from the British.

2. Patrick Henry proclaimed that he was not a Virginian, but rather an American. What unified the colonists and what divided them at the time of the Revolution?

3. Discuss the ramifications of using slaves in the British and Continental Armies. Why did the British authorize the use of slaves? Why did the Americans? How did the slaves benefit?

4. Why did the colonists reach the conclusion that membership in the empire threatened their freedoms, rather than guaranteed them?

5. Describe how *Common Sense* and the Declaration of Independence reflected the ideas put forth by philosophers such as John Locke that liberty was a natural right. Why did they have such an appeal to colonists of all social classes?

6. How would you justify the British view that the colonists owed loyalty to the existing government and gratitude for past actions?

7. Summarize the difference of opinion between British officials and colonial leaders over the issues of taxation and representation.

8. Trace the growth of colonial cooperation against the British government and the development of an "American" identity.

FREEDOM QUESTIONS

1. The grand ideas of liberty and freedom are contagious and often spread rapidly. Why were many colonial elites, who held one definition of liberty, alarmed by the actions and claims of average citizens in the decade before independence?

2. Almost every colonist—even those like Thomas Hutchinson who later became loyalists—opposed the Stamp Act. Identify the many ways colonists identified the Stamp Act as a threat to their freedoms.

3. Explain how each of the following could be viewed as a threat to freedom by different groups of colonists: the growing debt of Virginia planters, a lack of courts in the Carolina backcountry, imports of British manufactured goods, and imports of low-priced tea.

4. Why did some Americans view freedom as dependent upon their remaining loyal to the British government and remaining part of the empire?

5. Many historians say that the Declaration of Independence is the most important document in U.S. history. How did it permanently change the meaning of American freedom? What concepts make it so appealing to people of all social classes, across time and the globe?

KEY TERMS

Loyal Nine (p. 184)

"virtual representation" (p. 186)

writs of assistance (p. 186)

Sugar Act (p. 186)

Committees of Correspondence (p. 189)

Sons of Liberty (p. 189)

Regulators (p. 190)

Daughters of Liberty (p. 191)

Boston Massacre (p. 192)

Crispus Attucks (p. 192)

"Wilkes and Liberty" (p. 194)

Boston Tea Party (p. 194)

Quebec Act (p. 195)

Suffolk Resolves (p. 195)

Committees of Safety (p. 196)

Lord Dunmore's proclamation (p. 198)

Olive Branch Petition (p. 199)

Common Sense (p. 199)

Declaration of Independence (p. 202)

"American exceptionalism" (p. 204)

The American Crisis (p. 208)

Valley Forge (p. 210)

Benedict Arnold (p. 210)

Treaty of Paris (p. 214)

REVIEW TABLE

British Acts Imposed on the Colonies

Act	Date	Function
Proclamation of 1763	1763	To halt colonial settlement west of the Appalachian Mountains and prevent warfare with Indians
Sugar Act	1764	To collect revenue by reducing the tax on molasses and discouraging smuggling
Stamp Act	1765	To directly tax all printed materials
Declaratory Act	1766	To declare that the British Parliament had the power to make laws for its colonies
Townshend Act	1767	To tax imported goods such as paper, glass, paint, lead, and tea
Tea Act	1773	To tax tea as part of an effort to help the failing East India Company
Intolerable Acts	1774	To close the port of Boston and restrict the colony's political autonomy
Quebec Act	1774	To grant religious toleration for Catholics in Canada

CHAPTER 6

The Revolution Within

In Side of the Old Lutheran Church in 1800, York, Pa. *A watercolor by a local artist depicts the interior of one of the numerous churches that flourished after independence. While the choir sings, a man chases a dog out of the building and another man stokes the stove. The institutionalization of religious liberty was one of the most important results of the American Revolution.*

FOCUS QUESTIONS

- How did equality become a stronger component of American freedom after the Revolution?

- How did the expansion of religious liberty after the Revolution reflect the new American ideal of freedom?

- How did the definition of economic freedom change after the Revolution, and who benefited from the changes?

- How did the Revolution diminish the freedoms of both Loyalists and Native Americans?

- What was the impact of the Revolution on slavery?

- How did the Revolution affect the status of women?

Born in Massachusetts in 1744, Abigail Adams became one of the revolutionary era's most articulate and influential women. At a time when educational opportunities for girls were extremely limited, she taught herself by reading books in the library of her father, a Congregational minister. In 1764, she married John Adams, a young lawyer about to emerge as a leading advocate of resistance to British taxation and, eventually, of American independence. During the War of Independence, with her husband away in Philadelphia and Europe serving the American cause, she stayed behind at their Massachusetts home, raising their four children and managing the family's farm. The letters they exchanged form one of the most remarkable correspondences in American history. She addressed John as "Dear friend," and signed her letters "Portia"—after Brutus's devoted wife in Shakespeare's play *Julius Caesar*. Though denied an official role in politics, Abigail Adams was a keen observer of public affairs. She kept her husband informed of events in Massachusetts and offered opinions on political matters. Later, when Adams served as president, he relied on her advice more than on members of his cabinet.

In March 1776, a few months before the Second Continental Congress declared American independence, Abigail Adams wrote her best-known letter to her husband. She began by commenting indirectly on the evils of slavery. How strong, she wondered, could the "passion for Liberty" be among those "accustomed to deprive their fellow citizens of theirs." She went on to urge Congress, when it drew up a "Code of Laws" for the new republic, to "remember the ladies." All men, she warned, "would be tyrants if they could." Women, she playfully suggested, "will not hold ourselves bound by any laws in which we have no voice or representation."

It was the leaders of colonial society who initiated resistance to British taxation. But, as Abigail Adams's letter illustrates, the struggle for American liberty emboldened other colonists to demand more liberty for themselves. All revolutions enlarge the public sphere, inspiring previously marginalized groups to express their own dreams of freedom. At a time when so many Americans—slaves, indentured servants, women, Indians, apprentices, propertyless men—were denied full freedom, the struggle against Britain threw into question many forms of authority and inequality.

Abigail Adams did not believe in female equality in a modern sense. She accepted the prevailing belief that a woman's primary responsibility was to her family. But she resented the "absolute power" husbands exercised over their wives. "Put it out of the power of husbands," she wrote, "to use us as they will"—a discreet reference to men's legal control over the bodies of their wives, and their right to inflict physical punishment on them. Her letter is widely remembered today. Less familiar is

John Adams's response, which illuminated how the Revolution had unleashed challenges to all sorts of inherited ideas of deference and authority: "We have been told that our struggle has loosened the bands of government everywhere; that children and apprentices were disobedient; that schools and colleges were grown turbulent; that Indians slighted their guardians, and negroes grew insolent to their masters." To John Adams, this upheaval, including his wife's claim to greater freedom, was an affront to the natural order of things. To others, it formed the essence of the American Revolution.

Abigail Adams, *a portrait by Gilbert Stuart, painted over several years beginning in 1800. Stuart told a friend that, as a young woman, Adams must have been a "perfect Venus."*

DEMOCRATIZING FREEDOM

THE DREAM OF EQUALITY

The American Revolution took place at three levels simultaneously. It was a struggle for national independence, a phase in a century-long global battle among European empires, and a conflict over what kind of nation an independent America should be.

With its wide distribution of property, lack of a legally established hereditary aristocracy, and established churches far less powerful than in Britain, colonial America was a society with deep democratic potential. But it took the struggle for independence to transform it into a nation that celebrated equality and opportunity. The Revolution unleashed public debates and political and social struggles that enlarged the scope of freedom and challenged inherited structures of power within America. In rejecting the crown and the principle of hereditary aristocracy, many Americans also rejected the society of privilege, patronage, and fixed status that these institutions embodied. To be sure, the men who led the Revolution from start to finish were by and large members of the American elite. The lower classes did not rise to power as a result of independence. Nonetheless, the idea of liberty became a revolutionary rallying cry, a standard by which to judge and challenge home-grown institutions as well as imperial ones.

Jefferson's seemingly straightforward assertion in the Declaration of Independence that "all men are created equal" announced a radical principle whose full implications no one could anticipate. In both Britain and its colonies, a well-ordered society was widely thought to depend on obedience to authority—the power of rulers over their subjects, husbands over wives, parents over children, employers over servants and apprentices, slaveholders over slaves. Inequality had been fundamental to the colonial social order; the Revolution challenged it in many ways. Henceforth, American freedom would be forever linked with the idea of equality—equality before the law, equality in political rights, equality of economic opportunity, and, for some, equality of condition. "Whenever I use the words *freedom* or *rights*," wrote Thomas Paine, "I desire to be understood to mean a perfect equality of them. . . . The floor of Freedom is as level as water."

CÉRÉMONIE DU SACRE
DE LOUIS XVI
1775.

Americans have frequently defined the idea of freedom in relation to its opposite, which in the eighteenth century meant the highly unequal societies of the Old World. This engraving, The Coronation of Louis XVI of France, *reveals the splendor of the royal court, but also illustrates the world of fixed, unequal classes and social privilege repudiated by American revolutionaries.*

EXPANDING THE POLITICAL NATION

With liberty and equality as their rallying cries, previously marginalized groups advanced their demands. Long-accepted relations of dependency and restrictions on freedom suddenly appeared illegitimate—a process not intended by most of the leading patriots. In political, social, and religious life, Americans challenged the previous domination by a privileged few. In the end, the Revolution did not undo the obedience to which male heads of household were entitled from their wives and children, and, at least in the southern states, their slaves. For free men, however, the democratization of freedom was dramatic. Nowhere was this more evident than in challenges to the traditional limitation of political participation to those who owned property.

In the political thought of the eighteenth century, "democracy" had several meanings. One, derived from the writings of Aristotle, defined democracy as a system in which the entire people governed directly. However, this was thought to mean mob rule. Another definition viewed democracy as the condition of primitive societies, which was not appropriate for the complex modern world. British thinkers sometimes used the word when referring to the House of Commons, the "democratic" branch of a mixed government. Yet another understanding revolved less around the structure of government than the fact that a government served the interests of the people rather than an elite. In the wake of the American Revolution, the term came into wider use to express the popular aspirations for greater equality inspired by the struggle for independence.

"We are all, from the cobbler up to the senator, become politicians," declared a Boston letter writer in 1774. Throughout the colonies, election campaigns became freewheeling debates on the fundamentals of government. Universal male suffrage, religious toleration, and even the abolition of slavery were discussed not only by the educated elite but by artisans, small farmers, and laborers, now emerging as a self-conscious element in politics. In many colonies-turned-states, the militia, composed largely of members of the "lower orders," became a "school of political democracy." Its members demanded the right to elect all their officers and to vote for public officials whether or not they met age and property qualifications. They thereby established the tradition that service in the army enabled excluded groups to stake a claim to full citizenship.

THE REVOLUTION IN PENNSYLVANIA

The Revolution's radical potential was more evident in Pennsylvania than in any other state. Elsewhere, the established leadership either embraced independence by the spring of 1776 or split into pro-British and pro-independence factions (in New York, for example, the Livingstons and their supporters ended up as patriots, the De Lanceys as Loyalists). But in Pennsylvania nearly the entire prewar elite opposed independence, fearing that severing the tie with Britain would lead to rule by the "rabble" and to attacks on property.

The vacuum of political leadership opened the door for the rise of a new pro-independence grouping, based on the artisan and lower-class communities of Philadelphia, and organized in extralegal committees and the local militia. Their leaders included Thomas Paine (the author of *Common Sense*), Benjamin Rush (a local physician), Timothy Matlack (the son of a local brewer), and Thomas Young (who had already been involved in the Sons of Liberty in Albany and Boston). As a group, these were men of modest wealth who stood outside the merchant elite, had little political influence before 1776, and believed strongly in democratic reform. Paine and Young had only recently arrived in Philadelphia. They formed a temporary alliance with supporters of independence in the Second Continental Congress (then meeting in Philadelphia), who disapproved of their strong belief in equality but hoped to move Pennsylvania toward a break with Britain.

As the public sphere expanded far beyond its previous boundaries, equality became the rallying cry of Pennsylvania's radicals. They particularly attacked property qualifications for voting. "God gave mankind freedom by nature," declared the anonymous author of the pamphlet *The People the Best Governors*, "and made every man equal to his neighbors." The people, therefore, were "the best guardians of their own liberties," and every free man should be eligible to vote and hold office. In June 1776, a broadside (a printed sheet posted in public places) warned citizens to distrust "great and over-grown rich men" who were inclined "to be framing distinctions in society." Three months after independence, Pennsylvania adopted a new state constitution that sought to institutionalize democracy by concentrating power in a one-house legislature elected annually by all men over age twenty-one who paid taxes. It abolished the office of governor, dispensed with property qualifications for officeholding, and provided that

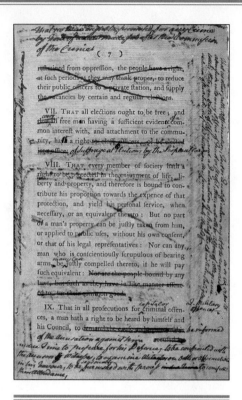

John Dickinson's copy of the Pennsylvania constitution of 1776, with handwritten proposals for changes. Dickinson, one of the more conservative advocates of independence, felt the new state constitution was far too democratic. He crossed out a provision that all "free men" should be eligible to hold office, and another declaring the people not bound by laws that did not promote "the common good."

schools with low fees be established in every county. It also included clauses guaranteeing "freedom of speech, and of writing," and religious liberty.

THE NEW CONSTITUTIONS

Like Pennsylvania, every state adopted a new constitution in the aftermath of independence. Nearly all Americans now agreed that their governments must be republics, meaning that their authority rested on the consent of the governed, and that there would be no king or hereditary aristocracy. The essence of a republic, Paine wrote, was not the "particular form" of government, but its object: the "public good." But as to how a republican government should be structured so as to promote the public good, there was much disagreement.

Pennsylvania's new constitution reflected the belief that since the people had a single set of interests, a single legislative house was sufficient to represent it. In part to counteract what he saw as Pennsylvania's excessive radicalism, John Adams in 1776 published *Thoughts on Government*, which insisted that the new constitutions should create "balanced governments" whose structure would reflect the division of society between the wealthy (represented in the upper house) and ordinary men (who would control the lower). A powerful governor and judiciary would ensure that neither class infringed on the liberty of the other. Adams's call for two-house legislatures was followed by every state except Pennsylvania, Georgia, and Vermont. But only his own state, Massachusetts, gave the governor an effective veto over laws passed by the legislature. Americans had come to believe that excessive royal authority had undermined British liberty. They had long resented efforts by appointed governors to challenge the power of colonial assemblies. They preferred power to rest with the legislature.

THE RIGHT TO VOTE

The issue of requirements for voting and officeholding proved far more contentious. Conservative patriots struggled valiantly to reassert the rationale for the old voting restrictions. It was ridiculous, wrote one pamphleteer, to think that "every silly clown and illiterate mechanic [artisan]" deserved a voice in government. To John Adams, as conservative on the internal affairs of America as he had been radical on independence, freedom and equality were opposites. Men without property, he believed, had no "judgment of their own," and the removal of property qualifications, therefore, would "confound and destroy all distinctions, and prostrate all ranks to one common level." Eliminating traditional social ranks, however, was precisely the aim of the era's radical democrats, including the most influential promoter of independence, Thomas Paine.

The provisions of the new state constitutions reflected the balance of power between advocates of internal change and those who feared excessive democracy. The least democratization occurred in the southern states, whose highly deferential political traditions enabled the landed gentry to retain their control of political affairs. In Virginia and South Carolina, the new constitutions retained property qualifications for voting and authorized the gentry-dominated legislature to choose the governor.

Maryland combined a low property qualification for voting with high requirements for officeholding, including £5,000—a veritable fortune—for the governor.

The most democratic new constitutions moved much of the way toward the idea of voting as an entitlement rather than a privilege, but they generally stopped short of universal suffrage, even for free men. Vermont's constitution of 1777 was the only one to sever voting completely from financial considerations, eliminating not only property qualifications but the requirement that voters pay taxes. Pennsylvania's constitution no longer required ownership of property, but it retained the taxpaying qualification. As a result, it enfranchised nearly all of the state's free male population but left a small number, mainly paupers and domestic servants, still barred from voting. Nonetheless, even with the taxpaying requirement, it represented a dramatic departure from the colonial practice of restricting the suffrage to those who could claim to be economically independent. It elevated "personal liberty," in the words of one essayist, to a position more important than property ownership in defining the boundaries of the political nation.

DEMOCRATIZING GOVERNMENT

Overall, the Revolution led to a great expansion of the right to vote. By the 1780s, with the exceptions of Virginia, Maryland, and New York, a large majority of the adult white male population could meet voting requirements. New Jersey's new state constitution, of 1776, granted the suffrage to all "inhabitants" who met a property qualification. Until the state added the word "male" (along with "white") in 1807, property-owning women, mostly widows, did cast ballots. The new constitutions also expanded the number of legislative seats, with the result that numerous men of lesser property assumed political office. The debate over the suffrage would, of course, continue for many decades. For white men, the process of democratization did not run its course until the Age of Jackson; for women and non-whites, it would take much longer.

Even during the Revolution, however, in the popular language of politics if not in law, freedom and an individual's right to vote had become interchangeable. "The suffrage," declared a 1776 petition of disenfranchised North Carolinians, was "a right essential to and inseparable from freedom." Without it, Americans could not enjoy "equal liberty." A proposed new constitution for Massachusetts was rejected by a majority of the towns in 1778, partly because it contained a property qualification for voting. "All men were born equally free and independent," declared the town of Lenox. How could they defend their "life and liberty and property" without a voice in electing public officials? A new draft, which retained a substantial requirement for voting in state elections but allowed virtually all men to vote for town officers, was approved in 1780. And every state except South Carolina provided for annual legislative elections, to ensure that representatives remained closely accountable to the people. Henceforth, political freedom would mean not only, as in the past, a people's right to be ruled by their chosen representatives but also an individual's right to political participation.

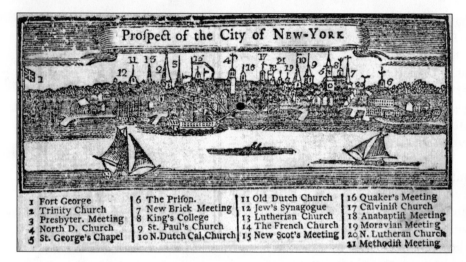

Prospect of the City of NEW-YORK

1 Fort George	6 The Prison.	11 Old Dutch Church	16 Quaker's Meeting
2 Trinity Church	7 New Brick Meeting	12 Jew's Synagogue	17 Calvinist Church
3 Presbyter. Meeting	8 King's College	13 Lutherian Church	18 Anabaptist Meeting
4 North D. Church	9 St. Paul's Church	14 The French Church	19 Moravian Meeting
5 St. George's Chapel	10 N. Dutch Cal. Church	15 New Scot's Meeting	20 N. Lutheran Church
			21 Methodist Meeting

A 1771 image of New York City lists some of the numerous churches visible from the New Jersey shore, illustrating the diversity of religions practiced in the city.

TOWARD RELIGIOUS TOLERATION

As remarkable as the expansion of political freedom was the Revolution's impact on American religion. Religious toleration, declared one Virginia patriot, was part of "the common cause of Freedom." In Britain, Dissenters—Protestants who belonged to other denominations than the Anglican Church—had long invoked the language of liberty in seeking repeal of the laws that imposed various disabilities on non-Anglicans. (Few, however, included Catholics in their ringing calls for religious freedom.) We have already seen that some colonies, like Rhode Island and Pennsylvania, had long made a practice of toleration. But freedom of worship before the Revolution arose more from the reality of religious pluralism than from a well-developed theory of religious liberty. Apart from Rhode Island, New England had little homegrown experience of religious pluralism. Indeed, authorities in England had occasionally pressed the region's rulers to become more tolerant. Before the Revolution, most colonies supported religious institutions with public funds and discriminated in voting and officeholding against Catholics, Jews, and even dissenting Protestants. On the very eve of independence, Baptists who refused to pay taxes to support local Congregational ministers were still being jailed in Massachusetts. "While our country are pleading so high for liberty," the victims complained, "yet they are denying of it to their neighbors."

CATHOLIC AMERICANS

The War of Independence weakened the deep tradition of American anti-Catholicism. The First Continental Congress denounced the Quebec Act of 1774, which, as noted in the previous chapter, allowed Canadian Catholics to worship freely, as part of a plot to establish "popery" in North America. But a year later, when the Second Continental Congress decided on an ill-fated invasion of Canada, it invited the inhabitants of Quebec to join in the struggle against Britain, assuring them that Protestants and Catholics could readily cooperate. However, predominantly Catholic Quebec preferred being ruled from distant London rather than from Boston or Philadelphia. In 1778, the United States formed an alliance with France, a Catholic nation. Benedict Arnold justified his treason, in part, by saying that an alliance with "the enemy of the protestant faith" was too much for him to bear. But the indispensable assistance provided by France to American victory strengthened the idea that Catholics had a role to play in the newly independent nation. In fact, this represented a marked departure from the traditional notion that the full rights of Englishmen only applied to Protestants. When America's first Roman Catholic bishop, James Carroll of Maryland, visited Boston in 1791, he received a cordial welcome.

THE FOUNDERS AND RELIGION

The end of British rule immediately threw into question the privileged position enjoyed by the Anglican Church in many colonies. In Virginia, for example, backcountry Scotch-Irish Presbyterian farmers demanded relief from taxes supporting the official Anglican Church. "The free exercise of our rights of conscience," one patriotic meeting resolved, formed an essential part of "our liberties."

Many of the leaders of the Revolution considered it essential for the new nation to shield itself from the unruly passions and violent conflicts that religious differences had inspired during the past three centuries. Men like Thomas Jefferson, John Adams, James Madison, and Alexander Hamilton believed religion necessary as a foundation of public morality. But they viewed religious doctrines through the Enlightenment lens of rationalism and skepticism. They believed in a benevolent Creator but not in supernatural interventions into the affairs of men. Jefferson wrote a version of the Bible and a life of Jesus that insisted that while Jesus had lived a deeply moral life, he was not divine and performed no miracles. In discussing the natural history of the Blue Ridge Mountains in his book *Notes on the State of Virginia*, he rejected the biblical account of creation in favor of a prolonged process of geological change.

SEPARATING CHURCH AND STATE

The drive to separate church and state brought together Deists like Jefferson, who hoped to erect a "wall of separation" that would free politics and the exercise of the intellect from religious control, with members of evangelical sects, who sought to protect religion from the corrupting embrace of government. Religious leaders continued to adhere to the traditional definition of Christian liberty—submitting to God's will and leading a moral life—but increasingly felt this could be achieved without the support of government. Christ's kingdom, as Isaac Backus, the Baptist leader, put it, was "not of this world."

The movement toward religious freedom received a major impetus during the revolutionary era. Throughout the new nation, states disestablished their established churches—that is, deprived them of public funding and special legal privileges—although in some cases they appropriated money for the general support of Protestant denominations. The seven state constitutions that began with declarations of rights all declared a commitment to "the free exercise of religion."

To be sure, every state but New York—whose constitution of 1777 established complete religious liberty—kept intact colonial provisions barring Jews from voting and holding public office. Seven states limited officeholding to Protestants. Massachusetts retained its Congregationalist establishment well into the nineteenth century. Its new constitution declared church attendance compulsory while guaranteeing freedom of individual worship. It would not end public financial support for religious institutions until 1833. Throughout the country, however, Catholics gained the right to worship without persecution. Maryland's constitution of 1776 restored to the large Catholic population the civil and political rights that had been denied them for nearly a century.

A BILL for establishing RELIGIOUS FREEDOM,
printed for the consideration of the PEOPLE.

WELL aware that the opinions and belief of men depend not on their own will, but follow involuntarily the evidence proposed to their minds, that Almighty God hath created the mind free, and manifested his Supreme will that free it shall remain, by making it altogether insusceptible of restraint: That all attempts to influence it by temporal punishments or burthens, or by civil incapacitations, tend only to beget habits of hypocrisy and meanness, and are a departure from the plan of the holy author of our religion, who being Lord both of body and mind, yet chose not to propagate it by coercions on either, as was in his Almighty power to do, but to extend it by its influence on reason alone: That the impious presumption of legislators and rulers, civil as well as ecclesiastical, who, being themselves but fallible and uninspired men, have assumed dominion over the faith of others, setting up their own opinions and modes of thinking, as the only true and infallible, and as such, endeavouring to impose them on others, hath established and maintained false religions over the greatest part of the world, and through all time: That to compel a man to furnish contributions of money for the propagation of opinions which he disbelieves and abhors, is sinful and tyrannical: That even the forcing him to support this or that teacher of his own religious persuasion, is depriving him of the comfortable liberty of giving his contributions to the particular pastor whose morals he would make his pattern, and whose powers he feels most persuasive to righteousness, and is withdrawing from the Ministry those temporal rewards which, proceeding from an approbation of their personal conduct, are an additional incitement to earnest and unremitting labour for the instruction of mankind: That our civil rights have no dependance on our religious opinions, any more than on our opinions in physicks or geometry: That therefore the proscribing any citizen as unworthy the publick confidence, by laying upon him an incapacity of being called to offices of trust and emolument, unless he profess or renounce this or that religious opinion, is depriving him injuriously of those privileges and advantages to which, in common with his fellow citizens he has a natural right: That it tends also to corrupt the principles of that very religion it is meant to encourage, by bribing with a monopoly of worldly honours and emoluments, those who will externally profess and conform to it: That though indeed these are criminal who do not withstand such temptation, yet neither are those innocent who lay the bait in their way: That the opinions of men are not the object of civil government, nor under its jurisdiction: That to suffer the civil Magistrate to intrude his powers into the field of opinion, and to restrain the profession or propagation of principles on supposition of their ill tendency, is a dangerous fallacy, which at once destroys all religious liberty; because he being of course Judge of that tendency will make his own opinions the rule of judgment, and approve or condemn the sentiments of others only as they shall square with, or differ from his own: That it is time enough for the rightful purposes of civil government for its officers to interfere when principles break out into overt acts against peace and good order: And finally, that truth is great and will prevail if left to herself; that she is the proper and sufficient antagonist to errour, and has nothing to fear from the conflict, unless by human interposition, disarmed of her natural weapons, free argument and debate; errours ceasing to be dangerous when it is permitted freely to contradict them

WE the General Assembly of *Virginia* do enact, that no man shall be compelled to frequent or support any religous Worship place or Ministry whatsoever, nor shall be enforced, restrained, molested, or burthened in his body or goods, nor shall otherwise suffer on account of his religious opinions or belief, but that all men shall be free to profess, and by argument to maintain their opinions in matters of religion, and that the same shall in no wise diminish, enlarge, or affect their civil capacities.

AND though we well know that this Assembly, elected by the people for the ordinary purposes of legislation only, have no power to restrain the acts of succeeding Assemblies, constituted with powers equal to our own, and that therefore to declare this act irrevocable would be of no effect in law; yet we are free to declare, and do declare, that the rights hereby asserted are of the natural rights of mankind, and that if any act shall be hereafter passed to repeal the present, or to narrow its operation, such act will be an infringement of natural right.

A draft of Thomas Jefferson's Virginia Bill for Establishing Religious Freedom, published in 1779 in order to encourage public discussion of the issue. The bill was enacted in 1786.

JEFFERSON AND RELIGIOUS LIBERTY

In Virginia, Thomas Jefferson drew up a Bill for Establishing Religious Freedom, which was introduced in the House of Burgesses in 1779 and adopted, after considerable controversy, in 1786. "I have sworn on the altar of God," he would later write, "eternal hostility against every form of tyranny over the mind of man." Jefferson viewed established churches as a major example of such despotism and, as his statement reveals, believed that religious liberty served God's will. Jefferson's bill, whose preamble declared that God "hath created the mind free," eliminated religious requirements for voting and officeholding and government financial support for churches, and barred the state from "forcing" individuals to adopt one or

How did the expansion of religious liberty after the Revolution reflect the new American ideal of freedom?

229

another religious outlook. Late in life, Jefferson would list this measure, along with the Declaration of Independence and the founding of the University of Virginia, as the three accomplishments (leaving out his two terms as president) for which he wished to be remembered.

Religious liberty became the model for the revolutionary generation's definition of "rights" as private matters that must be protected from governmental interference. In an overwhelmingly Christian (though not necessarily churchgoing) nation, the separation of church and state drew a sharp line between public authority and a realm defined as "private," reinforcing the idea that rights exist as restraints on the power of government. It also offered a new justification for the idea of the United States as a beacon of liberty. In successfully opposing a Virginia tax for the general support of Christian churches, James Madison insisted that one reason for the complete separation of church and state was to reinforce the principle that the new nation offered "asylum to the persecuted and oppressed of every nation and religion."

THE REVOLUTION AND THE CHURCHES

Thus, the Revolution enhanced the diversity of American Christianity and expanded the idea of religious liberty. But even as the separation of church and state created the social and political space that allowed all kinds of religious institutions to flourish, the culture of individual rights of which that separation was a part threatened to undermine church authority.

One example was the experience of the Moravian Brethren, who had emigrated from Germany to North Carolina on the eve of independence. To the dismay of the Moravian elders, younger members of the community, like so many other Americans of the revolutionary generation, insisted on asserting "their alleged freedom and human rights." Some became unruly and refused to obey the orders of town leaders. Many rejected the community's tradition of arranged marriages, insisting on choosing their own husbands and wives. To the elders, the idea of individual liberty—which they called, disparagingly, "the American freedom"—was little more than "an opportunity for temptation," a threat to the spirit of self-sacrifice and communal loyalty essential to Christian liberty.

But despite such fears, the Revolution did not end the influence of religion on American society—quite the reverse. American churches, in the words of one Presbyterian leader, learned to adapt to living at a time when "a spirit of liberty prevails." Thanks to religious freedom, the early republic witnessed an amazing proliferation of religious denominations. The most well-established churches—Anglican, Presbyterian, and Congregationalist—found themselves constantly challenged by upstarts like Free-Will Baptists and Universalists. Today, even as debate continues over the

Ezra Stiles, the president of Yale College, drew this sketch of a flag in his diary on April 24, 1783, shortly after Congress ratified the Treaty of Paris. Thirteen stars surround the coat of arms of Pennsylvania. The banner text illustrates the linkage among virtue, liberty, and American independence.

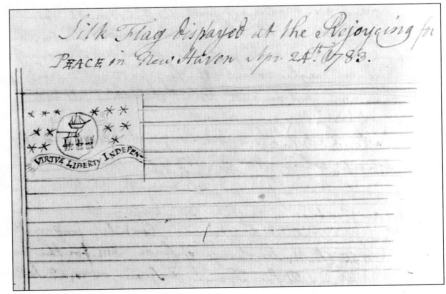

Silk Flag displayed at the Rejoyqing for PEACE in New Haven Apr. 24th 1783.

VIRTUE LIBERTY INDEPEN-

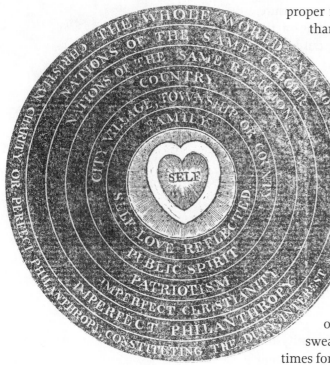

The Self, *an engraving in* The Columbian Magazine, *1789, illustrates various admirable qualities radiating outward from the virtuous citizen, including love for one's family, community, and nation.*

proper relationship between spiritual and political authority, more than 1,300 religions are practiced in the United States.

A VIRTUOUS CITIZENRY

Despite the separation of church and state, colonial leaders were not hostile to religion. Most were devout Christians, and even Deists who attended no organized church believed religious values reinforced the moral qualities necessary for a republic to prosper. Public authority continued to support religious values, in laws barring non-Christians from office and in the continued prosecution of blasphemy and breaches of the Sabbath. Pennsylvania's new democratic constitution required citizens to acknowledge the existence of God, and it directed the legislature to enact "laws for the prevention of vice and immorality." In the nineteenth century, Pennsylvania's lawmakers took this mandate so seriously that the state became as famous for its laws against swearing and desecrating the Sabbath as it had been in colonial times for religious freedom.

Patriot leaders worried about the character of future citizens, especially how to encourage the quality of "virtue," the ability to sacrifice self-interest for the public good. Some, like Jefferson, John Adams, and Benjamin Rush, put forward plans for the establishment of free, state-supported public schools. These would instruct future citizens in what Adams called "the principles of freedom," equipping them for participation in the now-expanded public sphere and for the wise election of representatives. A broad diffusion of knowledge was essential for a government based on the will of the people to survive and for America to avoid the fixed class structure of Europe. No nation, Jefferson wrote, could "expect to be ignorant and free."

DEFINING ECONOMIC FREEDOM

TOWARD FREE LABOR

In economic as well as political and religious affairs, the Revolution rewrote the definition of freedom. In colonial America, slavery was one part of a broad spectrum of kinds of unfree labor. In the generation after independence, with the rapid decline of indentured servitude and apprenticeship and the transformation of paid domestic service into an occupation for blacks and white females, the halfway houses between slavery and freedom disappeared, at least for white men. The decline of these forms of labor had many causes. Wage workers became more available as indentured servants completed their terms of required labor, and considerable numbers of servants and apprentices took advantage of the turmoil of the Revolution to escape from their masters.

The democratization of freedom contributed to these changes. The lack of freedom inherent in apprenticeship and servitude increasingly came to be seen as incompatible with republican citizenship. Ebenezer Fox, a young apprentice on a Massachusetts farm, later recalled how he and other youths "made a direct application of the doctrines we heard daily, in relation to the oppression of the mother country, to our own circumstance.... I thought that I was doing myself a great injustice by remaining in bondage, when I ought to go free." Fox became one of many apprentices during the Revolution who decided to run away—or, as he put it, to "liberate myself." On the eve of the battles of Lexington and Concord in 1775, Fox and a friend set off for Rhode Island. After briefly working as a sailor, Fox, still a teenager, joined the Continental army.

In 1784, a group of "respectable" New Yorkers released a newly arrived shipload of indentured servants on the grounds that their status was "contrary to ... the idea of liberty this country has so happily established." By 1800, indentured servitude had all but disappeared from the United States. This development sharpened the distinction between freedom and slavery and between a northern economy relying on what would come to be called "free labor" (that is, working for wages or owning a farm or shop) and a southern economy ever more heavily dependent on the labor of slaves.

THE SOUL OF A REPUBLIC

Americans of the revolutionary generation were preoccupied with the social conditions of freedom. Could a republic survive with a sizable dependent class of citizens? "A general and tolerably equal distribution of landed property," proclaimed the educator and newspaper editor Noah Webster, "is the whole basis of national freedom." "Equality," he added, was "the very soul of a republic." It outstripped in importance liberty of the press, trial by jury, and other "palladia of freedom." Even a conservative like John Adams, who distrusted the era's democratic upsurge, hoped that every member of society could acquire land, "so that the multitude may be

View from Bushongo Tavern, *an engraving from* The Columbian Magazine, *1788, depicts the landscape of York County, Pennsylvania, exemplifying the kind of rural independence many Americans thought essential to freedom.*

possessed of small estates" and the new nation could avoid the emergence of fixed and unequal social classes. At the Revolution's radical edge, some patriots believed that government had a responsibility to limit accumulations of property in the name of equality. To most free Americans, however, "equality" meant equal opportunity, rather than equality of condition. Many leaders of the Revolution nevertheless assumed that in the exceptional circumstances of the New World, with its vast areas of available land and large population of independent farmers and artisans, the natural workings of society would produce justice, liberty, and equality.

Like many other Americans of his generation, Thomas Jefferson believed that to lack economic resources was to lack freedom. Jefferson favored a limited state, but he also believed that government could help create freedom's institutional framework. His proudest achievements included laws passed by Virginia abolishing entail (the limitation of inheritance to a specified line of heirs to keep an estate within a family) and primogeniture (the practice of passing a family's land entirely to the eldest son). These measures, he believed, would help to prevent the rise of a "future aristocracy." To the same end, Jefferson proposed to award fifty acres of land to "every person of full age" who did not already possess it, another way government could enhance the liberty of its subjects. Of course, the land Jefferson hoped would secure American liberty would have to come from Indians.

THE POLITICS OF INFLATION

The Revolution thrust to the forefront of politics debates over whether local or national authorities should take steps to bolster household independence and protect Americans' livelihoods by limiting price increases. Economic dislocations sharpened the controversy. To finance the war, Congress issued hundreds of millions of dollars in paper money. Coupled with wartime disruption of agriculture and trade and the hoarding of goods by some Americans hoping to profit from shortages, this produced an enormous increase in prices. The country, charged a letter to a Philadelphia newspaper in 1778, had been "reduced to the brink of ruin by the infamous practices of monopolizers." "Hunger," the writer warned, "will break through stone walls."

Between 1776 and 1779, more than thirty incidents took place in which crowds confronted merchants accused of holding scarce goods off the market. Often, they seized stocks of food and sold them at the traditional "just price," a form of protest common in eighteenth-century England. In one such incident, a crowd of 100 Massachusetts women accused an "eminent, wealthy, stingy merchant" of hoarding coffee, opened his warehouse, and carted off the goods. "A large concourse of men," wrote Abigail Adams, "stood amazed, silent spectators of the whole transaction."

A broadside printed by the extralegal Philadelphia price-control committee, setting the retail prices of various goods such as coffee, sugar, and rum. Advocates of a free market strongly opposed the committee's efforts.

THE DEBATE OVER FREE TRADE

In 1779, with inflation totally out of control (in one month, prices in Philadelphia jumped 45 percent), Congress urged states to adopt measures to fix wages and prices. The policy embodied the belief that the task of republican government was to promote the public good, not individuals' self-interest. Bitter comments appeared in the Philadelphia press about the city's elite expending huge sums on "public dinners and other extravaganzas" while many in the city were "destitute of the necessities of life." But when a Committee of Safety tried to enforce price controls, it met spirited opposition from merchants and other advocates of a free market.

In opposition to the traditional view that men should sacrifice for the public good, believers in freedom of trade argued that economic development arose from economic self-interest. Just as Newton had revealed the inner workings of the natural universe, so the social world also followed unchanging natural laws, among them that supply and demand regulated the prices of goods. Adam Smith's great treatise on economics, *The Wealth of Nations*, published in England in 1776, was beginning to become known in the United States. Smith's argument that the "invisible hand" of the free market directed economic life more effectively and fairly than governmental intervention offered intellectual justification for those who believed that the economy should be left to regulate itself.

Advocates of independence had envisioned America, released from the British Navigation Acts, trading freely with all the world. Opponents of price controls advocated free trade at home as well. "Let trade be as free as air," wrote one merchant. "Natural liberty" would regulate prices. Here were two competing conceptions of economic freedom—one based on the traditional view that the interests of the community took precedence over the property rights of individuals, the other that unregulated economic freedom would produce social harmony and public gain. After 1779, the latter view gained ascendancy. In 1780, Robert Morris, a Philadelphia merchant and banker, became director of congressional fiscal policy. State and federal efforts to regulate prices ceased. But the clash between these two visions of economic freedom would continue long after independence had been achieved.

"Yield to the mighty current of American freedom." So a member of the South Carolina legislature implored his colleagues in 1777. The current of freedom swept away not only British authority but also the principle of hereditary rule, the privileges of established churches, long-standing habits of deference and hierarchy, and old limits on the political nation. Yet in other areas, the tide of freedom encountered obstacles that did not yield as easily to its powerful flow.

THE LIMITS OF LIBERTY

COLONIAL LOYALISTS

Not all Americans shared in the democratization of freedom brought on by the American Revolution. Loyalists—those who retained their allegiance to the crown—experienced the conflict and its aftermath as a loss of liberty. Many leading Loyalists had supported American resistance in the 1760s but drew back at the prospect of independence and war. Loyalists included some of the most prominent Americans and some of the most humble. Altogether, an estimated 20 to 25 percent of free Americans remained loyal to the British, and nearly 20,000 fought on their side. At some points in the war, Loyalists serving with the British outnumbered Washington's army.

There were Loyalists in every colony, but they were most numerous in New York, Pennsylvania, and the backcountry of the Carolinas and Georgia.

Some were wealthy men whose livelihoods depended on close working relationships with Britain—lawyers, merchants, Anglican ministers, and imperial officials. Many feared anarchy in the event of an American victory. "Liberty," one wrote, "can have no existence without obedience to the laws."

The struggle for independence heightened existing tensions between ethnic groups and social classes within the colonies. Some Loyalist ethnic minorities, like Highland Scots in North Carolina, feared that local majorities would infringe on their freedom to enjoy cultural autonomy. In the South, many backcountry farmers who had long resented the domination of public affairs by wealthy planters sided with the British. So did tenants on the New York estates of patriot landlords like the Livingston family. Robert Livingston had signed the Declaration of Independence. When the army of General Burgoyne approached Livingston's manor in 1777, tenants rose in revolt, hoping the British would confiscate his land and distribute it among themselves. Their hopes were dashed by Burgoyne's defeat at Saratoga. In the South, numerous slaves sided with the British, hoping an American defeat would bring them freedom.

THE LOYALISTS' PLIGHT

The War of Independence was in some respects a civil war among Americans. "This country," wrote a German colonel fighting with the British, "is the scene of the most cruel events. Neighbors are on opposite sides, children are against their fathers." Freedom of expression is often a casualty of war, and many Americans were deprived of basic rights in the name of liberty. After Dr. Abner Beebe, of East Haddam, Connecticut, spoke "very freely" in favor of the British, a mob attacked his house and destroyed his gristmill. Beebe himself was "assaulted, stripped naked, and hot pitch [tar] was poured upon him." The new state governments, or in other instances crowds of patriots, suppressed newspapers thought to be loyal to Britain.

Pennsylvania arrested and seized the property of Quakers, Mennonites, and Moravians—pacifist denominations who refused to bear arms because of their religious beliefs. With the approval of Congress, many states required residents to take oaths of allegiance to the new nation. Those who refused were denied the right to vote and in many cases forced into exile. "The flames of discord," wrote one British observer, "are sprouting from the seeds of liberty." Some wealthy Loyalists saw their land confiscated and sold at auction. Twenty-eight estates belonging to New Hampshire governor John Wentworth and his family were seized, as were the holdings of great New York Loyalist landlords like the De Lancey and Philipse families. Most of the buyers of this land were merchants, lawyers, and established landowners. Unable to afford the purchase price, tenants had no choice but to continue to labor for the new owners.

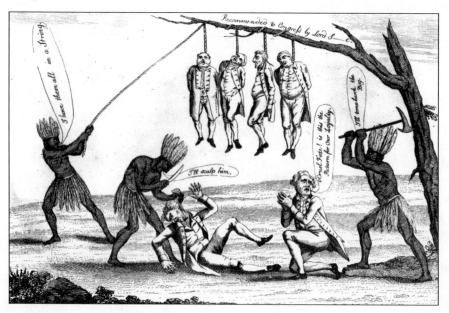

A 1780 British cartoon commenting on the "cruel fate" of American Loyalists. Pro-independence colonists are likened to savage Indians.

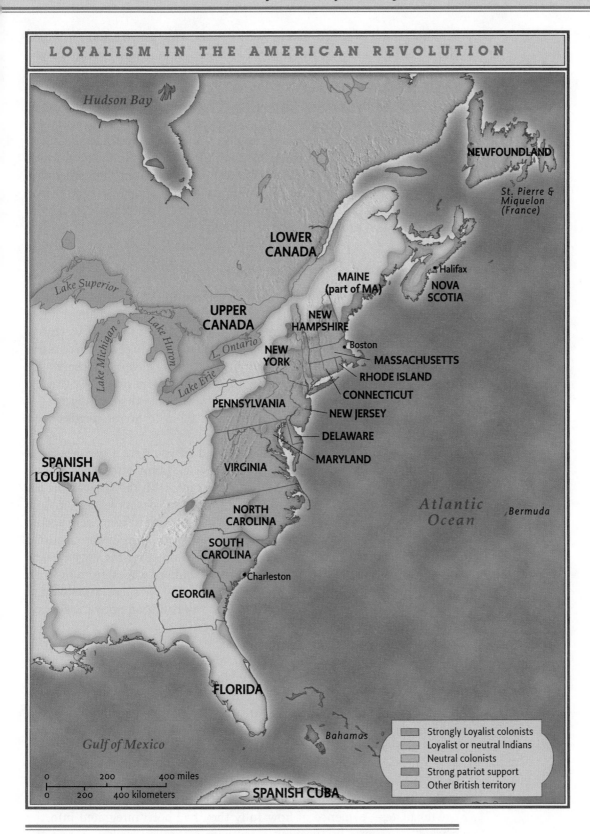

LOYALISM IN THE AMERICAN REVOLUTION

Legend:
- Strongly Loyalist colonists
- Loyalist or neutral Indians
- Neutral colonists
- Strong patriot support
- Other British territory

The Revolutionary War was, in some ways, a civil war within the colonies. There were Loyalists in every colony; they were most numerous in New York and North and South Carolina.

When the war ended, as many as 100,000 Loyalists (including 20,000 slaves) were banished from the United States or emigrated voluntarily—mostly to Britain, Canada, or the West Indies—rather than live in an independent United States. But for those who remained, hostility proved to be short-lived. In the Treaty of Paris of 1783, as noted in Chapter 5, Americans pledged to end the persecution of Loyalists by state and local governments and to restore property seized during the war. American leaders believed the new nation needed to establish an international reputation for fairness and civility. States soon repealed their test oaths for voting and officeholding. Loyalists who did not leave the country were quickly reintegrated into American society, although despite the promise of the Treaty of Paris, confiscated Loyalist property was not returned.

THE INDIANS' REVOLUTION

Another group for whom American independence spelled a loss of freedom—the Indians—was less fortunate. Despite the Proclamation of 1763, discussed in Chapter 4, colonists had continued to move westward during the 1760s and early 1770s, leading Indian tribes to complain of intrusions on their land. Lord Dunmore, Virginia's royal governor, observed in 1772 that he had found it impossible "to restrain the Americans. . . . They do not conceive that government has any right to forbid their taking possession of a vast tract of country" or to force them to honor treaties with Indians.

Kentucky, the principal hunting ground of southern Cherokees and numerous Ohio Valley Indians, became a flash point of conflict among settlers, land speculators, and Native Americans, with the faraway British government seeking in vain to impose order. Many patriot leaders, including George Washington, Patrick Henry, and Thomas Jefferson, were deeply involved in western land speculation. Washington himself had acquired over 60,000 acres of land in western Pennsylvania after the Seven Years' War by purchasing land vouchers (a form of soldiers' wages) from his men at discount rates. Indeed, British efforts to restrain land speculation west of the line specified by the Proclamation of 1763 had been one of the many grievances of Virginia's revolutionary generation.

About 200,000 Native Americans lived east of the Mississippi River in 1790. Like white Americans, Indians divided in allegiance during the War of Independence. Some, like the Stockbridge tribe in Massachusetts, suffered heavy losses fighting the British. Many tribes tried to maintain neutrality, only to see themselves break into pro-American and pro-British factions. Most of the Iroquois nations sided with the British, but the Oneida joined the Americans. Despite strenuous efforts to avoid conflict, members of the Iroquois Confederacy for the first time faced each other in battle. (After the war, the Oneida submitted to Congress claims for losses suffered during the war, including sheep, hogs, kettles, frying pans, plows, and pewter plates—evidence of how fully they had been integrated into the market economy.) In the South, younger Cherokee leaders joined the British while older chiefs tended to favor the Americans. Other southern tribes like the Choctaw and Creek remained loyal to the crown.

Among the grievances listed by Jefferson in the Declaration of Independence was Britain's enlisting "savages" to fight on its side. But in the

war that raged throughout the western frontier, savagery was not confined to either combatant. In the Ohio country, the British encouraged Indian allies to burn frontier farms and settlements. For their part, otherwise humane patriot leaders ignored the traditional rules of warfare when it came to Indians. William Henry Drayton, a leader of the patriot cause in South Carolina and the state's chief justice in 1776, advised officers marching against the Cherokees to "cut up every Indian cornfield, burn every Indian town," and enslave all Indian captives. Three years later, Washington dispatched an expedition, led by General John Sullivan, against hostile Iroquois, with the aim of "the total destruction and devastation of their settlements and the capture of as many prisoners of every age and sex as possible." After his campaign ended, Sullivan reported that he had burned forty Indian towns, destroyed thousands of bushels of corn, and uprooted a vast number of fruit trees and vegetable gardens. Many Iroquois communities faced starvation. In the Ohio Valley, as we will see in Chapter 7, fighting did not end until the 1790s.

A cartoon depicting a British officer buying the scalps of patriots from Indians. Jefferson listed British incitement of Indians against the colonists as one of Americans' grievances in the Declaration of Independence.

WHITE FREEDOM, INDIAN FREEDOM

Independence created governments democratically accountable to voters who coveted Indian land. Indeed, to many patriots, access to Indian land was one of the fruits of American victory. Driving the Indians from the Ohio Valley, wrote Jefferson, would "add to the Empire of Liberty an extensive and fertile country." But liberty for whites meant loss of liberty for Indians. "The whites were no sooner free themselves," a Pequot, William Apess, would later write, than they turned on "the poor Indians." Independence offered the opportunity to complete the process of dispossessing Indians of their rich lands in upstate New York, the Ohio Valley, and the southern backcountry. The only hope for the Indians, Jefferson wrote, lay in their "removal beyond the Mississippi." Even as the war raged, Americans forced defeated tribes like the Cherokee to cede most of their land.

American independence, a group of visiting Indians told the Spanish governor at St. Louis, was "the greatest blow that could have been dealt us." The Treaty of Paris marked the culmination of a century in which the balance of power in eastern North America shifted away from the Indians and toward white Americans. The displacement of British power to Canada, coming twenty years after the departure of the French, left Indians with seriously diminished white support. Some Indian leaders, like Joseph Brant, a young Mohawk in upstate New York, hoped to create an Indian confederacy lying between Canada and the new United States. He sided with the British to try to achieve this goal. But in the Treaty of Paris, the British abandoned their Indian allies, agreeing to recognize American sovereignty over the entire region east of the Mississippi River, completely ignoring the Indian presence.

To Indians, freedom meant defending their own independence and retaining possession of their land. Like other Americans, they appropriated the language of the Revolution and interpreted it according to their own experiences and for their own purposes. The Iroquois, declared one spokesman, were "a free people subject to no power on earth." Creeks and Choctaws denied having done anything to forfeit their "independence and natural rights." When Massachusetts established a system of state "guardianship" over previously self-governing tribes, a group of Mashpees petitioned the legislature, claiming for themselves "the rights of man" and complaining of this "infringement of freedom."

"Freedom" had not played a major part in Indians' vocabulary before the Revolution. By the early nineteenth century, dictionaries of Indian languages for the first time began to include the word. In a sense, Indians' definition of their rights was becoming Americanized. But there seemed to be no permanent place for the descendants of the continent's native population in a new nation bent on creating an empire in the West.

SLAVERY AND THE REVOLUTION

While Indians experienced American independence as a real threat to their own liberty, African-Americans saw in the ideals of the Revolution and the reality of war an opportunity to claim freedom. When the United States declared its independence in 1776, the slave population had grown to 500,000, about one-fifth of the new nation's inhabitants. Slaveowning and slave trading were accepted routines of colonial life. Advertisements announcing the sale of slaves and seeking the return of runaways filled colonial newspapers. Sometimes, the same issues of patriotic newspapers that published accounts of the activities of the Sons of Liberty or arguments against the Stamp Act also contained slave sale notices.

THE LANGUAGE OF SLAVERY AND FREEDOM

Slavery played a central part in the language of revolution. Apart from "liberty," it was the word most frequently invoked in the era's legal and political literature. Eighteenth-century writers frequently juxtaposed freedom and slavery as "the two extremes of happiness and misery in society." Yet in the era's debates over British rule, slavery was primarily a political category, shorthand for the denial of one's personal and political rights by arbitrary government. Those who lacked a voice in public affairs, declared a 1769 petition demanding an expansion of the right to vote in Britain, were "enslaved." By the eve of independence, the contrast between Britain, "a kingdom of slaves," and America, a "country of free men," had become a standard part of the language of resistance. Such language was employed without irony even in areas where nearly half the population in fact consisted of slaves. South Carolina, one writer declared in 1774, was a "sacred land" of freedom, where it was impossible to believe that "slavery shall soon be permitted to erect her throne."

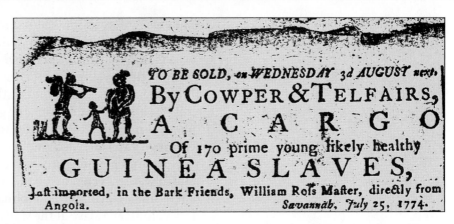

Advertisement for newly arrived slaves, in a Savannah newspaper, 1774. Even as colonists defended their own liberty against the British, the buying and selling of slaves continued.

Colonial writers of the 1760s occasionally made a direct connection between slavery as a reality and slavery as a metaphor. Few were as forthright as James Otis of Massachusetts, whose pamphlets did much to popularize the idea that Parliament lacked the authority to tax the colonies and regulate their commerce. Freedom, Otis insisted, must be universal: "What man is or ever was born free if every man is not?" Otis wrote of blacks not as examples of the loss of rights awaiting free Americans, but as flesh and blood British subjects "entitled to all the civil rights of such."

Otis was hardly typical of patriot leaders. But the presence of hundreds of thousands of slaves powerfully affected the meaning of freedom for the leaders of the American Revolution. In a famous speech to Parliament warning against attempts to intimidate the colonies, the British statesman Edmund Burke suggested that familiarity with slavery made colonial leaders unusually sensitive to threats to their own liberties. Where freedom was a privilege, not a common right, he observed, "those who are free are by far the most proud and jealous of their freedom." On the other hand, many British observers could not resist pointing out the colonists' apparent hypocrisy. "How is it," asked Dr. Samuel Johnson, "that we hear the loudest yelps for liberty from the drivers of negroes?"

OBSTACLES TO ABOLITION

The contradiction between freedom and slavery seems so self-evident that it is difficult today to appreciate the power of the obstacles to abolition. At the time of the Revolution, slavery was already an old institution in America. It existed in every colony and formed the basis of the economy and social structure from Maryland southward. At least 40 percent of Virginia's population and even higher proportions in Georgia and South Carolina were slaves.

Virtually every founding father owned slaves at one point in his life, including not only southern planters but northern merchants, lawyers, and farmers. (John Adams and Tom Paine were notable exceptions.)

Thomas Jefferson owned more than 100 slaves when he wrote of mankind's unalienable right to liberty, and everything he cherished in his own manner of life, from lavish entertainments to the leisure that made possible the pursuit of arts and sciences, ultimately rested on slave labor.

Some patriots, in fact, argued that slavery for blacks made freedom possible for whites. Eliminating the great bulk of the dependent poor from the political nation left the public arena to men of propertied independence. Owning slaves offered a route to the economic autonomy widely deemed necessary for genuine freedom, a point driven home by a 1780 Virginia law that rewarded veterans of the War of Independence with 300 acres of land—and a slave. South Carolina and Georgia promised every white military volunteer a slave at the war's end.

So, too, the Lockean vision of the political community as a group of individuals contracting together to secure their natural rights could readily be invoked to defend bondage. Nothing was more essential to freedom, in this view, than the right of self-government and the protection of property against outside interference. These principles suggested that for the government to seize property—including slave property—against the owner's will would be an infringement on liberty. If government by the consent of the governed formed the essence of political freedom, then to require owners to give up their slave property would reduce *them* to slavery.

THE CAUSE OF GENERAL LIBERTY

Nonetheless, by imparting so absolute a value to liberty and defining freedom as a universal entitlement rather than a set of rights specific to a particular place or people, the Revolution inevitably raised questions about the status of slavery in the new nation. Before independence, there had been little public discussion of the institution, even though enlightened opinion in the Atlantic world had come to view slavery as morally wrong and economically inefficient, a relic of a barbarous past.

As early as 1688, a group of German Quakers issued a "protest" regarding the rights of blacks, declaring it as unjust "to have them slaves, as it is to have other white ones." Samuel Sewall, a Boston merchant, published *The Selling of Joseph* in 1700, the first antislavery tract printed in America. All "the sons of Adam," Sewall insisted, were entitled to "have equal right unto liberty." Slavery, as noted in Chapter 4, had initially been banned in Georgia (although it later came to sustain the rice-based plantation economy in that colony). During the course of the eighteenth century, antislavery sentiments had spread among Pennsylvania's Quakers, whose belief that all persons possessed the divine "inner light" made them particularly receptive.

But it was during the revolutionary era that slavery for the first time became a focus of public debate. The Pennsylvania patriot Benjamin Rush in 1773 called upon "advocates for American liberty" to "espouse the cause of . . . general liberty" and warned that slavery was one of those

A 1775 notice in The Massachusetts Spy *reporting a resolution of the Committees of Correspondence of Worcester County that advocated the abolition of slavery.*

WHEREAS the NEGROES in the counties of Briſtol and Worceſter, the 24th of March laſt, petitioned the Committees of Correſpondence for the county of Worceſter (then convened in Worceſter) to aſſiſt them in obtaining their freedom.   THEREFORE,
In County Convention, *June 14th, 1775.*
RESOLVED, That we abhor the enſlaving of any of the human race, and particularly of the NEGROES in this country.   And that whenever there ſhall be a door opened, or opportunity preſent, for any thing to be done toward the emancipating the NEGROES; we will uſe our influence and endeavour that ſuch a thing may be effected,   *Atteſt.* WILLIAM HENSHAW, *Clerk.*

"national crimes" that one day would bring "national punishment." Jefferson, as mentioned in the previous chapter, unsuccessfully tried to include criticism of slavery in the Declaration of Independence. Although a slaveholder himself, in private he condemned slavery as a system that every day imposed on its victims "more misery, than ages of that which [the colonists] rose in rebellion to oppose."

PETITIONS FOR FREEDOM

The Revolution inspired widespread hopes that slavery could be removed from American life. Most dramatically, slaves themselves appreciated that by defining freedom as a universal right, the leaders of the Revolution had devised a weapon that could be used against their own bondage. The language of liberty echoed in slave communities, North and South. Living amid freedom but denied its benefits, slaves appropriated the patriotic ideology for their own purposes. The most insistent advocates of freedom as a universal entitlement were African-Americans, who demanded that the leaders of the struggle for independence live up to their self-proclaimed creed. As early as 1766, white Charlestonians had been shocked when their opposition to the Stamp Act inspired a group of blacks to parade about the city crying "Liberty." Nine years later, the Provincial Congress of South Carolina felt compelled to investigate the "high notions of liberty" the struggle against Britain had inspired among the slaves.

The first concrete steps toward emancipation in revolutionary America were "freedom petitions"—arguments for liberty presented to New England's courts and legislatures in the early 1770s by enslaved African-Americans. How, one such petition asked, could America "seek release from English tyranny and not seek the same for disadvantaged Africans in her midst?" Some slaves sued in court for being "illegally detained in slavery." The turmoil of war offered other avenues to freedom. Many slaves ran away from their masters and tried to pass as freeborn. The number of fugitive slave advertisements in colonial newspapers rose dramatically in the 1770s and 1780s. As one owner put it in accounting for his slave Jim's escape, "I believe he has nothing in view but freedom."

In 1776, the year of American independence, Lemuel Haynes, a black member of the Massachusetts militia and later a celebrated minister, urged that Americans "extend" their conception of freedom. If liberty were truly "an innate principle" for all mankind, Haynes insisted, "even an African [had] as equally good a right to his liberty in common with Englishmen." Throughout the revolutionary period, petitions, pamphlets, and sermons by blacks expressed "astonishment" that white patriots failed to realize that "every principle from which America has acted" demanded emancipation. Blacks sought to make white Americans understand slavery as a concrete reality—the denial of all the essential elements of freedom—not merely as a metaphor for the loss of political self-determination. Petitioning for their freedom in 1773, a group of New England slaves exclaimed, "We have no property! We have no wives! No children! We have no city! No country!"

Most slaves of the revolutionary era were only one or two generations removed from Africa. They did not need the ideology of the Revolution to persuade them that freedom was a birthright—the experience of their par-

A portrait of the poet Phillis Wheatley (1753–1784).

ents and grandparents suggested as much. "My love of freedom," wrote the black poet Phillis Wheatley in 1783, arose from the "cruel fate" of being "snatch'd from Afric's" shore. Brought as a slave to Boston in 1761, Wheatley learned to read and published her first poem in a New England newspaper in 1765, when she was around twelve years old. The fact that a volume of her poems had to be printed with a testimonial from prominent citizens, including patriot leader John Hancock, affirming that she was in fact the author, illustrates that many whites found it difficult to accept the idea of blacks' intellectual ability. Yet by invoking the Revolution's ideology of liberty to demand their own rights and by defining freedom as a universal entitlement, blacks demonstrated how American they had become, even as they sought to redefine what American freedom in fact represented.

BRITISH EMANCIPATORS

As noted in the previous chapter, some 5,000 slaves fought for American independence and many thereby gained their freedom. Yet far more slaves obtained liberty from the British. Lord Dunmore's proclamation of 1775, and the Phillipsburgh Proclamation of General Henry Clinton issued four years later, offered sanctuary to slaves who escaped to British lines. Numerous signers of the Declaration of Independence lost slaves as a result. Thirty of Thomas Jefferson's slaves ran away to the British, as did slaves owned by Patrick Henry and James Madison. All told, nearly 100,000 slaves, including one-quarter of all the slaves in South Carolina and one-third of those in Georgia, deserted their owners and fled to British lines. This was by far the largest exodus from the plantations until the outbreak of the Civil War.

Some of these escaped slaves were recaptured as the tide of battle turned in the patriots' favor. But at the war's end, some 20,000 were living in three enclaves of British control—New York, Charleston, and Savannah. George Washington insisted they must be returned. Sir Guy Carleton, the British commander in New York, replied that to do so would be "a dishonorable violation of the public faith," since they had been promised their freedom. In the end, more than 15,000 black men, women, and children accompanied the British out of the country. They ended up in Nova Scotia, England, and Sierra Leone, a settlement for former slaves from the United States established by the British on the coast of West Africa. Some were re-enslaved in the West Indies. A number of their stories were indeed remarkable. Harry Washington, an African-born slave of George Washington, had run away from Mount Vernon in 1771 but was recaptured. In 1775, he fled to join Lord Dunmore and eventually became a corporal in a black British regiment, the Black Pioneers. He eventually ended up in Sierra Leone, where in 1800 he took part in an unsuccessful uprising by black settlers against the British-appointed government.

The issue of compensation for the slaves who departed with the British poisoned relations between Britain and the new United States for decades to come. Finally, in 1827, Britain agreed to make payments to 1,100 Americans who claimed they had been improperly deprived of their slave property.

The Book of Negroes, *compiled by British commanders when they evacuated New York City in 1783, lists some 3,000 African-Americans who had sought their freedom behind British lines and departed with the British army. Many ended up in Nova Scotia; some eventually made their way to Sierra Leone in West Africa. This page includes an entry for Deborah, formerly a slave of George Washington (sixth from bottom).*

VOLUNTARY EMANCIPATIONS

For a brief moment, the revolutionary upheaval appeared to threaten the continued existence of slavery. During the War of Independence, nearly every state prohibited or discouraged the further importation of slaves

VOICES OF FREEDOM

FROM ABIGAIL ADAMS TO JOHN ADAMS, Braintree, Mass. (March 31, 1776)

From their home in Massachusetts, Abigail Adams maintained a lively correspondence with her husband while he was in Philadelphia serving in the Continental Congress. In this letter, she suggests some of the limits of the patriots' commitment to liberty.

I wish you would write me a letter half as long as I write you, and tell me if you may where your fleet have gone? What sort of defense Virginia can make against our common enemy? Whether it is so situated as to make an able defense? . . . I have sometimes been ready to think that the passion for Liberty cannot be equally strong in the breasts of those who have been accustomed to deprive their fellow creatures of theirs. Of this I am certain, that it is not founded upon that generous and Christian principle of doing to others as we would that others should do unto us. . . .

I long to hear that you have declared an independency, and by the way in the new Code of Laws which I suppose it will be necessary for you to make I desire you would Remember the Ladies, and be more generous and favorable to them than your ancestors. Do not put such unlimited power into the hands of the husbands. Remember all men would be tyrants if they could. If particular care and attention is not paid to the Ladies we are determined to foment a Rebellion, and will not hold ourselves bound by any such laws in which we have no voice, or representation.

That your sex are naturally tyrannical is a truth so thoroughly established as to admit of no dispute, but such of you as wish to be happy willingly give up the harsh title of Master for the more tender and endearing one of Friend. Why then, not put it out of the power of the vicious and the lawless to use us with cruelty and indignity with impunity? Men of sense in all ages abhor those customs which treat us only as the vassals of your sex. Regard us then as beings placed by providence under your protection and in imitation of the Supreme Being make use of that power only for our happiness.

From Petitions of Slaves to
the Massachusetts Legislature (1773 and 1777)

Many slaves saw the struggle for independence as an opportunity to assert their own claims to freedom. Among the first efforts toward abolition were petitions by Massachusetts slaves to their legislature.

The efforts made by the legislative of this province in their last sessions to free themselves from slavery, gave us, who are in that deplorable state, a high degree of satisfaction. We expect great things from men who have made such a noble stand against the designs of their *fellow-men* to enslave them. We cannot but wish and hope Sir, that you will have the same grand object, we mean civil and religious liberty, in view in your next session. The divine spirit of *freedom*, seems to fire every breast on this continent. . . .

* * *

Your petitioners apprehend that they have in common with all other men a natural and unalienable right to that freedom which the great parent of the universe hath bestowed equally on all mankind and which they have never forfeited by any compact or agreement whatever but [they] were unjustly dragged by the hand of cruel power from their dearest friends and . . . from a populous, pleasant, and plentiful country and in violation of laws of nature and of nations and in defiance of all the tender feelings of humanity brought here . . . to be sold like beast[s] of burden . . . among a people professing the mild religion of Jesus. . . .

In imitation of the laudable example of the good people of these states your petitioners have long and patiently waited the event of petition after petition by them presented to the legislative body. . . . They cannot but express their astonishment that it has never been considered that every principle from which America has acted in the course of their unhappy difficulties with Great Britain pleads stronger than a thousand arguments in favor of your petitioners [and their desire] to be restored to the enjoyment of that which is the natural right of all men.

QUESTIONS

1. What does Abigail Adams have in mind when she refers to the "unlimited power" husbands exercise over their wives?

2. How do the slaves employ the principles of the Revolution for their own aims?

3. What do these documents suggest about the boundaries of freedom in the era of the American Revolution?

from Africa. The war left much of the plantation South in ruins. During the 1780s, a considerable number of slaveholders, especially in Virginia and Maryland, voluntarily emancipated their slaves. In 1796, Robert Carter III, a member of one of Virginia's wealthiest families, provided for the gradual emancipation of the more than 400 slaves he owned. In the same year, Richard Randolph, a member of another prominent Virginia family, drafted a will that condemned slavery as an "infamous practice," provided for the freedom of about 90 slaves, and set aside part of his land for them to own.

Farther south, however, the abolition process never got under way. When the British invaded South Carolina during the war, John Laurens, whose father Henry was Charleston's leading merchant and revolutionary-era statesman, proposed to "lead a corps of emancipated blacks in the defense of liberty." South Carolina's leaders rejected the idea. They would rather lose the war than lose their slaves. (However, black soldiers from the colony of Saint Domingue, some free and some slave, fought on the American side as part of a French contingent in the unsuccessful defense of Savannah, Georgia, in 1778.)

ABOLITION IN THE NORTH

Between 1777 (when Vermont drew up a constitution that banned slavery) and 1804 (when New Jersey acted), every state north of Maryland took steps toward emancipation, the first time in recorded history that legislative power had been invoked to eradicate slavery. But even here, where slavery was peripheral to the economy, the method of abolition reflected how property rights impeded emancipation. Generally, abolition laws did not free living slaves. Instead, they provided for the liberty of any child born in the future to a slave mother, but only after he or she had served the mother's master until adulthood as compensation for the owner's future economic loss. Children born to slave mothers in Pennsylvania after passage of the state's emancipation act of 1780 had to serve the owner for twenty-eight years, far longer than had been customary for white indentured servants. These laws gave indentured servitude, rapidly declining among whites, a new lease on life in the case of northern blacks.

Abolition in the North was a slow, drawn-out process. For slaves alive when the northern laws were passed, hopes for freedom rested on their own ability to escape and the voluntary actions of their owners. And many northern slaveholders proved reluctant indeed when it came to liberating their slaves. New York City, where one-fifth of the white families owned at least one slave in 1790, recorded only seventy-six such voluntary acts between 1783 and 1800. The first national census, in 1790, recorded 21,000 slaves still living in New York and 11,000 in New Jersey. New Yorker John Jay, chief justice of the United States, owned five slaves in 1800. As late as 1830, the census revealed that there were still 3,500 slaves in the North. The last slaves in Connecticut did not become free until 1848. In 1860, eighteen elderly slaves still resided in New Jersey.

FREE BLACK COMMUNITIES

All in all, the Revolution had a contradictory impact on American slavery and, therefore, on American freedom. Gradual as it was, the abolition of slav-

An engraving from a commemorative pitcher presented to the abolitionist Joseph Curtis by the New York Manumission Society in 1819 depicts Liberty releasing slaves from bondage. Curtis holds aloft a mirror reflecting the rising sun. Founded in 1785 by Alexander Hamilton, John Jay, and others, the Society was instrumental in the passage of New York's 1799 law providing for the gradual abolition of slavery.

VISIONS OF FREEDOM

Liberty Displaying the Arts and Sciences. *This 1792 painting by Samuel Jennings is one of the few visual images of the early republic explicitly to link slavery with tyranny and liberty with abolition. The female figure offers books to newly freed slaves. Other forms of knowledge depicted include a globe, an artist's palette, and the top of a column, evoking the republic of ancient Rome. Beneath her left foot lies a broken chain. In the background, free slaves enjoy some leisure time. Painted at the same time as the Haitian Revolution was spreading fear of a slave rebellion, the work celebrates emancipation rather than seeing it as threatening.*

QUESTIONS

1. What attributes of freedom does the artist emphasize most strongly in the painting?

2. How do the figures in the painting convey ideas about race?

A tray painted by an unknown artist in the early nineteenth century portrays Lemuel Haynes, a celebrated black preacher and critic of slavery.

ery in the North drew a line across the new nation, creating the dangerous division between free and slave states. Abolition in the North, voluntary emancipation in the Upper South, and the escape of thousands from bondage created, for the first time in American history, a sizable free black population (many of whose members took new family names like Freeman or Freeland).

On the eve of independence, virtually every black person in America had been a slave. Now, free communities, with their own churches, schools, and leaders, came into existence. They formed a standing challenge to the logic of slavery, a haven for fugitives, and a springboard for further efforts at abolition. In 1776, fewer than 10,000 free blacks resided in the United States. By 1810, their numbers had grown to nearly 200,000, most of them living in Maryland and Virginia. In all the states except Virginia, South Carolina, and Georgia, free black men who met taxpaying or property qualifications enjoyed the right to vote under new state constitutions. As the widespread use of the term "citizens of color" suggests, the first generation of free blacks, at least in the North, formed part of the political nation.

For many Americans, white as well as black, the existence of slavery would henceforth be recognized as a standing affront to the ideal of American freedom, a "disgrace to a free government," as a group of New Yorkers put it. In 1792, when Samuel Jennings of Philadelphia painted *Liberty Displaying the Arts and Sciences*, he included among the symbols of freedom a slave's broken chain, graphically illustrating how freedom had become identified not simply with political independence, but with emancipation. Nonetheless, the stark fact is that slavery survived the War of Independence and, thanks to the natural increase of the slave population, continued to grow. The national census of 1790 revealed that despite all those who had become free through state laws, voluntary emancipation, and escape, the number of slaves in the United States had grown to 700,000—200,000 more than in 1776.

DAUGHTERS OF LIBERTY

REVOLUTIONARY WOMEN

The revolutionary generation included numerous women who contributed to the struggle for independence. Deborah Sampson, the daughter of a poor Massachusetts farmer, disguised herself as a man and in 1782, at age twenty-one, enlisted in the Continental army. Sampson displayed remarkable courage, participating in several battles and extracting a bullet from her own leg so as not to have a doctor discover her identity. Ultimately, her commanding officer discovered her secret but kept it to himself, and she was honorably discharged at the end of the war. Years later, Congress awarded her a soldier's pension. Other patriotic women participated in crowd actions against merchants accused of seeking profits by holding goods off the market until their prices rose, contributed homespun goods to the army, and passed along information about British army movements.

In Philadelphia, Esther Reed, the wife of patriot leader Joseph Reed, and Sarah Franklin Bache, the daughter of Benjamin Franklin, organized a Ladies' Association to raise funds to assist American soldiers. They issued public broadsides calling for the "women of America" to name a "Treasuress" in each county in the United States who would collect funds and forward them to the governor's wife or, if he were unmarried, to "Mistress Washington." Referring to themselves as "brave Americans" who had been "born for liberty," the Ladies' Association illustrated how the Revolution was propelling women into new forms of public activism.

Within American households, women participated in the political discussions unleashed by independence. "Was not every fireside," John Adams later recalled, "a theater of politics?" Adams's own wife, Abigail Adams, as has been mentioned, was a shrewd analyst of public affairs. Mercy Otis Warren—the sister of James Otis and wife of James Warren, a founder of the Boston Committee of Correspondence—was another commentator on politics. She promoted the revolutionary cause in poems and dramas and later published a history of the struggle for independence.

In this painting from 1797, Deborah Sampson, who donned men's clothes to fight in the War of Independence, is portrayed in genteel female attire.

GENDER AND POLITICS

Gender, nonetheless, formed a boundary limiting those entitled to the full blessings of American freedom. Lucy Knox, the wife of General Henry Knox, wrote her husband during the war that when he returned home he should not consider himself "commander in chief of your own house, but be convinced that there is such a thing as equal command." But the winning of independence did not alter the family law inherited from Britain. The principle of "coverture" (described in Chapter 1) remained intact in the new

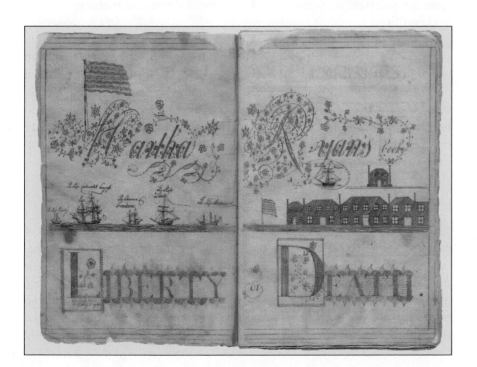

The 1781 cipher book (a notebook for mathematics exercises) of Martha Ryan, a North Carolina girl, contains images of ships and a port town and the patriotic slogan "Liberty or Death," illustrating how women shared in the political culture of the revolutionary era.

Keep within Compass, *a late-eighteenth-century engraving, illustrates the happiness of a "virtuous woman" if she remains within the world of the home and family, and some of the "troubles" awaiting her if she ventures outside. The woman appears in a space marked off by a compass, an instrument for drawing a circle.*

nation. The husband still held legal authority over the person, property, and choices of his wife. The words "to have and to hold" appeared in deeds conveying land from one owner to another, and in common marriage vows. Despite the expansion of democracy, politics remained overwhelmingly a male realm.

For men, political freedom meant the right to self-government, the power to consent to the individuals and political arrangements that ruled over them. For women, however, the marriage contract superseded the social contract. A woman's relationship to the larger society was mediated through her relationship with her husband. In both law and social reality, women lacked the essential qualification of political participation—the opportunity for autonomy based on ownership of property or control of one's own person. Since the common law included women within the legal status of their husbands, women could not be said to have property in themselves in the same sense as men.

Men took pride in qualities like independence and masculinity that distinguished them from women, and still considered control over their families an element of freedom. Among the deprivations of slavery cited by a group of black male petitioners in 1774 was that it prevented their wives from "submitting themselves to husbands in all things," as the natural order of the universe required. Many women who entered public debate felt the need to apologize for their forthrightness. A group of Quaker women who petitioned Congress during the War of Independence protesting the mistreatment of men who would not take an oath of loyalty hoped the lawmakers would "take no offense at the freedom of women."

Most men considered women to be naturally submissive and irrational, and therefore unfit for citizenship. While public debate in the revolutionary era viewed men's rights as natural entitlements, discussions of women's roles emphasized duty and obligations, not individual liberty. Their rights were nonpolitical, deriving from their roles as wives and mothers.

Overall, the republican citizen was, by definition, male. In a notable case, a Massachusetts court returned to James Martin confiscated property previously owned by his mother, who had fled the state during the Revolution with her Loyalist husband. Like other states, Massachusetts seized the land of those who had supported the British. But, the court ruled, it was unreasonable to expect a wife to exercise independent political judgment. To rebel against the king was one thing, but one could hardly ask Mrs. Martin to rebel against her husband. Therefore, the court reasoned, she should not have been punished for taking the British side.

REPUBLICAN MOTHERHOOD

The Revolution nonetheless did produce an improvement in status for many women. According to the ideology of "republican motherhood" that emerged as a result of independence, women played an indispensable role by training future citizens. The "foundation of national morality," wrote John Adams, "must be laid in private families." Even though republican motherhood ruled out direct female involvement in politics, it encouraged the expansion of educational opportunities for women, so that they could impart political wisdom to their children. Women, wrote Benjamin Rush, needed to have a "suitable education," to enable them to "instruct their sons in the principles of liberty and government."

The idea of republican motherhood reinforced the trend, already evident in the eighteenth century, toward the idea of "companionate" marriage, a voluntary union held together by affection and mutual dependency rather than male authority. In her letter to John Adams quoted above, Abigail Adams recommended that men should willingly give up "the harsh title of Master for the more tender and endearing one of Friend."

The structure of family life itself was altered by the Revolution. In colonial America, those living within the household often included indentured servants, apprentices, and slaves. After independence, southern slaves remained, rhetorically at least, members of the owner's "family." In the North, however, with the rapid decline of various forms of indentured servitude and apprenticeship, a more modern definition of the household as consisting of parents and their children took hold. Hired workers, whether domestic servants or farm laborers, were not considered part of the family.

Like slaves, some free women adapted the rhetoric of the Revolution to their own situation. Ann Baker Carson later recalled how she became estranged from the tyrannical husband she had married at age sixteen. "I was an American," she wrote. "A land of liberty had given me birth. I felt myself his equal." She left the marriage rather than continue as a "female slave." But unlike the case of actual slaves, the subordination of women did not become a major source of public debate until long after American independence.

THE ARDUOUS STRUGGLE FOR LIBERTY

The Revolution changed the lives of virtually every American. As a result of the long struggle against British rule, the public sphere, and with it the

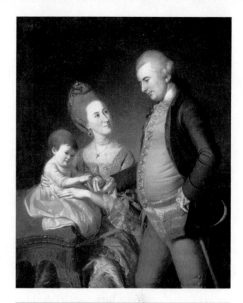

Portrait of John and Elizabeth Lloyd Cadwalader and Their Daughter Anne. *This 1772 portrait of a prominent Philadelphia businessman and his family by the American artist Charles Willson Peale illustrates the emerging ideal of the "companionate" marriage, which is based on affection rather than male authority.*

A little Boy and Girl reading.

ALL good Boys and Girls take Care to learn their Lessons, and read in a pretty Manner; which makes every Body admire them.

A little Boy and Girl bestowing their Charity.

ALL good Boys and Girls, when they see a poor Man, or Woman, or a Child in Want, will give them either Money or such Meat and Drink as they have to spare; which makes the whole World love them.

Two pages from A Little Pretty Pocket-Book, Intended for the Instruction and Amusement of Little Master Tommy and Pretty Miss Polly *(1787), which taught virtuous behavior to young children. The Revolution stimulated interest in improving female education.*

America Triumphant and Britannia in Distress. *An elaborate allegory representing American independence as a triumph of liberty, from an almanac published in Boston in 1781. An accompanying key explains the symbolism: (1) America [on the right] holds an olive branch of peace and invites all nations to trade with her. (2) News of America's triumph is broadcast around the world. (3) Britain, seated next to the devil, laments the loss of trade with America. (4) The British flag falls from a fortress. (5) European ships in American waters. (6) Benedict Arnold, the traitor, hangs himself in New York City [in fact, Arnold died of natural causes in London in 1801].*

right to vote, expanded markedly. Bound labor among whites declined dramatically, religious groups enjoyed greater liberty, blacks mounted a challenge to slavery in which many won their freedom, and women in some ways enjoyed a higher status. On the other hand, for Indians, many Loyalists, and the majority of slaves, American independence meant a deprivation of freedom.

In the words of one British admirer, "the genuine liberty on which America is founded is totally and entirely a new system of things and men." A new nation, which defined itself as an embodiment of freedom, had taken its place on the world stage. "Not only Britain, but all Europe are spectators of the conflict, the arduous struggle for liberty," wrote Ezra Stiles, a future president of Yale College, in 1775. "We consider ourselves as laying the foundation of a glorious future empire, and acting a part for the contemplation of the ages."

Like Stiles, many other Americans were convinced that their struggle for independence had worldwide significance. American independence, indeed, formed part of a larger set of movements that transformed the Atlantic world. The year 1776 saw not only Paine's *Common Sense* and Jefferson's Declaration but also the publication in England of Adam Smith's *The Wealth of Nations*, which attacked the British policy of closely regulating trade, and Jeremy Bentham's *Fragment on Government*, which criticized the nature of British government.

The winds of change were sweeping across the Atlantic world. The ideals of the American Revolution helped to inspire countless subsequent struggles for social equality and national independence, from the French Revolution, which exploded in 1789, to the uprising that overthrew the slave system in Haiti in the 1790s, to the Latin American wars for independence in the early nineteenth century, and numerous struggles of colonial peoples for nationhood in the twentieth. But within the new republic, the debate over who should enjoy the blessings of liberty would continue long after independence had been achieved.

SUGGESTED READING

BOOKS

Berkin, Carol. *Revolutionary Mothers: Women in the Struggle for American Independence* (2005). Presents profiles of women who took part in the movement for independence.

Boulton, Terry. *Taming Democracy: "The People," the Founders, and the Troubled Ending of the American Revolution* (2007). Argues that the democratic impulse unleashed by the War of Independence was to some extent reversed by the events of the 1780s.

Brown, Wallace. *The Good Americans: The Loyalists in the American Revolution* (1969). A study of Americans who remained loyal to Great Britain during the War of Independence.

Calloway, Colin. *The American Revolution in Indian Country* (1995). Examines how the Revolution affected Indians in each region of the United States.

Davis, David Brion. *The Problem of Slavery in the Age of Revolution* (1975). An influential study of the emergence of slavery as a major public issue in the Atlantic world.

Doerflinger, Thomas M. *A Vigorous Spirit of Enterprise: Merchants and Economic Development in Revolutionary Philadelphia* (1986). Explores how Philadelphia merchants participated in and reacted to the upheavals of the revolutionary era.

Frey, Sylvia R. *Water from the Rock: Black Resistance in a Revolutionary Age* (1991). A study of the many ways blacks sought to gain freedom for themselves during the Revolution.

Hatch, Nathan O. *The Democratization of American Christianity* (1989). A comprehensive account of the Revolution's impact on religion, and its aftermath.

Holton, Woody. *Forced Founders: Indians, Debtors, Slaves and the Making of the American Revolution in Virginia* (1999). Explores how the struggles of those outside Virginia's elite contributed to the movement for independence.

Kruman, Marc. *Between Authority and Liberty: State Constitution Making in Revolutionary America* (1997). The most detailed account of how state constitutions were changed during the era.

Nash, Gary. *The Unknown American Revolution: The Unruly Birth of Democracy and the Struggle to Create America* (2005). Emphasizes the role of ordinary Americans in the struggle for independence.

Schama, Simon. *Rough Crossing: Britain, the Slaves and the American Revolution* (2006). A detailed look at the experience of the thousands of slaves who escaped to British lines and their fate after the end of the War of Independence.

Taylor, Alan. *The Divided Ground: Indians, Settlers, and the Northern Borderland of the American Revolution* (2006). Examines the Revolution and its consequence in the Iroquois region of upstate New York.

Wood, Gordon. *The Radicalism of the American Revolution* (1992). An influential work that sees the Revolution as transforming a hierarchical society into a democratic one.

WEBSITES

Creating the United States: http://myloc.gov/exhibitions/creatingtheus/Pages/default.aspx

Religion and the Founding of the American Republic: www.loc.gov/exhibits/religion/religion.html

The Geography of Slavery in Virginia: www2.vcdh.virginia.edu/gos/

REVIEW QUESTIONS

1. Colonial society was based on inequality and obedience to authority. How did the American Revolution challenge the existing order of society?

2. Why did the Revolution cause more radical changes in Pennsylvania than elsewhere, and how was this radicalism demonstrated in the new state constitution?

3. Even after the American Revolution, conservatives denied that freedom and equality were synonymous, and opposed the growth of democracy. How did conservatives resist democratization in the South?

4. What role did the founders forsee for religion in American government and society?

5. What was the impact of the American Revolution on Native Americans?

6. What were the most important features of the new state constitutions?

7. How did popular views of property rights and the marriage contract prevent women and slaves from enjoying all the freedoms of the social contract?

8. What was "republican motherhood," and why was it significant?

FREEDOM QUESTIONS

1. Revolutions create change, challenge authority, and embolden marginalized groups to apply revolutionary ideals to their own situation. How did slaves, indentured servants, women, and Native Americans use the ideals of freedom to further their causes?

2. Wartime patriots insisted that freedom of conscience was a key part of liberty. What steps were taken to protect religious freedom, and did this freedom apply to everyone?

3. Before the American Revolution, Americans commonly held that the role of government was to promote the public good. After the war, merchants and other leaders advocated free trade and free markets, ruled by self-interest, as an expression of freedom. How did this new concept of freedom for some Americans deprive others of their freedoms?

4. Patriots claimed to be fighting a war to protect liberty and freedom in America, yet these ideas did not apply to everyone. How did Loyalists and Native Americans suffer, and why were their "natural rights" not protected?

5. "Slavery" and "liberty" were the two most frequently used terms in the debate over freedom. How did they apply to the political rights of white property owners, but then mean something entirely different when referring to African-Americans held as property?

KEY TERMS

one-house legislature (p. 223)

Thoughts on Government (p. 224)

balanced government (p. 224)

suffrage (p. 225)

"wall of separation" (p. 227)

Bill for Establishing Religious
   Freedom (p. 228)

free labor (p. 231)

free trade (p. 232)

inflation (p. 232)

Loyalists (p. 233)

Stockbridge Indians (p. 236)

General John Sullivan (p. 237)

abolition (p. 239)

freedom petitions (p. 241)

Lemuel Haynes (p. 241)

free blacks (p. 248)

"citizens of color" (p. 248)

republican motherhood (p. 250)

"suitable education" (p. 251)

REVIEW TABLE

Freedom and the State Constitutions

Provision	States
Eliminated property qualification for voting	All states except Virginia, Maryland, South Carolina
Eliminated all property and tax qualifications for voting	Vermont
Granted vote to free blacks who met qualifications	All states except Virginia, South Carolina, Georgia
One-house state government	Pennsylvania, Georgia, Vermont
Two-house state government	All states except Pennsylvania, Georgia, Vermont
Guaranteed complete religious liberty	New York
Deprived governor of veto power	All states except Massachusetts
Established annual elections to increase accountability	All states except North Carolina

CHAPTER 7

Founding a Nation, 1783–1789

In this late eighteenth-century engraving, Americans celebrate the signing of the Constitution beneath a temple of liberty.

- What were the achievements and problems of the Confederation government?

- What major disagreements and compromises molded the final content of the Constitution?

- How did Anti-Federalist concerns raised during the ratification process lead to the creation of the Bill of Rights?

- How did the definition of citizenship in the new republic exclude Native Americans and African-Americans?

During June and July of 1788, civic leaders in cities up and down the Atlantic coast organized colorful pageants to celebrate the ratification of the United States Constitution. For one day, Benjamin Rush commented of Philadelphia's parade, social class "forgot its claims," as thousands of marchers—rich and poor, businessman and apprentice—joined in a common public ceremony. New York's Grand Federal Procession was led by farmers, followed by the members of every craft in the city from butchers and coopers (makers of wooden barrels) to bricklayers, blacksmiths, and printers. Lawyers, merchants, and clergymen brought up the rear. The parades testified to the strong popular support for the Constitution in the nation's cities. And the prominent role of skilled artisans reflected how the Revolution had secured their place in the American public sphere. Elaborate banners and floats gave voice to the hopes inspired by the new structure of government. "May commerce flourish and industry be rewarded," declared Philadelphia's mariners and shipbuilders.

Throughout the era of the Revolution, Americans spoke of their nation as a "rising empire," destined to populate and control the entire North American continent. While Europe's empires were governed by force, America's would be different. In Jefferson's phrase, it would be "an empire of liberty," bound together by a common devotion to the principles of the Declaration of Independence. Already, the United States exceeded in size Great Britain, Spain, and France combined. As a new nation, it possessed many advantages, including physical isolation from the Old World (a significant asset between 1789 and 1815, when European powers were almost constantly at war), a youthful population certain to grow much larger, and a broad distribution of property ownership and literacy among white citizens.

On the other hand, while Americans dreamed of economic prosperity and continental empire, the nation's prospects at the time of independence were not entirely promising. Control of its vast territory was by no means secure. Nearly all of the 3.9 million Americans recorded in the first national census of 1790 lived near the Atlantic coast. Large areas west of the Appalachian Mountains remained in Indian hands. The British retained military posts on American territory near the Great Lakes, and there were fears that Spain might close the port of New Orleans to American commerce on the Mississippi River.

Away from navigable waterways, communication and transportation were primitive. The country was overwhelmingly rural—fewer than one American in thirty lived in a place with 8,000 inhabitants or more. The population consisted of numerous ethnic and religious groups and some 700,000 slaves, making unity difficult to achieve. No republican government had ever been established over so vast a territory or with so diverse a population. Local loyalties outweighed national patriotism. "We have no Americans in America," commented John Adams. It would take time for consciousness of a common nationality to sink deep roots.

Today, with the United States the most powerful country on earth, it is difficult to recall that in 1783 the future seemed precarious indeed for the fragile nation seeking to make its way in a world of hostile great powers. Profound questions needed to be answered. What course of development should the United States follow? How could the competing claims of local self-government, sectional interests, and national authority be balanced? Who should be considered full-fledged members of the American people, entitled to the blessings of liberty? These issues became the focus of heated debate as the first generation of Americans sought to consolidate their new republic.

AMERICA UNDER THE CONFEDERATION

THE ARTICLES OF CONFEDERATION

The first written constitution of the United States was the Articles of Confederation, drafted by Congress in 1777 and ratified by the states four years later. The Articles sought to balance the need for national coordination of the War of Independence with widespread fear that centralized political power posed a danger to liberty. It explicitly declared the new national government to be a "perpetual union." But it resembled less a blueprint for a common government than a treaty for mutual defense—in its own words, a "firm league of friendship" among the states. Under the Articles, the thirteen states retained their individual "sovereignty, freedom, and independence." The national government consisted of a one-house Congress, in which each state, no matter how large or populous, cast a single vote. There was no president to enforce the laws and no judiciary to interpret them. Major decisions required the approval of nine states rather than a simple majority.

The only powers specifically granted to the national government by the Articles of Confederation were those essential to the struggle for independence—declaring war, conducting foreign affairs, and making treaties with other governments. Congress had no real financial resources. It could coin money but lacked the power to levy taxes or regulate commerce. Its revenue came mainly from contributions by the individual states. To amend the Articles required the unanimous consent of the states, a formidable obstacle to change. Various amendments to strengthen the national government were proposed during the seven years (1781–1788) when the Articles of Confederation were in effect, but none received the approval of all the states.

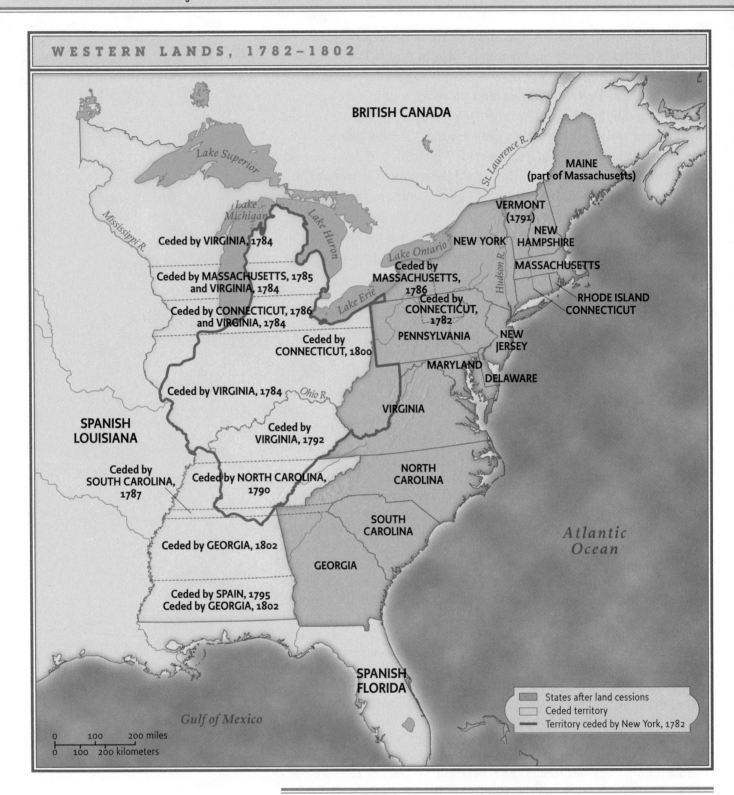

WESTERN LANDS, 1782–1802

BRITISH CANADA

Lake Superior

Lake Michigan

Lake Huron

Mississippi R.

St. Lawrence R.

MAINE
(part of Massachusetts)

VERMONT
(1791)

NEW
HAMPSHIRE

NEW YORK

Lake Ontario

MASSACHUSETTS

Hudson R.

RHODE ISLAND
CONNECTICUT

Ceded by VIRGINIA, 1784

Ceded by MASSACHUSETTS, 1785
and VIRGINIA, 1784

Ceded by CONNECTICUT, 1786
and VIRGINIA, 1784

Lake Erie

Ceded by
MASSACHUSETTS,
1786

Ceded by
CONNECTICUT,
1782

PENNSYLVANIA

NEW
JERSEY

Ceded by
CONNECTICUT, 1800

MARYLAND

DELAWARE

Ceded by VIRGINIA, 1784

Ohio R.

VIRGINIA

SPANISH
LOUISIANA

Ceded by
VIRGINIA, 1792

Ceded by
SOUTH CAROLINA,
1787

Ceded by NORTH CAROLINA,
1790

NORTH
CAROLINA

Ceded by GEORGIA, 1802

SOUTH
CAROLINA

GEORGIA

*Atlantic
Ocean*

Ceded by SPAIN, 1795
Ceded by GEORGIA, 1802

SPANISH
FLORIDA

Gulf of Mexico

States after land cessions
Ceded territory
Territory ceded by New York, 1782

0   100   200 miles
0   100   200 kilometers

*The creation of a nationally controlled public domain from western land ceded
by the states was one of the main achievements of the federal government under the
Articles of Confederation.*

The Articles made energetic national government impossible. But Congress in the 1780s did not lack for accomplishments. The most important was establishing national control over land to the west of the thirteen states and devising rules for its settlement. Disputes over access to western land almost prevented ratification of the Articles in the first place. Citing their original royal charters, which granted territory running all the way to the "South Sea" (the Pacific Ocean), states like Virginia, the Carolinas, and Connecticut claimed immense tracts of western land. Land speculators, politicians, and prospective settlers from states with clearly defined boundaries insisted that such land must belong to the nation at large. Only after the land-rich states, in the interest of national unity, ceded their western claims to the central government did the Articles win ratification.

CONGRESS AND THE WEST

Establishing rules for the settlement of this national domain—the area controlled by the federal government, stretching from the western boundaries of existing states to the Mississippi River—was by no means easy. Although some Americans spoke of it as if it were empty, some 100,000 Indians in fact inhabited the region. In the immediate aftermath of independence, Congress took the position that by aiding the British, Indians had forfeited the right to their lands. Little distinction was made among tribes that had sided with the enemy, those that had aided the patriots, and those in the interior that had played no part in the war at all. At peace conferences at Fort Stanwix, New York, in 1784 and Fort McIntosh near Pittsburgh the following year, American representatives demanded and received large surrenders of Indian land north of the Ohio River. Similar treaties soon followed with the Cherokee, Choctaw, and Chickasaw tribes in the South, although here Congress guaranteed the permanency of the Indians' remaining, much-reduced holdings. The treaties secured national control of a large part of the country's western territory.

When it came to disposing of western land and regulating its settlement, the Confederation government faced conflicting pressures. Many leaders believed that the economic health of the new republic required that farmers have access to land in the West. But they also saw land sales as a potential source of revenue and worried that unregulated settlement would produce endless conflicts with the Indians. Land companies, which lobbied Congress vigorously, hoped to profit by purchasing real estate and reselling it to settlers. The government, they insisted, should step aside and allow private groups to take control of the West's economic development.

SETTLERS AND THE WEST

The arrival of peace meanwhile triggered a large population movement from settled parts of the original states into frontier areas like upstate New York and across the Appalachian Mountains into Kentucky and Tennessee. To settlers, the right to take possession of western lands and use them as they saw fit was an essential element of American freedom. When a group of Ohioans petitioned Congress in 1785, assailing landlords and speculators

An engraving from The Farmer's and Mechanics Almanac *shows farm families moving west along a primitive road.*

who monopolized available acreage and asking that preference in land ownership be given to "actual settlements," their motto was "Grant us Liberty." Indeed, settlers paid no heed to Indian land titles and urged the government to set a low price on public land or give it away. They frequently occupied land to which they had no legal title. By the 1790s, Kentucky courts were filled with lawsuits over land claims, and many settlers lost land they thought they owned. Eventually, disputes over land forced many early settlers (including the parents of Abraham Lincoln) to leave Kentucky for opportunities in other states.

At the same time, however, like British colonial officials before them, many leaders of the new nation feared that an unregulated flow of population across the Appalachian Mountains would provoke constant warfare with Indians. Moreover, they viewed frontier settlers as disorderly and lacking in proper respect for authority—"our debtors, loose English people, our German servants, and slaves," Benjamin Franklin had once called them. Establishing law and order in the West and strict rules for the occupation of land there seemed essential to attracting a better class of settlers to the West and avoiding discord between the settled and frontier parts of the new nation.

THE LAND ORDINANCES

A series of measures approved by Congress during the 1780s defined the terms by which western land would be marketed and settled. Drafted by Thomas Jefferson, the Ordinance of 1784 established stages of self-government for the West. The region would be divided into districts initially governed by Congress and eventually admitted to the Union as member states. By a single vote, Congress rejected a clause that would have prohibited slavery

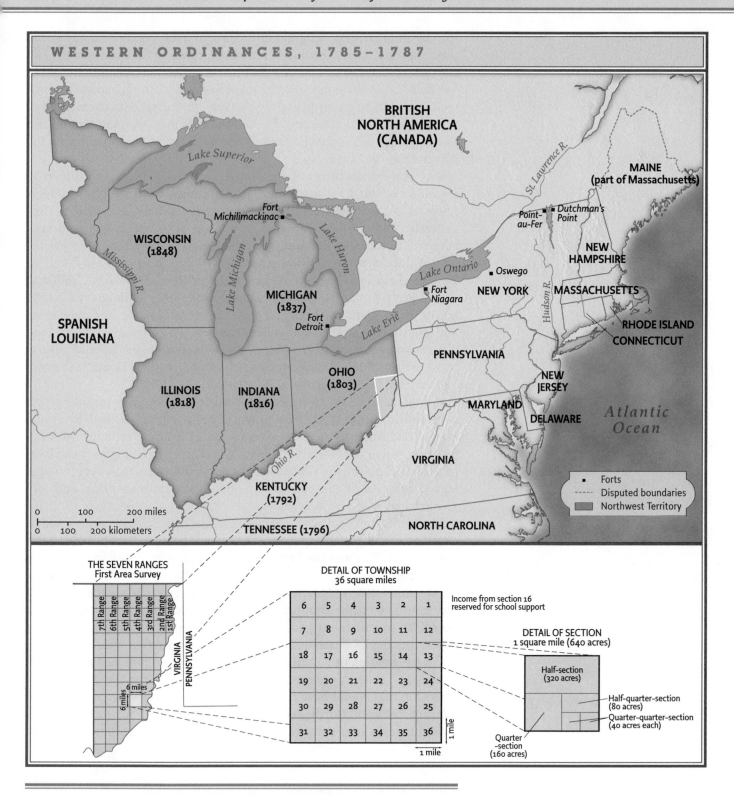

WESTERN ORDINANCES, 1785–1787

BRITISH NORTH AMERICA (CANADA)

Lake Superior

MAINE (part of Massachusetts)

Fort Michilimackinac

Point-au-Fer   Dutchman's Point

WISCONSIN (1848)

Lake Huron

NEW HAMPSHIRE

Lake Michigan

Lake Ontario   Oswego

St. Lawrence R.

MICHIGAN (1837)

Fort Niagara   NEW YORK   MASSACHUSETTS

Mississippi R.

Fort Detroit   Lake Erie

Hudson R.

RHODE ISLAND
CONNECTICUT

SPANISH LOUISIANA

PENNSYLVANIA

NEW JERSEY

ILLINOIS (1818)

INDIANA (1816)

OHIO (1803)

MARYLAND

DELAWARE

Atlantic Ocean

Ohio R.

VIRGINIA

KENTUCKY (1792)

■ Forts
- - - Disputed boundaries
Northwest Territory

TENNESSEE (1796)

NORTH CAROLINA

0   100   200 miles
0   100   200 kilometers

THE SEVEN RANGES
First Area Survey

7th Range
6th Range
5th Range
4th Range
3rd Range
2nd Range
1st Range

VIRGINIA
PENNSYLVANIA

6 miles
6 miles

DETAIL OF TOWNSHIP
36 square miles

6	5	4	3	2	1
7	8	9	10	11	12
18	17	16	15	14	13
19	20	21	22	23	24
30	29	28	27	26	25
31	32	33	34	35	36

Income from section 16 reserved for school support

DETAIL OF SECTION
1 square mile (640 acres)

Half-section (320 acres)

Half-quarter-section (80 acres)

Quarter-quarter-section (40 acres each)

Quarter-section (160 acres)

1 mile

1 mile

A series of ordinances in the 1780s provided for both the surveying and sale of lands in the public domain north of the Ohio River and the eventual admission of states carved from the area as equal members of the Union.

throughout the West. A second ordinance, in 1785, regulated land sales in the region north of the Ohio River, which came to be known as the Old Northwest. Land would be surveyed by the government and then sold in "sections" of a square mile (640 acres) at $1 per acre. In each township, one section would be set aside to provide funds for public education. The system promised to control and concentrate settlement and raise money for Congress. But settlers violated the rules by pressing westward before the surveys had been completed.

Like the British before them, American officials found it difficult to regulate the thirst for new land. The minimum purchase price of $640, however, put public land out of the financial reach of most settlers. They generally ended up buying smaller parcels from speculators and land companies. In 1787, Congress decided to sell off large tracts to private groups, including 1.5 million acres to the Ohio Company, organized by New England land speculators and army officers. (This was a different organization from the Ohio Company of the 1750s, mentioned in Chapter 4.) For many years, national land policy benefited private land companies and large buyers more than individual settlers. And for many decades, actual and prospective settlers pressed for a reduction in the price of government-owned land, a movement that did not end until the Homestead Act of 1862 offered free land on the public domain.

A final measure, the Northwest Ordinance of 1787, called for the eventual establishment of from three to five states north of the Ohio River and east of the Mississippi. Thus was enacted the basic principle of what Jefferson called the "empire of liberty"—rather than ruling over the West as a colonial power, the United States would admit the area's population as equal members of the political system. Territorial expansion and self-government would grow together.

The Northwest Ordinance pledged that "the utmost good faith" would be observed toward local Indians and that their land would not be taken without consent. This was the first official recognition that Indians continued to own their land. Congress realized that allowing settlers and state government simply to seize Indian lands would produce endless, expensive military conflicts on the frontier. "It will cost much less," one congressman noted, "to conciliate the good opinion of the Indians than to pay men for destroying them." But national land policy assumed that whether through purchase, treaties, or voluntary removal, the Indian presence would soon disappear. The Ordinance also prohibited slavery in the Old Northwest, a provision that would have far-reaching consequences when the sectional conflict between North and South developed. But for years, owners brought slaves into the area, claiming that they had voluntarily signed long-term labor contracts.

THE CONFEDERATION'S WEAKNESSES

Whatever the achievements of the Confederation government, in the eyes of many influential Americans they were outweighed by its failings. Both the national government and the country at large faced worsening economic problems. To finance the War of Independence, Congress had borrowed large sums of money by selling interest-bearing bonds and paying soldiers and suppliers in notes to be redeemed in the future. Lacking a secure source of revenue, it found itself unable to pay either interest or the debts themselves. With the United States now outside the British empire, American ships were barred from trading with the West Indies. Imported goods, however, flooded the market, undercutting the business of many craftsmen, driving down wages, and draining money out of the country.

With Congress unable to act, the states adopted their own economic policies. Several imposed tariff duties on goods imported from abroad. Indebted farmers, threatened with the loss of land because of failure to meet tax or mortgage payments, pressed state governments for relief, as did urban craftsmen who owed money to local merchants. In order to increase the amount of currency in circulation and make it easier for individuals to pay their debts, several states printed large sums of paper money. Others enacted laws postponing debt collection. Creditors considered such measures attacks on their property rights. In a number of states, legislative elections produced boisterous campaigns in which candidates for office denounced creditors for oppressing the poor and importers of luxury goods for undermining republican virtue.

SHAYS'S REBELLION

In late 1786 and early 1787, crowds of debt-ridden farmers closed the courts in western Massachusetts to prevent the seizure of their land for failure to pay taxes. They called themselves "regulators"—a term already used by protesters in the Carolina backcountry in the 1760s. The uprising came to be known as Shays's Rebellion, a name affixed to it by its opponents, after Daniel Shays, one of the leaders and a veteran of the War for Independence. Massachusetts had firmly resisted pressure to issue paper money or in other ways assist needy debtors. The participants in Shays's Rebellion believed they were acting in the spirit of the Revolution. They modeled their tactics on the crowd activities of the 1760s and 1770s and employed liberty trees and liberty poles as symbols of their cause. They received no sympathy from Governor James Bowdoin, who dispatched an army headed by former revolutionary war general Benjamin Lincoln. The rebels were dispersed in January 1787, and more than 1,000 were arrested. Without adherence to the rule of law, Bowdoin declared, Americans would descend into "a state of anarchy, confusion and slavery."

Observing Shays's Rebellion from Paris where he was serving as ambassador, Thomas Jefferson refused to be alarmed. "A little rebellion now and then is a good thing," he wrote to a friend. "The tree of liberty must be refreshed from time to time with the blood of patriots and tyrants." But the uprising was the culmination of a series of events in the 1780s that persuaded an influential group of Americans that the national government must be strengthened so that it could develop uniform economic policies and protect property owners from infringements on their rights by local majorities. The actions of state legislatures (most of them elected annually by an expanded voting population), followed by Shays's Rebellion, produced fears that the Revolution's democratic impulse had gotten out of hand.

"Our government," Samuel Adams wrote in 1785, "at present has liberty for its object." But among proponents of stronger national authority, liberty had lost some of its luster. The danger to individual rights, they came to

A Bankruptcy Scene. *Creditors repossess the belongings of a family unable to pay its debts, while a woman weeps in the background. Popular fears of bankruptcy led several states during the 1780s to pass laws postponing the collection of debts.*

James Madison, "father of the Constitution," in a miniature portrait painted by Charles Willson Peale in 1783. Madison was only thirty-six years old when the Constitutional Convention met.

Alexander Hamilton, another youthful leader of the nationalists of the 1780s, was born in the West Indies in 1755. This portrait was painted by Charles Willson Peale in the early 1790s.

believe, now arose not from a tyrannical central government, but from the people themselves. "Liberty," declared James Madison, "may be endangered by the abuses of liberty as well as the abuses of power." To put it another way, private liberty, especially the secure enjoyment of property rights, could be endangered by public liberty—unchecked power in the hands of the people.

NATIONALISTS OF THE 1780S

Madison, a diminutive, colorless Virginian and the lifelong disciple and ally of Thomas Jefferson, thought deeply and creatively about the nature of political freedom. He was among the group of talented and well-organized men who spearheaded the movement for a stronger national government. Another was Alexander Hamilton, who had come to North America as a youth from the West Indies, served at the precocious age of twenty as an army officer during the War of Independence, and married into a prominent New York family. Hamilton was perhaps the most vigorous proponent of an "energetic" government that would enable the new nation to become a powerful commercial and diplomatic presence in world affairs. Genuine liberty, he insisted, required "a proper degree of authority, to make and exercise the laws." Men like Madison and Hamilton were nation-builders. They came to believe during the 1780s that Americans were squandering the fruits of independence and that the country's future greatness depended on enhancing national authority.

The concerns voiced by critics of the Articles found a sympathetic hearing among men who had developed a national consciousness during the Revolution. Nationalists included army officers, members of Congress accustomed to working with individuals from different states, and diplomats who represented the country abroad. In the army, John Marshall (later a chief justice of the Supreme Court) developed "the habit of considering America as my country, and Congress as my government." Influential economic interests also desired a stronger national government. Among these were bondholders who despaired of being paid so long as Congress lacked a source of revenue, urban artisans seeking tariff protection from foreign imports, merchants desiring access to British markets, and all those who feared that the states were seriously interfering with property rights. While these groups did not agree on many issues, they all believed in the need for a stronger national government.

In September 1786, delegates from six states met at Annapolis, Maryland, to consider ways for better regulating interstate and international commerce. The delegates proposed another gathering, in Philadelphia, to amend the Articles of Confederation. Shays's Rebellion greatly strengthened the nationalists' cause. "The late turbulent scenes in Massachusetts," wrote Madison, underscored the need for a new constitution. "No respect," he complained, "is paid to the federal authority." Without a change in the structure of government, either anarchy or monarchy was the likely outcome, bringing to an end the experiment in republican government. Every state except Rhode Island, which had gone the farthest in developing its own debtor relief and trade policies, decided to send delegates to the Philadelphia convention. When they assembled in

May 1787, they decided to scrap the Articles of Confederation entirely and draft a new constitution for the United States.

A NEW CONSTITUTION

The fifty-five men who gathered for the Constitutional Convention included some of the most prominent Americans. Thomas Jefferson and John Adams, serving as diplomats in Europe, did not take part. But among the delegates were George Washington (whose willingness to lend his prestige to the gathering and to serve as presiding officer was an enormous asset), George Mason (author of Virginia's Declaration of Rights of 1776), and Benjamin Franklin (who had returned to Philadelphia after helping to negotiate the Treaty of Paris of 1783, and was now eighty-one years old). John Adams described the convention as a gathering of men of "ability, weight, and experience." He might have added, "and wealth." Few men of ordinary means attended. Although a few, like Alexander Hamilton, had risen from humble origins, most had been born into propertied families. They earned their livings as lawyers, merchants, planters, and large farmers. Nearly all were quite prosperous by the standards of the day.

At a time when fewer than one-tenth of 1 percent of Americans attended college, more than half the delegates had college educations. A majority had participated in interstate meetings of the 1760s and 1770s, and twenty-two had served in the army during the Revolution. Their shared social status and political experiences bolstered their common belief in the need to strengthen national authority and curb what one called "the excesses of democracy." To ensure free and candid debate, the deliberations took place in private. Madison, who believed the outcome would have great consequences for "the cause of liberty throughout the world," took careful notes. They were not published, however, until 1840, four years after he became the last delegate to pass away.

THE STRUCTURE OF GOVERNMENT

It quickly became apparent that the delegates agreed on many points. The new Constitution would create a legislature, an executive, and a national judiciary. Congress would have the power to raise money without relying on the states. States would be prohibited from infringing on the rights of property. And the government would represent the people. Hamilton's proposal for a president and Senate serving life terms, like the king and House of Lords of England, received virtually no support. The "rich and well-born," Hamilton told the convention, must rule, for the masses "seldom judge or determine right." Most delegates, however, hoped to find a middle ground between the despotism of monarchy and aristocracy and what they considered the excesses of popular self-government. "We had been

A fifty-dollar note issued by the Continental Congress during the War of Independence. Congress's inability to raise funds to repay such paper money in gold or silver was a major reason why nationalists desired a stronger federal government.

The Philadelphia State House (now called Independence Hall), where the Declaration of Independence was signed in 1776 and the Constitutional Convention took place in 1787.

too democratic," observed George Mason, but he warned against the danger of going to "the opposite extreme." The key to stable, effective republican government was finding a way to balance the competing claims of liberty and power.

Differences quickly emerged over the proper balance between the federal and state governments and between the interests of large and small states. Early in the proceedings, Madison presented what came to be called the Virginia Plan. It proposed the creation of a two-house legislature with a state's population determining its representation in each. Smaller states, fearing that populous Virginia, Massachusetts, and Pennsylvania would dominate the new government, rallied behind the New Jersey Plan. This called for a single-house Congress in which each state cast one vote, as under the Articles of Confederation. In the end, a compromise was reached—a two-house Congress consisting of a Senate in which each state had two members, and a House of Representatives apportioned according to population. Senators would be chosen by state legislatures for six-year terms. They were thus insulated from sudden shifts in public opinion. Representatives were to be elected every two years directly by the people.

THE LIMITS OF DEMOCRACY

Under the Articles of Confederation, no national official had been chosen by popular vote. Thus, the mode of choosing the House of Representatives represented an expansion of democracy. Popular election of at least one part of the political regime, Madison declared, was "essential to every plan of free government." The Constitution, moreover, imposed neither property nor religious qualifications for voting, leaving it to the states to set voting rules.

Overall, however, the new structure of government was less than democratic. The delegates sought to shield the national government from the popular enthusiasms that had alarmed them during the 1780s and to ensure that the right kind of men held office. The people would remain sovereign, but they would choose among the elite to staff the new government. The delegates assumed that the Senate would be composed of each state's most distinguished citizens. They made the House of Representatives quite small (initially 65 members, at a time when the Massachusetts assembly had 200), on the assumption that only prominent individuals could win election in large districts.

Nor did the delegates provide for direct election of either federal judges or the president. Members of the Supreme Court would be appointed by the president for life terms. The president would be chosen either by members of an electoral college or by the House of Representatives. The number of electors for each state was determined by adding together its allocation of senators and representatives. A state's electors would be chosen either by its legislature or by popular vote. In either case, the delegates assumed, electors would be prominent, well-educated individuals better qualified than ordinary voters to choose the head of state.

The actual system of election seemed a recipe for confusion. Each elector was to cast votes for two candidates for president, with the second-place finisher becoming vice president. If no candidate received a majority of the electoral ballots—as the delegates seem to have assumed would normally be the case—the president would be chosen from among the top three finishers by the House of Representatives, with each state casting one vote. The Senate would then elect the vice president. The delegates devised this extremely cumbersome system of indirect election because they did not trust ordinary voters to choose the president and vice president directly.

THE DIVISION AND SEPARATION OF POWERS

Hammered out in four months of discussion and compromise, the Constitution is a spare document of only 4,000 words that provides only the briefest outline of the new structure of government. (See the Appendix for the full text.) It embodies two basic political principles—federalism, sometimes called the "division of powers," and the system of "checks and balances" between the different branches of the national government, also known as the "separation of powers."

Federalism refers to the relationship between the national government and the states. Compared to the Articles of Confederation, the Constitution significantly strengthened national authority. It charged the president with enforcing the law and commanding the military. It empowered Congress to levy taxes, borrow money, regulate commerce, declare war, deal with foreign nations and Indians, and promote the "general welfare." Madison proposed to allow Congress to veto state laws, but this proved too far-reaching for most delegates. The Constitution did, however, declare national legislation the "supreme Law of the Land." And it included strong provisions to prevent the states from infringing on property rights. They were barred from issuing paper money, impairing contracts, interfering with interstate commerce, and levying their own import or export duties. On the other hand, most day-to-day affairs of government, from education to law enforcement, remained in the hands of the states. This principle of divided sovereignty was a recipe for debate, which continues to this day, over the balance of power between the national government and the states.

The "separation of powers," or the system of "checks and balances," refers to the way the Constitution seeks to prevent any branch of the national government from dominating the other two. To prevent an accumulation of power dangerous to liberty, authority within the government is diffused and balanced against itself. Congress enacts laws, but the president can veto them, and a two-thirds majority is required to pass legislation over his objection. Federal judges are nominated by the president and approved by Congress, but to ensure their independence, the judges then serve for life. The president can be impeached by the House and removed from office by the Senate for "high crimes and misdemeanors."

THE DEBATE OVER SLAVERY

The structure of government was not the only source of debate at the Constitutional Convention. As Madison recorded, "the institution of slavery and its implications" divided the delegates at many sessions. Those who gathered in Philadelphia included numerous slaveholders, as well as some dedicated advocates of abolition. Madison, like Jefferson a Virginia slaveholder who detested slavery, told the convention that the "distinction of color" had become the basis for "the most oppressive dominion ever exercised by man over man." Yet he later assured the Virginia ratifying convention that the Constitution offered slavery "better security than any that now exists."

The words "slave" and "slavery" did not appear in the Constitution—a concession to the sensibilities of delegates who feared they would "contaminate the glorious fabric of American liberty." As Luther Martin of Maryland wrote, his fellow delegates "anxiously sought to avoid the admission of expressions which might be odious to the ears of Americans." But, he continued, they were "willing to admit into their system those *things* which the *expressions signified.*" The document prohibited Congress from abolishing the African slave trade for twenty years. It required states to return to their owners fugitives from bondage. And it provided that three-fifths of the slave population would be counted in determining each state's representation in the House of Representatives and its electoral votes for president.

South Carolina's delegates had come to Philadelphia determined to defend slavery, and they had a powerful impact on the final document. They originated the fugitive slave clause, the three-fifths clause, and the electoral college. They insisted on strict limits on the power of Congress to levy taxes within the states, fearing future efforts to raise revenue by taxing slave property. They threatened disunion if the Atlantic slave trade were prohibited immediately, as the New England states and Virginia, with its abundance of native-born slaves, demanded. Their threats swayed many delegates. Gouverneur Morris, one of Pennsylvania's delegates, declared that he was being forced to decide between offending the southern states or doing injustice to "human nature." For the sake of national unity, he said, he would choose the latter.

This advertisement for the sale of 100 slaves from Virginia to states farther south appeared in a Richmond newspaper only a few months after the signing of the Constitution. Slavery was a major subject of debate at the Constitutional Convention.

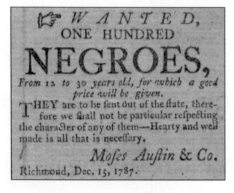

The Signing of the Constitution, *by mid-nineteenth-century American artist Thomas Pritchard Rossiter, depicts the conclusion of the Constitutional Convention of 1787. Among the founding fathers depicted are James Wilson, signing the document at the table in the center, and George Washington, presiding from the dais with an image of the sun behind him.*

SLAVERY IN THE CONSTITUTION

The Constitution's slavery clauses were compromises, efforts to find a middle ground between the institution's critics and defenders. Taken together, however, they embedded slavery more deeply than ever in American life and politics. The slave trade clause allowed a commerce condemned by civilized society—one that had been suspended during the War of Independence—to continue until 1808. On January 1, 1808, the first day that Congress was allowed under the Constitution, it prohibited the further importation of slaves. But in the interim, partly to replace slaves who had escaped to the British and partly to provide labor for the expansion of slavery to fertile land away from the coast, some 170,000 Africans were brought to the new nation as slaves. South Carolina and Georgia imported 100,000. This number represented more than one-quarter of all the slaves brought to mainland North America after 1700.

The fugitive slave clause accorded slave laws "extraterritoriality"—that is, the condition of bondage remained attached to a person even if he or she escaped to a state where slavery had been abolished. John Jay, while serving in Spain on a diplomatic mission, once wrote of how he missed the "free air" of America. Jay was probably unaware of the phrase's full implications. In the famous *Somerset* case of 1772, the lawyer for a West Indian slave brought to Britain had obtained his client's freedom by invoking the memorable words, "the air of England is too pure for a slave to breathe" (that is, the moment any person sets foot on British soil, he or she becomes free). Yet the new federal Constitution required all the states, North and South, to recognize and help police the institution of slavery. For slaves, there was no "free air" in America.

The Constitution gave the national government no power to interfere with slavery in the states. And the three-fifths clause allowed the white South to exercise far greater power in national affairs than the size of its

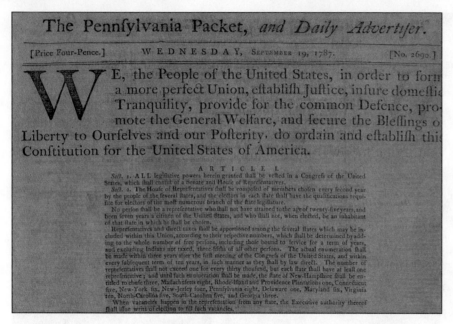

The preamble to the Constitution, as printed in a Pennsylvania newspaper two days after the Constitutional Convention adjourned.

free population warranted. The clause greatly enhanced the number of southern votes in the House of Representatives and therefore in the electoral college (where, as noted above, the number of electors for each state was determined by adding together its number of senators and representatives). Of the first sixteen presidential elections, between 1788 and 1848, all but four placed a southern slaveholder in the White House.

Even the initial failure to include a Bill of Rights resulted, in part, from the presence of slavery. As South Carolina delegate Charles C. Pinckney explained, "such bills generally begin with declaring that all men are by nature born free," a declaration that would come "with a very bad grace, when a large part of our property consists in men who are actually born slaves."

But some slaveholders detected a potential threat buried in the Constitution. Patrick Henry, who condemned slavery but feared abolition, warned that, in time of war, the new government might take steps to arm and liberate the slaves. "May Congress not say," he asked, "that every black man must fight? Did we not see a little of this [in the] last war?" What Henry could not anticipate was that the war that eventually destroyed slavery would be launched by the South itself to protect the institution.

THE FINAL DOCUMENT

Gouverneur Morris put the finishing touches on the final draft of the new Constitution, trying to make it, he explained, "as clear as our language would permit." For the original preamble, which began, "We the people of the States of New Hampshire, Massachusetts," etc., he substituted the far more powerful, "We the people of the United States." He added a statement of the Constitution's purposes, including to "establish justice," promote "the general welfare," and "secure the blessings of liberty"—things the Articles of Confederation, in the eyes of most of the delegates, had failed to accomplish.

The last session of the Constitutional Convention took place on September 17, 1787. Benjamin Franklin urged the delegates to put aside individual objections and approve the document, whatever its imperfections. "The older I grow," he remarked, "the more apt I am to . . . pay more respect to the judgment of others." Of the forty-five delegates who remained in Philadelphia, thirty-nine signed the Constitution. It was then sent to the states for ratification.

The Constitution created a new framework for American development. By assigning to Congress power over tariffs, interstate commerce, the coining of money, patents, rules for bankruptcy, and weights and measures, and by prohibiting states from interfering with property rights, it made possible a national economic market. It created national political institutions, reduced the powers of the states, and sought to place limits on popular

This satirical engraving by Amos Doolittle (who created the image of the Battle of Concord in Chapter 5) depicts some of the issues in the debate over the ratification of the Constitution. The wagon in the center is carrying Connecticut and sinking into the mud under the weight of debts and paper money as "Federals" and "Antifederals" try to pull it out. Federals call for the state to "comply with Congress" (that is, to pay money requisitioned by the national government); the Antifederals reply "tax luxury" and "success to Shays," a reference to Shays's Rebellion. The Connecticut shoreline and the buildings of Manhattan are on the right. Underneath the three merchant ships is a phrase criticizing the tariffs that states were imposing on imports from one another (which the Constitution prohibited). At the bottom is the biblical motto, "A house divided against itself cannot stand," later made famous by Abraham Lincoln.

democracy. "The same enthusiasm, *now* pervades all classes in favor of *government*," observed Benjamin Rush, "that actuated us in favor of *liberty* in the years 1774 and 1775." Whether "all classes" truly agreed may be doubted, for the ratification process unleashed a nationwide debate over the best means of preserving American freedom.

THE RATIFICATION DEBATE AND THE ORIGIN OF THE BILL OF RIGHTS

THE FEDERALIST

Even though the Constitution provided that it would go into effect when nine states, not all thirteen as required by the Articles of Confederation, had given their approval, ratification was by no means certain. Each state held an election for delegates to a special ratifying convention. A fierce public battle ensued, producing hundreds of pamphlets and newspaper articles and spirited campaigns to elect delegates. To generate support, Hamilton, Madison, and Jay composed a series of eighty-five essays that appeared in newspapers under the pen name Publius and were gathered as a book, *The Federalist*, in 1788. Hamilton wrote fifty, Madison thirty, and Jay the remainder. Today, the essays are regarded as among the most important American contributions to political thought. At the time, however, they represented only one part of a much larger national debate over ratification, reflected in innumerable pamphlets, newspaper articles, and public meetings.

Again and again, Hamilton and Madison repeated that rather than posing a danger to Americans' liberties, the Constitution in fact protected them. Hamilton's essays sought to disabuse Americans of their fear of political power. Government, he insisted, was an expression of freedom, not its enemy. Any government could become oppressive, but with its checks and balances and division of power, the Constitution made political tyranny almost impossible. Hamilton insisted that he was "as zealous an advocate for liberty as any man whatever." But "want of power" had been the fatal flaw of the Articles. At the New York ratifying convention, Hamilton assured the delegates that the Constitution had created "the perfect balance between liberty and power."

"EXTEND THE SPHERE"

Madison, too, emphasized how the Constitution was structured to prevent abuses of authority. But in several essays, especially *Federalist* nos. 10 and 51, he moved beyond such assurances to develop a strikingly new vision of the relationship between government and society in the United States. Madison identified the essential dilemma, as he saw it, of the new republic—government must be based on the will of the people, yet the people had shown themselves susceptible to dangerous enthusiasms. Most worrisome, they had threatened property rights, whose protection was the "first object of government." The problem of balancing democracy and respect for property would only grow in the years ahead because, he warned, economic development would inevitably increase the numbers of poor. What was to prevent them from using their political power to secure "a more equal distribution" of wealth?

The answer, Madison explained, lay not simply in the way power balanced power in the structure of government, but in the nation's size and diversity. Previous republics had existed only in small territories—the Dutch republic, or Italian city-states of the Renaissance. But, argued Madison, the very size of the United States was a source of stability, not, as many feared, weakness. "Extend the sphere," he wrote. The multiplicity of religious denominations, he argued, offered the best security for religious liberty. Likewise, in a nation as large as the United States, so many distinct interests—economic, regional, and political—would arise, that no single one would ever be able to take over the government and oppress the rest. Every majority would be a coalition of minorities, and thus "the rights of individuals" would be secure.

Madison's writings did much to shape the early nation's understanding of its new political institutions. In arguing that the size of the republic helped to secure Americans' rights, they reinforced the tradition that saw continuous westward expansion as essential to freedom. And in basing the preservation of freedom on the structure of government and size of the republic, not the character of the people, his essays represented a major shift away from the "republican" emphasis on a virtuous citizenry devoted to the common good as the foundation of proper government. Madison helped to popularize the "liberal" idea that men are generally motivated by self-interest, and that the good of society arises from the clash of these private interests.

THE ANTI-FEDERALISTS

Opponents of ratification, called Anti-Federalists, insisted that the Constitution shifted the balance between liberty and power too far in the direction of the latter. Anti-Federalists lacked the coherent leadership of the Constitution's defenders. They included state politicians fearful of seeing their influence diminish, among them such revolutionary heroes as Samuel Adams, John Hancock, and Patrick Henry. Small farmers, many of whom supported the state debtor-relief measures of the 1780s that the Constitution's supporters deplored, also saw no need for a stronger central government. Some opponents of the Constitution denounced the document's protections for slavery; others warned that the powers of Congress were so broad that it might enact a law for abolition.

Anti-Federalists repeatedly predicted that the new government would fall under the sway of merchants, creditors, and others hostile to the interests of ordinary Americans. Repudiating Madison's arguments in *Federalist* nos. 10 and 51, Anti-Federalists insisted that "a very extensive territory cannot be governed on the principles of freedom." Popular self-government, they claimed, flourished best in small communities, where rulers and ruled interacted daily. Only men of wealth, "ignorant of the sentiments of the middling and lower class of citizens," would have the resources to win election to a national government. The result of the Constitution, warned Melancton Smith of New York, a member of Congress under the Articles of Confederation, would be domination of the "common people" by the "well-born." "This," Smith predicted, "will be a government of oppression."

Liberty was the Anti-Federalists' watchword. America's happiness, they insisted, "arises from the freedom of our institutions and the limited nature of our government," both threatened by the new Constitution. Maryland Anti-Federalists had caps manufactured bearing the word "Liberty," to wear to the polls when members of the state's ratification convention were elected. To the vision of the United States as an energetic great power, Anti-Federalists counterposed a way of life grounded in local, democratic institutions. "What is Liberty?" asked James Lincoln of South Carolina. "The power of governing yourselves. If you adopt this constitution, have you this power? No."

Anti-Federalists also pointed to the Constitution's lack of a Bill of Rights, which left unprotected rights such as trial by jury and freedom of speech and the press. The absence of a Bill of Rights, declared Patrick Henry, was "the most absurd thing to mankind that ever the world saw." State constitutions had bills of rights, yet the states, Henry claimed, were now being

Order of Procession,
In honor of the Constitution of the United States.

THIS DAY.

AT 8 o'clock this morning, 23d of July, 10 guns will fire, when the Procession will parade, and proceed by the following rout, viz.
———Down Broad-way to Great Dock-Street, thence through Hanover-square, Queen, Chatham, Division and Arundel-streets; and from thence through Bullock-street to Bayard's-house.

2 Horsemen with Trumpets.
1 piece of Artillery.
First Division.
Foresters in frocks, carrying axes.
Columbus in his ancient dress, on horseback.
6 Foresters, &c.
A Plough.
A Harrow.
Farmers.

Fourth Division.
Carpenters.
Farriers.
Hatters.
Peruke-makers and Hair-dressers.
Fifth Division.
White Smiths.
Cutlers.
Stone Masons.
Brick Layers.
Painters and Glaziers.
Cabinet Makers.
Windsor Chair Makers.
Upholsterers.
Fringe Makers.
Paper Stainers.
Civil Engineers.
Sixth Division.
Ship Wrights.
Black Smiths.
Ship Joiners.
Boat Builders.

In New York City's Grand Federal Procession of 1788, celebrating the ratification of the Constitution, members of each trade and occupation marched together. This document illustrates the variety of crafts in the pre-industrial city.

VOICES OF FREEDOM

FROM DAVID RAMSAY,
The History of the American Revolution (1789)

A member of the Continental Congress from South Carolina, David Ramsay published his history of the Revolution the year after the Constitution was ratified. In this excerpt, he lauds the principles of representative government and the right of future amendment, embodied in the state constitutions and adopted in the national one, as unique American political principles and the best ways of securing liberty.

The world has not hitherto exhibited so fair an opportunity for promoting social happiness. It is hoped for the honor of human nature, that the result will prove the fallacy of those theories that mankind are incapable of self government. The ancients, not knowing the doctrine of representation, were apt in their public meetings to run into confusion, but in America this mode of taking the sense of the people, is so well understood, and so completely reduced to system, that its most populous states are often peaceably convened in an assembly of deputies, not too large for orderly deliberation, and yet representing the whole in equal proportion. These popular branches of legislature are miniature pictures of the community, and from their mode of election are likely to be influenced by the same interests and feelings with the people whom they represent....

In no age before, and in no other country, did man ever possess an election of the kind of government, under which he would choose to live. The constituent parts of the ancient free governments were thrown together by accident. The freedom of modern European governments was, for the most part, obtained by concessions, or liberality of monarchs, or military leaders. In America alone, reason and liberty concurred in the formation of constitutions ... In one thing they were all perfect. They left the people in the power of altering and amending them, whenever they pleased. In this happy peculiarity they placed the science of politics on a footing with the other sciences, by opening it to improvements from experience, and the discoveries of future ages. By means of this power of amending American constitutions, the friends of mankind have fondly hoped that oppression will one day be no more.

From James Winthrop,
Anti-Federalist Essay Signed "Agrippa" (1787)

A local official in Middlesex, Massachusetts, James Winthrop published sixteen public letters between November 1787 and February 1788 opposing ratification of the Constitution.

It is the opinion of the ablest writers on the subject, that no extensive empire can be governed upon republican principles, and that such a government will degenerate into a despotism, unless it be made up of a confederacy of smaller states, each having the full powers of internal regulation. This is precisely the principle which has hitherto preserved our freedom. No instance can be found of any free government of considerable extent which has been supported upon any other plan. Large and consolidated empires may indeed dazzle the eyes of a distant spectator with their splendor, but if examined more nearly are always found to be full of misery. . . . It is under such tyranny that the Spanish provinces languish, and such would be our misfortune and degradation, if we should submit to have the concerns of the whole empire managed by one empire. To promote the happiness of the people it is necessary that there should be local laws; and it is necessary that those laws should be made by the representatives of those who are immediately subject to [them]. . . .

It is impossible for one code of laws to suit Georgia and Massachusetts. They must, therefore, legislate for themselves. Yet there is, I believe, not one point of legislation that is not surrendered in the proposed plan. Questions of every kind respecting property are determinable in a continental court, and so are all kinds of criminal causes. The continental legislature has, therefore, a right to make rules in all cases. . . . No rights are reserved to the citizens. . . . This new system is, therefore, a consolidation of all the states into one large mass, however diverse the parts may be of which it is composed. . . .

A bill of rights . . . serves to secure the minority against the usurpation and tyranny of the majority. . . . The experience of all mankind has proved the prevalence of a disposition to use power wantonly. It is therefore as necessary to defend an individual against the majority in a republic as against the king in a monarchy.

QUESTIONS

1. Why does Ramsay feel that the power to amend the Constitution is so important a political innovation?

2. Why does Winthrop believe that a Bill of Rights is essential in the Constitution?

3. How do Ramsay and Winthrop differ concerning how the principle of representation operates in the United States?

asked to surrender most of their powers to the federal government, with no requirement that it respect Americans' basic liberties.

In general, pro-Constitution sentiment flourished in the nation's cities and in rural areas closely tied to the commercial marketplace. The Constitution's most energetic supporters were men of substantial property. But what George Bryan of Pennsylvania, a supporter of ratification, called the "golden phantom" of prosperity also swung urban artisans, laborers, and sailors behind the movement for a government that would use its "energy and power" to revive the depressed economy. Anti-Federalism drew its support from small farmers in more isolated rural areas such as the Hudson Valley of New York, western Massachusetts, and the southern back-country.

In the end, the supporters' energy and organization, coupled with their domination of the colonial press, carried the day. Ninety-two newspapers and magazines existed in the United States in 1787. Of these, only twelve published a significant number of Anti-Federalist pieces. Madison also won support for the new Constitution by promising that the first Congress would enact a Bill of Rights. By mid-1788, the required nine states had ratified. Although there was strong dissent in Massachusetts, New York, and Virginia, only Rhode Island and North Carolina voted against ratification, and they subsequently had little choice but to join the new government. Anti-Federalism died. But as with other movements in American history that did not immediately achieve their goals—for example, the Populists of the late nineteenth century—some of the Anti-Federalists' ideas eventually entered the political mainstream. To this day, their belief that a too-powerful central government is a threat to liberty continues to influence American political culture.

THE BILL OF RIGHTS

Ironically, the parts of the Constitution Americans most value today—the freedoms of speech, the press, and religion; protection against unjust criminal procedures; equality before the law—were not in the original document. All of these but the last (which was enshrined in the Fourteenth Amendment after the Civil War) were contained in the first ten amendments, known as the Bill of Rights. Madison was so convinced that the balances of the Constitution would protect liberty that he believed a Bill of Rights "redundant or pointless." Amendments restraining federal power, he believed, would have no effect on the danger to liberty posed by unchecked majorities in the states, and no list of rights could ever anticipate the numerous ways that Congress might operate in the future. "Parchment barriers" to the abuse of authority, he observed, would prove least effective when most needed. Madison's prediction would be amply borne out at future times of popular hysteria, such as during the Red Scare following World War I and the McCarthy era of the 1950s, when all branches of government joined in trampling on freedom of expression, and during World War II, when hatred of a foreign enemy led to the internment of more than 100,000 Japanese-Americans, most of them citizens of the United States.

Nevertheless, every new state constitution contained some kind of declaration of citizens' rights, and large numbers of Americans—Federalist

VISIONS OF FREEDOM

SOCIETY of PEWTERERS

SOLID AND PURE.

Banner of the Society of Pewterers. *A banner carried by one of the many artisan groups that took part in New York City's Grand Federal Procession of 1788 celebrating the ratification of the Constitution. The banner depicts artisans at work in their shop and some of their products. The words "Solid and Pure," and the inscription at the upper right, link the quality of their pewter to their opinion of the new frame of government and hopes for the future. The inscription reads:*

> *The Federal Plan Most Solid and Secure*
> *Americans Their Freedom Will Endure*
> *All Arts Shall Flourish in Columbia's Land*
> *And All Her Sons Join as One Social Band*

QUESTIONS

1. Why do you think the pewterers believed that the new Constitution would promote Americans' freedom and prosperity, as stated in the inscription?

2. How does the banner reflect the pewterers' pride in their craft?

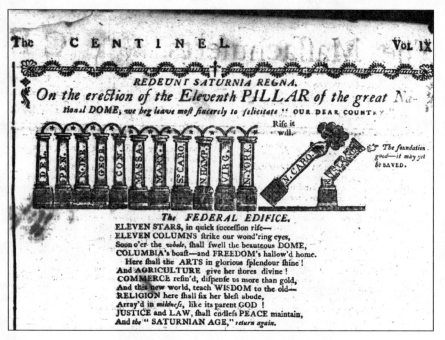

An engraving and poem, published in 1788 in an American newspaper, after New York became the eleventh state to ratify the new Constitution. North Carolina would ratify in 1789 and Rhode Island in 1790.

and Anti-Federalist alike—believed the new national Constitution should also have one. In order to "conciliate the minds of the people," as Madison put it, he presented to Congress a series of amendments that became the basis of the Bill of Rights, which was ratified by the states in 1791. The First Amendment prohibited Congress from legislating with regard to religion or infringing on freedom of speech, freedom of the press, or the right of assembly. The Second upheld the people's right to "keep and bear arms" in conjunction with "a well-regulated militia." Others prohibited abuses such as arrests without warrants and forcing a person accused of a crime to testify against himself, and reaffirmed the right to trial by jury.

In a sense, the Bill of Rights offered a definition of the "unalienable rights" Jefferson had mentioned in the Declaration of Independence—rights inherent in the human condition. Not having been granted by government in the first place, they could not be rescinded by government. In case any had been accidentally omitted, the Ninth Amendment declared that rights not specifically mentioned in the Constitution were "retained by the people." Its suggestion that the Constitution was not meant to be complete opened the door to future legal recognition of rights not grounded in the actual text (such as the right to privacy). The Tenth Amendment, meant to answer fears that the federal government would ride roughshod over the states, affirmed that powers not delegated to the national government or prohibited to the states continued to reside with the states.

The roots and even the specific language of some parts of the Bill of Rights lay far back in English history. The Eighth Amendment, prohibiting excessive bail and cruel and unusual punishments, incorporates language that originated in a declaration by the House of Lords in 1316 and was repeated centuries later in the English Bill of Rights and the constitutions of a number of American states.

Other provisions reflected the changes in American life brought about by the Revolution. The most remarkable of these was constitutional recognition of religious freedom. Unlike the Declaration of Independence, which invokes the blessing of divine providence, the Constitution is a purely secular document that contains no reference to God and bars religious tests for federal officeholders. The First Amendment prohibits the federal government from legislating on the subject of religion—a complete departure from British and colonial precedent. Under the Constitution it was and remains possible, as one critic complained, for "a papist, a Mohomatan, a deist, yea an atheist" to become president of the United States. Madison was so adamant about separating church and state that he even opposed the appointment of chaplains to serve Congress and the military.

Today, when Americans are asked to define freedom, they instinctively

RATIFICATION OF THE CONSTITUTION

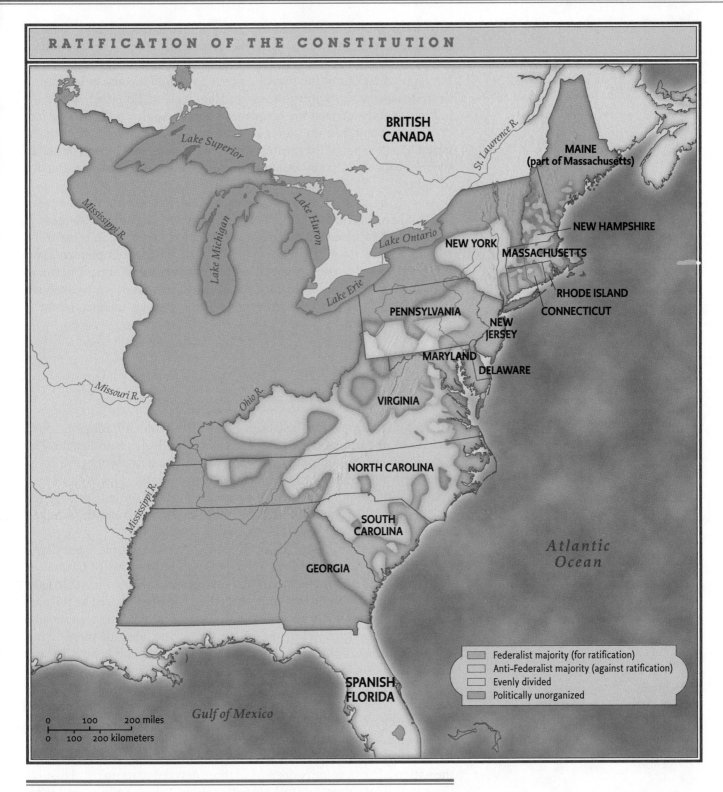

Federalists—those who supported the new Constitution—tended to be concentrated in cities and nearby rural areas, while backcountry farmers were more likely to oppose the new frame of government.

turn to the Bill of Rights and especially the First Amendment, with its guarantees of freedom of speech, the press, and religion. Yet the Bill of Rights aroused little enthusiasm on ratification and for decades was all but ignored. Not until the twentieth century would it come to be revered as an indispensable expression of American freedom. Nonetheless, the Bill of Rights subtly affected the language of liberty. Applying only to the federal government, not the states, it reinforced the idea that concentrated national power posed the greatest threat to freedom. And it contributed to the long process whereby freedom came to be discussed in the vocabulary of rights.

Among the most important rights were freedom of speech and the press, vital building blocks of a democratic public sphere. Once an entitlement of members of Parliament and colonial assemblies, free speech came to be seen as a basic right of citizenship. Although the legal implementation remained to be worked out, and serious infringements would occur at many points in American history, the Bill of Rights did much to establish freedom of expression as a cornerstone of the popular understanding of American freedom.

"WE THE PEOPLE"

NATIONAL IDENTITY

The colonial population had been divided by ethnicity, religion, class, and status and united largely by virtue of their allegiance to Britain. The Revolution created not only a new nation but also a new collective body, the American people, whose members were to enjoy freedom as citizens in a new political community. Since government in the United States rested on the will of the people, it was all the more important to identify who the people were.

The Constitution opens with the words, "We the People," describing those who, among other things, are to possess "the Blessings of Liberty" as a birthright and pass them on to "Posterity." (Abraham Lincoln would later cite these words to argue that since the nation had been created by the people, not the states, the states could not dissolve it.) Although one might assume that the "people" of the United States included all those living within the nation's borders, the text made clear that this was not the case. The Constitution identifies three populations inhabiting the United States: Indians, treated as members of independent tribes and not part of the American body politic; "other persons"—that is, slaves; and the "people." Only the third were entitled to American freedom.

Every nation confronts the task of defining its identity. Historians have traditionally distinguished between "civic nationalism," which envisions the nation as a community open to all those devoted to its political institutions and social values, and "ethnic nationalism," which defines the nation as a community of descent based on a shared ethnic heritage, language, and culture. At first glance, the United States appears to conform to the civic model. It lacked a clear ethnic identity or long-established national boundaries—the political principles of the Revolution held Americans together. To be an American, all one had to do was commit oneself to an ideology of liberty, equality, and democracy. From the outset, however,

A medal issued to Red Jacket, a Seneca chief, during his visit to Philadelphia (then the national capital) in 1792. It depicts George Washington offering an Indian a peace pipe. The agricultural scene in the background was intended to suggest that Indians should take up farming.

GEORGE WASHINGTON
PRESIDENT.
1792.

American nationality combined both civic and ethnic definitions. For most of our history, American citizenship has been defined by blood as well as by political allegiance.

INDIANS IN THE NEW NATION

The early republic's policies toward Indians and African-Americans illustrate the conflicting principles that shaped American nationality. American leaders agreed that the West should not be left in Indian hands, but they disagreed about the Indians' ultimate fate. The government hoped to encourage the westward expansion of white settlement, which implied one of three things: the removal of the Indian population to lands even farther west, their total disappearance, or their incorporation into white "civilization" with the expectation that they might one day become part of American society.

Many white Americans, probably most, deemed Indians savages unfit for citizenship. Indian tribes had no representation in the new government, and the Constitution excluded Indians "not taxed" from being counted in determining each state's number of congressmen. The treaty system gave them a unique status within the American political system. But despite this recognition of their sovereignty, treaties were essentially ways of transferring land from Indians to the federal government or the states. Often, a

The signing of the Treaty of Greenville of 1795, painted by an unknown member of General Anthony Wayne's staff. In the treaty, a group of tribes ceded most of the area of the current state of Ohio, along with the site that became the city of Chicago, to the United States.

INDIAN TRIBES, 1790

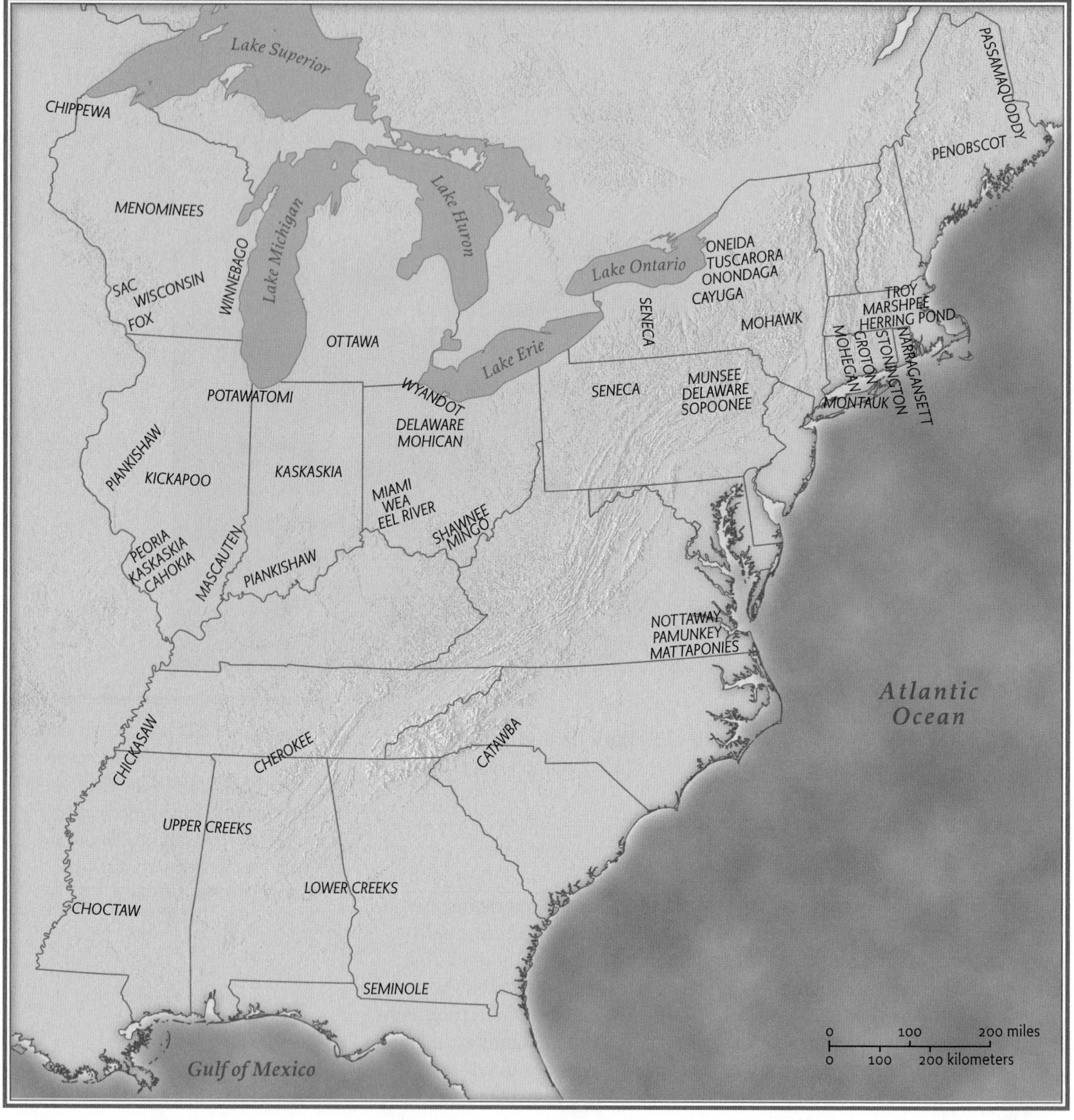

CHIPPEWA

MENOMINEES

SAC
WISCONSIN
FOX

Lake Superior

Lake Michigan

Lake Huron

WINNEBAGO

OTTAWA

POTAWATOMI

WYANDOT
DELAWARE
MOHICAN

PIANKISHAW

KICKAPOO

KASKASKIA

MIAMI
WEA
EEL RIVER

SHAWNEE
MINGO

PEORIA
KASKASKIA
CAHOKIA

MASCAUTEN

PIANKISHAW

Lake Ontario

ONEIDA
TUSCARORA
ONONDAGA
CAYUGA

SENECA

MOHAWK

SENECA

MUNSEE
DELAWARE
SOPOONEE

Lake Erie

PASSAMAQUODDY

PENOBSCOT

TROY
MARSHPEE
HERRING POND
NARRAGANSETT
STONINGTON
CROTON
MOHEGAN
MONTAUK

NOTTAWAY
PAMUNKEY
MATTAPONIES

Atlantic
Ocean

CHICKASAW

CHEROKEE

CATAWBA

UPPER CREEKS

LOWER CREEKS

CHOCTAW

SEMINOLE

Gulf of Mexico

| 0 | 100 | 200 miles |
| 0 | 100 | 200 kilometers |

By 1790, the Indian population had declined significantly from the early colonial era, but the area west of the Appalachian Mountains was still known as "Indian country."

How did the definition of citizenship in the new republic exclude
Native Americans and African-Americans?

285

treaty was agreed to by only a small portion of a tribe, but the whole tribe
was then forced to accept its legitimacy.

During Washington's administration, Secretary of War Henry Knox
hoped to deal with Indians with a minimum of warfare and without undermining the new nation's honor. He recognized, he said in 1794, that
American treatment of the continent's native inhabitants had been even
"more destructive to the Indian" than Spain's conduct in Mexico and Peru.
His conciliatory policy had mixed results. Congress forbade the transfer of
Indian land without federal approval. But several states ignored this directive and continued to negotiate their own agreements.

Open warfare continued in the Ohio Valley. In 1791, Little Turtle, leader
of the Miami Confederacy, inflicted a humiliating defeat on American
forces led by Arthur St. Clair, the American governor of the Northwest
Territory. With 630 dead, this was the costliest loss ever suffered by the
United States Army at the hands of Indians. In 1794, 3,000 American troops
under Anthony Wayne defeated Little Turtle's forces at the Battle of Fallen
Timbers. This led directly to the Treaty of Greenville of 1795, in which
twelve Indian tribes ceded most of Ohio and Indiana to the federal government. The treaty also established the "annuity" system—yearly grants of
federal money to Indian tribes that institutionalized continuing government influence in tribal affairs and gave outsiders considerable control
over Indian life.

Many prominent figures, however, rejected the idea that Indians were
innately inferior to white Americans. Thomas Jefferson believed that
Indians merely lived at a less advanced stage of civilization. Indians could
become full-fledged members of the republic by abandoning communal
landholding and hunting in favor of small-scale farming. Once they "possessed property," Jefferson told one Indian group, they could "join us in our
government" and, indeed, "mix your blood with ours."

To pursue the goal of assimilation, Congress in the 1790s authorized
President Washington to distribute agricultural tools and livestock to
Indian men and spinning wheels and looms to Indian women. To whites,
the adoption of American gender norms, with men working the land and
women tending to their homes, would be a crucial sign that the Indians
were becoming "civilized." But the American notion of civilization
required so great a transformation of Indian life that most tribes rejected it.
One missionary was told, "If we want to work, we know how to do it
according to our own way and as it pleases us." To Indians, freedom meant
retaining tribal autonomy and identity, including the ability to travel widely in search of game. "Since our acquaintance with our brother white people," declared a Mohawk speaker at a 1796 treaty council, "that which we
call freedom and liberty, becomes an entire stranger to us." There was no
room for Indians who desired to retain their traditional way of life in the
American empire of liberty.

BLACKS AND THE REPUBLIC

By 1790, the number of African-Americans far exceeded the Indian population within the United States. The status of free blacks was somewhat indeterminate. Nowhere does the original Constitution define who in fact are

Table 7.1 TOTAL POPULATION AND BLACK POPULATION OF THE UNITED STATES, 1790

State	Total Population	Slaves	Free Blacks
New England:			
New Hampshire	141,899	158	630
Vermont*	85,341	0	271
Massachusetts	378,556	0	5,369
Connecticut	237,655	2,764	2,771
Rhode Island	69,112	948	3,484
Maine**	96,643	0	536
Middle States:			
New York	340,241	21,324	4,682
New Jersey	184,139	11,423	2,762
Pennsylvania	433,611	3,737	6,531
South:			
Delaware	59,096	8,887	3,899
Maryland	319,728	103,036	8,043
Virginia	747,610	292,627	12,866
North Carolina	395,005	100,572	5,041
South Carolina	249,073	107,094	1,801
Georgia	82,548	29,264	398
Kentucky*	73,677	12,430	114
Tennessee*	35,691	3,417	361
Total	3,929,625	697,624	59,557

*Vermont, Kentucky, and Tennessee were territories that had not yet been admitted as states.
**Maine was part of Massachusetts in 1790.

citizens of the United States. The individual states were left free to determine the boundaries of liberty. The North's gradual emancipation acts assumed that former slaves would remain in the country, not be colonized abroad. Northern statesmen like Hamilton, Jay, and Franklin worked for abolition, and some helped to establish schools for black children. During the era of the Revolution, free blacks enjoyed at least some of the legal rights accorded to whites, including, in most states, the right to vote. Some cast ballots in the election of delegates to conventions that ratified the Constitution. The large majority of blacks, of course, were slaves, and slavery rendered them all but invisible to those imagining the American community. Slaves, as Edmund Randolph, the nation's first attorney general, put it, were "not . . . constituent members of our society," and the language of liberty did not apply to them.

One of the era's most widely read books, *Letters from an American Farmer*, published in France in 1782 by Hector St. John de Crèvecoeur, strikingly illustrated this process of exclusion. Born in France, Crèvecoeur had taken part in the unsuccessful defense of Quebec during the Seven Years' War. Instead of returning home, he came to New York City in 1759. As a trader and explorer, he visited most of the British mainland colonies, as well as the Ohio and Mississippi Valleys. Crèvecoeur eventually married the daughter of a prominent New York landowner and lived with his own family on a farm in Orange County. Seeking to remain neutral during the War of Independence, he suffered persecution by both patriots and the British, and eventually returned to France.

In *Letters from an American Farmer*, Crèvecoeur popularized the idea, which would become so common in the twentieth century, of the United States as a melting pot. "Here," he wrote, "individuals of all nations are melted into a new one." The American left behind "all his ancient prejudices and manners [and received] new ones from the new mode of life he has embraced." Crèvecoeur was well aware of what he called "the horrors of slavery." But when he posed the famous question, "What then is the American, this new man?" he answered, "a mixture of English, Scotch, Irish, French, Dutch, Germans, and Swedes. . . . He is either a European, or the descendant of a European." This at a time when fully one-fifth of the population (the highest proportion in U.S. history) consisted of Africans and their descendants.

Like Crèvecoeur, many white Americans excluded blacks from their conception of the American people. The Constitution empowered Congress to create a uniform system by which immigrants became citizens, and the Naturalization Act of 1790 offered the first legislative definition of American nationality. With no debate, Congress restricted the process of becoming a citizen from abroad to "free white persons."

The law initiated a policy that some historians, with only partial accuracy, call "open immigration." For Europeans, the process was indeed open. Only in the last quarter of the nineteenth century were groups of whites, beginning with prostitutes, convicted felons, lunatics, and persons likely to become a "public charge," barred from entering the country. For the first century of the republic, virtually the only white persons in the entire world ineligible to claim American citizenship were those unwilling to renounce hereditary titles of nobility, as required in an act of

1795. And yet, the word "white" in the Naturalization Act excluded a large majority of the world's population from emigrating to the "asylum for mankind" and partaking in the blessings of American freedom. For eighty years, no non-white immigrant could become a naturalized citizen. Africans were allowed to do so in 1870, but not until the 1940s did persons of Asian origin become eligible. (Native Americans were granted American citizenship in 1924.)

JEFFERSON, SLAVERY, AND RACE

Man's liberty, John Locke had written, flowed from "his having reason." To deny liberty to those who were not considered rational beings did not seem to be a contradiction. White Americans increasingly viewed blacks as permanently deficient in the qualities that made freedom possible—the capacity for self-control, reason, and devotion to the larger community. These were the characteristics that Jefferson, in a famous comparison of the races in his book *Notes on the State of Virginia*, published in 1785, claimed blacks lacked, partly due to natural incapacity and partly because the bitter experience of slavery had (quite understandably, he felt) rendered them disloyal to the nation. Jefferson was reluctant to "degrade a whole race of men from the rank in the scale of beings which their Creator may perhaps have given them." He therefore voiced the idea "as a suspicion only," that blacks "are inferior to the whites in the endowments both of body and mind." Yet this "unfortunate" circumstance, he went on, "is a powerful obstacle to the emancipation of these people."

Jefferson was obsessed with the connection between heredity and environment, race and intelligence. His belief that individuals' abilities and achievements are shaped by social conditions inclined him to hope that no group was fixed permanently in a status of inferiority. He applied this principle, as has been noted, to Indians, whom he believed naturally the equal of whites in intelligence. In the case of blacks, however, he could not avoid the "suspicion" that nature had permanently deprived them of the qualities that made republican citizenship possible. Benjamin Banneker, a free African-American from Maryland who had taught himself the principles of mathematics, sent Jefferson a copy of an astronomical almanac he had published, along with a plea for the abolition of slavery. Jefferson replied, "Nobody wishes more than I do to see such proofs as you exhibit, that nature has given to our black brethren, talents equal to the other colors of men." To his friend Joel Barlow, however, Jefferson suggested that a white person must have helped Banneker with his calculations.

"Nothing is more certainly written in the book of fate," wrote Jefferson, "than that these people are to be free." Yet he felt that America should have a homogeneous citizenry with common experiences, values, and inborn abilities. Americans' essential sameness would underpin the ideal of equal rights for all, making it possible to realize the idea of the public good. Black Americans, Jefferson affirmed, should eventually enjoy the natural rights enumerated in the Declaration of Independence, but in Africa or the Caribbean, not in the United States. He foresaw Indians merging with whites into a single people, but he was horrified by the idea of miscegenation between blacks and whites. Unlike Indians, blacks, he believed, were unfit

The artist John Singleton Copley, best known for his portraits of prominent Americans and Britons, painted this young African-American in the late 1770s. The subject probably worked on a New England fishing boat. This is one of the era's very few portraits of a black person.

for economic independence and political self-government. Freeing the slaves without removing them from the country would endanger the nation's freedom. In his will, Tadeusz Kosciuszko, a Polish aristocrat who fought for American independence, left funds for Jefferson to purchase and free slaves, "giving them liberty in my name." But when his friend died in 1817, Jefferson transferred the money to an official of the American Colonization Society, an organization dedicated to sending freed slaves to Africa. Eventually, the funds were divided among Kosciuszko's heirs in Europe.

Jefferson reflected the divided mind of his generation. Some prominent Virginians assumed that blacks could become part of the American nation. Edward Coles, an early governor of Illinois, brought his slaves from Virginia, freed them, and settled them on farms. Washington, who died in 1799, provided in his will that his 277 slaves would become free after the death of his wife, Martha. (Feeling uncomfortable living among men and women who looked forward to her death, she emancipated them the following year.) Jefferson thought of himself as a humane owner. The slave cabins at his estate, Monticello, one visitor wrote, "are all much better than I have seen on any other plantation," although he could not help adding that "their cabins form a most unpleasant contrast with the palace that rises so near them." Believing the slave trade immoral, Jefferson tried to avoid selling slaves to pay off his mounting debts. But his will provided for the freedom of only five, all relatives of his slave Sally Hemings, with whom he appears to have had fathered one or more children. When he died in 1826, Jefferson owed so much money that his property, including the majority of his more than 200 slaves, was sold at auction, thus destroying the slave community he had tried to keep intact.

PRINCIPLES OF FREEDOM

Even as the decline of apprenticeship and indentured servitude narrowed the gradations of freedom among the white population, the Revolution widened the divide between free Americans and those who remained in slavery. Race, one among many kinds of legal and social inequality in colonial America, now emerged as a convenient justification for the existence of slavery in a land that claimed to be committed to freedom. Blacks' "natural faculties," Alexander Hamilton noted in 1779, were "probably as good as ours." But the existence of slavery, he added, "makes us fancy many things that are founded neither in reason or experience."

"We the people" increasingly meant only white Americans. "Principles of freedom, which embrace only half mankind, are only half systems," declared the anonymous author of a Fourth of July speech in Hartford, Connecticut, in 1800. "Declaration of Independence," he wondered, "where art thou now?" The answer came from a Richmond newspaper: "Tell us not of principles. Those principles have been annihilated by the existence of slavery among us."

SUGGESTED READING

BOOKS

Amar, Akhil Reed. *Bill of Rights: Creation and Reconstruction* (1998). Presents the history of the Bill of Rights from its ratification through the Reconstruction era.

Berkin, Carol. *A Brilliant Solution: Inventing the American Constitution* (2002). A lively account of the proceedings of the Constitutional Convention.

Cornell, Saul. *The Other Founders: Anti-Federalism and the Dissenting Tradition in America, 1788–1828* (1999). A careful examination of the ideas of those who opposed ratification of the Constitution.

Dowd, Gregory E. *A Spirited Resistance: The North American Indian Struggle for Unity, 1745–1815* (1992). Contains an important discussion of the place of Indians in the new American nation.

Holton, Woody. *Unruly Americans and the Origins of the Constitution* (2007). Argues that the political activities of ordinary Americans helped to shape the Constitution.

Kettner, James T. *The Development of American Citizenship, 1608–1870* (1978). Traces the development of the definition of American citizenship from early colonization to the aftermath of the Civil War.

Levy, Leonard. *The Establishment Clause: Religion and the First Amendment* (1994). A historical account of one of the key components of the Bill of Rights.

MacLeod, Duncan J. *Slavery, Race, and the American Revolution* (1974). A British scholar's interpretation of the role of race and slavery in the revolutionary era.

McMillin, James A. *The Final Victims: Foreign Slave Trade to North America, 1783–1810* (2004). A study of the last phase of the American slave trade, as made possible by the new Constitution.

Morris, Richard B. *The Forging of the Union, 1781–1789* (1987). A comprehensive account of the nation's history under the Articles of Confederation.

Nash, Gary. *The Forgotten Fifth: African Americans in the Age of Revolution* (2006). A comprehensive survey of the Revolution's impact on blacks, slave and free.

Nedelsky, Jennifer. *Private Property and the Limits of American Constitutionalism* (1990). Analyzes how the protection of private property shaped the writing of the Constitution.

Rakove, Jack. *Original Meanings: Politics and Ideas in the Making of the Constitution* (1996). An influential interpretation of the ideas that went into the drafting of the Constitution.

Richards, Leonard L. *Shays's Rebellion: The American Revolution's Final Battle* (2002). The most recent study of the uprising that helped to produce the Constitution.

Wood, Gordon S. *The Creation of the American Republic, 1776–1789* (1969). Presents the evolution of American political ideas and institutions from the Declaration of Independence to the ratification of the Constitution.

WEBSITES

Creating the United States: http://myloc.gov/exhibitions/creatingtheus/Pages/default.aspx

Explore the Constitution: www.constitutioncenter.org

REVIEW QUESTIONS

1. How did the limited central government created by the Articles of Confederation reflect the issues behind the Revolution and fears for individual liberties?

2. Explain the importance of the Land Ordinances of 1784 and 1785, as well as the Northwest Ordinance of 1787, both for the early republic and future generations.

3. Who were the nationalists of the late 1780s, and why did they believe a new national constitution was necessary?

4. The Constitution has been described as a "bundle of compromises." Which compromises were the most significant in shaping the direction of the new nation and why?

5. What were the major arguments against the Constitution put forth by the Anti-Federalists?

6. How accurate was Hector St. John de Crèvecoeur's description of America as a melting pot?

FREEDOM QUESTIONS

1. Why did settlers believe that the right to take possession of western lands and use them as they saw fit was an essential part of American freedom? Why did this same freedom not apply to the Native Americans already on the land?

2. James Madison argued that "Liberty may be endangered by the abuses of liberty as well as the abuse of power." Explain what Madison meant, and how this statement affected the ideas of freedom for the participants at the Constitutional Convention.

3. Why and how did the framers of the Constitution design a government that protected slavery and its advocates?

4. How important was the Bill of Rights at the time it was enacted, and how important is it now?

5. Why does the Constitution never use the word "slavery"?

KEY TERMS

Land Ordinances of 1784 and 1785 (pp. 262–263)

Shays's Rebellion (p. 265)

Northwest Ordinance of 1787 (p. 266)

international commerce (p. 266)

checks and balances (p. 269)

separation of powers (p. 269)

"high crimes and misdemeanors" (p. 270)

three-fifths clause (p. 270)

The Federalist (p. 273)

Anti-Federalists (p. 275)

Bill of Rights (p. 275)

civic nationalism (p. 282)

ethnic nationalism (p. 282)

Miami Confederacy (p. 285)

Battle of Fallen Timbers (p. 285)

Treaty of Greenville (p. 285)

"annuity" system (p. 285)

gradual emancipation (p. 286)

Letters from an American Farmer (p. 286)

"open immigration" (p. 286)

Notes on the State of Virginia (p. 287)

REVIEW TABLE

Debates Surrounding the Constitutional Convention

Interests at Stake	Issue	Resolution
Big v. small states	Representation in Congress • Virginia plan • New Jersey plan	• Proportional representation in House • Equal representation in Senate
Slave v. non-slave states	• Size of population in determining proportional representation • When to stop the slave trade	• Three-fifths clause • Twenty years after ratification Congress could ban the slave trade
Advocates of strong v. weak central government	• Preventing one branch of the government from dominating the others • Preventing the federal government from dominating state governments	• Separation of powers • Division of powers
Common people v. wealthy elite	The role of citizens in the new government	Voters excluded from direct election of Senate and president

CHAPTER 8

Securing the Republic, 1790–1815

This colorful image from around the time of the War of 1812 contains numerous symbols of freedom, among them the goddess of liberty with her liberty cap, a broken chain at the sailor's feet, the fallen crown (under his left foot), a broken royal scepter, and the sailor himself, since English interference with American shipping was one of the war's causes.

☞ FOCUS QUESTIONS

• What issues made the politics of the 1790s so divisive?

• How did competing views of freedom and global events promote the political divisions of the 1790s?

• What were the achievements and failures of Jefferson's presidency?

• What were the causes and significant results of the War of 1812?

An early American coin, bearing an image of liberty and the word itself, as directed by Congress in a 1792 law.

On April 30, 1789, in New York City, the nation's temporary capital, George Washington became the first president under the new Constitution. All sixty-nine electors had awarded him their votes. Dressed in a plain suit of "superfine American broad cloth" rather than European finery, Washington took the oath of office on the balcony of Federal Hall before a large crowd that reacted with "loud and repeated shouts" of approval. He then retreated inside to deliver his inaugural address before members of Congress and other dignitaries.

Washington's speech expressed the revolutionary generation's conviction that it had embarked on an experiment of enormous historical importance, whose outcome was by no means certain. "The preservation of the sacred fire of liberty and the destiny of the republican model of government," Washington proclaimed, depended on the success of the American experiment in self-government. Most Americans seemed to agree that freedom was the special genius of American institutions. In a resolution congratulating Washington on his inauguration, the House of Representatives observed that he had been chosen by "the freest people on the face of the earth." When the time came to issue the nation's first coins, Congress directed that they bear the image not of the head of state (as would be the case in a monarchy) but "an impression emblematic of liberty," with the word itself prominently displayed.

American leaders believed that the success of the new government depended, above all, on maintaining political harmony. They were especially anxious to avoid the emergence of organized political parties, which had already appeared in several states. Parties were considered divisive and disloyal. "They serve to organize faction," Washington would later declare, and to substitute the aims of "a small but artful" minority for the "will of the nation." The Constitution makes no mention of political parties, and the original method of electing the president assumes that candidates will run as individuals, not on a party ticket (otherwise, the second-place finisher would not have become vice president). Nonetheless, national political parties quickly arose. Originating in Congress, they soon spread to the general populace. Instead of harmony, the 1790s became, in the words of one historian, an "age of passion," with each party questioning the loyalty of the other and lambasting its opponent in the most extreme terms. Political rhetoric became inflamed because the stakes seemed so high—nothing less than the legacy of the Revolution, the new nation's future, and the survival of American freedom.

POLITICS IN AN AGE OF PASSION

President Washington provided a much-needed symbol of national unity. Having retired to private life after the War of Independence (despite some army officers' suggestion that he set himself up as a dictator), he was a model of self-sacrificing republican virtue. His vice president, John Adams, was widely respected as one of the main leaders in the drive for independence. Washington brought into his cabinet some of the new nation's most prominent political leaders, including Thomas Jefferson as secretary of state and Alexander Hamilton to head the Treasury Department. He also appointed a Supreme Court of six members, headed by John Jay of New York. But harmonious government proved short-lived.

HAMILTON'S PROGRAM

Political divisions first surfaced over the financial plan developed by Secretary of the Treasury Hamilton in 1790 and 1791. Hamilton's immediate aims were to establish the nation's financial stability, bring to the government's support the country's most powerful financial interests, and encourage economic development. His long-term goal was to make the United States a major commercial and military power. Hamilton's model was Great Britain. The goal of national greatness, he believed, could never be realized if the government suffered from the same weaknesses as under the Articles of Confederation.

Hamilton's program had five parts. The first step was to establish the new nation's credit-worthiness—that is, to create conditions under which persons would loan money to the government by purchasing its bonds, confident that they would be repaid. Hamilton proposed that the federal government assume responsibility for paying off at its full face value the national debt inherited from the War of Independence, as well as outstanding debts of the states. Second, he called for the creation of a new national debt. The old debts would be replaced by new interest-bearing bonds issued to the government's creditors. This would give men of economic substance a stake in promoting the new nation's stability, since the stronger and more economically secure the federal government, the more likely it would be to pay its debts.

The third part of Hamilton's program called for the creation of a Bank of the United States, modeled on the Bank of England, to serve as the nation's main financial agent. A private corporation rather than a branch of the government, it would hold public funds, issue bank notes that would serve as currency, and make loans to the government when necessary, all the while returning a tidy profit to its stockholders. Fourth, to raise revenue, Hamilton proposed a tax on producers of whiskey. Finally, in a Report on Manufactures delivered to Congress in December 1791, Hamilton called for the imposition of a tariff (a tax on imported foreign goods) and government subsidies to encourage the development of factories that could manufacture products currently purchased from abroad. Privately, Hamilton promoted an unsuccessful effort to build an industrial city at present-day Paterson, New Jersey. He also proposed the creation of a national army to deal with uprisings like Shays's Rebellion.

Liberty and Washington, *painted by an unknown artist around 1800, depicts a female figure of liberty placing a wreath on a bust of the first president. She carries an American flag and stands on a royal crown, which has been thrown to the ground. In the background is a liberty cap. Washington had died in 1799 and was now immortalized as a symbol of freedom, independence, and national pride.*

The Bank of Pennsylvania, Philadelphia. Designed by the architect Benjamin Latrobe and built between 1798 and 1801, this elegant structure with Greek columns housed one of the country's first banks. Hamilton's program was intended to give the country's financial leaders a stake in the stability of the federal government.

THE EMERGENCE OF OPPOSITION

Hamilton's vision of a powerful commercial republic won strong support from American financiers, manufacturers, and merchants. But it alarmed those who believed the new nation's destiny lay in charting a different path of development. Hamilton's plans hinged on close ties with Britain, America's main trading partner. To James Madison and Thomas Jefferson, the future lay in westward expansion, not connections with Europe. They had little desire to promote manufacturing or urban growth or to see economic policy shaped in the interests of bankers and business leaders. Their goal was a republic of independent farmers marketing grain, tobacco, and other products freely to the entire world. Free trade, they believed, not a system of government favoritism through tariffs and subsidies, would promote American prosperity while fostering greater social equality. Jefferson and Madison quickly concluded that the greatest threat to American freedom lay in the alliance of a powerful central government with an emerging class of commercial capitalists, such as Hamilton appeared to envision.

To Jefferson, Hamilton's system "flowed from principles adverse to liberty, and was calculated to undermine and demolish the republic." Hamilton's plans for a standing army seemed to his critics a bold threat to freedom. The national bank and assumption of state debts, they feared, would introduce into American politics the same corruption that had undermined British liberty, and enrich those already wealthy at the expense of ordinary Americans. During the 1780s, speculators had bought up at great discounts (often only a few cents on the dollar) government bonds and paper notes that had been used to pay those who fought in the Revolution or supplied the army. Under Hamilton's plan, speculators would reap a windfall by being paid at face value while the original holders received nothing. Because transportation was so poor, moreover, many backcountry farmers were used to distilling their grain harvest into whiskey, which could then be carried more easily to market. Hamilton's whiskey tax seemed to single them out unfairly in order to enrich bondholders.

THE JEFFERSON-HAMILTON BARGAIN

At first, opposition to Hamilton's program arose almost entirely from the South, the region that had the least interest in manufacturing development and the least diversified economy. It also had fewer holders of federal bonds than the Middle States and New England. (Virginia had pretty much paid off its war debt; it did not see why it should be taxed to benefit states like Massachusetts that had failed to do so.) Hamilton insisted that all his plans were authorized by the Constitution's ambiguous clause empowering Congress to enact laws for the "general welfare." As a result, many southerners who had supported the new Constitution now became "strict constructionists," who insisted that the federal government could only exercise powers specifically listed in the document. Jefferson, for example, believed the new national bank unconstitutional, since the right of Congress to create a bank was not mentioned in the Constitution.

Opposition in Congress threatened the enactment of Hamilton's plans. Behind-the-scenes negotiations followed. They culminated at a famous dinner in 1790 at which Jefferson brokered an agreement whereby southerners accepted Hamilton's fiscal program (with the exception of subsidies to manufacturers) in exchange for the establishment of the permanent national capital on the Potomac River between Maryland and Virginia. Southerners hoped that the location would enhance their own power in the government while removing it from the influence of the northern financiers and merchants with whom Hamilton seemed to be allied. Major Pierre-Charles L'Enfant, a French-born veteran of the War of Independence, designed a grandiose plan for the "federal city" modeled on the great urban centers of Europe, with wide boulevards, parks, and fountains. The job of surveying was done, in part, by Benjamin Banneker, the free African-American scientist mentioned in the previous chapter. When it came to constructing public buildings in the nation's new capital, most of the labor was done by slaves.

THE IMPACT OF THE FRENCH REVOLUTION

Political divisions began over Hamilton's fiscal program, but they deepened in response to events in Europe. When it began in 1789, nearly all Americans welcomed the French Revolution, inspired in part by the example of their own rebellion. John Marshall, a Virginian who would become chief justice of the Supreme Court, later recalled, "I sincerely believed human liberty to depend in a great measure on the success of the French Revolution." But in 1793, the Revolution took a more radical turn with the execution of King Louis XVI along with numerous aristocrats and other foes of the new government, and war broke out between France and Great Britain.

Events in France became a source of bitter conflict in America. Jefferson and his followers believed that despite its excesses the Revolution marked a historic victory for the idea of popular self-government, which must be defended at all costs. Enthusiasm for France inspired a rebirth of symbols of liberty. Liberty poles and caps reappeared on the streets of American towns and cities. To Washington, Hamilton, and their supporters, however, the Revolution raised the specter of anarchy. America, they believed, had no choice but to draw closer to Britain.

Venerate the Plough, *a medal of the Philadelphia Society for the Promotion of Agriculture, 1786. Americans like Jefferson and Madison believed that farmers were the most virtuous citizens and therefore agriculture must remain the foundation of American life.*

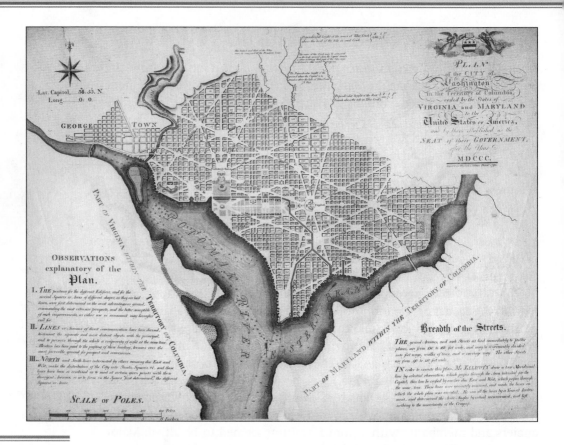

Pierre-Charles L'Enfant's 1791 plan for Washington, D.C., includes broad avenues that crisscross the city and that are named for the thirteen states, and a long mall stretching from the Potomac River to the Capitol building, slightly to the right of center.

American leaders feared being divided into parties "swayed by rival European powers," in the words of John Quincy Adams. But the rivalry between Britain and France did much to shape early American politics. The "permanent" alliance between France and the United States, which dated to 1778, complicated the situation. No one advocated that the United States should become involved in the European war, and Washington in April 1793 issued a proclamation of American neutrality. But that spring the French Revolution's American admirers organized tumultuous welcomes for Edmond Genet, a French envoy seeking to arouse support for his beleaguered government. When Genet began commissioning American ships to attack British vessels under the French flag, the Washington administration asked for his recall. (Deeming the situation in France too dangerous, he decided to remain in America and married the daughter of George Clinton, the governor of New York.)

Meanwhile, the British seized hundreds of American ships trading with the French West Indies and resumed the hated practice of impressment—kidnapping sailors, including American citizens of British origin, to serve in their navy. Sent to London to present objections, while still serving as chief justice, John Jay negotiated an agreement in 1794 that produced the greatest public controversy of Washington's presidency. Jay's Treaty contained no British concessions on impressment or the rights of American shipping. Britain did agree to abandon outposts on the western frontier, which it was supposed to have done in 1783. In return, the United States guaranteed favored treatment to British imported goods. In effect, the treaty canceled the American-French alliance and recognized British economic and naval supremacy as unavoidable facts of life. Critics of the

administration charged that it aligned the United States with monarchical Britain in its conflict with republican France. Ultimately, Jay's Treaty sharpened political divisions in the United States and led directly to the formation of an organized opposition party.

Infant Liberty Nursed by Mother Mob, *a Federalist cartoon from 1807, illustrates the party's fear that the spirit of liberty was degenerating into anarchy. In the background, a mob assaults a building, while in the foreground a pile of books burn.*

POLITICAL PARTIES

By the mid-1790s, two increasingly coherent parties had appeared in Congress, calling themselves Federalists and Republicans. (The latter had no connection with today's Republican Party, which was founded in the 1850s.) Both parties laid claim to the language of liberty, and each accused its opponent of engaging in a conspiracy to destroy it.

The Federalists, supporters of the Washington administration, favored Hamilton's economic program and close ties with Britain. Prosperous merchants, farmers, lawyers, and established political leaders (especially outside the South) tended to support the Federalists. Their outlook was generally elitist, reflecting the traditional eighteenth-century view of society as a fixed hierarchy and of public office as reserved for men of economic substance—the "rich, the able, and the well-born," as Hamilton put it. Freedom, Federalists insisted, rested on deference to authority. It did not mean the right to stand up in opposition to government. Federalists feared that the "spirit of liberty" unleashed by the American Revolution was degenerating into anarchy and "licentiousness." When the New York Federalist leader Rufus King wrote an essay on the "words . . . with wrong meaning" that had "done great harm" to American society, his first example was "Liberty."

THE WHISKEY REBELLION

The Federalists may have been the only major party in American history forthrightly to proclaim democracy and freedom dangerous in the hands of

GENERAL GEORGE WASHINGTON.
Reviewing the Western army at Fort Cumberland the 18th of October 1794.

A 1794 painting by the Baltimore artist and sign painter Frederick Kemmelmayer depicting President George Washington as commander-in-chief of the army dispatched to put down the Whiskey Rebellion.

ordinary citizens. The Whiskey Rebellion of 1794, which broke out when back-country Pennsylvania farmers sought to block collection of the new tax on distilled spirits, reinforced this conviction. The "rebels" invoked the symbols of 1776, displaying liberty poles and banners reading "Liberty or Death." "The citizens of the western country," one group wrote to the president, "consider [the tax] as repugnant to liberty, [and] an invasion of those privileges which the revolution bestowed upon them." But Washington dispatched 13,000 militiamen to western Pennsylvania (a larger force than he had commanded during the Revolution). He accompanied them part of the way to the scene of the disturbances, the only time in American history that the president has actually commanded an army in the field. The "rebels" offered no resistance. His vigorous response, Washington wrote, was motivated in part by concern for "the impression" the restoration of public order "will make on others"—the "others" being Europeans who did not believe the American experiment in self-government could survive.

THE REPUBLICAN PARTY

Republicans, led by Madison and Jefferson, were more sympathetic to France than the Federalists and had more faith in democratic self-government. They drew their support from an unusual alliance of wealthy southern planters and ordinary farmers throughout the country. Enthusiasm for the French Revolution increasingly drew urban artisans into Republican ranks as well. Republicans preferred what a New Hampshire editor called the "boisterous sea of liberty" to the "calm of despotism." They were far more critical than the Federalists of social and economic inequality, and more accepting of broad democratic participation as essential to freedom.

Each emerging party considered itself the representative of the nation and the other an illegitimate "faction." As early as 1792, Madison composed an imaginary dialogue between spokesmen for the two groups. The Federalist described ordinary people as "stupid, suspicious, licentious" and accused the Republican of being "an accomplice of atheism and anarchy." The latter called the Federalist an opponent of liberty and "an idolater of tyranny."

In real life, too, political language became more and more heated. Federalists denounced Republicans as French agents, anarchists, and traitors. Republicans called their opponents monarchists intent on transforming the new national government into a corrupt, British-style aristocracy. Each charged the other with betraying the principles of the War of Independence and of American freedom. Washington himself received mounting abuse. When he left office, a Republican newspaper declared that his name had become synonymous with "political iniquity" and "legalized corruption." One contemporary complained that the American press, "one of the great safeguards of free government," had become "the most scurrilous in the civilized world."

AN EXPANDING PUBLIC SPHERE

The debates of the 1790s produced not only one of the most intense periods of partisan warfare in American history but also an enduring expansion of the public sphere, and with it the democratic content of American freedom. More and more citizens attended political meetings and became avid readers of pamphlets and newspapers. The establishment of nearly 1,000 post offices made possible the wider circulation of personal letters and printed materials. The era witnessed the rapid growth of the American press—the number of newspapers rose from around 100 to 260 during the 1790s, and reached nearly 400 by 1810.

A print shop in the early republic. The increasing number of newspapers played a major role in the expansion of the public sphere.

Hundreds of "obscure men" wrote pamphlets and newspaper essays and formed political organizations. The decade's democratic ferment was reflected in writings like *The Key of Liberty* by William Manning, a self-educated Massachusetts farmer who had fought at the battle of Concord that began the War of Independence. Although not published until many years later, Manning's work, addressed to "friends to liberty and free government," reflected the era's popular political thought. The most important division in society, Manning declared, was between the "few" and the "many." He called for the latter to form a national political association to prevent the "few" from destroying "free government" and "tyrannizing over" the people.

THE DEMOCRATIC-REPUBLICAN SOCIETIES

Inspired by the Jacobin clubs of Paris, supporters of the French Revolution and critics of the Washington administration in 1793 and 1794 formed nearly fifty Democratic-Republican societies. The Republican press publicized their meetings, replete with toasts to French and American liberty. The declaration of the Democratic Society of Addison County, Vermont, was typical: "That all men are naturally free, and possess equal rights. That all legitimate government originates in the voluntary social compact of the people."

Federalists saw the societies as another example of how liberty was getting out of hand. The government, not "self-created societies," declared the president, was the authentic voice of the American people. Forced to justify their existence, the societies developed a defense of the right of the people to debate political issues and organize to affect public policy. To the societies, "free inquiry" and "free communication" formed the first line of defense of "the unalienable rights of free men." Political liberty meant not simply voting at elections but constant involvement in public affairs. "We make no apology for thus associating ourselves," declared the Addison

VOICES OF FREEDOM

FROM Address of the Democratic-Republican Society of Pennsylvania (December 18, 1794)

The creation of around fifty Democratic-Republican societies in 1793 and 1794 reflected the expansion of the public sphere. The Pennsylvania society issued an address defending itself against critics who questioned its right to criticize the administration of George Washington.

The principles and proceedings of our Association have lately been caluminated [tarred by malicious falsehoods]. We should think ourselves unworthy to be ranked as Freemen, if awed by the name of any man, however he may command the public gratitude for past services, we could suffer in silence so sacred a right, so important a principle, as the freedom of opinion to be infringed, by attack on Societies which stand on that constitutional basis.

Freedom of thought, and a free communication of opinions by speech through the medium of the press, are the safeguards of our Liberties. . . . By the freedom of opinion, cannot be meant the right of

thinking merely; for of this right the greatest Tyrant cannot deprive his meanest slave; but, it is freedom in the communication of sentiments [by] speech or through the press. This liberty is an imprescriptable [unlimitable] right, independent of any Constitution or social compact; it is as complete a right as that which any man has to the enjoyment of his life. These principles are eternal—they are recognized by our Constitution; and that nation is already enslaved that does not acknowledge their truth. . . .

If freedom of opinion, in the sense we understand it, is the right of every Citizen, by what mode of reasoning can that right be denied to an assemblage of Citizens? . . . The Society are free to declare that they never were more strongly impressed with . . . the importance of associations . . . than at the present time. The germ of an odious Aristocracy is planted among us—it has taken root. . . . Let us remain firm in attachment to principles. . . . Let us be particularly watchful to preserve inviolate the freedom of opinion, assured that it is the most effectual weapon for the protection of our liberty.

From Judith Sargent Murray, "On the Equality of the Sexes" (1790)

A prominent writer of plays, novels, and poetry, Judith Sargent Murray of Massachusetts was one of the first women to demand equal educational opportunities for women.

Is it upon mature consideration we adopt the idea, that nature is thus partial in her distributions? Is it indeed a fact, that she hath yielded to one half of the human species so unquestionable a mental superiority? I know that to both sexes elevated understandings, and the reverse, are common. But, suffer me to ask, in what the minds of females are so notoriously deficient, or unequal. . . .

Are we deficient in reason? We can only reason from what we know, and if an opportunity of acquiring knowledge hath been denied us, the inferiority of our sex cannot fairly be deduced from thence. . . . Will it be said that the judgment of a male of two years old, is more sage than that of a female's of the same age? I believe the reverse is generally observed to be true. But from that period what partiality! How is the one exalted, and the other depressed, by the contrary modes of education which are adopted! The one is taught to aspire, and the other is early confined and limited. As their years increase, the sister must be wholly domesticated, while the brother is led by the hand through all the flowery paths of science. Grant that their minds are by nature equal, yet who shall wonder at the *apparent* superiority. . . . At length arrived at womanhood, the uncultivated fair one feels a void, which the employments allotted her are by no means capable of filling. . . . She herself is most unhappy; she feels the want of a cultivated mind. . . . Should it . . . be vociferated, 'Your domestic employments are sufficient'—I would calmly ask, is it reasonable, that a candidate for immortality, for the joys of heaven, an intelligent being, who is to spend an eternity in contemplating the works of Deity, should at present be so degraded, as to be allowed no other ideas, than those which are suggested by the mechanism of a pudding, or the sewing the seams of a garment? . . .

Yes, ye lordly, ye haughty sex, our souls are by nature *equal* to yours.

QUESTIONS

1. Why does the Democratic-Republican society insist on the centrality of "free communication of opinions" in preserving American liberty?

2. How does Murray answer the argument that offering education to women will lead them to neglect their "domestic employments"?

3. How do these documents reflect expanding ideas about who should enjoy the freedom to express one's ideas in the early republic?

An engraving from The Lady's Magazine and Repository of Entertaining Knowledge, *published in Philadelphia in 1792. A woman identified as the "Genius of the Ladies Magazine" kneels before Liberty, presenting a petition for the "Rights of Women." In the foreground are symbols of the arts, science, and literature—knowledge that should be available to women as well as men.*

Mary Wollstonecraft, author of the pioneering work A Vindication of the Rights of Woman, *in a 1797 portrait.*

County society. "Political freedom" included the right to "exercise watchfulness and inspection, upon the conduct of public officers." Blamed by Federalists for helping to inspire the Whiskey Rebellion, the societies disappeared by the end of 1795. But much of their organization and outlook was absorbed into the emerging Republican Party. They helped to legitimize the right of "any portion of the people," regardless of station in life, to express political opinions and take an active role in public life.

The Republicans also gained support from immigrants from the British Isles, where war with France inspired a severe crackdown on dissent. Thomas Paine had returned to Britain in 1787. Five years later, after publishing *The Rights of Man*, a defense of the French Revolution and a stirring call for democratic change at home, he was forced to flee to France one step ahead of the law. But his writings inspired the emergence of a mass movement for political and social change, which authorities brutally suppressed. Threatened with arrest for treason, a number of British and Irish radicals emigrated to America. They included journalists like Joseph Gales and John D. Burk, who soon found themselves editing Republican newspapers that condemned social privilege on both sides of the Atlantic and charged the Federalists with attempting to introduce European tyranny in America.

THE RIGHTS OF WOMEN

The democratic ferment of the 1790s inspired renewed discussion about women's rights. In 1792, Mary Wollstonecraft published in England her extraordinary pamphlet, *A Vindication of the Rights of Woman*. Inspired by Paine's *Rights of Man*, she asserted that the "rights of humanity" should not be "confined to the male line." Wollstonecraft did not directly challenge traditional gender roles. Her call for greater access to education and to paid employment for women rested on the idea that this would enable single women to support themselves and married women to perform more capably as wives and mothers. But she did "drop a hint," as she put it, that women "ought to have representation" in government. Within two years, American editions of Wollstonecraft's work had appeared, along with pamphlets defending and attacking her arguments. A short-lived women's rights magazine was published in 1795 in New York City.

The expansion of the public sphere offered new opportunities to women. Increasing numbers began expressing their thoughts in print. Hannah Adams of Massachusetts became the first American woman to support herself as an author, publishing works on religious history and the history of New England. Other women took part in political discussions, read newspapers, and listened to orations, even though outside of New Jersey none could vote. In 1792, Sarah W. Morton of Boston published *The African Chief*, a lengthy poem recounting the enslavement of an African.

Judith Sargent Murray, one of the era's most accomplished American women, wrote essays for the *Massachusetts Magazine* under the pen name "The Gleaner." Murray's father, a prosperous Massachusetts merchant, had taken an enlightened view of his daughter's education. Although Judith could not attend college because of her sex, she studied alongside her brother with a tutor preparing the young man for admission to Harvard. In her essay "On the Equality of the Sexes," written in 1779 and published in

1790, Murray insisted that women had as much right as men to exercise all their talents and should be allowed equal educational opportunities to enable them to do so. Women's apparent mental inferiority to men, she insisted, simply reflected the fact that they had been denied "the opportunity of acquiring knowledge." "The idea of the incapability of women," she maintained, was "totally inadmissable in this enlightened age."

WOMEN AND THE REPUBLIC

Were women part of the new body politic? Until after the Civil War, the word "male" did not appear in the Constitution. Women were counted fully in determining representation in Congress, and there was nothing explicitly limiting the rights outlined in the Constitution to men. A few contributors to the pamphlet debate on women's rights admitted that, according to the logic of democracy, women ought to have a voice in government. The Constitution's use of the word "he" to describe officeholders, however, reflected an assumption so widespread that it scarcely required explicit defense: politics was a realm for men. The time had not yet arrived for a broad assault on gender inequality. But like the activities of the Democratic-Republican societies, the discussion of women's status helped to popularize the language of rights in the new republic.

The men who wrote the Constitution did not envision the active and continuing involvement of ordinary citizens in affairs of state. But the rise of political parties seeking to mobilize voters in hotly contested elections, the emergence of the "self-created societies," the stirrings of women's political consciousness, and even armed uprisings like the Whiskey Rebellion broadened and deepened the democratization of public life set in motion by the American Revolution.

This sampler was made by Peggy Castleman, a student in Frederick County, Virginia, in 1802. It includes an American eagle, a symbol of patriotism, along with more conventional decorations and domestic imagery. Women as well as men shared in the enthusiasm for early American nationalism.

THE ADAMS PRESIDENCY

In 1792, Washington won unanimous reelection. Four years later, he decided to retire from public life, in part to establish the precedent that the presidency is not a life office. In his Farewell Address (mostly drafted by Hamilton and published in the newspapers rather than delivered orally; see the Appendix for excerpts from the speech), Washington defended his administration against criticism, warned against the party spirit, and advised his countrymen to steer clear of international power politics by avoiding "permanent alliances with any portion of the foreign world."

THE ELECTION OF 1796

George Washington's departure unleashed fierce party competition over the choice of his successor. In this, the first contested presidential election, two tickets presented themselves: John Adams, with Thomas Pinckney of South Carolina for vice president, representing the Federalists, and Thomas Jefferson, with Aaron Burr of New York, for the Republicans. In a majority of the sixteen states (Vermont, Kentucky, and Tennessee had been added to the original thirteen during Washington's presidency), the legislature still chose presidential electors. But in the six states where the people voted for electors directly, intense campaigning took place. Adams received seventy-one electoral votes to Jefferson's sixty-eight. Because of factionalism among the Federalists, Pinckney received only fifty-nine votes, so Jefferson, the leader of the opposition party, became vice president. Voting fell almost entirely along sectional lines: Adams carried New England, New York, and New Jersey, while Jefferson swept the South, along with Pennsylvania.

In 1797, John Adams assumed leadership of a divided nation. Brilliant but austere, stubborn, and self-important, he was disliked even by those who honored his long career of service to the cause of independence. His presidency was beset by crises.

On the international front, the country was nearly dragged into the ongoing European war. As a neutral nation, the United States claimed the right to trade nonmilitary goods with both Britain and France, but both countries seized American ships with impunity. In 1797, American diplomats were sent to Paris to negotiate a treaty to replace the old alliance of 1778. French officials presented them with a demand for bribes before negotiations could proceed. When Adams made public the envoys' dispatches, the French officials were designated by the last three letters of the alphabet. This "XYZ affair" poisoned America's relations with its former ally. By 1798, the United States and France were engaged in a "quasi-war" at sea, with French ships seizing American vessels in the Caribbean and a newly enlarged American navy harassing the French. In effect, the United States had become a military ally of Great Britain. Despite pressure from Hamilton, who desired a declaration of war, Adams in 1800 negotiated peace with France.

Adams was less cautious in domestic affairs. Unrest continued in many rural areas. In 1799, farmers in southeastern Pennsylvania obstructed the assessment of a tax on land and houses that Congress had imposed to help fund an expanded army and navy. A crowd led by John Fries, a local militia leader and auctioneer, released arrested men from prison. No shots were fired in what came to be called Fries's Rebellion, but Adams dispatched units of the federal army to the area. The army arrested Fries for treason and proceeded to terrorize his supporters, tear down liberty poles, and whip Republican newspaper editors. Adams pardoned Fries in 1800, but the area, which had supported his election in 1796, never again voted Federalist.

THE "REIGN OF WITCHES"

But the greatest crisis of the Adams administration arose over the Alien and Sedition Acts of 1798. Confronted with mounting opposition, some of it voiced by immigrant pamphleteers and editors, Federalists moved to silence their critics. A new Naturalization Act extended from five to fourteen years the residency requirement for immigrants seeking American citizenship. The Alien Act allowed the deportation of persons from abroad deemed "dangerous" by federal authorities. The Sedition Act (which was set to expire in 1801, by which time Adams hoped to have been reelected) authorized the prosecution of virtually any public assembly or publication critical of the government. While more lenient than many such measures in Europe (it did not authorize legal action before publication and allowed for trials by jury), the new law meant that opposition editors could be prosecuted for almost any political comment they printed. The main target was the Republican press, seen by Federalists as a group of upstart workingmen (most editors had started out as printers) whose persistent criticism of the administration fomented popular rebelliousness and endangered "genuine liberty."

The passage of these measures launched what Jefferson—recalling events in Salem, Massachusetts, a century earlier—termed a "reign of witches." Eighteen individuals, including several Republican newspaper editors, were charged under the Sedition Act. Ten were convicted for spreading "false, scandalous, and malicious" information about the government. Matthew Lyon, a member of Congress from Vermont and editor of a Republican newspaper, *The Scourge of Aristocracy*, received a sentence of four months in prison and a fine of $1,000. (Lyon had been the first former printer and most likely the first former indentured servant elected to Congress.) The government also imprisoned Thomas Cooper, a lawyer and physician in Pennsylvania who had emigrated from England in 1794, for writings accusing the Adams administration of pro-British bias. In Massachusetts, authorities indicted several men for erecting a liberty pole bearing the inscription, "No Stamp Act, no Sedition, no Alien Bill, no Land Tax; Downfall to the Tyrants of America."

Congressional Pugilists, *a 1798 cartoon depicting a fight on the floor of Congress between Connecticut Federalist Roger Griswold and Matthew Lyon, a Republican from Vermont. Lyon would soon be jailed under the Sedition Act for criticizing the Adams administration in his newspaper.*

THE VIRGINIA AND KENTUCKY RESOLUTIONS

The Alien and Sedition Acts failed to silence the Republican press. Some newspapers ceased publication, but new ones, with names like *Sun of Liberty* and *Tree of Liberty*, entered the field. The Sedition Act thrust freedom of expression to the center of discussions of American liberty. Madison and Jefferson mobilized opposition, drafting resolutions adopted by the Virginia and Kentucky legislatures. Both resolutions attacked the Sedition Act as an unconstitutional violation of the First Amendment. Virginia's, written by Madison, called on the federal courts to protect free speech. The original version of Jefferson's Kentucky resolution went further, asserting that states could nullify laws of Congress that violated the Constitution— that is, states could unilaterally prevent the enforcement of such laws within their borders. The legislature prudently deleted this passage. The resolutions were directed against assaults on freedom of expression by the federal government, not the states. Jefferson took care to insist that the states "fully possessed" the authority to punish "seditious" speech, even if the national government did not. Indeed, state-level prosecutions of newspapers for seditious libel did not end when the Sedition Act expired in 1801.

An 1800 campaign banner, with a portrait of Thomas Jefferson and the words, "John Adams is no more."

No other state endorsed the Virginia and Kentucky resolutions. Many Americans, including many Republicans, were horrified by the idea of state action that might endanger the Union. But the "crisis of freedom" of the late 1790s strongly reinforced the idea that "freedom of discussion" was an indispensable attribute of American liberty and of democratic government. Free speech, as Massachusetts Federalist Harrison Gray Otis noted, had become the people's "darling privilege." The broad revulsion against the Alien and Sedition Acts contributed greatly to Jefferson's election as president in 1800.

THE "REVOLUTION OF 1800"

"Jefferson and Liberty" became the watchword of the Republican campaign. By this time, Republicans had developed effective techniques for mobilizing voters, such as printing pamphlets, handbills, and newspapers and holding mass meetings to promote their cause. The Federalists, who viewed politics as an activity for a small group of elite men, found it difficult to match their opponents' mobilization. Nonetheless, they still dominated New England and enjoyed considerable support in the Middle Atlantic states. Jefferson triumphed, with seventy-three electoral votes to Adams's sixty-five.

Before assuming office, Jefferson was forced to weather an unusual constitutional crisis. Each party arranged to have an elector throw away one of his two votes for president, so that its presidential candidate would come out a vote ahead of the vice presidential. But the designated Republican elector failed to do so. As a result, both Jefferson and his running mate, Aaron Burr, received seventy-three electoral votes. With no candidate having a majority, the election was thrown into the House of Representatives that had been elected in 1798, where the Federalists enjoyed a slight majority. For thirty-five ballots, neither man received a majority of the votes. Finally, Hamilton intervened. He disliked Jefferson but believed him enough of a statesman to recognize that the Federalist financial system could not be dismantled. Burr, he warned, was obsessed with power, "an embryo Caesar."

Hamilton's support for Jefferson tipped the balance. To avoid a repetition of the crisis, Congress and the states soon adopted the Twelfth Amendment to the Constitution, requiring electors to cast separate votes for president and vice president. The election of 1800 also set in motion a chain of events that culminated four years later when Burr killed Hamilton in a duel. Burr appears to have subsequently engaged in a plot to form a new nation in the West from land detached from the United States and the Spanish empire. Acquitted of treason in 1807, he went into exile in Europe, eventually returning to New York, where he practiced law until his death in 1836.

The events of the 1790s demonstrated that a majority of Americans believed ordinary people had a right to play an active role in politics, express their opinions freely, and contest the policies of their government. His party, wrote Samuel Goodrich, a prominent Connecticut Federalist, was overthrown because democracy had become "the watchword of popular liberty." To their credit, Federalists never considered resistance to the election result. Adams's acceptance of defeat established the vital precedent of a peaceful transfer of power from a defeated party to its successor.

SLAVERY AND POLITICS

Lurking behind the political battles of the 1790s lay the potentially divisive issue of slavery. Jefferson, after all, received every one of the South's forty-one electoral votes. He always referred to his victory as the "Revolution of 1800" and saw it not simply as a party success but as a vindication of American freedom, securing for posterity the fruits of independence. Yet the triumph of "Jefferson and Liberty" would not have been possible without slavery. Had three-fifths of the slaves not been counted in apportionment, John Adams would have been reelected in 1800.

The issue of slavery would not disappear. The very first Congress under the new Constitution received petitions calling for emancipation. One bore the weighty signature of Benjamin Franklin, who in 1787 had agreed to serve as president of the Pennsylvania Abolition Society. The blessings of liberty, Franklin's petition insisted, should be available "without distinction of color to all descriptions of people."

A long debate followed, in which speakers from Georgia and South Carolina vigorously defended the institution and warned that behind northern criticism of slavery they heard "the trumpets of civil war." Madison found their forthright defense of slavery an embarrassment. But he concluded that the slavery question was so divisive that it must be kept out of national politics. He opposed Congress's even receiving a petition from North Carolina slaves on the grounds that they were not part of the American people and had "no claim" on the lawmakers' "attention." In 1793, to implement the Constitution's fugitive slave clause, Congress enacted a law providing for federal and state judges and local officials to facilitate the return of escaped slaves.

THE HAITIAN REVOLUTION

Events during the 1790s underscored how powerfully slavery defined and distorted American freedom. The same Jeffersonians who hailed the French Revolution as a step in the universal progress of liberty reacted in horror against the slave revolution that began in 1791 in Saint Domingue, the jewel of the French overseas empire situated not far from the southern coast of the United States. Toussaint L'Ouverture, an educated slave on a sugar plantation, forged the rebellious slaves into an army able to defeat British forces seeking to seize the island and then an expedition hoping to reestablish French authority. The slave uprising led to the establishment of Haiti as an independent nation in 1804.

Although much of the country was left in ruins by years of warfare, the Haitian Revolution affirmed the universality of the revolutionary era's creed of liberty. It inspired hopes for freedom among slaves in the United States. Throughout the nineteenth century, black Americans would look to

THE PROVIDENTIAL DETECTION

The Providential Detection, *a Federalist political cartoon from 1800 attacking Thomas Jefferson. An eagle rescues the Constitution and Declaration of Independence before Jefferson can burn them on an "altar to Gallic [French] despotism." Feeding the flames are writings despised by Federalists, including Thomas Paine's* The Age of Reason, *which attacked organized religion, and the* Aurora, *a Jeffersonian newspaper. Jefferson drops a 1796 letter to his Italian friend Philip Mazzei that criticized President Washington.*

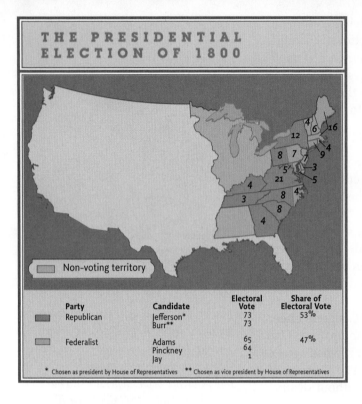

THE PRESIDENTIAL ELECTION OF 1800

Non-voting territory

Party	Candidate	Electoral Vote	Share of Electoral Vote
Republican	Jefferson*	73	53%
	Burr**	73	
Federalist	Adams	65	47%
	Pinckney	64	
	Jay	1	

* Chosen as president by House of Representatives ** Chosen as vice president by House of Representatives

Toussaint as a hero and celebrate the winning of Haitian independence. During the 1820s, several thousand free African-Americans emigrated to Haiti, whose government promised newcomers political rights and economic opportunity they did not enjoy in the United States.

Among white Americans, the response to the Haitian Revolution was different. Thousands of refugees from Haiti poured into the United States, fleeing the upheaval. Many spread tales of the massacres of slaveowners and the burning of their plantations, which reinforced white Americans' fears of slave insurrection at home. To most whites, the rebellious slaves seemed not men and women seeking liberty in the tradition of 1776, but a danger to American institutions. That the slaves had resorted to violence was widely taken to illustrate blacks' unfitness for republican freedom. Ironically, the Adams administration, which hoped that American merchants could replace their French counterparts in the island's lucrative sugar trade, encouraged the independence of black Haiti. When Jefferson became president, on the other hand, he sought to quarantine and destroy the hemisphere's second independent republic.

GABRIEL'S REBELLION

The momentous year of 1800 witnessed not only the "revolution" of Jefferson's election but an attempted real one, a plot by slaves in Virginia itself to gain their freedom. It was organized by a Richmond blacksmith, Gabriel, and his brothers Solomon, also a blacksmith, and Martin, a slave preacher. The conspirators planned to march on the city, which had recently become the state capital, from surrounding plantations. They would kill some white inhabitants and hold the rest, including Governor James Monroe, hostage until their demand for the abolition of slavery was met. Gabriel hoped that "poor white people" would join the insurrection, and he ordered that Quakers and Methodists (many of whom were critics of slavery) and "French people" (whose country was engaged in the "quasi-war" with the United States described earlier) be spared. On the night when the slaves were to gather, a storm washed out the roads to Richmond. The plot was soon discovered and the leaders arrested. Twenty-six slaves, including Gabriel, were hanged and dozens more transported out of the state.

Blacks in 1800 made up half of Richmond's population. One-fifth were free. A black community had emerged in the 1780s and 1790s, and the conspiracy was rooted in its institutions. Gabriel gathered recruits at black Baptist churches, funerals, barbecues, and other gatherings. In cities like Richmond, many skilled slave craftsmen, including Gabriel himself, could read and write and enjoyed the privilege of hiring themselves out to employers—that is, negotiating their own labor arrangements, with their owner receiving their "wages." Their relative autonomy helps account for slave artisans' prominent role in the conspiracy.

Gabriel's Rebellion was a product of its age. Gabriel himself had been born in 1776. Like other Virginians, the participants in the conspiracy spoke the language of liberty forged in the American Revolution and reinvigorated during the 1790s. The rebels even planned to carry a banner emblazoned with the slogan, reminiscent of Patrick Henry, "Death or Liberty." "We have as much right," one conspirator declared, "to fight for our liberty as any men." Another likened himself to George Washington, who had rebelled against established authority to "obtain the liberty of [his] countrymen." (This analogy carried the disturbing implication that Virginia officials had now replaced the British as enemies of freedom.)

If Gabriel's conspiracy demonstrated anything, commented the prominent Virginian George Tucker, it was that slaves possessed "the love of freedom" as fully as other men. Gabriel's words, he added, reflected "the advance of knowledge" among Virginia's slaves, including knowledge of the American language of liberty. When slaves escaped to join Lord Dunmore during the War of Independence, he wrote, "they sought freedom merely as a good; now they also claim it as a right." Tucker believed Virginians should emancipate their slaves and settle them outside of the state. The legislature, however, moved in the opposite direction. It tightened controls over the black population—making it illegal for them to congregate on Sundays without white supervision—and severely restricted the possibility of masters voluntarily freeing their slaves. Any slave freed after 1806 was required to leave Virginia or be sold back into slavery. The door to emancipation, thrown open during the American Revolution, had been slammed shut.

Toussaint L'Ouverture, leader of the slave revolution in Saint Domingue, in a portrait from a history of the island published in 1805.

JEFFERSON IN POWER

The first president to begin his term in Washington, D.C., Jefferson assumed office on March 4, 1801. The city, with its unpaved streets, impoverished residents, and unfinished public buildings, scarcely resembled L'Enfant's grand plan. At one point, part of the roof of the Capitol collapsed, narrowly missing the vice president. The capital's condition seemed to symbolize Jefferson's intention to reduce the importance of the national government in American life.

Jefferson's inaugural address was conciliatory toward his opponents. "Every difference of opinion," he declared, "is not a difference of principle. . . . We are all Republicans, we are all Federalists." He went on to expound the policies his administration would follow—economy in government, unrestricted trade, freedom of religion and the press, friendship to all nations but "entangling alliances" with none. America, "the world's best hope," would flourish if a limited government allowed its citizens to be "free to regulate their own pursuits."

Jefferson hoped to dismantle as much of the Federalist system as possible. Among his first acts as president was to pardon all those imprisoned under the Sedition Act. During his eight years as president, he reduced the number of government employees and slashed the army and navy. He abolished all taxes except the tariff, including the hated tax on whiskey, and paid off part of the national debt. He aimed to minimize federal power and eliminate government oversight of the economy. His policies ensured that the United States would not become a centralized state on a European model, as Hamilton had envisioned.

A watercolor by the artist William Russell Birch depicts the Capitol in 1800, the year Congress first occupied the building. Washington, D.C., was clearly a small community at the time.

JUDICIAL REVIEW

Nonetheless, as Hamilton predicted, it proved impossible to uproot national authority entirely. Jefferson distrusted the unelected judiciary and always believed in the primacy of local self-government. But during his presidency, and for many years thereafter, Federalist John Marshall headed the Supreme Court. Marshall had served John Adams as secretary of state and was appointed by the president to the Court shortly before Jefferson took office. A strong believer in national supremacy, Marshall established the Court's power to review laws of Congress and the states.

The first landmark decision of the Marshall Court came in 1803, in the case of *Marbury v. Madison.* On the eve of leaving office, Adams had appointed a number of justices of the peace for the District of Columbia. Madison, Jefferson's secretary of state, refused to issue commissions (the official documents entitling them to assume their posts) to these "midnight judges." Four, including William Marbury, sued for their offices. Marshall's decision declared unconstitutional the section of the Judiciary Act of 1789 that allowed the courts to order executive officials to deliver judges' commissions. It exceeded the power of Congress as outlined in the Constitution and was therefore void. Marbury, in other words, may have been entitled to his commission, but the Court had no power under the Constitution to order Madison to deliver it. On the immediate issue, therefore, the administration got its way. But the cost, as Jefferson saw it, was high. The Supreme Court had assumed the right to determine whether an act of Congress violates the Constitution—a power known as "judicial review."

Seven years later, in *Fletcher v. Peck*, the Court extended judicial review to state laws. In 1794, four land companies had paid nearly every member of the state legislature, Georgia's two U.S. senators, and a number of federal judges, to secure their right to purchase land in present-day Alabama and Mississippi claimed by Georgia. They then sold the land to individual buyers at a large profit. Two years later, many of the corrupt lawmakers were defeated for reelection and the new legislature rescinded the land grant and subsequent sales. Whatever the circumstances of the legislature's initial action, Marshall declared, the Constitution forbade Georgia from taking any action that impaired a contract. Therefore, the individual purchasers could keep their land and the legislature could not repeal the original grant.

THE LOUISIANA PURCHASE

But the greatest irony of Jefferson's presidency involved his greatest achievement, the Louisiana Purchase. This resulted not from astute

American diplomacy but because the rebellious slaves of Saint Domingue defeated forces sent by the ruler of France, Napoleon Bonaparte, to reconquer the island. Moreover, to take advantage of the sudden opportunity to purchase Louisiana, Jefferson had to abandon his conviction that the federal government was limited to powers specifically mentioned in the Constitution, since the document said nothing about buying territory from a foreign power.

This vast Louisiana Territory, which stretched from the Gulf of Mexico to Canada and from the Mississippi River to the Rocky Mountains, had been ceded by France to Spain in 1762 as part of the reshuffling of colonial possessions at the end of the Seven Years' War. France secretly reacquired it in 1800. Soon after taking office, Jefferson learned of the arrangement. He had long been concerned about American access to the port of New Orleans, which lay within Louisiana at the mouth of the Mississippi River. The right to trade through New Orleans, essential to western farmers, had been acknowledged in the Treaty of San Lorenzo (also known as Pinckney's Treaty) of 1795 between the United States and Spain. But Jefferson feared that the far more powerful French might try to interfere with American commerce. He dispatched envoys to France offering to purchase the city. Needing money for military campaigns in Europe and with his dreams of American empire in ruins because of his inability to reestablish control over Saint Domingue, Napoleon offered to sell the entire Louisiana Territory. The cost, $15 million (the equivalent of perhaps $250 million in today's money), made the Louisiana Purchase one of history's greatest real-estate bargains.

In a stroke, Jefferson had doubled the size of the United States and ended the French presence in North America. Federalists were appalled. "We are to give money, of which we have too little," one declared, "for land, of which we already have too much." Jefferson admitted that he had "done an act beyond the Constitution." But he believed the benefits justified his transgression. Farmers, Jefferson had written, were "the chosen people of God," and the country would remain "virtuous" as long as it was "chiefly agricultural." Madison, in *Federalist* no. 10, had explained that

White Hall Plantation, *painted around 1800, depicts a Louisiana plantation and the dynamism of the region's economy on the eve of its acquisition by the United States. Black oarsmen man a boat carrying bales of cotton for sale in New Orleans.*

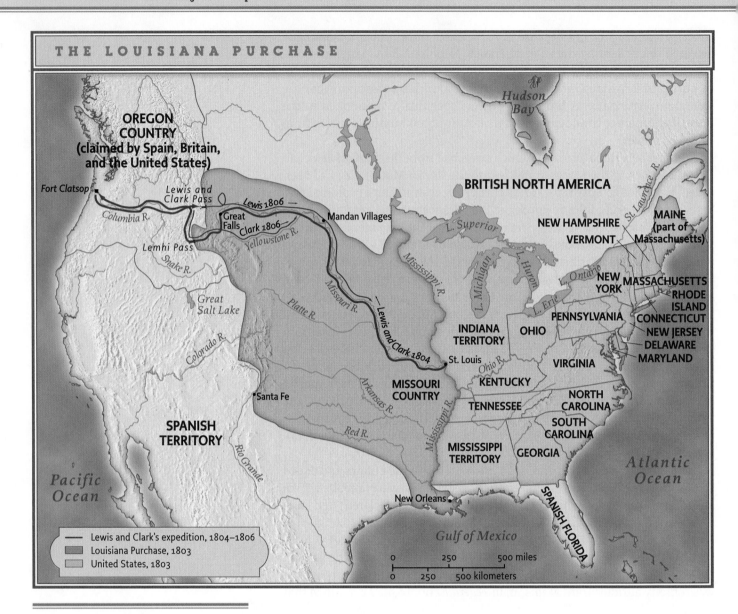

THE LOUISIANA PURCHASE

The Louisiana Purchase of 1803 doubled the land area of the United States.

the large size of the republic made self-government possible—"extend the sphere," he had proclaimed. Now, Jefferson believed, he had ensured the agrarian character of the United States and its political stability for centuries to come.

LEWIS AND CLARK

Within a year of the purchase, Jefferson dispatched an expedition led by Meriwether Lewis and William Clark, two Virginia-born veterans of Indian wars in the Ohio Valley, to explore the new territory. Their objects were both scientific and commercial—to study the area's plants, animal life, and geography, and to discover how the region could be exploited economically. Jefferson hoped the explorers would establish trading relations with western Indians and locate a water route to the Pacific Ocean—an updated version of the old dream of a Northwest Passage that could facilitate commerce with Asia.

In the spring of 1804, Lewis and Clark's fifty-member "corps of discovery" set out from St. Louis on the most famous exploring party in American history. They spent the winter in the area of present-day North Dakota and then resumed their journey in April 1805. They were now accompanied by a fifteen-year-old Shoshone Indian woman, Sacajawea, the wife of a French fur trader, who served as their guide and interpreter. After crossing the Rocky Mountains, the expedition reached the Pacific Ocean in the area of present-day Oregon (which lay beyond the nation's new boundaries) in November 1805. They returned in 1806, bringing with them an immense amount of information about the region as well as numerous plant and animal specimens. Reports about geography, plant and animal life, and Indian cultures filled their daily journals. Although Lewis and Clark failed to find a commercial route to Asia, they demonstrated the possibility of overland travel to the Pacific coast. They found Indians in the trans-Mississippi West accustomed to dealing with European traders and already connected to global markets. The success of their journey helped to strengthen the idea that American territory was destined to reach all the way to the Pacific.

INCORPORATING LOUISIANA

The only part of the Louisiana Purchase with a significant non-Indian population in 1803 was the region around New Orleans. When the United States took control, the city had around 8,000 inhabitants, including nearly 3,000 slaves and 1,300 free persons of color. Incorporating this diverse population into the United States was by no means easy. French and Spanish law accorded free blacks, many of whom were the offspring of unions between white military officers and slave women, nearly all the rights of white citizens. Slaves in Louisiana, as in Florida and Texas under Spanish rule, enjoyed legal protections unknown in the United States. Spain made it easy for slaves to obtain their freedom through purchase or voluntary emancipation by the owners. Slave women had the right to go to court for protection against cruelty or rape by their owners.

The treaty that transferred Louisiana to the United States promised that all free inhabitants would enjoy "the rights, advantages, and immunities of citizens." Spanish and French civil codes, unlike British and American law, recognized women as co-owners of family property. Under American rule, Louisiana retained this principle of "community property" within marriage. But free blacks suffered a steady decline in status. And the local legislature soon adopted one of the most sweeping slave codes in the South, forbidding blacks to "ever consider themselves the equal of whites" and limiting the practice of manumission and access to the courts. Louisiana's slaves had enjoyed far more freedom under the rule of tyrannical Spain than as part of the liberty-loving United States.

THE BARBARY WARS

Among other things, the Louisiana Purchase demonstrated that despite its vaunted isolation from the Old World, the United States continued to be deeply affected by events throughout the Atlantic world. At a time when Americans still relied on British markets to purchase their farm produce

A page from William Clark's journal of the Lewis and Clark expedition, depicting a salmon. Among their tasks was to record information about the West's plants, animal life, and geography.

New Orleans in 1803, at the time of the Louisiana Purchase. The painting shows a view of the city from a nearby plantation. The town houses of merchants and plantation owners line the broad promenade along the waterfront. At the lower center, a slave goes about his work. An eagle holds aloft a banner that suggests the heady optimism of the young republic: Under My Wings Every Thing Prospers.

and British suppliers for imported manufactured goods, European wars directly influenced the livelihood of American farmers, merchants, and artisans. Jefferson hoped to avoid foreign entanglements, but he found it impossible as president to avoid being drawn into the continuing wars of Europe. Even as he sought to limit the power of the national government, foreign relations compelled him to expand it. The first war fought by the United States was to protect American commerce in a dangerous world.

Only a few months after taking office, Jefferson employed the very navy whose expansion by John Adams he had strongly criticized. The Barbary states on the northern coast of Africa had long preyed on shipping in the Mediterranean and Atlantic, receiving tribute from several countries, including the United States, to protect their vessels. Between 1785 and 1796, pirates captured thirteen American ships and held more than 100 sailors as "slaves," paralyzing American trade with the Mediterranean. The federal government paid hundreds of thousands of dollars in ransom and agreed to annual sums to purchase peace. In 1801, Jefferson refused demands for increased payments and the pasha of Tripoli declared war on the United States. The naval conflict lasted until 1804, when an American squadron won a victory at Tripoli harbor (a victory commemorated in the official hymn of the Marine Corps, which mentions fighting on "the shores of Tripoli"). The treaty ending the war guaranteed the freedom of American commerce, but Tripoli soon resumed harassing American ships. Only after the War of 1812 and one final American show of force did Barbary interference with American shipping end.

The Barbary Wars were the new nation's first encounter with the Islamic world. In the 1790s, as part of an attempt to establish peaceful relations, the federal government declared that the United States was "not, in any sense, founded on the Christian religion." But the conflicts helped to establish a long-lasting pattern in which Americans viewed Muslims as an exotic people whose way of life did not adhere to Western standards. In the eyes of many Americans, Islam joined monarchy and aristocracy as forms of Old World despotism that stood as opposites to freedom.

THE EMBARGO

Far more serious in its impact on the United States was warfare between Britain and France, which resumed in 1803 after a brief lull. According to international law, neutral nations had a right to trade nonmilitary goods with countries at war. By 1806, however, each combatant had declared the other under blockade, seeking to deny trade with America to its rival. The Royal Navy resumed the practice of impressment. By the end of 1807, it had seized more than 6,000 American sailors (claiming they were British citizens and deserters), including men from the U.S. warship *Chesapeake*, which the British frigate *Leopard* bombarded and boarded in American waters off the coast of Maryland.

To Jefferson, the economic health of the United States required freedom of trade with which no foreign government had a right to interfere. American farmers needed access to markets in Europe and the Caribbean. As colonial patriots had done in the 1760s and 1770s, he decided to use trade as weapon. In December 1807, he persuaded Congress to enact the Embargo, a ban on all American vessels sailing for foreign ports. For a believer in limited government, this was an amazing exercise of federal power.

Enforcement of the Embargo brought back memories of the Intolerable Acts of 1774, with the navy sealing off ports and seizing goods without warrants and the army arresting accused smugglers. Jefferson hoped it would lead Europeans to stop their interference with American shipping and also reduce the occasion for impressment. In 1808, American exports plummeted by 80 percent. Unfortunately, neither Britain nor France, locked in a death struggle, took much notice. But the Embargo devastated the economies of American port cities. Just before his term ended, in March 1809, Jefferson signed the Non-Intercourse Act, banning trade only with Britain and France but providing that if either side rescinded its edicts against American shipping, commerce with that country would resume.

MADISON AND PRESSURE FOR WAR

Jefferson left office at the lowest point of his career. He had won a sweeping reelection in 1804, receiving 162 electoral votes to only 14 for the Federalist candidate, Charles C. Pinckney. With the exception of Connecticut, he even carried the Federalist stronghold of New England. Four years later, his handpicked successor, James Madison, also won an easy victory. The Embargo, however, had failed to achieve its diplomatic aims and was increasingly violated by American shippers and resented by persons whose livelihoods depended on trade. In 1810, Madison adopted a new policy. Congress enacted a measure known as Macon's Bill No. 2, which allowed trade to resume but provided that if either France or Britain ceased interfering with American rights, the president could reimpose an embargo on the other. With little to lose, since Britain controlled the seas, the French emperor Napoleon announced that he had repealed his decrees against neutral shipping. But the British continued to attack American vessels and, with their navy hard-pressed for manpower, stepped up the impressment

O-Grab-Me, or, the American Snapping-Turtle, *a cartoon criticizing Jefferson's Embargo (spelled backward as o-grab-me), which banned all American shipping to foreign ports.*

of American sailors. In the spring of 1812, Madison reimposed the embargo on trade with Britain.

Meanwhile, a group of younger congressmen, mostly from the West, were calling for war with Britain. Known as the War Hawks, this new generation of political leaders had come of age after the winning of independence and were ardent nationalists. Their leaders included Henry Clay of Kentucky, elected Speaker of the House of Representatives in 1810, and John C. Calhoun of South Carolina. The War Hawks spoke passionately of defending the national honor against British insults, but they also had more practical goals in mind, notably the annexation of Canada. "Agrarian cupidity [greed], not maritime rights," declared Congressman John Randolph of Virginia, "urges the war. We have heard but one word . . . Canada! Canada! Canada!" Randolph exaggerated, for many southern War Hawks also pressed for the conquest of Florida, a haven for fugitive slaves owned by Britain's ally Spain. Members of Congress also spoke of the necessity of upholding the principle of free trade and liberating the United States once and for all from European infringements on its independence. Unimpeded access to overseas markets was essential if the agrarian republic were to prosper.

THE "SECOND WAR OF INDEPENDENCE"

The growing crisis between the United States and Britain took place against the background of deteriorating Indian relations in the West, which also helped propel the United States down the road to war. Jefferson had long favored the removal beyond the Mississippi River of Indian tribes who refused to cooperate in "civilizing" themselves. The Louisiana Purchase made this policy more feasible. "The acquisition of Louisiana," he wrote, "will, it is hoped, put in our power the means of inducing all the Indians on this side [of the Mississippi River] to transplant themselves to the other side." Jefferson enthusiastically pursued efforts to purchase Indian lands west of the Appalachian Mountains. He encouraged traders to lend money to Indians, in the hope that accumulating debt would force them to sell some of their holdings, thus freeing up more land for "our increasing numbers." On the other hand, the government continued President Washington's policy of promoting settled farming among the Indians. Benjamin Hawkins, a friend of Jefferson who served as American agent for Indian affairs south of the Ohio River, also encouraged the expansion of African-American slavery among the tribes as one of the elements of advancing civilization.

THE INDIAN RESPONSE

By 1800, nearly 400,000 American settlers lived west of the Appalachian Mountains. They far outnumbered the remaining Indians, whose seemingly irreversible decline in power led some Indians to rethink their opposition to assimilation. Among the Creek and Cherokee, a group led by men of mixed Indian-white ancestry like Major Ridge and John Ross enthusiastically endorsed the federal policy of promoting "civilization." Many had established businesses as traders and slaveowning farmers with the help of their white fathers. Their views, in turn, infuriated "nativists," who wished to root out European influences and resist further white encroachment on Indian lands.

The period from 1800 to 1812 was an "age of prophecy" among the Indians. Movements for the revitalization of Indian life arose among the Creeks, Cherokees, Shawnees, Iroquois, and other tribes. Handsome Lake of the Seneca, who had overcome an earlier addiction to alcohol, preached that Indians must refrain from fighting, gambling, drinking, and sexual promiscuity. He believed Indians could regain their autonomy without directly challenging whites or repudiating all white ways, and he urged his people to take up farming and attend school.

TECUMSEH'S VISION

A more militant message was expounded by two Shawnee brothers—Tecumseh, a chief who had refused to sign the Treaty of Greenville in 1795, and Tenskwatawa, a religious prophet who called for complete separation from whites, the revival of traditional Indian culture, and resistance to federal policies. White people, Tenskwatawa preached, were the source of all evil in the world, and Indians should abandon American alcohol, clothing, food, and manufactured goods. His followers gathered at Prophetstown, located on the Wabash River in Indiana.

Tecumseh meanwhile traversed the Mississippi Valley, seeking to revive Neolin's pan-Indian alliance of the 1760s (discussed in Chapter 4). The alternative to resistance was extermination. "Where today are the Pequot?" he asked. "Where are the Narragansett, the Mohican, the Pocanet, and other powerful tribes of our people? They have vanished before the avarice [greed] and oppression of the white man, as snow before the summer sun." Indians, he proclaimed, must recognize that they were a single people and unite in claiming "a common and equal right in the land." He repudiated chiefs who had sold land to the federal government: "Sell a country! Why not sell the air, the great sea, as well as the earth? Did not the Great Spirit make them all for the use of his children?" In 1810, Tecumseh called for attacks on American frontier settlements. In November 1811, while he was absent, American forces under William Henry Harrison destroyed Prophetstown in the Battle of Tippecanoe.

THE WAR OF 1812

In 1795, James Madison had written that war is the greatest enemy of "true liberty." "War," he explained, "is the parent of armies; from these proceed debts and taxes, and armies, and debts, and taxes are the known instruments for bringing the many under the domination of the few." Nonetheless, Madison became a war president. Reports that the British were encouraging Tecumseh's efforts contributed to the coming of the War of 1812. In June 1812, with assaults on American shipping continuing,

VISIONS OF FREEDOM

Benjamin Hawkins Trading with the Creek Indians. *Painted around 1805 by an unidentified artist, this work depicts Hawkins explaining the advantages of settled agriculture as part of a plan to promote "civilization" among Native Americans. Having served in the Continental army during the War of Independence and as a senator from North Carolina, Hawkins was appointed in 1795 Superintendent of Indian Affairs for the southeastern United States. He supplied the Creeks, Cherokees, and Choctaws with agricultural training and farm implements and married a Creek woman.*

QUESTIONS

1. In what ways does the artist depict Indians having adopted the kind of social order Hawkins is encouraging?

2. What elements of traditional Indian culture remain?

Madison asked Congress for a declaration of war. American nationality, the president declared, was at stake—would Americans remain "an independent people" or become "colonists and vassals" of Great Britain? The vote revealed a deeply divided country. Both Federalists and Republicans representing the states from New Jersey northward, where most of the mercantile and financial resources of the country were concentrated, voted against war. The South and West were strongly in favor. The bill passed the House by a vote of 79–49 and the Senate by 19–13. It was the first time the United States declared war on another country, and was approved by the smallest margin of any declaration of war in American history.

In retrospect, it seems remarkably foolhardy for a disunited and militarily unprepared nation to go to war with one of the world's two major powers. And with the expiration in 1811 of the charter of the Bank of the United States and the refusal of northern merchants and bankers to loan money, the federal government found it increasingly difficult to finance the war. Before the conflict ended, it was essentially bankrupt. Fortunately for the United States, Great Britain at the outset was preoccupied with the struggle in Europe. But it easily repelled two feeble American invasions of Canada and imposed a blockade that all but destroyed American commerce. In 1814, having finally defeated Napoleon, Britain invaded the United States. Its forces seized Washington, D.C., and burned the White House, while the government fled for safety.

Americans did enjoy a few military successes. In August 1812, the American frigate *Constitution* defeated the British warship *Guerriere*. Commodore Oliver H. Perry defeated a British naval force in September 1813 on Lake Erie (a startling result considering that Britain prided itself on having the world's most powerful navy—although the Americans outgunned them on the Great Lakes). In the following year, a British assault on Baltimore was repulsed when Fort McHenry at the entrance to the harbor withstood a British bombardment. This was the occasion when Francis Scott Key composed "The Star-Spangled Banner," an ode to the "land of the free and home of the brave" that became the national anthem during the 1930s.

Like the War of Independence, the War of 1812 was a two-front struggle—against the British and against the Indians. The war produced significant victories over western Indians who sided with the British. In 1813, pan-Indian forces led by Tecumseh (who had been commissioned a general in the British army) were defeated, and he himself was killed, at the Battle of the Thames, near Detroit, by an American force led by William Henry Harrison. In March 1814, an army of Americans and pro-assimilation Cherokees and Creeks under the command of Andrew Jackson defeated hostile Creeks known as the Red Sticks at the Battle of Horseshoe Bend in Alabama, killing more than 800 of them. "The power of the Creeks is forever broken," Jackson wrote, and he dictated terms of surrender that

The lid of a chest decorated with scenes from the War of 1812. Images of Hope, on the left, and Liberty flank a picture of the naval battle in which the USS Constitution *defeated a British warship. Liberty holds a paper that reads, "Free Trade and Sailors Rights," two of the issues that drew the United States into the war.*

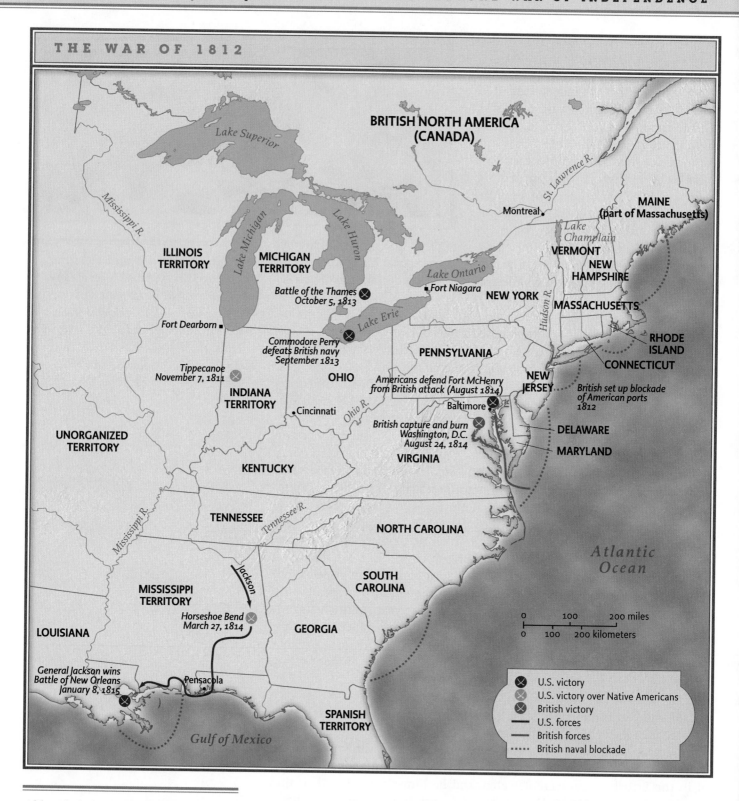

THE WAR OF 1812

Although the British burned the nation's capital, the War of 1812 essentially was a military draw.

required the Indians, hostile and friendly alike, to cede more than half their land, over 23 million acres in all, to the federal government.

Jackson then proceeded to New Orleans, where he engineered the war's greatest American victory, fighting off a British invasion in January 1815. Although a slaveholder, Jackson recruited the city's free men of color into his forces, appealing to them as "sons of freedom" and promising them the same pay and land bounties as white recruits. A number of prominent political careers flowed from American victories. Jackson and Harrison would ride their reputations as military heroes all the way to the White House. Colonel Richard M. Johnson, who claimed to have actually killed Tecumseh, would later be elected vice president.

With neither side wishing to continue the conflict, the United States and Britain signed the Treaty of Ghent, ending the war. Although the treaty was signed in December 1814, ships carrying news of the agreement did not reach America until after the Battle of New Orleans had been fought. The treaty restored the previous status quo. No territory exchanged hands, nor did any provisions relate to impressment or neutral shipping rights. Considering that the war had not been a military success for the United States, the Treaty of Ghent was about as good an outcome as could be expected.

The Taking of the City of Washington, an 1814 engraving produced in London, portrays the assault during which British forces captured the undefended city and burned the White House, the Capitol, and several warships.

THE WAR'S AFTERMATH

A number of contemporaries called the War of 1812 the Second War of Independence. Despite widespread opposition to the conflict, it confirmed the ability of a republican government to conduct a war without surrendering its institutions. Jackson's victory at New Orleans not only made him a national hero but also became a celebrated example of the ability of virtuous citizens of a republic to defeat the forces of despotic Europe.

Moreover, the war completed the conquest of the area east of the Mississippi River, which had begun during the Revolution. Never again would the British or Indians pose a threat to American control of this vast region. The war also broke the remaining power of Indians in the Old Northwest and significantly reduced their holdings in the South, opening rich new lands to American settlers. In its aftermath, white settlers poured into Indiana, Michigan, Alabama, and Mississippi, bringing with them their distinctive forms of social organization. "I have no doubt," Jackson wrote to his wife, "but in a few years the banks of the Alabama will present a beautiful view of elegant mansions and extensive rich and productive farms." He did not mention that those mansions would be built and the farms worked by slaves.

Britain's defeat of Napoleon inaugurated a long period of peace in Europe. With diplomatic affairs playing less and less of a role in American public life, Americans' sense of separateness from the Old World grew ever stronger. The war also strengthened a growing sense of nationalism in Canada, based in part on separateness from the United States. As in 1775, Canadians did not rise up to welcome an invading army from the south, to the puzzlement of Americans who could not understand why they did not wish to become part of the empire of liberty.

The bombardment of Baltimore's Fort McHenry in September 1814 was of minor military importance, but it is remembered as the inspiration for Francis Scott Key's poem "The Star-Spangled Banner."

THE END OF THE FEDERALIST PARTY

Jefferson and Madison succeeded in one major political aim—the elimination of the Federalist Party. At first, the war led to a revival of Federalist fortunes. With antiwar sentiment at its peak in 1812, Madison had been reelected by the relatively narrow margin of 128 electoral votes to 89 over his Federalist opponent, DeWitt Clinton of New York. But then came a self-inflicted blow. In December 1814, a group of New England Federalists gathered at Hartford, Connecticut, to give voice to their party's long-standing grievances, especially the domination of the federal government by Virginia presidents and their own region's declining influence as new western states entered the Union. They called for amending the Constitution to eliminate the three-fifths clause that strengthened southern political power, and to require a two-thirds vote of Congress for the admission of new states, declarations of war, and laws restricting trade. Contrary to later myth, the Hartford Convention did not call for secession or disunion. But it affirmed the right of a state to "interpose" its authority if the federal government violated the Constitution.

The Hartford Convention had barely adjourned before Jackson electrified the nation with his victory at New Orleans. "Rising Glory of the American Republic," one newspaper exulted. In speeches and sermons, political and religious leaders alike proclaimed that Jackson's triumph revealed, once again, that a divine hand oversaw America's destiny. The Federalists could not free themselves from the charge of lacking patriotism. Within a few years, their party no longer existed. Its stance on the war was only one cause of the party's demise. The urban commercial and financial interests it championed represented a small minority in an expanding agricultural nation. Their elitism and distrust of popular self-government placed Federalists more and more at odds with the new nation's democratic ethos. Yet in their dying moments Federalists had raised an issue—southern domination of the national government—that would long outlive their political party. And the country stood on the verge of a profound economic and social transformation that strengthened the very forces of commercial development that Federalists had welcomed and many Republicans feared.

SUGGESTED READING

BOOKS

Appleby, Joyce. *Capitalism and a New Social Order: The Republican Vision of the 1790s* (1984). Explores how the Jeffersonians sought simultaneously to expand economic enterprise and equality of opportunity.

Banning, Lance. *The Jeffersonian Persuasion: Evolution of a Party Ideology* (1978). A careful examination of Jeffersonian ideas, relating them to the ideological origins of the American Revolution.

Egerton, Douglas R. *Gabriel's Rebellion: The Virginia Slave Conspiracies of 1800 and 1802* (1993). The most comprehensive account of one the most important slave conspiracies in American history.

Elkins, Stanley, and Eric L. McKitrick. *The Age of Federalism* (1993). A detailed account of the politics of the 1790s.

Hofstadter, Richard. *The Idea of a Party System: The Rise of Legitimate Opposition in the United States, 1780–1840* (1969). Considers how Americans began by rejecting the idea of organized political parties and ended up accepting their legitimacy.

Kerber, Linda K. *Women of the Republic: Intellect and Ideology in Revolutionary America* (1980). A study of prevailing ideas about women's place in the new republic.

Lambert, Frank. *The Barbary Wars: American Independence in the Atlantic World* (2005). An account of the first foreign military conflict conducted by the newly independent United States.

McCoy, Drew. *The Elusive Republic: Political Economy in Jeffersonian America* (1980). An influential study of the economic and political outlooks and policies of Federalists and Jeffersonians.

Miller, John C. *Crisis in Freedom: The Alien and Sedition Acts* (1952). Examines how the Adams administration sought to use the power of the federal government to stifle dissent and the free press.

Ronda, James P. *Lewis and Clark among the Indians* (1984). An account of the most famous exploring party in American history.

Rothman, Adam. *Slave Country: American Expansion and the Origins of the Deep South* (2005). A pioneering study of how the United States secured control of what are now the Gulf states, opening the door for the expansion of slavery.

Smelser, Marshall. *The Democratic Republic, 1801–1815* (1968). Still the best narrative history of the presidencies of Jefferson and Madison.

Sugden, John. *Tecumseh's Last Stand* (1985). Relates the rise and fall of the era's most prominent Indian leader.

Waldstreicher, David. *In the Midst of Perpetual Fetes: The Making of American Nationalism, 1776–1820* (1997). Explores how Americans celebrated and thought about their nation's independence in the years of the early republic.

WEBSITES

Rivers, Edens, Empires: Lewis and Clark and the Revealing of America: www
.loc.gov/exhibits/lewisandclark/lewisandclark.html

REVIEW QUESTIONS

1. Identify the major parts of Hamilton's financial plan, who supported these proposals, and why they created such passionate opposition.

2. How did the French Revolution and ensuing global struggle between Great Britain and France shape early American politics?

3. How did each of the following demonstrate a growing U.S. involvement in the world: Washington's Farewell Address, Jefferson's response to the Haitian Revolution, and the Barbary Wars.

4. How did the expansion of the public sphere offer new opportunities to women?

5. How did the Virginia and Kentucky resolutions of 1798 threaten government stability and the future of the republic?

6. Thomas Jefferson spoke of creating an "Empire of Liberty." What actions did he take to achieve such a goal, and was a universal expansion of freedom the result?

7. Why did contemporaries refer to the War of 1812 as the Second War of Independence, and was this name accurate?

8. Whose status was changed the most by the War of 1812—Great Britain, the United States, or Native Americans?

FREEDOM QUESTIONS

1. Why did Jefferson believe Hamilton's financial plan would destroy both freedom and the republic?

2. Identify the key components of liberty endorsed by the Democratic-Republican societies. Why did Federalists view such societies and ideas as evidence that liberty was getting "out of hand"?

3. Why were the Alien and Sedition Acts of 1798 viewed as assaults on freedom by Jefferson's supporters, but justified as a defense of a stable republic by the Federalists?

4. The divide between the ideals of American liberty and the institution of slavery grew during the first quarter century of the American republic. Explain how and why, using examples.

KEY TERMS

REVIEW TABLE

Growing Global Involvement

Event	Date	National Issue	Response
French Revolution and war in Europe	1789–1815	Uphold alliance and go to war, or benefit economically by neutrality	Neutrality proclamation
Haitian Revolution	1791–1804	Increased fear of slave insurrections	Quarantine trade with Haiti
British seizure of ships and impressments	1793–1796	War or peace	Jay's Treaty keeps peace until 1812
Barbary Wars	1801–1804	Pirates seizing ships and enslaving Americans; forcing ransom payments	Naval war v. Tripoli

CHAPTER 9

The Market Revolution, 1800–1840

Painted around 1850, this work depicts the city of Lowell, Massachusetts, the most famous of the early factory towns and a center of the cotton textile industry. The factories sit alongside the Merrimack River, which supplies them with water power. The artist's prominent depiction of trees suggests that nature and industry can coexist harmoniously.

Focus Questions

- What were the main elements of the market revolution?

- How did the market revolution spark social change?

- How did the meanings of American freedom change in this period?

- How did the market revolution affect the lives of workers, women, and African-Americans?

In 1824, the Marquis de Lafayette visited the United States. Nearly fifty years had passed since, as a youth of twenty, the French nobleman fought at Washington's side in the War of Independence. Now, his thirteen-month tour became a triumphant Jubilee of Liberty. Americans had good reason to celebrate Lafayette's visit and their own freedom. Since 1784, when he had last journeyed to the United States, the nation's population had tripled to nearly 12 million, its land area had more than doubled, and its political institutions had thrived. Lafayette's tour demonstrated how profoundly the nation had changed. The thirteen states of 1784 had grown to twenty-four, and he visited every one—a journey that would have been almost impossible forty years earlier. Lafayette traveled up the Mississippi and Ohio Rivers by steamboat, a recent invention that was helping to bring economic development to the trans-Appalachian West, and crossed upstate New York via the Erie Canal, the world's longest man-made waterway, which linked the region around the Great Lakes with the Atlantic coast via the Hudson River.

Americans in the first half of the nineteenth century were fond of describing liberty as the defining quality of their new nation, the unique genius of its institutions. The poet Walt Whitman wrote of his countrymen's "deathless attachment to freedom." Likenesses of the goddess of Liberty, a familiar figure in eighteenth-century British visual imagery, became even more common in the United States, appearing in paintings and sculpture and on folk art from weather vanes to quilts and tavern signs. Never, declared President Andrew Jackson in his farewell address in 1837, had any population "enjoyed so much freedom and happiness as the people of these United States." The celebration of freedom could be found in sermons, newspaper editorials, and political pronouncements in every region of the country. In *Democracy in America*, the French historian and politician Alexis de Tocqueville wrote of the "holy cult of freedom" he encountered on his own visit to the United States during the early 1830s. "For fifty years," he wrote, "the inhabitants of the United States have been repeatedly and constantly told that they are the only religious, enlightened, and free people. They . . . have an immensely high opinion of themselves and are not far from believing that they form a species apart from the rest of the human race."

Even as Lafayette, Tocqueville, and numerous other visitors from abroad toured the United States, however, Americans' understandings of freedom were changing. Three historical processes unleashed by the Revolution accelerated after the War of 1812: the spread of market relations, the westward movement of the population, and the rise of a vigorous political democracy. (The first two will be discussed in this chapter, the third in Chapter 10.) All powerfully affected the development of American society. They also helped to reshape the idea of freedom, identifying it ever more closely with economic opportunity, physical mobility, and participation in a vibrantly democratic political system.

But American freedom also continued to be shaped by the presence of slavery. Lafayette, who had purchased a plantation in the West Indies and freed its slaves, once wrote, "I would never have drawn my sword in the cause of America if I could have conceived that thereby I was founding a land of slavery." Yet slavery was moving westward with the young republic. The same steamboats and canals that enabled millions of farm families to send their goods to market also facilitated the growth of slave-based cotton plantations in the South. And slavery drew a strict racial boundary around American democracy, making voting, officeholding, and participation in the public sphere privileges for whites alone. In several southern cities, public notices warned "persons of color" to stay away from the ceremonies honoring Lafayette. Half a century after the winning of independence, the coexistence of liberty and slavery, and their simultaneous expansion, remained the central contradiction of American life.

A NEW ECONOMY

In the first half of the nineteenth century, an economic transformation known to historians as the market revolution swept over the United States. Its catalyst was a series of innovations in transportation and communication. American technology had hardly changed during the colonial era. No important alterations were made in sailing ships, no major canals were built, and manufacturing continued to be done by hand, with skills passed on from artisan to journeyman and apprentice. At the dawn of the nineteenth century, most roads were little more than rutted paths through the woods. Apart from sailing ships plying the Atlantic coast and flatboats floating downstream on major rivers, trade within the new nation faced insuperable barriers. Transporting goods thirty miles inland by road cost as much as shipping the same cargo from England. In 1800, it took fifty days to move goods from Cincinnati to New York City, via a flatboat ride down the Mississippi River to New Orleans and then a journey by sail along the Gulf and Atlantic coasts.

The market revolution represented an acceleration of developments already under way in the colonial era. As noted in previous chapters, southern planters were marketing the products of slave labor in the international market as early as the seventeenth century. By the eighteenth, many colonists had been drawn into Britain's commercial empire. Consumer goods like

An 1810 advertisement for a stagecoach route linking Boston and Sandwich, Massachusetts, reveals the slow speed and high cost of land transportation in the early nineteenth century. It took the entire day (beginning at 5 A.M.), and cost around fifty dollars in today's money to travel the fifty-seven miles between the towns, with stops along the way for breakfast and lunch.

sugar and tea, and market-oriented tactics like the boycott of British goods, had been central to the political battles leading up to independence.

Nonetheless, as Americans moved across the Appalachian Mountains, and into interior regions of the states along the Atlantic coast, they found themselves more and more isolated from markets. In 1800, American farm families produced at home most of what they needed, from clothing to farm implements. What they could not make themselves, they obtained by bartering with their neighbors or purchasing from local stores and from rural craftsmen like blacksmiths and shoemakers. Those farmers not located near cities or navigable waterways found it almost impossible to market their produce.

The early life of Abraham Lincoln was typical of those who grew up in the pre-market world. Lincoln was born in Kentucky in 1809 and seven years later moved with his family to Indiana, where he lived until 1831. His father occasionally took pork down the Ohio and Mississippi Rivers to market in New Orleans, and Lincoln himself at age nineteen traveled by flatboat to that city to sell the goods of a local merchant. But essentially, the Lincoln family was self-sufficient. They hunted game for much of their food and sewed most of their clothing at home. They relied little on cash; Lincoln's father sometimes sent young Abraham to work for neighbors as a way of settling debts. As an adult, however, Lincoln embraced the market revolution. In the Illinois legislature in the 1830s, he eagerly promoted the improvement of rivers to facilitate access to markets. As a lawyer, he eventually came to represent the Illinois Central Railroad, which opened large areas of Illinois to commercial farming.

Many Americans devoted their energies to solving the technological problems that inhibited commerce within the country. Thomas Paine spent the 1780s and 1790s not only promoting democracy in America and Europe but also developing a design for an iron bridge, so that rivers could be crossed in all seasons of the year without impeding river traffic.

An 1837 copy of a color drawing that accompanied a patent application for a type of raft designed in 1818. For many years, rafts like this were used to transport goods to market on western rivers.

A view of New York City, in 1849, by the noted lithographer Nathaniel Currier. Steamships and sailing vessels of various sizes crowd the harbor of the nation's largest city and busiest port.

ROADS AND STEAMBOATS

In the first half of the nineteenth century, in rapid succession, the steamboat, canal, railroad, and telegraph wrenched America out of its economic past. These innovations opened new land to settlement, lowered transportation costs, and made it far easier for economic enterprises to sell their products. They linked farmers to national and world markets and made them major consumers of manufactured goods. Americans, wrote Tocqueville, had "annihilated space and time."

The first advance in overland transportation came through the construction of toll roads, or "turnpikes," by localities, states, and private companies. Between 1800 and 1830, the New England and Middle Atlantic states alone chartered more than 900 companies to build new roads. In 1806, Congress authorized the construction of the paved National Road from Cumberland, Maryland, to the Old Northwest. It reached Wheeling, on the Ohio River, in 1818 and by 1838 extended to Illinois, where it ended.

Because maintenance costs were higher than expected and many towns built "shunpikes"—short detours that enabled residents to avoid tollgates, most private toll roads never turned a profit. Even on the new roads, horse-drawn wagons remained an inefficient mode of getting goods to market, except over short distances. It was improved water transportation that most dramatically increased the speed and lowered the expense of commerce.

Robert Fulton, a Pennsylvania-born artist and engineer, had experimented with steamboat designs while living in France during the 1790s. He even launched a steamboat on the Seine River in Paris in 1803. But not until 1807, when Fulton's ship, the *Clermont*, navigated the Hudson River from New York City to Albany, was the steamboat's technological and commercial feasibility demonstrated. The invention made possible upstream commerce (that is, travel against the current) on the country's major rivers as well as rapid transport across the Great Lakes and, eventually, the Atlantic Ocean. By 1811, the first steamboat had been introduced on the Mississippi River; twenty years later some 200 plied its waters.

THE ERIE CANAL

The completion in 1825 of the 363-mile Erie Canal across upstate New York (a remarkable feat of engineering at a time when America's next largest canal was only twenty-eight miles long) allowed goods to flow between the Great Lakes and New York City. Almost instantaneously, the canal attracted an influx of farmers migrating from New England, giving birth to cities like Buffalo, Rochester, and Syracuse along its path. Its water, wrote the novelist Nathaniel Hawthorne after a trip on the canal, served as a miraculous "fertilizer," for "it causes towns with their masses of brick and stone, their churches and theaters, their business . . . to spring up."

New York governor DeWitt Clinton, who oversaw the construction of the state-financed canal, predicted that it would make New York City "the granary of the world, the emporium of commerce, the seat of manufactures, the focus of great moneyed operations." And, indeed, the canal gave New York City primacy over competing ports in access to trade with the Old Northwest. In its financing by the state government, the Erie Canal typified the developing transportation infrastructure. With the federal government generally under the control of political leaders hostile to federal funding for internal improvements, the burden fell on the states. Between 1787 and 1860, the federal government spent about $60 million building roads and canals and improving harbors; the states spent nearly ten times that sum.

The completion of the Erie Canal set off a scramble among other states to match New York's success. Several borrowed so much money to finance elaborate programs of canal construction that they went bankrupt during the economic depression that began in 1837. By then, however, more than 3,000 miles of canals had been built, creating a network linking the Atlantic states with the Ohio and Mississippi Valleys and drastically reducing the cost of transportation.

A watercolor from 1830 depicts the Erie Canal five years after it opened. Boats carrying passengers and goods traverse the waterway, along whose banks farms and villages have sprung up.

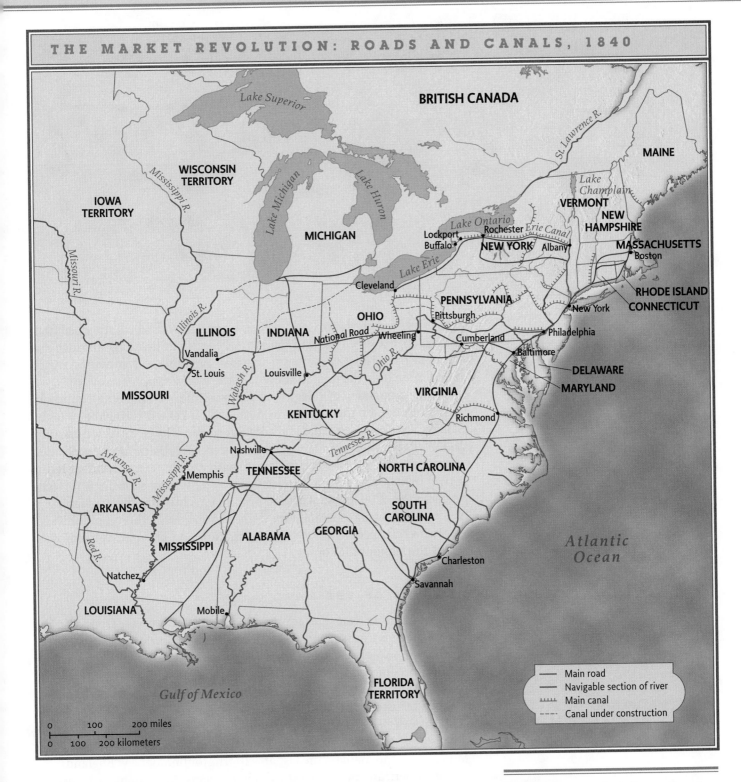

THE MARKET REVOLUTION: ROADS AND CANALS, 1840

Legend:
— Main road
— Navigable section of river
⊥⊥⊥ Main canal
- - - Canal under construction

RAILROADS AND THE TELEGRAPH

Canals connected existing waterways. The railroad opened vast new areas of the American interior to settlement, while stimulating the mining of coal for fuel and the manufacture of iron for locomotives and rails. Work on the Baltimore and Ohio, the nation's first commercial railroad, began in 1828.

The improvement of existing roads and building of new roads and canals sharply reduced transportation times and costs and stimulated the growth of the market economy.

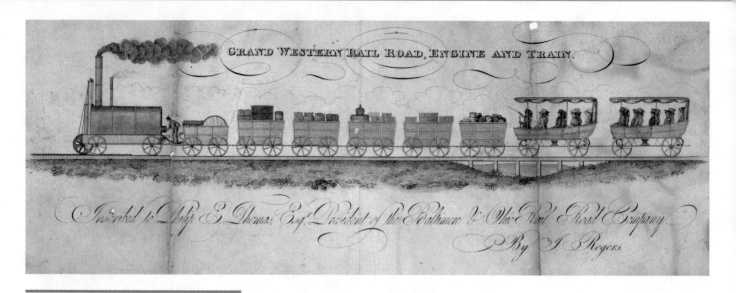

An 1827 engraving designed to show the feasibility of railroads driven by steam-powered locomotives, and dedicated to the president of the Baltimore and Ohio Railroad, which began construction in the following year. The engraver placed passengers as far from the locomotive as possible to ensure their safety in case of an explosion.

Five years later, the South Carolina Canal and Railroad, which stretched from Charleston across the state to Hamburg, became the first long-distance line to begin operation. By 1860, the railroad network had grown to 30,000 miles, more than the total in the rest of the world combined.

At the same time, the telegraph made possible instantaneous communication throughout the nation. The device was invented during the 1830s by Samuel F. B. Morse, an artist and amateur scientist living in New York City, and it was put into commercial operation in 1844. Using Morse code, messages could be sent over electric wires, with each letter and number represented by its own pattern of electrical pulses. Within sixteen years, some 50,000 miles of telegraph wire had been strung. Initially, the telegraph was a service for businesses, and especially newspapers, rather than individuals. It helped speed the flow of information and brought uniformity to prices throughout the country.

THE RISE OF THE WEST

Improvements in transportation and communication made possible the rise of the West as a powerful, self-conscious region of the new nation. Between 1790 and 1840, some 4.5 million people crossed the Appalachian Mountains—more than the entire U.S. population at the time of Washington's first inauguration. Most of this migration took place after the end of the War of 1812, which unleashed a flood of land-hungry settlers moving from eastern states. In the six years following the end of the war in 1815, six new states entered the Union (Indiana, Illinois, Missouri, Alabama, Mississippi, and Maine—the last an eastern frontier for New England).

Few Americans moved west as lone pioneers. More frequently, people traveled in groups and, once they arrived in the West, cooperated with each other to clear land, build houses and barns, and establish communities. One stream of migration, including both small farmers and planters with their slaves, flowed out of the South to create the new Cotton Kingdom of Alabama, Mississippi, Louisiana, and Arkansas. Many farm families from the Upper South crossed into southern Ohio, Indiana, and Illinois. A third population stream moved from New England across New York to the

Upper Northwest—northern Ohio, Indiana, and Illinois, and Michigan and Wisconsin.

Some western migrants became "squatters," setting up farms on unoccupied land without a clear legal title. Those who purchased land acquired it either from the federal government, at the price, after 1820, of $1.25 per acre payable in cash, or from land speculators on long-term credit. By 1840, settlement had reached the Mississippi River and two large new regions—the Old Northwest and Old Southwest—had entered the Union. The West became the home of regional cultures very much like those the migrants had left behind. Upstate New York and the Upper Northwest resembled New England, with its small towns, churches, and schools, while the Lower South replicated the plantation-based society of the southern Atlantic states.

As population moved west, the nation's borders expanded. National boundaries made little difference to territorial expansion—in Florida, and later in Texas and Oregon, American settlers rushed in to claim land under the jurisdiction of foreign countries (Spain, Mexico, and Britain) or Indian tribes, confident that American sovereignty would soon follow in their wake. Nor did the desire of local inhabitants to remain outside the American republic deter the nation's expansion. Florida, for example, fell into American hands despite the resistance of local Indians and Spain's rejection of American offers to buy the area. In 1810, American residents of West Florida rebelled and seized Baton Rouge, and the United States soon annexed the area. The drive for the acquisition of East Florida was spurred by Georgia and Alabama planters who wished to eliminate a refuge for fugitive slaves and hostile Seminole Indians. Andrew Jackson led troops into the area in 1818. While on foreign soil, he created an international crisis by executing two British traders and a number of Indian chiefs. Although Jackson withdrew, Spain, aware that it could not defend the territory, sold it to the United States in the Adams-Onís Treaty of 1819.

Successive censuses told the remarkable story of western growth. In 1840, by which time the government had sold to settlers and land companies nearly 43 million acres of land, 7 million Americans—two-fifths of the

A watercolor by the artist Edwin Whitefield depicts a squatter's cabin in the Minnesota woods.

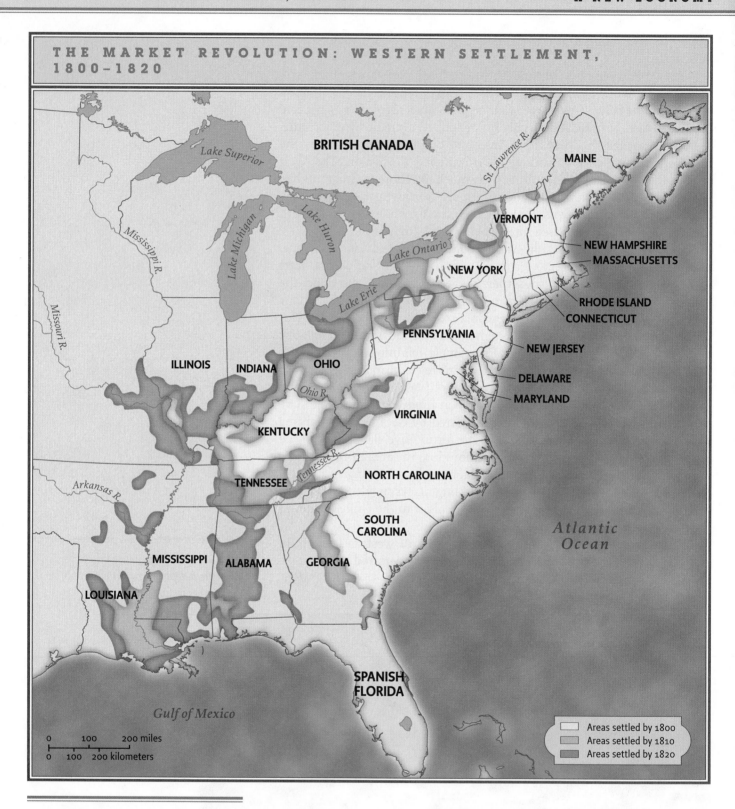

THE MARKET REVOLUTION: WESTERN SETTLEMENT, 1800–1820

Areas settled by 1800
Areas settled by 1810
Areas settled by 1820

In the first two decades of the nineteenth century, the westward movement of the population brought settlement to and across the Mississippi River. Before canals—and later, railroads—opened previously landlocked areas to commercial farming, settlement was concentrated near rivers.

total population—lived beyond the Appalachian Mountains. Between 1810 and 1830, Ohio's population grew from 231,000 to more than 900,000. It reached nearly 2 million in 1850, when it ranked third among all the states. The careers of the era's leading public figures reflected the westward movement. Andrew Jackson, Henry Clay, and many other statesmen had been born in states along the Atlantic coast but made their mark in politics after moving west.

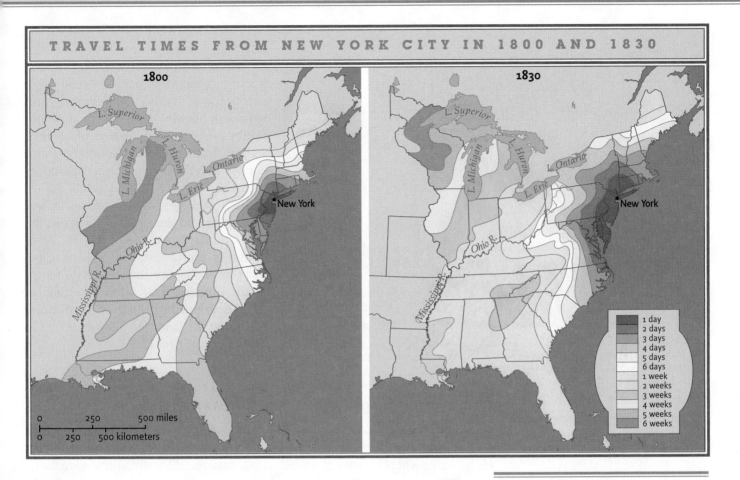

TRAVEL TIMES FROM NEW YORK CITY IN 1800 AND 1830

1800 · 1830

1 day	
2 days	
3 days	
4 days	
5 days	
6 days	
1 week	
2 weeks	
3 weeks	
4 weeks	
5 weeks	
6 weeks	

These maps illustrate how the transportation revolution of the early nineteenth century made possible much more rapid travel within the United States.

THE COTTON KINGDOM

Although the market revolution and westward expansion occurred simultaneously in the North and the South, their combined effects heightened the nation's sectional divisions. In some ways, the most dynamic feature of the American economy in the first thirty years of the nineteenth century was the rise of the Cotton Kingdom. The early industrial revolution, which began in England and soon spread to parts of the North, centered on factories producing cotton textiles with water-powered spinning and weaving machinery. These factories generated an immense demand for cotton, a crop the Deep South was particularly suited to growing because of its climate and soil fertility. Until 1793, the marketing of cotton had been slowed by the laborious task of removing seeds from the plant itself. But in that year, Eli Whitney, a Yale graduate working in Georgia as a private tutor, invented the cotton gin. A fairly simple device consisting of rollers and brushes, the gin quickly separated the seed from the cotton. It made possible the growing and selling of cotton on a large scale.

Coupled with rising demand for cotton and the opening of new lands in the West to settlement, Whitney's invention revolutionized American slavery. An institution that many Americans had expected to die out because its major crop, tobacco, exhausted the soil, now embarked on a period of unprecedented expansion. In the first decade of the nineteenth century, cotton plantations spread into the South Carolina upcountry (the region inland from the Atlantic coast previously dominated by small farms), a major reason why the state reopened the African slave trade between

Table 9.1 POPULATION GROWTH OF SELECTED WESTERN STATES, 1800–1850 (EXCLUDING INDIANS)

State	1810	1830	1850
Alabama	9,000	310,000	772,000
Illinois	12,000	157,000	851,000
Indiana	25,000	343,000	988,000
Louisiana	77,000	216,000	518,000
Mississippi	31,000	137,000	607,000
Missouri	20,000	140,000	682,000
Ohio	231,000	938,000	1,980,000

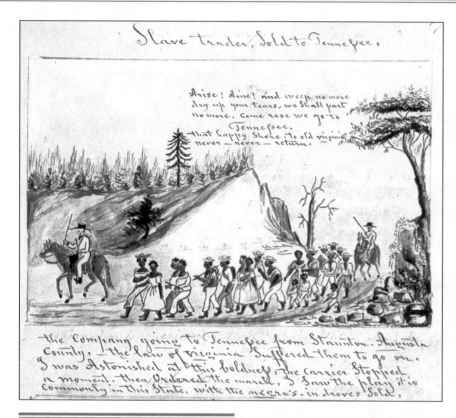

Slave Trader, Sold to Tennessee, *a watercolor sketch by the artist Lewis Miller from the mid-1850s. Miller depicts a group of slaves being marched from Virginia to Tennessee. Once Congress voted to prohibit the further importation of slaves into the country, slaveowners in newly opened areas of the country had to obtain slaves from other parts of the United States.*

1803 and 1808. After the War of 1812, the federal government moved to consolidate American control over the Deep South, forcing defeated Indians to cede land, encouraging white settlement, and acquiring Florida. With American sovereignty came the expansion of slavery. Settlers from the older southern states flooded into the region. Planters monopolized the most fertile land, while poorer farmers were generally confined to less productive and less accessible areas in the "hill country" and piney woods. After Congress prohibited the Atlantic slave trade in 1808—the earliest date allowed by the Constitution—a massive trade in slaves developed within the United States, supplying the labor force required by the new Cotton Kingdom.

THE UNFREE WESTWARD MOVEMENT

Historians estimate that around 1 million slaves were shifted from the older slave states to the Deep South between 1800 and 1860. Some traveled with their owners to newly established plantations, but the majority were transported by slave traders to be sold at auction for work in the cotton fields. Slave trading became a well-organized business, with firms gathering slaves in Maryland, Virginia, and South Carolina and shipping them to markets in Mobile, Natchez, and New Orleans. Slave coffles—groups chained to one another on forced marches to the Deep South—became a common sight. A British visitor to the United States in the 1840s encountered what he called a "disgusting and hideous spectacle," a file of "about two hundred slaves, manacled and chained together," being marched from Virginia to Louisiana. A source of greater freedom for many whites, the westward movement meant to African-Americans the destruction of family ties, the breakup of long-standing communities, and receding opportunities for liberty.

In 1793, when Whitney designed his invention, the United States produced 5 million pounds of cotton. By 1820, the crop had grown to nearly 170 million pounds. Thomas Jefferson had believed that European demand for American grain would underpin the nation's economic growth and the small farmer's independence. But as the southern economy expanded westward, it was cotton produced on slave plantations, not grain grown by sturdy yeomen, that became the linchpin of southern development and by far the most important export of the empire of liberty.

MARKET SOCIETY

Since cotton was produced solely for sale in national and international markets, the South was in some ways the most commercially oriented

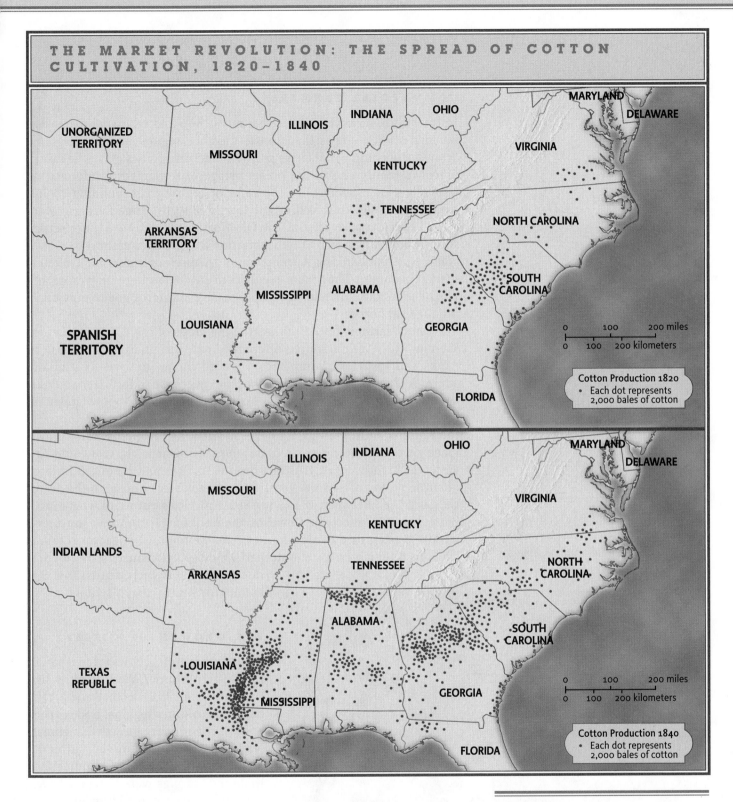

THE MARKET REVOLUTION: THE SPREAD OF COTTON CULTIVATION, 1820–1840

region of the United States. Yet rather than spurring economic change, the South's expansion westward simply reproduced the same agrarian, slave-based social order of the older states. The region remained overwhelmingly rural. In 1860, roughly 80 percent of southerners worked the land—the same proportion as in 1800. The South's transportation and banking systems remained adjuncts of the plantation economy, geared largely to

Maps of cotton production graphically illustrate the rise of the Cotton Kingdom stretching from South Carolina to Louisiana.

transporting cotton and other staple crops to market and financing the purchase of land and slaves.

COMMERCIAL FARMERS

In the North, however, the market revolution and westward expansion set in motion changes that transformed the region into an integrated economy of commercial farms and manufacturing cities. As in the case of Lincoln's family, the initial pioneer stage of settlement reinforced the farmer's self-sufficiency, for the tasks of felling trees, building cabins, breaking the soil, and feeding the family left little time for agriculture geared to the market. But as the Old Northwest became a more settled society, bound by a web of transportation and credit to eastern centers of commerce and banking, farmers found themselves drawn into the new market economy. They increasingly concentrated on growing crops and raising livestock for sale, while purchasing at stores goods previously produced at home.

Western farmers found in the growing cities of the East a market for their produce and a source of credit. Loans originating with eastern banks and insurance companies financed the acquisition of land and supplies and, in the 1840s and 1850s, the purchase of fertilizer and new agricultural machinery to expand production. The steel plow, invented by John Deere in 1837 and mass-produced by the 1850s, made possible the rapid subduing of the western prairies. The reaper, a horse-drawn machine that greatly increased the amount of wheat a farmer could harvest, was invented by Cyrus McCormick in 1831 and produced in large quantities soon afterward. Tens of thousands were in use on the eve of the Civil War. Between 1840 and 1860, America's output of wheat nearly tripled. Unlike cotton, however, the bulk of the crop was consumed within the country. Eastern farmers, unable to grow wheat and corn as cheaply as their western counterparts, increasingly concentrated on producing dairy products, fruits, and vegetables for nearby urban centers.

Lagonda Agricultural Works, *a color lithograph from 1859 advertising an Ohio manufacturer of agricultural machinery, in this case a horse-drawn reaper.*

THE GROWTH OF CITIES

From the beginning, cities formed part of the western frontier. Western cities like Cincinnati and St. Louis that stood at the crossroads of inter-regional trade experienced extraordinary growth. Cincinnati was known as "porkopolis," after its slaughterhouses where hundreds of thousands of pigs were butchered each year and processed for shipment to eastern consumers of meat. The greatest of all the western cities was Chicago. In the early 1830s, it was a tiny settlement on the shore of Lake Michigan. By 1860, thanks to the railroad, Chicago had become the nation's fourth largest city,

A painting of Cincinnati, self-styled Queen City of the West, from 1835. Steamboats line the Ohio River waterfront.

where farm products from throughout the Northwest were gathered to be sent east.

Like rural areas, urban centers witnessed dramatic changes due to the market revolution. The number of cities with populations exceeding 5,000 rose from 12 in 1820 to nearly 150 three decades later, by which time the urban population numbered more than 6 million. Urban merchants, bankers, and master craftsmen took advantage of the economic opportunities created by the expanding market among commercial farmers. The drive among these businessmen to increase production and reduce labor costs fundamentally altered the nature of work. Traditionally, skilled artisans had manufactured goods at home, where they controlled the pace and intensity of their own labor. Now, entrepreneurs gathered artisans into large workshops in order to oversee their work and subdivide their tasks. Craftsmen who traditionally produced an entire pair of shoes or piece of furniture saw the labor process broken down into numerous steps requiring far less skill and training. They found themselves subjected to constant supervision by their employers and relentless pressure for greater output and lower wages.

THE FACTORY SYSTEM

In some industries, most notably textiles, the factory superceded traditional craft production altogether. Factories gathered large groups of workers under central supervision and replaced hand tools with power-driven machinery. Samuel Slater, an immigrant from England, established America's first factory in 1790 at Pawtucket, Rhode Island. Since British law made it illegal to export the plans for industrial machinery, Slater, a skilled mechanic, built from memory a power-driven spinning jenny, one of the key inventions of the early industrial revolution.

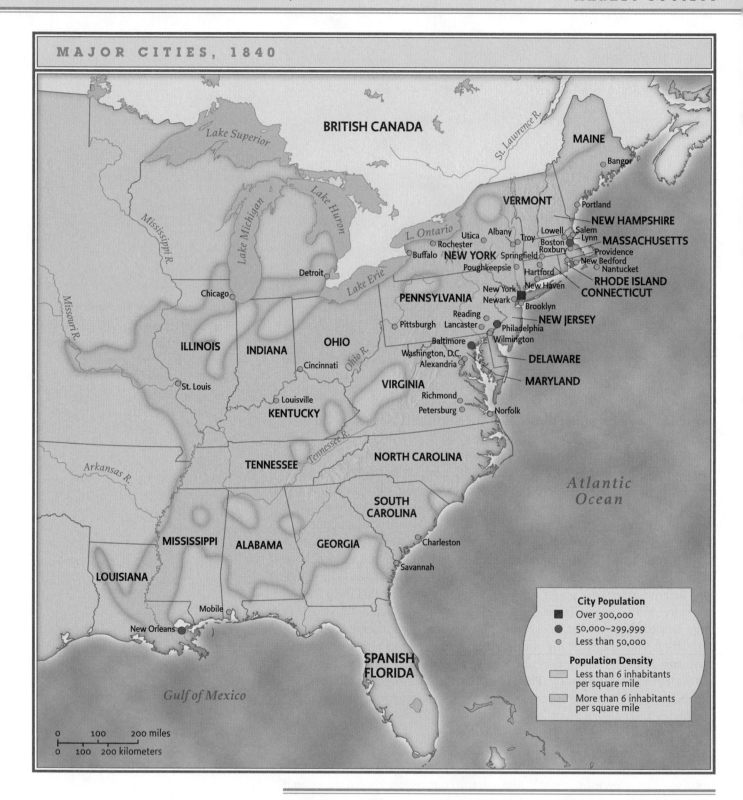

MAJOR CITIES, 1840

City Population
- ■ Over 300,000
- ● 50,000–299,999
- ○ Less than 50,000

Population Density
- Less than 6 inhabitants per square mile
- More than 6 inhabitants per square mile

Although the United States was still predominantly agricultural, by 1840 major cities had arisen in the northern and northwestern states. The South lagged far behind in urban growth. Most cities were located on navigable waterways—either the Atlantic coast or inland rivers—or on rivers that provided water power for early factories.

Spinning factories such as Slater's produced yarn, which was then sent to traditional hand-loom weavers and farm families to be woven into cloth. This "outwork" system, in which rural men and women earned money by taking in jobs from factories, typified early industrialization. Before shoe production was fully mechanized, for example, various parts of the shoe were produced in factories, then stitched together in nearby homes, and then returned to the factories for finishing. Eventually, however, the entire manufacturing process in textiles, shoes, and many other products was brought under a single factory roof.

The cutoff of British imports because of the Embargo of 1807 and the War of 1812 stimulated the establishment of the first large-scale American factory utilizing power looms for weaving cotton cloth. This was constructed in 1814 at Waltham, Massachusetts, by a group of merchants who came to be called the Boston Associates. In the 1820s, they expanded their enterprise by creating an entirely new factory town (incorporated as the city of Lowell in 1836) on the Merrimack River, twenty-seven miles from Boston. Here they built a group of modern textile factories that brought together all phases of production from the spinning of thread to the weaving and finishing of cloth. By 1850, Lowell's fifty-two mills employed more than 10,000 workers. Across New England, small industrial cities sprang up pat-

A group of shoemakers with their tools, photographed in 1837. Artisan production survived in many crafts, but shoemakers found themselves in dire straits as factories began industrializing shoe production.

Mill on the Brandywine, *an 1830 watercolor of a Pennsylvania paper mill. Because it relied on water power, much early manufacturing took place in the countryside.*

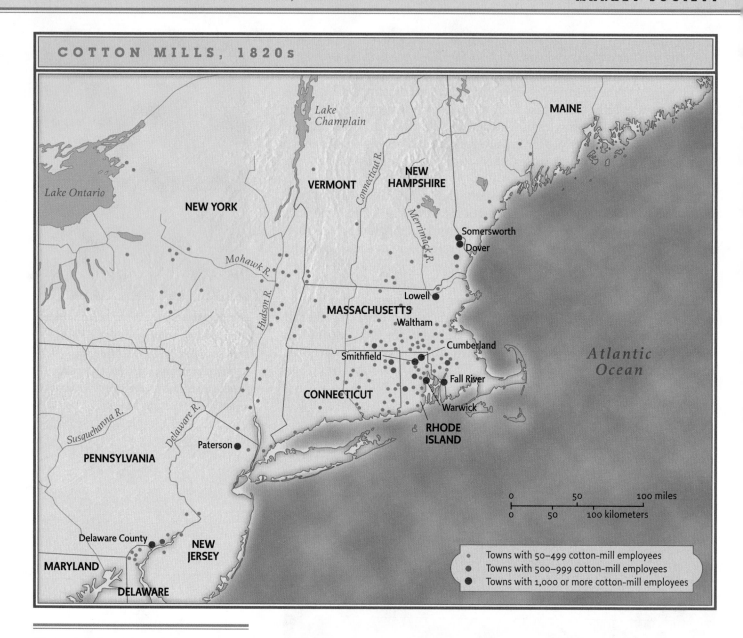

COTTON MILLS, 1820s

Towns with 50–499 cotton-mill employees
Towns with 500–999 cotton-mill employees
Towns with 1,000 or more cotton-mill employees

The early industrial revolution was concentrated in New England, where factories producing textiles from raw cotton sprang up along the region's many rivers, taking advantage of water power to drive their machinery.

terned on Waltham and Lowell. Massachusetts soon became the second most industrialized region of the world, after Great Britain.

The earliest factories, including those at Pawtucket, Waltham, and Lowell, were located along the "fall line," where waterfalls and river rapids could be harnessed to provide power for spinning and weaving machinery. By the 1840s, steam power made it possible for factory owners to locate in towns like New Bedford nearer to the coast, and in large cities like Philadelphia and Chicago with their immense local markets. In 1850, manufacturers produced in factories not only textiles but also a wide variety of other goods, including tools, firearms, shoes, clocks, ironware, and agricultural machinery. What came to be called the "American system of manufactures" relied on the mass production of interchangeable parts that could be rapidly assembled into standardized finished products. This technique was first perfected in the manufacture of clocks by Eli Terry, a

Connecticut craftsman, and in small-arms production by Eli Whitney, who had previously invented the cotton gin. More impressive, in a way, than factory production was the wide dispersion of mechanical skills throughout northern society. Every town, it seemed, had its sawmill, paper mill, iron works, shoemaker, hatmaker, tailor, and a host of other such small enterprises.

The early industrial revolution was largely confined to New England and a few cities outside it. Lacking a strong internal market, and with its slaveholding class generally opposed to industrial development, the South lagged in factory production. And outside New England, most northern manufacturing was still done in small-scale establishments employing a handful of workers, not in factories. In Cincinnati, for example, most workers in 1850 still labored in small unmechanized workshops.

THE INDUSTRIAL WORKER

The market revolution helped to change Americans' conception of time itself. Farm life continued to be regulated by the rhythms of the seasons. But in cities, clocks became part of daily life, and work time and leisure time came to be clearly marked off from one another. In artisan workshops of the colonial and early national eras, bouts of intense work alternated with periods of leisure. Artisans would set down their tools to enjoy a drink at a tavern or attend a political discussion. As the market revolution accelerated, work in factories, workshops, and even for servants in Americans' homes, took place for a specified number of hours per day. In colonial America, an artisan's pay was known as his "price," since it was linked to the goods he produced. In the nineteenth century, pay increasingly became a "wage," paid according to an hourly or daily rate. The increasing reliance on railroads, which operated according to fixed schedules, also made Americans more conscious of arranging their lives according to "clock time."

Closely supervised work tending a machine for a period determined by a clock seemed to violate the independence Americans considered an essential element of freedom. Consequently, few native-born men could be attracted to work in the early factories. Employers turned instead to those who lacked other ways of earning a living.

THE "MILL GIRLS"

While some factories employed entire families, the early New England textile mills relied largely on female and child labor. At Lowell, the most famous center of early textile manufacturing, young unmarried women from Yankee farm families dominated the workforce that tended the spinning machines. To persuade parents to allow their daughters to leave home to work in the mills, Lowell owners set up boarding houses with strict rules regulating personal behavior. They also established lecture halls, churches, and even a periodical edited by factory workers, the *Lowell Offering*, to occupy the women's free time.

The constant supervision of the workers' private lives seems impossibly restrictive from a modern point of view. But this was the first time in history that large numbers of women left their homes to participate in the pub-

A broadside from 1853, illustrating the long hours of work (twelve hours per day, with thirty minutes for lunch) in the Lowell mills and the way factory labor was strictly regulated by the clock.

Women at work tending machines in the Lowell textile mills.

A photograph from around 1860 of four anonymous working women. Their stance and gaze suggest a spirit of independence.

lic world. Most valued the opportunity to earn money independently at a time when few other jobs were open to women. Home life, Lucy Larcom later recalled, was narrow and confining, while living and working at Lowell gave the "mill girls" a "larger, firmer idea of womanhood," teaching them "to go out of themselves and enter into the lives of others. . . . It was like a young man's pleasure in entering upon business for himself." But women like Larcom did not become a permanent class of factory workers. They typically remained in the factories for only a few years, after which they left to return home, marry, or move west. Larcom herself migrated to Illinois, where she became a teacher and writer. The shortage of industrial labor continued, easing only when large-scale immigration began in the 1840s and 1850s.

THE GROWTH OF IMMIGRATION

Economic expansion fueled a demand for labor, which was met, in part, by increased immigration from abroad. Between 1790 and 1830, immigrants contributed only marginally to American population growth. But between 1840 and 1860, over 4 million people (more than the entire population of 1790) entered the United States, the majority from Ireland and Germany. About 90 percent headed for the northern states, where job opportunities were most abundant and the new arrivals would not have to compete with slave labor. Immigrants were virtually unknown in the slave states, except in cities on the periphery of the South, such as New Orleans, St. Louis, and Baltimore. In the North, however, they became a visible presence in both urban and rural areas. In 1860, the 814,000 residents of New York City, the major port of entry, included more than 384,000 immigrants, and one-third of the population of Wisconsin was foreign-born.

Numerous factors inspired this massive flow of population across the Atlantic. In Europe, the modernization of agriculture and the industrial revolution disrupted centuries-old patterns of life, pushing peasants off the land and eliminating the jobs of traditional craft workers. The introduction of the ocean-going steamship and the railroad made long-distance travel more practical. The Cunard Line began regular sailings with inexpensive fares from Britain to Boston and New York City in the 1840s. Beginning around 1840, emigration from Europe accelerated, not only to the United States but to Canada and Australia as well. Frequently, a male family member emigrated first; he would later send back money for the rest of the family to follow.

IRISH AND GERMAN NEWCOMERS

To everyone discontented in Europe, commented the *New York Times*, "thoughts come of the New Free World." America's political and religious freedoms attracted Europeans who chafed under the continent's repressive governments and rigid social hierarchies, including political refugees from

Table 9.2 TOTAL NUMBER OF IMMIGRANTS BY FIVE-YEAR PERIOD	
Years	**Number of Immigrants**
1841–1845	430,000
1846–1850	1,283,000
1851–1855	1,748,000
1856–1860	850,000

the failed revolutions of 1848. "In America," wrote a German newcomer, "there aren't any masters, here everyone is a free agent."

The largest number of immigrants, however, were refugees from disaster—Irish men and women fleeing the Great Famine of 1845–1851, when a blight destroyed the potato crop on which the island's diet rested. An estimated 1 million persons starved to death and another million emigrated in those years, most of them to the United States. Lacking industrial skills and capital, these impoverished agricultural laborers and small farmers ended up filling the low-wage unskilled jobs native-born Americans sought to avoid. Male Irish immigrants built America's railroads, dug canals, and worked as common laborers, servants, longshoremen, and factory operatives. Irish women frequently went to work as servants in the homes of native-born Americans, although some preferred factory work to domestic service. "It's the freedom that we want when the day's work is done," one Irish woman explained. "Our day is ten hours long, but when it's done it's done"; however, servants were on call at any time. By the end of the 1850s, the Lowell textile mills had largely replaced Yankee farm women with immigrant Irish families. Four-fifths of Irish immigrants remained in the Northeast. In Boston, New York, and smaller industrial cities, they congregated in overcrowded urban ghettos notorious for poverty, crime, and disease.

The second-largest group of immigrants, Germans, included a considerably larger number of skilled craftsmen than the Irish. Germans also settled in tightly knit neighborhoods in eastern cities, but many were able to move to the West, where they established themselves as craftsmen, shopkeepers, and farmers. The "German triangle," as the cities of Cincinnati, St. Louis, and Milwaukee were sometimes called, all attracted large German populations. A vibrant German-language culture, with its own schools, newspapers, associations, and churches, developed wherever large numbers of Germans settled. "As one passes along the Bowery," one observer

Although our image of the West emphasizes the lone pioneer, many migrants settled in tightly knit communities and worked cooperatively. This painting by Olof Krans, who came to the United States from Sweden with his family in 1850 at the age of twelve, shows a group of women preparing to plant corn at the immigrant settlement of Bishop Hill, Illinois.

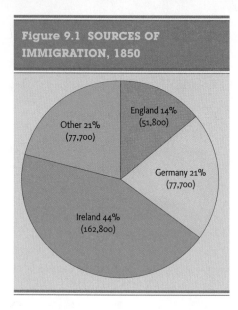

Figure 9.1 SOURCES OF IMMIGRATION, 1850

England 14% (51,800)

Germany 21% (77,700)

Ireland 44% (162,800)

Other 21% (77,700)

noted of a part of New York City known as Kleindeutschland (Little Germany), "almost everything is German."

Some 40,000 Scandinavians also emigrated to the United States in these years, most of whom settled on farms in the Old Northwest. The continuing expansion of industry and the failure of the Chartist movement of the 1840s, which sought to democratize the system of government in Britain, also inspired many English workers to emigrate to the United States.

THE RISE OF NATIVISM

Immigrants from England (whose ranks included the actor Junius Brutus Booth, father of John Wilkes Booth) were easily absorbed, but those from Ireland encountered intense hostility. As Roman Catholics, they faced discrimination in a largely Protestant society in which the tradition of "anti-popery" still ran deep. The Irish influx greatly enhanced the visibility and power of the Catholic Church, previously a minor presence in most parts of the country. During the 1840s and 1850s, Archbishop John Hughes of New York City made the Church a more assertive institution. Hughes pressed Catholic parents to send their children to an expanding network of parochial schools, and he sought government funding to pay for them. He aggressively attempted to win converts from Protestantism.

The idea of the United States as a refuge for those seeking economic opportunity or as an escape from oppression has always coexisted with suspicion of and hostility to foreign newcomers. American history has witnessed periods of intense anxiety over immigration. The Alien Act of 1798 reflected fear of immigrants with radical political views. During the early twentieth century, as will be discussed below, there was widespread hostility to the "new immigration" from southern and eastern Europe. In the early twenty-first century, the question of how many persons should be allowed to enter the United States, and under what circumstances, remains a volatile political issue.

The Irish influx of the 1840s and 1850s thoroughly alarmed many native-born Americans. Those who feared the impact of immigration on American political and social life were called "nativists." They blamed immigrants for urban crime, political corruption, and a fondness for intoxicating liquor, and they accused them of undercutting native-born skilled laborers by working for starvation wages. The Irish were quickly brought into the urban political machines of the Democratic Party, whose local bosses provided jobs and poor relief to struggling newcomers. Nativists contended that the Irish, supposedly unfamiliar with American conceptions of liberty and subservient to the Catholic Church, posed a threat to democratic institutions, social reform, and public education. Stereotypes similar to those directed at blacks flourished regarding the Irish as well—childlike, lazy, and slaves of their passions, they were said to be unsuited for republican freedom.

Nativism would not become a national political movement until the 1850s, as we will see in Chapter 13. But in the 1840s, New York City and Philadelphia witnessed violent anti-immigrant riots. Appealing mainly to skilled native-born workers who feared that immigrants were taking their jobs and undercutting their wages, a nativist candidate was elected New York City's mayor in 1844.

THE TRANSFORMATION OF LAW

American law increasingly supported the efforts of entrepreneurs to participate in the market revolution, while shielding them from interference by local governments and liability for some of the less desirable results of economic growth. The corporate form of business organization became central to the new market economy. A corporate firm enjoys special privileges and powers granted in a charter from the government, among them that investors and directors are not personally liable for the company's debts. Unlike companies owned by an individual, family, or limited partnership, in other words, a corporation can fail without ruining its directors and stockholders. Corporations were therefore able to raise far more capital than the traditional forms of enterprise. By the 1830s, many states had replaced the granting of charters through specific acts of legislation with "general incorporation laws," allowing any company to obtain a corporate charter if it paid a specified fee.

Many Americans distrusted corporate charters as a form of government-granted special privilege. But the courts upheld their validity, while opposing efforts by established firms to limit competition from newcomers. In *Dartmouth College v. Woodward* (1819), John Marshall's Supreme Court defined corporate charters issued by state legislatures as contracts, which future lawmakers could not alter or rescind. Five years later, in *Gibbons v. Ogden*, the Court struck down a monopoly the New York legislature had granted for steamboat navigation. And in 1837, with Roger B. Taney now the chief justice, the Court ruled that the Massachusetts legislature did not infringe the charter of an existing company that had constructed a bridge over the Charles River when it empowered a second company to build a competing bridge. The community, Taney declared, had a legitimate interest in promoting transportation and prosperity.

Local judges, meanwhile, held businessmen blameless for property damage done by factory construction (such as the flooding of upstream farmlands and the disruption of fishing when dams were built to harness water power). Numerous court decisions also affirmed employers' full authority over the workplace and invoked the old common law of conspiracy to punish workers who sought to strike for higher wages. Not until 1842, in *Commonwealth v. Hunt*, did Massachusetts chief justice Lemuel Shaw decree that there was nothing inherently illegal in workers organizing a union or a strike. Like changes in work and time, changes in the law illustrated the comment of Horace Bushnell, a Connecticut minister, that the market economy had produced a "complete revolution" in Americans' "life and manners."

THE FREE INDIVIDUAL

By the 1830s, the market revolution and westward expansion had produced a society that amazed European visitors: energetic, materialistic, and seemingly in constant motion. Arriving in Chicago in 1835, the British writer Harriet Martineau found the streets "crowded with land speculators, hurrying from one sale to another.... As the gentlemen of our party walked the streets, store-keepers hailed them from their doors, with offers of farms, and all manner of land-lots, advising them to speculate before the price of land rose higher." Alexis de Tocqueville was struck by Americans' restless energy and apparent lack of attachment to place. "No sooner do you set foot on American soil," he observed, "than you find yourself in a sort of tumult. All around you, everything is on the move." Westward migration and urban development created a large mobile population no longer tied to local communities who sought to seize the opportunities offered by economic change. "In the United States," wrote Tocqueville, "a man builds a house in which to spend his old age, and sells it before the roof is on; he plants a garden and [rents] it just as the trees are coming into bearing; he brings a field into tillage and leaves other men to gather the crops."

THE WEST AND FREEDOM

Westward expansion and the market revolution profoundly affected the lives of all Americans. They reinforced some older ideas of freedom and helped to create new ones. American freedom, for example, had long been linked with the availability of land in the West. A New York journalist, John L. O'Sullivan, first employed the phrase "manifest destiny," meaning that the United States had a divinely appointed mission, so obvious as to be beyond dispute, to occupy all of North America. Americans, he proclaimed, had a far better title to western lands than could be provided by any international treaty, right of discovery, or long-term settlement. Their right to the continent was provided by the nation's mission to extend the area of freedom. Other peoples' claims, O'Sullivan wrote, must give way to "our manifest destiny to overspread and to possess the whole of the continent which providence has given us for the development of the great experiment in liberty." Those who stood in the way of expansion—European powers like Great Britain and Spain, Native Americans, Mexicans—were by definition obstacles to the progress of freedom.

O'Sullivan wrote these words in 1845, but the essential idea was familiar much earlier. As the population moved across the Appalachian Mountains, so did the linkage between westward expansion and freedom. "The Goddess of Liberty," declared Senator John Breckinridge of Kentucky, was not "governed by geographical limits." A sense of spatial openness, of the constant opportunity to pick up and move when the pursuit of happiness seemed to demand it, became more and more a central component of American freedom. Like its predecessors, this generation of Americans believed that the United States had been selected by God for the greatest experiment in human history, the achievement of liberty, and that westward expansion was part and parcel of this destiny. Freedom in the United States, wrote the French historian Michel Chevalier, one of the many Europeans who visited the country in the 1830s, was a "practical idea" as much as a "mystical one"—it meant "a liberty of action and motion which the American uses to expand over the vast territory that Providence has given him and to subdue it to his uses."

In national myth and ideology, the West would long remain, as the writer Wallace Stegner would later put it, "the last home of the freeborn American." The settlement and economic exploitation of the West promised to prevent the United States from following down the path of Europe and becoming a society with fixed social classes and a large group of wage-earning poor. In the West, land was more readily available and oppressive factory labor far less common. With population and the price of land rising dramatically in the older states and young men's prospects for acquiring a farm or setting up an independent artisan shop declining, the West still held out the chance to achieve economic independence, the social condition of freedom.

THE TRANSCENDENTALISTS

The restless, competitive world of the market revolution strongly encouraged the identification of American freedom with the absence of restraints on self-directed individuals seeking economic advancement and personal development. The "one important revolution" of the day, the philosopher Ralph Waldo Emerson wrote in the 1830s, was "the new value of the private man." The opportunity for personal growth offered a new definition of Jefferson's pursuit of happiness, one well suited to a world in which territorial expansion and the market revolution had shattered traditional spatial and social boundaries and made moving from place to place and status to status common features of American life.

In a widely reprinted 1837 address, "The American Scholar," Emerson called on the person engaged in writing and thinking to "feel all confidence in himself, . . . to never defer to the popular cry," and to find and trust his own "definition of freedom." In Emerson's definition, rather than a preexisting set of rights or privileges, freedom was an open-ended process of self-realization by which individuals could remake themselves and their own lives. The keynote of the times, he declared, was "the new importance given to the single person" and the "emancipation" of the individual, the "American idea."

Emerson was perhaps the most prominent member of a group of New England intellectuals known as the transcendentalists, who insisted on the primacy of individual judgment over existing social traditions and institutions. Emerson's Concord, Massachusetts, neighbor, the writer Henry David Thoreau, echoed his call for individual self-reliance. "Any man more right than his neighbors," Thoreau wrote, "is a majority of one."

The daguerreotype, an early form of photography, required the sitter to remain perfectly still for twenty seconds or longer. The philosopher Ralph Waldo Emerson, depicted here, did not like the result. He complained in his journal that in his "zeal not to blur the image," every muscle had become "rigid" and his face was fixed in a frown as "in madness, or in death."

INDIVIDUALISM

Ironies abounded in the era's "individualism" (a term that first entered the language in the 1820s). For even as the market revolution promoted commercial connections between far-flung people, the idea of the "sovereign individual" proclaimed that Americans should depend on no one but themselves. Of course, personal independence had long been associated with American freedom. But eighteenth-century thinkers generally saw no contradiction between private happiness and self-sacrificing public virtue, defined as devotion to the common good. Now, Tocqueville observed, individualism led "each member of the community to sever himself from the mass of his fellows and to draw apart with his family and his

FROM RALPH WALDO EMERSON, "The American Scholar" (1837)

Ralph Waldo Emerson was perhaps the most prominent intellectual in mid-nineteenth-century America. In this famous address, delivered at Harvard College, he insisted on the primacy of individual judgment over existing social traditions as the essence of freedom.

Perhaps the time is already come, when . . . the sluggard intellect of this continent will look from under its iron lids and fill the postponed expectation of the world with something better than the exertions of mechanical skill. Our day of dependence, our long apprenticeship to the learning of other lands, draws to a close. . . .

In self-trust, all the virtues are comprehended. Free should the scholar be,–free and brave. Free even to the definition of freedom. . . . Not he is great who can alter matter, but he who can alter my state of mind. They are the kings of the world who give the color of their present thought to all nature and all art. . . .

[A] sign of the times . . . is the new importance given to the single individual. Every thing that tends to insulate the individual,–to surround him with barriers of natural respect, so that each man shall feel the world is his, and man shall treat with man as a sovereign state with a sovereign state:–tends to true union as well as greatness. 'I learned,' said the melancholy Pestalozzi [a Swiss educator], "that no man in God's wide earth is either willing or able to help any other man." Help must come from his bosom alone. . . .

We have listened too long to the courtly muses of Europe. The spirit of the American freeman is already suspected to be timid, imitative, tame. . . . The scholar is decent, indolent, complaisant. See already the tragic consequence. The mind of this country taught to aim at low objects, eats upon itself. Young men . . . do not yet see, that if the single man [should] plant himself indomitably on his instincts, and there abide, the huge world will come round to him. . . . We will walk on our own feet; we will work with our own hands; we will speak our own minds.

FROM "Factory Life as It Is, by an Operative" (1845)

Beginning in the 1830s, young women who worked in the cotton textile factories in Lowell, Massachusetts, organized to demand shorter hours of work and better labor conditions. In this pamphlet from 1845, a factory worker details her grievances as well as those of female domestic workers, the largest group of women workers.

Philanthropists of the nineteenth century!—shall not the operatives of our country be permitted to speak for themselves? Shall they be compelled to listen in silence to [those] who speak for gain, and are the mere echo of the will of the corporations? Shall the worthy laborer be awed into silence by wealth and power, and for fear of being deprived of the means of procuring his daily bread? Shall tyranny and cruel oppression be allowed to rivet the chains of physical and mental slavery on the millions of our country who are the real producers of all its improvements and wealth, and they fear to speak out in noble self-defense? Shall they fear to appeal to the sympathies of the people, or the justice of this far-famed republican nation? God forbid!

Much has been written and spoken in woman's behalf, especially in America; and yet a large class of females are, and have been, destined to a state of servitude as degrading as unceasing toil can make it. I refer to the female operatives of New England—the free states of our union—the states where no colored slave can breathe the balmy air, and exist as such;—but yet there are those, a host of them, too, who are in fact nothing more nor less than slaves in every sense of the word! Slaves to a system of labor which requires them to toil from five until seven o'clock, with one hour only to attend to the wants of nature, allowed—slaves to the will and requirements of the "powers that be," however they may infringe on the rights or conflict with the feelings of the operative—slaves to

ignorance—and how can it be otherwise? What time has the operative to bestow on moral, religious or intellectual culture? How can our country look for aught but ignorance and vice, under the existing state of things? When the whole system is exhausted by unremitting labor during twelve and thirteen hours per day, can any reasonable being expect that the mind will retain its vigor and energy? Impossible! Common sense will teach every one the utter impossibility of improving the mind under these circumstances, however great the desire may be for knowledge.

Again, we hear much said on the subject of benevolence among the wealthy and so called, Christian part of community. Have we not cause to question the sincerity of those who, while they talk benevolence in the parlor, compel their help to labor for a mean, paltry pittance in the kitchen? And while they manifest great concern for the souls of the heathen in distant lands, care nothing for the bodies and intellects of those within their own precincts? . . .

In the strength of our united influence we will soon show these drivelling cotton lords, this mushroom aristocracy of New England, who so arrogantly aspire to lord it over God's heritage, that our rights cannot be trampled upon with impunity; that we WILL not longer submit to that arbitrary power which has for the last ten years been so abundantly exercised over us.

QUESTIONS

1. How does Emerson define the freedom of what he calls "the single individual"?

2. Why does the female factory worker compare her conditions with those of slaves?

3. What does the contrast between these two documents suggest about the impact of the market revolution on American thought?

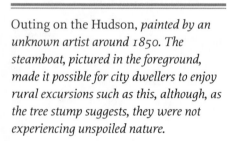

Outing on the Hudson, *painted by an unknown artist around 1850. The steamboat, pictured in the foreground, made it possible for city dwellers to enjoy rural excursions such as this, although, as the tree stump suggests, they were not experiencing unspoiled nature.*

friends . . . [leaving] society at large to itself." Americans increasingly understood the realm of the self—which came to be called "privacy"—as one with which neither other individuals nor government had a right to interfere. As will be discussed in the next chapter, individualism also helped to inspire the expansion of democracy. Ownership of one's self rather than ownership of property now made a person capable of exercising the right to vote.

Looking back from the 1880s, Emerson would recall the era before the Civil War as a time when "social existence" gave way to "the enlargement and independency of the individual, . . . driven to find all his resources, hopes, rewards, society, and deity within himself." In his own life, Thoreau illustrated Emerson's point about the primacy of individual conscience in matters political, social, and personal, and the need to find one's own way rather than following the crowd. Like other transcendentalists, he did not approve of the way individuals in a market economy engaged in this pursuit of happiness. Thoreau became persuaded that modern society stifled individual judgment by making men "tools of their tools," trapped in stultifying jobs by their obsession with acquiring wealth. Even in "this comparatively free country," he wrote, most persons were so preoccupied with material things that they had no time to contemplate the beauties of nature.

To escape this fate, Thoreau retreated for two years to a cabin on Walden Pond near Concord, where he could enjoy the freedom of isolation from the "economical and moral tyranny" he believed ruled American society. He subsequently published *Walden* (1854), an account of his experiences and a critique of how the market revolution was, in his opinion, degrading both Americans' values and the natural environment. An area that had been covered with dense forest in his youth, he observed, had been so transformed by woodcutters and farmers that it had become almost completely devoid of trees and wild animals. In one famous passage, Thoreau noted how his enjoyment of nature was disturbed by the distant sound of a locomotive whistle—a symbol of how it seemed impossible to escape the market revolution. Thoreau appealed to Americans to "simplify" their lives rather than become obsessed with the accumulation of wealth. Genuine freedom, he insisted, lay within.

THE SECOND GREAT AWAKENING

The popular religious revivals that swept over the country during the Second Great Awakening added a religious underpinning to the celebration of personal self-improvement, self- reliance, and self-determination. These revivals, which began at the turn of the century, were originally organized by established religious leaders alarmed by low levels of church attendance in the young republic (perhaps as few as 10 percent of white Americans regularly attended church during the 1790s). But they quickly expanded far beyond existing churches. They reached a crescendo in the 1820s and early 1830s, when the Reverend Charles Grandison Finney held months-long revival meetings in upstate New York and New York City.

The son of Connecticut farmers, Finney had been inspired to preach after attending a religious revival in 1821. Like the evangelists (traveling preachers) of the first Great Awakening of the mid-eighteenth century, discussed in Chapter 4, Finney warned of hell in vivid language while offering the promise of salvation to converts who abandoned their sinful ways. He became a national celebrity after his success in Oneida County in upstate New York. After Finney's preaching, according to one report, the area had

Religious Camp Meeting, *a watercolor from the late 1830s depicting an evangelical preacher at a revival meeting. Some of the audience members seem inattentive, while others are moved by his fiery sermon.*

Das neue Jerusalem (*The New Jerusalem*), an early-nineteenth-century watercolor, in German, illustrates the narrow gateway to heaven and the fate awaiting sinners in hell. These were common themes of preachers in the Second Great Awakening.

been "completely overthrown by the Holy Ghost" so that "the theater has been deserted, the tavern sanctified . . . and far higher and purer enjoyment has been found in exercises of devotion."

The Second Great Awakening democratized American Christianity, making it a truly mass enterprise. At the time of independence, fewer than 2,000 Christian ministers preached in the United States. In 1845, they numbered 40,000. Evangelical denominations like the Methodists and Baptists enjoyed explosive growth in membership, and smaller sects proliferated. By the 1840s, Methodism, with more than 1 million members, had become the country's largest denomination. Deism, a form of religious belief hostile to organized churches, had been prominent among the generation of the founding fathers. It now waned, and Christianity became even more central to American culture. Americans, wrote Tocqueville, "combine the notions of Christianity and of liberty so intimately in their minds that it is impossible to make them conceive the one without the other."

New religious prophets seemed to appear regularly in early-nineteenth-century America, determined, in novelist Herman Melville's phrase, to "gospelize the world anew." At large camp meetings, especially prominent on the frontier, fiery revivalist preachers rejected the idea that man is a sinful creature with a preordained fate, promoting instead the doctrine of human free will. At these gatherings, rich and poor, male and female, and in some instances whites and blacks worshiped alongside one another and pledged to abandon worldly sins in favor of the godly life.

THE AWAKENING'S IMPACT

Even more than its predecessor of several decades earlier, the Second Great Awakening stressed the right of private judgment in spiritual matters and the possibility of universal salvation through faith and good works. Every

VISIONS OF FREEDOM

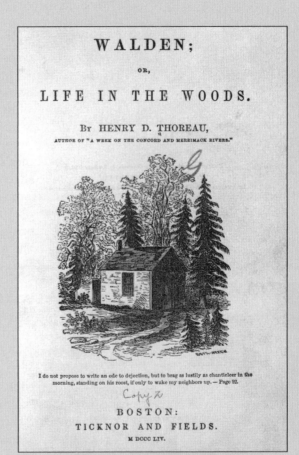

Official Seal of Arkansas and Title Page of Walden. *These images offer two responses to the market revolution. The official seal of Arkansas (1836) juxtaposes a woman holding a cap of liberty with symbols of technological progress (an iron plow and a steamboat) and material prosperity (horns of plenty). The sketch of Henry David Thoreau's cabin on Walden Pond illustrates his belief that Americans could enjoy what he called "absolute freedom" by rejecting market society and retreating into the wilderness. Only in this way, he insisted, could they preserve both individual independence and the natural environment.*

QUESTIONS

1. What does each vision of freedom offer that the other lacks?

2. Why do you think that the seal of Arkansas, a slave state, includes no image of slavery?

person, Finney insisted, was a "moral free agent"—that is, a person free to choose between a Christian life and sin. Sinners could experience a "change of heart" and embrace spiritual freedom, defined, in the words of evangelical minister Jonathan Blanchard, as "Christ ruling in and over rational creatures who are obeying him freely and from choice."

Revivalist ministers seized the opportunities offered by the market revolution to spread their message. They raised funds, embarked on lengthy preaching tours by canal, steamboat, and railroad, and flooded the country with mass-produced, inexpensive religious tracts. The revivals' opening of religion to mass participation and their message that ordinary Americans could shape their own spiritual destinies resonated with the spread of market values.

To be sure, evangelical preachers can hardly be described as cheerleaders for a market society. They regularly railed against greed and indifference to the welfare of others as sins. Finney called selfishness—an extreme form of individualism encouraged by the scramble for wealth produced by the market revolution—"the law of Satan's empire," not God's. Yet the revivals thrived in areas caught up in the rapid expansion of the market economy, such as the region of upstate New York along the path of the Erie Canal. Most of Finney's converts here came from the commercial and professional classes. Evangelical ministers promoted what might be called a controlled individualism as the essence of freedom. In stressing the importance of industry, sobriety, and self-discipline as examples of freely chosen moral behavior, evangelical preachers promoted the very qualities necessary for success in a market culture.

THE LIMITS OF PROSPERITY

LIBERTY AND PROSPERITY

As the market revolution progressed, the right to compete for economic advancement became a touchstone of American freedom. "The whole question of freedom or slavery for man," argued Henry C. Carey, perhaps the era's most prominent economist, was bound up with economic achievement. Official imagery linked the goddess of liberty ever more closely to emblems of material wealth. New Jersey, whose official seal, adopted in 1776, had paired liberty with Ceres, the Roman goddess of agriculture, in 1821 added the motto "Liberty and Prosperity." The state seal of Arkansas, admitted to the Union in 1836, pictured liberty atop an image of a steamboat and two overflowing horns of plenty.

Many enterprising Americans seized the opportunities offered by the market revolution to enrich themselves. John Jacob Astor, the son of a poor German butcher who emigrated to the United States at the end of the War of Independence, earned large profits in the early nineteenth century by shipping furs to China and importing teas and silk. Astor invested his wealth in Manhattan real estate, which was rapidly rising in value, and built Astor House, which quickly became the nation's most famous hotel. He died in 1848 the richest man in the United States, leaving a fortune of perhaps $10 million, the equivalent of hundreds of millions of dollars today.

Astor's story seemed to exemplify the opportunities open to the "self-made man," a term that came into use during his lifetime. According to this

Pat Lyon at the Forge, *an 1826–1827 painting of a prosperous blacksmith. Proud of his accomplishments as a self-made man who had achieved success through hard work and skill rather than inheritance, Lyon asked the artist to paint him in his shop wearing his work clothes.*

idea, those who achieved success in America did so not as a result of hereditary privilege or government favoritism as in Europe, but through their own intelligence and hard work. In the extent of his wealth, of course, Astor was hardly typical. But the market revolution and the quickening of commercial life enriched numerous bankers, merchants, industrialists, and planters. It produced a new middle class—an army of clerks, accountants, and other office employees who staffed businesses in Boston, New York, and elsewhere. It created new opportunities for farmers who profited from the growing demand at home and abroad for American agricultural products, and for skilled craftsmen like Thomas Rodgers, a machine builder who established a successful locomotive factory in Paterson, New Jersey. New opportunities for talented men opened in professions like law, medicine, and teaching. By the early 1820s, there were an estimated 10,000 physicians in the United States.

RACE AND OPPORTUNITY

The market revolution affected the lives of all Americans. But not all were positioned to take advantage of its benefits. Most blacks, of course, were slaves, but even free blacks found themselves excluded from the new economic opportunities. The 220,000 blacks living in the free states on the eve of the Civil War (less than 2 percent of the North's population) suffered discrimination in every phase of their lives. Although virtually every northern county east of the Mississippi River reported some black residents, the majority of blacks lived in the poorest, unhealthiest sections of cities like New York, Philadelphia, and Cincinnati. And even these neighborhoods were subjected to occasional violent assault by white mobs, like the armed bands that attacked blacks and destroyed their homes and businesses in Cincinnati in 1829.

Barred from schools and other public facilities, free blacks laboriously constructed their own institutional life, centered on mutual aid and educational societies, as well as independent churches, most notably the African Methodist Episcopal Church. Richard Allen of Philadelphia, a Methodist preacher, had been spurred to found the church after being forcibly removed from his former church for praying at the altar rail, a place reserved for whites.

While many white Americans could look forward to a life of economic accumulation and individual advancement, large numbers of free blacks experienced downward mobility. As noted in Chapter 6, northern free blacks were the last large group to experience indentured servitude, since the terms of emancipation generally required children of slave mothers to work for their owners before being freed. At the time of abolition, because of widespread slave ownership among eighteenth-century artisans, a considerable number of northern blacks possessed craft skills. But it became more and more difficult for blacks to utilize these skills once they became free. Although many white artisans criticized slavery, most viewed the freed slaves as low-wage competitors and sought to bar them from skilled employment. "They are leaders in the cause of equal rights for themselves," a black editor commented of New York City's artisans in the 1830s.

Hostility from white craftsmen, however, was only one of many obstacles that kept blacks confined to the lowest ranks of the labor market. White

Juliann Jane Tillman, a preacher in the African Methodist Episcopal Church, in an 1844 engraving. Many Protestant denominations allowed women to preach, although their presence also aroused much criticism.

The Crowning of Flora, *a painting from 1816, depicts idealized women of virtue and modesty. These were the qualities the nineteenth century's cult of domesticity emphasized as essential to proper womanhood.*

employers refused to hire them in anything but menial positions, and white customers did not wish to be served by them. The result was a rapid decline in economic status, until by mid-century, the vast majority of northern blacks labored for wages in unskilled jobs and as domestic servants. The state census of 1855 revealed 122 black barbers and 808 black servants in New York City, but only 1 lawyer and 6 doctors. Nor could free blacks take advantage of the opening of the West to improve their economic status, a central component of American freedom. Federal law barred them from access to public land, and by 1860 four states—Indiana, Illinois, Iowa, and Oregon—prohibited them from entering their territory altogether.

THE CULT OF DOMESTICITY

Women, too, found many of the opportunities opened by the market revolution closed to them. As the household declined as a center of economic production, many women saw their traditional roles undermined by the availability of mass-produced goods previously made at home. Some women, as noted above, followed work as it moved from household to factory. Others embraced a new definition of femininity, which glorified not a woman's contribution to the family's economic well-being, but her ability to create a private environment shielded from the competitive tensions of the market economy. Woman's "place" was in the home, a site increasingly emptied of economically productive functions as work moved from the household to workshops and factories. Her role was to sustain nonmarket values like love, friendship, and mutual obligation, providing men with a shelter from the competitive marketplace.

The earlier ideology of "republican motherhood," which allowed women a kind of public role as mothers of future citizens, subtly evolved into the mid-nineteenth-century "cult of domesticity." "Virtue," which in the eighteenth century was a political characteristic of men essential to the success of republican government, came to be redefined as a personal moral quality associated more and more closely with women. "Virtue" for a woman meant not only sexual innocence but beauty, frailty, and dependence on men. "In whatever situation of life a woman is placed from her cradle to her grave," declared *The Young Lady's Book*, one of numerous popular magazines addressed to female audiences of the 1820s and 1830s, "a spirit of obedience and submission, pliability of temper, and humility of mind, are required from her." These magazines carried articles such as "Woman, a Source of Comfort," "Woman, a Being to Come Home To," and "Woman—Man's Best Friend."

With more and more men leaving the home for work, women did exercise considerable power over personal affairs within the family. The rapid decline in the American birthrate during the nineteenth century (from an average of seven children per woman in 1800 to four in 1900) cannot be explained except by the conscious decision of millions of women to limit the number of children they bore. But the idea of domesticity minimized women's even indirect participation in the outside world. For both sexes, freedom meant fulfilling their respective "inborn" qualities. Men were rational, aggressive, and domineering, while women were nurturing, selfless, ruled by the emotions, and thus less fitted for public life. If submission to the will of another increasingly seemed inadmissible for free men, it remained a condition natural to women and expected of them. Men moved freely between the public and private "spheres"; women were supposed to remain cloistered in the private realm of the family.

A woman with a sewing machine, in an undated photograph. It is not clear if she is sewing for herself and family, or for income as a seamstress.

An image from a female infant's 1830 birth and baptismal certificate depicts a domestic scene, with women at work while men relax.

WOMEN AND WORK

Prevailing ideas concerning gender bore little relation to the experience of those women who worked for wages at least some time in their lives. They did so despite severe disadvantages. Women could not compete freely for employment, since only low-paying jobs were available to them. Married women still could not sign independent contracts or sue in their own name, and not until after the Civil War did they, not their husbands, control the wages they earned. Nonetheless, for poor city dwellers and farm families, the labor of all family members was essential to economic survival. Thousands of poor women found jobs as domestic servants, factory workers, and seamstresses. Early industrialization enhanced the availability of paid work for northern women, as the spread of the putting-out system in such indus-

tries as shoemaking, hatmaking, and clothing manufacture allowed women laboring at home to contribute to family income even as they retained responsibility for domestic chores.

For the expanding middle class, however, it became a badge of respectability for wives to remain at home, outside the disorderly new market economy, while husbands conducted business in their offices, shops, and factories. In larger cities, where families of different social classes had previously lived alongside one another, fashionable middle-class neighborhoods populated by merchants, factory owners, and professionals like lawyers and doctors began to develop. Work in middle-class homes was done by domestic servants, the largest employment category for women in nineteenth-century America. The freedom of the middle-class woman—defined in part as freedom from labor—rested on the employment of other women within her household.

Even though most women were anything but idle, in a market economy where labor increasingly meant work that created monetary value, it became more and more difficult to think of labor as encompassing anyone but men. Lydia Maria Child wrote a popular book, *The Frugal Housewife*, published in 1829, that sought to prepare women for the ups and downs of the market revolution (one chapter was entitled "How to Endure Poverty"). Child supported her family by her writing and became a prominent advocate of antislavery and of greater rights for women. Her diary reveals that in a single year she also sewed thirty-six pieces of clothing, prepared more than 700 meals, and spent much time supervising household help.

By any reasonable definition, Child worked—at home and as a writer. But discussions of labor rarely mentioned housewives, domestic servants, and female outworkers, except as an indication of how the spread of capitalism was degrading men. The idea that the male head of household should command a "family wage" that enabled him to support his wife and children became a popular definition of social justice. It sank deep roots

No More Grinding the Poor—But Liberty and the Rights of Man, *a labor movement cartoon of the 1830s. The devil and a millionaire conspire to buy an election with money (in the box at the lower left), while an honest workingman hands his ballot to a female figure of liberty. The worker's motto is "Liberty, Equity, Justice, and The Rights of Man."*

not only among middle-class Americans but among working-class men as well. Capitalism, said the newspaper *Workingman's Advocate*, tore women from their role as "happy and independent mistresses" of the domestic sphere and forced them into the labor market, thereby undermining the natural order of the household and the authority of its male head.

THE EARLY LABOR MOVEMENT

As this complaint suggests, although many Americans welcomed the market revolution, others felt threatened by its consequences. Surviving members of the revolutionary generation feared that the obsession with personal economic gain was undermining devotion to the public good. "Commerce, luxury, and avarice," warned John Adams, "have destroyed every republican government." In the 1820s, as he neared the end of his life, Jefferson was denouncing "stockjobbers," financiers, speculators, and others for leading the nation away from his idealized virtuous agrarian republic.

The Shoemakers' Strike in Lynn—Procession in the Midst of a Snow-Storm, of Eight Hundred Women Operatives, *an engraving from* Frank Leslie's Illustrated Newspaper, *March 17, 1860. The striking women workers carry a banner comparing their condition to that of slaves.*

Many Americans experienced the market revolution not as an enhancement of the power to shape their own lives, but as a loss of freedom. The period between the War of 1812 and 1840 witnessed a sharp economic downturn in 1819, a full-fledged depression starting in 1837, and numerous ups and downs in between, during which employment was irregular and numerous businesses failed. For every aspiring American who rode the tide of economic progress, another seemed to sink beneath the waves. The economic transformation produced an explosive growth in the nation's output and trade and a rise in the general standard of living. But especially in the growing cities of the Northeast, it significantly widened the gap between wealthy merchants and industrialists on the one hand and impoverished factory workers, unskilled dockworkers, and seamstresses laboring at home on the other. In Massachusetts, the most industrialized state in the country, the richest 5 percent of the population owned more than half the wealth. Inequality was even more pronounced in Philadelphia, where the top 1 percent possessed more wealth than the rest of the population combined. Bankruptcy was a common fact of life, and men unable to pay their debts filled the prisons of major cities.

Alarmed at the erosion of traditional skills and the threat of being reduced to the status of dependent wage earners, skilled craftsmen in the late 1820s created the world's first Workingmen's Parties, short-lived political organizations that sought to mobilize lower-class support for candidates who would press for free public education, an end to imprisonment for debt, and legislation limiting work to ten hours per day. In the 1830s, a time of rapidly rising prices, union organization spread and strikes became commonplace. Along with demands for higher wages and shorter hours, the early labor movement called for free homesteads for settlers on public land and an end to the imprisonment of union leaders for conspiracy.

THE "LIBERTY OF LIVING"

But over and above these specific issues, workers' language of protest drew on older ideas of freedom linked to economic autonomy, public-spirited virtue, and social equality. The conviction of twenty New York tailors in 1835 under the common law of conspiracy for combining to seek higher wages inspired a public procession marking the "burial of liberty." Such actions and language were not confined to male workers. The young mill women of Lowell walked off their jobs in 1834 to protest a reduction in wages and again two years later when employers raised rents at their boardinghouses. They carried banners affirming their rights as "daughters of free men," and, addressing the factory owners, they charged, "the oppressive hand of avarice [greed] would enslave us." Freedom, Noah Webster's *American Dictionary* declared in 1828, was "a state of exemption from the power or control of another." The labor movement asked how many wage earners truly enjoyed such "exemption."

Some labor spokesmen, like Langdon Byllesby of Philadelphia, went so far as to describe wage labor itself as the "very essence of slavery," since dependence on another person for one's economic livelihood was incompatible with freedom. The idea that permanent wage work bore some resemblance to slavery was not confined to labor radicals. In Herman Melville's short story *The Tartarus of Maids*, workers in a New England paper mill stand by their machines "mutely and cringingly as the slave."

Rooted in the traditions of the small producer and the identification of freedom with economic independence, labor's critique of the market economy directly challenged the idea that individual improvement—Emerson's "self-trust, self-reliance, self-control, self-culture"—offered an adequate response to social inequality. "Wealth and labor," wrote Orestes Brownson in his influential essay "The Laboring Classes" (1840), were at war. Workers' problems, he went on, must be understood as institutional, not individual. They had their root in "the constitution of society," and their solution required not a more complete individualism, but a "radical change [in] existing social arrangements" so as to produce "equality between man and man."

"We are free," wrote Peter Rödel, an immigrant German shoemaker, "but not free enough. . . . We want the liberty of living." Here lay the origins of the idea, which would become far more prominent in the late nineteenth and twentieth centuries, that economic security—a standard of life below which no person would fall—formed an essential part of American freedom.

Thus, the market revolution transformed and divided American society and its conceptions of freedom. It encouraged a new emphasis on individualism and physical mobility among white men, while severely limiting the options available to women and African-Americans. It opened new opportunities for economic freedom for many Americans, while leading others to fear that their traditional economic independence was being eroded. In a democratic society, it was inevitable that the debate over the market revolution and its consequences for freedom would be reflected in American politics.

SUGGESTED READING

BOOKS

Arieli, Yehoshua. *Individualism and Nationalism in American Ideology* (1964). A study of the rise of individualism and other key ideas in American thought.

Boydston, Jeanne. *Home and Work: Housework, Wages, and the Ideology of Work in the Early Republic* (1990). Examines how the market revolution affected ideas relating to women's work.

Butler, Jon. *Awash in a Sea of Faith: Christianizing the American People* (1990). A history of American religion with emphasis on evangelical movements, including the Second Great Awakening.

Clark, Christopher. *The Roots of Rural Capitalism: Western Massachusetts, 1780–1860* (1990). Considers how the market revolution transformed economic and social life in one region of the North.

Deyle, Steven. *Carry Me Back: The Domestic Slave Trade in American Life* (2005). The most comprehensive history of the internal slave trade, by which millions of slaves were transported to the Deep South.

Dublin, Thomas. *Women at Work: The Transformation of Work in Lowell, Massachusetts, 1826–1860* (1975). A pioneering study of the working and non-working lives of Lowell "factory girls."

Faragher, John M. *Sugar Creek: Life on the Illinois Prairie* (1986). Traces the growth of a frontier community from early settlement to market society.

Harris, Leslie. *In the Shadow of Slavery: African-Americans in New York City, 1626–1863* (2003). A study that emphasizes the exclusion of African-Americans from the economic opportunities offered by the market revolution.

Howe, Daniel W. *What Hath God Wrought: The Transformation of America, 1815–1848* (2007). A comprehensive account of social and political changes in this era, emphasizing the significance of the communications revolution.

Johnson, Paul E. *A Shopkeeper's Millennium: Society and Revivals in Rochester, New York, 1815–1837* (1978). Explores the impact of religious revivals on a key city of upstate New York.

Kasson, John F. *Civilizing the Machine: Technology and Republican Values in America, 1776–1900* (1976). Examines how Americans tried to incorporate the emerging factory system into their concepts of freedom and equality.

Miller, Kerby A. *Exiles and Emigrants: Ireland and the Irish Exodus to North America* (1985). An examination of Irish immigration over the course of American history.

Ryan, Mary P. *Cradle of the Middle Class: The Family in Oneida County, New York, 1790–1865* (1981). Examines how economic change helped to produce a new kind of middle-class family structure centered on women's dominance of the household.

Stansell, Christine. *City of Women: Sex and Class in New York, 1789–1860* (1986). Considers how gender conventions and economic change shaped the lives of working-class women.

Wilentz, Sean. *Chants Democratic: New York City and the Rise of the American Working Class, 1788–1850* (1984). A study of the early labor movement in one of its key centers in antebellum America.

WEBSITES

American Transcendentalism: www.vcu.edu/engweb/transcendentalism/

Erie Canal Time Machine: www.archives.nysed.gov/projects/eriecanal/

Women in America, 1820–1842: http://xroads.virginia.edu/~HYPER/ DETOC/FEM/ home.htm

REVIEW QUESTIONS

1. Identify the major transportation improvements in this period and explain how they influenced the market economy.

2. How did state and local governments promote the national economy in this period?

3. How did the market economy increase the nation's sectional differences?

4. Explain how the market economy promoted the growth of cities in the East and along the frontier.

5. What role did immigrants play in the new market society?

6. What were the main changes in American law during this period?

7. As it democratized American Christianity, the Second Great Awakening both took advantage of the market revolution and criticized its excesses. Explain.

8. What was the "cult of domesticity" and how was it a result of the market revolution?

FREEDOM QUESTIONS

1. Explain how the growth of the Cotton Kingdom benefited planters and other slaveowners, but reduced the liberties of poorer southern farmers and African-Americans.

2. How did the growth of the factory system limit the traditional freedoms of American artisans, and how did they respond?

3. The market revolution added new terminology to the American lexicon. Explain how each of the following concepts is related to a change in individual freedom: wages, clock time, self-made man, privacy, and middle class.

4. The 1828 edition of Noah Webster's *American Dictionary* defined freedom as "a state of exemption from the power and control of another." Using this definition, assess the impact of the market revolution on the freedoms of white women, African-Americans, immigrants, and wage workers.

5. Explain how the market revolution changed the meanings of American freedom, both by reinforcing older ideas and creating new ones.

KEY TERMS

turnpikes (p. 333)

Erie Canal (p. 334)

telegraph (p. 335)

squatters (p. 337)

cotton gin (p. 339)

Cotton Kingdom (p. 339)

slave coffles (p. 340)

John Deere steel plow (p. 342)

Cyrus McCormick reaper (p. 342)

factory system (p. 343)

"American system of manufactures" (p. 346)

mill girls (p. 348)

nativism (p. 350)

Gibbons v. Ogden (p. 351)

Charles River Bridge case (p. 351)

manifest destiny (p. 352)

transcendentalists (p. 353)

camp meetings (p. 358)

"self-made man" (p. 360)

cult of domesticity (p. 362)

REVIEW TABLE

Landmarks of the Market Revolution

Event	Date	Accomplishment
Congress approves funds for a National Road	1806	Cumberland Road reaches Ohio River in 1818 and Illinois in 1838
Robert Fulton's steamboat, the *Clermont*, navigates the Hudson River	1807	Makes possible upstream commerce on the country's major rivers
Waltham textile mills open	1814	By 1850, the area's 52 mills employ 10,000 workers
Dartmouth College case	1819	Court defines corporate charters issued by states as contracts
Erie Canal completed	1825	Connects New York City to the Great Lakes
Work begun on B&O railroad, the nation's first commercial railroad	1828	National railroad network grows to 30,000 miles by 1860
Invention of McCormick reaper and Deere steel plow	1830s	Made mass-production of grain crops possible
Commonwealth v. Hunt	1842	Affirmed legality of workers' unions and strikes
Telegraph put into commercial operation	1844	50,000 miles of telegraph wire is strung by 1860

CHAPTER 10

Democracy in America, 1815–1840

The House of Representatives in 1822, in a painting by Samuel F. B. Morse (who also invented the telegraph). By this time, most adult white men could vote for members of the House, a far wider franchise than was known in Europe at the time.

☞ FOCUS QUESTIONS

• What were the social bases for the flourishing democracy of the early mid-nineteenth century?

• What efforts were made in this period to strengthen the economic integration of the nation, and what major crises hindered these efforts?

• What were the major areas of conflict between nationalism and sectionalism?

• In what ways did Andrew Jackson embody the contradictions of democratic nationalism?

• How did the Bank War influence the economy and party competition?

he inauguration of Andrew Jackson on March 4, 1829, made it clear that something had changed in American politics. The swearing-in of the president had previously been a small, dignified event. Jackson's inauguration attracted a crowd of some 20,000 people who poured into the White House after the ceremony, ruining furniture and breaking china and glassware in the crush. It was "the reign of King Mob," lamented Justice Joseph Story of the Supreme Court.

Jackson aroused powerful feelings, pro and con. His supporters viewed his election as the advent of genuine democracy, the coming to power of the "common man." Philip Hone, a New York political leader who kept a detailed diary for more than thirty years, recorded that Jackson was "the most popular man we have ever known." Hone had voted for President John Quincy Adams in 1828, but he recognized that Jackson's democratic bearing and beliefs "suit [the people] exactly." Jackson's critics, on the other hand, considered him a tyrant. They called him King Andrew I, and when they organized politically they borrowed their name, the Whig Party, from the opponents of royal power in eighteenth-century England.

Andrew Jackson's career embodied the major developments of his era—the market revolution, the westward movement, the expansion of slavery, and the growth of democracy. He was a symbol of the self-made man. Unlike previous presidents, Jackson rose to prominence from a humble background, reflecting his era's democratic opportunities. Born in 1767 on the South Carolina frontier, he had been orphaned during the American Revolution. Early on, Jackson displayed the courage and impetuousness for which he would later become famous. While still a youth, he served as a courier for patriotic forces during the War of Independence. Captured and imprisoned, he was almost killed when a British officer struck him with a sword after Jackson refused an order to polish the officer's boots.

As a young man, Jackson moved to Tennessee, where he studied law, became involved in local politics, and in the 1790s won election to the House of Representatives and the Senate, and became a judge on the state supreme court. His military campaigns against the British and Indians helped to consolidate American control over the Deep South, making possible the rise of the Cotton Kingdom. He himself acquired a large plantation in Tennessee. But more than anything else, to this generation of Americans Andrew Jackson symbolized one of the most crucial features of national life—the triumph of political democracy.

Americans pride themselves on being the world's oldest democracy. New Zealand, whose constitution of 1893 gave women and Maoris (the native population) the right to vote, may have a better claim. Even in the nineteenth century, when democracy meant male suffrage, some Latin American nations extended the right to vote to free blacks and the descendants of the indigenous population well before the United States. Europe lagged far behind. Britain did not achieve universal male suffrage until the 1880s. France instituted it in 1793, abandoned it in 1799, reintroduced it in 1848, and abandoned it again a few years later. More to the point, perhaps, democracy became part of the definition of American nationality and the American idea of freedom.

THE TRIUMPH OF DEMOCRACY

PROPERTY AND DEMOCRACY

The market revolution and territorial expansion were intimately connected with a third central element of American freedom—political democracy. The challenge to property qualifications for voting, begun during the American Revolution, reached its culmination in the early nineteenth century. Not a single state that entered the Union after the original thirteen required ownership of property to vote. In the older states, constitutional conventions during the 1820s and 1830s reconsidered democracy's economic basis. Even as the expansion of industry and commercial agriculture increased the number of wage earners in cities and older rural areas, men who could not meet property requirements insisted that they were as fit as others to exercise the rights of citizens. Their insistent pressure did much to democratize American politics.

Owning property, declared a petition by "Non-Freeholders" [landless men] of Richmond to the Virginia constitutional convention of 1829, did not necessarily mean the possession of "moral or intellectual endowments" superior to those of the poor. "They alone deserve to be called free," they continued, "who participate in the formation of their political institutions." By this time, only North Carolina, Rhode Island, and Virginia still retained property requirements. The large slaveholders who dominated Virginia politics successfully resisted demands for changes in voting qualifications in 1829, but a subsequent constitutional convention, in 1850, eliminated the property requirement. Although the speed of the process varied from state to state, by 1860 all but one had ended property requirements for voting (although several continued to bar persons accepting poor relief, on the grounds that they lacked genuine independence). The personal independence necessary in the citizen now rested not on ownership of property, but on ownership of one's self—a reflection of the era's individualism.

THE DORR WAR

The lone exception to the trend toward democratization was Rhode Island, which required voters to own real estate valued at $134 or rent property for at least $7 per year. A center of factory production, Rhode Island had a steadily growing population of propertyless wage earners

An anti-Jackson cartoon from 1832 portrays Andrew Jackson as an aspiring monarch, wielding the veto power while trampling on the Constitution.

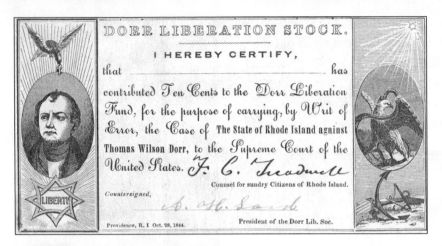

Dorr Liberation Stock, *a certificate indicating that a person has helped to finance Thomas Dorr's appeal to the U.S. Supreme Court of his conviction for treason against the state of Rhode Island because of his role in the Dorr War. The Court ruled against him, and Dorr served two years in prison.*

unable to vote. Leaders of the state's labor movement complained repeatedly about the absence of "free suffrage." In October 1841, proponents of democratic reform organized a People's Convention, which drafted a new state constitution. It enfranchised all adult white men while eliminating entirely blacks, who previously could vote if they owned the required amount of property (another illustration of how the expansion of white freedom sometimes went hand in hand with restrictions on the freedom of non-whites). When the reformers ratified their constitution in an extralegal referendum and proceeded to inaugurate Thomas Dorr, a prominent Rhode Island lawyer, as governor, President John Tyler dispatched federal troops to the state. The movement collapsed, and Dorr subsequently served nearly two years in prison for treason. The Dorr War demonstrated the passions aroused by the continuing exclusion of any group of white men from voting. And the legislature soon eliminated the property qualification for native-born men, black as well as white, although it retained it for immigrants until 1888.

TOCQUEVILLE ON DEMOCRACY

By 1840, more than 90 percent of adult white men were eligible to vote. A flourishing democratic system had been consolidated. American politics was boisterous, highly partisan, and sometimes violent, and it engaged the energies of massive numbers of citizens. In a country that lacked more traditional bases of nationality—a powerful and menacing neighbor, historic ethnic, religious, and cultural unity—democratic political institutions came to define the nation's sense of its own identity.

Alexis de Tocqueville, the French writer who visited the United States in the early 1830s, returned home to produce *Democracy in America*, a classic account of a society in the midst of a political transformation. Tocqueville had come to the United States to study prisons. But he soon realized that to understand America, one must understand democracy (which as a person of aristocratic background he rather disliked). His key insight was that democracy by this time meant far more than either the right to vote or a particular set of political institutions. It was what scholars call a "habit of the heart," a culture that encouraged individual initiative, belief in equality, and an active public sphere populated by numerous voluntary organizations that sought to improve society. Democracy, Tocqueville saw, had become an essential attribute of American freedom.

As Tocqueville recognized, the rise of democracy represented a profound political transformation. The idea that sovereignty belongs to the mass of ordinary citizens was a new departure in Western thought. As long ago as Aristotle, political philosophers had warned that democracy inevitably degenerated into anarchy and tyranny. For centuries, doctrines of divine right and hierarchical authority had dominated political thought. The founders of the republic, who believed that government must rest on the consent of the governed, also sought to shield political authority from excessive influence by ordinary people (hence the Electoral College, Supreme Court, and other undemocratic features of the Constitution). Nonetheless, thanks to persistent pressure from those originally excluded from political participation, democracy—for white males—had triumphed by the Age of Jackson.

Democracy reinforced a sense of equality among those who belonged to the political nation, and it deepened the divide separating them from those who did not. Participation in elections and the pageantry surrounding them—parades, bonfires, mass meetings, party conventions—helped to define the "people" of the United States. The right to vote increasingly became the emblem of American citizenship. In law, voting was still, strictly speaking, a privilege rather than a right, subject to regulation by the individual states. But Noah Webster's *American Dictionary* noted that according to common usage and understanding in America (but not in Europe), the term "citizen" had become synonymous with the right to vote. The suffrage, said one advocate of democratic reform, was "the first mark of liberty, the only true badge of the freeman."

THE INFORMATION REVOLUTION

The market revolution and political democracy produced a large expansion of the public sphere and an explosion in printing sometimes called the "information revolution." The application of steam power to newspaper printing led to a great increase in output and the rise of the mass-circulation "penny press," priced at one cent per issue instead of the traditional six. Newspapers like the *New York Sun* and *New York Herald* introduced a new style of journalism, appealing to a mass audience by emphasizing sensationalism, crime stories, and exposés of official misconduct. By 1840, according to one estimate, the total weekly circulation of newspapers in the United States, whose population was 17 million, exceeded that of Europe, with 233 million people.

Thanks to low postal rates, many newspapers circulated far beyond their places of publication. Indeed, by the 1830s, newspapers accounted for most postal traffic, outstripping private letters. The emergence of organized political parties also spurred newspaper publication. Each major party needed to have newspapers supporting its views in every part of the country, and government printing contracts were essential to most newspapers' survival. The publication of all sorts of magazines, travel guides, advice manuals, religious titles, and other reading materials rose dramatically.

The reduction in the cost of printing also made possible the appearance of "alternative" newspapers in the late 1820s and early 1830s, including *Freedom's Journal* (the first black newspaper), *Philadelphia Mechanic's Advocate* and other labor publications, the abolitionist weekly *The Liberator*, and *Cherokee Phoenix*, the first Native American newspaper.

The growth of the reading public, yet another facet of the democratization of American life, opened the door for the rise of a new generation of women writers. Lydia Maria Child, Catharine Maria Sedgwick, Catharine Beecher, and others published stories, poetry, essays, and guides to domestic life. By the 1830s, moreover, through participation in religious and reform movements, thousands of women would establish a public presence,

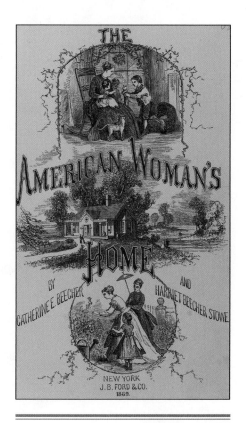

The American Woman's Home, *a guide to domestic life by the sisters Catharine Beecher and Harriet Beecher Stowe. Even though works like this were meant to instruct middle-class women on how to meet their domestic responsibilities, their popularity allowed talented women to take on a new public role as writers.*

as will be described in Chapter 12. Nonetheless, once New Jersey added the word "male" to its voting requirements in 1807, women everywhere, whether married or single, propertied or dependent, were denied the right to vote.

THE LIMITS OF DEMOCRACY

By the 1830s, the time of Andrew Jackson's presidency, the axiom that "the people" ruled had become a universally accepted part of American politics. Those who opposed this principle, wrote Tocqueville, "hide their heads." But the very centrality of democracy to the definition of both freedom and nationality made it all the more necessary to define the boundaries of the political nation. As older economic exclusions fell away, others survived and new ones were added. The vigorous public life of antebellum America was simultaneously expansive and exclusive, and its limits were as essential to its nature as its broad scope. Democracy in America could absorb native-born poor white men as well as waves of immigrants, yet it erected impenetrable barriers to the participation of women and non-white men— groups also excluded, as noted in the previous chapter, from full participation in the market revolution.

The "principle of universal suffrage," declared the *United States Magazine and Democratic Review* in 1851, meant that "white males of age constituted the political nation." How could the word "universal" be reconciled with barring blacks and women from political participation? As democracy triumphed, the intellectual grounds for exclusion shifted from economic dependency to natural incapacity. Gender and racial differences were widely understood as part of a single, natural hierarchy of innate endowments. A boundary drawn by nature itself was not really exclusion at all. "How did woman first become subject to man, as she now is all over the world?" asked the *New York Herald* in 1852. "By her nature, her sex, just as the negro is and always will be, to the end of time, inferior to the white race, and, therefore, doomed to subjection." Paradoxically, therefore, while freedom for white men involved an open-ended process of personal transformation, developing to the fullest the potential inherent within each human being, the limits of American democracy rested on the belief that the character and abilities of non-whites and women were forever fixed by nature.

The debate over which people are and are not qualified to take part in American democracy lasted well into the twentieth century. Not until 1920 was the Constitution amended to require states to allow women to vote. The Voting Rights Act of 1965 swept away restrictions on black voting imposed by many southern states. Even today, controversy persists over the voting rights of immigrants, persons who have served prison terms, and the poor.

The political world of the nineteenth century, so crucial an arena for the exercise of American freedom, was in part defined in contrast to the feminine sphere of the home. Freedom in the public realm in no way implied freedom in private life. The "most rabid Radical," Ralph Waldo Emerson remarked in his journal in 1841, was likely to be conservative "in relation to the theory of Marriage." Beyond the right to "decent treatment" by her husband and to whatever property the law allowed her to control, declared the *New York Herald*, a woman had "no rights ... with which the public have any concern."

A RACIAL DEMOCRACY

If the exclusion of women from political freedom continued a long-standing practice, the increasing identification of democracy and whiteness marked something of a departure. Tocqueville noted that by the 1830s, "equality" had become an American obsession. In contrast to the highly stratified societies of Europe, white Americans of all social classes dressed the same, traveled in the same stagecoaches and railroad cars, and stayed in the same hotels. Yet at the same time, blacks were increasingly considered a group apart.

Racist imagery became the stock-in-trade of popular theatrical presentations like minstrel shows, in which white actors in blackface entertained the audience by portraying African-Americans as stupid, dishonest, and altogether ridiculous. With the exception of Herman Melville, who portrayed complex, sometimes heroic black characters in works like *Moby Dick* and *Benito Cereno* (the latter a fictionalized account of a shipboard slave rebellion), American authors either ignored blacks entirely or presented them as stereotypes—happy slaves prone to superstition or long-suffering but devout Christians. Meanwhile, the somewhat tentative thinking of the revolutionary era about the status of non-whites flowered into an elaborate ideology of racial superiority and inferiority, complete with "scientific" underpinnings. These developments affected the boundaries of the political nation.

In the revolutionary era, only Virginia, South Carolina, and Georgia explicitly confined the vote to whites, although elsewhere, custom often made it difficult for free blacks to exercise the franchise. As late as 1800, no northern state barred blacks from voting. But every state that entered the Union after that year, with the single exception of Maine, limited the right to vote to white males. And, beginning with Kentucky in 1799 and Maryland two years later, states that had allowed blacks to vote rescinded the privilege.

"Dandy Jim," a piece of sheet music from 1843. Minstrel shows were a form of nineteenth-century entertainment in which white actors impersonated blacks. Here, the actor makes fun of a black man attempting to adopt the style of middle-class white Americans.

RACE AND CLASS

In 1821, the same New York constitutional convention that removed property qualifications for white voters raised the requirement for blacks to $250, a sum beyond the reach of nearly all of the state's black residents. North Carolina disenfranchised free blacks in 1835, and Pennsylvania, home of an articulate, economically successful black community in Philadelphia, did the same three years later. One delegate to the Pennsylvania constitutional convention refused to sign the completed document because of its provision limiting suffrage to whites. This was Thaddeus Stevens, who would later become a leader in the drive for equal rights for African-Americans after the Civil War. By 1860, blacks could vote on the same basis as whites in only five New England states, which contained only 4 percent of the nation's free black population. A delegate to the Pennsylvania convention of 1837 described the United States as "a political community of white persons."

Despite racial inequalities, many whites of the revolutionary generation had thought of African-Americans as "citizens of color," potential members of the body politic. But in the nineteenth century, the definition of the political nation became more and more associated with race. The federal government barred free blacks from service in state militias and the army (although the navy did enroll some black sailors). No state accorded free blacks what today would be considered full equality before the law. In Illinois, for example, blacks could not vote, testify or sue in court, serve in the militia, or attend public schools. Blacks were aliens, not Americans, "intruders among us," declared a political leader in Minnesota.

In effect, race had replaced class as the boundary between those American men who were entitled to enjoy political freedom and those who were not. Even as this focus on race limited America's political community as a whole, it helped to solidify a sense of national identity among the diverse groups of European origin. In a country where the right to vote had become central to the meaning of freedom, it is difficult to overstate the importance of the fact that white male immigrants could vote in some states almost from the moment they landed in America, while nearly all free blacks (and, of course, slaves), whose ancestors had lived in the country for centuries, could not vote at all.

NATIONALISM AND ITS DISCONTENTS

THE AMERICAN SYSTEM

The War of 1812, which the United States and Great Britain—the world's foremost military power—fought to a draw, inspired an outburst of nationalist pride. But the war also revealed how far the United States still was from being a truly integrated nation. With the Bank of the United States having gone out of existence when its charter expired in 1811, the country lacked a uniform currency and found it almost impossible to raise funds for the war effort. Given the primitive state of transportation, it proved very difficult to move men and goods around the country. One shipment of supplies from New England had taken seventy-five days to reach New Orleans. With the coming of peace, the manufacturing enterprises that sprang up while trade with Britain had been suspended faced intense competition from low-cost imported goods. A younger generation of Republicans, led by Henry Clay and John C. Calhoun, believed these "infant industries" deserved national protection. While retaining their Jeffersonian belief in an agrarian republic, they insisted that agriculture must be complemented by a manufacturing sector if the country were to become economically independent of Britain.

In 1806, Congress, as noted in the previous chapter, had approved using

An image from a broadside from the campaign of 1824, promoting the American System of government-sponsored economic development. The illustrations represent industry, commerce, and agriculture. The ship at the center is named the John Quincy Adams. *Its flag, "No Colonial Subjection," suggests that without a balanced economy, the United States will remain economically dependent on Great Britain.*

FREE TRADE & SAILORS RIGHTS
NO COLONIAL SUBJECTION
SPEED THE PLOUGH

National Industry is National Wealth.

Agriculture is the Source of Prosperity.

public funds to build a paved National Road from Cumberland, Maryland, to the Ohio Valley. Two years later, Albert Gallatin, Jefferson's Secretary of the treasury, outlined a plan for the federal government to tie the vast nation together by constructing roads and canals up and down the eastern seaboard, and by connecting the Atlantic coast with the Great Lakes and Ohio and Mississippi Rivers. Gallatin's proposal fell victim to regional rivalries and fears of excessive national power. But the idea revived after the War of 1812.

In his annual message (now known as the State of the Union address) to Congress in December 1815, President James Madison put forward a blueprint for government-promoted economic development that came to be known as the American System, a label coined by Henry Clay. (It should not be confused with the "American system of manufactures" mentioned in the previous chapter, which referred to a way of mass-producing goods with interchangeable parts, not a political program for economic growth.) The plan rested on three pillars: a new national bank, a tariff on imported manufactured goods to protect American industry, and federal financing of improved roads and canals. The last was particularly important to those worried about the dangers of disunity. "Let us bind the nation together, with a perfect system of roads and canals," John C. Calhoun implored Congress in 1815. "Let us conquer space." When believers in strict construction of the Constitution objected, Calhoun replied: "If we are restricted in the use of money to the enumerated powers, on what principle can the purchase of Louisiana be justified?"

Government-sponsored "internal improvements," as the construction of roads and canals was called, proved to be the most controversial part of the plan. Congress enacted an internal-improvements program drafted by Calhoun only to be astonished when the president, on the eve of his retirement from office in March 1817, vetoed the bill. Since calling for its enactment, Madison had become convinced that allowing the national government to exercise powers not mentioned in the Constitution would prove dangerous to individual liberty and southern interests. A constitutional amendment would be necessary, he declared, before the federal government could build roads and canals. The other two parts of his plan, however, became law. The tariff of 1816 offered protection to goods that could be produced in the United States, especially cheap cotton textiles, while admitting tax-free those that could not be manufactured at home. Many southerners supported the tariff, believing that it would enable their region to develop a manufacturing base to rival New England's. And in 1816, a new Bank of the United States was created, with a twenty-year charter from Congress.

John C. Calhoun in an 1822 portrait by the artist Charles Bird King. Calhoun would evolve from a nationalist into the most prominent spokesman for state sovereignty and the right of nullification.

BANKS AND MONEY

The Second Bank of the United States soon became the focus of public resentment. Like its predecessor, it was a private, profit-making corporation that served as the government's financial agent, issuing paper money, collecting taxes, and paying the government's debts. It was also charged with ensuring that paper money issued by local banks had real value. The number of local banks had risen to more than 200—a sign of the accelerating market revolution. They promoted economic growth by helping to finance manufacturing and commerce and extending loans to farmers for the purchase of land, tools, consumer goods, and, in the South, slaves. They also printed paper money.

Today, only the federal government issues paper money, and the amount is determined by the Federal Reserve Bank, not the amount of gold held at the repository at Fort Knox. But in the nineteenth century, paper money consisted of notes promising to pay the bearer on demand a specified amount of "specie" (gold or silver). The value of the currency issued by individual banks depended on their reputation for stability. Since banks often printed far more money than the specie in their vaults, the value of paper currency fluctuated wildly. The Bank of the United States was supposed to prevent the overissuance of money. Because it held all the funds of the federal government, it accumulated a large amount of paper money issued by local banks, which had been used to purchase public land. The Bank of the United States could demand payment in gold and silver from a local bank in exchange for that bank's paper money. This prospect was supposed to prevent local banks from acting improperly, for if it could not provide the specie when asked, it would have to suspend operations.

THE PANIC OF 1819

But instead of effectively regulating the currency and loans issued by local banks, the Bank of the United States participated in a speculative fever that swept the country after the end of the War of 1812. The resumption of trade with Europe created a huge overseas market for American cotton and grain. Coupled with the rapid expansion of settlement into the West, this stimulated demand for loans to purchase land, which local banks and branches of the Bank of the United States were only too happy to meet by printing more money. The land boom was especially acute in the South, where the Cotton Kingdom was expanding.

Early in 1819, as European demand for American farm products returned to normal levels, the economic bubble burst. The demand for land plummeted, and speculators lost millions as the price of western land fell. At this time, loans tended to be of short duration and banks could demand repayment at any time. The Bank of the United States, followed by state banks, began asking for payments from those to whom it had loaned money. Farmers and businessmen who could not repay declared bankruptcy, and unemployment rose in eastern cities.

THE POLITICS OF THE PANIC

The Panic of 1819 lasted little more than a year, but it severely disrupted the political harmony of the previous years. Those suffering from the economic downturn pressed the state and national governments for assistance. To the consternation of creditors, many states, especially in the West, responded by suspending the collection of debts. Kentucky went even further, establishing a state bank that flooded the state with paper money that creditors were required to accept in repayment of loans. This eased the burden on indebted farmers, but injured those who had loaned them the money. Overall, the Panic deepened many Americans' traditional distrust of banks. It undermined the reputation of the Second Bank of the United States,

What efforts were made in this period to strengthen the economic integration of the nation, and what major crises hindered these efforts?

381

which was widely blamed for causing the Panic. Several states retaliated against the national bank by taxing its local branches.

These tax laws produced another of John Marshall's landmark Supreme Court decisions, in the case of *McCulloch v. Maryland* (1819). Reasserting his broad interpretation of governmental powers, Marshall declared the Bank a legitimate exercise of congressional authority under the Constitution's clause that allowed Congress to pass "necessary and proper" laws. Marshall's interpretation of the Constitution directly contradicted the "strict construction" view that limited Congress to powers specifically granted in the Constitution. Marshall acknowledged that the Constitution nowhere mentions the right of lawmakers to issue corporate charters. But, he wrote, where the aim of legislation—in this case to promote the "general welfare"—was legitimate, "all means which are . . . not prohibited . . . are constitutional." Maryland, the chief justice continued, could not tax the Bank. "The power to tax," Marshall remarked, "involves the power to destroy," and the states lacked the authority to destroy an agency created by the national government.

THE MISSOURI CONTROVERSY

In 1816, James Monroe handily defeated Federalist candidate Rufus King, becoming the last of the Virginia presidents. By 1820, the Federalists fielded electoral tickets in only two states, and Monroe carried the entire country. (One elector, William Plumer of New Hampshire, however, cast his vote for John Quincy Adams, whom he deemed more qualified than Monroe to be president. The legend later arose that Plumer voted as he did because he wished George Washington to remain the only president elected unanimously.) Monroe's two terms in office were years of one-party government, sometimes called the Era of Good Feelings. Plenty of bad feelings, however, surfaced during his presidency. In the absence of two-party competition, politics was organized along lines of competing sectional interests.

Even as political party divisions faded and John Marshall aligned the Supreme Court with the aggressive nationalism of Clay, Calhoun, and others, the troublesome issue of slavery again threatened to disrupt the nation's unity. In 1819, Congress considered a request from Missouri, an area carved out of the Louisiana Purchase, to form a constitution in preparation for admission to the Union as a state. Missouri's slave population already exceeded 10,000. James Tallmadge, a Republican congressman from New York, moved that the introduction of further slaves be prohibited and that children of those already in Missouri be freed at age twenty-five.

Tallmadge's proposal sparked two years of controversy, during which Republican unity shattered along sectional lines. His restriction passed the House, where most northern congressmen supported it over the objections of southern representatives. It died in the Senate, however. When Congress reconvened in 1820, Senator Jesse Thomas of Illinois proposed a compromise with three parts. Missouri would be authorized to draft a constitution without Tallmadge's restriction. Maine, which prohibited slavery, would be admitted to the Union to maintain the sectional balance between free and slave states. And slavery would be prohibited in all remaining territory within the Louisiana Purchase north of latitude 36°309 (Missouri's southern boundary). Congress adopted Thomas's plan as the Missouri Compromise.

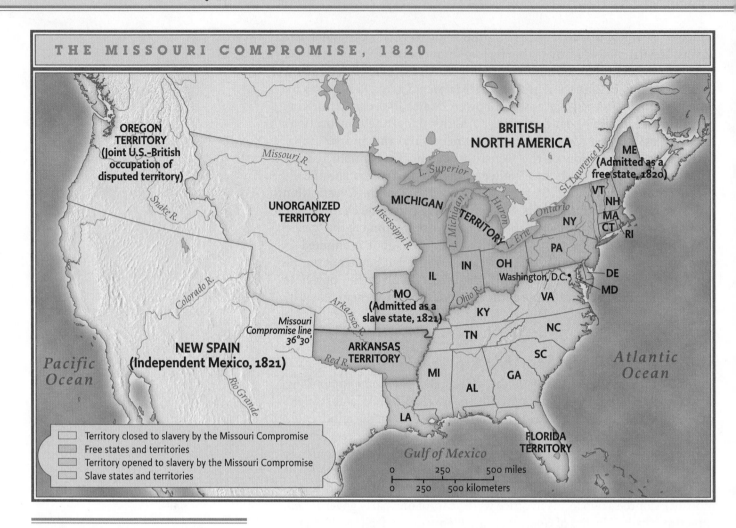

THE MISSOURI COMPROMISE, 1820

The Missouri Compromise temporarily settled the question of the expansion of slavery by dividing the Louisiana Purchase into free and slave areas.

A year later, Missouri presented to Congress its new constitution, which not only protected slavery but prohibited free blacks from entering the state. Since some northern states still considered blacks citizens, this seemed to violate the federal Constitution's "comity" clause, which requires each state to recognize the rights of citizens of other states. Henry Clay engineered a second Missouri Compromise, according to which Congress accepted the state's constitution as written, but instructed Missouri that it could not deprive the citizens of any states of their rights under the U.S. Constitution. Missouri, however, largely ignored this provision.

THE SLAVERY QUESTION

Thomas Jefferson, who had drafted the clause of the Northwest Ordinance of 1787 prohibiting slavery north of the Ohio River, strenuously opposed efforts to keep the institution out of Missouri. He saw the entire controversy as an attempt by Federalists to revive their party by setting northern and southern Republicans against each other. Jefferson was correct that political power, not moral scruples, motivated most northern congressmen. But Republicans, not the few remaining Federalists, provided the bulk of the votes against slavery in Missouri. By 1820, New York had surpassed Virginia in population, and

What efforts were made in this period to strengthen the economic integration of the nation, and what major crises hindered these efforts?

383

New York Republicans were among the leading advocates of emancipation in Missouri. Twenty-eight years of Virginia presidents, interrupted only by the single term of John Adams of Massachusetts, had persuaded many northerners that the South exercised undue influence in Washington. More slave states meant more southern congressmen and electoral votes.

The Missouri controversy raised for the first time what would prove to be a fatal issue—the westward expansion of slavery. The sectional division it revealed aroused widespread feelings of dismay. "This momentous question," wrote Jefferson, "like a fire bell in the night, awakened and filled me with terror. I considered it at once as the knell of the union." John Quincy Adams wrote of the debate in his diary:

> [It] disclosed a secret: it revealed the basis for a new organization of parties. . . . Here was a new party really formed . . . terrible to the whole Union, but portentously terrible to the South—threatening in its progress the emancipation of all their slaves, threatening in its immediate effect that southern domination which has swayed the Union for the last twenty years.

The "dissolution of the Union" over the issue of slavery, Adams mused, disastrous as that might be, would result in civil war and the "extirpation of slavery from this whole continent." It would take more than forty years for Adams's prediction to be fulfilled. For the moment, the slavery issue faded once again from national debate.

NATION, SECTION, AND PARTY

THE UNITED STATES AND THE LATIN AMERICAN WARS OF INDEPENDENCE

Between 1810 and 1822, Spain's Latin American colonies rose in rebellion and established a series of independent nations, including Mexico, Venezuela, Ecuador, and Peru. By 1825, Spain's once vast American empire had been reduced to the islands of Cuba and Puerto Rico. The uprisings inspired a wave of sympathy in the United States. In 1822, the Monroe administration became the first government to extend diplomatic recognition to the new Latin American republics.

Parallels existed between the Spanish-American revolutions and the one that had given birth to the United States. In both cases, the crisis of empire was precipitated by programs launched by the imperial country aimed in large measure at making the colonies contribute more to its finances. The government in Spain had been trying to strengthen its hold on the empire since the late eighteenth century. A French army under Napoleon occupied Spain in 1808 and overthrew the monarchy, inspiring assertions of local control throughout Spanish America. A new constitution adopted by Spain in 1812 granted greater local rights in Spain and the colonies. When the king was restored in 1814, he repudiated the constitution and moved to reassert control over the colonies. But the colonists had become used to autonomy. As had happened in British North America, local elites demanded status and treatment equal to residents of the imperial power. The

VOICES OF FREEDOM

FROM PRESIDENT JAMES MONROE,
Annual Message to Congress (1823)

In the wake of the Latin American struggle for independence, President James Monroe included in his annual message a passage that became known as the Monroe Doctrine. It outlined principles that would help to govern the country's relations with the rest of the world for nearly a century—that the Western Hemisphere was no longer open to European colonization, and that the United States would remain uninvolved in the wars of Europe.

[This] occasion has been judged proper for asserting, as a principle . . . , that the American continents, by the free and independent condition which they have assumed and maintain, are henceforth not to be considered as subjects for future colonization by any European powers. . . .

It was stated at the commencement of the last session that a great effort was then making in Spain and Portugal to improve the condition of the people of those countries, and that it appeared to be conducted with extraordinary moderation. It need scarcely be remarked that the results have been so far very different from what was then anticipated. Of events in that quarter of the globe, with which we have so much intercourse and from which we derive our origin, we have always been anxious and interested spectators. The citizens of the United States cherish sentiments the most friendly in favor of the liberty and happiness of their fellow-men on that side of the Atlantic. In the wars of the European powers in matters relating to themselves we have never taken any part, nor does it comport with our policy to do so. It is only when our rights are invaded or seriously menaced that we resent injuries or make preparation for our defense. With the movements in this hemisphere we are of necessity more immediately connected, and by causes which must be obvious to all enlightened and impartial observers. The political system of the allied powers [of Europe] is essentially different in this respect from that of America. . . .

We owe it, therefore, to candor and to the amicable relations existing between the United States and those powers to declare that we should consider any attempt on their part to extend their system to any portion of this hemisphere as dangerous to our peace and safety. With the existing colonies or dependencies of any European power we have not interfered and shall not interfere. But with the Governments who have declared their independence and maintain it, and whose independence we have, on great consideration and on just principles, acknowledged, we could not view any interposition for the purpose of oppressing them, or controlling in any other manner their destiny, by any European power in any other light than as the manifestation of an unfriendly disposition toward the United States.

FROM JOHN C. CALHOUN, "A Disquisition on Government" (ca. 1845)

The most prominent political philosopher in the pre–Civil War South, John C. Calhoun sought to devise ways that the South could retain the power to protect its interests within the Union (especially the institution of slavery) as it fell behind the North in population and political power.

There are two different modes in which the sense of the community may be taken; one, simply by the right of suffrage, unaided; the other, by the right through a proper organism. Each collects the sense of the majority. But one regards numbers only, and considers the whole community as a unit, having but one common interest throughout; and collects the sense of the greater number of the whole, as that of the community. The other, on the contrary, regards interests as well as numbers;–considering the community as made up of different and conflicting interests, as far as the action of the government is concerned; and takes the sense of each, through its majority or appropriate organ, and the united sense of all, as the sense of the entire community. The former of these I shall call the numerical, or absolute majority; and the latter, the concurrent, or constitutional majority. I call it the constitutional majority, because it is an essential element in every constitutional government,–be whatever form it takes. So great is the difference, politically speaking, between the two majorities, that they cannot be confounded, without leading to great and fatal errors; and yet the distinction between them has been so entirely overlooked, that when the term *majority* is used in political discussions, it is applied exclusively to designate the numerical,–as if there were no other. . . .

The first and leading error which naturally arises from overlooking the distinction referred to, is, to confound the numerical majority with the people, and this is so completely as to regard them as identical. This is a consequence that necessarily results from considering the numerical as the only majority. All admit, that a popular government, or democracy, is the government of the people. . . . Those who regard the numerical as the only majority . . . [are] forced to regard the numerical majority as, in effect, the entire people. . . .

The necessary consequence of taking the sense of the community by the concurrent majority is . . . to give to each interest or portion of the community a negative on the others. It is this mutual negative among its various conflicting interests, which invests each with the power of protecting itself; . . . Without this, there can be no constitution.

QUESTIONS

1. Why does Monroe think that the "systems" of Europe and the Western Hemisphere are fundamentally different?

2. Which Americans would be most likely to object to Calhoun's political system?

3. How do the two documents differ in their conception of how powerful the national government ought to be?

Spanish-American declarations of independence borrowed directly from that of the United States. The first, issued in 1811, even before the restoration of the monarchy in Spain, declared that the "United Provinces" of Venezuela now enjoyed "among the sovereign nations of the earth the rank which the Supreme Being and nature has assigned us"—language strikingly similar to Jefferson's.

Unlike the British empire, Spain's dissolved into seventeen different nations. The Spanish empire was too vast and disconnected for a common sense of nationhood to emerge. The Spanish government had imposed severe restrictions on printing, thereby making communication between the various parts of the empire more difficult than in the British colonies. The first printing press in Bogotá, a major city in South America, was not established until the 1770s. Nonetheless, imported books had circulated widely, spreading the era's revolutionary ideas.

In some ways, the new Latin American constitutions were more democratic than that of the United States. Most sought to implement the trans-Atlantic ideals of rights and freedom by creating a single national "people" out of the diverse populations that made up the Spanish empire. To do so, they extended the right to vote to Indians and free blacks. The Latin American wars of independence, in which black soldiers participated on both sides, also set in motion the gradual abolition of slavery. But the Latin American wars of independence lasted longer—sometimes more than a decade—and were more destructive than the one in the United States had been. In some countries, independence was followed by civil war. As a result, it proved far more difficult for the new Latin American republics to achieve economic development than the United States.

THE MONROE DOCTRINE

John Quincy Adams, who was serving as James Monroe's secretary of state, was devoted to consolidating the power of the national government at home and abroad. Adams feared that Spain would try to regain its Latin American colonies. In 1823, he drafted a section of the president's annual message to Congress that became known as the Monroe Doctrine. It expressed three principles. First, the United States would oppose any further efforts at colonization by European powers in the Americas (a statement aimed not only against Spain but also at France, which had designs on Cuba, and at Russia, which was seeking to expand its holdings on the Pacific coast). Second, the United States would abstain from involvement in the wars of Europe. Finally, Monroe warned European powers not to interfere with the newly independent states of Latin America.

The Monroe Doctrine is sometimes called America's diplomatic declaration of independence. For many decades, it remained a cornerstone of American foreign policy. Based on the assumption that the Old and New Worlds formed separate political and diplomatic systems, it claimed for the United States the role of dominant power in the Western Hemisphere. For Adams, the commercial implications were as important as the political ones. In 1823, Latin America was a major market for British goods, and British citizens were heavily involved in mining, banking, and commercial enterprises there. Adams hoped that the United States could eventually assume Britain's economic role.

THE AMERICAS, 1830

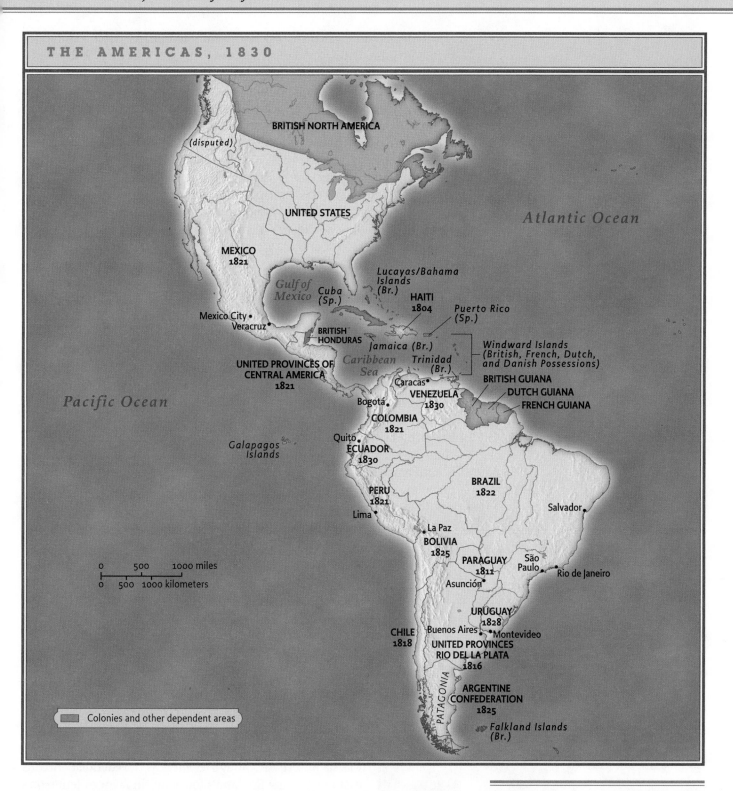

BRITISH NORTH AMERICA

(disputed)

UNITED STATES

Atlantic Ocean

MEXICO
1821

Gulf of Mexico

Lucayas/Bahama
Islands
(Br.)

Cuba
(Sp.)

HAITI
1804

Puerto Rico
(Sp.)

Mexico City •
Veracruz •

BRITISH
HONDURAS

Jamaica (Br.)

Windward Islands
(British, French, Dutch,
and Danish Possessions)

UNITED PROVINCES OF
CENTRAL AMERICA
1821

*Caribbean
Sea*

Trinidad
(Br.)

BRITISH GUIANA
DUTCH GUIANA
FRENCH GUIANA

Caracas •

Pacific Ocean

Bogotá •

VENEZUELA
1830

COLOMBIA
1821

Quito •

*Galapagos
Islands*

ECUADOR
1830

BRAZIL
1822

PERU
1821

Salvador •

Lima •

La Paz •

BOLIVIA
1825

0   500   1000 miles
0 500 1000 kilometers

PARAGUAY
1811

São
Paulo

Rio de Janeiro •

Asunción •

URUGUAY
1828

CHILE
1818

Buenos Aires •
• Montevideo

UNITED PROVINCES
RIO DEL LA PLATA
1816

PATAGONIA

ARGENTINE
CONFEDERATION
1825

Falkland Islands
(Br.)

☐ Colonies and other dependent areas

THE ELECTION OF 1824

The Monroe Doctrine reflected a rising sense of American nationalism. But sectionalism seemed to rule domestic politics. As the election of 1824 approached, only Andrew Jackson could claim truly national support. Jackson's popularity rested not on any specific public policy—few voters knew his views—but on military victories over the British at the Battle of

This map depicts the Western Hemisphere after most of Spain's colonies achieved their independence.

New Orleans, and over the Creek and Seminole Indians. Other candidates included John Quincy Adams, Secretary of the Treasury William H. Crawford of Georgia, and Henry Clay of Kentucky. Adams's support was concentrated in New England and, more generally, in the North, where Republican leaders insisted the time had come for the South to relinquish the presidency. Crawford represented the South's Old Republicans, who wanted the party to reaffirm the principles of states' rights and limited government. Clay was one of the era's most popular politicians, but his support in 1824 lay primarily in the West. A caucus of Republican congressmen traditionally chose the party's nominee for president. The caucus selected Crawford, but this did not deter the other candidates, a sign that at a time of expanding democracy a small group of officials could no longer determine who ran for office.

Jackson received 153,544 votes and carried states in all the regions outside of New England. But with four candidates in the field, none received a majority of the electoral votes. As required by the Constitution, Clay, who finished fourth, was eliminated, and the choice among the other three fell to the House of Representatives. Sincerely believing Adams to be the most qualified candidate and the one most likely to promote the American System, and probably calculating that the election of Jackson, a westerner, would impede his own presidential ambitions, Clay gave his support to Adams, helping to elect him. He soon became secretary of state in Adams's cabinet. The charge that he had made a "corrupt bargain"—bartering critical votes in the presidential contest for a public office—clung to Clay for the rest of his career, making it all but impossible for him to reach the White House. The election of 1824 laid the groundwork for a new system of political parties. Supporters of Jackson and Crawford would soon unite in a new organization, the Democratic Party, determined to place Jackson in the White House in 1828. The alliance of Clay and Adams became the basis for the Whig Party of the 1830s.

THE NATIONALISM OF JOHN QUINCY ADAMS

John Quincy Adams enjoyed one of the most distinguished pre-presidential careers of any American president. The son of John Adams, he had witnessed the Battle of Bunker Hill at age eight and at fourteen had worked as private secretary and French interpreter for an American envoy in Europe. He had gone on to serve as ambassador to Prussia, the Netherlands, Britain, and Russia, and as senator from Massachusetts. Although elected as a Federalist, Adams cast one of New England's few votes in favor of Jefferson's embargo policy, arguing that his region must rise above sectional self-interest to defend the national good. Given the intense political passions of the time, he had been forced to resign his seat as a result of his vote, and he soon abandoned the Federalist Party.

Adams was not an engaging figure. He described himself

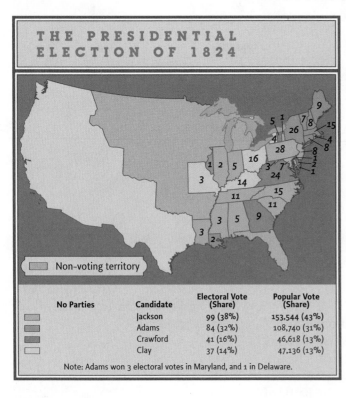

THE PRESIDENTIAL ELECTION OF 1824

Non-voting territory

No Parties	Candidate	Electoral Vote (Share)	Popular Vote (Share)
	Jackson	99 (38%)	153,544 (43%)
	Adams	84 (32%)	108,740 (31%)
	Crawford	41 (16%)	46,618 (13%)
	Clay	37 (14%)	47,136 (13%)

Note: Adams won 3 electoral votes in Maryland, and 1 in Delaware.

as "a man of cold, austere, and foreboding manners." But he had a clear vision of national greatness. At home, he strongly supported the American System of government-sponsored economic development. Abroad, he hoped to encourage American commerce throughout the world and, as illustrated by his authorship of the Monroe Doctrine, enhance American influence in the Western Hemisphere. As Monroe's secretary of state, he had been the only cabinet member to oppose reprimanding Andrew Jackson for his violent incursion into Florida. In 1819, as noted in the previous chapter, Adams negotiated a treaty by which the United States acquired Florida from Spain. He also concluded an agreement with Great Britain fixing the Canadian-American border at the northern boundary of the Louisiana Purchase. An ardent expansionist, Adams was certain that the United States would eventually, and peacefully, absorb Canada, Cuba, and at least part of Mexico. Indeed, he once said, the "proper domain" of the United States was "the entire continent of North America."

John Quincy Adams in an 1843 daguerreotype.

"LIBERTY IS POWER"

Adams held a view of federal power far more expansive than most of his contemporaries. In his first message to Congress, in December 1825, he set forth a comprehensive program for an activist national state. "The spirit of improvement is abroad in the land," Adams announced, and the federal government should be its patron. He called for legislation promoting agriculture, commerce, manufacturing, and "the mechanical and elegant arts." His plans included the establishment of a national university, an astronomical observatory, and a naval academy. At a time when many Americans felt that governmental authority posed the greatest threat to freedom, Adams astonished many listeners with the bold statement "liberty is power." The United States, the freest nation on earth, would also, he predicted, become the mightiest.

Adams's proposals alarmed all believers in strict construction of the Constitution. His administration spent more on internal improvements than his five predecessors combined, and it enacted a steep increase in tariff rates in 1828. But the rest of Adams's ambitious ideas received little support in Congress. Not until the twentieth century would the kind of national economic and educational planning envisioned by Adams be realized. Some of his proposals, like the adoption by the United States of the metric system of weights and measures used by nearly every other nation in the world, and the building of a national university, have yet to be implemented.

MARTIN VAN BUREN AND THE DEMOCRATIC PARTY

Adams's program handed his political rivals a powerful weapon. With individual liberty, states' rights, and limited government as their rallying cries, Jackson's supporters began to organize for the election of 1828 almost as soon as Adams assumed office. Martin Van Buren, a senator from New York, oversaw the task. The clash between Adams and Van Buren demonstrated how democracy was changing the nature of American politics. Adams typified the old politics—he was the son of a president and, like Jefferson and Madison, a man of sterling intellectual accomplishments. Van Buren represented the new political era. The son of a tavern keeper, he was a talented party manager, not a person of great vision or intellect.

But Van Buren did have a compelling idea. Rather than being dangerous and divisive, as the founding generation had believed, political parties, he insisted, were a necessary and indeed desirable element of political life. Party competition provided a check on those in power and offered voters a real choice in elections. And by bringing together political leaders from different regions in support of common candidates and principles, national parties could counteract the sectionalism that had reared its head during the 1820s. Like many of his contemporaries, Van Buren had been alarmed when politics divided along sectional lines in the Missouri debates and again in the election of 1824. He attributed this in part to a loss of discipline within the ruling Republican Party. "Party attachment," Van Buren wrote to Virginia editor Thomas Ritchie, "in former times furnished a complete antidote for sectional prejudices by producing counteracting feelings. It was not until that defense had been broken down that the clamor against southern influence and African slavery could be made effectual in the North." National political parties, Van Buren realized, formed a bond of unity in a divided nation. He set out to reconstruct the Jeffersonian political alliance between "the planters of the South and the plain republicans [the farmers and urban workers] of the North."

THE ELECTION OF 1828

By 1828, Van Buren had established the political apparatus of the Democratic Party, complete with local and state party units overseen by a national committee and a network of local newspapers devoted to the party. Adams, for his part, disdained political organization. Despite Clay's urging, he refused to dismiss federal officeholders who campaigned for Jackson and did little to promote his own reelection.

Apart from a general commitment to limited government, Jackson's supporters made few campaign promises, relying on their candidate's popularity and the workings of party machinery to get out the vote. The 1828 election campaign was scurrilous. Jackson's supporters accused Adams of having had a series of mistresses while serving as a diplomat in Europe. They praised their candidate's frontier manliness and ridiculed Adams's intellectual attainments. ("Vote for Andrew Jackson who can fight, not John Quincy Adams who can write," declared one campaign slogan.) Jackson's opponents condemned him as a murderer for having executed army deserters and killing men in duels. They questioned the morality of his wife, Rachel, because she had married Jackson before her divorce from her first husband had become final. Jackson always believed his opponents' slanders had contributed to his wife's death shortly after the election.

By 1828, voters, not the legislature, chose presidential electors in every state except South Carolina, a fact that helped to encourage vigorous campaigning and high turnout. Nearly 57 percent of the eligible electorate cast ballots, more than double the percentage four years earlier. Jackson won a resounding victory, with around 650,000 votes to 500,000 for Adams. He carried the entire South and West, along with Pennsylvania. Jackson's

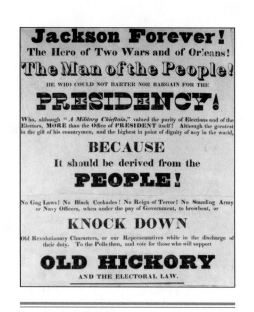

A broadside from the 1828 campaign illustrates how Andrew Jackson's supporters promoted him as a military hero and "man of the people."

election was the first to demonstrate how the advent of universal white male voting, organized by national political parties, had transformed American politics. For better or worse, the United States had entered the Age of Jackson.

THE AGE OF JACKSON

Andrew Jackson was a man of many contradictions. Although he had little formal education (Adams called him "a barbarian who could not write a sentence of grammar"), Jackson was capable of genuine eloquence in his public statements. A self-proclaimed champion of the common man, his vision of democracy excluded any role for Indians, who he believed should be pushed west of the Mississippi River, and African-Americans, who should remain as slaves or be freed and sent abroad. Although he rose from modest beginnings on the South Carolina frontier to become one of the richest men in Tennessee, he had an abiding suspicion of banks and paper money, and he shared the fears of many Americans that the market revolution was a source of moral decay rather than progress. A strong nationalist, Jackson nonetheless believed that the states, not Washington, D.C., should be the focal point of governmental activity. He opposed federal efforts to shape the economy or interfere in individuals' private lives.

THE PRESIDENTIAL ELECTION OF 1828

Non-voting territory

Party	Candidate	Electoral Vote (Share)	Popular Vote (Share)
Democrat	Jackson	178 (68%)	647,286 (56%)
National Republican	Adams	83 (32%)	508,064 (44%)

THE PARTY SYSTEM

By the time of Jackson's presidency, politics had become more than a series of political contests—it was a spectacle, a form of mass entertainment, a part of Americans' daily lives. Every year witnessed elections to some office—local, state, or national—and millions took part in the parades and rallies organized by the parties. Politicians were popular heroes with mass followings and popular nicknames. Jackson was Old Hickory, Clay was Harry of the West, and Van Buren the Little Magician (or, to his critics, the Sly Fox). Thousands of Americans willingly attended lengthy political orations and debates. An audience of 100,000 was said to have gathered on a Massachusetts hillside to hear a speech by the great Whig orator Daniel Webster.

"Politics," one newspaper editor remarked, "seems to enter into everything." Indeed, party machines, headed by professional politicians, reached into every neighborhood, especially in cities. They provided benefits like jobs to constituents and ensured that voters went to the polls on election day. Party functionaries were rewarded with political offices. Government posts, Jackson declared, should be open to the people, not reserved for a privileged class of permanent bureaucrats. He introduced the principle of rotation in office (called the "spoils system" by opponents) into national government, making loyalty to the party the main qualification for jobs like postmaster and customs official.

Large national conventions where state leaders gathered to hammer out a platform now chose national candidates. Newspapers played a greater and greater role in politics. Nearly 400 were published in 1830, compared

VISIONS OF FREEDOM

Stump Speaking. *In this painting from the 1850s, George Caleb Bingham depicts a candidate in a county election addressing a group of voters, an illustration of grassroots democracy in action. One of the listeners appears about to question or challenge the speaker. Bingham's paintings generally depict scenes in the American West, including exploration, landscapes, and life on the Missouri and Mississippi Rivers. But he was also fascinated by democratic politics. A founder of the Whig Party in Missouri, Bingham himself ran for office several times and was elected to the state legislature in 1848.*

QUESTIONS

1. What does the painting tell us about the extent and limits of American democracy in the mid-nineteenth century?

2. What does the clothing of those in the painting indicate about their occupations or status?

Procession of Victuallers, *a lithograph commemorating a parade of butchers through the streets of Philadelphia in 1821. Their banner, "We Feed the Hungry," illustrates the belief among members of the "producing classes" that their work led to practical benefits for society, unlike the activities of "nonproducers" like bankers.*

to 90 in 1790. Every significant town, it seemed, had its Democratic and Whig papers whose job was not so much to report the news as to present the party's position on issues of the day. Jackson's Kitchen Cabinet—an informal group of advisers who helped to write his speeches and supervise communication between the White House and local party officials—mostly consisted of newspaper editors.

DEMOCRATS AND WHIGS

There was more to party politics, however, than spectacle and organization. Jacksonian politics revolved around issues spawned by the market revolution and the continuing tension between national and sectional loyalties. The central elements of political debate were the government's stance toward banks, tariffs, currency, and internal improvements, and the balance of power between national and local authority. Although both parties were coalitions of groups with varied, sometimes contradictory approaches to the issues of the day, the market revolution did much to determine their views and makeup. Democrats tended to be alarmed by the widening gap between social classes. They warned that "nonproducers"—bankers, merchants, and speculators—were seeking to use connections with government to enhance their wealth to the disadvantage of the "producing classes" of farmers, artisans, and laborers. They believed the government should adopt a hands-off attitude toward the economy and not award special favors to entrenched economic interests.

"All bank charters, all acts of incorporation," declared a Democratic newspaper, "are calculated to enhance the power of wealth, produce inequalities among the people and to subvert liberty." If the national government removed itself from the economy, ordinary Americans could test their abilities in the fair competition of the self-regulating market. The Democratic Party attracted aspiring entrepreneurs who resented govern-

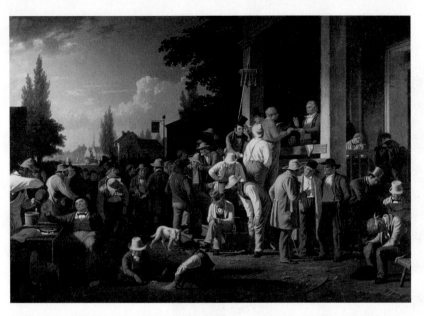

County Election, *another painting by George Caleb Bingham depicting American democracy in action. In this 1852 work, a voter takes an oath while party workers dispense liquor, seek to persuade voters, and keep track of who has cast ballots. The banner on the pole reads, "The Will of the People the Supreme Law." The slogan is meant to be ironic. Bingham includes a number of Democratic politicians he accused of cheating him in a recent election.*

ment aid to established businessmen, as well as large numbers of farmers and city working-men suspicious of new corporate enterprises. Poorer farming regions isolated from markets, like the lower Northwest and the southern backcountry, tended to vote Democratic.

Whigs united behind the American System, believing that via a protective tariff, a national bank, and aid to internal improvements, the federal government could guide economic development. They were strongest in the Northeast, the most rapidly modernizing region of the country. Most established businessmen and bankers supported their program of government-promoted economic growth, as did farmers in regions near rivers, canals, and the Great Lakes, who benefited from economic changes or hoped to do so. The counties of upstate New York along the Erie Canal, for example, became a Whig stronghold, while more isolated rural communities tended to vote Democratic. Many slaveholders supported the Democrats, believing states' rights to be slavery's first line of defense. But like well-to-do merchants and industrialists in the North, the largest southern planters generally voted Whig.

PUBLIC AND PRIVATE FREEDOM

The party battles of the Jacksonian era reflected the clash between "public" and "private" definitions of American freedom and their relationship to governmental power, a persistent tension in the nation's history. For Democrats, liberty was a private entitlement best secured by local governments and endangered by powerful national authority. "The limitation of power, in every branch of our government," wrote a Democratic newspaper in 1842, "is the only safeguard of liberty." A "splendid" government was always "built upon the ruins of popular rights."

Under Jackson, even as democracy expanded, the power of the national government waned. Weak national authority, in the Democratic view, was essential to both private freedom and states' rights—"the freedom of the individual in the social union, [and] the freedom of the State in the Federative Union." Ralph Waldo Emerson called antebellum Americans "fanatics in freedom," whose obsession expressed itself in hatred of "tolls, taxes, turnpikes, banks, hierarchies, governors, yea, almost laws." Democrats regularly condemned the faraway federal government as the greatest "danger to liberty" in America and identified government-granted privilege as the root cause of social inequality. During Jackson's presidency, Democrats reduced expenditures, lowered the tariff, killed the national bank, and refused pleas for federal aid to internal improvements. By 1835, Jackson had even managed to pay off the national debt. As a result, states replaced the federal government as the country's main economic actors, planning systems of canals and roads and chartering banks and other corporations.

POLITICS AND MORALITY

Democrats, moreover, considered individual morality a private matter, not a public concern. They opposed attempts to impose a unified moral vision on society, such as "temperance" legislation, which restricted or outlawed the production and sale of liquor, and laws prohibiting various kinds of entertainment on Sundays. As noted in Chapter 9, Catholic Irish and German immigrants who began arriving in significant numbers in the 1830s flocked to the Democratic Party. One reason was that they did not wish to have Protestant moral standards enforced by the government. "In this country," declared the New York *Journal of Commerce* in 1848, "liberty is understood to be the *absence* of government from private affairs." The test of public policies was not whether they enhanced the common good, but the extent to which they allowed scope for "free agency"—that is, for individuals to make decisions, pursue their interests, and cultivate their unique talents without outside interference.

Whigs, for their part, insisted that liberty and power reinforced each other. "A weak government," wrote Francis Lieber, the founding father of American political science, was "a negation of liberty." An activist national government, on the other hand, could enhance the realm of freedom. Liberty, Whigs believed, required a prosperous and moral America. The government should create the conditions for balanced and regulated economic development, thereby promoting a prosperity in which all classes and regions would share. Like the Federalists before them, wealthy Whigs tended to view society as a hierarchy of social classes, in contrast to the disorderly world of unrestrained individual competition embraced by many Democrats. But unlike most Federalists, they insisted that in the United States class status was not fixed, since any individual could achieve upward mobility.

Whigs, moreover, rejected the premise that the government must not interfere in private life. To function as free—that is, self-directed and self-disciplined—moral agents, individuals required certain character traits, which government could help to instill. The role of government, declared one New York Whig, was not simply to stand aside but actively to "promote the welfare of the people." Many evangelical Protestants supported the Whigs, convinced that via public education, the building of schools and asylums, temperance legislation, and the like, democratic governments could inculcate the "principles of morality." And during the Jacksonian era, popularly elected local authorities enacted numerous laws, ordinances, and regulations that tried to shape public morals by banning prostitution and the consumption of alcohol, and regulating other kinds of personal behavior. Pennsylvania was as renowned in the nineteenth century for its stringent laws against profanity and desecrating the Sabbath as it had been in the colonial era for its commitment to religious liberty.

SOUTH CAROLINA AND NULLIFICATION

Andrew Jackson, it has been said, left office with many more principles than he came in with. Elected as a military hero backed by an efficient party machinery, he was soon forced to define his stance on public issues. Despite his commitment to states' rights, Jackson's first term was dominated by a battle to uphold the supremacy of federal over state law. The tariff of 1828, which raised taxes on imported manufactured goods made of wool as well as on raw materials like iron, had aroused considerable opposition in the South, nowhere more than in South Carolina, where it was called the "tariff of abominations." The state's leaders no longer believed it possible or desirable to compete with the North in industrial development. Insisting that the tariff on imported manufactured goods raised the prices paid by southern consumers to benefit the North, the legislature threatened to "nullify" it—that is, declare it null and void within their state.

The state with the largest proportion of slaves in its population (55 percent in 1830), South Carolina was controlled by a tightly knit group of large planters. They maintained their grip on power by a state constitution that gave plantation counties far greater representation in the legislature than their population warranted, as well as through high property qualifications for officeholders. They had been thoroughly alarmed by the Missouri crisis and by the steady strengthening of national authority by John Marshall's Supreme Court. Behind their economic complaints against the tariff lay the conviction that the federal government must be weakened lest it one day take action against slavery.

CALHOUN'S POLITICAL THEORY

John C. Calhoun soon emerged as the leading theorist of nullification. As the South began to fall behind the rest of the country in population, Calhoun had evolved from the nationalist of 1812 into a powerful defender of southern sectionalism. Having been elected vice president in 1828, Calhoun at first remained behind the scenes, secretly drafting the *Exposition and Protest* in which the South Carolina legislature justified nullification. The document drew on the arguments in the Virginia and Kentucky resolutions of 1798 (discussed in Chapter 8). The national government, Calhoun insisted, had been created by an agreement among sovereign states, each of which retained the right to prevent the enforcement within its borders of acts of Congress that exceeded the powers specifically spelled out in the Constitution.

Almost from the beginning of Jackson's first term, Calhoun's influence in the administration waned, while Secretary of State Martin Van Buren emerged as the president's closest adviser. One incident that helped set Jackson against Calhoun occurred a few weeks after the inauguration. Led by Calhoun's wife, Floride, Washington society women ostracized Peggy Eaton, the wife of Jackson's secretary of war, because she was the daughter of a Washington tav-

A cartoon published in 1833, at the height of the nullification controversy, shows John C. Calhoun climbing steps, including those marked "nullification," "treason," and "civil war," toward the goal of "despotism." He is flanked by James H. Hammond and Robert Y. Hayne, two of South Carolina's political leaders. On the right, President Andrew Jackson threatens to hang them.

ern keeper and, allegedly, a woman of "easy virtue." Van Buren, a widower, stood by her, as did Jackson, who identified criticism of Peggy Eaton with the abuse his own wife had suffered during the campaign of 1828.

Far weightier matters soon divided Jackson and Calhoun. Debate over nullification raged in Washington. In a memorable exchange in the Senate in January 1830, Daniel Webster responded to South Carolina senator Robert Y. Hayne, a disciple of Calhoun. The people, not the states, declared Webster, created the Constitution, making the federal government sovereign. He called nullification illegal, unconstitutional, and treasonous. Webster's ending was widely hailed throughout the country—"Liberty *and* Union, now and forever, one and inseparable." A few weeks later, at a White House dinner, Jackson delivered a toast while fixing his gaze on Calhoun: "Our Federal Union—it must be preserved." Calhoun's reply came immediately: "The Union—next to our liberty most dear." By 1831, Calhoun had publicly emerged as the leading theorist of states' rights.

An 1834 print portrays the United States as a Temple of Liberty. At the center, a figure of liberty rises from the flames, holding the Bill of Rights and a staff with a liberty cap. Justice and Minerva (Roman goddess of war and wisdom) flank the temple, above which flies a banner, "The Union Must and Shall Be Preserved."

THE NULLIFICATION CRISIS

Nullification was not a purely sectional issue. South Carolina stood alone during the crisis, and several southern states passed resolutions condemning its action. Nonetheless, the elaboration of the compact theory of the Constitution gave the South a well-developed political philosophy to which it would turn when sectional conflict became more intense. Calhoun denied that nullification was a step toward disunion. On the contrary, the only way to ensure the stability of a large, diverse nation was for each state to be assured that national actions would never trample on its rights or vital interests. According to Calhoun's theory of the "concurrent majority," each major interest, including slaveholders, should have a veto over all measures that affected it.

To Jackson, however, nullification amounted to nothing less than disunion. He dismissed Calhoun's constitutional arguments out of hand: "Can anyone of common sense believe the absurdity, that a faction of any state, or a state, has a right to secede and destroy this union, and the liberty of the country with it?" The issue came to a head in 1832, when a new tariff was enacted. Despite a reduction in tariff rates, South Carolina declared the tax on imported goods null and void in the state after the following February. In response, Jackson persuaded Congress to enact a Force Bill authorizing him to use the army and navy to collect customs duties.

To avert a confrontation, Henry Clay, with Calhoun's assistance, engineered the passage of a new tariff, in 1833, further reducing duties. South Carolina then rescinded the ordinance of nullification, although it proceeded to "nullify" the Force Act. Calhoun abandoned the Democratic Party for the Whigs, where, with Clay and Webster, he became part of a formida-

Black Hawk and His Son, Whirling Thunder, *painted in 1833 by the artist John Wesley Jarvis shortly after the Black Hawk War. Jarvis hoped that traditional Indian ways, symbolized by the son's dress, would be replaced by Black Hawk's "civilized" appearance.*

A lithograph from 1836 depicts Sequoia, with the alphabet of the Cherokee language that he developed. Because of their written language and constitution, the Cherokee were considered by many white Americans to be a "civilized tribe."

ble trio of political leaders (even though the three agreed on virtually nothing except hostility to Jackson). It is perhaps ironic that Andrew Jackson, a firm believer in states' rights and limited government, did more than any other individual to give an emotional aura to the idea of Union and to offer an example of willingness to go to war, if necessary, to preserve what he considered the national government's legitimate powers.

INDIAN REMOVAL

The nullification crisis underscored Jackson's commitment to the sovereignty of the nation. His exclusion of Indians from the era's assertive democratic nationalism led to the final act in the centuries-long conflict between white Americans and Indians east of the Mississippi River. The last Indian resistance to the advance of white settlement in the Old Northwest came in 1832, when federal troops and local militiamen routed the Sauk leader Black Hawk, who, with about 1,000 followers, attempted to reclaim ancestral land in Illinois. One of the Illinois militiamen was the young Abraham Lincoln, although, as he later remarked, he saw no action, except against mosquitoes.

In the slave states, the onward march of cotton cultivation placed enormous pressure on remaining Indian holdings. "Extending the area of slavery," proclaimed Thomas Hart Benton, who represented Missouri in the Senate for thirty years, required "converting Indian soil into slave soil." During the 1820s, Missouri forced its Indian population to leave the state. Soon, the policy of expulsion was enacted in the older slave states. One of the early laws of Jackson's administration, the Indian Removal Act of 1830, provided funds for uprooting the so-called Five Civilized Tribes—the Cherokee, Chickasaw, Choctaw, Creek, and Seminole—with a population of around 60,000 living in North Carolina, Georgia, Florida, Alabama, and Mississippi.

The law marked a repudiation of the Jeffersonian idea that "civilized" Indians could be assimilated into the American population. These tribes had made great efforts to become everything republican citizens should be. The Cherokee had taken the lead, establishing schools, adopting written laws and a constitution modeled on that of the United States, and becoming successful farmers, many of whom owned slaves. But in his messages to Congress, Jackson repeatedly referred to them as "savages" and supported Georgia's effort to seize Cherokee land and nullify the tribe's laws.

"Free citizens of the Cherokee nation" petitioned Congress for aid in remaining "in peace and quietude upon their ancient territory." In good American fashion, Cherokee leaders also went to court to protect their rights, guaranteed in treaties with the federal government. Their appeals forced the Supreme Court to clarify the unique status of American Indians.

THE SUPREME COURT AND THE INDIANS

In a crucial case involving Indians in 1823, *Johnson v. M'Intosh*, the Court had proclaimed that Indians were not in fact owners of their land, but merely had a "right of occupancy." Chief Justice John Marshall, himself a speculator in western lands, claimed that from the early colonial era, Indians had lived as nomads and hunters, not farmers. Entirely inaccurate

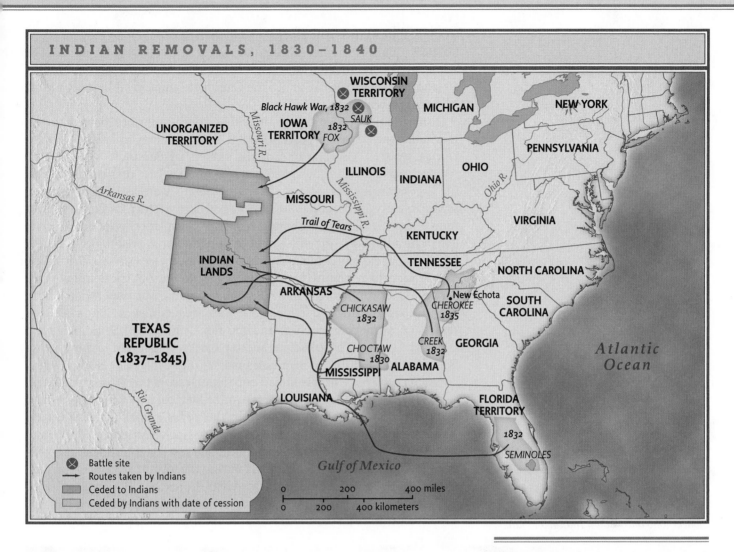

INDIAN REMOVALS, 1830–1840

The removal of the so-called Five Civilized Tribes from the Southeast all but ended the Indian presence east of the Mississippi River.

as history, the decision struck a serious blow against Indian efforts to retain their lands. In *Cherokee Nation v. Georgia* (1831), Marshall described Indians as "wards" of the federal government. They deserved paternal regard and protection, but they lacked the standing as citizens that would allow the Supreme Court to enforce their rights. The justices could not, therefore, block Georgia's effort to extend its jurisdiction over the tribe.

Marshall, however, believed strongly in the supremacy of the federal government over the states. In 1832, in *Worcester v. Georgia*, the Court seemed to change its mind, holding that Indian nations were a distinct people with the right to maintain a separate political identity. They must be dealt with by the federal government, not the states, and Georgia's actions violated the Cherokees' treaties with Washington. But despite his strong assertion of national supremacy in the nullification crisis, Jackson refused to recognize the validity of the *Worcester* ruling. "John Marshall has made his decision," he supposedly declared, "now let him enforce it."

With legal appeals exhausted, one faction of the tribe agreed to cede their lands, but the majority, led by John Ross, who had been elected "principal chief" under the Cherokee constitution, adopted a policy of passive resistance. Federal soldiers forcibly removed them during the presidency of Jackson's successor, Martin Van Buren. The army herded 18,000 men, women, and children into stockades and then forced them to move west. At least one-quarter perished during the winter of 1838–1839 on the Trail of Tears, as the removal route from Georgia to the area of present-day Oklahoma came to be called. (In the Cherokee language, it literally meant "the trail on which we cried.")

During the 1830s, most of the other southern tribes bowed to the inevitable and departed peacefully. But the Seminoles of sparsely settled Florida resisted. Osceola, one of the leaders of Seminole resistance to removal, was a Red Stick who had survived Andrew Jackson's assault on hostile Creeks during the War of 1812. The Indians were assisted by escaped slaves. As early as colonial times, Florida had been a refuge for fugitive slaves from South Carolina and Georgia, to whom Spanish officials offered freedom. The administration of George Washington attempted to persuade the Seminoles to expel the fugitives, but they refused. Georgia sent the militia into Florida to recapture them, but it was driven out by Seminole and African-American fighters. In the Second Seminole War, which lasted from 1835 to 1842 (the first had followed American acquisition of Florida in 1819), some 1,500 American soldiers and the same number of Seminoles were killed, and perhaps 3,000 Indians and 500 blacks were forced to move to the West. A small number of Seminoles managed to remain in Florida, a tiny remnant of the once sizable Indian population east of the Mississippi River.

In 1831, William Apess, a descendant of Metacom, or King Philip, who had battled New England colonists in the 1670s, published *A Son of the Forest*, the first significant autobiography by a Native American. The son of a white man and an Indian woman, Apess had served with American forces in an unsuccessful attack on Canada during the War of 1812. He later converted to Methodism and became a revivalist preacher. His book appealed for harmony between white Americans and Indians. "How much better it

The Trapper and His Family *(1845), by the artist Charles Deas, depicts a white pioneer who married an Indian woman.*

Buffalo Chase over Prairie Bluffs, a painting from the 1830s by George Catlin, who created dozens of works depicting Native Americans in the trans-Mississippi West. Catlin saw himself as recording for posterity a vanishing way of life. At the time, millions of buffalo inhabited the West, providing food and hides for Native Americans.

would be if the whites would act like civilized people [and] give every one his due," Apess wrote. "What do they, the Indians, want? You have only to look at the unjust laws made for them and say, 'They want what I want.'"

Removal was the alternative to the coexistence championed by Apess. It powerfully reinforced the racial definition of American nationhood and freedom. At the time of independence, Indians had been a familiar presence in many parts of the United States. John Adams once recalled how, when he was young, local Indians "were frequent visitors in my father's house," and how he would visit a nearby Indian family, "where I never failed to be treated with whortleberries, blackberries, strawberries or apples, plums, peaches, etc." By 1840, in the eyes of most whites east of the Mississippi River, they were simply a curiosity, a relic of an earlier period of American history. Although Indians still dominated the trans-Mississippi West, as American settlement pushed relentlessly westward it was clear that their days of freedom there also were numbered.

THE BANK WAR AND AFTER

BIDDLE'S BANK

The central political struggle of the Age of Jackson was the president's war on the Bank of the United States. The Bank symbolized the hopes and fears inspired by the market revolution. The expansion of banking helped to finance the nation's economic development. But many Americans, including Jackson, distrusted bankers as "nonproducers" who contributed nothing to the nation's wealth but profited from the labor of others. The tendency of banks to overissue paper money, whose deterioration in value reduced the real income of wage earners, reinforced this conviction. Jackson himself had

The Downfall of Mother Bank, *a Democratic cartoon celebrating the destruction of the Second Bank of the United States. President Andrew Jackson topples the building by brandishing his order removing federal funds from the Bank. Led by Nicholas Biddle, with the head of a demon, the Bank's corrupt supporters flee, among them Henry Clay, Daniel Webster, and newspaper editors allegedly paid by the institution.*

long believed that "hard money"—gold and silver—was the only honest currency. Nonetheless, when he assumed office there was little reason to believe that the Bank War would become the major event of his presidency.

Heading the Bank was Nicholas Biddle of Pennsylvania, who during the 1820s had effectively used the institution's power, discussed earlier in this chapter, to curb the overissuing of money by local banks and to create a stable currency throughout the nation. A snobbish, aristocratic Philadelphian, Biddle was as strong-willed as Jackson and as unwilling to back down in a fight. In 1832, he told a congressional committee that his Bank had the ability to "destroy" any state bank. He hastened to add that he had never "injured" any of them. But Democrats wondered whether any institution, public or private, ought to possess such power. Many called it the Monster Bank, an illegitimate union of political authority and entrenched economic privilege. The issue of the Bank's future came to a head in 1832. Although the institution's charter would not expire until 1836, Biddle's allies persuaded Congress to approve a bill extending it for another twenty years. Jackson saw the tactic as a form of blackmail—if he did not sign the bill, the Bank would use its considerable resources to oppose his reelection. "The Bank," he told Van Buren, "is trying to destroy me, but I will kill it."

Jackson's veto message is perhaps the central document of his presidency. Its argument resonated with popular values. In a democratic government, Jackson insisted, it was unacceptable for Congress to create a source of concentrated power and economic privilege unaccountable to the people. "It is to be regretted," he declared, "that the rich and powerful too often bend the acts of government to their selfish purposes." Exclusive privileges like the Bank's charter widened the gap between the wealthy and "the humble members of society—the farmers, mechanics, and laborers." Jackson presented himself as the defender of these "humble" Americans.

The Bank War reflected how Jackson enhanced the power of the presidency during his eight years in office, proclaiming himself the symbolic representative of all the people. He was the first president to use the veto power as a major weapon and to appeal directly to the public for political support, over the head of Congress. Whigs denounced him for usurping the power of the legislature. They insisted that Congress, not the president, represented the will of the people and that the veto power, while created by the Constitution, should only be used in extraordinary circumstances. But Jackson's effective appeal to democratic popular sentiments helped him win a sweeping reelection victory in 1832 over the Whig candidate, Henry Clay. His victory ensured the death of the Bank of the United States. (Ironically, Jackson's image today adorns the twenty-dollar bill issued by the Federal Reserve Bank, in some respects a successor of the Bank of the United States.)

THE PET BANKS AND THE ECONOMY

What, however, would take the Bank's place? Two very different groups applauded Jackson's veto—state bankers who wished to free themselves from Biddle's regulations and issue more paper currency (called "soft money"), and "hard money" advocates who opposed all banks, whether chartered by the states or the federal government, and believed that gold and silver formed the only reliable currency.

During Jackson's second term, state bankers were in the ascendancy. Not content to wait for the charter of the Bank of the United States to expire in 1836, Jackson authorized the removal of federal funds from its vaults and their deposit in local banks. Not surprisingly, political and personal connections often determined the choice of these "pet banks." The director of the Maine Bank of Portland, for example, was the brother-in-law of Levi Woodbury, a member of Jackson's cabinet. A justice of the Supreme Court recommended the Planters Bank of Savannah. Two secretaries of the Treasury refused to transfer federal money to the pet banks, since the law creating the Bank had specified that government funds could not be removed except for a good cause as communicated to Congress. Jackson finally appointed Attorney General Roger B. Taney, a loyal Maryland Democrat, to the Treasury post, and he carried out the order. When John Marshall died in 1835, Jackson rewarded Taney by appointing him chief justice.

Without government deposits, the Bank of the United States lost its ability to regulate the activities of state banks. They issued more and more paper money, partly to help finance the rapid expansion of industrial development in New England, agriculture in the South and West, and canal and railroad systems planned by the states. The value of bank notes in circulation rose from $10 million in 1833 to $149 million in 1837.

Prices rose dramatically, and even though wages also increased, they failed to keep pace. As a result, workers' "real wages"—the actual value of their pay—declined. Numerous labor unions emerged, which attempted to protect the earnings of urban workers. Speculators hastened to cash in on rising land prices. Using paper money, they bought up huge blocks of public land, which they resold to farmers or to eastern purchasers of lots in entirely nonexistent western towns. States projected tens of millions of dollars in internal improvements.

THE PANIC OF 1837

Inevitably, the speculative boom collapsed. The government sold 20 million acres of federal land in 1836, ten times the amount sold in 1830, nearly all of

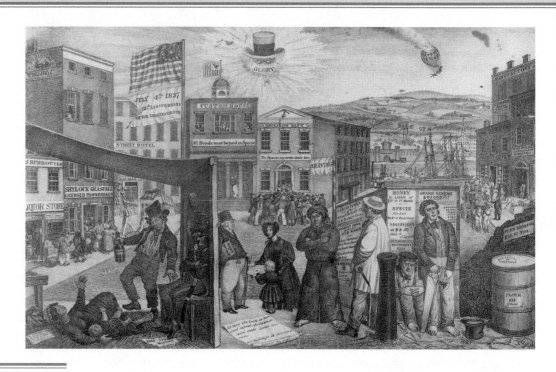

The Times, *an 1837 engraving that blames Andrew Jackson's policies for the economic depression. The Custom House is idle, while next door a bank is mobbed by worried depositors. Beneath Jackson's hat, spectacles, and clay pipe (with the ironic word "glory"), images of hardship abound.*

it paid for in paper money, often of questionable value. In July 1836, the Jackson administration issued the Specie Circular, declaring that henceforth it would only accept gold and silver as payment for public land. At the same time, the Bank of England, increasingly suspicious about the value of American bank notes, demanded that American merchants pay their creditors in London in gold or silver. Then, an economic downturn in Britain dampened demand for American cotton, the country's major export.

Taken together, these events triggered an economic collapse in the United States, the Panic of 1837, followed by a depression that lasted to 1843. Prices fell by 25 percent in the first year of the downturn. Businesses throughout the country failed, and many farmers, unable to meet mortgage payments because of declining income, lost their land. Tens of thousands of urban workers saw their jobs disappear. The fledgling labor movement collapsed as strikes became impossible given the surplus of unemployed labor. By 1842, nine states had defaulted on their debts, mostly incurred to finance ambitious internal improvement projects. During the 1840s, states amended their constitutions to prohibit legislatures from borrowing money, issuing corporate charters, and buying stock in private enterprises. For the time being, the Jacksonians had succeeded in separating government—both federal and state—from the economy.

VAN BUREN IN OFFICE

The president forced to deal with the depression was Martin Van Buren, who had been elected in 1836 over three regional candidates put forward by the Whigs in an attempt to maximize the party's electoral vote and throw the election into the House of Representatives. Under Van Buren, the hard money, anti-bank wing of the Democratic Party came to power. In

1837, the administration announced its intention to remove federal funds from the pet banks and hold them in the Treasury Department in Washington, under the control of government officials. Not until 1840 did Congress approve the new policy, known as the Independent Treasury, which completely separated the federal government from the nation's banking system. It would be repealed in 1841 when the Whigs returned to power, but it was reinstated under President James K. Polk in 1846. Making federal funds unavailable for banks to use for investment would have dampened future economic growth had not the discovery of gold in California in 1848 poured new money into the economy.

The Independent Treasury split the Democratic Party. Business-oriented Democrats, often connected with the state banks, strongly opposed Van Buren's policy and shifted wholesale to the Whigs. Meanwhile, the party's "agrarian" wing—small farmers and urban laborers opposed to all banking and paper money and uncomfortable with the market revolution in general, rallied to Van Buren. Many advocates of state sovereignty who had joined the Whigs after the nullification crisis now returned to the Democratic fold, including Van Buren's old nemesis, John C. Calhoun.

THE ELECTION OF 1840

Despite his reputation as a political magician, Van Buren found that without Jackson's personal popularity he could not hold the Democratic coalition together. In 1840, he also discovered that his Whig opponents had mastered the political techniques he had helped to pioneer. Confronting an unprecedented opportunity for victory because of the continuing economic depression, the Whigs abandoned their most prominent leader, Henry Clay, and nominated William Henry Harrison. Like Jackson when he first sought the presi-

A political cartoon from the 1840 presidential campaign shows public opinion as the "almighty lever" of politics in a democracy. Under the gaze of the American eagle, "Loco-Foco" Democrats slide into an abyss, while the people are poised to lift William Henry Harrison, the Whig candidate, to victory.

THE ALMIGHTY LEVER

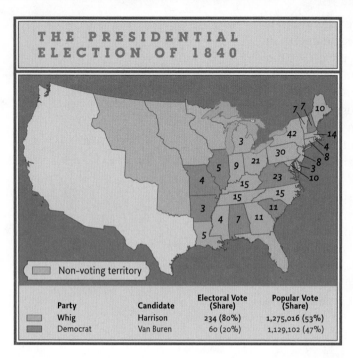

THE PRESIDENTIAL ELECTION OF 1840

Non-voting territory

Party	Candidate	Electoral Vote (Share)	Popular Vote (Share)
Whig	Harrison	234 (80%)	1,275,016 (53%)
Democrat	Van Buren	60 (20%)	1,129,102 (47%)

dency, Harrison's main claim to fame was military success against the British and Indians during the War of 1812.

The party nominated Harrison without a platform. In a flood of publications, banners, parades, and mass meetings, they promoted him as the "log cabin" candidate, the champion of the common man. This tactic proved enormously effective, even though it bore little relationship to the actual life of the wealthy Harrison. The Whigs also denounced Van Buren as an aristocrat who had squandered the people's hard-earned money on "expensive furniture, china, glassware, and gold spoons" for the White House. Harrison's running mate was John Tyler, a states'-rights Democrat from Virginia who had joined the Whigs after the nullification crisis and did not follow Calhoun back to the Democrats. On almost every issue of political significance, Tyler held views totally opposed to those of other Whigs. But party leaders hoped he could expand their base in the South.

By 1840, the mass democratic politics of the Age of Jackson had absorbed the logic of the marketplace. Selling candidates and their images was as important as the positions for which they stood. With two highly organized parties competing throughout the country, voter turnout soared to 80 percent of those eligible, a level at which it remained for the rest of the nineteenth century. Harrison won a sweeping victory. "We have taught them how to conquer us," lamented a Democratic newspaper.

HIS ACCIDENCY

Whig success proved short-lived. Immediately upon assuming office, Harrison contracted pneumonia. He died a month later, and John Tyler succeeded him. When the Whig majority in Congress tried to enact the American System into law, Tyler vetoed nearly every measure, including a new national bank and higher tariff. Most of the cabinet resigned, and his party repudiated him. Whig newspapers were soon calling the president His Accidency and The Executive Ass.

Tyler's four years in office were nearly devoid of accomplishment. If the campaign that resulted in the election of Harrison and Tyler demonstrated how a flourishing system of democratic politics had come into existence, Tyler's lack of success showed that political parties had become central to American government. Without a party behind him, a president could not govern. But a storm was now gathering that would test the stability of American democracy and the statesmanship of its political leaders.

SUGGESTED READING

BOOKS

Ashworth, John. *"Agrarians" and "Aristocrats": Party Ideology in the United States, 1837–1846* (1983). A careful study of political ideas in the last years of Jacksonian politics, stressing increasing class divisions between the parties.

Cott, Nancy. *The Bonds of Womanhood: "Woman's Sphere" in New England, 1780–1835* (1977). A pioneering study of the emergence of the ideological separation between gender-defined "public" and "private" spheres.

Forbes, Robert. *The Missouri Compromise and Its Aftermath: Slavery and the Meaning of America* (2007). Places the Missouri controversy in the context of the long national debate over slavery.

Formisano, Ronald P. *The Transformation of Political Culture: Massachusetts Parties, 1790–1840s* (1983). A study of politics in one key state, stressing the importance of ethnocultural divisions in shaping political alignments.

Freehling, William G. *Prelude to Civil War: The Nullification Controversy in South Carolina, 1816–1836* (1966). Still the standard account of the nullification crisis during Jackson's presidency.

Howe, Daniel W. *The Political Culture of the American Whigs* (1979). Illuminates the key ideas that held the Whig Party together.

Keyssar, Alexander. *The Right to Vote: The Contested History of Democracy in the United States* (2000). The most up-to-date history of the right to vote in America from the colonial era to the present.

Kinsbrunner, Jay. *Independence in Spanish America: Civil Wars, Revolutions, and Underdevelopment* (2000). A history of the Latin American wars of independence and their aftermath.

McFaul, James. *The Politics of Jacksonian Finance* (1972). A careful examination of party differences on currency and banking questions.

Remini, Robert. *Martin Van Buren and the Making of the Democratic Party* (1959). Examines how Van Buren created the structure of party organization that elected Andrew Jackson in 1828.

Schlesinger, Arthur M., Jr. *The Age of Jackson* (1945). An influential account of Jacksonian ideas and politics, which shaped debate among a generation of historians.

Starr, Paul. *Creation of the Media: Political Origins of Modern Communications* (2004). Contains an illuminating account of the "information revolution" in Jacksonian America.

Wallace, Anthony. *The Long, Bitter Trail: Andrew Jackson and the Indians* (1993). A brief history of Jackson's Indian policies, especially Indian Removal in the southern states.

Watson, Harry. *Liberty and Power: The Politics of Jacksonian America* (1990). A valuable brief account of the politics of the 1820s and 1830s.

Wilentz, Sean. *The Rise of American Democracy: Jefferson to Lincoln* (2005). A comprehensive history of democratic ideas and politics from the American Revolution to the Civil War.

WEBSITES

Democracy in America, Alexis de Tocqueville: http://xroads.virginia.edu/~HYPER/DETOC/home.html

George Catlin and His Indian Gallery: http://americanart.si.edu/exhibitions/online/catlin/index.html

Legacy: Spain and the United States in the Age of Independence, 1763–1848: http://latino.si.edu/SpainLegacy/Archive/index.html

REVIEW QUESTIONS

1. John Quincy Adams was an ardent expansionist. What actions did he support to help the United States become the "first and mightiest nation in the world"?

2. How did Andrew Jackson represent all of the major developments of the era: a self-made man, the westward movement, the market revolution, and the growth of democracy?

3. How did the expansion of white male democracy run counter to the ideals of the founders, who believed government should be sheltered from excessive influence by ordinary people?

4. What were the components of the American System, and how were they designed to promote the national economy under the guidance of the federal government?

5. How did the Missouri Compromise and the nullification crisis demonstrate increasing sectional competition and disagreements over slavery?

6. According to Martin Van Buren, why were political parties a desirable element of public life?

7. What were the major economic, humanitarian, political, and social arguments for and against Indian removal?

8. What actions by Andrew Jackson prompted charges of tyranny and led to the growth of the Whig Party?

9. Explain the causes and effects of the Panic of 1837.

FREEDOM QUESTIONS

1. How did freedom become more democratic in the period, and what were the limits to that development?

2. How did the three-fifths clause of the Constitution enter into the debates over the expansion of slavery into Missouri?

3. Considering economic policies and the balance of power between national and local authority, how did Whigs and Democrats differ in their definitions of American freedom and its relationship to government authority?

4. Whigs denounced Andrew Jackson as a tyrant. What actions did they see as a threat to American freedom and why?

KEY TERMS

the Dorr War (p. 373)

Democracy in America (p. 374)

"information revolution" (p. 375)

"infant industries" (p. 378)

American System (p. 378)

internal improvements (p. 379)

Second Bank of the United States (p. 379)

Panic of 1819 (p. 380)

McCulloch v. Maryland (p. 381)

Missouri controversy (p. 381)

Monroe Doctrine (p. 384)

"spoils system" (p. 391)

Eaton affair (p. 396)

Exposition and Protest (p. 396)

Force Act (p. 397)

Indian Removal Act (p. 398)

Worcester v. Georgia (p. 399)

the Bank War (p. 401)

"hard money" v. "soft money" (pp. 402-403)

"pet banks" (p. 403)

Panic of 1837 (p. 403)

REVIEW TABLE

Major Events of the Jackson Administration, 1829–1836

Event	Dates	Origin of Crisis	Resolution
Nullification crisis	1830–1833	South Carolina's opposition to a tariff becomes a battle to uphold the supremacy of federal over state law	Force Bill authorizes Jackson to use the military to collect customs duties after South Carolina nullifies the tariff
Bank War	1833–1836	Jackson opposes attempt of Congress to extend the Bank of the United State's charter another twenty years	Jackson vetoes Congress's resolution to grant the extension, effectively killing the Bank
Indian removal	1830–1838	Georgians want Cherokee land for expansion of cotton agriculture	Indian Removal Act of 1830 calls for the relocation of 46,000 Southeastern Indians to west of the Mississippi

Part 3

SLAVERY, FREEDOM, AND THE CRISIS OF THE UNION, 1840–1877

During the middle part of the nineteenth century, the United States confronted its greatest crisis, as the division between slave and free societies tore the country apart. A new nation emerged from the Civil War, with slavery abolished and the meaning of freedom transformed for all Americans.

Despite the hope of some of the founders that slavery might die out, the institution grew in size and economic importance as the nineteenth century progressed. Slavery expanded westward with the young republic, and the slave population grew to nearly 4 million by 1860. After the northern states abolished slavery, it became the "peculiar institution" of the South, the basis of a society growing ever more different from the rest of the country in economic structure and social values. Planters who dominated southern life also exerted enormous influence in national affairs. They developed a defense of slavery that insisted the institution was the foundation of genuine freedom for white citizens. Slaves, meanwhile, created their own semiautonomous culture that nurtured from one generation to the next their hope for liberation from bondage. Nonetheless, slavery was in some ways a national institution. Slave-grown cotton, a source of wealth to slaveowners, also provided the raw material for the North's growing textile industry and became the country's most important export.

During the 1820s and 1830s, numerous social movements arose that worked to reform American society. Their inspiration lay primarily in the Second Great Awakening, the religious revivals that swept both North and South and offered salvation to sinners and

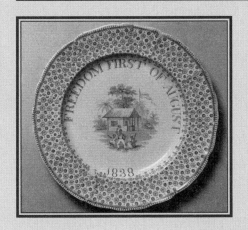

improvement to society at large. While some reform movements were national in scope, others existed only in the North. Most notable among the latter was a new, militant movement demanding the immediate abolition of slavery and the incorporation of blacks as equal citizens of the republic. The abolitionists helped to focus discussions of freedom on the sharp contradiction between liberty and slavery. They promoted an understanding of freedom as control over one's self and participation as an equal member in social and political life. They not only helped to place the issue of slavery squarely on the national agenda but also inspired the stirrings of protest among a number of northern women, whose work in the antislavery movement led them to resent their own lack of legal rights and educational and economic opportunities.

In the 1840s, the conflict between free and slave societies moved to the center stage of American politics. It did so as a result of the nation's territorial expansion. The acquisition of a vast new area of land as the result of the Mexican War raised the question of whether slavery would be able to expand further westward. By the 1850s, this issue had destroyed the Whig Party, weakened the Democrats, and led to the creation of an entirely new party, the Republicans, dedicated to confining slavery to the states where

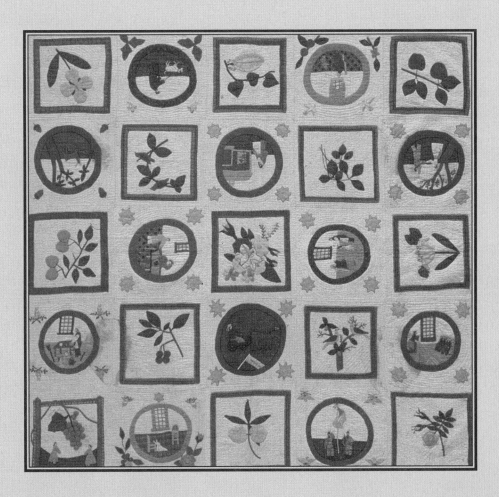

it already existed. Exalting the superiority of northern society, based on "free labor," to southern society, based on slavery, Republicans elected Abraham Lincoln as president in 1860, even though he did not receive a single vote in most of the southern states. In response, seven slave states seceded from the Union and formed a new nation, the Confederate States of America. When southern forces fired on Fort Sumter, an enclave of Union control in Charleston Harbor, they inaugurated the Civil War, by far the bloodiest conflict in American history.

Begun as a struggle to preserve the Union, the Civil War eventually became a crusade for emancipation, which brought the nation what President Lincoln called "a new birth of freedom." The North's failure to achieve military victory in the first two years of the war, coupled with the actions of slaves who by the thousands abandoned the plantations to flee to Union lines, propelled the Lincoln administration down the road to emancipation. Although it freed few slaves on the day it was issued, January 1, 1863, Lincoln's Emancipation Proclamation proved to be the turning point of the Civil War, for it announced that, henceforth, the Union army would serve as an agent of freedom. And by authorizing, for the first time, the enlistment of black men into the Union army, the Proclamation raised the question of black citizenship in the postwar world.

The era of Reconstruction that followed the Civil War was a time of intense political and social conflict, in which the definition of freedom and the question of who was entitled to enjoy it played a central role. Former slaves claimed that freedom meant full incorporation into

PUBLISHED BY THE SUPERVISORY COMMITTEE FOR RECRUITING COLORED REGIMENTS
1210 CHESTNUT ST. PHILADELPHIA.

American society, with the same rights and opportunities whites enjoyed. They also demanded that the government guarantee them access to land, to provide an economic foundation for their freedom. Most southern whites believed that blacks should go back to work on the plantations, enjoying very few political and civil rights. Andrew Johnson, who succeeded Lincoln as president, shared their view. But the majority of northern Republicans came to believe that the emancipated slaves should enjoy the same legal rights as whites. In 1867, they granted black men in the South the right to vote. During Reconstruction, northern Republicans rewrote the laws and Constitution to incorporate the ideal of equal citizenship for all Americans, regardless of race. This was a dramatic expansion of the meaning of freedom.

In the South, Reconstruction witnessed a short-lived period in which former slaves voted and held office alongside whites, a remarkable experiment in interracial democracy. On the other hand, the former slaves failed to achieve the economic freedom they desired, since the North proved unwilling to distribute land. As a result, most former slaves, and increasing numbers of whites in the war-devastated South, found themselves confined to working as sharecroppers on land owned by others. But the genuine advances achieved during Reconstruction, such as improved access to education, exercise of political rights, and the creation of new black institutions like independent churches, produced a violent reaction by upholders of white supremacy. During the 1870s, the North retreated from its commitment to equality. In 1877, Reconstruction came to an end. Many of the rights guaranteed to the former slaves were violated in the years that followed.

Although Reconstruction only lasted from 1865 to 1877, the issues debated then forecast many of the controversies that would envelop American society in the decades that followed. The definition of American citizenship, the power of the federal government and its relationship to the states, the future of political democracy in a society marked by increasing economic inequality—all these were Reconstruction issues, and all reverberated in the Gilded Age and Progressive era that followed.

The Civil War era resolved the contradiction of the existence of slavery in a land that celebrated freedom. But just as the American Revolution left to nineteenth-century Americans the problem of slavery, the Civil War and Reconstruction left to future generations the challenge of bringing genuine freedom to the descendants of slavery.

CHAPTER 11

The Peculiar Institution

An American Slave Market, *painted in 1852 by the unknown artist Taylor, depicts the sale of slaves, including one who had attempted to run away.*

FOCUS QUESTIONS

- How did slavery shape social and economic relations in the Old South?

- What were the legal and material constraints on slaves' lives and work?

- How did family, gender, religion, and values combine to create distinct slave cultures in the Old South?

- What were the major forms of resistance to slavery?

A photograph of Frederick Douglass, the fugitive slave who became a prominent abolitionist, taken between 1847 and 1852. As a fellow abolitionist noted at the time, "The very look and bearing of Douglass are an irresistible logic against the oppression of his race."

In an age of "self-made" men, no American rose more dramatically from humble origins to national and international distinction than Frederick Douglass. Born into slavery in 1818, he became a major figure in the crusade for abolition, the drama of emancipation, and the effort during Reconstruction to give meaning to black freedom.

Douglass was the son of a slave mother and an unidentified white man, possibly his owner. As a youth in Maryland, he gazed out at the ships in Chesapeake Bay, seeing them as "freedom's swift-winged angels." In violation of Maryland law, Douglass learned to read and write, initially with the assistance of his owner's wife and then, after her husband forbade her to continue, with the help of local white children. "From that moment," he later wrote, he understood that knowledge was "the pathway from slavery to freedom." Douglass experienced slavery in all its variety, from work as a house servant and as a skilled craftsman in a Baltimore shipyard to labor as a plantation field hand. When he was fifteen, Douglass's owner sent him to a "slave breaker" to curb his independent spirit. After numerous whippings, Douglass defiantly refused to allow himself to be disciplined again. This confrontation, he recalled, was "the turning-point in my career as a slave." It rekindled his desire for freedom. In 1838, having borrowed the free papers of a black sailor, he escaped to the North.

Frederick Douglass went on to become the most influential African-American of the nineteenth century and the nation's preeminent advocate of racial equality. "He who has endured the cruel pangs of slavery," he wrote, "is the man to advocate liberty." Douglass lectured against slavery throughout the North and the British Isles, and he edited a succession of antislavery publications. He published a widely read autobiography that offered an eloquent condemnation of slavery and racism. Indeed, his own accomplishments testified to the incorrectness of prevailing ideas about blacks' inborn inferiority. Douglass was also active in other reform movements, including the campaign for women's rights. During the Civil War, he advised Abraham Lincoln on the employment of black soldiers and became an early advocate of giving the right to vote to the emancipated slaves. Douglass died in 1895, as a new system of white supremacy based on segregation and disenfranchisement was being fastened upon the South.

Throughout his career, Douglass insisted that slavery could only be overthrown by continuous resistance. "Those who profess to favor freedom, and yet deprecate agitation," he declared, "are men who want crops without plowing up the ground, they want rain without thunder and lightning, they want the ocean without the awful roar of its many waters." In effect, Douglass argued that in their desire for freedom, the slaves were truer to the nation's underlying principles than the white Americans who annually celebrated the Fourth of July while allowing the continued existence of slavery.

THE OLD SOUTH

When Frederick Douglass was born, slavery was already an old institution in America. Two centuries had passed since the first twenty Africans were landed in Virginia from a Dutch ship. After abolition in the North, slavery had become the "peculiar institution" of the South—that is, an institution unique to southern society. The Mason-Dixon Line, drawn by two surveyors in the eighteenth century to settle a boundary dispute between Maryland and Pennsylvania, eventually became the dividing line between slavery and freedom.

Despite the hope of some of the founders that slavery might die out, in fact the institution survived the crisis of the American Revolution and rapidly expanded westward. During the first thirty years of Douglass's life, the number of slaves and the economic and political importance of slavery continued to grow. On the eve of the Civil War, the slave population had risen to nearly 4 million, its high rate of natural increase more than making up for the prohibition in 1808 of further slave imports from Africa. In the South as a whole, slaves made up one-third of the total population, and in the cotton-producing states of the Deep South, around half. By the 1850s, slavery had crossed the Mississippi River and was expanding rapidly in Arkansas, Louisiana, and eastern Texas. In 1860, one-third of the nation's cotton crop was grown west of the Mississippi.

COTTON IS KING

In the nineteenth century, cotton replaced sugar as the world's major crop produced by slave labor. And although slavery survived in Brazil and the Spanish and French Caribbean, its abolition in the British empire in 1833 made the United States indisputably the center of New World slavery.

Table 11.1 GROWTH OF THE SLAVE POPULATION	
Year	*Slave Population*
1790	697,624
1800	893,602
1810	1,191,362
1820	1,538,022
1830	2,009,043
1840	2,487,355
1850	3,204,313
1860	3,953,760

An engraving from just after the Civil War shows a cotton gin in use. Black laborers bring cotton to the machine, which runs it through a series of pronged wheels, to separate the seeds from the fiber.

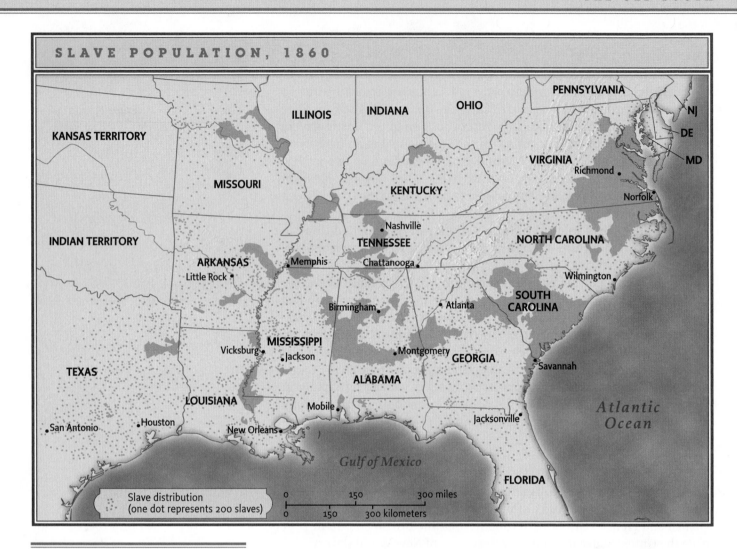

SLAVE POPULATION, 1860

Slave distribution
(one dot represents 200 slaves)

Rather than being evenly distributed throughout the South, the slave population was concentrated in areas with the most fertile soil and easiest access to national and international markets. By 1860, a significant percentage of the slave population had been transported from the Atlantic coast to the Deep South via the internal slave trade.

When measured by slavery's geographic extent, the numbers held in bondage, and the institution's economic importance both regionally and nationally, the Old South was the largest and most powerful slave society the modern world has known. Its strength rested on a virtual monopoly of cotton, the South's "white gold." Cotton had been grown for thousands of years in many parts of the globe. The conquistador Hernán Cortés was impressed by the high quality of woven cotton clothing worn by the Aztecs. But in the nineteenth century, cotton assumed an unprecedented role in the world economy.

Because the early industrial revolution centered on factories using cotton as the raw material to manufacture cloth, cotton had become by far the most important commodity in international trade. And three-fourths of the world's cotton supply came from the southern United States. Throughout the world, hundreds of thousands of workers loaded, unloaded, spun, and wove cotton, and thousands of manufacturers and merchants owed their wealth to the cotton trade. Textile manufacturers in places as far-flung as Massachusetts, Lancashire in Great Britain, Normandy in France, and the suburbs of Moscow depended on a regular supply of American cotton.

As early as 1803, cotton had become the most important American export. Cotton sales earned the money from abroad that allowed the United States to pay for imported manufactured goods. On the eve of the Civil War, it represented well over half of the total value of American exports. In 1860, the economic investment represented by the slave population exceeded the value of the nation's factories, railroads, and banks combined.

THE SECOND MIDDLE PASSAGE

As noted in Chapter 9, to replace the slave trade from Africa, which had been prohibited by Congress in 1808, a massive trade in slaves developed within the United States. More than 2 million slaves were sold between 1820 and 1860, a majority to local buyers but hundreds of thousands from older states to "importing" states of the Lower South. Slave trading was a visible, established business. The main business districts of southern cities contained the offices of slave traders, complete with signs reading "Negro Sales" or "Negroes Bought Here." Auctions of slaves took place at public slave markets, as in New Orleans, or at courthouses. Southern newspapers carried advertisements for slave sales, southern banks financed slave trading, southern ships and railroads carried slaves from buyers to sellers, and southern states and municipalities earned revenue by taxing the sale of slaves. Virtually every slaveowner at one time or another bought and sold slaves. The Cotton Kingdom could not have arisen without the internal slave trade, and the economies of older states like Virginia came increasingly to rely on the sale of slaves.

A slave dealer's place of business in Atlanta. The buying and selling of slaves was a regularized part of the southern economy, and such businesses were a common sight in every southern town.

SLAVERY AND THE NATION

Slavery, Henry Clay proclaimed in 1816, "forms an exception . . . to the general liberty prevailing in the United States." But Clay, like many of his contemporaries, underestimated slavery's impact on the entire nation. The "free states" had ended slavery, but they were hardly unaffected by it. The Constitution, as we have seen, enhanced the power of the South in the House of Representatives and electoral college and required all states to return fugitives from bondage. Slavery shaped the lives of all Americans, white as well as black. It helped to determine where they lived, how they worked, and under what conditions they could exercise their freedoms of speech, assembly, and the press.

Northern merchants and manufacturers participated in the slave economy and shared in its profits. Money earned in the cotton trade helped to finance industrial development and internal improvements in the North. Northern ships carried cotton to New York and Europe, northern bankers financed cotton plantations, northern companies insured slave property, and northern factories turned cotton into cloth. New York City's rise to commercial prominence depended as much on the establishment of shipping lines that gathered the South's cotton and transported it to Europe, as on the Erie Canal. The Lords of the Loom (New England's early factory owners) relied on cotton supplied by the Lords of the Lash (southern slaveowners). Northern manufacturers like Brooks Brothers supplied cheap fabrics (called "Negro cloth") to clothe the South's slaves.

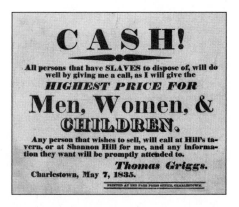

An advertisement by a slave trader seeking owners wishing to sell slaves. Dealers like Griggs played a crucial role in moving slaves from the Upper South to the burgeoning Cotton Kingdom of the Gulf Coast states.

This 1860 view of New Orleans captures the size and scale of the cotton trade in the South's largest city. More than 3,500 steamboats arrived in New Orleans in 1860.

THE SOUTHERN ECONOMY

There was no single South before the Civil War. In the eight slave states of the Upper South, slaves and slaveowners made up a smaller percentage of the total population than in the seven Deep South states that stretched from South Carolina west to Texas. The Upper South had major centers of industry in Baltimore, Richmond, and St. Louis, and its economies were more diversified than those in the Deep South, which was heavily dependent on cotton. Not surprisingly, during the secession crisis of 1860–1861, the Deep South states were the first to leave the Union. Even after the war began, four Upper South states (Delaware, Maryland, Kentucky, and Missouri) refused to join the Confederacy.

Nonetheless, slavery led the South down a very different path of economic development than the North's, limiting the growth of industry, discouraging immigrants from entering the region, and inhibiting technological progress. The South did not share in the urban growth experienced by the rest of the country. Most southern cities were located on the region's periphery and served mainly as centers for gathering and shipping cotton. Southern banks existed primarily to help finance the plantations. They loaned money for the purchase of land and slaves, not manufacturing development. Southern railroads mostly consisted of short lines that brought cotton from the interior to coastal ports.

In the Cotton Kingdom, the only city of significant size was New Orleans. With a population of 168,000 in 1860, New Orleans ranked as the nation's sixth-largest city. As the gathering point for cotton grown along the Mississippi River and sugar from the plantations of southeastern Louisiana, it was the world's leading exporter of slave-grown crops. Unlike other cities with slavery (apart from St. Louis and Baltimore, on the periphery of the South), New Orleans also attracted large numbers of European immigrants. In 1860, 40 percent of its population was foreign-born. And New Orleans's rich French heritage and close connections with the Caribbean produced a local culture quite different from that of the rest of the United States, reflected in the city's distinctive music, dance, religion, and cuisine.

In 1860, the South produced less than 10 percent of the nation's manufactured goods. Many northerners viewed slavery as an obstacle to American economic progress. But as New Orleans showed, slavery and economic growth could go hand in hand. In general, the southern economy was hardly stagnant, and slavery proved very profitable for most owners. The profits produced by slavery for the South and the nation as a whole formed a powerful obstacle to abolition. Speaking of cotton, Senator James Henry Hammond of South Carolina declared, "No power on earth dares to make war upon it. Cotton is king."

PLAIN FOLK OF THE OLD SOUTH

The foundation of the Old South's economy, slavery powerfully shaped race relations, politics, religion, and the law. Its influence was pervasive: "Nothing escaped," writes one historian, "nothing and no one." This was true despite the fact that the majority of white southerners—three out of four white families—owned no slaves. Since planters monopolized the best land, most small white farmers lived outside the plantation belt in hilly areas unsuitable for cotton production. They worked the land using family labor rather than slaves or hired workers.

Many southern farmers lived lives of economic self-sufficiency remote from the market revolution. They raised livestock and grew food for their families, purchasing relatively few goods at local stores. Those residing on marginal land in isolated hill areas and the Appalachian Mountains were often desperately poor and, since nearly all the southern states lacked systems of free public education, were more often illiterate than their north-

An upcountry family, dressed in homespun, in Cedar Mountain, Virginia. Many white families in the pre–Civil War South were largely isolated from the market economy. This photograph was taken in 1862 but reflects the prewar way of life.

ern counterparts. Not until the arrival of railroads and coal mining later in the nineteenth century would such areas become integrated into the market economy. Most yeoman farmers enjoyed a comfortable standard of living, and many owned a slave or two. But even successful small farmers relied heavily on home production to supply their basic needs. Unlike northern farmers, therefore, they did not provide a market for manufactured goods. This was one of the main reasons why the South did not develop an industrial base.

Some poorer whites resented the power and privileges of the great planters. Politicians like Andrew Johnson of Tennessee and Joseph Brown of Georgia rose to power as self-proclaimed spokesmen of the common man against the "slaveocracy." But most poor whites made their peace with the planters in whose hands economic and social power was concentrated. Racism, kinship ties, common participation in a democratic political culture, and regional loyalty in the face of outside criticism all served to cement bonds between planters and the South's "plain folk." In the plantation regions, moreover, small farmers manned the slave patrols that kept a lookout for runaway slaves and those on the roads without permission. Non-slaveholders frequently rented slaves from planters and regularly elected slaveowners to public offices in the South. Like other white southerners, most small farmers believed their economic and personal freedom rested on slavery. Not until the Civil War would class tensions among the white population threaten the planters' domination.

THE PLANTER CLASS

Even among slaveholders, the planter was far from typical. In 1850, a majority of slaveholding families owned five or fewer slaves. Less than 40,000 families possessed the twenty or more slaves that qualified them as planters. Fewer than 2,000 families owned a hundred slaves or more. Nonetheless, even though the planter was not the typical slaveholder or white southerner, his values and aspirations dominated southern life. The plantation, wrote Frederick Douglass, was "a little nation by itself, with its own language, its own rules, regulations, and customs." These rules and customs set the tone for southern society.

Ownership of slaves provided the route to wealth, status, and influence. Planters not only held the majority of slaves, but they controlled the most fertile land, enjoyed the highest incomes, and dominated state and local offices and the leadership of both political parties. Small slaveholders aspired to move up into the ranks of the planter class. Those who acquired wealth almost always invested it in land and slaves. But as the price of a "prime field hand" rose from $1,000 in 1840 to $1,800 in 1860 (the latter figure equivalent to around $40,000 today), it became more and more difficult for poorer white southerners to become slaveholders.

Slavery, of course, was a profit-making system, and slave-owners kept close watch on world prices for their products, invested in enterprises such as railroads and canals, and carefully supervised their plantations. Their wives—the "planta-tion mistresses" idealized in southern lore for femininity, beauty, and dependence on men—were hardly idle. They cared for sick slaves, directed the domestic servants, and supervised the entire plantation when their husbands were away. The wealthiest Americans before the Civil War were planters in the South Carolina low country and the cotton region around Natchez, Mississippi. Frederick Stanton, a cotton broker turned planter in the Natchez area, owned 444 slaves and more than 15,000 acres of land in Mississippi and Louisiana.

Nonetheless, Alexis de Tocqueville observed that "the northerner loves to make money, the southerner to spend it." Many of the richest planters squandered their wealth in a lifestyle complete with lavish entertain-ments and summer vacations in Newport and Saratoga. House slaves were so numerous in Charleston, wrote one visitor to the city, that "the Charlestonians are obliged to exercise their wits to devise sufficient variety to keep them employed." On the cotton

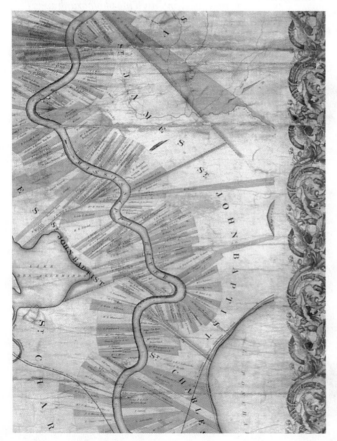

A detail from Norman's Chart of the Lower Mississppi River *(1858) shows slave plantations laid out so that each fronted on the river and, therefore, had easy access to the market.*

frontier, many planters lived in crude log homes. But in the older slave states, and as settled society developed in the Deep South, they constructed elegant mansions adorned with white columns in the Greek Revival style of architecture. Planters discouraged their sons from entering "lowly" trades like commerce and manufacturing, one reason why the South remained overwhelmingly agricultural.

THE PATERNALIST ETHOS

The slave plantation was deeply embedded in the world market, and planters sought to accumulate land, slaves, and profits. Many invested in railroads and banks as well as slaves. But planters' values glorified not the competitive capitalist marketplace, but a hierarchical, agrarian society in which slaveholding gentlemen took personal responsibility for the physical and moral well-being of their dependents—women, children, and slaves. "The master," wrote one planter, "as the head of the system, has a right to the obedience and labor of the slave, but the slave has also his mutual rights in the master; the right of protection, the right of counsel and guidance, the right of subsistence, the right of care and attention in sickness and old age."

This outlook, known as "paternalism" (from the Latin word for "father"), had been a feature of American slavery even in the eighteenth century. But it became more ingrained after the closing of the African slave trade in 1808, which narrowed the cultural gap between master and slave and gave owners an economic interest in the survival of their human property. Unlike the absentee planters of the West Indies, many of whom resided in Great Britain, southern slaveholders lived on their plantations and thus had year-round contact with their slaves.

The paternalist outlook both masked and justified the brutal reality of slavery. It enabled slaveowners to think of themselves as kind, responsible masters even as they bought and sold their human property—a practice at odds with the claim that slaves formed part of the master's "family." Some slaveowners tried to reform the system to eliminate its most oppressive features. The Reverend Charles C. Jones, a wealthy planter of Liberty County, Georgia, organized his neighbors to promote the religious instruction of slaves, improve slave housing, diet, and medical care, and discourage severe punishments. But even Jones believed his slaves so "degraded" and lacking in moral self-discipline that he could not contemplate an end to slavery.

THE CODE OF HONOR

As time went on, the dominant southern conception of the good society diverged more and more sharply from that of the egalitarian, competitive, individualistic North. In the South, for example, both upper- and lower-class whites adhered to a code of personal honor, in which men were expected to defend, with violence if necessary, their own reputation and that of their families. Although dueling was illegal, many prominent southerners took part in duels to avenge supposed insults. In 1826, Henry Clay and John Randolph, two of the most important southern political leaders, fought a duel with pistols after Clay took exception to criticisms by Randolph on the floor of Congress. Fortunately, each missed the other. Twenty years later, however, John H. Pleasants, editor of the *Richmond Whig*, died in a duel with the son of a rival newspaperman.

Table 11.2 SLAVEHOLDING, 1850 (IN ROUND NUMBERS)	
Number of Slaves Owned	*Slaveholders*
1	68,000
2–4	105,000
5–9	80,000
10–19	55,000
20–49	30,000
50–99	6,000
100–199	1,500
200 +	250

A pre–Civil War engraving depicting the paternalist ideal. The old slave in the foreground says, "God Bless you massa! you feed and clothe us, . . . and when too old to work, you provide for us!" The master replies, "These poor creatures are a sacred legacy from my ancestors and while a dollar is left me, nothing shall be spared to increase their comfort and happiness."

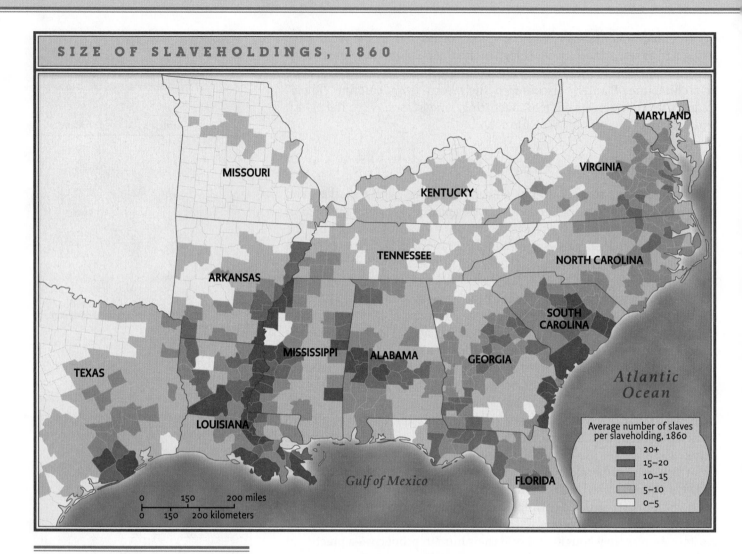

SIZE OF SLAVEHOLDINGS, 1860

Average number of slaves per slaveholding, 1860
20+
15–20
10–15
5–10
0–5

Most southern slaveholders owned fewer than five slaves. The largest plantations were concentrated in coastal South Carolina and along the Mississippi River.

Just as southern men had a heightened sense of their own honor and masculinity, white southern women, even more than in the North, were confined within the "domestic circle." "A man loves his children," wrote George Fitzhugh, a Virginia lawyer and author of numerous books and articles on social issues, "because they are weak, helpless, and dependent. He loves his wife for similar reasons." As will be discussed in the next chapter, many northern women before the Civil War became part of a thriving female culture centered on voluntary religious and reform organizations. Few parallels existed in the South, and plantation mistresses often complained of loneliness and isolation.

THE PROSLAVERY ARGUMENT

Some southerners worried about their standing in the eyes of the world, especially how others viewed the intellectual life of their region. "We of the South," one wrote, "must, to Europe, continue to appear inferior to the North in intellectual cultivation." The free states outstripped the slave states in public education, the number of colleges, and in newspapers, literary journals, and other publications. Nonetheless, the life of the mind flourished in the Old South, and the region did not lack for novelists, political philosophers, scientists, and the like.

In the thirty years before the outbreak of the Civil War, however, even as northern criticism of the "peculiar institution" began to deepen, proslavery thought came to dominate southern public life. Fewer and fewer white southerners shared the view, common among the founding fathers, that slavery was, at best, a "necessary evil." "Many in the South," John C. Calhoun proclaimed in 1837, "once believed that [slavery] was a moral and political evil. . . . That folly and delusion are gone; we see it now in its true light, and regard it as the most safe and stable basis for free institutions in the world."

Even those who had no direct stake in slavery shared with planters a deep commitment to white supremacy. Indeed, racism—the belief that blacks were innately inferior to whites and unsuited for life in any condition other than slavery—formed one pillar of the proslavery ideology. Most slaveholders also found legitimation for slavery in biblical passages such as the injunction that servants should obey their masters. Others argued that slavery was essential to human progress. Had not the ancient republics of Greece and Rome and the great European empires of the seventeenth and eighteenth centuries rested on slave labor? Without slavery, planters would be unable to cultivate the arts, sciences, and other civilized pursuits.

Still other defenders of slavery insisted that the institution guaranteed equality for whites by preventing the growth of a class doomed to a life of unskilled labor. Like northerners, they claimed to be committed to the ideal of freedom. Slavery for blacks, they declared, was the surest guarantee of "perfect equality" among whites, liberating them from the "low, menial" jobs like factory labor and domestic service performed by wage laborers in the North. Slavery made possible the considerable degree of economic autonomy (the social condition of freedom) enjoyed not only by planters but by non-slaveholding whites. Because of slavery, claimed one congressman, white southerners were as "independent as the bird which cleaves the air." And because independence was necessary for citizenship, slavery was the "cornerstone of our republican edifice."

St. John Plantation, *an 1861 painting by Marie Adrien Persac, a French-born artist who originally came to the United States to hunt buffalo. This was a Louisiana sugar plantation; the sugar mill can be seen on the extreme right. In Persac's romanticized depiction, whites enjoy themselves on horseback, while slaves appear to have little to do but watch.*

ABOLITION IN THE AMERICAS

American slaveowners were well aware of developments in slave systems elsewhere in the Western Hemisphere. As noted in Chapter 8, the slave revolution in Haiti sent shock waves of fear throughout the American South. White southerners were further alarmed by slave uprisings early in the nineteenth century in Barbados, British Guiana, and Jamaica. And they observed carefully the results of the wave of emancipations that swept the

VISIONS OF FREEDOM

Slavery as It Exists in America; Slavery as It Exists in England. *Published in Boston in 1850, this lithograph illustrates one aspect of proslavery thought. The artist depicts southern slaves as happy and carefree, while English workers, including children, are victims of the oppressive system of "factory slavery." The portrait at the bottom is of George Thompson, an English abolitionist who lectured against slavery in the United States. At the rear of the top image, a northerner addresses a slaveowner, suggesting that people in the North had been "deceived by false reports" about slavery and therefore had caused unnecessary "trouble" between the regions. In the bottom image, a poor woman exclaims, "Oh Dear! What wretched slaves this factory life makes me and my children."*

QUESTIONS

1. To whom do you think this image is addressed, and is the audience likely to be convinced that slaves enjoy more freedom than English laborers?

2. Why do you think the artist chose to compare the condition of slaves with that of English, not American, free laborers?

hemisphere in the first four decades of the century. In these years, slavery was abolished in most of Spanish America and in the British empire.

In most Latin American nations, the end of slavery followed the pattern established earlier in the northern United States—gradual emancipation accompanied by some kind of recognition of the owners' legal right to property in slaves. These "laws of the free womb" allowed slaveholders to retain ownership of existing slaves while freeing their slaves' children after they worked for the mother's owner for a specified number of years. Such laws, wrote one official, "respected the past and corrected only the future." Abolition was far swifter in the British empire, where Parliament in 1833 mandated almost immediate emancipation, with a seven-year transitional period of "apprenticeship." This system produced so much conflict between former master and former slave that Britain decreed complete freedom in 1838. The law appropriated 20 million pounds to compensate the owners.

The experience of emancipation in other parts of the hemisphere strongly affected debates over slavery in the United States. Southern slaveowners judged the vitality of the Caribbean economy by how much sugar and other crops it produced for the world market. Since many former slaves preferred to grow food for their own families, defenders of slavery in the United States charged that British emancipation had been a failure. Abolitionists disagreed, pointing to the rising standard of living of freed slaves, the spread of education among them, and other improvements in their lives. But the stark fact remained that, in a hemispheric perspective, slavery was a declining institution. By 1840, slavery had been outlawed in Mexico, Central America, and Chile, and only small numbers of aging slaves remained in Venezuela, Colombia, and Peru. During the European revolutions of 1848, France and Denmark emancipated their colonial slaves. At mid-century, significant New World slave systems remained only in Cuba, Puerto Rico, Brazil—and the United States.

SLAVERY AND LIBERTY

Many white southerners declared themselves the true heirs of the American Revolution. They claimed to be inspired by "the same spirit of freedom and independence" that motivated the founding generation. Like their ancestors of the 1760s and 1770s, their political language was filled with contrasts between liberty and slavery and complaints that outsiders proposed to reduce them to "slaves" by interfering with their local institutions. Southern state constitutions enshrined the idea of equal rights for free men, and the South participated fully in the movement toward political democracy for whites.

Beginning in the 1830s, however, proslavery writers began to question the ideals of liberty, equality, and democracy so widely shared elsewhere in the nation. South Carolina, the only southern state where a majority of white families owned slaves, became the home of an aggressive defense of slavery that repudiated the idea that freedom and equality were universal entitlements. The language of the Declaration of Independence—that all men were created equal and entitled to liberty—was "the most false and dangerous of all political errors," insisted John C. Calhoun. Proslavery

A plate manufactured in England to celebrate emancipation in the British empire. After a brief period of apprenticeship, the end of slavery came on August 1, 1838. At the center, a family of former slaves celebrates outside their cabin.

spokesmen returned to the older definition of freedom as a privilege rather than a universal entitlement, a "reward to be earned, not a blessing to be gratuitously lavished on all alike."

As the sectional controversy intensified after 1830, a number of southern writers and politicians came to defend slavery less as the basis of equality for whites than as the foundation of an organic, hierarchical society. Many southern clergymen, in the course of offering a religious defense of slavery, argued that inequality and hence the submission of inferior to superior—black to white, female to male, lower classes to upper classes—was a "fundamental law" of human existence. A hierarchy of "ranks and orders in human society," insisted John B. Alger, a Presbyterian minister in South Carolina, formed part of the "divine arrangement" of the world.

SLAVERY AND CIVILIZATION

The Virginia writer George Fitzhugh took the argument to its most radical conclusion, repudiating not only Jeffersonian ideals but the notion of America's special mission in the world. Far from being the natural condition of mankind, Fitzhugh wrote, "universal liberty" was the exception, an experiment carried on "for a little while" in "a corner of Europe" and the northern United States. Taking the world and its history as a whole, slavery, "without regard to race and color," was "the general, . . . normal, natural" basis of "civilized society." Indeed, wrote Fitzhugh, slaveowners and slaves shared a "community of interest" unknown in "free society." Since they lacked economic cares, he contended, "the Negro slaves of the South are the happiest, and, in some degree, the freest people in the world." White workers in both the North and South, according to Fitzhugh, would fare better having individual owners, rather than living as "slaves" of the economic marketplace.

It seems safe to assume that few non-slaveholding white southerners agreed that enslavement would offer them greater freedom than they already enjoyed. Nor was Fitzhugh entirely consistent. Sometimes, he argued that all free laborers would be better off as slaves. On other occasions, he spoke of slavery only for blacks—perpetual "children" for whom liberty would be "a curse."

Abraham Lincoln would later observe that the essential function of the proslavery argument was to serve the interests of those who benefited from a system of extreme inequality. He imagined Dr. Frederick A. Ross, a leading proslavery clergyman, considering whether he should free his slave Sambo. God's view of the subject, Lincoln noted, was not entirely clear, and "no one thinks of asking Sambo's opinion." Therefore, it fell to Dr. Ross to decide the question. "If he decides that God wills Sambo to continue a slave," Lincoln wrote, "he thereby retains his own comfortable position; but if he decides that God wills Sambo to be free, he thereby has to walk out of the shade, take off his gloves, and [work] for his own bread." Under these circumstances, it was hardly surprising that Dr. Ross found the argument that Sambo should remain a slave very persuasive.

After 1830, southern writers, newspaper editors, politicians, and clergymen increasingly devoted themselves to spreading the defense of slavery. The majority of white southerners came to believe that freedom for whites rested on the power to command the labor of blacks. In the words of the Richmond *Enquirer*, "freedom is not possible without slavery."

LIFE UNDER SLAVERY

SLAVES AND THE LAW

For slaves, the "peculiar institution" meant a life of incessant toil, brutal punishment, and the constant fear that their families would be destroyed by sale. Before the law, slaves were property. Although they had a few legal rights (all states made it illegal to kill a slave except in self-defense, and slaves accused of serious crimes were entitled to their day in court, before all-white judges and juries), these were haphazardly enforced. Slaves could be sold or leased by their owners at will and lacked any voice in the governments that ruled over them. They could not testify in court against a white person, sign contracts or acquire property, own firearms, hold meetings unless a white person was present, or leave the farm or plantation without the permission of their owner. By the 1830s, it was against the law to teach a slave to read or write.

Not all of these laws were rigorously enforced. Some members of slaveholding families taught slave children to read (although rather few, since well over 90 percent of the slave population was illiterate in 1860). In the South Carolina rice fields, owners allowed some slaves to carry shotguns, in defiance of the law, to scare off birds feasting on rice seeds. It was quite common throughout the South for slaves to gather without white supervision at crossroads villages and country stores on Sunday, their day of rest. But the extent to which authorities enforced or bent the law depended on the decisions of the individual owners.

The slave, declared a Louisiana law, "owes to his master . . . a respect without bounds, and an absolute obedience." Not only did the owner have the legal right to what Alabama's legal code called the "time, labor, and services" of his slaves, but no aspect of their lives, from the choice of marriage partners to how they spent their free time, was immune from his interference. The entire system of southern justice, from the state militia and courts down to armed patrols in each locality, was designed to enforce the master's control over the person and labor of his slaves.

In one famous case, a Missouri court considered the "crime" of Celia, a slave who had killed her master in 1855 while resisting a sexual assault. State law deemed "any woman" in such circumstances to be acting in self-defense. But Celia, the court ruled, was not a "woman" in the eyes of the law. She was a slave, whose master had complete power over her person. The court sentenced her to death. However, since Celia was pregnant, her execution was postponed until the child was born, so as not to deprive her owner's heirs of their property rights.

CONDITIONS OF SLAVE LIFE

As the nineteenth century progressed, some southern states enacted laws to prevent the mistreatment of slaves, and their material living conditions improved. Food supplies and wild game were abundant in the South, and many slaves supplemented the food provided by their owners (primarily cornmeal and pork or bacon) with chickens and vegetables they raised themselves, animals they hunted in the forests, and, not infrequently, items they stole from the plantation smokehouse. Compared with their counter-

Metal shackles, from around 1850. Slaves were shackled as a form of punishment, or to prevent escape when being transported from one place to another.

VOICES OF FREEDOM

From Letter by Joseph Taper to Joseph Long (1840)

No one knows how many slaves succeeded in escaping from bondage before the Civil War. Some settled in northern cities like Boston, Cincinnati, and New York. But because the Constitution required that fugitives be returned to slavery, many continued northward until they reached Canada.

One successful fugitive was Joseph Taper, a slave in Frederick County, Virginia, who in 1837 ran away to Pennsylvania with his wife and children. Two years later, learning that a "slave catcher" was in the neighborhood, the Tapers fled to Canada. In 1840, Taper wrote to a white acquaintance in Virginia recounting some of his experiences.

The biblical passage to which Taper refers reads: "And I will come near to you to judgment; and I will be a swift witness against the sorcerers, and against the adulterers, and against false swearers, and against those that oppress the hireling in his wages, the widow, and the father-less, and that turn aside the stranger from his right, and fear not me, saith the Lord of hosts."

Dear sir,

I now take the opportunity to inform you that I am in a land of liberty, in good health. . . . Since I have been in the Queen's dominions I have been well contented, Yes well contented for Sure, man is as God intended he should be. That is, all are born free and equal. This is a wholesome law, not like the Southern laws which puts man made in the image of God, on level with brutes. O, what will become of the people, and where will they stand in the day of Judgment. Would that the 5th verse of the 3d chapter of Malachi were written as with the bar of iron, and the point of a diamond upon every oppressor's heart that they might repent of this evil, and let the oppressed go free. . . .

We have good schools, and all the colored population supplied with schools. My boy Edward who will be six years next January, is now reading, and I intend keeping him at school until he becomes a good scholar.

I have enjoyed more pleasure within one month here than in all my life in the land of bondage. . . . My wife and self are sitting by a good comfortable fire happy, knowing that there are none to molest [us] or make [us] afraid. God save Queen Victoria. The Lord bless her in this life, and crown her with glory in the world to come is my prayer,

Yours With much respect
most obt, Joseph Taper

From the Rules of Highland Plantation (1838)

A wealthy Louisiana slaveholder, Bennet H. Barrow considered himself a model of planter paternalism who, by his own standards, treated his slaves well. An advocate of rigorous plantation discipline, he drew up a series of strict rules, which he recommended to other owners.

No Negro shall leave the place at any time without my permission.... No Negro shall be allowed to marry out of the plantation.

No Negro shall be allowed to sell anything without my express permission. I have ever maintained the doctrine that my Negroes have no time whatever, that they are always liable to my call without questioning for a moment the propriety, of it. I adhere to this on the grounds of expediency and right. The very security of the plantation requires that a general and uniform control over the people of it should be exercised.... You must ... make him as comfortable at home as possible, affording him what is essentially necessary for his happiness—you must provide for him yourself and by that means create in him a habit of perfect dependence on you. Allow it once to be understood by a Negro that he is to provide for himself, and you that moment give him an undeniable claim on you for a portion of his time to make this provision, and should you from necessity, or any other cause, encroach upon his time, disappointment and discontent are seriously felt.

If I employ a laborer to perform a certain quantum of work per day and I agree to pay him a certain amount for the performance of said work, when he has accomplished it I of course have no further claim on him for his time or services—but how different is it with a slave.... If I furnish my Negro with every necessary of life, without the least care on his part—if I support him in sickness, however long it may be, and pay all his expenses, though he does nothing—if I maintain him in his old age, ... am I not entitled to an exclusive right in his time?

No rule that I have stated is of more importance than that relating to Negroes marrying out of the plantation.... It creates a feeling of independence, from being, of right, out of the control of the masters for a time.

Never allow any man to talk to your Negroes, nothing more injurious.

QUESTIONS

1. How does Taper's letter reverse the rhetoric, common among white Americans, which saw the United States as a land of freedom and the British empire as lacking in liberty?

2. Why does Barrow feel that his slaves owe him complete obedience?

3. What do these documents suggest about whether masters and slaves shared the same values?

parts in the West Indies and Brazil, American slaves enjoyed better diets, lower rates of infant mortality, and longer life expectancies. Many factors contributed to improving material conditions. One was the growing strength of the planters' paternalist outlook. Douglass himself noted that "not to give a slave enough to eat, is regarded as the most aggravated development of meanness, even among slaveholders." Most of the South, moreover, lies outside the geographical area where tropical diseases like malaria, yellow fever, and typhoid fever flourish, so health among all southerners was better than in the Caribbean. And with the price of slaves rising dramatically after the closing of the African slave trade, it made economic sense for owners to become concerned with the health and living conditions of their human property.

Improvements in the slaves' living conditions were meant to strengthen slavery, not undermine it. Even as the material lives of the majority of slaves improved, the South drew tighter and tighter the chains of bondage. If slaves in the United States enjoyed better health and diets than elsewhere in the Western Hemisphere, they had far less access to freedom. In Brazil, it was not uncommon for an owner to free slaves as a form of celebration—on the occasion of a wedding in the owner's family, for example—or to allow slaves to purchase their freedom. Although slavery in Brazil lasted until 1888, more than half the population of African descent was already free in 1850. (The comparable figure in the American South was well below 10 percent.) In the nineteenth-century South, more and more states set limits on voluntary manumission, requiring that such acts be approved by the legislature. "All the powers of earth," declared Abraham Lincoln in 1857, seemed to be "rapidly combining" to fasten bondage ever more securely upon American slaves. Few slave societies in history have so systematically closed off all avenues to freedom as the Old South.

FREE BLACKS IN THE OLD SOUTH

The existence of slavery helped to define the status of those blacks who did enjoy freedom. On the eve of the Civil War, nearly half a million free blacks lived in the United States, a majority in the South. Most were the descendants of slaves freed by southern owners in the aftermath of the Revolution or by the gradual emancipation laws of the northern states. Their numbers were supplemented by slaves who had been voluntarily liberated by their masters, who had been allowed to purchase their freedom, or who succeeded in running away.

When followed by "black" or "Negro," the word "free" took on an entirely new meaning. Whites defined their freedom, in part, by their distance from slavery. But among blacks, wrote Douglass, "the distinction between the slave and the free is not great." Northern free blacks, as noted in Chapter 10, generally could not vote and enjoyed few economic opportunities. Free blacks in the South could legally own property and marry and, of course, could not be bought and sold. But many regulations restricting the lives of slaves also applied to them. Free blacks had no voice in selecting public officials. Like slaves, they were prohibited from owning dogs, firearms, or liquor, and they could not strike a white person, even in self-defense. They were not allowed to testify in court or serve on juries, and they had to carry at all times a certificate of freedom. Poor free blacks who required public assistance could be bound out to labor alongside slaves. "Free negroes," declared a South Carolina judge in 1848, "belong to a degraded caste of society" and should learn to conduct themselves "as inferiors."

As noted above, nineteenth-century Brazil had a large free black population. In the West Indies, many children of white owners and female slaves gained their freedom, becoming part of a "free colored" population sharply distinguished from both whites above them and slaves below. In the absence of a white lower middle class, free blacks in Jamaica and other Caribbean islands operated shops and worked as clerks in government offices.

In the United States, a society that equated "black" and "slave" and left little room for a mulatto group between them, free blacks were increasingly considered an undesirable group, a potential danger to the slave system. By the 1850s, most southern states prohibited free blacks from entering their territory and a few states even moved to expel them altogether, offering the choice of enslavement or departure. Nonetheless, a few free blacks managed to prosper within slave society. William Johnson, a Natchez barber, acquired enough money to purchase a plantation with fifteen slaves; he hunted with upper-class whites and loaned them money. But he suffered from the legal disadvantages common to his race. He could not, for example, testify against his debtors in court when they failed to pay. In Virginia, the slaves freed and given land by the will of Richard Randolph (noted in Chapter 6) established a vibrant community they called Israel Hill. Despite the legal restrictions on free blacks in the state, they prospered as farmers and skilled craftsmen, and they learned to defend their rights in court, even winning lawsuits against whites who owed them money.

Table 11.3 FREE BLACK POPULATION, 1860		
Region	*Free Black Population*	*Percentage of Total Black Population*
North	226,152	100%
South	261,918	6.2
Upper South	224,963	12.8
Lower South	36,955	1.5
Delaware	19,829	91.7
Washington, D.C.	11,131	77.8
Kentucky	10,684	4.5
Maryland	83,942	49.1
Missouri	3,572	3.0
North Carolina	30,463	8.4
Tennessee	7,300	2.6
Virginia	58,042	10.6
Alabama	2,690	0.6
Arkansas	144	0.1
Florida	932	1.5
Georgia	3,500	0.8
Louisiana	18,647	5.3
Mississippi	773	0.2
South Carolina	9,914	2.4
Texas	355	0.2

THE UPPER AND LOWER SOUTH

Very few free blacks (around 37,000 persons, or less than 2 percent of the area's black population) lived in the Lower South in 1860. Like William Johnson, a majority of them resided in cities. Mississippi, an overwhelmingly rural state with no real urban centers, had fewer than 800 free blacks on the eve of the Civil War. In New Orleans and Charleston, on the other hand, relatively prosperous free black communities developed, mostly composed of mixed-race descendants of unions between white men and slave women. Some became truly wealthy—Antoine Dubuclet of Louisiana, for example, owned 100 slaves. Many free blacks in these cities acquired an education and worked as skilled craftsmen such as tailors, carpenters, and mechanics. They established churches for their communities

Slaves were an ever-present part of southern daily life. In this 1826 portrait of the five children of Commodore John Daniel Daniels, a wealthy Baltimore shipowner, a young slave lies on the floor at their side, holding the soap for a game of blowing bubbles, while another hovers in the background, almost depicted as part of the room's design.

and schools for their children. Some New Orleans free blacks sent their children to France for an education. These elite free blacks did everything they could to maintain a separation from the slave population. The Brown Fellowship Society of Charleston, for example, would not even allow dark-skinned free men to join. Even in these cities, however, most free blacks were poor unskilled laborers.

In the Upper South, where the large majority of southern free blacks lived, they generally worked for wages as farm laborers. Here, where tobacco had exhausted the soil, many planters shifted to grain production, which required less year-round labor. They sold off many slaves to the Lower South and freed others. By 1860, half the African-American population of Maryland was free. Planters hired local free blacks to work alongside their slaves at harvest time. Free blacks in Virginia and Maryland were closely tied to the slave community and often had relatives in bondage. Some owned slaves, but usually these were free men who had purchased their slave wives and children but could not liberate them because the law required any slave who became free to leave the state. Overall, in the words of Willis A. Hodges, a member of a free Virginia family that helped runaways to reach the North, free blacks and slaves were "one man of sorrow."

SLAVE LABOR

First and foremost, slavery was a system of labor; "from sunup to first dark," with only brief interruptions for meals, work occupied most of the slaves' time. Large plantations were diversified communities, where slaves performed all kinds of work. The 125 slaves on one plantation, for instance, included a butler, two waitresses, a nurse, a dairymaid, a gardener, ten carpenters, and two shoemakers. Other plantations counted among their slaves engineers, blacksmiths, and weavers, as well as domestic workers from cooks to coachmen.

Slaves cut wood to provide fuel for steamboats, worked in iron and coal mines, manned the docks in southern seaports, and laid railroad track. They were set to work by local authorities to construct and repair bridges, roads, and other facilities and by the federal government to build forts and other public buildings in the South. Businessmen, merchants, lawyers, and civil servants owned slaves, and by 1860 some 200,000 worked in industry, especially in the ironworks and tobacco factories of the Upper South. In southern cities, thousands were employed as unskilled laborers and skilled artisans. Reliance on unfree labor, moreover, extended well beyond the ranks of slaveholders, for, as noted earlier, many small farmers and manufacturers rented slaves from plantation owners. A few owners gave trusted slaves extensive responsibilities. Simon Gray's owner made him the head of a riverboat crew on the Mississippi. Gray supervised both white and slave workers, sold his owner's lumber at urban markets, and handled large sums of money.

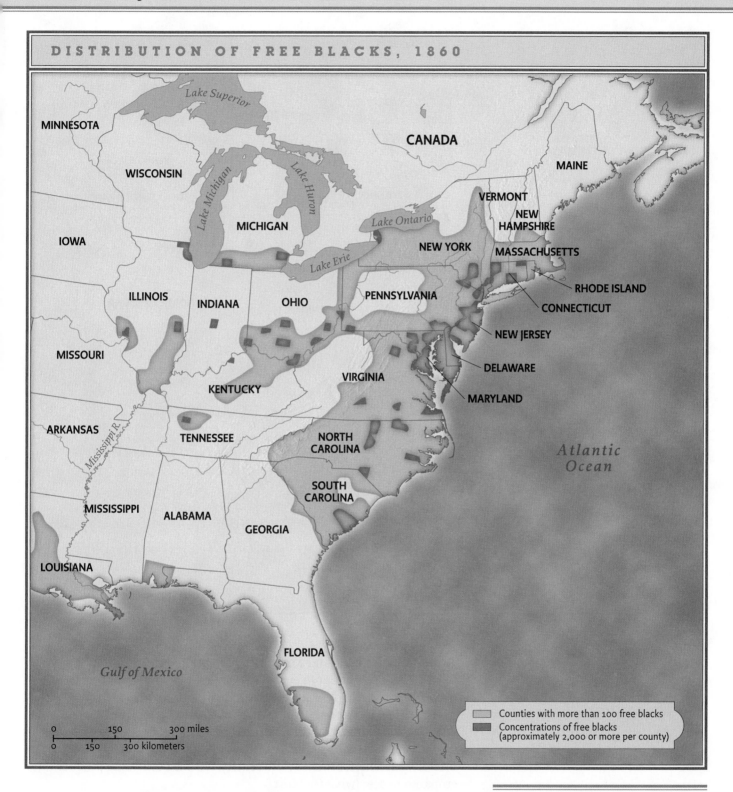

DISTRIBUTION OF FREE BLACKS, 1860

Legend:
- Counties with more than 100 free blacks
- Concentrations of free blacks (approximately 2,000 or more per county)

The nation's population in 1860 included nearly 500,000 free blacks. The majority lived in the slave states, especially Maryland and Virginia.

GANG LABOR AND TASK LABOR

Gray's experience, of course, was hardly typical. The large majority of slaves—75 percent of women and nearly 90 percent of men, according to one study—worked in the fields. The precise organization of their labor varied according to the crop and the size of the holding. On small farms, the owner often toiled side-by-side with his slaves. The largest concentration of

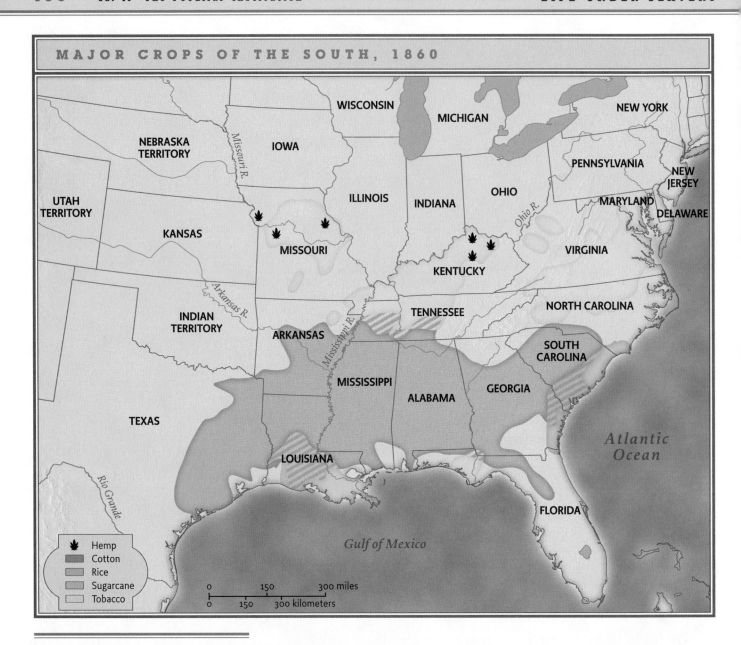

MAJOR CROPS OF THE SOUTH, 1860

Legend:
- Hemp
- Cotton
- Rice
- Sugarcane
- Tobacco

Cotton was the major agricultural crop of the South, and, indeed, the nation, but slaves also grew rice, sugarcane, tobacco, and hemp.

slaves, however, lived and worked on plantations in the Cotton Belt, where men, women, and children labored in gangs, often under the direction of an overseer and perhaps a slave "driver" who assisted him. Among slaves, overseers had a reputation for meting out harsh treatment. "The requisite qualifications for an overseer," wrote Solomon Northup, a free black who spent twelve years in slavery after being kidnapped from the North, "are utter heartlessness, brutality, and cruelty. It is his business to produce large crops, no matter [what the] cost."

The 150,000 slaves who worked in the sugar fields of southern Louisiana also labored in large gangs. Conditions here were among the harshest in the South, for the late fall harvest season required round-the-clock labor to cut and process the sugarcane before it spoiled. On the rice plantations of South Carolina and Georgia, the system of task labor, which had originated in the colonial era, prevailed. With few whites willing to venture into the malaria-infested swamps, slaves were assigned daily tasks and allowed to set their own pace of work. Once a slave's task had been completed, he or she could spend the rest of the day hunting, fishing, or cultivating garden crops.

SLAVERY IN THE CITIES

From the slaves' point of view, slavery in the different regions of the South could be "worse" in some respects and "better" in others. Slaves in the rice fields, for example, endured harsh working conditions but enjoyed more independence than other rural slaves because of the task system of labor and the absence of a large resident white population. Skilled urban craftsmen also enjoyed considerable autonomy. Most city slaves were servants, cooks, and other domestic laborers. But owners sometimes allowed those with craft skills to "hire their own time." This meant that they could make work arrangements individually with employers, with most of the wages going to the slave's owner. Many urban slaves even lived on their own. But slaveholders increasingly became convinced that, as one wrote, the growing independence of skilled urban slaves "exerts a most injurious influence upon the relation of master and servant." For this reason, many owners in the 1850s sold city slaves to the countryside and sought replacements among skilled white labor.

During his time in Baltimore, Frederick Douglass "sought my own employment, made my own contracts, and collected my own earnings." Compared to conditions on the plantation, he concluded, "I was really well off." Douglass hastened to add, however, that his favored treatment in no way lessened his desire for freedom—"it was *slavery*, not its mere incidents, that I hated."

MAINTAINING ORDER

Slaveowners employed a variety of means in their attempts to maintain order and discipline among their human property and persuade them to labor productively. At base, the system rested on force. Masters had almost complete discretion in inflicting punishment, and rare was the slave who went through his or her life without experiencing a whipping. Josiah Henson, who escaped to the North and published an autobiography, wrote that he could never erase from his memory the traumatic experience of seeing his father brutally whipped for striking a white man. Any infraction of plantation rules, no matter how minor, could be punished by the lash. One Georgia planter recorded in his journal that he had whipped a slave "for not bringing over milk for my coffee, being compelled to take it without."

Subtler means of control supplemented violence. Owners encouraged and

A female slave drying cotton on a plantation in the South Carolina Sea Islands, 1862. Slave men, women, and children all worked in the cotton fields.

In this undated photograph, men, women, and children pick cotton under the watchful eye of an overseer. Unlike sugarcane, cotton does not grow to a great height, allowing an overseer to supervise a large number of slaves.

A Public Whipping of Slaves in Lexington, Missouri, in 1856, *an illustration from the abolitionist publication* The Suppressed Book about Slavery. *Whipping was a common form of punishment for slaves.*

exploited divisions among the slaves, especially between field hands and house servants. They created systems of incentives that rewarded good work with time off or even money payments. One Virginia slaveholder gave his slaves ten cents per day for good work and reported that this made them labor "with as much steadiness and cheerfulness as whites," thereby "saving all the expense of overseers." Probably the most powerful weapon wielded by slaveowners was the threat of sale, which separated slaves from their immediate families and from the communities that, despite overwhelming odds, African-Americans created on plantations throughout the South.

SLAVE CULTURE

Slaves never abandoned their desire for freedom or their determination to resist total white control over their lives. In the face of grim realities, they succeeded in forging a semi-independent culture, centered on the family and church. This enabled them to survive the experience of bondage without surrendering their self-esteem and to pass from generation to generation a set of ideas and values fundamentally at odds with those of their masters.

Slave culture drew on the African heritage. African influences were evident in the slaves' music and dances, style of religious worship, and the use of herbs by slave healers to combat disease. (Given the primitive nature of professional medical treatment, some whites sought out slave healers instead of trained physicians.) Unlike the plantation regions of the Caribbean and Brazil, where the African slave trade continued into the nineteenth century and the black population far outnumbered the white, most slaves in the United States were American-born and lived amidst a white majority. Slave culture was a new creation, shaped by African traditions and American values and experiences.

THE SLAVE FAMILY

At the center of the slave community stood the family. On the sugar plantations of the West Indies, the number of males far exceeded that of females, the workers lived in barracks-type buildings, and settled family life was nearly impossible. The United States, where the slave population grew from natural increase rather than continued importation from Africa, had an even male-female ratio, making the creation of families far more possible. To be sure, the law did not recognize the legality of slave marriages. The master had to consent before a man and woman could "jump over the broomstick" (the slaves' marriage ceremony), and families stood in constant danger of being broken up by sale.

Nonetheless, most adult slaves married, and their unions, when not disrupted by sale, typically lasted for a lifetime. To solidify a sense of family continuity, slaves frequently named children after cousins, uncles, grandparents, and other relatives. Nor did the slave family simply mirror kinship patterns among whites. Slaves, for example, did not marry first cousins, a practice common among white southerners. Most slaves lived in two-parent families. But because of constant sales, the slave community had a significantly higher number of female-headed households than among whites, as well as families in which grandparents, other relatives, or even non-kin assumed responsibility for raising children.

Kitchen Ball at White Sulphur Springs, Virginia, *an 1838 painting by the German-born American artist Christian Mayr. Fashionably dressed domestic slaves celebrate the wedding of a couple, dressed in white at the center.*

THE THREAT OF SALE

As noted above, the threat of sale, which disrupted family ties, was perhaps the most powerful disciplinary weapon slaveholders possessed. As the domestic slave trade expanded with the rise of the Cotton Kingdom, about one slave marriage in three in slave-selling states like Virginia was broken by sale. Many children were separated from their parents by sale. According to one estimate, at least 10 percent of the teenage slaves in the Upper South were sold in the interstate slave trade. Fear of sale permeated slave life, especially in the Upper South. "Mother, is Massa going to sell us tomorrow?" ran a line in a popular slave song. As a reflection of their paternalist responsibilities, some owners encouraged slaves to marry. Others, however, remained unaware of their slaves' family connections, and their interest in slave children was generally limited to the children's ability to work in the fields. The federal census broke down the white population by five-year age categories, but it divided slaves only once, at age ten, the point at which they became old enough to enter the plantation labor force.

Slave traders gave little attention to preserving family ties. A public notice, "Sale of Slaves and Stock," announced the 1852 auction of property belonging to a recently deceased Georgia planter. It listed thirty-six individuals ranging from an infant to a sixty-nine-year old woman and ended with the proviso: "Slaves will be sold separate, or in lots, as best suits the purchaser." Sales like this were a human tragedy. "My dear wife," a Georgia slave wrote in 1858, "I take the pleasure of writing you these few [lines] with much regret to inform you that I am sold. . . . Give my love to my father and mother and tell them good bye for me, and if we shall not meet

Sale of Slaves and Stock.

The Negroes and Stock listed below, are a Prime Lot, and belong to the ESTATE OF THE LATE LUTHER McGOWAN, and will be sold on Monday, Sept. 22nd, 1852, at the Fair Grounds, in Savannah, Georgia, at 1:00 P. M. The Negroes will be taken to the grounds two days previous to the Sale, so that they may be inspected by prospective buyers.

On account of the low prices listed below, they will be sold for cash only, and must be taken into custody within two hours after sale.

No.	Name	Age	Remarks	Price
1	Lunesta	27	Prime Rice Planter,	$1,275.00
2	Violet	16	Housework and Nursemaid,	900.00
3	Lizzie	30	Rice, Unsound,	300.00
4	Minda	27	Cotton, Prime Woman,	1,200.00
5	Adam	28	Cotton, Prime Young Man,	1,100.00
6	Abel	41	Rice Hand, Eyesight Poor,	675.00
7	Tanney	22	Prime Cotton Hand,	950.00
8	Flementina	39	Good Cook, Stiff Knee,	400.00
9	Lanney	34	Prime Cottom Man,	1,000.00
10	Sally	10	Handy in Kitchen,	675.00
11	Maccabey	35	Prime Man, Fair Carpenter,	980.00
12	Dorcas Judy	25	Seamstress, Handy in House,	800.00
13	Happy	60	Blacksmith,	575.00
14	Mowden	15	Prime Cotton Boy,	700.00
15	Bills	21	Handy with Mules,	900.00
16	Theopolis	39	Rice Hand, Gets Fits,	575.00
17	Coolidge	29	Rice Hand and Blacksmith,	1,275.00
18	Bessie	69	Infirm, Sews,	250.00
19	Infant	1	Strong Likely Boy	400.00
20	Samson	41	Prime Man, Good with Stock,	975.00
21	Callie May	27	Prime Woman, Rice,	1,000.00
22	Honey	14	Prime Girl, Hearing Poor,	850.00
23	Angelina	16	Prime Girl, House or Field,	1,000.00
24	Virgil	21	Prime Field Hand,	1,100.00
25	Tom	40	Rice Hand, Lame Leg,	750.00
26	Noble	11	Handy Boy,	900.00
27	Judge Lesh	55	Prime Blacksmith,	800.00
28	Booster	43	Fair Mason, Unsound,	600.00
29	Big Kate	37	Housekeeper and Nurse,	950.00
30	Melie Ann	19	Housework, Smart Yellow Girl,	1,250.00
31	Deacon	26	Prime Rice Hand,	1,000.00
32	Coming	19	Prime Cotton Hand,	1,000.00
33	Mabel	47	Prime Cotton Hand,	800.00
34	Uncle Tim	60	Fair Hand with Mules,	600.00
35	Abe	27	Prime Cotton Hand,	1,000.00
36	Tennes	29	Prime Rice Hand and Coachman,	1,250.00

There will also be offered at this sale, twenty head of Horses and Mules with harness, along with thirty head of Prime Cattle. Slaves will be sold separate, or in lots, as best suits the purchaser. Sale will be held rain or shine.

A broadside advertising the public sale of slaves, along with horses, mules, and cattle, after the death of their owner. The advertisement notes that the slaves will be sold individually or in groups "as best suits the purchaser," an indication that families were likely to be broken up. The prices are based on each slave's sex, age, and skill.

in this world I hope to meet in heaven. My dear wife for you and my children my pen cannot express the grief I feel to be parted from you all."

GENDER ROLES AMONG SLAVES

In some ways, gender roles under slavery differed markedly from those in the larger society. Slave men and women experienced, in a sense, the equality of powerlessness. The nineteenth century's "cult of domesticity," which defined the home as a woman's proper sphere, did not apply to slave women, who regularly worked in the fields. Slave men could not act as the economic providers for their families. Nor could they protect their wives from physical or sexual abuse by owners and overseers (a frequent occurrence on many plantations) or determine when and under what conditions their children worked.

When slaves worked "on their own time," however, more conventional gender roles prevailed. Slave men chopped wood, hunted, and fished, while women washed, sewed, and assumed primary responsibility for the care of children. Some planters allowed their slaves small plots of land on which to grow food to supplement the rations provided by the owner; women usually took charge of these "garden plots." But whatever its internal arrangements, the family was central to the slave community, allowing for the transmission of values, traditions, and survival strategies—in a word, of slave culture—from one generation to the next.

SLAVE RELIGION

A distinctive version of Christianity also offered solace to slaves in the face of hardship and hope for liberation from bondage. Some blacks, free and slave, had taken part in the Great Awakening of the colonial era, and even more were swept into the South's Baptist and Methodist churches during

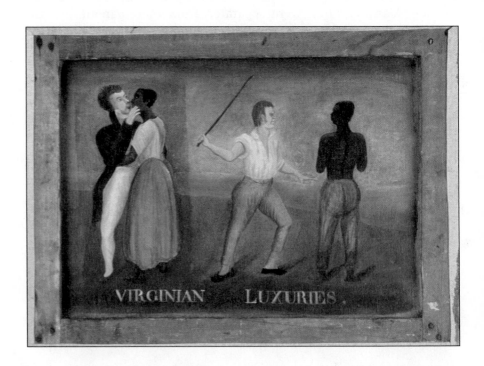

Virginian Luxuries. *Originally painted on the back panel of a formal portrait, this image illustrates two "luxuries" of a Virginia slaveowner—the power to sexually abuse slave women and to whip slaves.*

the religious revivals of the late eighteenth and early nineteenth centuries. As one preacher recalled of the great camp meeting that drew thousands of worshipers to Cane Ridge, Kentucky, in 1801, no distinctions were made "as to age, sex, color, or anything of a temporary nature; old and young, male and female, black and white, had equal privilege to minister the light which they received, in whatever way the Spirit directed."

Even though the law prohibited slaves from gathering without a white person present, every plantation, it seemed, had its own black preacher. Usually the preacher was a "self-called" slave who possessed little or no formal education but whose rhetorical abilities and familiarity with the Bible made him one of the most respected members of the slave community. Especially in southern cities, slaves also worshiped in biracial congregations with white ministers, where they generally were required to sit in the back pews or in the balcony. Urban free blacks established their own churches, sometimes attended by slaves.

To masters, Christianity offered another means of social control. Many required slaves to attend services conducted by white ministers, who preached that theft was immoral and that the Bible required servants to obey their masters. One slave later recalled being told in a white minister's sermon "how good God was in bringing us over to this country from dark and benighted Africa, and permitting us to listen to the sound of the gospel." Several slaves walked out of the service during a sermon by Charles C. Jones stressing that God had commanded servants to obey their masters and that they should not try to run away. One man came up to Jones at the end and said, "the doctrine is *one-sided*."

THE GOSPEL OF FREEDOM

The slaves transformed the Christianity they had embraced, turning it to their own purposes. A blend of African traditions and Christian belief, slave religion was practiced in secret nighttime gatherings on plantations and in "praise meetings" replete with shouts, dances, and frequent emotional interchanges between the preacher and the congregation. One former slave later recalled typical secret religious gatherings: "We used to slip off into the woods in the old slave days on Sunday evening way down in the swamps to sing and pray to our own liking. We prayed for this day of freedom."

The biblical story of Exodus, in which God chose Moses to lead the enslaved Jews of Egypt into a promised land of freedom, played a central role in black Christianity. Slaves identified themselves as a chosen people, whom God in the fullness of time would deliver from bondage. At the same time, the figure of Jesus Christ represented to slaves a personal redeemer, one who truly cared for the oppressed. Slaves found other heroes and symbols in the Bible as well: Jonah, who overcame hard luck and escaped from the belly of a whale; David, who vanquished the more powerful Goliath; and Daniel, who escaped from the lion's den. And the Christian

A black preacher, as portrayed in Harper's Weekly, *February 2, 1867. Although engraved after the Civil War, the scene is the same as religious services under slavery.*

PRAYER MEETING

Plantation Burial, *a painting from around 1860 by John Antrobus, an English artist who emigrated to New Orleans in 1850 and later married the daughter of a plantation owner. A slave preacher conducts a funeral service while black men, women, and children look on. The well-dressed white man and woman on the far right are, presumably, the plantation owner and his wife. This is a rare eyewitness depiction of black culture under slavery.*

message of brotherhood and the equality of all souls before the Creator, in the slaves' eyes, offered an irrefutable indictment of the institution of slavery.

THE DESIRE FOR LIBERTY

If their masters developed an elaborate ideology defending the South's "peculiar institution," slave culture rested on a conviction of the unjustness of bondage and the desire for freedom. "Nobody," the British political philosopher Edmund Burke had written during the American Revolution, "will be argued into slavery." Frederick Douglass called the proslavery argument "flimsy nonsense," which men would be "ashamed to remember" once slavery had been abolished. Whatever proslavery writers asserted and ministers preached, blacks thought of themselves as a working people unjustly deprived of the fruits of their labor by idle planters who lived in luxury. "We bake the bread / they give us the crust," said a line from one slave song.

Most slaves fully understood the impossibility of directly confronting the system. Their folk tales had no figures equivalent to Paul Bunyan, the powerful, larger-than-life backwoodsman popular in white folklore. Slaves' folklore, such as the Brer Rabbit stories, glorified the weak hare who outwitted stronger foes like the bear and fox, rather than challenging them directly. Their religious songs, or spirituals, spoke of lives of sorrow ("I've been 'buked and I've been scorned"), while holding out hope for ultimate liberation ("Didn't my Lord deliver Daniel?"). When they sang, "I'm bound for the land of Canaan," slaves meant not only relief from worldly woes in an afterlife but also escaping to the North or, in God's good time, witnessing the breaking of slavery's chains.

"Freedom," declared a black minister after emancipation, "burned in the black heart long before freedom was born." A fugitive who reached the North later recalled that the "desire for freedom" was the "constant theme" of conversations in the slave quarters. Even the most ignorant slave, observed Solomon Northup, could not "fail to observe the difference between their own condition and the meanest white man's, and to realize the injustice of laws which place it within [the owner's] power not only to appropriate the profits of their industry, but to subject them to unmediated and unprovoked punishment without remedy."

The world of most rural slaves was bounded by their local communities and kin. They became extremely familiar with the local landscape, crops, and population, but had little knowledge of the larger world. Nonetheless, slaves could not remain indifferent to the currents of thought unleashed by the American Revolution or to the language of freedom in the society around them. "I am in a land of liberty," wrote Joseph Taper, a Virginia slave who escaped to Canada around 1840. "Here man is as God intended he should be . . . not like the southern laws which put man, made in the image of God, on level with brutes." The social and political agenda African-Americans would put forward in the Reconstruction era that followed emancipation—stressing civil and political equality, the strengthening of the black community, and autonomy in their working lives—flowed directly out of their experience in slavery.

RESISTANCE TO SLAVERY

Confronted with federal, state, and local authorities committed to preserving slavery, and outnumbered within the South as a whole by the white population, slaves could only rarely express their desire for freedom by outright rebellion. Compared to Brazil and the West Indies, which experienced numerous uprisings, involving hundreds or even thousands of slaves, revolts in the United States were smaller and less frequent. There was no parallel, of course, to the successful slave revolution in Haiti discussed in Chapter 8 or to the unsuccessful 1831 rebellion in Jamaica that appears to have involved as many as 20,000 slaves. This does not, however, mean that slaves in the United States placidly accepted the system under which they were compelled to live. Resistance to slavery took many forms in the Old South, from individual acts of defiance to occasional uprisings. These actions posed a constant challenge to the slaveholders' self-image as benign paternalists and their belief that slaves were obedient subjects grateful for their owners' care.

FORMS OF RESISTANCE

The most widespread expression of hostility to slavery was "day-to-day resistance" or "silent sabotage"—doing poor work, breaking tools, abusing animals, and in other ways disrupting the plantation routine. Frederick Law Olmsted, a northerner who toured the South in the 1850s, took note of "gates left open, rails removed from fences by the negroes, mules lamed and implements broken, a flat boat set adrift in the river, men ordered to cart rails for a new fence, depositing them so that a double expense of labor would be required to lay them." Many slaves made believe that they were ill to avoid work (although almost no slaves reported themselves sick on Sunday, their only day of rest). Then there was the theft of food, a form of resistance so common that one southern physician diagnosed it as a hereditary disease unique to blacks. Less frequent, but more dangerous, were serious crimes committed by slaves, including arson, poisoning, and armed assaults against individual whites.

FUGITIVE SLAVES

Even more threatening to the stability of the slave system were slaves who ran away. Formidable obstacles confronted the prospective fugitive. As Solomon Northup recalled, "Every white man's hand is raised against him, the patrollers are watching for him, the hounds are ready to follow in his track." Slaves had little or no knowledge of geography, apart from understanding that following the north star led to freedom. No one knows how many slaves succeeded in reaching the North or Canada—the most common rough estimate is around 1,000 per year. Not surprisingly, most of those who succeeded lived, like Frederick Douglass, in the Upper South,

SLAVE RESISTANCE IN THE NINETEENTH-CENTURY ATLANTIC WORLD

Insurrections and major conspiracies

MICHIGAN

NEW YORK

Boston MASSACHUSETTS

New Haven Newport

ILLINOIS INDIANA OHIO PENNSYLVANIA RHODE ISLAND
CONECTICUT

Philadelphia New York

MISSOURI NEW JERSEY

Baltimore DELAWARE

VIRGINIA MARYLAND

Richmond, 1800 (Gabriel's Rebellion)

KENTUCKY

Southampton County, 1831 (Nat Turner's Rebellion)

TENNESSEE NORTH CAROLINA

ARKANSAS

Atlantic Ocean

SOUTH CAROLINA Wilmington

MISSISSIPPI ALABAMA GEORGIA

Charleston, 1822 (Denmark Vesey Conspiracy)

Louisiana, 1811 Savannah

LOUISIANA

FLORIDA

Insurrection aboard the slave ship Creole, 1841

Gulf of Mexico

Bahama Islands

Insurrection aboard the slave ship Amistad, 1839

CUBA

Haiti, 1791–1804

HAITI

Jamaica, 1831

St. Kitts Antigua
Nevis

MEXICO

Caribbean Sea

St. Vincent

Barbados, 1816

Trinidad

Pacific Ocean

SOUTH AMERICA

Denemarra, 1823

0   250   500 miles
0   250   500 kilometers

Instances of slave resistance occurred throughout the Western Hemisphere, on land and at sea. This map shows the location of major events in the nineteenth century.

especially Maryland, Virginia, and Kentucky, which bordered on the free states. Douglass, who escaped at age twenty, was also typical in that the large majority of fugitives were young men. Most slave women were not willing to leave children behind, and to take them along on the arduous escape journey was nearly impossible.

In the Deep South, fugitives tended to head for cities like New Orleans or Charleston, where they hoped to lose themselves in the free black community. Other escapees fled to remote areas like the Great Dismal Swamp of Virginia or the Florida Everglades, where the Seminole Indians offered refuge before they were forced to move west. Even in Tennessee, a study of newspaper advertisements for runaways finds that around 40 percent were thought to have remained in the local neighborhood, 30 percent to have headed to other locations in the South, while only 25 percent tried to reach the North.

The Underground Railroad, a loose organization of sympathetic abolitionists who hid fugitives in their homes and sent them on to the next "station," assisted some runaway slaves. A few courageous individuals made forays into the South to liberate slaves. The best known was Harriet Tubman. Born in Maryland in 1820, Tubman escaped to Philadelphia in 1849 and during the next decade risked her life by making some twenty trips back to her state of birth to lead relatives and other slaves to freedom. But most who managed to reach the North did so on their own initiative, sometimes showing remarkable ingenuity. William and Ellen Craft impersonated a sickly owner traveling with her slave. Henry "Box" Brown packed himself inside a crate and literally had himself shipped from Georgia to freedom in the North.

A typical broadside offering a reward for the capture of a runaway slave.

THE AMISTAD

In a few instances, large groups of slaves collectively seized their freedom. The most celebrated instance involved fifty-three slaves who in 1839 took control of the *Amistad*, a ship transporting them from one port in Cuba to another, and tried to force the navigator to steer it to Africa. The *Amistad* wended its way up the Atlantic coast, until an American vessel seized it off the coast of Long Island. President Martin Van Buren favored returning the slaves to Cuba. But abolitionists brought their case to the Supreme Court, where former president John Quincy Adams argued that since they had been recently brought from Africa in violation of international treaties banning the slave trade, the captives should be freed. The Court accepted Adams's reasoning, and most of the captives made their way back to Africa.

The *Amistad* case had no legal bearing on slaves within the United States. But it may well have inspired a similar uprising in 1841, when 135 slaves being transported by sea from Norfolk, Virginia, to New Orleans seized control of the ship *Creole* and sailed for Nassau in the British Bahamas. Their leader had the evocative name Madison Washington. To the dismay of the Tyler administration, the British gave refuge to the *Creole* slaves.

SLAVE REVOLTS

Resistance to slavery occasionally moved beyond such individual and group acts of defiance to outright rebellion. The four largest conspiracies in American history occurred within the space of thirty-one years in the early nineteenth century. The first, organized by the Virginia slave Gabriel in 1800, was discussed in Chapter 8. It was followed eleven years later by an uprising on sugar plantations upriver from New Orleans. Somewhere between 200 and 500 men and women, armed with sugarcane knives, axes, clubs, and a few guns, marched toward the city, destroying property as they proceeded. The white population along the route fled in panic to New

A lithograph depicting Joseph Cinqué, leader of the slave revolt on the Spanish ship Amistad *off the coast of Cuba in 1839. The ship was eventually seized near Long Island. After a long legal battle, the Supreme Court allowed the slaves to return to Africa.*

Orleans. Within two days, the militia and regular army troops met the rebels and dispersed them in a pitched battle, killing sixty-six. Soon afterwards, the principal leaders were executed. Captured rebels offered little explanation for their revolt other than the desire, as one put it, "to kill the white." But they seem to have been inspired by the recent success of the slave revolution in Haiti.

The next major conspiracy was organized in 1822 by Denmark Vesey, a slave carpenter in Charleston, South Carolina, who had purchased his freedom after winning a local lottery. An outspoken, charismatic leader, Vesey rebuked blacks who stepped off the city's sidewalks to allow whites to pass and took a leading role in the local African Methodist Church. His conspiracy reflected the combination of American and African influences then circulating in the Atlantic world and coming together in black culture. "He studied the Bible a great deal," recalled one of his followers, "and tried to prove from it that slavery and bondage is against the Bible." Vesey also quoted the Declaration of Independence, pored over newspaper reports of the debates in Congress regarding the Missouri Compromise, and made pronouncements like "all men had equal rights, blacks as well as whites." And he read to his co-conspirators accounts of the successful slave revolution in Haiti. The African heritage was present in the person of Vesey's lieutenant Gullah Jack, a religious "conjurer" from Angola who claimed to be able to protect the rebels against injury or death. The plot was discovered before it could reach fruition.

As in the case of many slave conspiracies, evidence about the Vesey plot is contradictory and disputed. Much of it comes from a series of trials in which the court operated in secret and failed to allow the accused to confront those who testified against them. South Carolina's governor, Thomas Bennett Jr., a number of whose slaves were among the accused, complained to Robert Y. Hayne, the state's attorney general, that the court proceedings violated "the rules which universally obtain among civilized nations." Hayne replied that to try a "free white man" under such circumstances would clearly violate his fundamental rights. But, he added, "slaves are not entitled to these rights," since "all the provisions of our constitution in favor of liberty are intended for freemen only." In the end, thirty-five slaves and free blacks, among them Vesey and three slaves belonging to the governor, were executed and an equal number banished from the state.

NAT TURNER'S REBELLION

The best known of all slave rebels was Nat Turner, a slave preacher and religious mystic in Southampton County, Virginia, who came to believe that God had chosen him to lead a black uprising. Turner traveled widely in the county conducting religious services. He told of seeing black and white angels fighting in the sky and the heavens running red with blood. Perhaps from a sense of irony, Turner initially chose July 4, 1831, for his rebellion only to fall ill on the appointed day. On August 22, he and a handful of followers marched from farm to farm assaulting the white inhabitants. Most of their victims were women and children, for many of the area's men were attending a religious revival across the border in North Carolina. By the time the militia put down the uprising, about eighty slaves had joined Turner's band, and some sixty whites had been killed. Turner was subsequently captured and, with seventeen other rebels, condemned to die. Asked before his execution whether he regretted what he had done, Turner responded, "Was not Christ crucified?"

Nat Turner's was the last large-scale rebellion in southern history. Like Gabriel's and Vesey's conspiracies, Turner's took place outside the heart of the plantation South, where slavery was most rigidly policed. Because Turner began with only a handful of followers, he faced less chance of discovery or betrayal than Gabriel or Vesey. Nonetheless, his revolt demonstrated conclusively that in a region where whites outnumbered blacks and the white community was armed and united, slaves stood at a fatal disadvantage in any violent encounter. Only an outside force could alter the balance of power within the South. Slave resistance, however, hardly disappeared. Turner's uprising, in fact, demonstrated the connection between outright rebellion and less dramatic forms of resistance. For in its aftermath, numerous reports circulated of "insubordinate" behavior by slaves on Virginia's farms and plantations.

Turner's rebellion sent shock waves through the entire South. "A Nat Turner," one white Virginian warned, "might be in any family." In the panic that followed the revolt, hundreds of innocent slaves were whipped and scores executed. For one last time, Virginia's leaders openly debated whether steps ought to be taken to do away with the "peculiar institution." "The blood of Turner and his innocent victims," declared a Richmond newspaper, "has opened the doors which have been shut for fifty years." But a proposal to commit the state to gradual emancipation and the removal of the black population from the state failed to win legislative approval. The measure gained overwhelming support in the western part of Virginia, where slaves represented less than 10 percent of the population, but it failed to win sufficient votes in the eastern counties where slavery was centered.

Instead of moving toward emancipation, the Virginia legislature of 1832 decided to fasten even more tightly the chains of bondage. New laws prohibited blacks, free or slave, from acting as preachers (a measure that proved impossible to enforce), strengthened the militia and patrol systems, banned free blacks from owning firearms, and prohibited teaching slaves

An engraving depicting Nat Turner's slave rebellion of 1831, from a book published soon after the revolt.

to read. Other southern states followed suit. In the debate's aftermath, Thomas R. Dew, a professor at the College of William and Mary in Virginia, published an influential pamphlet pointing to the absurdity of deporting the bulk of the state's labor force. The state, he insisted, faced a stark choice—retain slavery, or free the slaves and absorb them into Virginia society. Few critics of slavery were willing to accept the latter alternative.

In some ways, 1831 marked a turning point for the Old South. In that year, Parliament launched a program for abolishing slavery throughout the British empire (a process completed in 1838), underscoring the South's growing isolation in the Western world. Turner's rebellion, following only a few months after the appearance in Boston of William Lloyd Garrison's abolitionist journal, *The Liberator* (discussed in the next chapter), suggested that American slavery faced enemies both within and outside the South. The proslavery argument increasingly permeated southern intellectual and political life, while dissenting opinions were suppressed. Some states made membership in an abolitionist society a criminal offense, while mobs drove critics of slavery from their homes. The South's "great reaction" produced one of the most thoroughgoing suppressions of freedom of speech in American history. Even as reform movements arose in the North that condemned slavery as contrary to Christianity and to basic American values, and national debate over the peculiar institution intensified, southern society closed in defense of slavery.

SUGGESTED READING

BOOKS

Aptheker, Herbert. *American Negro Slave Revolts* (1943). Still the fullest account of slave rebellions in the United States.

Berlin, Ira. *Slaves without Masters: The Free Negro in the Antebellum South* (1974). A careful study of the status of free blacks, stressing differences between the Upper and Lower South.

Clinton, Catherine. *The Plantation Mistress: Woman's World in the Old South* (1982). Explores how the institution of slavery affected the lives of planters' wives and daughters.

Davis, David Brion. *Inhuman Bondage: The Rise and Fall of Slavery in the New World* (2006). Places the history of slavery in the United States firmly in a hemispheric context.

Genovese, Eugene D. *Roll, Jordan, Roll: The World the Slaves Made* (1974). A classic study of the paternalist ethos and the culture that developed under slavery.

Gutman, Herbert G. *The Black Family in Slavery and Freedom* (1976). A pioneering examination of how slaves created and sustained families under the harsh conditions of slavery.

Johnson, Walter. *Soul by Soul: Life inside the Antebellum Slave Market* (1999). Considers the operations of the New Orleans slave market as a window into slavery as a whole.

Joyner, Charles D. *Down by the Riverside: A South Carolina Slave Community* (1984). Studies slave communities in coastal South Carolina, emphasizing the blend of African and American influences.

Kolchin, Peter. *American Slavery, 1619–1877* (rev. ed., 2003). A careful, up-to-date survey of the history of slavery in North America from its beginning through emancipation.

McCurry, Stephanie. *Masters of Small Worlds: Yeoman Households, Gender Relations, and the Political Culture of Antebellum South Carolina* (1995). Studies the lives of men and women in non-slaveholding families, to explore their links with the planter class.

O'Brien, Michael. *Conjectures of Order: Intellectual Life and the American South* (2004). A comprehensive study of intellectual life in the Old South.

Rugemer, Edward B. *The Problem of Emancipation: The Caribbean Roots of the American Civil War* (2008). Explores how developments in the West Indies affected the outlook of American slaveholders.

Stevenson, Brenda. *Life in Black and White: Family and Community in the Slave South* (1996). Focusing on Virginia, an examination of how slaves adapted to the rise of the interstate slave trade.

Wade, Richard. *Slavery in the Cities: The South, 1820–1860* (1964). An examination of slavery in southern cities, and growing white fears of lack of control of the urban slave population.

Wright, Gavin. *The Political Economy of the Cotton South: Households, Markets, and Wealth in the Nineteenth Century* (1978). Presents the economic development and structure of the cotton South, by a prominent economic historian.

WEBSITES

Born in Slavery: Slave Narratives from the Federal Writers' Project: http://lcweb2.loc. gov/ammem/snhtml/snhome.html

Documenting the American South: http://docsouth.unc.edu

Gilder Lehrman Center for the Study of Slavery, Resistance, and Abolition: www.yale.edu/glc/index.htm

Slaves and the Courts, 1740–1860: http://memory.loc.gov/ammem/sthtml/sthome.html

REVIEW QUESTIONS

1. Given that by 1860 the economic investment represented by the slave population exceeded the value of the nation's factories, railroads, and banks combined, explain how important slavery was to the national economy and the emergence of the United States as a great power.

2. While some poor southern whites resented the dominance of the "slavocracy" most supported the institution and accepted the power of the planter class. Why did the "plain folk" continue to support slavery?

3. Describe the paternalistic ethos the planters embraced, and explain how it both masked and justified the brutal realities of slavery.

4. Identify the basic elements of the proslavery defense and those points aimed especially at non-southern audiences.

5. Compare slaves in the Old South with those elsewhere in the world, focusing on health, diet, and opportunities for freedom.

6. Describe the difference between gang labor and task labor for slaves, and explain how slaves' tasks varied by region across the Old South.

7. Enslaved African-Americans developed their own culture. What were the different sources of this culture, and how did it vary by region?

8. Identify the different types of resistance to slavery. Which ones were the most common, the most effective, and the most demonstrative?

FREEDOM QUESTIONS

1. In Frederick Douglass's view, how were slaves, in their desire for freedom, closer to the founding ideals than the whites who celebrated the Fourth of July but preserved slavery?

2. How did slavery affect the lives and freedoms of both black and white Americans?

3. How did the defenders of slavery handle the founding ideas that freedom and equality were natural rights?

4. What constraints were there on the rights of free blacks in the antebellum South?

5. How did slaves think of freedom, and what were the sources for their beliefs?

KEY TERMS

the "peculiar institution" (p. 417)

"Cotton Is King" (p. 417)

Lords of the Loom and Lords of the Lash (p. 419)

"plain folk" (p. 422)

southern paternalism (p. 423)

the proslavery argument (p. 424)

slave religion (p. 441)

"silent sabotage" (p. 443)

Underground Railroad (p. 445)

runaways (p. 445)

Harriet Tubman (p. 445)

Denmark Vesey's conspiracy (p. 446)

Nat Turner's Rebellion (p. 447)

REVIEW TABLE

Slave Rebellions and the Old South

Rebellion	Date	Result
Gabriel's Rebellion	1800	Virginia prohibits blacks from congregating on Sundays without white supervision and restricts masters voluntarily freeing their slaves
Denmark Vesey's conspiracy	1822	Vesey is executed in South Carolina, and the state increases restrictions on free blacks
Nat Turner's Rebellion	1831	The only large-scale rebellion in the South, it causes Virginia to further tighten its grip on slavery
Amistad	1839	Slaves aboard the ship win their freedom, increasing southern fear of federal power to attack slavery

CHAPTER 12

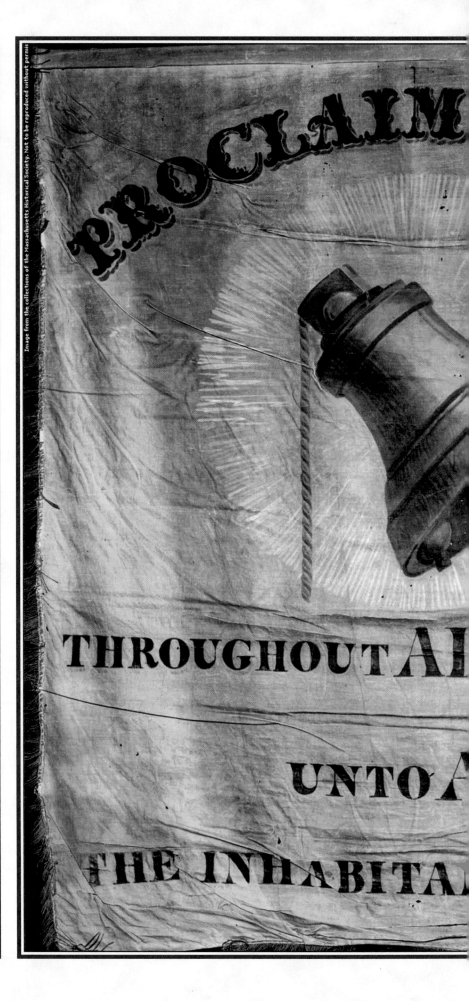

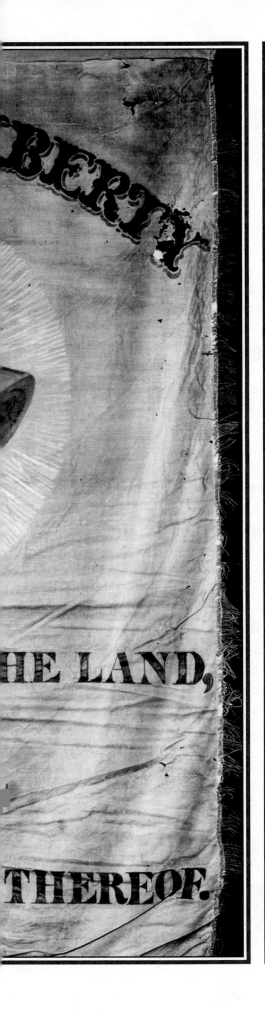

An Age of Reform, 1820–1840

An abolitionist banner. Antislavery organizations adopted the Liberty Bell as a symbol of their campaign to extend freedom to black Americans. Previously, the bell, forged in Philadelphia in the eighteenth century, had simply been known as the Old State House Bell.

FOCUS QUESTIONS

- What were the major movements and goals of antebellum reform?

- What were the different varieties of abolitionism?

- How did abolitionism challenge barriers to racial equality and free speech?

- What were the diverse sources of the antebellum women's rights movement and its significance?

Among the many Americans who devoted their lives to the crusade against slavery, few were as selfless or courageous as Abby Kelley. Born in Massachusetts in 1811, she was educated at a Quaker boarding school in Rhode Island. As a teacher in Lynn, Massachusetts, she joined the Female Anti-Slavery Society and, like thousands of other northern women, threw herself into the abolitionist movement. In 1838, Kelley began to give public speeches about slavery. Her first lecture outside of Lynn was literally a baptism of fire. Enraged by reports that abolitionists favored "amalgamation" of the races—that is, sexual relations between whites and blacks—residents of Philadelphia stormed the meeting hall and burned it to the ground.

For two decades, Kelley traveled throughout the North, speaking almost daily in churches, public halls, and antislavery homes on "the holy cause of human rights." Her career illustrated the interconnections of the era's reform movements. In addition to abolitionism, she was active in pacifist organizations—which opposed the use of force, including war, to settle disputes—and was a pioneer in the early struggle for women's rights. "In striving to strike [the slave's] irons off," she wrote, women "found most surely that we were manacled ourselves." Kelley was not the first American woman to speak in public. But she covered more miles and gave more speeches than any other female orator. She forthrightly challenged her era's assumption that woman's "place" was in the home. More than any other individual, remarked Lucy Stone, another women's rights advocate, Kelley "earned for us all the right of free speech."

Abby Kelley's private life was as unconventional as her public career. She enjoyed a long and happy marriage to Stephen S. Foster, a strong-willed abolitionist given to interrupting Sunday sermons to denounce ministers who failed to condemn slavery. She gave birth to a daughter in 1847 but soon returned to lecturing. When criticized for not devoting herself to the care of her infant, Kelley replied: "I have done it for the sake of the mothers whose babies are sold away from them. The most precious legacy I can leave my child is a free country."

THE REFORM IMPULSE

"In the history of the world," wrote Ralph Waldo Emerson in 1841, "the doctrine of reform has never such hope as at the present hour." Abolitionism was only one of the era's numerous efforts to improve American society. During his visit in the early 1830s, Alexis de Tocqueville noted how in the absence of a powerful national government, Americans' political and

A rare photograph of an abolitionist meeting in New York State around 1850. The woman at the center wearing a bonnet may be Abby Kelley. Frederick Douglass sits immediately to her right.

social activities were organized through voluntary associations—churches, fraternal orders, political clubs, and the like. The reform impulse was part of this proliferation of voluntary groups. Americans established organizations that worked to prevent the manufacture and sale of liquor, end public entertainments and the delivery of the mail on Sunday, improve conditions in prisons, expand public education, uplift the condition of wage laborers, and reorganize society on the basis of cooperation rather than competitive individualism.

Nearly all these groups worked to convert public opinion to their cause. They sent out speakers, gathered signatures on petitions, and published pamphlets. Like Abby Kelley, many reformers were active in more than one crusade. Some reform movements, like restraining the consumption of liquor and alleviating the plight of the blind and insane, flourished throughout the nation. Others, including women's rights, labor unionism, and educational reform, were weak or nonexistent in the South, where they were widely associated with antislavery sentiment. Reform was an international crusade. Peace, temperance, women's rights, and antislavery advocates regularly crisscrossed the Atlantic to promote their cause.

Reformers adopted a wide variety of tactics to bring about social change. Some relied on "moral suasion" to convert people to their cause. Others, like opponents of the "demon rum," sought to use the power of the government to force sinners to change their ways. Some reformers decided to withdraw altogether from the larger society and establish their own cooperative settlements. They hoped to change American life by creating "heavens on earth," where they could demonstrate by example the superiority of a collective way of life. Reformers never amounted to anything like a majority of the population, even in the North, but they had a profound impact on both politics and society.

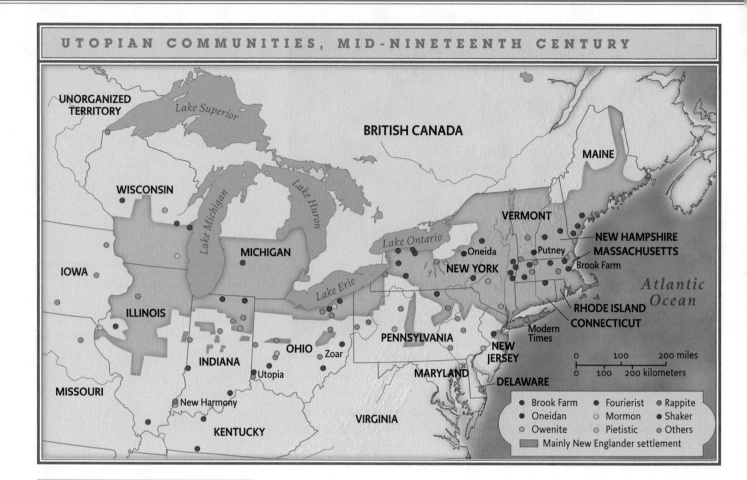

UTOPIAN COMMUNITIES, MID-NINETEENTH CENTURY

In the first half of the nineteenth century, dozens of utopian communities were established in the United States, where small groups of men and women attempted to establish a more perfect social order within the larger society.

UTOPIAN COMMUNITIES

About 100 reform communities were established in the decades before the Civil War. Historians call them "utopian" after Thomas More's sixteenth-century novel *Utopia*, an outline of a perfect society. (The word has also come to imply that such plans are impractical and impossible to realize.) These communities differed greatly in structure and motivation. Some were subject to the iron discipline of a single leader, while others operated in a democratic fashion. Most arose from religious conviction, but others were inspired by the secular desire to counteract the social and economic changes set in motion by the market revolution.

Nearly all the communities set out to reorganize society on a coopera-tive basis, hoping to restore social harmony to a world of excessive individ-ualism and to narrow the widening gap between rich and poor. Through their efforts, the words "socialism" and "communism," meaning a social organization in which productive property is owned by the community rather than private individuals, entered the language of politics. Most utopian communities also tried to find substitutes for conventional gender relations and marriage patterns. Some prohibited sexual relations between men and women altogether; others allowed them to change partners at will. But nearly all insisted that the abolition of private property must be accompanied by an end to men's "property" in women.

THE SHAKERS

Religious communities attracted those who sought to find a retreat from a society permeated by sin, "a refuge from the evils of this Sodom," as the founders of Zoar, in Ohio, put it. But the Shakers, the most successful of the religious communities, also had a significant impact on the outside world. At their peak during the 1840s, cooperative Shaker settlements, which stretched from Maine to Kentucky, included more than 5,000 members. The Shakers were founded in the late eighteenth century by Mother Ann Lee, the daughter of an English blacksmith, who became a religious exhorter and claimed that Christ had directed her to emigrate with her followers to America. The first Shaker community was established in upstate New York in 1787.

God, the Shakers believed, had a "dual" personality, both male and female, and thus the two sexes were spiritually equal. Their work was deemed equally important (although each man was assigned a "sister" to take care of his washing and sewing). "Virgin purity" formed a pillar of the Shakers' faith. They completely abandoned traditional family life. Men and women lived separately in large dormitory-like structures and ate in communal dining rooms. Their numbers grew by attracting converts and adopting children from orphanages, rather than through natural increase. Numerous outsiders visited Shaker communities to observe the religious services that gave the group its name, in which men and women, separated by sex, engaged in frenzied dancing. Although they rejected the individual accumulation of private property, the Shakers proved remarkably successful economically. They were among the first to market vegetable and flower seeds and herbal medicines commercially and to breed cattle for profit. Their beautifully crafted furniture is still widely admired today.

An engraving of a Shaker dance, drawn by Benson Lossing, an artist who visited a Shaker community and reported on life there for Harper's Magazine *in 1857.*

THE MORMONS' TREK

Another migration brought thousands of members of the Church of Jesus Christ of Latter-Day Saints, or Mormons, to modern-day Utah. One of the era's numerous religious sects that hoped to create a Kingdom of God on earth, the Mormons had been founded in the 1820s by Joseph Smith, a young farmer in upstate New York. Smith claimed to have been led by an angel to a set of golden plates covered with strange writing, which he translated as the Book of Mormon. It claimed that ancient Hebrews had emigrated to the New World and become the ancestors of the American Indians.

The absolute authority Smith exercised over his followers, as well as the refusal of the Mormons to separate church and state, alarmed many neighbors. Even more outrageous to the general community was the Mormon practice of polygamy, which allows one man to have more than one wife, a repudiation of traditional Christian teaching and nineteenth-century morality. Mobs drove Smith and his followers out of New York, Ohio, and Missouri before they settled in 1839 in Nauvoo, Illinois, where they hoped to await the Second Coming of Christ. There, five years later, Smith was arrested on the charge of inciting a riot that destroyed an anti-Mormon newspaper. While in jail awaiting trial, Smith was murdered by a group of intruders. His successor as Mormon leader, Brigham Young, led more than 10,000 followers across the Great Plains and Rocky Mountains to the shores of the Great Salt Lake in present-day Utah, seeking a refuge where they could practice their faith undisturbed. The Mormons' plight revealed the limits of religious toleration in nineteenth-century America.

ONEIDA

Another influential and controversial community was Oneida, founded in 1848 in upstate New York by John Humphrey Noyes, the Vermont-born son of a U.S. congressman. After graduating from Dartmouth College, Noyes briefly studied law but soon experienced a conversion at a religious revival and decided to become a minister. Noyes took the revivalists' message that man could achieve moral perfection to an atypical extreme. He preached that he and his followers had become so perfect that they had achieved a state of complete "purity of heart," or sinlessness.

In 1836, Noyes and his followers formed a small community in Putney, Vermont. Like the Shakers, Noyes did away with private property and abandoned traditional marriage. But in contrast to Shaker celibacy, he taught that all members of his community formed a single "holy family" of equals. His community became notorious for what Noyes called "complex marriage," whereby any man could propose sexual relations to any woman, who had the right to reject or accept his invitation, which would then be registered in a public record book. The great danger was "exclusive affections," which, Noyes felt, destroyed the harmony of the community.

After being indicted for adultery by local officials, Noyes in 1848 moved his community to Oneida, where it survived until 1881. Oneida was an extremely dictatorial environment. To become a member of the community, one had to demonstrate command of Noyes's religious teachings and live according to his rules. Members carefully observed each other's conduct and publicly criticized those who violated Noyes's regulations. By the 1860s, a committee was even determining which couples would be permitted to have children—an early example of "eugenics," as the effort to improve the human race by regulating reproduction came to be known.

WORLDLY COMMUNITIES

To outside observers, utopian communities like Oneida seemed a case of "voluntary slavery." But because of their members' selfless devotion to the teachings and rules laid down by their leader, spiritually oriented communities often achieved remarkable longevity. The Shakers survived well into the twentieth century. Communities with a more worldly orientation tended to be beset by internal divisions and therefore lasted for much shorter periods.

In 1841, New England transcendentalists established Brook Farm not far from Boston, where they hoped to demonstrate that manual and intellectual labor could coexist harmoniously. They modeled the community in part on the ideas of the French social reformer Charles Fourier, who envisioned communal living and working arrangements, while retaining private property. Fourier's blueprint for "phalanxes," as he called his settlements, planned everything to the last detail, from the number of residents (2,000) to how much income would be generated by charging admission to sightseers. With leisure time devoted to music, dancing, dramatic readings, and intellectual discussion, Brook Farm was like an exciting miniature university. But it attracted mostly writers, teachers, and ministers, some of whom disliked farm labor. The novelist Nathaniel Hawthorne, a resident for a time, complained about having to shovel manure. Brook Farm disbanded after a few years, and Hawthorne offered a skeptical view of life there in his 1852 novel *The Blithedale Romance*.

THE OWENITES

The most important secular communitarian (meaning a person who plans or lives in a cooperative community) was Robert Owen, a British factory owner. Appalled by the degradation of workers in the early industrial revolution, Owen created a model factory village at New Lanark, Scotland, which combined strict rules of work discipline with comfortable housing and free public education. Around 1815, its 1,500 employees made New Lanark the largest center of cotton manufacturing in the world. Convinced that the "rich and the poor, the governors and the governed, have really but one interest," Owen promoted communitarianism as a peaceful means of ensuring that workers received the full value of their labor. In 1824, he purchased the Harmony community in Indiana—originally founded by the German Protestant religious leader George Rapp, who had emigrated to America with his followers at the beginning of the nineteenth century. Here, Owen established New Harmony, where he hoped to create a "new moral world."

"The character of man is, without a single exception, always formed for him," Owen declared. Individuals could be transformed by changing the

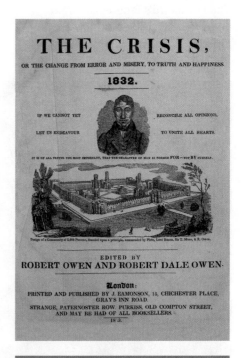

The Crisis, *a publication by the communitarian Robert Owen and his son, Robert Dale Owen. The cover depicts Owen's vision of a planned socialist community.*

circumstances in which they lived. In Owen's scheme, children would be removed at an early age from the care of their parents to be educated in schools where they would be trained to subordinate individual ambition to the common good. Owen also defended women's rights, especially access to education and the right to divorce. At New Harmony, he promised, women would no longer be "enslaved" to their husbands, and "false notions" about innate differences between the sexes would be abandoned.

Harmony eluded the residents of New Harmony. They squabbled about everything from the community's constitution to the distribution of property. Owen's settlement survived for only a few years, but it strongly influenced the labor movement, educational reformers, and women's rights advocates. Owen's vision resonated with the widely held American belief that a community of equals could be created in the New World.

Quite different from Owen's planned system were the short-lived secular communities founded by Josiah Warren, an early American anarchist (one who believes that all institutions that exercise power over individuals, including government, are illegitimate). At Utopia, Ohio, and Modern Times, New York, Warren established totally unregulated voluntary settlements. Like other communitarians, Warren tried to address the sources of labor unrest and women's inequality. In an attempt to solve the labor problem, he created stores where goods were exchanged according to the amount of work that had gone into producing them, thus preventing middlemen like bankers and merchants from sharing in the hard-earned income of farmers, laborers, and manufacturers. Marriage in Warren's communities was a purely voluntary arrangement, since no laws regulated personal behavior. In effect, Warren took American individualism to its logi-

The Drunkard's Progress, *an 1826 anti-liquor broadside illustrating how drinking leads a respectable man and his family to ruin.*

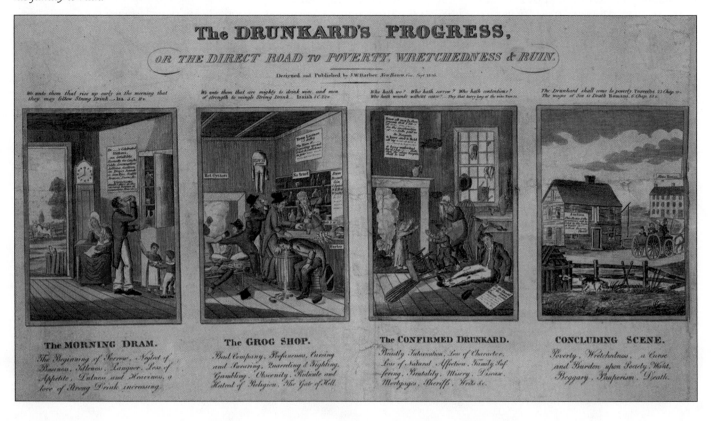

cal extreme. Freedom, he declared, meant "allowing each individual to be absolute despot or sovereign" over himself.

RELIGION AND REFORM

Most Americans saw the ownership of property as the key to economic independence—and, therefore, to freedom—and marriage as the foundation of the social order. Few were likely to join communities that required them to surrender both. Far more typical of the reform impulse were movements that aimed at liberating men and women either from restraints external to themselves, such as slavery and war, or from forms of internal "servitude" like drinking, illiteracy, and a tendency toward criminality. Drinkers, proclaimed one reformer, could not be considered free: they were "chained to alcohol, bound to the demon rum." Many of these reform movements drew their inspiration from the religious revivalism of the Second Great Awakening, discussed in Chapter 9. If, as the revivalist preachers maintained, God had created man as a "free moral agent," sinners could not only reform themselves but could also remake the world.

The revivals popularized the outlook known as "perfectionism," which saw both individuals and society at large as capable of indefinite improvement. Regions like upstate New York and northern Ohio became known as "burned-over districts" because of the intense revivals they experienced in the 1820s and 1830s. Such areas became fertile soil for the era's reform movements and their vision of a society freed from sin. Under the impact of the revivals, older reform efforts moved in a new, radical direction. Temperance (which literally means moderation in the consumption of liquor) was transformed into a crusade to eliminate drinking entirely. Criticism of war became outright pacifism. And, as will be related below, critics of slavery now demanded not gradual emancipation but immediate and total abolition.

THE TEMPERANCE MOVEMENT

To members of the North's emerging middle-class culture, reform became a badge of respectability, an indication that individuals had taken control of their own lives and had become morally accountable human beings. The American Temperance Society, founded in 1826, directed its efforts to redeeming not only habitual drunkards but also the occasional drinker. It claimed by the 1830s to have persuaded hundreds of thousands of Americans to renounce liquor. By 1840, the consumption of alcohol per person had fallen to less than half the level of a decade earlier. (It had peaked in 1830 at seven gallons per person per year, compared to around two gallons today.) During the 1840s, the Washingtonian Society gathered reformed drinkers in "experience meetings" where they offered public testimony about their previous sins.

The temperance crusade and other reform movements aroused considerable hostility. One person's sin is another's pleasure or cherished custom. Those Americans who enjoyed Sunday recreation or a stiff drink from time to time did not think they were any less moral than those who had been reborn at a religious camp meeting, had abandoned drinking, and devoted the Sabbath to religious observances.

A temperance banner from around 1850 depicts a young man torn between a woman in white, who illustrates female purity, and a temptress, who offers him a drink of liquor.

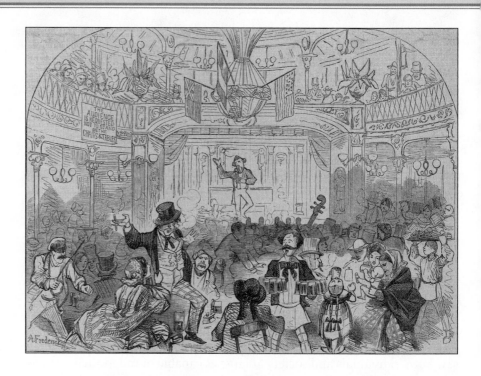

A German Beer Garden on Sunday Evening, *an engraving from* Harper's Weekly, *October 15, 1858. German and Irish immigrants resented efforts of temperance reformers to prohibit the sale of alcoholic beverages.*

CRITICS OF REFORM

Many Americans saw the reform impulse as an attack on their own freedom. Drinking was a prominent feature of festive celebrations and events like militia gatherings. As in the colonial era, taverns were popular meeting places for workingmen in early-nineteenth-century towns and cities, sites not only of drinking but also of political discussions, organizational meetings, and popular recreations. A "Liberty Loving Citizen" of Worcester, Massachusetts, wondered what gave one group of citizens the right to dictate to others how to conduct their personal lives.

American Catholics, their numbers growing because of Irish and German immigration, proved hostile to the reform impulse. Catholics understood freedom in ways quite different from Protestant reformers. They viewed sin as an inescapable burden of individuals and society. The perfectionist idea that evil could be banished from the world struck them as an affront to genuine religion, and they bitterly opposed what they saw as reformers' efforts to impose their own version of Protestant morality on their neighbors. While reformers spoke of man as a free moral agent, Catholics tended to place less emphasis on individual independence and more on the importance of communities centered on family and church. "Man," declared Archbishop John Hughes of New York, the nation's most prominent Catholic leader, was not an autonomous creature but "by his nature, a being of society."

REFORMERS AND FREEDOM

Reformers had to reconcile their desire to create moral order and their quest to enhance personal freedom. They did this through a vision of freedom that was liberating and controlling at the same time. On the one hand, reformers insisted that their goal was to enable Americans to enjoy genuine liberty. In a world in which personal freedom increasingly meant the opportunity to compete for economic gain and individual self-improvement, they spoke of liberating Americans from various forms of "slavery" that made it impossible to succeed—slavery to drink, to poverty, to sin.

On the other hand, reformers insisted that self-fulfillment came through self-discipline. Their definition of the free individual was the person who internalized the practice of self-control. Philip Schaff, a German minister who emigrated to Pennsylvania in 1843, wrote that "true national freedom, in the American view," was "anything but an absence of restraint." Rather, it "rests upon a moral groundwork, upon the virtue of self-possession and self-control in individual citizens." In some ways, reformers believed, American society suffered from an excess of liberty—the anarchic "natural liberty" John Winthrop had warned against in the early days of Puritan Massachusetts, as opposed to the "Christian liberty" of the morally upright citizen.

Many religious groups in the East worried that settlers in the West and immigrants from abroad lacked self-control and led lives of vice, exhibited by drinking, violations of the Sabbath, and lack of Protestant devotion. They formed the American Tract Society, the American Bible Society, and other groups that flooded eastern cities and the western frontier with copies of the gospel and pamphlets promoting religious virtue. Between 1825 and 1835, the pamphlets distributed by the Tract Society amounted to more than 500 million pages. Both their understanding of freedom and their ability to take advantage of the new printing technologies influenced the era's reform movements.

THE INVENTION OF THE ASYLUM

The tension between liberation and control in the era's reform movements was vividly evident in the proliferation of new institutions that reformers hoped could remake human beings into free, morally upright citizens. In colonial America, crime had mostly been punished by whipping, fines, or banishment. The poor received relief in their own homes, orphans lived with neighbors, and families took care of mentally ill members.

The New York House of Refuge, one of many institutions established in the 1820s and 1830s to address social ills by assisting and reforming criminals and the poor. Young boys and girls convicted of petty theft were assigned to the House of Refuge, where they performed supervised labor and received some educational instruction.

During the 1830s and 1840s, Americans embarked on a program of institution building—jails for criminals, poorhouses for the destitute, asylums for the insane, and orphanages for children without families. These institutions differed in many respects, but they shared with communitarians and religious believers in "perfectionism" the idea that social ills once considered incurable could in fact be eliminated. The way to "cure" undesirable elements of society was to place afflicted persons and impressionable youths in an environment where their character could be transformed. Prisons and asylums would eventually become overcrowded places where rehabilitating the inmates seemed less important than simply holding them at bay, away from society. At the outset, however, these institutions were inspired by the conviction that those who passed through their doors could eventually be released to become productive, self-disciplined citizens.

THE COMMON SCHOOL

The largest effort at institution building before the Civil War came in the movement to establish common schools—that is, tax-supported state school systems open to all children. In the early nineteenth century, most children were educated in locally supported schools, private academies, charity schools, or at home, and many had no access to learning at all. School reform reflected the numerous purposes that came together in the era's reform impulse. Horace Mann, a Massachusetts lawyer and Whig politician who served as director of the state's board of education, was the era's leading educational reformer. His annual reports, widely read throughout the country, combined conservatism and radicalism, liberation and social control.

This daguerreotype from around 1850 depicts a classroom in a school for girls presided over by a male teacher.

Mann embraced the new industrial order of his state. But he hoped that universal public education could restore equality to a fractured society by bringing the children of all classes together in a common learning experience and equipping the less fortunate to advance in the social scale. Education would "equalize the conditions of men"—in effect, it would serve as industrial society's alternative to moving west to acquire a farm. This view of free public education as an avenue to social advancement was also shared by the early labor movement, which made the establishment of common schools one of its goals. At the same time, Mann argued that the schools would reinforce social stability by rescuing students from the influence of parents who failed to instill the proper discipline. Character building was as important a function of education as reading, writing, and arithmetic. To some extent, the schools' "silent curriculum"—obedience to authority, promptness in attendance, organizing one's day according to predetermined time periods that changed at the ringing of a bell—helped to prepare students for work in the new industrial economy.

The schools, Mann believed, were training free individuals—meaning persons who internalized self-discipline. But he encountered persistent opposition from parents who did not wish to surrender the moral education of their children to teachers and bureaucrats. Nonetheless, with labor organizations, factory owners, and middle-class reformers all supporting the idea, every northern state by 1860 had established tax-supported school systems for its children. The common school movement created the first real career opportunity for women, who quickly came to dominate the ranks of teachers. The South, where literate blacks were increasingly viewed as a danger to social order and planters had no desire to tax themselves to pay for education for poor white children, lagged far behind in public education. This was one of many ways in which North and South seemed to be growing apart.

THE CRUSADE AGAINST SLAVERY

Compared with drinking, Sabbath-breaking, and illiteracy, the greatest evil in American society at first appeared to attract the least attention from reformers. For many years, it seemed that the only Americans willing to challenge the existence of slavery were Quakers, slaves, and free blacks. After the antislavery impulse spawned by the Revolution died out, the slavery question faded from national life, with occasional eruptions like the Missouri controversy of 1819–1821.

COLONIZATION

Before the 1830s, those white Americans willing to contemplate an end to bondage almost always coupled calls for abolition with the "colonization" of freed slaves—their deportation to Africa, the Caribbean, or Central America. In 1816, proponents of this idea founded the American Colonization Society, which promoted the gradual abolition of slavery and the settlement of black Americans in Africa. It soon established Liberia on the coast of West Africa, an outpost of American influence whose capital, Monrovia, was named for President James Monroe.

Colonization struck many observers as totally impractical. When the English writer Harriet Martineau visited the United States in the 1830s, she was amazed that former president James Madison endorsed the idea. "How such a mind as his" could be convinced that slavery would not end unless blacks were deported from the country she could not understand. In her account of her travels, *Society in America* (1837), she called colonization a way in which "slave-owners who had scruples about holding men as property might, by sending their slaves away over sea, relieve their consciences without annoying their neighbors."

Nonetheless, numerous prominent political leaders of the Jacksonian era—including Henry Clay, John Marshall, Daniel Webster, and Jackson himself—supported the Colonization Society. Many northerners saw colonization as the only way to rid the nation of slavery. Southern supporters of colonization devoted most of their energy to persuading those African-Americans who were already free to leave the United States. Free blacks, they insisted, were a "degraded" group whose presence posed a danger to white society. Other colonizationists believed that slavery and racism were so deeply embedded in American life, that blacks could never

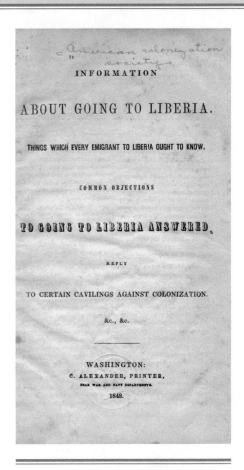

A pamphlet issued in 1848 by the American Colonization Society urging free blacks to emigrate to Liberia, in West Africa, and defending the Society against "certain cavilings"—that is, abolitionist criticism.

achieve equality if freed and allowed to remain in the country. Like Indian removal, colonization rested on the premise that America is fundamentally a white society.

BLACKS AND COLONIZATION

In the decades before the Civil War, several thousand black Americans did emigrate to Liberia with the aid of the Colonization Society. Some were slaves emancipated by their owners on the condition that they depart, while others left voluntarily, motivated by a desire to spread Christianity in Africa or to enjoy rights denied them in the United States. Having experienced "the legal slavery of the South and the social slavery of the North," wrote one emigrant on leaving for Liberia, he knew he could "never be a free man in this country."

But most African-Americans adamantly opposed the idea of colonization. In fact, the formation of the American Colonization Society galvanized free blacks to claim their rights as Americans. Early in 1817, some 3,000 free blacks assembled in Philadelphia for the first national black convention. Their resolutions insisted that blacks were Americans, entitled to the same freedom and rights enjoyed by whites. "We have no wish to separate from our present homes," they declared. In the years that followed, a number of black organizations removed the word "African" from their names to eliminate a possible reason for being deported from the land of their birth.

MILITANT ABOLITIONISM

The abolitionist movement that arose in the 1830s differed profoundly from its genteel, conservative predecessor. Drawing on the religious conviction that slavery was an unparalleled sin and the secular one that it contradicted the values enshrined in the Declaration of Independence, a new generation of reformers rejected the traditional approach of gradual emancipation and demanded immediate abolition. Also unlike their predecessors, they directed explosive language against slavery and slaveholders and insisted that blacks, once free, should be incorporated as equal citizens of the republic rather than being deported. White abolitionists themselves were hardly free of the racism that pervaded American society. Some, indeed, wondered whether the slaves were too "feminine" in character to revolt against oppression, which they claimed manly Anglo-Saxons would surely do. Nonetheless, nearly all abolitionists insisted that economic, civil, and political rights in the United States should be equally enjoyed without regard to race. Perfecting American society, they insisted, meant rooting out not just slavery, but racism in all its forms.

The first indication of the new spirit of abolitionism came in 1829 with the appearance of *An Appeal to the Coloured Citizens of the World* by David Walker, a free black who had been born in North Carolina and now operated a used-clothing store in Boston. A passionate indictment of slavery and racial prejudice, the *Appeal* called on black Americans to mobilize for abolition—by force if necessary—and warned whites that the nation faced divine punishment if it did not mend its sinful ways. Walker invoked the

William Lloyd Garrison, editor of The Liberator *and probably the nation's most prominent abolitionist, in a daguerreotype from around 1850.*

The masthead of William Lloyd Garrison's The Liberator, *with engravings of scenes of slavery and freedom.*

Bible and the Declaration of Independence, but he went beyond these familiar arguments to call on blacks to take pride in the achievements of ancient African civilizations and to claim all their rights as Americans. "Tell us no more about colonization," Walker wrote, addressing white readers, "for America is as much our country as it is yours."

THE EMERGENCE OF GARRISON

Walker's language alarmed both slaveholders and many white critics of slavery. When free black sailors secretly distributed the pamphlet in the South, some southern states put a price on Walker's head. Walker, however, did not create an abolitionist organization, and he died in mysterious circumstances in 1830. Not until the appearance in 1831 of *The Liberator*, William Lloyd Garrison's weekly journal published in Boston, did the new breed of abolitionism find a permanent voice. "I will be as harsh as truth," Garrison announced, "and as uncompromising as justice. On this subject, I do not wish to think, or speak, or write, with moderation. . . . I will not equivocate—I will not excuse—I will not retreat a single inch—and I will be heard."

And heard he was, partly because southerners, outraged by his inflammatory rhetoric (one editorial called slaveowners "an adulterous and perverse generation, a brood of vipers"), reprinted Garrison's editorials in their own newspapers in order to condemn them, thus providing him with instant notoriety. Some of Garrison's ideas, such as his suggestion that the North abrogate the Constitution and dissolve the Union to end its complicity in the evil of slavery, were rejected by many abolitionists. But his call for the immediate abolition of slavery echoed throughout antislavery circles. Garrison's pamphlet, *Thoughts on African Colonization*, persuaded many foes of slavery that blacks must be recognized as part of American society, not viewed as aliens to be shipped overseas. Other antislavery publications soon emerged, but *The Liberator* remained the preeminent abolitionist journal.

SPREADING THE ABOLITIONIST MESSAGE

Beginning with a handful of activists, the abolitionist movement expanded rapidly throughout the North. Antislavery leaders took advantage of the rapid development of print technology and the expansion of literacy due to common school education to spread their message. Like radical pamphlet-

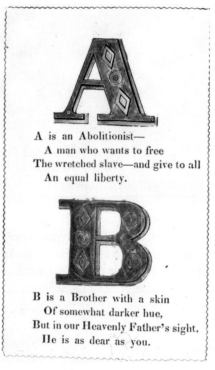

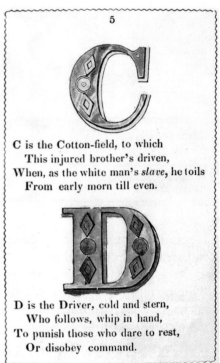

A is an Abolitionist—
   A man who wants to free
The wretched slave—and give to all
   An equal liberty.

B is a Brother with a skin
   Of somewhat darker hue,
But in our Heavenly Father's sight,
   He is as dear as you.

C is the Cotton-field, to which
   This injured brother's driven,
When, as the white man's *slave*, he toils
   From early morn till even.

D is the Driver, cold and stern,
   Who follows, whip in hand,
To punish those who dare to rest,
   Or disobey command.

Pages from an abolitionist book for children. Abolitionists sought to convince young and old of the evils of slavery.

eers of the American Revolution and evangelical ministers of the Second Great Awakening, they recognized the democratic potential in the production of printed material. Abolitionists seized upon the recently invented steam printing press to produce millions of copies of pamphlets, newspapers, petitions, novels, and broadsides. Between the formation of the American Anti-Slavery Society in 1833 and the end of the decade, some 100,000 northerners joined local groups devoted to abolition. Most were ordinary citizens—farmers, shopkeepers, craftsmen, laborers, along with a few prominent businessmen like the merchants Arthur and Lewis Tappan of New York.

If Garrison was the movement's most notable propagandist, Theodore Weld, a young minister who had been converted by the evangelical preacher Charles G. Finney, helped to create its mass constituency. A brilliant orator, Weld trained a band of speakers who brought the abolitionist message into the heart of the rural and small-town North. Their methods were those of the revivals—fervent preaching, lengthy meetings, calls for individuals to renounce their immoral ways—and their message was a simple one: slavery was a sin. "In discussing the subject of slavery," wrote Weld, "I have always presented it as preeminently a moral question, arresting the conscience of the nation. As a question of politics and national economy, I have passed it with scarce a look or a word."

There was far more to Weld's moralistic approach than a concern for religious righteousness. Identifying slavery as a sin was essential to replacing the traditional strategies of gradual emancipation and colonization with immediate abolition. The only proper response to the sin of slavery, abolitionist speakers proclaimed, was the institution's immediate elimination. Weld also supervised the publication of abolitionist pamphlets, including his own *Slavery As It Is* (1839), a compilation of accounts of the maltreatment of slaves. Since Weld took all his examples from the southern press, they could not be dismissed as figments of the northern imagination.

SLAVERY AND MORAL SUASION

Many southerners feared that the abolitionists intended to spark a slave insurrection, a belief strengthened by the outbreak of Nat Turner's Rebellion a few months after *The Liberator* made its appearance. Yet not only was Garrison completely unknown to Turner, but nearly all abolitionists, despite their militant language, rejected violence as a means of ending slavery. Many were pacifists or "non-resistants," who believed that coercion should be eliminated from all human relationships and institutions. Their strategy was "moral suasion" and their arena the public sphere. Slaveholders must be convinced of the sinfulness of their ways, and the North of its complicity in the peculiar institution. (Some critics charged that this approach left nothing for the slaves to do in seeking their own liberation but await the nation's moral regeneration.)

Standing outside established institutions, abolitionists adopted the role of radical social critics. Among the first to appreciate the key role of public opinion in a mass democracy, they focused their efforts not on infiltrating the existing political parties, but on awakening the nation to the moral evil of slavery. Their language was deliberately provocative, calculated to seize public attention. "Slavery," said Garrison, "will not be overthrown without excitement, without a most tremendous excitement."

ABOLITIONISTS AND THE IDEA OF FREEDOM

The abolitionist crusade both reinforced and challenged common understandings of freedom in Jacksonian America. Abolitionists helped to popularize the concept, fortified by the market revolution, that personal freedom derived not from the ownership of productive property such as land

Slave Market of America, an engraving produced by the American Anti-Slavery Society in 1836, illustrates how abolitionists sought to identify their cause with American traditions, even as they mocked the nation's claim to be a "land of the free."

but from ownership of one's self and the ability to enjoy the fruits of one's labor. Abolitionists repudiated the idea of "wage slavery," which had been popularized by the era's labor movement. Compared with the slave, the person working for wages, they insisted, was an embodiment of freedom: the free laborer could change jobs if he wished, accumulate property, and enjoy a stable family life. Only slavery, wrote the abolitionist William Goodell, deprived human beings of their "grand central right—the inherent right of self-ownership."

On the other hand, abolitionists argued that slavery was so deeply embedded in American life that its destruction would require fundamental changes in the North as well as the South. They insisted that the inherent, natural, and absolute right to personal liberty, regardless of race, took precedence over other forms of freedom, such as the right of citizens to accumulate and hold property or self-government by local political communities.

A NEW VISION OF AMERICA

In a society in which the rights of citizenship had become more and more closely associated with whiteness, the antislavery movement sought to reinvigorate the idea of freedom as a truly universal entitlement. The origins of the idea of an American people unbounded by race lies not with the founders, who by and large made their peace with slavery, but with the abolitionists. The antislavery crusade viewed slaves and free blacks as members of the national community, a position summarized in the title of Lydia Maria Child's popular treatise of 1833, *An Appeal in Favor of That Class of Americans Called Africans*. Child's text insisted that blacks were fellow countrymen, not foreigners or a permanently inferior caste. They should no more be considered Africans than whites were Englishmen. The idea that birthplace alone, not race, should determine who was an American, later enshrined in the Fourteenth Amendment, represented a radical departure from the traditions of American life. "We do not admit," declared the *New England Magazine* in 1832, "that America is as much the country of the blacks, bound and free, as it is ours." But abolitionists maintained that the slaves, once freed, should be empowered to participate fully in the public life of the United States. Abolitionists also pioneered the modern idea that human rights took precedence over national sovereignty. They urged the United States to participate in the courts that brought together judges from Britain and other countries to punish those who violated the ban on the Atlantic slave trade. These courts were perhaps the first example of transnational human rights enforcement. But with southerners exerting powerful influence in Washington, the United States did not join the court system until 1862, in the midst of the Civil War.

The crusade against slavery, wrote Angelina Grimké, who became a leading abolitionist speaker, was the nation's preeminent "school in which human rights are . . . investigated." Abolitionists debated the Constitution's relationship to slavery. William Lloyd Garrison burned the document, calling it a covenant with the devil; Frederick Douglass came to believe that it offered no national protection to slavery. But despite this difference of opin-

One of many popular lithographs illustrating scenes from Harriet Beecher Stowe's novel Uncle Tom's Cabin, *the most widely read of all antislavery writings. This depicts the slave Eliza escaping with her child across the ice floes of the Ohio River.*

ion, abolitionists developed an alternative, rights-oriented view of constitutional law, grounded in their universalistic understanding of liberty. Seeking to define the core rights to which all Americans were entitled—the meaning of freedom in concrete legal terms—abolitionists invented the concept of equality before the law regardless of race, one all but unknown in American life before the Civil War. Abolitionist literature also helped to expand the definition of cruelty. The graphic descriptions of the beatings, brandings, and other physical sufferings of the slaves helped to popularize the idea of bodily integrity as a basic right that slavery violated.

Despite being denounced by their opponents as enemies of American principles, abolitionists consciously identified their movement with the revolutionary heritage. The Declaration of Independence was not as fundamental to public oratory in the early republic as it would later become. Abolitionists seized upon it, interpreting the document's preamble as a condemnation of slavery. The Liberty Bell, later one of the nation's most venerated emblems of freedom, did not achieve that status until abolitionists adopted it as a symbol and gave it its name, as part of an effort to identify their principles with those of the founders. (Prior to the 1830s, it was simply the Old State House Bell, used at various times to mark the death of prominent citizens, summon students at the University of Pennsylvania to their classes, and celebrate patriotic holidays.) Of course, Americans of all regions and political beliefs claimed the Revolution's legacy. Mobs that disrupted abolitionist meetings invoked the "spirit of '76," as did southern defenders of slavery. Abolitionists never represented more than a small part of the North's population. But as the slavery controversy intensified, the belief spread far beyond abolitionist circles that slavery contradicted the nation's heritage of freedom.

Harriet Beecher Stowe, author of the abolitionist novel Uncle Tom's Cabin.

BLACK AND WHITE ABOLITIONISM

BLACK ABOLITIONISTS

Blacks played a leading role in the antislavery movement. Even before the appearance of *The Liberator*, as we have seen, northern free blacks had organized in opposition to the Colonization Society. James Forten, a successful black sailmaker in Philadelphia, helped to finance *The Liberator* in its early years. As late as 1834, northern blacks, attracted by Garrison's rejection of colonization and his demand for equal rights for black Americans, made up a majority of the journal's subscribers. Several blacks served on the board of directors of the American Anti-Slavery Society, and northern-born blacks and fugitive slaves quickly emerged as major organizers and speakers.

Frederick Douglass was only one among many former slaves who published accounts of their lives in bondage; these accounts convinced thousands of northerners of the evils of slavery. Indeed, the most effective piece of antislavery literature of the entire period, Harriet Beecher Stowe's novel *Uncle Tom's Cabin*, was to some extent modeled on the autobiography of fugitive slave Josiah Henson. Serialized in 1851 in a Washington antislavery newspaper and published as a book the following year, *Uncle Tom's*

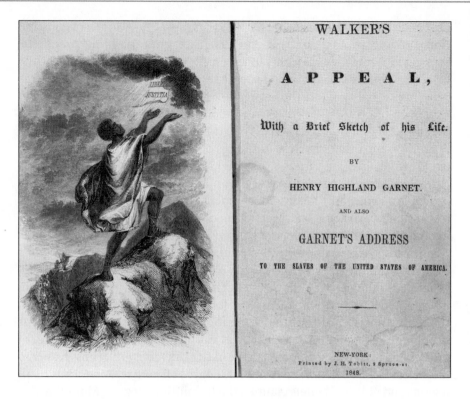

The frontispiece of the 1848 edition of David Walker's Appeal *and Henry Highland Garnet's* Address to the Slaves *depicts a black figure receiving "liberty" and "justice" from heaven.*

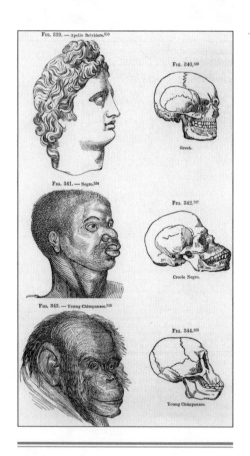

An illustration from Types of Mankind, *an 1854 book by the physicians and racial theorists Josiah C. Nott and George R. Gliddon, who argued that blacks formed a separate species, midway between whites and chimpanzees. Abolitionists sought to counter the pseudoscientific defenses of slavery and racism.*

Cabin sold more than 1 million copies by 1854, and it also inspired numerous stage versions. By portraying slaves as sympathetic men and women, and as Christians at the mercy of slaveholders who split up families and set bloodhounds on innocent mothers and children, Stowe's melodrama gave the abolitionist message a powerful human appeal.

ABOLITIONISM AND RACE

The first racially integrated social movement in American history and the first to give equal rights for blacks a central place in its political agenda, abolitionism was nonetheless a product of its time and place. Racism, as we have seen, was pervasive in nineteenth-century America, North as well as South. White abolitionists could not free themselves entirely from this prejudice. They monopolized the key decision-making posts, charged black spokesman Martin R. Delany, relegating blacks to "a mere secondary, underling position." By the 1840s, black abolitionists sought an independent role within the movement, regularly holding their own conventions. The black abolitionist Henry Highland Garnet, who as a child had escaped from slavery in Maryland with his father, proclaimed at one such gathering in 1843 that slaves should rise in rebellion to throw off their shackles. His position was so at odds with the prevailing belief in moral suasion that the published proceedings entirely omitted the speech. Not until 1848 did Garnet's speech appear in print, along with David Walker's *Appeal*, in a pamphlet partially financed by a then-obscure abolitionist named John Brown.

What is remarkable, however, is not that white abolitionists reflected the prejudices of their society, but the extent to which they managed to rise above them. "While the word 'white' is on the statute-book of Massachusetts," declared Edmund Quincy, an active associate of William Lloyd Garrison, "Massachusetts is a slave state." Defying overwhelming odds, abolitionists launched legal and political battles against racial discrimination in the North. They achieved occasional victories, such as the end of school segregation in Massachusetts in 1855. Not only did abolitionists struggle to overturn northern laws discriminating against blacks but they refused to compromise the principle that the slave was a moral being, created in the image of God. The abolitionist emblem—a portrait of a slave in chains coupled with the motto "Am I Not a Man and a Brother?"—challenged white Americans to face up to the reality that men and women no different from themselves were being held in bondage.

Most adamant in contending that the struggle against slavery required a redefinition of both freedom and Americanness were black members of the abolitionist crusade. Black abolitionists developed an understanding of freedom that went well beyond the usage of most of their white contemporaries. They worked to attack the intellectual foundations of racism, seeking to disprove pseudoscientific arguments for black inferiority. They challenged the prevailing image of Africa as a continent without civilization. Many black abolitionists called on free blacks to seek out skilled and dignified employment in order to demonstrate the race's capacity for advancement.

SLAVERY AND AMERICAN FREEDOM

At every opportunity, black abolitionists rejected the nation's pretensions as a land of liberty. Many free blacks dramatically reversed the common association of the United States with the progress of freedom. Black communities in the North devised an alternative calendar of "freedom celebrations" centered on January 1, the date in 1808 on which the slave trade became illegal, and August 1, the anniversary of West Indian emancipation, rather than July 4. (Many localities forcibly barred them from Independence Day festivities.) In doing so, they offered a stinging rebuke to white Americans' claims to live in a land of freedom. Thanks to its embrace of emancipation in the 1830s, declared a group of black abolitionists in Philadelphia, Britain had become a model of liberty and justice, while the United States remained a land of tyranny.

Even more persistently than their white counterparts, black abolitionists articulated the ideal of color-blind citizenship. "The real battleground between liberty and slavery," wrote Samuel Cornish, "is prejudice against color." (Cornish, a Presbyterian minister, had helped to establish the nation's first black newspaper, *Freedom's Journal*, in New York City in 1827. The first editor, John B. Russwurm, closed the paper after two years and moved to Liberia, explaining, "we consider it a waste of mere words to talk of ever enjoying citizenship in this country.") Black abolitionists also identified the widespread poverty of the free black population as a consequence of slavery and insisted that freedom possessed an economic dimension. It must be part of the "great work" of the antislavery crusade, insisted Charles L. Reason, "to abolish not only chattel slavery, but that other kind of slavery, which, for generation after generation, dooms an oppressed people to a condition of dependence and pauperism."

Am I Not a Man and a Brother? *The most common abolitionist depiction of a slave, this image not only presents African-Americans as unthreatening individuals seeking white assistance but also calls upon white Americans to recognize blacks as fellow men unjustly held in bondage.*

The greatest oration on American slavery and American freedom was delivered in Rochester in 1852 by Frederick Douglass. Speaking just after the annual Independence Day celebration, Douglass posed the question, "What, to the Slave, is the Fourth of July?" (see p. 481 and the Appendix for excerpts from the speech). He answered that Fourth of July festivities revealed the hypocrisy of a nation that proclaimed its belief in liberty yet daily committed "practices more shocking and bloody" than any other country on earth. Like other abolitionists, however, Douglass also laid claim to the founders' legacy. The Revolution had left a "rich inheritance of justice, liberty, prosperity, and independence," from which subsequent generations had tragically strayed. Only by abolishing slavery and freeing the "great doctrines" of the Declaration of Independence from the "narrow bounds" of race could the United States recapture its original mission.

GENTLEMEN OF PROPERTY AND STANDING

At first, abolitionism aroused violent hostility from northerners who feared that the movement threatened to disrupt the Union, interfere with profits wrested from slave labor, and overturn white supremacy. Led by "gentlemen of property and standing" (often merchants with close commercial ties to the South), mobs disrupted abolitionist meetings in northern cities. In 1835, a Boston crowd led William Lloyd Garrison through the streets with a rope around his neck. The editor barely escaped with his life. In the following year, a Cincinnati mob destroyed the printing press of James G. Birney, a former slaveholder who had been converted to abolitionism by Theodore Weld and had been forced to flee Kentucky for the North.

In 1837, antislavery editor Elijah P. Lovejoy became the movement's first martyr when he was killed by a mob in Alton, Illinois, while defending his

A New Method of Assorting the Mail, As Practised by Southern Slave-Holders, *an engraving criticizing the burning of abolitionist materials taken from the U.S. Post Office in Charleston in 1835.*

Destruction by Fire of Pennsylvania Hall, *a lithograph depicting the burning of the abolitionist meeting hall by a Philadelphia mob in 1838.*

press. A native of Maine and a Presbyterian minister, Lovejoy had begun his editorial career in the slave state of Missouri but had soon been forced to move to Illinois. His message, that "the system of Negro slavery is an awful evil and sin," won few converts in Alton, then the state's largest city, which enjoyed a flourishing trade with the South. Four times, mobs destroyed his printing press, only to see Lovejoy resume publication. The fifth attack ended in his death. In 1838, a mob in Philadelphia burned to the ground Pennsylvania Hall, which abolitionists had built to hold their meetings. Before starting the fire, however, the mob patriotically carried a portrait of George Washington to safety.

Elsewhere, crowds of southerners, with the unspoken approval of Andrew Jackson's postmaster general, Amos Kendall, burned abolitionist literature that they had removed from the mails. In 1836, when abolitionists began to flood Washington with petitions calling for emancipation in the nation's capital, the House of Representatives adopted the notorious "gag rule," which prohibited their consideration. The rule was repealed in 1844, thanks largely to the tireless opposition of former president John Quincy Adams, who since 1831 had represented Massachusetts in the House.

SLAVERY AND CIVIL LIBERTIES

Far from stemming the movement's growth, however, mob attacks and attempts to limit abolitionists' freedom of speech convinced many northerners that slavery was incompatible with the democratic liberties of white Americans. In a speech after Lovejoy's murder, Theodore Weld commented on the contrast between Americans' self-confident claims to freedom and the reality of anti-abolitionist violence: "The empty name is everywhere—*free* government, *free* men, *free* speech, *free* schools, and *free* churches. Hollow counterfeits all! . . . The substance has gone." It was the murder of Lovejoy that led Wendell Phillips, who became one of the movement's greatest orators, to associate himself with the abolitionist cause. "We commenced the present struggle," announced abolitionist William Jay, "to obtain the freedom of the slave; we are compelled to continue it to preserve our own. We are now contending . . . for the liberty of speech, of the press, and of conscience."

The abolitionist movement now broadened its appeal so as to win the support of northerners who cared little about the rights of blacks but could be convinced that slavery endangered their own cherished freedoms. The gag rule aroused considerable resentment in the North. "If the government once begins to discriminate as to what is orthodox and what heterodox in opinion," wrote the *New York Evening Post*, hardly a supporter of abolitionism, "farewell, a long farewell to our freedom."

For many years, the American public sphere excluded discussion of slavery. Tocqueville had noted that in a democracy, individual dissenters found it difficult to stand up against the overwhelming power of majority opinion. Americans valued free speech, he wrote, but he did "not know any country where, in general, less independence of mind and genuine freedom of discussion reign than in America." The fight for the right to debate slavery openly and without reprisal led abolitionists to elevate "free opinion"—freedom of speech and of the press and the right of petition—to a central place in what Garrison called the "gospel of freedom." In defending free speech, abolitionists claimed to have become custodians of the "rights of every freeman."

THE ORIGINS OF FEMINISM

THE RISE OF THE PUBLIC WOMAN

"When the true history of the antislavery cause shall be written," Frederick Douglass later recalled, "women will occupy a large space in its pages." Much of the movement's grassroots strength derived from northern women, who joined by the thousands. Most were evangelical Protestants, New England Congregationalists, or Quakers convinced, as Martha Higginson of Vermont wrote, that slavery was "a disgrace in this land of Christian light and liberty." A few became famous, but most antislavery women remain virtually unknown to history. One such activist was Lucy Colman, whose mother sang her antislavery songs when she was a child. Colman's career illustrated how the era's reform movements often overlapped. She became an abolitionist lecturer, a teacher at a school for blacks in upstate New York, an advocate of women's rights, and an opponent of capital punishment.

The public sphere was open to women in ways government and party politics were not. Long before they could vote, women circulated petitions, attended meetings, marched in parades, and delivered public lectures. They became active in the temperance movement, the building of asylums, and other reform activities. Dorothea Dix, a Massachusetts schoolteacher, for example, was the leading advocate of more humane treatment of the insane, who at the time generally were placed in jails alongside debtors and hardened criminals. Thanks to her efforts, twenty-eight states constructed

VISIONS OF FREEDOM

A Women's Rights Quilt. *Made by an unknown woman only a few years after the Seneca Falls Convention of 1848, this quilt embodies an unusual form of political expression. It includes scenes visualizing a woman engaged in various activities that violated the era's cult of domesticity, and it illustrates some of the demands of the early women's rights movement. The individual blocks show a woman driving her own buggy and a banner advocating "women's rights," another dressing to go out while her husband remains at home wearing an apron, and a third addressing a public meeting with a mixed male-female audience.*

QUESTIONS

1. Which aspects of freedom does the quiltmaker emphasize?

2. What aspects of women's rights are not depicted in the quilt?

The May Session of the Woman's Rights Convention, *a cartoon published in* Harper's Weekly, *June 11, 1859. A female orator addresses the audience of men and women, while hecklers in the balcony disrupt the proceedings.*

mental hospitals before the Civil War. In 1834, middle-class women in New York City organized the Female Moral Reform Society, which sought to redeem prostitutes from lives of sin and to protect the morality of single women. They attacked the era's sexual double standard by publishing lists of men who frequented prostitutes or abused women. By 1840, the society had been replicated in hundreds of American communities.

WOMEN AND FREE SPEECH

All these activities enabled women to carve out a place in the public sphere. But it was participation in abolitionism that inspired the early movement for women's rights. In working for the rights of the slave, not a few women developed a new understanding of their own subordinate social and legal status. The daughters of a prominent South Carolina slaveholder, Angelina and Sarah Grimké had been converted first to Quakerism and then abolitionism while visiting Philadelphia. During the 1830s, they began to deliver popular lectures that offered a scathing condemnation of slavery from the perspective of those who had witnessed its evils firsthand.

The Grimké sisters were neither the first women to lecture in public nor the first to be feverishly condemned by self-proclaimed guardians of female modesty. Frances Wright, a Scottish-born follower of reformer Robert Owen, spoke at New York's Hall of Science in the late 1820s and early 1830s, on subjects ranging from communitarianism to slavery, women's rights, and the plight of northern laborers. One New York newspaper called Wright a "female monster" for "shamefully obtruding herself upon the public." Maria Stewart, a black Bostonian, in 1832 became the first American woman to lecture to mixed male and female audiences. She, too, received intense criticism. "I have made myself contemptible in the eyes of many," Stewart wrote. "This is the land of freedom," she added, "and we claim our rights," including the right to speak in public.

Stewart left Boston in 1833 and rarely lectured again. The Grimké sisters, however, used the controversy over their speeches as a springboard for a vigorous argument against the idea that taking part in assemblies, demonstrations, and lectures was unfeminine. Outraged by the sight of females sacrificing all "modesty and delicacy" by appearing on the public lecture platform, a group of Massachusetts clergymen denounced the sisters. In reply, they forthrightly defended not only the right of women to take part in political debate but also their right to share the social and educational privileges enjoyed by men. "Since I engaged in the investigation of the rights of the slave," declared Angelina Grimké, "I have necessarily been led to a better understanding of my own." Her sister Sarah proceeded to publish *Letters on the Equality of the Sexes* (1838), a powerful call for equal rights for women and a critique of the notion of separate spheres. The book raised numerous issues familiar even today, including what later generations would call "equal pay for equal work." Why, Sarah Grimké wondered, did male teachers invariably receive higher wages than women, and a male tailor earn "two or three times as much" as a female counterpart "although the work done by each may be equally good?"

WOMEN'S RIGHTS

The Grimkés were the first to apply the abolitionist doctrine of universal freedom and equality to the status of women. When the prominent writer Catharine Beecher reprimanded the sisters for stepping outside "the domestic and social sphere," urging them to accept the fact that "heaven" had designated man "the superior" and woman "the subordinate," Angelina Grimké issued a stinging answer. "I know nothing," she wrote, "of men's rights and women's rights. My doctrine, then is, that whatever it is morally right for man to do, it is morally right for woman to do." Like their predecessors Frances Wright and Maria Stewart, the Grimké sisters soon retired from the fray, unwilling to endure the intense criticism to which they were subjected. But their writings helped to spark the movement for women's rights, which arose in the 1840s.

Elizabeth Cady Stanton and Lucretia Mott, the key organizers of the Seneca Falls Convention of 1848, were veterans of the antislavery crusade. In 1840, they had traveled to London as delegates to the World Anti-Slavery Convention, only to be barred from participating because of their sex. The Seneca Falls Convention, a gathering on behalf of women's rights held in the upstate New York town where Stanton lived, raised the issue of woman's suffrage for the first time. Stanton, the principal author, modeled the Seneca Falls Declaration of Sentiments on the Declaration of Independence (see the Appendix for the full text). But the document added "women" to Jefferson's axiom "all men are created equal," and in place of a list of injustices committed by George III, it condemned the "injuries and usurpations on the part of man toward woman." The first to be listed was denying her the right to vote. As Stanton told the convention, only the vote would make woman "free as man is free," since in a democratic society, freedom was impossible without access to the ballot. The argument was

VOICES OF FREEDOM

FROM ANGELINA GRIMKÉ,
Letter in *The Liberator* (August 2, 1837)

The daughters of a prominent South Carolina slaveholder, Angelina and Sarah Grimké became abolitionists after being sent to Philadelphia for education. In this article, Angelina Grimké explains how participation in the movement against slavery led her to a greater recognition of women's lack of basic freedoms.

Since I engaged in the investigation of the rights of the slave, I have necessarily been led to a better understanding of my own; for I have found the Anti-Slavery cause to be . . . the school in which human rights are more fully investigated, and better understood and taught, than in any other [reform] enterprise. . . . Here we are led to examine why human beings have any rights. It is because they are moral beings. . . . Now it naturally occurred to me, that if rights were founded in moral being, then the circumstance of sex could not give to man higher rights and responsibilities, than to woman. . . .

When I look at human beings as moral beings, all distinction in sex sinks to insignificance and nothingness; for I believe it regulates rights and responsibilities no more than the color of the skin or the eyes. My doctrine, then is, that whatever it is morally right for man to do, it is morally right for woman to do. . . . This regulation of duty by the mere circumstance of sex . . . has led to all that [numerous] train of evils flowing out of the anti-christian doctrine of masculine and feminine virtues. By this doctrine, man has been converted into the warrior, and clothed in sternness . . . whilst woman has been taught to lean upon an arm of flesh, to . . . be admired for her personal charms, and caressed and humored like a spoiled child, or converted into a mere drudge to suit the convenience of her lord and master. . . . It has robbed woman of . . . the right to think and speak and act on all great moral questions, just as men think and speak and act. . . .

The discussion of the wrongs of slavery has opened the way for the discussion of other rights, and the ultimate result will most certainly be . . . the letting of the oppressed of every grade and description go free.

FROM FREDERICK DOUGLASS,
Speech on July 5, 1852, Rochester, New York

One of the most prominent reform leaders of his era, Frederick Douglass escaped from slavery in 1838 and soon became an internationally known writer and orator against slavery. His speech of July 1852 condemned the hypocrisy of a nation that proclaimed its devotion to freedom while practicing slavery. It was reprinted in 1855 in his autobiography, *My Bondage and My Freedom.*

Fellow-citizens, pardon me, allow me to ask, why am I called upon to speak here to-day? What have I, or those I represent, to do with your national independence? Are the great principles of political freedom and of natural justice, embodied in that Declaration of Independence, extended to us? . . . Such is not the case. I say it with a sad sense of the disparity between us. I am not included within the pale of this glorious anniversary! Your high independence only reveals the immeasurable distance between us. . . . The rich inheritance of justice, liberty, prosperity and independence, bequeathed by your fathers, is shared by you, not by me. . . .

For the present, it is enough to affirm the equal manhood of the negro race. Is it not astonishing that, while we are ploughing, planting and reaping, using all kinds of mechanical tools, erecting houses, constructing bridges, building ships, . . . acting as clerks, merchants and secretaries . . . confessing and worshiping the Christian's God, and looking hopefully for life and immortality beyond the grave, we are called upon to prove that we are men! . . .

Would you have me argue that man is entitled to liberty? That he is the rightful owner of his body? You have already declared it. Must I argue the wrongfulness of slavery? . . . that men have a natural right to freedom? . . . To do so, would be to make myself ridiculous, and to offer an insult to your understanding. There is not a man beneath the canopy of heaven, that does not know that slavery is wrong *for him.* . . .

What, to the American slave, is your 4th of July? I answer: a day that reveals to him, more than all other days in the year, the gross injustice and cruelty to which he is the constant victim. To him, your celebration is a sham; your boasted liberty, an unholy license; your national greatness, swelling vanity; your sounds of rejoicing are empty and heartless; your denunciations of tyrants, brass fronted impudence; your shouts of liberty and equality, hollow mockery—a thin veil to cover up crimes that would disgrace a nation of savages. There is not a nation on the earth guilty of practices, more shocking and bloody, than are the people of these United States, at this very hour.

====

QUESTIONS

1. What consequences does Grimké believe follow from the idea of rights being founded in the individual's "moral being"?

2. How does Douglass turn the ideals proclaimed by white Americans into weapons against slavery?

3. What do these documents suggest about the language and arguments employed by abolitionists?

Portrait of feminist Margaret Fuller (1810–1850) from an undated daguerreotype.

simple and irrefutable: in the words of Lydia Maria Child, "either the theory of our government [the democratic principle that government rests on the will of the people] is *false*, or women have a right to vote."

Seneca Falls marked the beginning of the seventy-year struggle for woman's suffrage. The vote, however, was hardly the only issue raised at the convention. The Declaration of Sentiments condemned the entire structure of inequality that denied women access to education and employment, gave husbands control over the property and wages of their wives and custody of children in the event of divorce, deprived women of independent legal status after they married, and restricted them to the home as their "sphere of action." Equal rights became the rallying cry of the early movement for women's rights, and equal rights meant claiming access to all the prevailing definitions of freedom.

FEMINISM AND FREEDOM

Like abolitionism, temperance, and other reforms, women's rights was an international movement. Lacking broad backing at home, early feminists found allies abroad. "Women alone will say what freedom they want," declared an article in *The Free Woman*, a journal established in Paris in 1832. With their household chores diminished because of the availability of manufactured goods and domestic servants, many middle-class women chafed at the restrictions that made it impossible for them to gain an education, enter the professions, and in other ways exercise their talents. Whether married or not, early feminists insisted, women deserved the range of individual choices—the possibility of self-realization—that constituted the essence of freedom.

Women, wrote Margaret Fuller, had the same right as men to develop their talents, to "grow . . . to live freely and unimpeded." The daughter of a Jeffersonian congressman, Fuller was educated at home, at first under her father's supervision (she learned Latin before the age of six) and later on her own. She became part of New England's transcendentalist circle (discussed in Chapter 9) and from 1840 to 1842 edited *The Dial*, a magazine that reflected the group's views. In 1844, Fuller became literary editor of the *New York Tribune*, the first woman to achieve so important a position in American journalism.

In *Woman in the Nineteenth Century*, published in 1845, Fuller sought to apply to women the transcendentalist idea that freedom meant a quest for personal development. "Every path" to self-fulfillment, she insisted, should be "open to woman as freely as to man." Fuller singled out Abby Kelley as a "gentle hero" for continuing to speak in public despite being denounced by men for venturing "out of her sphere." Fearing that marriage to an American would inevitably mean subordination to male dictation, Fuller traveled to Europe as a correspondent for the *Tribune*. There she married an Italian patriot. Along with her husband and baby, she died in a shipwreck in 1850 while returning to the United States.

WOMEN AND WORK

Women also demanded the right to participate in the market revolution. At an 1851 women's rights convention, the black abolitionist Sojourner Truth

Woman's Emancipation, *a satirical engraving from* Harper's Monthly, *August 1851, illustrating the much-ridiculed "Bloomer" costume.*

insisted that the movement devote attention to the plight of poor and working-class women and repudiate the idea that women were too delicate to engage in work outside the home. Born a slave in New York State around 1799, Truth did not obtain her freedom until the state's emancipation law of 1827. A listener at her 1851 speech (which was not recorded at the time) later recalled that Truth had spoken of her years of hard physical labor, had flexed her arm to show her strength, and exclaimed, "and aren't I a woman?"

Although those who convened at Seneca Falls were predominantly from the middle class—no representatives of the growing number of "factory girls" and domestic servants took part—the participants rejected the identification of the home as the women's "sphere." Women, wrote Pauline Davis in 1853, "must go *to work*" to emancipate themselves from "bondage." During the 1850s, some feminists tried to popularize a new style of dress, devised by Amelia Bloomer, consisting of a loose-fitting tunic and trousers. In her autobiography, published in 1898, Elizabeth Cady Stanton recalled that women who adopted Bloomer's attire were ridiculed by the press and insulted by "crowds of boys in the streets." They found that "the physical freedom enjoyed did not compensate for the persistent persecution and petty annoyances suffered at every turn." The target of innumerable male jokes, the "bloomer" costume attempted to make a serious point—that the long dresses, tight corsets, and numerous petticoats considered to be appropriate female attire were so confining that they made it almost impossible for women to claim a place in the public sphere or to work outside the home.

In one sense, feminism demanded an expansion of the boundaries of freedom rather than a redefinition of the idea. Women, in the words of one reformer, should enjoy "the rights and liberties that every 'free white male citizen' takes to himself as God-given." But even as it sought to apply prevailing notions of freedom to women, the movement posed a fundamental challenge to some of society's central beliefs—that the capacity for independence and rationality were male traits, that the world was properly

Am I Not a Woman and a Sister?, *an illustration from* The Liberator, *1849. Identifying with the plight of the female slave enabled free women to see more clearly the inequalities they themselves faced.*

divided into public and private realms, and that issues of justice and freedom did not apply to relations within the family. In every realm of life, including the inner workings of the family, declared Elizabeth Cady Stanton, there could be "no happiness without freedom."

THE SLAVERY OF SEX

The dichotomy between freedom and slavery powerfully shaped early feminists' political language. Just as the idea of "wage slavery" enabled northern workers to challenge the inequalities inherent in market definitions of freedom, the concept of the "slavery of sex" empowered the women's movement to develop an all-encompassing critique of male authority and their own subordination. Feminists of the 1840s and 1850s pointed out that the law of marriage made nonsense of the description of the family as a "private" institution independent of public authority. When the abolitionists and women's rights activitists Lucy Stone and Henry Blackwell married, they felt obliged to repudiate New York's laws that clothed the husband "with legal powers which . . . no man should possess."

Feminist abolitionists did not invent the analogy between marriage and slavery. The English writer Mary Wollstonecraft had invoked it as early as the 1790s in *A Vindication of the Rights of Woman* (discussed in Chapter 8). But the analogy between free women and slaves gained prominence as it was swept up in the accelerating debate over slavery. "Woman is a slave, from the cradle to the grave," asserted Ernestine Rose. "Father, guardian, husband—master still. One conveys her, like a piece of property, over to the other." For their part, southern defenders of slavery frequently linked slavery and marriage as natural and just forms of inequality. Eliminating the former institution, they charged, would threaten the latter.

Marriage was not, literally speaking, equivalent to slavery. The married woman, however, did not enjoy the fruits of her own labor—a central element of freedom. Beginning with Mississippi in 1839, numerous states enacted married women's property laws, shielding from a husband's creditors property brought into a marriage by his wife. Such laws initially aimed not to expand women's rights as much as to prevent families from losing their property during the depression that began in 1837. But in 1860, New York enacted a more far-reaching measure, allowing married women to sign contracts, buy and sell property, and keep their own wages. In most states, however, property accumulated after marriage, as well as wages earned by the wife, still belonged to the husband.

"SOCIAL FREEDOM"

Influenced by abolitionism, women's rights advocates turned another popular understanding of freedom—self-ownership, or control over one's own person—in an entirely new direction. The emphasis in abolitionist literature on the violation of the slave woman's body by her master helped to give the idea of self-ownership a concrete reality that encouraged application to free women as well. The law of domestic relations presupposed the husband's right of sexual access to his wife and to inflict corporal punishment on her. Courts proved reluctant to intervene in cases of physical abuse so long as it was not "extreme" or "intolerable." "Women's Rights," declared a Boston meeting in 1859, included "freedom and equal rights in the family." The demand that women should enjoy the rights to regulate their own sexual activity and procreation and to be protected by the state against violence at the hands of their husbands challenged the notion that claims for justice, freedom, and individual rights should stop at the household's door.

The issue of women's private freedom revealed underlying differences within the movement for women's rights. Belief in equality between the sexes and in the sexes' natural differences coexisted in antebellum feminist thought. Even as they entered the public sphere and thereby challenged some aspects of the era's "cult of domesticity" (discussed in Chapter 9), many early feminists accepted other elements. Allowing women a greater role in the public sphere, many female reformers argued, would bring their "inborn" maternal instincts to bear on public life, to the benefit of the entire society.

Even feminists critical of the existing institution of marriage generally refrained from raising in public the explosive issue of women's "private" freedom. The question frequently arose, however, in the correspondence of feminist leaders. "Social Freedom," Susan B. Anthony observed to Lucy Stone, "lies at the bottom of all—and until woman gets that, she must continue the slave of men in all other things." Women like Anthony, who never married, and Stone, who with her husband created their own definition of marriage, reflected the same dissatisfactions with traditional family life as the women who joined communitarian experiments. Not until the twentieth century would the demand that freedom be extended to intimate aspects of life inspire a mass movement. But the dramatic fall in the birthrate over the course of the nineteenth century suggests that many women were quietly exercising "personal freedom" in their most intimate relationships.

THE ABOLITIONIST SCHISM

Even in reform circles, the demand for a greater public role for women remained extremely controversial. Massachusetts physician Samuel Gridley Howe pioneered humane treatment of the blind and educational reform, and he was an ardent abolitionist. But Howe did not support his wife's participation in the movement for female suffrage, which, he complained, caused her to "neglect domestic relations." When organized abolitionism split into two wings in 1840, the immediate cause was a dispute over the proper role of women in antislavery work. Abby Kelley's appointment to the business committee of the American Anti-Slavery Society sparked the formation of a rival abolitionist organization, the American and Foreign Anti-Slavery Society, which believed it wrong for a woman to occupy so prominent a position. The antislavery poet John Greenleaf Whittier compared Kelley to Eve, Delilah, and Helen of Troy, women who had sown the seeds of male destruction.

Behind the split lay the fear among some abolitionists that Garrison's radicalism on issues like women's rights, as well as his refusal to support the idea of abolitionists voting or running for public office, impeded the movement's growth. Determined to make abolitionism a political movement, the seceders formed the Liberty Party, which nominated

This image appeared on the cover of the sheet music for "Get Off the Track!", a song popularized by the Hutchinson singers, who performed antislavery songs. The trains Immediate Emancipation *(with* The Liberator *as its front wheel) and* Liberty Party *pull into a railroad station. The* Herald of Freedom *and* American Standard *were antislavery newspapers. The song's lyrics praised William Lloyd Garrison and criticized various politicians, among them Henry Clay. The chorus went: "Roll it along! Through the nation / Freedom's car, Emancipation."*

James G. Birney as its candidate for president. He received only 7,000 votes (about one-third of 1 percent of the total). In 1840, antislavery northerners saw little wisdom in "throwing away" their ballots on a third-party candidate.

While the achievement of most of their demands lay far in the future, the women's rights movement succeeded in making "the woman question" a permanent part of the transatlantic discussion of social reform. As for abolitionism, although it remained a significant presence in northern public life until emancipation was achieved, by 1840 the movement had accomplished its most important work. More than 1,000 local antislavery societies were now scattered throughout the North, representing a broad constituency awakened to the moral issue of slavery. The "great duty of freedom," Ralph Waldo Emerson had declared in 1837, was "to open our halls to discussion of this question." The abolitionists' greatest achievement lay in shattering the conspiracy of silence that had sought to preserve national unity by suppressing public debate over slavery.

SUGGESTED READING

BOOKS

Bestor, Arthur E. *Backwoods Utopias: The Sectarian and Owenite Phases of Communitarian Socialism in America* (1948). An account of some of the numerous communitarian experiments in pre–Civil War America.

Boylan, Anne M. *The Origins of Women's Activism: New York and Boston, 1797–1840* (2002). Considers how middle-class urban women organized numerous associations for social improvement and thereby gained a place in the public sphere.

Burin, Eric. *Slavery and the Peculiar Solution: A History of the American Colonization Society* (2005). A history of the movement to send black Americans, free and slave, to Africa.

Bushman, Claudia L. and Richard L. Bushman. *Building the Kingdom: A History of Mormons in America* (2001). A survey of the history of American Mormons.

Goodman, Paul. *Of One Blood: Abolitionists and the Origins of Racial Equality* (1998). Explores the origins of racial egalitarianism in the movement against slavery.

Harding, Vincent. *There Is a River: The Black Struggle for Freedom in America* (1981). A study that links slave resistance and black abolitionism as phases of a common struggle for freedom.

Jeffrey, Julie R. *The Great Silent Army of Abolitionism: Ordinary Women in the Antislavery Movement* (1998). The role of women as the grassroots foot soldiers of the abolitionist movement.

Kaestle, Carl F. *Pillars of the Republic: Common Schools and American Society, 1780–1860* (1983). Surveys the movement to introduce free public education in the United States.

Kraditor, Aileen S. *Means and Ends in American Abolitionism* (1969). An influential discussion of the political strategies of Garrisonian abolitionists.

McGreevy, John T. *Catholicism and American Freedom* (2003). Contains an illuminating discussion of how Catholics responded to Protestant-based reform movements.

Nye, Russell B. *Fettered Freedom: Civil Liberties and the Slavery Controversy, 1830–1860* (1949). Examines the impact of mob activities and other violations of civil liberties on the growth of abolitionism.

Rothman, David J. *The Discovery of the Asylum: Social Order and Disorder in the New Republic* (1971). Relates the rise of prisons, orphanages, and asylums and their common characteristics.

Stewart, James B. *Holy Warriors: The Abolitionists and American Slavery* (rev. ed., 1996). A recent survey of the history of the antislavery movement.

Tyrrell, Ian. *Sobering Up: From Temperance to Prohibition in Antebellum America, 1800–1860* (1979). Traces the movement against the sale and use of liquor and how it changed in the first part of the nineteenth century.

WEBSITES

Samuel J. May Anti-Slavery Collection: http://dlxs.library.cornell.edu/m/mayanti slavery/

Women and Social Movements in the United States, 1600–2000: http://asp6new .alexanderstreet.com/wam2/wam2.index.map.aspx

REVIEW QUESTIONS

1. To what degree was antebellum reform international in scope?

2. What were the aims of prisons, asylums, and other institutions in this period of social change?

3. Why did Horace Mann believe that universal public education would return both equality and stability to a society fractured by the market revolution?

4. Why did so many prominent Americans, from both the North and South, support the colonization of freed slaves?

5. What was the strategy of "moral suasion" and why did most early abolitionists advocate this policy? How successful was it?

6. How was racism evident even in the abolitionist movement, and what steps did some abolitionists take to fight racism in American society?

7. How could antebellum women participate in the public sphere even though they were excluded from government and politics?

8. How did women's participation in the abolitionist movement enable them to raise issues of their own natural rights and freedoms?

9. How did the feminism of this period challenge traditional gender beliefs and social structures?

FREEDOM QUESTIONS

1. What freedoms did the Shakers and Mormons seek for their members?

2. Compare the limitations to freedom for slaves and white women in this period.

3. How did the physical and legal assaults on abolitionists become perceived as attacks on the liberties of all white Americans in the North?

4. How did the abolitionist movement promote the idea of freedom as universal, and thus alter the national definition of liberty?

5. Some reformers believed that government power could be a force for freedom. Other groups saw the reform movements as attacks on freedom and the community. Explain both views.

KEY TERMS

utopian communities (p. 456)

polygamy (p. 458)

secular communitarian (p. 459)

"perfectionism" (p. 461)

temperance movement (p. 461)

self-discipline (p. 462)

common school (p. 464)

public education (p. 464)

American Colonization Society
(p. 465)

American Anti-Slavery Society
(p. 468)

"moral suasion" (p. 469)

Uncle Tom's Cabin (p. 471)

"Am I Not a Man and a Brother?"
(p. 473)

"gentlemen of property and
standing" (p. 474)

gag rule (p. 476)

Dorothea Dix (p. 476)

woman suffrage (p. 479)

Woman in the Nineteenth Century
(p. 482)

Liberty Party (p. 485)

REVIEW TABLE

Reform Organizations

Society	Date	Purpose
American Colonization Society	1816	To promote the gradual abolition of slavery and the settlement of black Americans in Africa
American Temperance Society	1826	To redeem all drinkers
American Anti-Slavery Society	1833	To abolish slavery immediately
Female Moral Reform Society	1834	To redeem prostitutes from lives of sin and protect the morality of single women

Chapter 13

A House Divided, 1840–1861

Abraham Lincoln's nickname, "The Railsplitter," recalled his humble origins. An unknown artist created this larger-than-life portrait. The White House is visible in the distance. The painting is said to have been displayed during campaign rallies in 1860.

FOCUS QUESTIONS

- What were the major factors contributing to U.S. territorial expansion in the 1840s?

- Why did the expansion of slavery become the most divisive political issue in the 1840s and 1850s?

- What combination of issues and events fueled the creation of the Republican Party in the 1850s?

- What enabled Lincoln to emerge as president from the divisive party politics of the 1850s?

- What were the final steps on the road to secession?

In 1855, Thomas Crawford, one of the era's most prominent American sculptors, was asked to design a statue to adorn the Capitol's dome, still under construction in Washington, D.C. He proposed a statue of Freedom, a female figure wearing a liberty cap. Secretary of War Jefferson Davis of Mississippi, one of the country's largest slaveholders, objected to Crawford's plan. A familiar symbol in the colonial era, the liberty cap had fallen into disfavor among some Americans after becoming closely identified with the French Revolution. Davis's disapproval, however, rested on other grounds. Ancient Romans, he noted, regarded the cap as "the badge of the freed slave." Its use, he feared, might suggest that there was a connection between the slaves' longing for freedom and the liberty of free-born Americans. Davis ordered the liberty cap replaced with a less controversial military symbol, a feathered helmet.

Crawford died in Italy, where he had spent most of his career, in 1857. Two years later, the colossal Statue of Freedom, which weighed 15,000 pounds, was transported to the United States in several pieces and assembled at a Maryland foundry under the direction of Philip Reed, a slave craftsman. In 1863, it was installed atop the Capitol, where it can still be seen today. By the time it was put in place, the country was immersed in the Civil War and Jefferson Davis had become president of the Confederate States of America. The dispute over the Statue of Freedom

The original and final designs for Thomas Crawford's Statue of Freedom *for the dome of the Capitol building. Secretary of War Jefferson Davis of Mississippi insisted that the liberty cap in the first design, a symbol of the emancipated slave in ancient Rome, be replaced.*

offers a small illustration of how, by the mid-1850s, nearly every public question was being swept up into the gathering storm over slavery.

FRUITS OF MANIFEST DESTINY

CONTINENTAL EXPANSION

In the 1840s, slavery moved to the center stage of American politics. It did so not in the moral language or with the immediatist program of abolitionism, but as a result of the nation's territorial expansion. By 1840, with the completion of Indian removal, virtually all the land east of the Mississippi River was in white hands. The depression that began in 1837 sparked a large migration of settlers further west. Some headed to Oregon, whose Willamette Valley was reputed to be one of the continent's most beautiful and fertile regions. Until the 1840s, the American presence in the area had been limited to a few fur traders and explorers. But between 1840 and 1845, some 5,000 emigrants made the difficult 2,000-mile journey by wagon train to Oregon from jumping-off places on the banks of the Missouri River. By 1860, nearly 300,000 men, women, and children had braved disease, starvation, the natural barrier of the Rocky Mountains, and occasional Indian attacks to travel overland to Oregon and California.

During most of the 1840s, the United States and Great Britain jointly administered Oregon, and Utah was part of Mexico. This did not stop Americans from settling in either region. National boundaries meant little to those who moved west. The 1840s witnessed an intensification of the old belief that God intended the American nation to reach all the way to the Pacific Ocean. As noted in Chapter 9, the term that became a shorthand for this expansionist spirit was "manifest destiny."

A rare photograph of wagons on their way to Oregon during the 1840s.

VISIONS OF FREEDOM

American Progress. *This 1872 painting by John Gast, commissioned by the author of a travel guide to the Pacific coast, reflects the ebullient spirit of manifest destiny. A female figure descended from earlier representations of the goddess of liberty wears the star of empire and leads the movement westward while Indians retreat before her. Symbols of civilization abound: the eastern city in the upper right corner, railroads, fenced animals, stagecoaches, and telegraph wires and a "school book" held by the central figure.*

QUESTIONS

1. How does Gast explain the conquest of the West by white Americans?

2. What elements of Indian–white relations does the artist leave out?

THE MEXICAN FRONTIER: NEW MEXICO AND CALIFORNIA

Settlement of Oregon did not directly raise the issue of slavery. But the nation's acquisition of part of Mexico did. When Mexico achieved its independence from Spain in 1821 it was nearly as large as the United States and its population of 6.5 million was about two-thirds that of its northern neighbor. Mexico's northern provinces—California, New Mexico, and Texas—however, were isolated and sparsely settled outposts surrounded by Indian country. New Mexico's population at the time of Mexican independence consisted of around 30,000 persons of Spanish origin, 10,000 Pueblo Indians, and an indeterminate number of "wild" Indians—nomadic bands of Apaches, Comanches, Navajos, and Utes. With the opening in 1821 of the Santa Fe Trail linking that city with Independence, Missouri, New Mexico's commerce with the United States eclipsed trade with the rest of Mexico.

California's non-Indian population in 1821, some 3,200 missionaries, soldiers, and settlers, was vastly outnumbered by about 20,000 Indians living and working on land owned by religious missions and by 150,000 members of unsubdued tribes in the interior. In 1834, in the hope of reducing the power of the Catholic Church and attracting Mexican and foreign settlers to California, the Mexican government dissolved the great mission landholdings and emancipated Indians working for the friars. Most of the land ended up in the hands of a new class of Mexican cattle ranchers, the *Californios*, who defined their own identity in large measure against the surrounding Indian population. *Californios* referred to themselves as *gente de razón* (people capable of reason) as opposed to the *indios*, whom they called *gente sin razón* (people without reason). For the "common good," Indians were required to continue to work for the new landholders.

A watercolor of a scene on a ranch near Monterey, California, in 1849 depicts Californios *supervising the work of Native Americans.*

THE TRANS-MISSISSIPPI WEST, 1830s–1840s

Westward migration in the early and mid-1840s took American settlers across Indian country into the Oregon Territory, ownership of which was disputed with Great Britain. The Mormons migrated west to Salt Lake City, then part of Mexico.

By 1840, California was already linked commercially with the United States. New England ships were trading with the region, as illustrated in Richard Henry Dana's popular novel *Two Years before the Mast* (1840), an account of a young man's voyage to California and his experiences there. California also attracted a small number of American newcomers. In 1846, Alfred Robinson, who had moved from Boston, published *Life in California*. "In this age of annexation," he wondered, "why not extend the 'area of freedom' by the annexation of California?"

THE TEXAS REVOLT

The first part of Mexico to be settled by significant numbers of Americans was Texas, whose non-Indian population of Spanish origin (called *Tejanos*) numbered only about 2,000 when Mexico became independent. In order to develop the region, the Mexican government accepted an offer by Moses Austin, a Connecticut-born farmer, to colonize it with Americans. In 1820, Austin received a large land grant. He died soon afterward and his son

Stephen continued the plan, reselling land in smaller plots to American settlers at twelve cents per acre. By 1830, the population of American origin had reached around 7,000, considerably exceeding the number of *Tejanos.*

Alarmed that its grip on the area was weakening, the Mexican government in 1830 annulled existing land contracts and barred future emigration from the United States. Led by Stephen Austin, American settlers demanded greater autonomy within Mexico. Part of the area's tiny *Tejano* elite joined them. Mostly ranchers and large farmers, they had welcomed the economic boom that accompanied the settlers and had formed economic alliances with American traders. The issue of slavery further exacerbated matters. Mexico had abolished slavery, but local authorities allowed American settlers to bring slaves with them. When Mexico's ruler, General Antonio López de Santa Anna, sent an army in 1835 to impose central authority, a local committee charged that his purpose was "to give liberty to our slaves and make slaves of ourselves."

The appearance of Santa Anna's army sparked a chaotic revolt in Texas. The rebels formed a provisional government that soon called for Texan independence. On March 6, 1836, Santa Anna's army stormed the Alamo, a mission compound in San Antonio, killing its 187 American and *Tejano* defenders. "Remember the Alamo" became the Texans' rallying cry. In April, forces under Sam Houston, a former governor of Tennessee, routed Santa Anna's army at the Battle of San Jacinto and forced him to recognize Texan independence. Houston was soon elected the first president of the Republic of Texas. In 1837, the Texas Congress called for union with the United States. But fearing the political disputes certain to result from an attempt to add another slave state to the Union, Presidents Andrew Jackson and Martin Van

A flag carried at the Battle of San Jacinto during the Texas revolt of 1836 portrays a female figure displaying the rallying cry "Liberty or Death."

The plaza in San Antonio not long after the United States annexed Texas in 1845.

Buren shelved the question. Settlers from the United States nonetheless poured into the region, many of them slaveowners taking up fertile cotton land. By 1845, the population of Texas had reached nearly 150,000.

THE ELECTION OF 1844

Texas annexation remained on the political back burner until President John Tyler revived it in the hope of rescuing his failed administration and securing southern support for renomination in 1844. In April 1844, a letter by John C. Calhoun, whom Tyler had appointed secretary of state, was leaked to the press. It linked the idea of absorbing Texas directly to the goal of strengthening slavery in the United States. Some southern leaders, indeed, hoped that Texas could be divided into several states, thus further enhancing the South's power in Congress. Late that month, Henry Clay and former president Van Buren, the prospective Whig and Democratic candidates for president and two of the party system's most venerable leaders, met at Clay's Kentucky plantation. They agreed to issue letters rejecting immediate annexation on the grounds that it might provoke war with Mexico. Clay and Van Buren were reacting to the slavery issue in the traditional manner—by trying to keep it out of national politics.

Clay went on to receive the Whig nomination, but for Van Buren the letters proved to be a disaster. At the Democratic convention, southerners bent on annexation deserted Van Buren's cause, and he failed to receive the two-thirds majority necessary for nomination. The delegates then turned to the little-known James K. Polk, a former governor of Tennessee whose main assets were his support for annexation and his close association with Andrew Jackson, still the party's most popular figure. Like nearly all the presidents before him, Polk was a slaveholder. He owned substantial cotton plantations in Tennessee and Mississippi, where conditions were so brutal that only half of the slave children lived to the age of fifteen, and adults frequently ran away. To soothe injured feelings among northern Democrats over the rejection of Van Buren, the party platform called not only for the "reannexation" of Texas (implying that Texas had been part of the Louisiana Purchase and therefore once belonged to the United States) but also the "reoccupation" of all of Oregon. "Fifty-four forty or fight"—American control of Oregon all the way to its northern boundary at north latitude 54°40'—became a popular campaign slogan. But the bitterness of the northern Van Burenites over what they considered to be a betrayal on the part of the South would affect American politics for years to come.

Polk was the first "dark horse" candidate for president—that is, one whose nomination was completely unexpected. In the fall, he defeated Clay in an extremely close election. Polk's margin in the popular vote was less than 2 percent. Had not James G. Birney, running again as the Liberty Party candidate, received 16,000 votes in New York, mostly from antislavery Whigs, Clay would have been elected. In March 1845, only days before Polk's inauguration, Congress declared Texas part of the United States.

THE ROAD TO WAR

James K. Polk may have been virtually unknown, but he assumed the presidency with a clearly defined set of goals: to reduce the tariff, reestablish the independent Treasury system, settle the dispute over ownership of Oregon, and bring California into the Union. Congress soon enacted the first two goals, and the third was accomplished in an agreement with Great Britain dividing Oregon at the forty-ninth parallel. Many northerners were bitterly disappointed by this compromise, considering it a betrayal of Polk's campaign promise not to give up any part of Oregon without a fight. But the president secured his main objectives, the Willamette Valley and the magnificent harbor of Puget Sound.

War News from Mexico, an 1848 painting by Richard C. Woodville, shows how Americans received war news through the popular press.

Acquiring California proved more difficult. Polk dispatched an emissary to Mexico offering to purchase the region, but the Mexican government refused to negotiate. By the spring of 1846, Polk was planning for military action. In April, American soldiers under Zachary Taylor moved into the region between the Nueces River and the Rio Grande, land claimed by both countries on the disputed border between Texas and Mexico. This action made conflict with Mexican forces inevitable. When fighting broke out, Polk claimed that the Mexicans had "shed blood upon American soil" and called for a declaration of war.

THE WAR AND ITS CRITICS

The Mexican War was the first American conflict to be fought primarily on foreign soil and the first in which American troops occupied a foreign capital. Inspired by the expansionist fervor of manifest destiny, a majority of Americans supported the war. They were convinced, as Herman Melville put it in his novel *White-Jacket* (1850), that since Americans "bear the ark of Liberties" for all mankind, "national selfishness is unbounded philanthropy . . . to the world." But a significant minority in the North dissented, fearing that far from expanding the "great empire of liberty," the administration's real aim was to acquire new land for the expansion of slavery. Ulysses S. Grant, who served with distinction in Mexico, later called the war "one of the most unjust ever waged by a stronger nation against a weaker nation," an indication that the United States was beginning to behave like "European monarchies," not a democratic republic. Henry David Thoreau was jailed in Massachusetts in 1846 for refusing to pay taxes as a protest against the war. Defending his action, Thoreau wrote an important essay, "On Civil Disobedience," which inspired such later advocates of nonviolent resistance to unjust laws as Martin Luther King Jr. "Under a government which imprisons any unjustly," wrote Thoreau, "the true place of a just man is also a prison."

Among the war's critics was Abraham Lincoln, who had been elected to Congress in 1846 from Illinois. Like many Whigs, Lincoln questioned whether the Mexicans had actually inflicted casualties on American soil, as Polk claimed, and in 1847 he introduced a resolution asking the president to specify the precise "spot" where blood had first been shed. But Lincoln was also disturbed by Polk's claiming the right to initiate an invasion of Mexico. "Allow the president to invade a neighboring country whenever he shall deem it necessary to repel an invasion," he declared, "and you allow him to make war at pleasure. . . . If today he should choose to say he thinks it necessary to invade Canada to prevent the British from invading us, how could you stop him?" Lincoln's stance proved unpopular in Illinois. He had already agreed to serve only one term in Congress, but when Democrats captured his seat in 1848, many blamed the result on Lincoln's criticism of the war. But the concerns he raised regarding the president's power to "make war at pleasure" would continue to echo in the twentieth and twenty-first centuries.

COMBAT IN MEXICO

More than 60,000 volunteers enlisted and did most of the fighting. Combat took place on three fronts. In June 1846, a band of American insurrectionists proclaimed California freed from Mexican control and named Captain John C. Frémont, head of a small scientific expedition in the West, its ruler. Their aim was California's incorporation into the United States, but for the moment they adopted a flag depicting a large bear as the symbol of the area's independence. A month later, the U.S. Navy sailed into Monterey and San Francisco Harbors, raised the American flag, and put an end to the "bear flag republic." At almost the same time, 1,600 American troops under General Stephen W. Kearney occupied Sante Fe without resistance and then set out for southern California, where they helped to put down a Mexican uprising against American rule.

The bulk of the fighting occurred in central Mexico. In February 1847, Taylor defeated Santa Anna's army at the Battle of Buena Vista. When the Mexican government still refused to negotiate, Polk ordered American forces under Winfield Scott to march inland from the port of Vera Cruz toward Mexico City. Scott's forces routed Mexican defenders and in September occupied the country's capital. In February 1848, the two governments agreed to the Treaty of Guadalupe Hidalgo, which confirmed the annexation of Texas and ceded California and present-day New Mexico,

THE MEXICAN WAR, 1846-1848

Legend:
- ⊗ American victory
- ⊗ Mexican victory
- — American forces
- ···· American naval blockade
- — Mexican forces
- — Treaty of Guadalupe Hidalgo
- ▨ Lands disputed by United States and Mexico
- ☐ Lands ceded by Mexico

The Mexican War was the first in which an American army invaded another country and occupied its capital. As a result of the war, the United States acquired a vast new area in the modern-day Southwest.

Arizona, Nevada, and Utah to the United States. In exchange, the United States paid Mexico $15 million. The Mexican Cession, as the land annexed from Mexico was called, established the present territorial boundaries on the North American continent except for the Gadsden Purchase, a parcel of additional land bought from Mexico in 1853, and Alaska, acquired from Russia in 1867.

The Mexican War is only a footnote in most Americans' historical memory. Unlike other wars, few public monuments celebrate the conflict. Mexicans, however, regard the war (or "the dismemberment," as it is called in that country) as a central event of their national history and a source of continued resentment over a century and a half after it was fought. As the

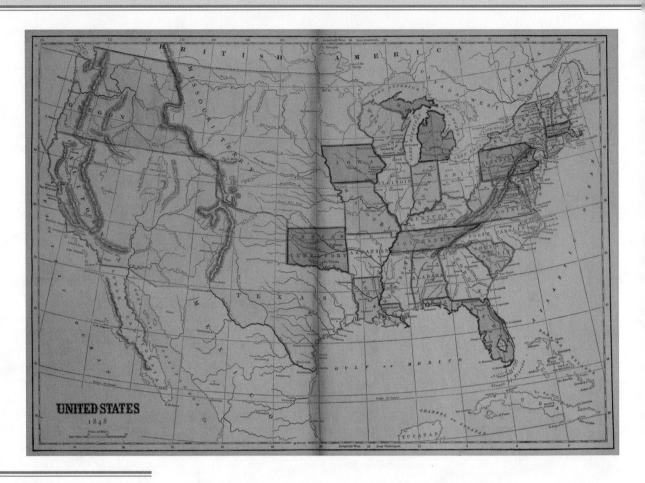

A map of the United States from 1848 reveals how the size of the country had grown during the past four years: Texas (its western boundary still unfixed) had been annexed in 1845; the dispute with Great Britain over Oregon was settled in 1846; and the Mexican Cession—the area of present-day Arizona, New Mexico, Utah, Nevada, and California—was added in 1848 at the end of the Mexican War.

Mexican negotiators of 1848 complained, it was unprecedented to launch a war because a country refused to sell part of its territory to a neighbor.

RACE AND MANIFEST DESTINY

With the end of the Mexican War, the United States absorbed half a million square miles of Mexico's territory, one-third of that nation's total area. A region that for centuries had been united was suddenly split in two, dividing families and severing trade routes. An estimated 75,000 to 100,000 Spanish-speaking Mexicans and more than 150,000 Indians inhabited the Mexican Cession. The Treaty of Guadalupe Hidalgo guaranteed to "male citizens" of the area "the free enjoyment of their liberty and property" and "all the rights" of Americans—a provision designed to protect the property of large Mexican landowners in California. As to Indians whose homelands and hunting grounds suddenly became part of the United States, the treaty referred to them only as "savage tribes" whom the United States must prevent from launching incursions into Mexico across the new border.

The spirit of manifest destiny gave a new stridency to ideas about racial superiority. During the 1840s, territorial expansion came to be seen as proof of the innate superiority of the "Anglo-Saxon race" (a mythical construct defined largely by its opposites: blacks, Indians, Hispanics, and Catholics). "*Race*," declared John L. O'Sullivan's *Democratic Review*, was the "key" to the "history of nations" and the rise and fall of empires.

"Race" in the mid-nineteenth century was an amorphous notion involving color, culture, national origin, class, and religion. Newspapers, magazines, and scholarly works popularized the link between American freedom and the supposedly innate liberty-loving qualities of Anglo-Saxon Protestants. The annexation of Texas and conquest of much of Mexico became triumphs of civilization, progress, and liberty over the tyranny of the Catholic Church and the innate incapacity of "mongrel races." Indeed, calls by some expansionists for the United States to annex all of Mexico failed in part because of fear that the nation could not assimilate its large non-white Catholic population, supposedly unfit for citizenship in a republic.

REDEFINING RACE

The imposition of the American system of race relations proved detrimental to many inhabitants of the newly acquired territories. Texas had already demonstrated as much. Mexico had abolished slavery and declared persons of Spanish, Indian, and African origin equal before the law. The Texas constitution adopted after independence not only included protections for slavery but also denied civil rights to Indians and persons of African origin. Only whites were permitted to purchase land, and the entrance of free blacks into the state was prohibited altogether. "Every privilege dear to a free man is taken away," one free black resident of Texas complained.

Local circumstances affected racial definitions in the former Mexican territories. Texas defined "Spanish" Mexicans, especially those who occupied important social positions, as white. The residents of New Mexico of both Mexican and Indian origin, on the other hand, were long deemed "too Mexican" for democratic self-government. With white migration lagging, Congress did not allow New Mexico to become a state until 1912.

GOLD-RUSH CALIFORNIA

California had a non-Indian population of less than 15,000 when the Mexican War ended. For most of the 1840s, ten times as many Americans emigrated to Oregon as to California. But this changed dramatically after January 1848, when gold was discovered in the foothills of the Sierra Nevada Mountains at a sawmill owned by the Swiss immigrant Johann A. Sutter. A mania for gold spread throughout the world, fanned by newspaper accounts of instant wealth acquired by early migrants. By ship and land, newcomers poured into California. The non-Indian population rose to 200,000 by 1852 and more than 360,000 eight years later.

California's gold-rush population was incredibly diverse. Experienced miners flooded in from Mexico and South America. Tens of thousands of Americans who had never seen a mine arrived from the East, and from overseas came Irish, Germans, Italians, and Australians. Nearly

The gold rush brought thousands of fortune seekers, from nearly every corner of the globe, to California.

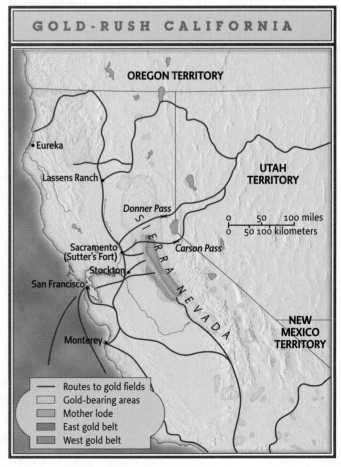

GOLD-RUSH CALIFORNIA

A contemporary depiction of mining operations during the California gold rush shows Native Americans, Mexicans, and numerous other miners all searching for gold.

25,000 Chinese landed between 1849 and 1852, almost all of them young men who had signed long-term labor contracts with Chinese merchants, who in turn leased them to mining and railroad companies and other employers. San Francisco, a town of 1,000 in 1848, became the gateway to the *El Dorado* of northern California. By 1850, it had 30,000 residents and had become perhaps the world's most racially and ethnically diverse city. Unlike farming frontiers settled by families, most of the gold-rush migrants were young men. Women played many roles in western mining communities, running restaurants and boardinghouses and working as laundresses, cooks, and prostitutes. But as late as 1860, California's male population outnumbered females by nearly three to one.

CALIFORNIA AND THE BOUNDARIES OF FREEDOM

As early surface mines quickly became exhausted, they gave way to underground mining that required a large investment of capital. This economic development worsened conflicts among California's many racial and ethnic groups engaged in fierce competition for gold. The law was very fragile in gold-rush California. In 1851 and 1856, "committees of vigilance" took control of San Francisco, sweeping aside established courts to try and execute those accused of crimes. White miners organized extralegal groups that expelled "foreign miners"—Mexicans, Chileans, Chinese, French, and American Indians—from areas with gold. The state legislature imposed a tax of twenty dollars per month on foreign miners, driving many of them from the state.

California would long remain in the American imagination a place of infinite opportunity, where newcomers could start their lives anew. But the boundaries of freedom there were tightly drawn. The state constitution of 1850 limited voting and the right to testify in court to whites, excluding Indians, Asians, and the state's few blacks (who numbered only 962 persons). California landowners who claimed Spanish descent or had intermarried with American settlers were deemed to be white. But with land titles derived from Mexican days challenged in court, many sold out to newcomers from the East.

For California's Indians, the gold rush and absorption into the United States proved to be disastrous. Gold seekers overran Indian communities. Miners, ranchers, and vigilantes murdered thousands of Indians. Determined to reduce the native population, state officials paid millions in bounties to private militias that launched attacks on the state's Indians. Although California was a free state, thousands of Indian children, declared orphans or vagrants by local courts, were bought and sold as slaves. By 1860, California's Indian population, nearly 150,000 when the Mexican War ended, had been reduced to around 30,000.

THE OTHER GOLD RUSH

In a remarkable coincidence, the California gold rush took place almost simultaneously with another located halfway around the world. In 1851, gold was discovered in Australia, then a collection of British colonies. During the 1850s, California and Australia together produced 80 percent of the world's gold. Like California, Australia attracted gold-seekers from across the globe. The population of Victoria, the colony where gold was found, grew from 77,000 in 1851 to 411,000 six years later. Like San Francisco, the Australian city of Melbourne rose to prominence on the basis of its proximity to the gold fields.

As in California, the gold rush was a disaster for the aboriginal peoples (as native Australians are called), whose population, already declining, fell precipitously. In Australia, like California, significant numbers of Chinese miners took part in the gold rush, only to face persistent efforts by miners of European origin to drive them from the fields. Indeed, Australians frequently modeled anti-Chinese legislation—especially their tax on foreign miners—on measures that had been pioneered in California.

OPENING JAPAN

The Mexican War ended with the United States in possession of the magnificent harbors of San Diego and San Francisco, long seen as jumping off points for trade with the Far East. In the 1850s, the United States took the lead in opening Japan, a country that had closed itself to nearly all foreign contact for more than two centuries. In 1853 and 1854, American warships under the command of Commodore Matthew Perry (the younger brother of Oliver Perry, a hero of the War of 1812) sailed into Tokyo Harbor. Perry, who had been sent by President Millard Fillmore to negotiate a trade treaty, demanded that the Japanese deal with him. Alarmed by European intrusions into China and impressed by Perry's armaments as well as a musical pageant he presented that included a blackface minstrel show, Japanese leaders agreed to do so. In 1854, they opened two ports to American shipping. Two years later, Townsend Harris, a mer-

Transportation of Cargo by Westerners at the Port of Yokohama, 1861, by the Japanese artist Utagawa Sadahide, depicts ships in port, including an American one on the left, eight years after Commodore Perry's first voyage to Japan.

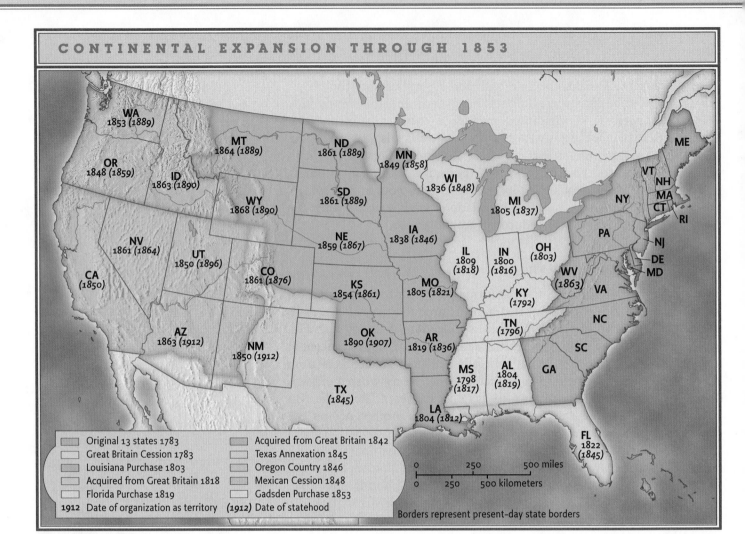

CONTINENTAL EXPANSION THROUGH 1853

WA 1853 (1889)
OR 1848 (1859)
ID 1863 (1890)
MT 1864 (1889)
ND 1861 (1889)
MN 1849 (1858)
WI 1836 (1848)
MI 1805 (1837)
ME
VT
NH
MA
CT
NY
RI
WY 1868 (1890)
SD 1861 (1889)
NV 1861 (1864)
UT 1850 (1896)
CO 1861 (1876)
NE 1859 (1867)
IA 1838 (1846)
IL 1809 (1818)
IN 1800 (1816)
OH 1803
PA
NJ
DE
MD
WV 1863
VA
CA (1850)
KS 1854 (1861)
MO 1805 (1821)
KY 1792
AZ 1863 (1912)
NM 1850 (1912)
OK 1890 (1907)
AR 1819 (1836)
TN 1796
NC
SC
TX (1845)
MS 1798 (1817)
AL 1804 (1819)
GA
LA 1804 (1812)
FL 1822 (1845)

Original 13 states 1783
Great Britain Cession 1783
Louisiana Purchase 1803
Acquired from Great Britain 1818
Florida Purchase 1819
1912 Date of organization as territory

Acquired from Great Britain 1842
Texas Annexation 1845
Oregon Country 1846
Mexican Cession 1848
Gadsden Purchase 1853
(1912) Date of statehood

0   250   500 miles
0   250   500 kilometers

Borders represent present-day state borders

By 1853, with the Gadsden Purchase, the present boundaries of the United States in North America, with the exception of Alaska, had been created.

chant from New York City, arrived as the first American consul (and, according to some accounts, was the inspiration for Puccini's great opera, *Madame Butterfly*, about an American who marries and then abandons a Japanese woman). Harris persuaded the Japanese to allow American ships into additional ports and to establish full diplomatic relations between the two countries. As a result, the United States acquired refueling places on the route to China—seen as Asia's most important trading partner. And Japan soon launched a process of modernization that transformed it into the region's major military power.

A DOSE OF ARSENIC

Victory over Mexico added more than 1 million square miles to the United States—an area larger than the Louisiana Purchase. But the acquisition of this vast territory raised the fatal issue that would disrupt the political system and plunge the nation into civil war—whether slavery should be allowed to expand into the West. Events soon confirmed Ralph Waldo Emerson's prediction that if the United States gobbled up part of Mexico, "it will be as the man who swallows arsenic. . . . Mexico will poison us."

THE WILMOT PROVISO

Before 1846, the status of slavery in all parts of the United States had been settled, either by state law or by the Missouri Compromise, which determined slavery's status in the Louisiana Purchase. The acquisition of new land reopened the question of slavery's expansion. The divisive potential of this issue became clear in 1846, when Congressman David Wilmot of Pennsylvania proposed a resolution prohibiting slavery from all territory acquired from Mexico. Party lines crumbled as every northerner, Democrat and Whig alike, supported what came to be known as the Wilmot Proviso, while nearly all southerners opposed it. The measure passed the House, where the more populous North possessed a majority, but failed in the Senate, with its even balance of free and slave states. The Proviso, said one newspaper, "as if by magic, brought to a head the great question that is about to divide the American people."

In 1848, opponents of slavery's expansion organized the Free Soil Party and nominated Martin Van Buren for president and Charles Francis Adams, the son of John Quincy Adams, as his running mate. Democrats nominated Lewis Cass of Michigan, who proposed that the decision on whether to allow slavery should be left to settlers in the new territories (an idea later given the name "popular sovereignty"). Van Buren was motivated in part by revenge against the South for jettisoning him in 1844. But his campaign struck a chord among northerners opposed to the expansion of slavery, and he polled some 300,000 votes, 14 percent of the northern total. Victory in 1848 went to the Whig candidate, Zachary Taylor, a hero of the Mexican War and a Louisiana sugar planter. But the fact that a former president and the son of another abandoned their parties to run on a Free Soil platform showed that antislavery sentiment had spread far beyond abolitionist ranks. "Antislavery," commented Senator William H. Seward of New York, "is at length a respectable element in politics."

THE FREE SOIL APPEAL

The Free Soil position had a popular appeal in the North that far exceeded the abolitionists' demand for immediate emancipation and equal rights for blacks. While Congress possessed no constitutional power to abolish slavery within a state, well-known precedents existed for keeping territories (areas that had not yet entered the Union as states) free from slavery. Congress had done this in 1787 in the Northwest Ordinance and again in the Missouri Compromise of 1820–1821. Many northerners had long resented what they considered southern domination of the federal government. The idea of preventing the creation of new slave states appealed to those who favored policies, such as the protective tariff and government aid to internal improvements, that the majority of southern political leaders opposed.

For thousands of northerners, moreover, the ability to move to the new western territories held out the promise of economic betterment. The depression of the early 1840s had reinforced the traditional equation of land ownership with economic freedom. The labor movement promoted access to western land as a way of combating unemployment and low wages in the East. "Freedom of the soil," declared George Henry Evans, the editor of a pro-labor newspaper, offered the only alternative to permanent economic dependence for American workers.

Such views merged easily with opposition to the expansion of slavery. If slave plantations were to occupy the fertile lands of the West, northern migration would be effectively blocked. The term "free soil" had a double meaning. The Free Soil platform of 1848 called both for barring slavery from western territories and for the federal government to provide free homesteads to settlers in the new territories. Unlike abolitionism, the "free soil" idea also appealed to the racism so widespread in northern society. Wilmot himself insisted that his controversial Proviso was motivated not by "morbid sympathy for the slaves" but to advance "the cause and rights of the free white man," in part by preventing him from having to compete with "black labor."

To white southerners, the idea of barring slavery from territory acquired from Mexico seemed a violation of their equal rights as members of the Union. Southerners had fought and died to win these territories; surely they had a right to share in the fruits of victory. To single out slavery as the one form of property barred from the West would be an affront to the South and its distinctive way of life. A majority of slaves in 1848 lived in states that had not even existed when the Constitution was adopted. Many older plantation areas already suffered from soil exhaustion. Just as northerners believed westward expansion essential to their economic well-being, southern leaders became convinced that slavery must expand or die. Moreover, the admission of new free states would overturn the delicate political balance between the sections and make the South a permanent minority. Southern interests would not be secure in a Union dominated by non-slaveholding states.

CRISIS AND COMPROMISE

In world history, the year 1848 is remembered as the "springtime of nations," a time of democratic uprisings against the monarchies of Europe and demands by ethnic minorities for national independence. American principles of liberty and self-government appeared to be triumphing in the Old World. The Chartist movement in Great Britain organized massive demonstrations in support of a proposed Charter that demanded democratic reforms. The French replaced their monarchy with a republic. Hungarians proclaimed their independence from Austrian rule. Patriots in Italy and Germany, both divided into numerous states, demanded national unification. But the revolutionary tide receded. Chartism faded away. In France, the Second Republic was soon succeeded by the reign of Emperor Napoleon III. Revolts in Budapest, Rome, and other cities were crushed. Would their own experiment in self-government, some Americans wondered, suffer the same fate as the failed revolutions of Europe?

With the slavery issue appearing more and more ominous, established party leaders moved to resolve differences between the sections. Some disputes were of long standing, but the immediate source of controversy arose from the acquisition of new lands after the Mexican War. In 1850, California asked to be admitted to the Union as a free state. Many southerners opposed the measure, fearing that it would upset the sectional balance in Congress. Senator Henry Clay offered a plan with four main provisions

Senator Daniel Webster of Massachusetts in a daguerreotype from 1850, the year his speech in support of the Compromise of 1850 contributed to its passage.

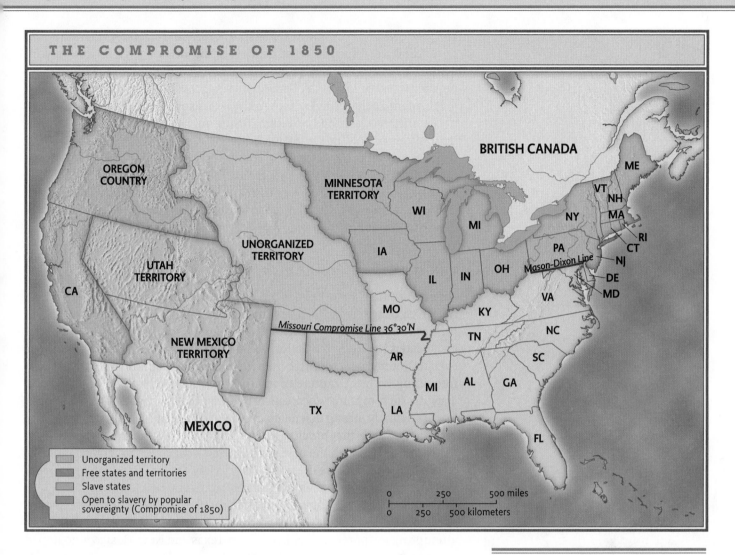

THE COMPROMISE OF 1850

that came to be known as the Compromise of 1850. California would enter the Union as a free state. The slave trade, but not slavery itself, would be abolished in the nation's capital. A stringent new law would allow southerners to reclaim runaway slaves. And the status of slavery in the remaining territories acquired from Mexico would be left to the decision of the local white inhabitants. The United States would also agree to pay off the massive debt Texas had accumulated while independent.

The Compromise of 1850 attempted to settle issues arising from the acquisition of territory from Mexico by admitting California as a free state and providing that the status of slavery in Utah and New Mexico would be determined by the settlers.

THE GREAT DEBATE

In the Senate debate on the Compromise, the divergent sectional positions received eloquent expression. Powerful leaders spoke for and against compromise. Daniel Webster of Massachusetts announced his willingness to abandon the Wilmot Proviso and accept a new fugitive slave law if this were the price of sectional peace. John C. Calhoun, again representing South Carolina, was too ill to speak. A colleague read his remarks rejecting the very idea of compromise. Slavery, Calhoun insisted, must be protected by the national government and extended into all the new territories. The North must yield or the Union could not survive. William H. Seward of New

York also opposed compromise. To southerners' talk of their constitutional rights, Seward responded that a "higher law" than the Constitution condemned slavery—the law of morality. Here was the voice of abolitionism, now represented in the U.S. Senate.

President Zachary Taylor, like Andrew Jackson a southerner but a strong nationalist, was alarmed by talk of disunion. He accused southern leaders in Congress of holding California hostage to their own legislative aims and insisted that all Congress needed to do was admit California to the Union. But Taylor died suddenly of an intestinal infection on July 9, 1850. His successor, Millard Fillmore of New York, threw his support to Clay's proposals. Fillmore helped to break the impasse in Congress and secure adoption of the Compromise of 1850.

THE FUGITIVE SLAVE ISSUE

For one last time, political leaders had removed the dangerous slavery question from congressional debate. The new Fugitive Slave Act, however, made further controversy inevitable. The law allowed special federal commissioners to determine the fate of alleged fugitives without benefit of a jury trial or even testimony by the accused individual. It prohibited local authorities from interfering with the capture of fugitives and required individual citizens to assist in such capture when called upon by federal agents. Thus, southern leaders, usually strong defenders of states' rights and local autonomy, supported a measure that brought federal agents into communities throughout the North, armed with the power to override local law enforcement and judicial procedures to secure the return of runaway slaves. The security of slavery was more important to them than states'-rights consistency.

The fugitive slave issue affected all the free states, not just those that bordered on the South. Slave catchers, for example, entered California attempting to apprehend fugitives from Texas and New Mexico who hoped to reach freedom in British Columbia. The issue drew into politics individuals like Ralph Waldo Emerson, who, although antislavery, had previously remained aloof from the abolitionist crusade. Emerson and others influenced by transcendentalism viewed the Fugitive Slave Act as a dangerous example of how a government doing the bidding of the South could override an individual's ability to act according to his conscience—the foundation, for Emerson, of genuine freedom.

During the 1850s, federal tribunals heard more than 300 cases and ordered 157 fugitives returned to the South, many at the government's expense. But the law further widened sectional divisions. In a series of dramatic confrontations, fugitives, aided by abolitionist allies, violently resisted recapture. A large crowd in 1851 rescued the escaped slave Jerry from jail in Syracuse, New York, and spirited him off to Canada. In the same year, an owner who attempted to recapture a fugitive was killed in Christiana, Pennsylvania. Later in the decade, Margaret Garner, a Kentucky slave who had escaped with her family to Ohio, killed her own young daughter rather than see her returned to slavery by federal marshals. (At the end of the twentieth century, this incident would become the basis for Toni Morrison's celebrated novel *Beloved*.)

In the North, several thousand fugitives and free-born blacks, worried

An 1855 broadside depicting the life of Anthony Burns, a runaway slave captured in Boston and returned to the South in 1854 by federal officials enforcing the Fugitive Slave Act.

that they might be swept up in the stringent provisions of the Fugitive Slave Act, fled to safety in Canada. The sight of so many refugees seeking liberty in a foreign land challenged the familiar image of the United States as an asylum for freedom. "Families are separating," reported a Toronto newspaper in October 1850, "leaving their homes, and flying in all directions to seek in Canada, under the British flag, the protection denied to them in the free republic."

DOUGLAS AND POPULAR SOVEREIGNTY

At least temporarily, the Compromise of 1850 seemed to have restored sectional peace and party unity. In the 1852 presidential election, Democrat Franklin Pierce won a sweeping victory over the Whig Winfield Scott on a platform that recognized the Compromise as a final settlement of the slavery controversy. Pierce received a broad popular mandate, winning 254 electoral votes to Scott's 42. Yet his administration turned out to be one of the most disastrous in American history. It witnessed the collapse of the party system inherited from the Age of Jackson.

In 1854, the old political order finally succumbed to the disruptive pressures of sectionalism. Early in that year, Illinois senator Stephen A. Douglas introduced a bill to provide territorial governments for Kansas and Nebraska, located within the Louisiana Purchase. With Calhoun, Clay, and Webster (the "great triumvirate") all having died between 1850 and 1852, Douglas, although only forty-one, saw himself as the new leader of the Senate. A strong believer in western development, he hoped that a transcontinental railroad could be constructed through Kansas or Nebraska. But he feared that this could not be accomplished unless formal governments had been established in these territories. Southerners in Congress, however, seemed adamant against allowing the organization of new free territories that might further upset the sectional balance. Douglas hoped to satisfy them by applying the principle of popular sovereignty, whereby the status of slavery would be determined by the votes of local settlers, not Congress. To Douglas, popular sovereignty embodied the idea of local self-government and offered a middle ground between the extremes of North and South. It was a principle on which all parts of the Democratic Party could unite, and which might enable him to capture the presidential nomination in 1856 to succeed the ineffectual Pierce.

THE KANSAS-NEBRASKA ACT

Unlike the lands taken from Mexico, Kansas and Nebraska lay in the nation's heartland, directly in the path of westward migration. Slavery, moreover, was prohibited there under the terms of the Missouri Compromise, which Douglas's bill repealed. In response to Douglas's proposal, a group of antislavery congressmen issued the *Appeal of the Independent Democrats*. Written by two abolitionists from Ohio—Congressman Joshua Giddings and Senator Salmon P. Chase—the *Appeal* proved to be one of the most effective pieces of political persuasion in American history. It arraigned Douglas's bill as a "gross violation of a sacred pledge," part and parcel of "an atrocious

THE KANSAS-NEBRASKA ACT, 1854

WASHINGTON TERRITORY
OREGON TERRITORY
UTAH TERRITORY
CA
NEW MEXICO TERRITORY
NEBRASKA TERRITORY
MINNESOTA TERRITORY
KANSAS TERRITORY
see inset
INDIAN TERRITORY
Missouri Compromise Line 36°30′N
BRITISH CANADA
WI **MI** **IA** **MO** **IL** **IN** **OH** **KY** **TN** **AR** **MI** **AL** **GA** **LA** **FL** **TX** **NC** **SC** **VA** **MD** **DE** **NJ** **PA** **NY** **ME** **VT** **NH** **MA** **RI** **CT**
Mason-Dixon Line

BLEEDING KANSAS
Atchison •
Leavenworth •
Lecompton •   • Lawrence   **MISSOURI**
KANSAS TERRITORY
Missouri R.
✕ Osawatomie
Pottawatomie Massacre ✕

0   250   500 miles
0   250   500 kilometers

Free states and territories
Slave states
Indian territory (unorganized)
Open to slavery by popular sovereignty under the Compromise of 1850
Open to slavery by popular sovereignty under the Kansas-Nebraska Act, 1854

The Kansas-Nebraska Act opened a vast area in the nation's heartland to the possible spread of slavery by repealing the Missouri Compromise and providing that settlers would determine the status of slavery in these territories.

plot" to convert free territory into a "dreary region of despotism, inhabited by masters and slaves." It helped to convince millions of northerners that southern leaders aimed at nothing less than extending their peculiar institution throughout the West.

Thanks to Douglas's energetic leadership, the Kansas-Nebraska Act became law. But it shattered the Democratic Party's unity. Even as Congress debated, protest meetings sprang up throughout the North. Fearing that the bill's unpopularity among their constituents would harm their chances for reelection, half the northern Democrats in the House cast negative votes. Loyalty to Pierce, Douglas, and their party led the other half to support the measure. It is difficult to think of a piece of legislation in American history that had a more profound impact on national life. In the wake of the bill's passage, American politics underwent a profound reorganization. During the next two years, the Whig Party, unable to develop a unified response to the political crisis, collapsed. From a region divided between the two parties, the South became solidly Democratic. Most northern Whigs, augmented by thousands of disgruntled Democrats, joined a new organization, the Republican Party, dedicated to preventing the further expansion of slavery.

THE RISE OF THE REPUBLICAN PARTY

THE NORTHERN ECONOMY

The disruptive impact of slavery on the traditional parties was the immediate cause of political transformation in the mid-1850s. But the rise of the Republican Party also reflected underlying economic and social changes, notably the completion of the market revolution and the beginning of mass immigration from Europe. The period from 1843, when prosperity returned, to 1857, when another economic downturn hit, witnessed explosive economic growth, especially in the North. The catalyst was the completion of the railroad network. From 5,000 miles in 1848, railroad track mileage grew to 30,000 by 1860, with most of the construction occurring in Ohio, Illinois, and other states of the Old Northwest. Four great trunk railroads now linked eastern cities with western farming and commercial centers. The railroads completed the reorientation of the Northwest's trade from the South to the East. As late as 1850, most western farmers still shipped their produce down the Mississippi River. Ten years later, however, railroads transported nearly all their crops to the East, at a fraction of the previous cost. By 1860, for example, 60 million bushels of wheat were passing through Buffalo on their way to market in eastern cities and abroad. The economic integration of the Northwest and Northeast created the groundwork for their political unification in the Republican Party.

By 1860, the North had become a complex, integrated economy, with eastern industrialists marketing manufactured goods to the commercial farmers of the West, while residents of the region's growing cities consumed the food westerners produced. Northern society stood poised between old and new ways. The majority of the population still lived not in large cities but in small towns and rural areas, where the ideal of economic independence—owning one's own farm or shop—still lay within reach. Yet the majority of the northern workforce no longer labored in agriculture, and the industrial revolution was spreading rapidly.

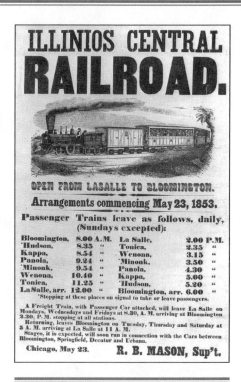

An 1853 broadside for one section of the Illinois Central Railroad. One of the most important new lines of the 1850s, the Illinois Central opened parts of the Old Northwest to settlement and commercial agriculture, and it helped to cement Chicago's place as the region's foremost city.

The Lackawanna Valley, *an 1855 painting by George Inness commissioned by the president of the Delaware, Lackawanna, and Western Railroad. In the background is the roundhouse at Scranton, Pennsylvania. Like* The Mill on the Brandywine *in Chapter 9, the scene emphasizes the harmony of technological progress and nature. The factory on the right is almost entirely hidden by trees. Yet the tree stumps in the foreground suggest some regret that the natural environment is giving way to progress.*

THE RAILROAD NETWORK, 1850s

The rapid expansion of the railroad network in the 1850s linked the Northeast and Old Northwest in a web of commerce. The South's rail network was considerably less developed, accounting for only 30 percent of the nation's track mileage.

Two great areas of industrial production had arisen. One, along the Atlantic coast, stretched from Boston to Philadelphia and Baltimore. A second was centered on or near the Great Lakes, in inland cities like Buffalo, Cleveland, Pittsburgh, and Chicago. Driven by railroad expansion, coal mining and iron manufacturing were growing rapidly. Chicago, the old Northwest's major rail center and the jumping-off place for settlers heading for the Great Plains, had become a complex manufacturing center, producing 5,000 reapers each year, along with barbed wire, windmills, and prefabricated "balloon frame" houses, all of which facilitated further western settlement. New York City by 1860 had become the nation's preeminent financial, commercial, and manufacturing center. Although the southern economy was also growing and the continuing expansion of cotton production brought wealth to slaveholders, the South did not share in these broad economic changes.

THE RISE AND FALL OF THE KNOW-NOTHINGS

As noted in Chapter 9, nativism—hostility to immigrants, especially Catholics—emerged as a local political movement in the 1840s. But in 1854, with the party system in crisis, it burst on the national political scene with the sudden appearance of the American, or Know-Nothing, Party (so called because it began as a secret organization whose members, when asked about its existence, were supposed to respond, "I know nothing"). The party trumpeted its dedication to reserving political office for native-born Americans and to resisting the "aggressions" of the Catholic Church, such as its supposed efforts to undermine public school systems. The Know-Nothings swept the 1854 state elections in Massachusetts, electing the governor, all of the state's congressmen, and nearly every member of the state legislature. They captured the mayor's office in cities like Philadelphia, Chicago, and San Francisco as well. In many states, nativists emerged as a major component of victorious "anti-Nebraska" coalitions of voters opposed to the Kansas-Nebraska Act. In the North, the Know-Nothings' appeal combined anti-Catholic and antislavery sentiment, with opposition to the sale of liquor often added to the equation. After all, most Catholics, as noted in the previous chapter, vigorously opposed the reform move-

George Catlin's 1827 painting Five Points *depicts a working-class immigrant neighborhood in New York City that gained a reputation for crime, drinking, and overcrowding.*

ments inspired by evangelical Protestantism, especially antislavery and temperance. The 1854 elections, said one observer, revealed "a deep seated feeling in favor of human freedom and also a fine determination that hereafter none but Americans shall rule America."

Despite severe anti-Irish discrimination in jobs, housing, and education, however, it is remarkable how little came of demands that immigrants be barred from the political nation. All European immigrants benefited from being white. During the 1850s, free blacks found immigrants pushing them out of even the jobs as servants and common laborers previously available to them. The newcomers had the good fortune to arrive after white male suffrage had become the norm and automatically received the right to vote. Even as New England states sought to reduce immigrant political power (Massachusetts and Connecticut made literacy a voting requirement, and Massachusetts mandated a two-year waiting period between becoming a naturalized citizen and voting), western states desperate for labor allowed immigrants to vote well before they became citizens. In a country where the suffrage had become essential to understandings of freedom, it is significant that many white male immigrants could vote almost from the moment they landed in America, while non-whites, whose ancestors had lived in the country for centuries, could not.

Political Chart of the United States, *an 1856 chart graphically illustrating the division between slave and free states and providing statistics to demonstrate the superiority of free to slave society. The image underscores the Republican contention that it is essential to prevent slavery from spreading into the western territories. John C. Frémont, Republican presidential candidate, is pictured at the top.*

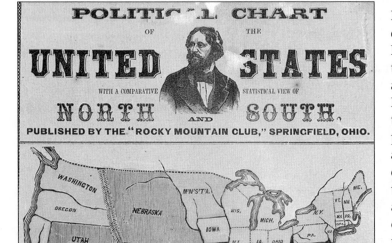

THE FREE LABOR IDEOLOGY

By 1856, it was clear that the Republican Party—a coalition of antislavery Democrats, northern Whigs, Free Soilers, and Know-Nothings opposed to the further expansion of slavery—would become the major alternative to the Democratic Party in the North. Republicans managed to convince most northerners that the Slave Power, as they called the South's proslavery political leadership, posed a more immediate threat to their liberties and aspirations than "popery" and immigration. The party's appeal rested on the idea of "free labor." In Republican hands, the antithesis between "free society" and "slave society" coalesced into a comprehensive worldview that glorified the North as the home of progress, opportunity, and freedom.

The defining quality of northern society, Republicans declared, was the opportunity it offered each laborer to move up to the status of landowning farmer or independent craftsman, thus achieving the economic independence essential to freedom. Slavery, by contrast, spawned a social order consisting of degraded slaves, poor whites with no hope of advancement, and idle aristocrats. The struggle over the territories was a contest about which of two antagonistic labor systems would dominate the West and, by implication, the nation's future. If slavery were to spread into the West, northern free laborers would be barred, and their chances for social advancement severely diminished. Slavery,

Republicans insisted, must be kept out of the territories so that free labor could flourish.

To southern claims that slavery was the foundation of liberty, Republicans responded with the rallying cry "freedom national"—meaning not abolition, but ending the federal government's support of slavery. Under the banner of free labor, northerners of diverse backgrounds and interests rallied in defense of the superiority of their own society. Republicans acknowledged that some northern laborers, including most Irish immigrants, were locked into jobs as factory workers and unskilled laborers and found it extremely difficult to rise in the social scale. But Republicans concluded that it was their "dependent nature"—a lack of Protestant, middle-class virtues—that explained the plight of the immigrant poor.

Republicans were not abolitionists—they focused on preventing the spread of slavery, not attacking it where it existed. Nonetheless, many party leaders viewed the nation's division into free and slave societies as an "irrepressible conflict," as Senator William H. Seward of New York put it in 1858, that eventually would have to be resolved. These "two systems" of society, Seward insisted, were "incompatible" within a single nation. The market revolution, Seward argued, by drawing the entire nation closer together in a web of transportation and commerce, heightened the tension between freedom and slavery. The United States, he predicted, "must and will, sooner or later, become either entirely a slaveholding nation, or entirely a free-labor nation."

BLEEDING KANSAS AND THE ELECTION OF 1856

Their free labor outlook, which resonated so effectively with deeply held northern values, helps to explain the Republicans' rapid rise to prominence. But dramatic events in 1855 and 1856 also fueled the party's growth. When Kansas held elections in 1854 and 1855, hundreds of proslavery Missourians crossed the border to cast fraudulent ballots. President Franklin Pierce recognized the legitimacy of the resulting proslavery legislature and replaced the territorial governor, Andrew H. Reeder of Pennsylvania, when he dissented. Settlers from free states soon established a rival government, and a sporadic civil war broke out in Kansas in which some 200 persons eventually lost their lives. In one incident, in May 1856, a proslavery mob attacked the free-soil stronghold of Lawrence, burning public buildings and pillaging private homes.

"Bleeding Kansas" seemed to discredit Douglas's policy of leaving the decision on slavery up to the local population, thus aiding the Republicans. The party also drew strength from an unprecedented incident in the halls of Congress. South Carolina representative Preston Brooks, wielding a gold-tipped cane, beat

A contemporary print denounces South Carolina congressman Preston S. Brooks's assault on Massachusetts senator Charles Sumner in May 1856. The attack on the floor of the Senate was in retaliation for Sumner's speech accusing Senator Andrew P. Butler (Brooks's distant cousin) of having taken "the harlot slavery" as his mistress.

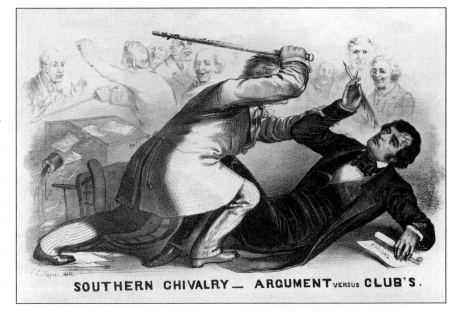

SOUTHERN CHIVALRY — ARGUMENT versus CLUB'S.

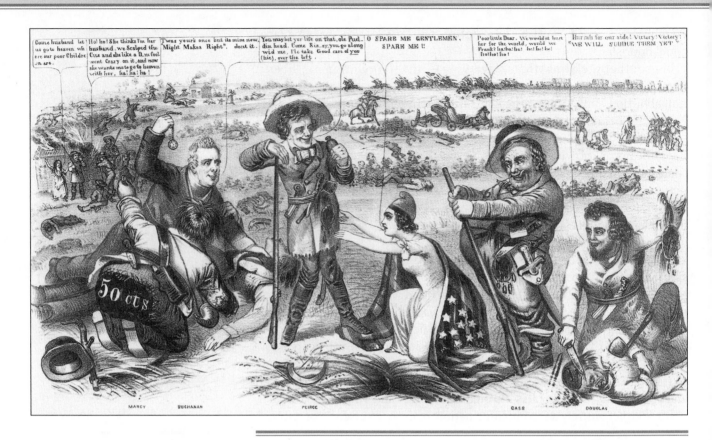

Liberty, the Fair Maid of Kansas, in the Hands of the "Border Ruffians," a cartoon blaming the Democratic Party for violence in Kansas in 1856. Leading Democrats surround the maid of liberty—from left to right, Secretary of State William L. Marcy, Democratic presidential candidate James Buchanan, President Franklin Pierce, Lewis Cass, the party's candidate for president in 1848, and Stephen A. Douglas, author of the Kansas-Nebraska Act, shown scalping an Indian.

the antislavery senator Charles Sumner of Massachusetts unconscious after Sumner delivered a denunciation of "The Crime against Kansas." Many southerners applauded Brooks, sending him canes emblazoned with the words "Hit him again!"

In the election of 1856, the Republican Party chose as its candidate John C. Frémont and drafted a platform that strongly opposed the further expansion of slavery. Stung by the northern reaction to the Kansas-Nebraska Act, the Democrats nominated James Buchanan, who had been minister to Great Britain in 1854 and thus had no direct connection with that divisive measure. The Democratic platform endorsed the principle of popular sovereignty as the only viable solution to the slavery controversy. Meanwhile, the Know-Nothings presented ex-president Millard Fillmore as their candidate. Frémont outpolled Buchanan in the North, carrying eleven of sixteen free states—a remarkable achievement for an organization that had existed for only two years. But Buchanan won the entire South and the key northern states of Illinois, Indiana, and Pennsylvania, enough to ensure his victory. Fillmore carried only Maryland. But he ran well among former Whig voters in the Upper South and more conservative areas of the North, who were reluctant to join the Democrats but feared Republican victory might threaten the Union.

The 1856 election returns made starkly clear that parties had reoriented themselves along sectional lines. One major party had been destroyed, another seriously weakened, and a new one had arisen, devoted entirely to the interests of the North.

THE EMERGENCE OF LINCOLN

The final collapse of the party system took place during the administration of a president who epitomized the old political order. Born during George Washington's presidency, James Buchanan had served in Pennsylvania's legislature, in both houses of Congress, and as secretary of state under James K. Polk. A staunch believer in the Union, he committed himself to pacifying inflamed sectional emotions. Few presidents have failed more disastrously in what they set out to accomplish.

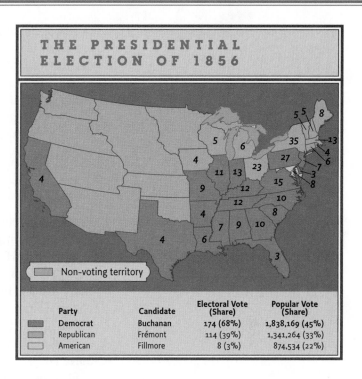

THE PRESIDENTIAL ELECTION OF 1856

	Non-voting territory		

Party	Candidate	Electoral Vote (Share)	Popular Vote (Share)
Democrat	Buchanan	174 (68%)	1,838,169 (45%)
Republican	Frémont	114 (39%)	1,341,264 (33%)
American	Fillmore	8 (3%)	874,534 (22%)

THE DRED SCOTT DECISION

Even before his inauguration, Buchanan became aware of an impending Supreme Court decision that held out the hope of settling the slavery controversy once and for all. This was the case of Dred Scott. During the 1830s, Scott had accompanied his owner, Dr. John Emerson of Missouri, to Illinois, where slavery had been prohibited by the Northwest Ordinance of 1787 and by state law, and to Wisconsin Territory, where it was barred by the Missouri Compromise. After returning to Missouri, Scott sued for his freedom, claiming that residence on free soil had made him free.

The Dred Scott decision, one of the most famous—or infamous—rulings in the long history of the Supreme Court, was announced in March 1857, two days after Buchanan's inauguration. The justices addressed three questions. Could a black person be a citizen and therefore sue in federal court? Did residence in a free state make Scott free? Did Congress possess the power to prohibit slavery in a territory? All nine justices issued individual opinions. But essentially, the Court divided 6-3 (with Justice Robert C. Grier of Pennsylvania, at Buchanan's behind-the-scenes urging, joining a southern majority). Speaking for the majority, Chief Justice Roger B. Taney declared that only white persons could be citizens of the United States. The nation's founders, Taney insisted, believed that blacks "had no rights which the white man was bound to respect." Descended from different ancestors and lacking a history of freedom, blacks, he continued, could never be part of the nation's "political family."

The case could have ended there, since Scott had no right to sue, but inspired by the idea of resolving the slavery issue, Taney pressed on. Scott, he declared, remained a slave. Illinois law had no effect on him after his return to Missouri. As for his residence in Wisconsin, Congress possessed no power under the Constitution to bar slavery from a territory. The Missouri Compromise, recently repealed by the Kansas-Nebraska Act, had

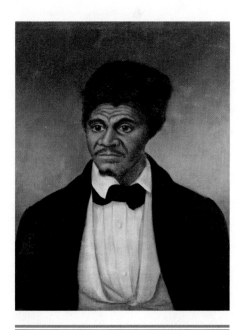

Dred Scott as painted in 1857, the year the Supreme Court ruled that he and his family must remain in slavery. (Collection of the New York Historical Society)

been unconstitutional and so was any measure interfering with southerners' right to bring slaves into the western territories. The decision in effect declared unconstitutional the Republican platform of restricting slavery's expansion. It also seemed to undermine Douglas's doctrine of popular sovereignty. For if Congress lacked the power to prohibit slavery in a territory, how could a territorial legislature created by Congress do so? The Court, a Georgia newspaper exulted, "covers every question regarding slavery and settles it in favor of the South."

THE DECISION'S AFTERMATH

Perhaps the person least directly affected by the Dred Scott decision was the plaintiff himself, for a new master immediately emancipated Scott and his wife, Harriet. Both died on the eve of the Civil War, having enjoyed their freedom for only a few years. The impact on the party system was more far-reaching. Among the decision's casualties was the reputation of the Court itself, which, in the North, sank to the lowest level in all of American history. Rather than abandoning their opposition to the expansion of slavery, Republicans now viewed the Court as controlled by the Slave Power.

Slavery, announced President Buchanan, henceforth existed in all the territories, "by virtue of the Constitution." In 1858, his administration attempted to admit Kansas as a slave state under the Lecompton Constitution, which had been drafted by a pro-southern convention and never submitted to a popular vote. Outraged by this violation of popular sovereignty, Douglas formed an unlikely alliance with congressional Republicans to block the attempt. Kansas remained a territory; it would join the Union as a free state on the eve of the Civil War. The Lecompton battle convinced southern Democrats that they could not trust their party's most popular northern leader.

LINCOLN AND SLAVERY

The depth of Americans' divisions over slavery were brought into sharp focus in 1858 in one of the most storied election campaigns in the nation's history. Seeking reelection to the Senate as both a champion of popular sovereignty and the man who had prevented the administration from forcing slavery on the people of Kansas, Douglas faced an unexpectedly strong challenge from Abraham Lincoln, then little known outside of Illinois. Born into a modest farm family in Kentucky in 1809, Lincoln had moved as a youth to frontier Indiana and then Illinois. Although he began running for public office at the age of twenty-one, until the mid-1850s his career hardly seemed destined for greatness. He had served four terms as a Whig in the state legislature and one in Congress from 1847 to 1849.

Lincoln reentered politics in 1854 as a result of the Kansas-Nebraska Act. He once said that he "hated slavery as much as any abolitionist." Unlike abolitionists, however, Lincoln was willing to compromise with the South to preserve the Union. "I hate to see the poor creatures hunted down," he once wrote of fugitive slaves, "but I bite my lip and keep silent." But on one question he was inflexible—stopping the expansion of slavery.

Lincoln developed a critique of slavery and its expansion that gave voice to the central values of the emerging Republican Party and the millions of northerners whose loyalty it commanded. His speeches combined the moral fervor of the abolitionists with the respect for order and the Constitution of more conservative northerners. "I hate it," he said in 1854 of the prospect of slavery's expansion, "because of the monstrous injustice of slavery itself. I hate it because it deprives our republican example of its just influence in the world—enables the enemies of free institutions, with plausibility, to taunt us as hypocrites—causes the real friends of freedom to doubt our sincerity." If slavery were allowed to expand, he warned, the "love of liberty" would be extinguished and with it America's special mission to be a symbol of democracy for the entire world.

Even though Lincoln lived in a society firmly in the grasp of the market revolution and worked on occasion as an attorney for the Illinois Central Railroad, one of the nation's largest corporations, his America was the world of the small producer. In a sense, his own life personified the free labor ideology and the opportunities northern society offered to laboring men. During the 1850s, property-owning farmers, artisans, and shopkeepers far outnumbered wage earners in Illinois. Lincoln was fascinated and disturbed by the writings of proslavery ideologues like George Fitzhugh (discussed in Chapter 11), and he rose to the defense of northern society. "I want every man to have the chance," said Lincoln, "and I believe a black man is entitled to it, in which he *can* better his condition." Blacks might not be the equal of whites in all respects, but in their "natural right" to the fruits of their labor, they were "my equal and the equal of all others."

Abraham Lincoln in 1858, the year of the Lincoln-Douglas debates.

THE LINCOLN-DOUGLAS CAMPAIGN

The campaign against Douglas, the North's preeminent political leader, created Lincoln's national reputation. Accepting his party's nomination for the Senate in June 1858, Lincoln etched sharply the differences between them. "A house divided against itself," he announced, "cannot stand. I believe this government cannot endure, permanently half *slave* and half *free*." Lincoln's point was not that civil war was imminent, but that Americans must choose between favoring and opposing slavery. There could be no middle ground. Douglas's policy of popular sovereignty, he insisted, reflected a moral indifference that could only result in the institution's spread throughout the entire country.

The Lincoln-Douglas debates, held in seven Illinois towns and attended by tens of thousands of listeners, remain classics of American political oratory. Clashing definitions of freedom lay at their heart. To Lincoln, freedom meant opposition to slavery. The nation needed to rekindle the spirit of the founding fathers, who, he claimed, had tried to place slavery on the path to "ultimate extinction." Douglas argued that the essence of freedom lay in local self-government and individual self-determination. A large and diverse nation could only survive by respecting the right of each locality to determine its own institutions. In response to a question posed by Lincoln during the Freeport debate, Douglas insisted that popular sovereignty was not incompatible with the Dred Scott decision. Although territorial legislatures could no longer exclude slavery directly, he argued, if the people

Stephen A. Douglas in a daguerreotype from around 1853.

VOICES OF FREEDOM

FROM THE LINCOLN-DOUGLAS DEBATES (1858)

The most famous political campaign in American history, the 1858 race for the U.S. Senate between Senator Stephen A. Douglas (a former Illinois judge) and Abraham Lincoln was highlighted by seven debates in which they discussed the politics of slavery and contrasting understandings of freedom.

DOUGLAS: Mr. Lincoln says that this government cannot endure permanently in the same condition in which it was made by its framers—divided into free and slave states. He says that it has existed for about seventy years thus divided, and yet he tells you that it cannot endure permanently on the same principles and in the same relative conditions in which our fathers made it.... One of the reserved rights of the states, was the right to regulate the relations between master and servant, on the slavery question.

Now, my friends, if we will only act conscientiously upon this great principle of popular sovereignty which guarantees to each state and territory the right to do as it pleases on all things local and domestic instead of Congress interfering, we will continue to be at peace one with another.

LINCOLN: Judge Douglas says, "Why can't this Union endure permanently, half slave and half free?" "Why can't we let it stand as our fathers placed it?" That is the exact difficulty between us.... I say when this government was first established it was the policy of its founders to prohibit the spread of slavery into the new territories of the United States, where it had not existed. But Judge Douglas and his friends have broken up that policy and placed it upon a new basis by which it is to become national and perpetual. All I have asked or desired anywhere is that it should be placed back again upon the basis that the founders of our government originally placed it—restricting it from the new territories. . . .

Judge Douglas assumes that we have no interest in them—that we have no right to interfere. . . . Do we not wish for an outlet for our surplus population, if I may so express myself? Do we not feel an interest in getting to that outlet with such institutions as we would like to have prevail there? Now irrespective of the moral aspect of this question as to whether there is a right or wrong in enslaving a negro, I am still in favor of our new territories being in such a condition that white men may find a home. I am in favor of this not merely for our own people, but as an outlet for *free white people everywhere*, the world over—in which Hans and Baptiste and Patrick, and all other men from all the world, may find new homes and better their conditions in life.

DOUGLAS: For one, I am opposed to negro citizenship in any and every form. I believe this government was made on the white basis. I believe it was made by white men, for the benefit of white men and their posterity forever . . . I do not believe that the Almighty made the negro capable of self-government. I say to you, my fellow-citizens, that in my opinion the signers of the Declaration of Independence had no reference to the negro whatever when they declared all men to be created equal. They desired to express by that phrase, white men, men of European birth and European descent . . . when they spoke of the equality of men.

LINCOLN: I have no purpose to introduce political and social equality between the white and the black races. There is a physical difference between the two, which in my judgment will probably forever forbid their living together upon the footing of perfect equality, and inasmuch as it becomes a necessity that there must be a difference, I, as well as Judge Douglas, am in favor of the race to which I belong, having the superior position. . . . But I hold that notwithstanding all this, there is no reason in the world why the negro is not entitled to all the natural rights enumerated in the Declaration of Independence, the right to life, liberty, and the pursuit of happiness. I hold that he is as much entitled to these as the white man. I agree with Judge Douglas he is not my equal in many respects—certainly not in color, perhaps not in moral or intellectual endowment. But in the right to eat the bread, without leave of anybody else, which his own hand earns, *he is my equal and the equal of Judge Douglas, and the equal of every living man.*

DOUGLAS: He tells you that I will not argue the question whether slavery is right or wrong. I tell you why I will not do it. . . . I hold that the people of the slaveholding states are civilized men as well as ourselves, that they bear consciences as well as we, and that they are accountable to God and their posterity and not to us. It is for them to decide therefore the moral and religious right of the slavery question for themselves within their own limits. . . . He says that he looks forward to a time when slavery shall be abolished everywhere. I look forward to a time when each state shall be allowed to do as it pleases.

LINCOLN: I suppose that the real difference between Judge Douglas and his friends, and the Republicans, is that the Judge is not in favor of making any difference between slavery and liberty . . . and consequently every sentiment he utters discards the idea that there is any wrong in slavery. . . . That is the real issue. That is the issue that will continue in this country when these poor tongues of Judge Douglas and myself shall be silent. It is the eternal struggle between these two principles—right and wrong—throughout the world.

QUESTIONS

1. How do Lincoln and Douglas differ on what rights black Americans are entitled to enjoy?

2. Why does Lincoln believe the nation cannot exist forever half slave and half free, whereas Douglas believes it can?

3. How does each of the speakers balance the right of each state to manage its own affairs against the right of every person to be free?

wished to keep slaveholders out all they needed to do was refrain from giving the institution legal protection.

In a critique not only of the antislavery movement but of the entire reform impulse deriving from religious revivalism, Douglas insisted that politicians had no right to impose their own moral standards on society as a whole. "I deny the right of Congress," he declared, "to force a good thing upon a people who are unwilling to receive it." If a community wished to own slaves, it had a right to do so. Of course, when Douglas spoke of the "people," he meant whites alone. He spent much of his time in the debates attempting to portray Lincoln as a dangerous radical whose positions threatened to degrade white Americans by reducing them to equality with blacks. The United States government, Douglas proclaimed, had been created "by white men for the benefit of white men and their posterity for ever."

Lincoln shared many of the racial prejudices of his day. He opposed giving Illinois blacks the right to vote or serve on juries and spoke frequently of colonizing blacks overseas as the best solution to the problems of slavery and race. Yet, unlike Douglas, Lincoln did not use appeals to racism to garner votes. And he refused to exclude blacks from the human family. No less than whites, they were entitled to the inalienable rights of the Declaration of Independence, which applied to "all men, in all lands, everywhere," not merely to Europeans and their descendants.

The Illinois election returns revealed a state sharply divided, like the nation itself. Southern Illinois, settled from the South, voted strongly Democratic, while the rapidly growing northern part of the state was firmly in the Republican column. Until the adoption of the Seventeenth Amendment in the early twentieth century, each state's legislature chose its U.S. senators. In 1858, Republican candidates for the legislature won more votes statewide than Democrats. But because the apportionment of seats, based on the census of 1850, did not reflect the growth of northern Illinois since then, the Democrats emerged with a narrow margin in the legislature. Douglas was reelected. His victory was all the more remarkable because elsewhere in the North Republicans swept to victory in 1858. Resentment over the administration's Kansas policy split the Democratic Party, sometimes producing two Democratic candidates (pro-Douglas and pro-Buchanan) running against a single Republican. Coupled with the impact of the economic recession that began in 1857, this helped to produce Republican victories even in Indiana and Pennsylvania, which Democrats had carried two years earlier.

JOHN BROWN AT HARPERS FERRY

An armed assault by the abolitionist John Brown on the federal arsenal at Harpers Ferry, Virginia, further heightened sectional tensions. Brown had a long career of involvement in antislavery activities. In the 1830s and 1840s, he had befriended fugitive slaves and, although chronically in debt, helped to finance antislavery publications. Like other abolitionists, Brown was a deeply religious man. But his God was not the forgiving Jesus of the revivals, who encouraged men to save themselves through conversion, but the vengeful Father of the Old Testament. During the civil war in Kansas,

John Brown in an 1847 portrait by Augustus Washington, a black photographer.

An 1835 painting of the federal arsenal at Harpers Ferry, Virginia (now West Virginia). John Brown's raid on Harpers Ferry in October 1859 helped to bring on the Civil War.

Brown traveled to the territory. In May 1856, after the attack on Lawrence, he and a few followers murdered five proslavery settlers at Pottawatomie Creek. For the next two years, he traveled through the North and Canada, raising funds and enlisting followers for a war against slavery.

On October 16, 1859, with twenty-one men, seven of them black, Brown seized Harpers Ferry. Militarily, the plan made little sense. Brown's band was soon surrounded and killed or captured by a detachment of federal soldiers headed by Colonel Robert E. Lee. Placed on trial for treason to the state of Virginia, Brown conducted himself with dignity and courage, winning admiration from millions of northerners who disapproved of his violent deeds. When Virginia's governor, Henry A. Wise, spurned pleas for clemency and ordered Brown executed, he turned Brown into a martyr to much of the North. Henry David Thoreau pronounced him "a crucified hero." Since Brown's death, radicals of both the left and right have revered Brown as a man willing to take action against an institution he considered immoral. Black leaders have long hailed him as a rare white person willing to sacrifice himself for the cause of racial justice.

To the South, the failure of Brown's assault seemed less significant than the adulation he seemed to arouse from much of the northern public. His raid and execution further widened the breach between the sections. Brown's last letter was a brief, prophetic statement: "I, John Brown, am quite certain that the crimes of this guilty land will never be purged away but with blood."

THE RISE OF SOUTHERN NATIONALISM

With the Republicans continuing to gain strength in the North, Democrats might have been expected to put a premium on party unity as the election of 1860 approached. By this time, however, a sizable group of southerners now viewed their region's prospects as more favorable outside the Union than within it. Throughout the 1850s, influential writers and political leaders kept up a drumbeat of complaints about the South's problems. The sky-high price of slaves made it impossible for many planters' sons and upwardly mobile small farmers to become planters in their own right. Many white southerners felt that the opportunity was eroding for economic independence through ownership of land and slaves—liberty as they understood it. The North, secessionists charged, reaped the benefits of the cotton trade, while southerners fell deeper and deeper into debt. To remain in the Union meant to accept "bondage" to the North. But an independent South could become the foundation of a slave empire ringing the Caribbean and embracing Cuba, other West Indian islands, Mexico, and parts of Central America.

More and more southerners were speaking openly of southward expansion. In 1854, Pierre Soulé of Louisiana, the American ambassador to Spain, had persuaded the ministers to Britain and France to join him in signing the Ostend Manifesto, which called on the United States to purchase or seize Cuba, where slavery was still legal, from Spain. Meanwhile, the military adventurer William Walker led a series of "filibustering" expeditions (the term derived from the Spanish word for pirate, *filibustero*) in Central America.

Born in Tennessee, Walker had headed to California to join the gold rush. Failing to strike it rich, he somehow decided to try to become the leader of a Latin American country. In 1853, he led a band of men who "captured" Baja California—a peninsula owned by Mexico south of California—and named himself president of an independent republic. The arrival of Mexican naval vessels forced Walker and his men to beat a hasty retreat. Walker next decided to establish himself as ruler of Nicaragua in Central America, and to open that country to slavery. Nicaragua at the time was engaged in a civil war, and one faction invited Walker to assist it by bringing 300 armed men. In 1855, Walker captured the city of Granada and in the following year proclaimed himself president. The administration of Franklin Pierce recognized Walker's government, but neighboring countries sent in troops, who forced Walker to flee. His activities represented clear violations of American neutrality laws. But Walker won acclaim in the South, and when federal authorities placed him on trial in New Orleans in 1858, the jury acquitted him.

By the late 1850s, southern leaders were bending every effort to strengthen the bonds of slavery. "Slavery is our king," declared a South Carolina politician in 1860. "Slavery is our truth, slavery is our divine right." New state laws further restricted access to freedom. One in Louisiana stated simply: "After the passage of this act, no slave shall be emancipated in this state." Some southerners called for the reopening of the African slave trade, hoping that an influx of new slaves would lower the price, thereby increasing the number of whites with a vested interest in the peculiar institution. By early 1860, seven states of the Deep South had gone on record demanding that the Democratic Platform pledge to protect slavery in all the territories that had not yet been admitted to the Union as states. Virtually no northern politician could accept this position. For southern leaders to insist on it would guarantee the destruction of the Democratic Party as a national institution. But southern nationalists, known as "fire-eaters," hoped to split the party and the country and form an independent Southern Confederacy.

THE DEMOCRATIC SPLIT

When the Democratic convention met in April 1860, Douglas's supporters commanded a majority but not the two-thirds required for a presidential nomination. Because of his fight against Kansas's Lecompton Constitution and his refusal to support congressional laws imposing slavery on all the territories, Douglas had become unacceptable to political leaders of the Deep South. They were still determined to bring Kansas into the Union as a slave state. When the convention adopted a platform reaffirming the doctrine of popular sovereignty, delegates from the seven slave states of the Lower South walked out and the gathering recessed in confusion. Six weeks later, it reconvened, replaced the bolters with Douglas supporters, and nominated him for president. In response, southern Democrats placed their own ticket in the field, headed by John C. Breckinridge of Kentucky. Breckinridge insisted that slavery must be protected in the western territories.

The Democratic Party, the last great bond of national unity, had been shattered. National conventions had traditionally been places where party managers, mindful of the need for unity in the fall campaign, reconciled their differences. But in 1860, neither northern nor southern Democrats were interested in conciliation. Southern Democrats no longer trusted their northern counterparts. Douglas's backers, for their part, would not accept a platform that doomed their party to certain defeat in the North.

THE NOMINATION OF LINCOLN

Meanwhile, Republicans gathered in Chicago and chose Lincoln as their standard-bearer. Although he entered the convention with fewer delegates than William H. Seward, Lincoln did not suffer from Seward's political liabilities. Former Know-Nothings, a majority of whom had by now joined Republican ranks, bitterly resented Seward's efforts as governor of New York to channel state funds to Catholic schools. Seward had a not entirely deserved reputation for radicalism as a result of his "higher law" and "irrepressible conflict" speeches, discussed earlier.

Lincoln's devotion to the Union appealed to moderate Republicans, and his emphasis on the moral dimension of the sectional controversy made him acceptable to Republicans from abolitionist backgrounds. Having never associated with the Know-Nothings, he could appeal to immigrant voters, and nativists preferred him to the hated Seward. Most important, coming from Illinois, Lincoln was better positioned to carry the pivotal "doubtful states" essential for Republican victory. On the third ballot, he was nominated. The party platform denied the validity of the Dred Scott decision, reaffirmed Republicans' opposition to slavery's expansion, and added economic planks designed to appeal to a broad array of northern voters—free homesteads in the West, a protective tariff, and government aid in building a transcontinental railroad.

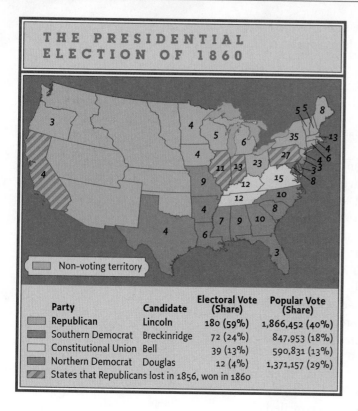

THE PRESIDENTIAL ELECTION OF 1860

Non-voting territory

Party	Candidate	Electoral Vote (Share)	Popular Vote (Share)
Republican	Lincoln	180 (59%)	1,866,452 (40%)
Southern Democrat	Breckinridge	72 (24%)	847,953 (18%)
Constitutional Union	Bell	39 (13%)	590,831 (13%)
Northern Democrat	Douglas	12 (4%)	1,371,157 (29%)
States that Republicans lost in 1856, won in 1860			

THE ELECTION OF 1860

In effect, two presidential campaigns took place in 1860. In the North, Lincoln and Douglas were the combatants. In the South, the Republicans had no presence and three candidates contested the election—Douglas, Breckinridge, and John Bell of Tennessee, the candidate of the hastily organized Constitutional Union Party. A haven for Unionist former Whigs, this new party adopted a platform consisting of a single pledge—to preserve "the Constitution as it is [that is, with slavery] and the Union as it was [without sectional discord]."

The most striking thing about the election returns was their sectional character. Lincoln carried all of the North except New Jersey, receiving 1.8 million popular votes (54 percent of the regional total and 40 percent of the national) and 180 electoral votes (a clear majority). Breckinridge captured most of the slave states, although Bell carried three Upper South states and about 40 percent of the southern vote as a whole. Douglas placed first only in Missouri, but his 1.3 million popular votes were second in number only to Lincoln's. Douglas was the only candidate with significant support in all parts of the country, a vindication, in a sense, of his long effort to transcend sectional divisions. But his failure to carry either section suggested that a traditional political career based on devotion to the Union was no longer possible. Without a single vote in ten southern states, Lincoln was elected the nation's sixteenth president. He failed to secure a majority of the national popular vote. But because of the North's superiority in population, Lincoln would still have carried the electoral college and thus been elected president even if the votes of his three opponents had all been cast for a single candidate.

THE IMPENDING CRISIS

THE SECESSION MOVEMENT

In the eyes of many white southerners, Lincoln's victory placed their future at the mercy of a party avowedly hostile to their region's values and interests. Those advocating secession did not believe Lincoln's administration would take immediate steps against slavery in the states. But if, as seemed quite possible, the election of 1860 marked a fundamental shift in power, the beginning of a long period of Republican rule, who could say what the North's antislavery sentiment would demand in five years, or ten? Slaveowners, moreover, feared Republican efforts to extend their party into the South by appealing to non-slaveholders. Rather than accept permanent minority status in a nation governed by their opponents, Deep South political leaders boldly struck for their region's independence. At stake, they believed, was not a single election, but an entire way of life.

An 1860 engraving of a mass meeting in Savannah, Georgia, shortly after Lincoln's election as president, which called for the state to secede from the Union. The banner on the obelisk at the center reads, "Our Motto State's Rights, Equality of the States, Don't Tread on Me"—the last a slogan from the American Revolution.

In the months that followed Lincoln's election, seven states stretching from South Carolina to Texas seceded from the Union. These were the states of the Cotton Kingdom, where slaves represented a larger part of the total population than in the Upper South. First to secede was South Carolina, the state with the highest percentage of slaves in its population and a long history of political radicalism. On December 20, 1860, the legislature unanimously voted to leave the Union. Its *Declaration of the Immediate Causes of Secession* placed the issue of slavery squarely at the center of the crisis. The North had "assumed the right of deciding upon the propriety of our domestic institutions." Lincoln was a man "whose opinions and purposes are hostile to slavery." Experience had proved "that slaveholding states cannot be safe in subjection to nonslaveholding states." Secessionists equated their movement with the struggle for American independence. Proslavery ideologue George Fitzhugh, however, later claimed that southern secession was even more significant than the "commonplace affair" of 1776, since the South rebelled not merely against a particular government but against the erroneous modern idea of freedom based on "human equality" and "natural liberty."

THE SECESSION CRISIS

As the Union unraveled, President Buchanan seemed paralyzed. He denied that a state could secede, but he also insisted that the federal government had no right to use force against it. Other political leaders struggled to find a formula to resolve the crisis. Senator John J. Crittenden of Kentucky, a slave state on the border between North and South, offered the most widely supported compromise plan of the secession winter. Embodied in a series of unamendable constitutional amendments, Crittenden's proposal would

A Richmond, Virginia, cartoonist in April 1861 depicts Lincoln as a cat seeking to catch the southern states as mice fleeing the Union, which lies dead on the left.

have guaranteed the future of slavery in the states where it existed, and extended the Missouri Compromise line to the Pacific Ocean, dividing between slavery and free soil all territories "now held, or hereafter acquired." The seceding states rejected the compromise as too little, too late. But many in the Upper South and North saw it as a way to settle sectional differences and prevent civil war.

Crittenden's plan, however, foundered on the opposition of Abraham Lincoln. Willing to conciliate the South on issues like the return of fugitive slaves, Lincoln took an unyielding stand against the expansion of slavery. Here, he informed one Republican leader, he intended to "hold firm, as with a chain of steel." A fundamental principle of democracy, Lincoln believed, was at stake. "We have just carried an election," he wrote, "on principles fairly stated to the people. Now we are told in advance that the government shall be broken up unless we surrender to those we have beaten, before we take the offices. . . . If we surrender, it is the end of us and the end of the government." Lincoln, moreover, feared that Crittenden's reference to land "hereafter acquired" offered the South a thinly veiled invitation to demand the acquisition of Cuba, Mexico, and other territory suited to slavery.

Before Lincoln assumed office on March 4, 1861, the seven seceding states formed the Confederate States of America, adopted a constitution, and chose as their president Jefferson Davis of Mississippi. With a few alterations—the president served a single six-year term; cabinet members, as in Britain, could sit in Congress—the Confederate constitution was modeled closely on that of the United States. It departed from the federal Constitution, however, in explicitly guaranteeing slave property both in the states and in any territories the new nation acquired. The "cornerstone" of the Confederacy, announced Davis's vice president, Alexander H. Stephens of Georgia, was "the great truth that the negro is not equal to the white man, that slavery, subordination to the superior race, is his natural and normal condition."

Inauguration of Mr. Lincoln, a photograph taken on March 4, 1861. The unfinished dome of the Capitol building symbolizes the precarious state of the Union at the time Lincoln assumed office.

AND THE WAR CAME

Even after rejecting the Crittenden Compromise, Lincoln did not believe war inevitable. When he became president, eight slave states of the Upper South remained in the Union. Here, slaves and slaveholders made up a considerably lower proportion of the population than in the Deep South, and large parts of the white population did not believe Lincoln's election justified dissolving the Union. Even within the Confederacy, whites had divided over secession, with considerable numbers of non-slaveholding farmers in opposition. In time, Lincoln believed, secession might collapse from within.

In his inaugural address, delivered on March 4, 1861, Lincoln tried to be conciliatory. He rejected the right of secession but denied any intention of interfering with slavery in the states. He said nothing of retaking the forts, arsenals, and customs houses the Confederacy had seized, although he did promise to "hold" remaining federal property in the seceding states. But Lincoln also issued a veiled warning: "In your hands, my dissatisfied fellow countrymen, and not in mine, is the momentous issue of civil war."

In his first month as president, Lincoln walked a tightrope. He avoided any action that might drive more states from the Union, encouraged southern Unionists to assert themselves within the Confederacy, and sought to quiet a growing clamor in the North for forceful action against secession. Knowing that the risk of war existed, Lincoln strove to ensure that if hostilities did break out, the South, not the Union, would fire the first shot. And that is precisely what happened on April 12, 1861, at Fort Sumter, an enclave of Union control in the harbor of Charleston, South Carolina.

A few days earlier, Lincoln had notified South Carolina's governor that he intended to replenish the garrison's dwindling food supplies. Viewing Fort Sumter's presence as an affront to southern nationhood, and perhaps

Bombardment of Fort Sumter, *a lithograph by Nathaniel Currier and James Ives depicting the beginning of the Civil War.*

hoping to force the wavering Upper South to join the Confederacy, Jefferson Davis ordered batteries to fire on the fort. On April 14, its commander surrendered. The following day, Lincoln proclaimed that an insurrection existed in the South and called for 75,000 troops to suppress it. Civil war had begun. Within weeks, Virginia, North Carolina, Tennessee, and Arkansas joined the Confederacy. "Both sides deprecated war," Lincoln later said, "but one of them would *make* war rather than let the nation survive; and the other would *accept* war rather than let it perish. And the war came."

In 1842, Henry Wadsworth Longfellow published *Poems on Slavery*, a collection that included a work entitled simply "The Warning." In it, Longfellow compared the American slave to the mighty biblical figure of Samson, who after being blinded and chained, managed to destroy the temple of his tormentors:

> There is a poor, blind Samson in this land,
> Shorn of his strength, and bound in bonds of steel,
> Who may, in some grim revel, raise his hand,
> And shake the pillars of this Commonweal,
> Till the vast Temple of our liberties
> A shapeless mass of wreck and rubbish lies.

In 1861, Longfellow's warning came to pass. The Union created by the founders lay in ruins. The struggle to rebuild it would bring about a new birth of American freedom.

SUGGESTED READING

BOOKS

Anbinder, Tyler. *Nativism and Slavery: The Northern Know-Nothings and the Politics of the 1850s* (1992). A detailed study of the relationship between nativism and antislavery politics in the North.

Cronon, William. *Nature's Metropolis: Chicago and the Great West* (1992). An influential account of the rise of Chicago and the city's relationship to its agricultural hinterland.

Current, Richard N. *Lincoln and the First Shot* (1963). Examines the decisions and strategy of both Lincoln and Jefferson Davis that produced the firing on Fort Sumter that began the Civil War.

Davis, William C. *Lone Star Rising: The Revolutionary Birth of the Texas Republic* (2004). An up-to-date history of the Texas war for independence.

Earle, Jonathan H. *Jacksonian Antislavery and the Politics of Free Soil, 1824–1854* (2004). Emphasizes the role of northern Jacksonians in antislavery politics.

Foner, Eric. *Free Soil, Free Labor, Free Men: The Ideology of the Republican Party before the Civil War* (1970). A discussion of the basic ideas that united Republicans in the 1850s, especially their "free labor ideology."

Goodman, David. *Gold Seeking: Victoria and California in the 1850s* (1994). A comparative history of the two gold rushes.

Haas, Lisbeth. *Conquests and Historical Identities in California, 1769–1936* (1995). Contains a detailed description of how California's acquisition by the United States affected the state's diverse population groups.

Johannsen, Robert W. *To the Halls of Montezuma: The Mexican War in the American Imagination* (1985). A history of the Mexican War and how it was remembered after its conclusion.

Levine, Bruce. *Half Slave and Half Free: The Roots of the Civil War* (1992). A survey of the coming of the Civil War, stressing irreconcilable differences between North and South.

Potter, David M. *The Impending Crisis, 1848–1861* (1976). Still the standard account of the nation's history in the years before the Civil War.

Sinha, Manisha. *The Counterrevolution of Slavery: Politics and Ideology in Antebellum South Carolina* (2002). A detailed study of how a vigorous defense of slavery developed in South Carolina, which justified the decision for secession.

Stampp, Kenneth. *And the War Came: The North and the Secession Crisis, 1860–61* (1950). An examination of Northern actions and attitudes during the secession crisis.

Stephanson, Anders. *Manifest Destiny: American Expansionism and the Empire of Right* (1995). Considers how the idea of an American mission to spread freedom and democracy has affected American foreign policy throughout the country's history.

WEBSITES

Getting the Message Out: National Campaign Materials, 1840–1860: http://dig.lib.niu.edu/message/

Gold Rush!: www.museumca.org/goldrush/

The Mexican-American War and the Media: www.history.vt.edu/MxAmWar/INDEX.HTM#

The Oregon Trail: www.isu.edu/~trinmich/Oregontrail.html

Uncle Tom's Cabin and American Culture: http://jefferson.village.virginia.edu/utc/

REVIEW QUESTIONS

1. Explain the justifications for the doctrine of manifest destiny, including material and idealistic motivations.

2. What economic forces promoted continental expansion in the 1830s and 1840s?

3. Why did many Americans criticize the Mexican War? How did they see expansion as a threat to American liberties?

4. How did the concept of "race" develop by the mid-nineteenth century, and how did it enter into the manifest destiny debate?

5. Explain the factors behind the creation of the Republican Party.

6. What three questions did the Supreme Court address in the Dred Scott case? Assess the Court's arguments.

7. Based on the Lincoln-Douglas debates, how did the views of both men differ on the expansion of slavery, equal rights, and the role of the national government?

8. What were the international implications of southern nationalism?

9. Explain how sectional voting patterns in the 1860 presidential election allowed southern "fire-eaters" to justify secession.

FREEDOM QUESTIONS

1. How did Americans argue that conquering Texas and other parts of Mexico was "extending the area of freedom"?

2. Explain how both northerners and southerners believed winning the struggle over the expansion of slavery was the key to preserving their freedoms and to preventing their domination by the other section of the nation.

3. According to the Republican Party, how was "free labor" the key to preserving American freedoms, and the free society threatened by the Slave Power?

4. How did southern nationalists justify independence as "freedom" from northern "bondage"?

KEY TERMS

Santa Fe Trail (p. 495)

Tejanos (p. 496)

the Texas revolt (p. 496)

Santa Anna (p. 497)

"reannexation" of Texas and "reoccupation" of Oregon (p. 499)

Wilmot Proviso (p. 507)

Free Soil Party (p. 507)

Fugitive Slave Act of 1850 (p. 510)

popular sovereignty (p. 511)

Kansas-Nebraska Act of 1854 (p. 511)

"balloon frame" houses (p. 515)

Know-Nothing Party (p. 515)

the Slave Power (p. 516)

"Bleeding Kansas" (p. 517)

the caning of Charles Sumner (p. 517)

Dred Scott decision (p. 519)

Lecompton Constitution (p. 527)

Harpers Ferry (p. 524)

"filibustering" expeditions (p. 526)

"fire-eaters" (p. 527)

REVIEW TABLE

Road Toward War

Event	Date	Explanation	Result
Compromise of 1850	1850	Southerners are concerned that congressional balance would be disrupted by California's request for free-state status	California becomes a free state; the Fugitive Slave Act is passed; and slavery in the New Mexico territory is to be decided by locals
Kansas-Nebraska Act	1854	A bill that provides for slavery to be decided by popular sovereignty	"Bleeding Kansas"—civil war in Kansas over the issue of slavery in 1856
Dred Scott decision	1857	Supreme Court rules that only white persons are citizens and that Congress possesses no power to bar slavery from a territory	It in effect declared unconstitutional the Republican platform of restricting slavery's expansion
John Brown and Harpers Ferry	1859	Brown raids a federal arsenal to launch a slave rebellion and is executed for his crime	Brown becomes a martyr to many in the North
1860 Election	1860	Abraham Lincoln wins with no votes in the South, ending decades of southern control of the presidency	Seven southern states secede from the Union before Lincoln is inaugurated

Chapter 14

A New Birth of Freedom: The Civil War, 1861–1865

Departure of the 7th Regiment, *a lithograph from 1861 illustrating the departure of a unit of the New York State militia for service in the Civil War. A contemporary writer captured the exuberant spirit of the early days of the war: "New York was certainly raving mad with excitement. The ladies laughed, smiled, sighed, sobbed, and wept. The men cheered and shouted as never men cheered and shouted before."*

☞

FOCUS QUESTIONS

- Why is the Civil War considered the first modern war?

- How did a war to preserve the Union become a war to end slavery?

- How did the Civil War transform the national economy and create a stronger nation-state?

- How did the war effort and leadership problems affect the society and economy of the Confederacy?

- What were the military and political turning points of the war?

- What were the most important wartime "rehearsals for Reconstruction"?

ike hundreds of thousands of other Americans, Marcus M. Spiegel volunteered in 1861 to fight in the Civil War. Born into a Jewish family in Germany in 1829, Spiegel took part in the failed German revolution of 1848. In the following year he emigrated to Ohio, where he married the daughter of a local farmer. When the Civil War broke out, the nation's 150,000 Jews represented less than 1 percent of the total population. But Spiegel shared wholeheartedly in American patriotism. He went to war, he wrote to his brother-in-law, to defend "the flag that was ever ready to protect you and me and every one who sought its protection from oppression."

Spiegel rose to the rank of colonel in the 120th Ohio Infantry and saw action in Virginia, Mississippi, and Louisiana. He corresponded frequently with his wife, Caroline. "I have seen and learned much," he wrote in 1863. "I have seen men dying of disease and mangled by the weapons of death; I have witnessed hostile armies arrayed against each other, the charge of infantry, [and] cavalry hunting men down like beasts." But he never wavered in his commitment to the "glorious cause" of preserving the Union and its heritage of freedom.

What one Pennsylvania recruit called "the magic word *Freedom*" shaped how many Union soldiers understood the conflict. The war's purpose, wrote Samuel McIlvaine, a sergeant from Indiana, was to preserve the American nation as "the beacon light of liberty and freedom to the human race." But as the war progressed, prewar understandings of liberty gave way to something new. Millions of northerners who had not been abolitionists became convinced that preserving the Union as an embodiment of liberty required the destruction of slavery.

Marcus Spiegel's changing views mirrored the transformation of a struggle to save the Union into a war to end slavery. Spiegel was an ardent Democrat. He shared the era's racist attitudes and thought Lincoln's Emancipation Proclamation a serious mistake. Yet as the Union army penetrated the heart of the Deep South, Spiegel became increasingly opposed to slavery. "Since I am here," he wrote to his wife from Louisiana in January 1864, "I have learned and seen . . . the horrors of slavery. You know it takes me long to say anything that sounds antidemocratic [opposed to Democratic Party policies], but . . . never hereafter will I either speak or vote in favor of slavery."

Marcus Spiegel was killed in a minor engagement in Louisiana in May 1864, one of 620,000 Americans to perish in the Civil War.

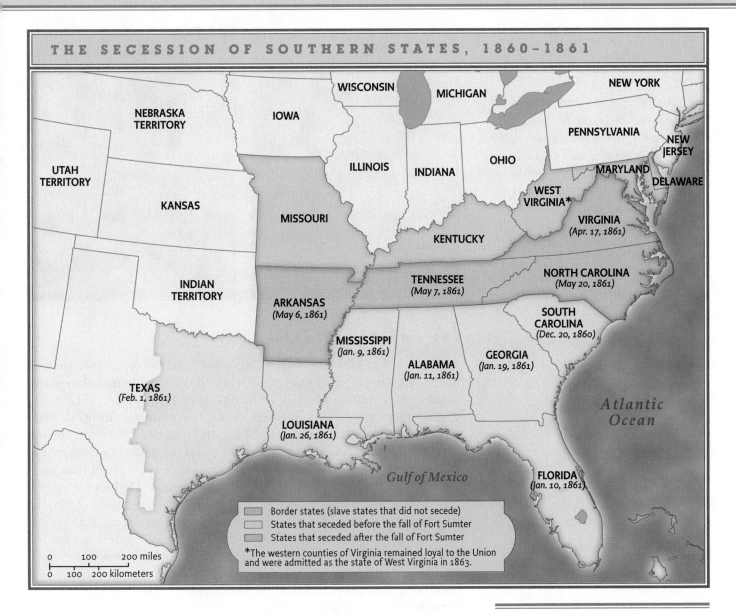

THE SECESSION OF SOUTHERN STATES, 1860-1861

Border states (slave states that did not secede)
States that seceded before the fall of Fort Sumter
States that seceded after the fall of Fort Sumter

*The western counties of Virginia remained loyal to the Union and were admitted as the state of West Virginia in 1863.

By the time secession ran its course, eleven slave states had left the Union.

THE FIRST MODERN WAR

The American Civil War is often called the first modern war. Never before had mass armies confronted each other on the battlefield with the deadly weapons created by the industrial revolution. The resulting casualties dwarfed anything in the American experience. Beginning as a battle of army versus army, the war became a conflict of society against society, in which the distinction between military and civilian targets often disappeared. In a war of this kind, the effectiveness of political leadership, the ability to mobilize economic resources, and a society's willingness to keep up the fight despite setbacks are as crucial to the outcome as success or failure on individual battlefields.

Sergeant James W. Travis, Thirty-eighth Illinois Infantry, Union army, and Private Edwin Francis Jemison, Second Louisiana Regiment, Confederate army, two of the nearly 3 million Americans who fought in the Civil War. Before going off to war, many soldiers sat for photographs like these, reproduced on small cards called cartes de visite, *which they distributed to friends and loved ones. Jemison was killed in the Battle of Malvern Hill in July 1862.*

THE TWO COMBATANTS

Almost any comparison between Union and Confederacy seemed to favor the Union. The population of the North and the loyal border slave states numbered 22 million in 1860, while only 9 million persons lived in the Confederacy, 3.5 million of them slaves. In manufacturing, railroad mileage, and financial resources, the Union far outstripped its opponent. On the other hand, the Union confronted by far the greater task. To restore the shattered nation, it had to invade and conquer an area larger than western Europe. Confederate soldiers were highly motivated fighters defending their homes and families. Like Washington's forces during the American Revolution, southern armies could lose most of the battles and still win the war if their opponent tired of the struggle. "No people," Confederate general P. G. T. Beauregard later claimed, "ever warred for independence with more relative advantages than the Confederacy."

On both sides, the outbreak of war stirred powerful feelings of patriotism. Recruits rushed to enlist, expecting a short, glorious war. Later, as enthusiasm waned, both sides resorted to a draft. The Confederacy in the spring of 1862 passed the first draft law in American history, and the North soon followed. By 1865, more than 2 million men had served in the Union army and 900,000 in the Confederate army. Each was a cross section of its society: the North's was composed largely of farm boys, shopkeepers, artisans, and urban workers, while the South's consisted mostly of non-slaveholding small farmers, with slaveowners dominating the officer corps.

Few recruits had any military experience. Fifteen years had passed since the Mexican War. Ideas about war were highly romantic, based on novels, magazine articles, and lithographs of soldiers covering themselves with glory. One private wrote home in 1862 that his notion of combat had come from the pictures of battles he had seen: "they would all be in a line, all standing in a nice level field fighting, a number of ladies taking care of the wounded, etc. But it isn't so." Nor were the recruits ready for military regimentation. "It comes rather hard at first to be deprived of liberty," wrote an Illinois soldier. Initially, the constant round of drilling, ditch digging, and other chores were only occasionally interrupted by fierce bursts of fighting on the battlefield. According to one estimate, during the first two years of the war the main Union force, the Army of the Potomac, spent only thirty days in actual combat.

THE TECHNOLOGY OF WAR

Neither the soldiers nor their officers were prepared for the way technology had transformed warfare. The Civil War was the first major conflict in which the railroad transported troops and supplies and the first to see railroad junctions such

Battle of the Iron-clads *Monitor and Merrimac*, painted in 1877 by William Torgerson, depicts the first clash between ironclad ships, which took place off the coast of Virginia on March 9, 1862. Precursors of modern battleships, ironclads were among the numerous technological advances introduced during the Civil War. The masts of a wooden naval vessel are visible on the horizon.

as Atlanta and Petersburg become major military objectives. The famous sea battle between the Union vessel *Monitor* and the Confederate *Merrimac* in 1862 was the first demonstration of the superiority of ironclads over wooden ships, revolutionizing naval warfare. The war saw the use of the telegraph for military communication, the introduction of observation balloons to view enemy lines, and even primitive hand grenades and submarines.

Perhaps most important, a revolution in arms manufacturing had replaced the traditional musket, accurate at only a short range, with the more modern rifle, deadly at 600 yards or more because of its grooved (or "rifled") barrel. This development changed the nature of combat, emphasizing the importance of heavy fortifications and elaborate trenches and giving those on the defensive—usually southern armies—a significant advantage over attacking forces. "My men," said Confederate general Thomas "Stonewall" Jackson, "sometimes fail to drive the enemy from his position, but to hold one, never." The war of rifle and trench produced the appalling casualty statistics of Civil War battles. The 620,000 who perished in the war represent the equivalent, in terms of today's population, of more

Confederate dead at Spotsylvania, Virginia, the site of a bloody battle in 1864.

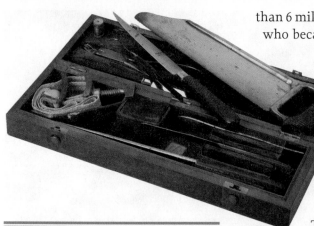

A surgeon's kit used in the Civil War, containing amputation instruments, knives, and tourniquets. With medical knowledge and practices primitive at best, far more men died from wounds, infections, and disease than in battle.

than 6 million men. These figures do not include the thousands of civilians who became victims of battles or who perished in disease-ridden camps for runaway slaves or in conflicts between Unionist and Confederate families that raged in parts of the South. The death toll in the Civil War nearly equals the total number of Americans who died in all the nation's other wars, from the Revolution to the war in Iraq.

Nor was either side ready for other aspects of modern warfare. Medical care remained primitive. "I believe the doctors kill more than they cure," wrote an Alabama private in 1862. Diseases like measles, dysentery, malaria, and typhus swept through army camps, killing more men than did combat. The Civil War was the first war in which large numbers of Americans were captured by the enemy and held in dire conditions in military prisons. Some 50,000 men died in these prisons, victims of starvation and disease, including 13,000 Union soldiers at Andersonville, Georgia.

Everywhere in the world, war was becoming more destructive. The scale of Civil War bloodshed was unique in American history, but not in the nineteenth-century world. The Taiping Rebellion in China (1850–1864) resulted in 23 million deaths. The War of the Triple Alliance in South America (1864–1870), which pitted Argentina, Brazil, and Uruguay against Paraguay, caused the death of half of Paraguay's prewar population of around 525,000. Napoleon III's military destruction of the Paris Commune in 1871 resulted in the death of more than 20,000 of his fellow countrymen in a single city.

THE PUBLIC AND THE WAR

Another modern feature of the Civil War was that both sides were assisted by a vast propaganda effort to mobilize public opinion. In the Union, an

Confederate prisoners of war at Camp Douglas, Chicago, in 1864.

outpouring of lithographs, souvenirs, sheet music, and pamphlets issued by patriotic organizations and the War Department reaffirmed northern values, tarred the Democratic Party with the brush of treason, and accused the South of numerous crimes against Union soldiers and loyal civilians. Comparable items appeared in the Confederacy.

At the same time, the war's brutal realities were brought home with unprecedented immediacy to the public at large. War correspondents accompanied the armies, and newspapers reported the results of battles on the following day and quickly published long lists of casualties. The infant art of photography carried images of war into millions of American living rooms. Beginning in 1862, when photographers entered the battlefield to take shocking pictures of the dead at Antietam, the camera, in the words of one journalist, "brought the bodies and laid them in our door-yards." Mathew Brady, who organized a corps of photographers to cover the war, found the conflict a passport to fame and wealth. For photography itself, it was a turning point in its growth as an art and business enterprise.

MOBILIZING RESOURCES

The outbreak of the war found both sides unprepared. In 1861, there was no national railroad gauge (the distance separating the two tracks), so trains built for one line could not run on another. There was no national banking system, no tax system capable of raising the enormous funds needed to finance the war, and not even accurate maps of the southern states. Soon after the firing on Fort Sumter, Lincoln proclaimed a naval blockade of the South, part of the so-called Anaconda Plan, which aimed to strangle the South economically. But the navy charged with patrolling the 3,500-mile coastline consisted of only ninety vessels, fewer than half of them steam-powered. Not until late in the war did the blockade become effective.

Then there was the problem of purchasing and distributing the food, weapons, and other supplies required by the soldiers. The Union army eventually became the best-fed and best-supplied military force in history. By the war's third year, on the other hand, southern armies were suffering from acute shortages of food, uniforms, and shoes. Yet the chief of the Confederacy's Ordnance Bureau, Josiah Gorgas (a transplanted northerner), proved brilliantly resourceful in arming southern troops. Under his direc-

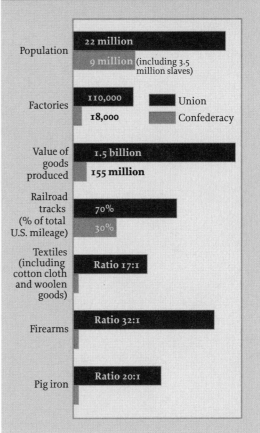

Figure 14.1 RESOURCES FOR WAR: UNION VERSUS CONFEDERACY

	Union	Confederacy
Population	22 million	9 million (including 3.5 million slaves)
Factories	110,000	18,000
Value of goods produced	1.5 billion	155 million
Railroad tracks (% of total U.S. mileage)	70%	30%
Textiles (including cotton cloth and woolen goods)	Ratio 17:1	
Firearms	Ratio 32:1	
Pig iron	Ratio 20:1	

In nearly every resource for warfare, the Union enjoyed a distinct advantage. But this did not make Union victory inevitable; as during the War of Independence, the stronger side sometimes loses.

Union army wagons crossing the Rapidan River in Virginia in May 1864. Supplying Civil War armies required an immense mobilization of economic resources.

tion, the Confederate government imported weapons from abroad and established arsenals of its own to turn out rifles, artillery, and ammunition.

MILITARY STRATEGIES

Each side tried to find ways to maximize its advantages. Essentially, the Confederacy adopted a defensive strategy, with occasional thrusts into the North. General Robert E. Lee, the leading southern commander, was a brilliant battlefield tactician who felt confident of his ability to fend off attacks by larger Union forces. He hoped that a series of defeats would weaken the North's resolve and lead it eventually to abandon the conflict and recognize southern independence.

Lincoln's early generals found it impossible to bring the Union's advantages in manpower and technology to bear on the battlefield. In April 1861, the regular army numbered little more than 15,000 men, most of whom were stationed west of the Mississippi River. Its officers had been trained to lead small, professional forces into battle, not the crowds of untrained men who assembled in 1861. The North also suffered from narrowness of military vision. Its generals initially concentrated on occupying southern territory and attempting to capture Richmond, the Confederate capital. They attacked sporadically and withdrew after a battle, thus sacrificing the North's manpower superiority and allowing the South to concentrate its smaller forces when an engagement impended.

Well before his generals did, Lincoln realized that simply capturing and occupying territory would not win the war, and that defeating the South's armies, not capturing its capital, had to be the North's battlefield objective. And when he came to adopt the policy of emancipation, Lincoln acknowledged what Confederate vice president Alexander H. Stephens had already affirmed: slavery was the "cornerstone" of the Confederacy. To win the war, therefore, the Union must make the institution that lay at the economic and social foundation of southern life a military target.

THE WAR BEGINS

In the East, most of the war's fighting took place in a narrow corridor between Washington and Richmond—a distance of only 100 miles—as a succession of Union generals led the Army of the Potomac (as the main northern force in the East was called) toward the Confederate capital, only to be turned back by southern forces. The first significant engagement, the first Battle of Bull Run, took place in northern Virginia on July 21, 1861. It ended with the chaotic retreat of the Union soldiers, along with the sightseers and politicians who had come to watch the battle. Almost 800 men died at Bull Run, a toll eclipsed many times in the years to come, but more Americans than had been killed in any previous battle in the nation's history. The encounter disabused both sides of the idea that the war would be a brief lark.

In the wake of Bull Run, George B. McClellan, an army engineer who had recently won a minor engagement with Confederate troops in western Virginia, assumed command of the Union's Army of the Potomac. A brilliant organizer, McClellan succeeded in welding his men into a superb fighting force. He seemed reluctant, however, to commit them to battle,

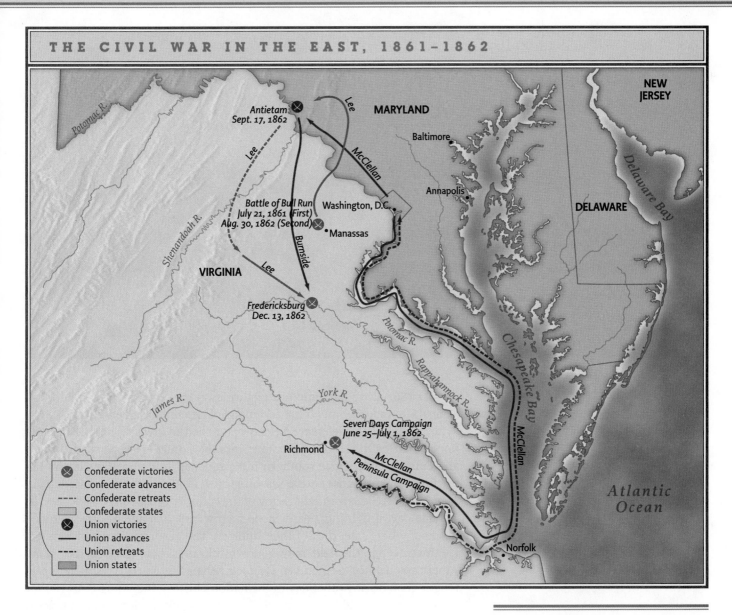

THE CIVIL WAR IN THE EAST, 1861–1862

since he tended to overestimate the size of enemy forces. And as a Democrat, he hoped that compromise might end the war without large-scale loss of life or a weakening of slavery. Months of military inactivity followed.

During the first two years of the war, most of the fighting took place in Virginia and Maryland.

THE WAR IN THE EAST, 1862

Not until the spring of 1862, after a growing clamor for action by Republican newspapers, members of Congress, and an increasingly impatient Lincoln, did McClellan lead his army of more than 100,000 men into Virginia. Here they confronted the smaller Army of Northern Virginia under the command of the Confederate general Joseph E. Johnston, and after he was wounded, Robert E. Lee. A brilliant battlefield tactician, Lee had been offered a command in the Union army but chose to fight for the Confederacy because of his devotion to Virginia. In the Seven Days' Campaign, a series of engagements in June 1862 on the peninsula south of Richmond, Lee blunted McClellan's attacks and forced him to withdraw back to the vicinity of Washington, D.C. In

The Battle of Antietam, *a painting of a Union advance by Captain James Hope of the Second Vermont Volunteers. More than 4,000 men died on September 17, 1862, when the Battle of Antietam was fought.*

August 1862, Lee again emerged victorious at the second Battle of Bull Run against Union forces under the command of General John Pope.

Successful on the defensive, Lee now launched an invasion of the North. He hoped to bring the border slave states into the Confederacy, persuade Britain and France to recognize southern independence, influence the North's fall elections, and perhaps capture Washington, D.C. At the Battle of Antietam, in Maryland, McClellan and the Army of the Potomac repelled Lee's advance. In a single day of fighting, nearly 4,000 men were killed and 18,000 wounded (2,000 of whom later died of their injuries). The dead, one survivor recalled, lay three deep in the field, mowed down "like grass before the scythe." More Americans died on September 17, 1862, when the Battle of Antietam was fought, than on any other day in the nation's history, including Pearl Harbor and D-Day in World War II and the terrorist attacks of September 11, 2001. Indeed, more American soldiers perished at Antietam than in all the other wars fought by the United States in the nineteenth century combined.

Since Lee was forced to retreat, the North could claim Antietam as a victory. It was to be the Union's last success in the East for some time. In December 1862, the Union suffered one of its most disastrous defeats of the war when General Ambrose E. Burnside, who had replaced McClellan as the head of the Army of the Potomac, assaulted Lee's army, which was entrenched on heights near Fredericksburg, Virginia. "It was not a fight," wrote one Union soldier to his mother, "it was a massacre."

THE WAR IN THE WEST

While the Union accomplished little in the East in the first two years of the war, events in the West followed a different course. Here, the architect of early success was Ulysses S. Grant. A West Point graduate who had resigned from the army in 1854 in part because of allegations of excessive drinking, Grant had been notably unsuccessful in civilian life. When the war broke out, he was working as a clerk in his brother's leather store in Galena, Illinois. But after being commissioned as a colonel in an Illinois regiment, Grant quickly displayed the daring, the logical mind, and the grasp of strategy he would demonstrate throughout the war.

In February 1862, Grant won the Union's first significant victory when he captured Forts Henry and Donelson in Tennessee. In April, naval forces under Admiral David G. Farragut steamed into New Orleans, giving the

Most of the Union's victories in the first two years of the war occurred in the West, especially at Shiloh and New Orleans.

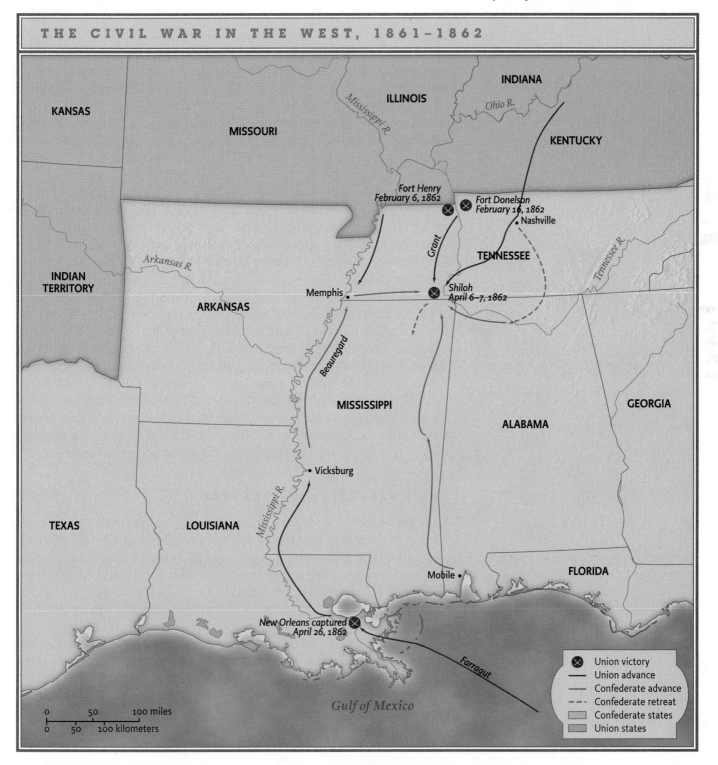

THE CIVIL WAR IN THE WEST, 1861–1862

Union control of the South's largest city and the rich sugar plantation parishes to its south and west. At the same time, Grant withstood a surprise Confederate attack at Shiloh, Tennessee. But Union momentum in the West then stalled.

THE COMING OF EMANCIPATION

SLAVERY AND THE WAR

War, it has been said, is the midwife of revolution. And the Civil War produced far-reaching changes in American life. The most dramatic of these was the destruction of slavery, the central institution of southern society. Between 1831, when the British abolished slavery in their empire, and 1888, when emancipation came to Brazil, some 6 million slaves gained their freedom in the Western Hemisphere. Of these, nearly 4 million, two-thirds of the total, lived in the southern United States. In numbers, scale, and the economic power of the institution of slavery, American emancipation dwarfed that of any other country (although far more people were liberated in 1861 when Czar Alexander II abolished serfdom in the Russian empire).

At the outset of the war, Lincoln invoked time-honored northern values to mobilize public support. In a message to Congress, he identified the Union cause with the fate of democracy for the "whole family of man." He identified the differences between North and South in terms of the familiar free labor ideology: "This is essentially a people's struggle. On the side of the Union, it is a struggle for maintaining in the world, that form and substance of government, whose leading object is to elevate the condition of men . . . to afford all, an unfettered start, and a fair chance, in the race of life."

But while appealing to free labor values, Lincoln initially insisted that slavery was irrelevant to the conflict. In the war's first year, his paramount concerns were to keep the border slave states—Delaware, Maryland, Kentucky, and Missouri—in the Union and to build the broadest base of support in the North for the war effort. Action against slavery, he feared, would drive the border, with its white population of 2.6 million and nearly 500,000 slaves, into the Confederacy and alienate conservative northerners.

THE UNRAVELING OF SLAVERY

Thus, in the early days of the war, a nearly unanimous Congress adopted a resolution proposed by Senator John J. Crittenden of Kentucky, which affirmed that the Union had no intention of interfering with slavery. Northern military commanders even returned fugitive slaves to their owners, a policy that raised an outcry in antislavery circles. Yet as the Confederacy set slaves to work as military laborers and blacks began to escape to Union lines, the policy of ignoring slavery unraveled. By the end of 1861, the military had adopted the plan, begun in Virginia by General Benjamin F. Butler, of treating escaped blacks as contraband of war—that is, property of military value subject to confiscation. Butler's order added a word to the war's vocabulary. Escaping slaves became known as "the contrabands." They were housed by the army in "contraband camps" and educated in new "contraband schools."

Meanwhile, slaves themselves took actions that helped propel a reluctant white America down the road to emancipation. Whatever the policies of the administration, blacks saw the outbreak of fighting as heralding the long-awaited end of bondage. Well before Lincoln made emancipation a war aim, blacks, in the North and the South, were calling the conflict the "freedom war." In 1861 and 1862, as the federal army occupied Confederate territory, slaves by the thousands headed for Union lines. Unlike fugitives before the war, these runaways included large numbers of women and children, as entire families abandoned the plantations. Not a few passed along military intelligence and detailed knowledge of the South's terrain. "The most valuable and reliable information of the enemy's movements in our vicinity that we have been able to get," noted the Union general Daniel E. Sickles, "derived from Negroes who came into our lines." In southern Louisiana, the arrival of the Union army in 1862 led slaves to sack plantation houses and refuse to work unless wages were paid. Slavery there, wrote a northern reporter, "is forever destroyed and worthless, no matter what Mr. Lincoln or anyone else may say on the subject."

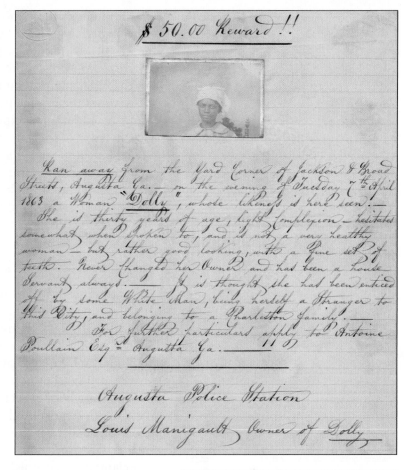

An 1863 advertisement for a runaway domestic slave circulated by Louis Manigault, a member of a prominent Georgia and South Carolina planter family. Manigault blamed an unknown white man for enticing her away, but she most likely escaped with a male slave who had begun to court her. Slaves fled to Union lines from the first days of the Civil War.

STEPS TOWARD EMANCIPATION

At first, blacks' determination to seize the opportunity presented by the war proved a burden to the army and an embarrassment to the administration. But the failure of traditional strategies to produce victory strengthened the hand of antislavery northerners. Since slavery stood at the foundation of the southern economy, they insisted, emancipation was necessary to weaken the South's ability to sustain the war.

The most uncompromising opponents of slavery before the war, abolitionists and Radical Republicans, quickly concluded that the institution must become a target of the Union war effort. "It is plain," declared Thaddeus Stevens, a Radical Republican congressman from Pennsylvania, "that nothing approaching the present policy will subdue the rebels." Outside of Congress, few pressed the case for emancipation more eloquently than Frederick Douglass. From the outset, he insisted that it was futile to "separate the freedom of the slave from the victory of the government." "Fire must be met with water," Douglass declared, "darkness with light, and war for the destruction of liberty must be met with war for the destruction of slavery."

These appeals won increasing support in a Congress frustrated by lack of military success. In March 1862, Congress prohibited the army from returning fugitive slaves. Then came abolition in the District of Columbia (with monetary compensation for slaveholders) and the territories, followed in July by the Second Confiscation Act, which liberated slaves of disloyal owners in Union-occupied territory, as well as slaves who escaped to Union lines.

Throughout these months, Lincoln struggled to retain control of the emancipation issue. In August 1861, John C. Frémont, commanding Union forces in Missouri, a state racked by a bitter guerrilla war between pronorthern and pro-southern bands, decreed the freedom of its slaves. Fearful of the order's impact on the border states, Lincoln swiftly rescinded it. In November, the president proposed that the border states embark on a program of gradual emancipation with the federal government paying owners for their loss of property. He also revived the idea of colonization. In August 1862, Lincoln met at the White House with a delegation of black leaders and urged them to promote emigration from the United States. "You and we are different races," he declared. "It is better for us both to be separated." As late as December, the president signed an agreement with a shady entrepreneur to settle former slaves on an island off the coast of Haiti.

LINCOLN'S DECISION

Sometime during the summer of 1862, Lincoln concluded that emancipation had become a political and military necessity. Many factors contributed to his decision—lack of military success, hope that emancipated slaves might help meet the army's growing manpower needs, changing northern public opinion, and the calculation that making slavery a target of the war effort would counteract sentiment in Britain for recognition of the Confederacy. But on the advice of Secretary of State William H. Seward, Lincoln delayed his announcement until after a Union victory, lest it seem an act of desperation. On September 22, 1862, five days after McClellan's army forced Lee to retreat at Antietam, Lincoln issued the Preliminary Emancipation Proclamation. It warned that unless the South laid down its arms by the end of 1862, he would decree abolition.

The initial northern reaction was not encouraging. In the fall elections of 1862, Democrats made opposition to emancipation the centerpiece of their campaign, warning that the North would be "Africanized"—inundated by freed slaves who would compete for jobs and seek to marry white women. The Republicans suffered sharp reverses. They lost control of the legislatures of Indiana and Illinois and the governorship of New York, and saw their majorities dangerously reduced in other states. In his annual message to Congress, early in December, Lincoln tried to calm northerners' racial fears, reviving the ideas of gradual emancipation and colonization. He concluded, however, on a higher note: "Fellow citizens, we cannot escape history. . . . The fiery trial through which we pass, will light us down, in honor or dishonor, to the latest generation. . . . In giving freedom to the slave, we assure freedom to the free—honorable alike in what we give, and what we preserve."

Abe Lincoln's Last Card, *an engraving from the British magazine* Punch, *October 18, 1862, portrays the Preliminary Emancipation Proclamation as the last move of a desperate gambler.*

THE EMANCIPATION PROCLAMATION

On January 1, 1863, after greeting visitors at the annual White House New Year's reception, Lincoln retired to his study to sign the Emancipation Proclamation. The document did not liberate all the slaves—indeed, on the day it was issued, it applied to very few. Because its legality derived from the president's authority as military commander-in-chief to combat the South's rebellion, the Proclamation exempted areas firmly under Union control (where the war, in effect, had already ended). Thus, it did not apply to the loyal border slave states that had never seceded or to areas of the Confederacy occupied by Union soldiers, such as Tennessee and parts of Virginia and Louisiana. But the vast majority of the South's slaves—more than 3 million men, women, and children—it declared "henceforward shall be free." Since most of these slaves were still behind Confederate lines, however, their liberation would have to await Union victories.

Despite its limitations, the Proclamation set off scenes of jubilation among free blacks and abolitionists in the North and "contrabands" and slaves in the South. "Sound the loud timbrel o'er Egypt's dark sea," intoned a black preacher at a celebration in Boston. "Jehovah hath triumphed, his people are free." By making the Union army an agent of emancipation and wedding the goals of Union and abolition, the Proclamation sounded the eventual death knell of slavery.

Not only did the Emancipation Proclamation alter the nature of the Civil War and the course of American history, but it also represented a turning point in Lincoln's own thinking. It contained no reference to compensation to slaveholders or to colonization of the freed people. For the first time, it committed the government to enlisting black soldiers in the Union army. Lincoln now became in his own mind the Great Emancipator—that is, he assumed the role that history had thrust upon him, and he tried to live up

Freed Negroes Celebrating President Lincoln's Decree of Emancipation, *a fanciful engraving from the French periodical* Le Monde Illustré, *March 21, 1863.*

VISIONS OF FREEDOM

Freedom to the Slave. *This hand-colored lithograph from 1863 celebrates the promise of emancipation and also links the American flag—the symbol of nationality—with freedom by placing a liberty cap atop it. On the left are symbols of freedom including a school, a church, a plow, and a black man reading a newspaper. A broken chain lies in the right foreground. The image conveys the optimism inspired by the Emancipation Proclamation. But many former slaves would never fully enjoy the kinds of freedom imagined in this lithograph.*

QUESTIONS

1. What does the image tell us about how emancipation was achieved?

2. In what ways does the artist suggest that freedom differed from life under slavery?

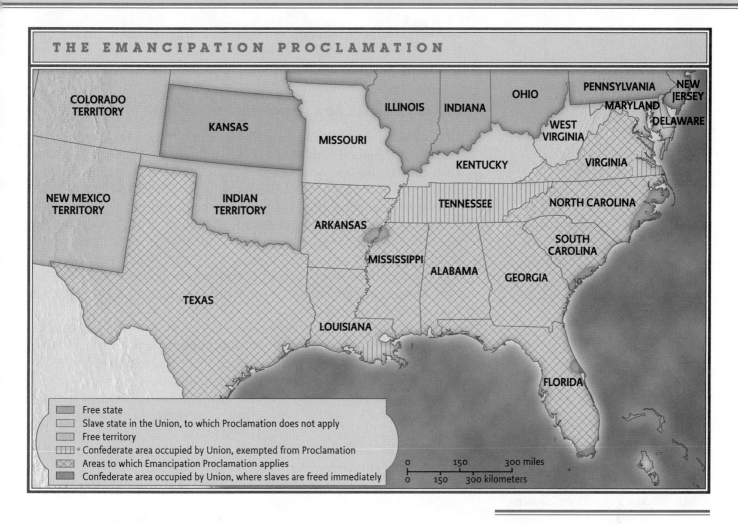

THE EMANCIPATION PROCLAMATION

Legend:
- Free state
- Slave state in the Union, to which Proclamation does not apply
- Free territory
- Confederate area occupied by Union, exempted from Proclamation
- Areas to which Emancipation Proclamation applies
- Confederate area occupied by Union, where slaves are freed immediately

With the exception of a few areas, the Emancipation Proclamation applied only to slaves in parts of the Confederacy not under Union control on January 1, 1863. Lincoln did not "free the slaves" with a stroke of his pen, but the Proclamation did change the nature of the Civil War.

to it. He would later refuse suggestions that he rescind or modify the Proclamation in the interest of peace. Were he to do so, he told one visitor, "I should be damned in time and eternity."

Like the end of slavery in Haiti and mainland Latin America, abolition in the United States came about as the result of war. But emancipation in the United States differed from its counterparts elsewhere in the Western Hemisphere—it was immediate, not gradual, and offered no compensation to slaveholders for their loss of property (with the exception of those in Washington, D.C.) It also foretold the inevitable end of slavery in Cuba, Puerto Rico, and Brazil. Not until 1888, however, when Brazil abolished the institution, did slavery come to an end in the entire Western Hemisphere.

The Civil War, which was begun to preserve the prewar Union, now portended a far-reaching transformation in southern life and a redefinition of American freedom. Decoupling emancipation from colonization meant that the freed slaves would become part of American life. A new system of labor, politics, and race relations would have to replace the shattered institution of slavery. "Up to now," wrote the socialist thinker Karl Marx, observing events from London, "we have witnessed only the first act of the Civil War—the constitutional waging of war. The second act, the revolutionary waging of war, is at hand." The evolution of

Lincoln's emancipation policy displayed the hallmarks of his wartime leadership—his capacity for growth and his ability to develop broad public support for his administration.

ENLISTING BLACK TROOPS

Of the Proclamation's provisions, few were more radical in their implications than the enrollment of blacks into military service. Since sailor had been one of the few occupations open to free blacks before the war, Secretary of the Navy Gideon Welles had already allowed African-Americans to serve on Union warships. But as during the American Revolution, when George Washington initially excluded blacks from the Continental army, blacks in the Civil War had to fight for the right to fight on land. Early in the war, Harry Jarvis, a Virginia slave, escaped to Fortress Monroe and offered to enlist in the Union army. General Benjamin F. Butler, Jarvis later recalled, "said *it wasn't a black man's war*. I told him it *would* be a black man's war before they got through."

At the outset, the Union army refused to accept northern black volunteers. The administration feared that whites would not be willing to fight alongside blacks, and that enlisting black soldiers would alienate the border slave states that remained in the Union. By the end of 1861, however, the army was employing escaped slaves as cooks, laundresses, and laborers. Preliminary steps to enlist combat troops were taken in a few parts of the South in 1862. White abolitionist Thomas Wentworth Higginson was sent to the South Carolina Sea Islands, which the Union navy had seized early in the war, to enroll slaves in the First South Carolina Volunteers. But only after the Emancipation Proclamation did the recruitment of black soldiers begin in earnest.

This widely reprinted recruiting poster urged African-American men to join the Union army after Congress and the president changed the policy of allowing only whites to serve.

By the end of the war, more than 180,000 black men had served in the Union army, and 24,000 in the navy. One-third died in battle, or of wounds or disease. Fifteen black soldiers and eight sailors received the Medal of Honor, the highest award for military valor. Some black units won considerable notoriety, among them the Fifty-fourth Massachusetts Volunteers, a company of free blacks from throughout the North commanded by Robert Gould Shaw, a young reformer from a prominent Boston family. The bravery of the Fifty-fourth in the July 1863 attack on Fort Wagner, South Carolina, where nearly half the unit, including Shaw, perished, helped to dispel widespread doubts about blacks' ability to withstand the pressures of the Civil War battlefield. (The exploits of Shaw and the Fifty-fourth Massachusetts were popularized in the 1989 film *Glory.*)

Photographs of four anonymous black Civil War soldiers, including a sergeant (with three stripes on his uniform).

Most black soldiers were emancipated slaves who joined the army in the South. After Union forces in 1863 seized control of the rich plantation lands of the Mississippi Valley, General Lorenzo Thomas raised fifty regiments of black soldiers—some 76,000 men in all. Another large group hailed from the border states exempted from the Emancipation Proclamation, where enlistment was, for most of the war, the only route to freedom. Here black military service undermined slavery, for Congress expanded the Emancipation Proclamation to liberate black soldiers and their families.

THE BLACK SOLDIER

For black soldiers themselves, military service proved to be a liberating experience. "No negro who has ever been a soldier," wrote a northern official in 1865, "can again be imposed upon; they have learned what it is to be free and they will infuse their feelings into others." Service in the army established men as community leaders and opened a door to political advancement. Out of the army came many of the leaders of the Reconstruction era. At least 130 former soldiers served in political office after the Civil War. In time, the memory of black military service would fade from white America's collective memory. Of the hundreds of Civil War monuments that still dot the northern landscape, fewer than a dozen contain an image of a black soldier. But well into the twentieth century, it remained a point of pride in black families throughout the United States that their fathers and grandfathers had fought for freedom.

The Union navy treated black sailors pretty much the same as white sailors. Conditions on ships made racial segregation impossible. Black and white sailors lived and dined together in the same quarters. They received equal pay and had the same promotion opportunities. Within the army, however, black soldiers received treatment that was anything but equal to their white counterparts. Organized into segregated units under sometimes abusive white officers, they initially received lower pay (ten dollars per month, compared to sixteen dollars for white soldiers). They were disproportionately assigned to labor rather than combat, and they could not rise to the rank of commissioned officer until the very end of the war. If captured by Confederate forces, they faced the prospect of sale into slavery or immediate execution. In a notorious incident in 1864, 200 of 262 black soldiers died when southern troops under the command of Nathan B. Forrest overran Fort Pillow in Tennessee. Some of those who perished were killed after surrendering.

Nonetheless, black soldiers played a crucial role not only in winning the Civil War but in defining the war's consequences. "Once let a black man get upon his person the brass letters U.S.," wrote Frederick Douglass in urging blacks to enlist, "and there is no power on earth which can deny that he has earned the right to citizenship in the United States." As Douglass predicted, thanks in part to black military service many Republicans in the last two years of the war came to believe that emancipation must bring with it equal protection of the laws regardless of race. One of the first acts of the federal government to recognize this principle was the granting of retroactive equal pay to black soldiers early in 1865. Racism was hardly eliminated from national life. But, declared George William Curtis, the editor of *Harper's Weekly*, the war and emancipation had transformed a government "for white men" into one "for mankind."

The service of black soldiers affected Lincoln's own outlook. He insisted that they must be treated the same as whites when captured and suspended prisoner-of-war exchanges when the Confederacy refused to include black troops. In 1864, Lincoln, who before the war had never supported suffrage for African-Americans, urged the governor of Union-occupied Louisiana to work for the partial enfranchisement of blacks, singling out soldiers as especially deserving. At some future time, he observed, they might again be called upon to "keep the *jewel of Liberty* in the family of freedom."

The illustration accompanying "The American Flag," a piece of patriotic Civil War sheet music, exemplifies how the war united the ideals of liberty and nationhood.

THE SECOND AMERICAN REVOLUTION

"Old things are passing away," wrote a black resident of California in 1862, "and eventually old prejudices must follow. The revolution has begun, and time alone must decide where it is to end." The changing status of black Americans was only one dramatic example of what some historians call the Second American Revolution—the transformation of American government and society brought about by the Civil War.

LIBERTY AND UNION

Never was freedom's contested nature more evident than during the Civil War. "We all declare for liberty," Lincoln observed in 1864, "but in using the same *word* we do not all mean the same *thing*." To the North, he continued, freedom meant for "each man" to enjoy "the product of his labor." To southern whites, it conveyed mastership—the power to do "as they please with other men, and the product of other men's labor." The Union's triumph consolidated the northern understanding of freedom as the national norm.

The attack on Fort Sumter crystallized in northern minds the direct conflict between freedom and slavery that abolitionists had insisted upon for decades. The war, as Frederick Douglass recognized as early as 1862, merged "the cause of the slaves and the cause of the country." "Liberty and Union," he continued, "have become identical." As during the American Revolution, religious and secular understandings of freedom joined in a celebration of national destiny. "As He died to make men holy, let us die to make men free," proclaimed the popular song "Battle Hymn of the Republic," written by Julia Ward Howe and published in 1862. Emancipation offered proof of the progressive nature and global significance of the country's history. For the first time, wrote the *Chicago Tribune*, the United States could truly exist as "our fathers designed it—the home of freedom, the asylum of the oppressed, the seat of justice, the land of equal rights under the law."

LINCOLN'S VISION

But it was Lincoln himself who linked the conflict with the deepest beliefs of northern society. It is sometimes said that the American Civil War was part of a broader nineteenth-century process of nation building. Throughout the world, powerful, centralized nation-states developed in old countries, and new nations emerged where none had previously existed. The Civil War took place as modern states were consolidating their power and reducing local autonomy. The Meiji Restoration in Japan saw the emperor reclaim power from local lords, or shoguns. Argentina in the 1850s adopted a new constitution that abolished slavery, established universal male suffrage, and gave the national government the right to intervene in local affairs. As in the United States, economic development quickly followed national unification. Japan soon emerged as a major economic power, and Argentina embarked on a policy of railroad construction, centralization of banking, industrial development, and the encouragement of European immigration, which soon made it the world's sixth largest economy.

Lincoln has been called the American equivalent of Giuseppe Mazzini or Otto von Bismarck, who during this same era created nation-states in Italy and Germany from disunited collections of principalities. But Lincoln's nation was different from those being constructed in Europe. They were based on the idea of unifying a particular people with a common ethnic, cultural, and linguistic heritage. To Lincoln, the American nation embodied a set of universal ideas, centered on political democracy and human liberty. The United States represented to the world the principle that government should rest on popular consent and that all men should be free. These ideals, Lincoln declared, allowed immigrants from abroad, who could not "trace their connection by blood" to the nation's birth, nonetheless to become fully American.

Lincoln summarized his conception of the war's meaning in November 1863 in brief remarks at the dedication of a military cemetery at the site of the war's greatest battle. The Gettysburg Address is considered his finest speech (see the Appendix for the full text). In less than three minutes, he identified the nation's mission with the principle that "all men are created equal," spoke of the war as bringing about a "new birth of freedom," and defined the essence of democratic government. The sacrifices of Union soldiers, he declared, would ensure that "government of the people, by the people, for the people, shall not perish from the earth."

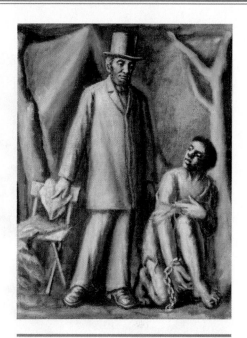

Lincoln and the Female Slave, *by the free black artist David B. Bowser. Working in Philadelphia, Bowser painted flags for a number of black Civil War regiments. Lincoln confers freedom on a kneeling slave, an image that downplays blacks' role in their own emancipation.*

The Eagle's Nest, *an 1861 antisecession cartoon promising "annihilation to traitors." The eggs representing seceding states have become rotten and are hatching monsters.*

FROM UNION TO NATION

The mobilization of the Union's resources for modern war brought into being a new American nation-state with greatly expanded powers and responsibilities. The United States remained a federal republic with sovereignty divided between the state and national governments. But the war forged a new national self-consciousness, reflected in the increasing use of the word "nation"—a unified political entity—in place of the older "Union" of separate states. In his inaugural address in 1861, Lincoln used the word "Union" twenty times, while making no mention of the "nation." By 1863, "Union" does not appear at all in the 269-word Gettysburg Address, while Lincoln referred five times to the "nation."

"Liberty, . . . true liberty," the writer Francis Lieber proclaimed, "requires a country." This was the moral of one of the era's most popular works of fiction, Edward Everett Hale's short story "The Man Without a Country," published in 1863. Hale's protagonist, Philip Nolan, in a fit of anger curses the land of his birth. As punishment, he is condemned to live on a ship, never to set foot on American soil or hear the name "the United States" spoken. He learns that to be deprived of national identity is to lose one's sense of self.

THE WAR AND AMERICAN RELIGION

The upsurge of patriotism, and of national power, was reflected in many aspects of American life. Even as the war produced unprecedented casualties, the northern Protestant clergy strove to provide it with a religious justification and to reassure their congregations that the dead had not died in vain. The religious press now devoted more space to military and political developments than to spiritual matters. In numerous wartime sermons, Christianity and patriotism were joined in a civic religion that saw the war as God's mechanism for ridding the United States of slavery and enabling it to become what it had never really been—a land of freedom. Lincoln, one of the few American presidents who never joined a church, shrewdly marshaled religious symbolism to generate public support, declaring days of Thanksgiving after northern victories and encouraging northern clergymen to support Republican candidates for office.

Religious beliefs also enabled Americans to cope with the unprecedented mass death the war involved. Of course, equating death with eternal life

is a central tenet of Christianity. But the war led to what one historian calls a "transformation of heaven," as Americans imagined future celestial family reunions that seemed more and more like gatherings in middle-class living rooms. Some Americans could not wait until their own deaths to see the departed. Spiritualism—belief in the ability to communicate with the dead—grew in popularity. Mary Todd Lincoln held seances in the White House to experience again the presence of her young son Willie, who succumbed to disease in 1862.

Coping with death also required unprecedented governmental action, from notifying next of kin to accounting for the dead and missing. Both the Union and Confederacy established elaborate systems for gathering statistics and maintaining records of dead and wounded soldiers, an effort supplemented by private philanthropic organizations. After the war ended, the federal government embarked on a program to locate and re-bury hundreds of thousands of Union soldiers in national military cemeteries. Between 1865 and 1871, the government reinterred more than 300,000 Union (but not Confederate) soldiers—including black soldiers, who were buried, as they had fought, in segregated sections of military cemeteries.

LIBERTY IN WARTIME

This intense new nationalism made criticism of the war effort—or of the policies of the Lincoln administration—seem to Republicans equivalent to treason. Although there had been sporadic persecution of opponents of the Mexican War, the Civil War presented, for the first time since the Revolution, the issue of the limits of wartime dissent. During the conflict, declared the Republican *New York Times*, "the safety of the nation is the supreme law." Arbitrary arrests numbered in the thousands. They included opposition newspaper editors, Democratic politicians, individuals who discouraged enlistment in the army, and ordinary civilians like the Chicago man briefly imprisoned for calling the president a "damned fool." With the Constitution unclear as to who possessed the power to suspend the writ of habeas corpus (thus allowing prisoners to be held without charge),

This image adorned a printed version of a popular Civil War song, "The Dying Soldier." It illustrates how Americans sought solace in religion in the face of the war's enormous death toll. At the left, an angel receives the dying soldier, while at the right his wife, mother, or sweetheart prays for his soul.

VOICES OF FREEDOM

FROM SPEECH of ALEXANDER H. STEPHENS,
Vice President of the Confederacy (March 21, 1861)

A Whig leader in Georgia, Alexander H. Stephens opposed secession until his state voted to leave the Union. He then accepted the vice presidency of the Confederacy, and in a speech in Savannah in March 1861 he explained the basic premises of the new government.

The [Confederate] Constitution has put at rest forever all the agitating questions relating to our peculiar institutions—African slavery as it exists among us—the proper status of the negro in our form of civilization. This was the immediate cause of the late rupture and present revolution. . . . The prevailing ideas entertained by [Jefferson] and most of the leading statesmen at the time of the formation of the old Constitution, were, that the enslavement of the African was in violation of the laws of nature; that it was wrong in principle, socially, morally and politically. . . .

These ideas, however, were fundamentally wrong. They rested on the assumption of the equality of races. This was an error. . . . Our new Government is founded upon exactly the opposite ideas; its foundations are laid, its cornerstone rests, upon the great truth that the negro is not equal to the white man; that slavery, subordination to the superior race, is his natural and moral condition. This, our new Government, is the first, in the history of the world, based upon this great physical, philosophical, and moral truth. . . .

It is the first Government ever instituted upon principles in strict conformity to nature, and the ordination of Providence, in furnishing the materials of human society. Many Governments have been founded upon the principles of certain classes; but the classes thus enslaved, were of the same race, and in violation of the laws of nature. Our system commits no such violation of nature's laws. The negro by nature, or by the curse against Canaan, is fitted for that condition which he occupies in our system. . . . The substratum of our society is made of the material fitted by nature for it, and by experience we know that it is the best, not only for the superior but for the inferior race, that it should be so.

FROM ABRAHAM LINCOLN,
Address at Sanitary Fair, Baltimore (April 18, 1864)

Abraham Lincoln's speech at a Sanitary Fair (a grand bazaar that raised money for the care of Union soldiers) offers a dramatic illustration of the contested meaning of freedom during the Civil War.

The world has never had a good definition of the word liberty, and the American people, just now, are much in want of one. We all declare for liberty; but in using the same *word* we do not all mean the same *thing*. With some the word liberty may mean for each man to do as he pleases with himself, and the product of his labor; while with others the same word may mean for some men to do as they please with other men, and the product of other men's labor. Here are two, not only different, but incompatible things, called by the same name—liberty. And it follows that each of the things is, by the respective parties, called by two different and incompatible names—liberty and tyranny.

The shepherd drives the wolf from the sheep's throat, for which the sheep thanks the shepherd as a *liberator*, while the wolf denounces him for the same act as the destroyer of liberty, especially as the sheep was a black one. Plainly the sheep and the wolf are not agreed upon a definition of the word liberty; and precisely the same difference prevails today among us human creatures, even in the North, and all professing to love liberty. Hence we behold the process by which thousands are daily passing from under the yoke of bondage, hailed by some as the advance of liberty, and bewailed by others as the destruction of all liberty. Recently, as it seems, the people of Maryland have been doing something to define liberty [abolishing slavery in the state]; and thanks to them that, in what they have done, the wolf's dictionary, has been repudiated.

QUESTIONS

1. Why does Stephens argue that slavery in the South differs from slavery as it has existed in previous societies?

2. What does Lincoln identify as the essential difference between northern and southern definitions of freedom?

3. How do Lincoln and Stephens differ in their definition of liberty and whether it applies to African-Americans?

Lincoln claimed the right under the presidential war powers and twice suspended the writ throughout the entire Union for those accused of "disloyal activities."

The courts generally gave the administration a free hand. They refused to intervene when a military court convicted Clement L. Vallandigham, a leading Ohio Democrat known for his blistering antiwar speeches, of treason. On Lincoln's order, Vallandigham was banished to the Confederacy. In 1861, Chief Justice Roger B. Taney had ordered the president to release John Merryman, a civilian who had been arrested by military authorities in Maryland, but the president ignored him. Not until 1866, after the fighting had ended, did the Supreme Court, in the case *Ex parte Milligan*, declare it unconstitutional to bring accused persons before military tribunals where civil courts were operating. The Constitution, declared Justice David Davis, is not suspended in wartime—it remains "a law for rulers and people, equally in time of war and peace."

Lincoln was not a despot. Most of those arrested were quickly released, the Democratic press continued to flourish, and contested elections were held throughout the war. But the policies of the Lincoln administration offered proof—to be repeated during later wars—of the fragility of civil liberties in the face of assertive patriotism and wartime demands for national unity.

THE NORTH'S TRANSFORMATION

Even as he invoked traditional values, Lincoln presided over far-reaching changes in northern life. The effort to mobilize the resources of the Union greatly enhanced the power not only of the federal government but also of a rising class of capitalist entrepreneurs. Unlike the South, which suffered economic devastation, the North experienced the war as a time of prosperity.

Nourished by wartime inflation and government contracts, the profits of industry boomed. New England mills worked day and night to supply the army with blankets and uniforms, and Pennsylvania coal mines and ironworks rapidly expanded their production. Mechanization proceeded apace in many industries, especially those like boot and shoe production and meatpacking that supplied the army's ever-increasing needs. Agriculture also flourished, for even as farm boys by the hundreds of thousands joined the army, the frontier of cultivation pushed westward, with machinery and immigrants replacing lost labor. Wisconsin furnished 90,000 men to the Union army, yet its population, grain production, and farm income continued to grow.

GOVERNMENT AND THE ECONOMY

As in contemporary Germany and Japan, the new American nation-state that emerged during the Civil War was committed to rapid economic development. Congress adopted policies that promoted economic growth and permanently altered the nation's financial system. With the South now unrepresented, the lawmakers adopted policies long advocated by many northerners. To spur agricultural development, the Homestead Act offered 160 acres of free public land to settlers in the West. It took effect on January 1, 1863, the same day as the Emancipation Proclamation, and like the Proclamation, tried to implement a vision of freedom. By the 1930s,

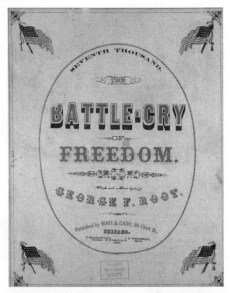

Sheet music for two of the best-known patriotic songs written during the Civil War.

more than 400,000 families had acquired farms under its provisions. In addition, the Land Grant College Act assisted the states in establishing "agricultural and mechanic colleges."

BUILDING THE TRANSCONTINENTAL RAILROAD

Congress also made huge grants of money and land for internal improvements, including up to 100 million acres to the Union Pacific and Central Pacific, two companies chartered in 1862 and charged with building a railroad from the Missouri River to the Pacific coast. (These were the first corporate charters issued by the federal government since the Second Bank of the United States in 1816.)

When first proposed by entrepreneur Asa Whitney in 1846, the idea of a transcontinental railroad had been considered by Congress "too gigantic" and "entirely impracticable." And, indeed, the project was monumental. The Central Pacific progressed only twenty miles a year for the first three years of construction because the Sierra Nevada range was almost impassable. It required some 20,000 men to lay the tracks across prairies and mountains, a substantial number of them immigrant Chinese contract laborers, called "coolies" by many Americans. Hundreds of Chinese workers died blasting tunnels and building bridges through this treacherous terrain. When it was completed in 1869, the transcontinental railroad, which ran from Omaha, Nebraska, to San Francisco, expanded the national market, facilitated the spread of settlement and investment in the West, and heralded the doom of the Plains Indians.

THE WAR AND NATIVE AMERICANS

One of Lincoln's first orders as president was to withdraw federal troops from the West so that they could protect Washington, D.C. Recognizing that this would make it impossible for the army to keep white interlopers from intruding on Indian land, as treaties required it to do, Indian leaders begged Lincoln to reverse this decision, but to no avail. Inevitably, conflict flared in the West between Native Americans and white settlers, with disastrous results. During the Civil War, the Sioux killed hundreds of white farmers in Minnesota before being subdued by the army. After a military court sentenced more than 300 Indians to death, Lincoln commuted the sentences of all but 38. But their hanging in December 1862 remains the largest official execution in American history. In 1864, a unit of Colorado soldiers under the command of Colonel John Chivington attacked a village of Cheyenne and Arapaho Indians at Sand Creek, killing perhaps 400 men, women, and children.

The Union army also launched a campaign against the Navajo in the Southwest, destroying their orchards and sheep and forcing 8,000 people to move to a reservation set aside by the government. The Navajo's Long Walk became as central to their historical experience as the Trail of Tears to the Cherokee (see Chapter 10). Unlike the eastern Indians, however, the Navajo were eventually allowed to return to a portion of their lands.

Ironically, the Confederacy, although defending slavery, treated Native Americans more fairly than the Union. The Confederate Constitution provided for Indian tribes to elect representatives to Congress, and the Davis

A Union soldier stands guard over a group of Indians during the Navajo's Long Walk, in which the army removed them from their New Mexico homeland to a reservation hundreds of miles away.

administration removed state jurisdiction over Indian reservations, allowing them complete self-government. Some tribes that owned slaves, like the Cherokee, sided with the Confederacy. After 1865, they were forced to cede much of their land to the federal government and to give some land to their former slaves (the only slaveowners required to do so).

A NEW FINANCIAL SYSTEM

The need to pay for the war produced dramatic changes in financial policy. To raise money, the government increased the tariff to unprecedented heights (thus promoting the further growth of northern industry), imposed new taxes on the production and consumption of goods, and enacted the nation's first income tax. It also borrowed more than $2 billion by selling interest-bearing bonds, thus creating an immense national debt. And it printed more than $400 million worth of paper money, called "greenbacks," declared to be legal tender—that is, money that must be accepted for nearly all public and private payments and debts. To rationalize the banking system, Congress established a system of nationally chartered banks, which were required to purchase government bonds and were given the right to issue bank notes as currency. A heavy tax drove money issued by state banks out of existence. Thus, the United States, whose money supply before the war was a chaotic mixture of paper notes issued by state and local banks, now had essentially two kinds of national paper currency—greenbacks printed directly by the federal government, and notes issued by the new national banks.

Along with profitable contracts to supply goods for the military effort, wartime economic policies greatly benefited northern manufacturers, railroad men, and financiers. Numerous Americans who would take the lead in reshaping the nation's postwar economy created or consolidated their fortunes during the Civil War, among them iron and steel entrepreneur Andrew Carnegie, oil magnate John D. Rockefeller, financiers Jay Gould and J. P. Morgan, and Philip D. Armour, who earned millions supplying beef to the Union army. These and other "captains of industry" managed to escape military service, sometimes by purchasing exemptions or hiring substitutes, as allowed by the draft law.

Taken together, the Union's economic policies vastly increased the power and size of the federal government. The federal budget for 1865 exceeded $1 billion—nearly twenty times that of 1860. With its new army of clerks, tax collectors, and other officials, the government became the nation's largest employer. And while much of this expansion proved temporary, the government would never return to its weak and fragmented condition of the prewar period.

WOMEN AND THE WAR

For many northern women, the conflict opened new doors of opportunity. Women took advantage of the wartime labor shortage to move into jobs in factories and into certain largely male professions, particularly nursing. The expansion of the activities of the national government opened new jobs for women as clerks in government offices. Many of these wartime gains were short-lived, but in white-collar government jobs, retail sales, and nursing, women found a permanent place in the workforce.

Some northern women took a direct part in military campaigns. Clara Barton, a clerk in the Patent Office in Washington, D.C., when the war began, traveled with the Army of Northern Virginia, helping to organize supply lines and nursing wounded soldiers. Barton worked alone rather than as a part of the Department of Female Nurses, and she never received compensation from the government.

Hundreds of thousands of northern women took part in organizations that gathered money and medical supplies for soldiers and sent books, clothing, and food to freedmen. The United States Sanitary Commission emerged as a centralized national relief agency to coordinate donations on the northern home front. Although control at the national level remained in male hands, patriotic women did most of the grassroots work. Women played the leading role in organizing Sanitary Fairs—

Filling Cartridges at the U. S. Arsenal of Watertown, Massachusetts, *an engraving from* Harper's Weekly, *September 21, 1861. Both men and women were drawn to work in the booming war-related industries of the North.*

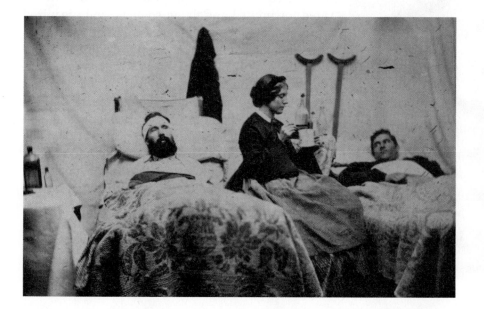

A female nurse photographed between two wounded Union soldiers in a Nashville military hospital in 1862. Many northern women served the army as nurses during the war.

Whimsical potholders expressing hope for a better life for emancipated slaves were sold at the Chicago Sanitary Fair of 1865, to raise money for soldiers' aid.

grand bazaars that displayed military banners, uniforms, and other relics of the war and sold goods to raise money for soldiers' aid. New York City's three-week fair of 1864 attracted a crowd of 30,000 and raised more than $1 million.

Many men understood women's war work as an extension of their "natural" capacity for self-sacrifice. But the very act of volunteering to work in local soldiers' aid societies brought many northern women into the public sphere and offered them a taste of independence. The suffrage movement suspended operations during the war to devote itself to the Union and emancipation. But women's continuing lack of the vote seemed all the more humiliating as their involvement in war work increased.

From the ranks of this wartime mobilization came many of the leaders of the postwar movement for women's rights. Mary Livermore, the wife of a Chicago minister, for example, toured military hospitals to assess their needs, cared for injured and dying soldiers, and organized two Sanitary Fairs. She emerged from the war with a deep resentment of women's legal and political subordination and organized her state's first woman suffrage convention. Women, she had concluded, must "think and act for themselves." After the war, Clara Barton not only became an advocate of woman suffrage but, as president of the American National Red Cross, lobbied for the United States to endorse the First Geneva Convention of 1864, which mandated the humane treatment of battlefield casualties. Largely as a result of Barton's efforts, the Senate ratified the convention in 1882. (Subsequent Geneva Conventions in the twentieth century would deal with the treatment of prisoners of war and civilians during wartime.)

Camp of Thirty-first Pennsylvania Infantry, Near Washington, D.C., *an 1862 photograph by the Mathew Brady studio. Many women worked for the army as laundresses. Some accompanied their husbands and even brought their children.*

The Riots in New York: The Mob Lynching a Negro in Clarkson Street, *an engraving from the British magazine* Illustrated London News, *August 8, 1863, reveals how the New York City draft riots escalated from an attempt to obstruct the draft into an assault on the city's black population.*

THE DIVIDED NORTH

Despite Lincoln's political skills, the war and his administration's policies divided northern society. Republicans labeled those opposed to the war Copperheads, after a poisonous snake that strikes without warning. Mounting casualties and rapid societal changes divided the North. Disaffection was strongest among the large southern-born population of states like Ohio, Indiana, and Illinois and working-class Catholic immigrants in eastern cities.

As the war progressed, it heightened existing social tensions and created new ones. The growing power of the federal government challenged traditional notions of local autonomy. The Union's draft law, which allowed individuals to provide a substitute or buy their way out of the army, caused widespread indignation. Workers resented manufacturers and financiers who reaped large profits while their own real incomes dwindled because of inflation. The war witnessed the rebirth of the northern labor movement, which organized numerous strikes for higher wages. The prospect of a sweeping change in the status of blacks called forth a racist reaction in many parts of the North. Throughout the war, the Democratic Party subjected Lincoln's policies to withering criticism, although it remained divided between "War Democrats," who supported the military effort while criticizing emancipation and the draft, and those who favored immediate peace.

On occasion, dissent degenerated into outright violence. In July 1863, the introduction of the draft provoked four days of rioting in New York City. The mob, composed largely of Irish immigrants, assaulted symbols of the new order being created by the war—draft offices, the mansions of wealthy Republicans, industrial establishments, and the city's black population, many of whom fled to New Jersey or took refuge in Central Park. Only the arrival of Union troops quelled the uprising, but not before more than 100 persons had died.

THE CONFEDERATE NATION

LEADERSHIP AND GOVERNMENT

The man charged with the task of rallying public support for the Confederacy proved unequal to the task. Born in 1808 in Kentucky, within eight months and 100 miles of Lincoln's birth, Jefferson Davis had moved to Mississippi as a youth, attended West Point, and acquired a large plantation. Aloof, stubborn, and humorless, he lacked Lincoln's common touch and political flexibility. Although known before the war as the "Cicero of the Senate" for his eloquent speeches, Davis, unlike Lincoln, proved unable to communicate the war's meaning effectively to ordinary men and women. Moreover, the Confederacy's lack of a party system proved to be a political liability. Like the founders of the American republic, southern leaders saw parties as threats to national unity. As a result, Davis lacked a counterpart to the well-organized Republican Party, which helped to mobilize support for the Lincoln administration.

Under Davis, the Confederate nation became far more centralized than the Old South had been. The government raised armies from scratch, took control of southern railroads, and built manufacturing plants. But it failed to find an effective way of utilizing the South's major economic resource, cotton. In the early part of the war, the administration tried to suppress cotton production, urging planters to grow food instead and banning cotton exports. This, it was hoped, would promote economic self-sufficiency and force Great Britain, whose textile mills could not operate without southern cotton, to intervene on the side of the Confederacy.

The centrality of slavery to the Confederacy is illustrated by the paper money issued by state governments and private banks, which frequently juxtaposed scenes of slaves at work with other revered images. The ten-dollar note of the Eastern Bank of Alabama depicts slaves working in the field and at a port, along with an idealized portrait of southern white womanhood. Alabama's five-dollar bill includes an overseer directing slaves in the field, and a symbol of liberty.

"King Cotton diplomacy" turned out to be ineffective. Large crops in 1859 and 1860 had created a huge stockpile in English warehouses. By the time distress hit the manufacturing districts in 1862, the government of Prime Minister Palmerston had decided not to intervene, partly because Britain needed northern wheat almost as much as southern cotton. But the Confederate policy had far-reaching global consequences. Recognizing their overdependence on southern cotton, other nations moved to expand production. Britain promoted cultivation of the crop in Egypt and India, and Russia did the same in parts of Central Asia. As a result, the resumption of American cotton production after the war led directly to a worldwide crisis of overproduction that drove down the price of cotton, impoverishing farmers around the world.

Nor did Davis deal effectively with obstructionist governors like Joseph E. Brown of Georgia, who denounced the Confederate draft as "a dangerous usurpation" of states' rights and individual liberty. All in all, Davis was so inferior to Lincoln as a wartime leader that one historian has suggested that had the North and South exchanged presidents, the South would have won the war.

A drawing by Langdon Cheves III, the teenage grandson of a prominent South Carolina political leader, depicts a Confederate killing a Yankee officer.

THE INNER CIVIL WAR

As the war progressed, social change and internal turmoil engulfed much of the Confederacy. At the outset, most white southerners rallied to the Confederate cause. No less fervently than northern troops, southern soldiers spoke of their cause in the language of freedom. "We are fighting for our liberty," wrote one volunteer, without any sense of contradiction, "against tyrants of the North . . . who are determined to destroy slavery." But public disaffection eventually became an even more serious problem for the Confederacy than for the Union.

Even as it waged a desperate struggle for independence, the South found itself increasingly divided. One grievance was the draft. Like the Union, the Confederacy allowed individuals to provide a substitute. Because of the accelerating disintegration of slavery, it also exempted one white male for every twenty slaves on a plantation (thus releasing many overseers and planters' sons from service). The "twenty-negro" provision convinced many yeomen that the struggle for southern independence had become "a rich man's war and a poor man's fight."

ECONOMIC PROBLEMS

Economic deprivation also sparked disaffection. As the blockade tightened, areas of the Confederacy came under Union occupation, and production by

An engraving in the New York Illustrated News *depicts the bread riot that took place in Mobile, Alabama, in the fall of 1863.*

slaves declined, shortages arose of essential commodities such as salt, corn, and meat. The war left countless farms, plantations, businesses, and railroads in ruins. The economic crisis, which stood in glaring contrast to the North's boom, was an unavoidable result of the war. But Confederate policies exaggerated its effects. War requires sacrifice, and civilian support for war depends, in part, on the belief that sacrifice is being fairly shared. Many non-slaveholders, however, became convinced that they were bearing an unfair share of the war's burdens.

Like the Union, the Confederacy borrowed heavily to finance the war. Unlike federal lawmakers, however, the planter-dominated Confederate Congress proved unwilling to levy heavy taxes that planters would have to pay. It relied on paper money, of which it issued $1.5 billion, far more than the North's greenbacks. Congress also authorized military officers to seize farm goods to supply the army, paying with increasingly worthless Confederate money. Small farmers deeply resented this practice, known as "impressment." "The Rebel army treated us a heap worse than [Union general William T.] Sherman did," a Georgia farmer later recalled. "I had hogs, and a mule, and a horse, and they took them all." Numerous yeoman families, many of whom had gone to war to preserve their economic independence, sank into poverty and debt. Food riots broke out in many places, including Richmond, Virginia, and Mobile, Alabama, where in 1863 large crowds of women plundered army food supplies.

In 1862, Joshua B. Moore, a slaveholder in northern Alabama, commented on how slavery threatened the Confederate war effort: "Men who have no interest in it," he wrote, "are not going to fight through a long war to save it—never. They will tire of it and quit." As the war progressed, desertion became what one officer called a "crying evil" for the southern armies. By the war's end, more than 100,000 men had deserted, almost entirely from among "the poorest class of nonslaveholders whose labor is indispensable to the daily support of their families." Men, another official noted, "cannot be expected to fight for the government that permits their wives and children to starve."

SOUTHERN UNIONISTS

By 1864, organized peace movements had appeared in several southern states, and secret societies such as the Heroes of America were actively promoting disaffection. Confederate military tribunals imprisoned hundreds of Unionists. Others were violently driven from their homes, and a few were executed by the army or civilian authorities. But southerners loyal to the Union made a significant contribution to northern victory. By the end of the war, an estimated 50,000 white southerners had fought in the Union armies.

One of the most celebrated Union heroes of the war was Elizabeth Van Lew of Richmond, who had persuaded her mother to free the family's slaves when her father died in 1843. During the war she frequently visited Libby Prison in the Confederate capital, bringing supplies to Union prisoners of war and helping some of them to escape. With the aid of Mary Elizabeth Bowser, a former slave of the Van Lew family who worked as a servant in the southern White House, Van Lew passed information about Confederate plans to Union forces.

WOMEN AND THE CONFEDERACY

Even more than in the North, the war placed unprecedented burdens on southern white women. Left alone on farms and plantations, they were often forced to manage business affairs and discipline slaves, previously the responsibility of men. As in the North, women mobilized to support soldiers in the field and stepped out of their traditional "sphere" to run commercial establishments and work in arms factories. In Richmond, "government girls" staffed many of the clerkships in the new Confederate bureaucracy. Rose Greenhow, the widow of a former American diplomat, headed an espionage ring in Washington, D.C., that passed valuable information about Union troop movements to the Confederacy early in the war. Even after her arrest and jailing, she managed to smuggle out intelligence until she was exiled to Richmond in 1862. Jefferson Davis rewarded Greenhow with $2,500 for her services.

Southern women's self-sacrificing devotion to the cause became legendary. But as the war went on and the death toll mounted, increasing numbers of women came to believe that the goal of independence was not worth the cost. The growing disaffection of southern white women, conveyed in letters to loved ones at the front, contributed to the decline in civilian morale and encouraged desertion from the army.

BLACK SOLDIERS FOR THE CONFEDERACY

The growing shortage of white manpower eventually led Confederate authorities to a decision no one could have foreseen when the war began: they authorized the arming of slaves to fight for the South. As early as September 1863, a Mississippi newspaper had argued for freeing and enlisting able-bodied black men. "Let them," it wrote, "be declared free, placed in the ranks, and told to fight for their homes and country." But many slaveholders fiercely resisted this idea, and initially, the Confederate Senate rejected it. Not until March 1865, after Robert E. Lee had endorsed the plan, did the Confederate Congress authorize the arming of slaves.

The war ended before the recruitment of black soldiers actually began. But the Confederate army did employ numerous blacks, nearly all of them slaves, as laborers. This later led to some confusion over whether blacks actually fought for the Confederacy—apart from a handful who "passed" for white, none in fact did. But the South's decision to raise black troops illustrates how the war undermined not only slavery but also the proslavery ideology. "The day you make soldiers of them is the beginning of the end of the revolution," declared Howell Cobb, a Georgia planter and politician. "If slaves make good soldiers, our whole theory of slavery is wrong."

TURNING POINTS

GETTYSBURG AND VICKSBURG

Despite the accelerating demise of slavery and the decline of morale in the South, the war's outcome remained very much in doubt for much of its third and fourth years. In April 1863, "Fighting Joe" Hooker, who had succeeded Ambrose E. Burnside as the Union commander in the East, brought the Army of the Potomac into central Virginia to confront Lee. Outnumbered two to one, Lee repelled Hooker's attack at Chancellorsville, although he lost his ablest lieutenant, "Stonewall" Jackson, mistakenly killed by fire from his own soldiers.

Lee now gambled on another invasion of the North, although his strategic objective remains unclear. Perhaps he believed a defeat on its own territory would destroy the morale of the northern army and public. In any event, the two armies, with Union soldiers now under the command of

In July 1863, the Union won major victories at Gettysburg and Vicksburg.

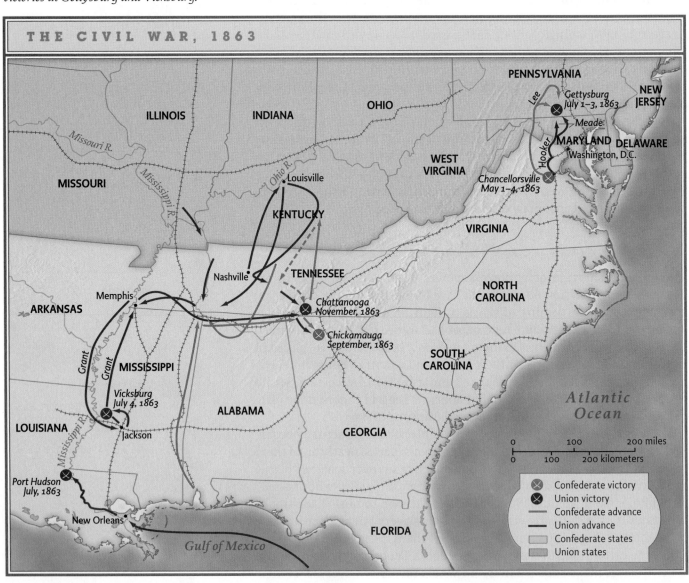

THE CIVIL WAR, 1863

General George G. Meade, met at Gettysburg, Pennsylvania, on the first three days of July 1863. With 165,000 troops involved, Gettysburg remains the largest battle ever fought on the North American continent. Lee found himself in the unusual position of confronting entrenched Union forces. After two days of failing to dislodge them, he decided to attack the center of the Union line. On July 3, Confederate forces, led by Major General George E. Pickett's crack division, marched across an open field toward Union forces. Withering artillery and rifle fire met the charge, and most of Pickett's soldiers never reached Union lines. Of the 14,000 men who made the advance—the flower of Lee's army—fewer than half returned. Later remembered as "the high tide of the Confederacy," Pickett's Charge was also Lee's greatest blunder. His army retreated to Virginia, never again to set foot on northern soil.

On the same day that Lee began his retreat from Gettysburg, the Union achieved a significant victory in the West. Late in 1862, Grant had moved into Mississippi toward the city of Vicksburg. From its heights, defended by miles of trenches and earthworks, the Confederacy commanded the central Mississippi River. When direct attacks failed, as did an attempt to divert the river by digging a canal, Grant launched a siege. On July 4, 1863, Vicksburg surrendered, and with it John C. Pemberton's army of 30,000 men, a loss the Confederacy could ill afford. The entire Mississippi Valley now lay in Union hands. The simultaneous defeats at Gettysburg and Vicksburg dealt a heavy blow to southern morale. "Today absolute ruin seems our portion," one official wrote in his diary. "The Confederacy totters to its destruction."

1864

Nearly two years, however, would pass before the war ended. Brought east to take command of Union forces, Grant in 1864 began a war of attrition against Lee's army in Virginia. That is, he was willing to accept high numbers of casualties, knowing that the North could replace its manpower losses while the South could not. Grant understood that to bring the North's manpower advantage into play, he must attack continuously "all along the line," thereby preventing the enemy from concentrating its forces or retreating to safety after an engagement.

In May 1864, the 115,000-man Army of the Potomac crossed the Rapidan River to do battle with Lee's forces in Virginia. A month of the war's bloodiest fighting followed. Grant and Lee first encountered each other in the Wilderness, a wild, shrub-covered region where, one participant recalled, "it was as though Christian men had turned to fiends, and hell itself had usurped the place of earth." Grant's army suffered 18,000 casualties, while Lee's far smaller forces incurred 7,500. Previous Union generals had broken off engagements after losses of this magnitude. But Grant continued to press forward, attacking again at Spotsylvania and then at Cold Harbor. At the end of six weeks of fighting, Grant's casualties stood at 60,000—almost the size of Lee's entire army—while Lee had lost 30,000 men. The sustained fighting in Virginia was a turning point in modern warfare. With daily combat and a fearsome casualty toll, it had far more in common with the trench warfare of World War I (discussed in Chapter 19) than the almost gentlemanly fighting with which the Civil War began.

Generals Robert E. Lee and Ulysses S. Grant, leaders of the opposing armies in the East, 1864–1865.

Grant had become the only Union general to maintain the initiative against Lee, but at a cost that led critics to label him a "butcher of men." Victory still eluded him. Grant attempted to capture Petersburg, which controlled the railway link to Richmond, but Lee got to Petersburg first, and Grant settled in for a prolonged siege. Meanwhile, General William T. Sherman, who had moved his forces into Georgia from Tennessee, encountered dogged resistance from Confederate troops. Not until September 1864 did he finally enter Atlanta, seizing Georgia's main railroad center.

As casualty rolls mounted in the spring and summer of 1864, northern morale sank to its lowest point of the war. Lincoln for a time believed he would be unable to win reelection. In May, hoping to force Lincoln to step aside, Radical Republicans nominated John C. Frémont on a platform calling for a constitutional amendment to abolish slavery, federal protection of the freedmen's rights, and confiscation of the land of leading Confederates. The Democratic candidate for president, General George B. McClellan, was hampered from the outset of the campaign by a platform calling for an immediate cease-fire and peace conference—a plan that even war-weary northerners viewed as equivalent to surrender. In the end, Frémont withdrew, and buoyed by Sherman's capture of Atlanta, Lincoln won a sweeping victory. He captured every state but Kentucky, Delaware, and New Jersey. The result ensured that the war would continue until the Confederacy's defeat.

REHEARSALS FOR RECONSTRUCTION AND THE END OF THE WAR

As the war drew toward a close and more and more parts of the Confederacy came under Union control, federal authorities found themselves presiding over the transition from slavery to freedom. In South Carolina, Louisiana, and other parts of the South, debates took place over issues—access to land, control of labor, and the new structure of political power—that would reverberate in the postwar world.

THE SEA ISLAND EXPERIMENT

The most famous "rehearsal for Reconstruction" took place on the Sea Islands just off the coast of South Carolina. The war was only a few months old when, in November 1861, the Union navy occupied the islands. Nearly the entire white population fled, leaving behind some 10,000 slaves. The navy was soon followed by other northerners—army officers, Treasury agents, prospective investors in cotton land, and a group known as Gideon's Band, which included black and white reformers and teachers committed to uplifting the freed slaves. Each of these groups, in addition to the islands' black population, had its own view of how the transition to freedom should be organized. And journalists reported every development on the islands to an eager reading public in the North.

Convinced that education was the key to making self-reliant, productive citizens of the former slaves, northern-born teachers like Charlotte Forten, a member of one of Philadelphia's most prominent black families, and Laura M. Towne, a white native of Pittsburgh, devoted themselves to teaching the freed blacks. Towne, who in 1862 helped to establish Penn school on

Long Abraham Lincoln a Little Longer, Harper's Weekly's *comment on Lincoln's reelection in 1864. At six feet four inches, Lincoln was the tallest American president.*

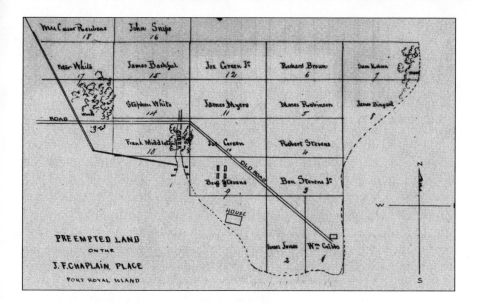

Diagram of plots selected by former slaves on Port Royal Island, South Carolina, January 25, 1864. Taking advantage of a sale of abandoned property, eighteen blacks (seventeen men and one woman) selected plots on a Sea Island plantation for purchase.

St. Helena Island, remained there as a teacher until her death in 1901. Like many of the Gideonites, Towne and Forten assumed that blacks needed outside guidance to appreciate freedom. But they sympathized with the former slaves' aspirations, central to which was the desire for land.

Other northerners, however, believed that the transition from slave to free labor meant not giving blacks land but enabling them to work for wages in more humane conditions than under slavery. When the federal government put land on the islands up for sale, most was acquired not by former slaves but by northern investors bent upon demonstrating the superiority of free wage labor and turning a tidy profit at the same time. By 1865, the Sea Island experiment was widely held to be a success. Black families were working for wages, acquiring education, and enjoying better shelter and clothing and a more varied diet than under slavery. But the experiment also bequeathed to postwar Reconstruction the contentious issue of whether land ownership should accompany black freedom.

WARTIME RECONSTRUCTION IN THE WEST

A very different rehearsal for Reconstruction, involving a far larger area and population than the Sea Islands, took place in Louisiana and the Mississippi Valley. After the capture of Vicksburg, the Union army established regulations for plantation labor. Military authorities insisted that the emancipated slaves must sign labor contracts with plantation owners who took an oath of loyalty. But, unlike before the war, they would be paid wages and provided with education, physical punishment was prohibited, and their families were safe from disruption by sale.

Neither side was satisfied with the new labor system. Blacks resented having to resume working for whites and being forced to sign labor contracts. Planters complained that their workers were insubordinate. Without the whip, they insisted, discipline could not be enforced. But only occasionally did army officers seek to implement a different vision of freedom. At Davis Bend, Mississippi, site of the cotton plantations of Jefferson Davis and his brother Joseph, General Grant decided to establish a "negro para-

Teachers in the Freedmen's Schools in Norfolk, 1863, *a photograph of a group of black and white teachers who brought education to former slaves in a Union-occupied part of Virginia.*

dise." Here, rather than being forced to labor for white owners, the emancipated slaves saw the land divided among themselves. In addition, a system of government was established that allowed the former slaves to elect their own judges and sheriffs.

THE POLITICS OF WARTIME RECONSTRUCTION

As the Civil War progressed, the future political status of African-Americans emerged as a key dividing line in public debates. Events in Union-occupied Louisiana brought the issue to national attention. Hoping to establish a functioning civilian government in the state, Lincoln in 1863 announced his Ten-Percent Plan of Reconstruction. He essentially offered an amnesty and full restoration of rights, including property except for slaves, to nearly all white southerners who took an oath affirming loyalty to the Union and support for emancipation. When 10 percent of the voters of 1860 had taken the oath, they could elect a new state government, which would be required to abolish slavery. Lincoln's plan offered no role to blacks in shaping the post-slavery order. His leniency toward southern whites seems to have been based on the assumption that many former slaveholders would come forward to accept his terms, thus weakening the Confederacy, shortening the war, and gaining white support for the ending of slavery.

Another group now stepped onto the stage of politics—the free blacks of New Orleans, who saw the Union occupation as a golden opportunity to press for equality before the law and a role in government for themselves. Their complaints at being excluded under Lincoln's Reconstruction plan won a sympathetic hearing from Radical Republicans in Congress. By the summer of 1864, dissatisfaction with events in Louisiana helped to inspire the Wade-Davis Bill, named for two leading Republican members of Congress. This bill required a majority (not one-tenth) of white male southerners to pledge support for the Union before Reconstruction could begin in any state, and it guaranteed blacks equality before the law, although not the right to vote. The bill passed Congress only to die when Lincoln refused to sign it and Congress adjourned. As the war drew to a close, it was clear that while slavery was dead, no agreement existed as to what social and political system should take its place.

VICTORY AT LAST

After Lincoln's reelection, the war hastened to its conclusion. In November 1864, Sherman and his army of 60,000 set out from Atlanta on their March to the Sea. Cutting a sixty-mile-wide swath through the heart of Georgia, they destroyed railroads, buildings, and all the food and supplies they could not use. His aim, Sherman wrote, was "to whip the rebels, to humble their pride, to follow them to their innermost recesses, and make them fear and dread us." Here was modern war in all its destructiveness, even though few civilians were physically harmed. In January 1865, after capturing Savannah, Sherman moved into South Carolina, bringing even greater destruction. Anarchy reigned on the plantations as slaves drove off remaining overseers, destroyed planters' homes, plundered smokehouses and storerooms, and claimed the land for themselves.

General William T. Sherman photographed in 1864.

On January 31, 1865, Congress approved the Thirteenth Amendment, which abolished slavery throughout the entire Union—and in so doing, introduced the word "slavery" into the Constitution for the first time. In March, in his second inaugural address, Lincoln called for reconciliation: "with malice toward none, with charity for all, . . . let us . . . bind up the nation's wounds." Yet he also leveled a harsh judgment on the nation's past.

The military defeat of the Confederacy came in the East, with Sherman's March to the Sea, Grant's occupation of Richmond, and the surrender of Robert E. Lee's army.

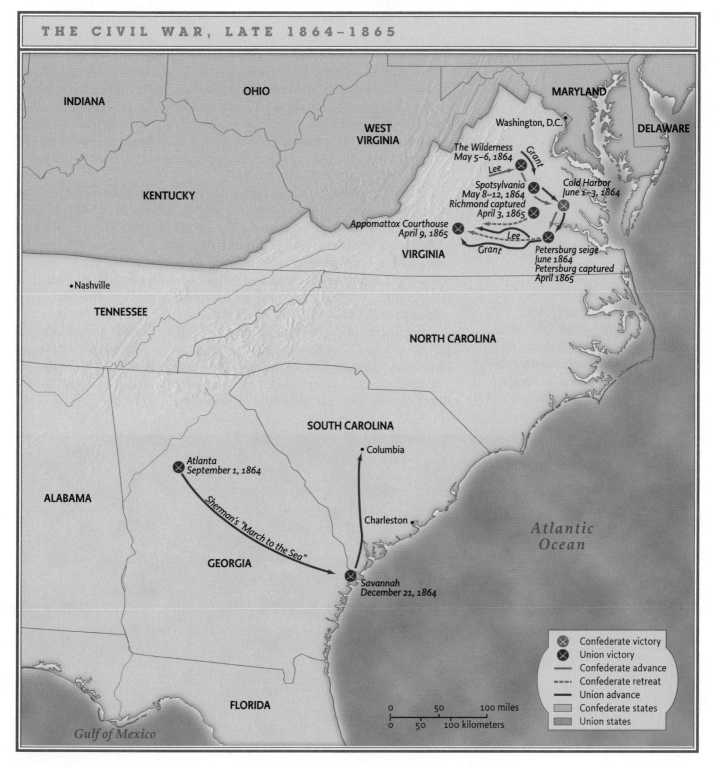

THE CIVIL WAR, LATE 1864–1865

INDIANA

OHIO

MARYLAND

WEST VIRGINIA

Washington, D.C.

DELAWARE

The Wilderness
May 5–6, 1864

Grant

Lee

KENTUCKY

Spotsylvania
May 8–12, 1864

Cold Harbor
June 1–3, 1864

Richmond captured
April 3, 1865

Appomattox Courthouse
April 9, 1865

Lee

VIRGINIA

Grant

Petersburg seige
June 1864
Petersburg captured
April 1865

• Nashville

TENNESSEE

NORTH CAROLINA

SOUTH CAROLINA

• Columbia

Atlanta
September 1, 1864

ALABAMA

Sherman's "March to the Sea"

Charleston

*Atlantic
Ocean*

GEORGIA

Savannah
December 21, 1864

FLORIDA

Gulf of Mexico

⊗	Confederate victory
⊗	Union victory
——	Confederate advance
- - -	Confederate retreat
——	Union advance
	Confederate states
	Union states

0   50   100 miles
0   50   100 kilometers

Unlike the northern clergy, who were sure of what God intended, Lincoln suggested that man does not know God's will—a remarkably modest statement on the eve of Union victory. Perhaps, Lincoln suggested, God had brought on the war to punish the entire nation, not just the South, for the sin of slavery. And if God willed that the war continue until all the wealth created by 250 years of slave labor had been destroyed, and "every drop of blood drawn with the lash shall be paid by another drawn with the sword," this too would be an act of justice (see the Appendix for the full text).

April 1865 brought some of the most momentous events in American history. On April 2, Grant finally broke through Lee's lines at Petersburg, forcing the Army of Northern Virginia to abandon the city and leaving Richmond defenseless. The following day, Union soldiers occupied the southern capital. At the head of one black army unit marched its chaplain, Garland H. White, a former fugitive from slavery. Called upon by a large crowd to make a speech, White, as he later recalled, proclaimed "for the first time in that city freedom to all mankind." Then the "doors of all the slave pens were thrown open and thousands came out shouting and praising God, and Father, or Master Abe."

On April 4, heedless of his own safety, Lincoln walked the streets of Richmond accompanied only by a dozen sailors. At every step he was besieged by former slaves, some of whom fell on their knees before the embarrassed president, who urged them to remain standing. Meanwhile, Lee and his army headed west, only to be encircled by Grant's forces. Realizing that further resistance was useless, Lee surrendered at Appomattox Courthouse, Virginia, on April 9. Although some Confederate units remained in the field, the Civil War was over.

Lincoln did not live to savor victory. On April 11, in what proved to be his last speech, he called publicly for the first time for limited black suffrage. Three days later, while attending a performance at Ford's Theatre in Washington, D.C., the president was mortally wounded by John Wilkes Booth, one of the nation's most celebrated actors. Lincoln died the next

The Evacuation of Richmond, *a Currier and Ives lithograph from 1865, dramatically depicts the last days of the Civil War. Residents flee the Confederate capital as fires set by retreating troops to destroy ammunition supplies consume parts of the city.*

The ruins of Richmond, in an 1865 photograph by Alexander Gardner.

morning. A train carried the president's body to its final resting place in Illinois on a winding 1,600-mile journey that illustrated how tightly the railroad now bound the northern states. Grieving crowds lined the train route, and solemn processions carried the president's body to lie in state in major cities so that mourners could pay their respects. It was estimated that 300,000 persons passed by the coffin in Philadelphia, 500,000 in New York, and 200,000 in Chicago. On May 4, 1865, Lincoln was laid to rest in Springfield.

THE WAR AND THE WORLD

In 1877, soon after retiring as president, Ulysses S. Grant embarked with his wife on a two-year tour of the world. At almost every location, he was greeted as a modern-day hero. What did America in the aftermath of the Civil War represent to the world? In England, the son of the duke of Wellington greeted Grant as a military genius, the primary architect of victory in one of the greatest wars in human history, and a fitting successor to his own father, the general who had vanquished Napoleon. In Newcastle, parading English workers hailed him as the man whose military prowess had saved the world's leading experiment in democratic government, and as a "Hero of Freedom," whose commander-in-chief, Abraham Lincoln, had vindicated the principles of free labor by emancipating America's slaves. In Berlin, Otto von Bismarck, the chancellor of Germany, welcomed Grant as a nation-builder, who had accomplished on the battlefield something—national unity—that Bismarck was attempting to create for his own people. "You had to save the Union," Bismarck commented, "just as we had to save Germany."

A redesign of the American flag proposed in 1863 illustrates the linkage of nationalism and freedom that was solidified by the Civil War. The thirty-five stars forming the word "FREE" include the eleven Confederate states.

THE WAR IN AMERICAN HISTORY

The Civil War laid the foundation for modern America, guaranteeing the Union's permanence, destroying slavery, and shifting power in the nation from the South to the North (and, more specifically, from slaveowning planters to northern capitalists). It dramatically increased the power of the federal government and accelerated the modernization of the northern economy. And it placed on the postwar agenda the challenge of defining and protecting African-American freedom.

Paradoxically, both sides lost something they had gone to war to defend. Slavery was the cornerstone of the Confederacy, but the war led inexorably to slavery's destruction. In the North, the war hastened the transformation of Lincoln's America—the world of free labor, of the small shop and independent farmer—into an industrial giant. Americans, in the words of the abolitionist Wendell Phillips, would "never again . . . see the republic in which we were born."

Late in May 1865, a little over a month after Lincoln's death, some 200,000 veterans paraded through Washington, D.C., for the Grand Review of the Union armies, a final celebration of the nation's triumph. The scene inspired the poet Bret Harte to imagine a very different parade—a "phantom army" of the Union dead:

> The martyred heroes of Malvern Hill,
> Of Gettysburg and Chancellorsville,
> The men whose wasted figures fill
> The patriot graves of the nation . . .
> And marching beside the others,
> Came the dusky martyrs of Pillow's fight.

To Harte, the war's meaning ultimately lay in the sacrifices of individual soldiers. He included in his reverie the black troops, including those massacred at Fort Pillow. Blacks, Harte seemed to be saying, had achieved equality in death. Could the nation give it to them in life?

Here was the problem that confronted the United States as the postwar era known as Reconstruction began. "Verily," as Frederick Douglass declared, "the work does not *end* with the abolition of slavery, but only *begins.*"

SUGGESTED READING

BOOKS

Ayers, Edward L. *In the Presence of Mine Enemies: War in the Heart of America, 1859–1863* (2003). A study of the experiences of Americans in two counties—one in Pennsylvania, one in Virginia—in the early years of the Civil War.

Berlin, Ira, ed. *Slaves No More: Three Essays on Emancipation and the Civil War* (1992). A careful account of the causes and consequences of emancipation during the war.

Faust, Drew G. *This Republic of Suffering* (2008). A powerful account of how the experience of mass death affected American culture, religion, and politics.

Freehling, William W. *The South vs. the South: How Anti-Confederate Southerners Shaped the Course of the Civil War* (2001). An examination of internal disunion within the Confederacy and how it affected the struggle for southern independence.

Glatthaar, Joseph T. *Forged in Battle: The Civil War Alliance of Black Soldiers and White Officers* (1990). Relates the complex experience of black Civil War soldiers and their officers.

Lawson, Melinda. *Patriot Fires: Forging a New Nationalism in the Civil War North* (2002). Considers how both public and private groups, in order to mobilize support for the war effort, promoted a new idea of American nationalism.

McPherson, James M. *Battle Cry of Freedom: The Civil War Era* (1988). The standard account of the coming of the war, its conduct, and its consequences.

Mitchell, Reid. *Civil War Soldiers* (1988). A look at the Civil War from the point of view of the experience of ordinary soldiers.

Neely, Mark E. *The Fate of Liberty: Abraham Lincoln and Civil Liberties* (1991). Explores how the Lincoln administration did and did not meet the challenge of preserving civil liberties while fighting the war.

Quarles, Benjamin. *Lincoln and the Negro* (1962). A judicious account of the evolution of Lincoln's policies regarding slavery, emancipation, and the rights of African-Americans.

Richardson, Heather C. *Greatest Nation of the Earth: Republican Economic Policies during the Civil War* (1997). Considers the far-reaching impact of the economic measures adopted by the Union during the war.

Rose, Willie Lee. *Rehearsal for Reconstruction: The Port Royal Experiment* (1964). Traces the unfolding of the issues of Reconstruction in the Sea Islands of South Carolina in the midst of the war.

Rubin, Anne S. *Shattered Nation: The Rise and Fall of the Confederacy, 1861–1868* (2005). An up-to-date account of the Confederate experience.

Silber, Nina. *Daughters of the Union: Northern Women Fight the Civil War* (2005). Examines the participation of northern women in the war effort and how this did and did not alter their lives.

Stout, Harry S. *Upon the Altar of the Nation: A Moral History of the Civil War* (2006). Examines the role of religion in mobilizing support for the war effort.

WEBSITES

A House Divided: America in the Age of Lincoln: www.digitalhistory.uh.edu/ahd/index.html

Civil War Women: http://library.duke.edu/specialcollections/collections/digitized/civil-war-women/

The American Civil War Homepage: http://sunsite.utk.edu/civil-war/

The Valley of the Shadow: Two Communities in the American Civil War: http://valley.vcdh.virginia.edu

REVIEW QUESTIONS

1. What made the American Civil War the first modern war?

2. Explain how the North won the war by considering its material resources, military strategy, and effective political and military leadership.

3. Describe how President Lincoln's war aims evolved between 1861 and 1863, changing from simply preserving the Union to also ending slavery.

4. How did the Emancipation Proclamation, northern military successes, and actions by the slaves themselves combine to finally end slavery?

5. What role did blacks play in both winning the Civil War and in defining the war's consequences?

6. What major policies did the wartime Congress pass that transformed the nation's economic and financial systems?

7. How was the American Civil War part of a global trend toward more destructive and deadly wars?

8. Compare the end of slavery in the United States to emancipation elsewhere in the world.

9. In what ways did the outcome of the Civil War change the United States's status in the world?

FREEDOM QUESTIONS

1. How did Lincoln's Gettysburg Address express the new connection between freedom, liberty, and nation?

2. Explain how both northern and southern soldiers could claim they were fighting for "freedom" and "liberty."

3. Explain how both northern and southern governments restricted liberties during the war. How were such actions justified?

4. Describe how the Civil War permanently altered the national definition of freedom and linked it to the survival of the nation

KEY TERMS

first modern war (p. 539)

Monitor v. Merrimac (p. 541)

Army of the Potomac (p. 541)

Army of Northern Virginia (p. 545)

Battle of Antietam (p. 546)

contraband of war (p. 548)

Radical Republicans (p. 549)

Emancipation Proclamation
   (p. 550)

black soldiers and sailors
   (p. 551)

Second American Revolution
   (p. 556)

Ex parte Milligan (p. 562)

transcontinental railroad (p. 563)

national banking system (p. 564)

women and war work (p. 565)

"King Cotton diplomacy" (p. 568)

southern Unionist (p. 571)

women in the Confederacy
   (p. 571)

Sea Island experiment (p. 574)

REVIEW TABLE

Rehearsals for Reconstruction

Event	Explanation	Result
Sea Island experiment, 1861–1865	Union takes islands and northerners bring their ideas for education, land distribution, and employment for blacks	Black families work for wages, get an education, and enjoy better food and shelter than under slavery
"Negro paradise"	General Grant seizes the cotton plantations of Jefferson Davis and his brother	Grant divides the land among the freed slaves, rather than have them work for white owners
Ten-Percent Plan	Lincoln's lenient plan toward the South, which offered no role for blacks	Rejected by many black southerners and the Radical Republicans in Congress
Wade-Davis Bill	Stricter reconstruction plan that guarantees blacks equality before the law	Pocket vetoed by Lincoln

CHAPTER 15

FROM THE PLANTATION TO THE

"What Is Freedom?": Reconstruction, 1865–1877

From the Plantation to the Senate, *an 1883 lithograph celebrating African-American
progress during Reconstruction. Among the black leaders pictured at the top are
Reconstruction congressmen Benjamin S. Turner, Josiah T. Walls, and Joseph H. Rainey;
Hiram Revels of Mississippi, the first African-American senator; religious leader Richard
Allen; and abolitionists Frederick Douglass and William Wells Brown. At the center,
emancipated slaves work in a cotton field. At the bottom, children attend school
and a black family stands outside their home.*

- What visions of freedom did the former slaves and slaveholders pursue in the postwar South?

- What were the sources, goals, and competing visions for Reconstruction?

- What were the social and political effects of Radical Reconstruction in the South?

- What were the main factors, in both the North and South, for the abandonment of Reconstruction?

On the evening of January 12, 1865, less than a month after Union forces captured Savannah, Georgia, twenty leaders of the city's black community gathered for a discussion with General William T. Sherman and Secretary of War Edwin M. Stanton. Mostly Baptist and Methodist ministers, the group included several men who within a few years would assume prominent positions during the era of Reconstruction that followed the Civil War. Ulysses S. Houston, pastor of the city's Third African Baptist Church, and James Porter, an episcopal religious leader who had operated a secret school for black children before the war, in a few years would win election to the Georgia legislature. James D. Lynch, who had been born free in Baltimore and educated in New Hampshire, went on to serve as secretary of state of Mississippi.

The conversation revealed that the black leaders brought out of slavery a clear definition of freedom. Asked what he understood by slavery, Garrison Frazier, a Baptist minister chosen as the group's spokesman, responded that it meant one person's "receiving by irresistible power the work of another man, and not by his consent." Freedom he defined as "placing us where we could reap the fruit of our own labor, and take care of ourselves." The way to accomplish this was "to have land, and turn it and till it by our own labor." Frazier insisted that blacks possessed "sufficient intelligence" to maintain themselves in freedom and enjoy the equal protection of the laws.

Sherman's meeting with the black leaders foreshadowed some of the radical changes that would take place during the era known as Reconstruction (meaning, literally, the rebuilding of the shattered nation). In the years following the Civil War, former slaves and their white allies, North and South, would seek to redefine the meaning and boundaries of American freedom. Previously an entitlement of whites, freedom would be expanded to include black Americans. The laws and Constitution would be rewritten to guarantee African-Americans, for the first time in the nation's history, recognition as citizens and equality before the law. Black men would be granted the right to vote, ushering in a period of interracial democracy throughout the South. Black schools, churches, and other institutions would flourish, laying the foundation for the modern African-American community. Many of the advances of Reconstruction would prove temporary, swept away during a campaign of violence in the South, and the North's retreat from the ideal of equality. But Reconstruction laid the foundation for future struggles to extend freedom to all Americans.

All this, however, lay in the future in January 1865. Four days after the meeting, Sherman responded to the black delegation by issuing Special Field Order 15. This set aside the Sea Islands and a large area along the South Carolina and Georgia coasts for the settlement of black families on forty-acre plots of land. He also offered them broken-down mules that the army could no longer use. In Sherman's order lay the origins of the phrase, "forty acres and a mule," that would reverberate across the South in the next few years. By June, some 40,000 freed slaves had been settled on "Sherman land." Among the emancipated slaves, Sherman's order raised hopes that the end of slavery would be accompanied by the economic independence that they, like other Americans, believed essential to genuine freedom.

THE MEANING OF FREEDOM

With the end of the Civil War, declared an Illinois congressman in 1865, the United States was a "new nation," for the first time "wholly free." The destruction of slavery, however, made the definition of freedom the central question on the nation's agenda. "What is freedom?" asked Congressman James A. Garfield in 1865. "Is it the bare privilege of not being chained? If this is all, then freedom is a bitter mockery, a cruel delusion." Did freedom mean simply the absence of slavery, or did it imply other rights for the former slaves, and if so, which ones: equal civil rights, the vote, ownership of property? During Reconstruction, freedom became a terrain of conflict, its substance open to different, often contradictory interpretations. Out of the conflict over the meaning of freedom arose new kinds of relations between black and white southerners, and a new definition of the rights of all Americans.

Family Record, *a lithograph marketed to former slaves after the Civil War, centers on an idealized portrait of a middle-class black family, with scenes of slavery and freedom.*

BLACKS AND THE MEANING OF FREEDOM

African-Americans' understanding of freedom was shaped by their experiences as slaves and their observation of the free society around them. To begin with, freedom meant escaping the numerous injustices of slavery—punishment by the lash, the separation of families, denial of access to education, the sexual exploitation of black women by their owners—and sharing in the rights and opportunities of American citizens. "If I cannot do like a white man," Henry Adams, an emancipated slave in Louisiana, told his former master in 1865, "I am not free."

Blacks relished the opportunity to demonstrate their liberation from the regulations, significant and trivial, associated with slavery. They openly held mass meetings and religious services free of white supervision, and they acquired dogs, guns, and liquor, all barred to them under slavery. No longer required to obtain a pass from their owners to travel, former slaves throughout the South left the plantations in search of better jobs, family members, or simply a taste of personal liberty. Many moved to southern towns and cities, where, it seemed, "freedom was free-er."

A post–Civil War photograph of an unidentified black family, seated before their humble home, possibly a former slave cabin.

Mother and Daughter Reading, Mt. Meigs, Alabama, *an 1890 photograph by Rudolph Eickemeyer. During Reconstruction and for years thereafter, former slaves exhibited a deep desire for education, and learning took place outside of school as well as within.*

FAMILIES IN FREEDOM

With slavery dead, institutions that had existed before the war, like the black family, free blacks' churches and schools, and the secret slave church, were strengthened, expanded, and freed from white supervision. The family was central to the postemancipation black community. Former slaves made remarkable efforts to locate loved ones from whom they had been separated under slavery. One northern reporter in 1865 encountered a freedman who had walked more than 600 miles from Georgia to North Carolina, searching for the wife and children from whom he had been sold away before the war. Meanwhile, widows of black soldiers successfully claimed survivors' pensions, forcing the federal government to acknowledge the validity of prewar relationships that slavery had attempted to deny.

But while Reconstruction witnessed the stabilization of family life, freedom subtly altered relationships within the family. Emancipation increased the power of black men and brought to many black families the nineteenth-century notion that men and women should inhabit separate "spheres." Immediately after the Civil War, planters complained that freedwomen had "withdrawn" from field labor and work as house servants. Many black women preferred to devote more time to their families than had been possible under slavery, and men considered it a badge of honor to see their wives remain at home. Eventually, the dire poverty of the black community would compel a far higher proportion of black women than white women to go to work for wages.

CHURCH AND SCHOOL

At the same time, blacks abandoned white-controlled religious institutions to create churches of their own. On the eve of the Civil War, 42,000 black Methodists worshiped in biracial South Carolina churches; by the end of Reconstruction, only 600 remained. The rise of the independent black church, with Methodists and Baptists commanding the largest followings, redrew the religious map of the South. As the major institution independent of white control, the church played a central role in the black community. A place of worship, it also housed schools, social events, and political gatherings. Black ministers came to play a major role in politics. Some 250 held public office during Reconstruction.

Another striking example of the freedpeople's quest for individual and community improvement was their desire for education. Education, declared a Mississippi freedman, was "the next best thing to liberty." The thirst for learning sprang from many sources—a desire to read the Bible, the need to prepare for the economic marketplace, and the opportunity, which arose in 1867, to take part in politics. Blacks of all ages flocked to the schools established by northern missionary societies, the Freedmen's

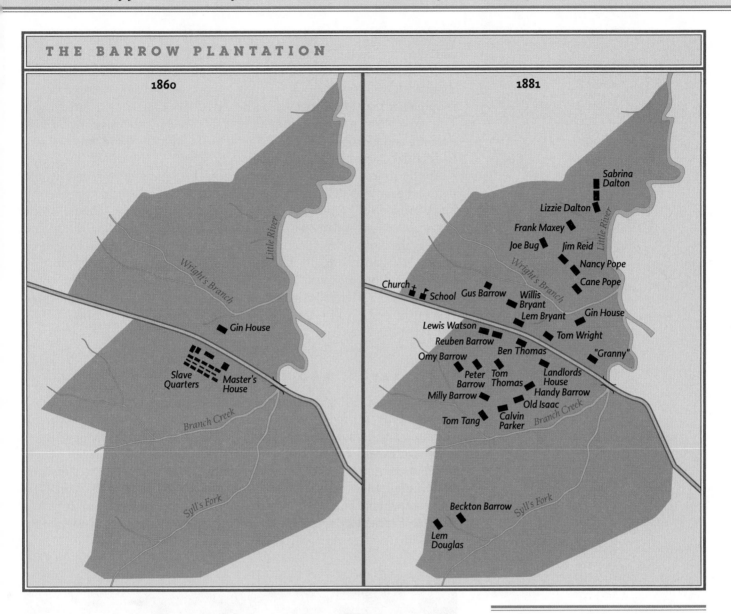

THE BARROW PLANTATION

1860

Little River

Wright's Branch

Gin House

Slave Quarters   Master's House

Branch Creek

Syll's Fork

1881

Sabrina Dalton

Lizzie Dalton

Frank Maxey

Joe Bug   Jim Reid

Nancy Pope

Cane Pope

Little River

Wright's Branch

Church   School   Gus Barrow   Willis Bryant

Lem Bryant   Gin House

Lewis Watson   Tom Wright

Reuben Barrow   Ben Thomas   "Granny"

Omy Barrow

Peter   Tom   Landlords
Barrow   Thomas   House

Milly Barrow   Handy Barrow

Old Isaac

Tom Tang   Calvin   Branch Creek
Parker

Beckton Barrow   Syll's Fork

Lem Douglas

Two maps of the Barrow plantation illustrate the effects of emancipation on rural life in the South. In 1860, slaves lived in communal quarters near the owner's house. Twenty years later, former slaves working as sharecroppers lived scattered across the plantation and had their own church and school.

Bureau, and groups of ex-slaves themselves. Northern journalist Sidney Andrews, who toured the South in 1865, was impressed by how much education also took place outside of the classroom: "I had occasion very frequently to notice that porters in stores and laboring men in warehouses, and cart drivers on the streets, had spelling books with them, and were studying them during the time they were not occupied with their work." Reconstruction also witnessed the creation of the nation's first black colleges, including Fisk University in Tennessee, Hampton Institute in Virginia, and Howard University in the nation's capital.

POLITICAL FREEDOM

In a society that had made political participation a core element of freedom, the right to vote inevitably became central to the former slaves' desire for empowerment and equality. As Frederick Douglass put it soon after the South's surrender in 1865, "Slavery is not abolished until the black man has the ballot." In a "monarchial government," Douglass explained, no "special" disgrace applied to those denied the right to vote. But in a democracy, "where universal suffrage is the rule," excluding any group meant branding them with "the stigma of inferiority." As soon as the Civil War ended, and in some parts of the South even earlier, free blacks and emancipated slaves claimed a place in the public sphere. They came together in conventions, parades, and petition drives to demand the right to vote and, on occasion, to organize their own "freedom ballots."

Anything less than full citizenship, black spokesmen insisted, would betray the nation's democratic promise and the war's meaning. Speakers at black conventions reminded the nation of Crispus Attucks, who fell at the Boston Massacre, and of black soldiers' contribution to the War of 1812 and during "the bloody struggle through which we have just passed." To demonstrate their patriotism, blacks throughout the South organized Fourth of July celebrations. For years after the Civil War, white southerners would "shut themselves within doors" on Independence Day, as a white resident of Charleston recorded in her diary, while former slaves commemorated the holiday themselves.

LAND, LABOR, AND FREEDOM

Like rural people throughout the world, former slaves' ideas of freedom were directly related to land ownership. Only land, wrote Merrimon Howard, a freedman from Mississippi, would enable "the poor class to enjoy the sweet boon of freedom." On the land they would develop independent communities free of white control. Many former slaves insisted that through their unpaid labor, they had acquired a right to the land. "The property which they hold," declared an Alabama black convention, "was nearly all earned by the sweat of *our* brows." In some parts of the South, blacks in 1865 seized property, insisting that it belonged to them. On one

Winslow Homer's 1876 painting, A Visit from the Old Mistress, *depicts an imaginary meeting between a southern white woman and her former slaves. Their stance and gaze suggest the tensions arising from the birth of a new social order. Homer places his subjects on an equal footing, yet maintains a space of separation between them. He exhibited the painting to acclaim at the Paris Universal Exposition in 1878.*

Tennessee plantation, former slaves claimed to be "joint heirs" to the estate and, the owner complained, took up residence "in the rooms of my house."

In its individual elements and much of its language, former slaves' definition of freedom resembled that of white Americans—self-ownership, family stability, religious liberty, political participation, and economic autonomy. But these elements combined to form a vision very much their own. For whites, freedom, no matter how defined, was a given, a birthright to be defended. For African-Americans, it was an open-ended process, a transformation of every aspect of their lives and of the society and culture that had sustained slavery in the first place. Although the freedpeople failed to achieve full freedom as they understood it, their definition did much to shape national debate during the turbulent era of Reconstruction.

MASTERS WITHOUT SLAVES

Most white southerners reacted to military defeat and emancipation with dismay, not only because of the widespread devastation but also because they must now submit to northern demands. "The demoralization is complete," wrote a Georgia girl. "We are whipped, there is no doubt about it." The appalling loss of life, a disaster without parallel in the American experience, affected all classes of southerners. Nearly 260,000 men died for the Confederacy—more than one-fifth of the South's adult male white population. The widespread destruction of work animals, farm buildings, and machinery ensured that economic revival would be slow and painful. In 1870, the value of property in the South, not counting that represented by slaves, was 30 percent lower than before the war.

Planter families faced profound changes in the war's aftermath. Many lost not only their slaves but their life savings, which they had patriotically invested in now-worthless Confederate bonds. Some, whose slaves departed the plantation, for the first time found themselves compelled to do physical labor. General Braxton Bragg returned to his "once prosperous" Alabama home to find "*all, all* was lost, except my debts." Bragg and his wife, a woman "raised in affluence," lived for a time in a slave cabin.

Southern planters sought to implement an understanding of freedom quite different from that of the former slaves. As they struggled to accept the reality of emancipation, most planters defined black freedom in the narrowest manner. As journalist Sidney Andrews discovered late in 1865, "The whites seem wholly unable to comprehend that freedom for the negro means the same thing as freedom for them. They readily enough admit that the government has made him free, but appear to believe that they have the right to exercise the same old control." Southern leaders sought to revive

The Great Labor Question from a Southern Point of View, *a cartoon by the artist Winslow Homer, published in Harper's Weekly, July 29, 1865. Homer satirizes the attitudes of many white southerners. While blacks labor in the fields, an idle planter warns a former slave, "My boy, we've toiled and taken care of you long enough—now you've got to work!"*

the antebellum definition of freedom as if nothing had changed. Freedom still meant hierarchy and mastery; it was a privilege not a right, a carefully defined legal status rather than an open-ended entitlement. Certainly, it implied neither economic autonomy nor civil and political equality. "A man may be free and yet not independent," Mississippi planter Samuel Agnew observed in his diary in 1865. A Kentucky newspaper summed up the stance of much of the white South: the former slave was "*free*, but free only to labor."

THE FREE LABOR VISION

Along with former slaves and former masters, the victorious Republican North tried to implement its own vision of freedom. Central to its definition was the antebellum principle of free labor, now further strengthened as a definition of the good society by the Union's triumph. In the free labor vision of a reconstructed South, emancipated blacks, enjoying the same opportunities for advancement as northern workers, would labor more productively than they had as slaves. At the same time, northern capital and migrants would energize the economy. The South would eventually come to resemble the "free society" of the North, complete with public schools, small towns, and independent farmers. Unified on the basis of free labor, proclaimed Carl Schurz, a refugee from the failed German revolution of 1848 who rose to become a leader of the Republican Party, America would become "a republic, greater, more populous, freer, more prosperous, and more powerful" than any in history.

With planters seeking to establish a labor system as close to slavery as possible, and former slaves demanding economic autonomy and access to land, a long period of conflict over the organization and control of labor followed on plantations throughout the South. It fell to the Freedmen's Bureau, an agency established by Congress in March 1865, to attempt to establish a working free labor system.

THE FREEDMEN'S BUREAU

Under the direction of O. O. Howard, a graduate of Bowdoin College in Maine and a veteran of the Civil War, the Bureau took on responsibilities that can only be described as daunting. The Bureau was an experiment in government social policy that seems to belong more comfortably to the New Deal of the 1930s or the Great Society of the 1960s (see Chapters 21 and 25, respectively) than to nineteenth-century America. Bureau agents were supposed to establish schools, provide aid to the poor and aged, settle disputes between whites and blacks and among the freedpeople, and secure for former slaves and white Unionists equal treatment before the courts. "It is not . . . in your power to fulfill one-tenth of the expectations of those who framed the Bureau," General William T. Sherman wrote to Howard. "I fear you have Hercules' task."

The Bureau lasted from 1865 to 1870. Even at its peak, there were fewer than 1,000 agents in the entire South. Nonetheless, the Bureau's achievements in some areas, notably education and health care, were striking. While the Bureau did not establish schools itself, it coordinated and helped to finance the activities of northern societies committed to black education.

By 1869, nearly 3,000 schools, serving more than 150,000 pupils in the South, reported to the Bureau. Bureau agents also assumed control of hospitals established by the army during the war, and expanded the system into new communities. They provided medical care and drugs to both black and white southerners. In economic relations, however, the Bureau's activities proved far more problematic.

The Freedmen's Bureau, *an engraving from* Harper's Weekly, *July 25, 1868, depicts the Bureau agent as a promoter of racial peace in the violent postwar South.*

THE FAILURE OF LAND REFORM

The idea of free labor, wrote one Bureau agent, was "the noblest principle on earth." All that was required to harmonize race relations in the South was fair wages, good working conditions, and the opportunity to improve the laborer's situation in life. But blacks wanted land of their own, not jobs on plantations. One provision of the law establishing the Bureau gave it the authority to divide abandoned and confiscated land into forty-acre plots for rental and eventual sale to the former slaves.

In the summer of 1865, however, President Andrew Johnson, who had succeeded Lincoln, ordered nearly all land in federal hands returned to its former owners. A series of confrontations followed, notably in South Carolina and Georgia, where the army forcibly evicted blacks who had settled on "Sherman land." When O. O. Howard, head of the Freedmen's Bureau, traveled to the Sea Islands to inform blacks of the new policy, he was greeted with disbelief and protest. A committee of former slaves drew up petitions to Howard and President Johnson. "We want Homesteads," they declared, "we were promised Homesteads by the government." Land, the freedmen insisted, was essential to the meaning of freedom. Without it, they declared, "we have not bettered our condition" from the days of slavery—"you will see, this is not the condition of really free men."

Because no land distribution took place, the vast majority of rural freed-people remained poor and without property during Reconstruction. They

A black family in the cotton fields after the Civil War, photographed in 1867.

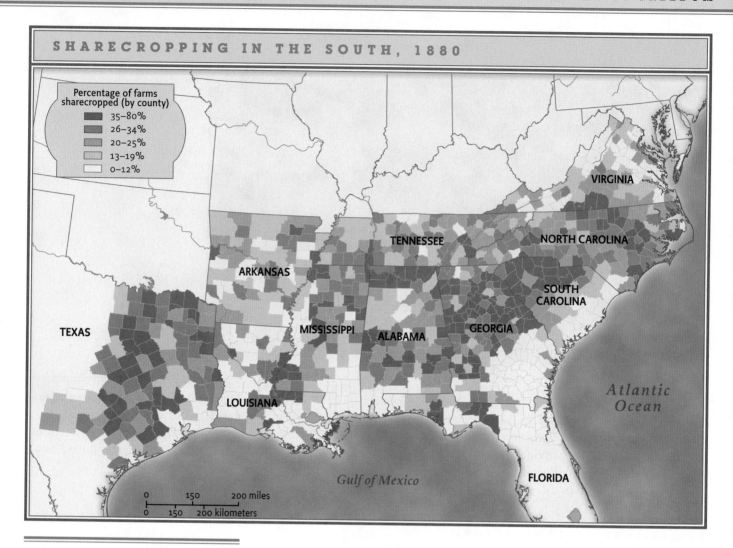

SHARECROPPING IN THE SOUTH, 1880

Percentage of farms
sharecropped (by county)

- 35–80%
- 26–34%
- 20–25%
- 13–19%
- 0–12%

By 1880, sharecropping had become the dominant form of agricultural labor in large parts of the South. The system involved both white and black farmers.

had no alternative but to work on white-owned plantations, often for their former owners. Far from being able to rise in the social scale through hard work, black men were largely confined to farm work, unskilled labor, and service jobs, and black women to positions in private homes as cooks and maids. Their wages remained too low to allow for any accumulation. By the turn of the century, a significant number of southern African-Americans had managed to acquire small parcels of land. But the failure of land reform produced a deep sense of betrayal that survived among the former slaves and their descendants long after the end of Reconstruction. "No sir," Mary Gaffney, an elderly ex-slave, recalled in the 1930s, "we were not given a thing but freedom."

TOWARD A NEW SOUTH

Out of the conflict on the plantations, new systems of labor emerged in the different regions of the South. The task system, under which workers were assigned daily tasks, completion of which ended their responsibilities for that day, survived in the rice kingdom of South Carolina and Georgia. Closely supervised wage labor predominated on the sugar plantations of southern Louisiana. Sharecropping came to dominate the Cotton Belt and much of the Tobacco Belt of Virginia and North Carolina.

Sharecropping initially arose as a compromise between blacks' desire for land and planters' demand for labor discipline. The system allowed each black family to rent a part of a plantation, with the crop divided between worker and owner at the end of the year. Sharecropping guaranteed the planters a stable resident labor force. Former slaves preferred it to gang labor because it offered them the prospect of working without day-to-day white supervision. But as the years went on, sharecropping became more and more oppressive. Sharecroppers' economic opportunities were severely limited by a world market in which the price of farm products suffered a prolonged decline.

THE WHITE FARMER

The plight of the small farmer was not confined to blacks in the postwar South. Wartime devastation set in motion a train of events that permanently altered the independent way of life of white yeomen, leading to what they considered a loss of freedom. Before the war, most small farmers had concentrated on raising food for their families and grew little cotton. With much of their property destroyed, many yeomen saw their economic condition worsened by successive crop failures after the war. To obtain supplies from merchants, farmers were forced to take up the growing of cotton and pledge a part of the crop as collateral (property the creditor can seize if a debt is not paid). This system became known as the "crop lien." Since interest rates were extremely high and the price of cotton fell steadily, many farmers found themselves still in debt after marketing their portion of the crop at year's end. They had no choice but to

Farmers with Cotton in the Courthouse Square, *an 1880 photograph of Marietta, Georgia. After the Civil War, more and more white farmers began growing cotton to support their families, permanently altering their formerly self-sufficient way of life.*

VOICES OF FREEDOM

In the summer of 1865, President Andrew Johnson ordered land that had been distributed to freed slaves in South Carolina and Georgia returned to its former owners. A committee of freedmen drafted a petition asking for the right to obtain land. Johnson did not, however, change his policy.

We the freedmen of Edisto Island, South Carolina, have learned from you through Major General O. O. Howard . . . with deep sorrow and painful hearts of the possibility of [the] government restoring these lands to the former owners. We are well aware of the many perplexing and trying questions that burden your mind, and therefore pray to god (the preserver of all, and who has through our late and beloved President [Lincoln's] proclamation and the war made us a free people) that he may guide you in making your decisions and give you that wisdom that cometh from above to settle these great and important questions for the best interests of the country and the colored race.

Here is where secession was born and nurtured. Here is where we have toiled nearly all our lives as slaves and treated like dumb driven cattle. This is our home, we have made these lands what they were, we are the only true and loyal people that were found in possession of these lands. We have been always ready to strike for liberty and humanity, yea to fight if need be to preserve this glorious Union. Shall not we who are freedmen and have always been true to this Union have the same rights as are enjoyed by others? . . . Are not our rights as a free people and good citizens of these United States to be considered before those who were found in rebellion against this good and just government? . . .

[Are] we who have been abused and oppressed for many long years not to be allowed the privilege of purchasing land but be subject to the will of these large land owners? God forbid. Land monopoly is injurious to the advancement of the course of freedom, and if government does not make some provision by which we as freedmen can obtain a homestead, we have not bettered our condition. . . .

We look to you . . . for protection and equal rights with the privilege of purchasing a homestead— a homestead right here in the heart of South Carolina.

From a Sharecropping Contract (1866)

Few former slaves were able to acquire land in the post–Civil War South. Most ended up as sharecroppers, working on white-owned land for a share of the crop at the end of the growing season. This contract, typical of thousands of others, originated in Tennessee. The laborers signed with an X, as they were illiterate.

Thomas J. Ross agrees to employ the Freedmen to plant and raise a crop on his Rosstown Plantation.... On the following Rules, Regulations and Remunerations.

The said Ross agrees to furnish the land to cultivate, and a sufficient number of mules & horses and feed them to make and house said crop and all necessary farming utensils to carry on the same and to give unto said Freedmen whose names appear below one half of all the cotton, corn and wheat that is raised on said place for the year 1866 after all the necessary expenses are deducted out that accrues on said crop. Outside of the Freedmen's labor in harvesting, carrying to market and selling the same the said Freedmen ... covenant and agrees to and with said Thomas J. Ross that for and in consideration of one half of the crop before mentioned that they will plant, cultivate, and raise under the management control and Superintendence of said Ross, in good faith, a cotton, corn and oat crop under his management for the year 1866. And we the said Freedmen agrees to furnish ourselves & families in provisions, clothing, medicine and medical bills and all, and every kind of other expenses that we may incur on said plantation for the year 1866 free of charge to said Ross. Should the said Ross furnish us any of the above supplies or any other kind of expenses, during said year, are to settle and pay him out of the net proceeds of our part of the crop the retail price of the county at time of sale or any price we may agree upon—The said Ross shall keep a regular book account, against each and every one or the head of every family to be adjusted and settled at the end of the year.

We furthermore bind ourselves to and with said Ross that we will do good work and labor ten hours a day on an average, winter and summer.... We further agree that we will lose all lost time, or pay at the rate of one dollar per day, rainy days excepted. In sickness and women lying in childbed are to lose the time and account for it to the other hands out of his or her part of the crop....

We furthermore bind ourselves that we will obey the orders of said Ross in all things in carrying out and managing said crop for said year and be docked for disobedience. All is responsible for all farming utensils that is on hand or may be placed in care of said Freedmen for the year 1866 to said Ross and are also responsible to said Ross if we carelessly, maliciously maltreat any of his stock for said year to said Ross for damages to be assessed out of our wages.

Samuel (X) Johnson, Thomas (X) Richard, Tinny (X) Fitch, Jessie (X) Simmons, Sophe (X) Pruden, Henry (X) Pruden, Frances (X) Pruden, Elijah (X) Smith

---

QUESTIONS

1. Why do the black petitioners believe that owning land is essential to the enjoyment of freedom?

2. In what ways does the contract limit the freedom of the laborers?

3. What do these documents suggest about competing definitions of black freedom in the aftermath of slavery?

continue to plant cotton to obtain new loans. By the mid-1870s, white farmers, who cultivated only 10 percent of the South's cotton crop in 1860, were growing 40 percent, and many who had owned their land had fallen into dependency as sharecroppers, who now rented land owned by others.

Both black and white farmers found themselves caught in the sharecropping and crop-lien systems. A far higher percentage of black than white farmers in the South rented land rather than owned it. But every census from 1880 to 1940 counted more white than black sharecroppers. The workings of sharecropping and the crop-lien system are illustrated by the case of Matt Brown, a Mississippi farmer who borrowed money each year from a local merchant. He began 1892 with a debt of $226 held over from the previous year. By 1893, although he produced cotton worth $171, Brown's debt had increased to $402, because he had borrowed $33 for food, $29 for clothing, $173 for supplies, and $112 for other items. Brown never succeeded in getting out of debt. He died in 1905; the last entry under his name in the merchant's account book is a coffin.

THE URBAN SOUTH

Even as the rural South stagnated economically, southern cities experienced remarkable growth after the Civil War. As railroads penetrated the interior, they enabled merchants in market centers like Atlanta to trade directly with the North, bypassing coastal cities that had traditionally monopolized southern commerce. A new urban middle class of merchants, railroad promoters, and bankers reaped the benefits of the spread of cotton production in the postwar South.

Thus, Reconstruction brought about profound changes in the lives of southerners, black and white, rich and poor. In place of the prewar world of master, slave, and self-sufficient yeoman, the postwar South was peopled by new social classes—landowning employers, black and white sharecroppers, cotton-producing white farmers, wage-earning black laborers, and urban entrepreneurs. Each of these groups turned to Reconstruction politics in an attempt to shape to its own advantage the aftermath of emancipation.

AFTERMATHS OF SLAVERY

The United States, of course, was not the only society to confront the problem of the transition from slavery to freedom. Indeed, many parallels exist between the debates during Reconstruction and struggles that followed slavery in other parts of the Western Hemisphere over the same issues of land, control of labor, and political power. In every case, former planters (or, in Haiti, where the planter class had been destroyed, the government itself) tried to encourage or require former slaves to go back to work on plantations to grow the same crops as under slavery. Planters elsewhere held the same stereotypical views of black laborers as were voiced by their counterparts in the United States—former slaves were supposedly lazy, lacking in ambition, and thought that freedom meant an absence of labor.

For their part, former slaves throughout the hemisphere tried to carve out as much independence as possible, both in their daily lives and in their labor. They attempted to reconstruct family life by withdrawing women and children from field labor (in the West Indies, women turned to marketing their families' crops to earn income). Wherever possible, former slaves acquired land of their own and devoted more time to growing food for their families than crops for the international market. On small Caribbean islands like Barbados, where no unoccupied land existed, former slaves had no alternative but to return to plantation labor. Elsewhere, the plantations either fell to pieces, as in Haiti, or continued operating with a new labor force composed of indentured servants from India and China, as in Jamaica, Trinidad, and British Guiana. As slavery ended between the years 1838 and 1865, more than 100,000 Indian laborers were introduced into the British Caribbean—a process that could not have taken place without the consolidation of British control over India as part of its nineteenth-century empire. Southern planters in the United States brought in a few Chinese laborers in an attempt to replace freedmen, but since the federal government opposed such efforts, the Chinese remained only a tiny proportion of the southern workforce.

But if struggles over land and labor united its postemancipation experience with that of other societies, in one respect the United States was unique. Only in the United States were former slaves, within two years of the end of slavery, granted the right to vote and, thus, given a major share of political power. Few anticipated this development when the Civil War ended. It came about as the result of one of the greatest political crises of American history—the battle between President Andrew Johnson and Congress over Reconstruction. The struggle resulted in profound changes in the nature of citizenship, the structure of constitutional authority, and the meaning of American freedom.

Chinese laborers at work on a Louisiana plantation during Reconstruction.

THE MAKING OF RADICAL RECONSTRUCTION

ANDREW JOHNSON

To Lincoln's successor, Andrew Johnson, fell the task of overseeing the restoration of the Union. Born in poverty in North Carolina, as a youth Johnson worked as a tailor's apprentice. After moving to Tennessee, he achieved success through politics. Beginning as an alderman (a town official), he rose to serve in the state legislature, the U.S. Congress, and for two terms as governor of Tennessee. Johnson identified himself as the champion of his state's "honest yeomen" and a foe of large planters, whom he described as a "bloated, corrupted aristocracy." A strong defender of the Union, he became the only senator from a seceding state to remain at his post in Washington, D.C., when the Civil War began in 1861. When northern forces occupied Tennessee, Abraham Lincoln named him military governor. In 1864, Republicans nominated him to run for vice president as a symbol of the party's hope of extending its organization into the South.

In personality and outlook, Johnson proved unsuited for the responsibilities he shouldered after Lincoln's death. A lonely, stubborn man, he was intolerant of criticism and unable to compromise. He lacked Lincoln's political skills and keen sense of public opinion. A fervent believer in states' rights, Johnson insisted that since secession was illegal, the southern states had never actually left the Union or surrendered the right to govern their own affairs. Moreover, while Johnson had supported emancipation once Lincoln made it a goal of the war effort, he held deeply racist views. African-Americans, Johnson believed, had no role to play in Reconstruction.

THE FAILURE OF PRESIDENTIAL RECONSTRUCTION

A little over a month after Lee's surrender at Appomattox, and with Congress out of session until December, Johnson in May 1865 outlined his plan for reuniting the nation. He issued a series of proclamations that began the period of Presidential Reconstruction (1865–1867). Johnson offered a pardon (which restored political and property rights, except for slaves) to nearly all white southerners who took an oath of allegiance. He excluded Confederate leaders and wealthy planters whose prewar property had been valued at more than $20,000. This exemption suggested at first that Johnson planned a more punitive Reconstruction than Lincoln had intended. Most of those exempted, however, soon received individual pardons from the president. Johnson also appointed provisional governors and ordered them to call state conventions, elected by whites alone, that would establish loyal governments in the South. Apart from the requirement that they abolish slavery, repudiate secession, and refuse to pay the Confederate debt—all unavoidable consequences of southern defeat—he granted the new governments a free hand in managing local affairs.

At first, most northerners believed Johnson's policy deserved a chance to succeed. The conduct of the southern governments elected under his program, however, turned most of the Republican North against the president. By and large, white voters returned prominent Confederates and members of the old elite to power. Reports of violence directed against former slaves and northern visitors in the South further alarmed Republicans.

THE BLACK CODES

But what aroused the most opposition to Johnson's Reconstruction policy were the Black Codes, laws passed by the new southern governments that attempted to regulate the lives of the former slaves. These laws granted blacks certain rights, such as legalized marriage, ownership of property, and limited access to the courts. But they denied them the rights to testify against whites, to serve on juries or in state militias, or to vote. And in response to planters' demands that the freedpeople be required to work on the plantations, the Black Codes declared that those who failed to sign yearly labor contracts could be arrested and hired out to white landowners. Some states limited the occupations open to blacks and barred them from acquiring land, and others provided that judges could assign black children to work for their former owners without the consent of the parents. "We are not permitted to own the land whereon to build a schoolhouse or a church," complained a black convention in Mississippi. "Where is justice? Where is freedom?"

Clearly, the death of slavery did not automatically mean the birth of freedom. But the Black Codes so completely violated free labor principles that they called forth a vigorous response from the Republican North. Wars—especially civil wars—often generate hostility and bitterness. But few groups of rebels in history have been treated more leniently than the defeated Confederates. A handful of southern leaders were arrested but most were quickly released. Only one was executed—Henry Wirz, the commander of Andersonville prison, where thousands of Union prisoners of war had died. Most of the Union army was swiftly demobilized. What motivated the North's turn against Johnson's policies was not a desire to "punish" the white South, but the inability of the South's political leaders to accept the reality of emancipation. "We must see to it," announced

Selling a Freeman to Pay His Fine at Monticello, Florida, *an engraving from Frank Leslie's Illustrated Newspaper, January 19, 1867. Under the Black Codes enacted by southern legislatures immediately after the Civil War, blacks convicted of "vagrancy"—often because they refused to sign contracts to work on plantations—were fined and, if unable to pay, auctioned off to work for the person who paid the fine.*

Thaddeus Stevens, leader of the Radical Republicans in the House of Representatives during Reconstruction.

Republican senator William Stewart of Nevada, "that the man made free by the Constitution of the United States is a freeman indeed."

THE RADICAL REPUBLICANS

When Congress assembled in December 1865, Johnson announced that with loyal governments functioning in all the southern states, the nation had been reunited. In response, Radical Republicans, who had grown increasingly disenchanted with Johnson during the summer and fall, called for the dissolution of these governments and the establishment of new ones with "rebels" excluded from power and black men guaranteed the right to vote. Radicals tended to represent constituencies in New England and the "burned-over" districts of the rural North that had been home to religious revivalism, abolitionism, and other reform movements. Although they differed on many issues, Radicals shared the conviction that Union victory created a golden opportunity to institutionalize the principle of equal rights for all, regardless of race.

The Radicals fully embraced the expanded powers of the federal government born during the Civil War. Traditions of federalism and states' rights, they insisted, must not obstruct a sweeping national effort to protect the rights of all Americans. The most prominent Radicals in Congress were Charles Sumner, a senator from Massachusetts, and Thaddeus Stevens, a lawyer and iron manufacturer who represented Pennsylvania in the House of Representatives. Before the Civil War, both had been outspoken foes of slavery and defenders of black rights. Early in the Civil War, both had urged Lincoln to free and arm the slaves, and both in 1865 favored black suffrage in the South. "The same national authority," declared Sumner, "that destroyed slavery must see that this other pretension [racial inequality] is not permitted to survive."

Thaddeus Stevens's most cherished aim was to confiscate the land of disloyal planters and divide it among former slaves and northern migrants to the South. "The whole fabric of southern society," he declared, "*must* be changed. Without this, this Government can never be, as it has never been, a true republic." But his plan to make "small independent landholders" of the former slaves proved too radical even for many of his Radical colleagues. Congress, to be sure, had already offered free land to settlers in the West in the Homestead Act of 1862. But this land had been in the possession of the federal government, not private individuals (although originally, of course, it had been occupied by Indians). Most congressmen believed too deeply in the sanctity of property rights to be willing to take land from one group of owners and distribute it to others. Stevens's proposal failed to pass.

THE ORIGINS OF CIVIL RIGHTS

With the South unrepresented, Republicans enjoyed an overwhelming majority in Congress. But the party was internally divided. Most Republicans were moderates, not Radicals. Moderates believed that Johnson's plan was flawed, but they desired to work with the president to modify it. They feared that neither northern nor southern whites would accept black suffrage. Moderates and Radicals joined in refusing to seat the southerners recently elected to Congress, but moderates broke with the Radicals by leaving the Johnson governments in place.

Early in 1866, Senator Lyman Trumbull of Illinois proposed two bills, reflecting the moderates' belief that Johnson's policy required modification. The first extended the life of the Freedmen's Bureau, which had originally been established for only one year. The second, the Civil Rights Bill, was described by one congressman as "one of the most important bills ever presented to the House for its action." It defined all persons born in the United States as citizens and spelled out rights they were to enjoy without regard to race. Equality before the law was central to the measure—no longer could states enact laws like the Black Codes discriminating between white and black citizens. So were free labor values. According to the law, no state could deprive any citizen of the right to make contracts, bring lawsuits, or enjoy equal protection of one's person and property. These, said Trumbull, were the "fundamental rights belonging to every man as a free man." The bill made no mention of the right to vote for blacks. In constitutional terms, the Civil Rights Bill represented the first attempt to give concrete meaning to the Thirteenth Amendment, which had abolished slavery, to define in law the essence of freedom.

To the surprise of Congress, Johnson vetoed both bills. Both, he said, would centralize power in the national government and deprive the states of the authority to regulate their own affairs. Moreover, he argued, blacks did not deserve the rights of citizenship. By acting to secure their rights, Congress was discriminating "against the white race." The vetoes made a breach between the president and nearly the entire Republican Party inevitable. Congress failed by a single vote to muster the two-thirds majority necessary to override the veto of the Freedmen's Bureau Bill (although later in 1866, it did extend the Bureau's life to 1870). But in April 1866, the Civil Rights Bill became the first major law in American history to be passed over a presidential veto.

President Andrew Johnson, in an 1868 lithograph by Currier and Ives. Because of Johnson's stubborn opposition to the congressional Reconstruction policy, one disgruntled citizen drew a crown on his head with the words, "I am King."

THE FOURTEENTH AMENDMENT

Congress now proceeded to adopt its own plan of Reconstruction. In June, it approved and sent to the states for ratification the Fourteenth Amendment, which placed in the Constitution the principle of citizenship for all persons born in the United States, and which empowered the federal government to protect the rights of all Americans. The amendment prohibited the states from abridging the "privileges and immunities" of citizens or denying them the "equal protection of the law." This broad language opened the door for future Congresses and the federal courts to breathe meaning into the guarantee of legal equality.

In a compromise between the radical and moderate positions on black suffrage, the amendment did not grant blacks the right to vote. But it did provide that if a state denied the vote to any group of men, that state's representation in Congress would be reduced. (This provision did not apply when states barred women from voting.) The abolition of slavery threatened to increase southern political power, since now all blacks, not merely three-fifths as in the case of slaves, would be counted in determining a state's representation in Congress. The Fourteenth Amendment offered the leaders of the white South a choice—allow black men to vote and keep their

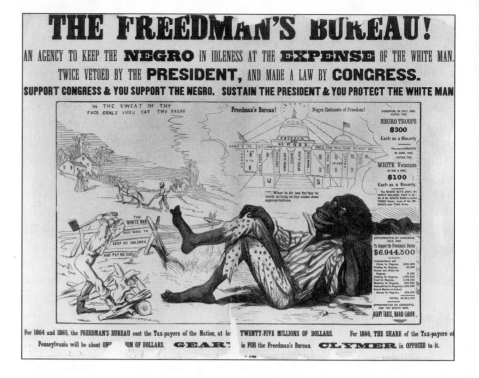

A Democratic Party broadside from the election of 1866 in Pennsylvania uses racist imagery to argue that government assistance aids lazy former slaves at the expense of hardworking whites.

state's full representation in the House of Representatives, or limit the vote to whites and sacrifice part of their political power.

The Fourteenth Amendment produced an intense division between the parties. Not a single Democrat in Congress voted in its favor, and only 4 of 175 Republicans were opposed. Radicals, to be sure, expressed their disappointment that the amendment did not guarantee black suffrage. (It was far from perfect, Stevens told the House, but he intended to vote for it, "because I live among men and not among angels.") Nonetheless, by writing into the Constitution the principle that equality before the law regardless of race is a fundamental right of all American citizens, the amendment made the most important change in that document since the adoption of the Bill of Rights.

THE RECONSTRUCTION ACT

The Fourteenth Amendment became the central issue of the political campaign of 1866. Johnson embarked on a speaking tour of the North, called by journalists the "swing around the circle," to urge voters to elect members of Congress committed to his own Reconstruction program. Denouncing his critics, the president made wild accusations that the Radicals were plotting to assassinate him. His behavior further undermined public support for his policies, as did riots that broke out in Memphis and New Orleans, in which white policemen and citizens killed dozens of blacks.

In the northern congressional elections that fall, Republicans opposed to Johnson's policies won a sweeping victory. Nonetheless, at the president's urging, every southern state but Tennessee refused to ratify the Fourteenth Amendment. The intransigence of Johnson and the bulk of the white South pushed moderate Republicans toward the Radicals. In March 1867, over Johnson's veto, Congress adopted the Reconstruction Act, which temporarily divided the South into five military districts and called for the creation of new state governments, with black men given the right to vote. Thus began the period of Radical Reconstruction, which lasted until 1877.

A variety of motives combined to produce Radical Reconstruction—demands by former slaves for the right to vote, the Radicals' commitment to the idea of equality, widespread disgust with Johnson's policies, the desire to fortify the Republican Party in the South, and the determination to keep ex-Confederates from office. But the conflict between President Johnson and Congress did not end with the passage of the Reconstruction Act.

IMPEACHMENT AND THE ELECTION OF GRANT

In March 1867, Congress adopted the Tenure of Office Act, barring the president from removing certain officeholders, including cabinet members, without the consent of the Senate. Johnson considered this an unconstitutional restriction on his authority. In February 1868, he removed Secretary of War Edwin M. Stanton, an ally of the Radicals. The House of Representatives responded by approving articles of impeachment—that is, it presented charges against Johnson to the Senate, which had to decide whether to remove him from office.

That spring, for the first time in American history, a president was placed on trial before the Senate for "high crimes and misdemeanors." By this point, virtually all Republicans considered Johnson a failure as president. But some moderates disliked Benjamin F. Wade, a Radical who, as temporary president of the Senate, would become president if Johnson were removed. Others feared that conviction would damage the constitutional separation of powers between Congress and the executive. Johnson's lawyers assured moderate Republicans that, if acquitted, he would stop interfering with Reconstruction policy. The final tally was 35-19 to convict Johnson, one vote short of the two-thirds necessary to remove him. Seven Republicans had joined the Democrats in voting to acquit the president.

A few days after the vote, Republicans nominated Ulysses S. Grant, the Union's most prominent military hero, as their candidate for president. Grant's Democratic opponent was Horatio Seymour, the former governor of New York. Reconstruction became the central issue of the bitterly fought 1868 campaign. Republicans identified their opponents with secession and treason, a tactic known as "waving the bloody shirt." Democrats denounced Reconstruction as unconstitutional and condemned black suffrage as a violation of America's political traditions. They appealed openly to racism. Seymour's running mate, Francis P. Blair Jr., charged Republicans with placing the South under the rule of "a semi-barbarous race" who longed to "subject the white women to their unbridled lust."

THE FIFTEENTH AMENDMENT

Grant won the election of 1868, although by a margin—300,000 of 6 million votes cast—that many Republicans

A Democratic ribbon from the election of 1868, with Horatio Seymour and Francis P. Blair Jr., the party's candidates for president and vice president. The ribbon illustrates the explicit appeals to racism that marked the campaign.

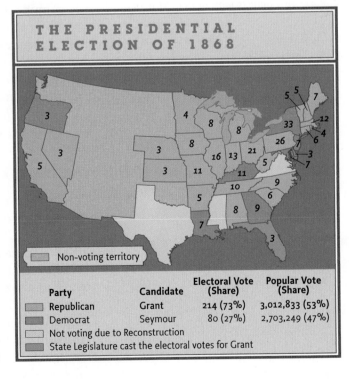

THE PRESIDENTIAL ELECTION OF 1868

Non-voting territory

Party	Candidate	Electoral Vote (Share)	Popular Vote (Share)
Republican	Grant	214 (73%)	3,012,833 (53%)
Democrat	Seymour	80 (27%)	2,703,249 (47%)
Not voting due to Reconstruction			
State Legislature cast the electoral votes for Grant			

The Fifteenth Amendment, *an 1870 lithograph marking the ratification of the constitutional amendment prohibiting states from denying citizens the right to vote because of race. Surrounding an image of a celebration parade are portraits of Abraham Lincoln; President Ulysses S. Grant and his vice president, Schuyler Colfax; abolitionists John Brown, Martin R. Delany, and Frederick Douglass; and Hiram Revels, the first black to serve in the U.S. Senate. At the bottom are scenes of freedom—education, family, political representation, and church life.*

found uncomfortably slim. The result led Congress to adopt the era's third and final amendment to the Constitution. In February 1869, it approved the Fifteenth Amendment, which prohibited the federal and state governments from denying any citizen the right to vote because of race. Bitterly opposed by the Democratic Party, it was ratified in 1870.

Although the Fifteenth Amendment opened the door to suffrage restrictions not explicitly based on race—literacy tests, property qualifications, and poll taxes—and did not extend the right to vote to women, it marked the culmination of four decades of abolitionist agitation. As late as 1868, even after Congress had enfranchised black men in the South, only eight northern states allowed African-American men to vote. With the Fifteenth Amendment, the American Anti-Slavery Society disbanded, its work, its members believed, now complete. "Nothing in all history," exclaimed veteran abolitionist William Lloyd Garrison, equaled "this wonderful, quiet, sudden transformation of four millions of human beings from . . . the auction-block to the ballot-box."

THE "GREAT CONSTITUTIONAL REVOLUTION"

The laws and amendments of Reconstruction reflected the intersection of two products of the Civil War era—a newly empowered national state, and the idea of a national citizenry enjoying equality before the law. What Republican leader Carl Schurz called the "great Constitutional revolution" of Reconstruction transformed the federal system and with it, the language of freedom so central to American political culture.

Before the Civil War, American citizenship had been closely linked to race. The first Congress, in 1790, had limited to whites the right to become a naturalized citizen when immigrating from abroad. No black person, free or slave, the Supreme Court had declared in the *Dred Scott* decision of 1857, could be a citizen of the United States. The laws and amendments of Reconstruction repudiated the idea that citizenship was an entitlement of whites alone. The principle of equality before the law, moreover, did not apply only to the South. The Reconstruction amendments voided many northern laws discriminating on the basis of race. And, as one congressman noted, the amendments expanded the liberty of whites as well as blacks, including "the millions of people of foreign birth who will flock to our shores."

The new amendments also transformed the relationship between the federal government and the states. The Bill of Rights had linked civil liberties to the autonomy of the states. Its language—"Congress shall make no law"—reflected the belief that concentrated national power posed the greatest threat to freedom. The authors of the Reconstruction amendments assumed that rights required national power to enforce them. Rather than a threat to liberty, the federal government, in Charles Sumner's words, had become "the custodian of freedom."

The Reconstruction amendments transformed the Constitution from a document primarily concerned with federal-state relations and the rights of property into a vehicle through which members of vulnerable minorities could stake a claim to freedom and seek protection against misconduct by all levels of government. In the twentieth century, many of the Supreme Court's most important decisions expanding the rights of American citizens were based on the Fourteenth Amendment, perhaps most notably the 1954 *Brown* ruling that outlawed school segregation (see Chapter 24).

BOUNDARIES OF FREEDOM

Reconstruction redrew the boundaries of American freedom. Lines of exclusion that limited the privileges of citizenship to white men had long been central to the practice of American democracy. Only in an unparalleled crisis could they have been replaced, even temporarily, by the vision

Uncle Sam's Thanksgiving Dinner, *an engraving by Thomas Nast from* Harper's Weekly, *November 20, 1868, shortly after the election of Ulysses S. Grant, graphically illustrates how the boundaries of freedom had expanded during Reconstruction. The guests include, among others, African-Americans, Asian-Americans, and Native Americans, men and women, all enjoying a harmonious feast. The table's centerpiece contains the slogan, "universal suffrage."*

of a republic of equals embracing black Americans as well as white. That the United States was a "white man's government" had been a widespread belief before the Civil War. It is not difficult to understand why Andrew Johnson, in one of his veto messages, claimed that federal protection of blacks' civil rights violated "all our experience as a people."

Reconstruction Republicans' belief in universal rights also had its limits. In his remarkable "Composite Nation" speech of 1869, Frederick Douglass condemned prejudice against immigrants from China. America's destiny, he declared, was to transcend race by serving as an asylum for people "gathered here from all corners of the globe by a common aspiration for national liberty." A year later, Charles Sumner moved to strike the word "white" from naturalization requirements. Senators from the western states objected. At their insistence, the naturalization law was amended to make Africans eligible to obtain citizenship when migrating from abroad. But Asians remained ineligible. The racial boundaries of nationality had been redrawn, but not eliminated. The juxtaposition of the amended naturalization law and the Fourteenth Amendment created a significant division in the Asian-American community. Well into the twentieth century, Asian immigrants could not become citizens, but their native-born children automatically did so.

THE RIGHTS OF WOMEN

"The contest with the South that destroyed slavery," wrote the Philadelphia lawyer Sidney George Fisher in his diary, "has caused an immense increase in the popular passion for liberty and equality." But advocates of women's rights encountered the limits of the Reconstruction commitment to equality. Women activists saw Reconstruction as the moment to claim their own emancipation. No less than blacks, proclaimed Elizabeth Cady Stanton, women had arrived at a "transition period, from slavery to freedom." The rewriting of the Constitution, declared suffrage leader Olympia Brown, offered the opportunity to sever the blessings of freedom from sex as well as race and to "bury the black man and the woman in the citizen."

The destruction of slavery led feminists to search for ways to make the promise of free labor real for women. Every issue of the new women's rights journal, *The Agitator*, edited by Mary Livermore, who had led fund-raising efforts for aid to Union soldiers during the war, carried stories complaining of the limited job opportunities and unequal pay for females who entered the labor market. Other feminists debated how to achieve "liberty for married women." Demands for liberalizing divorce laws (which generally required evidence of adultery, desertion, or extreme abuse to termi-

A Delegation of Advocates of Woman Suffrage Addressing the House Judiciary Committee, *an engraving from* Frank Leslie's Illustrated Newspaper, *February 4, 1871. The group includes Elizabeth Cady Stanton, seated just to the right of the speaker, and Susan B. Anthony, at the table on the extreme right.*

nate a marriage) and for recognizing "woman's control over her own body" (including protection against domestic violence and access to what later generations would call birth control) moved to the center of many feminists' concerns. "Our rotten marriage institution," one Ohio woman wrote, "is the main obstacle in the way of woman's freedom."

FEMINISTS AND RADICALS

Talk of woman suffrage and redesigning marriage found few sympathetic male listeners. Even Radical Republicans insisted that Reconstruction was the "Negro's hour" (the hour, that is, of the black male). The Fourteenth Amendment for the first time introduced the word "male" into the Constitution, in its clause penalizing a state for denying any group of men the right to vote. The Fifteenth Amendment outlawed discrimination in voting based on race but not gender. These measures produced a bitter split both between feminists and Radical Republicans, and within feminist circles.

Some leaders, like Stanton and Susan B. Anthony, opposed the Fifteenth Amendment because it did nothing to enfranchise women. They denounced their former abolitionist allies and moved to sever the women's rights movement from its earlier moorings in the antislavery tradition. On occasion, they appealed to racial and ethnic prejudices, arguing that native-born white women deserved the vote more than non-whites and immigrants. "Patrick and Sambo and Hans and Yung Tung, who do not know the difference between a monarchy and a republic," declared Stanton, had no right to be "making laws for [feminist leader] Lucretia Mott." But other abolitionist-feminists, like Abby Kelley and Lucy Stone, insisted that despite their limitations, the Reconstruction amendments represented steps in the direction of truly universal suffrage and should be supported. The result was a split in the movement and the creation in 1869 of two hostile women's rights organizations—the National Woman Suffrage Association, led by Stanton, and the American Woman Suffrage Association, with Lucy Stone as president. They would not reunite until the 1890s.

Thus, even as it rejected the racial definition of freedom that had emerged in the first half of the nineteenth century, Reconstruction left the gender boundary largely intact. When women tried to use the rewritten legal code and Constitution to claim equal rights, they found the courts unreceptive. Myra Bradwell invoked the idea of free labor in challenging an Illinois statute limiting the practice of law to men, but the Supreme Court in 1873 rebuffed her claim. Free labor principles, the justices declared, did not apply to women, since "the law of the Creator" had assigned them to "the domestic sphere."

Despite their limitations, the Fourteenth and Fifteenth Amendments and the Reconstruction Act of 1867 marked a radical departure in American and world history. Alone among the nations that abolished slavery in the nineteenth century, the United States, within a few years of emancipation, clothed its former slaves with citizenship rights equal to those of whites. "We have cut loose from the whole dead past," wrote Timothy Howe, a Republican senator from Wisconsin, "and have cast our anchor out a hundred years" into the future. The Reconstruction Act of 1867 inaugurated America's first real experiment in interracial democracy.

Electioneering at the South, *an engraving from* Harper's Weekly, *July 25, 1868, depicts a speaker at a political meeting in the rural South. Women as well as men took part in these grassroots gatherings.*

RADICAL RECONSTRUCTION IN THE SOUTH

"THE TOCSIN OF FREEDOM"

Among the former slaves, the passage of the Reconstruction Act inspired an outburst of political organization. At mass political meetings—community gatherings attended by men, women, and children—African-Americans staked their claim to equal citizenship. Blacks, declared an Alabama meeting, deserved "exactly the same rights, privileges and immunities as are enjoyed by white men. We ask for nothing more and will be content with nothing less."

These gatherings inspired direct action to remedy long-standing grievances. Hundreds took part in sit-ins that integrated horse-drawn public streetcars in cities across the South. Plantation workers organized strikes for higher wages. Speakers, male and female, fanned out across the South. Frances Ellen Watkins Harper, a black veteran of the abolitionist movement, embarked on a two-year tour, lecturing on "Literacy, Land, and Liberation." James D. Lynch, a member of the group that met with General Sherman in 1865, organized Republican meetings. He became known, in the words of a white contemporary, as "a great orator, fluid and graceful," who "stirred the emotions" of his listeners "as no other man could do."

Determined to exercise their new rights as citizens, thousands joined the Union League, an organization closely linked to the Republican Party, and the vast majority of eligible African-Americans registered to vote. James K. Green, a former slave in Hale County, Alabama, and a League organizer, went on to serve eight years in the Alabama legislature. In the 1880s, Green looked back on his political career. Before the war, he declared, "I was entirely ignorant; I knew nothing more than to obey my master; and there were thousands of us in the same attitude. . . . But the tocsin [warning bell] of freedom sounded and knocked at the door and we walked out like free men and shouldered the responsibilities."

By 1870, all the former Confederate states had been readmitted to the Union, and in a region where the Republican Party had not existed before the war, nearly all were under Republican control. Their new state constitutions, drafted in 1868 and 1869 by the first public bodies in American history with substantial black representation, marked a considerable improvement over those they replaced. The constitutions greatly expanded public responsibilities. They established the region's first state-funded systems of free public education, and they created new penitentiaries, orphan asylums, and homes for the insane. The constitutions guaranteed equality of civil and political rights and abolished practices of the antebellum era such as whipping as a punishment for crime, property qualifications for officeholding, and imprisonment for debt. A few states initially barred former Confederates from voting, but this policy was quickly abandoned by the new state governments.

THE BLACK OFFICEHOLDER

Throughout Reconstruction, black voters provided the bulk of the Republican Party's support. But African-Americans did not control Reconstruction politics, as their opponents frequently charged. The highest offices remained almost entirely in white hands, and only in South Carolina, where blacks made up 60 percent of the population, did they form a majority of the legislature. Nonetheless, the fact that some 2,000 African-Americans occupied public offices during Reconstruction represented a fundamental shift of power in the South and a radical departure in American government.

African-Americans were represented at every level of government. Fourteen were elected to the national House of Representatives. Two blacks

The First Vote, *an engraving from* Harper's Weekly, *November 16, 1867, depicts the first biracial elections in southern history. The voters represent key sources of the black political leadership that emerged during Reconstruction—the artisan carrying his tools, the well-dressed city person (probably free before the war), and the soldier.*

Black and white members of the Mississippi Senate, 1874–1875, shortly before the end of Reconstruction in the state. The woman in the bottom row is a postmistress.

The Operations of the Registration Laws and Negro Suffrage in the South, *an engraving in* Frank Leslie's Illustrated *Newspaper, November 30, 1867, shows blacks and whites for the first time serving together on a southern jury.*

served in the U.S. Senate during Reconstruction, both representing Mississippi. Hiram Revels, who had been born free in North Carolina, was educated in Illinois, and served as a chaplain in the wartime Union army, in 1870 became the first black senator in American history. The second, Blanche K. Bruce, a former slave, was elected in 1875. Since then, only four African-Americans—Edward W. Brooke of Massachusetts (who served 1967–1978), Carol Moseley Braun of Illinois (1993–1998), Barack Obama of Illinois (2005–2008) and Roland Burris (2009–November 29, 2010) have held seats in the Senate.

Pinckney B. S. Pinchback of Louisiana, the Georgia-born son of a white planter and a free black woman, served briefly during the winter of 1872–1873 as America's first black governor. More than a century would pass before L. Douglas Wilder of Virginia, elected in 1989, became the second. Some 700 blacks sat in state legislatures during Reconstruction, and scores held local offices ranging from justice of the peace to sheriff, tax assessor, and policeman. The presence of black officeholders and their white allies made a real difference in southern life, ensuring that blacks accused of crimes would be tried before juries of their peers and enforcing fairness in such aspects of local government as road repair, tax assessment, and poor relief.

In South Carolina and Louisiana, homes of the South's wealthiest and best-educated free black communities, most prominent Reconstruction officeholders had never experienced slavery. In addition, a number of black Reconstruction officials, like Pennsylvania-born Jonathan J. Wright, who served on the South Carolina Supreme Court, had come from the North after the Civil War. The majority, however, were former slaves who had established their leadership in the black community by serving in the Union army, working as ministers, teachers, or skilled craftsmen, or engaging in Union League organizing. Among the most celebrated black officeholders was Robert Smalls, who had worked as a slave on the Charleston docks before the Civil War and who won national fame in 1862 by secretly guiding the *Planter*, a Confederate vessel, out of the harbor and delivering it to Union forces. Smalls became a powerful political leader on the South Carolina Sea Islands and was elected to five terms in Congress.

VISIONS OF FREEDOM

The Shackle Broken—by the Genius of Freedom.
This 1874 lithograph depicts the progress of black freedom during the Civil War and Reconstruction. At the center, Robert B. Elliott, a black congressman from South Carolina, delivers a celebrated speech supporting the bill that became the Civil Rights Act of 1875.

QUESTIONS

1. What does the artist suggest about the foundations of blacks' claim to equal rights, and what they anticipated as the results of freedom?

2. What aspects of freedom does the artist include that are absent in the Visions of Freedom image in Chapter 14?

Emancipation, *an 1865 lithograph, is unusual because along with the familiar images of Lincoln and emancipated slaves, it also portrays a poor white family, suggesting that all Americans will benefit from the end of slavery and Reconstruction.*

CARPETBAGGERS AND SCALAWAGS

The new southern governments also brought to power new groups of whites. Many Reconstruction officials were northerners who for one reason or another had made their homes in the South after the war. Their opponents dubbed them "carpetbaggers," implying that they had packed all their belongings in a suitcase and left their homes in order to reap the spoils of office in the South. Some carpetbaggers were undoubtedly corrupt adventurers. The large majority, however, were former Union soldiers who decided to remain in the South when the war ended, before there was any prospect of going into politics. Others were investors in land and railroads who saw in the postwar South an opportunity to combine personal economic advancement with a role in helping to substitute, as one wrote, "the civilization of freedom for that of slavery." Teachers, Freedmen's Bureau officers, and others who came to the region genuinely hoping to assist the former slaves represented another large group of "carpetbaggers."

Most white Republicans, however, had been born in the South. Former Confederates reserved their greatest scorn for these "scalawags," whom they considered traitors to their race and region. Some southern-born Republicans were men of stature and wealth, like James L. Alcorn, the owner of one of Mississippi's largest plantations and the state's first Republican governor.

Most "scalawags," however, were non-slaveholding white farmers from the southern upcountry. Many had been wartime Unionists, and they now cooperated with the Republicans in order to prevent "rebels" from returning to power. Others hoped Reconstruction governments would help them recover from wartime economic losses by suspending the collection of debts and enacting laws protecting small property holders from losing their homes to creditors. In states like North Carolina, Tennessee, and Arkansas, Republicans initially commanded a significant minority of the white vote. Even in the Deep South, the small white Republican vote was important, because the population remained almost evenly divided between blacks (almost all of whom voted for the party of Lincoln) and whites (overwhelmingly Democratic).

SOUTHERN REPUBLICANS IN POWER

In view of the daunting challenges they faced, the remarkable thing is not that Reconstruction governments in many respects failed, but how much they did accomplish. Perhaps their greatest achievement lay in establishing the South's first state-supported public schools. The new educational systems served both black and white children, although generally in schools segregated by race. Only in New Orleans were the public schools integrated during Reconstruction, and only in South Carolina did the state university admit black students (elsewhere, separate colleges were established). By the 1870s, in a region whose prewar leaders had made it illegal for slaves to learn and had done little to provide education for poorer whites, more than half the children, black and white, were attending public schools. The new governments also pioneered civil rights legislation. Their laws made it illegal for railroads, hotels, and other institutions to discriminate on the basis of race. Enforcement varied considerably from locality to locality, but Reconstruction established for the first time at the state

Black students outside a schoolhouse in a post–Civil War photograph. The teacher is seated at the far right.

level a standard of equal citizenship and a recognition of blacks' right to a share of public services.

Republican governments also took steps to strengthen the position of rural laborers and promote the South's economic recovery. They passed laws to ensure that agricultural laborers and sharecroppers had the first claim on harvested crops, rather than merchants to whom the landowner owed money. South Carolina created a state Land Commission, which by 1876 had settled 14,000 black families and a few poor whites on their own farms.

THE QUEST FOR PROSPERITY

Rather than land distribution, however, the Reconstruction governments pinned their hopes for southern economic growth and opportunity for African-Americans and poor whites alike on regional economic development. Railroad construction, they believed, was the key to transforming the South into a society of booming factories, bustling towns, and diversified agriculture. "A free and living republic," declared a Tennessee Republican, would "spring up in the track of the railroad." Every state during Reconstruction helped to finance railroad construction, and through tax reductions and other incentives tried to attract northern manufacturers to invest in the region. The program had mixed results. Economic development in general remained weak. With abundant opportunities existing in the West, few northern investors ventured to the Reconstruction South.

To their supporters, the governments of Radical Reconstruction presented a complex pattern of disappointment and accomplishment. A revitalized southern economy failed to materialize, and most African-Americans remained locked in poverty. On the other hand, biracial democratic government, a thing unknown in American history, for the first time functioned effectively in many parts of the South. Public facilities were rebuilt and expanded, school systems established, and legal codes purged of racism. The conservative elite that had dominated southern government from colonial

Murder of Louisiana, *an 1873 cartoon, illustrates the intensity of the opposition to Reconstruction. President Ulysses S. Grant, depicted as an emperor advised by Attorney General George H. Williams in the form of the devil, prepares to sacrifice the state on the "altar of radicalism." The victim, held by two black men, has already had her heart cut out by Republican governor William P. Kellogg. The other southern states, with South Carolina kneeling in chains, look on.*

times to 1867 found itself excluded from political power, while poor whites, newcomers from the North, and former slaves cast ballots, sat on juries, and enacted and administered laws. "We have gone through one of the most remarkable changes in our relations to each other," declared a white South Carolina lawyer in 1871, "that has been known, perhaps, in the history of the world." It is a measure of how far change had progressed that the reaction against Reconstruction proved so extreme.

THE OVERTHROW OF RECONSTRUCTION

RECONSTRUCTION'S OPPONENTS

The South's traditional leaders—planters, merchants, and Democratic politicians—bitterly opposed the new governments. They denounced them as corrupt, inefficient, and examples of "black supremacy." "Intelligence, virtue, and patriotism" in public life, declared a protest by prominent southern Democrats, had given way to "ignorance, stupidity, and vice." Corruption did exist during Reconstruction, but it was confined to no race, region, or party. The rapid growth of state budgets and the benefits to be gained from public aid led in some states to a scramble for influence that produced bribery, insider dealing, and a get-rich-quick atmosphere. Southern frauds, however, were dwarfed by those practiced in these years by the Whiskey Ring, which involved high officials of the Grant administration, and by New York's Tweed Ring, controlled by the Democrats, whose thefts ran into the tens of millions of dollars. (These are discussed in the next chapter.) The rising taxes needed to pay for schools and other new public facilities and to assist railroad development were another cause of opposition to Reconstruction. Many poor whites who had initially supported the Republican Party turned against it when it became clear that their economic situation was not improving.

The most basic reason for opposition to Reconstruction, however, was that most white southerners could not accept the idea of former slaves voting, holding office, and enjoying equality before the law. In order to restore white supremacy in southern public life and to ensure planters a disciplined, reliable labor force, they believed, Reconstruction must be overthrown. Opponents launched a campaign of violence in an effort to end Republican rule. Their actions posed a fundamental challenge both for Reconstruction governments in the South and for policymakers in Washington, D.C.

"A REIGN OF TERROR"

The Civil War ended in 1865, but violence remained widespread in large parts of the postwar South. In the early years of Reconstruction, violence was mostly local and unorganized. Blacks were assaulted and murdered for refusing to give way to whites on city sidewalks, using "insolent" language, challenging end-of-year contract settlements, and attempting to buy land. The violence that greeted the advent of Republican governments after 1867, however, was far more pervasive and more directly motivated by politics. In wide areas of the South, secret societies sprang up with the aim of preventing blacks from voting and destroying the organization of the Republican Party by assassinating local leaders and public officials.

The most notorious such organization was the Ku Klux Klan, which in effect served as a military arm of the Democratic Party in the South. From its founding in 1866 in Tennessee, the Klan was a terrorist organization. It quickly spread into nearly every southern state. Led by planters, merchants, and Democratic politicians, men who liked to style themselves the South's "respectable citizens," the Klan committed some of the most brutal criminal acts in American history. In many counties, it launched what one victim called a "reign of terror" against Republican leaders, black and white.

The Klan's victims included white Republicans, among them wartime Unionists and local officeholders, teachers, and party organizers. William Luke, an Irish-born teacher in a black school, was lynched in 1870. But African-Americans—local political leaders, those who managed to acquire land, and others who in one way or another defied the norms of white supremacy—bore the brunt of the violence. In York County, South Carolina, where nearly the entire white male population joined the Klan (and women participated by sewing the robes and hoods Klansmen wore as disguises), the organization committed eleven murders and hundreds of whippings.

On occasion, violence escalated from assaults on individuals to mass terrorism and even local insurrections. In Meridian, Mississippi, in 1871, some thirty blacks were murdered in cold blood, along with a white Republican judge. The bloodiest act of violence during Reconstruction took place in Colfax, Louisiana, in 1873, where armed whites assaulted the town with a small cannon. Hundreds of former slaves were murdered, including fifty members of a black militia unit after they had surrendered.

Unable to suppress the Klan, the new southern

A Prospective Scene in the City of Oaks, a cartoon in the September 1, 1868, issue of the Independent Monitor, *a Democratic newspaper published in Tuscaloosa, Alabama. The cartoon sent a warning to the Reverend A. S. Lakin, who had moved from Ohio to become president of the University of Alabama, and Dr. N. B. Cloud, a southern-born Republican serving as Alabama's superintendent of public education. The Ku Klux Klan forced both men from their positions.*

Two Members of the Ku Klux Klan in Their Disguises, *from* Harper's Weekly, *December 19, 1868. The Klan did not adopt its familiar white robes until after Reconstruction.*

governments appealed to Washington for help. In 1870 and 1871, Congress adopted three Enforcement Acts, outlawing terrorist societies and allowing the president to use the army against them. These laws continued the expansion of national authority during Reconstruction. They defined crimes that aimed to deprive citizens of their civil and political rights as federal offenses rather than violations of state law. In 1871, President Grant dispatched federal marshals, backed up by troops in some areas, to arrest hundreds of accused Klansmen. Many Klan leaders fled the South. After a series of well-publicized trials, the Klan went out of existence. In 1872, for the first time since the Civil War, peace reigned in most of the former Confederacy.

THE LIBERAL REPUBLICANS

Despite the Grant administration's effective response to Klan terrorism, the North's commitment to Reconstruction waned during the 1870s. Many Radicals, including Thaddeus Stevens, who died in 1868, had passed from the scene. Within the Republican Party, their place was taken by politicians less committed to the ideal of equal rights for blacks. Northerners increasingly felt that the South should be able to solve its own problems without constant interference from Washington. The federal government had freed the slaves, made them citizens, and given them the right to vote. Now, blacks should rely on their own resources, not demand further assistance.

In 1872, an influential group of Republicans, alienated by corruption within the Grant administration and believing that the growth of federal power during and after the war needed to be curtailed, formed their own party. They included Republican founders like Lyman Trumbull and prominent editors and journalists such as E. L. Godkin of *The Nation*. Calling themselves Liberal Republicans, they nominated Horace Greeley, editor of the *New York Tribune*, for president.

The Old Plantation Home, *a lithograph from 1872 produced by the prominent firm of Currier and Ives in New York City, illustrates how a nostalgic image of slavery as a time of carefree happiness for African-Americans was being promoted even as Reconstruction took place.*

The Liberals' alienation from the Grant administration initially had little to do with Reconstruction. They claimed that corrupt politicians had come to power in the North by manipulating the votes of immigrants and workingmen, while men of talent and education like themselves had been pushed aside. Democratic criticisms of Reconstruction, however, found a receptive audience among the Liberals. As in the North, they became convinced, the "best men" of the South had been excluded from power while "ignorant" voters controlled politics, producing corruption and misgovernment. Power in the South should be returned to the region's "natural leaders." During the campaign of 1872, Greeley repeatedly called on Americans to "clasp hands across the bloody chasm" by putting the Civil War and Reconstruction behind them.

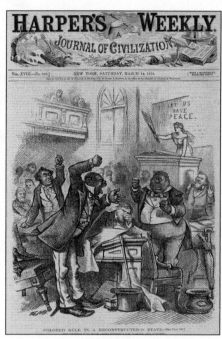

Changes in graphic artist Thomas Nast's depiction of blacks in Harper's Weekly *mirrored the evolution of Republican sentiment in the North.* And Not This Man? *August 5, 1865, shows the black soldier as an upstanding citizen deserving of the vote.* Colored Rule in a Reconstructed (?) State, *March 14, 1874, suggests that Reconstruction legislatures had become travesties of democratic government.*

Greeley had spent most of his career, first as a Whig and then as a Republican, denouncing the Democratic Party. But with the Republican split presenting an opportunity to repair their political fortunes, Democratic leaders endorsed Greeley as their candidate. Many rank and file Democrats, unable to bring themselves to vote for Greeley, stayed at home on election day. As a result, Greeley suffered a devastating defeat by Grant, whose margin of more than 700,000 popular votes was the largest in a nineteenth-century presidential contest. But Greeley's campaign placed on the northern agenda the one issue on which the Liberal reformers and the Democrats could agree—a new policy toward the South.

THE NORTH'S RETREAT

The Liberal attack on Reconstruction, which continued after 1872, contributed to a resurgence of racism in the North. Journalist James S. Pike, a leading Greeley supporter, in 1874 published *The Prostrate State*, an influential account of a visit to South Carolina. The book depicted a state engulfed by political corruption, drained by governmental extravagance, and under the control of "a mass of black barbarism." The South's problems, he insisted, arose from "Negro government." The solution was to restore leading whites to political power. Newspapers that had long supported Reconstruction now began to condemn black participation in southern government. They expressed their views visually as well. Engravings depicting the former slaves as heroic Civil War veterans, upstanding citizens, or victims of violence were increasingly replaced by caricatures presenting them as little more than unbridled animals. Resurgent racism offered a convenient explanation for the alleged "failure" of Reconstruction.

Other factors also weakened northern support for Reconstruction. In 1873, the country plunged into a severe economic depression. Distracted by economic problems, Republicans were in no mood to devote further attention to the South. The depression dealt the South a severe blow and further weakened the prospect that Republicans could revitalize the region's economy. Democrats made substantial gains throughout the nation in the elections of 1874. For the first time since the Civil War, their party took control of the House of Representatives. Before the new Congress met, the old one enacted a final piece of Reconstruction legislation, the Civil Rights Act of 1875. This outlawed racial discrimination in places of public accommodation like hotels and theaters. But it was clear that the northern public was retreating from Reconstruction.

The Supreme Court whittled away at the guarantees of black rights Congress had adopted. In the *Slaughterhouse Cases* (1873), butchers excluded from a state-sponsored monopoly in Louisiana went to court, claiming that their right to equality before the law guaranteed by the Fourteenth Amendment had been violated. The justices rejected their claim, ruling that the amendment had not altered traditional federalism. Most of the rights of citizens, it declared, remained under state control. Three years later, in *United States v. Cruikshank*, the Court gutted the Enforcement Acts by throwing out the convictions of some of those responsible for the Colfax Massacre of 1873.

THE TRIUMPH OF THE REDEEMERS

By the mid-1870s, Reconstruction was clearly on the defensive. Democrats had already regained control of states with substantial white voting majorities such as Tennessee, North Carolina, and Texas. The victorious Democrats called themselves Redeemers, since they claimed to have "redeemed" the white South from corruption, misgovernment, and northern and black control.

In those states where Reconstruction governments survived, violence again erupted. This time, the Grant administration showed no desire to intervene. In contrast to the Klan's activities—conducted at night by disguised men—the violence of 1875 and 1876 took place in broad daylight, as if to underscore Democrats' conviction that they had nothing to fear from Washington. In Mississippi, in 1875, white rifle clubs drilled in public and openly assaulted and murdered Republicans. When Governor Adelbert Ames, a Maine-born Union general, frantically appealed to the federal government for assistance, President Grant responded that the northern public was "tired out" by southern problems. On election day, armed Democrats destroyed ballot boxes and drove former slaves from the polls. The result was a Democratic landslide and the end of Reconstruction in Mississippi. "A revolution has taken place," wrote Ames, "and a race are disfranchised—they are to be returned to . . . an era of second slavery."

Similar events took place in South Carolina in 1876. Democrats nominated for governor former Confederate general Wade Hampton. Hampton promised to respect the rights of all citizens of the state, but his supporters, inspired by Democratic tactics in Mississippi, launched a wave of intimidation. Democrats intended to carry the election, one planter told a black official, "if we have to wade in blood knee-deep."

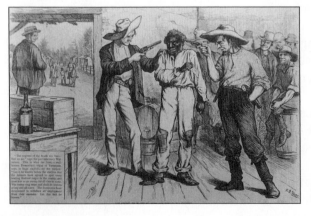

Of Course He Wants to Vote the Democratic Ticket, a cartoon from Harper's Weekly, *October 21, 1876, comments on the campaign of terror launched by South Carolina Democrats in an attempt to carry the election of 1876.*

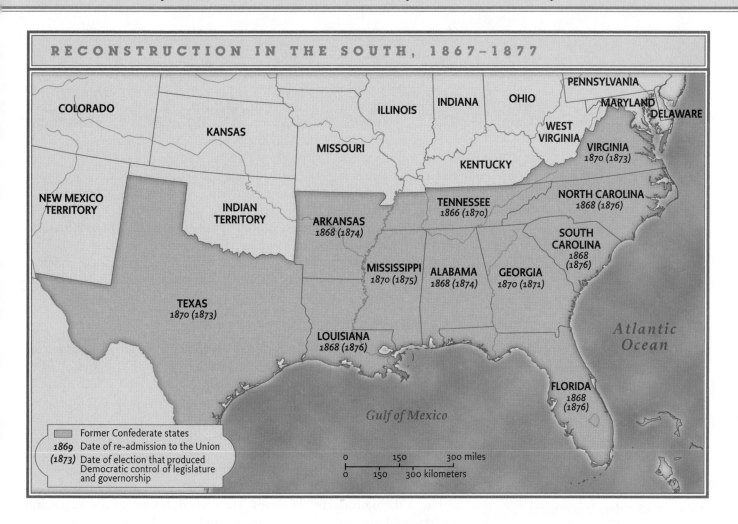

RECONSTRUCTION IN THE SOUTH, 1867–1877

Former Confederate states
1869 Date of re-admission to the Union
(1873) Date of election that produced Democratic control of legislature and governorship

THE DISPUTED ELECTION AND BARGAIN OF 1877

Events in South Carolina directly affected the outcome of the presidential campaign of 1876. To succeed Grant, the Republicans nominated Governor Rutherford B. Hayes of Ohio. Democrats chose as his opponent New York's governor, Samuel J. Tilden. By this time, only South Carolina, Florida, and Louisiana remained under Republican control. The election turned out to be so close that whoever captured these states—which both parties claimed to have carried—would become the next president.

Unable to resolve the impasse on its own, Congress in January 1877 appointed a fifteen-member Electoral Commission, composed of senators, representatives, and Supreme Court justices. Republicans enjoyed an 8-7 majority on the commission, and to no one's surprise, the members decided by that margin that Hayes had carried the disputed southern states and had been elected president. Even as the commission deliberated, however, behind-the-scenes negotiations took place between leaders of the two parties. Hayes's representatives agreed to recognize

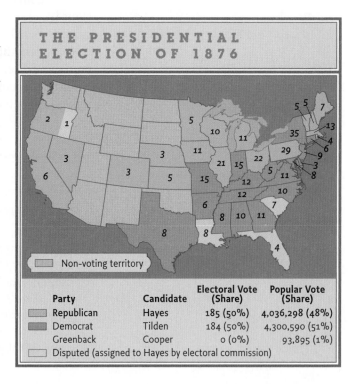

THE PRESIDENTIAL ELECTION OF 1876

Non-voting territory

Party	Candidate	Electoral Vote (Share)	Popular Vote (Share)
Republican	Hayes	185 (50%)	4,036,298 (48%)
Democrat	Tilden	184 (50%)	4,300,590 (51%)
Greenback	Cooper	0 (0%)	93,895 (1%)
Disputed (assigned to Hayes by electoral commission)			

Is This a Republican Form of Government?, *a cartoon by Thomas Nast in* Harper's Weekly, *September 2, 1876, illustrates his conviction that the overthrow of Reconstruction meant that the United States was not prepared to live up to its democratic ideals or protect the rights of black citizens threatened by violence.*

Democratic control of the entire South and to avoid further intervention in local affairs. They also pledged that Hayes would place a southerner in the cabinet position of postmaster general and that he would work for federal aid to the Texas and Pacific railroad, a transcontinental line projected to follow a southern route. For their part, Democrats promised not to dispute Hayes's right to office and to respect the civil and political rights of blacks.

Thus was concluded the Bargain of 1877. Not all of its parts were fulfilled. But Hayes became president, and he did appoint David M. Key of Tennessee as postmaster general. Hayes quickly ordered federal troops to stop guarding the state houses in Louisiana and South Carolina, allowing Democratic claimants to become governor. (Contrary to legend, Hayes did not remove the last soldiers from the South—he simply ordered them to return to their barracks.) But the Texas and Pacific never did get its land grant. Of far more significance, the triumphant southern Democrats failed to live up to their pledge to recognize blacks as equal citizens.

THE END OF RECONSTRUCTION

As a historical process—the nation's adjustment to the destruction of slavery—Reconstruction continued well after 1877. Blacks continued to vote and, in some states, hold office into the 1890s. But as a distinct era of national history—when Republicans controlled much of the South, blacks exercised significant political power, and the federal government accepted the responsibility for protecting the fundamental rights of all American citizens—Reconstruction had come to an end. Despite its limitations, Reconstruction was a remarkable chapter in the story of American freedom. Nearly a century would pass before the nation again tried to bring equal rights to the descendants of slaves. The civil rights era of the 1950s and 1960s would sometimes be called the Second Reconstruction.

Even while it lasted, however, Reconstruction revealed some of the tensions inherent in nineteenth-century discussions of freedom. The policy of granting black men the vote while denying them the benefits of land ownership strengthened the idea that the free citizen could be a poor, dependent laborer. Reconstruction placed on the national agenda a problem that would dominate political discussion for the next half-century—how, in a modern society, to define the economic essence of freedom.

SUGGESTED READING

BOOKS

Carter, Dan T. *When the War Was Over: The Failure of Self-Reconstruction in the South, 1865–1867* (1985). A careful study of the South during the period of Presidential Reconstruction.

DuBois, Ellen C. *Feminism and Suffrage: The Emergence of an Independent Women's Movement in America, 1848–1869* (1978). Explores how the split over the exclusion of women from the Fourteenth and Fifteenth Amendments gave rise to a movement for woman suffrage no longer tied to the abolitionist tradition.

Edwards, Laura. *Gendered Strife and Confusion: The Political Culture of Reconstruction* (1997). Considers how issues relating to gender relations affected the course of southern Reconstruction.

Fields, Barbara J. *Slavery and Freedom on the Middle Ground: Maryland during the Nineteenth Century* (1985). A study of slavery and emancipation in a key border state.

Foner, Eric. *Nothing but Freedom: Emancipation and Its Legacy* (1983). Includes a comparison of the emancipation experience in different parts of the Western Hemisphere.

Foner, Eric. *Reconstruction: America's Unfinished Revolution, 1863–1877* (1988). A comprehensive account of the Reconstruction era.

Hahn, Steven. *A Nation under Our Feet: Black Political Struggles in the Rural South from Slavery to the Great Migration* (2003). A detailed study of black political activism, stressing nationalist consciousness and emigration movements.

Hyman, Harold M. *A More Perfect Union: The Impact of the Civil War and Reconstruction on the Constitution* (1973). Analyzes how the laws and constitutional amendments of Reconstruction changed the Constitution and the rights of all Americans.

Jung, Moon-Ho. *Coolies and Cane: Race, Labor, and Sugar in the Age of Emancipation* (2006). Tells the story of Chinese laborers brought to work in the sugar fields after the end of slavery.

Litwack, Leon F. *Been in the Storm So Long: The Aftermath of Slavery* (1979). A detailed look at the immediate aftermath of the end of slavery and the variety of black and white responses to emancipation.

Rable, George C. *But There Was No Peace: The Role of Violence in the Politics of Reconstruction* (1984). The only full-scale study of violence in the Reconstruction South.

Richardson, Heather C. *West from Appomattox* (2007). An account that fully integrates the West into the history of the Reconstruction era.

Rodrigue, John C. *Reconstruction in the Cane Fields: From Slavery to Free Labor in Louisiana's Sugar Parishes, 1862–1880* (2001). A study of how an often-neglected part of the South experienced the aftermath of slavery.

Summers, Mark W. *Railroads, Reconstruction, and the Gospel of Prosperity: Aid under the Radical Republicans, 1865–1877* (1984). A detailed look at southern governments' efforts to promote economic development, and the political corruption that sometimes accompanied it.

Trefousse, Hans L. *The Radical Republicans: Lincoln's Vanguard for Racial Justice* (1969). An account of the political history of the Radical Republicans, from the pre–Civil War period through the end of Reconstruction.

WEBSITES

After Slavery: Race, Labor, and Politics in the Post-Emancipation Carolinas: www.afterslavery.com

America's Reconstruction: People and Politics after the Civil War: www.digitalhistory.uh.edu/reconstruction/index.html

Freedmen and Southern Society Project: www.history.umd.edu/Freedmen/

The Andrew Johnson Impeachment Trial: www.law.umkc.edu/faculty/projects/ftrials/impeach/impeachmt.htm

REVIEW QUESTIONS

1. In 1865, former Confederate general Robert Richardson remarked that "the emancipated slaves own nothing, because nothing but freedom has been given to them." Explain whether this would be an accurate assessment of Reconstruction twelve years later.

2. The women's movement split into two separate national organizations in part because the Fifteenth Amendment did not give women the vote. Explain why the two groups split.

3. Explain how important black families, churches, schools, and other institutions were to the development of African-American culture and political activism in this period.

4. Why did ownership of land and control of labor become major points of contention between former slaves and whites in the South?

5. By what methods did southern whites seek to limit African-American civil rights and liberties?

6. How did the failure of land reform and continued poverty lead to new forms of servitude for both blacks and whites?

7. What caused the confrontation between President Johnson and Congress over Reconstruction policies?

8. What national issues and attitudes combined to bring an end to Reconstruction by 1877?

9. By 1877, how did the condition of former slaves in the United States compare with that of freedmen around the globe?

FREEDOM QUESTIONS

1. After the Civil War, how did the definitions of freedom change for the nation, for the freedmen, and for southern whites?

2. Identify and explain the key elements of freedom according to the former slaves.

3. In the text we see that "Reconstruction redrew the boundaries of American freedom." How did these boundaries expand for some citizens but remain closed or restricted for others?

KEY TERMS

black families (p. 588)

the Freedmen's Bureau (p. 588)

sharecropping (p. 594)

crop-lien system (p. 598)

Black Codes (p. 601)

Civil Rights Bill of 1866 (p. 603)

Fourteenth Amendment (p. 603)

"swing around the circle" (p. 604)

"waving the bloody shirt" (p. 605)

Fifteenth Amendment (p. 605)

literacy tests (p. 606)

Bradwell v. Illinois (p. 609)

carpetbaggers and scalawags
    (p. 614)

Enforcement Acts (p. 618)

Civil Rights Act of 1875 (p. 620)

Slaughterhouse Cases (p. 620)

Redeemers (p. 620)

Bargain of 1877 (p. 622)

REVIEW TABLE

Reconstruction Constitutional Amendments		
Amendment	Date Ratified	Provisions
Thirteenth	1865	Ends slavery
Fourteenth	1868	Guarantees federal protection of citizenship and equal rights under the law
Fifteenth	1870	Prohibits voting restrictions based on race, color, or previous conditions of servitude

Part 4

TOWARD A GLOBAL PRESENCE, 1870–1920

Between the era of Reconstruction and the end of World War I, the United States underwent a profound social and economic revolution that affected all aspects of Americans' lives. By 1900, the country had emerged as the world's major industrial power and, thanks to the Spanish-American War of 1898, the possessor of a small overseas empire. Giant new corporations now dominated the economy. They introduced new forms of labor control and new methods of mass production, manufacturing a seemingly endless array of industrial and consumer goods. Immigrants arrived from abroad in unprecedented numbers, providing labor for the expanding economy and fueling the growth of the nation's cities. In 1920, residents of cities for the first time outnumbered those living in rural areas.

In the first two decades of the twentieth century, the United States became a major participant in world affairs. It repeatedly sent troops to direct the affairs of Caribbean and Central American countries. During World War I, President Woodrow Wilson not only dispatched American soldiers, for the first time, to fight in Europe but also called for continuous American involvement in the creation and preservation of a peaceful, economically interconnected world order.

These changes increased the economic opportunities of many Americans. The middle class of clerks, managers, and other white-collar workers expanded significantly. Economic growth drew large numbers of women into the workforce. When the outbreak of World War I cut off immigration from Europe, hundreds of thousands of blacks moved from southern farms to jobs in northern cities, gaining access to the industrial economy and changing the country's racial configuration.

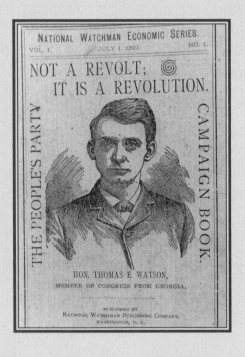

What is sometimes called "the second industrial revolution" also led to an era of persistent and often violent labor conflict. To many Americans, social life seemed increasingly polarized between those at the top, who reaped most of the benefits of economic expansion, and workers struggling to make ends meet on low wages and living in desperate conditions in city slums. Democracy itself seemed threatened by the political influence of the large corporations and the corrupt activities of city bosses. In the early twentieth century, increasing numbers of Americans concluded that only the reform of politics and increased government intervention in economic life could curb the powers of the new corporations, ensure safe working conditions, and provide economic security for ordinary men and women.

Throughout these years, divergent views of the country's course of development, and the proper role of government in shaping and reshaping it, found expression in debates over American freedom. Many Americans held to a traditional understanding of freedom as the absence of external restraints on free individuals operating in a competitive marketplace. In this view, known as "liberty of contract," any government interference with economic relationships represented an infringement on property rights and, therefore, on freedom.

Others turned to collective action, economic and political, to try to reverse what they considered a decline of traditional freedoms. Workers flocked into unions that promised not only higher wages but also "industrial freedom"—a share in basic economic decision making. During the 1890s, millions of farmers joined the Populist movement in an attempt to reverse their declining economic prospects and rescue the government from what they saw as control by powerful corporate interests. In the Progressive era of the early twentieth century, urban reformers sought to expand economic and political freedom by increasing workers' rights, weakening the power of city bosses, and using the power of the state and national governments to regulate corporate behavior.

In many cities and states, and at the national level under Presidents Theodore Roosevelt, William Howard Taft, and Woodrow Wilson, government took on new roles in Progressive America. It sought to protect workers, especially women and children, from economic hardship, established

agencies to determine rules for corporate behavior, and set aside parks and forests to preserve them from commercial exploitation. To Progressives, freedom was a positive idea, the effective power to achieve personal and social goals. At the same time, the expansion of the consumer economy and the new freedoms for women offered by city life encouraged the growth of an idea of personal freedom based on individual fulfillment, including self-determination in the most intimate areas of life.

Even as definitions of freedom expanded, the number of Americans who enjoyed genuine freedom contracted. In the 1890s and the early twentieth century, the political leaders of the white South imposed on the region's African-Americans a comprehensive system of second-class citizenship that rested on racial segregation, denial of the right to vote, lack of economic opportunities, and the ever-present threat of violence. Many native-born Americans considered immigrants, especially the large numbers arriving from southern and eastern Europe, as unfit for American citizenship. They sought to restrict their numbers and to force those already here to "Americanize" themselves by abandoning traditional cultures for mainstream values.

The country's emergence as a world power intensified these debates over freedom. To its supporters, the new American empire represented a continuation of the country's traditional self-image of promoting liberty and democracy throughout the world. President Wilson envisioned American involvement in World War I as a crusade not for national aggrandizement, but to "make the world safe for democracy." Yet critics of the acquisition of foreign colonies questioned whether an empire could still be considered a democracy. This question gained new urgency during World War I. On the one hand, the war ushered in the final success of the long struggle for woman suffrage, the greatest expansion of democracy in American history. On the other, the federal government and private patriotic organizations embarked on the most extensive campaign in American history to stifle criticism of administration policies and the economic status quo. By 1920, the United States was the world's foremost economic and military power. But the role it would play in world affairs in the future, and the fate of freedom at home, remained unresolved.

Chapter 16

America's Gilded Age, 1870–1890

A quilt created by a Sioux woman who lived on a reservation in South Dakota around 1900, possibly as a gift for a nearby white family. It depicts scenes of traditional daily life among the Indians, including hunting buffalo and cooking game. The bird's eggs at the top left corner have hatched at the bottom right.

FOCUS QUESTIONS

- What factors combined to make the United States a mature industrial society after the Civil War?

- How was the West transformed economically and socially in this period?

- Was the Gilded Age political system effective in meeting its goals?

- How did the economic development of the Gilded Age affect American freedom?

- How did reformers of the period approach the problems of an industrial society?

An immense crowd gathered in New York Harbor on October 28, 1886, for the dedication of *Liberty Enlightening the World*, a fitting symbol for a nation now wholly free. The idea for the statue originated in 1865 with Édouard de Laboulaye, a French educator and the author of several books on the United States, as a response to the assassination of Abraham Lincoln. The statue, de Laboulaye hoped, would celebrate both the historic friendship between France and the United States and the triumph, through the Union's victory in the Civil War, of American freedom. Measuring more than 150 feet from torch to toe and standing atop a huge pedestal, the edifice was the tallest man-made structure in the Western Hemisphere. It exceeded in height, newspapers noted with pride, the Colossus of Rhodes, a wonder of the ancient world.

In time, the Statue of Liberty, as it came to be called, would become Americans' most revered national icon. For over a century it has stood as a symbol of freedom. The statue has offered welcome to millions of immigrants—the "huddled masses yearning to breathe free" celebrated in a poem by Emma Lazarus inscribed on its base in 1903. In the years since its dedication, the statue's familiar image has been reproduced by folk artists in every conceivable medium and has been used by advertisers to promote everything from cigarettes and lawn mowers to war bonds. As its use by Chinese students demanding democracy in the Tiananmen Square protests of 1989 showed, it has become a powerful international symbol as well.

The year of the statue's dedication, 1886, also witnessed the "great upheaval," a wave of strikes and labor protests that touched every part of the nation. Six months before the unveiling of the Statue of Liberty, police had killed four striking workers who attempted to prevent strikebreakers

The dedication of the Statue of Liberty, October 28, 1886.

from entering a Chicago factory. This was only one of many violent clashes that accompanied labor unrest between the end of Reconstruction in 1877 and the turn of the twentieth century. The 600 dignitaries (598 of them men) who gathered on what is now called Liberty Island for the dedication hoped the Statue of Liberty would inspire renewed devotion to the nation's political and economic system. But for all its grandeur, the statue could not conceal the deep social divisions and fears about the future of American freedom that accompanied the country's emergence as the world's leading industrial power. Nor did the celebrations address the crucial questions that moved to the center stage of American public life during the 1870s and 1880s and remained there for decades to come: What are the social conditions that make freedom possible, and what role should the national government play in defining and protecting the liberty of its citizens?

The Strike, *an 1886 painting by the German-born artist Robert Koehler, who had grown up in a working-class family in Milwaukee. Koehler depicts a confrontation between a factory owner, dressed in a silk top hat, and angry workers. A woman and her children, presumably members of a striker's family, watch from the side while another woman, at the center, appears to plead for restraint. The threat of violence hangs in the air, and a striker in the lower right-hand corner reaches for a stone. The painting was inspired by events in Pittsburgh during the Great Railroad Strike of 1877, although Koehler was living in New York City at the time.*

THE SECOND INDUSTRIAL REVOLUTION

Between the end of the Civil War and the early twentieth century, the United States underwent one of the most rapid and profound economic revolutions any country has ever experienced. There were numerous causes for this explosive economic growth. The country enjoyed abundant natural resources, a growing supply of labor, an expanding market for manufactured goods, and the availability of capital for investment. In addition, the federal government actively promoted industrial and agricultural

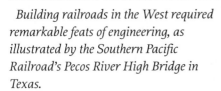

Building railroads in the West required remarkable feats of engineering, as illustrated by the Southern Pacific Railroad's Pecos River High Bridge in Texas.

development. It enacted high tariffs that protected American industry from foreign competition, granted land to railroad companies to encourage construction, and used the army to remove Indians from western lands desired by farmers and mining companies.

THE INDUSTRIAL ECONOMY

The rapid expansion of factory production, mining, and railroad construction in all parts of the country except the South signaled the transition from Lincoln's America—a world centered on the small farm and artisan workshop—to a mature industrial society. Americans of the late nineteenth century marveled at the triumph of the new economy. "One can hardly believe," wrote the philosopher John Dewey, "there has been a revolution in history so rapid, so extensive, so complete."

By 1913, the United States produced one-third of the world's industrial output—more than the total of Great Britain, France, and Germany combined. Small-scale craft production still flourished in many trades, and armies of urban workers, male and female, toiled in their own homes or in the households of others as outworkers and domestics. But half of all industrial workers now labored in plants with more than 250 employees. On the eve of the Civil War, the first industrial revolution, centered on the textile industry, had transformed New England into a center of manufacturing. But otherwise, the United States was still primarily an agricultural nation. By 1880, for the first time, the Census Bureau found a majority of the workforce engaged in non-farming jobs. The traditional dream of economic independence seemed obsolete. By 1890, two-thirds of Americans worked for wages, rather than owning a farm, business, or craft shop. Drawn to factories by the promise of employment, a new working class emerged in these years. Between 1870 and 1920, almost 11 million Americans moved from farm to city, and another 25 million immigrants arrived from overseas.

Most manufacturing now took place in industrial cities. New York, with its new skyscrapers and hundreds of thousands of workers in all sorts of manufacturing establishments, symbolized dynamic urban growth. After merging

Table 16.1 INDICATORS OF ECONOMIC CHANGE, 1870–1920

	1870	*1900*	*1920*
Farms (millions)	2.7	5.7	6.4
Land in farms (million acres)	408	841	956
Wheat grown (million bushels)	254	599	843
Employment (millions)	14	28.5	44.5
In manufacturing (millions)	2.5	5.9	11.2
Percentage in workforce[a]			
Agricultural	52		27
Industry[b]	29		44
Trade, service, administration[c]	20		27
Railroad track (thousands of miles)	53	258	407
Steel produced (thousands of tons)	0.8	11.2	46
GNP (billions of dollars)	7.4	18.7	91.5
Per capita (in 1920 dollars)	371	707	920
Life expectancy at birth (years)	42	47	54

[a] Percentages are rounded and do not total 100.
[b] Includes manufacturing, transportation, mining, construction.
[c] Includes trade, finance, public administration.

with Brooklyn in 1898, its population exceeded 3.4 million. The city financed industrialization and westward expansion, its banks and stock exchange funneling capital to railroads, mines, and factories. But the heartland of the second industrial revolution was the region around the Great Lakes, with its factories producing iron and steel, machinery, chemicals, and packaged foods. Pittsburgh had become the world's center of iron and steel manufacturing. Chicago, by 1900 the nation's second-largest city, with 1.7 million inhabitants, was home to factories producing steel and farm machinery and giant stockyards where cattle were processed into meat products for shipment east in refrigerated rail cars. Smaller industrial cities also proliferated, often concentrating on a single industry—cast-iron stoves in Troy, New York, silk in Paterson, New Jersey, furniture in Grand Rapids, Michigan.

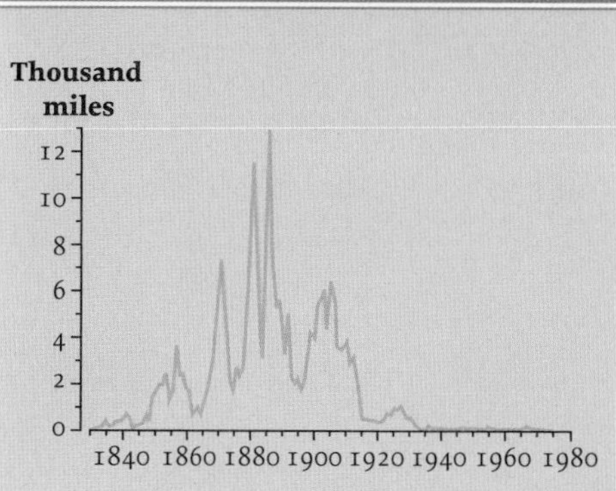

RAILROADS AND THE NATIONAL MARKET

The railroad made possible what is sometimes called the "second industrial revolution." Spurred by private investment and massive grants of land and money by federal, state, and local governments, the number of miles of railroad track in the United States tripled between 1860 and 1880 and tripled again by 1920, opening vast new areas to commercial farming and creating a truly national market for manufactured goods. In 1886, the railroads adopted a standard national gauge (the distance separating the two tracks), making it possible for the first time for trains of one company to travel on any other company's track. By the 1890s, five transcontinental lines trans-

Figure 16.1 RAILROAD MILEAGE BUILT, 1830–1975

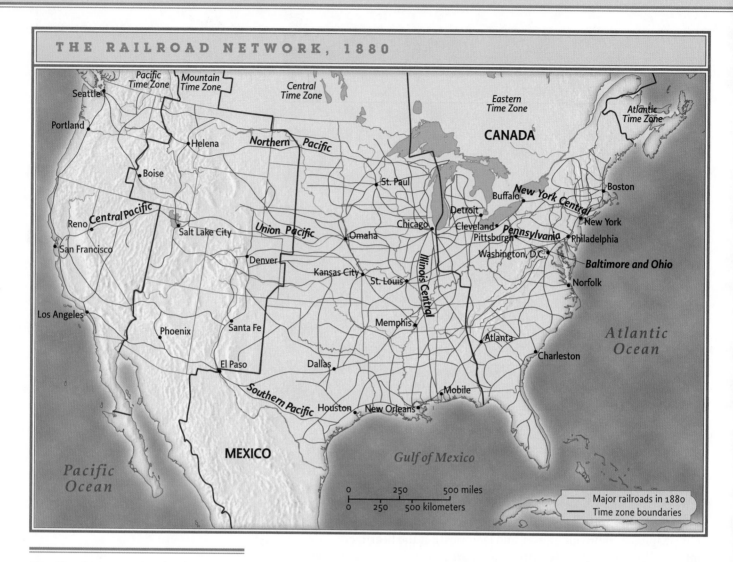

THE RAILROAD NETWORK, 1880

By 1880, the transnational rail network made possible the creation of a truly national market for goods.

ported the products of western mines, farms, ranches, and forests to eastern markets and carried manufactured goods to the West. The railroads reorganized time itself. In 1883, the major companies divided the nation into the four time zones still in use today. Indeed, the centrality of railroads to the national market meant that when railroads experienced financial crises, the entire economy suffered.

The growing population formed an ever-expanding market for the mass production, mass distribution, and mass marketing of goods, essential elements of a modern industrial economy. The spread of national brands like Ivory soap and Quaker Oats symbolized the continuing integration of the economy. So did the growth of national chains, most prominently the Atlantic and Pacific Tea Company, better known as A & P grocery stores. Based in Chicago, the national mail-order firms Montgomery Ward and Sears, Roebuck & Co. sold clothing, jewelry, farm equipment, and numerous other goods to rural families throughout the country.

THE SPIRIT OF INNOVATION

A remarkable series of technological innovations spurred rapid communication and economic growth. The opening of the Atlantic cable in 1866

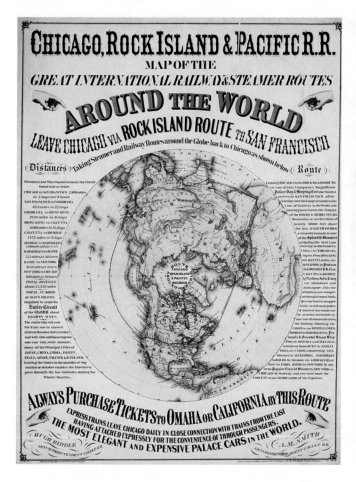

(Left) Travel became globalized in the second half of the nineteenth century. This advertisement promotes an around-the-world route by railroad and steamboat, beginning in Chicago. (Right) The cover of the 1897 Sears, Roebuck & Co. catalog. One of the country's largest mail-order companies, Sears, Roebuck processed 100,000 orders per day at the end of the nineteenth century. The cornucopia at the center suggests the variety of items one could order by mail: furniture, a piano, a bicycle, and farm tools.

made it possible to send electronic telegraph messages instantaneously between the United States and Europe. During the 1870s and 1880s, the telephone, typewriter, and handheld camera came into use.

Scientific breakthroughs poured forth from research laboratories in Menlo Park and Orange, New Jersey, created by the era's greatest inventor, Thomas A. Edison. Born in Ohio in 1847, Edison had little formal education, but as a teenager he read popular books on science and began doing chemistry experiments. During the course of his life, Edison helped to establish entirely new industries that transformed private life, public entertainment, and economic activity, including the phonograph, light-bulb, motion picture, and a system for generating and distributing electric power. He opened the first electric generating station in Manhattan in 1882 to provide power to streetcars, factories, and private homes, and he established, among other companies, the forerunner of General Electric to market electrical equipment. The spread of electricity was essential to industrial and urban growth, providing a more reliable and flexible source of power than water or steam. However, it was not Edison but another inventor, Nikola Tesla, an ethnic Serb born in modern-day Croatia who emigrated to the United States at the age of twenty-eight, who developed an electric motor using the system of alternating current that overcame many of the challenges of using electricity for commercial and industrial purposes.

Thomas Edison's laboratory at Menlo Park, New Jersey, and some of the employees of the great inventor.

COMPETITION AND CONSOLIDATION

Economic growth was dramatic but highly volatile. The combination of a market flooded with goods and the federal monetary policies (discussed later) that removed money from the national economy led to a relentless fall in prices. The world economy suffered prolonged downturns in the 1870s and 1890s. Indeed, before the 1930s, the years from 1873 to 1897 were known throughout the world as the Great Depression.

Businesses engaged in ruthless competition. Railroads and other companies tried various means of bringing order to the chaotic marketplace. They formed "pools" that divided up markets between supposedly competing firms and fixed prices. They established "trusts"—legal devices whereby the affairs of several rival companies were managed by a single director. Such efforts to coordinate the economic activities of independent companies generally proved short-lived, disintegrating as individual firms continued their intense pursuit of profits.

To avoid cutthroat competition, more and more corporations battled to control entire industries. Many companies fell by the wayside or were gobbled up by others. The process of economic concentration culminated between 1897 and 1904, when some 4,000 firms vanished into larger corporations that served national markets and exercised an unprecedented degree of control over the marketplace. By the time the wave of mergers had been completed, giant corporations like U.S. Steel (created by financier J. P. Morgan in 1901 by combining eight large steel companies into the first billion-dollar economic enterprise), Standard Oil, and International Harvester (a manufacturer of agricultural machinery) dominated major parts of the economy.

THE RISE OF ANDREW CARNEGIE

In an era without personal or corporate income taxes, some business leaders accumulated enormous fortunes and economic power. Under the aggressive leadership of Thomas A. Scott, the Pennsylvania Railroad—for a time the nation's largest corporation—forged an economic empire that stretched across the continent and included coal mines and oceangoing steamships. With an army of professional managers to oversee its far-flung activities, the railroad pioneered modern techniques of business organization.

Another industrial giant was Andrew Carnegie, who emigrated with his family from his native Scotland at the age of thirteen and as a teenager worked in a Pennsylvania textile factory. During the 1850s, Scott hired Carnegie as his private telegraph operator and, by the eve of the Civil War, had promoted him to one of the Pennsylvania Railroad's major management positions. During the depression that began in 1873, Carnegie set out to establish a "vertically integrated" steel company—that is, one that controlled every phase of the business from raw materials to transportation, manufacturing, and distribution. By the 1890s, he dominated the steel industry and had accumulated a fortune worth hundreds of millions of dollars. Carnegie's complex of steel factories at Homestead, Pennsylvania, were the most technologically advanced in the world.

Carnegie's father, an immigrant Scottish weaver who had taken part in popular efforts to open the British political system to working-class participation, had instilled in his son a commitment to democracy and social equality. From his mother, Carnegie learned that life was a ceaseless struggle in which one must strive to get ahead or sink beneath the waves. His life reflected the tension between these elements of his upbringing. Believing that the rich had a moral obligation to promote the advancement of society, Carnegie denounced the "worship of money" and distributed much of his wealth to various philanthropies, especially the creation of public libraries in towns throughout the country. But he ran his companies with a dictatorial hand. His factories operated nonstop, with two twelve-hour shifts every day of the year except the Fourth of July.

THE TRIUMPH OF JOHN D. ROCKEFELLER

If any single name became a byword for enormous wealth, it was John D. Rockefeller, who began his working career as a clerk for a Cleveland merchant and rose to dominate the oil industry. He drove out rival firms through cutthroat competition, arranging secret deals with railroad companies, and fixing prices and production quotas. Rockefeller began with "horizontal" expan-

The Electricity Building at the Chicago World's Fair of 1893, *painted by Childe Hassam. The electric lighting at the fair astonished visitors and illustrated how electricity was changing the visual landscape.*

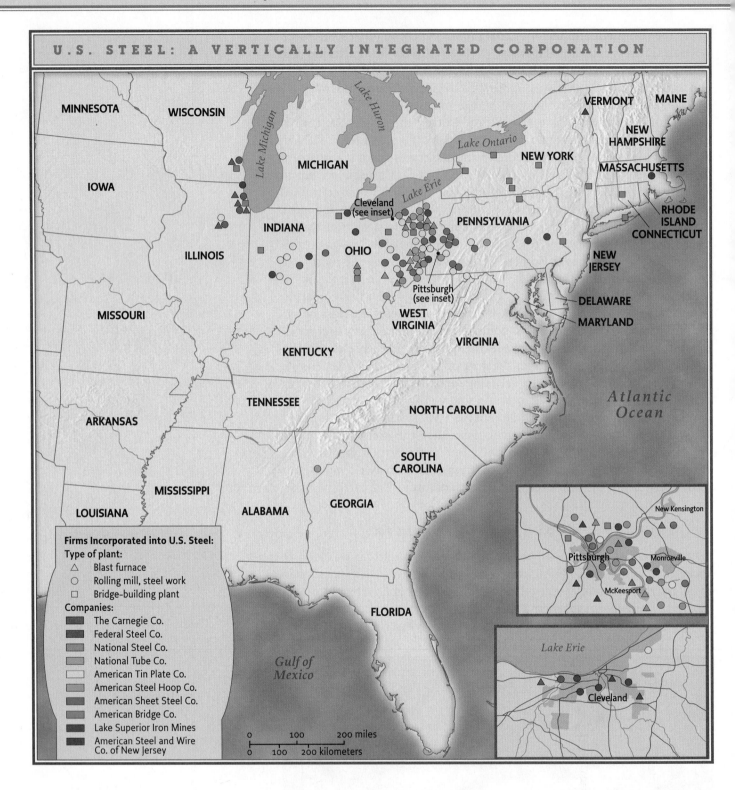

U.S. STEEL: A VERTICALLY INTEGRATED CORPORATION

Firms Incorporated into U.S. Steel:
Type of plant:
△ Blast furnace
○ Rolling mill, steel work
□ Bridge-building plant
Companies:
The Carnegie Co.
Federal Steel Co.
National Steel Co.
National Tube Co.
American Tin Plate Co.
American Steel Hoop Co.
American Sheet Steel Co.
American Bridge Co.
Lake Superior Iron Mines
American Steel and Wire Co. of New Jersey

sion—buying out competing oil refineries. But like Carnegie, he soon established a vertically integrated monopoly, which controlled the drilling, refining, storage, and distribution of oil. By the 1880s, his Standard Oil Company controlled 90 percent of the nation's oil industry. Like Carnegie, Rockefeller gave much of his fortune away, establishing foundations to promote education and medical research. And like Carnegie, he bitterly fought his employees' efforts to organize unions.

These and other industrial leaders inspired among ordinary Americans a combination of awe, admiration, and hostility. Depending on one's point of view, they were "captains of industry," whose energy and vision pushed the economy forward, or "robber barons," who wielded power without any accountability in an unregulated market-place. Most rose from modest backgrounds and seemed examples of how inventive genius and business sense enabled Americans to seize opportunities for success. But their dictatorial attitudes, unscrupulous methods, repressive labor policies, and exercise of power without any democratic control led to fears that they were undermining political and economic freedom. Concentrated wealth degraded the political process, declared Henry Demarest Lloyd in *Wealth against Commonwealth* (1894), an exposé of how Rockefeller's Standard Oil Company made a mockery of economic competition and political democracy by manipulating the market and bribing legislators. "Liberty and monopoly," Lloyd concluded, "cannot live together."

Next!, a cartoon from the magazine Puck, *September 7, 1904, depicts the Standard Oil Company as an octopus with tentacles wrapped around the copper, steel, and shipping industries, as well as a state house and Congress. One tentacle reaches for the White House.*

WORKERS' FREEDOM IN AN INDUSTRIAL AGE

Striking as it was, the country's economic growth distributed its benefits very unevenly. For a minority of workers, the rapidly expanding industrial system created new forms of freedom. In some industries, skilled workers commanded high wages and exercised considerable control over the production process. A worker's economic independence now rested on technical skill rather than ownership of one's own shop and tools as in earlier times. What was known as "the miner's freedom" consisted of elaborate work rules that left skilled underground workers free of managerial supervision on the job. Through their union, skilled iron- and steelworkers fixed output quotas and controlled the training of apprentices in the technique of iron rolling. These workers often knew more about the details of production than their employers did.

Such "freedom," however, applied only to a tiny portion of the industrial labor force and had little bearing on the lives of the growing army of semi-skilled workers who tended machines in the new factories. For most workers, economic insecurity remained a basic fact of life. During the depressions of the 1870s and 1890s, millions of workers lost their jobs or were forced to accept reductions of pay. The "tramp" became a familiar figure on the social landscape as thousands of men took to the roads in search of work. Many industrial workers labored sixty-hour weeks with no pensions, compensation for injuries, or protections against unemployment. Although American workers received higher wages than their counterparts in Europe, they also experienced more dangerous working conditions. Between 1880 and 1900, an average of 35,000 workers perished each year in factory and mine accidents, the highest rate in the industrial world. Most strikes for higher wages

A turn-of-the-century photograph of the Casino Grounds, Newport, Rhode Island, an exclusive country club for rich socialites of the Gilded Age.

The opening image in Matthew Smith's book, Sunshine and Shadow in New York *(1868), contrasts the living conditions of the city's rich and poor.*

failed, as employers found it easy to call on the unemployed to take the strikers' jobs, and to bring in public and private police forces to intimidate workers.

Much of the working class remained desperately poor and to survive needed income from all family members. In 1888, the Chicago *Times* published a series of articles by reporter Nell Cusack under the title "City Slave Girls," exposing wretched conditions among the growing number of women working for wages in the city's homes, factories, and sweatshops. The articles unleashed a flood of letters to the editor from women workers. One woman singled out domestic service—still the largest employment category for women—as "a slave's life," with "long hours, late and early, seven days in the week, bossed and ordered about as before the war."

SUNSHINE AND SHADOW: INCREASING WEALTH AND POVERTY

At the other end of the economic spectrum, the era witnessed an unprecedented accumulation of wealth. Class divisions became more and more visible. In frontier days, all classes in San Francisco, for example, lived near the waterfront. In the late nineteenth century, upper-class families built mansions on Nob Hill and Van Ness Avenue (known as "millionaire's row"). In eastern cities as well, the rich increasingly resided in their own exclusive neighborhoods and vacationed among members of their own class at exclusive resorts like Newport, Rhode Island. The growing urban middle class of professionals, office workers, and small businessmen moved to new urban and suburban neighborhoods linked to central business districts by streetcars and commuter railways. "Passion for money," wrote the novelist Edith Wharton in *The House of Mirth* (1905) dominated society. Wharton's book traced the difficulties of Lily Bart, a young woman of modest means pressured by her mother and New York high society to "barter" her beauty for marriage to a rich husband in a world where "to be poor . . . amounted to disgrace."

By 1890, the richest 1 percent of Americans received the same total income as the bottom half of the population and owned more property than the remaining 99 percent. Many of the wealthiest Americans consciously pursued an aristocratic lifestyle, building palatial homes, attending exclusive social clubs, schools, and colleges, holding fancy-dress balls, and marrying into each other's families. In 1899, the economist and social historian Thorstein Veblen published *The Theory of the Leisure Class*, a devastating critique of an upper-class culture focused on "conspicuous consumption"—that is, spending money not on needed or even desired goods, but simply to demonstrate the possession of wealth. One of the era's most widely publicized spectacles was an elaborate costume ball organized in 1897 by Mrs. Bradley Martin, the daughter of a New York railroad financier. The theme was the royal court of prerevolutionary France. The Waldorf-Astoria Hotel was decorated to look like the palace of Versailles, the guests wore the dress of the French nobility, and the hostess bedecked herself with the actual jewels of Queen Marie Antoinette.

Not that far from the Waldorf, much of the working class lived in desperate conditions. Matthew Smith's 1868 best-seller *Sunshine and Shadow in New York* opened with an engraving that contrasted department store magnate Alexander T. Stewart's two-million-dollar mansion with housing in the city's slums. Two decades later, Jacob Riis, in *How the Other Half Lives* (1890), offered a shocking account of living conditions among the urban poor, complete with photographs of apartments in dark, airless, overcrowded tenement houses.

Baxter Street Court, *1890, one of numerous photographs by Jacob Riis depicting living conditions in New York City's slums.*

THE TRANSFORMATION OF THE WEST

Nowhere did capitalism penetrate more rapidly or dramatically than in the trans-Mississippi West, whose "vast, trackless spaces," as the poet Walt Whitman called them, were now absorbed into the expanding economy. At the close of the Civil War, the frontier of settlement did not extend far beyond the Mississippi River. To the west lay millions of acres of fertile and mineral-rich land roamed by giant herds of buffalo whose meat and hides provided food, clothing, and shelter for a population of more than 250,000 Indians.

In 1893, the historian Frederick Jackson Turner gave a celebrated lecture, "The Significance of the Frontier in American History," in which he argued that on the western frontier the distinctive qualities of American culture were forged: individual freedom, political democracy, and economic mobility. The West, he added, acted as a "safety valve," drawing off those dissatisfied with their situation in the East and therefore counteracting the threat of social unrest. Turner's was one of the most influential interpretations of American history ever developed. But his lecture summarized attitudes toward the West that had been widely shared among Americans long before 1893. Ever since the beginning of colonial settlement in British North America, the West—a region whose definition shifted as the popula-

The family of David Hilton on their Nebraska homestead in 1887. The Hiltons insisted on being photographed with their organ, away from the modest sod house in which they lived, to better represent their aspiration for prosperity.

tion expanded—had been seen as a place of opportunity for those seeking to improve their condition in life.

Many Americans did indeed experience the westward movement in the way Turner described it. From farmers moving into Ohio, Indiana, and Illinois in the decades after the American Revolution to prospectors who struck it rich in the California gold rush of the mid-nineteenth century, millions of Americans and immigrants from abroad found in the westward movement a path to economic opportunity. But Turner offered only a partial account of western history. Most settlers moved west in family groups or as members of immigrant communities, not as lone pioneers. Turner seemed to portray the West as an empty space before the coming of white settlers. In fact, of course, it was already inhabited by Native Americans, whose dispossession was essential to the opening of land for settlement by others. Moreover, the West was hardly a uniform paradise of small, independent farmers. Beginning in the eighteenth century, for example, California was the site of forced Indian labor on missions established by members of religious orders, a system that helped establish the pattern of large agricultural land holdings in that region. Landlords, railroads, and mining companies in the West also utilized Mexican migrant and indentured labor, Chinese working on long-term contracts, and, until the the end of the Civil War, African-American slaves.

A DIVERSE REGION

The West, of course, was hardly a single area. West of the Mississippi River lay a variety of regions, all marked by remarkable physical beauty—the "vast, trackless" Great Plains, the Rocky Mountains, the desert of the Southwest, the Sierra Nevada, and the valleys and coastline of California and the Pacific Northwest. It would take many decades before individual settlers and corporate business enterprises penetrated all these areas. But the process was far advanced by the end of the nineteenth century.

The political and economic incorporation of the American West was part of a global process. In many parts of the world, indigenous inhabitants— the Mapuche in Chile, the Zulu in South Africa, aboriginal peoples in Australia, American Indians—were pushed aside (often after fierce resistance) as centralizing governments brought large interior regions under their control. In the United States, the incorporation of the West required the active intervention of the federal government, which acquired Indian land by war and treaty, administered land sales, regulated territorial politics, and distributed land and money to farmers, railroads, and mining companies.

In the twentieth century, the construction of federally financed irrigation systems and dams would open large areas to commercial farming. Ironically, the West would become known (not least to its own inhabitants) as a place of rugged individualism and sturdy independence. But without active governmental assistance, the region could never have been settled and developed.

FARMING ON THE MIDDLE BORDER

Even as sporadic Indian wars raged, settlers poured into the West. Territorial and state governments eager for population, and railroad companies anxious to sell land they had acquired from the government, flooded European countries and eastern cities with promotional literature promising easy access to land. More land came into cultivation in the thirty years after the Civil War than in the previous two and a half centuries of American history. Hundreds of thousands of families acquired farms under the Homestead Act, and even more purchased land from speculators and from railroad companies that had been granted immense tracts of public land by the federal government. A new agricultural empire producing wheat and corn for national and international markets arose on the Middle Border (Minnesota, the Dakotas, Nebraska, and Kansas), whose population rose from 300,000 in 1860 to 5 million in 1900. The farmers were a diverse group, including native-born easterners, blacks escaping the post-Reconstruction South, and immigrants from Canada, Germany, Scandinavia, and Great Britain. Although ethnic diversity is generally associated with eastern cities, in the late nineteenth century the most multicultural state in the Union was North Dakota.

Despite the promises of promotional pamphlets, farming on the Great Plains was not an easy task. Difficulties came in many forms—from the poisonous rattlesnakes that lived in the tall prairie grass to the blizzards and droughts that periodically afflicted the region. Much of the burden fell on women. Farm families generally invested in the kinds of labor-saving machinery that would bring in cash, not machines that would ease women's burdens in the household (like the back-breaking task of doing laundry). While husbands and sons tended to devote their labor to cash

An engraving from the early 1880s of a California farm adjacent to the Southern Pacific Railroad. Having been granted vast tracts of land by the federal government, the railroad encouraged settlement along its lines.

crops, farm wives cared for animals, grew crops for food, and cooked and cleaned. A farm woman in Arizona described her morning chores in her diary: "Get up, turn out my chickens, draw a pail of water . . . make a fire, put potatoes to cook, brush and sweep half inch of dust off floor, feed three litters of chickens, then mix biscuits, get breakfast, milk, besides work in the house, and this morning had to go half mile after calves." On far-flung homesteads, many miles from schools, medical care, and sources of entertainment, farm families suffered from loneliness and isolation—a problem especially severe for women when their husbands left, sometimes for weeks at a time, to market their crops.

BONANZA FARMS

John Wesley Powell, the explorer and geologist who surveyed the Middle Border in the 1870s, warned that because of the region's arid land and limited rainfall, development there required large-scale irrigation projects. The model of family farming envisioned by the Homestead Act of 1862 could not apply: no single family could do all the work required on irrigated farms— only cooperative, communal farming could succeed, Powell maintained.

Despite the emergence of a few "bonanza farms" that covered thousands of acres and employed large numbers of agricultural wage workers, family farms still dominated the trans-Mississippi West. Even small farmers, however, became increasingly oriented to national and international markets, specializing in the production of single crops for sale in faraway places. At the same time, railroads brought factory-made goods to rural people, replacing items previously produced in farmers' homes. Farm families became more and more dependent on loans to purchase land, machinery, and industrial products, and more and more vulnerable to the ups and downs of prices for agricultural goods in the world market. Agriculture reflected how the international economy was becoming more integrated. The combination of economic depressions and expanding agricultural pro-

California Harvest Scene—Dr. Glenn's Farm in Colusa County, *an engraving from 1876, illustrates the large scale of operations and heavy investment in machinery common on western "bonanza" farms.*

duction in places like Argentina, Australia, and the American West pushed prices of farm products steadily downward. From Italy and Ireland to China, India, and the American South, small farmers throughout the world suffered severe difficulties in the last quarter of the nineteenth century. Many joined the migration to cities within their countries or the increasing international migration of labor.

LARGE-SCALE AGRICULTURE IN CALIFORNIA

The future of western farming ultimately lay with giant agricultural enterprises relying heavily on irrigation, chemicals, and machinery—investments far beyond the means of family farmers. A preview of the agricultural future was already evident in California, where, as far back as Spanish and Mexican days, landownership had been concentrated in large units. In the late nineteenth century, California's giant fruit and vegetable farms, owned by corporations like the Southern Pacific Railroad, were tilled not by agricultural laborers who could expect to acquire land of their own, but by migrant laborers from China, the Philippines, Japan, and Mexico, who tramped from place to place following the ripening crops. "California is not a country of farms, but . . . of plantations and estates," wrote the young journalist Henry George in 1871, urging the government to take action against "land monopoly" and to "give all men an equal chance" to achieve economic independence.

THE COWBOY AND THE CORPORATE WEST

The two decades following the Civil War also witnessed the golden age of the cattle kingdom. The Kansas Pacific Railroad's stations at Abilene, Dodge City, and Wichita, Kansas, became destinations for the fabled drives of millions of cattle from Texas. A collection of white, Mexican, and black men who conducted the cattle drives, the cowboys became symbols of a life of freedom on the open range. Their exploits would later serve as the theme of many a Hollywood movie, and their clothing inspired fashions that remain popular today. But there was nothing romantic about the life of the cowboys, most of whom were low-paid wage workers. (Texas cowboys even went on strike for higher pay in 1883.) The days of the long-distance cattle drive ended in the mid-1880s, as farmers enclosed more and more of the open range with barbed-wire fences, making it difficult to graze cattle on the grasslands of the Great Plains, and two terrible winters destroyed millions of cattle. When the industry recuperated, it was reorganized in large, enclosed ranches close to rail connections.

The West was more than a farming empire. By 1890, a higher percentage of its population lived in cities than was the case in other regions. The economic focus of California's economy remained San Francisco, a major manufacturing and trading center. The explosive growth of southern California began in the 1880s, first with tourism, heavily promoted by railroad companies, followed by the discovery of oil in Los Angeles in 1892. Large corporate enterprises appeared throughout the West. The lumber industry, dominated by small-scale producers in 1860, came under the control of corporations that acquired large tracts of forest and employed armies of loggers. Western mining, from Michigan iron ore and copper to gold and silver in California,

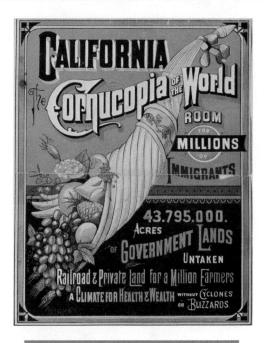

In the late 1800s, California tried to attract immigrants by advertising its pleasant climate and the availability of land, although large-scale corporate farms were coming to dominate the state's agriculture.

Nevada, and Colorado, fell under the sway of companies that mobilized eastern and European investment to introduce advanced technology. Gold and silver rushes took place in the Dakotas in 1876, Idaho in 1883, and Alaska at the end of the century. But as in California after 1848, the independent prospector working a surface mine with his pick and shovel quickly gave way to deep-shaft corporate mining employing wage workers.

A similar process occurred in New Mexico, where traditional life based on sheep farming on land owned in common by Mexican villagers had continued more or less unchanged after the United States acquired the area in the Mexican War. Railroads reached the area in the 1870s, bringing with them eastern mining companies and commercial ranchers and farmers. Because courts only recognized Mexican-era land titles to individual plots of land, communal landholdings were increasingly made available for sale to newcomers. By 1880, three-quarters of New Mexico's sheep belonged to just twenty families. Unable to continue as sheep raisers, more and more Hispanic residents went to work for the new mines and railroads.

THE SUBJUGATION OF THE PLAINS INDIANS

The incorporation of the West into the national economy spelled the doom of the Plains Indians and their world. Their lives had already undergone profound transformations. In the eighteenth century, the spread of horses, originally introduced by the Spanish, led to a wholesale shift from farming and hunting on foot to mounted hunting of buffalo. New Indian groups migrated to the Great Plains to take advantage of the horse, coalescing into the great tribes of the nineteenth century—the Cheyenne, Comanche, Crow, Kiowa, and Sioux. Persistent warfare took place between the more established tribes and newcomers, including Indians removed from the East, who sought access to their hunting grounds.

Most migrants on the Oregon and California Trails before the Civil War

Albert Bierstadt's 1863 painting, The Rocky Mountains, Lander's Peak, *depicts Indians as an integral part of the majestic landscape of the West.*

Hunters shooting buffalo as the Kansas-Pacific Railroad cuts across the West, 1870s.

encountered little hostility from Indians, often trading with them for food and supplies. But as settlers encroached on Indian lands, bloody conflict between the army and Plains tribes began in the 1850s and continued for decades.

In 1869, President Ulysses S. Grant announced a new "peace policy" in the West, but warfare soon resumed. Drawing on methods used to defeat the Confederacy, Civil War generals like Philip H. Sheridan set out to destroy the foundations of the Indian economy—villages, horses, and especially the buffalo. Hunting by mounted Indians had already reduced the buffalo population—estimated at 30 million in 1800—but it was army campaigns and the depredations of hunters seeking buffalo hides that rendered the vast herds all but extinct. By 1886, an expedition from the Smithsonian Institution in Washington had difficulty finding twenty-five "good specimens." "A cold wind blew across the prairie when the last buffalo fell," said the Sioux leader Sitting Bull, "a death-wind for my people."

"LET ME BE A FREE MAN"

The army's relentless attacks broke the power of one tribe after another. In 1877, troops commanded by former Freedmen's Bureau commissioner O. O. Howard pursued the Nez Percé Indians on a 1,700-mile chase across the Far West. The Nez Percé (whose name was given them by Lewis and Clark in 1805 and means "pierced noses" in French) were seeking to escape to Canada after fights with settlers who had encroached on tribal lands in Oregon and Idaho. After four months, Howard forced the Indians to surrender, and they were removed to Oklahoma.

Two years later, the Nez Percé leader, Chief Joseph, delivered a speech in Washington to a distinguished audience that included President Rutherford B. Hayes. Condemning the policy of confining Indians to reservations, Joseph adopted the language of freedom and equal rights before the law so powerfully reinforced by the Civil War and Reconstruction. "Treat all men alike," he pleaded. "Give them the same law. . . . Let me be a free man—free to travel, free to stop, free to work, free to trade where I

Chief Joseph of the Nez Percé Indians in 1877, the year he surrendered to the U.S. Army.

VOICES OF FREEDOM

FROM CHIEF JOSEPH OF THE NEZ PERCÉ INDIANS, Speech in Washington, D.C. (1879)

Chief Joseph, leader of the Nez Percé Indians, led his people on a 1,700-mile trek from their homes in Oregon and Idaho through the Far West in 1877 in an unsuccessful effort to escape to Canada. Two years later, he addressed an audience in Washington, D.C., that included President Rutherford B. Hayes, appealing for the freedom and equal rights enshrined in the law after the Civil War.

My friends, I have been asked to show you my heart. I am glad to have a chance to do so. I want the white people to understand my people. Some of you think an Indian is like a wild animal. This is a great mistake. I will tell you all about our people, and then you can judge whether an Indian is a man or not. . . . I will tell you in my way how the Indian sees things. The white man has more words to tell you how they look to him, but it does not require many words to speak the truth. . . .

I have heard talk and talk, but nothing is done. Good words do not last long unless they amount to something. Words do not pay for my dead people. They do not pay for my country, now overrun by white men . . . . Good words will not get my people a home where they can live in peace and take care of themselves. I am tired of talk that comes to nothing. It makes my heart sick when I remember all the . . . broken promises. . . .

If the white man wants to live in peace with the Indian he can live in peace. There need be no trouble. Treat all men alike. Give them the same law. Give them all an even chance to live and grow. All men were made by the same Great Spirit Chief. They are all brothers. The earth is the mother of all people, and all people should have equal rights upon it. You might as well expect the rivers to run backward as that any man who was born a free man should be contented when penned up and denied liberty to go where he pleases. . . .

When I think of our condition my heart is heavy. I see men of my race treated as outlaws and driven from country to country, or shot down like animals. I know that my race must change. We cannot hold our own with the white men as we are. We only ask an even chance to live as other men live. . . .

Let me be a free man—free to travel, free to stop, free to work, free to trade where I choose, free to choose my own teachers, free to follow the religion of my fathers, free to think and talk and act for myself— and I will obey every law, or submit to the penalty.

From Ira Steward,
"A Second Declaration
of Independence" (1879)

At a Fourth of July celebration in Chicago in 1879, Ira Steward, the most prominent labor leader associated with the movement for the eight-hour day, invoked the legacy of the Declaration of Independence and the abolition of slavery during the Civil War to discuss labor's grievances.

Resolved, That the practical question for an American Fourth of July is not between freedom and slavery, but between wealth and poverty. For if it is true that laborers ought to have as little as possible of the wealth they produce, South Carolina slaveholders were right and the Massachusetts abolitionists were wrong. Because, when the working classes are denied everything but the barest necessities of life, they have no decent use for liberty. . . .

Slavery is . . . the child of poverty, instead of poverty the child of slavery: and freedom is the child of wealth, instead of wealth the child of freedom. The only road, therefore, to universal freedom is the road that leads to universal wealth.

Resolved, That while the Fourth of July was heralded a hundred years ago in the name of Liberty, we now herald this day in behalf of the great economic measure of Eight Hours, or shorter day's work for wageworkers everywhere . . . because more leisure, rest and thought will cultivate habits, customs, and expenditures that mean higher wages: and the world's highest paid laborers now furnish each other with vastly more occupations or days' work than the lowest paid workers can give to one another. . . . [And] if the worker's power to buy increases with his power to do, granaries and warehouses will empty their pockets, and farms and factories fill up with producers. . . .

And we call to the workers of the whole civilized world, especially those of France, Germany, and Great Britain, to join hands with the laborers of the United States in this mighty movement. . . .

On the . . . issue of eight hours, therefore, or less hours, we join hands with all, regardless of politics, nationality, color, religion, or sex; knowing no friends or foes except as they aid or oppose this long-postponed and world-wide movement.

And for the soundness of our political economy, as well as the rectitude of our intentions, we confidently and gladly appeal to the wiser statesmanship of the civilized world.

QUESTIONS

1. What are Chief Joseph's complaints about the treatment of his people?

2. Why does Ira Steward appeal to other countries for assistance and understanding?

3. In what ways do the definitions of freedom in the two documents agree and disagree?

choose, free to . . . think and talk and act for myself." The government eventually transported the surviving Nez Percé to another reservation in Washington Territory. Until his death in 1904, Joseph would unsuccessfully petition successive presidents for his people's right to return to their beloved Oregon homeland.

Indians occasionally managed to inflict costly delay and even defeat on army units. The most famous Indian victory took place in June 1876 at Little Bighorn, when General George A. Custer and his entire command of 250 men perished. The Sioux and Cheyenne warriors, led by Sitting Bull and Crazy Horse, were defending tribal land in the Black Hills of the Dakota Territory. Reserved for them in an 1868 treaty "for as long as the grass shall grow," their lands had been invaded by whites after the discovery of gold. In the Southwest, Cochise, Geronimo, and other leaders of the Apache, who had been relocated by the government a number of times, led bands that crossed and recrossed the border with Mexico, evading the army and occasionally killing civilians. They would not surrender until the mid-1880s.

Another casualty was the Comanche empire, centered in modern-day New Mexico and Colorado. Beginning in the mid-eighteenth century, the Comanche dominated much of the Great Plains and Southwest. The Comanche had subordinated local Indian groups to their power, imposed a toll on trade routes like the Santa Fe Trail, and dealt for a time as an equal with the Spanish, French, and American governments. Their power was not finally broken until the 1870s.

These events delayed only temporarily the onward march of white soldiers, settlers, and prospectors. Between the end of the Civil War and 1890, eight new western states entered the Union (Nebraska, Colorado, North and South Dakota, Montana, Washington, Idaho, and Wyoming). Railroads now crisscrossed the Great Plains, farmers and cattlemen exploited land formerly owned by Indians, and the Plains tribes had been concentrated on

The Battle of the Little Bighorn, June 25–26, 1876, in which General George A. Custer and his entire command were killed, as drawn by Red Horse, a Sioux chief.

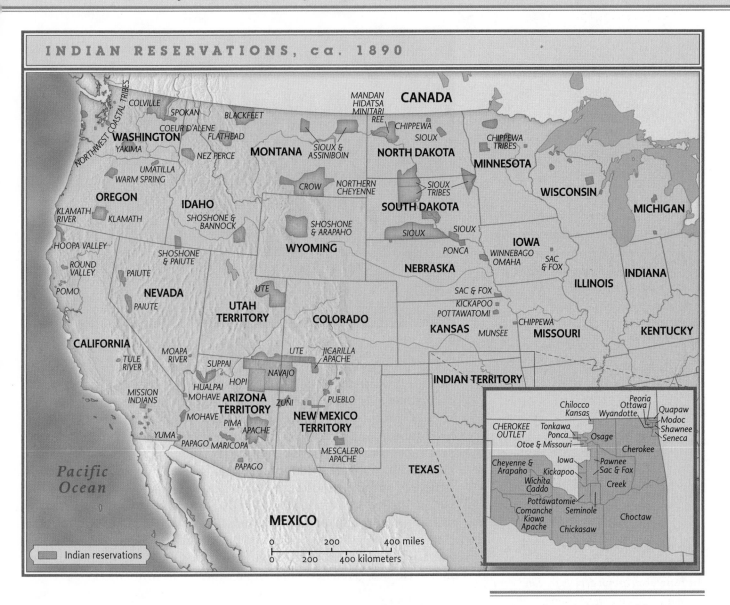

INDIAN RESERVATIONS, ca. 1890

By 1890, the vast majority of the remaining Indian population had been removed to reservations scattered across the western states.

reservations, where they lived in poverty, preyed upon by unscrupulous traders and government agents. A strong opponent of the reservation system, Sitting Bull escaped to Canada after the army defeated the Sioux, but he returned and was imprisoned in 1881. He was released in 1883 and for a time became part of Buffalo Bill's Wild West Show, a popular traveling extravaganza complete with mock Indian attacks and shooting and riding exhibitions. For most Americans, Indians were now simply objects of curiosity or entertainment.

REMAKING INDIAN LIFE

"The life my people want is a life of freedom," Sitting Bull declared. The Indian idea of freedom, however, which centered on preserving their cultural and political autonomy and control of ancestral lands, conflicted with the interests and values of most white Americans. Nearly all officials believed that the federal government should persuade or force the Plains Indians to surrender most of their land and to exchange their religion, com-

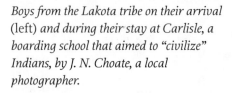

Boys from the Lakota tribe on their arrival (left) *and during their stay at Carlisle, a boarding school that aimed to "civilize" Indians, by J. N. Choate, a local photographer.*

An 1893 photograph depicts the land rush when a portion of Cherokee land in the Oklahoma Territory was opened to white settlement under the provisions of the Dawes Act.

munal property, nomadic way of life, and gender relations for Christian worship, private ownership, and small farming on reservations with men tilling the fields and women working in the home.

In 1871, Congress eliminated the treaty system that dated back to the revolutionary era, by which the federal government negotiated agreements with Indians as if they were independent nations. This step was supported by railroad companies that found tribal sovereignty an obstacle to construction and by Republicans who believed that it contradicted the national unity born of the Civil War. The federal government pressed forward with its assault on Indian culture. The Bureau of Indian Affairs established boarding schools where Indian children, removed from the "negative" influences of their parents and tribes, were dressed in non-Indian clothes, given new names, and educated in white ways.

THE DAWES ACT

The crucial step in attacking "tribalism" came in 1887 with the passage of the Dawes Act, named for Senator Henry L. Dawes of Massachusetts, chair of the Senate's Indian Affairs Committee. The Act broke up the land of nearly all tribes into small parcels to be distributed to Indian families, with the remainder auctioned off to white purchasers. Indians who accepted the farms and "adopted the habits of civilized life" would become full-fledged American citizens. The policy proved to be a disaster, leading to the loss of much tribal land and the erosion of Indian cultural traditions. Whites, however, benefited enormously. On the Nez Percé reservation, for example, 172,000 acres were divided into farms for Indians, but white ranchers and land speculators purchased 500,000 acres. When the government made 2 million acres of Indian land available in Oklahoma, 50,000 white settlers poured into the territory to claim farms on the single day of

April 22, 1889. Further land rushes followed in the 1890s. In the half century after the passage of the Dawes Act, Indians lost 86 million of the 138 million acres of land in their possession in 1887.

INDIAN CITIZENSHIP

Many laws and treaties in the nineteenth century offered Indians the right to become an American citizen if they left the tribal setting and assimilated into American society. But tribal identity was the one thing nearly every Indian wished to maintain, and very few took advantage of these offers. Thus, few Indians were recognized as American citizens. Western courts ruled that the citizenship rights guaranteed by the Fourteenth and Fifteenth Amendments did not apply to them, and in *Elk v. Wilkins* (1884) the U.S. Supreme Court agreed, even though John Elk had left his tribe in Oklahoma and lived among white settlers in Nebraska. The Court questioned whether any Indian had achieved the degree of "civilization" required of American citizens.

By 1900, roughly 53,000 Indians had become American citizens by accepting land allotments under the Dawes Act. The following year, Congress granted citizenship to 100,000 residents of Indian Territory (in present-day Oklahoma). The remainder would have to wait until 1919 (for those who fought in World War I) and 1924, when Congress made all Indians American citizens.

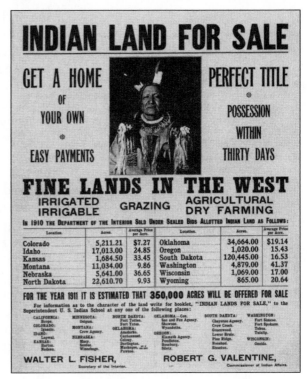

A 1911 poster advertising the federal government's sale of land formerly possessed by Indians. Under the Dawes Act of 1887, Indian families were allotted individual farms and the remaining land on reservations, so-called surplus land, was made available to whites.

THE GHOST DANCE AND WOUNDED KNEE

Some Indians sought solace in the Ghost Dance, a religious revitalization campaign reminiscent of the pan-Indian movements led by earlier prophets like Neolin and Tenskwatawa (discussed in Chapters 4 and 8). Its leaders foretold a day when whites disappear, the buffalo would return, and Indians could once again practice their ancestral customs "free from misery, death, and disease." Large numbers of Indians gathered for days of singing, dancing, and religious observances. Fearing a general uprising, the government sent troops to the reservations. On December 29, 1890, soldiers opened fire on Ghost Dancers encamped near Wounded Knee Creek in South Dakota, killing between 150 and 200 Indians, mostly women and children.

The Wounded Knee massacre marked the end of four centuries of armed conflict between the continent's native population and European settlers and their descendants. By 1900, the Indian population had fallen to 250,000, the lowest point in American history. A children's book about Indians published around this time stated flatly, "the Indian pictured in these pages no longer exists." Yet despite everything, Indians survived, and in the twentieth century their numbers once again would begin to grow.

SETTLER SOCIETIES AND GLOBAL WESTS

The conquest of the American West was part of a global process whereby settlers moved boldly into the interior of regions in temperate climates around the world, bringing their familiar crops and livestock and establishing mining and other industries. Countries such as Argentina, Australia, Canada, and New Zealand, as well as the United States, are often called "settler societies," because immigrants from overseas quickly outnumbered and displaced the original inhabitants—unlike in India and most parts of colonial Africa, where fewer Europeans ventured and those who did relied on the labor of the indigenous inhabitants. South Africa combined the characteristics of these two forms of Western expansion. The descendants of European immigrants grew to a substantial population and fully controlled politics and the economy, but they still remained far fewer in number than the native Africans, who did most of the work in the region's mines and rural areas.

In the late nineteenth century, even as the population of the American West grew dramatically, the Argentine military occupied the Pampas, opening a vast area for cattle raising and wheat cultivation. In 1885, Canada marked the completion of its first transcontinental railroad, although the more severe climate limited the number of western settlers to a much smaller population than in the American West (and as a result, the displacement of Indians did not produce as much conflict and bloodshed). In many settler societies, native peoples were subjected to cultural reconstruction similar to policies in the United States. In Australia, the government gathered the Aboriginal populations—their numbers devastated by disease—in "reserves" reminiscent of American Indian reservations. Australia went further than the United States in the forced assimilation of surviving Aboriginal peoples. The government removed large numbers of children from their families to be adopted by whites—a policy only abandoned in the 1970s and for which the prime minister formally apologized in 2008 in a national moment of reconciliation called Sorry Day.

POLITICS IN A GILDED AGE

The era from 1870 to 1890 is the only period of American history commonly known by a derogatory name—the Gilded Age, after the title of an 1873 novel by Mark Twain and Charles Dudley Warner. "Gilded" means covered with a layer of gold, but it also suggests that the glittering surface covers a core of little real value and is therefore deceptive. Twain and Warner were referring not only to the remarkable expansion of the economy in this period but also to the corruption caused by corporate dominance of politics and to the oppressive treatment of those left behind in the scramble for wealth. "Get rich, dishonestly if we can, honestly if we must," was the era's slogan, according to *The Gilded Age*.

THE CORRUPTION OF POLITICS

As they had earlier in the nineteenth century, Americans during the Gilded Age saw their nation as an island of political democracy in a world still dominated by undemocratic governments. In Europe, only France and Switzerland enjoyed universal male suffrage. Even in Britain, which prided itself on its tradition of political liberty, most of the working class could not

The Bosses of the Senate, *a cartoon from* Puck, *January 23, 1889, shows well-fed monopolists towering over the obedient senators. Above them, a sign rewrites the closing words of Lincoln's Gettysburg Address: "This is the Senate of the Monopolists, by the Monopolists, and for the Monopolists."*

vote until the passage of the Reform Act of 1884. As late as the eve of World War I, the House of Lords, an unelected body of hereditary aristocrats, could veto any legislation passed by the House of Commons.

Nonetheless, the power of the new corporations, seemingly immune to democratic control, raised disturbing questions for the American understanding of political freedom as popular self-government. Political corruption was rife. "The galleries and lobbies of every legislature," observed an Illinois Republican leader, "are thronged with men seeking to procure an advantage" for one corporation or another. In Pennsylvania's legislature, the "third house" of railroad lobbyists supposedly exerted as much influence as the elected chambers. In the West, many lawmakers held stock or directorships in lumber companies and railroads that received public aid.

Urban politics fell under the sway of corrupt political machines like New York's Tweed Ring, which plundered the city of tens of millions of dollars. "Boss" William M. Tweed's organization reached into every neighborhood. He forged close ties with railroad men and labor unions, and he won support from the city's immigrant poor by fashioning a kind of private welfare system that provided food, fuel, and jobs in hard times. A combination of political reformers and businessmen tired of paying tribute to the ring ousted Tweed in the early 1870s, although he remained popular among the city's poor, who considered him an urban Robin Hood.

At the national level, many lawmakers supported bills aiding companies in which they had invested money or from which they received stock or salaries. The most notorious example of corruption came to light during Grant's presidency. This was Crédit Mobilier, a corporation formed by an inner ring of Union Pacific Railroad stockholders to oversee the line's government-assisted construction. Essentially, it enabled the participants to sign contracts with themselves, at an exorbitant profit, to build the new line. The arrangement was protected by the distribution of stock to influential politicians, including Speaker of the House Schuyler Colfax, who was elected vice president in 1868. In another example of corruption, the Whiskey Ring of the Grant administration united Republican officials, tax collectors, and whiskey manufacturers in a massive scheme that defrauded the federal government of millions of tax dollars.

THE POLITICS OF DEAD CENTER

In national elections, party politics bore the powerful imprint of the Civil War. Republicans controlled the industrial North and Midwest and the agrarian West and were particularly strong among members of revivalist churches, Protestant immigrants, and blacks. Organizations of Union veterans formed a bulwark of Republican support. Every Republican candidate for president from 1868 to 1900 had fought in the Union army. (In the 1880 campaign, all four candidates—Republican James A. Garfield, Democrat Winfield Scott Hancock, Prohibitionist Neal Dow, and James B. Weaver of the Greenback-Labor Party, discussed later—had been Union generals during the war.) By 1893, a lavish system of pensions for Union soldiers and their widows and children consumed more than 40 percent of the federal budget. Democrats, after 1877, dominated the South and did well among Catholic voters, especially Irish-Americans, in the nation's cities.

The parties were closely divided. In three of the five presidential elections between 1876 and 1892, the margin separating the major candidates was less than 1 percent of the popular vote. Twice, in 1876 and 1888, the candidate with an electoral-college majority trailed in the popular vote. The congressional elections of 1874, when Democrats won control of the House of Representatives, ushered in two decades of political stalemate. A succession of one-term presidencies followed: Rutherford B. Hayes (elected in 1876), James A. Garfield (succeeded after his assassination in 1881 by Chester A. Arthur), Grover Cleveland in 1884, Benjamin Harrison in 1888, and Cleveland, elected for the second time, in 1892. Only for brief periods did the same party control the White House and both houses of Congress. More than once, Congress found itself paralyzed as important bills shuttled back and forth between House and Senate, and special sessions to complete legislation became necessary. Gilded Age presidents made little effort to mobilize public opinion or exert executive leadership. Their staffs were quite small. Grover Cleveland himself answered the White House doorbell.

In some ways, American democracy in the Gilded Age seemed remarkably healthy. Elections were closely contested, party loyalty was intense, and 80 percent or more of eligible voters turned out to cast ballots. It was an era of massive party rallies and spellbinding political oratory. James G. Blaine was among the members of Congress tainted by the Crédit Mobilier scandal, but Robert G. Ingersoll's speech before the Republican national convention of 1876 nearly secured Blaine's nomination for president by depicting him as a "plumed knight" who had raised his "shining lance" against the country's enemies.

POLITICAL STALEMATE, 1876–1892

Non-voting territory

Elections of 1876–1892

Voted Democrat 4–5 times
Voted Republican 4–5 times
Voted more irregularly

GOVERNMENT AND THE ECONOMY

The nation's political structure, however, proved ill equipped to deal with the problems created by the economy's rapid growth. Despite its expanded scope and powers arising from the Civil War, the federal government remained remarkably small by modern standards. Activities from education to medical care, business regulation, civil and criminal prosecutions, and many others were almost entirely under the control of local and state governments or private institutions. The federal workforce in 1880 numbered 100,000 (today, it exceeds 2.5 million).

Nationally, both parties came under the control of powerful political managers with close ties to business interests. Republicans strongly supported a high tariff to protect American industry, and throughout the 1870s they pursued a fiscal policy based on reducing federal spending, repaying much of the national debt, and withdrawing greenbacks—the paper money issued by the Union during the Civil War—from circulation. Democrats opposed the high tariff, but the party's national leadership remained closely linked to New York bankers and financiers and resisted demands from debt-ridden agricultural areas for an increase in the money supply. In 1879, for the first time since the war, the United States returned to the gold standard—that is, paper currency became exchangeable for gold at a fixed rate.

By reducing competition from foreign manufactured goods and leaving the banks, not the government, in control of issuing money, Republican economic policies strongly favored the interests of eastern industrialists and bankers. These policies worked to the disadvantage of southern and western farmers, who had to pay a premium for manufactured goods while the prices they received for their produce steadily declined.

A political cartoon shows Grover Cleveland leading the Democratic Party in an assault against Republican high taxes.

REFORM LEGISLATION

Gilded Age national politics did not entirely lack accomplishments. Inspired in part by President Garfield's assassination by a disappointed office seeker, the Civil Service Act of 1883 created a merit system for federal employees, with appointment via competitive examinations rather than political influence. Although it applied at first to only 10 percent of the more than 100,000 government workers, the act marked the first step in establishing a professional civil service and removing officeholding from the hands of political machines. (However, since funds raised from political appointees had helped to finance the political parties, civil service reform had the unintended result of increasing politicians' dependence on donations from business interests.)

In 1887, in response to public outcries against railroad practices, Congress established the Interstate Commerce Commission (ICC) to ensure that the rates railroads charged farmers and merchants to transport their goods were "reasonable" and did not offer more favorable treatment to some shippers over others. The ICC was the first federal agency intended to regulate economic activity, but since it lacked the power to establish rates on its own—it could only sue companies in court—it had little impact on railroad practices. Three years later, Congress passed the Sherman Antitrust Act, which banned combinations and practices that restrained free trade. But the language was so vague that the act proved almost impossible to enforce. Weak as they were, these laws helped to establish the precedent that the national government could regulate the economy to promote the public good.

POLITICAL CONFLICT IN THE STATES

The nation had to weather the effects of drastic economic change and periodic economic crises without leadership from Washington. At the state and local level, however, the Gilded Age was an era of political ferment and conflict over the proper uses of governmental authority. In the immediate aftermath of the Civil War, state governments in the North, like those in the Reconstruction South, greatly expanded their responsibility for public health, welfare, and education, and cities invested heavily in public works such as park construction and improved water and gas services. Those who suffered from economic change called on the activist state created by the war to redress their own grievances.

Third parties enjoyed significant if short-lived success in local elections. The Greenback-Labor Party proposed that the federal government stop taking "greenback" money out of circulation. This, it argued, would make more funds available for investment and give the government, not private bankers, control of the money supply. It also condemned the use of militias and private police against strikes. In the late 1870s, the party controlled local government in a number of industrial and mining communities and contributed to the election of twenty-one members of Congress independent of the two major parties.

The policies of railroad companies produced a growing chorus of protest, especially in the West. Farmers and local merchants complained of excessively high freight rates, discrimination in favor of large producers and shippers, and high fees charged by railroad-controlled grain warehouses. Critics of the railroads came together in the Patrons of Husbandry, or Grange, which moved to establish cooperatives for storing and marketing farm output in the hope of forcing the carriers "to take our produce at a fair price." Founded in 1867, the Grange claimed more than 700,000 members by the mid-1870s. Its members called on state governments to establish fair freight rates and warehouse charges. In several states, the Grange succeeded in having commissions established to investigate—and, in some cases, regulate—railroad practices.

At the same time, the labor movement, revitalized during the Civil War, demanded laws establishing eight hours as a legal day's work. Seven northern legislatures passed such laws, but since most lacked strong means of enforcement they remained dead letters. But the efforts of farmers and workers to use the power of the state to

Laying Tracks at Union Square for a Railroad, *an 1890 painting, depicts one of the era's many public works assisted by state and local governments.*

counteract the inequalities of the Gilded Age inspired a far-reaching debate on the relationship between political and economic freedom in an industrial society.

FREEDOM IN THE GILDED AGE

THE SOCIAL PROBLEM

As the United States matured into an industrial economy, Americans struggled to make sense of the new social order. Debates over political economy engaged the attention of millions of Americans, reaching far beyond the tiny academic world into the public sphere inhabited by self-educated workingmen and farmers, reformers of all kinds, newspaper editors, and politicians. This broad public discussion produced thousands of books, pamphlets, and articles on such technical issues as land taxation and currency reform, as well as widespread debate over the social and ethical implications of economic change.

Many Americans sensed that something had gone wrong in the nation's social development. Talk of "better classes," "respectable classes," and "dangerous classes" dominated public discussion, and bitter labor strife seemed to have become the rule. During the Gilded Age, Congress and a number of states established investigating committees to inquire into the relations between labor and capital. Their hearings produced powerful evidence of distrust between employees and employers. In 1881, the Massachusetts Bureau of Labor Statistics reported that virtually every worker it interviewed in Fall River, the nation's largest center of textile production, complained of overwork, poor housing, and tyrannical employers. For their part, manufacturers claimed their workingmen were "the scum of the English and Irish," whose complaints reflected nothing more than a "hereditary feeling of discontent."

FREEDOM, INEQUALITY, AND DEMOCRACY

The appearance of what Massachusetts cotton manufacturer Edward Atkinson called "a permanent factory population" living on the edge of poverty alongside a growing class of millionaires posed a sharp challenge to traditional definitions of freedom. Did America's promise still lie in the opportunity it offered ordinary citizens to achieve economic autonomy? "The great curse of the Old World—the division of society into classes," declared *The Nation*, had come to America. It became increasingly difficult to view wage labor as a temporary resting place on the road to economic independence, or the West as a haven for the dispossessed small producers of the East.

Given the vast expansion of the nation's productive capacity, many Americans viewed the concentration of wealth as inevitable, natural, and justified by progress. By the turn of the century, advanced economics taught that wages were determined by the iron law of supply and demand and that wealth rightly flowed not to those who worked the hardest but to men with business skills and access to money. The close link between freedom and equality, forged in the Revolution and reinforced during the Civil

War, appeared increasingly out of date. The task of social science, wrote iron manufacturer Abram Hewitt, was to devise ways of making "men who are equal in liberty" content with the "inequality in . . . distribution" inevitable in modern society.

Among the first to take up this challenge were the self-styled "liberal" reformers. (Their beliefs were quite different from those called liberals in modern America, who advocate that an activist government try to address social needs.) This group of editors and professionals broke with the Republican Party in 1872 and helped to bring about a change in northern opinion regarding Reconstruction. But their program was not confined to the South. Like the men who led the movement for a new constitution in the 1780s, Gilded Age reformers feared that with lower-class groups seeking to use government to advance their own interests, democracy was becoming a threat to individual liberty and the rights of property. Some urged a return to the long-abandoned principle that voting should be limited to property owners. During the 1830s, Alexis de Tocqueville had reported that opponents of democracy "hide their heads." By the 1870s, wrote one observer, "expressions of doubt and distrust in regard to universal suffrage are heard constantly . . . [at] the top of our society."

SOCIAL DARWINISM IN AMERICA

The idea of the natural superiority of some groups to others, which before the Civil War had been invoked to justify slavery in an otherwise free society, now reemerged in the vocabulary of modern science to explain the success and failure of individuals and social classes. In 1859, the British scientist Charles Darwin published *On the Origin of Species*. One of the most influential works of science ever to appear, it expounded the theory of evolution whereby plant and animal species best suited to their environment took the place of those less able to adapt.

In a highly oversimplified form, language borrowed from Darwin, such as "natural selection," "the struggle for existence," and "the survival of the fittest," entered public discussion of social problems in the Gilded Age. According to what came to be called Social Darwinism, evolution was as natural a process in human society as in nature, and government must not interfere. Especially misguided, in this view, were efforts to uplift those at the bottom of the social order, such as laws regulating conditions of work or public assistance to the poor. The giant industrial corporation, Social Darwinists believed, had emerged because it was better adapted to its environment than earlier forms of enterprise. To restrict its operations by legislation would reduce society to a more primitive level.

Even the depressions of the 1870s and 1890s did not shake the widespread view that the poor were essentially responsible for their own fate. Charity workers and local governments spent much time and energy distinguishing the "deserving" poor (those, like widows and orphans, destitute through no fault of their own) from the "undeserving," a far larger number. Failure to advance in society was widely thought to indicate a lack of character, an absence of self-reliance and determination in the face of adversity. As late as 1900, half the nation's largest cities offered virtually no public relief, except to persons living in poorhouses. To improve their lot,

VISIONS OF FREEDOM

Detail from Capital and Labor. Capital and Labor, *a cotton textile from around 1870, illustrates the free labor ideal, with an employer and employee shaking hands and laborers enjoying dignity at work and a "happy home." One image and its caption ("The Two Powers in Accord") illustrates the idea of a harmony of interests between worker and employer, a key tenet of free-labor thought. Others stress the dignity of the workingman, based partly on his skill and partly on his ability to provide a comfortable home for his family. The portrait of American industry here stands in stark contrast to the widespread labor strife of the Gilded Age.*

QUESTIONS

1. Why did many Americans in the Gilded Age worry that this vision of harmony no longer described American life?

2. Give some examples of how the images here misrepresent the realities of the period.

according to the philosophy of Social Darwinism, workers should practice personal economy, keep out of debt, and educate their children in the principles of the marketplace, not look to the government for aid.

The era's most influential Social Darwinist was Yale professor William Graham Sumner. For Sumner, freedom meant "the security given to each man" that he can acquire, enjoy, and dispose of property "exclusively as he chooses," without interference from other persons or from government. Freedom thus defined required frank acceptance of inequality. Society faced two and only two alternatives: "liberty, inequality, survival of the fittest; not-liberty, equality, survival of the unfittest." In 1883, Sumner published *What Social Classes Owe to Each Other*. His answer, essentially, was nothing: "In a free state," no one was entitled to claim "help from, and cannot be charged to [offer] help to, another." Government, Sumner believed, existed only to protect "the property of men and the honor of women," not to upset social arrangements decreed by nature.

LIBERTY OF CONTRACT

The growing influence of Social Darwinism helped to popularize an idea that would be embraced by the business and professional classes in the last quarter of the nineteenth century—a "negative" definition of freedom as limited government and an unrestrained free market. Central to this social vision was the idea of contract. "The laws of contract," wrote one reformer, "are the foundation of civilization." Labor contracts reconciled freedom and authority in the workplace. So long as labor relations were governed by contracts freely arrived at by independent individuals, neither the government nor unions had a right to interfere with working conditions, and Americans had no grounds to complain of a loss of freedom.

Demands by workers that the government enforce an eight-hour day, provide relief to the unemployed, or in other ways intervene in the economy struck liberals as an example of how the misuse of political power posed a threat to liberty. "The right of each man to labor as much or as little as he chooses, and to enjoy his own earnings, is the very foundation stone of . . . freedom," wrote Chicago newspaper editor Horace White. The principle of free labor, which originated as a celebration of the independent small producer in a society of broad equality and social harmony, was transformed into a defense of the unrestrained operations of the capitalist marketplace.

THE COURTS AND FREEDOM

In elevating liberty of contract from one element of freedom to its very essence, the courts played a significant role. The Fourteenth Amendment had empowered the federal government to overturn state laws that violated citizens' rights. By the 1880s, liberty of contract, not equality before the law for former slaves, came to be defined as the amendment's true meaning. State and federal courts regularly struck down state laws regulating economic enterprise as an interference with the right of the free laborer to choose his employment and working conditions, and of the entrepreneur to utilize his property as he saw fit. For decades, the courts viewed state regulation of business—especially laws establishing maximum hours of work and safe working conditions—as an insult to free labor.

The Ironworkers' Noontime, *painted in 1880–1881 by Thomas Anshutz, an artist born in West Virginia, whose family owned iron factories. Unlike artists who depicted factories and workers earlier in the century, Anshutz does not try to reconcile nature and industry (there are no reminders of the natural environment). Nor does he emphasize the dignity of labor. The workers seem dwarfed by the factory, and some seem exhausted.*

At first, the Supreme Court was willing to accept laws regulating enterprises that represented a significant "public interest." In *Munn v. Illinois*, an 1877 decision, it upheld the constitutionality of an Illinois law that established a state board empowered to eliminate railroad rate discrimination and set maximum charges. Nine years later, however, in *Wabash v. Illinois*, the Court essentially reversed itself, ruling that only the federal government, not the states, could regulate railroads engaged in interstate commerce, as all important lines were. The decision led directly to the passage of the Interstate Commerce Act of 1887. But on virtually every occasion when cases brought by the ICC against railroads made their way to the Supreme Court, the company emerged victorious.

The courts generally sided with business enterprises that complained of a loss of economic freedom. In 1885, the New York Court of Appeals invalidated a state law that prohibited the manufacture of cigars in tenement dwellings on the grounds that such legislation deprived the worker of the "liberty" to work "where he will." Although women still lacked political rights, they were increasingly understood to possess the same economic "liberty," defined in this way, as men. On the grounds that it violated women's freedom, the Illinois Supreme Court in 1895 declared unconstitutional a state law that outlawed the production of garments in sweatshops and established a forty-eight-hour work week for women and children. In the same year, in *United States v. E. C. Knight Co.*, the U.S. Supreme Court ruled that the Sherman Antitrust Act of 1890, which barred combinations in restraint of trade, could not be used to break up a sugar refining monopoly, since the Constitution empowered Congress to regulate commerce, but not manufacturing. Their unwillingness to allow regulation of the economy, however, did not prevent the courts from acting to impede labor organization. The Sherman Act, intended to prevent business mergers that stifled competition, was used by judges primarily to issue injunctions prohibiting strikes on the grounds that they illegally interfered with the freedom of trade.

In a 1905 case that became almost as notorious as *Dred Scott* and gave the name "Lochnerism" to the entire body of liberty of contract decisions, the Supreme Court in *Lochner v. New York* voided a state law establishing ten hours per day or sixty per week as the maximum hours of work for bakers. The law, wrote Associate Justice Rufus Peckham for the 5-4 majority, "interfered with the right of contract between employer and employee" and therefore infringed upon individual freedom. By this time, the Court was invoking "liberty" in ways that could easily seem absurd. In one case, it overturned as a violation of "personal liberty" a Kansas law prohibiting "yellow-dog" contracts, which made nonmembership in a union a condition of employment. In another, it struck down state laws requiring payment of coal miners in money rather than paper usable only at company-owned stores. Workers, observed mine union leader John P. Mitchell, could not but feel that "they are being guaranteed the liberties they do not want and denied the liberty that is of real value to them."

LABOR AND THE REPUBLIC

"THE OVERWHELMING LABOR QUESTION"

As Mitchell's remark suggests, public debate in the late nineteenth century more than at almost any other moment in American history divided along class lines. The shift from the slavery controversy to what one politician called "the overwhelming labor question" was dramatically illustrated in 1877, the year of both the end of Reconstruction and also the first national labor walkout—the Great Railroad Strike. When workers protesting a pay cut paralyzed rail traffic in much of the country, militia units tried to force them back to work. After troops fired on strikers in Pittsburgh, killing twenty people, workers responded by burning the city's railroad yards, destroying millions of dollars in property. General strikes paralyzed Chicago and St. Louis. The strike revealed both a strong sense of solidarity among workers and the close ties between the Republican Party and the new class of industrialists. President Rutherford B. Hayes, who a few months earlier had ordered federal troops in the South to end their involvement in local politics, ordered the army into the North. The workers, the president wrote in his diary, were "put down by force."

"The days are over," declared the *New York Times*, "in which this country could rejoice in its freedom from the elements of social strife which have long abounded in the old countries." In the aftermath of 1877, the federal government constructed armories in major cities to ensure that troops would be on hand in the event of further labor difficulties. Henceforth, national power would be used not to protect beleaguered former slaves, but to guarantee the rights of property.

THE KNIGHTS OF LABOR AND THE "CONDITIONS ESSENTIAL TO LIBERTY"

The 1880s witnessed a new wave of labor organizing. At its center stood the Knights of Labor. The Knights were the first group to try to organize unskilled workers as well as skilled, women alongside men, and blacks as well as whites (although even the Knights excluded the despised Asian immigrants on the West Coast). The group reached a peak membership of

Ruins of the Pittsburgh Round House, *a photograph published in the July 1895 issue of* Scribner's Magazine, *shows the widespread destruction of property during the Great Railroad Strike of July 1877.*

nearly 800,000 in 1886 and involved millions of workers in strikes, boycotts, political action, and educational and social activities.

Caught between nostalgia for the era of small production and acknowledgment of the factory's triumph, labor reformers of the Gilded Age put forward a wide array of programs, from the eight-hour day to public employment in hard times, currency reform, anarchism, socialism, and the creation of a vaguely defined "cooperative commonwealth." All these ideas arose from the conviction that the social conditions of the 1880s needed drastic change. Americans, declared Terence V. Powderly, head of the Knights of Labor, were not "the free people that we imagine we are."

The labor movement launched a sustained assault on the understanding of freedom grounded in Social Darwinism and liberty of contract. Because of unrestrained economic growth and political corruption, the Knights charged, ordinary Americans had lost control of their economic livelihoods and their own government. Reaching back across the divide of the Civil War, labor defined employers as a new "slave power." Concentrated capital, warned George E. McNeill, a shoemaker and factory worker who became one of the movement's most eloquent writers, had become "a greater power than that of the state." "Extremes of wealth and poverty," he warned, threatened the very existence of democratic government. The remedy was to "engraft republican principles into our industrial system" by guaranteeing a basic set of economic rights for all Americans.

Labor raised the question whether meaningful freedom could exist in a situation of extreme economic inequality. On July 4, 1886, the Federated Trades of the Pacific Coast rewrote the Declaration of Independence. Workers, the new Declaration claimed, had been subjected not to oppressive government but to "the unjust domination of a special class." It went on to list among mankind's inalienable rights, "Life and the means of living, Liberty and the conditions essential to liberty."

An engraving from Frank Leslie's Illustrated Newspaper, *October 16, 1886, shows black delegate Frank J. Farrell introducing Terence V. Powderly, leader of the Knights of Labor, at the labor organization's national convention in Richmond, Virginia. The Knights were among the few nineteenth-century labor groups to recruit black members.*

MIDDLE-CLASS REFORMERS

Dissatisfaction with social conditions in the Gilded Age extended well beyond aggrieved workers. Supreme Court justice John Marshall Harlan in the late 1880s spoke of a "deep feeling of unease," a widespread fear that the country "was in real danger of another kind of slavery that would result from the aggregation of capital in the hands of a few individuals." Alarmed by fear of class warfare and the growing power of concentrated capital, social thinkers offered numerous plans for change. In the last quarter of the century, more than 150 utopian or cataclysmic novels appeared, predicting that social conflict would end either in a new, harmonious social order or in total catastrophe. One popular novel of the era, *Caesar's Column* (1891) by Ignatius Donnelly, ended with civilized society destroyed in a savage civil war between labor and capital.

Of the many books proposing more optimistic remedies for the unequal distribution of wealth, the most popular were *Progress and Poverty* (1879) by Henry George, *The Cooperative Commonwealth* (1884) by Laurence Gronlund, and Edward Bellamy's *Looking Backward* (1888). All three were among the century's greatest best-sellers, their extraordinary success testifying to what George called "a wide-spread consciousness . . . that there is something *radically* wrong in the present social organization." All three

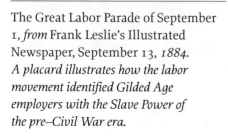

The Great Labor Parade of September 1, *from* Frank Leslie's Illustrated Newspaper, September 13, *1884.* *A placard illustrates how the labor movement identified Gilded Age employers with the Slave Power of the pre–Civil War era.*

writers, though in very different ways, sought to reclaim an imagined golden age of social harmony and American freedom.

PROGRESS AND POVERTY

Although it had no direct impact on government policy, *Progress and Poverty* probably commanded more public attention than any book on economics in American history. An antislavery newspaper editor in California in the 1850s and 1860s, Henry George had witnessed firsthand the rapid monopolization of land in the state. His book began with a famous statement of "the problem" suggested by its title—the growth of "squalor and misery" alongside material progress. His solution was the "single tax," which would replace other taxes with a levy on increases in the value of real estate. The single tax would be so high that it would prevent speculation in both urban and rural land. No one knows how many of Henry George's readers actually believed in this way of solving the nation's ills. But millions responded to his clear explanation of economic relationships and his stirring account of how the "social distress" long thought to be confined to the Old World had made its appearance in the New.

Freedom lay at the heart of George's analysis. The "proper name" for the political movement spawned by his book, he once wrote, was "freedom men," who would "do for the question of industrial slavery" what the Republican Party had done for the slavery of blacks. George rejected the traditional equation of liberty with ownership of land (since the single tax in effect made land the "common property" of the entire society). In other ways, however, his definition of freedom was thoroughly in keeping with mainstream thought. Despite calling for a single massive public intervention in the economy, George saw government as a "repressive power," whose functions in the "co-operative society" of the future would be limited to enhancing the quality of life—building "public baths, museums, libraries, gardens," and the like.

THE COOPERATIVE COMMONWEALTH

Quite different in outlook was *The Cooperative Commonwealth*, the first book to popularize socialist ideas for an American audience. Its author, Laurence Gronlund, was a lawyer who had emigrated from Denmark in 1867. Socialism—the belief that private control of economic enterprises should be replaced by government ownership in order to ensure a fairer distribution of the benefits of the wealth produced—became a major political force in western Europe in the late nineteenth century. In the United States, however, where access to private property was widely considered essential to individual freedom, socialist beliefs were largely confined to immigrants, whose writings, frequently in foreign languages, attracted little attention.

Gronlund began the process of socialism's Americanization. While Karl Marx, the nineteenth century's most influential socialist theorist, had predicted that socialism would come into being via a working-class revolution, Gronlund portrayed it as the end result of a process of peaceful evolution, not violent upheaval. He thus made socialism seem more acceptable to middle-class Americans who desired an end to class conflict and the restoration of social harmony.

BELLAMY'S UTOPIA

Not until the early twentieth century would socialism become a significant presence in American public life. As Gronlund himself noted, the most important result of *The Cooperative Commonwealth* was to prepare an audience for Edward Bellamy's *Looking Backward*, which promoted socialist ideas while "ignoring that name" (Bellamy wrote of nationalism, not socialism). Bellamy lived virtually his entire life in the small industrial city of Chicopee Falls, Massachusetts. In *Looking Backward*, his main character falls asleep in the late nineteenth century only to awaken in the year 2000, in a world where cooperation has replaced class strife, "excessive individualism," and cutthroat competition. Inequality has been banished and with it the idea of liberty as a condition to be achieved through individual striving free of governmental restraint. Freedom, Bellamy insisted, was a social condition, resting on interdependence, not autonomy.

From today's vantage point, Bellamy's utopia—with citizens obligated to labor for years in an Industrial Army controlled by a single Great Trust—seems a chilling social blueprint. Yet the book inspired the creation of hundreds of nationalist clubs devoted to bringing into existence the world of 2000 and left a profound mark on a generation of reformers and intellectuals. Bellamy held out the hope of retaining the material abundance made possible by industrial capitalism while eliminating inequality. In proposing that the state guarantee economic security to all, Bellamy offered a far-reaching expansion of the idea of freedom. "I am aware that you called yourself free in the nineteenth century," a resident of the year 2000 tells Bellamy's Rip Van Winkle. But "the meaning of the word could not then have been at all what it is at present," or it could not have been applied to a

Edward Bellamy, author of the utopian novel Looking Backward.

society in which so many lived in a state of "galling personal dependence upon others as to the very means of life."

A SOCIAL GOSPEL

By 1888, when *Looking Backward* appeared, Social Darwinism and the laissez-faire definition of freedom were under attack from many quarters, including the labor movement and middle-class writers like George and Bellamy, as well as clergymen shocked by the inequities in the emerging industrial order. Most of the era's Protestant preachers concentrated on attacking individual sins like drinking and Sabbath-breaking and saw nothing immoral about the pursuit of riches. Their Gospel of Wealth gave a moral underpinning to the "liberty of contract" outlook. But the outlines of what came to be called the Social Gospel were taking shape in the writings of Walter Rauschenbusch, a Baptist minister in New York City, Washington Gladden, a Congregational clergyman in Columbus, Ohio, and others. They insisted that freedom and spiritual self-development required an equalization of wealth and power and that unbridled competition mocked the Christian ideal of brotherhood.

The Social Gospel movement originated as an effort to reform Protestant churches by expanding their appeal in poor urban neighborhoods and making them more attentive to the era's social ills. The movement's adherents established missions and relief programs in urban areas that attempted to alleviate poverty, combat child labor, and encourage the construction of better working-class housing. They worked with the Knights of Labor and other groups demanding health and safety laws. Some suggested that a more cooperative organization of the economy should replace competitive capitalism. Within American Catholicism, as well, a group of priests and bishops emerged who attempted to alter the Church's traditional hostility to movements for social reform and its isolation from contemporary currents of social thought. With most of its parishioners working men and women, they argued, the Church should lend its support to the labor movement. These developments suggested the existence of widespread dissatisfaction with the "liberty of contract" understanding of freedom.

THE HAYMARKET AFFAIR

The year of the dedication of the Statue of Liberty, 1886, also witnessed an unprecedented upsurge in labor activity. Inspired by a successful strike by western railroad unions against lines controlled by the powerful financier Jay Gould, workers flooded into the Knights of Labor. Its membership, only 100,000 in 1885, rose more than sevenfold in the following year. On May 1, 1886, some 350,000 workers in cities across the country demonstrated for an eight-hour day. Having originated in the United States, May 1, or May Day as it came to be called, soon became an annual date of parades, picnics, and protests, celebrated around the world by organized labor.

The most dramatic events of 1886 took place in Chicago, a city with a large and vibrant labor movement that brought together native-born and immigrant workers, whose outlooks ranged from immigrant socialism and anarchism to American traditions of equality and anti-monopoly. In 1885, the iron moulders union—one of the most powerful organizations of skilled industrial workers in the country—had organized a strike against a wage reduction at the great McCormick plant that produced agricultural machinery. The company brought in strikebreakers and private police, who battled in the streets with the strikers. Fearing chaos, the mayor and prominent business leaders persuaded the company to settle on the union's terms. But in February 1886, after the company installed new machinery that reduced its dependence on the iron moulders' traditional skills, it announced that henceforth the factory would operate on a nonunion basis. The result was a bitter, prolonged strike.

This time, Chicago's city government sided with the company. On May 3, 1886, four strikers were killed by police when they attempted to prevent strikebreakers from entering the factory. The next day, a rally was held in Haymarket Square to protest the killings. Near the end of the speeches, someone—whose identity has never been determined—threw a bomb into the crowd, killing a policeman. The panicked police opened fire, shooting several bystanders and a number of their own force. Soon after, police raided the offices of labor and radical groups and arrested of their leaders. Employers took the opportunity to paint the labor movement as a dangerous and un-American force, prone to violence and controlled by foreign-born radicals. The McCormick strike was defeated and the union local destroyed. Eight anarchists were charged with plotting and carrying out the bombing. Even though the evidence against them was extremely weak, a jury convicted the "Haymarket martyrs." Four were hanged, one committed suicide in prison, and the remaining three were imprisoned until John Peter Altgeld, a pro-labor governor of Illinois, commuted their sentences in 1893.

Seven of the eight men accused of plotting the Haymarket bombing were foreign-born—six Germans and an English immigrant. The last was Albert Parsons, a native of Alabama who had served in the Confederate army in the Civil War and edited a Republican newspaper in Texas during Reconstruction. Fearing violence because of his political views and the fact that his wife, Lucy Parsons, was black, Albert Parsons moved to Chicago during the 1870s. Having survived the Ku Klux Klan in Reconstruction Texas, Parsons perished on the Illinois gallows for a crime that he, like the other "Haymarket martyrs," did not commit.

A cartoon from the 1880s depicts radicals as foreigners attempting to destroy the foundations of American society. A caterpillar labeled "comunism" gnaws at the leaf "capital" beneath which are the fruits of American society—among them education, industry, business, law, order, and peace.

LABOR AND POLITICS

The Haymarket affair took place amid an outburst of independent labor political activity. One study has identified more than 100 local political tickets associated with the Knights of Labor between 1886 and 1888, from

In this pro-labor cartoon from 1888, a workingman rescues liberty from the stranglehold of monopolies and the pro-business major parties.

Anniston, Alabama, to Whitewater, Wisconsin. Their major aim was to end the use of public and private police forces and court injunctions against strikes and labor organizations. At least sixty achieved some kind of electoral success. In Kansas City, a coalition of black and Irish-American workers and middle-class voters elected Tom Hanna as mayor. He proceeded to side with unions rather than employers in industrial disputes.

The most celebrated labor campaign took place in New York City, where in 1886, somewhat to his own surprise, Henry George found himself thrust into the role of labor's candidate for mayor. George's aim in running was to bring attention to the single tax on land. The labor leaders who organized the United Labor Party had more immediate goals in mind, especially stopping the courts from barring strikes and jailing unionists for conspiracy. George ran a spirited campaign, speaking at factories, immigrant associations, and labor parades and rallies. A few days after the dedication of the Statue of Liberty, New Yorkers flocked to the polls to elect their mayor. Nearly 70,000 voted for George, who finished second, eclipsing the total of the Republican candidate, Theodore Roosevelt, and coming close to defeating Democrat Abram Hewitt.

In a political system that within living memory had witnessed the disappearance of the Whig Party, the rise and fall of the Know-Nothings, and the emergence of the Republicans, the events of 1886 suggested that labor might be on the verge of establishing itself as a permanent political force. In fact, that year marked the high point of the Knights of Labor. Facing increasing employer hostility and with a poorly organized structure that could not assimilate the great spurt in new members, the Knights soon declined. The major parties, moreover, proved remarkably resourceful in appealing to labor voters.

Thus, America's Gilded Age witnessed deep and sometimes violent divisions over the definition of freedom in a rapidly industrializing society. The battle between upholders of Social Darwinism and laissez-faire, who saw freedom as the right of individuals to pursue their economic interests without outside restraint, and those who believed in collective efforts to create "industrial freedom" for ordinary Americans, would continue for many decades. In the early twentieth century, reformers would turn to new ways of addressing the social conditions of freedom and new means of increasing ordinary Americans' political and economic liberty. But before this, in the 1890s, the nation would face its gravest crisis since the Civil War, and the boundaries of freedom would once again be redrawn.

SUGGESTED READING

BOOKS

Bensel, Richard F. *The Political Economy of American Industrialization, 1877–1900* (2000). A study of the policies and political divisions that contributed to and resulted from the second industrial revolution.

Blackhawk, Ned. *Violence Over the Land: Indians and Empires in the Early American West* (2006). A history of the long conflict between Native Americans and the federal government for control of the trans-Mississippi West.

Chandler, Alfred. *The Visible Hand: The Managerial Revolution in American Business* (1977). Examines how railroads pioneered techniques of modern business management that other corporations then adopted.

De Leon, Arnoldo. *Racial Frontiers: Africans, Chinese, and Mexicans in Western America, 1848–1890* (2002). Emphasizes the diversity of the West's population and the different experiences of its racial minorities.

Deutsch, Sarah. *No Separate Refuge: Culture, Class, and Gender on the Anglo-Hispanic Frontier in the American Southwest, 1880–1940* (1987). A careful analysis of the changing experience of people of Hispanic origin in the Southwest during these years.

Fink, Leon. *Workingmen's Democracy: The Knights of Labor and American Politics* (1983). Examines the rise of the Knights of Labor and their forays into local politics in the mid-1880s.

Hamalainen, Pekka. *The Comanche Empire* (2008). The rise and fall of Comanche domination over much of the southwestern United States.

Hofstadter, Richard. *Social Darwinism in American Thought* (1944). A classic study of a major tendency in American thought during the Gilded Age.

Isenberg, Andrew C. *The Destruction of the Bison: An Environmental History, 1750–1920* (2000). Examines the numerous causes for the decimation of buffalo herds, from climate change to commercial hunting.

Jeffrey, Julie R. *Frontier Women: "Civilizing" the West? 1840–1880* (rev. ed., 1998). A study, based on letters and diaries, of the experience of women on the western frontier.

Keller, Morton. *Affairs of State: Public Life in Late Nineteenth-Century America* (1977). A comprehensive account of the activities of government during the Gilded Age.

Morgan, H. Wayne. *From Hayes to McKinley: National Party Politics, 1877–1896* (1969). The standard narrative of national politics during these years.

Shannon, Fred A. *The Farmer's Last Frontier: Agriculture 1860–1897* (1945). Remains an excellent introduction to the experience of farmers in the last four decades of the nineteenth century.

Sproat, John G. *"The Best Men": Liberal Reformers in the Gilded Age* (1968). Traces the origins, outlook, and political impact of reformers dissatisfied with the corruption of national politics.

Thomas, John L. *Alternative Americas: Henry George, Edward Bellamy, Henry Demarest Lloyd and the Adversary Tradition* (1983). A thorough exposition of the thought of three critics of Gilded Age society.

Trachtenberg, Alan. *The Incorporation of America: Culture and Society in the Gilded Age* (1982). An influential survey of how economic change affected American life during the Gilded Age.

WEBSITES

Indian Peoples of the Northern Great Plains: www.lib.montana.edu/digital/nadb/
The Dramas of Haymarket: www.chicagohistory.org/dramas/overview/over.htm
Western History Photography Collection: http://photoswest.org/presearch.html

REVIEW QUESTIONS

1. The American economy thrived because of federal involvement, not the lack of it. How did the federal government actively promote industrial and agricultural development in this period?

2. Describe the importance of the nation's railroads in the rise of America's second industrial revolution.

3. How did the development of an urban, industrial society exacerbate inequalities in U.S. society and promote class violence?

4. Describe the involvement of American family farmers in the global economy after 1870 and its effects on their independence.

5. According to *The Gilded Age* by Mark Twain and Charles Dudley Warner, the era's slogan was "Get rich, dishonestly if we can, honestly if we must." Explain how this was true of the politics of the era.

6. How successfully did third parties lead movements for reform at the state level?

7. Explain how social thinkers misapplied Charles Darwin's ideas to justify massive disparities in wealth and power and to deny government a role in equalizing opportunity.

8. How do the ideas of Henry George, Edward Bellamy, and other authors conflict with Social Darwinism?

9. Compare William Graham Sumner's comments in *What Social Classes Owe to Each Other* to those of the Federated Trades of the Pacific Coast's "rewrite" of the Declaration of Independence. What two positions are laid out?

FREEDOM QUESTIONS

1. How would the elite differ from the urban and rural poor on the following questions: What social conditions make freedom possible, and what role should the government play in defining and protecting the liberties of its citizens?

2. How did Native American ideas of freedom differ from those of settlers and government officials in this period?

3. How did the creation of a poor population of factory workers threaten traditional American ideas about freedom, equality, and democracy?

4. Explain how the courts, by embracing Social Darwinism and a "negative" idea of freedom through the liberty of contract ideal, eroded the freedoms of workers and others.

KEY TERMS

"great upheaval" of 1886 (p. 632)

standard gauge (p. 635)

railroad time zones (p. 636)

vertical integration (p. 639)

Standard Oil Company (p. 640)

"captains of industry" v. "robber barons" (p. 641)

"The Significance of the Frontier in American History" (p. 643)

bonanza farming (p. 646)

Dawes Act (p. 654)

Ghost Dance (p. 655)

greenbacks (p. 659)

Civil Service Act of 1883 (p. 659)

Interstate Commerce Commission (p. 659)

Patrons of Husbandry (p. 660)

iron law of supply and demand (p. 661)

Social Darwinism (p. 662)

liberty of contract (p. 664)

Lochner v. New York (p. 666)

Great Railroad Strike of 1877 (p. 666)

Knights of Labor (p. 666)

Social Gospel (p. 670)

REVIEW TABLE

Landmarks in Indian Relations, 1876–1890

Event	Date	Outcome
Battle at Little Bighorn	**1876**	General Custer's army is massacred
Chief Joseph's trek toward freedom	**1877**	Nez Percé tribe is captured and placed on a reservation
Dawes Act	**1887**	Indian lands are divided into small family plots, and the rest is sold off
Massacre at Wounded Knee	**1890**	Final defeat, ending the Indian Wars

CHAPTER 17

Freedom's Boundaries, at Home and Abroad, 1890–1900

A Trifle Embarrassed, *a cartoon from the magazine* Puck *in 1898, depicts Uncle Sam and a female figure of liberty standing at the gate of a Foundling [Orphan] Asylum and being presented with orphans representing Puerto Rico, Hawaii, Cuba, and the Philippines. These were the territories acquired by the United States during the Spanish-American War (all but Cuba remained American possessions). The artist seems to question whether the United States is prepared to assume the role of imperial power.*

• What were the origins and the significance of Populism?

• How did the liberties of blacks after 1877 give way to legal segregation across the South?

• In what ways did the boundaries of American freedom grow narrower in this period?

• How did the United States emerge as an imperial power in the 1890s?

One of the most popular songs of 1892 bore the title "Father Was Killed by a Pinkerton Man." It was inspired by an incident during a bitter strike at Andrew Carnegie's steelworks at Homestead, Pennsylvania, the nineteenth century's most widely publicized confrontation between labor and capital. The strike pitted one of the nation's leading industrial corporations against a powerful union, the Amalgamated Association, which represented the skilled iron- and steelworkers among the complex's 3,800 employees.

Homestead's twelve steel mills were the most profitable and technologically advanced in the world. The union contract gave the Amalgamated Association a considerable say in their operation, including the right to approve the hiring of new workers and to regulate the pace of work. To Carnegie and Henry Clay Frick, his local supervisor, the union's power increasingly seemed an intolerable infringement on management's rights. In 1892, they decided to operate the plant on a nonunion basis. Frick surrounded the factory with a fence topped by barbed wire, constructed barracks to house strikebreakers, and fired the entire workforce. Henceforth, only workers who agreed not to join the union could work at Homestead. In response, the workers, including the unskilled laborers not included in the Amalgamated Association, blockaded the steelworks and mobilized support from the local community. The battle memorialized in song took place on July 6, 1892, when armed strikers confronted 300 private policemen from the Pinkerton Detective Agency. Seven workers and three Pinkerton agents were killed, and the Pinkertons were forced to retreat. Four days later, the governor of Pennsylvania dispatched 8,000 militiamen to open the complex on management's terms. The strikers held out until November, but the union's defeat was now inevitable. In the end, the Amalgamated Association was destroyed.

The Carnegie corporation's tactics and the workers' solidarity won the strikers widespread national sympathy. "Ten thousand Carnegie libraries," declared the *St. Louis Post-Dispatch*, "would not compensate the country for the evils resulting from Homestead." The strike became an international cause célèbre as well. British newspapers pointed out that their country restricted the use of private police forces far more severely than the United States. Britons, they claimed, understood economic liberty better than Americans.

Homestead demonstrated that neither a powerful union nor public opinion could influence the conduct of the largest corporations. The writer Hamlin Garland, who visited Homestead two years after the strike, found the workforce sullen and bitter. He described a town "as squalid and unlovely as could be imagined," with dingy houses over which hung dense clouds of black smoke. It was "American," he wrote, "only in the sense in which [it] represents the American idea of business."

In fact, two American ideas of freedom collided at Homestead—the employers' definition, based on the idea that property rights, unrestrained by union rules or public regulation, sustained the public good, and the workers' conception, which stressed economic security and independence from what they considered the "tyranny" of employers. The strife at Homestead also reflected broader battles over American freedom during the 1890s. Like the Homestead workers, many Americans came to believe that they were being denied economic independence and democratic self-government, long central to the popular understanding of freedom.

Andrew Carnegie's ironworks at Homestead, Pennsylvania.

During the 1890s, millions of farmers joined the Populist movement in an attempt to reverse their declining economic prospects and to rescue the government from what they saw as control by powerful corporate interests. The 1890s witnessed the imposition of a new racial system in the South that locked African-Americans into the status of second-class citizenship, denying them many of the freedoms white Americans took for granted. Increasing immigration produced heated debates over whether the country should reconsider its traditional self-definition as a refuge for foreigners seeking greater freedom on American shores. At the end of the 1890s, in the Spanish-American War, the United States for the first time acquired overseas possessions and found itself ruling over subject peoples from Puerto Rico to the Philippines. Was the democratic republic, many Americans wondered, becoming an empire like those of Europe? Rarely has the country experienced at one time so many debates over both the meaning of freedom and freedom's boundaries.

THE POPULIST CHALLENGE

THE FARMERS' REVOLT

Even as labor unrest crested, a different kind of uprising was ripening in the South and the trans-Mississippi West, a response to falling agricultural prices and growing economic dependency in rural areas. Like industrial workers, small farmers faced increasing economic insecurity. In the South, the sharecropping system, discussed in Chapter 15, locked millions of tenant farmers, white and black, into perpetual poverty. The interruption of cotton exports during the Civil War had led to the rapid expansion of production in India, Egypt, and Brazil. The glut of cotton on the world market led to declining prices (from 11 cents a pound in 1881 to 4.6 cents in 1894), throwing millions of small farmers deep into debt and threatening them with the loss of their land. In the West, farmers who had mortgaged their property to purchase seed, fertilizer, and equipment faced the prospect of losing their farms when unable to repay their bank loans. Farmers increasingly believed that their plight derived from the high freight rates charged by railroad companies, excessive interest rates for loans from merchants and bankers, and the fiscal policies of the federal government (discussed in the previous chapter) that reduced the supply of money and helped to push down farm prices.

Through the Farmers' Alliance, the largest citizens' movement of the nineteenth century, farmers sought to remedy their condition. Founded in Texas in the late 1870s, the Alliance spread to forty-three states by 1890. The farmers' alternatives, said J. D. Fields, a Texas Alliance leader, were "success and freedom, or failure and servitude." At first, the Alliance remained aloof from politics, attempting to improve rural conditions by the cooperative financing and marketing of crops. Alliance "exchanges" would loan money to farmers and sell their produce. But it soon became clear that farmers on their own could not finance this plan, and banks refused to extend loans to the exchanges. The Alliance therefore proposed that the federal government establish warehouses where farmers could store their crops until they were sold. Using the crops as collateral, the government would then issue loans to farmers at low interest rates, thereby ending their dependence on bankers and merchants. Since it would have to be enacted by Congress, the "subtreasury plan," as this proposal was called, led the Alliance into politics.

THE PEOPLE'S PARTY

In the early 1890s, the Alliance evolved into the People's Party (or Populists), the era's greatest political insurgency. The party did not just appeal to farmers. It sought to speak for all the "producing classes" and achieved some of its greatest successes in states like Colorado and Idaho, where it won the support of miners and industrial workers. It attracted veterans of the Knights of Labor by condemning the use of court injunctions and private police forces against strikers. But its major base lay in the cotton and wheat belts of the South and West.

Building on the Farmers' Alliance network of local institutions, the Populists embarked on a remarkable effort of community organization and education. To spread their message they published numerous pamphlets on political and economic questions, established more than 1,000 local newspapers, and sent traveling speakers throughout rural America. Wearing "a huge black sombrero and a black Prince Albert coat," Texas Populist orator "Cyclone" Davis traveled the Great Plains accompanied by the writings of Thomas Jefferson, which he quoted to demonstrate the evils of banks and large corporations. At great gatherings on the western plains, similar in some ways to religious revival meetings, and in small-town southern country stores, one observer wrote, "people commenced to think

A group of Kansas Populists, perhaps on their way to a political gathering, in a photograph from the 1890s.

who had never thought before, and people talked who had seldom spoken. . . . Little by little they commenced to theorize upon their condition."

Here was the last great political expression of the nineteenth-century vision of America as a commonwealth of small producers whose freedom rested on the ownership of productive property and respect for the dignity of labor. "Day by day," declared the *People's Party Paper* of Georgia in 1893, "the power of the individual sinks. Day by day the power of the classes, or the corporations, rises. . . . In all essential respects, the republic of our fathers is dead."

But although the Populists used the familiar language of nineteenth-century radicalism, they were hardly a backward-looking movement. They embraced the modern technologies that made large-scale cooperative enterprise possible—the railroad, the telegraph, and the national market—while looking to the federal government to regulate them in the public interest. They promoted agricultural education and believed farmers should adopt modern scientific methods of cultivation. They believed the federal government could move beyond partisan conflict to operate in a businesslike manner to promote the public good—a vision soon to be associated with the Progressive movement and, many years later, politicians like Jimmy Carter and Barack Obama.

THE POPULIST PLATFORM

The Populist platform of 1892, adopted at the party's Omaha convention, remains a classic document of American reform (see the Appendix for the full text). Written by Ignatius Donnelly, a Minnesota editor and former Radical Republican congressman during Reconstruction, it spoke of a nation "brought to the verge of moral, political, and material ruin" by political corruption and economic inequality. "The fruits of the toil of millions," the platform declared, "are boldly stolen to build up colossal fortunes . . . while their possessors despise the republic and endanger liber-

Tom Watson, the Georgia Populist leader, on the cover of the party's "campaign book" for 1892.

ty." The platform put forth a long list of proposals to restore democracy and economic opportunity, many of which would be adopted during the next half-century: the direct election of U.S. senators, government control of the currency, a graduated income tax, a system of low-cost public financing to enable farmers to market their crops, and recognition of the right of workers to form labor unions. In addition, Populists called for public ownership of the railroads to guarantee farmers inexpensive access to markets for their crops. A generation would pass before a major party offered so sweeping a plan for political action to create the social conditions of freedom.

THE POPULIST COALITION

In some southern states, the Populists made remarkable efforts to unite black and white small farmers on a common political and economic program. The obstacles to such an alliance were immense—not merely the heritage of racism and the political legacy of the Civil War, but the fact that many white Populists were landowning farmers while most blacks were tenants and agricultural laborers. Unwelcome in the southern branches of the Farmers' Alliance, black farmers formed their own organization, the Colored Farmers' Alliance. In 1891, it tried to organize a strike of cotton pickers on plantations in South Carolina, Arkansas, and Texas. The action was violently suppressed by local authorities and landowners, some of them sympathetic to the white Alliance but unwilling to pay higher wages to their own laborers.

In general, southern white Populists' racial attitudes did not differ significantly from those of their non-Populist neighbors. Nonetheless, recognizing the need for allies to break the Democratic Party's stranglehold on power in the South, some white Populists insisted that black and white

In a cartoon from Tom Watson's People's Party Paper, *February 25, 1892, northern and southern Civil War veterans bury their past antagonism and unite in the Populist campaign.*

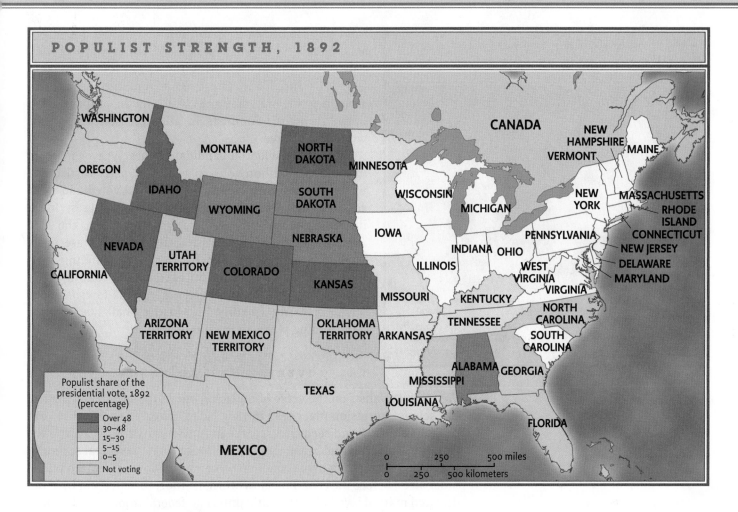

POPULIST STRENGTH, 1892

Populist share of the presidential vote, 1892 (percentage)

- Over 48
- 30–48
- 15–30
- 5–15
- 0–5
- Not voting

farmers shared common grievances and could unite for common goals. Tom Watson, Georgia's leading Populist, worked the hardest to forge a black-white alliance. "You are kept apart," he told interracial audiences, "that you may be separately fleeced of your earnings. . . . This race antagonism perpetuates a monetary system which beggars both." While many blacks refused to abandon the party of Lincoln, others were attracted by the Populist appeal. In 1894, a coalition of white Populists and black Republicans won control of North Carolina, bringing to the state a "second Reconstruction" complete with increased spending on public education and a revival of black officeholding. In most of the South, however, Democrats fended off the Populist challenge by resorting to the tactics they had used to retain power since the 1870s—mobilizing whites with warnings about "Negro supremacy," intimidating black voters, and stuffing ballot boxes on election day.

The Populist movement also engaged the energies of thousands of reform-minded women from farm and labor backgrounds. Some, like Mary Elizabeth Lease, a former homesteader and one of the first female lawyers in Kansas, became prominent organizers, campaigners, and strategists. Lease was famous for her speeches urging farmers to "raise less corn and more hell" (although she apparently never actually uttered those exact words, which would have been considered inappropriate for a woman in public). "We fought England for our liberty," Lease declared,

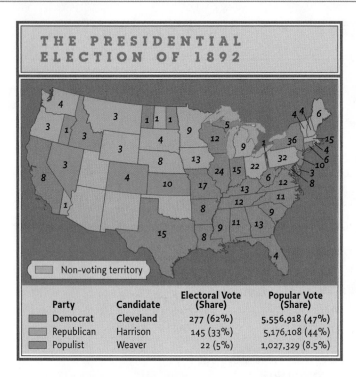

THE PRESIDENTIAL ELECTION OF 1892

Non-voting territory

Party	Candidate	Electoral Vote (Share)	Popular Vote (Share)
Democrat	Cleveland	277 (62%)	5,556,918 (47%)
Republican	Harrison	145 (33%)	5,176,108 (44%)
Populist	Weaver	22 (5%)	1,027,329 (8.5%)

"and put chains on four million blacks. We wiped out slavery and . . . began a system of white wage slavery worse than the first." During the 1890s, referendums in Colorado and Idaho approved extending the vote to women, while in Kansas and California the proposal went down in defeat. Populists in all these states endorsed women's suffrage.

Populist presidential candidate James Weaver received more than 1 million votes in 1892. The party carried five western states, with twenty-two electoral votes, and elected three governors and fifteen members of Congress. In his inaugural address in 1893, Lorenzo Lewelling, the new Populist governor of Kansas, anticipated a phrase made famous seventy years later by Martin Luther King Jr.: "I have a dream. . . . In the beautiful vision of a coming time I behold the abolition of poverty. A time is foreshadowed when . . . liberty, equality, and justice shall have permanent abiding places in the republic."

THE GOVERNMENT AND LABOR

Were the Populists on the verge of replacing one of the two major parties? The severe depression that began in 1893 led to increased conflict between capital and labor and seemed to create an opportunity for expanding the Populist vote. Time and again, employers brought state or federal authority to bear to protect their own economic power or put down threats to public order. Even before the economic downturn, in 1892, the governor of Idaho declared martial law and sent militia units and federal troops into the mining region of Coeur d'Alene to break a strike. In May 1894, the federal government deployed soldiers to disperse Coxey's Army—a band of several hundred unemployed men led by Ohio businessman Jacob Coxey, who marched to Washington demanding economic relief.

Coxey's Army on the march in 1894.

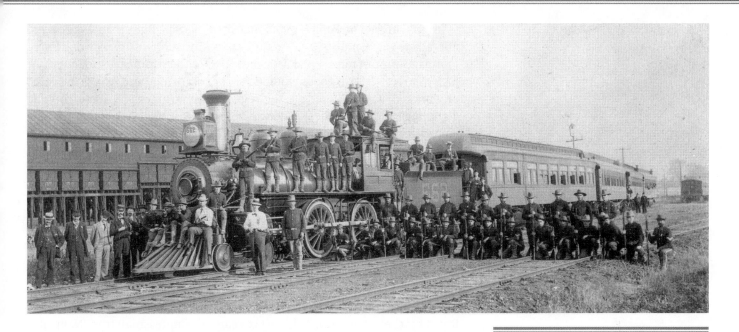

Federal troops pose atop a railroad engine after being sent to Chicago to help suppress the Pullman strike of 1894.

DEBS AND THE PULLMAN STRIKE

Also in 1894, workers in the company-owned town of Pullman, Illinois, where railroad sleeping cars were manufactured, called a strike to protest a reduction in wages. The American Railway Union, whose 150,000 members included both skilled and unskilled railroad laborers, announced that its members would refuse to handle trains with Pullman cars. When the boycott crippled national rail service, President Grover Cleveland's attorney general, Richard Olney (himself on the board of several railroad companies), obtained a federal court injunction ordering the strikers back to work. Federal troops and U.S. marshals soon occupied railroad centers like Chicago and Sacramento. Violent clashes between troops and workers erupted from Maine to California, leaving thirty-four persons dead.

The strike collapsed when the union's leaders, including its charismatic president, Eugene V. Debs, were jailed for contempt of court for violating the judicial order. In the case of *In re Debs*, the Supreme Court unanimously confirmed the sentences and approved the use of injunctions against striking labor unions. On his release from prison in November 1895, more than 100,000 persons greeted Debs at a Chicago railroad depot. Hailing the crowd of well-wishers as "lovers of liberty," Debs charged that concentrated economic power, now aligned with state and national governments, was attempting to "wrest from the weak" their birthright of freedom.

POPULISM AND LABOR

In 1894, Populists made determined efforts to appeal to industrial workers. Populist senators supported the demand of Coxey's Army for federal unemployment relief, and Governor Davis Waite of Colorado, who had edited a labor newspaper before his election, sent the militia to protect striking miners against company police. In the state and congressional elections of that year, as the economic depression deepened, voters by the millions abandoned the Democratic Party of President Cleveland.

In rural areas, the Populist vote increased in 1894. But urban workers did not rally to the Populists, whose core issues—the subtreasury plan and lower mortgage interest rates—had little meaning for them and whose demand for higher prices for farm goods would raise the cost of food and reduce the value of workers' wages. Moreover, the revivalist atmosphere of many Populist gatherings and the biblical cadences of Populist speeches were alien to the largely immigrant and Catholic industrial working class. Urban working-class voters in 1894 instead shifted en masse to the Republicans, who claimed that raising tariff rates (which Democrats had recently reduced) would restore prosperity by protecting manufacturers and industrial workers from the competition of imported goods and cheap foreign labor. In one of the most decisive shifts in congressional power in American history, the Republicans gained 117 seats in the House of Representatives.

BRYAN AND FREE SILVER

In 1896, Democrats and Populists joined to support William Jennings Bryan for the presidency. A thirty-six-year-old congressman from Nebraska, Bryan won the Democratic nomination after delivering to the national convention an electrifying speech that crystallized the farmers' pride and grievances. "Burn down your cities and leave our farms," Bryan proclaimed, "and your cities will spring up again as if by magic; but destroy our farms and grass will grow in the streets of every city in the country." Bryan called for the "free coinage" of silver—the unrestricted minting of silver money. In language ringing with biblical imagery, Bryan condemned the gold standard: "You shall not press down upon the brow of labor this crown of thorns. You shall not crucify mankind upon a cross of gold."

At various points in the nineteenth century, from debates over "hard" versus "soft" money in the Jacksonian era to the greenback movement after the Civil War, the "money question" had played a central role in American politics. Bryan's demand for "free silver" was the latest expression of the view that increasing the amount of currency in circulation would raise the prices farmers received for their crops and make it easier to pay off their debts. His nomination wrested control of the Democratic Party from long-dominant leaders like President Grover Cleveland, who were closely tied to eastern businessmen.

There was more to Bryan's appeal, however, than simply free silver. A devoutly religious man, he was strongly influenced by the Social Gospel movement (discussed in the previous chapter) and tried to apply the teachings of Jesus Christ to uplifting the "little people" of the United States. He championed a vision of the government helping ordinary Americans that anticipated provisions of the New Deal of the 1930s, including a progressive income tax, banking regulation, and the right of workers to form unions.

Many Populists were initially cool to Bryan's campaign. Their party had been defrauded time and again by Democrats in the South. Veteran Populists feared that their broad program was in danger of being reduced to "free silver." But realizing that they could not secure victory alone, the party's leaders endorsed Bryan's candidacy. Bryan broke with tradition and embarked on a nationwide speaking tour, seeking to rally farmers and workers to his cause.

A cartoon from the magazine Judge, *September 14, 1896, condemns William Jennings Bryan and his "cross of gold" speech for defiling the symbols of Christianity. Bryan tramples on the Bible while holding his golden cross; a vandalized church is visible in the background.*

A Republican cartoon, entitled Dubious, *from the 1896 campaign, suggests that Bryan's platform would reduce the United States to the status of poor countries that utilized silver money.*

THE CAMPAIGN OF 1896

Republicans met the silverite challenge head on, insisting that gold was the only "honest" currency. Abandoning the gold standard, they insisted, would destroy business confidence and prevent recovery from the depression by making creditors unwilling to extend loans, since they could not be certain of the value of the money in which they would be repaid. The party nominated for president Ohio governor William McKinley, who as a congressman in 1890 had shepherded to passage the strongly protectionist McKinley Tariff.

The election of 1896 is sometimes called the first modern presidential campaign because of the amount of money spent by the Republicans and the efficiency of their national organization. Eastern bankers and industrialists, thoroughly alarmed by Bryan's call for monetary inflation and his fiery speeches denouncing corporate arrogance, poured millions of dollars into Republican coffers. (McKinley's campaign raised some $10 million; Bryan's around $300,000.) While McKinley remained at his Ohio home, where he addressed crowds of supporters from his front porch, his political manager Mark Hanna created a powerful national political machine that flooded the country with pamphlets, posters, and campaign buttons.

The results revealed a nation as divided along regional lines as in 1860. Bryan carried the South and West and received 6.5 million votes. McKinley swept the more populous industrial states of the Northeast and Midwest, attracting 7.1 million. The Republican candidate's electoral margin was even greater: 271 to 176. The era's bitter labor strife did not carry over into the electoral arena; indeed, party politics seemed to mute class conflict rather than to reinforce it. Industrial America, from financiers

THE PRESIDENTIAL ELECTION OF 1896

Non-voting territory

Party	Candidate	Electoral Vote (Share)	Popular Vote (Share)
Republican	McKinley	271 (61%)	7,104,779 (51%)
Democrat	Bryan	176 (39%)	6,502,925 (47%)
Minor parties			315,398 (2%)

and managers to workers, now voted solidly Republican, a loyalty reinforced when prosperity returned after 1897.

According to some later critics, the popular children's classic *The Wonderful Wizard of Oz*, published by L. Frank Baum in 1900, offered a commentary on the election of 1896 and its aftermath. In this interpretation, the Emerald City (where everything is colored green, for money) represents Washington, D.C., and the Wizard of Oz, who remains invisible in his palace and rules by illusion, is President McKinley. The only way to get to the city is via a Yellow Brick Road (the color of gold). The Wicked Witches of the East and West represent oppressive industrialists and mine owners. In the much-beloved film version made in the 1930s, Dorothy, the all-American girl from the heartland state of Kansas, wears ruby slippers. But in the book her shoes are silver, supposedly representing the money preferred by ordinary people.

Whatever Baum's symbolism, one thing was clear. McKinley's victory shattered the political stalemate that had persisted since 1876 and created one of the most enduring political majorities in American history. During McKinley's presidency, Republicans placed their stamp on economic policy by passing the Dingley Tariff of 1897, raising rates to the highest level in history, and the Gold Standard Act of 1900. Not until 1932, in the midst of another economic depression, would the Democrats become the nation's majority party. The election of 1896 also proved to be the last presidential election with extremely high voter turnout (in some states, over 90 percent of those eligible). From then on, with the South solidly Democratic and the North overwhelmingly Republican, few states witnessed vigorous two-party campaigns. Voter participation began a downhill trend, although it rose again from the mid-1930s through the 1960s. Today, only around half the electorate casts ballots.

THE SEGREGATED SOUTH

THE REDEEMERS IN POWER

The failure of Populism in the South opened the door for the full imposition of a new racial order. The coalition of merchants, planters, and business entrepreneurs who dominated the region's politics after 1877 called themselves Redeemers, since they claimed to have redeemed the region from the alleged horrors of misgovernment and "black rule." On achieving power, they had moved to undo as much as possible of Reconstruction. State budgets were slashed, taxes, especially on landed property, reduced, and public facilities like hospitals and asylums closed. Hardest hit were the new public school systems. Louisiana spent so little on education that it became the only state in the Union in which the percentage of whites unable to read and write actually increased between 1880 and 1900. Black schools, however, suffered the most, as the gap between expenditures for black and white pupils widened steadily. "What I want here is Negroes who can make cotton," declared one planter, "and they don't need education to help them make cotton."

New laws authorized the arrest of virtually any person without employment and greatly increased the penalties for petty crimes. "They send [a man] to the penitentiary if he steals a chicken," complained a former slave

A group of Florida convict laborers. Southern states notoriously used convicts for public labor, or leased them out to work in dire conditions for private employers.

in North Carolina. As the South's prison population rose, the renting out of convicts became a profitable business. Every southern state placed at least a portion of its convicted criminals, the majority of them blacks imprisoned for minor offenses, in the hands of private businessmen. Railroads, mines, and lumber companies competed for this new form of cheap, involuntary labor. Conditions in labor camps were often barbaric, with disease rife and the death rates high. "One dies, get another" was the motto of the system's architects. The Knights of Labor made convict labor a major issue in the South. In 1892, miners in Tennessee burned the stockade where convict workers were housed and shipped them out of the region. Tennessee abolished the convict lease system three years later but replaced it with a state-owned coal mine using prison labor that reaped handsome profits for decades.

Coal miners, in a photograph by Lewis Hine. Mining was one occupation in which blacks and whites often worked side by side.

THE FAILURE OF THE NEW SOUTH DREAM

During the 1880s, Atlanta editor Henry Grady tirelessly promoted the promise of a New South, an era of prosperity based on industrial expansion and agricultural diversification. In fact, while planters, merchants, and industrialists prospered, the region as a whole sank deeper and deeper into poverty. Some industry did develop, including mining in the Appalachians, textile production in the Carolinas and Georgia, and furniture and cigarette manufacturing in certain southern cities. The new upcountry cotton factories offered jobs to entire families of poor whites from the surrounding countryside. But since the main attractions for investors were the South's low wages and taxes and the availability of convict labor, these enterprises made little contribution to regional economic development. With the exception of Birmingham, Alabama, which by 1900 had developed into an important center for the manufacture of iron and steel, southern cities were mainly export centers for cotton, tobacco, and rice, with little industry or skilled labor. Overall, the region remained dependent on the North for capital and manufactured goods. In 1900, southern per capita income amounted to only 60 percent of the national average. As late as the 1930s, President Franklin D. Roosevelt would declare the South the nation's "number one" economic problem.

BLACK LIFE IN THE SOUTH

As the most disadvantaged rural southerners, black farmers suffered the most from the region's condition. In the Upper South, economic development offered some opportunities—mines, iron furnaces, and tobacco factories employed black laborers, and a good number of black farmers managed to acquire land. In the rice kingdom of coastal South Carolina and Georgia, planters found themselves unable to acquire the capital necessary to repair irrigation systems and machinery destroyed by the war. By the turn of the century, most of the great plantations had fallen to pieces, and many blacks

Black women washing laundry, one of the few jobs open to them in the New South.

acquired land and took up self-sufficient farming. In most of the Deep South, however, African-Americans owned a smaller percentage of the land in 1900 than they had at the end of Reconstruction.

In southern cities, the network of institutions created after the Civil War—schools and colleges, churches, businesses, women's clubs, and the like—served as the foundation for increasingly diverse black urban communities. They supported the growth of a black middle class, mostly professionals like teachers and physicians, or businessmen like undertakers and shopkeepers serving the needs of black customers. But the labor market was rigidly divided along racial lines. Black men were excluded from supervisory positions in factories and workshops and white-collar jobs such as clerks in offices. A higher percentage of black women than white worked for wages, but mainly as domestic servants. They could not find employment among the growing numbers of secretaries, typists, and department store clerks.

Even after the demise of the Knights of Labor, some local unions, mainly of dockworkers and mine laborers, had significant numbers of black members. But in most occupations, the few unions that existed in the South excluded blacks, forming yet another barrier to their economic advancement.

THE KANSAS EXODUS

Overall, one historian has written, the New South was "a miserable landscape dotted only by a few rich enclaves that cast little or no light upon the poverty surrounding them." Trapped at the bottom of a stagnant economy, some blacks sought a way out through emigration from the South. In 1879 and 1880, an estimated 40,000 to 60,000 African-Americans migrated to Kansas, seeking political equality, freedom from violence, access to education, and economic opportunity. The name participants gave to this migration—the Exodus, derived from the biblical account of the Jews

An 1878 poster seeking recruits for the Kansas Exodus.

Benjamin "Pap" Singleton (on the left), who helped to organize the "Exodus" of 1879, superimposed on a photograph of a boat carrying African-Americans emigrating from the South to Kansas.

escaping slavery in Egypt—indicated that its roots lay in deep longings for the substance of freedom. Those promoting the Exodus, including former fugitive slave Benjamin "Pap" Singleton, the organizer of a real estate company, distributed flyers and lithographs picturing Kansas as an idyllic land of rural plenty. Lacking the capital to take up farming, however, most black migrants ended up as unskilled laborers in towns and cities. But few chose to return to the South. In the words of one minister active in the movement, "We had rather suffer and be free."

Despite deteriorating prospects in the South, most African-Americans had little alternative but to stay in the region. The real expansion of job opportunities was taking place in northern cities. But most northern employers refused to offer jobs to blacks in the expanding industrial economy, preferring to hire white migrants from rural areas and immigrants from Europe. Not until the outbreak of World War I in Europe in 1914 cut off immigration did northern employers open industrial jobs to blacks, setting in motion the Great Migration discussed in Chapter 19. Until then, the vast majority of African-Americans remained in the South.

THE DECLINE OF BLACK POLITICS

Neither black voting nor black officeholding came to an abrupt end in 1877. Blacks continued to cast ballots in large numbers, although Democrats solidified their control of state and local affairs by redrawing district lines and substituting appointive for elective officials in counties with black majorities. A few blacks even served in Congress in the 1880s and 1890s. Nonetheless, political opportunities became more and more restricted. Not until the 1990s would the number of black legislators in the South approach the level seen during Reconstruction.

For black men of talent and ambition, other avenues—business, the law, the church—increasingly seemed to offer greater opportunities for personal advancement and community service than politics. The banner of political leadership passed to black women activists. The National Association of Colored Women, founded in 1896, brought together local and regional women's clubs to press for both women's rights and racial uplift. Most female activists emerged from the small urban black middle class and preached the necessity of "respectable" behavior as part and parcel of the struggle for equal rights. They aided poor families, offered lessons in home life and childrearing, and battled gambling and drinking in black communities. Some poor blacks resented middle-class efforts to instruct them in proper behavior. But by insisting on the right of black women to be considered as "respectable" as their white counterparts, the women reformers challenged the racial ideology that consigned all blacks to the status of degraded second-class citizens.

For nearly a generation after the end of Reconstruction, despite fraud and violence, black southerners continued to cast ballots. In some states, the Republican Party remained competitive. In Virginia, a coalition of mostly black Republicans and anti-Redeemer Democrats formed an alliance known as the Readjuster movement (the name derived from their plan to scale back, or "readjust," the state debt). They governed the state between 1879 and 1883. Tennessee and Arkansas also witnessed the formation of biracial political coalitions that challenged Democratic Party rule. Despite the limits of the Populists' interracial alliance, the threat of a biracial political insurgency frightened the ruling Democrats and contributed greatly to the disenfranchisement movement. In North Carolina, for example, the end of the Populist-Republican coalition government in 1898—accomplished by a violent campaign that culminated in a riot in Wilmington in which scores of blacks were killed—was quickly followed by the elimination of black voting.

THE ELIMINATION OF BLACK VOTING

Between 1890 and 1906, every southern state enacted laws or constitutional provisions meant to eliminate the black vote. Since the Fifteenth Amendment prohibited the use of race as a qualification for the suffrage, how were such measures even possible? Southern legislatures drafted laws that on paper appeared color-blind, but that were actually designed to end black voting. The most popular devices were the poll tax (a fee that each citizen had to pay in order to retain the right to vote), literacy tests, and the requirement that a prospective voter demonstrate to election officials an "understanding" of the state constitution. Six southern states also adopted a "grandfather clause," exempting from the new requirements descendants of persons eligible to vote before the Civil War (when only whites, of course, could cast ballots in the South). The racial intent of the grandfather clause was so clear that the Supreme Court in 1915 invalidated such laws for violating the Fifteenth Amendment. The other methods of limiting black voting, however, remained on the books.

Some white leaders presented disenfranchisement as a "good government" measure—a means of purifying politics by ending the fraud, violence, and manipulation of voting returns regularly used against Republicans and Populists. But ultimately, as a Charleston newspaper declared, the aim was to make clear that the white South "does not desire or intend ever to include black men among its citizens." Democrats persistently raised the threat of "Negro domination" to justify the denial of the right to vote. Although election officials often allowed whites who did not meet the new qualifications to register, numerous poor and illiterate whites also lost the right to vote, a result welcomed by many planters and urban reformers. Louisiana, for example, reduced the number of blacks registered to vote from 130,000 in 1894 to 1,342 a decade later. But 80,000 white voters also lost the right. Disenfranchisement led directly to the rise of a generation of southern "demagogues," who mobilized white voters by extreme appeals to racism. Tom Watson, who as noted before had tried to forge an interracial Populist coalition in the 1890s, reemerged early in the twentieth century as a power in Georgia public life through vicious speeches whipping up prejudice against blacks, Jews, and Catholics.

As late as 1940, only 3 percent of adult black southerners were registered to vote. The elimination of black and many white voters, which reversed the nineteenth-century trend toward more inclusive suffrage, could not have been accomplished without the approval of the North. In 1891, the Senate defeated a proposal for federal protection of black voting rights in the South. Apart from the grandfather clause, the Supreme Court gave its approval to disenfranchisement laws. According to the Fourteenth Amendment, any state that deprived male citizens of the franchise was supposed to lose part of its representation in Congress. But like much of the Constitution, this provision was consistently violated so far as African-Americans were concerned. As a result, southern congressmen wielded far greater power on the national scene than their tiny electorates warranted. As for blacks, for decades thereafter, they would regard "the loss of suffrage as being the loss of freedom."

THE LAW OF SEGREGATION

Along with disenfranchisement, the 1890s saw the widespread imposition of segregation in the South. Laws and local customs requiring the separation of the races had numerous precedents. They had existed in many parts

African-Americans of all ages were required to abide by segregation laws. Here, in a twentieth-century photograph, a youth is about to drink from a "colored" water fountain.

of the pre–Civil War North. Southern schools and many other institutions had been segregated during Reconstruction. In the 1880s, however, southern race relations remained unsettled. Some railroads, theaters, and hotels admitted blacks and whites on an equal basis while others separated them by race or excluded blacks altogether.

In 1883, in the *Civil Rights Cases*, the Supreme Court invalidated the Civil Rights Act of 1875, which had outlawed racial discrimination by hotels, theaters, railroads, and other public facilities. The Fourteenth Amendment, the Court insisted, prohibited unequal treatment by state authorities, not private businesses. In 1896, in the landmark decision in *Plessy v. Ferguson*, the Court gave its approval to state laws requiring separate facilities for blacks and whites. The case arose in Louisiana, where the legislature had required railroad companies to maintain a separate car or section for black passengers. A Citizens Committee of black residents of New Orleans came together to challenge the law. To create a test case, Homer Plessy, a light-skinned African-American, refused a conductor's order to move to the "colored only" part of his railroad car and was arrested.

To argue the case before the Supreme Court, the Citizens Committee hired Albion W. Tourgée, who as a judge in North Carolina during Reconstruction had waged a courageous battle against the Ku Klux Klan. "Citizenship is national and knows no color," he insisted, and racial segregation violated the Fourteenth Amendment's guarantee of equal protection before the law. But in an 8-1 decision, the Court upheld the Louisiana law, arguing that segregated facilities did not discriminate so long as they were "separate but equal." The lone dissenter, John Marshall Harlan, reprimanded the majority with an oft-quoted comment: "Our constitution is color-blind." Segregation, he insisted, sprang from whites' conviction that they were the "dominant race" (a phrase used by the Court's majority), and it violated the principle of equal liberty. To Harlan, freedom for the former slaves meant the right to participate fully and equally in American society.

SEGREGATION AND WHITE DOMINATION

As Harlan predicted, states reacted to the *Plessy* decision by passing laws mandating racial segregation in every aspect of southern life, from schools to hospitals, waiting rooms, toilets, and cemeteries. Some states forbade taxi drivers to carry members of different races at the same time. Despite the "thin disguise" (Harlan's phrase) of equality required by the Court's "separate but equal" doctrine, facilities for blacks were either nonexistent or markedly inferior. In 1900, no public high school for blacks existed in the entire South. Black elementary schools, one observer reported, occupied buildings "as bad as stables."

More than a form of racial separation, segregation was one part of an all-encompassing system of white domination, in which each component—disenfranchisement, unequal economic status, inferior education—reinforced the others. The point was not so much to keep the races apart as to ensure that when they came into contact with each other, whether in politics, labor relations, or social life, whites held the upper hand. For example, many blacks could be found in "whites-only" railroad cars. But they entered as servants and nurses, not as paying customers entitled to equal treatment.

An elaborate social etiquette developed, with proper behavior differentiated by race. One sociologist who studied the turn-of-the-century South reported that in places of business, blacks had to stand back and wait until whites had been served. They could not raise their voices or in other ways act assertively in the presence of whites, and they had to "give way" on the streets. In shops, whites but not blacks were allowed to try on clothing.

Segregation affected other groups as well as blacks. In some parts of Mississippi where Chinese laborers had been brought in to work the fields after the Civil War, three separate school systems—white, black, and Chinese—were established. In California, black, Hispanic, and American Indian children were frequently educated alongside whites, but state law required separate schools for those of "mongolian or Chinese descent." In Texas and California, although Mexicans were legally considered "white," they found themselves barred from many restaurants, places of entertainment, and other public facilities.

THE RISE OF LYNCHING

Those blacks who sought to challenge the system, or who refused to accept the demeaning behavior that was a daily feature of southern life, faced not only overwhelming political and legal power but also the threat of violent reprisal. In every year between 1883 and 1905, more than fifty persons, the vast majority of them black men, were lynched in the South—that is, murdered by a mob. Lynching continued well into the twentieth century. By mid-century, the total number of victims since 1880 had reached nearly 5,000. Some lynchings occurred secretly at night; others were advertised

Part of the crowd of 10,000 that watched the 1893 lynching of Henry Smith in Paris, Texas. Smith was accused of raping and murdering a four-year-old girl. The word "justice" was painted on the platform.

Table 17.1 STATES WITH OVER 200 LYNCHINGS, 1889–1918

State	Number of Lynchings
Georgia	386
Mississippi	373
Texas	335
Louisiana	313
Alabama	276
Arkansas	214

in advance and attracted large crowds of onlookers. Mobs engaged in activities that shocked the civilized world. In 1899, Sam Hose, a plantation laborer who killed his employer in self-defense, was brutally murdered near Newman, Georgia, before 2,000 onlookers, some of whom arrived on a special excursion train from Atlanta. A crowd including young children watched as his executioners cut off Hose's ears, fingers, and genitals, burned him alive, and then fought over pieces of his bones as souvenirs. Law enforcement authorities made no effort to prevent the lynching or to bring those who committed the crime to justice.

Like many victims of lynchings, Hose was accused after his death of having raped a white woman. Many white southerners considered preserving the purity of white womanhood a justification for extralegal vengeance. Yet in nearly all cases, as activist Ida B. Wells argued in a newspaper editorial after a Memphis lynching in 1892, the charge of rape was a "bare lie." Born a slave in Mississippi in 1862, Wells had become a schoolteacher and editor. Her essay condemning the lynching of three black men in Memphis led a mob to destroy her newspaper, the *Memphis Free Press*, while she was out of the city. Wells moved to the North, where she became the nation's leading antilynching crusader. She bluntly insisted that given the conditions of southern blacks, the United States had no right to call itself the "land of the free."

Although many countries have witnessed outbreaks of violence against minority racial, ethnic, or religious groups, widespread lynching of individuals over so long a period was a phenomenon unknown elsewhere. Canada, for example, has experienced only one lynching in its history—in 1884, when a mob from the United States crossed the border into British Columbia to lynch an Indian teenager who had fled after being accused of murder.

Years later, black writer Blyden Jackson recalled growing up in early-twentieth-century Louisville, Kentucky, a city in many ways typical of the New South. It was a divided society. There was the world "where white folks lived . . . the Louisville of the downtown hotels, the lower floors of the big movie houses . . . the inner sanctums of offices where I could go only as a humble client or a menial custodian." Then there was the black world, "the homes, the people, the churches, and the schools," where "everything was black." "I knew," Jackson later recalled, "that there were two Louisvilles and . . . two Americas."

THE POLITICS OF MEMORY

As the white North and South moved toward reconciliation in the 1880s and 1890s, one cost was the abandonment of the dream of racial equality spawned by the Civil War and written into the laws and Constitution during Reconstruction. In popular literature and memoirs by participants, at veterans' reunions and in public memorials, the Civil War came to be remembered as a tragic family quarrel among white Americans in which blacks had played no significant part. It was a war of "brother against brother" in which both sides fought gallantly for noble causes—local rights on the part of the South, preservation of the Union for the North. Slavery increasingly came to be viewed as a minor issue, not the war's fundamental cause, and Reconstruction as a regrettable period of "Negro rule" when former slaves had power thrust upon them by a vindictive North. This outlook gave legitimacy to southern efforts to eliminate black voting, lest the region once again suffer the alleged "horrors" of Reconstruction.

Southern governments erected monuments to the Lost Cause, school history textbooks emphasized happy slaves and the evils of Reconstruction, and the role of black soldiers in winning the war was all but forgotten. In fact, when a group of black veterans attempted to participate in a Florida ceremony commemorating the fiftieth anniversary of the outbreak of the Civil War in 1911, a white mob tore the military insignias off their jackets and drove them away.

REDRAWING THE BOUNDARIES

The effective nullification of the laws and amendments of Reconstruction and the reduction of blacks to the position of second-class citizens reflected nationwide patterns of thought and policy. As the nineteenth century drew to a close, American society seemed to be fracturing along lines of both class and race. The result, commented economist Simon Patten, was a widespread obsession with redrawing the boundary of freedom by identifying and excluding those unworthy of the blessings of liberty. "The South," he wrote, "has its negro, the city has its slums. . . . The friends of American institutions fear the ignorant immigrant, and the workingman dislikes the Chinese." As Patten suggested, many Americans embraced a more and more restricted definition of nationhood. The new exclusiveness was evident in the pages of popular periodicals, filled with derogatory imagery depicting blacks and other "lesser" groups as little more than savages and criminals incapable of partaking in American freedom.

A cartoon from the magazine Judge *illustrates anti-immigrant sentiment. A tide of newcomers representing the criminal element of other countries washes up on American shores, to the consternation of Uncle Sam.*

THE HIGH TIDE OF IMMIGRATION—A NATIONAL MENACE.

THE NEW IMMIGRATION AND THE NEW NATIVISM

The 1890s witnessed a major shift in the sources of immigration to the United States. Despite the prolonged depression, 3.5 million newcomers entered the United States during the decade, seeking jobs in the industrial centers of the North and Midwest. Over half arrived not from Ireland, England, Germany, and Scandinavia, the traditional sources of immigration, but from southern and eastern Europe, especially Italy and the Russian and Austro-Hungarian empires. The "new immigrants" were widely described by native-born Americans as members of distinct "races," whose lower level of civilization explained everything from their willingness to work for substandard wages to their supposed inborn tendency toward criminal behavior. They were "beaten men from beaten races," wrote economist Francis Amasa Walker, representing "the worst failures in the struggle for existence." American cities, said an Ohio newspaper, were being overrun by foreigners who "have no true appreciation of the meaning of liberty" and therefore posed a danger to democratic government.

Founded in 1894 by a group of Boston professionals, the Immigration Restriction League called for reducing immigration by barring the illiterate from entering the United States. Such a measure was adopted by Congress early in 1897 but was vetoed by President Cleveland. Like the South, northern and western states experimented with ways to eliminate undesirable voters. Nearly all the states during the 1890s adopted the secret or "Australian" ballot, meant both to protect voters' privacy and to limit the participation of illiterates (who could no longer receive help from party officials at polling places). Several states ended the nineteenth-century practice of allowing immigrants to vote before becoming citizens and adopted stringent new residency and literacy requirements. None of these measures approached the scope of black disenfranchisement in the South or the continued denial of voting rights to women. But suffrage throughout the country was increasingly becoming a privilege, not a right.

CHINESE EXCLUSION AND CHINESE RIGHTS

The boundaries of nationhood, expanded so dramatically in the aftermath of the Civil War, slowly contracted. Leaders of both parties expressed vicious opinions regarding immigrants from China—they were "odious, abominable, dangerous, revolting," declared Republican leader James G. Blaine. Between 1850 and 1870, nearly all Chinese immigrants had been unattached men, brought in by labor contractors to work in western gold fields, railroad construction, and factories. In the early 1870s, entire Chinese families began to immigrate, leading Congress in 1875 to exclude Chinese women from entering the country. California congressman Horace Page, the bill's author, insisted that it was intended to preserve the health of white citizens by barring Chinese prostitutes. But immigration authorities enforced the Page law so as to keep out as well the wives and daughters of arriving men and of those already in the country.

Beginning in 1882, Congress temporarily excluded immigrants from China from entering the country altogether. Although non-whites had long been barred from becoming naturalized citizens, this was the first

Chinese agricultural laborers in southern California around 1880.

Result of an anti-Chinese riot in Seattle, Washington.

time that race had been used to exclude an entire group of people from entering the United States. Congress renewed the restriction ten years later and made it permanent in 1902.

At the time of exclusion, 105,000 persons of Chinese descent lived in the United States. Nearly all of them resided on the West Coast, where they suffered intense discrimination and periodic mob violence. In the late-nineteenth-century West, thousands of Chinese immigrants were expelled from towns and mining camps, and mobs assaulted Chinese residences and businesses. Drawing on the legislation of the Reconstruction era, Chinese victims sued local governments for redress when their rights were violated and petitioned Congress for indemnity. Their demands for equal rights forced the state and federal courts to define the reach of the Fourteenth Amendment. For example, between 1871 and 1885, San Francisco provided no public education for Chinese children. In 1885, the California Supreme Court, in *Tape v. Hurley*, ordered the city to admit Chinese students to public schools. The state legislature responded by passing a law authorizing segregated education, and the city established a school for Chinese. But Joseph and Mary Tape, who had lived in the United States since the 1860s, insisted that their daughter be allowed to attend her neighborhood school like other children. "Is it a disgrace to be born a Chinese?" Mary Tape wrote. "Didn't God make us all!" But her protest failed. Not until 1947 did California repeal the law authorizing separate schools for the Chinese.

The U.S. Supreme Court also considered the status of Chinese-Americans. In *Yick Wo v. Hopkins* (1886), the Court unanimously ordered San Francisco to grant licenses to Chinese-operated laundries, which the city government had refused to do. To deny a person the opportunity to earn a living, the Court declared, was "intolerable in any country where freedom prevails." Twelve years later, in *United States v. Wong Kim Ark*, the Court ruled that the

Booker T. Washington, advocate of industrial education and economic self-help.

Fourteenth Amendment awarded citizenship to children of Chinese immigrants born on American soil.

Yet the Justices also affirmed the right of Congress to set racial restrictions on immigration. And in its decision in *Fong Yue Ting* (1893), the Court authorized the federal government to expel Chinese aliens without due process of law. In his dissent, Justice David J. Brewer acknowledged that the power was now directed against a people many Americans found "obnoxious." But "who shall say," he continued, "it will not be exercised tomorrow against other classes and other people?" Brewer proved to be an accurate prophet. In 1904, the Court cited *Fong Yue Ting* in upholding a law barring anarchists from entering the United States, demonstrating how restrictions on the rights of one group can become a precedent for infringing on the rights of others.

Exclusion profoundly shaped the experience of Chinese-Americans, long stigmatizing them as incapable of assimilation and justifying their isolation from mainstream society. Congress for the first time also barred groups of whites from entering the country, beginning in 1875 with prostitutes and convicted felons, and in 1882 adding "lunatics" and those likely to become a "public charge." "Are we still a [place of refuge] for the oppressed of all nations?" wondered James B. Weaver, the Populist candidate for president in 1892.

THE EMERGENCE OF BOOKER T. WASHINGTON

The social movements that had helped to expand the nineteenth-century boundaries of freedom now redefined their objectives so that they might be realized within the new economic and intellectual framework. Prominent black leaders, for example, took to emphasizing economic self-help and individual advancement into the middle class as an alternative to political agitation.

Symbolizing the change was the juxtaposition, in 1895, of the death of Frederick Douglass with Booker T. Washington's widely praised speech at the Atlanta Cotton Exposition that urged blacks to adjust to segregation and abandon agitation for civil and political rights. Born a slave in 1856, Washington had studied as a young man at Hampton Institute, Virginia. He adopted the outlook of Hampton's founder, General Samuel Armstrong, who emphasized that obtaining farms or skilled jobs was far more important to African-Americans emerging from slavery than the rights of citizenship. Washington put this view into practice when he became head of Tuskegee Institute in Alabama, a center for vocational education (education focused on training for a job rather than broad learning).

In his Atlanta speech, Washington repudiated the abolitionist tradition that stressed ceaseless agitation for full equality. He urged blacks not to try to combat segregation: "In all the things that are purely social we can be as separate as the fingers, yet one as the hand in all things essential to mutual progress." Washington advised his people to seek the assistance of white employers who, in a land racked by labor turmoil, would prefer a docile, dependable black labor force to unionized whites. Washington's ascendancy rested in large part on his success in channeling aid from wealthy northern whites to Tuskegee and to black politicians and newspapers who backed his program. But his support in the black community also arose from a widespread sense that in the world of the late nineteenth century, frontal assaults on white power were impossible and that blacks should concentrate on building up their segregated communities.

THE RISE OF THE AFL

Within the labor movement, the demise of the Knights of Labor and the ascendancy of the American Federation of Labor (AFL) during the 1890s reflected a similar shift away from a broadly reformist past to more limited goals. As the Homestead and Pullman strikes demonstrated, direct confrontations with the large corporations were likely to prove suicidal. Unions, declared Samuel Gompers, the AFL's founder and longtime president, should not seek economic independence, pursue the Knights' utopian dream of creating a "cooperative commonwealth," or form independent parties with the aim of achieving power in government. Rather, the labor movement should devote itself to negotiating with employers for higher wages and better working conditions for its members. Like Washington, Gompers spoke the language of the era's business culture. Indeed, the AFL policies he pioneered were known as "business unionism." Gompers embraced the idea of "freedom of contract," shrewdly turning it into an argument against interference by judges with workers' right to organize unions.

During the 1890s, union membership rebounded from its decline in the late 1880s. But at the same time, the labor movement became less and less inclusive. Abandoning the Knights' ideal of labor solidarity, the AFL restricted membership to skilled workers—a small minority of the labor force—effectively excluding the vast majority of unskilled workers and, therefore, nearly all blacks, women, and new European immigrants. AFL membership centered on sectors of the economy like printing and building construction that were dominated by small competitive businesses with workers who frequently were united by craft skill and ethnic background. AFL unions had little presence in basic industries like steel and rubber, or in the large-scale factories that now dominated the economy.

THE WOMEN'S ERA

Changes in the women's movement reflected the same combination of expanding activities and narrowing boundaries. The 1890s launched what would later be called the "women's era"—three decades during which women, although still denied the vote, enjoyed larger opportunities than in the past for economic independence and played a greater and greater role in public life. By now, nearly every state had adopted laws giving married women control over their own wages and property and the right to sign separate contracts and make separate wills. Nearly 5 million women worked for wages in 1900. Although most were young, unmarried, and concentrated in traditional jobs such as domestic service and the garment industry, a generation of college-educated women was beginning to take its place in better-paying clerical and professional positions.

Through a network of women's clubs, temperance associations, and social reform organizations, women exerted a growing influence on public affairs. Founded in 1874, the Women's Christian Temperance Union (WCTU) grew to become the era's largest female organization, with a

Woman's Holy War, *a lithograph from 1874, the year the Women's Christian Temperance Union was founded, portrays an advocate of prohibition as an armed crusader against hard liquor.*

A drawing for the 1896 meeting of the National American Woman Suffrage Association depicts Elizabeth Cady Stanton (with the Woman's Bible, which she wrote, on her lap) and Susan B. Anthony seated on either side of George Washington. They, in turn, are flanked by Utah and Wyoming, which as territories had been the first parts of the United States to give women the right to vote. Although the image might lead viewers to assume that Stanton and Anthony had joined Washington in heaven, they were both still alive in 1896.

membership by 1890 of 150,000. Under the banner of Home Protection, it moved from demanding the prohibition of alcoholic beverages (blamed for leading men to squander their wages on drink and treat their wives abusively) to a comprehensive program of economic and political reform, including the right to vote. Women, insisted Frances Willard, the group's president, must abandon the idea that "weakness" and dependence were their nature and join assertively in movements to change society. "A wider freedom is coming to the women of America," she declared in an 1895 speech to male and female strikers in a Massachusetts shoe factory. "Too long has it been held that woman has no right to enter these movements. So much for the movements. Politics is the place for woman."

At the same time, the center of gravity of feminism shifted toward an outlook more in keeping with prevailing racial and ethnic norms. The earlier "feminism of equal rights," which claimed the ballot as part of a larger transformation of women's status, was never fully repudiated. The movement continued to argue for women's equality in employment, education, and politics. But with increasing frequency, the native-born, middle-class women who dominated the suffrage movement claimed the vote as educated members of a "superior race."

A new generation of suffrage leaders suggested that educational and other voting qualifications did not conflict with the movement's aims, so long as they applied equally to men and women. Immigrants and former slaves had been enfranchised with "ill-advised haste," declared Carrie Chapman Catt, president of the National American Woman Suffrage Association (created in 1890 to reunite the rival suffrage organizations formed after the Civil War). Indeed, Catt suggested, extending the vote to native-born white women would help to counteract the growing power of the "ignorant foreign vote" in the North and the dangerous potential for a second Reconstruction in the South. Elitism within the movement was reinforced when many advocates of suffrage blamed the "slum vote" for the defeat of a women's suffrage referendum in California. In 1895, the same year that Booker T. Washington delivered his Atlanta address, the National American Woman Suffrage Association held its annual convention in that segregated city. Like other American institutions, the organized movement for women's suffrage had made its peace with nativism and racism.

BECOMING A WORLD POWER

THE NEW IMPERIALISM

In the last years of the 1890s, the narrowed definition of nationhood was projected abroad, as the United States took its place as an imperial power on the international stage. In world history, the last quarter of the nineteenth century is known as the age of imperialism, when rival European empires carved up large parts of the world among themselves. For most of this period, the United States remained a second-rate power. In 1880, the sultan of Turkey decided to close three foreign embassies to reduce expenses. He chose those in Sweden, Belgium, and the United States. In that year, the American navy was smaller than Denmark's or Chile's. When European powers met at the Berlin Congress of 1884–1885 to divide most of Africa among themselves, the United States attended because of its relationship with Liberia but did not sign the final agreement.

Throughout the nineteenth century, large empires dominated much of the globe. Some were land-based, like the Russian, Ottoman, and Chinese empires, and others included territories on several continents linked by sea, such as the British, French, and Spanish. After 1870, a "new imperialism" arose, dominated by European powers and Japan. Belgium, Great Britain, and France consolidated their hold on colonies in Africa, and newly unified Germany acquired colonies there as well. The British and Russians sought to increase their influence in Central Asia, and all the European powers struggled to dominate parts of China. By the early twentieth century, most of Asia, Africa, the Middle East, and the Pacific had been divided among these empires. The justification for this expansion of imperial power was that it would bring modern "civilization" to the supposedly backward peoples of the non-European world. The natives, according to their colonial occupiers, would be instructed in Western values, labor practices, and the Christian religion. Eventually, they would be accorded the right of self-government, although no one could be sure how long this would take. In the meantime, "empire" was another word for "exploitation."

AMERICAN EXPANSIONISM

Territorial expansion, of course, had been a feature of American life from well before independence. But the 1890s marked a major turning point in America's relationship with the rest of the world. Americans were increasingly aware of themselves as an emerging world power. "We are a great imperial Republic destined to exercise a controlling influence upon the actions of mankind and to affect the future of the world," proclaimed Henry Watterson, an influential newspaper editor.

Until the 1890s, American expansion had taken place on the North American continent. Ever since the Monroe Doctrine (see Chapter 10), to be sure, many Americans had considered the Western Hemisphere an American sphere of influence. There was persistent talk of acquiring Cuba, and President Grant had sought to annex the Dominican Republic, only to see the Senate reject the idea. The last territorial acquisition before the 1890s had been Alaska, purchased from Russia by Secretary of State William H. Seward in 1867, to much derision from those who could not see the purpose of American ownership of "Seward's icebox." Seward, however, was mostly interested in the Aleutian Islands, a part of Alaska that stretched much of the way to Asia (see the map on p. 711) and that, he believed, could be the site of coaling stations for merchant ships plying the Pacific.

Most Americans who looked overseas were interested in expanded trade, not territorial possessions. The country's agricultural and industrial production could no longer be entirely absorbed at home. By 1890, companies like Singer Sewing Machines and John D. Rockefeller's Standard Oil Company aggressively marketed their products abroad. Especially during economic downturns, business leaders insisted on the necessity of greater access to foreign customers.

THE LURE OF EMPIRE

One group of Americans who spread the nation's influence overseas were religious missionaries, thousands of whom ventured abroad in the late nineteenth century to spread Christianity, prepare the world for the second coming of Christ, and uplift the poor. Inspired by Dwight Moody, a Methodist evangelist, the Student Volunteer Movement for Foreign Missions sent more than 8,000 missionaries to "bring light to heathen worlds" across the globe. Missionary work offered employment to those with few opportunities at home, including blacks and women, who made up a majority of the total.

A small group of late-nineteenth-century thinkers actively promoted American expansionism, warning that the country must not allow itself to be shut out of the scramble for empire. In *Our Country* (1885), Josiah Strong, a prominent Congregationalist clergyman, sought to update the idea of manifest destiny. Having demonstrated their special aptitude for liberty and self-government on the North American continent, Strong announced, Anglo-Saxons should now spread their institutions and values to "inferior races" throughout the world. The economy would benefit, he insisted, since one means of civilizing "savages" was to turn them into consumers of American goods.

Naval officer Alfred T. Mahan, in *The Influence of Sea Power upon History* (1890), argued that no nation could prosper without a large fleet of ships engaged in international trade, protected by a powerful navy operating from overseas bases. Mahan published his book in the same year that the census bureau announced that there was no longer a clear line separating settled from unsettled land. Thus, the frontier no longer existed. "Americans," wrote Mahan, "must now begin to look outward." His arguments influenced the outlook of James G. Blaine, who served as secretary of state during Benjamin Harrison's presidency (1889–1893). Blaine urged the president to try to acquire Hawaii, Puerto Rico, and Cuba as strategic naval bases.

Although independent, Hawaii was already closely tied to the United States through treaties that exempted imports of its sugar from tariff duties and provided for the establishment of an American naval base at Pearl Harbor. Hawaii's economy was dominated by American-owned sugar plantations that employed a workforce of native islanders and Chinese, Japanese, and Filipino laborers under long-term contracts. Early in 1893, a group of American planters organized a rebellion that overthrew the Hawaii government of Queen Liliuokalani. On the eve of leaving office, Harrison submitted a treaty of annexation to the Senate. After determining that a majority of Hawaiians did not favor the treaty, Harrison's successor, Grover Cleveland, withdrew it. In July 1898, in the midst of the Spanish-American War, the United States finally annexed the Hawaiian Islands. In 1993, the U.S. Congress passed, and President Bill Clinton signed, a resolution expressing regret to native Hawaiians for "the overthrow of the Kingdom of Hawaii . . . with the participation of agents and citizens of the United States."

The depression that began in 1893 heightened the belief that a more aggressive foreign policy was necessary to stimulate American exports. Fears of economic and ethnic disunity fueled an assertive nationalism. In the face of social conflict and the new immigration, government and private organizations in the 1890s promoted a unifying patriotism. These were the years when rituals like the Pledge of Allegiance and the practice of standing for the playing of "The Star-Spangled Banner" came into existence. Americans had long honored the Stars and Stripes, but the "cult of the flag," including an official Flag Day, dates to the 1890s. New, mass-circulation newspapers also promoted nationalistic sentiments. By the late 1890s, papers like William Randolph Hearst's *New York Journal* and Joseph Pulitzer's *New York World*—dubbed the "yellow press" by their critics after the color in which Hearst printed a popular comic strip—were selling a million copies each day by mixing sensational accounts of crime and political corruption with aggressive appeals to patriotic sentiments.

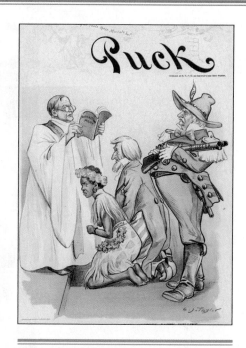

A cartoon in Puck, *December 1, 1897, imagines the annexation of Hawaii by the United States as a shotgun wedding. The minister, President McKinley, reads from a book entitled* Annexation Policy. *The Hawaiian bride appears to be looking for a way to escape. Most Hawaiians did not support annexation.*

THE "SPLENDID LITTLE WAR"

All these factors contributed to America's emergence as a world power in the Spanish-American War of 1898. But the immediate origins of the war lay not at home but in the long Cuban struggle for independence from Spain. Ten years of guerrilla war had followed a Cuban revolt in 1868. The movement for independence resumed in 1895. As reports circulated of widespread suffering caused by the Spanish policy of rounding up civilians and moving them into detention camps, the Cuban struggle won growing support in the United States.

The destruction of the battleship Maine *in Havana Harbor (later found to have been an accident) provided the occasion for patriotic pageants like "Remember the Maine," by William H. West's Big Minstrel Jubilee.*

Demands for intervention escalated after February 15, 1898, when an explosion—probably accidental, a later investigation concluded—destroyed the American battleship *Maine* in Havana Harbor, with the loss of nearly 270 lives. The yellow press blamed Spain and insisted on retribution. After Spain rejected an American demand for a cease-fire on the island and eventual Cuban independence, President McKinley in April asked Congress for a declaration of war. The purpose, declared Senator Henry Teller of Colorado, was to aid Cuban patriots in their struggle for "liberty and freedom." To underscore the government's humanitarian intentions, Congress adopted the Teller Amendment, stating that the United States had no intention of annexing or dominating the island.

Secretary of State John Hay called the Spanish-American conflict a "splendid little war." It lasted only four months and resulted in fewer than 400 American combat deaths. Having shown little interest in imperial expansion before 1898, McKinley now embraced the idea. The war's most decisive engagement, in fact, took place not in Cuba but at Manila Bay, a strategic harbor in the Philippine Islands in the distant Pacific Ocean. Here, on May 1, the American navy under Admiral George Dewey defeated a Spanish fleet. Soon afterward, soldiers went ashore, becoming the first American army units to engage in combat outside the Western Hemisphere. July witnessed another naval victory off Santiago, Cuba, and the landing of American troops on Cuba and Puerto Rico.

ROOSEVELT AT SAN JUAN HILL

The most highly publicized land battle of the war took place in Cuba. This was the charge up San Juan Hill, outside Santiago, by Theodore Roosevelt's

Rough Riders. An ardent expansionist, Roosevelt had long believed that a war would reinvigorate the nation's unity and sense of manhood, which had suffered, he felt, during the 1890s. A few months shy of his fortieth birthday when war broke out, Roosevelt resigned his post as assistant secretary of the navy to raise a volunteer cavalry unit, which rushed to Cuba to participate in the fighting. Roosevelt envisioned his unit as a cross section of American society and enrolled athletes from Ivy League colleges, western cowboys, representatives of various immigrant groups, and even some American Indians. But with the army still segregated, he excluded blacks from his regiment. Ironically, when the Rough Riders reached the top of San Juan Hill, they found that black units had preceded them— a fact Roosevelt omitted in his reports of the battle, which were widely reproduced in the popular press. His heroic exploits made Roosevelt a national hero. He was elected governor of New York that fall and in 1900 became McKinley's vice president.

Charge of the Rough Riders at San Juan Hill, a painting by Frederic Remington, depicts the celebrated unit, commanded by Theodore Roosevelt, in action in Cuba during the Spanish-American War of 1898. Roosevelt, on horseback, leads the troops. Remington had been sent to the island the previous year by publisher William Randolph Hearst to provide pictures of Spanish atrocities during the Cuban war for independence in the hope of boosting the New York Journal's *circulation.*

AN AMERICAN EMPIRE

With the backing of the yellow press, the war quickly escalated from a crusade to aid the suffering Cubans to an imperial venture that ended with the United States in possession of a small overseas empire. McKinley became convinced that the United States could neither return the Philippines to Spain nor grant them independence, for which he believed the inhabitants unprepared. In an interview with a group of Methodist ministers, the president spoke of receiving a divine revelation that Americans had a duty to "uplift and civilize" the Filipino people and to train them for self-government. In the treaty with Spain that ended the war, the United States acquired the Philippines, Puerto Rico, and the Pacific island of Guam. As for Cuba, before recognizing its independence, McKinley forced the island's new government to approve the Platt Amendment to the new Cuban constitution (drafted by Senator Orville H. Platt of Connecticut), which authorized the United States to intervene militarily whenever it saw fit. The United States also acquired a permanent lease on naval stations in Cuba, including what is now the facility at Guantánamo Bay.

The Platt Amendment passed the Cuban Congress by a single vote. Cuban patriots were terribly disappointed. José Martí had fomented revolution in Cuba from exile in the United States and then traveled to the island to take part in the uprising, only to be killed in a battle with Spanish soldiers in 1895. "To change masters is not to be free," Martí had written. And the memory of the betrayal of 1898 would help to inspire another Cuban revolution half a century later.

American interest in its new possessions had more to do with trade than gaining wealth from natural resources or large-scale American settlement. Puerto Rico and Cuba were gateways to Latin America, strategic outposts from which American naval and commercial power could be projected throughout the hemisphere. The Philippines, Guam, and Hawaii lay astride shipping routes to the markets of Japan and China. In 1899, soon after the end of the Spanish-American War, Secretary of State John Hay announced the Open Door policy, demanding that European powers that had recently

In both the Caribbean and the Pacific, the United States achieved swift victories over Spain in the Spanish-American War.

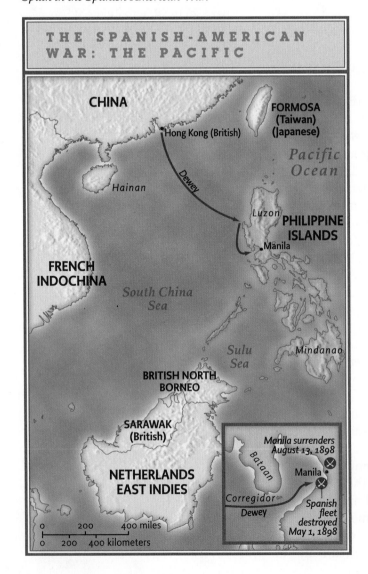

THE SPANISH-AMERICAN WAR: THE PACIFIC

THE SPANISH-AMERICAN WAR: THE CARIBBEAN

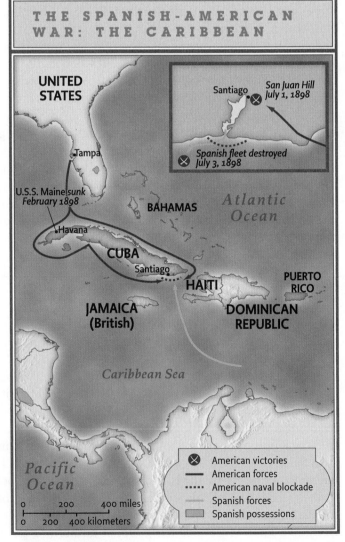

VISIONS OF FREEDOM

"CIVILIZATION BEGINS AT HOME."

Civilization Begins at Home. *This cartoon from the New York World, a Democratic newspaper, was published in November 1898, not long after the end of the Spanish-American War. It depicts a figure representing justice urging President William McKinley to turn his attention from the Philippines to domestic problems in the United States.*

QUESTIONS

1. What problems within the United States does the cartoonist draw attention to, and what point is he trying to make?

2. What position does the cartoonist appear to take on the question of annexing the Philippines?

In this cartoon comment on the American effort to suppress the movement for Philippine independence, Uncle Sam tries to subdue a knife-wielding insurgent.

Emilio Aguinaldo, leader of the Philippine War against American occupation, in a more dignified portrayal than in the cartoon above.

divided China into commercial spheres of influence grant equal access to American exports. The Open Door referred to the free movement of goods and money, not people. Even as the United States banned the immigration of Chinese into this country, it insisted on access to the markets and investment opportunities of Asia. Such economic ambitions could easily lead to military intervention. When Chinese nationalists in the 1900 Boxer Rebellion killed thousands of Christian Chinese and beseiged foreign embassies in Beijing, the United States contributed over 3,000 soldiers to the international force that helped to suppress the rebellion.

THE PHILIPPINE WAR

Many Cubans, Filipinos, and Puerto Ricans had welcomed American intervention as a way of breaking Spain's long hold on these colonies. Large planters looked forward to greater access to American markets, and local elites hoped that the American presence would fend off radical changes proposed by rebellious nationalist movements. Nationalists and labor leaders admired America's democratic ideals and believed that American participation in the destruction of Spanish rule would lead to social reform and political self-government.

But the American determination to exercise continued control, direct or indirect, led to a rapid change in local opinion, nowhere more so than in the Philippines. Filipinos had been fighting a war against Spain since 1896. After Dewey's victory at Manila Bay, their leader, Emilio Aguinaldo, established a provisional government with a constitution modeled on that of the United States. But once McKinley decided to retain possession of the islands, the Filipino movement turned against the United States. The result was a second war, far longer (it lasted from 1899 to 1903) and bloodier (it cost the lives of well more than 100,000

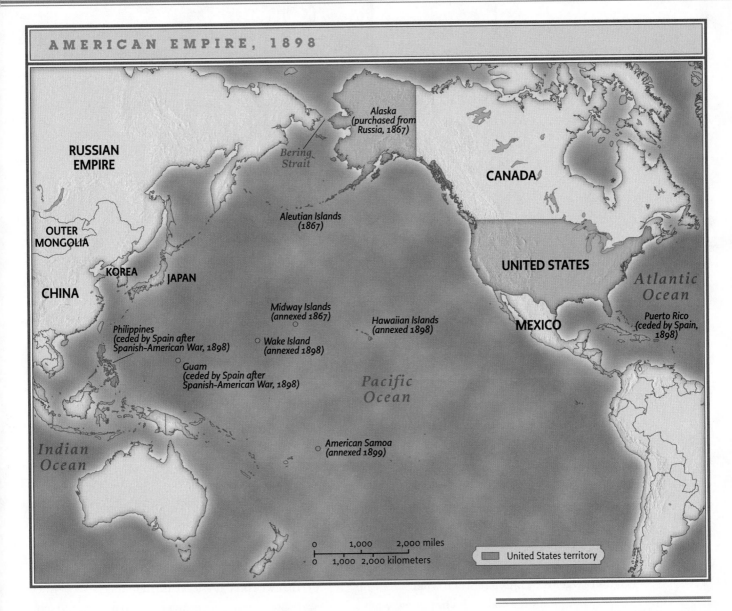

AMERICAN EMPIRE, 1898

As a result of the Spanish-American War, the United States became the ruler of a far-flung overseas empire.

Filipinos and 4,200 Americans) than the Spanish-American conflict. Today, this is perhaps the least remembered of all American wars. At the time, however, it was closely followed and widely debated in the United States. Press reports of atrocities committed by American troops—the burning of villages, torture of prisoners of war, and rape and execution of civilians—tarnished the nation's self-image as liberators. "We do not intend to free the people of the Philippines," complained Mark Twain. "We have gone there to conquer."

The McKinley administration justified its policies on the grounds that its aim was to "uplift and civilize and Christianize" the Filipinos (although most residents of the islands were already Roman Catholics). William Howard Taft, who became governor-general of the Philippines in 1901, believed it might take a century to raise Filipinos to the condition where they could appreciate "what Anglo-Saxon liberty is."

Once in control of the Philippines, the colonial administration took seriously the idea of modernizing the islands. It expanded railroads and

VOICES OF FREEDOM

FROM Interview with President McKinley (1899)

In 1899, soon after the end of the Spanish-American War, President William McKinley met with a group of Methodist Church leaders to discuss his decision to annex the Philippines. McKinley offered a defense of American empire as being in the best interests of Americans and Filipinos.

Before you go I would like to say just a word about the Philippine business. I have been criticized a good deal about the Philippines, but don't deserve it. The truth is I didn't want the Philippines, and when they came to us, as a gift from the gods, I did not know what to do with them. When the Spanish War broke out [Admiral] Dewey was at Hong Kong, and I ordered him to go to Manila and to capture or destroy the Spanish fleet, and he had to; because, if defeated, he had no place to refit on that side of the globe, and if the Dons [Spanish] were victorious they would likely cross the Pacific and ravage our Oregon and California coasts. And so he had to destroy the Spanish fleet, and did it! But that was as far as I thought then.

When I next realized that the Philippines had dropped into our laps I confess I did not know what to do with them. I sought counsel from all sides—Democrats as well as Republicans—but got little help. I thought first we would take only Manila; then Luzon; then other islands perhaps also. I walked the floor of the White House night after night until midnight; and I am not ashamed to tell you, gentlemen, that I went down on my knees and prayed [to] Almighty God for light and guidance more than one night. And one night late it came to me this way—I don't know how it was, but it came: (1) That we could not give them back to Spain—that would be cowardly and dishonorable; (2) that we could not turn them over to France and Germany—our commercial rivals in the Orient—that would be bad business and discreditable; (3) that we could not leave them to themselves—they were unfit for self-government—and they would soon have anarchy and misrule over there worse than Spain's was; and (4) that there was nothing left for us to do but to take them all, and to educate the Filipinos, and uplift and civilize and Christianize them, and by God's grace do the very best we could by them, as our fellow-men for whom Christ also died. And then I went to bed, and went to sleep, and slept soundly, and the next morning I sent for the chief engineer of the War Department (our map-maker), and I told him to put the Philippines on the map of the United States (pointing to a large map on the wall of his office), and there they are, and there they will stay while I am President!

From "Aguinaldo's Case against the United States" (1899)

Emilio Aguinaldo, who led the Filipino armed struggle for independence against Spain and then another war against the United States when President McKinley decided to annex the Philippines, explained his reasons for opposing American imperialism in an article in the widely read magazine, the *North American Review*. He contrasted American traditions of self-government with the refusal to grant this right to the Philippines.

We Filipinos have all along believed that if the American nation at large knew exactly, as we do, what is daily happening in the Philippine Islands, they would rise en masse, and demand that this barbaric war should stop [and] . . . she would cease to be the laughing stock of other civilized nations, as she became when she abandoned her traditions and set up a double standard of government—government by consent in America, government by force in the Philippine Islands. . . .

You have been deceived all along the line. You have been greatly deceived in the personality of my countrymen. You went to the Philippines under the impression that their inhabitants were ignorant savages. . . . We have been represented by your popular press as if we were Africans or Mohawk Indians. . . .

You repeat constantly the dictum that we cannot govern ourselves. . . . With equal reason, you might have said the same thing some fifty or sixty years ago of Japan; and, little over a hundred years ago, it was extremely questionable, when you, also, were rebels against the English Government, if you could govern yourselves. . . . Now, the moral of all this obviously is: Give us the chance; treat us exactly as you demanded to be treated at the hands of England when you rebelled against her autocratic methods.

Now, here is a unique spectacle—the Filipinos fighting for liberty, the American people fighting them to give them liberty. . . . You entered into an alliance with our chiefs at Hong Kong and at Singapore, and you promised us your aid and protection in our attempt to form a government on the principles and after the model of the government of the United States. . . . In combination with our forces, you compelled Spain to surrender. . . . Joy abounded in every heart, and all went well . . . until . . . the Government at Washington . . . commenc[ed] by ignoring all promises that had been made and end[ed] by ignoring the Philippine people, their personality and rights, and treating them as a common enemy. . . . In the face of the world you emblazon humanity and Liberty upon your standard, while you cast your political constitution to the winds and attempt to trample down and exterminate a brave people whose only crime is that they are fighting for their liberty.

QUESTIONS

1. How persuasive is McKinley's account of how and why he decided to annex the Philippines?

2. Why does Aguinaldo think that the United States is betraying its own values?

3. How do these documents reflect different definitions of liberty in the wake of the Spanish-American War?

harbors, brought in American schoolteachers and public health officials, and sought to modernize agriculture (although efforts to persuade local farmers to substitute corn for rice ran afoul of Filipino climate and cultural traditions). The United States, said President McKinley, had an obligation to its "little brown brothers." Yet in all the new possessions, American policies tended to serve the interests of land-based local elites—native-born landowners in the Philippines, American sugar planters in Hawaii and Puerto Rico—and such policies bequeathed enduring poverty to the majority of the rural population. Under American rule, Puerto Rico, previously an island of diversified small farmers, became a low-wage plantation economy controlled by absentee corporations. By the 1920s, its residents were among the poorest in the entire Caribbean.

CITIZENS OR SUBJECTS?

American rule also brought with it American racial attitudes. In an 1899 poem, the British writer Rudyard Kipling urged the United States to take up the "white man's burden" of imperialism. American proponents of empire agreed that the domination of non-white peoples by whites formed part of the progress of civilization. Among the soldiers sent to the Philippines to fight Aguinaldo were a number of black regiments. Their letters from the front suggested that American atrocities arose from white troops applying to the Filipino population the same "treatment for colored peoples" practiced at home. "Is America any better than Spain?" wondered George W. Prioleau, a black cavalryman who had fought at San Juan Hill.

America's triumphant entry into the ranks of imperial powers sparked an intense debate over the relationship among political democracy, race, and American citizenship. The American system of government had no provision for permanent colonies. The right of every people to self-government was one of the main principles of the Declaration of Independence. The idea of an "empire of liberty" assumed that new territories would eventually be admitted as equal states and their residents would be American citizens. In the aftermath of the Spanish-American War, however, nationalism, democracy, and American freedom emerged more closely identified than ever with notions of Anglo-Saxon superiority.

Leaders of both parties, while determined to retain the new overseas possessions, feared that people of what one congressman called "an alien race and foreign tongue" could not be incorporated into the Union. The Foraker Act of 1900 declared Puerto Rico an "insular territory," different from previous territories in the West. Its 1 million inhabitants were defined as citizens of Puerto Rico, not the United States, and denied a future path to statehood. Filipinos occupied a similar status. In a series of cases decided between 1901 and 1904 and known collectively as the Insular Cases, the Supreme Court held that the Constitution did not fully apply to the territories recently acquired by the United States—a significant limitation of the scope of American freedom. Congress, the Court

William Howard Taft, the rotund American governor-general of the Philippines, astride a local water buffalo.

Some of the 1,200 Filipinos exhibited at the 1904 Louisiana Purchase Exposition in St. Louis. The federal government displayed the Filipinos in a "native" setting in order to win public support for the annexation of the Philippines.

declared, must recognize the "fundamental" personal rights of residents of the Philippines and Puerto Rico. But otherwise it could govern them as it saw fit for an indefinite period of time. Thus, two principles central to American freedom since the War of Independence—no taxation without representation, and government based on the consent of the governed—were abandoned when it came to the nation's new possessions.

In the twentieth century, the territories acquired in 1898 would follow different paths. Hawaii, which had a sizable population of American missionaries and planters, became a traditional territory. Its population, except for Asian immigrant laborers, became American citizens, and it was admitted as a state in 1959. After nearly a half-century of American rule, the Philippines achieved independence in 1946. Until 1950, the U.S. Navy administered Guam, which remains today an "unincorporated" territory. As for Puerto Rico, it is sometimes called "the world's oldest colony," because ever since the Spanish conquered the island in 1493 it has lacked full self-government. Congress extended American citizenship to Puerto Ricans in 1917. Puerto Rico today remains in a kind of political limbo, poised on the brink of statehood or independence. The island has the status of a commonwealth. It elects its own government but lacks a voice in Congress (and in the election of the U.S. president) and key issues such as defense and environmental policy are controlled by the United States.

DRAWING THE GLOBAL COLOR LINE

Just as American ideas about liberty and self-government had circulated around the world in the Age of Revolution, American racial attitudes had a global impact in the age of empire. The turn of the twentieth century was a time of worldwide concern about immigration, race relations, and the "white man's burden," all of which inspired a global sense of fraternity

School Begins, an *1899 cartoon from Puck, suggests doubts about the project of "civilizing" non-whites in new American possessions. Uncle Sam lectures four unkempt black children, labeled "Philippines," "Hawaii," "Porto Rico," and "Cuba," while neatly dressed pupils representing various states study quietly. In the background, an American Indian holds a book upside down, while a black man washes the window. A Chinese student, apparently hoping for instruction, waits at the door.*

among "Anglo-Saxon" nations. Chinese exclusion in the United States strongly influenced anti-Chinese laws adopted in Canada, and American segregation and disenfranchisement became models for Australia and South Africa as they formed new governments; they read in particular the proceedings of the Mississippi constitutional convention of 1890, which pioneered ways to eliminate black voting rights.

One "lesson" these countries learned from the United States was that the "failure" of Reconstruction demonstrated the impossibility of multiracial democracy. The extremely hostile account of Reconstruction by the British writer James Bryce in his widely read book *The American Commonwealth* (published in London in 1888) circulated around the world. Bryce called African-Americans "children of nature" and insisted that giving them the right to vote had been a terrible mistake, which had produced all kinds of corruption and misgovernment. His book was frequently cited by the founders of the Australian Commonwealth (1901) to justify their "white Australia" policy, which barred the further immigration of Asians. The Union of South Africa, inaugurated in 1911, saw its own policy of racial separation—later known as apartheid—as following in the footsteps of segregation in the United States. South Africa, however, went much further, enacting laws that limited skilled jobs to whites and dividing the country into areas where black Africans could and could not live. Even American proposals that did not become law, such as the literacy test for immigrants vetoed by President Cleveland, influenced measures adopted overseas. The United States, too, learned from other countries. The Gentleman's Agreement that limited Japanese immigration early in the twentieth century (see Chapter 19) followed a similar arrangement between Japan and Canada.

"REPUBLIC OR EMPIRE?"

The emergence of the United States as an imperial power sparked intense debate. Opponents formed the Anti-Imperialist League. It united writers and social reformers who believed American energies should be directed at home, businessmen fearful of the cost of maintaining overseas outposts, and racists who did not wish to bring non-white populations into the United States. Among its prominent members were E. L. Godkin, the editor of *The Nation*, the novelist William Dean Howells, and the labor leader George E. McNeill. The League held meetings throughout the country and published pamphlets called Liberty Tracts, warning that empire was incompatible with democracy. America's historic mission, the League declared, was to "help the world by an example of successful self-government," not to conquer other peoples. A "republic of free men," anti-imperialists proclaimed, should assist the people of Puerto Rico and the Philippines in their own "struggles for liberty," rather than subjecting them to colonial rule.

In 1900, Democrats again nominated William Jennings Bryan to run against McKinley. The Democratic platform opposed the Philippine War for placing the United States in the "un-American" position of "crushing with military force" another people's desire for "liberty and self-government." George S. Boutwell, president of the Anti-Imperialist League, declared that the most pressing question in the election was the nation's future character—"republic or empire?"

But without any sense of contradiction, proponents of an imperial foreign policy also adopted the language of freedom. Anti-imperialists were the real "infidels to the gospel of liberty," claimed Senator Albert Beveridge of Indiana, because America ventured abroad not for material gain or national power, but to bring "a new day of freedom" to the peoples of the world. America's was a "benevolent" imperialism, rooted in a national mission to uplift backward cultures and spread liberty across the globe. Beveridge did not, however, neglect more practical considerations. American trade, he insisted, "henceforth must be with Asia. The Pacific is our ocean.... Where shall we turn for consumers of our surplus? Geography answers the question. China is our natural customer." And the Philippines held the key to "the commercial situation of the entire East." Riding the wave of patriotic sentiment inspired by the war, and with the economy having recovered from the depression of 1893–1897, McKinley in 1900 repeated his 1896 triumph.

At the dawn of the twentieth century, the United States seemed poised to take its place among the world's great powers. Writers at home and overseas confidently predicted that American influence would soon span the globe. In his 1902 book *The New Empire*, Brooks Adams, a grandson of John Quincy Adams, predicted that because of its economic power, the United States would soon "outweigh any single empire, if not all empires combined." Years would pass before this prediction was fulfilled. But in 1900, many features that would mark American life for much of the twentieth century were already apparent. The United States had surpassed Britain, France, and Germany in industrial production. The merger movement of 1897–1904 (discussed in the previous chapter) left broad sections of the economy under the control of giant corporations. The political system had stabilized. The white North and South had achieved reconciliation, while

A Republican campaign poster from the election of 1900 links prosperity at home and benevolent imperialism abroad as achievements of William McKinley's first term in office.

rigid lines of racial exclusion—the segregation of blacks, Chinese exclusion, Indian reservations—limited the boundaries of freedom and citizenship.

Yet the questions central to nineteenth-century debates over freedom—the relationship between political and economic liberty, the role of government in creating the conditions of freedom, and the definition of those entitled to enjoy the rights of citizens—had not been permanently answered. Nor had the dilemma of how to reconcile America's role as an empire with traditional ideas of freedom. These were the challenges bequeathed by the nineteenth century to the first generation of the twentieth.

SUGGESTED READING

BOOKS

Aleinikoff, Alexander. *Semblances of Sovereignty: The Constitution, the State, and American Citizenship* (2002). Includes a careful discussion of the citizenship status of American minorities and residents of overseas possessions.

Blight, David. *Race and Reunion: The Civil War in American Memory* (2001). Examines how a memory of the Civil War that downplayed the issue of slavery played a part in sectional reconciliation and the rise of segregation.

Brands, H. W. *The Reckless Decade: America in the 1890s* (2002). A lively account of the decade.

Factor, Robert L. *The Black Response to America: Men, Ideals, and Organization from Frederick Douglass to the NAACP* (1970). Discusses black social and political thought, including that of Booker T. Washington and his critics.

Goodwyn, Lawrence. *The Populist Moment: A Short History of the Agrarian Revolt in America* (1978). A sympathetic account of the rise and fall of Populism.

Higginbotham, Evelyn. *Righteous Discontent: The Women's Movement in the Black Baptist Church, 1880–1920* (1993). Explains how black women developed ways of exerting their influence in public life even as black men were losing the right to vote.

Kraditor, Aileen S. *The Ideas of the Woman Suffrage Movement, 1890–1920* (1962). A careful examination of various tendencies in the movement for the right to vote for women.

Krause, Paul. *The Battle for Homestead, 1880–1892: Politics, Culture, and Steel* (1992). An account of the era's most celebrated conflict between capital and labor.

LaFeber, Walter. *The New Empire: An Interpretation of American Expansion, 1860–1898* (1963). A classic examination of the forces that led the United States to acquire an overseas empire.

Lake, Marilyn, and Henry Reynolds. *Drawing the Global Color Line* (2008). Traces the global transmission of ideas about white supremacy in the late nineteenth century.

Linn, Brian M. *The Philippine War, 1899–1902* (2000). A detailed history of America's "forgotten war."

McClain, Charles J. *In Search of Equality: The Chinese Struggle against Discrimination in Nineteenth-Century America* (1994). Explores how Chinese-Americans worked to combat the discrimination to which they were subjected and to assert their rights.

McMillen, Neil R. *Dark Journey: Black Mississippians in the Age of Jim Crow* (1989). A powerful account of black life in the segregation era and the boundaries within which it operated.

Perez, Louis A. *The War of 1898: The United States and Cuba in History and Historiography* (1998). Presents the Cuban side of the Spanish-American War, including a detailed discussion of the Cuban movement for independence and how American intervention affected it.

Postel, Charles. *The Populist Vision* (2007). A history of the Populist movement that stresses how it anticipated many public policies of the twentieth century.

Sanders, Elizabeth. *Roots of Reform: Farmers, Workers, and the American State, 1877–1917* (1999). Emphasizes the role of farmers' movements in putting forth many of the proposals associated with political reform in the late nineteenth and early twentieth centuries.

Woodward, C. Vann. *Origins of the New South, 1877–1913* (1951). A classic treatment of the New South, emphasizing how its rulers failed to meet the needs of most southerners, white as well as black.

WEBSITES

1896: The Presidential Campaign: http://projects.vassar.edu/1896/1896home.html

The Chinese in California, 1850–1925: http://lcweb2.loc.gov/ammem/award99/cubhtml/cichome.html

The History of Jim Crow: www.jimcrowhistory.org

The World of 1898: The Spanish-American War: www.loc.gov/rr/hispanic/1898

REVIEW QUESTIONS

1. What economic issues gave rise to the Populist Party, and what political and economic changes did the party advocate?

2. How did employers use state and federal forces to protect their own economic interests, and what were the results?

3. Why is the election of 1896 called the first modern presidential election?

4. Who were the Redeemers, and how did they change society and politics in the New South?

5. Using political, economic, and social examples, explain how the freedoms of Southern blacks were reduced after 1877.

6. How does the politics of memory, focusing on the Civil War and Reconstruction, demonstrate how whites removed blacks from a significant role in U.S. history?

7. What ideas and interests motivated the United States to create an empire in the late nineteenth century?

8. Compare the arguments for and against U.S. imperialism. Be sure to consider the views of President McKinley and Emilio Aguinaldo.

9. Explain the impact of American racial attitudes and practices on other nations during the age of empire.

FREEDOM QUESTIONS

1. Describe the debate sparked by the Spanish-American War over the relationships between political democracy, race, citizenship, and freedom.

2. Since the Age of Jackson, the meanings of freedom included economic independence and democratic self-government. Why did workers, farmers, and women feel excluded from these freedoms between 1877 and 1900?

3. Explain Eugene V. Debs's argument that the government was being used to deprive workers of their birthright of freedom.

4. How did political leaders and the courts justify the erosion of black rights in the name of freedom?

5. What restrictions were placed on the freedoms of post–Civil War immigrants, and how were these limitations justified?

KEY TERMS

agricultural expansion and decline (pp. 679–680)

the People's Party (p. 680)

Coxey's Army (p. 684)

"free coinage" of silver (p. 686)

Kansas Exodus (p. 690)

elimination of black voting (p. 692)

Civil Rights Cases (p. 694)

Plessy v. Ferguson (p. 694)

"separate but equal" (p. 694)

lynching (p. 695)

politics of memory (p. 696)

Immigration Restriction League (p. 698)

Yick Wo v. Hopkins (p. 699)

United States v. Wong Kim Ark (p. 699)

Fong Yue Ting (p. 700)

Alfred T. Mahan (p. 704)

U.S.S. *Maine* (p. 706)

Platt Amendment (p. 708)

Emilio Aguinaldo (p. 710)

Foraker Act (p. 714)

Anti-Imperialist League (p. 717)

REVIEW TABLE

Facing the Limits of Freedom

Group Affected	Challenge Faced	Response	Explanation
Family farmers	Low crop prices, high costs, loss of family farms	Farmers Alliance, Populist Party	Advocated federal government restore democracy and economic opportunity for all
Blacks	Jim Crow laws; lynching	Booker T. Washington's "Atlanta Compromise"	Advocated a policy of accommodation and vocational education
Labor	Viewed as radical	Samuel Gompers's "business unionism"	Concentrated on wages, hours, not social reform
Women	Denied the right to vote	Organizations like the Women's Christian Temperance Union	Allowed women to exert more influence on public affairs
Chinese	1882 Chinese Exclusion Act	*United States v. Wong Kim Ark*	Decision held that the Fourteenth Amendment awarded citizenship to American-born children of Chinese immigrants
Filipinos	Controlled and denied rights by colonial powers	Wars against Spain and the United States	Wanted independence from foreign powers

CHAPTER 18

The Progressive Era, 1900–1916

A rare color photograph from around 1900 shows the teeming street life of Mulberry Street, on New York City's densely populated Lower East Side. The massive immigration of the early twentieth century transformed the life of urban centers throughout the country and helped to spark the Progressive movement.

FOCUS QUESTIONS

• Why was the city such a central element in Progressive America?

• How did the labor and women's movements challenge the nineteenth-century meanings of American freedom?

• In what ways did Progressivism include both democratic and anti-democratic impulses?

• How did the Progressive presidents foster the rise of the nation-state?

It was late afternoon on March 25, 1911, when fire broke out at the Triangle Shirtwaist Company. The factory occupied the top three floors of a ten-story building in the Greenwich Village neighborhood of New York City. Here some 500 workers, mostly young Jewish and Italian immigrant women, toiled at sewing machines producing ladies' blouses, some earning as little as three dollars per week. Those who tried to escape the blaze discovered that the doors to the stairwell had been locked—the owners' way, it was later charged, of discouraging theft and unauthorized bathroom breaks. The fire department rushed to the scene with high-pressure hoses. But their ladders reached only to the sixth floor. As the fire raged, onlookers watched in horror as girls leapt from the upper stories. By the time the blaze had been put out, 46 bodies lay on the street and 100 more were found inside the building.

The Triangle Shirtwaist Company was typical of manufacturing in the nation's largest city, a beehive of industrial production in small, crowded factories. New York was home to 30,000 manufacturing establishments with more than 600,000 employees—more industrial workers than the entire state of Massachusetts. Triangle had already played a key role in the era's labor history. When 200 of its workers tried to join the International Ladies' Garment Workers Union (ILGWU), the owners responded by firing them. This incident helped to spark a general walkout of female garment workers in 1909—the Uprising of the 20,000. Among the strikers' demands was better safety in clothing factories. The impoverished immigrants forged an alliance with middle- and upper-class female supporters, including members of the Women's Trade Union League, which had been founded in 1903 to help bring women workers into unions. Alva Belmont, the ex-wife of railroad magnate William Vanderbilt, contributed several of her cars to a parade in support of the striking workers. By the time the walkout ended early in 1911, the ILGWU had won union contracts with more than 300 firms. But the Triangle Shirtwaist Company was not among them.

The Triangle fire was not the worst fire disaster in American history (seven years earlier, over 1,000 people had died in a blaze on the *General Slocum* excursion boat in New York Harbor). But it had an unrivaled impact on public consciousness. More than twenty years later, Franklin D. Roosevelt would refer to it in a press conference as an example of why the government needed to regulate industry. In its wake, efforts to organize the city's workers accelerated, and the state legislature passed new factory inspection laws and fire safety codes.

Triangle focused attention on the social divisions that plagued American society during the first two decades of the twentieth century, a period known as the Progressive era. These were years when economic expansion produced millions of new jobs and brought an unprecedented array of goods within reach of American consumers. Cities expanded rapidly—by 1920, for the first time, more Americans lived in towns and

Policemen stare up as the Triangle fire of 1911 rages, while the bodies of factory workers who plunged to their deaths to escape the blaze lie on the sidewalk.

cities than in rural areas. Yet severe inequality remained the most visible feature of the urban landscape, and persistent labor strife raised anew the question of government's role in combating social inequality. The fire and its aftermath also highlighted how traditional gender roles were changing as women took on new responsibilities in the workplace and in the making of public policy.

The word "Progressive" came into common use around 1910 as a way of describing a broad, loosely defined political movement of individuals and groups who hoped to bring about significant change in American social and political life. Progressives included forward-looking businessmen who realized that workers must be accorded a voice in economic decision making, and labor activists bent on empowering industrial workers. Other major contributors to Progressivism were members of female reform organizations who hoped to protect women and children from exploitation, social scientists who believed that academic research would help to solve social problems, and members of an anxious middle class who feared that their status was threatened by the rise of big business.

Everywhere in early-twentieth-century America the signs of economic and political consolidation were apparent—in the power of a small directorate of Wall Street bankers and corporate executives, the manipulation of democracy by corrupt political machines, and the rise of new systems of managerial control in workplaces. In these circumstances, wrote Benjamin P. DeWitt, in his 1915 book *The Progressive Movement*, "the individual could not hope to compete . . . . Slowly, Americans realized that they were not free."

As this and the following chapter will discuss, Progressive reformers responded to the perception of declining freedom in varied, contradictory ways. The era saw the expansion of political and economic freedom

City of Ambition, 1910, by the photographer Alfred Stieglitz, captures the stark beauty of New York City's new skyscrapers.

through the reinvigoration of the movement for woman suffrage, the use of political power to expand workers' rights, and efforts to improve democratic government by weakening the power of city bosses and giving ordinary citizens more influence on legislation. It witnessed the flowering of understandings of freedom based on individual fulfillment and personal self-determination—the ability to participate fully in the ever-expanding consumer marketplace and, especially for women, to enjoy economic and sexual freedoms long considered the province of men. At the same time, many Progressives supported efforts to limit the full enjoyment of freedom to those deemed fit to exercise it properly. The new system of white supremacy born in the 1890s became fully consolidated in the South. Growing numbers of native-born Americans demanded that immigrants abandon their traditional cultures and become fully "Americanized." And efforts were made at the local and national levels to place political decision making in the hands of experts who did not have to answer to the electorate. Even as the idea of freedom expanded, freedom's boundaries contracted in Progressive America.

AN URBAN AGE AND A CONSUMER SOCIETY

FARMS AND CITIES

The Progressive era was a period of explosive economic growth, fueled by increasing industrial production, a rapid rise in population, and the continued expansion of the consumer marketplace. In the first decade of the twentieth century, the economy's total output rose by about 85 percent. For the last time in American history, farms and cities grew together. As farm prices recovered from their low point during the depression of the 1890s, American agriculture entered what would later be remembered as its "golden age." The expansion of urban areas stimulated demand for farm goods. Farm families poured into the western Great Plains. More than 1 million claims for free government land were filed under the Homestead Act of 1862—more than in the previous forty years combined. Between 1900 and 1910, the combined population of Texas and Oklahoma rose by nearly 2 million people, and Kansas, Nebraska, and the Dakotas added 800,000. Irrigation transformed the Imperial Valley of California and parts of Arizona into major areas of commercial farming.

But it was the city that became the focus of Progressive politics and of a new mass-consumer society. Throughout the industrialized world, the number of great cities multiplied. The United States counted twenty-one cities whose population exceeded

	Table 18.1 RISE OF THE CITY, 1880–1920	
Year	Urban Population (percentage)	Number of Cities with 100,000+ Population
1880	20%	12
1890	28	15
1900	38	18
1910	50	21
1920	68	26

100,000 in 1910, the largest of them New York, with 4.7 million residents. The twenty-three square miles of Manhattan Island were home to over 2 million people, more than lived in thirty-three of the states. Fully a quarter of them inhabited the Lower East Side, an immigrant neighborhood more densely populated than Bombay or Calcutta in India.

The stark urban inequalities of the 1890s continued into the Progressive era. Immigrant families in New York's downtown tenements often had no electricity or indoor toilets. Three miles to the north stood the mansions of Fifth Avenue's Millionaire's Row. According to one estimate, J. P. Morgan's financial firm directly or indirectly controlled 40 percent of all financial and industrial capital in the United States. Alongside such wealth, reported the Commission on Industrial Relations, established by Congress in 1912, more than one-third of the country's mining and manufacturing workers lived in "actual poverty."

The city captured the imagination of artists, writers, and reformers. The glories of the American landscape had been the focal point of nineteenth-century painters (exemplified by the Hudson River school, which produced canvases celebrating the wonders of nature). The city and its daily life now

The mansion of Cornelius Vanderbilt II on New York City's Fifth Avenue, in a 1920 photograph. Designed in the style of a French château, it took up the entire block. Today, the Bergdorf Goodman department store occupies the site.

Six O'Clock, Winter, a 1912 painting by John Sloan, depicts a busy city street with an elevated railroad overhead. Sloan was one of a group of painters dubbed the Ashcan School because of their focus on everyday city life.

became their preoccupation. Painters like George W. Bellows and John Sloan and photographers such as Alfred Stieglitz and Edward Steichen captured the electric lights, crowded bars and theaters, and soaring skyscrapers of the urban landscape. With its youthful, exuberant energies, the city seemed an expression of modernity itself.

THE MUCKRAKERS

Others saw the city as a place where corporate greed undermined traditional American values. At a time when more than 2 million children under the age of fifteen worked for wages, Lewis Hine photographed child laborers to draw attention to persistent social inequality. A new generation of journalists writing for mass-circulation national magazines exposed the ills of industrial and urban life. *The Shame of the Cities* by Lincoln Steffens (published as a series in *McClure's Magazine* in 1901–1902 and in book form in 1904) showed how party bosses and business leaders profited from political corruption. *McClure's* also hired Ida Tarbell to expose the arrogance and economic machinations of John D. Rockefeller's Standard Oil Company. Published in two volumes in 1904, her *History of the Standard Oil Company* was the most substantial product of what Theodore Roosevelt disparaged as "muckraking"—the use of journalistic skills to expose the underside of American life.

Major novelists of the era took a similar unsparing approach to social ills. Theodore Dreiser's *Sister Carrie* (1900) traced a hopeful young woman's descent into prostitution in Chicago's harsh urban environment. Perhaps the era's most influential novel was Upton Sinclair's *The Jungle* (1906), whose description of unsanitary slaughterhouses and the sale of rotten meat stirred public outrage and led directly to the passage of the Pure Food and Drug Act and the Meat Inspection Act of 1906.

IMMIGRATION AS A GLOBAL PROCESS

If one thing characterized early-twentieth-century cities, it was their immigrant character. The "new immigration" from southern and eastern Europe

Two photographs by Lewis Hine, who used his camera to chronicle the plight of child laborers: a young spinner in a southern cotton factory and "breaker" boys who worked in a Pennsylvania coal mine.

(discussed in Chapter 17) had begun around 1890 but reached its peak during the Progressive era. Between 1901 and the outbreak of World War I in Europe in 1914, some 13 million immigrants came to the United States, the majority from Italy, Russia, and the Austro-Hungarian empire. In fact, Progressive-era immigration formed part of a larger process of worldwide migration set in motion by industrial expansion and the decline of traditional agriculture. Poles emigrated not only to Pittsburgh and Chicago but to work in German factories and Scottish mines. Italians sought jobs in Belgium, France, and Argentina as well as the United States. As many as 750,000 Chinese migrated to other countries each year.

During the years from 1840 to 1914 (when immigration to the United States would be virtually cut off, first by the outbreak of World War I and then by legislation), perhaps 40 million persons emigrated to the United States and another 20 million to other parts of the Western Hemisphere, including Canada, Argentina, Brazil, and the Caribbean. This population flow formed one part of a massive shifting of peoples throughout the world, much of which took place in Asia. Millions of persons migrated to Southeast Asia and the South Pacific, mainly from India and China. Millions more moved from Russia and northern Asia to Manchuria, Siberia, and Central Asia.

The century between 1815, when the Napoleonic Wars in Europe and the War of 1812 in the United States ended, and the outbreak of World War I in 1914, witnessed a series of massive shifts in the world's population. The 35 million people who crossed the Atlantic to North America formed the largest migration stream, but millions of migrants also moved to South America, eastern Russia, and various parts of Asia.

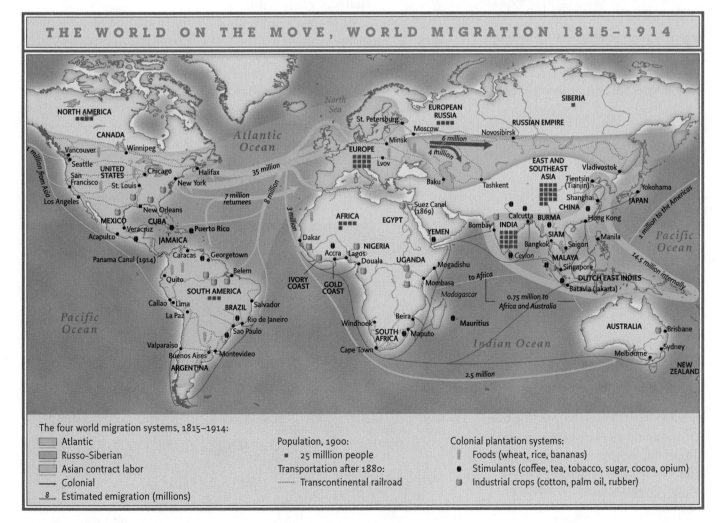

THE WORLD ON THE MOVE, WORLD MIGRATION 1815–1914

The four world migration systems, 1815–1914:
- Atlantic
- Russo-Siberian
- Asian contract labor
- → Colonial
- —8→ Estimated emigration (millions)

Population, 1900:
- ■ 25 milllion people

Transportation after 1880:
- ∙∙∙∙∙ Transcontinental railroad

Colonial plantation systems:
- Foods (wheat, rice, bananas)
- Stimulants (coffee, tea, tobacco, sugar, cocoa, opium)
- Industrial crops (cotton, palm oil, rubber)

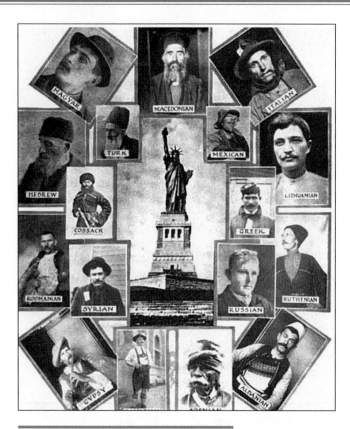

An illustration in the 1912 publication
The New Immigration *depicts the
various "types" entering the United States.*

Numerous causes inspired this massive uprooting of population. Rural southern and eastern Europe and large parts of Asia were regions marked by widespread poverty and illiteracy, burdensome taxation, and declining economies. Political turmoil at home, like the revolution that engulfed Mexico after 1911, also inspired emigration. Not all of these immigrants could be classified as "free laborers," however. Large numbers of Chinese, Mexican, and Italian migrants, including many who came to the United States, were bound to long-term labor contracts. These contracts were signed with labor agents, who then provided the workers to American employers. But all the areas attracting immigrants were frontiers of one kind or another—agricultural, mining, or industrial—with expanding job opportunities.

Most European immigrants to the United States entered through Ellis Island. Located in New York Harbor, this became in 1892 the nation's main facility for processing immigrants. Millions of Americans today trace their ancestry to an immigrant who passed through Ellis Island. The less fortunate, who failed a medical examination or were judged to be anarchists, prostitutes, or in other ways undesirable, were sent home.

At the same time, an influx of Asian and Mexican newcomers was taking place in the West. After the exclusion of immigrants from China in the late nineteenth century, a small number of Japanese arrived, primarily to work as agricultural laborers in California's fruit and vegetable fields and on Hawaii's sugar plantations. By 1910, the population of Japanese origin had grown to 72,000. Between 1910 and 1940, Angel Island in San Francisco Bay—the "Ellis Island of the West"—served as the main entry point for immigrants from Asia.

Far larger was Mexican immigration. Between 1900 and 1930, some 1 million Mexicans (more than 10 percent of that country's population)

Italian Family on Ferry Boat, Leaving
Ellis Island, *a 1905 photograph by Lewis
Hine. The family of immigrants has just
passed through the inspection process at
the gateway to the United States.*

entered the United States—a number exceeded by only a few European countries. Many Mexicans entered through El Paso, Texas, the main southern gateway into the United States. Many ended up in the San Gabriel Valley of California, where citrus growers searching for cheap labor had earlier experimented with Native American, South Asian, Chinese, and Filipino migrant workers.

By 1910, one-seventh of the American population was foreign-born, the highest percentage in the country's history. More than 40 percent of New York City's population had been born abroad. In Chicago and smaller industrial cities like Providence, Milwaukee, and San Francisco, the figure exceeded 30 percent. Although many newcomers moved west to take part in the expansion of farming, most clustered in industrial centers. By 1910, nearly three-fifths of the workers in the twenty leading manufacturing and mining industries were foreign-born.

THE IMMIGRANT QUEST FOR FREEDOM

Like their nineteenth-century predecessors, the new immigrants arrived imagining the United States as a land of freedom, where all persons enjoyed equality before the law, could worship as they pleased, enjoyed economic opportunity, and had been emancipated from the oppressive social hierarchies of their homelands. "America is a free country," one Polish immigrant wrote home. "You don't have to be a serf to anyone." Agents sent abroad by the American government to investigate the reasons for large-scale immigration reported that the main impetus was a desire to share in the "freedom and prosperity enjoyed by the people of the United States." Freedom, they added, was largely an economic ambition—a desire to escape from "hopeless poverty" and achieve a standard of living impossible at home. While some of the new immigrants, especially Jews fleeing religious persecution in the Russian empire, thought of themselves as permanent emigrants, the majority initially planned to earn enough money to return home and purchase land. Groups like Mexicans and Italians included many "birds of passage," who remained only temporarily in the United States. In 1908, a year of economic downturn in the United States, more Italians left the country than entered.

The new immigrants clustered in close-knit "ethnic" neighborhoods with their own shops, theaters, and community organizations, and often continued to speak their native tongues. As early as 1900, more than 1,000 foreign-language newspapers were published in the United

Table 18.2 IMMIGRANTS AND THEIR CHILDREN AS PERCENTAGE OF POPULATION, TEN MAJOR CITIES, 1920	
City	*Percentage*
New York City	76%
Cleveland	72
Boston	72
Chicago	71
Detroit	65
San Francisco	64
Minneapolis	63
Pittsburgh	59
Seattle	55
Los Angeles	45

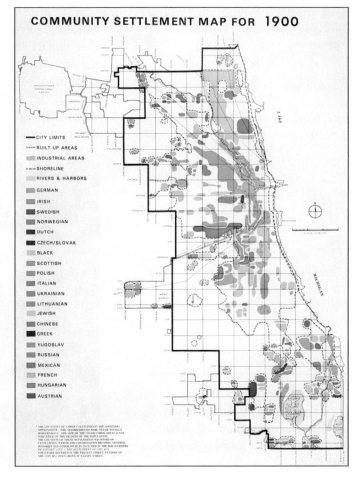

A community settlement map for Chicago in 1900 illustrates the immigrant and racial neighborhoods in the nation's second largest city.

An immigrant from Mexico, arriving around 1912 in a cart drawn by a donkey.

States. Churches were pillars of these immigrant communities. In New York's East Harlem, even anti-clerical Italian immigrants, who resented the close alliance in Italy between the Catholic Church and the oppressive state, participated eagerly in the annual festival of the Madonna of Mt. Carmel. After Italian-Americans scattered to the suburbs, they continued to return each year to reenact the festival.

Although most immigrants earned more than was possible in the impoverished regions from which they came, they endured low wages, long hours, and dangerous working conditions. In the mines and factories of Pennsylvania and the Midwest, eastern European immigrants performed low-wage unskilled labor, while native-born workers dominated skilled and supervisory jobs. The vast majority of Mexican immigrants became poorly paid agricultural, mine, and railroad laborers, with little prospect of upward economic mobility. "My people are not in America," remarked one Slavic priest, "they are under it."

CONSUMER FREEDOM

Cities, however, were also the birthplace of a mass-consumption society that added new meaning to American freedom. There was, of course, nothing unusual in the idea that the promise of American life lay, in part, in the enjoyment by the masses of citizens of goods available in other countries only to the well-to-do. Not until the Progressive era, however, did the advent of large downtown department stores, chain stores in urban neighborhoods, and retail mail-order houses for farmers and small-town resi-

In Hester Street, *painted in 1905, George Luks, a member of the Ashcan School of urban artists, captures the colorful street life of an immigrant neighborhood in New York City.*

VISIONS OF FREEDOM

Movie, 5 Cents. *In this 1907 painting, the artist John Sloan depicts the interior of a movie house. By this time, millions of people each week were flocking to see silent motion pictures. The audience includes different classes and races, as well as couples and women attending alone.*

QUESTIONS

1. What does the nature of the audience suggest about movie theaters as places of a new social freedom?

2. Does the painting help explain why some critics complained that movies promoted immorality?

Women at work in a shoe factory, 1908.

dents make available to consumers throughout the country the vast array of goods now pouring from the nation's factories. By 1910, Americans could purchase, among many other items, electric sewing machines, washing machines, vacuum cleaners, and record players. Low wages, the unequal distribution of income, and the South's persistent poverty limited the consumer economy, which would not fully come into its own until after World War II. But it was in Progressive America that the promise of mass consumption became the foundation for a new understanding of freedom as access to the cornucopia of goods made available by modern capitalism.

Leisure activities also took on the characteristics of mass consumption. Amusement parks, dance halls, and theaters attracted large crowds of city dwellers. The most popular form of mass entertainment at the turn of the century was vaudeville, a live theatrical entertainment consisting of numerous short acts typically including song and dance, comedy, acrobats, magicians, and trained animals. In the 1890s, brief motion pictures were already being introduced into vaudeville shows. As the movies became longer and involved more sophisticated plot narratives, separate theaters developed. By 1910, 25 million Americans per week, mostly working-class urban residents, were attending "nickelodeons"—motion-picture theaters whose five-cent admission charge was far lower than at vaudeville shows.

THE WORKING WOMAN

The new visibility of women in urban public places—at work, as shoppers, and in places of entertainment like cinemas and dance halls—indicated that traditional gender roles were changing dramatically in Progressive America. As the Triangle fire revealed, more and more women were working for wages. Black women still worked primarily as domestics or in southern cotton fields. Immigrant women were largely confined to low-paying factory employment. But for native-born white women, the kinds of jobs available expanded enormously. By 1920, around 25 percent of employed women were office workers or telephone operators, and only 15 percent worked in domestic service, the largest female job category of the nineteenth century. Female work was no longer confined to young, unmarried white women and adult black women. In 1920, of 8 million women working for wages, one-quarter were married and living with their husbands.

Table 18.3 PERCENTAGE OF WOMEN 14 YEARS AND OLDER IN THE LABOR FORCE			
Year	*All Women*	*Married Women*	*Women as % of Labor Force*
1900	20.4%	5.6%	18%
1910	25.2	10.7	24
1920	23.3	9.0	24
1930	24.3	11.7	25

The working woman—immigrant and native, working-class and professional—became a symbol of female emancipation. Women faced special limitations on their economic freedom, including wage discrimination and exclusion from many jobs. Yet almost in spite of themselves, union leader Abraham Bisno remarked, young immigrant working women developed a sense of independence: "They acquired the *right to a personality*," something alien to the highly patriarchal family structures of the old country. "We enjoy our independence and freedom" was the assertive statement of the Bachelor Girls Social Club, a group of female mail-order clerks in New York.

The growing number of younger women who desired a lifelong career, wrote Charlotte Perkins Gilman in her influential book *Women and Economics* (1898), offered evidence of a "spirit of personal independence" that pointed to a coming transformation of both economic and family life. Gilman's writings reinforced the claim that the road to woman's freedom lay through the workplace. In the home, she argued, women experienced not fulfillment but oppression, and the housewife was an unproductive parasite, little more than a servant to her husband and children. By condemning women to a life of domestic drudgery, prevailing gender norms made them incapable of contributing to society or enjoying freedom in any meaningful sense of the word.

The desire to participate in the consumer society produced remarkably similar battles within immigrant families of all nationalities between parents and their self-consciously "free" children, especially daughters. Contemporaries, native and immigrant, noted how "the novelties and frivolities of fashion" appealed to young working women, who spent part of their meager wages on clothing and makeup and at places of entertainment. Daughters considered parents who tried to impose curfews or to prevent them from going out alone to dances or movies as old-fashioned and not sufficiently "American." Immigrant parents found it very difficult to adapt to what one Mexican mother called "this terrible freedom in this United States." "The Mexican girls," she told a sociologist studying immigrant life in Los Angeles, "seeing American girls with freedom, they want it too."

THE RISE OF FORDISM

If any individual exemplified the new consumer society, it was Henry Ford. The son of an immigrant Irish farmer, Ford had worked as an apprentice in Michigan machine shops and later as an engineer for the Edison Illuminating Company. Ford did not invent the automobile, but he developed the techniques of production and marketing that brought it within the reach of ordinary Americans. In 1905, he established the Ford Motor Company, one of dozens of small automobile manufacturing firms that emerged in these years. Three years later, he introduced the Model T, a simple, light vehicle sturdy enough to navigate the country's poorly maintained roads. While early European models like the Mercedes aimed at an elite market and were superior in craftsmanship, Ford concentrated on standardizing output and lowering prices.

In 1913, Ford's factory in Highland Park, Michigan, adopted the method of production known as the moving assembly line, in which car frames were brought to workers on a continuously moving conveyor belt. The process enabled Ford to expand output by greatly reducing the time it took

Table 18.4 PERCENTAGE OF WOMEN WORKERS IN VARIOUS OCCUPATIONS		
Occupation	1900	1920
Professional, technical	8.2%	11.7%
Clerical	4.0	18.7
Sales workers	4.3	6.2
Unskilled and semiskilled manufacturing	23.7	20.2
Household workers	28.7	15.7

The Return from Toil, *a drawing by John Sloan for the radical magazine* The Masses, *pictures working women not as downtrodden but as independent-minded, stylish, and self-confident.*

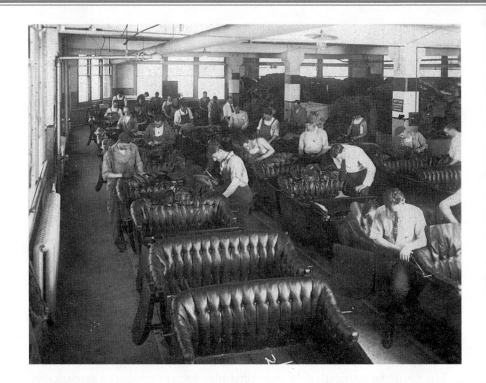

The assembly line at the Ford Motor Company factory in Highland Park, Michigan, around 1915.

to produce each car. In 1914, he raised wages at his factory to the unheard of level of five dollars per day (more than double the pay of most industrial workers), enabling him to attract a steady stream of skilled laborers. Labor conditions in the Ford plant were not as appealing as the wages, however: assembly-line work was monotonous (the worker repeated the same basic motions for the entire day), and Ford used spies and armed detectives to prevent unionization. When other businessmen criticized him for endangering profits by paying high wages, Ford replied that workers must be able to afford the goods being turned out by American factories. Ford's output rose from 34,000 cars, priced at $700 each, in 1910, to 730,000 Model T's that sold at a price of $316 (well within the reach of many workers) in 1916. The economic system based on mass production and mass consumption came to be called Fordism.

THE PROMISE OF ABUNDANCE

As economic production shifted from capital goods (steel, railroad equipment, etc.) to consumer products, the new advertising industry perfected ways of increasing sales, often by linking goods with the idea of freedom. Numerous products took "liberty" as a brand name or used an image of the Statue of Liberty as a sales device. The department-store magnate Edward Filene called consumerism a "school of freedom," since shoppers made individual choices on basic questions of living. Economic abundance would eventually come to define the "American way of life," in which personal fulfillment was to be found through acquiring material goods.

The promise of abundance shifted the quest for freedom to the realm of private life, but it also inspired political activism. Exclusion from the world of mass consumption would come to seem almost as great a denial of the

Table 18.5 SALES OF PASSENGER CARS	
Year	Number of Cars (in thousands)
1900	4.1
1905	24.2
1910	181.0
1915	895.9
1920	1,905.5
1925	3,735.1

One day's output of Model T Fords, in a 1913 photograph. The assembly line made mass production like this possible.

rights of citizenship as being barred from voting once had been. The desire for consumer goods led many workers to join unions and fight for higher wages. The argument that monopolistic corporations artificially raised prices at the expense of consumers became a weapon against the trusts. "Consumers' consciousness," wrote Walter Lippmann, who emerged in these years as one of the nation's most influential social commentators, was growing rapidly, with the "high cost of living" as its rallying cry.

AN AMERICAN STANDARD OF LIVING

The maturation of the consumer economy gave rise to concepts—a "living wage" and an "American standard of living"—that offered a new language for criticizing the inequalities of wealth and power in Progressive America. Father John A. Ryan's influential book *A Living Wage* (1906) described a decent standard of living (one that enabled a person to participate in the consumer economy) as a "natural and absolute" right of citizenship. Ryan had grown up in Minnesota in a family sympathetic to Henry George, the Knights of Labor, and the Populists. His book sought to translate into American terms Pope Leo XIII's powerful statement of 1894, *Rerum Novarum*, which criticized the divorce of economic life from ethical considerations, endorsed the right of workers to organize unions, and repudiated competitive individualism in favor of a more cooperative vision of the good society. Ryan's insistence that economic relationships should be governed by moral standards had a powerful influence on social thought among American Catholics.

The popularity of the idea of an American standard of living reflected, in part, the emergence of a mass-consumption society during the Progressive era. For the first time in the nation's history, mass consumption came to occupy a central place in descriptions of American society and its future. In the

One of the numerous advertisements of the early twentieth century that invoked the Statue of Liberty to market consumer goods, in this case a brand of crackers.

Picturesque America, *a 1909 cartoon by Harry Grant Dart, offers a satirical comment on how advertising was threatening to overwhelm public life. Dart also includes a political comment—"He would rather advertise than be president"—on Senator Robert LaFollette of Wisconsin, pictured at the top right delivering a speech.*

Gilded Age, social theorists like Henry George had wondered why economic progress produced both increased wealth and abject misery. The Progressive generation was strongly influenced by the more optimistic writings of Simon W. Patten, a prophet of prosperity. Patten announced the end of the "reign of want" and the advent of a society of abundance and leisure. In the dawning "new civilization," he proclaimed, Americans would enjoy economic equality in a world in which "every one is independent and free."

VARIETIES OF PROGRESSIVISM

For most Americans, however, Patten's "new civilization" lay far in the future. The more immediate task, in the Progressives' view, was to humanize industrial capitalism and find common ground in a society still racked by labor conflict and experiencing massive immigration from abroad. Some Progressives proposed to return to a competitive marketplace populated by small producers. Others accepted the permanence of the large corporation and looked to the government to reverse the growing concentration of wealth and to ensure social justice. Still others would relocate freedom from the economic and political worlds to a private realm of personal fulfillment and unimpeded self-expression. But nearly all Progressives agreed that freedom must be infused with new meaning to deal with the economic and social conditions of the early twentieth century. The "old democracy," wrote Walter Weyl, associate editor of *The New Republic*, a weekly magazine that became the "bible" of Progressive intellectuals, provided no answer to the problems of a world in which the "chief restrictions upon liberty" were economic, not political.

INDUSTRIAL FREEDOM

In Progressive America, complaints of a loss of freedom came not only from the most poorly paid factory workers but from better-off employees as well. Large firms in the automobile, electrical, steel, and other industries sought to implement greater control over the work process. Efficiency expert Frederick W. Taylor pioneered what he called "scientific management"—a program that sought to streamline production and boost profits by systematically controlling costs and work practices. Through scientific study, the "one best way" of producing goods could be determined and implemented. The role of workers was to obey the detailed instructions of supervisors. Not surprisingly, many skilled workers saw the erosion of their traditional influence over the work process as a loss of freedom. "Men and women," complained Samuel Gompers, whose American Federation of Labor (AFL) represented such skilled workers, "cannot live during working hours under autocratic conditions, and instantly become sons and daughters of freedom as they step outside the shop gates."

The great increase in the number of white-collar workers—the army of salespeople, bookkeepers, salaried professionals, and corporate managers that sprang up with the new system of management—also undermined the experience of personal autonomy. For although they enjoyed far higher social status and incomes than manual workers, many, wrote one commentator, were the kind of individuals who "under former conditions, would have been . . . managing their own businesses," not working for someone else.

These developments helped to place the ideas of "industrial freedom" and "industrial democracy," which had entered the political vocabulary in the Gilded Age, at the center of political discussion during the Progressive era. Lack of "industrial freedom" was widely believed to lie at the root of the much-discussed "labor problem." Since in an industrial age the prospect of managing one's own business seemed increasingly remote, many Progressives believed that the key to increasing industrial freedom lay in empowering workers to participate in economic decision making via strong unions. Louis D. Brandeis, an active ally of the labor movement whom President Woodrow Wilson appointed to the Supreme Court in 1916, maintained that unions embodied an essential principle of freedom—the right of people to govern themselves. The contradiction between "political liberty" and "industrial slavery," Brandeis insisted, was America's foremost social problem. Workers deserved a voice not only in establishing wages and working conditions but also in making such managerial decisions as the relocation of factories, layoffs, and the distribution of profits.

THE SOCIALIST PRESENCE

Economic freedom was also a rallying cry of American socialism, which reached its greatest influence during the Progressive era. Founded in 1901, the Socialist Party brought together surviving late-nineteenth-century radicals such as Populists and followers of Edward Bellamy, with a portion of the labor movement. The party called for immediate reforms such as free college education, legislation to improve the condition of laborers, and, as an ultimate goal, democratic control over the economy through public ownership of railroads and factories. It was the task of socialism, said western labor leader John O'Neill, to "gather together the shards of liberty"—the fragments of the American heritage of freedom—scattered by a government controlled by capitalist millionaires.

By 1912, the Socialist Party claimed 150,000 dues-paying members, published hundreds of newspapers, enjoyed substantial support in the American Federation of Labor, and had elected scores of local officials. Socialism flourished in diverse communities throughout the country. On the Lower East Side of New York City, it arose from the economic exploitation of immigrant workers and Judaism's tradition of social reform. Here, a vibrant socialist culture developed, complete with Yiddish-language newspapers and theaters, as well as large public meetings and street demonstrations. In 1914, the district elected socialist Meyer London to Congress. Another center of socialist strength was Milwaukee, where Victor Berger, a German-born teacher and newspaper editor, mobilized local AFL unions into a potent political force that elected Emil Seidel mayor in 1910. Seidel's administration provided aid to the unemployed, forced the police to recognize the rights of strikers, and won the respect of middle-class residents for its honesty and freedom from machine domination. Socialism also made

Roller skaters with socialist leaflets during a New York City strike in 1916. A "scab" is a worker who crosses the picket line during a strike.

VOICES OF FREEDOM

FROM CHARLOTTE PERKINS GILMAN, Women and Economics (1898)

Women and Economics, by the prolific feminist social critic and novelist Charlotte Perkins Gilman, influenced the new generation of women aspiring to greater independence. It insisted that how people earned a living shaped their entire lives, and that therefore women must free themselves from the home to achieve genuine freedom.

It is not motherhood that keeps the housewife on her feet from dawn till dark; it is house service, not child service. Women work longer and harder than most men. . . . A truer spirit is the increasing desire of young girls to be independent, to have a career of their own, at least for a while, and the growing objection of countless wives to the pitiful asking for money, to the beggary of their position. More and more do fathers give their daughters, and husbands their wives, a definite allowance,—a separate bank account,—something . . . all their own.

The spirit of personal independence in the women of today is sure proof that a change has come . . . . The radical change in the economic position of women is advancing upon us. . . . The growing individualization of democratic life brings inevitable change to our daughters as well as to our sons. . . . One of its most noticeable features is the demand in women not only for their own money, but for their own work for the sake of personal expression. Few girls today fail to manifest some signs of this desire for individual expression. . . .

Economic independence for women necessarily involves a change in the home and family relation. But, if that change is for the advantage of individual and race, we need not fear it. It does not involve a change in the marriage relation except in withdrawing the element of economic dependence, nor in the relation of mother to child save to improve it. But it does involve the exercise of human faculty in women, in social service and exchange rather than in domestic service solely. . . . [Today], when our still developing social needs call for an ever-increasing . . . freedom, the woman in marrying becomes the house-servant, or at least the housekeeper, of the man. . . . When women stand free as economic agents, they will [achieve a] much better fulfilment of their duties as wives and mothers and [contribute] to the vast improvement in health and happiness of the human race.

From John Mitchell, "The Workingman's Conception of Industrial Liberty" (1910)

During the Progressive era, the idea of "industrial liberty" moved to the center of political discussion. Progressive reformers and labor leaders like John Mitchell, head of the United Mine Workers, condemned the prevailing idea of liberty of contract in favor of a broader definition of economic freedom.

While the Declaration of Independence established civil and political liberty, it did not, as you all know, establish industrial liberty.... Liberty means more than the right to choose the field of one's employment. He is not a free man whose family must buy food today with the money that is earned tomorrow. He is not really free who is forced to work unduly long hours and for wages so low that he can not provide the necessities of life for himself and his family; who must live in a crowded tenement and see his children go to work in the mills, the mines, and the factories before their bodies are developed and their minds trained. To have freedom a man must be free from the harrowing fear of hunger and want; he must be in such a position that by the exercise of reasonable frugality he can provide his family with all of the necessities and the reasonable comforts of life. He must be able to educate his children and to provide against sickness, accident, and old age....

A number of years ago the legislatures of several coal producing States enacted laws requiring employers to pay the wages of their workmen in lawful money of the United States and to cease the practice of paying wages in merchandise. From time immemorial it had been the custom of coal companies to conduct general supply stores, and the workingmen were required, as a condition of employment, to accept products in lieu of money in return for services rendered. This system was a great hardship to the workmen.... The question of the constitutionality of this legislation was carried into the courts and by the highest tribunal it was declared to be an invasion of the workman's liberty to deny him the right to accept merchandise in lieu of money as payment of his wages.... [This is] typical of hundreds of instances in which laws that have been enacted for the protection of the workingmen have been declared by the courts to be unconstitutional, on the grounds that they invaded the liberty of the working people.... Is it not natural that the workingmen should feel that they are being guaranteed the liberties they do not want and denied the liberty that is of real value to them? May they not exclaim, with Madame Roland [of the French Revolution], "O Liberty! Liberty! How many crimes are committed in thy name!"

QUESTIONS

1. What does Gilman see as the main obstacles to freedom for women?

2. What does Mitchell believe will be necessary to establish "industrial liberty"?

3. How do the authors differ in their view of the relationship of the family to individual freedom?

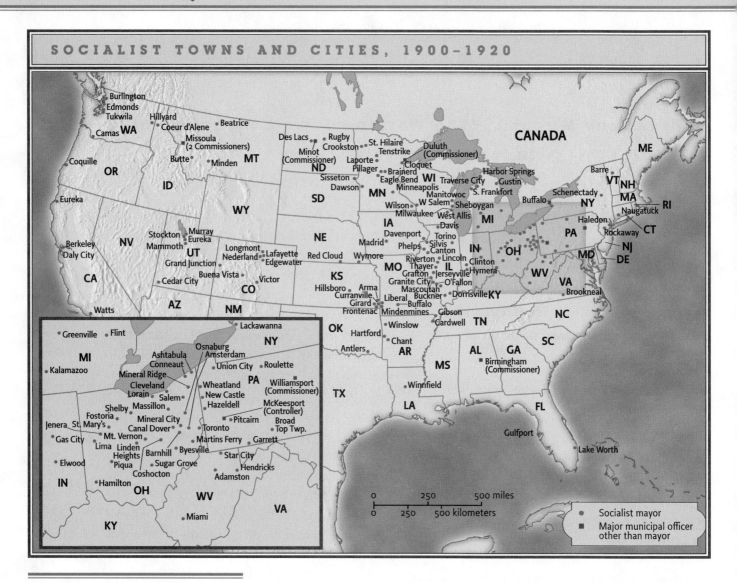

SOCIALIST TOWNS AND CITIES, 1900–1920

Although the Socialist Party never won more than 6 percent of the vote nationally, it gained control of numerous small and medium-sized cities between 1900 and 1920.

inroads among tenant farmers in old Populist areas like Oklahoma, and in the mining regions of Idaho and Montana.

THE GOSPEL OF DEBS

No one was more important in spreading the socialist gospel or linking it to ideals of equality, self-government, and freedom than Eugene V. Debs, the railroad union leader who, as noted in the previous chapter, had been jailed during the Pullman Strike of 1894. For two decades, Debs criss-crossed the country preaching that control of the economy by a democratic government held out the hope of uniting "political equality and economic freedom." As a champion of the downtrodden, Debs managed to bridge the cultural divide among New York's Jewish immigrants, prairie socialists of the West, and native-born intellectuals attracted to the socialist ideal. "While there is a lower class," proclaimed Debs, "I am in it, . . . while there is a soul in prison, I am not free."

Throughout the Atlantic world of the early twentieth century, socialism was a rising presence. Debs would receive more than 900,000 votes for president (6 percent of the total) in 1912. In that year, the socialist *Appeal to Reason*, published in Girard, Kansas, with a circulation of 700,000, was the largest weekly newspaper in the country, and socialist Max Hayes polled one-third of the vote when he challenged Samuel Gompers for the presidency of the AFL. In western Europe, socialism experienced even more pronounced growth. In the last elections before the outbreak of World War I in 1914, socialists in France, Germany, and Scandinavia won between one-sixth and one-third of the vote. "Socialism is coming," declared the *Appeal to Reason*. "It is coming like a prairie fire and nothing can stop it."

One Big Union, *the emblem of the Industrial Workers of the World.*

AFL AND IWW

Socialism was only one example of widespread discontent in Progressive America. The labor strife of the Gilded Age continued into the early twentieth century. Having survived the depression of the 1890s, the American Federation of Labor saw its membership triple to 1.6 million between 1900 and 1904. At the same time, it sought to forge closer ties with forward-looking corporate leaders willing to deal with unions as a way to stabilize employee relations. AFL president Gompers joined with George Perkins of the J. P. Morgan financial empire and Mark Hanna, who had engineered McKinley's election, in the National Civic Federation, which accepted the right of collective bargaining for "responsible" unions. It helped to settle hundreds of industrial disputes and encouraged improvements in factory safety and the establishment of pension plans for long-term workers. Most employers nonetheless continued to view unions as an intolerable interference with their authority, and resisted them stubbornly.

The AFL mainly represented the most privileged American workers—skilled industrial and craft laborers, nearly all of them white, male, and native-born. In 1905, a group of unionists who rejected the AFL's exclusionary policies formed the Industrial Workers of the World (IWW). Part trade union, part advocate of a workers' revolution that would seize the means of production and abolish the state, the IWW made solidarity its guiding principle, extending "a fraternal hand to every wage-worker, no matter what his religion, fatherland, or trade." The organization sought to mobilize those excluded from the AFL—the immigrant factory-labor force, migrant timber and agricultural workers, women, blacks, and even the despised Chinese on the West Coast. The IWW's most prominent leader was William "Big Bill" Haywood, who had worked in western mines as a youth. Dubbed by critics "the most dangerous man in America," Haywood became a national figure in 1906 when he was kidnapped and spirited off to Idaho, accused of instigating the murder of a former anti-union governor. Defended by labor lawyer Clarence Darrow, Haywood was found not guilty.

THE NEW IMMIGRANTS ON STRIKE

The Uprising of the 20,000 in New York's garment industry, mentioned earlier, was one of a series of mass strikes among immigrant workers that placed labor's demand for the right to bargain collectively at the forefront

Striking New York City garment workers carrying signs in multiple languages, 1913.

of the reform agenda. These strikes demonstrated that while ethnic divisions among workers impeded labor solidarity, ethnic cohesiveness could also be a basis of unity, so long as strikes were organized on a democratic basis. The IWW did not originate these confrontations but was sometimes called in by local unionists to solidify the strikers. IWW organizers printed leaflets, posters, and banners in multiple languages and insisted that each nationality enjoy representation on the committee coordinating a walkout. It drew on the sense of solidarity within immigrant communities to persuade local religious leaders, shopkeepers, and officeholders to support the strikes.

The labor conflict that had the greatest impact on public consciousness took place in Lawrence, Massachusetts. The city's huge woolen mills employed 32,000 men, women, and children representing twenty-five nationalities. They worked six days per week and earned an average of sixteen cents per hour. When the state legislature in January 1912 enacted a fifty-four-hour limit to the workweek, employers reduced the weekly take-home pay of those who had been laboring longer hours. Workers spontaneously went on strike, and called on the IWW for assistance.

In February, Haywood and a group of women strikers devised the idea of sending strikers' children out of the city for the duration of the walkout. Socialist families in New York City agreed to take them in. The sight of the children, many of whom appeared pale and half-starved, marching up Fifth Avenue from the train station led to a wave of sympathy for the strikers. "I have worked in the slums of New York," wrote one observer, "but I have never found children who were so uniformly ill-nourished, ill-fed, and ill-clothed." A few days later, city officials ordered that no more youngsters could leave Lawrence. When a group of mothers and children gathered at the railroad station in defiance of the order, club-wielding police drove them away, producing outraged headlines around the world. The governor of Massachusetts soon intervened, and the strike was settled on the workers' terms. A banner carried by the Lawrence strikers gave a new slogan to the labor movement: "We want bread and roses, too"—a declaration that workers sought not only higher wages but the opportunity to enjoy the finer things of life.

Another highly publicized labor uprising took place in New Orleans, where a 1907 strike of 10,000 black and white dockworkers prevented employers' efforts to eliminate their unions and reduce their wages. This was a remarkable expression of interracial solidarity at a time when segregation had become the norm throughout the South. Other strikes proved less successful. A six-month walkout of 25,000 silk workers in Paterson, New Jersey, in 1913 failed despite publicity generated by the Paterson pageant, in which the strikers reenacted highlights of their struggle before a sympathetic audience at New York's Madison Square Garden.

A strike against the Rockefeller-owned Colorado Fuel and Iron Company was also unsuccessful. Mostly recent immigrants from Europe and Mexico, the strikers demanded recognition of the United Mine Workers of America, wage increases, an eight-hour workday, and the right to shop and live in places not owned by the company. When the walkout began, in September 1913, the mine owners evicted 11,000 strikers and their families from company housing. They moved into tent colonies, which armed militia units soon surrounded. On April 20, 1914, the militia attacked the largest tent city, at Ludlow, and burned it to the ground, killing an estimated twenty to thirty men, women, and children. Seven months after the Ludlow Massacre, the strike was called off.

LABOR AND CIVIL LIBERTIES

The fiery organizer Mary "Mother" Jones, who at the age of eighty-three had been jailed after addressing the Colorado strikers, later told a New York audience that the union "had only the Constitution; the other side had the bayonets." Yet the struggle of workers for the right to strike and of labor radicals against restraints on open-air speaking made free speech a significant public issue in the early twentieth century. By and large, the courts rejected their claims. But these battles laid the foundation for the rise of civil liberties as a central component of freedom in twentieth-century America.

State courts in the Progressive era regularly issued injunctions prohibiting strikers from speaking, picketing, or distributing literature during labor disputes. Like the abolitionists before them, the labor movement, in the name of freedom, demanded the right to assemble, organize, and spread their views. The investigations of the Commission on Industrial Relations revealed the absence of free speech in many factory communities, with labor organizers prohibited from speaking freely under threat of either violence from private police or suppression by local authorities. "I don't think we live in a free country or enjoy civil liberties," Clarence Darrow told the commission.

The IWW's battle for civil liberties breathed new meaning into the idea of freedom of expression. Lacking union halls, its organizers relied on songs, street theater, impromptu organizing meetings, and street corner gatherings to spread their message and attract support. In response to IWW activities, officials in Los Angeles, Spokane, Denver, and more than a dozen other cities limited or prohibited outdoor meetings. To arouse popular support, the IWW filled the jails with members who defied local law by speaking in public. Sometimes, prisoners

The New York shirtwaist strike of 1909 inspired workers in other cities. Here women in Rochester, New York, boldly hold aloft a strike banner.

A sheet music cover, with a modern woman erasing the word "obey" from marriage vows.

Isadora Duncan brought a new freedom to an old art form.

were brutally treated, as in Spokane, where three died and hundreds were hospitalized after being jailed for violating a local law requiring prior approval of the content of public speeches. In nearly all the free-speech fights, however, the IWW eventually forced local officials to give way. "Whether they agree or disagree with its methods or aims," wrote one journalist, "all lovers of liberty everywhere owe a debt to this organization for . . . [keeping] alight the fires of freedom."

THE NEW FEMINISM

During the Progressive era, the word "feminism" first entered the political vocabulary. One organization, the Feminist Alliance, constructed apartment houses with communal kitchens, cafeterias, and daycare centers, to free women from the constraints of the home. In 1914, a mass meeting at New York's Cooper Union debated the question "What is Feminism?" The meeting was sponsored by Heterodoxy, a women's club located in Greenwich Village that brought together female professionals, academics, and reformers. Feminism, said one speaker, meant women's emancipation "both as a human being and a sex-being." Feminists' forthright attack on traditional rules of sexual behavior added a new dimension to the discussion of personal freedom.

Heterodoxy was part of a new radical "bohemia" (a social circle of artists, writers, and others who reject conventional rules and practices). Its definition of feminism merged issues like the vote and greater economic opportunities with open discussion of sexuality. In New York's Greenwich Village and counterparts in Chicago, San Francisco, and other cities, a "lyrical left" came into being in the prewar years. Its members formed discussion clubs, attended experimental theaters, and published magazines. They confidently expected to preside over the emancipation of the human spirit from the prejudices of the nineteenth century.

One symbol of the new era was Isadora Duncan, who brought from California a new, expressive dance based on the free movement of a body liberated from the constraints of traditional technique and costume. "I beheld the dance I had always dreamed of," wrote the novelist Edith Wharton on seeing a Duncan performance, "satisfying every sense as a flower does, or a phrase of Mozart's." Another sign of artistic revolution was the Armory Show of 1913, an exhibition that exposed New Yorkers to new cubist paintings from Europe by artists previously unknown in the United States, like Pablo Picasso.

The lyrical left made freedom the key to its vision of society. At the famed salon in heiress Mabel Dodge's New York living room, a remarkable array of talented radicals gathered to discuss with equal passion labor unrest, modern trends in the arts, and sexual liberation. Although many Progressives frequented the Dodge salon, there was a world of difference between the exuberant individualism of the lyrical left and most Progressives' preoccupation with order and efficiency. "What [women] are really after," explained Crystal Eastman, is *freedom*." A graduate of New York University Law School, Eastman had taken a leading role both in the suffrage movement and in investigating industrial accidents. But her definition of freedom went beyond the vote, beyond "industrial democracy," to encompass emotional and sexual self-determination.

THE RISE OF PERSONAL FREEDOM

During the Progressive era, as journalist William M. Reedy jested, it struck "sex o'clock" in America. The founder of psychiatry, Sigmund Freud, lectured at Clark University in Worcester, Massachusetts, in 1909, and discovered that his writings on infantile sexuality, repression, and the irrational sources of human behavior were widely known "even in prudish America." Issues of intimate personal relations previously confined to private discussion blazed forth in popular magazines and public debates.

For the generation of women who adopted the word "feminism" to express their demand for greater liberty, free sexual expression and reproductive choice emerged as critical definitions of women's emancipation. Greenwich Village became a center of sexual experimentation. The aura of tolerance attracted many homosexuals to the area, and although organized demands for gay rights lay far in the future, the gay community became an important element of the Village's lifestyle. But new sexual attitudes spread far beyond bohemia; they flourished among the young, unmarried, self-supporting women who made sexual freedom a hallmark of their oft-proclaimed personal independence.

THE BIRTH-CONTROL MOVEMENT

The growing presence of women in the labor market reinforced demands for access to birth control, an issue that gave political expression to changing sexual behavior. In the nineteenth century, the right to "control one's body" generally meant the ability to refuse sexual advances, including those of a woman's husband. Now, it suggested the ability to enjoy an active sexual life without necessarily bearing children. Emma Goldman, who had emigrated to the United States from Lithuania at the age of sixteen, toured the country lecturing on subjects from anarchism to the need for more enlightened attitudes toward homosexuality. She regularly included the right to birth control in her speeches and distributed pamphlets with detailed information about various contraceptive devices. "I demand freedom for both sexes," she proclaimed, "freedom of action, freedom in love and freedom in motherhood." Goldman constantly ran afoul of the law. By one count, she was arrested more than forty times for dangerous or "obscene" statements or simply to keep her from speaking.

By forthrightly challenging the laws banning contraceptive information and devices, Margaret Sanger, one of eleven children of an Irish-American working-class family, placed the issue of birth control at the heart of the new feminism. In 1911, she began a column on sex education, "What Every Girl Should Know," for *The Call*, a New York socialist newspaper. Postal officials barred one issue, containing a column on venereal disease, from the mails. The next issue of *The Call* included a blank page with the headline: "What Every Girl Should Know—Nothing; by order of the U. S. Post Office."

By 1914, the intrepid Sanger was openly advertising birth-control devices in her own journal, *The Woman Rebel*. "No woman can call herself free," she proclaimed, "who does not own and control her own body [and] can choose consciously whether she will or will not be a mother." In 1916, Sanger opened a clinic in a working-class neighborhood of Brooklyn and began distributing contraceptive devices to poor Jewish and Italian

The much-beloved and much-feared Emma Goldman, with a poster advertising a series of her lectures, illustrating the remarkable variety of topics on which she spoke.

Mothers with baby carriages wait outside Margaret Sanger's birth-control clinic in Brownsville, Brooklyn, 1916.

women, an action for which she was sentenced to a month in prison. Few Progressives rallied to her defense. But for a time, the birth-control issue became a crossroads where the paths of labor radicals, cultural modernists, and feminists intersected. The IWW and Socialist Party distributed Sanger's writings. Like the IWW free-speech fights and Goldman's persistent battle for the right to lecture, Sanger's travail was part of a rich history of dissent in the Progressive era that helped to focus enlightened opinion on the ways local authorities and national obscenity legislation set rigid limits to Americans' freedom of expression.

NATIVE AMERICAN PROGRESSIVISM

Many groups participated in the Progressive impulse. Founded in 1911, the Society of American Indians was a reform organization typical of the era. It brought together Indian intellectuals to promote discussion of the plight of Native Americans in the hope that public exposure would be the first step toward remedying injustice. Because many of the Society's leaders had been educated at government-sponsored boarding schools, the Society united Indians of many tribal backgrounds. It created a pan-Indian public space independent of white control.

Many of these Indian intellectuals were not unsympathetic to the basic goals of federal Indian policy, including the transformation of communal landholdings on reservations into family farms. But Carlos Montezuma, a founder of the Society of American Indians, became an outspoken critic. Born in Arizona, he had been captured as a child by members of a neighboring tribe and sold to a traveling photographer, who brought him to Chicago. There Montezuma attended school and eventually obtained a medical degree.

In 1916, Montezuma established a newsletter, *Wassaja* (meaning "signaling"), that condemned federal paternalism toward the Indians and called for the abolition of the Bureau of Indian Affairs. Convinced that outsiders exerted too much power over life on the reservations, he insisted that self-determination was the only way for Indians to escape poverty and marginalization: "We must free ourselves. . . . We must be independent."

But he also demanded that Indians be granted full citizenship and all the constitutional rights of other Americans. Montezuma's writings had little influence at the time on government policy, but Indian activists would later rediscover him as a forerunner of Indian radicalism.

THE POLITICS OF PROGRESSIVISM

EFFECTIVE FREEDOM

Progressivism was an international movement. In the early twentieth century, cities throughout the world experienced similar social strains arising from rapid industrialization and urban growth. In 1850, London and Paris were the only cities whose population exceeded 1 million. By 1900, there were twelve—New York, Chicago, and Philadelphia in the United States, and others in Europe, Latin America, and Asia. Facing similar social problems, reformers across the globe exchanged ideas and envisioned new social policies. Sun Yat-Sen, the Chinese leader, was influenced by the writings of Henry George and Edward Bellamy. The mayor of Osaka, Japan, called for a new "social economy" that replaced competition with cooperation.

As governments in Britain, France, and Germany instituted old age pensions, minimum wage laws, unemployment insurance, and the regulation of workplace safety, American reformers came to believe they had much to learn from the Old World. The term "social legislation," meaning governmental action to address urban problems and the insecurities of working-class life, originated in Germany but soon entered the political vocabulary of the United States.

Progressives believed that the modern era required a fundamental rethinking of the functions of political authority, whether the aim was to combat the power of the giant corporations, protect consumers, civilize the marketplace, or guarantee industrial freedom at the workplace. Drawing on the reform programs of the Gilded Age and the example of European legislation, Progressives sought to reinvigorate the idea of an activist, socially conscious government. Even in South Carolina, with its strong tradition of belief in local autonomy, Governor Richard I. Manning urged his constituents to modify their view of government as "a threat to individual liberty," to see it instead as "a means for solving the ills of the body politic."

Progressives could reject the traditional assumption that powerful government posed a threat to freedom, because their understanding of freedom was itself in flux. "Effective freedom," wrote the philosopher John Dewey, was far different from the "highly formal and limited concept of liberty" as protection from outside restraint. Freedom was a positive, not a negative, concept—the "power to do specific things." As such, it depended on "the *distribution* of powers that exists at a given time." Thus, freedom inevitably became a political question. "Freedom," wrote Dewey's brilliant young admirer, the writer Randolph Bourne, "means a democratic cooperation in determining the ideals and purposes and industrial and social institutions of a country."

STATE AND LOCAL REFORMS

Throughout the Western world, social legislation proliferated in the early twentieth century. In the United States, with a political structure more decentralized than in European countries, state and local governments

Children at play at the Hudson-Bank Gymnasium, built in 1898 in a New York immigrant neighborhood by the Outdoor Recreation League, one of many Progressive era groups that sought to improve life in urban centers.

enacted most of the era's reform measures. In cities, Progressives worked to reform the structure of government to reduce the power of political bosses, establish public control of "natural monopolies" like gas and water works, and improve public transportation. They raised property taxes in order to spend more money on schools, parks, and other public facilities.

Gilded Age mayors Hazen Pingree and Samuel "Golden Rule" Jones pioneered urban Progressivism. A former factory worker who became a successful shoe manufacturer, Pingree served as mayor of Detroit from 1889 to 1897. He battled the business interests that had dominated city government, forcing gas and telephone companies to lower their rates, and established a municipal power plant. Jones had instituted an eight-hour day and paid vacations at his factory that produced oil drilling equipment. As mayor of Toledo, Ohio, from 1897 to 1905, he founded night schools and free kindergartens, built new parks, and supported the right of workers to unionize.

Since state legislatures defined the powers of city government, urban Progressives often carried their campaigns to the state level. Pingree became governor of Michigan in 1896, in which post he continued his battle against railroads and other corporate interests. Hiram Johnson, who as public prosecutor had secured the conviction for bribery of San Francisco political boss Abraham Ruef, was elected governor of California in 1910. Having promised to "kick the Southern Pacific [Railroad] out of politics," he secured passage of the Public Utilities Act, one of the country's strongest railroad-regulation measures, as well as laws banning child labor and limiting the working hours of women.

The most influential Progressive administration at the state level was that of Robert M. La Follette, who made Wisconsin a "laboratory for democracy." After serving as a Republican member of Congress, La Follette became convinced that an alliance of railroad and lumber companies controlled state politics. Elected governor in 1900, he instituted a series of measures known as the Wisconsin Idea, including nominations of candidates for office through primary elections rather than by political bosses, the taxation of corporate wealth, and state regulation of railroads and public utilities. To staff his administration, he drew on nonpartisan faculty members from the University of Wisconsin.

PROGRESSIVE DEMOCRACY

"We are far from free," wrote Randolph Bourne in 1913, "but the new spirit of democracy is the angel that will free us." Progressives hoped to reinvigorate democracy by restoring political power to the citizenry and civic harmony to a divided society. Alarmed by the upsurge in violent class conflict and the unrestricted power of corporations, they believed that political reforms could help to create a unified "people" devoted to greater democracy and social reconciliation. Yet increasing the responsibilities of government made it all the more important to identify who was entitled to political participation and who was not.

The Progressive era saw a host of changes implemented in the political process, many seemingly contradictory in purpose. The electorate was simultaneously expanded and contracted, empowered and removed from direct influence on many functions of government. Democracy was enhanced by the Seventeenth Amendment—which provided that U.S. senators be chosen by popular vote rather than by state legislatures—by widespread adoption of the popular election of judges, and by the use of primary elections among party members to select candidates for office. Several states, including California under Hiram Johnson, adopted the initiative and referendum (the former allowed voters to propose legislation, the latter to vote directly on it) and the recall, by which officials could be removed from office by popular vote. The era culminated with a constitutional amendment enfranchising women—the largest expansion of democracy in American history.

But the Progressive era also witnessed numerous restrictions on democratic participation, most strikingly the disenfranchisement of blacks in the South, a process, as noted in Chapter 17, supported by many white southern Progressives as a way of ending election fraud. To make city government more honest and efficient, many localities replaced elected mayors with appointed nonpartisan commissions or city managers—a change that insulated officials from machine domination but also from popular control. New literacy tests and residency and registration requirements, common in northern as well as southern states, limited the right to vote among the poor. Taken as a whole, the electoral changes of the Progressive era represented a significant reversal of the idea that voting was an inherent right of American citizenship. And, as will be noted in the next chapter, most white Progressives proved remarkably indifferent to the plight of African-Americans. In the eyes of many Progressives, the "fitness" of voters, not their absolute numbers, defined a functioning democracy.

GOVERNMENT BY EXPERT

"He didn't believe in democracy; he believed simply in government." The writer H. L. Mencken's quip about Theodore Roosevelt came uncomfortably close to the mark for many Progressive advocates of an empowered state. Most Progressive thinkers were highly uncomfortable with the real world of politics, which seemed to revolve around the pursuit of narrow class, ethnic, and regional interests. Robert M. La Follette's reliance on college professors to staff important posts in his administration reflected a larger Progressive faith in expertise. The government could best exercise intelligent control over society through a democracy run by impartial experts who were in many respects unaccountable to the citizenry.

This impulse toward order, efficiency, and centralized management—all in the name of social justice—was an important theme of Progressive reform. The title of Walter Lippmann's influential 1914 work of social commentary, *Drift and Mastery*, posed the stark alternatives facing the nation.

A staff member greets an immigrant family at Hull House, the settlement house established in Chicago by Jane Addams.

"Drift" meant continuing to operate according to the outmoded belief in individual autonomy. "Mastery" required applying scientific inquiry to modern social problems. The new generation of educated professionals, Lippmann believed, could be trusted more fully than ordinary citizens to solve America's deep social problems. Political freedom was less a matter of direct participation in government than of qualified persons devising the best public policies.

JANE ADDAMS AND HULL HOUSE

But alongside this elitist politics, Progressivism also included a more democratic vision of the activist state. As much as any other group, organized women reformers spoke for the more democratic side of Progressivism. Still barred from voting and holding office in most states, women nonetheless became central to the political history of the Progressive era. Women challenged the barriers that excluded them from formal political participation and developed a democratic, grassroots vision of Progressive government. In so doing, they placed on the political agenda new understandings of female freedom. The immediate catalyst was a growing awareness among women reformers of the plight of poor immigrant communities and the emergence of the condition of women and child laborers as a major focus of public concern.

The era's most prominent female reformer was Jane Addams, who had been born in 1860, the daughter of an Illinois businessman. After graduating from college, Addams, who never married, resented the prevailing expectation that a woman's life should be governed by what she called the "family claim"—the obligation to devote herself to parents, husband, and children. In 1889, she founded Hull House in Chicago, a "settlement house" devoted to improving the lives of the immigrant poor. Hull House was modeled on Toynbee Hall, which Addams had visited after its establishment in a working-class neighborhood of London in 1884. Unlike previous reformers, who had aided the poor from afar, settlement house workers moved into poor neighborhoods. They built kindergartens and playgrounds for children, established employment bureaus and health clinics, and showed female victims of domestic abuse how to gain legal protection. By 1910, more than 400 settlement houses had been established in cities throughout the country.

"SPEARHEADS FOR REFORM"

Addams was typical of the Progressive era's "new woman." By 1900, there were more than 80,000 college-educated women in the United States. Many found a calling in providing social services, nursing, and education to poor families in the growing cities. The efforts of middle-class women to uplift the poor, and of laboring women to uplift themselves, helped to shift the center of gravity of politics toward activist government. Women like Addams discovered that even well-organized social work was not enough to alleviate the problems of inadequate housing, income, and health. Government action was essential. Hull House instigated an array of reforms in Chicago, soon adopted elsewhere, including stronger building and sanitation codes, shorter working hours and safer labor conditions, and the right of labor to organize.

Female activism spread throughout the country. Ironically, the exclusion of blacks from jobs in southern textile mills strengthened the region's movement against child labor. Reformers portrayed child labor as a menace to white supremacy, depriving white children of educations they would need as adult members of the dominant race. These reformers devoted little attention to the condition of black children. Women's groups in Alabama were instrumental in the passage of a 1903 state law restricting child labor. By 1915, every southern state had followed suit. But with textile mill owners determined to employ children and many poor families dependent on their earnings, these laws were enforced only sporadically.

Visiting nurse on a New York City rooftop, 1908. Efforts to uplift the immigrant poor offered new opportunities for professional employment to many women during the Progressive era.

The settlement houses have been called "spearheads for reform." They produced prominent Progressive figures like Julia Lathrop, the first woman to head a federal agency (the Children's Bureau, established in 1912 to investigate the conditions of mothers and children and advocate their interests). Florence Kelley, the daughter of Civil War–era Radical Republican congressman William D. Kelley and a veteran of Hull House, went on to mobilize women's power as consumers as a force for social change. In the Gilded Age, the writer Helen Campbell had brilliantly exposed the contradiction of a market economy in which fashionable women wore clothing produced by poor women in wretched sweatshops. "Emancipation on the one side," she pointedly observed, "has meant no corresponding emancipation for the other." A generation later, under Kelley's leadership, the National Consumers' League became the nation's leading advocate of laws governing the working conditions of women and children. Freedom of choice in the marketplace, Kelley insisted, enabled socially conscious consumers to "unite with wage earners" by refusing to purchase goods produced under exploitative conditions.

THE CAMPAIGN FOR WOMAN SUFFRAGE

After 1900, the campaign for women's suffrage moved beyond the elitism of the 1890s to engage a broad coalition ranging from middle-class members of women's clubs to unionists, socialists, and settlement house workers. For the first time, it became a mass movement. Membership in the National American Woman Suffrage Association grew from 13,000 in 1893 to more than 2 million by 1917. The group campaigned throughout the country for the right to vote and began to enjoy some success. By 1900, more than half the states allowed women to vote in local elections dealing with school issues, and Wyoming, Colorado, Idaho, and Utah had adopted full women's suffrage.

Cynics charged that Wyoming legislators used suffrage to attract more female migrants to their predominantly male state, while Utah hoped to

In this 1912 woman suffrage parade in New York City, a mother wheels a baby carriage to counteract the charge that allowing women to vote would undermine the family.

enhance the political power of husbands in polygamous marriages banned by law but still practiced by some Mormons. In Colorado and Idaho, however, the success of referendums in the 1890s reflected the power of the Populist Party, a strong supporter of votes for women. Between 1910 and 1914, seven more western states enfranchised women. In 1913, Illinois became the first state east of the Mississippi River to allow women to vote in presidential elections.

These campaigns, which brought women aggressively into the public sphere, were conducted with a new spirit of militancy. They also made effective use of the techniques of advertising, publicity, and mass entertainment characteristic of modern consumer society. California's successful 1911 campaign utilized automobile parades, numerous billboards and electric signs, and countless suffrage buttons and badges. Nonetheless, state campaigns were difficult, expensive, and usually unsuccessful. The movement increasingly focused its attention on securing a national constitutional amendment giving women the right to vote.

MATERNALIST REFORM

Ironically, the desire to exalt women's role within the home did much to inspire the reinvigoration of the suffrage movement. Many of the era's experiments in public policy arose from the conviction that the state had an obligation to protect women and children. Female reformers helped to launch a mass movement for direct government action to improve the living standards of poor mothers and children. Laws providing for mothers' pensions (state aid to mothers of young children who lacked male support) spread rapidly after 1910. The pensions tended to be less than generous, and local eligibility requirements opened the door to unequal treatment (white widows benefited the most, single mothers were widely discriminated against, and black women were almost entirely excluded). "Maternalist" reforms like mothers' pensions rested on the assumption that the government should encourage women's capacity for bearing and raising children

and enable them to be economically independent at the same time. Both feminists and believers in conventional domestic roles supported such measures. The former hoped that these laws would subvert women's dependence on men, the latter that they would strengthen traditional families and the mother-child bond.

Other Progressive legislation recognized that large numbers of women did in fact work outside the home, but defined them as a dependent group (like children) in need of state protection in ways male workers were not. In 1908, in the landmark case of *Muller v. Oregon*, Louis D. Brandeis filed a famous brief citing scientific and sociological studies to demonstrate that because they had less strength and endurance than men, long hours of labor were dangerous for women, while their unique ability to bear children gave the government a legitimate interest in their working conditions. Persuaded by Brandeis's argument, the Supreme Court unanimously upheld the constitutionality of an Oregon law setting maximum working hours for women.

Thus, three years after the notorious *Lochner* decision invalidating a New York law limiting the working hours of male bakers (discussed in Chapter 16), the Court created the first large breach in "liberty of contract" doctrine. But the cost was high: at the very time that women in unprecedented numbers were entering the labor market and earning college degrees, Brandeis's brief and the Court's opinion solidified the view of women workers as weak, dependent, and incapable of enjoying the same economic rights as men. By 1917, thirty states had enacted laws limiting the hours of labor of female workers. Many women derived great benefit from these laws; others saw them as an infringement on their freedom.

While the maternalist agenda built gender inequality into the early foundations of the welfare state, the very use of government to regulate working conditions called into question basic assumptions concerning liberty of contract. Although not all reformers were willing to take the step, it was easy to extend the idea of protecting women and children to demand that government better the living and working conditions of men as well, by insuring them against the impact of unemployment, old age, ill health, and disability. Brandeis himself insisted that government should concern itself with the health, income, and future prospects of all its citizens.

THE IDEA OF ECONOMIC CITIZENSHIP

Brandeis envisioned a different welfare state from that of the maternalist reformers, one rooted less in the idea of healthy motherhood than in the notion of universal economic entitlements, including the right to a decent income and protection against unemployment and work-related accidents. For him, the right to assistance derived from citizenship itself, not some special service to the nation (as in the case of mothers) or upstanding character (which had long differentiated the "deserving" from the "undeserving" poor).

This vision, too, enjoyed considerable support in the Progressive era. By 1913, twenty-two states had enacted workmen's compensation laws to benefit workers, male or female, injured on the job. This legislation was the first wedge that opened the way for broader programs of social insurance. To avoid the stigma of depending on governmental assistance, contributions from workers' own wages funded these programs in part, thus distinguishing them from charity dispensed by local authorities to the poor. But state minimum wage laws and most laws regulating working hours applied only to women. Women and children may have needed protection, but interference with the freedom of contract of adult male workers was still widely seen as degrading. The establishment of a standard of living and working conditions beneath which no American should be allowed to fall would await the coming of the New Deal.

THE PROGRESSIVE PRESIDENTS

Despite the ferment of Progressivism on the city and state levels, the most striking political development of the early twentieth century was the rise of the national state. The process of nationalization was occurring throughout American life. National corporations dominated the economy; national organizations like the American Medical Association came into being to raise the incomes and respect of professions. The process was even reflected in the consolidation of local baseball teams into the American and National Leagues and the advent in 1903 of the World Series. Only energetic national government, Progressives believed, could create the social conditions of freedom.

Despite creative experiments in social policy at the city and state levels, the tradition of localism seemed to most Progressives an impediment to a renewed sense of national purpose. Poverty, economic insecurity, and lack of industrial democracy were national problems that demanded national solutions. The democratic national state, wrote *New Republic* editor Herbert Croly, offered an alternative to control of Americans' lives by narrow interests that manipulated politics or by the all-powerful corporations. Croly proposed a new synthesis of American political traditions. To achieve the "Jeffersonian ends" of democratic self-determination and individual freedom, he insisted, the country needed to employ the "Hamiltonian means" of government intervention in the economy. Each in his own way, the

Louis D. Brandeis, Progressive reformer and advocate of the labor movement, was appointed to the Supreme Court in 1916 by President Woodrow Wilson.

Progressive presidents—Theodore Roosevelt, William Howard Taft, and Woodrow Wilson—tried to address this challenge.

THEODORE ROOSEVELT

In September 1901, the anarchist Leon Czolgosz assassinated William McKinley while the president visited the Pan-American Exposition in Buffalo, New York. At the age of forty-two, Vice President Theodore Roosevelt became the youngest man ever to hold the office of president. Roosevelt was an impetuous, energetic individual with a penchant for what he called the "strenuous life" of manly adventure. In many ways, he became the model for the twentieth-century president, an official actively and continuously engaged in domestic and foreign affairs. (The foreign policies of the Progressive presidents will be discussed in the next chapter.) Roosevelt regarded the president as "the steward of the public welfare." He moved aggressively to set the political agenda.

When the British writer H. G. Wells visited the United States soon after the turn of the century, he found that "the steady trend towards concentration" had become "the cardinal topic of thought and discussion in the American mind." Roosevelt's program, which he called the Square Deal, attempted to confront the problems caused by economic consolidation by distinguishing between "good" and "bad" corporations. The former, among which he included U.S. Steel and Standard Oil, served the public interest. The latter were run by greedy financiers interested only in profit, and had no right to exist.

Soon after assuming office, Roosevelt shocked the corporate world by announcing his intention to prosecute under the Sherman Antitrust Act the Northern Securities Company. Created by financier J. P. Morgan, this "holding company" owned the stock and directed the affairs of three major western railroads. It monopolized transportation between the Great Lakes and the Pacific. Morgan was outraged. "Wall Street is paralyzed," quipped one newspaper, "at the thought that a President of the United States should sink to enforce the law." In 1904, the Supreme Court ordered Northern Securities dissolved, a major victory for the antitrust movement.

ROOSEVELT AND ECONOMIC REGULATION

Roosevelt also believed that the president should be an honest broker in labor disputes, rather than automatically siding with employers as his predecessors had usually done. When a strike paralyzed the West Virginia and Pennsylvania coalfields in 1902, he summoned union and management leaders to the White House. By threatening a federal takeover of the mines, he persuaded the owners to allow the dispute to be settled by a commission he himself would appoint.

Reelected in 1904, Roosevelt pushed for more direct federal regulation of the economy. Appealing to the public for support, he condemned the misuse of the "vast power conferred by vast wealth." He proposed to strengthen the Interstate Commerce Commission, which the Supreme Court had essentially limited to collecting economic statistics. By this time, journalistic exposés, labor unrest, and the agitation of Progressive reformers had created significant public support for Roosevelt's regulatory program. In 1906,

President Theodore Roosevelt addressing a crowd in Evanston, Illinois, in 1902.

Putting the Screws on Him, *a 1904 cartoon, depicts President Theodore Roosevelt squeezing ill-gotten gains out of the trusts.*

Congress passed the Hepburn Act, giving the ICC the power to examine railroads' business records and to set reasonable rates, a significant step in the development of federal intervention in the corporate economy. That year, as has been noted, also saw the Pure Food and Drug Act, which established a federal agency to police the quality and labeling of food and drugs, and the Meat Inspection Act. Many businessmen supported these measures, recognizing that they would benefit from greater public confidence in the quality and safety of their products. But they were alarmed by Roosevelt's calls for federal inheritance and income taxes and the regulation of all interstate businesses.

THE CONSERVATION MOVEMENT

A dedicated outdoorsman who built a ranch in North Dakota in the 1880s, Roosevelt also moved to preserve parts of the natural environment from economic exploitation. If the United States lagged behind Europe in many areas of social policy, it led the way in the conservation of national resources. The first national park, Yellowstone in Wyoming, had been created in 1872—partly to preserve an area of remarkable natural beauty, and partly at the urging of the Northern Pacific Railroad, which was anxious to promote western tourism. In the 1890s, the Scottish-born naturalist John Muir organized the Sierra Club to help preserve forests, which he called "God's first temples," from uncontrolled logging by timber companies and other intrusions of civilization. Congress in that decade authorized the president to withdraw "forest reserves" from economic development.

It was under Roosevelt that conservation became a concerted federal policy. Relying for advice on Gifford Pinchot, the head of the U.S. Forest Service, he ordered that millions of acres be set aside as wildlife preserves and encouraged Congress to create new national parks. The creation of parks like Yellowstone, Yosemite, and Glacier required the removal of Indians who hunted and fished there as well as the reintroduction of animals that had previously disappeared. City dwellers who visited the national parks did not realize that these were to a considerable extent artificially created and managed environments, not primordial nature.

In some ways, conservation was a typical Progressive reform. Manned by experts, the government could stand above political and economic battles, serving the public good while preventing "special interests" from causing irreparable damage to the environment. The aim was less to end the economic utilization of natural resources than to develop responsible, scientific plans for their use. Pinchot halted timber companies' reckless assault on the nation's forests. But unlike Muir, he believed that development and conservation could go hand in hand and that logging, mining, and grazing on public lands should be controlled, not eliminated. Conservation also reflected the Progressive thrust toward efficiency and control—in this case, control of nature itself.

In the view of Progressive conservationists, the West's scarcest resource—water—cried out for regulation. Governments at all levels moved to control the power of western rivers, building dams and irrigation projects to regularize their flow, prevent waste, and provide water for large-scale agriculture and urban development. With such projects came political conflict, as cities like Los Angeles and San Francisco battled with rural areas for access to water. After secretly buying up large tracts of land in the Owens Valley east of the city, for example, the City of Los Angeles constructed a major aqueduct between 1908 and 1913, over the vigorous objections of the valley's residents. By the 1920s, so much water had been diverted to the city that the once thriving farming and ranching businesses of Owens Valley could no longer operate.

TAFT IN OFFICE

Having served nearly eight years as president, Roosevelt did not run again in 1908. His chosen successor was William Howard Taft, a federal judge from Ohio who had served as governor of the Philippines after the Spanish-American War. Taft defeated William Jennings Bryan, making his third unsuccessful race for the White House. Taft's inaugural address expressed the Progressive view of the state: "The scope of a modern government . . . has been widened far beyond the principles laid down by the old 'laissez-faire' school of political writers."

Although temperamentally more conservative than Roosevelt, Taft pursued antitrust policy even more aggressively. He persuaded the Supreme Court in 1911 to declare John D. Rockefeller's Standard Oil Company (one of Roosevelt's "good" trusts) in violation of the Sherman Antitrust Act and to order its breakup into separate marketing, producing, and refining companies. The government also won a case against American Tobacco, which the Court ordered to end pricing policies that were driving smaller firms out of business. In these decisions, the justices announced a new standard for judging large corporations—the "rule of reason"—which in effect implemented Roosevelt's old distinction between good and bad trusts. Big businesses were not, in and of themselves, antitrust violators, unless they engaged in policies that stifled competition.

Taft supported the Sixteenth Amendment to the Constitution, which authorized Congress to enact a graduated income tax (one whose rate of taxation is higher for wealthier citizens). It was ratified shortly before he left office. A 2 percent tax on incomes over $4,000 had been included in a tariff enacted in 1894 but had been quickly declared unconstitutional by the Supreme Court as a "communistic threat to property." The movement to resurrect the income tax united southern and western farmers who wished to reduce government dependence on revenue from the tariff, which they believed discriminated against nonindustrial states, and Progressives who believed that taxation should be based on the ability to pay. A key step in the modernization of the federal government, the income tax provided a reliable and flexible source of revenue for a national state whose powers, responsibilities, and expenditures were growing rapidly.

Despite these accomplishments, Taft seemed to gravitate toward the more conservative wing of the Republican Party. Only a few months after taking office, he signed the Payne-Aldrich Tariff, which reduced rates on imported goods but not nearly as much as reformers wished. Taft's rift with Progressives grew deeper when Richard A. Ballinger, the new secretary of the interior, concluded that Roosevelt had exceeded his authority in placing land in forest reserves. Ballinger decided to return some of this land to the public domain, where mining and lumber companies would have access to it. Gifford Pinchot accused Ballinger of colluding with business interests and

Theodore Roosevelt and the conservationist John Muir at Glacier Point, Yosemite Valley, California, in 1906. Yosemite was set aside as a national park in 1890.

Eugene V. Debs, the Socialist Party candidate, speaking in Chicago during the 1912 presidential campaign.

repudiating the environmental goals of the Roosevelt administration. When Taft fired Pinchot in 1910, the breach with party Progressives became irreparable. In 1912, Roosevelt challenged Taft for the Republican nomination. Defeated, Roosevelt launched an independent campaign as the head of the new Progressive Party.

THE ELECTION OF 1912

All the crosscurrents of Progressive era thinking about what *McClure's Magazine* called "the problem of the relation of the State and the corporation" came together in the presidential campaign of 1912. The four-way contest between Taft, Roosevelt, Democrat Woodrow Wilson, and Socialist Eugene V. Debs became a national debate on the relationship between political and economic freedom in the age of big business. At one end of the political spectrum stood Taft, who stressed that economic individualism could remain the foundation of the social order so long as government and private entrepreneurs cooperated in addressing social ills. At the other end was Debs. Relatively few Americans supported the Socialist Party's goal of abolishing the "capitalistic system" altogether, but its immediate demands—including public ownership of the railroads and banking system, government aid to the unemployed, and laws establishing shorter working hours and a minimum wage—summarized forward-looking Progressive thought.

But it was the battle between Wilson and Roosevelt over the role of the federal government in securing economic freedom that galvanized public attention in 1912. The two represented competing strands of Progressivism. Both believed government action necessary to preserve individual freedom, but they differed over the dangers of increasing the government's power and the inevitability of economic concentration. Though representing a party thoroughly steeped in states' rights and laissez-faire ideology, Wilson was deeply imbued with Progressive ideas. "Freedom today," he declared, "is something more than being let alone. The program of a government of freedom must in these days be positive, not negative merely." As governor of New Jersey, Wilson had presided over the implementation of a system of workmen's compensation and state regulation of utilities and railroads.

NEW FREEDOM AND NEW NATIONALISM

Strongly influenced by Louis D. Brandeis, with whom he consulted frequently during the campaign, Wilson insisted that democracy must be reinvigorated by restoring market competition and freeing government from domination by big business. Wilson feared big government as much as he feared the power of the corporations. The New Freedom, as he called his program, envisioned the federal government strengthening antitrust laws, protecting the right of workers to unionize, and actively encouraging small businesses—creating, in other words, the conditions for the renewal of economic competition without increasing government regulation of the economy. Wilson warned that corporations were as likely to corrupt government as to be managed by it, a forecast that proved remarkably accurate.

To Roosevelt's supporters, Wilson seemed a relic of a bygone era; his program, they argued, served the needs of small businessmen but ignored the inevitability of economic concentration and the interests of professionals, consumers, and labor. Wilson and Brandeis spoke of the "curse of bigness." What the nation actually needed, Walter Lippmann countered, was frank acceptance of the benefits of bigness, coupled with the intervention of government to counteract its abuses. Lippmann was expressing the core of the New Nationalism, Roosevelt's program of 1912. Only the "controlling and directing power of the government," Roosevelt insisted, could restore "the liberty of the oppressed." He called for heavy taxes on personal and corporate fortunes and federal regulation of industries, including railroads, mining, and oil.

The Progressive Party platform offered numerous proposals to promote social justice. Drafted by a group of settlement-house activists, labor reformers, and social scientists, the platform laid out a blueprint for a modern, democratic welfare state, complete with woman suffrage, federal supervision of corporate enterprise, national labor and health legislation for women and children, an eight-hour day and "living wage" for all workers, and a national system of social insurance covering unemployment, medical care, and old age. Described by Roosevelt as the "most important document" since the end of the Civil War, the platform brought together many of the streams of thought and political experiences that flowed into Progressivism. Roosevelt's campaign helped to give freedom a modern social and economic content and established an agenda that would define political liberalism for much of the twentieth century.

WILSON'S FIRST TERM

The Republican split ensured a sweeping victory for Wilson, who won about 42 percent of the popular vote, although Roosevelt humiliated Taft by winning about 27 percent to the president's 23 percent. In office, Wilson proved himself a strong executive leader. He established an office at the Capitol so that he could confer regularly with members of Congress about pending legislation, and he was the first president to hold regular press conferences in order to influence public opinion directly and continuously. He delivered messages personally to Congress rather than sending them in written form like all his predecessors since John Adams.

With Democrats in control of Congress, Wilson moved aggressively to implement his version of Progressivism. The first significant measure of his presidency was the Underwood Tariff, which substantially reduced duties on imports and, to make up for lost revenue, imposed a graduated income tax on the richest 5 percent of Americans. There followed the Clayton Act of 1914, which exempted labor unions from antitrust laws and barred courts from issuing injunctions curtailing the right to strike. In 1916 came the Keating-Owen Act outlawing child labor in the manufacture of goods sold in interstate commerce, the Adamson Act establishing an eight-hour workday on the

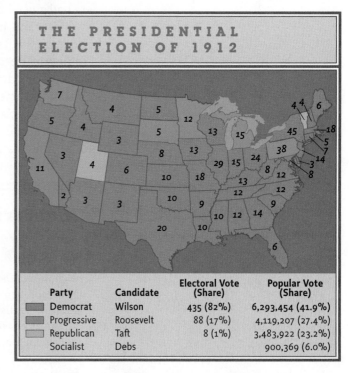

THE PRESIDENTIAL ELECTION OF 1912

Party	Candidate	Electoral Vote (Share)	Popular Vote (Share)
Democrat	Wilson	435 (82%)	6,293,454 (41.9%)
Progressive	Roosevelt	88 (17%)	4,119,207 (27.4%)
Republican	Taft	8 (1%)	3,483,922 (23.2%)
Socialist	Debs		900,369 (6.0%)

nation's railroads, and the Warehouse Act, reminiscent of the Populist sub-treasury plan, which extended credit to farmers when they stored their crops in federally licensed warehouses.

THE EXPANDING ROLE OF GOVERNMENT

Some of Wilson's policies seemed more in tune with Roosevelt's New Nationalism than the New Freedom of 1912. He abandoned the idea of aggressive trust-busting in favor of greater government supervision of the economy. Wilson presided over the creation of two powerful new public agencies. In 1913, Congress created the Federal Reserve System, consisting of twelve regional banks. They were overseen by a central board appointed by the president and empowered to handle the issuance of currency, aid banks in danger of failing, and influence interest rates so as to promote economic growth. The law was a delayed response to the Panic of 1907, when the failure of several financial companies threatened a general collapse of the banking system. With the federal government lacking a modern central bank, it had been left to J. P. Morgan to assemble the funds to prop up threatened financial institutions. Morgan's actions highlighted the fact that in the absence of federal regulation of banking, power over finance rested entirely in private hands.

A second expansion of national power occurred in 1914, when Congress established the Federal Trade Commission (FTC) to investigate and prohibit "unfair" business activities such as price-fixing and monopolistic practices. Both the Federal Reserve and FTC were welcomed by many business leaders as a means of restoring order to the economic marketplace and warding off more radical measures for curbing corporate power. But they reflected the remarkable expansion of the federal role in the economy during the Progressive era.

By 1916, the social ferment and political mobilizations of the Progressive era had given birth to a new American state. With new laws, administrative agencies, and independent commissions, government at the local, state, and national levels had assumed the authority to protect and advance "industrial freedom." Government had established rules for labor relations, business behavior, and financial policy, protected citizens from market abuses, and acted as a broker among the groups whose conflicts threatened to destroy social harmony. But a storm was already engulfing Europe that would test the Progressive faith in empowered government as the protector of American freedom.

SUGGESTED READING

BOOKS

Bodnar, John. *The Transplanted: A History of Immigrants in Urban America* (1985). A comprehensive account of American immigration.

Cameron, Ardis. *Radicals of the Worst Sort: Laboring Women in Lawrence, Massachusetts, 1860–1912* (1993). Describes the lives of working women in Lawrence and their role in the strike of 1912.

Cott, Nancy F. *The Grounding of Modern Feminism* (1987). A careful study of feminist ideas in the Progressive era.

Dawley, Alan. *Struggles for Justice: Social Responsibility and the Liberal State* (1991). Examines the varieties of Progressive reform and various efforts to use the power of government for social betterment.

Diner, Steven. *A Very Different Age: Americans of the Progressive Era* (1998). A survey of the main trends of the Progressive period.

Glickman, Lawrence B. *A Living Wage: Workers and the Making of American Consumer Society* (1997). Traces the origins and development of the idea that workers are entitled to a "living wage."

Hofstadter, Richard. *The Age of Reform: From Bryan to F. D. R.* (1955). A classic account of the ideas of reformers from Populism to the New Deal.

Johnston, Robert D. *The Radical Middle Class: Populist Democracy and the Question of Capitalism in Progressive Era Portland* (2003). Analyzes how Progressivism operated in one important city.

Maddox, Lucy. *Citizen Indians: Native American Intellectuals, Race, and Reform* (2005). A study of the Society of American Indians and other manifestations of Indian Progressivism.

Montgomery, David. *The Fall of the House of Labor: The Workplace, the State, and American Labor Activism, 1865–1925* (1987). An account of the labor battles of the era and the gradual decline of labor's power, especially at the workplace.

Orsi, Robert A. *The Madonna of 115th Street: Faith and Community in Italian Harlem, 1880–1950* (1985). An influential study of a single immigrant community and the role of religion in binding it together.

Peiss, Kathy. *Cheap Amusements: Working Women and Leisure in Turn-of-the-Century New York* (1986). Explores the rise of mass entertainment and how it affected women's lives in Progressive America.

Recchiuti, John L. *Civic Engagement: Social Science and Progressive-Era Reform in New York City* (2006). Examines the influence of a group of reform-minded scholars on the politics of the Progressive era.

Rodgers, Daniel T. *Atlantic Crossings: Social Politics in a Progressive Age* (1998). A comprehensive study of the flow of Progressive ideas and policies back and forth across the Atlantic.

Stansell, Christine. *American Moderns: Bohemian New York and the Creation of a New Century* (2000). A colorful account of the Greenwich Village radicals who expanded the idea of personal freedom in the Progressive era.

Stromquist, Shelton. *Re-Inventing "The People": The Progressive Movement, the Class Problem, and the Origins of Modern Liberalism* (2006). Discusses how the desire to re-create social harmony in an age of labor conflict shaped Progressivism.

WEBSITES

Evolution of the Conservation Movement, 1860–1920: http://lcweb2.loc.gov/ammem/amrvhtml/conshome.html

Immigration to the United States, 1789–1930: http://ocp.hul.harvard.edu/ immigration/

Triangle Shirtwaist Factory Fire: www.ilr.cornell.edu/trianglefire/

Urban Experience in Chicago: Hull House and Its Neighborhoods: www.uic.edu/jaddams/hull/urbanexp/index.htm

Votes for Women: http://memory.loc.gov/ammem/naw/nawshome.html

REVIEW QUESTIONS

1. Identify the main groups and ideas that drove the Progressive movement.

2. Explain how immigration to the United States in this period was part of a global movement of peoples.

3. Describe how Fordism transformed American industrial and consumer society.

4. Socialism was a rising force across the globe in the early twentieth century. How successful was the movement in the United States?

5. Explain why the Industrial Workers of the World (IWW) grew so rapidly and aroused so much opposition.

6. What did striking workers mean when they declared that they wanted "bread and roses, too"?

7. What did Progressive era feminists want to change in society, and how did their actions help to spearhead broader reforms?

8. Explain how and why Progressivism was an international movement.

9. How did each Progressive era president view the role of the federal government?

10. How democratic was the Progressive movement?

FREEDOM QUESTIONS

1. Immigrants came to the United States in search of freedom and economic opportunity. Describe to what extent they achieved and were denied these goals.

2. Explain the concept of "consumer freedom" and its connections to the growing women's movement and the new urban society.

3. How did workers and employers differ in their idea of "industrial freedom"?

4. How did the struggles of the Industrial Workers of the World and suffrage advocates promote a broader defense of freedom of expression?

5. Assess the record of the Progressive movement in promoting the expansion of freedom and democracy.

KEY TERMS

muckrakers (p. 728)

child labor (p. 728)

Ellis Island and Angel Island
(p. 730)

Mexican immigration (p. 730)

Fordism (p. 736)

American standard of living
(p. 737)

Rerum Novarum (p. 737)

"scientific management" (p. 738)

Industrial Workers of the World
(p. 743)

"New Feminism" (p. 746)

birth-control movement (p. 747)

Society of American Indians
(p. 748)

"effective freedom" (p. 749)

maternalist reform (p. 754)

Muller v. Oregon (p. 755)

workmen's compensation laws
(p. 756)

coal miners' strike of 1902 (p.
757)

Pure Food and Drug Act (p. 758)

Roosevelt and conservation
(p. 758)

Federal Reserve System (p. 762)

Federal Trade Commission
(p. 762)

REVIEW TABLE

Key Federal Legislation

Act	Date	Purpose
Hepburn Act	1906	To give the Interstate Commerce Commission the power to oversee railroad practices and rates
Pure Food and Drug Act	1906	To police the quality and labeling of food and drugs
Federal Reserve System	1913	To regulate interest rates and promote national economic growth
Federal Trade Commission	1914	To investigate and prohibit "unfair" business activities
Clayton Act	1914	To exempt labor unions from antitrust laws and allow unions the right to strike
Keating-Owen Act	1916	To outlaw child labor in manufacturing goods sold in interstate commerce
Adamson Act	1916	To establish an eight-hour work day on the nation's railroads

CHAPTER 19

Safe for Democracy: The United States and World War I, 1916–1920

A rather aggressive-looking Statue of Liberty directs Americans to purchase Liberty Bonds (that is, loan money to the federal government) during World War I. Symbols of liberty were widely used by the government in its efforts to mobilize popular support for the war. The bottom of the full image included the words, "Lest I perish."

FOCUS QUESTIONS

• In what ways did the Progressive presidents promote the expansion of American power overseas?

• How did the United States get involved in World War I?

• How did the United States mobilize resources and public opinion for the war effort?

• How did the war affect race relations in the United States?

• Why was 1919 such a watershed year for the United States and the world?

In 1902, W. T. Stead published a short volume with the arresting title *The Americanization of the World; or, the Trend of the Twentieth Century*. Stead was an English editor whose sensational writings included an exposé of London prostitution, *Maiden Tribute of Modern Babylon*. He would meet his death in 1912 as a passenger on the *Titanic*, the ocean liner that foundered after striking an iceberg in the North Atlantic. Impressed by Americans' "exuberant energies," Stead predicted that the United States would soon emerge as "the greatest of world-powers." But what was most striking about his work was that Stead located the source of American power less in the realm of military might or territorial acquisition than in the country's single-minded commitment to the "pursuit of wealth" and the relentless international spread of American culture—art, music, journalism, even ideas about religion and gender relations. He foresaw a future in which the United States promoted its interests and values through an unending involvement in the affairs of other nations. Stead proved to be an accurate prophet.

The Spanish-American War had established the United States as an international empire. Despite the conquest of the Philippines and Puerto Rico, however, the country's overseas holdings remained tiny compared to those of Britain, France, and Germany. And no more were added, except for a strip of land surrounding the Panama Canal, acquired in 1903, and the Virgin Islands, purchased from Denmark in 1917. In 1900, Great Britain ruled over more than 300 million people in possessions scattered across the globe, and France had nearly 50 million subjects in Asia and Africa. Compared with these, the American presence in the world seemed very small. As Stead suggested, America's empire differed significantly from those of European countries—it was economic, cultural, and intellectual, rather than territorial.

The world economy at the dawn of the twentieth century was already highly globalized. An ever-increasing stream of goods, investments, and people flowed from country to country. Although Britain still dominated world banking and the British pound remained the major currency of international trade, the United States had become the leading industrial power. By 1914, it produced more than one-third of the world's manufactured goods. Already, Europeans complained of an "American invasion" of steel, oil, agricultural equipment, and consumer goods. Spearheads of American culture like movies and popular music were not far behind.

Europeans were fascinated by American ingenuity and mass production techniques. Many feared American products and culture would overwhelm their own. "What are the chief new features of London life?" one British writer asked in 1901. "They are the telephone, the portable camera, the phonograph, the electric street car, the automobile, the typewriter. . . . In every one of these the American maker is supreme." Meanwhile, hundreds of thousands of Americans traveled abroad each year in the early twentieth century. And American racial and ethnic groups became heavily engaged in overseas politics. Through fraternal, religious, and political organizations based in their ethnic and racial communities, Irish-Americans supported Irish independence, American Jews protested the treatment of their co-religionists in Russia, and black Americans hoped to uplift Africa. American influence was growing throughout the world.

America's growing connections with the outside world led to increasing military and political involvement. In the two decades after 1900, many of the basic principles that would guide American foreign policy for the rest of the century were formulated. The "open door"—the free flow of trade, investment, information, and culture—emerged as a key principle of American foreign relations. "Since the manufacturer insists on having the world as a market," wrote Woodrow Wilson, "the flag of his nation must follow him and the doors of nations which are closed against him must be battered down."

Americans in the twentieth century often discussed foreign policy in the language of freedom. At least in rhetoric, the United States ventured abroad—including intervening militarily in the affairs of other nations—not to pursue strategic goals or to make the world safe for American economic interests, but to promote liberty and democracy. A supreme faith in America's historic destiny and in the righteousness of its ideals enabled the country's leaders to think of the United States simultaneously as an emerging great power and as the worldwide embodiment of freedom.

More than any other individual, Woodrow Wilson articulated this vision of America's relationship to the rest of the world. His foreign policy, called by historians "liberal internationalism," rested on the conviction that economic and political progress went hand in hand. Thus, greater worldwide freedom would follow inevitably from increased American investment and trade abroad. Frequently during the twentieth century, this conviction would serve as a mask for American power and self-interest. It would also inspire sincere efforts to bring freedom to other peoples. In either case, liberal internationalism represented a shift from the nineteenth-century tradition of promoting freedom primarily by example, to active intervention to remake the world in the American image.

American involvement in World War I provided the first great test of Wilson's belief that American power could "make the world safe for democracy." Most Progressives embraced the country's participation in the war, believing that the United States could help to spread Progressive values throughout the world. But rather than bringing Progressivism to

A Russian advertisement for the Singer Sewing Machine Company, one of the many American companies that marketed their goods worldwide in the early twentieth century. Singer established factories in Russia and also imported machines from the United States. The figure that appears to be the number "3" is actually the letter "Z" in the Cyrillic alphabet, representing the company's name in Russian, Zinger. European and American ads for sewing machines depicted women in modern dress; here, however, the operator wears the traditional attire of a peasant, part of the company's strategy of trying to sell sewing machines to Russia's vast rural population.

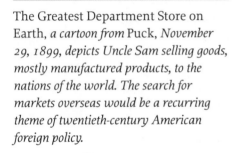

The Greatest Department Store on Earth, *a cartoon from* Puck, *November 29, 1899, depicts Uncle Sam selling goods, mostly manufactured products, to the nations of the world. The search for markets overseas would be a recurring theme of twentieth-century American foreign policy.*

other peoples, the war destroyed it at home. The government quickly came to view critics of American involvement not simply as citizens with a different set of opinions, but as enemies of the very ideas of democracy and freedom. As a result, the war produced one of the most sweeping repressions of the right to dissent in all of American history.

AN ERA OF INTERVENTION

Just as they expanded the powers of the federal government in domestic affairs, the Progressive presidents were not reluctant to project American power outside the country's borders. At first, their interventions were confined to the Western Hemisphere, whose affairs the United States had claimed a special right to oversee ever since the Monroe Doctrine of 1823. Between 1901 and 1920, U.S. marines landed in Caribbean countries more than twenty times. Usually, they were dispatched to create a welcoming economic environment for American companies that wanted stable access to raw materials like bananas and sugar, and for bankers nervous that their loans to local governments might not be repaid.

"I TOOK THE CANAL ZONE"

Like his distinction between good and bad trusts, Theodore Roosevelt divided the world into "civilized" and "uncivilized" nations. The former, he believed, had an obligation to establish order in an unruly world. Roosevelt became far more active in international diplomacy than most of his predecessors, helping, for example, to negotiate a settlement of the Russo-Japanese War of 1905, a feat for which he was awarded the Nobel Peace Prize. Closer to home, his policies were more aggressive. "I have always been fond of the West African proverb," he wrote, "'Speak softly and carry a big stick.'" And although he declared that the United States "has not the slightest desire for territorial aggrandizement at the expense of its southern neighbors," Roosevelt pursued a policy of intervention in Central America.

Between 1898 and 1934, the United States intervened militarily numerous times in Caribbean countries, generally to protect the economic interests of American banks and investors.

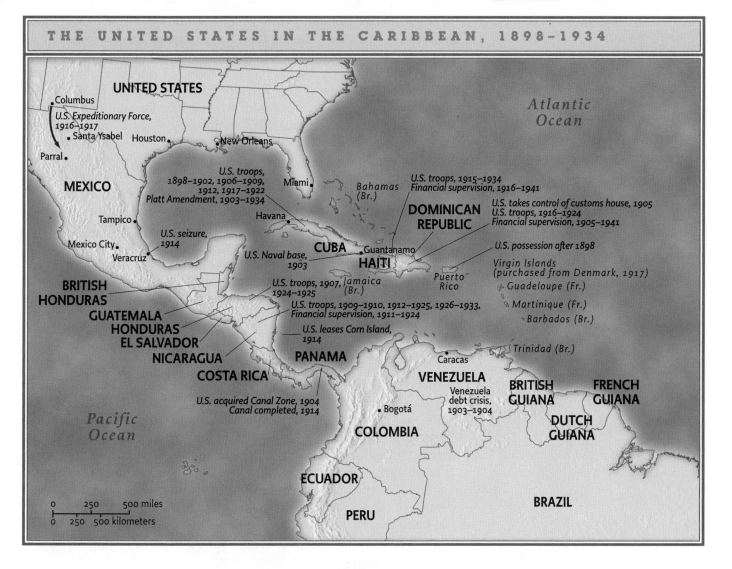

THE UNITED STATES IN THE CARIBBEAN, 1898–1934

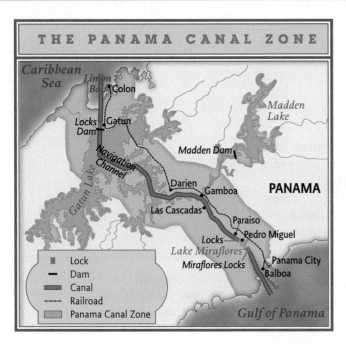

THE PANAMA CANAL ZONE

Caribbean Sea
Limón Bay — Colón
Locks — Gatún Dam
Navigation Channel
Gatún Lake
Madden Lake
Madden Dam
Darién
Gamboa
Las Cascadas
PANAMA
Paraíso
Locks — Pedro Miguel
Lake Miraflores
Miraflores Locks — Panama City
Balboa
Gulf of Panama

▪ Lock
— Dam
— Canal
∙∙∙∙ Railroad
▨ Panama Canal Zone

Constructed in the first years of the twentieth century, after Theodore Roosevelt helped engineer Panama's independence from Colombia, the Panama Canal drastically reduced the time it took for commercial and naval vessels to sail from the Atlantic to the Pacific Oceans.

In his first major action in the region, Roosevelt engineered the separation of Panama from Colombia in order to facilitate the construction of a canal linking the Atlantic and Pacific Oceans. The idea of a canal across the fifty-one-mile-wide Isthmus of Panama had a long history. In 1879–1881, the French engineer Ferdinand de Lesseps attempted to construct such a waterway but failed because of inadequate funding and the toll exacted on his workers by yellow fever and malaria. Roosevelt had long been a proponent of American naval development. He was convinced that a canal would facilitate the movement of naval and commercial vessels between the two oceans. In 1903, when Colombia, of which Panama was a part, refused to cede land for the project, Roosevelt helped to set in motion an uprising by conspirators led by Philippe Bunau-Varilla, a representative of the Panama Canal Company. An American gunboat prevented the Colombian army from suppressing the rebellion.

Upon establishing Panama's independence, Bunau-Varilla signed a treaty giving the United States both the right to construct and operate a canal and sovereignty over the Canal Zone, a ten-mile-wide strip of land through which the route would run. A remarkable feat of engineering, the canal was the largest construction project in history to that date. Like the building of the transcontinental railroad in the 1860s and much construction work today, it involved the widespread use of immigrant labor. Most of the 60,000 workers came from the Caribbean islands of Barbados and Jamaica, but others hailed from Europe, Asia, and the United States. In keeping with American segregation policies, the best jobs were reserved for white Americans, who lived in their own communities complete with schools, churches, and libraries. It also required a massive effort to eradicate the mosquitoes that carried the tropical diseases responsible, in part, for the failure of earlier French efforts. When completed in 1914, the canal reduced the sea voyage between the East and West Coasts of the United States by 8,000 miles. "I took the Canal Zone," Roosevelt exulted. But the manner in which the canal had been initiated, and the continued American rule over the Canal Zone, would long remain a source of tension. In 1977, President Jimmy Carter negotiated treaties that led to turning over the canal's operation and control of the Canal Zone to Panama in the year 2000 (see Chapter 26).

THE ROOSEVELT COROLLARY

Roosevelt's actions in Panama reflected a principle that came to be called the Roosevelt Corollary to the Monroe Doctrine. This held that the United States had the right to exercise "an international police power" in the Western Hemisphere—a significant expansion of Monroe's pledge to defend the hemisphere against European intervention. Early in Roosevelt's administration, British, Italian, and German naval forces blockaded Venezuela to ensure the payment of debts to European bankers. Roosevelt persuaded them to withdraw, but the incident convinced him that financial instability in the New World would invite intervention from the Old. In 1904, Roosevelt ordered American forces to seize the customs houses of

The World's Constable, *a cartoon commenting on Theodore Roosevelt's "new diplomacy," in* Judge, *January 14, 1905, portrays Roosevelt as an impartial policeman, holding in one hand the threat of force and in the other the promise of the peaceful settlement of disputes. Roosevelt stands between the undisciplined non-white peoples of the world and the imperialist powers of Europe and Japan.*

the Dominican Republic to ensure payment of its debts to European and American investors. He soon arranged an "executive agreement" giving a group of American banks control over Dominican finances. In 1906, he dispatched troops to Cuba to oversee a disputed election; they remained in the country until 1909. Roosevelt also encouraged investment by American corporations like the United Fruit Company, whose huge banana plantations soon dominated the economies of Honduras and Costa Rica.

Roosevelt's successor, William Howard Taft, landed marines in Nicaragua to protect a government friendly to American economic interests. In general, however, Taft emphasized economic investment and loans from American banks, rather than direct military intervention, as the best way to spread American influence. As a result, his foreign policy became known as Dollar Diplomacy. In Honduras, Nicaragua, the Dominican Republic, and even Liberia—the West African nation established in 1816 as a home for freed American slaves—Taft pressed for more efficient revenue collection, stable government, and access to land and labor by American companies.

MORAL IMPERIALISM

The son of a Presbyterian minister, Woodrow Wilson brought to the presidency a missionary zeal and a sense of his own and the nation's moral righteousness. He appointed as secretary of state William Jennings Bryan, a strong anti-imperialist. Wilson repudiated Dollar Diplomacy and promised a new foreign policy that would respect Latin America's independence and free it from foreign economic domination. But Wilson could not abandon the conviction that the United States had a responsibility to teach other peoples the lessons of democracy. Moreover, he believed, the export of American manufactured goods and investments went hand in hand with the spread of democratic ideals. To Wilson, expanding American economic influence served a higher purpose than mere profit. Americans, he told a

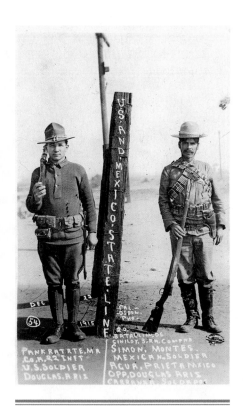

A 1915 postcard portrays two soldiers— one American, one Mexican—at the border between the two countries shortly before Woodrow Wilson ordered American troops into Mexico. The photograph is intended to show a difference in discipline between the two.

group of businessmen in 1916, were "meant to carry liberty and justice" throughout the world. "Go out and sell goods," he urged them, "that will make the world more comfortable and happy, and convert them to the principles of America."

Wilson's "moral imperialism" produced more military interventions in Latin America than any president before or since. In 1915, he sent marines to occupy Haiti after the government refused to allow American banks to oversee its financial dealings. In 1916, he established a military government in the Dominican Republic, with the United States controlling the country's customs collections and paying its debts. American soldiers remained in the Dominican Republic until 1924 and in Haiti until 1934. They built roads and schools, but did little or nothing to promote democracy. Wilson's foreign policy underscored a paradox of modern American history: the presidents who spoke the most about freedom were likely to intervene most frequently in the affairs of other countries.

WILSON AND MEXICO

Wilson's major preoccupation in Latin America was Mexico, where in 1911 a revolution led by Francisco Madero overthrew the government of dicta-

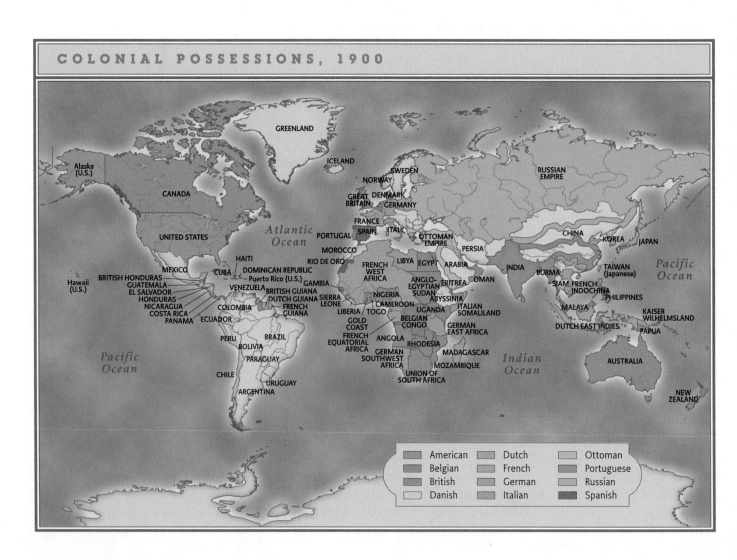

COLONIAL POSSESSIONS, 1900

tor Porfirio Díaz. Two years later, without Wilson's knowledge but with the backing of the U.S. ambassador and of American companies that controlled Mexico's oil and mining industries, military commander Victoriano Huerta assassinated Madero and seized power.

Wilson was appalled. The United States, he announced, would not extend recognition to a "government of butchers." He would "teach" Latin Americans, he added, "to elect good men." When civil war broke out in Mexico, Wilson ordered American troops to land at Vera Cruz to prevent the arrival of weapons meant for Huerta's forces. But to Wilson's surprise, Mexicans greeted the marines as invaders rather than liberators. Vera Cruz, after all, was where the forces of the conquistador Hernán Cortés had landed in the sixteenth century and those of Winfield Scott during the Mexican War. More than 100 Mexicans and 19 Americans died in the fighting that followed. Huerta left the presidency in 1914, but civil war continued, and neither side seemed grateful for Wilson's interference.

In 1916, the war spilled over into the United States when "Pancho" Villa, the leader of one faction, attacked Columbus, New Mexico, where he killed seventeen Americans. Wilson ordered 10,000 troops into northern Mexico on an expedition that unsuccessfully sought to arrest Villa. Mexico was a warning that it might be more difficult than Wilson assumed to use American might to reorder the internal affairs of other nations, or to apply moral certainty to foreign policy.

AMERICA AND THE GREAT WAR

In June 1914, a Serbian nationalist assassinated Archduke Franz Ferdinand, heir to the throne of the Austro-Hungarian empire, in Sarajevo, Bosnia. (Today, Sarajevo is the capital of Bosnia and Herzegovina.) This deed set in motion a chain of events that plunged Europe into the most devastating war the world had ever seen. In the years before 1914, European nations had engaged in a scramble to obtain colonial possessions overseas and had constructed a shifting series of alliances seeking military domination within Europe. In the aftermath of the assassination, Austria-Hungary, the major power in eastern Europe, declared war on Serbia. Within a little more than a month, because of the European powers' interlocking military alliances, Britain, France, Russia, and Japan (the Allies) found themselves at war with the Central Powers— Germany, Austria-Hungary, and the Ottoman empire, whose holdings included modern-day Turkey and much of the Middle East.

German forces quickly overran Belgium and part of northern France. The war then settled into a prolonged stalemate, with bloody, indecisive battles succeeding one another. New military technologies—submarines, airplanes, machine guns, tanks, and poison gas—produced unprecedented slaughter. In one five-month battle at Verdun, in 1916, 600,000 French and German soldiers perished—nearly as many combatants as in the entire

Wilbur Wright, who with his brother Orville made the first powered flight in 1903, circling the Statue of Liberty six years later. World War I would reveal the military uses for this new technology.

The liner Lusitania, *pictured on a "peace" postcard. Its sinking by a German submarine in 1915 strengthened the resolve of those who wished to see the United States enter the European war.*

American Civil War. By the time the war ended, an estimated 10 million soldiers, and uncounted millions of civilians, had perished. And the war was followed by widespread famine and a worldwide epidemic of influenza that killed an estimated 21 million people more.

The Great War, or World War I as it came to be called, dealt a severe blow to the optimism and self-confidence of Western civilization. For decades, philosophers, reformers, and politicians had hailed the triumph of reason and human progress. Despite increasingly bitter rivalries between European powers, especially Germany and Britain, as they competed for political and military dominance at home and carved up Asia and Africa into rival empires, mankind seemed to have moved beyond the time when disputes were settled by war. The conflict was also a shock to European socialist and labor movements. Of the two great ideologies that had arisen in the nineteenth century, nationalism and socialism, the former proved more powerful. Karl Marx had called on the "workers of the world" to unite against their oppressors. Instead, they marched off to kill each other.

NEUTRALITY AND PREPAREDNESS

As war engulfed Europe, Americans found themselves sharply divided. British-Americans sided with their nation of origin, as did many other Americans who associated Great Britain with liberty and democracy and Germany with repressive government. On the other hand, German-Americans identified with Germany. Irish-Americans bitterly opposed any aid to the British, a sentiment reinforced in 1916 when authorities in London suppressed the Easter Rebellion, an uprising demanding Irish independence, and executed several of its leaders. Immigrants from the Russian empire, especially Jews, had no desire to see the United States aid the czar's regime. Indeed, the presence of Russia, the world's largest despotic state, as an ally of Britain and France made it difficult to see the war as a clear-cut battle between democracy and autocracy. Many feminists, pacifists, and social reformers, moreover, had become convinced that peace was essential to further efforts to enhance social justice at home. They lobbied vigorously against American involvement.

When war broke out in 1914, President Wilson proclaimed American neutrality. But as in the years preceding the War of 1812, naval warfare in Europe reverberated in the United States. Britain declared a naval blockade of Germany and began to stop American merchant vessels. Germany launched submarine warfare against ships entering and leaving British ports. In May 1915, a German submarine sank the British liner *Lusitania* (which was carrying a large cache of arms) off the coast of Ireland, causing the death of 1,198 passengers, including 124 Americans. Wilson composed a note of protest so strong that Bryan resigned as secretary of state, fearing that the president was laying the foundation for military intervention. Bryan had advocated warning Americans not to travel on the ships of belligerents, but Wilson felt this would represent a retreat from the principle of freedom of the seas.

The sinking of the *Lusitania* outraged American public opinion and strengthened the hand of those who believed that the United States must prepare for possible entry into the war. These included longtime advocates of a stronger military establishment, like Theodore Roosevelt, and businessmen with close economic ties to Britain, the country's leading trading partner and the recipient of more than $2 billion in wartime loans from American banks. Wilson himself had strong pro-British sympathies and viewed Germany as "the natural foe of liberty." By the end of 1915, he had embarked on a policy of "preparedness"—a crash program to expand the American army and navy.

THE ROAD TO WAR

In May 1916, Germany announced the suspension of submarine warfare against noncombatants. Wilson's preparedness program seemed to have succeeded in securing the right of Americans to travel freely on the high seas without committing American forces to the conflict. "He kept us out of war" became the slogan of his campaign for reelection. With the Republican Party reunited after its split in 1912, the election proved to be one of the closest in American history. Wilson defeated Republican candidate Charles Evans Hughes by only twenty-three electoral votes and about 600,000 popular votes out of more than 18 million cast. Partly because he seemed to promise not to send American soldiers to Europe, Wilson carried ten of the twelve states that had adopted woman suffrage. Without the votes of women, Wilson would not have been reelected.

On January 22, 1917, Wilson called for a "peace without victory" in Europe and outlined his vision for a world order including freedom of the seas, restrictions

A 1916 Wilson campaign truck (a new development in political campaigning), promising peace, prosperity, and preparedness.

on armaments, and self-determination for nations great and small. Almost immediately, however, Germany announced its intention to resume submarine warfare against ships sailing to or from the British Isles, and several American merchant vessels were sunk. The German government realized that its actions would probably lead Wilson to intervene, but German strategists gambled that the blockade would strangle Britain economically before the arrival of American troops.

In March 1917, British spies intercepted and made public the Zimmerman Telegram, a message by German foreign secretary Arthur Zimmerman calling on Mexico to join in a coming war against the United States and promising to help it recover territory lost in the Mexican War of 1846–1848. A revolution in Russia that same month overthrew the czar and established a constitutional government, making it more plausible to believe that the United States would be fighting on the side of democracy. On April 2, Wilson went before Congress to ask for a declaration of war against Germany. "The world," he proclaimed, "must be made safe for democracy. Its peace must be planted upon the tested foundation of political liberty." The war resolution passed the Senate 82–6 and the House 373–50.

THE FOURTEEN POINTS

Not until the spring of 1918 did American forces arrive in Europe in large numbers. By then, the world situation had taken a dramatic turn. In November 1917, a communist revolution headed by Vladimir Lenin overthrew the Russian government that had come to power the previous spring. Shortly thereafter, Lenin withdrew Russia from the war and published the secret treaties by which the Allies had agreed to divide up conquered territory after the war—an embarrassment for Wilson, who had promised a just peace.

Partly to assure the country that the war was being fought for a moral cause, Wilson in January 1918 issued the Fourteen Points, the clearest statement of American war aims and of his vision of a new international order. Among the key principles were self-determination for all nations, freedom of the seas, free trade, open diplomacy (an end to secret treaties), the readjustment of colonial claims with colonized people given "equal weight" in deciding their futures, and the creation of a "general association of nations" to preserve the peace. Wilson envisioned this last provision, which led to the establishment after the war of the League of Nations, as a kind of global counterpart to the regulatory commissions Progressives had created at home to maintain social harmony and prevent the powerful from exploiting the weak. Although purely an American program, not endorsed by the other Allies, the Fourteen Points established the agenda for the peace conference that followed the war.

The United States threw its economic resources and manpower into the war. When American troops finally arrived in Europe, they turned the tide of battle. In the spring of 1918, they helped to repulse a German advance near Paris and by July were participating in a major Allied counteroffensive. In September, in the Meuse-Argonne campaign, more than 1 million American soldiers under General John J. Pershing helped to push back the outnumbered and exhausted German army. With his forces in full retreat,

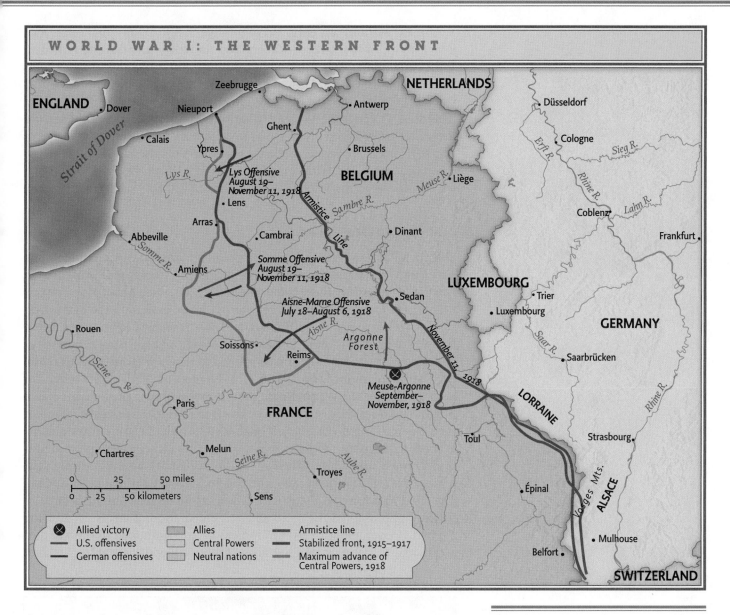

WORLD WAR I: THE WESTERN FRONT

the German kaiser abdicated on November 9. Two days later, Germany sued for peace. Over 100,000 Americans had died, a substantial number, but they were only 1 percent of the 10 million soldiers killed in the Great War.

After years of stalemate on the western front in World War I, the arrival of American troops in 1917 and 1918 shifted the balance of power and made possible the Allied victory.

THE WAR AT HOME

THE PROGRESSIVES' WAR

Looking back on American participation in the European conflict, Randolph Bourne summed up one of its lessons: "War is the health of the state." Bourne saw the expansion of government power as a danger, but it struck most Progressives as a golden opportunity. To them, the war offered the possibility of reforming American society along scientific lines, instilling a sense of national unity and self-sacrifice, and expanding social justice. That American power could now disseminate Progressive values around the globe heightened the war's appeal.

Almost without exception, Progressive intellectuals and reformers, joined by prominent labor leaders and native-born socialists, rallied to Wilson's support. The roster included intellectuals like John Dewey, journalists such as Walter Lippmann and Herbert Croly, AFL head Samuel Gompers, socialist writers like Upton Sinclair, and prominent reformers including Florence Kelley and Charlotte Perkins Gilman. In *The New Republic*, Dewey urged Progressives to recognize the "social possibilities of war." The crisis, he wrote, offered the prospect of attacking the "immense inequality of power" within the United States, thus laying the foundation for Americans to enjoy "effective freedom."

THE WARTIME STATE

Like the Civil War, World War I created, albeit temporarily, a national state with unprecedented powers and a sharply increased presence in Americans' everyday lives. Under the Selective Service Act of May 1917, 24 million men were required to register with the draft, and the army soon swelled from 120,000 to 5 million men. The war seemed to bring into being the New Nationalist state Theodore Roosevelt and so many Progressives had desired. New federal agencies moved to regulate industry, transportation, labor relations, and agriculture. Headed by Wall Street financier Bernard Baruch, the War Industries Board presided over all elements of war production from the distribution of raw materials to the prices of manufactured goods. To spur efficiency, it established standardized specifications for everything from automobile tires to shoe colors (three were permitted—black, brown, and white). The Railroad Administration took control of the nation's transportation system, and the Fuel Agency rationed coal and oil. The Food Administration instructed farmers on modern methods of cultivation and promoted the more efficient preparation of meals. Its director, Herbert Hoover, mobilized the shipment of American food to the war-devastated Allies, popularizing the slogan "Food will win the war."

World War I was the first war in which soldiers moved to the battlefront in motorized trucks. This photograph is from 1918.

These agencies generally saw themselves as partners of business as much as regulators. They guaranteed government suppliers a high rate of profit and encouraged cooperation among former business rivals by suspending antitrust laws. At the same time, however, the War Labor Board, which included representatives of government, industry, and the American Federation of Labor, pressed for the establishment of a minimum wage, eight-hour workday, and the right to form unions. During the war, wages rose substantially, working conditions in many industries improved, and union membership doubled. To finance the war, corporate and individual income taxes rose enormously. By 1918, the wealthiest Americans were paying 60 percent of their income in taxes. Tens of millions of Americans answered the call to demonstrate their patriotism by purchasing Liberty bonds. Once peace arrived, the wartime state quickly withered away. But for a time, the federal government seemed well on its way to fulfilling the Progressive task of promoting economic rationalization, industrial justice, and a sense of common national purpose.

THE PROPAGANDA WAR

During the Civil War, it had been left to private agencies—Union Leagues, the Loyal Publication Society, and others—to mobilize prowar public opinion. But the Wilson administration decided that patriotism was too important to leave to the private sector. Many Americans were skeptical about whether democratic America should enter a struggle between rival empires. Some vehemently opposed American participation, notably the Industrial Workers of the World (IWW) and the bulk of the Socialist Party, which in 1917 condemned the declaration of war as "a crime against the people of the United States" and called on "the workers of all countries" to refuse to fight. As the major national organization to oppose Wilson's policy, the Socialist Party became a rallying point for antiwar sentiment. In mayoral elections across the country in the fall of 1917, the Socialist vote averaged 20 percent, far above the party's previous total.

In April 1917, the Wilson administration created the Committee on Public Information (CPI) to explain to Americans and the world, as its director, George Creel, put it, "the cause that compelled America to take arms in defense of its liberties and free institutions." Enlisting academics, journalists, artists, and advertising men, the CPI flooded the country with prowar propaganda, using every available medium from pamphlets (of which it issued 75 million) to posters, newspaper advertisements, and motion pictures. It trained and dispatched across the country 75,000 Four-Minute Men, who delivered brief standardized talks (sometimes in Italian, Yiddish, and other immigrant languages) to audiences in movie theaters, schools, and other public venues.

Never before had an agency of the federal government attempted the "conscious and intelligent manipulation of the organized habits and opinions of the masses," in the words of young Edward Bernays, a member of Creel's staff who would later create the modern profession of public relations. The CPI's activities proved, one adman wrote, that it was possible to "sway the ideas of whole populations, change their habits of life, create belief, practically universal in any policy or idea." In the 1920s, advertisers

A poster addressed to Jewish immigrants by the U.S. Food Administration proclaims, "Food Will Win the War." It adds, "You came here seeking freedom, now you must help preserve it." Copies were also printed in other European languages.

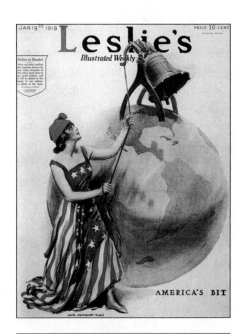

A female figure wearing a cap of liberty rings the liberty bell in this patriotic illustration from 1918.

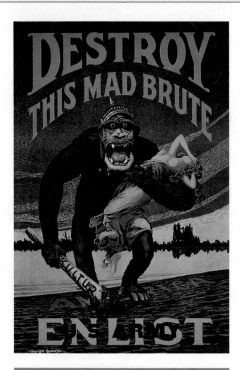

A vivid example of the anti-German propaganda produced by the federal government to encourage prowar sentiment during World War I.

would use what they had learned to sell goods. But the CPI also set a precedent for active governmental efforts to shape public opinion in later international conflicts, from World War II to the Cold War and Iraq.

"THE GREAT CAUSE OF FREEDOM"

The CPI couched its appeal in the Progressive language of social cooperation and expanded democracy. Abroad, this meant a peace based on the principle of national self-determination. At home, it meant improving "industrial democracy." A Progressive journalist, Creel believed the war would accelerate the movement toward solving the "age-old problems of poverty, inequality, oppression, and unhappiness." He took to heart a warning from historian Carl Becker that a simple contrast between German tyranny and American democracy would not seem plausible to the average worker: "You talk to him of our ideals of liberty and he thinks of the shameless exploitation of labor and of the ridiculous gulf between wealth and poverty." The CPI distributed pamphlets foreseeing a postwar society complete with a "universal eight-hour day" and a living wage for all.

While "democracy" served as the key term of wartime mobilization, "freedom" also took on new significance. The war, a CPI advertisement proclaimed, was being fought in "the great cause of freedom." Thousands of persons, often draftees, were enlisted to pose in giant human tableaus representing symbols of liberty. One living representation of the Liberty Bell at Fort Dix, New Jersey, included 25,000 people. The most common visual image in wartime propaganda was the Statue of Liberty, employed especially to rally support among immigrants. "You came here seeking Freedom," stated a caption on one Statue of Liberty poster. "You must now help preserve it." Buying Liberty bonds became a demonstration of patriotism. Wilson's speeches cast the United States as a land of liberty fighting alongside a "concert of free people" to secure self-determination for the oppressed peoples of the world. The idea of freedom, it seems, requires an antithesis, and the CPI found one in the German kaiser and, more generally, the German nation and people. Government propaganda whipped up hatred of the wartime foe by portraying it as a nation of barbaric Huns.

Women during World War I: two women hauling ice—a job confined to men before the war—and woman suffrage demonstrators in front of the White House.

THE COMING OF WOMAN SUFFRAGE

The enlistment of "democracy" and "freedom" as ideological war weapons inevitably inspired demands for their expansion at home. In 1916, Wilson had cautiously endorsed votes for women. America's entry into the war threatened to tear the suffrage movement apart, since many advocates had been associated with opposition to American involvement. Indeed, among those who voted against the declaration of war was the first woman member of Congress, the staunch pacifist Jeannette Rankin of Montana. "I want to stand by my country, but I cannot vote for war," she said. Although defeated in her reelection bid in 1918, Rankin would return to Congress in 1940. She became the only member to oppose the declaration of war against Japan in 1941, which ended her political career. In 1968, at the age of eighty-five, Rankin took part in a giant march on Washington to protest the war in Vietnam.

As during the Civil War, however, most leaders of woman suffrage organizations enthusiastically enlisted in the effort. Women sold war bonds, organized patriotic rallies, and went to work in war production jobs. Some 22,000 served as clerical workers and nurses with American forces in Europe. Many believed wartime service would earn them equal rights at home.

At the same time, a new generation of college-educated activists, organized in the National Women's Party, pressed for the right to vote with militant tactics many older suffrage advocates found scandalous. The party's leader, Alice Paul, had studied in England between 1907 and 1910 when the British suffrage movement adopted a strategy that included arrests, imprisonments, and vigorous denunciations of a male-dominated political system. How could the country fight for democracy abroad, Paul asked, while denying it to women at home? She compared Wilson to the Kaiser, and a group of her followers chained themselves to the White House fence,

A 1915 cartoon showing the western states where women had won the right to vote. Women in the East reach out to a western woman carrying a torch of liberty.

THE AWAKENING

resulting in a seven-month prison sentence. When they began a hunger strike, the prisoners were force-fed.

The combination of women's patriotic service and widespread outrage over the mistreatment of Paul and her fellow prisoners pushed the administration toward full-fledged support for woman suffrage. "We have made partners of the women in this war," Wilson proclaimed. "Shall we admit them only to a partnership of suffering and sacrifice and toil and not to a partnership of privilege and right?" In 1920, the long struggle ended with the ratification of the Nineteenth Amendment barring states from using sex as a qualification for the suffrage. The United States became the twenty-seventh country to allow women to vote.

PROHIBITION

The war gave a powerful impulse to other campaigns that had engaged the energies of many women in the Progressive era. Ironically, efforts to stamp out prostitution and protect soldiers from venereal disease led the government to distribute birth-control information and devices—the very action for which Margaret Sanger had recently been jailed, as noted in the previous chapter.

In the early years of the twentieth century, many states and localities in the South and West banned the manufacture and sale of alcoholic beverages. ("Wet" counties allowed alcoholic beverages, "dry" counties banned them.) Prohibition became national with the adoption of the Eighteenth Amendment in 1919.

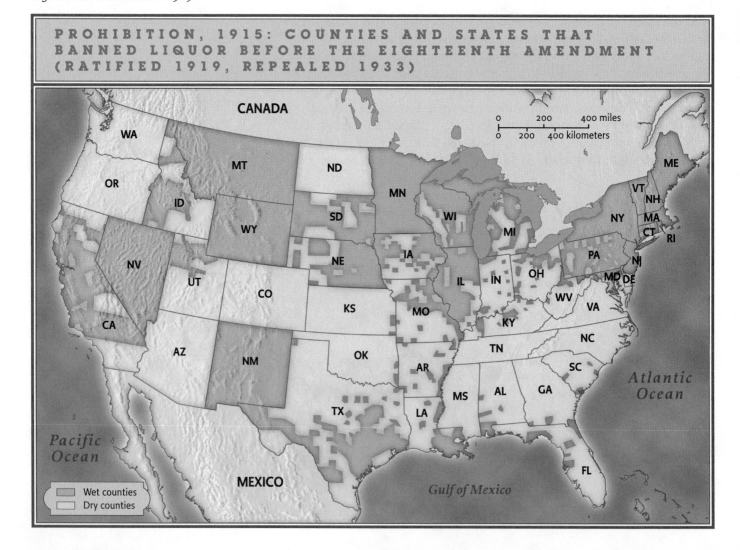

PROHIBITION, 1915: COUNTIES AND STATES THAT BANNED LIQUOR BEFORE THE EIGHTEENTH AMENDMENT (RATIFIED 1919, REPEALED 1933)

Prohibition, a movement inherited from the nineteenth century that had gained new strength and militancy in Progressive America, finally achieved national success during the war. Numerous impulses flowed into the renewed campaign to ban intoxicating liquor. Employers hoped it would create a more disciplined labor force. Urban reformers believed that it would promote a more orderly city environment and undermine urban political machines that used saloons as places to organize. Women reformers hoped Prohibition would protect wives and children from husbands who engaged in domestic violence when drunk or who squandered their wages at saloons. Many native-born Protestants saw Prohibition as a way of imposing "American" values on immigrants.

Like the suffrage movement, Prohibitionists first concentrated on state campaigns. By 1915, they had won victories in eighteen southern and midwestern states where the immigrant population was small and Protestant denominations like Baptists and Methodists strongly opposed drinking. But like the suffrage movement, Prohibitionists came to see national legislation as their best strategy. The war gave them added ammunition. Many prominent breweries were owned by German-Americans, making beer seem unpatriotic. The Food Administration insisted that grain must be used to produce food, not distilled into beer and liquor. In December 1917, Congress passed the Eighteenth Amendment, prohibiting the manufacture and sale of intoxicating liquor. It was ratified by the states in 1919 and went into effect at the beginning of 1920.

LIBERTY IN WARTIME

World War I raised questions already glimpsed during the Civil War that would trouble the nation again during the McCarthy era and in the aftermath of the terrorist attacks of 2001: What is the balance between security and freedom? Does the Constitution protect citizens' rights during wartime? Should dissent be equated with lack of patriotism? The conflict demonstrated that during a war, traditional civil liberties are likely to come under severe pressure.

In 1917, Randolph Bourne ridiculed Progressives who believed they could mold the war according to their own "liberal purposes." The conflict, he predicted, would empower not reformers but the "least democratic forces in American life." The accuracy of Bourne's prediction soon become apparent. Despite the administration's idealistic language of democracy and freedom, the war inaugurated the most intense repression of civil liberties the nation has ever known. Perhaps the very nobility of wartime rhetoric contributed to the massive suppression of dissent. For in the eyes of Wilson and many of his supporters, America's goals were so virtuous that disagreement could only reflect treason to the country's values. "It is a fearful thing to lead this great peaceful people into war," Wilson remarked in his speech asking Congress to bring America into the conflict. Even he could not have predicted how significant an impact the war would have on American freedom.

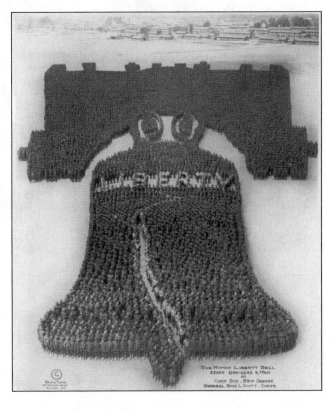

The Liberty Bell, formed by 25,000 soldiers at Camp Dix, New Jersey, in 1918, another example of the use of an image of liberty to inspire patriotic sentiment during World War I.

THE ESPIONAGE ACT

For the first time since the Alien and Sedition Acts of 1798, the federal government enacted laws to restrict freedom of speech. The Espionage Act of 1917 prohibited not only spying and interfering with the draft but also "false statements" that might impede military success. The postmaster general barred from the mails numerous newspapers and magazines critical of the administration. The victims ranged from virtually the entire socialist press and many foreign-language publications to *The Jeffersonian*, a newspaper owned by ex-Populist leader Tom Watson, which criticized the draft as a violation of states' rights. In 1918, the Sedition Act made it a crime to make spoken or printed statements that intended to cast "contempt, scorn, or disrepute" on the "form of government," or that advocated interference with the war effort. The government charged more than 2,000 persons with violating these laws. Over half were convicted. A court sentenced Ohio farmer John White to twenty-one months in prison for saying that the murder of innocent women and children by German soldiers was no worse than what the United States had done in the Philippines in the war of 1899–1903.

The most prominent victim was Eugene V. Debs, convicted in 1918 under the Espionage Act for delivering an antiwar speech. Before his sentencing, Debs gave the court a lesson in the history of American freedom, tracing the tradition of dissent from Thomas Paine to the abolitionists, and pointing out that the nation had never engaged in a war without internal opposition. Germany sent socialist leader Karl Liebknecht to prison for four years for opposing the war; in the United States, Debs's sentence was ten years. After the war's end, Wilson rejected the advice of his attorney general that he commute Debs's sentence. Debs ran for president while still in prison in 1920 and received 900,000 votes. It was left to Wilson's successor, Warren G. Harding, to release Debs from prison in 1921.

COERCIVE PATRIOTISM

Even more extreme repression took place at the hands of state governments and private groups. Americans had long displayed the flag (and used it in advertisements for everything from tobacco products to variety shows). But during World War I, attitudes toward the American flag became a test of patriotism. Persons suspected of disloyalty were forced to kiss the flag in public; those who made statements critical of the flag could be imprisoned. During the war, thirty-three states outlawed the possession or display of red or black flags (symbols, respectively, of communism and anarchism), and twenty-three outlawed a newly created offense, "criminal syndicalism," the advocacy of unlawful acts to accomplish political change or "a change in industrial ownership."

A 1917 antiwar cartoon from the radical magazine The Masses *depicts an editor, capitalist, politician, and minister celebrating American involvement in World War I and hoping to benefit from it. President Woodrow Wilson barred* The Masses *and other antiwar publications from the mails.*

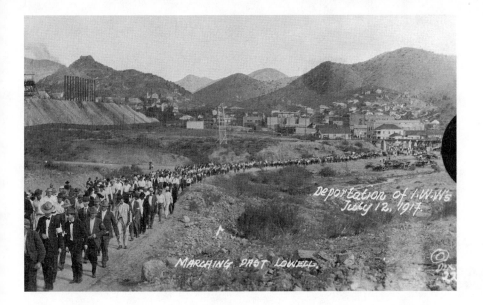

A long line of striking miners being led out of Bisbee, Arizona, in July 1917. Some 1,200 members of the Industrial Workers of the World were transported into the desert by armed vigilantes and abandoned there.

"Who is the real patriot?" Emma Goldman asked when the United States entered the war. She answered, those who "love America with open eyes," who were not blind to "the wrongs committed in the name of patriotism." But from the federal government to local authorities and private groups, patriotism came to be equated with support for the government, the war, and the American economic system, while antiwar sentiment, labor radicalism, and sympathy for the Russian Revolution became "un-American." Minnesota established a Commission of Public Safety to root out disloyalty from the state. Local authorities formally investigated residents who failed to subscribe to Liberty Loans. Throughout the country, schools revised their course offerings to ensure their patriotism and required teachers to sign loyalty oaths.

The 250,000 members of the newly formed American Protective League (APL) helped the Justice Department identify radicals and critics of the war by spying on their neighbors and carrying out "slacker raids" in which thousands of men were stopped on the streets of major cities and required to produce draft registration cards. Many private groups seized upon the atmosphere of repression as a weapon against domestic opponents. Employers cooperated with the government in crushing the Industrial Workers of the World (IWW), a move long demanded by business interests. In July 1917, vigilantes in Bisbee, Arizona, rounded up some 1,200 striking copper miners and their sympathizers, herded them into railroad boxcars, and transported them into the desert, where they were abandoned. New Mexico's governor ordered them housed in tents and provided with food and water. Few ever returned to Bisbee. In August, a crowd in Butte, Montana, lynched IWW leader Frank Little. The following month, operating under one of the broadest warrants in American history, federal agents swooped down on IWW offices throughout the country, arresting hundreds of leaders and seizing files and publications.

The war experience, commented Walter Lippmann, demonstrated "that the traditional liberties of speech and opinion rest on no solid foundation." Yet while some Progressives protested individual excesses, most

VOICES OF FREEDOM

FROM EUGENE V. DEBS,
Speech to the Jury before Sentencing under the Espionage Act (1918)

The most prominent spokesman for American socialism and a fervent opponent of American participation in World War I, Eugene V. Debs was arrested for delivering an antiwar speech and convicted of violating the Espionage Act. In his speech to the jury, he defended the right of dissent in wartime.

I wish to admit the truth of all that has been testified to in this proceeding.... Gentlemen, you have heard the report of my speech at Canton on June 16, and I submit that there is not a word in that speech to warrant the charges set out in the indictment.... In what I had to say there my purpose was to have the people understand something about the social system in which we live and to prepare them to change this system by perfectly peaceable and orderly means into what I, as a Socialist, conceive to be a real democracy.... I have never advocated violence in any form. I have always believed in education, in intelligence, in enlightenment; and I have always made my appeal to the reason and to the conscience of the people.

In every age there have been a few heroic souls who have been in advance of their time, who have been misunderstood, maligned, persecuted,

sometimes put to death.... Washington, Jefferson, Franklin, Paine, and their compeers were the rebels of their day.... But they had the moral courage to be true to their convictions....

William Lloyd Garrison, Wendell Phillips, Elizabeth Cady Stanton ... and other leaders of the abolition movement who were regarded as public enemies and treated accordingly, were true to their faith and stood their ground.... You are now teaching your children to revere their memories, while all of their detractors are in oblivion.

This country has been engaged in a number of wars and every one of them has been condemned by some of the people. The war of 1812 was opposed and condemned by some of the most influential citizens; the Mexican War was vehemently opposed and bitterly denounced, even after the war had been declared and was in progress, by Abraham Lincoln, Charles Sumner, Daniel Webster.... They were not indicted; they were not charged with treason....

I believe in the Constitution. Isn't it strange that we Socialists stand almost alone today in upholding and defending the Constitution of the United States? The revolutionary fathers ... understood that free speech, a free press and the right of free assemblage by the people were fundamental principles in democratic government.... I believe in the right of free speech, in war as well as in peace.

FROM W. E. B. DU BOIS, "Returning Soldiers," *The Crisis* (1919)

Scholar, poet, activist, founder of the National Association for the Advancement of Colored People and editor of its magazine, *The Crisis*, W. E. B. Du Bois was the most prominent black leader of the first half of the twentieth century. He supported black participation in World War I, but he insisted that black soldiers must now join in the struggle for freedom at home.

We are returning from war! *The Crisis* and tens of thousands of black men were drafted into a great struggle. For bleeding France and what she means and has meant and will mean to us and humanity and against the threat of German race arrogance, we fought gladly and to the last drop of blood; for America and her highest ideals, we fought in far-off hope; for the dominant southern oligarchy entrenched in Washington, we fought in bitter resignation. For the America that represents and gloats in lynching, disfranchisement, caste, brutality and devilish insult—for this, in the hateful upturning and mixing of things, we were forced by vindictive fate to fight, also.

But today we return! . . . We sing: This country of ours, despite all its better souls have done and dreamed, is yet a shameful land.

It *lynches*.

And lynching is barbarism of a degree of contemptible nastiness unparalleled in human history. Yet for fifty years we have lynched two Negroes a week, and we have kept this up right through the war.

It *disfranchises* its own citizens.

Disfranchisement is the deliberate theft and robbery of the only protection of poor against rich and black against white. The land that disfranchises its citizens and calls itself a democracy lies and knows it lies.

It encourages *ignorance*.

It has never really tried to educate the Negro. A dominate minority does not want Negroes educated. It wants servants. . . .

It *insults* us.

It has organized a nationwide and latterly a worldwide propaganda of deliberate and continuous insult and defamation of black blood wherever found. . . .

This is the country to which we Soldiers of Democracy return. This is the fatherland for which we fought! But it is *our* fatherland. It was right for us to fight. . . .

We *return fighting*.

Make way for Democracy!

QUESTIONS

1. Why does Debs relate the history of wartime dissent in America?

2. What connections does Du Bois draw between blacks fighting abroad in the war and returning to fight at home?

3. In what ways does each author point up the contradiction between America's professed values and its actual conduct?

failed to speak out against the broad suppression of freedom of expression. Civil liberties, by and large, had never been a major concern of Progressives, who had always viewed the national state as the embodiment of democratic purpose and insisted that freedom flowed from participating in the life of society, not standing in opposition. Strong believers in the use of national power to improve social conditions, Progressives found themselves ill prepared to develop a defense of minority rights against majority or governmental tyranny. From the AFL to *New Republic* intellectuals, moreover, supporters of the war saw the elimination of socialists and alien radicals as a necessary prelude to the integration of labor and immigrants into an ordered society, an outcome they hoped would emerge from the war.

WHO IS AN AMERICAN?

In many respects, Progressivism was a precursor to major developments of the twentieth century—the New Deal, the Great Society, the socially active state. But in accepting the idea of "race" as a permanent, defining characteristic of individuals and social groups, Progressives bore more resemblance to nineteenth-century thinkers than to later twentieth-century liberals, with whom they are sometimes compared.

THE "RACE PROBLEM"

Even before American participation in World War I, what contemporaries called the "race problem"—the tensions that arose from the country's increasing ethnic diversity—had become a major subject of public concern. "Race" referred to far more than black-white relations. The *Dictionary of Races of Peoples*, published in 1911 by the U.S. Immigration Commission, listed no fewer than forty-five immigrant "races," each supposedly with its own inborn characteristics. They ranged from Anglo-Saxons at the top down to Hebrews, Northern Italians, and, lowest of all, Southern Italians—supposedly violent, undisciplined, and incapable of assimilation.

In 1907, Congress had decreed that an American woman who married an alien automatically forfeited her American citizenship. Popular best-sellers like *The Passing of the Great Race*, published in 1916 by Madison Grant, president of the New York Zoological Society, warned that the influx of new immigrants and the low birthrate of native white women threatened the foundations of American civilization. The new science of eugenics, which studied the alleged mental characteristics of different races, gave anti-immigrant sentiment an air of professional expertise. If democracy could not flourish in the face of vast inequalities of economic power, neither, most Progressives believed, could it survive in a nation permanently divided along racial and ethnic lines.

AMERICANIZATION AND PLURALISM

Somehow, the very nationalization of politics and economic life served to heighten awareness of ethnic and racial difference and spurred demands for "Americanization"—the creation of a more homogeneous national culture.

VISIONS OF FREEDOM

An Americanization Celebration. *A photograph of a Catholic assembly on National Slavic Day, September 3, 1914, illustrates how immigrants strove to demonstrate their patriotism. Children wear Old World dress, but most of the adults are in American clothing or nurses' uniforms.*

QUESTIONS

1. What does this image suggest about whether these immigrants are seeking to assimilate into American society?

2. How does the image connect the ideas of liberty, war, and patriotism?

A 1908 play by the Jewish immigrant writer Israel Zangwill, *The Melting Pot*, gave a popular name to the process by which newcomers were supposed to merge their identity into existing American nationality. Public and private groups of all kinds—including educators, employers, labor leaders, social reformers, and public officials—took up the task of Americanizing new immigrants. The Ford Motor Company's famed sociological department entered the homes of immigrant workers to evaluate their clothing, furniture, and food preferences and enrolled them in English-language courses. Ford fired those who failed to adapt to American standards after a reasonable period of time. Americanization programs often targeted women as the bearers and transmitters of culture. In Los Angeles, teachers and religious missionaries worked to teach English to Mexican-American women so that they could then assimilate American values. Fearful that adult newcomers remained too stuck in their Old World ways, public schools paid great attention to Americanizing immigrants' children. The challenge facing schools, wrote one educator, was "to implant in their children, so far as can be done, the Anglo-Saxon conception of righteousness, law and order, and popular government."

A minority of Progressives questioned Americanization efforts and insisted on respect for immigrant subcultures. At Hull House, teachers offered English-language instruction but also encouraged immigrants to value their European heritage. Probably the most penetrating critique issued from the pen of Randolph Bourne, whose 1916 essay, "Trans-National America," exposed the fundamental flaw in the Americanization model. "There is no distinctive American culture," Bourne pointed out. Interaction between individuals and groups had produced the nation's music, poetry, and other cultural expressions. Bourne envisioned a democratic, cosmopolitan society in which immigrants and natives alike submerged their group identities in a new "trans-national" culture.

With President Wilson declaring that some Americans "born under foreign flags" were guilty of "disloyalty . . . and must be absolutely crushed," the federal and state governments demanded that immigrants demonstrate

Graduates of the Ford English School at the conclusion of their 1916 graduation ceremony. Dressed in their traditional national costumes, they disembarked from an immigrant ship into a giant melting pot. After teachers stirred the pot with ladles, the Ford workers emerged in American clothing, carrying American flags.

their unwavering devotion to the United States. The Committee on Public Information renamed the Fourth of July, 1918, Loyalty Day and asked ethnic groups to participate in patriotic pageants. New York City's celebration included a procession of 75,000 persons with dozens of floats and presentations linking immigrants with the war effort and highlighting their contributions to American society. Leaders of ethnic groups that had suffered discrimination saw the war as an opportunity to gain greater rights. Prominent Jewish leaders promoted enlistment and expressions of loyalty. The Chinese-American press insisted that even those born abroad and barred from citizenship should register for the draft, to "bring honor to the people of our race."

A 1919 Americanization pageant in Milwaukee, in which immigrants encounter Abraham Lincoln and the Statue of Liberty.

THE ANTI-GERMAN CRUSADE

German-Americans bore the brunt of forced Americanization. The first wave of German immigrants had arrived before the Civil War. By 1914, German-Americans numbered nearly 9 million, including immigrants and persons of German parentage. They had created thriving ethnic institutions including clubs, sports associations, schools, and theaters. On the eve of the war, many Americans admired German traditions in literature, music, and philosophy, and one-quarter of all the high school students in the country studied the German language. But after American entry into the war, the use of German and expressions of German culture became a target of prowar organizations. In Iowa, Governor William L. Harding issued a proclamation requiring that all oral communication in schools, public places, and over the telephone be conducted in English. Freedom of speech, he declared, did not include "the right to use a language other than the language of the country."

By 1919, the vast majority of the states had enacted laws restricting the teaching of foreign languages. Popular words of German origin were changed: "hamburger" became "liberty sandwich," and "sauerkraut" was renamed "liberty cabbage." Many communities banned the playing of German music. The government jailed Karl Müch, the director of the Boston Symphony and a Swiss citizen, as an enemy alien after he insisted on including the works of German composers like Beethoven in his concerts. The war dealt a crushing blow to German-American culture. By 1920, the number of German-language newspapers had been reduced to 276 (one-third the number twenty years earlier), and only 1 percent of high school pupils still studied German. The Census of 1920 reported a 25 percent drop in the number of Americans admitting to having been born in Germany.

A 1919 cartoon, Close the Gate, *warns that unrestricted immigration allows dangerous radicals to enter the United States.*

TOWARD IMMIGRATION RESTRICTION

Even as Americanization programs sought to assimilate immigrants into American society, the war strengthened the conviction that certain kinds of undesirable persons ought to be excluded altogether. The new immigrants, one advocate of restriction declared, appreciated the values of democracy and freedom far less than "the Anglo-Saxon," as evidenced by their attraction to "extreme political doctrines" like anarchism and socialism. Stanford University psychologist Lewis Terman introduced the term "IQ" (intelligence quotient) in 1916, claiming that this single number could measure an individual's mental capacity. Intelligence tests administered to recruits by the army seemed to confirm scientifically that blacks and the new immigrants stood far below native white Protestants on the IQ scale, further spurring demands for immigration restriction.

In 1917, over Wilson's veto, Congress required that immigrants be literate in English or another language. The war accelerated other efforts to upgrade the American population. Some were inspired by the idea of improving the human race by discouraging reproduction among less "desirable" persons. Indiana in 1907 had passed a law authorizing doctors to sterilize insane and "feeble-minded" inmates in mental institutions so that they would not pass their "defective" genes on to children. Numerous other states now followed suit. In *Buck v. Bell* (1927), the Supreme Court upheld the constitutionality of these laws. Justice Oliver Wendell Holmes's opinion included the famous statement, "three generations of imbeciles are enough." By the time the practice ended in the 1960s, some 63,000 persons had been involuntarily sterilized.

GROUPS APART: MEXICANS, PUERTO RICANS, AND ASIAN-AMERICANS

No matter how coercive, Americanization programs assumed that European immigrants and especially their children could eventually adjust to the conditions of American life, embrace American ideals, and become productive citizens enjoying the full blessings of American freedom. This assumption did not apply to non-white immigrants or to blacks. Although the melting-pot idea envisioned that newcomers from Europe would leave their ethnic enclaves and join the American mainstream, non-whites confronted ever-present boundaries of exclusion.

The war led to further growth of the Southwest's Mexican population. Wartime demand for labor from the area's mine owners and large farmers led the government to exempt Mexicans temporarily from the literacy test enacted in 1917. Mexicans were legally classified as white, and many Progressive reformers viewed the growing Mexican population as candidates for Americanization. Teachers and religious missionaries sought to instruct them in English, convert them to Protestantism, and in other ways promote their assimilation into the mainstream culture. Yet public officials in the Southwest treated them as a group apart. Segregation, by law and custom, was common in schools, hospitals, theaters, and other institutions in states with significant Mexican populations. By 1920, nearly all Mexican children in California and the Southwest were educated in their own schools or classrooms. Phoenix, Arizona, established separate public schools for Indians, Mexicans, blacks, and whites.

Puerto Ricans also occupied an ambiguous position within American society. On the eve of American entry into World War I, Congress terminated the status "citizen of Puerto Rico" and conferred American citizenship on residents of the island. The aim was to dampen support for Puerto Rican independence and to strengthen the American hold on a strategic outpost in the Caribbean. The change did not grant islanders the right to vote for president, or representation in Congress. Puerto Rican men, nonetheless, were subject to the draft and fought overseas. José de Diego, the Speaker of the House of the island's legislature, wrote the president in 1917 asking that Puerto Rico be granted the democracy the United States was fighting for in Europe.

Even more restrictive were policies toward Asian-Americans. In 1906, the San Francisco school board ordered all Asian students confined to a single public school. When the Japanese government protested, president Theodore Roosevelt persuaded the city to rescind the order. He then negotiated the Gentlemen's Agreement of 1907 whereby Japan agreed to end migration to the United States except for the wives and children of men already in the country. In 1913, California barred all aliens incapable of becoming naturalized citizens (that is, Asians) from owning or leasing land.

THE COLOR LINE

By far the largest non-white group, African-Americans, were excluded from nearly every Progressive definition of freedom described in Chapter 18. After their disenfranchisement in the South, few could participate in American democracy. Barred from joining most unions and from skilled employment, black workers had little access to "industrial freedom." A majority of adult black women worked outside the home, but for wages that offered no hope of independence. Predominantly domestic and agricultural workers, they remained unaffected by the era's laws regulating the hours and conditions of female labor. Nor could blacks, the majority desperately poor, participate fully in the emerging consumer economy, either as employees in the new department stores (except as janitors and cleaning women) or as purchasers of the consumer goods now flooding the marketplace.

Progressive intellectuals, social scientists, labor reformers, and suffrage advocates displayed a remarkable indifference to the black condition. Israel Zangwill did not include blacks in the melting-pot idea popularized by his Broadway play. Walter Weyl waited until the last fifteen pages of *The New Democracy* to introduce the "race problem." His comment, quoted in the previous chapter, that the chief obstacles to freedom were economic, not political, revealed little appreciation of how the denial of voting rights underpinned the comprehensive system of inequality to which southern blacks were subjected.

Most settlement house reformers accepted segregation as natural and equitable, assuming there should be white settlements for white neighborhoods and black settlements for black. White leaders of the woman suffrage movement said little about black disenfranchisement. In the South, members of upper-class white women's clubs sometimes raised funds for black schools and community centers. But suffrage leaders insisted that the vote was a racial entitlement, a "badge and synonym of freedom," in the words of Rebecca Felton of Georgia, that should not be denied to "free-born white women." During Reconstruction, women had been denied constitutional recognition because it was "the Negro's hour." Now, World War I's "woman's hour" excluded blacks. The amendment that achieved woman suffrage left the states free to limit voting by poll taxes and literacy tests. Living in the South, the vast majority of the country's black women did not enjoy its benefits.

ROOSEVELT, WILSON, AND RACE

The Progressive presidents shared prevailing attitudes concerning blacks. Theodore Roosevelt shocked white opinion by inviting Booker T. Washington to dine with him in the White House and by appointing a number of blacks to federal offices. But in 1906, when a small group of black soldiers shot off their guns in Brownsville, Texas, killing one resident, and none of their fellows would name them, Roosevelt ordered the dishonorable discharge of three black companies—156 men in all, including six winners of the Congressional Medal of Honor. Roosevelt's ingrained belief in Anglo-Saxon racial destiny (he called Indians "savages" and blacks "wholly unfit for the suffrage") did nothing to lessen Progressive intellectuals' enthusiasm for his New Nationalism. Even Jane Addams, one of the few Progressives to take a strong interest in black rights and a founder of the National Association for the Advancement of Colored People (NAACP), went along when the Progressive Party convention of 1912 rejected a civil rights plank in its platform and barred black delegates from the South.

Woodrow Wilson, a native of Virginia, could speak without irony of the South's "genuine representative government" and its exalted "standards of liberty." His administration imposed racial segregation in federal departments in Washington, D.C., and dismissed numerous black federal employees. Wilson allowed D. W. Griffith's film *Birth of a Nation*, which glorified the Ku Klux Klan as the defender of white civilization during Reconstruction, to have its premiere at the White House in 1915. "Have you a 'new freedom' for white Americans and a new slavery for your African-American fellow citizens?" William Monroe Trotter, the militant black editor of the *Boston Guardian* and founder of the all-black National Equal Rights League, asked the president.

Blacks subject to disenfranchisement and segregation were understandably skeptical of the nation's claim to embody freedom and fully appreciated the ways the symbols of liberty could coexist with brutal racial violence. In one of hundreds of lynchings during the Progressive era, a white mob in Springfield, Missouri, in 1906 falsely accused three black men of rape, hanged them from an electric light pole, and burned their bodies in a public orgy of violence. Atop the pole stood a replica of the Statue of Liberty.

W. E. B. DU BOIS AND THE REVIVAL OF BLACK PROTEST

Black leaders struggled to find a strategy to rekindle the national commitment to equality that had flickered brightly, if briefly, during Reconstruction. No one thought more deeply, or over so long a period, about the black

A cartoon from the St. Louis Post-Dispatch, *April 17, 1906, commenting on the lynching of three black men in Springfield, Missouri. The shadow cast by the Statue of Liberty forms a gallows on the ground.*

condition and the challenge it posed to American democracy than the scholar and activist W. E. B. Du Bois. Born in Great Barrington, Massachusetts, in 1868, and educated at Fisk and Harvard universities, Du Bois lived to his ninety-fifth year. The unifying theme of his career was Du Bois's effort to reconcile the contradiction between what he called "American freedom for whites and the continuing subjection of Negroes." His book *The Souls of Black Folk* (1903) issued a clarion call for blacks dissatisfied with the accommodationist policies of Booker T. Washington to press for equal rights. Du Bois believed that educated African-Americans like himself—the "talented tenth" of the black community—must use their education and training to challenge inequality.

In some ways, Du Bois was a typical Progressive who believed that investigation, exposure, and education would lead to solutions for social problems. As a professor at Atlanta University, he projected a grandiose plan for decades of scholarly study of black life in order to make the country aware of racism and point the way toward its elimination. But he also understood the necessity of political action.

W. E. B. Du Bois, founder of the NAACP and editor of its magazine, The Crisis, *in his New York office.*

In 1905, Du Bois gathered a group of black leaders at Niagara Falls (meeting on the Canadian side since no American hotel would provide accommodations) and organized the Niagara movement, which sought to reinvigorate the abolitionist tradition. "We claim for ourselves," Du Bois wrote in the group's manifesto, "every single right that belongs to a freeborn American, political, civil, and social; and until we get these rights we will never cease to protest and assail the ears of America." The Declaration of Principles adopted at Niagara Falls called for restoring to blacks the right to vote, an end to racial segregation, and complete equality in economic and educational opportunity. These would remain the cornerstones of the black struggle for racial justice for decades to come. Four years later, Du Bois joined with a group of mostly white reformers shocked by a lynching in Springfield, Illinois (Lincoln's adult home), to create the National Association for the Advancement of Colored People. The NAACP, as it was known, launched a long struggle for the enforcement of the Fourteenth and Fifteenth Amendments.

The NAACP's legal strategy won a few victories. In *Bailey v. Alabama* (1911), the Supreme Court overturned southern "peonage" laws that made it a crime for sharecroppers to break their labor contracts. Six years later, it ruled unconstitutional a Louisville zoning regulation excluding blacks from living in certain parts of the city (primarily because it interfered with whites' right to sell their property as they saw fit). Overall, however, the Progressive era witnessed virtually no progress toward racial justice. At a time when Americans' rights were being reformulated, blacks, said Moorfield Story, the NAACP's president, enjoyed a "curious citizenship." They shared obligations like military service, but not "the fundamental rights to which all men are entitled unless we repudiate . . . the Declaration of Independence."

CLOSING RANKS

Among black Americans, the wartime language of freedom inspired hopes for a radical change in the country's racial system. With the notable exception of William Monroe Trotter, most black leaders saw American participation in the war as an opportunity to make real the promise of freedom. To Trotter, much-publicized German atrocities were no worse than American lynchings; rather than making the world safe for democracy, the government should worry about "making the South safe for the Negroes." Yet the black press rallied to the war. Du Bois himself, in a widely reprinted editorial in the NAACP's monthly magazine, *The Crisis*, called on African-Americans to "close ranks" and enlist in the army, to help "make our own America a real land of the free."

Black participation in the Civil War had helped to secure the destruction of slavery and the achievement of citizenship. But during World War I, closing ranks did not bring significant gains. The navy barred blacks entirely, and the segregated army confined most of the 400,000 blacks who served in the war to supply units rather than combat. Wilson feared, as he noted in his diary, that the overseas experience would "go to their heads." And the U.S. Army campaigned strenuously to persuade the French not to treat black soldiers as equals—not to eat or socialize with them, or even shake their hands. Contact with African colonial soldiers fighting alongside the British and French did widen the horizons of black American soldiers. But while colonial troops marched in the victory parade in Paris, the Wilson administration did not allow black Americans to participate.

A 1918 poster celebrates black soldiers in World War I as "True Sons of Freedom." At the upper right, Abraham Lincoln looks on, with a somewhat modified quotation from the Gettysburg Address.

THE GREAT MIGRATION AND THE "PROMISED LAND"

Nonetheless, the war unleashed social changes that altered the contours of American race relations. The combination of increased wartime production and a drastic falloff in immigration from Europe once war broke out opened thousands of industrial jobs to black laborers for the first time, inspiring a large-scale migration from South to North. On the eve of World War I, 90 percent of the African-American population still lived in the South. Most northern cities had tiny black populations, and domestic and service work still predominated among both black men and women in the North. But between 1910 and 1920, half a million blacks left the South. The black population of Chicago more than doubled, New York City's rose 66 percent, and smaller industrial cities like Akron, Buffalo, and Trenton showed similar gains.

Many motives sustained the Great Migration—higher wages in northern factories than were available in the South (even if blacks remained confined to menial and unskilled positions), opportunities for educating their children, escape from the threat of lynching, and the prospect of exercising the right to vote. Migrants spoke of a Second Emancipation, of "crossing over Jordan," and of leaving the realm of pharaoh for the Promised Land. One group from Mississippi stopped to sing, "I am bound for the land of Canaan," after their train crossed the Ohio River into the North.

The black migrants, mostly young men and women, carried with them "a new vision of opportunity, of social and economic freedom," as Alain Locke explained in the preface to his influential book, *The New Negro* (1925). Yet the migrants encountered vast disappointments—severely restricted employment opportunities, exclusion from unions, rigid housing segregation, and outbreaks of violence that made it clear that no

City	Black Population, 1910	Black Population, 1920	Percent Increase
New York	91,709	152,467	66.3%
Philadelphia	84,459	134,229	58.9
Chicago	44,103	109,458	148.2
St. Louis	43,960	69,854	58.9
Detroit	5,741	40,838	611.3
Pittsburgh	25,623	37,725	47.2
Cleveland	8,448	34,451	307.8

Table 19.1 THE GREAT MIGRATION

region of the country was free from racial hostility. More white southerners than blacks moved north during the war, often with similar economic aspirations. But the new black presence, coupled with demands for change inspired by the war, created a racial tinderbox that needed only an incident to trigger an explosion.

RACIAL VIOLENCE, NORTH AND SOUTH

Dozens of blacks were killed during a 1917 riot in East St. Louis, Illinois, where employers had recruited black workers in an attempt to weaken unions (most of which excluded blacks from membership). In 1919, more than 250 persons died in riots in the urban North. Most notable was the violence in Chicago, touched off by the drowning by white bathers of a black teenager who accidentally crossed the unofficial dividing line between black and white beaches on Lake Michigan. The riot that followed raged for five days and involved pitched battles between the races throughout the city. By the time the National Guard restored order, 38 persons had been killed and more than 500 injured.

Violence was not confined to the North. In the year after the war ended, seventy-six persons were lynched in the South, including several returning black veterans wearing their uniforms. In Phillips County, Arkansas, attacks on striking black sharecroppers by armed white vigilantes left as many as 200 persons dead and required the intervention of the army to restore order. The worst race riot in American history occurred in Tulsa, Oklahoma, in 1921, when more than 300 blacks were killed and over 10,000 left homeless after a white mob, including police and National Guardsmen, burned an all-black section of the city to the ground. The violence erupted after a group of black veterans tried to prevent the lynching of a youth who had accidently tripped and fallen on a white female elevator operator, causing rumors of rape to sweep the city.

THE RISE OF GARVEYISM

World War I kindled a new spirit of militancy. The East St. Louis riot of 1917 inspired a widely publicized Silent Protest Parade on New York's

The silent parade down Fifth Avenue, July 28, 1917, in which 10,000 black marchers protested the East St. Louis race riot.

Fifth Avenue in which 10,000 blacks silently carried placards reading, "Mr. President, Why Not Make America Safe for Democracy?" In the new densely populated black ghettos of the North, widespread support emerged for the Universal Negro Improvement Association, a movement for African independence and black self-reliance launched by Marcus Garvey, a recent immigrant from Jamaica. Freedom for Garveyites meant national self-determination. Blacks, they insisted, should enjoy the same internationally recognized identity enjoyed by other peoples in the aftermath of the war. "Everywhere we hear the cry of freedom," Garvey proclaimed in 1921. "We desire a freedom that will lift us to the common standard of all men, . . . freedom that will give us a chance and opportunity to rise to the fullest of our ambition and that we cannot get in countries where other men rule and dominate." Du Bois and other established black leaders viewed Garvey as little more than a demagogue. They applauded when the government deported him after a conviction for mail fraud. But the massive following his movement achieved testified to the sense of betrayal that had been kindled in black communities during and after the war.

1919

A WORLDWIDE UPSURGE

The combination of militant hopes for social change and disappointment with the war's outcome was evident far beyond the black community. In the Union of Soviet Socialist Republics (or Soviet Union), as Russia had been renamed after the revolution, Lenin's government had nationalized landholdings, banks, and factories and proclaimed the socialist dream of a workers' government. The Russian Revolution and the democratic aspirations unleashed by World War I sent tremors of hope and fear throughout the world. Like 1848 and, in the future, 1968, 1919 was a year of worldwide social and political upheaval. Inspired by Lenin's call for revolution, communist-led governments came to power in Bavaria (a part of Germany) and Hungary. General strikes demanding the fulfillment of wartime promises of "industrial democracy" took place in Belfast, Glasgow, and Winnipeg. In Spain, anarchist peasants began seizing land. Crowds in India challenged British rule, and nationalist movements in other colonies demanded independence. "We are living and shall live all our lives in a revolutionary world," wrote Walter Lippmann.

The worldwide revolutionary upsurge produced a countervailing mobilization by opponents of radical change. Even as they fought the Germans, the Allies viewed the Soviet government as a dire threat and attempted to overturn it. In the summer of 1918, Allied expeditionary forces—British, French, Japanese, and Americans—landed in Russia to aid Lenin's opponents in the civil war that had engulfed the country. The last of them did not leave until 1920.

Wilson's policies toward the Soviet Union revealed the contradictions within the liberal internationalist vision. On the one hand, in keeping with the principles of the Fourteen Points and its goal of a worldwide economic open door, Wilson hoped to foster trade with the new government. On the other, fear of communism as a source of international instability and a threat to private property inspired military intervention in Russia. The Allies did not invite the Soviet Union to the Versailles peace conference, and Wilson refused to extend diplomatic recognition to Lenin's government. The Soviet regime survived, but in the rest of the world the tide of change receded. By the fall, the mass strikes had been suppressed and conservative governments had been installed in central Europe. Anticommunism would remain a pillar of twentieth-century American foreign policy.

UPHEAVAL IN AMERICA

In the United States, 1919 also brought unprecedented turmoil. It seemed all the more disorienting for occurring in the midst of a worldwide flu epidemic that killed between 20 and 40 million persons, including nearly 700,000 Americans. Racial violence, as noted above, was widespread. In June, bombs exploded at the homes of prominent Americans, including the attorney general, A. Mitchell Palmer, who escaped uninjured. Among aggrieved American workers, wartime language linking patriotism with democracy and freedom inspired hopes that an era of social justice and economic empowerment was at hand. In 1917, Wilson had told the AFL, "While we are fighting for freedom, we must see to it among other things that labor is free." Labor took him seriously—more seriously, it seems, than Wilson intended. The government, as one machinist put it, had "proclaimed to the World that the freedom and democracy we are fighting for shall be practiced in the industries of America."

By the war's end, many Americans believed that the country stood on the verge of what Herbert Hoover called "a new industrial order." Sidney Hillman, leader of the garment workers' union, was one of those caught up in the utopian dreams inspired by the war and reinforced by the Russian Revolution. "One can hear the footsteps of the Deliverer," he wrote. "Labor will rule and the World will be free." In 1919, more than 4 million workers engaged in strikes—the greatest wave of labor unrest in American history. There were walkouts, among many others, by textile workers, telephone operators, and Broadway actors. Throughout the country, workers appropriated the imagery and rhetoric of the war, parading in army uniforms with Liberty buttons, denouncing their employers as "kaisers," and demanding "freedom in the workplace." They were met by an unprecedented mobilization of employers, government, and private patriotic organizations.

The strike wave began in January 1919 in Seattle, where a walkout of shipyard workers mushroomed into a general strike that for once united

An advertisement placed by a steel company in a Pittsburgh newspaper announces, in several languages, that the steel strike of 1919 "has failed." The use of the figure of Uncle Sam illustrates how the companies clothed their anti-union stance in the language of patriotism.

Local police with literature seized from a Communist Party office in Cambridge, Massachusetts, November 1919.

AFL unions and the IWW. For five days, a committee of labor leaders oversaw city services, until federal troops arrived to end the strike. In September, Boston policemen struck for higher wages and shorter working hours. Declaring "there is no right to strike against the public safety," Massachusetts governor Calvin Coolidge called out the National Guard to patrol the city and fired the entire police force. In the nation's coalfields, a company manager observed, wartime propaganda had raised unrealistic expectations among workers, who took the promise of "an actual emancipation" too "literally." When the war ended, miners demanded an end to company absolutism. Their strike was ended by a court injunction obtained by Attorney General Palmer.

THE GREAT STEEL STRIKE

The wartime rhetoric of economic democracy and freedom helped to inspire the era's greatest labor uprising, the 1919 steel strike. Centered in Chicago, it united some 365,000 mostly immigrant workers in demands for union recognition, higher wages, and an eight-hour workday. Before 1917, the steel mills were little autocracies where managers arbitrarily established wages and working conditions and suppressed all efforts at union organizing. During the war, workers flooded into the Amalgamated Association, the union that had been nearly destroyed by its defeat at Homestead a generation earlier. By the end of 1918, they had won an eight-hour day. Employers' anti-union activities resumed following the armistice that ended the fighting. "For why this war?" asked one Polish immigrant steelworker at a union meeting. "For why we buy Liberty bonds? For the mills? No, for freedom and America—for everybody. No more [work like a] horse and wagon. For eight-hour day."

In response to the strike, steel magnates launched a concerted counterattack. Employers appealed to anti-immigrant sentiment among native-born workers, many of whom returned to work, and conducted a propaganda campaign that associated the strikers with the IWW, communism, and disloyalty. "Americanism vs. Alienism" was the issue of the strike, declared the *New York Tribune*. With middle-class opinion having turned against the labor movement and the police in Pittsburgh assaulting workers on the streets, the strike collapsed in early 1920.

THE RED SCARE

Many Progressives hoped to see the wartime apparatus of economic planning continue after 1918. The Wilson administration, however, quickly dismantled the agencies that had established controls over industrial production and the labor market, although during the 1930s they would serve as models for some policies of Franklin D. Roosevelt's New Deal. Wartime repression of dissent, however, continued. It reached its peak with the Red Scare of 1919–1920, a short-lived but intense period of political intolerance inspired by the postwar strike wave and the social tensions and fears generated by the Russian Revolution.

Convinced that episodes like the steel strike were part of a worldwide communist conspiracy, Attorney General A. Mitchell Palmer in November

1919 and January 1920 dispatched federal agents to raid the offices of radical and labor organizations throughout the country. They carried search warrants so broad that they reminded those with a sense of history of the writs of assistance against which James Otis had eloquently protested as being destructive of liberty in 1761. The Palmer Raids were overseen by the twenty-four-year-old director of the Radical Division of the Justice Department, J. Edgar Hoover. More than 5,000 persons were arrested, most of them without warrants, and held for months without charge. The government deported hundreds of immigrant radicals, including Emma Goldman, the prominent radical speaker mentioned in the previous chapter. Hoover also began compiling files on thousands of Americans suspected of holding radical political ideas, a practice he would later continue as head of the Federal Bureau of Investigation.

The abuse of civil liberties in early 1920 was so severe that Palmer came under heavy criticism from Congress and much of the press. Secretary of Labor Louis Post began releasing imprisoned immigrants, and the Red Scare collapsed. Even the explosion of a bomb outside the New York Stock Exchange in September 1920, which killed forty persons, failed to rekindle it. (The perpetrators of this terrorist explosion, the worst on American soil until the Oklahoma City bombing of 1995, were never identified.) The reaction to the Palmer Raids planted the seeds for a new appreciation of the importance of civil liberties that would begin to flourish during the 1920s. But in their immediate impact, the events of 1919 and 1920 dealt a devastating setback to radical and labor organizations of all kinds and kindled an intense identification of patriotic Americanism with support for the political and economic status quo. The IWW had been effectively destroyed, and many moderate unions lay in disarray. The Socialist Party crumbled under the weight of governmental repression (the New York legislature expelled five Socialist members, and Congress denied Victor Berger the seat to which he had been elected from Wisconsin) and internal differences over the Russian Revolution.

Part of the crowd that greeted President Woodrow Wilson in November 1918 when he traveled to Paris to take part in the peace conference. An electric sign proclaims "Long Live Wilson."

WILSON AT VERSAILLES

The beating back of demands for fundamental social change was a severe rebuke to the hopes with which so many Progressives had enlisted in the war effort. Wilson's inability to achieve a just peace based on the Fourteen Points compounded the sense of failure. Late in 1918, the president traveled to France to attend the Versailles peace conference. Greeted by ecstatic Paris crowds, he declared that American soldiers had come to Europe "as crusaders, not merely to win a war, but to win a cause . . . to lead the world on the way of liberty." But he proved a less adept negotiator than his British and French counterparts, David Lloyd George and Georges Clemenceau.

While the Fourteen Points had called for "open covenants openly arrived at," the negotiations were conducted in secret. The Versailles Treaty did accomplish some of Wilson's goals. It established the League of Nations, the body central to his vision of a new international order. It applied the principle of self-determination to eastern Europe and redrew the map of that region. From the ruins of the Austro-Hungarian empire and parts of Germany and czarist Russia, new European nations emerged from the war—Finland, Poland, Czechoslovakia, Austria, Hungary, Latvia, Lithuania, Estonia, and Yugoslavia. Some enjoyed ethno-linguistic unity, while others comprised unstable combinations of diverse nationalities.

Despite Wilson's pledge of a peace without territorial acquisitions or vengeance, the Versailles Treaty was a harsh document that all but guaranteed future conflict in Europe. Clemenceau won for France the right to occupy the Saar Basin and Rhineland—iron- and coal-rich parts of Germany. The treaty placed strict limits on the size of Germany's future

World War I and the Versailles Treaty redrew the map of Europe and the Middle East. The Austro-Hungarian and Ottoman empires ceased to exist, and Germany and Russia were reduced in size. A group of new states emerged in eastern Europe, embodying the principle of self-determination, one of Woodrow Wilson's Fourteen Points.

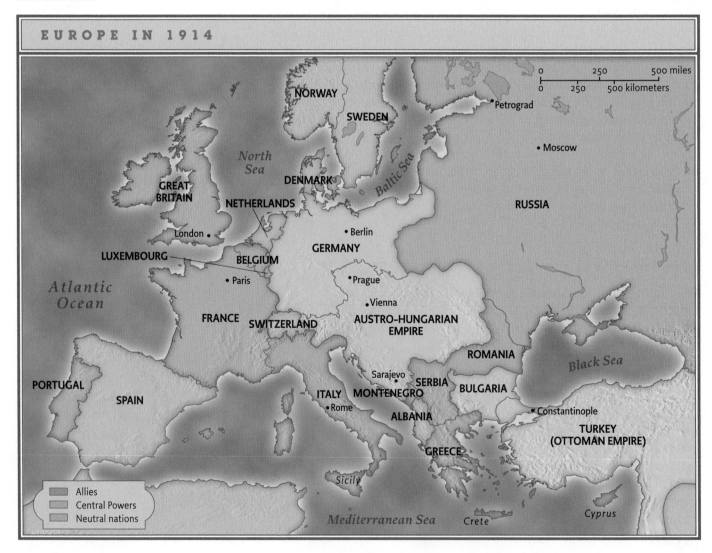

EUROPE IN 1914

army and navy. Lloyd George persuaded Wilson to agree to a clause declaring Germany morally responsible for the war and setting astronomical reparations payments (they were variously estimated at between $33 billion and $56 billion), which crippled the German economy.

THE WILSONIAN MOMENT

To many people around the world, the Great War seemed like a civil war among the nations of Europe. The carnage destroyed European claims that theirs was a higher civilization, which gave them the right to rule over more barbaric peoples. In this sense, it helped to heighten the international prestige of the United States, a latecomer to the war. Like the ideals of the American Revolution, the Wilsonian rhetoric of self-determination reverberated across the globe, especially among oppressed minorities (including blacks in the United States) and colonial peoples seeking independence. In fact, these groups took Wilson's rhetoric more seriously than he did. Despite his belief in self-determination, he had supported the American

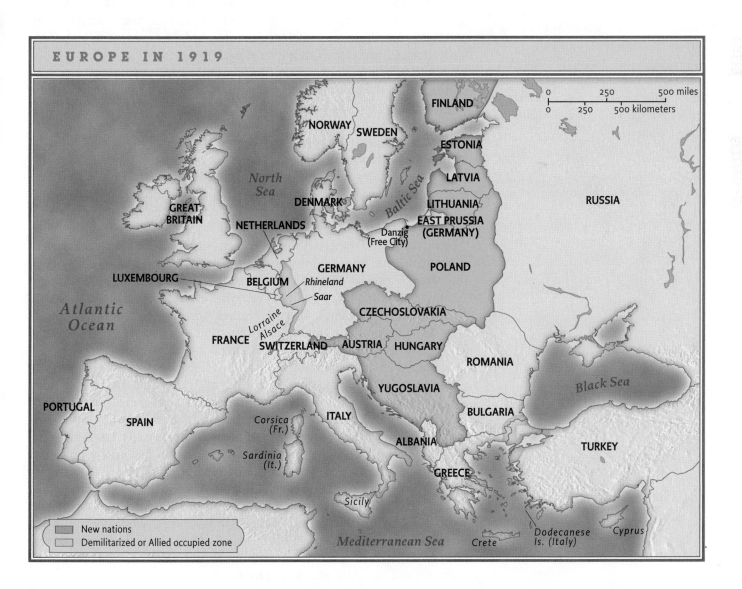

EUROPE IN 1919

Mahatma Ghandi, pictured here in 1919, became the leader of the nonviolent movement for independence for India. He was among those disappointed by the failure of the Versailles peace conference to apply the principle of self-determination to the colonial world.

annexation of the Philippines, believing that colonial peoples required a long period of tutelage before they were ready for independence.

Nonetheless, Wilsonian ideals quickly spread around the globe—not simply the idea that government must rest on the consent of the governed, but also Wilson's stress on the "equality of nations," large and small, and that international disputes should be settled by peaceful means rather than armed conflict. These stood in sharp contrast to the imperial ideas and practices of Europe. In Eastern Europe, whose people sought to carve new, independent nations from the ruins of the Austro-Hungarian and Ottoman empires, many considered Wilson a "popular saint." The leading Arabic newspaper *Al-Ahram*, published in Egypt, then under British rule, gave extensive coverage to Wilson's speech asking Congress to declare war in the name of democracy, and to the Fourteen Points, and translated the Declaration of Independence into Arabic for its readers. In Beijing, students demanding that China free itself of foreign domination gathered at the American embassy shouting, "Long live Wilson." Japan proposed to include in the charter of the new League of Nations a clause recognizing the equality of all people, regardless of race. Hundreds of letters, petitions, and declarations addressed to President Wilson made their way to the Paris headquarters of the American delegation to the peace conference. Few reached the president, as his private secretary, Gilbert Close, carefully screened his mail.

Outside of Europe, however, the idea of "self-determination" was stillborn. When the peace conference opened, Secretary of State Robert Lansing warned that the phrase was "loaded with dynamite" and would "raise hopes which can never be realized." Wilson's language, he feared, had put "dangerous" ideas "into the minds of certain races" and would inspire "impossible demands, and cause trouble in many lands." As Lansing anticipated, advocates of colonial independence descended on Paris to lobby the peace negotiators. Arabs demanded that a unified independent state be carved from the old Ottoman empire in the Middle East. Nguyen That Thanh, a young Vietnamese patriot working in Paris, pressed his people's claim for greater rights within the French empire. Citing the Declaration of Independence, he appealed unsuccessfully to Wilson to help bring an end to French rule in Vietnam. W. E. B. Du Bois organized a Pan-African Congress in Paris that put forward the idea of a self-governing nation to be carved out of Germany's African colonies. Koreans, Indians, Irish, and others also pressed claims for self-determination.

The British and French, however, had no intention of applying this principle to their own empires. They rebuffed the pleas of colonial peoples for self-rule. During the war, the British had encouraged Arab nationalism as a weapon against the Ottoman empire and had also pledged to create a homeland in Palestine for the persecuted Jews of Europe. In fact, the victors of World War I divided Ottoman territory into a series of new territories, including Syria, Lebanon, Iraq, and Palestine, controlled by the victorious Allies under League of Nations "mandates." South Africa, Australia, and Japan acquired former German colonies in Africa and Asia. Nor did Ireland achieve its independence at Versailles. Only at the end of 1921 did Britain finally agree to the creation of the Irish Free State, while continuing to rule the northeastern corner of the island. As for the Japanese proposal to establish the principle of racial equality, Wilson, with the support of Great Britain and Australia, engineered its defeat.

THE SEEDS OF WARS TO COME

Du Bois, as noted above, had hoped that black participation in the war effort would promote racial justice at home and self-government for colonies abroad. "We return," he wrote in *The Crisis* in May 1919, "we return from fighting, we return fighting. Make way for Democracy!" But the war's aftermath both in the United States and overseas left him bitterly disappointed. Du Bois concluded that Wilson had "never at any single moment meant to include in his democracy" black Americans or the colonial peoples of the world. "Most men today," he complained, "cannot conceive of a freedom that does not involve somebody's slavery." In 1903, in *The Souls of Black Folk*, Du Bois had made the memorable prediction that "the problem of the twentieth century is the problem of the color-line." He now forecast a "fight for freedom" that would pit "black and brown and yellow men" throughout the world against racism and imperialism.

Disappointment at the failure to apply the Fourteen Points to the non-European world created a pervasive cynicism about Western use of the language of freedom and democracy. Wilson's apparent willingness to accede to the demands of the imperial powers helped to spark a series of popular protest movements across the Middle East and Asia, and the rise of a new anti-Western nationalism. It inspired the May 4 movement in China, a mass protest against the decision at the Versailles peace conference to award certain German concessions (parts of China governed by foreign powers) to Japan. Some leaders, like Nguyen That Thanh, who took the name Ho Chi Minh, turned to communism, in whose name he would lead Vietnam's long and bloody struggle for independence. The Soviet leader Lenin, in fact, had spoken of "the right of nations to self-determination" before Wilson, and with the collapse of the Wilsonian moment, Lenin's reputation in the colonial world began to eclipse that of the American president. But whether communist or not, these movements announced the emergence of anticolonial nationalism as a major force in world affairs, which it would remain for the rest of the twentieth century.

"Your liberalness," one Egyptian leader remarked, speaking of Britain and America, "is only for yourselves." Yet ironically, when colonial peoples demanded to be recognized as independent members of the international community, they would invoke both the heritage of the American Revolution—the first colonial struggle that produced an independent nation—and the Wilsonian language whereby the self-governing nation-state is the most legitimate political institution, and all nations deserve equal respect.

As Du Bois recognized, World War I sowed the seeds not of a lasting peace but of wars to come. German resentment over the peace terms would help to fuel the rise of Adolf Hitler and the coming of World War II. In the breakup of Czechoslovakia and Yugoslavia, violence over the status of Northern Ireland, and the seemingly unending conflict in the Middle East between Arabs and Israelis, the world was still haunted by the ghost of Versailles.

THE TREATY DEBATE

One final disappointment awaited Wilson on his return from Europe. He viewed the new League of Nations as the war's finest legacy. But many

Interrupting the Ceremony, *a 1918 cartoon from the* Chicago Tribune, *depicts Senate opponents of the Versailles Treaty arriving just in time to prevent the United States from becoming permanently ensnared in "foreign entanglements" through the League of Nations.*

Americans feared that membership in the League would commit the United States to an open-ended involvement in the affairs of other countries. Wilson asserted that the United States could not save the world without being continually involved with it. His opponents, led by Senator Henry Cabot Lodge of Massachusetts, argued that the League threatened to deprive the country of its freedom of action.

A considerable majority of senators would have accepted the treaty with "reservations" ensuring that the obligation to assist League members against attack did not supercede the power of Congress to declare war. As governor of New Jersey and as president, Wilson had proved himself to be a skilled politician capable of compromising with opponents. In this case, however, convinced that the treaty reflected "the hand of God," Wilson refused to negotiate with congressional leaders. In October 1919, in the midst of the League debate, Wilson suffered a serious stroke. Although the extent of his illness was kept secret, he remained incapacitated for the rest of his term. In effect, his wife, Edith, headed the government for the next seventeen months. In November 1919 and again in March 1920, the Senate rejected the Versailles Treaty.

American involvement in World War I lasted barely nineteen months, but it cast a long shadow over the following decade—and, indeed, the rest of the century. In its immediate aftermath, the country retreated from international involvements. But in the long run, Wilson's combination of idealism and power politics had an enduring impact. His appeals to democracy, open markets, and a special American mission to instruct the world in freedom, coupled with a willingness to intervene abroad militarily to promote American interests and values, would create the model for twentieth-century American international relations.

On its own terms, the war to make the world safe for democracy failed. Even great powers cannot always bend the world to their purposes. The war brought neither stability nor democracy to most of the world, and it undermined freedom in the United States. It also led to the eclipse of Progressivism. Republican candidate Warren G. Harding, who had no connection with the party's Progressive wing, swept to victory in the presidential election of 1920. Harding's campaign centered on a "return to normalcy" and a repudiation of what he called "Wilsonism." He received 60 percent of the popular vote. Begun with idealistic goals and grand hopes for social change, American involvement in the Great War laid the foundation for one of the most conservative decades in the nation's history.

SUGGESTED READING

BOOKS

Bederman, Gail. *Manliness and Civilization: A Cultural History of Race and Gender in the United States, 1880–1917* (1995). Explores how ideas concerning civilization and gender affected American foreign policy.

Dawley, Alan. *Changing the World: American Progressives in War and Revolution* (2003). Presents the war as a fulfillment and betrayal of the Progressive impulse.

Gilmore, Glenda E. *Gender and Jim Crow: Women and the Politics of White Supremacy in North Carolina, 1896–1920* (1996). A careful study of how black and white women negotiated the boundaries of segregation in a southern state.

Green, Elna C. *Southern Strategies: Southern Women and the Woman Suffrage Question* (1997). Describes how southern women campaigned for the vote without challenging the subordinate status of African-Americans.

Greene, Julie. *The Canal Builders: Making American Empire at the Panama Canal* (2009). Tells the story of the construction of the Panama Canal and the tens of thousands of workers who did the work.

Grossman, James R. *Land of Hope: Chicago, Black Southerners, and the Great Migration* (1989). An in-depth study of the migration of blacks to one American city.

Healy, David. *Drive to Hegemony: The United States in the Caribbean, 1898–1917* (1988). Examines American foreign policy in the Caribbean from McKinley to Wilson.

Kennedy, David M. *Over Here: The First World War and American Society* (1980). A comprehensive account of how the war affected domestic life in the United States.

Knock, Thomas J. *To End All Wars: Woodrow Wilson and the Quest for a New World Order* (1992). Discusses Wilson's internationalist vision and how it led the United States into a successful war and a failed peace.

Manela, Erez. *The Wilsonian Moment* (2007). Details how the Wilsonian ideal of self-determination was received around the world, with results Wilson did not anticipate.

Meier, August. *Negro Thought in America, 1880–1915* (1966). A pioneering study of the ideas of black leaders, including W. E. B. Du Bois.

Mitchell, David J. *1919: Red Mirage* (1970). A global account of the upheavals of 1919.

Preston, William, Jr. *Aliens and Dissenters: Federal Suppression of Radicals, 1903–1933* (1963). An influential study of the federal government's efforts to suppress dissenting ideas, especially during and immediately after World War I.

Renda, Mary A. *Taking Haiti: Military Occupation and the Culture of U.S. Imperialism, 1915–1940* (2001). Examines the causes and consequences of the American occupation of Haiti.

Stein, Judith. *The World of Marcus Garvey: Race and Class in Modern Society* (1986). Places the Garvey movement in an Atlantic perspective linking Africa, the United States, and the West Indies.

Sullivan, Patricia. *Lift Every Voice: The NAACP and the Making of the Civil Rights Movement* (2009). A sweeping history of the country's preeminent civil rights organization, from its founding to the 1950s.

Tuttle, William. *Race Riot: Chicago in the Red Summer of 1919* (1970). A vivid account of the most violent racial upheaval of the era.

Weinstein, James. *The Decline of Socialism in America, 1912–1925* (1967). Explores how World War I and the Russian Revolution contributed to the demise of the American Socialist Party.

WEBSITES

Alcohol, Temperance, and Prohibition: http://dl.lib.brown.edu/temperance/

First World War.com: www.firstworldwar.com/index.htm

Red Scare: http://newman.baruch.cuny.edu/digital/redscare/

The Bisbee Deportation of 1917: www.library.arizona.edu/exhibits/bisbee/

REVIEW QUESTIONS

1. Explain the role of the United States in the global economy by 1920.

2. Explain how building the Panama Canal reflected American global expansion as well as U.S. racial attitudes.

3. What did President Wilson mean by "moral imperialism," and what measures were taken to apply this to Latin America?

4. Describe how World War I was a blow to the ideals of a "superior" Western civilization and to global socialism.

5. Why did Progressives see in the expansion of governmental powers in wartime an opportunity to reform American society?

6. What were the goals and methods of the Committee on Public Information during World War I?

7. Give some wartime examples of coercive patriotism and describe their effects.

8. Identify the goals of those pressing for global change in 1919, and of those who opposed them.

9. What were the major causes—both real and imaginary—of the Red Scare?

10. Describe how World War I and the U.S. failure to join the League of Nations sowed the seeds of future twentieth-century wars.

FREEDOM QUESTIONS

1. Explain how the Committee on Public Information supported the war effort by promoting freedom and democracy abroad while there were restrictions on both in the United States.

2. What were the effects of the war effort on the freedoms of people in the United States?

3. What were the experiences of the following groups during the war: German-Americans, Mexicans, Puerto Ricans, Asian-Americans, and African-Americans?

4. What were the major arguments made by W. E. B. Du Bois in his efforts to expand civil rights in America?

5. Explain how Wilsonian ideals and rhetoric spread around the globe, promoting calls for freedom and independence among colonial peoples.

KEY TERMS

"liberal internationalism" (p. 769)

Panama Canal Zone (p. 772)

yellow fever (p. 772)

Roosevelt Corollary (p. 772)

"moral imperialism" (p. 773)

sinking of the *Lusitania* (p. 777)

Zimmerman Telegram (p. 778)

Fourteen Points (p. 778)

Selective Service Act (p. 780)

War Industries Board (p. 780)

Committee on Public Information
    (p. 781)

Espionage Act (p. 786)

Sedition Act (p. 786)

American Protective League
    (p. 787)

intelligence quotient (IQ) (p. 794)

Brownsville affair (p. 796)

National Association for the
    Advancement of Colored
    People (p. 796)

Garveyites (p. 800)

United States in Russia (p. 801)

Red Scare (p. 802)

REVIEW TABLE

Wartime and Freedom

Event	Date	Consequences
Espionage Act	1917	Restricted freedom of speech by prohibiting "false statements" that might impede military success
American Protective League	1917–1919	Members spied on their neighbors in order to identify radicals and critics of the war to the federal government
Anti-German Crusade	1917–1919	Prowar organizations targeted the use of German and expressions of German culture, banning German music and changing German names
Red Scare and Palmer Raids	1919–1920	Over five thousand persons are arrested without warrants and held without charge, while hundreds of others are deported; government collects files on suspected radicals; IWW targeted by business and governmental opponents

Part 5

DEPRESSION AND WARS, 1920–1953

For the United States and the world at large, the decades between the end of World War I and the middle of the twentieth century marked one of the most painful eras in modern history. These years witnessed the Great Depression (1929–1939), World War II (1939–1945), and the advent of a Cold War that pitted the United States and the Soviet Union, former wartime allies, against each other in a global contest for power. These epochal events produced the deaths of tens of millions of people and wreaked economic havoc on hundreds of millions of others. By the end of this period, the United States and the world lived with the anxiety caused by the constant threat of nuclear war.

These developments could not have been anticipated in the immediate aftermath of World War I. After that conflict, the United States withdrew from active involvement in international affairs and enjoyed a decade of economic prosperity. During the 1920s, conservatism dominated the political arena. The labor movement suffered setback after setback, the government turned its back on many of the reforms of the Progressive era, and organized feminism faded from the public sphere. A nineteenth-century understanding of freedom based on liberty of contract in an unregulated marketplace, much criticized in the years before World War I, gained a new lease on life during the administrations of Warren G. Harding and Calvin Coolidge.

If political dissent faded during the 1920s, cultural differences seemed stronger than ever. In the name of personal freedom, many Americans embraced a new culture, centered in the nation's cities, based on consumption and enjoyment of new mass forms of leisure and entertainment, including radio

and motion pictures. Other Americans, living in rural areas of the South and West where traditional religion still held sway, saw the new urban culture not as an expansion of freedom, but as a threat to an understanding of freedom rooted in long-established moral values. During the 1920s, debates over immigration, Prohibition, the teaching of Darwin's theory of evolution in public schools, and the behavior of young, sexually liberated women in the nation's cities reflected the tension between older and newer cultures, each with its own definition of freedom.

The heady days of the 1920s came to an abrupt end with the stock market crash of 1929, which ushered in the Great Depression, the greatest economic crisis in American history. With the federal government unable to reverse the economic decline or relieve widespread distress, the election of 1932 brought to the presidency Franklin D. Roosevelt, who promised a New Deal for the American people. Roosevelt presided over a profound political and social transformation in government, society, and the understandings of freedom. During his presidency, the federal government undertook unprecedented initiatives in an attempt to stimulate economic recovery and expand Americans' economic liberties. The government determined what farmers could plant, required employers to deal with unions, insured bank deposits, regulated the stock market, loaned money to home owners, and provided payments to a majority of the elderly and unemployed. It transformed the physical environment through hydroelectric dams, reforestation projects, and rural electrification. Under Roosevelt's leadership, the Democratic Party was transformed into a coalition of farmers, white southerners, urban working-class voters representing numerous ethnic groups, and northern African-Americans. It dominated national politics for many years. The New Deal helped to inspire, and was powerfully influenced by, a popular upsurge that redefined the idea of freedom to include a public guarantee of economic security for ordinary citizens.

Even as the United States struggled with the economic crisis, events abroad drew the country into the largest war in human history. The rise of powerful dictatorships bent on military expansion—Germany in Europe and Japan in Asia—led inexorably to World War II. Most

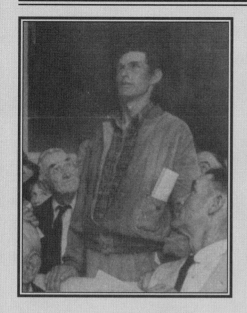

Americans hoped to remain aloof from the crisis. This "isolationism" restrained Roosevelt's efforts to aid those fighting Germany, even though he saw Hitler's conquests in Europe as a threat to American security. When the Japanese attacked the American naval base at Pearl Harbor, Hawaii, on December 7, 1941, the United States entered the war.

World War II expanded even further the size and power of the national government. War production finally ended the Depression and drew millions of Americans from rural areas into the army or to industrial centers in the North and West. The Four Freedoms—Roosevelt's statement of Allied war aims—became the wartime rallying cry. Unlike during World War I, the federal government promoted group equality as central to American freedom—although the internment of more than 100,000 Japanese-Americans revealed the limits of racial tolerance. The war also placed on the national agenda, for the first time since Reconstruction, the contradiction between the nation's rhetoric of freedom and the condition of its black population. It inspired an upsurge of black militancy, expressed in the slogan "double-V"—victory over enemies overseas, and over racial inequality at home.

No retreat into isolationism followed World War II. The United States had refused to join the League of Nations, but it became the leading member of the United Nations, which was established in 1945. However, the wartime alliance among the United States, Britain, and the Soviet Union soon shattered, replaced by the worldwide contest known as the Cold War. By the 1950s, through a series of global anticommunist alliances, the United States had taken on a permanent military presence throughout the world. As in previous wars, freedom both helped to mobilize public support for the Cold War and was subtly changed in the process. The defense of freedom—increasingly equated with "free enterprise"—became the rationale for the doctrine of "containment," or global opposition to the spread of communism. The Cold War also inspired an anticommunist crusade within the United States. In the late 1940s and early 1950s, thousands of Americans accused of holding "subversive" beliefs lost their jobs, and an atmosphere of political conformity dominated public life. The battle to defend the "free world" abroad produced severe infringements on freedom at home.

CHAPTER 20

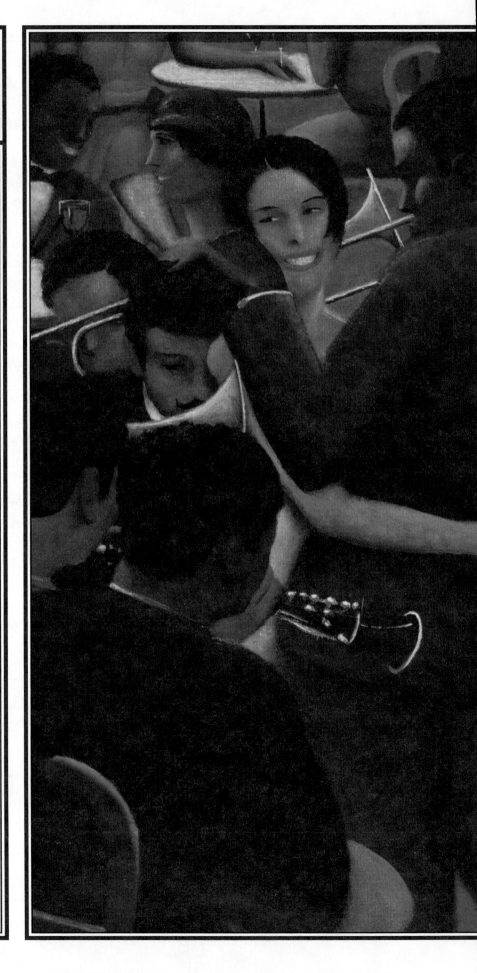

From Business Culture to Great Depression: The Twenties, 1920–1932

Blues, a 1929 painting by Archibald Motley Jr., depicts one side of the 1920s: dance halls, jazz bands, and drinking despite the advent of Prohibition.

☞ FOCUS QUESTIONS

• Who benefited and who suffered in the new consumer society of the 1920s?

• In what ways did the government promote business interests in the 1920s?

• Why did the protection of civil liberties gain importance in the 1920s?

• What were the major flash points between fundamentalism and pluralism in the 1920s?

• What were the causes of the Great Depression, and how effective were the government's responses by 1932?

▼
I
▲

n May 1920, at the height of the postwar Red Scare, police arrested two Italian immigrants accused of participating in a robbery at a South Braintree, Massachusetts, factory in which a security guard was killed. Nicola Sacco, a shoemaker, and Bartolomeo Vanzetti, an itinerant unskilled laborer, were anarchists who dreamed of a society in which government, churches, and private property had been abolished. They saw violence as an appropriate weapon of class warfare. But very little evidence linked them to this particular crime. One man claimed to have seen Vanzetti at the wheel of the getaway car, but all the other eyewitnesses described the driver quite differently. Disputed tests on one of the six bullets in the dead man's body suggested that it might have been fired from a gun owned by Sacco. Neither fingerprints nor possession of stolen money linked either to the crime. In the atmosphere of anti-radical and anti-immigrant fervor, however, their conviction was a certainty. "I have suffered," Vanzetti wrote from prison, "for things that I am guilty of. I am suffering because I am a radical and indeed I am a radical; I have suffered because I was an Italian, and indeed I am an Italian."

Although their 1921 trial had aroused little public interest outside the Italian-American community, the case of Sacco and Vanzetti attracted international attention during the lengthy appeals that followed. There were mass protests in Europe against their impending execution. In the United States, the movement to save their lives attracted the support of an impressive array of intellectuals, including the novelist John Dos Passos, the poet Edna St. Vincent Millay, and Felix Frankfurter, a professor at Harvard Law School and a future justice of the Supreme Court. In response to the mounting clamor, the governor of Massachusetts appointed a three-member commission to review the case, headed by Abbott Lawrence Lowell, the president of Harvard University (and for many years an official of the Immigration Restriction League). The commission upheld the verdict and death sentences, and on August 23, 1927, Sacco and Vanzetti died in the electric chair. "It is not every prisoner," remarked the journalist Heywood Broun, "who has a president of Harvard throw the switch for him."

The Sacco-Vanzetti case laid bare some of the fault lines beneath the surface of American society during the 1920s. The case, the writer Edmund Wilson commented, "revealed the whole anatomy of American life, with all its classes, professions and points of view and . . . it raised almost every fundamental question of our political and social system." It demonstrated how long the Red Scare extended into the 1920s and how powerfully it undermined basic American freedoms. It reflected the fierce cultural battles that raged in many communities during the decade. To many native-born Americans, the two men symbolized an alien threat to their way of life. To Italian-Americans, including respectable middle-class organizations like the Sons of Italy that raised money for the defense, the

A 1927 photograph shows Nicola Sacco and Bartolomeo Vanzetti outside the courthouse in Dedham, Massachusetts, surrounded by security agents and onlookers. They are about to enter the courthouse, where the judge will pronounce their death sentence.

outcome symbolized the nativist prejudices and stereotypes that haunted immigrant communities. To Dos Passos, the executions underscored the success of the anti-radical crusade: "They are stronger. They are rich. They hire and fire the politicians, the old judges, . . . the college presidents." Dos Passos's lament was a bitter comment on the triumph of pro-business conservatism during the 1920s.

In popular memory, the decade that followed World War I is recalled as the Jazz Age or the Roaring Twenties. With its flappers (young, sexually liberated women), speakeasies (nightclubs that sold liquor in violation of Prohibition), and a soaring stock market fueled by easy credit and a get-rich-quick outlook, it was a time of revolt against moral rules inherited from the nineteenth century. Observers from Europe, where class divisions were starkly visible in work, politics, and social relations, marveled at the uniformity of American life. Factories poured out standardized consumer goods, their sale promoted by national advertising campaigns. Conservatism dominated a political system from which radical alternatives seemed to have been purged. Radio and the movies spread mass culture throughout the nation. Americans seemed to dress alike, think alike, go to the same movies, and admire the same larger-than-life national celebrities.

Many Americans, however, did not welcome the new secular, commercial culture. They resented and feared the ethnic and racial diversity of America's cities and what they considered the lax moral standards of urban life. The 1920s was a decade of profound social tensions—between rural and urban Americans, traditional and "modern" Christianity, participants in the burgeoning consumer culture and those who did not fully share in the new prosperity.

Advertisements, like this one for a refrigerator, promised that consumer goods would enable Americans to fulfill their hearts' desires.

The spread of the telephone network hastened the nation's integration and opened further job opportunities for women. Lewis Hine photographed this telephone operator in the 1920s.

THE BUSINESS OF AMERICA

A DECADE OF PROSPERITY

"The chief business of the American people," said Calvin Coolidge, who became president after Warren G. Harding's sudden death from a heart attack in 1923, "is business." Rarely in American history had economic growth seemed more dramatic, cooperation between business and government so close, and business values so widely shared. After a sharp postwar recession that lasted into 1922, the 1920s was a decade of prosperity. Productivity and economic output rose dramatically as new industries—chemicals, aviation, electronics—flourished and older ones like food processing and the manufacture of household appliances adopted Henry Ford's moving assembly line.

The automobile was the backbone of economic growth. The most celebrated American factories now turned out cars, not textiles and steel as in the nineteenth century. Annual automobile production tripled during the 1920s, from 1.5 to 4.8 million. General Motors, which learned the secret of marketing numerous individual models and stylish designs, surpassed Ford with its cheap, standardized Model T (replaced in 1927 by the Model A). By 1929, half of all American families owned a car (a figure not reached in England until 1980). The automobile industry stimulated the expansion of steel, rubber, and oil production, road construction, and other sectors of the economy. It promoted tourism and the growth of suburbs (already, some commuters were driving to work) and helped to reduce rural isolation.

During the 1920s, American multinational corporations extended their sway throughout the world. With Europe still recovering from the Great War, American investment overseas far exceeded that of other countries. The dollar replaced the British pound as the most important currency of international trade. American companies produced 85 percent of the world's cars and 40 percent of its manufactured goods. General Electric and International Telephone and Telegraph bought up companies in other countries. International Business Machines (IBM) was the world's leader in office supplies. American oil companies built new refineries overseas. American companies took control of raw materials abroad, from rubber in Liberia to oil in Venezuela.

One of the more unusual examples of the global spread of American corporations was Fordlandia, an effort by the auto manufacturer Henry Ford to create a town in the heart of Brazil's Amazon rain forest. Ford hoped to secure a steady supply of rubber for car tires. But as in the United States, where he had compelled immigrant workers to adopt American dress and diet, he wanted to bring local inhabitants up to what he considered the proper standard of life (this meant, for example, forbidding his workers from using alcohol and tobacco and trying to get them to eat brown rice and whole wheat bread instead of traditional Brazilian foods). Eventually, the climate and local insects destroyed the rubber trees that Ford's engineers, lacking experience in tropical agriculture, had planted much too close together, while the workers rebelled against the long hours of labor and regimentation of the community.

A NEW SOCIETY

During the 1920s, consumer goods of all kinds proliferated, marketed by salesmen and advertisers who promoted them as ways of satisfying Americans' psychological desires and everyday needs. Frequently purchased on credit through new installment buying plans, they rapidly altered daily life. Telephones made communication easier. Vacuum cleaners, washing machines, and refrigerators transformed work in the home and reduced the demand for domestic servants. Boosted by Prohibition and an aggressive advertising campaign that, according to the company's sales director, made it "impossible for the consumer to *escape*" the product, Coca-Cola became a symbol of American life.

Americans spent more and more of their income on leisure activities like vacations, movies, and sporting events. By 1929, weekly movie attendance had reached 80 million, double the figure of 1922. Hollywood films now dominated the world movie market. Movies had been produced early in the century in several American cities, but shortly before World War I filmmakers gravitated to Hollywood, a district of Los Angeles, attracted by the open space, year-round sunshine for outdoor filming, and varied scenery. In 1910, two French companies, Pathé and Gaumont, had been the world's leading film producers. By 1925, American releases outnumbered French by eight to one. In the 1920s, both companies abandoned film production for the more profitable business of distributing American films in Europe.

Radios and phonographs brought mass entertainment into Americans' living rooms. The number of radios in Americans' homes rose from 190,000 in 1923 to just under 5 million in 1929. These developments helped to create and spread a new celebrity culture, in which recording, film, and sports stars moved to the top of the list of American heroes. During the 1920s, more than 100 million records were sold each year. RCA Victor sold so many recordings of the great opera tenor Enrico Caruso that he is sometimes called the first modern celebrity. He was soon joined by the film actor Charlie Chaplin, baseball player Babe Ruth, and boxer Jack Dempsey. Ordinary Americans followed every detail of their lives. Perhaps the decade's greatest celebrity, in terms of intensive press coverage, was the aviator Charles Lindbergh, who in 1927 made the first solo nonstop flight across the Atlantic.

André Siegfried, a Frenchman who had visited the United States four times since the beginning of the century, commented in 1928 that a "new society" had come into being, in which Americans considered their "standard of living" a "sacred acquisition, which they will defend at any price." In this new "mass

During the 1920s, radio penetrated virtually the entire country. In this photograph, a farmer tunes in to a program while milking his cow.

Electric washing machines and Hoover vacuum cleaners (demonstrated by a salesman) were two of the home appliances that found their way into many American homes during the 1920s. The woman on the right is a cardboard cutout.

civilization," widespread acceptance of going into debt to purchase consumer goods had replaced the values of thrift and self-denial, central to nineteenth-century notions of upstanding character. Work, once seen as a source of pride in craft skill or collective empowerment via trade unions, now came to be valued as a path to individual fulfillment through consumption and entertainment.

THE LIMITS OF PROSPERITY

"Big business in America," remarked the journalist Lincoln Steffens, "is producing what the socialists held up as their goal—food, shelter, and clothing for all." But signs of future trouble could be seen beneath the prosperity of the 1920s. The fruits of increased production were very unequally distributed. Real wages for industrial workers (wages adjusted to take account of inflation) rose by one-quarter between 1922 and 1929, but corporate profits rose at more than twice that rate. The process of economic concentration continued unabated. A handful of firms dominated numerous sectors of the economy. In 1929, 1 percent of the nation's banks controlled half of its financial resources. Most of the small auto companies that had existed earlier in the century had fallen by the wayside. General Motors, Ford, and Chrysler now controlled four-fifths of the industry.

At the beginning of 1929, the share of national income of the wealthiest 5 percent of American families exceeded that of the bottom 60 percent. A majority of families had no savings, and an estimated 40 percent of the population remained in poverty, unable to participate in the flourishing consumer economy. Improved productivity meant that goods could be produced with fewer workers. During the 1920s, more Americans worked in the professions, retailing, finance, and education, but the number of manufacturing workers declined by 5 percent, the first such drop in the nation's history. Parts of New England were already experiencing the

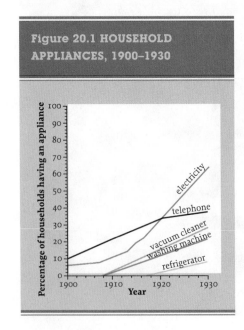

Figure 20.1 HOUSEHOLD APPLIANCES, 1900–1930

chronic unemployment caused by deindustrialization. Many of the region's textile companies failed in the face of low-wage competition from southern factories, or shifted production to take advantage of the South's cheap labor. Most advertisers directed their messages at businessmen and the middle class. At the end of the decade, 75 percent of American households still did not own a washing machine, and 60 percent had no radio.

THE FARMERS' PLIGHT

Nor did farmers share in the decade's prosperity. The "golden age" of American farming had reached its peak during World War I, when the need to feed war-torn Europe and government efforts to maintain high farm prices had raised farmers' incomes and promoted the purchase of more land on credit. Thanks to mechanization and the increased use of fertilizer and insecticides, agricultural production continued to rise even when government subsidies ended and world demand stagnated. As a result, farm incomes declined steadily and banks foreclosed tens of thousands of farms whose owners were unable to meet mortgage payments.

For the first time in the nation's history, the number of farms and farmers declined during the 1920s. For example, half the farmers in Montana lost their land to foreclosure between 1921 and 1925. Extractive industries, like mining and lumber, also suffered as their products faced a glut on the world market. During the decade, some 3 million persons migrated out of rural areas. Many headed for southern California, whose rapidly growing economy needed new labor. The population of Los Angeles, the West's leading industrial center, a producer of oil, automobiles, aircraft, and, of course, Hollywood movies, rose from 575,000 to 2.2 million during the decade, largely because of an influx of displaced farmers from the Midwest. Well before the 1930s, rural America was in an economic depression.

Farmers, like this family of potato growers in rural Minnesota, did not share in the prosperity of the 1920s.

THE IMAGE OF BUSINESS

Even as unemployment remained high in Britain throughout the 1920s, and inflation and war reparations payments crippled the German economy, Hollywood films spread images of "the American way of life" across the globe. America, wrote the historian Charles Beard, was "boring its way" into the world's consciousness. In high wages, efficient factories, and the mass production of consumer goods, Americans seemed to have discovered the secret of permanent prosperity. Businessmen like Henry Ford and engineers like Herbert Hoover were cultural heroes. Photographers like Lewis Hine and Margaret Bourke-White and painters like Charles Sheeler celebrated the beauty of machines and factories. *The Man Nobody Knows*, a 1925 best-seller by advertising executive Bruce Barton, portrayed Jesus Christ as "the greatest advertiser of his day, . . . a virile go-getting he-man of business," who "picked twelve men from the bottom ranks and forged a great organization."

After the Ludlow Massacre of 1914, discussed in Chapter 18, John D. Rockefeller himself had hired a public relations firm to repair his tarnished image. Now, persuaded by the success of World War I's Committee on Public Information that it was possible, as an advertising magazine put it, to "sway the minds of whole populations," numerous firms established public relations departments. They aimed to justify corporate practices to the public and counteract its long-standing distrust of big business.

They succeeded in changing popular attitudes toward Wall Street. Congressional hearings of 1912–1914 headed by Louisiana congressman Arsène Pujo had laid bare the manipulation of stock prices by a Wall Street "money trust." The Pujo investigation had reinforced the widespread view

River Rouge Plant, by the artist Charles Sheeler, exemplifies the "machine-age aesthetic" of the 1920s. Sheeler found artistic beauty in Henry Ford's giant automobile assembly factory.

of the stock market as a place where insiders fleeced small investors—as, indeed, they frequently did. But in the 1920s, as the steadily rising price of stocks made front-page news, the market attracted more investors. Many assumed that stock values would rise forever. By 1928, an estimated 1.5 million Americans owned stock—still a small minority of the country's 28 million families, but far more than in the past.

THE DECLINE OF LABOR

With the defeat of the labor upsurge of 1919 and the dismantling of the wartime regulatory state, business appropriated the rhetoric of Americanism and "industrial freedom" as weapons against labor unions. Some corporations during the 1920s implemented a new style of management. They provided their employees with private pensions and medical insurance plans, job security, and greater workplace safety. They established sports programs to occupy their employees' leisure time. They spoke of "welfare capitalism," a more socially conscious kind of business leadership, and trumpeted the fact that they now paid more attention to the "human factor" in employment.

At the same time, however, employers in the 1920s embraced the American Plan, at whose core stood the open shop—a workplace free of both government regulation and unions, except, in some cases, "company unions" created and controlled by management. Collective bargaining, declared one group of employers, represented "an infringement of personal liberty and a menace to the institutions of a free people." Prosperity, they insisted, depended on giving business complete freedom of action. This message was reinforced in a propaganda campaign that linked unionism and socialism as examples of the sinister influence of foreigners on American life. Even the most forward-looking companies continued to employ strikebreakers, private detectives, and the blacklisting of union organizers to prevent or defeat strikes.

During the 1920s, organized labor lost more than 2 million members, and unions agreed to demand after demand by employers in an effort to stave off complete elimination. In cities like Minneapolis, New Orleans, and Seattle, once centers of thriving labor movements, unions all but disappeared. Uprisings by the most downtrodden workers did occur sporadically throughout the decade. Southern textile mills witnessed desperate strikes by workers who charged employers with "making slaves out of the men and women" who labored there. Facing the combined opposition of business, local politicians, and the courts, as well as the threat of violence, such strikes were doomed to defeat.

THE EQUAL RIGHTS AMENDMENT

The idealistic goals of World War I, wrote the young Protestant minister Reinhold Niebuhr, seemingly had been abandoned: "We are rapidly becoming the most conservative nation on earth." Like the labor movement, feminists struggled to adapt to the new political situation. The achievement of suffrage in 1920 eliminated the bond of unity between various activists, each "struggling for her own conception of freedom," in the words of labor reformer Juliet Stuart Poyntz. Black feminists insisted that the movement must now demand enforcement of the Fifteenth Amendment in the South,

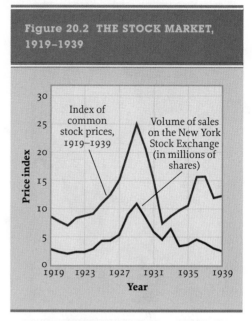

Figure 20.2 THE STOCK MARKET, 1919–1939

Index of common stock prices, 1919–1939

Volume of sales on the New York Stock Exchange (in millions of shares)

This graph illustrates the rapid rise and dramatic collapse of stock prices and the number of shares traded during the 1920s and early 1930s.

Tipsy, a 1930 painting by the Japanese artist Kobayakawa Kiyoshi, illustrates the global appeal of the "new woman" of the 1920s. The subject, a moga *("modern girl" in Japanese), sits alone in a nightclub wearing Western clothing, makeup, and hairstyle, accompanied by a cigarette and a martini. The title of the work suggests that Kiyoshi does not entirely approve of her behavior, but he presents her as self-confident and alluring. Japanese police took a dim view of "modern" women, arresting those who applied makeup in public.*

Many American authorities were no more welcoming to "new women." The superintendent of public buildings and grounds in Washington, D.C., decreed that women's bathing suits must fall no higher than six inches above the knee. Here, in 1922, he enforces his edict.

but they won little support from white counterparts. A few prominent feminists, including Elizabeth Cady Stanton's daughter Harriot Stanton Blatch, joined the rapidly diminishing Socialist Party, convinced that women should support an independent electoral force that promoted governmental protection of vulnerable workers.

The long-standing division between two competing conceptions of woman's freedom—one based on motherhood, the other on individual autonomy and the right to work—now crystallized in the debate over an Equal Rights Amendment (ERA) to the Constitution promoted by Alice Paul and the National Women's Party. This amendment proposed to eliminate all legal distinctions "on account of sex." In Paul's opinion, the ERA followed logically from winning the right to vote. Having gained political equality, she insisted, women no longer required special legal protection—they needed equal access to employment, education, and all the other opportunities of citizens. To supporters of mothers' pensions and laws limiting women's hours of labor, which the ERA would sweep away, the proposal represented a giant step backward. Apart from the National Women's Party, every major female organization, from the League of Women Voters to the Women's Trade Union League, opposed the ERA.

In the end, none of these groups achieved success in the 1920s. The ERA campaign failed, and only six states ratified a proposed constitutional amendment giving Congress the power to prohibit child labor, which farm groups and business organizations opposed. In 1929, Congress repealed the Sheppard-Towner Act of 1921, a major achievement of the maternalist reformers that had provided federal assistance to programs for infant and child health.

WOMEN'S FREEDOM

If political feminism faded, the prewar feminist demand for personal freedom survived in the vast consumer marketplace and in the actual behav-

ior of the decade's much-publicized liberated young women. Female liberation resurfaced as a lifestyle, the stuff of advertising and mass entertainment, stripped of any connection to political or economic radicalism. No longer one element in a broader program of social reform, sexual freedom now meant individual autonomy or personal rebellion. With her bobbed hair, short skirts, public smoking and drinking, and unapologetic use of birth-control methods such as the diaphragm, the young, single "flapper" epitomized the change in standards of sexual behavior, at least in large cities. She frequented dance halls and music clubs where white people now performed "wild" dances like the Charleston that had long been popular in black communities. She attended sexually charged Hollywood films featuring stars like Clara Bow, the provocative " 'It' Girl," and Rudolph Valentino, the original on-screen "Latin Lover." When Valentino died of a sudden illness in 1926, crowds of grieving women tried to storm the funeral home.

What had been scandalous a generation earlier—women's self-conscious pursuit of personal pleasure—became a device to market goods from automobiles to cigarettes. In 1904, a woman had been arrested for smoking in public in New York City. Two decades later, Edward Bernays, the "father" of modern public relations, masterminded a campaign to persuade women to smoke, dubbing cigarettes women's "torches of freedom." The new freedom, however, was available only during one phase of a woman's life. Once she married, what Jane Addams had called the "family claim" still ruled. And marriage, according to one advertisement, remained "the one pursuit that stands foremost in the mind of every girl and woman." Having found a husband, women were expected to seek freedom within the confines of the home, finding "liberation," according to the advertisements, in the use of new labor-saving appliances.

(Left) Advertisers marketed cigarettes to women as symbols of female independence. This 1929 ad for Lucky Strike reads: "Legally, politically and socially, woman has been emancipated from those chains which bound her. . . . Gone is that ancient prejudice against cigarettes." (Right) An ad for Procter & Gamble laundry detergent urges modern women to modernize the methods of their employees. The text relates how a white woman in the Southwest persuaded Felipa, her Mexican-American domestic worker, to abandon her "primitive washing methods." Felipa, according to the ad, agrees that the laundry is now "whiter, cleaner, and fresher."

BUSINESS AND GOVERNMENT

THE RETREAT FROM PROGRESSIVISM

In 1924, a social scientist remarked that the United States had just passed through "one of the most critical ten-year periods" in its history. Among the changes was the disintegration of Progressivism as a political movement and body of thought. The government's success in whipping up mass hysteria during the war seemed to undermine the very foundation of democratic thought—the idea of the rational, self-directed citizen. Followers of Sigmund Freud emphasized the unconscious, instinctual motivations of human behavior; scientists pointed to wartime IQ tests allegedly demonstrating that many Americans were mentally unfit for self-government. "The great bulk of people are stupid," declared one advertising executive, explaining why advertisements played on the emotions rather than providing actual information.

During the 1920s, Walter Lippmann published two of the most penetrating indictments of democracy ever written, *Public Opinion* and *The Phantom Public*, which repudiated the Progressive hope of applying "intelligence" to social problems in a mass democracy. Instead of acting out of careful consideration of the issues or even individual self-interest, Lippmann claimed, the American voter was ill-informed and prone to fits of enthusiasm. Not only were modern problems beyond the understanding of ordinary men and women (a sentiment that had earlier led Lippmann to favor administration by experts), but the independent citizen was nothing but a myth. Like advertising copywriters and journalists, he continued, the government had perfected the art of creating and manipulating public opinion—a process Lippmann called the "manufacture of consent."

In 1929, the sociologists Robert and Helen Lynd published *Middletown*, a classic study of life in Muncie, Indiana, a typical community in the American heartland. The Lynds found that new leisure activities and a new emphasis on consumption had replaced politics as the focus of public concern. Elections were no longer "lively centers" of public attention as in the nineteenth century, and voter participation had fallen dramatically. National statistics bore out their point; the turnout of eligible voters, over 80 percent in 1896, had dropped to less than 50 percent in 1924. Many factors helped to explain this decline, including the consolidation of one-party politics in the South, the long period of Republican dominance in national elections, and the enfranchisement of women, who for many years voted in lower numbers than men. But the shift from public to private concerns also played a part. "The American citizen's first importance to his country," declared a Muncie newspaper, "is no longer that of a citizen but that of a consumer."

The policies of President Calvin Coolidge were music to the ears of big business, according to one 1920s cartoonist.

THE REPUBLICAN ERA

Government policies reflected the pro-business ethos of the 1920s. Recalling the era's prosperity, one stockbroker later remarked, "God, J. P. Morgan and the Republican Party were going to keep everything going forever." Business lobbyists dominated national conventions of the

Republican Party. They called on the federal government to lower taxes on personal incomes and business profits, maintain high tariffs, and support employers' continuing campaign against unions. The administrations of Warren G. Harding and Calvin Coolidge obliged. "Never before, here or anywhere else," declared the *Wall Street Journal*, "has a government been so completely fused with business." The two presidents appointed so many pro-business members of the Federal Reserve Board, the Federal Trade Commission, and other Progressive era agencies that, complained Nebraska senator George W. Norris, they in effect repealed the regulatory system. The Harding administration did support Secretary of Commerce Herbert Hoover's successful effort to persuade the steel industry to reduce the workday from twelve to eight hours. But it resumed the practice of obtaining court injunctions to suppress strikes, as in a 1922 walkout of 250,000 railroad workers protesting a wage cut.

Under William Howard Taft, appointed chief justice in 1921, the Supreme Court remained strongly conservative. A resurgence of laissez-faire jurisprudence eclipsed the Progressive ideal of a socially active national state. The Court struck down a federal law that barred goods produced by child labor from interstate commerce. It even repudiated *Muller v. Oregon* (see Chapter 18) in a 1923 decision overturning a minimum wage law for women in Washington, D.C. Now that women enjoyed the vote, the justices declared, they were entitled to the same workplace freedom as men. "This," lamented Florence Kelley, "is a new Dred Scott decision," which, in the name of liberty of contract, "fills those words with the bitterest and most cruel mockery."

CORRUPTION IN GOVERNMENT

Warren G. Harding took office as president in 1921 promising a return to "normalcy" after an era of Progressive reform and world war. Reflecting the prevailing get-rich-quick ethos, his administration quickly became one of the most corrupt in American history. A likeable, somewhat ineffectual individual—he called himself "a man of limited talents from a small town"—Harding seemed to have little regard for either governmental issues or the dignity of the presidency. Prohibition did not cause him to curb his appetite for liquor. He continued a previous illicit affair with a young Ohio woman, Nan Britton. The relationship did not become known until 1927, when Britton published *The President's Daughter*, about their child to whom Harding had left nothing in his will.

Although his cabinet included men of integrity and talent, like Secretary of State Charles Evans Hughes and Secretary of Commerce Herbert Hoover, Harding also surrounded himself with cronies who used their offices for private gain. Attorney General Harry Daugherty accepted payments not to prosecute accused criminals. The head of the Veterans' Bureau, Charles Forbes, received kickbacks from the sale of government supplies. The most notorious scandal involved Secretary of the Interior Albert Fall, who accepted nearly $500,000 from private businessmen to whom he leased government oil reserves at Teapot Dome, Wyoming. Fall became the first cabinet member in history to be convicted of a felony.

"This decision affirms your constitutional right to starve." *A 1923 cartoon criticizes the Supreme Court decision declaring unconstitutional a Washington, D.C., law establishing a minimum wage for women. Justice George Sutherland, appointed to the Court the previous year by President Warren G. Harding, wrote the majority decision.*

VOICES OF FREEDOM

From André Siegfried,
"The Gulf Between," *Atlantic Monthly* (March 1928)

The French writer André Siegfried in 1928 commented on the rise of an industrial economy and consumer culture and the changes they produced in American society.

Never has Europe more eagerly observed, studied, discussed America; and never . . . have the two continents been wider apart in their aspirations and ideals. . . . Europe, after all, is not very different from what it was a generation ago; but there has been born since then a new America. . . .

The conquest of the continent has been completed, and—all recent American historians have noted the significance of the event—the western frontier has disappeared; the pioneer is no longer needed, and, with him, the mystic dream of the West . . . has faded away. Thus came the beginning of the era of organization: the new problem was not to conquer adventurously but to produce methodically. The great man of the new generation was no longer a pioneer like Lincoln . . . but . . . Henry Ford. From this time on, America has been no more an unlimited prairie with pure and infinite horizons, in which free men may sport like wild horses, but a huge factory of prodigious efficiency. . . .

In the last twenty-five or thirty years America has produced a new civilization. . . . From a *moral point of view*, it is obvious that Americans have come to consider their standard of living as a somewhat sacred acquisition, which they will defend at any price. This means that they would be ready to make many an intellectual or even moral concession in order to maintain that standard.

From a *political point of view*, it seems that the notion of efficiency of production is on the way to taking [precedence over] the very notion of liberty. In the name of efficiency, one can obtain, from the American, all sorts of sacrifices in relation to his personal and even to certain of his political liberties. . . .

Mass production and mass civilization, its natural consequence, are the true characteristics of the new American society. . . . Lincoln, with his Bible and classical tradition, was easier for Europe to understand than Ford, with his total absence of tradition and his proud creation of new methods and new standards, especially conceived for a world entirely different from our own.

FROM Majority Opinion, Justice James C. McReynolds, in *Meyer v. Nebraska* (1923)

A landmark in the development of civil liberties, the Supreme Court's decision in *Meyer v. Nebraska* rebuked the coercive Americanization impulse of World War I, overturning a Nebraska law that required all school instruction to take place in English.

The problem for our determination is whether the statute [prohibiting instruction in a language other than English] as construed and applied unreasonably infringes the liberty guaranteed . . . by the Fourteenth Amendment. . . .

The American people have always regarded education and acquisition of knowledge as matters of supreme importance which should be diligently promoted. . . . The calling always has been regarded as useful and honorable, essential, indeed, to the public welfare. Mere knowledge of the German language cannot reasonably be regarded as harmful. Heretofore it has been commonly looked upon as helpful and desirable. [Meyer] taught this language in school as part of his occupation. His right to teach and the right of parents to engage him so to instruct their children, we think, are within the liberty of the Amendment.

It is said the purpose of the legislation was to promote civil development by inhibiting training and education of the immature in foreign tongues and ideals before they could learn English and acquire American ideals. . . . It is also affirmed that the foreign born population is very large, that certain communities commonly use foreign words, follow foreign leaders, move in a foreign atmosphere, and that the children are therefore hindered from becoming citizens of the most useful type and the public safety is impaired.

That the State may do much, go very far, indeed, in order to improve the quality of its citizens, physically, mentally, and morally, is clear; but the individual has certain fundamental rights which must be respected. The protection of the Constitution extends to all, to those who speak other languages as well as to those born with English on the tongue. Perhaps it would be highly advantageous if all had ready understanding of our ordinary speech, but this cannot be coerced by methods which conflict with the Constitution. . . . No emergency has arisen which rendered knowledge by a child of some language other than English so clearly harmful as to justify its inhibition with the consequent infringement of rights long freely enjoyed.

QUESTIONS

1. Why does Siegfried feel Europeans no longer find America understandable?

2. How does the decision in *Meyer v. Nebraska* expand the definition of liberty protected by the Fourteenth Amendment?

3. How do the two excerpts reflect the changes American society experienced in the 1910s and 1920s?

A 1924 cartoon commenting on the scandals of the Harding administration. The White House, Capitol, and Washington Monument have been sold to the highest bidder.

THE ELECTION OF 1924

Harding's successor, Calvin Coolidge, who as governor of Massachusetts had won national fame for using state troops against striking Boston policemen in 1919, was a dour man of few words. But in contrast to his predecessor he seemed to exemplify Yankee honesty. The scandals subsided, but otherwise Coolidge continued his predecessor's policies. He twice vetoed the McNary-Haugen bill, the top legislative priority of congressmen from farm states. This bill sought to have the government purchase agricultural products for sale overseas in order to raise farm prices. Coolidge denounced it as an unwarranted interference with the free market. In 1924, Coolidge was reelected in a landslide, defeating John W. Davis, a Wall Street lawyer nominated on the 103rd ballot by a badly divided Democratic convention. (This was when the comedian Will Rogers made the quip, often repeated in future years, "I am a member of no organized political party; I am a Democrat.")

One-sixth of the electorate in 1924 voted for Robert La Follette, running as the candidate of a new Progressive Party, which called for greater taxation of wealth, the conservation of natural resources, public ownership of the railroads, farm relief, and the end of child labor. Although such ideas had been proposed many times before World War I, Coolidge described the platform as a blueprint for a "communistic and socialistic" America. Despite endorsements from veteran Progressives like Jane Addams and John Dewey and the American Federation of Labor, La Follette could raise no more than $250,000 for his campaign. He carried only his native Wisconsin. But his candidacy demonstrated the survival of some currents of dissent in a highly conservative decade.

ECONOMIC DIPLOMACY

Foreign affairs also reflected the close working relationship between business and government. "Any student of modern diplomacy," declared Huntington Wilson, a State Department official, "knows that in these days of competition, capital, trade, agriculture, labor and statecraft all go hand in hand if a country is to profit." The 1920s marked a retreat from Wilson's goal of internationalism in favor of unilateral American actions mainly designed to increase exports and investment opportunities overseas. Indeed, what is sometimes called the "isolationism" of the 1920s represented a reaction against the disappointing results of Wilson's military and diplomatic pursuit of freedom and democracy abroad. The United States did play host to the Washington Naval Arms Conference of 1922 that negotiated reductions in the navies of Britain, France, Japan, Italy, and the United States. But the country remained outside the League of Nations. Even as American diplomats continued to press for access to markets overseas, the Fordney-McCumber Tariff of 1922 raised taxes on imported goods to their highest levels in history, a repudiation of Wilson's principle of promoting free trade.

Much foreign policy was conducted through private economic relationships rather than governmental action. The United States emerged from World War I as both the world's foremost center of manufacturing and the major financial power, thanks to British and French debts for American loans that had funded their war efforts. During the 1920s, New York bankers, sometimes acting on their own and sometimes with the cooperation of the Harding and Coolidge administrations, solidified their international position by extending loans to European and Latin American governments. They advanced billions of dollars to Germany to enable the country to meet its World War I reparations payments. American industrial firms, especially in auto, agricultural machinery, and electrical equipment manufacturing, established plants overseas to supply the world market and take advantage of inexpensive labor. American investors gained control over raw materials such as copper in Chile and oil in Venezuela. In 1928, in the so-called Red Line Agreement, British, French, and American oil companies divided oil-producing regions in the Middle East and Latin America among themselves.

As before World War I, the government dispatched soldiers when a change in government in the Caribbean threatened American economic interests. Having been stationed in Nicaragua since 1912, American marines withdrew in 1925. But the troops soon returned in an effort to suppress a nationalist revolt headed by General Augusto César Sandino. Having created a National Guard headed by General Anastasio Somoza, the marines finally departed in 1933. A year later, Somoza assassinated Sandino and seized power. For the next forty-five years, he and his family ruled and plundered Nicaragua. Somoza was overthrown in 1978 by a popular movement calling itself the Sandinistas (see Chapter 26).

A German cartoon inspired by President Calvin Coolidge's dispatch of American troops to Nicaragua. While Coolidge insisted that the United States acted in the interest of preserving international order, residents of other countries often saw the United States as a grasping imperial power.

THE BIRTH OF CIVIL LIBERTIES

Among the casualties of World War I and the 1920s was Progressivism's faith that an active federal government embodied the national purpose and enhanced the enjoyment of freedom. Wartime and postwar repression, Prohibition, and the pro-business policies of the 1920s all illustrated, in the eyes of many Progressives, how public power could go grievously wrong.

This lesson opened the door to a new appreciation of civil liberties—rights an individual may assert even against democratic majorities—as essential elements of American freedom. Building on prewar struggles for freedom of expression by labor unions, socialists, and birth-control advocates, some reformers now developed a greater appreciation of the necessity of vibrant, unrestricted political debate. In the name of a "new freedom for the individual," the 1920s saw the birth of a coherent concept of civil liberties and the beginnings of significant legal protection for freedom of speech against the government.

THE "FREE MOB"

Wartime repression continued into the 1920s. Under the heading "Sweet Land of Liberty," *The Nation* magazine in 1923 detailed recent examples of the degradation of American freedom—lynchings in Alabama, Arkansas, and Florida; the beating by Columbia University students of an undergraduate who had written a letter defending freedom of speech and the press; the arrest of a union leader in New Jersey and 400 members of the IWW in California; refusal to allow a socialist to speak in Pennsylvania. Throughout the 1920s, artistic works with sexual themes were subjected to rigorous censorship. The Postal Service removed from the mails books it deemed obscene. The Customs Service barred works by the sixteenth-century French satirist Rabelais, the modern novelist James Joyce, and many others from entering the country. A local crusade against indecency made the phrase "Banned in Boston" a term of ridicule among upholders of artistic freedom. Boston's Watch and Ward Committee excluded sixty-five books from the city's bookstores, including works by the novelists Upton Sinclair, Theodore Dreiser, and Ernest Hemingway.

Hollywood producers feared that publicity over actress Mary Pickford's divorce, actor Wallace Reid's death from a drug overdose, and a murder trial involving actor Fatty Arbuckle would reinforce the belief that movies promoted immorality. In 1922, the film industry adopted the Hays code, a sporadically enforced set of guidelines that prohibited movies from depicting nudity, long kisses, and adultery, and barred scripts that portrayed clergymen in a negative light or criminals sympathetically. (The code in some ways anticipated recent efforts by television networks, music companies, and video game producers to adopt self-imposed guidelines to fend off governmental regulation.) Filmmakers hoped that self-censorship would prevent censorship by local governments, a not uncommon occurrence since the courts deemed movies a business subject to regulation, not a form of expression. Not until 1951, in a case involving *The Miracle*, a film many Catholics found offensive, would the Supreme Court declare movies an artistic form protected by the First Amendment.

Even as Europeans turned in increasing numbers to American popular culture and consumer goods, some came to view the country as a repressive cultural wasteland. Americans, commented the British novelist D. H. Lawrence, who lived for a time in the United States, prided themselves on being the "land of the free," but "the free mob" had destroyed the right to dissent. "I have never been in any country," he wrote, "where the individual has such an abject fear of his fellow countrymen." Disillusionment with the conservatism of American politics and the materialism of the culture inspired some American artists and writers to emigrate to Paris. The Lost Generation of cultural exiles included novelists and poets like Ernest Hemingway, Gertrude Stein, and F. Scott Fitzgerald. Europe, they felt, valued art and culture, and appreciated unrestrained freedom of expression (and, of course, allowed individuals to drink legally).

A "CLEAR AND PRESENT DANGER"

During World War I, the Unitarian minister John Haynes Holmes later recalled, "there suddenly came to the fore in our nation's life the new issue of civil liberties." The arrest of antiwar dissenters under the Espionage and Sedition Acts inspired the formation in 1917 of the Civil Liberties Bureau, which in 1920 became the American Civil Liberties Union (ACLU). For the rest of the century, the ACLU would take part in most of the landmark cases that helped to bring about a "rights revolution." Its efforts helped to give meaning to traditional civil liberties like freedom of speech and invented new ones, like the right to privacy. When it began, however, the ACLU was a small, beleaguered organization. A coalition of pacifists, Progressives shocked by wartime repression, and lawyers outraged at what they considered violations of Americans' legal rights, it saw its own pamphlets defending free speech barred from the mails by postal inspectors.

Prior to World War I, the Supreme Court had done almost nothing to protect the rights of unpopular minorities. Now, it was forced to address the question of the permissible limits on political and economic dissent. In its initial decisions, it dealt the concept of civil liberties a series of devastating blows. In 1919, the Court upheld the constitutionality of the Espionage Act and the conviction of Charles T. Schenck, a socialist who had distributed antidraft leaflets through the mails. Speaking for the Court, Justice Oliver Wendell Holmes declared that the First Amendment did not prevent Congress from prohibiting speech that presented a "clear and present danger" of inspiring illegal actions. Free speech, he observed, "would not protect a man in falsely shouting fire in a theater and causing a panic."

For the next half-century, Holmes's doctrine would remain the basic test in First Amendment cases. Since the Court usually allowed public officials to decide what speech was in fact "dangerous," it hardly provided a stable basis for the defense of free expression in times of crisis. A week after *Schenck v. United States*, the Court unanimously upheld the conviction of Eugene V. Debs for a speech condemning the war. It also affirmed the wartime jailing of the editor of a German-language newspaper whose editorials had questioned the draft's constitutionality.

THE COURT AND CIVIL LIBERTIES

Also in 1919, the Court upheld the conviction of Jacob Abrams and five other men for distributing pamphlets critical of American intervention in Russia after the Bolshevik revolution. This time, however, Holmes and Louis Brandeis dissented, marking the emergence of a court minority committed to a broader defense of free speech. Six years after *Abrams*, the two again dissented when the majority upheld the conviction of Benjamin Gitlow, a communist whose *Left-wing Manifesto* calling for revolution led to his conviction under a New York law prohibiting "criminal anarchy." "The only meaning of free speech," Holmes now declared, was that advocates of every set of beliefs, even "proletarian dictatorship," should have the right to convert the public to their views in the great "marketplace of ideas" (an apt metaphor for a consumer society). In approving Gitlow's conviction, the Court majority observed that the Fourteenth Amendment obligated the states to refrain from unreasonable restraints on freedom of speech and the press. The comment marked a major step in the long process by which the Bill of Rights was transformed from an ineffective statement of principle into a significant protection of Americans' freedoms.

The tide of civil-liberties decision making slowly began to turn. By the end of the 1920s, the Supreme Court had voided a Kansas law that made it a crime to advocate unlawful acts to change the political or economic system, and one from Minnesota authorizing censorship of the press. The new regard for free speech went beyond political expression. In 1930, the Court threw out the conviction of Mary Ware Dennett for sending a sex-education pamphlet, *The Sex Side of Life*, through the mails. Three years later, a federal court overturned the Customs Service's ban on James Joyce's novel *Ulysses*, a turning point in the battle against the censorship of works of literature.

Meanwhile, Brandeis was crafting an intellectual defense of civil liberties on grounds somewhat different from Holmes's model of a competitive market in ideas. In 1927, the Court upheld the conviction of the prominent California socialist and women's rights activist Anita Whitney for attending a convention of the Communist Labor Party where speakers advocated violent revolution. Brandeis voted with the majority on technical grounds. But he issued a powerful defense of freedom of speech as essential to active citizenship in a democracy: "Those who won our independence believed . . . that freedom to think as you will and to speak as you think are indispensable to the discovery and spread of political truth. . . . The greatest menace to freedom is an inert people." A month after the decision, the governor of California pardoned Whitney, terming freedom of speech the "indispensable birthright of every free American." The intrepid Mrs. Whitney was soon back in court for violating a California law making it a crime to display a red flag. In 1931, the Supreme Court overturned the law as "repugnant to the guaranty of liberty contained in the Fourteenth Amendment." A judicial defense of civil liberties was slowly being born.

THE CULTURE WARS

THE FUNDAMENTALIST REVOLT

Although many Americans embraced modern urban culture with its religious and ethnic pluralism, mass entertainment, and liberated sexual rules, others found it alarming. Many evangelical Protestants felt threatened by the decline of traditional values and the increased visibility of Catholicism and Judaism because of immigration. They also resented the growing presence within mainstream Protestant denominations of "modernists" who

VISIONS OF FREEDOM

City Activities with Dance Hall. *This mural, painted in 1930 by Thomas Hart Benton for the New School for Social Research in New York City, portrays aspects of 1920s urban life. On the left, hands reach for a bottle of liquor, a businessman reads a stock ticker, and patrons enjoy themselves at a dance hall and movie theater. Images on the right include a circus, a woman at a soda fountain, and scenes of family life.*

QUESTIONS

1. What kinds of freedom depicted by Benton alarmed moral traditionalists?

2. Does Benton seem to celebrate or criticize urban life, or both?

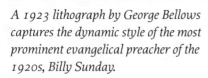

A 1923 lithograph by George Bellows captures the dynamic style of the most prominent evangelical preacher of the 1920s, Billy Sunday.

Federal agents pour confiscated liquor into a sewer in 1920, shortly after the advent of Prohibition.

sought to integrate science and religion and adapt Christianity to the new secular culture. "The day is past," declared Harry Emerson Fosdick, pastor of New York's First Presbyterian Church and a prominent modernist, "when you can ask thoughtful men to hold religion in one compartment of their minds and their modern world view in another."

Convinced that the literal truth of the Bible formed the basis of Christian belief, fundamentalists launched a campaign to rid Protestant denominations of modernism and to combat the new individual freedoms that seemed to contradict traditional morality. Their most flamboyant apostle was Billy Sunday, a talented professional baseball player who became a revivalist preacher. Between 1900 and 1930, Sunday drew huge crowds with a highly theatrical preaching style and a message denouncing sins ranging from Darwinism to alcohol. He was said to have preached to 100 million people during his lifetime—more than any other individual in history.

Much of the press portrayed fundamentalism as a movement of backwoods bigots. In fact, it was a national phenomenon. Even in New York City, the center of the new modern culture, Fosdick was removed from his ministry in 1924 (whereupon John D. Rockefeller Jr. built the interdenominational Riverside Church for him). Fundamentalism remained an important strain of 1920s culture and politics. Prohibition, which fundamentalists strongly supported, succeeded in reducing the consumption of alcohol as well as public drunkenness and drink-related diseases. Not until 1975 would per capita consumption of alcohol reach its pre-Prohibition level of 2.6 gallons per year.

Too many Americans, however, deemed Prohibition a violation of individual freedom for the flow of illegal liquor to stop. In urban areas, Prohibition led to large profits for the owners of illegal speakeasies and the "bootleggers" who supplied them. It produced widespread corruption as police and public officials accepted bribes to turn a blind eye to violations of the law. These developments reinforced fundamentalists' identification of urban life and modern notions of freedom with immorality and a decline of Christian liberty.

THE SCOPES TRIAL

In 1925, a trial in Tennessee threw into sharp relief the division between traditional values and modern, secular culture. John Scopes, a teacher in a Tennessee public school, was arrested for violating a state law that prohibited the teaching of Charles Darwin's theory of evolution. His trial became a national sensation. The proceedings were even carried live on national radio.

The Scopes trial reflected the enduring tension between two American definitions of freedom. Fundamentalist Christians, strongest in rural areas of the South and West, clung to the traditional idea of "moral" liberty—voluntary adherence to time-honored religious beliefs. The theory that man had evolved over millions of years from ancestors like apes contradicted the biblical account of creation. Those who upheld the Tennessee law identified evolutionists with feminists, socialists, and religious modernists, all of whom, they claimed, substituted human judgment for the word of God. To Scopes's defenders, including the American Civil Liberties Union, which had persuaded him to violate the law in order to test its constitutionality, freedom meant above all the right to independent thought and individual self-expression. To them, the Tennessee law offered a lesson in the dangers of religious intolerance and the merger of church and state.

The renowned labor lawyer Clarence Darrow defended Scopes. The trial's highlight came when Darrow called William Jennings Bryan to the stand as an "expert witness" on the Bible. Viewing the trial as a "duel to the death" between science and Christianity, he accepted Darrow's challenge. But Bryan revealed an almost complete ignorance of modern science and proved unable to respond effectively to Darrow's sarcastic questioning. Does the serpent really crawl on its belly as punishment for having tempted Eve in the Garden of Evil? When Bryan answered "yes," Darrow inquired how it got around before being cursed—on its tail? Asked whether God had actually created the world in six days, Bryan replied that these should be understood as ages, "not six days of twenty-four hours"—thus opening the door to the very nonliteral interpretation of the Bible fundamentalists rejected.

The jury found Scopes guilty, although the Tennessee supreme court later overturned the decision on a technicality. Shortly after the trial ended, Bryan died and the movement for anti-evolution laws disintegrated. Fundamentalists retreated for many years from battles over public education, preferring to build their own schools and colleges where teaching could be done as they saw fit and preachers were trained to spread their interpretation of Christianity. The battle would be rejoined, however, toward the end of the twentieth century, when fundamentalism reemerged as an important

The Anti-Evolution League selling its publications outside the Tennessee courthouse where the Scopes trial was taking place.

Because of extreme heat, some sessions of the Scopes trial were held outdoors, in front of the courthouse in Dayton, Tennessee. A photographer snapped this picture of the trial's climactic moment, when Clarence Darrow (standing at the center) questioned William Jennings Bryan (seated) about interpretation of the Bible.

force in politics. To this day, the teaching of the theory of evolution in public schools arouses intense debate in parts of the United States.

THE SECOND KLAN

Few features of urban life seemed more alien to rural and small-town native-born Protestants than their immigrant populations and cultures. The wartime obsession with "100 percent Americanism" continued into the 1920s, a decade of citizenship education programs in public schools, legally sanctioned visits to immigrants' homes to investigate their household arrangements, and vigorous efforts by employers to instill appreciation for "American values." Only "an agile and determined immigrant," commented the *Chicago Tribune*, could "hope to escape Americanization by at least one of the many processes now being prepared for his special benefit." In 1922, Oregon became the only state ever to require all students to attend public schools—a measure aimed, said the state's attorney general, at abolishing parochial education and preventing "bolshevists, syndicalists and communists" from organizing their own schools.

Perhaps the most menacing expression of the idea that enjoyment of American freedom should be limited on religious and ethnic grounds was the resurgence of the Ku Klux Klan in the early 1920s. The Klan had been reborn in Atlanta in 1915 after the lynching of Leo Frank, a Jewish factory manager accused of killing a teenage girl. By the mid-1920s, it claimed more than 3 million members, nearly all white, native-born Protestants, many of whom held respected positions in their communities. Unlike the Klan of Reconstruction, the organization now sank deep roots in parts of the North and West. It became the largest private organization in Indiana, and for a time controlled the state Republican Party. It was partly responsible for the Oregon law banning private schools. In southern California, its large marches and auto parades made the Klan a visible presence. The new Klan attacked a far broader array of targets than during Reconstruction.

American civilization, it insisted, was endangered not only by blacks but by immigrants (especially Jews and Catholics) and all the forces (feminism, unions, immorality, even, on occasion, the giant corporations) that endangered "individual liberty."

CLOSING THE GOLDEN DOOR

The Klan's influence faded after 1925, when its leader in Indiana was convicted of assaulting a young woman. But the Klan's attacks on modern secular culture and political radicalism and its demand that control of the nation be returned to "citizens of the old stock" reflected sentiments widely shared in the 1920s. The decade witnessed a flurry of legislation that offered a new answer to the venerable question "Who is an American?" Some new laws redrew the boundary of citizenship to include groups previously outside it. With women now recognized as part of the political nation, Congress in the Cable Act of 1922 overturned the 1907 law requiring American women who married foreigners to assume the citizenship of the husband—except in the case of those who married Asians, who still forfeited their nationality. Two years later, it declared all Indians born in the United States to be American citizens, although many western states continued to deny the vote to those living on reservations.

Far more sweeping was a fundamental change in immigration policy. Immigration restriction had a long history. The Naturalization Act of 1790 had barred blacks and Asians from naturalization, with the ban lifted for the former in 1870. Beginning in 1875, various classes of immigrants had been excluded, among them prostitutes, the mentally retarded, and those with contagious diseases. Nonetheless, prior to World War I virtually all the white persons who wished to pass through the "golden door" into the United States and become citizens were able to do so. During the 1920s, however, the pressure for wholesale immigration restriction became

A Ku Klux Klan gathering in Jackson, Michigan, in 1924. In the foreground is the Klan's drill team and band. Despite its rancor toward blacks, Catholics, and Jews, the Klan presented itself as part of mainstream America.

The Only Way to Handle It, *a cartoon endorsing immigration restriction.*

irresistible. One index of the changing political climate was that large employers dropped their traditional opposition. Fears of immigrant radicalism now outweighed the desire for cheap unskilled labor, especially since mechanization had halted the growth of the industrial labor force and the Great Migration of World War I had accustomed industrialists to employing African-Americans.

In 1921, a temporary measure restricted immigration from Europe to 357,000 per year (one-third of the annual average before the war). Three years later, Congress permanently limited European immigration to 150,000 per year, distributed according to a series of national quotas that severely restricted the numbers from southern and eastern Europe. The law aimed to ensure that descendants of the old immigrants forever outnumbered the children of the new. However, to satisfy the demands of large farmers in California who relied heavily on seasonal Mexican labor, the 1924 law established no limits on immigration from the Western Hemisphere.

The 1924 law did bar the entry of all those ineligible for naturalized citizenship—that is, the entire population of Asia, even though Japan had fought on the American side in World War I. The only Asians still able to enter the United States were residents of the Philippines, who were deemed to be "American nationals" (although not citizens) because the islands had been U.S. territory since the Spanish-American War. Largely to bar further Philippine immigration, Congress in 1934 established a timetable for the islands' independence, which was finally achieved in 1946. The 1934 law established an immigration quota of fifty Filipinos a year to the mainland United States, but allowed their continued entry into the Hawaiian Islands to work as plantation laborers.

Although a few Chinese had tried to enter the country in the past in spite of exclusion legislation, the law of 1924 established, in effect, for the first time a new category—the "illegal alien." With it came a new enforcement mechanism, the Border Patrol, charged with policing the land boundaries of the United States and empowered to arrest and deport persons who entered the country in violation of the new nationality quotas or other restrictions. Later associated almost exclusively with Latinos, "illegal aliens" at first referred mainly to southern and eastern Europeans who tried to sneak across the border from Mexico or Canada.

RACE AND THE LAW

The new immigration law reflected the heightened emphasis on "race" as a determinant of public policy. By the early 1920s, political leaders of both North and South agreed upon the relegation of blacks to second-class citizenship. In a speech in Alabama in 1921, President Harding unconsciously echoed W. E. B. Du Bois by affirming that the "problem" of race was a global one, not confined to the South. Unlike Du Bois, he believed the South showed the way to the problem's solution. "It would be helpful," he added, "to have that word 'equality' eliminated from this consideration." Clearly, the Republican Party of the Civil War era was dead.

But "race policy" meant far more than black-white relations. "America must be kept American," declared President Coolidge in signing the 1924 immigration law. His secretary of labor, James J. Davis, commented that immigration policy, once based on the need for labor and the notion of the

Table 20.1 SELECTED ANNUAL IMMIGRATION QUOTAS UNDER THE 1924 IMMIGRATION ACT

Country	Quota	Immigrants in 1914
Northern and Western Europe:		
Great Britain and Northern Ireland	65,721	48,729 (Great Britain only)
Germany	25,957	35,734
Ireland	17,853	24,688 (includes Northern Ireland)
Scandinavia (Sweden, Norway, Denmark, Finland)	7,241	29,391
Southern and Eastern Europe:		
Poland	6,524	(Not an independent state; included in Germany, Russia, and Austria-Hungary)
Italy	5,802	283,738
Russia	2,784	255,660
Other:		
Africa (total of various colonies and countries)	1,000	1,539
Western Hemisphere	No quota limit	122,695
Asia (China, India, Japan, Korea)	0	11,652

United States as an asylum of liberty, must now rest on a biological definition of the ideal population. Although enacted by a highly conservative Congress strongly influenced by nativism, the 1924 immigration law also reflected the Progressive desire to improve the "quality" of democratic citizenship and to employ scientific methods to set public policy. It revealed how these aims were overlaid with pseudo-scientific assumptions about the superiority and inferiority of particular "races."

The seemingly "scientific" calculation of the new quotas—based on the "national origins" of the American population dating back to 1790—involved a highly speculative analysis of past census returns, with the results altered to increase allowable immigration by politically influential groups like Irish-Americans. Non-whites (one-fifth of the population in 1790) were excluded altogether when calculating quotas—otherwise, Africa would have received a far higher quota than the tiny number allotted to it. But then, the entire concept of race as a basis for public policy lacked any rational foundation. The Supreme Court admitted as much in 1923 when it rejected the claim of Bhagat Singh Thind, an Indian-born World War I veteran, who asserted that as a "pure Aryan," he was actually white and could therefore become an American citizen. "White," the Court declared, was not a scientific concept at all, but part of "common speech, to be interpreted with the understanding of the common man" (a forthright statement of what later scholars would call the "social construction" of race).

PLURALISM AND LIBERTY

During the 1920s, some Americans challenged the idea that southern and eastern Europeans were unfit to become citizens, or could only do so by abandoning their traditions in favor of Anglo-Saxon ways. Horace Kallen, himself of German-Jewish origin, in 1924 coined the phrase "cultural pluralism" to describe a society that gloried in ethnic diversity rather than attempting to suppress it. Toleration of difference was part of the "American Idea," Kallen wrote. Anthopologists like Franz Boas, Alfred Kroeber, and Ruth Benedict insisted that no scientific basis existed for theories of racial superiority or for the notion that societies and races could be ranked on a fixed scale running from "primitive" to "civilized."

These writings, however, had little immediate impact on public policy. In the 1920s, the most potent defense of a pluralist vision of American society came from the new immigrants themselves. Every major city still contained ethnic enclaves with their own civic institutions, theaters, churches, and foreign-language newspapers. Their sense of separate identity had been heightened by the emergence of independent nation-states in eastern Europe after the war. It would be wrong, to be sure, to view ethnic communities as united in opposition to Americanization. In a society increasingly knit together by mass culture and a consumer economy, few could escape the pull of assimilation. The department store, dance hall, and motion picture theater were as much agents of Americanization as the school and workplace. From the perspective of many immigrant women, moreover, assimilation often seemed not so much the loss of an inherited culture as a loosening of patriarchal bonds and an expansion of freedom. But most immigrants resented the coercive aspects of Americanization programs, so often based on the idea of the superiority of Protestant mainstream culture.

PROMOTING TOLERANCE

In the face of immigration restriction, Prohibition, a revived Ku Klux Klan, and widespread anti-Semitism and anti-Catholicism, immigrant groups asserted the validity of cultural diversity and identified toleration of difference—religious, cultural, and individual—as the essence of American freedom. In effect, they reinvented themselves as "ethnic" Americans, claiming an equal share in the nation's life but, in addition, the right to remain in many respects culturally distinct. The Roman Catholic Church urged immigrants to learn English and embrace "American principles," but it continued to maintain separate schools and other institutions. In 1924, the Catholic Holy Name Society brought 10,000 marchers to Washington to challenge the Klan and to affirm Catholics' loyalty to the nation. Throughout the country, organizations like the Anti-Defamation League of B'nai B'rith (founded in 1916 to combat anti-Semitism) and the National Catholic Welfare Council lobbied, in the name of "personal liberty," for laws prohibiting discrimination against immigrants by employers, colleges, and government agencies. The Americanization movement, declared a Polish newspaper in Chicago, had "not the smallest particle of the true American spirit, the spirit of freedom, the brightest virtue of which is the broadest possible tolerance."

The Zion Lutheran Church in Nebraska where Robert Meyer was arrested for teaching a Bible lesson in German, in violation of state law. The case led to the landmark Supreme Court decision of Meyer v. Nebraska, *an important rebuke to World War I xenophobia.*

The efforts of immigrant communities to resist coerced Americanization and of the Catholic Church to defend its school system broadened the definition of liberty for all Americans. In landmark decisions, the Supreme Court struck down Oregon's law, mentioned earlier, requiring all students to attend public schools and Nebraska's prohibiting teaching in a language other than English—one of the anti-German measures of World War I. "The protection of the Constitution," the decision in *Meyer v. Nebraska* (1923) declared, "extends to all, to those who speak other languages as well as to those born with English on the tongue," a startling rebuke to enforced Americanization. The decision expanded the freedom of all immigrant groups. In its aftermath, federal courts overturned various Hawaii laws imposing special taxes and regulations on private Japanese-language schools. In these cases, the Court also interpreted the Fourteenth Amendment's guarantee of equal liberty to include the right to "marry, establish a home and bring up children" and to practice religion as one chose, "without interference from the state." The decisions gave pluralism a constitutional foundation and paved the way for the Court's elaboration, two generations later, of a constitutional right to privacy.

THE EMERGENCE OF HARLEM

The 1920s also witnessed an upsurge of self-consciousness among black Americans, especially in the North's urban ghettos. With European immigration all but halted, the Great Migration of World War I continued apace. Nearly 1 million blacks left the South during the 1920s, and the black population of New York, Chicago, and other urban centers more than doubled. New York's Harlem gained an international reputation as the "capital" of black America, a mecca for migrants from the South and immigrants from the West Indies, 150,000 of whom entered the United States between 1900 and 1930. Unlike the southern newcomers, most of whom had been agricultural workers, the West Indians included a large number of well-educated professional and white-collar workers. Their encounter with American racism appalled them. "I had heard of prejudice in America," wrote the poet

A black family arriving in Chicago in 1922, as part of the Great Migration from the rural South.

and novelist Claude McKay, who emigrated from Jamaica in 1912, "but never dreamed of it being so intensely bitter."

The 1920s became famous for "slumming," as groups of whites visited Harlem's dance halls, jazz clubs, and speakeasies in search of exotic adventure. The Harlem of the white imagination was a place of primitive passions, free from the puritanical restraints of mainstream American culture. The real Harlem was a community of widespread poverty, its residents confined to low-wage jobs and, because housing discrimination barred them from other neighborhoods, forced to pay exorbitant rents. Most Harlem businesses were owned by whites; even the famed Cotton Club excluded black customers and employed only light-skinned dancers in its renowned chorus line. Few blacks, North or South, shared in the prosperity of the 1920s.

THE HARLEM RENAISSANCE

But Harlem also contained a vibrant black cultural community that established links with New York's artistic mainstream. Poets and novelists like Countee Cullen, Langston Hughes, and Claude McKay were befriended and sponsored by white intellectuals and published by white presses. Broadway for the first time presented black actors in serious dramatic roles, as well as shows like *Dixie to Broadway* and *Blackbirds* that featured great entertainers like the singers Florence Mills and Ethel Waters and the tap dancer Bill Robinson. At the same time, the theater flourished in Harlem, freeing black writers and actors from the constraints imposed by white producers.

The term "New Negro," associated in politics with pan-Africanism and the militancy of the Garvey movement, in art meant the rejection of established stereotypes and a search for black values to put in their place. This quest led the writers of what came to be called the Harlem Renaissance to the roots of the black experience—Africa, the rural South's folk traditions, and the life of the urban ghetto. Claude McKay made the major character of

Segregated institutions sprang up to serve the expanding black communities created by the Great Migration. Here, black residents of the nation's capital enjoy an outing at Suburban Gardens, a black-owned amusement park.

his novel *Home to Harlem* (1928) a free spirit who wandered from one scene of exotic life to another in search of a beautiful girl he had known. W. E. B. Du Bois feared that a novel like McKay's, with its graphic sex and violence, actually reinforced white prejudices about black life. Harlem Renaissance writings, however, also contained a strong element of protest. This mood was exemplified by McKay's poem "If We Must Die," a response to the race riots of 1919. The poem affirmed that blacks would no longer allow themselves to be murdered defenselessly by whites:

> If we must die, let it not be like hogs
> Hunted and penned in an inglorious spot,
> While round us bark the mad and hungry dogs,
> Making their mock at our accursed lot. . . .
> Like men we'll face the murderous, cowardly pack,
> Pressed to the wall, dying, but fighting back!

Winston Churchill would invoke McKay's words to inspire the British public during World War II. The celebrated case of Ossian Sweet, a black physician who moved into a previously all-white Detroit neighborhood in 1925, reflected the new spirit of assertiveness among many African-Americans. When a white mob attacked his home, Sweet fired into the crowd, killing a man. Indicted for murder along with his two brothers, Sweet was defended by Clarence Darrow, fresh from his participation in the Scopes trial. The jury proved unable to agree on a verdict. A second prosecution, of Sweet's brother, ended in acquittal.

THE GREAT DEPRESSION

THE ELECTION OF 1928

Few men elected as president have seemed destined for a more successful term in office than Herbert Hoover. Born in Iowa in 1874, the son of a blacksmith and his schoolteacher wife, Hoover accumulated a fortune as a mining engineer working for firms in Asia, Africa, and Europe. During and

A *1928 campaign poster for the Republican ticket of Herbert Hoover and Charles Curtis.*

immediately after World War I, he gained international fame by coordinating overseas food relief. The British economist John Maynard Keynes, a severe critic of the 1919 Versailles Treaty, called Hoover "the only man" to emerge from the peace conference "with an enhanced reputation." He "had never known failure," wrote the novelist Sherwood Anderson. Hoover seemed to exemplify what was widely called the "new era" of American capitalism. In 1922, while serving as secretary of commerce, he published *American Individualism*, which condemned government regulation as an interference with the economic opportunities of ordinary Americans, but also insisted that self-interest should be subordinated to public service. Hoover considered himself a Progressive, although he preferred what he called "associational action," in which private agencies directed regulatory and welfare policies, to government intervention in the economy.

After "silent Cal" Coolidge in 1927 handed a piece of paper to a group of reporters that stated, "I do not choose to run for president in 1928," Hoover quickly emerged as his successor. Accepting the Republican nomination, Hoover celebrated the decade's prosperity and promised that poverty would "soon be banished from this earth." His Democratic opponent was Alfred E. Smith, the first Catholic to be nominated by a major party. Born into poverty on New York's Lower East Side, Smith had become a fixture in Tammany Hall politics. Although he had no family connection with the new immigrants from southern and eastern Europe (his grandparents had emigrated from Ireland), Smith emerged as their symbolic spokesman. The Triangle fire of 1911 made him an advocate of Progressive social legislation. He served three terms as governor of New York, securing passage of laws limiting the hours of working women and children and establishing widows' pensions. Smith denounced the Red Scare and called for the repeal of Prohibition. His bid for the Democratic nomination in 1924 had been blocked by delegates beholden to nativists and Klansmen, but he secured the nod four years later.

Given the prevailing prosperity and his own sterling reputation, Hoover's victory was inevitable. Other than on Prohibition, moreover, the Democratic platform did not differ much from the Republican one, leaving little to discuss except the candidates' personalities and religions. Smith's Catholicism became the focus of the race. Many Protestant ministers and religious publications denounced him for his faith. For the first time since Reconstruction, Republicans carried several southern states, reflecting the strength of anti-Catholicism and nativism among religious fundamentalists. "Hoover," wrote one previously Democratic southern newspaper editor, "is sprung from American soil and stock," while Smith represented "the aliens." On the other hand, Smith carried the nation's

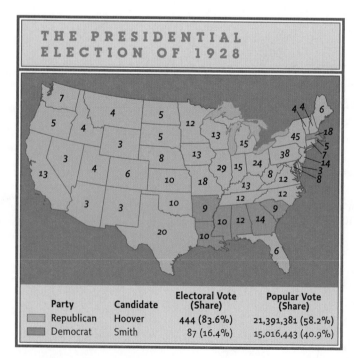

THE PRESIDENTIAL ELECTION OF 1928

Party	Candidate	Electoral Vote (Share)	Popular Vote (Share)
Republican	Hoover	444 (83.6%)	21,391,381 (58.2%)
Democrat	Smith	87 (16.4%)	15,016,443 (40.9%)

twelve largest cities and won significant support in economically struggling farm areas. With more than 58 percent of the vote, Hoover was elected by a landslide. But Smith's campaign helped to lay the foundation for the triumphant Democratic coalition of the 1930s, based on urban ethnic voters, farmers, and the South.

THE COMING OF THE DEPRESSION

On October 21, 1929, President Hoover traveled to Michigan to take part in the Golden Anniversary of the Festival of Light, organized by Henry Ford to commemorate the invention of the lightbulb by Thomas Edison fifty years earlier. Hoover's speech was a tribute to progress, and especially to the businessmen and scientists from whose efforts "we gain constantly in better standards of living, more stability of employment . . . and decreased suffering." Eight days later, on Black Tuesday, the stock market crashed. As panic selling set in, more than $10 billion in market value (equivalent to more than ten times that amount in today's money) vanished in five hours. Soon, the United States and, indeed, the entire world found itself in the grip of the Great Depression, the greatest economic disaster in modern history.

The stock market crash did not, by itself, cause the Depression. Even before 1929, signs of economic trouble had become evident. Southern California and Florida experienced frenzied real-estate speculation and then spectacular busts, with banks failing, land remaining undeveloped, and mortgages foreclosed. The highly unequal distribution of income and the prolonged depression in farm regions reduced American purchasing power. Sales of new autos and household consumer goods stagnated after 1926. European demand for American goods also declined, partly because industry there had recovered from wartime destruction.

A fall in the bloated stock market, driven ever higher during the 1920s by speculators, was inevitable. But it came with such severity that it destroyed many of the investment companies that had been created to buy and sell stock, wiping out thousands of investors, and it greatly reduced business and consumer confidence. Around 26,000 businesses failed in 1930. Those that survived cut back on further investment and began laying off workers. The global financial system, which was based on the gold standard, was ill-equipped to deal with the downturn. Germany defaulted on reparations payments to France and Britain, leading these governments to stop repaying debts to American banks. Throughout the industrial world, banks failed as depositors withdrew money, fearful that they could no longer count on the promise to redeem paper money in gold. Millions of families lost their life savings.

Although stocks recovered somewhat in 1930, they soon resumed their relentless downward slide. Between 1929 and 1932, the price of a share of U.S. Steel fell from $262 to $22, and General Motors from $73 to $8. Four-fifths of the Rockefeller family fortune disappeared. William C. Durant, one of the founders of General Motors, lost all his money and ended up

BUY! REPEATED BUY! PERSISTENT BUY! ADVICES

The American Institute of Finance *repeatedly* and *persistently* recommends the purchase of *the same* stock. This persistent repetition on the same stock makes it practically impossible for the advice to escape the attention of clients.

The following nine stocks have been definitely recommended for purchase no less than 113 times in a twenty-month period—an average of over five recommendations a month.

Have *YOU* made *REAL PROFITS* in These Stocks? Did *YOU* BUY

(14 advices in 18 mos.)	Allied Chemical	@	140	up—now	290
(12 advices in 19 mos.)	Air Reduction	@	138	up—now	330
(11 advices in 18 mos.)	American Smelting	@	155	up—now	360
(10 advices in 20 mos.)	Chicago, R. I. & Pacific	@	70	up—now	135
(10 advices in 18 mos.)	Gold Dust Corp.	@	45	up—now	150
(11 advices in 19 mos.)	Inter. Harvester	@	135	up—now	400
(10 advices in 18 mos.)	Jewel Tea	@	58	up—now	170*
(18 advices in 20 mos.)	Mathieson Alkali	@	86	up—now	190
(17 advices in 19 mos.)	Peoples Gas	@	128	up—now	250

* Price includes recent "rights."

Three months before the stock market crash, The Magazine of Wall Street *was avidly encouraging readers to purchase stocks.*

Oct. 29—Dies Irae, *a 1929 lithograph by James N. Rosenberg, depicts skyscrapers tottering, stockbrokers jumping from windows, and crowds panicking as the stock market crashes. The title means "Day of Wrath."*

Unemployed men, lined up at the New York Municipal Lodging House in 1930. Established in 1909 to provide food and shelter for the homeless, the Lodging House was overwhelmed by the advent of the Great Depression.

running a bowling alley in Flint, Michigan. In 1932, the economy hit rock bottom. Since 1929, the gross national product (the value of all the goods and services in the country) had fallen by one-third, prices by nearly 40 percent, and more than 11 million Americans—25 percent of the labor force—could not find work. U.S. Steel, which had employed 225,000 full-time workers in 1929, had none at the end of 1932, when it was operating at only 12 percent of capacity. Those who retained their jobs confronted reduced hours and dramatically reduced wages. Every industrial economy suffered, but the United States, which had led the way in prosperity in the 1920s, was hit hardest of all.

AMERICANS AND THE DEPRESSION

The Depression transformed American life. Hundreds of thousands of people took to the road in search of work. Hungry men and women lined the streets of major cities. In Detroit, 4,000 children stood in bread lines each day seeking food. Thousands of families, evicted from their homes, moved into ramshackle shantytowns, dubbed Hoovervilles, that sprang up in parks and on abandoned land. Cities quickly spent the little money they had available for poor relief. In Chicago, where half the working population was unemployed at the beginning of 1932, Mayor Anton Cermak telephoned people individually, begging them to pay their taxes. "We saw want and despair walking the streets," wrote a Chicago social worker, "and our friends, sensible, thrifty families, reduced to poverty." When the Soviet Union advertised its need for skilled workers, it received more than 100,000 applications from the United States.

The Depression actually reversed the long-standing movement of population from farms to cities. Many Americans left cities to try to grow food for their families. In 1935, 33 million people lived on farms—more than at any previous point in American history. But rural areas, already poor, saw families reduce the number of meals per day and children go barefoot.

A Hooverville—a shantytown created by homeless squatters—outside Seattle, Washington, in 1933.

With the future shrouded in uncertainty, the American suicide rate rose to the highest level in the nation's history, and the birthrate fell to the lowest.

"The American way of life," the confident slogan of the consumer culture, and common sayings like "safe as a bank" took on a hollow ring. The image of big business, carefully cultivated during the 1920s, collapsed as congressional investigations revealed massive irregularities committed by bankers and stockbrokers. Banks had knowingly sold worthless bonds. Prominent Wall Streeters had unloaded their own portfolios while advising small investors to maintain their holdings. Richard Whitney, the president of the New York Stock Exchange, was convicted of stealing funds from customers, including from a fund to aid widows and orphans. He ended up in jail.

RESIGNATION AND PROTEST

Many Americans reacted to the Depression with resignation or blamed themselves for economic misfortune. Others responded with protests that were at first spontaneous and uncoordinated, since unions, socialist organizations, and other groups that might have provided disciplined leadership had been decimated during the 1920s. In the spring of 1932, 20,000 unemployed World War I veterans descended on Washington to demand early payment of a bonus due in 1945, only to be driven away by federal soldiers led by the army's chief of staff, Douglas MacArthur. Throughout the country, the unemployed demonstrated for jobs and public relief. That summer, led by the charismatic Milo Reno, a former Iowa Populist, the National Farmers' Holiday Association protested low prices by temporarily blocking roads in the Midwest to prevent farm goods from getting to market.

Only the minuscule Communist Party seemed able to give a political focus to the anger and despair. "The most fully employed persons I met during the Depression," one labor leader later recalled, "were the Communists." They "brought misery out of hiding," forming unemployed councils, sponsoring marches and demonstrations for public assistance, and protesting the eviction of unemployed families from their homes. The press discussed the idea that the United States was on the verge of a revolution. The insurance

The celebrated photographer Dorothea Lange took this photograph of an unemployed man on a San Francisco breadline in 1933.

Police battling "bonus marchers" in Washington, D.C., July 1932. Soon afterward, President Hoover sent federal troops to evict the marchers.

Communist Party headquarters in New York City, 1932. The banners illustrate the variety of activities the party organized in the early 1930s.

firm Lloyd's of London reported an upsurge in American requests for riot insurance. The Hoover administration in 1931 opposed efforts to save money by reducing the size of the army, warning that this would "lessen our means of maintaining domestic peace and order."

HOOVER'S RESPONSE

In the eyes of many Americans, President Hoover's response to the Depression seemed inadequate and uncaring. Leading advisers, including Andrew Mellon, the wealthy secretary of the treasury, told Hoover that economic downturns were a normal part of capitalism, which weeded out unproductive firms and encouraged moral virtue among the less fortunate. Businessmen strongly opposed federal aid to the unemployed, and many publications called for individual "belt-tightening" as the road to recovery. Some initially saw a silver lining in the Depression. Wages had fallen so sharply, reported *Fortune* magazine, that "you can have your garden taken care of in Los Angeles for $1 a week" or hire an "affable Negro to fry your chicken and do your washing for $8 a month in Virginia."

The federal government had never faced an economic crisis as severe as the Great Depression. Few political leaders understood how important consumer spending had become in the American economy. Most held to the conventional view that government intervention to aid those who had lost their jobs would do little to spur economic recovery and would encourage Americans to rely on government charity to address misfortune. In 1931, Hoover quoted former president Grover Cleveland from four decades earlier: "The Government should not support the people. . . . Federal aid . . . weakens the sturdiness of our national character."

Strongly opposed on principle to direct federal intervention in the economy, Hoover remained committed to "associational action." He put his faith in voluntary steps by business to maintain investment and employment—something few found it possible to do—and efforts by local charity organizations to assist needy neighbors. He called numerous conferences of business and labor leaders and established commissions to encourage firms to cooperate in maintaining prices and wages without governmental dictation. Hoover attempted to restore public confidence, making frequent public statements that "the tide had turned." But these made him increasingly seem out of touch with reality. About the unemployed men who appeared on city streets offering apples at five cents apiece, Hoover would later write, "Many persons left their jobs for the more profitable one of selling apples."

THE WORSENING ECONOMIC OUTLOOK

Some administration remedies, like the Hawley-Smoot Tariff, which Hoover signed with some reluctance in 1930, made the economic situation worse. Raising the already high taxes on imported goods, it inspired similar increases abroad, further reducing international trade. A tax increase Hoover pushed through Congress in 1932 in an attempt to balance the federal budget further reduced Americans' purchasing power. Other initiatives inspired ridicule. When he approved funds to provide food for livestock, one observer remarked that the president would feed "jackasses but . . . not starving babies."

By 1932, Hoover had to admit that voluntary action had failed to stem the Depression. He signed laws creating the Reconstruction Finance Corporation, which loaned money to failing banks, railroads, and other businesses, and the Federal Home Loan Bank System, which offered aid to home owners threatened with foreclosure. Having vetoed previous

An unemployed man and woman selling apples on a city street during the Great Depression.

bills to create employment through public-works projects like road and bridge construction, he now approved a measure appropriating nearly $2 billion for such initiatives and helping to fund local relief efforts. These were dramatic departures from previous federal economic policy. But further than this, Hoover would not go. He adamantly opposed offering direct relief to the unemployed—it would do them a "disservice," he told Congress.

FREEDOM IN THE MODERN WORLD

In 1927, the New School for Social Research in New York City organized a series of lectures on the theme of Freedom in the Modern World. Founded eight years earlier as a place where "free thought and intellectual integrity" could flourish in the wake of wartime repression, the School's distinguished faculty included the philosopher John Dewey and historian Charles Beard (who had resigned from Columbia University in 1917 to protest the dismissal of antiwar professors). The lectures painted a depressing portrait of American freedom on the eve of the Great Depression. "The idea of freedom," declared economist Walton H. Hamilton, had become "an intellectual instrument for looking backward. . . . Liberty of contract has been made the be-all and end-all of personal freedom; . . . the domain of business has been defended against control from without in the name of freedom." The free exchange of ideas, moreover, had not recovered from the crisis of World War I. The "sacred dogmas of patriotism and Big Business," said the educator Horace Kallen, dominated teaching, the press, and public debate. A definition of freedom reigned supreme that celebrated the unimpeded reign of economic enterprise yet tolerated the surveillance of private life and individual conscience.

The prosperity of the 1920s had reinforced this definition of freedom. With the economic crash, compounded by the ineffectiveness of the Hoover administration's response, it would be discredited. By 1932, the seeds had already been planted for a new conception of freedom that combined two different elements in a sometimes uneasy synthesis. One was the Progressive belief in a socially conscious state making what Dewey called "positive and constructive changes" in economic arrangements. The other, which arose in the 1920s, centered on respect for civil liberties and cultural pluralism and declared that realms of life like group identity, personal behavior, and the free expression of ideas lay outside legitimate state concern. These two principles would become the hallmarks of modern liberalism, which during the 1930s would redefine American freedom.

SUGGESTED READING

BOOKS

Boyle, Kevin. *Arc of Justice: A Saga of Race, Civil Rights, and Murder in the Jazz Age* (2004). A history of the Sweet case, placing it in the context of postwar Detroit and the nation.

Cohen, Warren I. *Empire without Tears: America's Foreign Relations, 1921–1933* (1987). A careful examination of American foreign policy between the presidencies of Wilson and Roosevelt.

Dumenil, Lynn. *The Modern Temper: America in the Twenties* (1995). A brief survey of the main political and cultural trends of the decade.

Garraty, John A. *The Great Depression* (1986). Places the Depression in a global context and compares various governments' responses to it.

Gerstle, Gary. *American Crucible: Race and Nation in the Twentieth Century* (2002). A sweeping survey of how changing ideas of race have affected the concept of American nationality, with a strong account of the debates of the 1920s.

Gordon, Colin. *New Deals: Business, Labor, and Politics in America, 1920–1935* (1994). Examines how the federal government dealt with business and labor from the Republican era to the early New Deal.

Grandin, Greg. *Fordlandia: The Rise and Fall of Henry Ford's Forgotten Jungle City* (2009). Tells the fascinating story of Ford's effort to create a planned community in Brazil's Amazon rain forest.

Higham, John. *Strangers in the Land: Patterns of American Nativism, 1860–1925* (1955). A classic account of American hostility to immigrants, concluding with the immigration restriction of 1924.

Larson, Edward. *Summer for the Gods: The Scopes Trial and America's Continuing Debate over Science and Religion* (1998). A history of the famous trial and the enduring debate over evolution.

Lewis, David L. *When Harlem Was in Vogue* (1981). A lively account of the Harlem Renaissance of the 1920s.

Maclean, Nancy. *Behind the Mask of Chivalry: The Making of the Second Ku Klux Klan* (1994). A careful analysis of the membership and motivations of the Ku Klux Klan of the 1920s.

Marchand, Roland. *Advertising the American Dream: Making Way for Modernity, 1920–1940* (1985). Examines how advertisers responded to and helped to shape changes in American life between the two world wars.

Marsden, George M. *Fundamentalism and American Culture: The Shaping of Twentieth-Century Evangelicism, 1870–1925* (1980). Traces the ups and downs of American fundamentalism, culminating in the Scopes trial.

Murphy, Paul L. *World War I and the Origin of Civil Liberties in the United States* (1979). An analysis of how the repression of free speech during World War I paved the way for a heightened awareness of the importance of civil liberties.

Ngai, Mae. *Impossible Subjects: Illegal Aliens and the Making of Modern America* (2004). An influential examination of immigration policy toward Mexicans and Asians, and the development of the legal category of "illegal alien."

Ross, William G. *Forging New Freedoms: Nativism, Education, and the Constitution, 1917–1927* (1994). Discusses battles over cultural pluralism in the 1920s and how they laid the groundwork for an expanded definition of personal liberty.

WEBSITES

Emergence of Advertising in America: http://library.duke.edu/digitalcollections/eaa/

Harlem History: www.columbia.edu/cu/iraas/harlem/index.html

Pluralism and Unity: www.expo98.msu.edu

Prosperity and Thrift: Coolidge Era and the Consumer Economy: http://memory.loc.gov/ammem/coolhtml/coolhome.html

REVIEW QUESTIONS

1. How did consumerism affect the meaning of American freedom in the 1920s?

2. Which groups did not share in the prosperity of the 1920s and why?

3. How did observers explain the decrease in democracy and popular participation in government during the decade?

4. How did government actions reflect conservative business interests in this period? Give examples.

5. Explain the justifications for immigration restriction laws, as well as the reasons for specific exemptions to these laws.

6. Did U.S. society in the 1920s reflect the concept of cultural pluralism as explained by Horace Kallen? Why or why not?

7. Identify the causes of the Great Depression.

8. What principles guided President Hoover's response to the Great Depression, and how did this restrict his ability to help the American people?

9. To what degree was race a global issue in the 1920s?

FREEDOM QUESTIONS

1. How did business and government use the concept of personal liberty to attack unions and the freedoms of American labor?

2. How did the meanings of freedom change for American women in the 1920s?

3. Explain how debates over free speech and the First Amendment redefined freedom by the end of the 1920s.

4. Which groups and forces were the targets of fundamentalist opposition and why?

5. How did the actions of the Ku Klux Klan threaten American freedom in the 1920s?

KEY TERMS

Sacco-Vanzetti case (p. 818)

"the American way of life" (p. 824)

The Man Nobody Knows (p. 824)

rise of the stock market (p. 825)

"welfare capitalism" (p. 824)

Equal Rights Amendment (p. 825)

the "flapper" (p. 827)

Teapot Dome scandal (p. 829)

McNary-Haugen farm bill (p. 832)

Hays code (p. 834)

American Civil Liberties Union (p. 835)

"clear and present danger" (p. 835)

Scopes trial (p. 839)

"100 percent Americanism" (p. 840)

"illegal alien" (p. 842)

the "New Negro" (p. 846)

bonus marchers (p. 851)

REVIEW TABLE

The Fear of Modernization

Event	Date	Historical Significance
Reemergence of the Ku Klux Klan	**1915,** with the release of *Birth of a Nation* and the lynching of Leo Frank	Included anti-black, anti-immigrant, anti-Catholic, and anti-Jewish elements
Immigration Act	**1924**	Severely limited immigration from eastern and southern Europe and excluded all Asians
Scopes Trial	**1925**	Fundamentalists fought against teaching Darwin's theory of evolution in schools
"Free Mob" and repression	**1920s**	Censorship of speech; books banned by Postal Service and Customs Service; Hollywood adopts Hays code for self-censorship

CHAPTER 21

The New Deal, 1932–1940

THE FIRST NEW DEAL
FDR and the Election of 1932
The Coming of the New Deal
The Banking Crisis
The NRA
Government Jobs
Public-Works Projects
The New Deal and Agriculture
The New Deal and Housing
The Court and the New Deal

THE GRASSROOTS REVOLT
Labor's Great Upheaval
The Rise of the CIO
Labor and Politics
Voices of Protest

THE SECOND NEW DEAL
The WPA and the Wagner Act
The American Welfare State
The Social Security System

A RECKONING WITH LIBERTY
FDR and the Idea of Freedom
The Election of 1936
The Court Fight
The End of the Second New Deal

THE LIMITS OF CHANGE
The New Deal and American Women
The Southern Veto
The Stigma of Welfare
The Indian New Deal
The New Deal and Mexican-Americans
Last Hired, First Fired
A New Deal for Blacks
Federal Discrimination

A NEW CONCEPTION OF AMERICA
The Heyday of American Communism
Redefining the People
Promoting Diversity
Challenging the Color Line
Labor and Civil Liberties
The End of the New Deal
The New Deal in American History

This panel depicting the construction of a dam was painted in 1939 by William Gropper as part of a mural for the new Department of Interior building in Washington, D.C. Born on New York City's Lower East Side to a Jewish immigrant family, Gropper became a prominent "social realist" artist, whose works depicting scenes of American life included satirical cartoons of political and business leaders and paintings of labor struggles of the 1930s. Like other artists who found it difficult to obtain work during the Depression, he was hired by the Works Projects Administration, a New Deal agency, to paint murals for government buildings. This one was inspired by the construction of the Grand Coulee Dam on the Columbia River and the Davis Dam on the Colorado River, two of the many New Deal projects that expanded the nation's infrastructure and provided employment to victims of the Depression.

FOCUS QUESTIONS

• What were the major policy initiatives of the New Deal in the Hundred Days?

• Who were the main proponents of economic justice in the 1930s, and what measures did they advocate?

• What were the major initiatives of the Second New Deal, and how did they differ from the First New Deal?

• How did the New Deal recast the meaning of American freedom?

• How did New Deal benefits apply to women and minorities?

• How did the Popular Front influence American culture in the 1930s?

arly in 1941, the unemployed Woody Guthrie, soon to become one of the country's most popular songwriters and folk singers, brought his family to Portland, Oregon. He hoped to star in a film about the great public-works projects under way on the Columbia River. Given a temporary job by the Bonneville Power Authority, the public agency that controlled the Columbia dams, Guthrie produced a song every day for the next month. One, "Roll on, Columbia," became a popular statement of the benefits that resulted when government took the lead in economic planning and in improving the lot of ordinary citizens:

> And on up the river is the Grand Coulee Dam,
> The biggest thing built by the hand of a man,
> To run the great factories and water the land,
> So, roll on, Columbia, roll on. . . .
> Your power is turning our darkness to dawn.
> So, roll on, Columbia, roll on.©

The Columbia River winds its way on a 1,200-mile course from Canada through Washington and Oregon to the Pacific Ocean. Because of its steep descent from uplands to sea level, it produces an immense amount of energy. Residents of the economically underdeveloped Pacific Northwest had long dreamed of tapping this unused energy for electricity and irrigation. But not until the 1930s did the federal government launch the program of dam construction that transformed the region. The project created thousands of jobs for the unemployed, and the network of dams produced abundant cheap power.

When the Grand Coulee Dam went into operation in 1941, it was the largest man-made structure in world history. It eventually produced more than 40 percent of the nation's hydroelectric power. The dam provided the cheapest electricity in the country for towns that sprang up out of nowhere, farms on what had once been deserts in eastern Washington and Oregon, and factories that would soon be producing aluminum for World War II airplanes. The project also had less appealing consequences. From time immemorial, the Columbia River had been filled with salmon. But the Grand Coulee Dam made no provision for the passage of fish, and the salmon all but vanished. This caused little concern during the Depression but became a source of controversy later in the century as Americans became more concerned about preserving the natural environment.

The Grand Coulee Dam was part of what one scholar has called a "public works revolution" that transformed the American economy and landscape during the 1930s. The Roosevelt administration spent far more money on building roads, dams, airports, bridges, and housing than any other activity.

Franklin D. Roosevelt believed regional economic planning like that in the Northwest would promote economic growth, ease the domestic and working lives of ordinary Americans, and keep control of key natural resources in public rather than private hands. "It promises," one supporter wrote, "a world replete with more freedom and happiness than mankind has ever known."

The Columbia River project reflected broader changes in American life and thought during the New Deal of the 1930s. Roosevelt oversaw the transformation of the Democratic Party into a coalition of farmers, industrial workers, the reform-minded urban middle class, liberal intellectuals, northern African-Americans, and, somewhat incongruously, the white supremacist South, united by the belief that the federal government must provide Americans with protection against the dislocations caused by modern capitalism. "Liberalism," traditionally understood as limited government and free market economics, took on its modern meaning. Thanks to the New Deal, it now referred to active efforts by the national government to uplift less fortunate members of society.

Freedom, too, underwent a transformation during the 1930s. The Depression had discredited the ideas that social progress rests on the unrestrained pursuit of wealth and that, apart from unfortunates like widows and orphans, most poverty is self-inflicted. The New Deal elevated a public guarantee of economic security to the forefront of American discussions of freedom. The 1930s were a decade of dramatic social upheaval. Social and political activists, most notably a revitalized labor movement, placed new issues on the political agenda. When one writer in 1941 published a survey of democratic thought beginning in the ancient world, he concluded that what distinguished his own time was its awareness of "the social conditions of freedom." Thanks to the New Deal, he wrote, "economic security" had "at last been recognized as a political condition of personal freedom." Regional economic planning like that in the Northwest reflected this understanding of freedom. So did other New Deal measures, including the Social Security Act, which offered aid to the unemployed and aged, and the Fair Labor Standards Act, which established a national minimum wage.

Yet while the New Deal significantly expanded the meaning of freedom, it did not erase freedom's boundaries. Its benefits flowed to industrial workers but not tenant farmers, to men far more fully than women, and to white Americans more than blacks, who, in the South, still were deprived of the basic rights of citizenship.

Hydroelectric generators at the Grand Coulee Dam.

THE FIRST NEW DEAL

FDR AND THE ELECTION OF 1932

It is indeed paradoxical that Franklin D. Roosevelt, who had been raised in privilege on a New York country estate, came to be beloved as the symbolic representative of ordinary citizens. But like Lincoln, with whom he is

COLUMBIA RIVER BASIN PROJECT, 1949

A 1949 map of the Columbia River project, showing its numerous dams, including the Grand Coulee, the largest man-made structure in the world at the time of its opening in 1941.

often compared, Roosevelt's greatness lay in his willingness to throw off the "dogmas of the quiet past" (Lincoln's words) to confront an unprecedented national crisis. FDR, as he liked to be called, was born in 1882, a fifth cousin of Theodore Roosevelt. He graduated from Harvard in 1904 and six years later won election to the New York legislature from Duchess County, site of his family's home at Hyde Park. After serving as undersecretary of the navy during World War I, he ran for vice president on the ill-fated Democratic ticket of 1920 headed by James M. Cox. In 1921, he contracted polio and lost the use of his legs, a fact carefully concealed from the public in that pre-television era. Very few Americans realized that the president who projected an image of vigorous leadership during the 1930s and World War II was confined to a wheelchair.

In his speech accepting the Democratic nomination for president in 1932, Roosevelt promised a "new deal" for the American people. But his campaign offered only vague hints of what this might entail. Roosevelt spoke of the government's responsibility to guarantee "every man . . . a right to make a comfortable living." But he also advocated a balanced federal budget and criticized his opponent, President Hoover, for excessive government spending. The biggest difference between the parties during the campaign was the Democrats' call for the repeal of Prohibition. Battered by the economic crisis, Americans in 1932 were desperate for new leadership, and Roosevelt won a resounding victory. He received 57 percent of the popular vote, and Democrats swept to a commanding majority in Congress.

THE COMING OF THE NEW DEAL

The Depression did not produce a single pattern of international public response. For nearly the entire decade of the 1930s, conservative governments ruled Britain and France. They were more interested in preserving public order than relieving suffering or embarking on policy innovations. In Germany, Adolf Hitler, leader of the Nazi Party, established one of the most brutal dictatorships in human history. Hitler banned all political opposition and launched a reign of terror against Jews and others deemed to be "un-German." In the Soviet Union, another tyrant, Joseph Stalin, embarked on successive five-year plans that at great social cost produced rapid industrialization and claimed to have eliminated unemployment. The militarist government of Japan invaded China in 1937, and hoped to extend its rule throughout Asia.

THE PRESIDENTIAL ELECTION OF 1932			
Party	**Candidate**	**Electoral Vote (Share)**	**Popular Vote (Share)**
Democrat	Roosevelt	472 (88.9%)	22,821,857 (57.7%)
Republican	Hoover	59 (11.1%)	15,761,841 (39.8%)

Roosevelt conceived of the New Deal as an alternative to socialism on the left, Nazism on the right, and the inaction of upholders of unregulated capitalism. He hoped to reconcile democracy, individual liberty, and economic planning. "You have made yourself," the British economist John Maynard Keynes wrote to FDR, "the trustee for those in every country who seek to mend the evils of our condition by reasoned experiment within the framework of the existing social system." If Roosevelt failed, Keynes added, the only remaining choices would be "orthodoxy" (that is, doing nothing) or "revolution."

Roosevelt did not enter office with a blueprint for dealing with the Depression. At first, he relied heavily for advice on a group of intellectuals and social workers who took up key positions in his administration. They included Secretary of Labor Frances Perkins, a veteran of Hull House and the New York Consumers' League who had been among the eyewitnesses to the Triangle fire of 1911; Harry Hopkins, who had headed emergency relief efforts during Roosevelt's term as governor of New York; Secretary of the Interior Harold Ickes, a veteran of Theodore Roosevelt's Progressive campaign of 1912; and Louis Brandeis, who had advised Woodrow Wilson during the 1912 campaign and now offered political advice to FDR while serving on the Supreme Court.

The presence of these individuals reflected how Roosevelt drew on the reform traditions of the Progressive era. But Progressivism, as noted in Chapter 18, was hardly a unified movement, and Roosevelt's advisers did not speak with one voice. Brandeis believed that large corporations not only wielded excessive power but had contributed to the Depression by keeping prices artificially high and failing to increase workers' purchasing power. They should be broken up, he insisted, not regulated. But the "brains trust"—a group of academics that included a number of Columbia University professors—saw bigness as inevitable in a modern economy. The competitive marketplace, they argued, was a thing of the past, and large firms needed to be managed and directed by the government, not dismantled. Their view prevailed during what came to be called the First New Deal.

A celebrated cover of The New Yorker *depicts a morose Herbert Hoover and a jaunty Franklin D. Roosevelt riding to Roosevelt's inauguration in March 1933.*

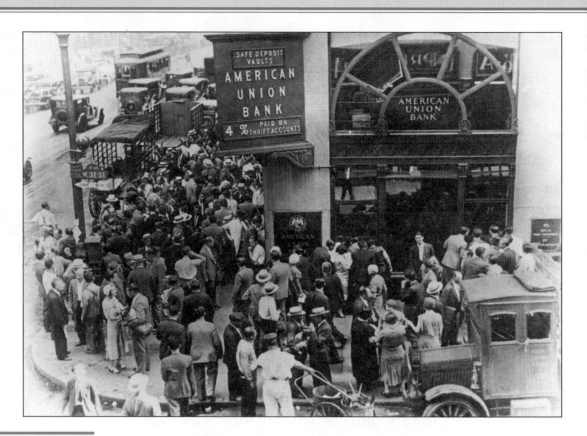

A "run" on a bank: crowds of people wait outside a New York City bank, hoping to withdraw their money.

THE BANKING CRISIS

"This nation asks for action and action now," Roosevelt announced on taking office on March 4, 1933. The country, wrote the journalist and political commentator Walter Lippmann, "was in such a state of confused desperation that it would have followed almost any leader anywhere he chose to go." FDR spent much of 1933 trying to reassure the public. In his inaugural address, he declared that "the only thing we have to fear is fear itself." (See the Appendix for the full text.)

Roosevelt confronted a banking system on the verge of collapse. As bank funds invested in the stock market lost their value and panicked depositors withdrew their savings, bank after bank had closed its doors. By March 1933, banking had been suspended in a majority of the states—that is, people could not gain access to money in their bank accounts. Roosevelt declared a "bank holiday," temporarily halting all bank operations, and called Congress into special session. On March 9, it rushed to pass the Emergency Banking Act, which provided funds to shore up threatened institutions.

Further measures soon followed that transformed the American financial system. The Glass-Steagall Act barred commercial banks from becoming involved in the buying and selling of stocks. Until its repeal in the 1990s, the law prevented many of the irresponsible practices that had contributed to the stock market crash. The same law established the Federal Deposit Insurance Corporation (FDIC), a government system that insured the accounts of individual depositors. And Roosevelt took the United States off the gold standard— that is, he severed the link between the country's currency and its gold reserves, thus making possible the issuance of more money in the hope of stimulating business activity. Together, these measures rescued the financial system and greatly increased the government's power over it. About 5,000 banks—one-third of the nation's total—had failed between 1929 and 1933, representing a loss of tens of millions of dollars to depositors. In 1936, not a single bank failed in the United States.

THE NRA

The Emergency Banking Act was the first of an unprecedented flurry of legislation during the first three months of Roosevelt's administration, a period known as the "Hundred Days." Seizing on the sense of crisis and the momentum of his electoral victory, Roosevelt won rapid passage of laws he hoped would promote economic recovery. He persuaded Congress to create a host of new agencies, whose initials soon became part of the language of politics—NRA, AAA, CCC. Never in American history had a president exercised such power or so rapidly expanded the role of the federal government in people's lives.

The centerpiece of Roosevelt's plan for combating the Depression, the National Industrial Recovery Act, was to a large extent modeled on the government–business partnership established by the War Industries Board of World War I. Roosevelt called it "the most important and far-reaching legislation ever enacted by the American Congress." The act established the National Recovery Administration (NRA), which would work with groups of business leaders to establish industry codes that set standards for output, prices, and working conditions. Thus, "cutthroat" competition (in which companies took losses to drive competitors out of business) would be ended. These industry-wide arrangements would be exempt from antitrust laws.

The NRA reflected how even in its early days, the New Deal reshaped understandings of freedom. In effect, FDR had repudiated the older idea of liberty based on the idea that the best way to encourage economic activity and ensure a fair distribution of wealth was to allow market competition to operate, unrestrained by the government. And to win support from labor, section 7a of the new law recognized the workers' right to organize unions—a departure from the "open shop" policies of the 1920s and a step toward government support for what workers called "industrial freedom."

Headed by Hugh S. Johnson, a retired general and businessman, the NRA quickly established codes that set standards for production, prices, and wages in the textile, steel, mining, and auto industries. Johnson launched a publicity campaign to promote the NRA and its symbol, the Blue Eagle, which stores and factories that abided by the codes displayed. But after initial public enthusiasm, the NRA became mired in controversy. Large companies dominated the code-writing process. An inquiry conducted by the labor lawyer Clarence Darrow in 1934 concluded that they used the NRA to drive up prices, limit production, lay off workers, and divide markets among themselves at the expense of smaller competitors. Many anti-union employers ignored section 7a. The government lacked the manpower to police the 750 codes in effect by 1935. The NRA produced neither economic recovery nor peace between employers and workers.

The Spirit of the New Deal, a 1933 cartoon in the Washington Star, *depicts the federal government, through the National Recovery Administration, promoting peace between workers and employers.*

GOVERNMENT JOBS

The Hundred Days also brought the government into providing relief to those in need. Roosevelt and most of his advisers shared the widespread fear that direct government payments to the unemployed would undermine individual self-reliance. Indeed, one of the first measures of the Hundred Days had been the Economy Act, which reduced federal spending in an attempt to win the confidence of the business community. But with nearly a quarter of the workforce unemployed, spending on relief was unavoidable. In May 1933, Congress created the Federal Emergency Relief Administration, to make grants to local agencies that aided those impoverished by the Depression. FDR, however, much preferred to create temporary jobs, thereby combating unemployment while improving the nation's infrastructure of roads, bridges, public buildings, and parks.

In March 1933, Congress established the Civilian Conservation Corps (CCC), which set unemployed young men to work on projects like forest preservation, flood control, and the improvement of national parks and wildlife preserves. By the time the program ended in 1942, more than 3 million persons had passed through CCC camps, where they received government wages of $30 per month.

PUBLIC-WORKS PROJECTS

One section of the National Industrial Recovery Act created the Public Works Administration (PWA), with an appropriation of $3.3 billion. Directed by Secretary of the Interior Harold Ickes, it built roads, schools, hospitals, and other public facilities, including New York City's Triborough Bridge and the Overseas Highway between Miami and Key West, Florida. In November, yet another agency, the Civil Works Administration (CWA), was launched. By January 1934, it employed more than 4 million persons in the construction of highways, tunnels, courthouses, and airports. But as the cost spiraled

A Civilian Conservation Corps workforce in Yosemite National Park, 1935.

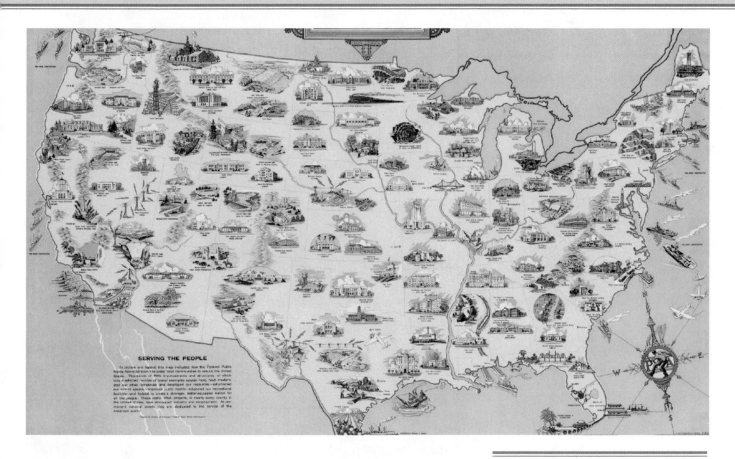

SERVING THE PEOPLE

upward and complaints multiplied that the New Deal was creating a class of Americans permanently dependent on government jobs, Roosevelt ordered the CWA dissolved.

Some New Deal public-works initiatives looked to government-planned economic transformation as much as economic relief. The Tennessee Valley Authority (TVA), another product of the Hundred Days, built a series of dams to prevent floods and deforestation along the Tennessee River and to provide cheap electric power for homes and factories in a seven-state region where many families still lived in isolated log cabins. The TVA put the federal government, for the first time, in the business of selling electricity in competition with private companies. It was a preview of the program of regional planning that spurred the economic development of the West.

A map published by the Public Works Administration in 1935 depicts some of the numerous infrastructure projects funded by the New Deal. Among the most famous public-works projects are the Triborough Bridge in New York City, the Key West Highway in Florida, and the Grand Coulee Dam in Washington. Overall, the New Deal spent $250 billion (in today's money) to construct, among other things, 40,000 public buildings, 72,000 schools, 80,000 bridges, and 8,000 parks.

THE NEW DEAL AND AGRICULTURE

Another policy initiative of the Hundred Days addressed the disastrous plight of American farmers. The Agricultural Adjustment Act (AAA) authorized the federal government to try to raise farm prices by setting production quotas for major crops and paying farmers not to plant more. Many crops already in the field were destroyed. In 1933, the government ordered more than 6 million pigs slaughtered as part of the policy, a step critics found strange at a time of widespread hunger.

The AAA succeeded in significantly raising farm prices and incomes. But not all farmers benefited. Benefits flowed to property-owning farmers,

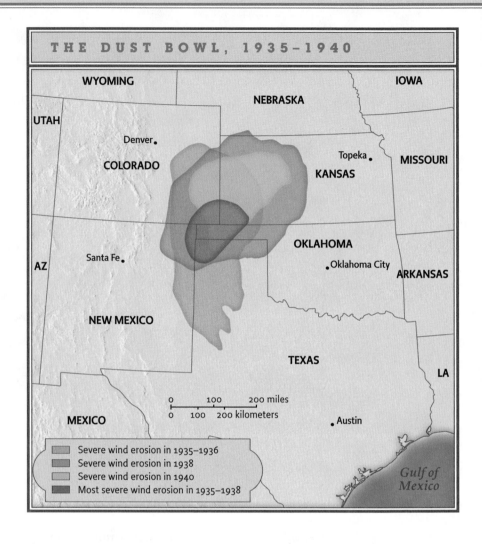

THE DUST BOWL, 1935–1940

Severe wind erosion in 1935–1936
Severe wind erosion in 1938
Severe wind erosion in 1940
Most severe wind erosion in 1935–1938

A giant dust storm engulfs a town in western Kansas on April 14, 1935, known as Black Sunday in the American West.

ignoring the large number who worked on land owned by others. The AAA policy of paying landowning farmers not to grow crops encouraged the eviction of thousands of poor tenants and sharecroppers. Many joined the rural exodus to cities or to the farms of the West Coast.

The onset in 1930 of a period of unusually dry weather in the nation's heartland worsened the Depression's impact on rural America. By mid-decade, the region suffered from the century's most severe drought. Mechanized agriculture in this semiarid region had pulverized the topsoil and killed native grasses that prevented erosion. Winds now blew much of the soil away, creating the Dust Bowl, as the affected areas of Oklahoma, Texas, Kansas, and Colorado were called. A local newspaper described the situation in Cimarron County, Oklahoma: "Not a blade of wheat; cattle dying on the range, ninety percent of the poultry dead because of the sand storms, milk cows gone dry." One storm in 1934 carried dust as far as Washington,

Sharecroppers evicted from the farms on which they had been working in New Madrid County, Missouri, as a result of government subsidies to farm owners to reduce crop production.

D.C. The drought and dust storms displaced more than 1 million farmers. John Steinbeck's novel *The Grapes of Wrath* (1939) and a popular film based on the book captured their plight, tracing a dispossessed family's trek from Oklahoma to California.

THE NEW DEAL AND HOUSING

Owning one's home had long been a widely shared American ambition. "A man is not a whole and complete man," Walt Whitman had written in the 1850s, "unless he owns a house and the ground it stands on." For many members of the middle class, home ownership had become a mark of respectability. For workers, it offered economic security at a time of low wages, erratic employment, and limited occupational mobility. On the eve of World War I, a considerably higher percentage of immigrant workers than the native-born middle class owned their homes.

The Depression devastated the American housing industry. The construction of new residences all but ceased, and banks and savings and loan associations that had financed home ownership collapsed or, to remain afloat, foreclosed on many homes (a quarter of a million in 1932 alone). In 1931, President Hoover convened a Conference on Home Building and Home Ownership to review the housing crisis. The president called owning a home an American "birthright," the embodiment of the spirit of "enterprise, of independence, and of . . . freedom." Rented apartments, he pointed out, did not inspire "immortal ballads" like *Home, Sweet Home* or *The Little Gray Home in the West.* Papers presented at the conference revealed that millions of Americans lived in overcrowded, unhealthy urban slums or in ramshackle rural dwellings. Private enterprise alone, it seemed clear, was unlikely to solve the nation's housing crisis.

Hoover's administration established a federally sponsored bank to issue home loans. Not until the New Deal, however, did the government systematically enter the housing market. Roosevelt spoke of "the security of the home" as a fundamental right akin to "the security of livelihood, and the security of social insurance." In 1933 and 1934, his administration

Figure 21.1 THE BUILDING BOOM AND ITS COLLAPSE, 1919–1939

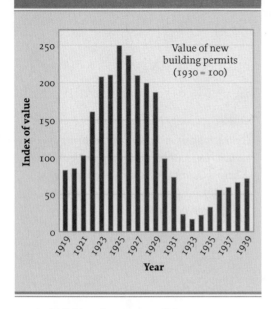

Value of new building permits
(1930 = 100)

As it did in other sectors of the economy, the Great Depression led to a collapse in the construction industry.

moved energetically to protect home owners from foreclosure and to stimulate new construction. The Home Owners Loan Corporation and Federal Housing Administration (FHA) insured millions of long-term mortgages issued by private banks. At the same time, the federal government itself built thousands of units of low-rent housing. New Deal housing policy represented a remarkable departure from previous government practice. Thanks to the FHA and, later, the Veterans' Administration, home ownership came within the reach of tens of millions of families. It became cheaper for most Americans to buy single-family homes than to rent apartments.

Other important measures of Roosevelt's first two years in office included the ratification of the Twenty-first Amendment to the Constitution, which repealed Prohibition; the establishment of the Federal Communications Commission to oversee the nation's broadcast airwaves and telephone communications; and the creation of the Securities and Exchange Commission to regulate the stock and bond markets. Taken together, the First New Deal was a series of experiments, some of which succeeded and some of which did not. They transformed the role of the federal government, constructed numerous public facilities, and provided relief to millions of needy persons. But they did not end the Depression. Some 10 million Americans—more than 20 percent of the workforce—remained unemployed when 1934 came to an end.

THE COURT AND THE NEW DEAL

In 1935, the Supreme Court, still controlled by conservative Republican judges who held to the nineteenth-century understanding of freedom as liberty of contract, began to invalidate key New Deal laws. First came the NRA, declared unconstitutional in May in a case brought by the Schechter Poultry Company of Brooklyn, which had been charged with violating the code adopted by the chicken industry. In a unanimous decision, the Court declared the NRA unlawful because in its codes and other regulations it delegated legislative powers to the president and attempted to regulate local businesses that did not engage in interstate commerce. In January

Russell Lee's 1939 photograph of a migrant family saying grace before eating by the side of the road near Fort Gibson, Oklahoma, shows how, even in the most difficult circumstances, families struggled to maintain elements of their normal lives.

1936, the AAA fell in *United States v. Butler*, which declared it an unconstitutional exercise of congressional power over local economic activities. In June, by a 5–4 vote, the justices ruled that New York could not establish a minimum wage for women and children.

Having failed to end the Depression or win judicial approval, the First New Deal ground to a halt. Meanwhile, pressures were mounting outside Washington that propelled the administration toward more radical departures in policy.

THE GRASSROOTS REVOLT

LABOR'S GREAT UPHEAVAL

The most striking development of the mid-1930s was the mobilization of millions of workers in mass-production industries that had successfully resisted unionization. "Labor's great upheaval," as this era of unprecedented militancy was called, came as a great surprise. Unlike in the past, however, the federal government now seemed to be on the side of labor, a commitment embodied in the National Industrial Recovery Act and in the Wagner Act (discussed later) of 1935, which granted workers the legal right to form unions. With the severe reduction of European immigration, ethnic differences among workers had diminished in importance. American-born children of the new immigrants now dominated the industrial labor force, and organizers no longer had to distribute materials in numerous languages as the IWW had done. And a cadre of militant labor leaders, many of them socialists and communists with long experience in organization, had survived the repression of the 1920s. They provided leadership to the labor upsurge.

American factories at the outset of the New Deal were miniature dictatorships in which unions were rare, workers could be beaten by supervisors and fired at will, and management determined the length of the workday and speed of the assembly line. In industrial communities scattered across the country, local government firmly supported the companies. "Jesus Christ couldn't speak in Duquesne for the union," declared the mayor of that Pennsylvania steel town. Workers' demands during the 1930s went beyond better wages. They included an end to employers' arbitrary power in the workplace, and basic civil liberties for workers, including the right to picket, distribute literature, and meet to discuss their grievances. All these goals required union recognition.

Roosevelt's election as president did much to rekindle hope among those who called themselves, in the words of a worker writing to Secretary of Labor Frances Perkins, "slaves of the depression." His inauguration unleashed a flood of poignant letters to the federal government describing what a Louisiana sugar laborer called the "terrible and inhuman condition" of many workers. Labor organizers spread the message that the "political liberty for which our forefathers fought" had been "made meaningless by economic inequality" and "industrial despotism." "We are free Americans," declared the Steel Workers Organizing Committee. "We shall exercise our inalienable rights to organize into a great industrial union."

Labor's great upheaval exploded in 1934, a year that witnessed no fewer than 2,000 strikes. Many produced violent confrontations between

The Illegal Act, *a cartoon critical of the Supreme Court's decision declaring the NRA unconstitutional. FDR tells a drowning Uncle Sam, "I'm sorry, but the Supreme Court says I must chuck you back in."*

Pennsylvania Steelworkers outside the Local Headquarters of the Steel Workers Organizing Committee, *a 1938 photograph by Arnold Rothstein.*

Signs carried by striking cotton mill workers in Lumberton, North Carolina, in 1937 illustrate how the labor movement revived the nineteenth-century language of "wage slavery" to demand union recognition.

workers and the local police. In Toledo, Ohio, 10,000 striking auto workers surrounded the Electric Auto-Lite factory, where managers had brought strikebreakers to take their jobs, leading to a seven-hour fight with police and the National Guard. In Minneapolis, where an organization of businessmen known as the Citizens Alliance controlled the city government, a four-month strike by truck drivers led to pitched battles in the streets and the governor declaring martial law. San Francisco experienced the country's first general strike since 1919. It began with a walkout of dockworkers led by the fiery communist Harry Bridges. Workers demanded recognition of the International Longshoremen's Association and an end to the hated "shape up" system in which they had to gather en masse each day to wait for work assignments. The year 1934 also witnessed a strike of 400,000 textile workers in states from New England to the Deep South, demanding recognition of the United Textile Workers. Many of these walkouts, including those in Toledo, Minneapolis, and San Francisco, won at least some of the workers' demands. But the textile strike failed.

THE RISE OF THE CIO

The labor upheaval posed a challenge to the American Federation of Labor's traditional policy of organizing workers by craft—welders or machine repairers, for example—rather than seeking to mobilize all the workers in a given industry, such as steel manufacturing. In 1934, thirty AFL leaders called for the creation of unions of industrial workers. When the AFL convention of 1935 refused, the head of the United Mine Workers, John L. Lewis, led a walkout that produced a new labor organization, the Congress of Industrial Organizations (CIO). It set out to create unions in the main bastions of the American economy. It aimed, said Lewis, at nothing less than to secure "economic freedom and industrial democracy" for American workers—a fair share in the wealth produced by their labor, and a voice in determining the conditions under which they worked.

In December 1936, the United Auto Workers (UAW), a fledgling CIO union, unveiled the sit-down, a strikingly effective tactic that the IWW had pioneered three decades earlier. Rather than walking out of a plant, thus enabling management to bring in strikebreakers, workers halted production but remained inside. In the UAW's first sit-down strike, 7,000 General Motors workers seized control of the Fisher Body Plant in Cleveland. Sit-downs soon spread to GM plants in Flint, Michigan, the nerve center of automobile production. When local police tried to storm the Flint plants, workers fought them off. Democratic governor Frank Murphy, who had been elected with strong support from the CIO, declared his unwillingness to use force to dislodge the strikers. The strikers demonstrated a remarkable spirit of unity. They cleaned the plant, oiled the idle machinery, settled disputes among themselves, prepared meals, and held concerts of labor songs. Workers' wives shuttled food into the plant. "They made a palace out of what had been their prison," wrote one reporter. On February 11, General Motors agreed to negotiate with the UAW. Not until 1941 would the bitterly anti-union Henry Ford sign a labor contract. But by the end of 1937, the UAW claimed 400,000 members.

The victory in the auto industry reverberated throughout industrial America. Steelworkers had suffered memorable defeats in the struggle for unionization, notably at Homestead in 1892 and in the Great Steel Strike of 1919. U.S. Steel, the country's single most important business firm, owner of an industrial empire that stretched across several states and employed more than 200,000 workers, had been among the strongest opponents of unionization. But in March 1937, fearing a sit-down campaign and aware that it could no longer count on the aid of state and federal authorities, the company agreed to recognize the Steel Workers Organizing Committee (forerunner of the United Steelworkers of America). Smaller steel firms, how-

Sit-down strike at a General Motors factory in Flint, Michigan, 1937.

ever, refused to follow suit. On Memorial Day, 1937, company guards and Chicago police fired on a picnic of striking Republic Steel workers, killing ten persons. Not until 1942 would Republic sign a labor contract.

Union membership nonetheless reached 9 million by 1940, more than double the number in 1930. The coming of the union, said a member of New York City's transit workers' organization, enabled workers "to go to our bosses and talk to them like men, instead of . . . like slaves." Unions frequently demanded and won a say in workplace management, including the right to contest the amount and pace of work and the introduction of new technology. They gained new grievance procedures and seniority systems governing hiring, firing, and promotions. The CIO unions helped to stabilize a chaotic employment situation and offered members a sense of dignity and freedom.

LABOR AND POLITICS

Throughout the industrial heartland, the labor upsurge altered the balance of economic power and propelled to the forefront of politics labor's goal of a fairer, freer, more equal America. Unlike the AFL, traditionally hostile to government intervention in labor-management relations, the CIO put forward an ambitious program for federal action to shield Americans from economic and social insecurity, including public housing, universal health care, and unemployment and old age insurance.

Building on the idea, so prominent in the 1920s, that the key to prosperity lay in an American standard of living based on mass consumption, CIO leaders explained the Depression as the result of an imbalance of wealth and income. The role of unions, in cooperation with the government, they argued, was to "create a consumer's demand" by raising wages and redistributing wealth. Only in this way could society absorb the products that rolled off modern assembly lines. The pathbreaking 1937 agreement between the UAW and General Motors spoke of a "rate of pay commensurate with an American standard of living." By mid-decade, many New Dealers accepted the "underconsumptionist" explanation of the Depression, which saw lack of sufficient consumer demand as its underlying cause. They concluded that the government must act to raise dramatically wage earners' share of the national income.

VOICES OF PROTEST

Other popular movements of the mid-1930s also placed the question of economic justice on the political agenda. In California, the novelist Upton Sinclair won the Democratic nomination for governor in 1934 as the head of the End Poverty in California movement. Sinclair called for the state to use idle factories and land in cooperative ventures that would provide jobs for the unemployed. He lost the election after being subjected to one of the first modern "negative" media campaigns. Sinclair's opponents circulated false newsreels showing armies of unemployed men marching to California to support his candidacy and a fake endorsement from the Communist Party.

The rise to national prominence of Huey Long offered another sign of popular dissatisfaction with the slow pace of economic recovery. Long's career embodied both Louisiana's Populist and Socialist traditions (Winn Parish, his home, had voted for both of these third parties) and the state's heritage of undemocratic politics. Driven by intense ambition and the desire to help uplift the state's "common people," Long won election as governor in 1928 and in 1930 took a seat in the U.S. Senate. From Washington, he dominated every branch of state government. He used his dictatorial power to build roads, schools, and hospitals and to increase the tax burden on Louisiana's oil companies.

One of the most colorful characters in twentieth-century American politics, Long was referred to by both admirers and critics as the "Kingfish." In 1934, he launched the Share Our Wealth movement, with the slogan

"Every Man a King." He called for the confiscation of most of the wealth of the richest Americans in order to finance an immediate grant of $5,000 and a guaranteed job and annual income for all citizens. In his inimitable style, Long explained his goal: "Let's pull down these huge piles of gold until there shall be a real job, not a little old sow-belly, black-eyed pea job but a real spending money, beefsteak and gravy . . . Ford in the garage . . . red, white, and blue job for every man." Long claimed a following of 5 million. He was on the verge of announcing a run for president when the son of a defeated political rival assassinated him in 1935.

A portrait of Huey Long, the "Kingfish" of Louisiana politics, towers over the inauguration of his supporter, Richard Leche, as governor in 1936.

Also in the mid-1930s, the "radio priest," Father Charles E. Coughlin, attracted millions of listeners with weekly broadcasts attacking Wall Street bankers and greedy capitalists, and calling for government ownership of key industries as a way of combating the Depression. Initially a strong supporter of FDR, Coughlin became increasingly critical of the president for what he considered the failure of the New Deal to promote social justice. His crusade would later shift to anti-Semitism and support for European fascism. Dr. Francis Townsend, a California physician, meanwhile won wide support for a plan by which the government would make a monthly payment of $200 to older Americans, with the requirement that they spend it immediately. This, he argued, would boost the economy. By the end of 1934, Townsend Clubs claimed more than 2 million members. Along with the rise of the CIO, these signs of popular discontent helped to spark the Second New Deal.

THE SECOND NEW DEAL

Spurred by the failure of his initial policies to pull the country out of the Depression and the growing popular clamor for greater economic equality, and buoyed by Democratic gains in the midterm elections of 1934, Roosevelt in 1935 launched the Second New Deal. The First had focused on economic recovery. The emphasis of the Second was economic security—a guarantee that Americans would be protected against unemployment and poverty. "Boys," Roosevelt's relief administrator, Harry Hopkins, told his staff, "this is our hour. We've got to get everything we want—a [public] works program, social security, wages and hours, everything—now or never."

The idea that lack of consumer demand caused the Depression had been popularized by Huey Long, Francis Townsend, and the CIO. By 1935, more and more New Dealers had concluded that the government should no longer try to plan business recovery but should try to redistribute the national income so as to sustain mass purchasing power in the consumer economy. A series of measures in 1935 attacked head-on the problem of weak demand and economic inequality. Congress levied a highly publicized tax on large fortunes and corporate profits—a direct response to the popularity of Huey Long's Share Our Wealth campaign. It created the Rural Electrification Agency (REA) to bring electric power to homes that lacked it—80 percent of farms were still without electricity in 1934—in part to enable more Americans to purchase household appliances.

The REA proved to be one of the Second New Deal's most successful programs. By 1950, 90 percent of the nation's farms had been wired for electricity, and almost all now possessed radios, electric stoves, refrigerators, and mechanical equipment to milk cows. In addition, the federal government under the Second New Deal tried to promote soil conservation and family farming. This effort resulted from the belief that the country would never achieve prosperity so long as farmers' standard of living lagged well behind that of city dwellers, and that rural poverty resulted mainly from the poor use of natural resources. Thus, farmers received federal assistance in reducing soil loss in their fields. The federal government also purchased significant amounts of marginal and eroded land and converted these areas from farms into national grasslands and parks. It encouraged more environmentally conscious agricultural techniques. These measures (like those of the AAA) mainly benefited landowners, not sharecroppers, tenants, or migrant workers. In the long run, the Second New Deal failed to arrest the trend toward larger farms and fewer farmers.

THE WPA AND THE WAGNER ACT

In 1934, Roosevelt had severely curtailed federal employment for those in need. Now, he approved the establishment of the Works Progress Administration (WPA), which hired some 3 million Americans, in virtually every walk of life, each year until it ended in 1943. Under Harry Hopkins's direction, the WPA changed the physical face of the United States. It constructed thousands of public buildings and bridges, more than 500,000 miles of roads, and 600 airports. It built stadiums, swimming pools, and sewage treatment plants. Unlike previous work relief programs, the WPA employed many out-of-work white-collar workers and professionals, even doctors and dentists.

Perhaps the most famous WPA projects were in the arts. The WPA set hundreds of artists to work decorating public buildings with murals. It hired writers to produce local histories and guidebooks to the forty-eight states and to record the recollections of ordinary Americans, including hundreds of former slaves. Its Federal Theater Project put on plays, including an all-black production of *Macbeth* and Sinclair Lewis's drama *It Can't Happen Here*, about fascism coming to the United States. The Federal Music Project established orchestras and choral groups, and the Federal Dance Project sponsored ballet and modern dance programs. Thanks to the WPA, audiences across the country enjoyed their first glimpse of live musical and theatrical performances and their first opportunity to view exhibitions of American art. Also in 1935, Congress created the National Youth Administration to provide relief to American teenagers and young adults.

Another major initiative of the Second New Deal, the Wagner Act, was known at the time as "Labor's Magna Carta" (a reference to an early landmark in the history of freedom). This brought democracy into the

A poster by the artist Vera Bock for the Federal Art Project of the Works Progress Administration depicts farmers and laborers joining hands to produce prosperity.

An art exhibit in a New York City alley in 1938. The Works Progress Administration tried to broaden the audience for art by displaying it in unusual venues.

American workplace by empowering the National Labor Relations Board to supervise elections in which employees voted on union representation. It also outlawed "unfair labor practices," including the firing and blacklisting of union organizers. The bill's main sponsor, Robert Wagner of New York, told the Senate that the ability of workers to pool their strength through collective bargaining represented the "next step" in "the evolution of American freedom." He also promised that unionization and higher wages would aid economic recovery by boosting the purchasing power of ordinary Americans.

THE AMERICAN WELFARE STATE

The centerpiece of the Second New Deal was the Social Security Act of 1935. It embodied Roosevelt's conviction that the national government had a responsibility to ensure the material well-being of ordinary Americans. It created a system of unemployment insurance, old age pensions, and aid to the disabled, the elderly poor, and families with dependent children.

None of these were original ideas. The Progressive platform of 1912 had called for old age pensions. Assistance to poor families with dependent children descended from the mothers' pensions promoted by maternalist reformers. Many European countries had already adopted national unemployment insurance plans. What was new, however, was that in the name of economic security, the American government would now supervise not simply temporary relief but a permanent system of social insurance.

The Social Security Act launched the American version of the welfare state—a term that originated in Britain during World War II to refer to a system of income assistance, health coverage, and social services for all citizens. The act illustrated both the extent and the limits of the changes ushered in by the Second New Deal. The American welfare state marked a radical departure from previous government policies, but compared with similar programs in Europe, it has always been far more decentralized, involved lower levels of public spending, and covered fewer citizens. The original Social Security bill, for example, envisioned a national system of health insurance. But Congress dropped this after ferocious opposition from the American Medical Association, which feared government regulation of doctors' activities and incomes.

THE SOCIAL SECURITY SYSTEM

Some New Dealers desired a program funded by the federal government's general tax revenues, and with a single set of eligibility standards administered by national officials. But Secretary of Labor Frances Perkins, along with powerful members of Congress, wished to keep relief in the hands of state and local authorities and believed that workers should contribute directly to the cost of their own benefits. Roosevelt himself preferred to fund Social Security by taxes on employers and workers, rather than out of general government revenues. He believed that paying such taxes gave contributors "a legal, moral, and political right" to collect their old age pensions and unemployment benefits, which no future Congress could rescind.

As a result, Social Security emerged as a hybrid of national and local funding, control, and eligibility standards. Old age pensions were administered nationally but paid for by taxes on employers and employees. Such taxes also paid for payments to the unemployed, but this program was highly decentralized, with the states retaining considerable control over the level of benefits. The states paid most of the cost of direct poor relief, under the program called Aid to Dependent Children, and eligibility and the level of payments varied enormously from place to place. As will be discussed later, the combination of local administration and the fact that domestic and agricultural workers were not covered by unemployment and old age benefits meant that Social Security at first excluded large numbers of Americans, especially unmarried women and non-whites.

Nonetheless, Social Security represented a dramatic departure from the traditional functions of government. The Second New Deal transformed the relationship between the federal government and American citizens. Before the 1930s, national political debate often revolved around the question of *whether* the federal government should intervene in the economy. After the New Deal, debate rested on *how* it should intervene. In addition, the government assumed a responsibility, which it has never wholly relinquished, for guaranteeing Americans a living wage and protecting them against economic and personal misfortune. "Laissez-faire is dead," wrote Walter Lippmann, "and the modern state has become responsible for the modern economy [and] the task of insuring . . . the standard of life for its people."

A RECKONING WITH LIBERTY

The Depression made inevitable, in the words of one writer, a "reckoning with liberty." For too many Americans, Roosevelt proclaimed, "life was no

A 1935 poster promoting the new Social Security system.

longer free; liberty no longer real; men could no longer follow the pursuit of happiness." The 1930s produced an outpouring of books and essays on freedom. The large majority took for granted the need for a new definition. In a volume entitled *Land of the Free* (1938), the poet Archibald MacLeish used photographs of impoverished migrants and sharecroppers to question the reality of freedom in desperate times. "We told ourselves we were free," he wrote. Now, "we wonder if the liberty is done . . . or if there's something different men can mean by Liberty."

Like the Civil War, the New Deal recast the idea of freedom by linking it to the expanding power of the national state. "Our democracy," wrote Father John A. Ryan, a prominent Catholic social critic, "finds itself . . . in a new age where not political freedom but social and industrial freedom is the most insistent cry." Influenced by Ryan, the National Catholic Welfare Conference in 1935 declared that "social justice" required a government guarantee of continuous employment and a "decent livelihood and adequate security" for all Americans. A 1935 survey by *Fortune* magazine found that among poor respondents, 90 percent believed that the government should guarantee that "every man who wants work has a job."

FDR delivering one of his "fireside chats" in 1938. Roosevelt was the first president to make effective use of the radio to promote his policies.

FDR AND THE IDEA OF FREEDOM

Along with being a superb politician, Roosevelt was a master of political communication. At a time when his political opponents controlled most newspapers, he harnessed radio's power to bring his message directly into American homes. By the mid-1930s, more than two-thirds of American families owned radios. They listened avidly to Roosevelt's radio addresses, known as "fireside chats."

Roosevelt adeptly appealed to traditional values in support of new policies. He gave the term "liberalism" its modern meaning. In the nineteenth century, liberalism had been a shorthand for limited government and free-market economics. Roosevelt consciously chose to employ it to describe a large, active, socially conscious state. He reclaimed the word "freedom" from conservatives and made it a rallying cry for the New Deal. In his second fireside chat, Roosevelt juxtaposed his own definition of liberty as "greater security for the average man" to the older notion of liberty of contract, which served the interests of "the privileged few." Henceforth, he would consistently link freedom with economic security and identify entrenched economic inequality as its greatest enemy. "The liberty of a democracy," he declared in 1938, was not safe if citizens could not "sustain an acceptable standard of living."

Even as Roosevelt invoked the word to uphold the New Deal, "liberty"—in the sense of freedom from powerful government—became the fighting slogan of his opponents. Their principal critique of the New Deal was that its "reckless spending" undermined fiscal responsibility and its new government regulations restricted American freedom. When conservative businessmen and politicians in 1934 formed an organization to mobilize opposition to Roosevelt's policies, they called it the American Liberty League. Robert Taft of Ohio, leader of the Republicans in Congress, accused Roosevelt of sacrificing "individual freedom" in a misguided effort to "improve the conditions of the poor."

VOICES OF FREEDOM

FROM FRANKLIN D. ROOSEVELT, "Fireside Chat" (1934)

President Roosevelt pioneered the use of the new mass medium of radio to speak directly to Americans in their homes. He used his "fireside chats" to mobilize support for New Deal programs, link them with American traditions, and outline his definition of freedom.

To those who say that our expenditures for public works and other means for recovery are a waste that we cannot afford, I answer that no country, however rich, can afford the waste of its human resources. Demoralization caused by vast unemployment is our greatest extravagance. Morally, it is the greatest menace to our social order. Some people try to tell me that we must make up our minds that in the future we shall permanently have millions of unemployed just as other countries have had them for over a decade. What may be necessary for those countries is not my responsibility to determine. But as for this country, I stand or fall by my refusal to accept as a necessary condition of our future a permanent army of unemployed. . . .

In our efforts for recovery we have avoided, on the one hand, the theory that business should and must be taken over into an all-embracing Government. We have avoided, on the other hand, the equally untenable theory that it is an interference with liberty to offer reasonable help when private enterprise is in need of help. The course we have followed fits the American practice of Government, a practice of taking action step by step, of regulating only to meet concrete needs, a practice of courageous recognition of change. I believe with Abraham Lincoln, that "the legitimate object of Government is to do for a community of people whatever they need to have done but cannot do at all or cannot do so well for themselves in their separate and individual capacities."

I am not for a return to that definition of liberty under which for many years a free people were being gradually regimented into the service of the privileged few. I prefer and I am sure you prefer that broader definition of liberty under which we are moving forward to greater freedom, to greater security for the average man than he has ever known before in the history of America.

FROM JOHN STEINBECK, *The Harvest Gypsies: On the Road to the Grapes of Wrath* (1938)

John Steinbeck's popular novel *The Grapes of Wrath* (1939), and the film version that followed shortly thereafter, focused national attention on the plight of homeless migrants displaced from their farms as a result of the Great Depression. Before that book appeared, Steinbeck had published a series of newspaper articles based on eyewitness accounts of the migrants, which became the basis for his novel.

In California, we find a curious attitude toward a group that makes our agriculture successful. The migrants are needed, and they are hated. . . . The migrants are hated for the following reasons, that they are ignorant and dirty people, that they are carriers of disease, that they increase the necessity for police and the tax bill for schooling in a community, and that if they are allowed to organize they can, simply by refusing to work, wipe out the season's crops. . . .

Let us see what kind of people they are, where they come from, and the routes of their wanderings. In the past they have been of several races, encouraged to come and often imported as cheap labor. Chinese in the early period, then Filipinos, Japanese and Mexicans. These were foreigners, and as such they were ostracized and segregated and herded about. . . . But in recent years the foreign migrants have begun to organize, and at this danger they have been deported in great numbers, for there was a new reservoir from which a great quantity of cheap labor could be obtained.

The drought in the middle west has driven the agricultural populations of Oklahoma, Nebraska and parts of Kansas and Texas westward. . . . Thousands of them are crossing the borders in ancient rattling automobiles, destitute and hungry and homeless, ready to accept any pay so that they may eat and feed their children. . . .

The earlier foreign migrants have invariably been drawn from a peon class. This is not the case with the new migrants. They are small farmers who have lost their farms, or farm hands who have lived with the family in the old American way. . . . They have come from the little farm districts where democracy was not only possible but inevitable, where popular government, whether practiced in the Grange, in church organization or in local government, was the responsibility of every man. And they have come into the country where, because of the movement necessary to make a living, they are not allowed any vote whatever, but are rather considered a properly unprivileged class. . . .

As one little boy in a squatter's camp said, "When they need us they call us migrants, and when we've picked their crop, we're bums and we got to get out."

QUESTIONS

1. What does Roosevelt mean by the difference between the definition of liberty that has existed in the past and his own "broader definition of liberty"?

2. According to Steinbeck, how do Depression-era migrant workers differ from those in earlier periods?

3. Do the migrant workers described by Steinbeck enjoy liberty as Roosevelt understands it?

This 1935 cartoon by William Gropper portrays Uncle Sam as Gulliver tied down by Lilliputians in the famous eighteenth-century novel Gulliver's Travels *by Jonathan Swift. In this case, the bonds are the numerous agencies and laws created by the New Deal, which, Gropper suggests, are inhibiting the country from getting back on its feet during the Great Depression.*

As the 1930s progressed, opponents of the New Deal invoked the language of liberty with greater and greater passion. The U.S. Chamber of Commerce charged FDR with attempting to "Sovietize" America. Even though his own administration had abandoned laissez-faire in the face of economic disaster, former president Hoover launched strident attacks on his successor for endangering "fundamental American liberties." In *The Challenge to Liberty* (1934), Hoover called the New Deal "the most stupendous invasion of the whole spirit of liberty" the nation had ever seen.

THE ELECTION OF 1936

By 1936, with working-class voters providing massive majorities for the Democratic Party and businesses large and small bitterly estranged from the New Deal, politics reflected class divisions more completely than at any other time in American history. Conceptions of freedom divided sharply as well. Americans, wrote George Soule, editor of *The New Republic*, confronted "two opposing systems of concepts about liberty," reflecting "the needs and purposes of two opposing [parts] of the population." One was the idea of "freedom for private enterprise," the other "socialized liberty" based on "an equitably shared abundance."

A fight for the possession of "the ideal of freedom," reported the *New York Times*, emerged as the central issue of the presidential campaign of 1936. The Democratic platform insisted that in a modern economy the government has an obligation to establish a "democracy of opportunity for all the people." In his speech accepting renomination, Roosevelt launched a blistering attack against "economic royalists" who, he charged, sought to establish a new tyranny over the "average man." Economic rights, he went on, were the precondition of liberty—poor men "are not free men." Throughout the campaign, FDR would insist that the threat posed to economic freedom by the "new despotism" of large corporations was the main issue of the election.

As Roosevelt's opponent, Republicans chose Kansas governor Alfred Landon, a former Theodore Roosevelt Progressive. Landon denounced Social Security and other measures as threats to individual liberty. Opposition to the New Deal planted the seeds for the later flowering of an antigovernment conservatism bent on upholding the free market and dismantling the welfare state. But in 1936 Roosevelt won a landslide reelection, with more than 60 percent of the popular vote. He carried every state except Maine and Vermont. Roosevelt's victory was all the more remarkable in view of the heavy support most of the nation's newspapers and nearly the entire business community gave to the Republicans. His success stemmed from strong backing from organized labor and his ability to unite southern white and northern black voters, Protestant farmers and urban Catholic and Jewish ethnics, industrial workers and middle-class home owners. These groups made up the so-called New Deal coalition, which would dominate American politics for nearly half a century.

THE COURT FIGHT

Roosevelt's second inaugural address was the first to be delivered on January 20. In order to lessen a newly elected president's wait before taking office, the recently ratified Twentieth Amendment had moved inauguration day from March 4. FDR called on the nation to redouble its efforts to aid those "who have too little." The Depression, he admitted, had not been conquered: "I see one-third of a nation ill-housed, ill-clad, and ill-nourished." Emboldened by his electoral triumph, Roosevelt now made what many considered a serious political miscalculation. On the pretense that several members of the Supreme Court were too old to perform their functions, he proposed that the president be allowed to appoint a new justice for each one who remained on the Court past age seventy (an age that six of the nine had already surpassed). FDR's aim, of course, was to change the balance of power on a Court that, he feared, might well invalidate Social Security, the Wagner Act, and other measures of the Second New Deal.

The plan aroused cries that the president was an aspiring dictator. Congress rejected it. But Roosevelt accomplished his underlying purpose. The Supreme Court, it is sometimes said, follows the election returns. Coming soon after Roosevelt's landslide victory of 1936, the threat of "court packing" inspired an astonishing about-face on the part of key justices. Beginning in March 1937, the Court suddenly revealed a new willingness to support economic regulation by both the federal government and the states. It upheld a minimum wage law of the state of Washington similar to the New York measure it had declared unconstitutional a year earlier. It turned aside challenges to Social Security and the Wagner Act. In subsequent cases, the Court affirmed federal power to regulate wages, hours, child labor, agricultural production, and numerous other aspects of economic life.

Announcing a new judicial definition of freedom, Chief Justice Charles Evans Hughes pointed out that the words "freedom of contract" did not

Fall In!, *a cartoon commenting on Roosevelt's proposal to "pack" the Supreme Court, from the* Richmond Times-Dispatch, *January 8, 1937.*

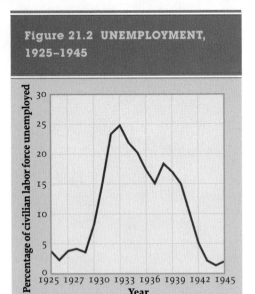

Figure 21.2 UNEMPLOYMENT, 1925-1945

The New Deal did not really solve the problem of unemployment, which fell below 10 percent only in 1941, as the United States prepared to enter World War II.

appear in the Constitution. "Liberty," however, did, and this, Hughes continued, required "the protection of law against the evils which menace the health, safety, morals, and welfare of the people." The Court's new willingness to accept the New Deal marked a permanent change in judicial policy. Having declared dozens of economic laws unconstitutional in the decades leading up to 1937, the justices have rarely done so since.

THE END OF THE SECOND NEW DEAL

Even as the Court made its peace with Roosevelt's policies, the momentum of the Second New Deal slowed. The landmark United States Housing Act did pass in 1937, initiating the first major national effort to build homes for the poorest Americans. But the Fair Labor Standards bill failed to reach the floor for over a year. When it finally passed in 1938, it banned goods produced by child labor from interstate commerce, set forty cents as the minimum hourly wage, and required overtime pay for hours of work exceeding forty per week. This last major piece of New Deal legislation established the practice of federal regulation of wages and working conditions, another radical departure from pre-Depression policies.

The year 1937 also witnessed a sharp downturn of the economy. With economic conditions improving in 1936, Roosevelt had reduced federal funding for farm subsidies and WPA work relief. The result was disastrous. As government spending fell, so did business investment, industrial production, and the stock market. Unemployment, still 14 percent at the beginning of 1937, rose to nearly 20 percent by year's end.

In 1936, in *The General Theory of Employment, Interest, and Money,* John Maynard Keynes had challenged economists' traditional belief in the sanctity of balanced budgets. Large-scale government spending, he insisted, was necessary to sustain purchasing power and stimulate economic activity during downturns. Such spending should be enacted even at the cost of a budget deficit (a situation in which the government spends more money than it takes in). By 1938, Roosevelt was ready to follow this prescription, which would later be known as Keynesian economics. In April, he asked Congress for billions more for work relief and farm aid. By the end of the year, the immediate crisis had passed. But the events of 1937–1938 marked a major shift in New Deal philosophy. Rather than economic planning, as in 1933–1934, or economic redistribution, as in 1935–1936, public spending would now be the government's major tool for combating unemployment and stimulating economic growth. The Second New Deal had come to an end.

THE LIMITS OF CHANGE

Roosevelt conceived of the Second New Deal, and especially Social Security, as expanding the meaning of freedom by extending assistance to broad groups of needy Americans—the unemployed, elderly, and dependent—as a right of citizenship, not charity or special privilege. But political realities, especially the power of inherited ideas about gender and black disenfranchisement in the South, powerfully affected the drafting of legislation. Different groups of Americans experienced the New Deal in radically different ways.

THE NEW DEAL AND AMERICAN WOMEN

The New Deal brought more women into government than ever before in American history. A number of talented women, including Secretary of Labor Frances Perkins, advised the president and shaped public policy. Most prominent of all was Eleanor Roosevelt, FDR's distant cousin whom he had married in 1905. She transformed the role of First Lady, turning a position with no formal responsibilities into a base for political action. She traveled widely, spoke out on public issues, wrote a regular newspaper column that sometimes disagreed openly with her husband's policies, and worked to enlarge the scope of the New Deal in areas like civil rights, labor legislation, and work relief.

But even as the New Deal increased women's visibility in national politics, organized feminism, already in disarray during the 1920s, disappeared as a political force. Indeed, the Depression inspired widespread demands for women to remove themselves from the labor market to make room for unemployed men. Because the Depression hit industrial employment harder than low-wage clerical and service jobs where women predominated, the proportion of the workforce made up of women rose. The government tried to reverse this trend. The Economy Act of 1932 prohibited both members of a married couple from holding federal jobs. Until its repeal in 1937, it led to the dismissal of numerous female civil service employees whose husbands worked for the government. Many states and localities prohibited the hiring of women whose husbands earned a "living wage," and employers from banks to public school systems barred married women from jobs. Although the CIO organized female workers, it, too, adhered to the idea that women should be supported by men. "The working wife whose husband is employed," said a vice president of the United Auto Workers, "should be barred from industry."

Eleanor Roosevelt transformed the role of First Lady by taking an active and visible part in public life. Here she visits a West Virginia coal mine in 1933.

Most New Deal programs did not exclude women from benefits (although the CCC restricted its camps to men). But the ideal of the male-headed household powerfully shaped social policy. Since paying taxes on one's wages made one eligible for the most generous Social Security programs—old age pensions and unemployment insurance—they left most women uncovered, since they did not work outside the home. The program excluded the 3 million mostly female domestic workers altogether. "Those who need protection most are completely overlooked," the sister of a household worker complained to Secretary of Labor Perkins. "What about the poor domestics, both in private homes and private institutions. What have you done for them? Nothing."

THE SOUTHERN VETO

Roosevelt made the federal government the symbolic representative of all the people, including racial and ethnic groups generally ignored by previous administrations. Yet the power of the Solid South helped to mold the New Deal welfare state into an entitlement of white Americans. After the South's blacks lost the right to vote around the turn of the century, Democrats enjoyed a political monopoly in the region. Democratic members of Congress were elected again and again. With results predetermined, many whites did not bother to vote (only about 20 percent of eligible southern voters cast ballots in the election of 1920). But this tiny electorate had an enormous impact on national policy. Committee chairmanships in Congress rest on seniority—how many years a member has served in office. Beginning in 1933, when Democrats took control of Congress, southerners took the key leadership positions. Despite his personal popularity, Roosevelt felt he could not challenge the power of southern Democrats if he wished legislation to pass. At their insistence, the Social Security law excluded agricultural and domestic workers, the largest categories of black employment.

Roosevelt spoke of Social Security's universality, but the demand for truly comprehensive coverage came from the political left and black organizations. Congressman Ernest Lundeen of Minnesota in 1935 introduced a bill establishing a federally controlled system of old age, unemployment, and health benefits for all wage workers, plus support for female heads of households with dependents. Black organizations like the Urban League and the NAACP supported the Lundeen bill and lobbied strenuously for a system that enabled agricultural and domestic workers to receive unemployment and old age benefits and that established national relief standards. The Social Security Act, however, not Lundeen's proposal, became law. Its limitations, complained the *Pittsburgh Courier*, a black newspaper, reflected the power of "reactionary elements in the South who cannot bear the thought of Negroes getting pensions and compensations" and who feared that the inclusion of black workers would disrupt the region's low-wage, racially divided labor system.

THE STIGMA OF WELFARE

Because of the "southern veto," the majority of black workers found themselves confined to the least generous and most vulnerable wing of the new welfare state. The public assistance programs established by Social Security, notably aid to dependent children and to the poor elderly, were open to all Americans who could demonstrate financial need. But they set benefits at extremely low levels and authorized the states to determine eligibility standards, including "moral" behavior as defined by local authorities. As a result, public assistance programs allowed for widespread discrimination in the distribution of benefits. Because recipients did not pay Social Security taxes, they soon came to bear the humiliating stigma of dependency on government handouts, which would soon come to be known as "welfare."

In 1942, the National Resources Planning Board noted that because of their exclusion from programs "which give aid under relatively favorable conditions," blacks were becoming disproportionately dependent on welfare, a program widely viewed with popular disfavor. The situation, the report concluded, seemed certain to stigmatize blacks as recipients of unearned government assistance, and welfare as a program for minorities, thus dooming it forever to inadequate "standards of aid." Over time, this is precisely what happened, until the federal government abolished its responsibility for welfare in 1996, during the presidency of Bill Clinton.

THE INDIAN NEW DEAL

Overall, the Depression and New Deal had a contradictory impact on America's racial minorities. Under Commissioner of Indian Affairs John Collier, the administration launched an "Indian New Deal." Collier ended the policy of forced assimilation and allowed Indians unprecedented cultural autonomy. He replaced boarding schools meant to eradicate the tribal heritage of Indian children with schools on reservations, and dramatically increased spending on Indian health. He secured passage of the Indian Reorganization Act of 1934, ending the policy, dating back to the Dawes Act of 1887, of dividing Indian lands into small plots for individual families and selling off the rest. Federal authorities once again recognized Indians' right to govern their own affairs, except where specifically limited by national laws. Such limitations, however, could weigh heavily on Indian tribes. The Navajos, the nation's largest tribe, refused to cooperate with the Reorganization Act as a protest against a federal soil conservation program that required them to reduce their herds of livestock.

The New Deal marked the most radical shift in Indian policy in the nation's history. But living conditions on the desperately poor reservations did not significantly improve, and New Deal programs often ignored Indians' interests. The building of the Grand Coulee Dam on the Columbia River flooded thousands of acres where Indians had hunted and fished for centuries. But the government did not make any of the irrigation water available to the region's reservations.

THE NEW DEAL AND MEXICAN-AMERICANS

For Mexican-Americans, the Depression was a wrenching experience. With demand for their labor plummeting, more than 400,000 (one-fifth of the population of Mexican origin) returned to Mexico, some voluntarily, others at the strong urging of local authorities in the Southwest. A majority of those "encouraged" to leave the country were recent immigrants, but they included perhaps 200,000 Mexican-American children who had been born

A large crowd of Mexican-Americans waiting to leave Los Angeles in 1932 as part of the repatriation campaign.

in the United States and were therefore citizens. Those who remained mostly worked in grim conditions in California's vegetable and fruit fields, whose corporate farms benefited enormously from New Deal dam construction that provided them with cheap electricity and water for irrigation. The Wagner and Social Security Acts did not apply to agricultural laborers. When the workers tried to organize a union as part of the decade's labor upsurge, they were brutally suppressed. In his 1939 book *Factories in the Field*, the writer Carey McWilliams exposed the low wages, inadequate housing, and political repression under which the migrant laborers suffered, which the New Deal did nothing to alleviate.

Mexican-American leaders struggled to develop a consistent strategy for their people. They sought greater rights by claiming to be white Americans—in order to not suffer the same discrimination as African-Americans—but also sought the backing of the Mexican government and promoted a mystical sense of pride and identification with Mexican heritage later given the name *la raza*.

LAST HIRED, FIRST FIRED

As the "last hired and first fired," African-Americans were hit hardest by the Depression. Even those who retained their jobs now faced competition from unemployed whites who had previously considered positions like waiter and porter beneath them. With an unemployment rate double that of whites, blacks benefited disproportionately from direct government relief and, especially in northern cities, jobs on New Deal public-works projects. Half of the families in Harlem received public assistance during the 1930s.

The Depression propelled economic survival to the top of the black agenda. Demonstrations in Harlem demanded jobs in the neighborhood's white-owned stores, with the slogan "Don't Buy Where You Can't Work." W. E. B. Du Bois abandoned his earlier goal of racial integration as unrealistic for the foreseeable future. Blacks, he wrote, must recognize themselves as "a nation within a nation." He called on blacks to organize for economic survival by building an independent, cooperative economy within their segregated communities, and to gain control of their own separate schools (a position reminiscent of that of Booker T. Washington, whom he had earlier condemned).

A NEW DEAL FOR BLACKS

Although Roosevelt seems to have had little personal interest in race relations or civil rights, he appointed Mary McLeod Bethune, a prominent black educator, as a special adviser on minority affairs and a number of other blacks to important federal positions. Key members of his administration, including his wife, Eleanor, and Secretary of the Interior Harold Ickes, a former president of the Chicago chapter of the NAACP, directed national attention to the injustices of segregation, disenfranchisement, and lynching. In 1939, Eleanor Roosevelt resigned from the Daughters of the American Revolution when the organization refused to allow the black singer Marian Anderson to present a concert at Constitution Hall in Washington. The president's wife arranged for Anderson to sing on the steps of the Lincoln Memorial and for the concert to be broadcast nationally on the radio.

Thanks to the New Deal, Bethune proclaimed, a "new day" had dawned when blacks would finally reach "the promised land of liberty." The decade witnessed a historic shift in black voting patterns. In the North and West, where they enjoyed the right to vote, blacks in 1934 and 1936 abandoned their allegiance to the party of Lincoln and emancipation in favor of Democrats and the New Deal. But their hopes for broad changes in the nation's race system were disappointed. Despite a massive lobbying campaign, southern congressmen prevented passage of a federal antilynching law. FDR offered little support. "I did not choose the tools with which I must work," he told Walter White of the NAACP; he could not jeopardize his economic programs by alienating powerful members of Congress. The CCC established segregated work camps. Because of the exclusion of agricultural and domestic workers, Social Security's old age pensions and unemployment benefits and the minimum wages established by the Fair Labor Standards Act left uncovered 60 percent of all employed blacks and 85 percent of black women.

FEDERAL DISCRIMINATION

Federal housing policy, which powerfully reinforced residential segregation, revealed the limits of New Deal freedom. As in the case of Social Security, local officials put national housing policy into practice in a way that reinforced existing racial boundaries. Nearly all municipalities, North as well as South, insisted that housing built or financially aided by the federal government be racially segregated. (In Texas, some communities financed three sets of housing projects—for whites, blacks, and Mexicans.) The Federal Housing Administration, moreover, had no hesitation about insuring mortgages that contained clauses barring future sales to non-white buyers, and it refused to channel money into integrated neighborhoods. In some cases, the presence of a single black family led the agency to declare an entire block off-limits for federal mortgage insurance. Along with discriminatory practices by private banks and real estate companies, federal policy became a major factor in further entrenching housing segregation in the United States.

Federal employment practices also discriminated on the basis of race. As late as 1940, of the 150,000 blacks holding federal jobs, only 2 percent occupied positions other than clerk or custodian. In the South, many New Deal construction projects refused to hire blacks at all. "They give all the work to white people and give us nothing," a black resident of Mississippi wrote to FDR in 1935. The New Deal began the process of modernizing southern agriculture, but tenants, black and white, footed much of the bill. Tens of thousands of sharecroppers, as noted earlier, were driven off the land as a result

A black clergyman carrying a sign outside Peoples Drugstore in Washington, D.C., in the late 1930s. The "Don't Buy Where You Can't Work" campaign targeted stores that served black customers but refused to hire black employees.

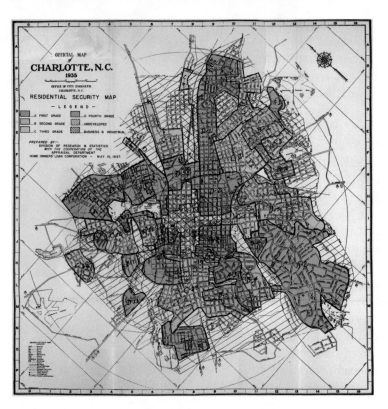

A map of Charlotte, North Carolina, prepared by the Home Owners' Loan Corporation, illustrates how federal agencies engaged in "redlining" of neighborhoods containing blue-collar and black residents. Wealthy areas, coded green, were given the best credit ratings, and white-collar districts, in blue, the second best. Residents of red districts found it almost impossible to obtain government housing loans.

of the AAA policy of raising crop prices by paying landowners to reduce cotton acreage.

Support for civil rights would eventually become a test of liberal credentials. But in the 1930s, one could advocate Roosevelt's economic program and oppose antilynching legislation and moves to incorporate black workers within Social Security. Theodore Bilbo, the notoriously racist senator from Mississippi, was one of the New Deal's most loyal backers. Not until the Great Society of the 1960s would those left out of Social Security and other New Deal programs—racial minorities, many women, migrants and other less privileged workers—win inclusion in the American welfare state.

A NEW CONCEPTION OF AMERICA

But if the New Deal failed to dismantle the barriers that barred non-whites from full participation in American life, the 1930s witnessed the absorption of other groups into the social mainstream. With Catholics and Jews occupying prominent posts in the Roosevelt administration and new immigrant voters forming an important part of its electoral support, the New Deal made ethnic pluralism a living reality in American politics. The election of the Italian-American Fiorello La Guardia as mayor of New York City in 1933 symbolized the coming to power of the new immigrants. Although elected as a Republican, La Guardia worked closely with FDR and launched his own program of spending on housing, parks, and public works. La Guardia's was one of numerous "little New Deals" that brought ethnic working-class voters to power in communities throughout the industrial heartland.

Thanks to the virtual cutoff of southern and eastern European immigration in 1924, the increasing penetration of movies, chain stores, and mass advertising into ethnic communities, and the common experience of economic crisis, the 1930s witnessed an acceleration of cultural assimilation. But the process had a different content from the corporate-sponsored Americanization plans of the preceding years. For the children of the new immigrants, labor and political activism became agents of a new kind of Americanization. One could participate fully in the broader society without surrendering one's ideals and ethnic identity. "Unionism is Americanism" became a CIO rallying cry. "The Mesabi Range," a Minnesota miner wrote to Secretary of Labor Perkins, complaining of low wages and management hostility to unions in the iron-rich region, "isn't Americanized yet."

THE HEYDAY OF AMERICAN COMMUNISM

In the mid-1930s, for the first time in American history, the left—an umbrella term for socialists, communists, labor radicals, and many New Deal liberals—enjoyed a shaping influence on the nation's politics and culture. The CIO and Communist Party became focal points for a broad social and intellectual impulse that helped to redraw the boundaries of American freedom. An obscure, faction-ridden organization when the Depression began, the Communist Party experienced remarkable growth during the 1930s. The party's membership never exceeded 100,000, but several times that number passed through its ranks.

The party's commitment to socialism resonated with a widespread belief that the Depression had demonstrated the bankruptcy of capitalism. But it was not so much the party's ideology as its vitality—its involvement in a mind-boggling array of activities, including demonstrations of the unemployed, struggles for industrial unionism, and a renewed movement for black civil rights—that for a time made it the center of gravity for a broad democratic upsurge. At the height of the Popular Front—a period during the mid-1930s when the Communist Party sought to ally itself with socialists and New Dealers in movements for social change, urging reform of the capitalist system rather than revolution—Communists gained an unprecedented respectability. Earl Browder, the party's leader, even appeared on the cover of *Time* magazine. It is one of the era's ironies that an organization with an undemocratic structure and closely tied to Stalin's dictatorial regime in Russia should have contributed to the expansion of freedom in the United States. But the Communist Party helped to imbue New Deal liberalism with a militant spirit and a more pluralistic understanding of Americanism.

REDEFINING THE PEOPLE

In theater, film, and dance, the Popular Front vision of American society sank deep roots and survived much longer than the political moment from which it sprang. In this broad left-wing culture, social and economic radicalism, not support for the status quo, defined true Americanism, ethnic and racial diversity was the glory of American society, and the "American way of life" meant unionism and social citizenship, not the unbridled pursuit of wealth. The American "people," viewed by many intellectuals in the 1920s as representing mean-spirited fundamentalism and crass commercialism, were suddenly rediscovered as embodiments of democratic virtue.

A card issued by the Communist Party during the 1936 campaign illustrates the party's attempt at "Americanization" (note the images of the American Revolution and Abraham Lincoln), as well as its emphasis on interracialism. James Ford, an African-American, was the party's vice-presidential candidate.

History of Southern Illinois, *a mural sponsored by the Illinois Federal Art Project, illustrates the widespread fascination during the 1930s with American traditions and the lives of ordinary Americans. On the left, a man strums a guitar, while workers labor on the waterfront.*

The "common man," Roosevelt proclaimed, embodied "the heart and soul of our country." During the 1930s, artists and writers who strove to create socially meaningful works eagerly took up the task of depicting the daily lives of ordinary farmers and city dwellers. Art about the people—such as Dorothea Lange's photographs of migrant workers and sharecroppers—and art created by the people—such as black spirituals—came to be seen as expressions of genuine Americanism. The Federal Music Project dispatched collectors with tape recorders to help preserve American folk music. Films celebrated populist figures who challenged and defeated corrupt business-men and politicians, as in *Mr. Deeds Goes to Town* (1936) and *Mr. Smith Goes to Washington* (1939). New immigrants, especially Jews and Italians, played a prominent role in producing and directing Hollywood films of the 1930s. Their movies, however, glorified not urban ethnic communities but ordinary small-town middle-class Americans.

PROMOTING DIVERSITY

"A new conception of America is necessary," wrote the immigrant labor radical Louis Adamic in 1938. Despite bringing ethnic and northern black voters into its political coalition, the Democratic Party said little about ethno-cultural issues, fearful of rekindling the divisive battles of the 1920s. But the Popular Front forthrightly sought to promote the idea that the country's strength lay in diversity, tolerance, and the rejection of ethnic prejudice and class privilege. The CIO avidly promoted the idea of ethnic and racial inclusiveness. It broke decisively with the AFL's tradition of exclusionary unionism. The CIO embraced cultural pluralism—an idea, as noted in Chapter 20, previously associated with intellectuals like Horace Kallen and the self-defense of ethnic and Catholic communities against enforced Americanization. "We are the only Americans who take them into our organ-ization as equals," wrote labor organizer Rose Pesotta, referring to the Mexican-Americans who flocked to the Cannery and Agricultural Workers union.

Popular Front culture presented a heroic but not uncritical picture of the country's past. Martha Graham's modern dance masterpiece *American*

VISIONS OF FREEDOM

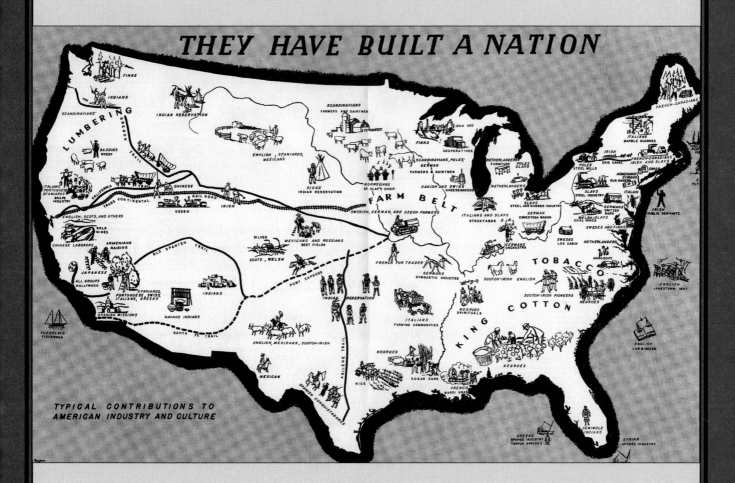

THEY HAVE BUILT A NATION

TYPICAL CONTRIBUTIONS TO
AMERICAN INDUSTRY AND CULTURE

Americans All, Immigrants All. *An image from a brochure that accompanied a twenty-six-week government-sponsored radio series (1938–1939) celebrating the history of various immigrant groups and their contributions to American society. One week was devoted to black Americans. The map highlights the distribution of members of racial and ethnic minorities throughout the country, and suggests some of their economic contributions.*

QUESTIONS

1. What does this map suggest about how the government was trying to shape public opinion during the 1930s?

2. How does the picture of American society presented here differ from the government's approach during World War I?

A Dorothea Lange photograph of a sharecropper and his family outside their modest home.

Document (1938), an embodiment of Popular Front aesthetics with its emphasis on America's folk traditions and multi-ethnic heritage, centered its account of history on the Declaration of Independence and the Gettysburg Address. Yet Graham did not neglect what her narrator called "things we are ashamed of," including the dispossession of the Indians and the plight of the unemployed. Graham's answer to Hector St. John de Crèvecoeur's old question, "What, then, is the American, this new man?" was that Americans were not only middle-class Anglo-Saxons but also blacks, immigrants, and the working class. Earl Robinson's song "Ballad for Americans," a typical expression of Popular Front culture that celebrated the religious, racial, and ethnic diversity of American society, became a national hit and was performed in 1940 at the Republican national convention.

CHALLENGING THE COLOR LINE

It was fitting that "Ballad for Americans" reached the top of the charts in a version performed by the magnificent black singer Paul Robeson. Popular Front culture moved well beyond New Deal liberalism in condemning racism as incompatible with true Americanism. In the 1930s, groups like the American Jewish Committee and the National Conference of Christians and Jews actively promoted ethnic and religious tolerance, defining pluralism as "the American way." But whether in Harlem or East Los Angeles, the Communist Party was the era's only predominantly white organization to make fighting racism a top priority. "The communists," declared Charles H. Houston, the NAACP's chief lawyer, "made it impossible for any aspirant to Negro leadership to advocate less than full economic, political and social equality."

Communist influence spread even to the South. The Communist-dominated International Labor Defense mobilized popular support for black defendants victimized by a racist criminal justice system. It helped to make

A scene from the Emancipation episode of Martha Graham's American Document, *photographed by Barbara Morgan. The dancers are Martha Graham and Eric Hawkins.*

the Scottsboro case an international cause célèbre. The case revolved around nine young black men arrested for the rape of two white women in Alabama in 1931. Despite the weakness of the evidence against the "Scottsboro boys" and the fact that one of the two accusers recanted, Alabama authorities three times put them on trial and three times won convictions. Landmark Supreme Court decisions overturned the first two verdicts and established legal principles that greatly expanded the definition of civil liberties—that defendants have a constitutional right to effective legal representation, and that states cannot systematically exclude blacks from juries. But the Court allowed the third set of convictions to stand, which led to prison sentences for five of the defendants. In 1937, a defense lawyer worked out a deal whereby Alabama authorities released nearly all the defendants on parole, although the last of the Scottsboro boys did not leave prison until thirteen years had passed.

Despite considerable resistance from white workers determined to preserve their monopoly of skilled positions and access to promotions, the CIO welcomed black members and advocated the passage of antilynching laws and the return of voting rights to southern blacks. The CIO brought large numbers of black industrial workers into the labor movement for the first time and ran extensive educational campaigns to persuade white workers to recognize the interests they shared with their black counterparts. Black workers, many of them traditionally hostile to unions because of their long experience of exclusion, responded with enthusiasm to CIO organizing efforts. The union offered the promise of higher wages, dignity in the workplace, and an end to the arbitrary power of often racist foremen. Ed McRea, a white CIO organizer in Memphis, Tennessee, reported that he had little difficulty persuading black workers of the value of unionization: "You didn't have any trouble explaining this to blacks, with the kinds of oppression and conditions they had. It was a question of freedom."

The "Scottsboro boys," flanked by two prison guards, with their lawyer, Samuel Liebowitz.

LABOR AND CIVIL LIBERTIES

Another central element of Popular Front public culture was its mobilization for civil liberties, especially the right of labor to organize. The struggle to launch industrial unions encountered sweeping local restrictions on freedom of speech as well as repression by private and public police forces. Nationwide publicity about the wave of violence directed against the Southern Tenant Farmers Union in the South and the CIO in industrial communities in the North elevated the rights of labor to a central place in discussions of civil liberties. The American Civil Liberties Union, primarily concerned in the 1920s with governmental repression, by 1934 concluded that "the masters of property" posed as great a danger to freedom of speech and assembly as political authorities.

Beginning in 1936, a Senate subcommittee headed by Robert M. La Follette Jr. exposed the methods employers used to combat unionization, including spies and private police forces. Workers had "no liberties at all," an employee of General Motors wrote to the committee from Saginaw, Michigan. The extensive violence unleashed against strikers in California's cotton and lettuce fields made that state, the committee report concluded, seem more like a "European dictatorship" than part of the United States.

Labor militancy helped to produce an important shift in the understanding of civil liberties. Previously conceived of as individual rights that must be protected against infringement by the government, the concept now expanded to include violations of free speech and assembly by powerful private groups. As a result, just as the federal government emerged as a guarantor of economic security, it also became a protector of freedom of expression.

By the eve of World War II, civil liberties had assumed a central place in the New Deal understanding of freedom. In 1939, Attorney General Frank Murphy established a Civil Liberties Unit in the Department of Justice. "For the first time in our history," Murphy wrote the president, "the full weight of the Department will be thrown behind the effort to preserve in this country the blessings of liberty." Meanwhile, the same Supreme Court that in 1937 relinquished its role as a judge of economic legislation moved to expand its authority over civil liberties. The justices insisted that constitutional guarantees of free thought and expression were essential to "nearly every other form of freedom" and therefore deserved special protection by the courts. Thus, civil liberties replaced liberty of contract as the judicial foundation of freedom. In 1937, the Court overturned on free speech grounds the conviction of Angelo Herndon, a Communist organizer jailed in Georgia for "inciting insurrection." Three years later, it invalidated an Alabama law that prohibited picketing in labor disputes. Since 1937, the large majority of state and national laws overturned by the courts have been those that infringe on civil liberties, not the property rights of business.

The new appreciation of free expression was hardly universal. In 1938, the House of Representatives established an Un-American Activities Committee to investigate disloyalty. Its expansive definition of "un-American" included communists, labor radicals, and the left of the Democratic Party, and its hearings led to the dismissal of dozens of federal employees on charges of subversion. Two years later, Congress enacted the Smith Act, which made it a federal crime to "teach, advocate, or encourage" the overthrow of the government. A similar pursuit of radical views took place at the state level. The New York legislature's Rapp-Coudert Committee held sweeping hearings investigating "subversive" influences in New York City's public colleges, resulting in the firing in 1941 of some sixty faculty members charged with communist sympathies.

THE END OF THE NEW DEAL

By then the New Deal, as an era of far-reaching social reform, had already begun to recede. One reason was that more and more southern Democrats were finding themselves at odds with Roosevelt's policies. In 1938, the administration released a "Report on Economic Conditions in the South," along with a letter by the president referring to the region as "the nation's No. 1 economic problem." The document revealed that the South lagged far behind other parts of the country in industrialization and investment in education and public health. Its per capita income stood at half that of the rest of the nation. Also in 1938, a new generation of homegrown radicals—southern New Dealers, black activists, labor leaders, communists, even a few elected officials—founded the Southern Conference for Human Welfare to work for unionization, unemployment relief, and racial justice.

Until the late 1930s, prominent southern Democrats had been strong supporters of the New Deal, while at the same time working to shape legislation to allow for the local administration of relief and the exclusion of most black workers. Now, southern business and political leaders feared that continuing federal intervention in their region would encourage unionization and upset race relations. Roosevelt concluded that the enactment of future New Deal measures required a liberalization of the southern Democratic Party. In 1938, he tried to persuade the region's voters to replace conservative congressmen with ones who would support his policies. The South's small electorate dealt him a stinging rebuke. In the North, where the economic downturn, the "Court-packing" plan, and the upsurge of CIO militancy alarmed many middle-class voters, Republicans increased their congressional representation.

A period of political stalemate followed the congressional election of 1938. For many years, a conservative coalition of southern Democrats and northern Republicans dominated Congress. Further reform initiatives became almost impossible, and Congress moved to abolish existing ones, beginning with the Federal Theater Project, which had alarmed conservatives because of the presence of radicals and homosexuals on its payroll. Congress repealed an earlier tax on corporate profits and rejected a proposed program of national medical insurance. The administration, moreover, increasingly focused its attention on the storm gathering in Europe. Even before December 1941, when the United States entered World War II, "Dr. Win the War," as Roosevelt put it, had replaced "Dr. New Deal."

THE NEW DEAL IN AMERICAN HISTORY

Given the scope of the economic calamity it tried to counter, the New Deal seems in many ways quite limited. Compared to later European welfare states, Social Security remained restricted in scope and modest in cost. The

New Deal failed to address the problem of racial inequality, which in some ways it actually worsened.

Yet even as the New Deal receded, its substantial accomplishments remained. It greatly expanded the federal government's role in the American economy and made it an independent force in relations between industry and labor. The government told farmers what they could and could not plant, required employers to deal with unions, insured bank deposits, regulated the stock market, loaned money to home owners, and provided payments to a majority of the elderly and unemployed. It transformed the physical environment through hydroelectric dams, reforestation projects, rural electrification, and the construction of innumerable public facilities. It restored faith in democracy and made the government an institution directly experienced in Americans' daily lives and directly concerned with their welfare. It redrew the map of American politics. It helped to inspire, and was powerfully influenced by, a popular upsurge that recast the idea of freedom to include a public guarantee of economic security for ordinary citizens and that identified economic inequality as the greatest threat to American freedom.

One thing the New Deal failed to do was generate sustained prosperity. More than 15 percent of the workforce remained unemployed in 1940. Only the mobilization of the nation's resources to fight World War II would finally end the Great Depression.

SUGGESTED READING

BOOKS

Brinkley, Alan. *Voices of Protest: Huey Long, Father Coughlin, and the Great Depression* (1982). An account of the political careers of two key figures of the New Deal era and their influence on national events.

Cohen, Lizabeth. *Making a New Deal: Industrial Workers in Chicago, 1919–1939* (1990). Describes how the assimilation of immigrants and their children paved the way for the creation of the New Deal political coalition.

Denning, Michael. *The Cultural Front: The Laboring of American Culture in the Twentieth Century* (1996). A comprehensive account of the rise of cultural activity associated with the political left and the New Deal.

Dickstein, Morris. *Dancing in the Dark: A Cultural History of the Great Depression* (2009). A comprehensive survey of how the Depression and New Deal affected the arts in the United States.

Goodman, James. *Stories of Scottsboro* (1994). Discusses how different participants viewed one of the most notorious legal cases of the 1930s.

Hawley, Ellis W. *The New Deal and the Problem of Monopoly: A Study in Economic Ambivalence* (1966). Explores the changing approach toward concentrated economic power adopted by the Roosevelt administration.

Katznelson, Ira. *When Affirmative Action Was White* (2005). An examination of the racial exclusion built into many New Deal policies, and their long-term consequences.

Kessler-Harris, Alice. *In Pursuit of Equity: Men, Women, and the Quest for Economic Citizenship in 20th-Century America* (2001). Explores how assumptions regarding the proper roles of men and women helped to shape New Deal measures such as Social Security.

Kirby, Jack T. *Rural Worlds Lost: The American South, 1920–1960* (1987). Traces the transformation of the South in these four decades, with emphasis on how the New Deal affected the southern states.

Leuchtenberg, William E. *Franklin D. Roosevelt and the New Deal, 1932–1940* (1963). Still the standard one-volume account of Roosevelt's first two terms as president.

Naison, Mark. *Communists in Harlem during the Depression* (1983). Examines the rise and decline of the Communist Party in a center of black life, and its impact on the movement for racial justice.

Phillips, Sarah T. *The Land, This Nation: Conservation, Rural America, and the New Deal* (2007). Examines New Deal policies regarding agricultural development, rural conservation, and land use, and its attempt to modernize and uplift rural life.

Sanchez, George. *Becoming Mexican American: Ethnicity, Culture, and Identity in Chicano Los Angeles, 1900–1945* (1995). A careful study of Mexican-Americans in Los Angeles, including their participation in the social unrest of the 1930s and the movement for deporting them during that decade.

Sitkoff, Harvard. *A New Deal for Blacks: The Emergence of Civil Rights as a National Issue* (1978). Discusses the changing approach of the Roosevelt administration toward black Americans.

Smith, Jason B. *Building New Deal Liberalism: The Political Economy of Public Works* (2006). Places the great construction projects of the 1930s at the center of New Deal economic policy.

Sullivan, Patricia. *Days of Hope: Race and Democracy in the New Deal Era* (1996). Analyzes how the New Deal inspired the emergence of a biracial movement for civil rights in the South.

Worster, Donald. *Dust Bowl: The Southern Plains in the 1930s* (1979). A social and environmental history of one of the key episodes in rural America during the 1930s.

Zieger, Robert H. *The CIO, 1935–1955* (1995). A comprehensive history of the Congress of Industrial Organizations, the major labor group to emerge during the New Deal.

WEBSITES

America from the Great Depression to World War II: http://memory.loc.gov/ammem/fsowhome.html

FDR Cartoon Archive: www.nisk.k12.ny.us/fdr/FDRcartoons.html

Flint Sit-Down Strike: www.historicalvoices.org/flint/

New Deal Network: http://newdeal.feri.org

REVIEW QUESTIONS

1. Discuss how regional planning such as the Tennessee Valley Authority and the Columbia River project reflected broader changes in American life during the New Deal.

2. What actions did President Roosevelt and Congress take to prevent the collapse of the banking system and reform its operations?

3. How did the actions of the AAA benefit many farmers, injure others, and provoke attacks by conservatives?

4. Explain what labor did in the 1930s to rise from being "slaves of the depression" to secure "economic freedom and industrial democracy" for American workers.

5. How did the emphasis of the Second New Deal differ from the First New Deal?

6. How did the entrenched power of southern conservatives limit women and blacks from enjoying the full benefits of the New Deal?

7. Analyze the effects of the Indian Reorganization Act of 1934 on Native Americans.

8. Explain how New Deal programs contributed to the stigma of blacks as welfare dependent.

9. Illustrate how labor militancy helped produce a shift in the legal understanding of civil liberties.

10. What were the major characteristics of liberalism by 1939?

FREEDOM QUESTIONS

1. How did the New Deal make economic security a vital element of American freedom?

2. Illustrate how FDR and the New Deal repudiated the 1920s idea that liberty was based on unrestrained marketplace competition.

3. What did Roosevelt mean when he said that for too many Americans during the Depression, "life was no longer free, liberty no longer real"?

4. Describe how the Popular Front redefined both popular culture and the concept of "the American people."

5. How did the New Deal link the idea of freedom to the expanding power of the national state?

KEY TERMS

"public works revolution" (p. 860)

bank holiday (p. 864)

the Hundred Days (p. 865)

National Recovery Administration (p. 865)

Public Works Administration (p. 866)

Agricultural Adjustment Act (p. 867)

Dust Bowl (p. 868)

sit-down strike (p. 873)

Share Our Wealth movement (p. 874)

Townsend plan (p. 875)

Rural Electrification Agency (p. 876)

Works Progress Administration (p. 876)

Social Security Act (p. 877)

court-packing plan (p. 883)

minimum wage laws (p. 883)

Indian New Deal (p. 887)

the Popular Front (p. 891)

"Scottsboro boys" (p. 895)

Smith Act (p. 896)

House Un-American Activities Committee (p. 897)

REVIEW TABLE

Landmark New Deal Legislation

Legislation	Date	Purpose
Federal Deposit Insurance Corporation	1933	To insure deposits, protecting customers against bank failures
National Recovery Administration	1933	To bring business and labor together to establish standards for output, prices, and working conditions
Agricultural Adjustment Act	1933	To authorize the federal government to raise farm prices by setting production quotas
Civilian Conservation Corps	1933	To employ young men to work on conservation projects
Tennessee Valley Authority	1933	To supply hydroelectric power to the Tennessee Valley
Works Project Administration	1935	To employ a significant number of blacks, white-collar workers, professionals, and artists
Social Security	1935	To create a system of unemployment insurance, old age pensions, and aid to the disabled, the elderly poor, and families with dependent children
Wagner Act	1935	To protect the rights of unions
Fair Labor Standards	1938	To set a minimum hourly wage and maximum hours of work

Chapter 22

1778

1943

Fighting for the Four Freedoms: World War II, 1941–1945

FIGHTING WORLD WAR II

Good Neighbors
The Road to War
Isolationism
War in Europe
Toward Intervention
Pearl Harbor
The War in the Pacific
The War in Europe

THE HOME FRONT

Mobilizing for War
Business and the War
Labor in Wartime
Fighting for the Four Freedoms
Freedom from Want
The Office of War Information
The Fifth Freedom
Women at War
Women at Work

VISIONS OF POSTWAR FREEDOM

Toward an American Century
"The Way of Life of Free Men"
An Economic Bill of Rights
The Road to Serfdom

THE AMERICAN DILEMMA

Patriotic Assimilation
The *Bracero* Program
Mexican-American Rights
Indians during the War
Asian-Americans in Wartime
Japanese-American Internment
Blacks and the War
Blacks and Military Service
Birth of the Civil Rights
  Movement
The Double-V
What the Negro Wants
An American Dilemma
Black Internationalism

THE END OF THE WAR

"The Most Terrible Weapon"
The Dawn of the Atomic Age
The Nature of the War
Planning the Postwar World
Yalta and Bretton Woods
The United Nations
Peace, but not Harmony

One of the patriotic war posters issued by the Office of War Information during World War II, linking modern-day soldiers with patriots of the American Revolution as fighters for freedom, a major theme of government efforts to mobilize support for the war. The caption on the original poster states: "Americans will always fight for liberty."

FOCUS QUESTIONS

• What steps led to American participation in World War II?

• How did the United States mobilize economic resources and promote popular support for the war effort?

• What visions of America's postwar role began to emerge during the war?

• How did American minorities face threats to their freedom at home and abroad during World War II?

• How did the end of the war begin to shape the postwar world?

By far the most popular works of art produced during World War II were paintings of the Four Freedoms by the magazine illustrator Norman Rockwell. In his State of the Union Address, delivered before Congress on January 6, 1941, President Roosevelt spoke eloquently of a future world order founded on the "essential human freedoms": freedom of speech, freedom of worship, freedom from want, and freedom from fear. The Four Freedoms became Roosevelt's favorite statement of Allied aims. At various times, he compared them with the Ten Commandments, the Magna Carta, and the Emancipation Proclamation. They embodied, Roosevelt declared in a 1942 radio address, the "rights of men of every creed and every race, wherever they live," and made clear "the crucial difference between ourselves and the enemies we face today."

Rockwell's paintings succeeded in linking the Four Freedoms with the defense of traditional American values. "Words like *freedom* or *liberty*," declared one wartime advertisement, "draw close to us only when we break them down into the homely fragments of daily life." This insight helps to explain Rockwell's astonishing popularity. Born in New York City in 1894, Rockwell had lived in the New York area until 1939, when he and his family moved to Arlington, Vermont, where they could enjoy, as he put it, "the clean, simple country life, as opposed to the complicated world of the city." Drawing on the lives of his Vermont neighbors, Rockwell translated the Four Freedoms into images of real people situated in small-town America. Each of the paintings focuses on an instantly recognizable situation. An ordinary citizen rises to speak at a town meeting; members of different religious groups are seen at prayer; a family enjoys a Thanksgiving dinner; a mother and father stand over a sleeping child.

The Four Freedoms paintings first appeared in the *Saturday Evening Post* early in 1943. Letters of praise poured in to the magazine's editors. The government produced and sold millions of reprints. The paintings toured the country as the centerpiece of the Four Freedoms Show, which included theatrical presentations, parades, and other events aimed at persuading Americans to purchase war bonds. By the end of its tour, the Four Freedoms Show had raised $133 million.

Even as Rockwell invoked images of small-town life to rally Americans to the war effort, however, the country experienced changes as deep as at any time in its history. Many of the economic trends and social movements that we associate with the last half of the twentieth century had their roots in the war years. As during World War I, but on a far larger scale, wartime mobilization expanded the size and scope of government and energized the economy. The gross national product more than doubled and unemployment disappeared as war production finally conquered the Depression. The demand for labor drew millions of women into the workforce and sent a tide of migrants from rural America to the industrial cities of the North and West, permanently altering the nation's social geography. Some 30 million Americans moved during the war, half going into military service and half taking up new jobs.

World War II gave the country a new and lasting international role and greatly strengthened the idea that American security was global in scope and could only be protected by the worldwide triumph of core American values. Government military spending sparked the economic development of the South and West, laying the foundation for the rise of the modern Sunbelt. The war created a close link between big business and a militarized federal government—a "military-industrial complex," as President Dwight D. Eisenhower would later call it—that long survived the end of fighting.

World War II also redrew the boundaries of American nationality. In contrast to World War I, the government recognized the "new

A draft of FDR's Four Freedoms speech of 1941 shows how he added the words "everywhere in the world," (8 and 13 lines down) indicating that the Four Freedoms should be truly international ideals.

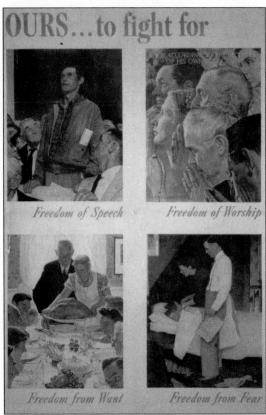

OURS...to fight for

Freedom of Speech   *Freedom of Worship*

Freedom from Want   *Freedom from Fear*

The immensely popular Office of War Information poster reproducing Norman Rockwell's paintings of the Four Freedoms, President Franklin D. Roosevelt's shorthand for American purposes in World War II.

immigrants" of the early twentieth century and their children as loyal Americans. Black Americans' second-class status assumed, for the first time since Reconstruction, a prominent place on the nation's political agenda. But toleration had its limits. With the United States at war with Japan, the federal government removed more than 100,000 Japanese-Americans, the majority of them American citizens, from their homes and placed them in internment camps.

As a means of generating support for the struggle, the Four Freedoms provided a crucial language of national unity. But this unity obscured divisions within American society that the war in some ways intensified, divisions reflected in debates over freedom. While some Americans looked forward to a worldwide New Deal, others envisioned "free enterprise" replacing government intervention in the economy. The war gave birth to the modern civil rights movement but strengthened the commitment of many white Americans to maintain the existing racial order. The movement of women into the labor force challenged traditional gender relations, but most men and not a few women longed for the restoration of family life with a male breadwinner and a wife responsible for the home.

Even Rockwell's popular paintings suggested some of the ambiguities within the idea of freedom. With the exception of *Freedom of Speech*, which depicts civic democracy in action, the paintings emphasized private situations. The message seemed to be that Americans were fighting to preserve freedoms enjoyed individually or within the family rather than in the larger public world. This emphasis on freedom as an element of private life would become more and more prominent in postwar America.

FIGHTING WORLD WAR II

GOOD NEIGHBORS

During the 1930s, with Americans preoccupied by the economic crisis, international relations played only a minor role in public affairs. From the outset of his administration, nonetheless, FDR embarked on a number of departures in foreign policy. In 1933, hoping to stimulate American trade, he exchanged ambassadors with the Soviet Union, whose government his Republican predecessors had stubbornly refused to recognize.

Roosevelt also formalized a policy initiated by Herbert Hoover by which the United States repudiated the right to intervene militarily in the internal affairs of Latin American countries. This Good Neighbor Policy, as it was called, had mixed results. During the 1930s, the United States withdrew its troops from Haiti and Nicaragua. FDR accepted Cuba's repeal of the Platt Amendment (discussed in Chapter 17), which had authorized American military interventions on that island. These steps offered a belated recognition of the sovereignty of America's neighbors. But while Roosevelt condemned "economic royalists" (wealthy businessmen) at home, like previous presidents he felt comfortable dealing with undemocratic governments friendly to American business interests abroad. The United States lent its support to dictators like Anastasio Somoza in Nicaragua, Rafael Trujillo Molina in the Dominican Republic, and Fulgencio Batista in Cuba. "He may be a son of a bitch, but he's *our* son of a bitch," FDR said of Somoza.

However, as the international crisis deepened in the 1930s, the Roosevelt administration took steps to counter German influence in Latin America by expanding hemispheric trade and promoting respect for American culture. Nelson Rockefeller, the head of an office that hoped to expand cultural relations in the hemisphere, sent the artists of the American Ballet Caravan and the NBC Symphony Orchestra on Latin American tours. This was a far different approach to relations with Central and South America than the military interventions of the first decades of the century.

THE ROAD TO WAR

Ominous developments in Asia and Europe quickly overshadowed events in Latin America. By the mid-1930s, it seemed clear that the rule of law was disintegrating in international relations and that war was on the horizon. In 1931, seeking to expand its military and economic power in Asia, Japan invaded Manchuria, a province of northern China. Six years later, its troops moved farther into China. When the Japanese overran the city of Nanjing, they massacred an estimated 300,000 Chinese prisoners of war and civilians.

An aggressive power threatened Europe as well. After brutally consolidating his rule in Germany, Adolf Hitler embarked on a campaign to control the entire continent. In violation of the Versailles Treaty, he feverishly pursued German rearmament. In 1936, he sent troops to occupy the Rhineland, a demilitarized zone between France and Germany established after World War I. The failure of Britain, France, and the United States to oppose this action convinced Hitler that the democracies could not muster the will to halt his aggressive plans. Italian leader Benito Mussolini, the founder of fascism, a movement similar to Hitler's Nazism, invaded and conquered Ethiopia. When General Francisco Franco in 1936 led an uprising against the democratically elected government of Spain, Hitler poured in arms, seeing the conflict as a testing ground for new weaponry. In 1939, Franco emerged victorious from a bitter civil war, establishing yet another fascist government in Europe. As part of a campaign to unite all Europeans of German origin in a single empire, Hitler in 1938 annexed Austria and the Sudetenland, an ethnically German part of Czechoslovakia. Shortly thereafter, he gobbled up all of that country.

As the 1930s progressed, Roosevelt became more and more alarmed at Hitler's aggression as well as his accelerating campaign against Germany's Jews, whom the Nazis stripped of citizenship and property and began to deport to concentration camps. In a 1937 speech in Chicago, FDR called for international action to "quarantine" aggressors. But no further steps followed. Roosevelt had little choice but to follow the policy of "appeasement"

This Hand Guides the Reich, *a Nazi propaganda poster from 1930s Germany. The bottom text reads: "German youth follow it in the ranks of Hitler Youth."*

In a 1940 cartoon, war clouds engulf Europe, while Uncle Sam observes that the Atlantic Ocean no longer seems to shield the United States from involvement.

adopted by Britain and France, who hoped that agreeing to Hitler's demands would prevent war. British prime minister Neville Chamberlain returned from the Munich conference of 1938, which awarded Hitler the Sudetenland, proclaiming that he had guaranteed "peace in our time."

ISOLATIONISM

To most Americans, the threat arising from Japanese and German aggression seemed very distant. Moreover, Hitler had more than a few admirers in the United States. Obsessed with the threat of communism, some Americans approved his expansion of German power as a counterweight to the Soviet Union. Businessmen did not wish to give up profitable overseas markets. Henry Ford did business with Nazi Germany throughout the 1930s. Indeed, Ford plants there employed slave labor provided by the German government. Trade with Japan also continued, including shipments of American trucks and aircraft and considerable amounts of oil. Until 1941, 80 percent of Japan's oil supply came from the United States.

Many Americans remained convinced that involvement in World War I had been a mistake. Senate hearings in 1934–1935 headed by Gerald P. Nye of North Dakota revealed that international bankers and arms exporters had pressed the Wilson administration to enter that war and had profited handsomely from it. Pacifism spread on college campuses, where tens of thousands of students took part in a "strike for peace" in 1935. Ethnic allegiances reinforced Americans' traditional reluctance to enter foreign conflicts. Many Americans of German and Italian descent celebrated the expansion of national power in their countries of origin, even when they disdained their dictatorial governments. Irish-Americans remained strongly anti-British.

Isolationism—the 1930s version of Americans' long-standing desire to avoid foreign entanglements—dominated Congress. Beginning in 1935, lawmakers passed a series of Neutrality Acts that banned travel on belligerents' ships and the sale of arms to countries at war. These policies, Congress hoped, would allow the United States to avoid the conflicts over freedom of the seas that had contributed to involvement in World War I. Despite the fact that the Spanish Civil War pitted a democratic government against an aspiring fascist dictator, the Western democracies, including the United States, imposed an embargo on arms shipments to both sides. Some 3,000 Americans volunteered to fight in the Abraham Lincoln Brigade on the side of the Spanish republic. But with Germany supplying the forces of Franco, the decision by democratic countries to abide by the arms embargo contributed substantially to his victory.

WAR IN EUROPE

In the Munich agreement of 1938, Britain and France had caved in to Hitler's aggression. In 1939, the Soviet Union proposed an international agreement to oppose further German demands for territory. Britain and

France, who distrusted Stalin and saw Germany as a bulwark against the spread of communist influence in Europe, refused. Stalin then astonished the world by signing a nonaggression pact with Hitler, his former sworn enemy. On September 1, immediately after the signing of the Nazi–Soviet pact, Germany invaded Poland. This time, Britain and France, who had pledged to protect Poland against aggression, declared war. But Germany appeared unstoppable. Within a year, the Nazi *blitzkrieg* (lightning war) had overrun Poland and much of Scandinavia, Belgium, and the Netherlands. On June 14, 1940, German troops occupied Paris. Hitler now dominated nearly all of Europe, as well as North Africa. In September 1940, Germany, Italy, and Japan created a military alliance known as the Axis.

For one critical year, Britain stood virtually alone in fighting Germany. Winston Churchill, who became prime minister in 1940, vowed to resist a threatened Nazi invasion. In the Battle of Britain of 1940–1941, the German air force launched devastating attacks on London and other cities. The Royal Air Force eventually turned back the air assault. But Churchill pointedly called on the "new world, with all its power and might," to step forward to rescue the old.

A newsreel theater in New York's Times Square announces Hitler's blitzkrieg *in Europe in the spring of 1940.*

TOWARD INTERVENTION

Roosevelt viewed Hitler as a mad gangster whose victories posed a direct threat to the United States. But most Americans remained desperate to remain out of the conflict. "What worries me, especially," FDR wrote to Kansas editor William Allen White, "is that public opinion over here is patting itself on the back every morning and thanking God for the Atlantic Ocean and the Pacific Ocean." After a tumultuous debate, Congress in 1940 agreed to allow the sale of arms to Britain on a "cash and carry" basis—that is, they had to be paid for in cash and transported in British ships. It also approved plans for military rearmament. But with a presidential election looming, Roosevelt was reluctant to go further. Opponents of involvement in Europe organized the America First Committee, with hundreds of thousands of members and a leadership that included well-known figures like Henry Ford, Father Coughlin, and Charles A. Lindbergh.

In 1940, breaking with a tradition that dated back to George Washington, Roosevelt announced his candidacy for a third term as president. The international situation was too dangerous and domestic recovery too fragile, he insisted, for him to leave office. Republicans chose as his opponent a political amateur, Wall Street businessman and lawyer Wendell Willkie. Differences between the candidates were far more muted than in 1936. Both supported the law, enacted in September 1940, that established the nation's first peacetime draft. Willkie endorsed New Deal social legislation. He captured more votes than Roosevelt's previous opponents, but FDR still emerged with a decisive victory.

During 1941, the United States became more and more closely allied with those fighting Germany and Japan. America, FDR declared, would be the "great arsenal of democracy." But with Britain virtually bankrupt, it could no longer pay for supplies. At Roosevelt's urging, Congress passed the Lend-Lease Act, which authorized military aid so long as countries promised somehow to return it all after the war. Under the law's provisions, the United States funneled billions of dollars worth of arms to Britain and

Walt Disney's program cover for the October 1941 "Fight for Freedom" rally at New York's Madison Square Garden, which demanded American intervention in the European war.

China, as well as the Soviet Union, after Hitler renounced his nonaggression pact and invaded that country in June 1941. FDR also froze Japanese assets in the United States, halting virtually all trade between the countries, including the sale of oil vital to Japan.

Those who believed that the United States must intervene to stem the rising tide of fascism tried to awaken a reluctant country to prepare for war. Interventionists popularized slogans that would become central to wartime mobilization. In June 1941, refugees from Germany and the occupied countries of Europe joined with Americans to form the Free World Association, which sought to bring the United States into the war against Hitler. The same year saw the formation of Freedom House. With a prestigious membership that included university presidents, ministers, businessmen, and labor leaders, Freedom House described the war raging in Europe as an ideological struggle between dictatorship and the "free world." In October 1941, it sponsored a "Fight for Freedom" rally at New York's Madison Square Garden, complete with a patriotic variety show entitled "It's Fun to Be Free." The rally ended by demanding an immediate declaration of war against Germany.

PEARL HARBOR

Until November 1941, the administration's attention focused on Europe. But at the end of that month, intercepted Japanese messages revealed that an assault in the Pacific was imminent. No one, however, knew where it would come. On December 7, 1941, Japanese planes, launched from aircraft carriers, bombed the naval base at Pearl Harbor in Hawaii, the first attack by a foreign power on American soil since the War of 1812. Pearl Harbor was a complete and devastating surprise. In a few hours, more than 2,000 American servicemen were killed, and 187 aircraft and 18 naval vessels, including 8 battleships, had been destroyed or damaged. By a stroke of fortune, no aircraft carriers—which would prove decisive in the Pacific war—happened to be docked at Pearl Harbor on December 7.

The battleships West Virginia *and* Tennessee *in flames during the Japanese attack on Pearl Harbor. Both were repaired and later took part in the Pacific war.*

Some of the 13,000 American troops forced to surrender to the Japanese on Corregidor Island in the Philippines in May 1942.

To this day, conspiracy theories abound suggesting that FDR knew of the attack and did nothing to prevent it so as to bring the United States into the war. No credible evidence supports this charge. Indeed, with the country drawing ever closer to intervention in Europe, Roosevelt hoped to keep the peace in the Pacific. But Secretary of Labor Frances Perkins, who saw the president after the attack, remarked that he seemed calm—"his terrible moral problem had been resolved." Terming December 7 "a date which will live in infamy," Roosevelt asked Congress for a declaration of war against Japan. The combined vote in Congress was 477 in favor and 1 against—pacifist Jeanette Rankin of Montana, who had also voted against American entry into World War I. The next day, Germany declared war on the United States. America had finally joined the largest war in human history.

Members of the U.S. Marine Corps, Navy, and Coast Guard taking part in an amphibious assault during the "island hopping" campaign in the Pacific theater of World War II.

THE WAR IN THE PACIFIC

World War II has been called a "gross national product war," meaning that its outcome turned on which coalition of combatants could outproduce the other. In retrospect, it appears inevitable that the entry of the United States, with its superior industrial might, would ensure the defeat of the Axis powers. But the first few months of American involvement witnessed an unbroken string of military disasters. Having earlier occupied substantial portions of French Indochina (now Vietnam, Laos, and

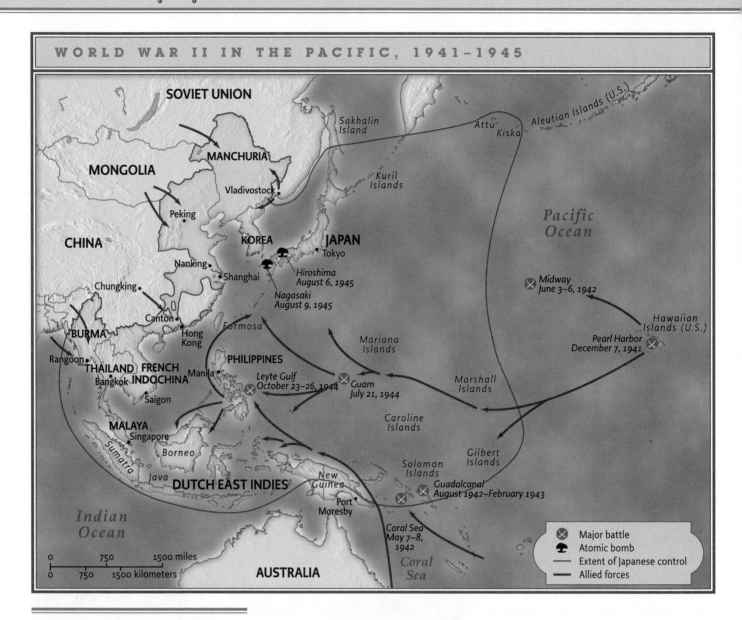

WORLD WAR II IN THE PACIFIC, 1941–1945

Although the Japanese navy never fully recovered from its defeats at the Coral Sea and Midway in 1942, it took three more years for American forces to near the Japanese homeland.

Cambodia), Japan in early 1942 conquered Burma (Myanmar) and Siam (Thailand). Japan also took control of the Dutch East Indies (Indonesia), whose extensive oil fields could replace supplies from the United States. And it occupied Guam, the Philippines, and other Pacific islands. At Bataan, in the Philippines, the Japanese forced 78,000 American and Filipino troops to lay down their arms—the largest surrender in American military history. Thousands perished on the ensuing "death march" to a prisoner-of-war camp, and thousands more died of disease and starvation after they arrived. At the same time, German submarines sank hundreds of Allied merchant and naval vessels during the Battle of the Atlantic.

Soon, however, the tide of battle began to turn. In May 1942, in the Battle of the Coral Sea, the American navy turned back a Japanese fleet intent on attacking Australia. The following month, it inflicted devastating losses on the Japanese navy in the Battle of Midway Island. These victories allowed American forces to launch the bloody campaigns that one by one drove the

Japanese from fortified islands like Guadalcanal and the Solomons in the western Pacific and brought American troops ever closer to Japan.

THE WAR IN EUROPE

In November 1942, British and American forces invaded North Africa and by May 1943 forced the surrender of the German army commanded by General Erwin Rommel. By the spring of 1943, the Allies also gained the upper hand in the Atlantic, as British and American destroyers and planes devastated the German submarine fleet. But even though Roosevelt was committed to liberating Europe from Nazi control, American troops did not immediately become involved on the European continent. As late as the end of 1944, more American military personnel were deployed in the Pacific than against Germany. In July 1943, American and British forces invaded Sicily, beginning the liberation of Italy. A popular uprising in Rome overthrew the Mussolini government, whereupon Germany occupied most of the country. Fighting there raged throughout 1944.

Ben Hurwitz, a soldier from New York City who fought in North Africa and Italy during World War II, made numerous sketches of his experiences. Here American troops pass a wrecked German tank in southern Italy in June 1944.

The major involvement of American troops in Europe did not begin until June 6, 1944. On that date, known as D-Day, nearly 200,000 American, British, and Canadian soldiers under the command of General Dwight D. Eisenhower landed in Normandy in northwestern France. More than a million troops followed them ashore in the next few weeks, in the most massive sea–land operation in history. After fierce fighting, German armies retreated eastward. By August, Paris had been liberated.

The crucial fighting in Europe, however, took place on the eastern front, the scene of an epic struggle between Germany and the Soviet Union. More than 3 million German soldiers took part in the 1941 invasion. After sweeping through western Russia, German armies in August 1942 launched a siege of Stalingrad, a city located deep inside Russia on the Volga River. This proved to be a catastrophic mistake. Bolstered by an influx of military supplies from the United States, the Russians surrounded the German troops and forced them to surrender. Some 800,000 Germans and 1.2 million Russians perished in the fighting. The German surrender at Stalingrad in January 1943 marked the turning point of the European war. Combined with a Russian victory at Kursk six months later in the greatest tank battle in history, the campaign in the east devastated Hitler's forces and sent surviving units on a long retreat back toward Germany.

Of 13.6 million German casualties in World War II, 10 million came on the Russian front. They represented only part of the war's vast toll in human lives. Millions of Poles and at least 20 million Russians, probably many more, perished—not only soldiers but civilian victims of starvation, disease,

WORLD WAR II IN EUROPE, 1942–1945

D-DAY

GREAT BRITAIN
London
Calais

Assembly Area
English Channel
Cherbourg
Le Havre
Rouen
Caen

FRANCE

Legend:
⊗ Major battles
— Allied offensives
Allied countries
Neutral countries
Axis countries
Extent of Axis control
Vichy France (controlled by Axis)

SWEDEN
FINLAND   1944
NORWAY
Leningrad
ESTONIA
1944
LATVIA
Moscow
1944
SOVIET UNION
LITHUANIA
EAST PRUSSIA
1945
Kursk July 1943
IRELAND
DENMARK
GREAT BRITAIN
NETHERLANDS
London
Berlin
Warsaw
1944
Stalingrad August 1942–February 1943
BELGIUM
GERMANY
1945
POLAND
1943
D-Day June 1944
Battle of the Bulge December 1944
1945
1943
1944
Paris
1944
LUXEMBOURG
FRANCE
CZECHOSLOVAKIA
1945
1944
SWITZERLAND
AUSTRIA
HUNGARY
1944
Vichy
1944
1945
ROMANIA
1944
PORTUGAL
YUGOSLAVIA
1944
SPAIN
1945
ITALY
BULGARIA
Rome
ALBANIA (It.)
1943
GREECE
TURKEY
1944
1942
SPANISH MOROCCO
Algiers
Oran
1942
Casablanca
1942
MOROCCO
1943
SYRIA (Fr.)
IRAQ (Br.)
LEBANON (Fr.)
Kasserine Pass February 1943
Mediterranean Sea
PALESTINE (Br.)
ALGERIA
TUNISIA
El Alamein October–November 1942
TRANSJORDAN (Br.)
1943
1942
SAUDI ARABIA
FRENCH NORTH AFRICA (Vichy France)
LIBYA (Italy)
EGYPT

0   250   500 miles
0   250   500 kilometers

Most of the land fighting in Europe during World War II took place on the eastern front between the German and Soviet armies.

and massacres by German soldiers. After his armies had penetrated eastern Europe in 1941, moreover, Hitler embarked on the "final solution"—the mass extermination of "undesirable" peoples—Slavs, gypsies, homosexuals, and, above all, Jews. By 1945, 6 million Jewish men, women, and children had died in Nazi death camps. What came to be called the Holocaust was the horrifying culmination of the Nazi belief that Germans constituted a "master race" destined to rule the world.

THE HOME FRONT

MOBILIZING FOR WAR

At home, World War II transformed the role of the national government. FDR created federal agencies like the War Production Board, the War Manpower Commission, and the Office of Price Administration to regulate the allocation of labor, control the shipping industry, establish manufacturing quotas, and fix wages, prices, and rents. The number of federal workers rose from 1 million to 4 million, part of a tremendous growth in new jobs that pushed the unemployment rate down from 14 percent in 1940 to 2 percent three years later.

The government built housing for war workers and forced civilian industries to retool for war production. Michigan's auto factories now turned out trucks, tanks, and jeeps for the army. By 1944, American factories produced a ship every day and a plane every five minutes. The gross national product rose from $91 billion to $214 billion during the war, and the federal government's expenditures amounted to twice the combined total of the previous 150 years. The government marketed billions of dollars worth of war bonds, increased taxes, and began the practice of withholding income tax directly from weekly paychecks. Before the war, only the 4 million wealthiest Americans paid income taxes; by 1945, more than 40 million did so. The government, one historian writes, moved during the war from "class taxation" to "mass taxation."

Prisoners at a German concentration camp liberated by Allied troops in 1945.

A list of jobs available in Detroit in July 1941 illustrates how war-related production ended the Great Depression even before the United States entered the conflict.

BUSINESS AND THE WAR

The relationship between the federal government and big business changed dramatically from the days of the Second New Deal. "If you are going to go to war in a capitalist country," observed Secretary of War Henry Stimson, "you had better let business make money out of the process." As corporate executives flooded into federal agencies concerned with war production, Roosevelt offered incentives to spur production—low-interest loans, tax concessions, and contracts with guaranteed profits. The great bulk of federal spending went to the largest corporations, furthering the long-term trend toward economic concentration. By the end of the war, the 200 biggest industrial companies accounted for almost half of all corporate assets in the United States.

Americans marveled at the achievements of wartime manufacturing. Thousands of aircraft, 100,000 armored vehicles, and 2.5 million trucks rolled off American assembly lines, and entirely new products like synthetic rubber replaced natural resources now controlled by Japan. Government-sponsored scientific research perfected inventions like radar, jet engines, and early computers that helped to win the war and would have a large impact on postwar life. These accomplishments not only made it possible to win a two-front war but also helped to restore the reputation of business and businessmen, which had reached a low point during the Depression.

Federal funds reinvigorated established manufacturing areas and created entirely new industrial centers. World War II saw the West Coast emerge as a focus of military-industrial production. The government invested billions of dollars in the shipyards of Seattle, Portland, and San Francisco and in the steel plants and aircraft factories of southern California. By the war's end, California had received one-tenth of all federal spending, and Los Angeles had become the nation's second largest manufacturing center. Nearly 2 million Americans moved to California for jobs in defense-related industries, and millions more passed through for military training and embarkation to the Pacific war.

In the South, the combination of rural out-migration and government investment in military-related factories and shipyards hastened a shift from agricultural to industrial employment. During the war, southern per capita income rose from 60 percent to 70 percent of the national average. But the South remained very poor when the war ended. Much of its rural population still lived in small wooden shacks with no indoor plumbing. The region had only two cities—Houston and New Orleans—with populations exceeding 500,000. Despite the expansion of war production, the South's

M-5 tanks on the assembly line at a Detroit Cadillac plant, in a 1942 photograph. During the war, General Motors and other automakers produced vehicles for the armed forces rather than cars for consumers.

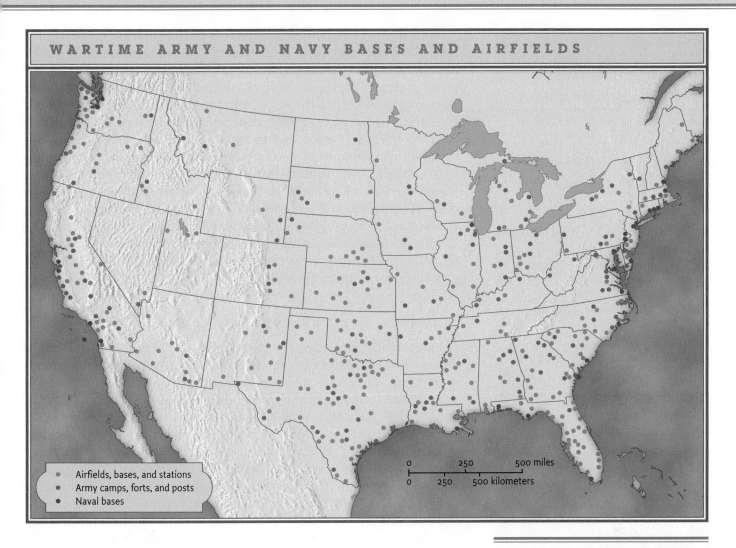

WARTIME ARMY AND NAVY BASES AND AIRFIELDS

- Airfields, bases, and stations
- Army camps, forts, and posts
- Naval bases

| 0 | 250 | 500 miles |
| 0 | 250 | 500 kilometers |

As this map indicates, the military and naval facilities built by the federal government during World War II were concentrated in the South and West, sparking the economic development of these regions.

economy still relied on agriculture and extractive industries—mining, lumber, oil—or manufacturing linked to farming, like the production of cotton textiles.

LABOR IN WARTIME

Organized labor repeatedly described World War II as a crusade for freedom that would expand economic and political democracy at home and abroad and win for unions a major voice in politics and industrial management. During the war, labor entered a three-sided arrangement with government and business that allowed union membership to soar to unprecedented levels. In order to secure industrial peace and stabilize war production, the federal government forced reluctant employers to recognize unions. In 1944, when Montgomery Ward, the large mail-order company, defied a pro-union order, the army seized its headquarters and physically evicted its president. For their part, union leaders agreed not to strike and conceded employers' right to "managerial prerogatives" and a "fair profit."

Despite the gains produced by labor militancy during the 1930s, unions only became firmly established in many sectors of the economy during

Table 22.1 LABOR UNION MEMBERSHIP	
Year	Number of Members
1933	2,857,000
1934	3,728,000
1935	3,753,000
1936	4,107,000
1937	5,780,000
1938	8,265,000
1939	8,980,000
1940	8,944,000
1941	10,489,000
1942	10,762,000
1943	13,642,000
1944	14,621,000
1945	14,796,000

In this recruitment poster for the Boy Scouts, a svelte Miss Liberty prominently displays the Bill of Rights, widely celebrated during World War II as the centerpiece of American freedom.

World War II. By 1945, union membership stood at nearly 15 million, one-third of the non-farm labor force and the highest proportion in American history. But if labor became a partner in government, it was very much a junior partner. The decline of the New Deal, already evident in the late 1930s, proceeded during the war. Congress continued to be dominated by a conservative alliance of Republicans and southern Democrats. They left intact core New Deal programs like Social Security but eliminated agencies thought to be controlled by leftists, including the Civilian Conservation Corps, National Youth Administration, and Works Progress Administration. Congress rejected Roosevelt's call for a cap on personal incomes and set taxes on corporate profits at a level far lower than FDR requested. Despite the "no-strike" pledge, 1943 and 1944 witnessed numerous brief walkouts in which workers protested the increasing speed of assembly-line production and the disparity between wages frozen by government order and expanding corporate profits.

FIGHTING FOR THE FOUR FREEDOMS

Previous conflicts, including the Mexican War and World War I, had deeply divided American society. In contrast, World War II came to be remembered as the Good War, a time of national unity in pursuit of indisputably noble goals. But all wars require the mobilization of patriotic public opinion. By 1940, "To sell *goods*, we must sell *words*" had become a motto of advertisers. Foremost among the words that helped to "sell" World War II was "freedom."

Talk of freedom pervaded wartime America. To Roosevelt, the Four Freedoms expressed deeply held American values worthy of being spread worldwide. Freedom from fear meant not only a longing for peace but a more general desire for security in a world that appeared to be out of control. Freedom of speech and religion scarcely required detailed explanation. But their prominent place among the Four Freedoms accelerated the process by which First Amendment protections of free expression moved to the center of Americans' definition of liberty. In 1941, the administration celebrated with considerable fanfare the 150th anniversary of the Bill of Rights (the first ten amendments to the Constitution). FDR described their protections against tyrannical government as defining characteristics of American life, central to the rights of "free men and free women." In 1943, the Supreme Court reversed a 1940 ruling and, on First Amendment grounds, upheld the right of Jehovah's Witnesses to refuse to salute the American flag in public schools. The decision stood in sharp contrast to the coercive patriotism of World War I, and it affirmed the sanctity of individual conscience as a bedrock of freedom, even in times of crisis. The justices contrasted the American system of constitutional protection for unpopular minorities with Nazi tyranny.

FREEDOM FROM WANT

The "most ambiguous" of the Four Freedoms, *Fortune* magazine remarked, was freedom from want. Yet this "great inspiring phrase," as a Pennsylvania steelworker put it in a letter to the president, seemed to strike the deepest chord in a nation just emerging from the Depression. Roosevelt initially meant it to refer to the elimination of barriers to international trade. But he

VISIONS OF FREEDOM

Patriotic Fan. *This fan, marketed to women during World War II, illustrates how freedom and patriotism were closely linked. At the far left and right, owners are instructed in ways to help win the war and preserve American freedom. The five middle panels suggest some of the era's definitions of freedom: freedom "to listen" (presumably without government censorship); self-government; freedom of assembly; the right to choose one's work; and freedom "to play."*

QUESTIONS

1. Compare the elements of freedom depicted on the fan with the Four Freedoms of President Roosevelt.

2. What aspects of freedom are not depicted in the fan?

quickly came to link freedom from want to an economic goal more relevant to the average citizen—protecting the future "standard of living of the American worker and farmer" by guaranteeing that the Depression would not resume after the war. This, he declared, would bring "real freedom for the common man."

When Norman Rockwell's paintings of the Four Freedoms first appeared in the *Saturday Evening Post*, each was accompanied by a brief essay. Three of these essays, by the celebrated authors Stephen Vincent Benét, Booth Tarkington, and Will Durant, emphasized that the values Rockwell depicted were essentially American and the opposite of those of the Axis powers. For *Freedom from Want*, the editors chose an unknown Filipino poet, Carlos Bulosan, who had emigrated to the United States at the age of sixteen. Bulosan's essay showed how the Four Freedoms could inspire hopes for a better future as well as nostalgia for Rockwell's imagined small-town past. Bulosan wrote of those Americans still outside the social mainstream— migrant workers, cannery laborers, black victims of segregation—for whom freedom meant having enough to eat, sending their children to school, and being able to "share the promise and fruits of American life."

THE OFFICE OF WAR INFORMATION

The history of the Office of War Information (OWI), created in 1942 to mobilize public opinion, illustrates how the political divisions generated by the New Deal affected efforts to promote the Four Freedoms. The liberal Democrats who dominated the OWI's writing staff sought to make the conflict "a 'people's war' for freedom." The OWI feared that Americans had only a vague understanding of the war's purposes and that the populace seemed more fervently committed to paying back the Japanese for their attack on Pearl Harbor than ridding the world of fascism. They utilized radio, film, the press, and other media to give the conflict an ideological meaning, while seeking to avoid the nationalist hysteria of World War I.

Wartime mobilization drew on deep-seated American traditions. The portrait of the United States holding aloft the torch of liberty in a world overrun by oppression reached back at least as far as the American Revolution. The description of a world half slave and half free recalled the Great Emancipator. But critics charged that the OWI seemed most interested in promoting the definition of freedom Roosevelt had emphasized during the 1930s. One of its first pamphlets listed as elements of freedom the right to a job at fair pay and to adequate food, clothing, shelter, and medical care. Concerned that the OWI was devoting as much time to promoting New Deal social programs as to the war effort, Congress eliminated most of its funding.

THE FIFTH FREEDOM

After Congress curtailed the OWI, the "selling of America" became overwhelmingly a private affair. Under the watchful eye of the War Advertising Council, private companies joined in the campaign to promote wartime patriotism, while positioning themselves and their brand names for the postwar world. Alongside advertisements urging Americans to purchase war bonds, guard against revealing military secrets, and grow "victory gardens" to allow food to be sent to the army, the war witnessed a burst of

In this patriotic war poster issued by the Office of War Information, the words of Abraham Lincoln are linked to the struggle against Nazi tyranny.

In this advertisement by the Liberty Motors and Engineering Corporation, published in the February 1944 issue of Fortune, *Uncle Sam offers the Fifth Freedom—"free enterprise"—to war-devastated Europe. To spread its message, the company offered free enlargements of its ad.*

messages marketing advertisers' definition of freedom. Without directly criticizing Roosevelt, they repeatedly suggested that he had overlooked a fifth freedom. The National Association of Manufacturers and individual companies bombarded Americans with press releases, radio programs, and advertisements attributing the amazing feats of wartime production to "free enterprise."

Americans on the home front enjoyed a prosperity many could scarcely remember. Despite the rationing of scarce consumer items like coffee, meat, and gasoline, consumers found more goods available in 1944 than when the war began. With the memory of the Depression still very much alive, businessmen predicted a postwar world filled with consumer goods, with "freedom of choice" among abundant possibilities assured if only private enterprise were liberated from government controls. One advertisement for Royal typewriters, entitled "What This War Is All About," explained that victory would "hasten the day when you . . . can once more walk into any store in the land and buy anything you want." Certainly, ads suggested, the war did not imply any alteration in American institutions. "I'm fighting for freedom," said a soldier in an ad by the Nash-Kelvinator Corporation. "So don't anybody tell me I'll find America changed."

WOMEN AT WAR

During the war, the nation engaged in an unprecedented mobilization of "womanpower" to fill industrial jobs vacated by men. OWI publications encouraged women to go to work, Hollywood films glorified the independent woman, and private advertising celebrated the achievements of Rosie the Riveter, the female industrial laborer depicted as muscular and self-reliant in Norman Rockwell's famous magazine cover. With 15 million men in the armed forces, women in 1944 made up more than one-third of the civilian labor force, and 350,000 served in auxiliary military units.

A female lathe operator in a Texas plant that produced transport planes.

This print, part of the America in the War *exhibition shown simultaneously in twenty-six American museums in 1943, offers a stylized image of women workers assembling shells in a factory while men march off to war.*

Even though most women workers still labored in clerical and service jobs, new opportunities suddenly opened in industrial, professional, and government positions previously restricted to men. On the West Coast, one-third of the workers in aircraft manufacturing and shipbuilding were women. For the first time in history, married women in their thirties outnumbered the young and single among female workers. Women forced unions like the United Auto Workers to confront issues like equal pay for equal work, maternity leave, and childcare facilities for working mothers. Defense companies sponsored swing bands and dances to boost worker morale and arranged dates between male and female workers. Having enjoyed what one wartime worker called "a taste of freedom"—doing "men's" jobs for men's wages and, sometimes, engaging in sexual activity while unmarried—many women hoped to remain in the labor force once peace returned.

WOMEN AT WORK

"We as a nation," proclaimed one magazine article, "must change our basic attitude toward the work of women." But change proved difficult. The government, employers, and unions depicted work as a temporary necessity, not an expansion of women's freedom. Advertisements assured women laboring in factories that they, too, were "fighting for freedom." But their language spoke of sacrifice and military victory, not rights, independence, or self-determination. One union publication even declared, "There should be a law requiring the women who have taken over men's jobs to be laid off after the war." When the war ended, most female war workers, especially those in better-paying industrial employment, did indeed lose their jobs.

Despite the upsurge in the number of working women, the advertisers' "world of tomorrow" rested on a vision of family-centered prosperity. Like

Norman Rockwell's Four Freedoms paintings, these wartime discussions of freedom simultaneously looked forward to a day of material abundance and back to a time when the family stood as the bedrock of society. The "American way of life" celebrated during the war centered on the woman with "a husband to meet every night at the door," and a home stocked with household appliances and consumer goods. Advertisements portrayed working women dreaming of their boyfriends in the army and emphasized that with the proper makeup, women could labor in a factory and remain attractive to men. Men in the army seem to have assumed that they would return home to resume traditional family life. In one wartime radio program, a young man described his goal for peacetime: "Havin' a home and some kids, and breathin' fresh air out in the suburbs ... livin' and workin' decent, like free people."

VISIONS OF POSTWAR FREEDOM

TOWARD AN AMERICAN CENTURY

The prospect of an affluent future provided a point of unity between New Dealers and conservatives, business and labor. And the promise of prosperity to some extent united two of the most celebrated blueprints for the postwar world. One was *The American Century*, publisher Henry Luce's 1941 effort to mobilize the American people both for the coming war and for an era of postwar world leadership. Americans, Luce's book insisted, must embrace the role history had thrust upon them as the "dominant power in the world." They must seize the opportunity to share with "all peoples" their "magnificent industrial products" and the "great American ideals," foremost among which stood "love of freedom." After the war, American power and American values would underpin a previously unimaginable prosperity—"the abundant life," Luce called it—produced by "free economic enterprise."

The idea of an American mission to spread democracy and freedom goes back to the Revolution. But traditionally, it had envisioned the country as an example, not an active agent imposing the American model throughout the globe. Luce's essay anticipated important aspects of the postwar world. But its bombastic rhetoric and a title easily interpreted as a call for an American imperialism aroused immediate opposition among liberals and the left. Henry Wallace offered their response in "The Price of Free World Victory," an address delivered in May 1942 to the Free World Association.

Wallace, secretary of agriculture during the 1930s and one of the more liberal New Dealers, had replaced Vice President John Nance Garner as Roosevelt's running mate in 1940. In contrast to Luce's American Century, a world of business dominance no less than of American power, Wallace predicted that the war would usher in a "century of the common man." The "march of freedom," said Wallace, would continue in the postwar world. That world, however, would be marked by international cooperation, not any single power's rule. Governments acting to "humanize" capitalism and redistribute economic resources would eliminate hunger, illiteracy, and poverty.

Luce and Wallace both spoke the language of freedom. Luce offered a confident vision of worldwide free enterprise, while Wallace anticipated a

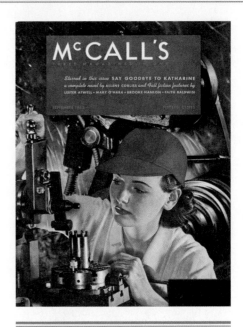

Unlike the lathe operator on the previous page, the woman operating industrial machinery on the cover of the September 1942 issue of McCall's *magazine remains glamorous, with makeup in place and hair unruffled.*

Despite the new independence enjoyed by millions of women, propaganda posters during World War II emphasized the male-dominated family as an essential element of American freedom.

global New Deal. But they had one thing in common—a new conception of America's role in the world, tied to continued international involvement, the promise of economic abundance, and the idea that the American experience should serve as a model for all other nations. Neither took into account the ideas that other countries might have developed as to how to proceed once the war had ended.

"THE WAY OF LIFE OF FREE MEN"

Even as Congress moved to dismantle parts of the New Deal, liberal Democrats and their left-wing allies unveiled plans for a postwar economic policy that would allow all Americans to enjoy freedom from want. In 1942 and 1943, the reports of the National Resources Planning Board (NRPB) offered a blueprint for a peacetime economy based on full employment, an expanded welfare state, and a widely shared American standard of living. Economic security and full employment were the Board's watchwords. It called for a "new bill of rights" that would include all Americans in an expanded Social Security system and guarantee access to education, health care, adequate housing, and jobs for able-bodied adults. Labor and farm organizations, church and civil rights groups, and liberal New Dealers hailed the reports as offering a "vision of freedom" for the postwar world. The NRPB's plan for a "full-employment economy" with a "fair distribution of income," said *The Nation*, embodied "the way of life of free men."

The reports continued a shift in liberals' outlook that dated from the late 1930s. Rather than seeking to reform the institutions of capitalism, liberals would henceforth rely on government spending to secure full employment, social welfare, and mass consumption, while leaving the operation of the economy in private hands. The reports appeared to reflect the views of British economist John Maynard Keynes, who, as noted in the previous chapter, had identified government spending as the best way to promote economic growth, even if it caused budget deficits. The war had, in effect, ended the Depression by implementing a military version of Keynesianism. In calling for massive spending on job creation and public works—urban redevelopment, rural electrification, an overhaul of the transportation system, and the like—the NRPB proposed the continuation of Keynesian spending in peacetime. But this went so far beyond what Congress was willing to support that it eliminated the NRPB's funding.

AN ECONOMIC BILL OF RIGHTS

Roosevelt had not publicized or promoted the NRPB reports of 1942 and 1943. Yet mindful that public-opinion polls showed a large majority of Americans favoring a guarantee of employment for those who could not find work, the president in 1944 called for an "Economic Bill of Rights." The original Bill of Rights restricted the power of government in the name of liberty. FDR proposed to expand its power in order to secure full employment, an adequate income, medical care, education, and a decent home for all Americans. "True individual freedom," he declared, "cannot exist without economic security and independence."

Already ill and preoccupied with the war, Roosevelt spoke only occasionally of the Economic Bill of Rights during the 1944 presidential campaign.

The replacement of Vice President Henry Wallace by Harry S. Truman, then a little-known senator from Missouri, suggested that the president did not intend to do battle with Congress over social policy. Congress did not enact the Economic Bill of Rights. But in 1944, it extended to the millions of returning veterans an array of benefits, including unemployment pay, scholarships for further education, low-cost mortgage loans, pensions, and job training. The Servicemen's Readjustment Act, or GI Bill of Rights, was one of the most far-reaching pieces of social legislation in American history. Aimed at rewarding members of the armed forces for their service and preventing the widespread unemployment and economic disruption that had followed World War I, it profoundly shaped postwar society. By 1946, more than 1 million veterans were attending college under its provisions, making up half of total college enrollment. Almost 4 million would receive home mortgages, spurring the postwar suburban housing boom.

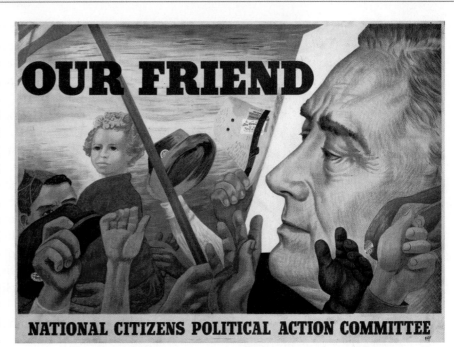

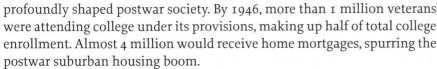

Ben Shahn's poster, Our Friend, *for the Congress of Industrial Organizations' political action committee, urges workers to vote for FDR during his campaign for a fourth term.*

During 1945, unions, civil rights organizations, and religious groups urged Congress to enact the Full Employment Bill, which tried to do for the entire economy what the GI Bill promised veterans. The measure established a "right to employment" for all Americans and required the federal government to increase its level of spending to create enough jobs in case the economy failed to do so. The target of an intense business lobbying campaign, the bill only passed in 1946 with the word "Full" removed from its title and after its commitment to governmental job creation had been eliminated. But as the war drew to a close, most Americans embraced the idea that the government must continue to play a major role in maintaining employment and a high standard of living.

THE ROAD TO SERFDOM

The failure of the Full Employment Bill confirmed the political stalemate that had begun with the elections of 1938. It also revealed the renewed intellectual respectability of fears that economic planning represented a threat to liberty. When the *New Republic* spoke of full employment as the "road to freedom," it subtly acknowledged the impact of *The Road to Serfdom* (1944), a surprise best-seller by Friedrich A. Hayek, a previously obscure Austrian-born economist. Hayek claimed that even the best-intentioned government efforts to direct the economy posed a threat to individual liberty. He offered a simple message—"planning leads to dictatorship."

Coming at a time when the miracles of war production had reinvigorated belief in the virtues of capitalism, and with the confrontation with Nazism highlighting the danger of merging economic and political power, Hayek offered a new intellectual justification for opponents of active government. In a complex economy, he insisted, no single person or group of experts could possibly possess enough knowledge to direct economic activity intelligently. A free market, he wrote, mobilizes the fragmented and partial knowledge scattered throughout society far more effectively than a planned economy.

Unlike many of his disciples, Hayek was not a doctrinaire advocate of laissez-faire. His book endorsed measures that later conservatives would denounce as forms of socialism—minimum wage and maximum hours laws, antitrust enforcement, and a social safety net guaranteeing all citizens a basic minimum of food, shelter, and clothing. Hayek, moreover, criticized traditional conservatives for fondness for social hierarchy and authoritarian government. "I am not a conservative," he would later write. But by equating fascism, socialism, and the New Deal and by identifying economic planning with a loss of freedom, he helped lay the foundation for the rise of modern conservatism and a revival of laissez-faire economic thought. As the war drew to a close, the stage was set for a renewed battle over the government's proper role in society and the economy, and the social conditions of American freedom.

THE AMERICAN DILEMMA

The unprecedented attention to freedom as the defining characteristic of American life had implications that went far beyond wartime mobilization. World War II reshaped Americans' understanding of themselves as a people. The struggle against Nazi tyranny and its theory of a master race discredited ethnic and racial inequality. Originally promoted by religious and ethnic minorities in the 1920s and the Popular Front in the 1930s, a pluralist vision of American society now became part of official rhetoric. What set the United States apart from its wartime foes, the government insisted, was not only dedication to the ideals of the Four Freedoms but also the principle that Americans of all races, religions, and national origins could enjoy those freedoms equally. Racism was the enemy's philosophy; Americanism rested on toleration of diversity and equality for all. By the end of the war, the new immigrant groups had been fully accepted as loyal ethnic Americans, rather than members of distinct and inferior "races." And the contradiction between the principle of equal freedom and the actual status of blacks had come to the forefront of national life.

PATRIOTIC ASSIMILATION

Among other things, World War II created a vast melting pot, especially for European immigrants and their children. Millions of Americans moved out of urban ethnic neighborhoods and isolated rural enclaves into the army and industrial plants where they came into contact with people of very different backgrounds. What one historian has called their "patriotic assimilation" differed sharply from the forced Americanization of World War I. While the Wilson administration had established

Arthur Poinier's cartoon for the Detroit Free Press, *June 19, 1941, illustrates how, during World War II, white ethnics (of British, German, Irish, French, Polish, Italian and Scandinanvian descent) were incorporated within the boundaries of American freedom.*

Anglo-Saxon culture as a national norm, Roosevelt promoted pluralism as the only source of harmony in a diverse society. The American way of life, wrote the novelist Pearl Buck in an OWI pamphlet, rested on brotherhood—the principle that "persons of many lands can live together . . . and if they believe in freedom they can become a united people."

Government and private agencies eagerly promoted equality as the definition of Americanism and a counterpoint to Nazism. Officials rewrote history to establish racial and ethnic tolerance as the American way. To be an American, FDR declared, had always been a "matter of mind and heart," and "never . . . a matter of race or ancestry"—a statement more effective in mobilizing support for the war than in accurately describing the nation's past. Mindful of the intolerance spawned by World War I, the OWI highlighted nearly every group's contributions to American life and celebrated the strength of a people united in respect for diversity. One OWI pamphlet described prejudice as a foreign import rather than a homegrown product and declared bigots more dangerous than spies—they were "fighting for the enemy."

Horrified by the uses to which the Nazis put the idea of inborn racial difference, biological and social scientists abandoned belief in a link among race, culture, and intelligence, an idea only recently central to their disciplines. Ruth Benedict's *Races and Racism* (1942) described racism as "a travesty of scientific knowledge." In the same year, Ashley Montagu's *Man's Most Dangerous Myth: The Fallacy of Race* became a best-seller. By the war's end, racism and nativism had been stripped of intellectual respectability, at least outside the South, and were viewed as psychological disorders.

Hollywood, too, did its part, portraying fighting units whose members, representing various regional, ethnic, and religious backgrounds, put aside group loyalties and prejudices for the common cause. *Air Force* featured a bomber crew that included an Anglo-Saxon officer, a Jewish sergeant, and a Polish-American gunner. In the film *Bataan*, the ethnically balanced platoon included a black soldier, even though the real army was racially segregated. The war's most popular motion picture, *This Is the Army*, starring, among others, future president Ronald Reagan, offered a vision of postwar society that celebrated the ethnic diversity of the American people.

Intolerance, of course, hardly disappeared from American life. One correspondent complained to Norman Rockwell that he included too many "foreign-looking" faces in his *Freedom of Worship* painting. Many business and government circles still excluded Jews. Along with the fact that early reports of the Holocaust were too terrible to be believed, anti-Semitism contributed to the government's unwillingness to allow more than a handful of European Jews (21,000 during the course of the war) to find refuge in the United States. Roosevelt himself learned during the war of the extent of Hitler's "final solution" to the Jewish presence in Europe. But he failed to authorize air strikes that might have destroyed German death camps.

Nonetheless, the war made millions of ethnic Americans, especially the children of the new immigrants, feel fully American for the first time. During the war, one New York "ethnic" recalled, "the Italo-Americans stopped being Italo and started becoming Americans." But the event that inspired this comment, the Harlem race riot of 1943, suggested that patriotic assimilation stopped at the color line.

THE *BRACERO* PROGRAM

The war had a far more ambiguous meaning for non-white groups than for whites. On the eve of Pearl Harbor, racial barriers remained deeply entrenched in American life. Southern blacks were still trapped in a rigid system of segregation. Asians could not emigrate to the United States or become naturalized citizens. As noted in the previous chapter, more than 400,000 Mexican-Americans had been "voluntarily" repatriated by local authorities in the Southwest during the Depression. Most American Indians still lived on reservations, in dismal poverty.

The war set in motion changes that would reverberate in the postwar years. Under the *bracero* program agreed to by the Mexican and American governments in 1942 (the name derives from *brazo*, the Spanish word for arm), tens of thousands of contract laborers crossed into the United States to take up jobs as domestic and agricultural workers. Initially designed as a temporary response to the wartime labor shortage, the program lasted until 1964. During the period of the *bracero* program, more than 4.5 million Mexicans entered the United States under government labor contracts (while a slightly larger number were arrested for illegal entry by the Border Patrol). *Braceros* were supposed to receive decent housing and wages. But since they could not become citizens and could be deported at any time, they found it almost impossible to form unions or secure better working conditions.

Although the *bracero* program reinforced the status of immigrants from Mexico as an unskilled labor force, wartime employment opened new opportunities for second-generation Mexican-Americans. Hundreds of thousands of men and women emerged from ethnic neighborhoods, or *barrios*, to work in defense industries and serve in the army (where, unlike blacks, they fought alongside whites). A new "Chicano" culture—a fusion of Mexican heritage and American experience—was being born. Contact with other groups led many to learn English and sparked a rise in interethnic marriages.

MEXICAN-AMERICAN RIGHTS

The "zoot suit" riots of 1943, in which club-wielding sailors and policemen attacked Mexican-American youths wearing flamboyant clothing on the streets of Los Angeles, illustrated the limits of wartime tolerance. "Our Latin American boys," complained one activist, "are not segregated at the front line.... They are dying that democracy may live." Yet when they return home, the activist continued, "they are not considered good enough to go into a café." But the contrast between the war's rhetoric of freedom and pluralism and the reality of continued discrimination inspired a heightened consciousness of civil rights. For example, Mexican-Americans brought complaints of discrimination before the Fair Employment Practices Commission (FEPC) to fight the practice in the Southwest of confining them to the lowest-paid work or paying them lower wages than white workers doing the same jobs.

Perhaps half a million Mexican-American men and women served in the armed forces. And with discrimination against Mexicans an increasing embarrassment in view of Roosevelt's Good Neighbor policy, Texas (the state with the largest population of Mexican descent) in 1943 unanimously passed the oddly named Caucasian Race—Equal Privileges resolution. It stated that since "all the nations of the North and South American continents" were united in the struggle against Nazism, "all persons of the Caucasian race" were entitled to equal treatment in places of public accommodation. Since Texas law had long defined Mexicans as white, the measure applied to them while not challenging the segregation of blacks. The resolution lacked an enforcement mechanism. Indeed, because of continued discrimination in Texas, the Mexican government for a time prohibited the state from receiving laborers under the *bracero* program.

INDIANS DURING THE WAR

The war also brought many American Indians closer to the mainstream of American life. Some 25,000 served in the army (including the famous Navajo "code-talkers," who transmitted messages in their complex native language, which the Japanese could not decipher). Insisting that the United States lacked the authority to draft Indian men into the army, the Iroquois issued their own declaration of war against the Axis powers. Tens of thousands of Indians left reservations for jobs in war industries. Exposed for the first time to urban life and industrial society, many chose not to return to the reservations after the war ended (indeed, the reservations did not share in wartime prosperity). Some Indian veterans took advantage of the GI Bill to attend college after the war, an opportunity that had been available to very few Indians previously.

ASIAN-AMERICANS IN WARTIME

Asian-Americans' war experience was paradoxical. More than 50,000—the children of immigrants from China, Japan, Korea, and the Philippines—fought in the army, mostly in all-Asian units. With China an ally in the Pacific war, Congress in 1943 ended decades of complete exclusion by establishing a nationality quota for Chinese immigrants. The annual limit of 105 hardly suggested a desire for a large-scale influx. But the image of the Chinese as gallant fighters defending their country against Japanese aggression called into question long-standing racial stereotypes. As in the case of Mexican-Americans, large numbers of Chinese-Americans moved out of ethnic ghettos to work alongside whites in jobs on the home front.

The experience of Japanese-Americans was far different. Many Americans viewed the war against Germany as an ideological struggle. But both sides saw the Pacific war as a race war. Japanese propaganda depicted Americans as a self-indulgent people contaminated by ethnic and racial diversity as opposed to the racially "pure" Japanese. In the United States, long-standing prejudices and the shocking attack on Pearl Harbor combined to produce an unprecedented hatred of Japan. "In all our history," according to one historian, "no foe has been detested as were the Japanese." Government propaganda and war films portrayed the Japanese foe as rats, dogs, gorillas, and snakes—bestial and subhuman. They blamed Japanese aggression on a violent racial or national character, not, as in the case of Germany and Italy, on tyrannical rulers.

On the one-year anniversary of the Pearl Harbor attack, the cover of Collier's *magazine depicts Japanese prime minister Hideki Tojo as a vampire bat—one of many wartime images that sought to dehumanize the Pacific foe.*

About 70 percent of Japanese-Americans in the continental United States lived in California, where they dominated vegetable farming in the Los Angeles area. One-third were first-generation immigrants, or *issei*, but a substantial majority were *nisei*—American-born, and therefore citizens. Many of the latter spoke only English, had never been to Japan, and had tried to assimilate despite prevailing prejudice. But the Japanese-American community could not remain unaffected by the rising tide of hatred. The government bent over backward to include German-Americans and Italian-Americans in the war effort. It ordered the arrest of only a handful of the more than 800,000 German and Italian nationals in the United States when the war began. But it viewed every person of Japanese ethnicity as a potential spy.

JAPANESE-AMERICAN INTERNMENT

California, as discussed in Chapter 19, had a long history of hostility toward the Japanese. Now, inspired by exaggerated fears of a Japanese invasion of the West Coast and pressured by whites who saw an opportunity to gain possession of Japanese-American property, the military persuaded FDR to issue Executive Order 9066. Promulgated in February 1942, this ordered the expulsion of all persons of Japanese descent from the West Coast. That spring and summer, authorities removed more than 110,000 men, women, and children—nearly two-thirds of them American citizens—to internment camps far from their homes. The order did not apply to persons of Japanese descent living in Hawaii, where they represented nearly 40 percent of the population. Despite Hawaii's vulnerability, its economy could not function without Japanese-American labor. But the treatment of mainland Japanese-Americans provided ammunition for Japan's claim that its aggressions in Asia were intended to defend the rights of non-white peoples against colonial rule and a racist United States.

The internees were subjected to a quasi-military discipline in the camps. Living in former horse stables, makeshift shacks, or barracks behind barbed wire fences, they were awakened for roll call at 6:45 each morning and ate their meals (which rarely included the Japanese cooking to which they were accustomed) in giant mess halls. Armed guards patrolled the camps, and searchlights shone all night. Privacy was difficult to come by, and medical facilities were often nonexistent. Nonetheless, the internees did their best to create an atmosphere of home, decorating their accommodations with pictures, flowers, and curtains, planting vegetable gardens, and setting up activities like sports clubs and art classes for themselves.

Internment revealed how easily war can undermine basic freedoms. There were no court hearings, no due process, and no writs of habeas corpus. One searches the wartime record in vain for public protests among non-Japanese against the gravest violation of civil liberties since the end of slavery. The press supported the policy almost unanimously. In Congress, only Senator Robert Taft of Ohio spoke out against it. Groups publicly committed to fighting discrimination, from the Communist Party to the NAACP and the American Jewish Committee, either defended the policy or remained silent.

The courts refused to intervene. In 1944, in *Korematsu v. United States*, the Supreme Court denied the appeal of Fred Korematsu, a Japanese-American

In this 1942 photograph by Dorothea Lange, members of a Japanese-American family await relocation to an internment camp.

possibly even invade China and use nuclear weapons against it. But Truman, fearing an all-out war on the Asian mainland, refused. MacArthur did not fully accept the principle of civilian control of the military. When he went public with criticism of the president, Truman removed him from command. The war then settled into a stalemate around the thirty-eighth parallel, the original boundary between the two Koreas. Not until 1953 was an armistice agreed to, essentially restoring the prewar status quo. There has never been a formal peace treaty ending the Korean War.

As this map indicates, when General Douglas MacArthur launched his surprise landing at Inchon, North Korean forces controlled nearly the entire Korean peninsula.

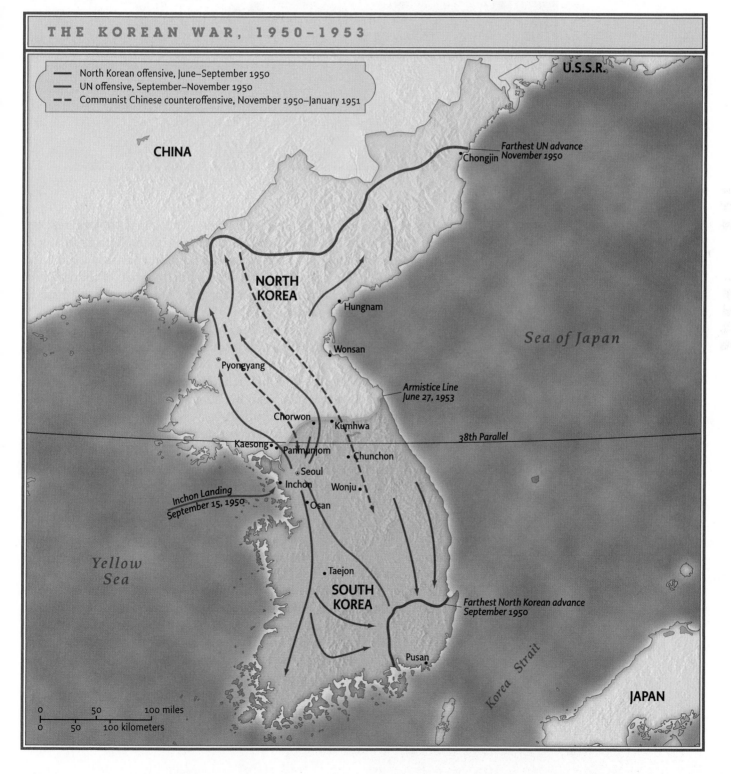

THE KOREAN WAR, 1950–1953

- North Korean offensive, June–September 1950
- UN offensive, September–November 1950
- - - Communist Chinese counteroffensive, November 1950–January 1951

U.S.S.R.

CHINA

Farthest UN advance November 1950
Chongjin

NORTH KOREA

Hungnam

Sea of Japan

Wonsan

Pyongyang

Armistice Line June 27, 1953

Chorwon
Kumhwa
Kaesong
Panmunjom
38th Parallel
Chunchon
Seoul
Inchon
Wonju
Inchon Landing September 15, 1950
Osan

Yellow Sea

Taejon

SOUTH KOREA

Farthest North Korean advance September 1950

Pusan

Korea Strait

JAPAN

0   50   100 miles
0   50   100 kilometers

A photograph of a street battle in Seoul, South Korea, during the Korean War illustrates the ferocity of the fighting.

More than 33,000 Americans died in Korea. The Asian death toll reached an estimated 1 million Korean soldiers and 2 million civilians (many of them victims of starvation after American bombing destroyed irrigation systems essential to rice cultivation), along with hundreds of thousands of Chinese troops. Korea made it clear that the Cold War, which began in Europe, had become a global conflict.

Taken together, the events of 1947–1953 showed that the world had moved very far from the hopes for global harmony symbolized by the founding of the United Nations in 1945. No longer did the United States speak of One World (the title of Wendell Willkie's influential wartime book). Instead, the world had been divided in two. The United States now stood as the undisputed leader of what was increasingly known as the West (although it included Japan, where permanent American military bases were established), or the Free World. NATO was soon followed by SEATO in Southeast Asia and CENTO in the Middle East, forming a web of military alliances that ringed the Soviet Union and China.

COLD WAR CRITICS

In the Soviet Union, Stalin had consolidated a brutal dictatorship that jailed or murdered millions of Soviet citizens. With its one-party rule, stringent state control of the arts and intellectual life, and government-controlled economy, the Soviet Union presented a stark opposite of democracy and "free enterprise." As a number of contemporary critics, few of them sympathetic to Soviet communism, pointed out, however, casting the Cold War in terms of a worldwide battle between freedom and slavery had unfortunate consequences. George Kennan, whose Long Telegram had inspired the policy of containment, observed that such language made it impossible to view international crises on a case-by-case basis, or to determine which genuinely involved either freedom or American interests.

In a penetrating critique of Truman's policies, Walter Lippmann, one of the nation's most prominent journalists, objected to turning foreign policy into an "ideological crusade." To view every challenge to the status quo as part of a contest with the Soviet Union, Lippmann correctly predicted, would require the United States to recruit and subsidize an "array of satellites, clients, dependents and puppets." It would have to intervene continuously in the affairs of nations whose political problems did not arise from Moscow and could not be easily understood in terms of the battle between freedom and slavery. World War II, he went on, had shaken the foundations of European empires. In the tide of revolutionary nationalism now sweeping the world, communists were certain to play an important role. It would be a serious mistake, Lippmann warned, for the United States to align itself against the movement for colonial independence in the name of anticommunism.

IMPERIALISM AND DECOLONIZATION

World War II had increased awareness in the United States of the problem of imperialism and had led many African-Americans to identify their own struggle for equality with the strivings of non-white colonial peoples overseas. Many movements for colonial independence borrowed the language of the American Declaration of Independence in demanding the right to self-government. Liberal Democrats and black leaders urged the Truman administration to take the lead in promoting worldwide decolonization, insisting that a Free World worthy of the name should not include colonies and empires. In 1946, the United States granted independence to the Philippines, a move hailed by nationalist movements in other colonies. But as the Cold War developed, the United States backed away from pressuring its European allies to move toward granting self-government to colonies like French Indochina, the Dutch East Indies, and British possessions like the Gold Coast and Nigeria in Africa and Malaya in Asia. Even after granting independence to India and Pakistan in 1947, Britain was determined to retain much of its empire.

In practice, geopolitical and economic interests shaped American foreign policy as powerfully as the idea of freedom. But American policymakers used the language of a crusade for freedom to justify actions around the world that had little to do with freedom by almost any definition. No matter how repressive to its own people, if a nation joined the worldwide anticommunist alliance led by the United States, it was counted as a member of the Free World. The Republic of South Africa, for example, was considered a part of the Free World even though its white minority had deprived the black population of nearly all their rights. Was there not some way, one critic asked, that the United States could accept "the aid of tyrants" on practical grounds "without corrupting our speeches by identifying tyranny with freedom"?

THE COLD WAR AND THE IDEA OF FREEDOM

Among other things, the Cold War was an ideological struggle, a battle, in a popular phrase of the 1950s, for the "hearts and minds" of people throughout the world. Like other wars, it required popular mobilization, in which the idea of freedom played a central role. During the 1950s, freedom became an inescapable theme of academic research, popular journalism, mass culture, and official pronouncements. Henry Luce, who had popularized the idea of an American Century, explained that freedom was the "one word out of the whole human vocabulary" through which *Time* magazine could best explain America to the rest of the world. In many ways, the Cold War established the framework for the discussion of freedom.

THE CULTURAL COLD WAR

One of the more unusual Cold War battlefields involved American history and culture. Many scholars read the American Creed of pluralism, tolerance, and equality back into the past as a timeless definition of Americanism, ignoring the powerful ethnic and racial strains with which it had always coexisted. Under the code name "Militant Liberty," national security agencies encouraged Hollywood to produce anticommunist movies, such as *The Red Menace* (1949) and *I Married a Communist* (1950), and urged that film scripts be changed to remove references to less-than-praiseworthy aspects of American history, such as Indian removal and racial discrimination.

The Central Intelligence Agency and Defense Department emerged as unlikely patrons of the arts. As noted in Chapter 21, the federal government had openly financed all sorts of artistic works during the 1930s. But Cold War funding for the arts remained top-secret—in part because Congress proved reluctant to spend money for this purpose, in part because Americans charged communist governments with imposing artistic conformity. In an effort to influence public opinion abroad, the Soviet Union sponsored tours of its world-famous ballet companies, folk dance troupes, and symphony orchestras. To counteract the widespread European view of the United States as a cultural backwater, the CIA secretly funded an array of overseas publications, conferences, publishing houses, concerts, and art exhibits. And to try to improve the international image of American race relations, the government sent jazz musicians and other black performers abroad, especially to Africa and Asia.

Works produced by artists who considered themselves thoroughly nonpolitical became weapons in the cultural Cold War. The CIA promoted the so-called New York school of painters, led by Jackson Pollock. For Pollock, the essence of art lay in the process of creation, not the final product. His "action" paintings, made by spontaneously dripping and pouring paint over large canvases, produced works of vivid color and energy but without any recognizable subject matter. Many members of Congress much preferred Norman Rockwell's readily understandable illustrations of small-town life to Pollock's "abstract expressionism." Some called Pollock's works un-American and wondered aloud if they were part of a communist plot. But the CIA funded the Museum of Modern Art in New York, which championed the New York school, and helped arrange for exhibitions overseas. It hoped to persuade Europeans not only that these paintings demonstrated that the United States represented artistic leadership as well as military power, but that such art embodied the free, individual expression denied to artists in communist countries. Pollock's paintings, John Cage's musical compositions, which incorporated chance sounds rather than a fixed score, and the "graceful freedom" of George Balanchine's choreography were all described as artistic reflections of the essence of American life.

A poster for The Red Menace, *one of numerous anticommunist films produced by Hollywood during the 1950s.*

Visitors to the Museum of Modern Art in New York City contemplate a work by Jackson Pollock, whose paintings exemplified the artistic school of abstract expressionism, promoted during the Cold War as a reflection of American freedom. The paintings had no recognizable subject other than reminding the viewer of how Pollock had created them, by flinging paint at the canvas. "I want to express my feelings, rather than illustrate them," Pollock declared.

FREEDOM AND TOTALITARIANISM

Along with freedom, the Cold War's other great mobilizing concept was "totalitarianism." The term originated in Europe between the world wars to describe fascist Italy and Nazi Germany—aggressive, ideologically driven states that sought to subdue all of civil society, including churches, unions, and other voluntary associations, to their control. Such states, according to the theory of totalitarianism, left no room for individual rights or alternative values and therefore could never change from within. By 1950, the year the McCarran Internal Security Act barred "totalitarians" from entering the United States, the term had become a shorthand way of describing those on the other side in the Cold War. As the eventual collapse of communist governments in eastern Europe and the Soviet Union would demonstrate, the idea of totalitarianism greatly exaggerated the totality of government control of private life and thought in these countries. But its widespread use reinforced the view that the greatest danger to freedom lay in an overly powerful government.

Just as the conflict over slavery redefined American freedom in the nineteenth century and the confrontation with the Nazis shaped understandings of freedom during World War II, the Cold War reshaped them once again. Russia had already conquered America, the poet Archibald MacLeish complained in 1949, since politics was conducted "under a kind of upside-down Russian veto." Whatever Moscow stood for was by definition the opposite of freedom, including anything to which the word "socialized" could be attached. In the largest public relations campaign in American history, the American Medical Association raised the specter of "socialized medicine" to discredit and defeat Truman's proposal for national health insurance. The real estate industry likewise mobilized against public housing, terming it "socialized housing," similar to policies undertaken by Moscow. The Soviets opposed organized religion, so to "strengthen our national resistance to communism," Congress in 1954 added the words "under God" to the Pledge of Allegiance.

Cartoonist Bill Mauldin illustrated the essence of the idea of totalitarianism in this 1946 cartoon—a dictatorial government that refuses to accept the legitimacy of difference of opinion.

THE RISE OF HUMAN RIGHTS

The Cold War also affected the emerging concept of human rights. The idea that there are rights that are applicable to all of humanity originated during the eighteenth century in the Enlightenment and the American and French Revolutions. The atrocities committed during World War II, as well as the global language of the Four Freedoms and the Atlantic Charter, forcefully raised the issue of human rights in the postwar world. After the war, the victorious Allies put numerous German officials on trial before special courts at Nuremberg for crimes against humanity. For the first time, individuals were held directly accountable to the international community for violations of human rights. The trials resulted in prison terms for many Nazi officials and the execution of ten leaders.

The United Nations Charter includes strong language prohibiting discrimination on the basis of race, sex, or religion. In 1948, the UN General Assembly approved a far more sweeping document, the Universal Declaration of Human Rights, drafted by a committee chaired by Eleanor Roosevelt. It identified a broad range of rights to be enjoyed by people everywhere, including freedom of speech, religious toleration, and protection against arbitrary government, as well as social and economic entitlements like the right to an adequate standard of living and access to housing, education, and medical care. The document had no enforcement mechanism. Some considered it an exercise in empty rhetoric. But the core principle—that a nation's treatment of its own citizens should be subject to outside evaluation—slowly became part of the language in which freedom was discussed.

AMBIGUITIES OF HUMAN RIGHTS

The American and French Revolutions of the late eighteenth century had introduced into international relations the idea of basic rights belonging to all persons simply because they are human. In a sense, this was the origin of the idea of "human rights"—principles so fundamental that no government has a right to violate them. The antislavery movement had turned this idea into a powerful weapon against the legitimacy of slavery. Yet the debates over the Universal Declaration of Human Rights revealed the tensions inherent in the idea, tensions that persist to the present day. To what extent do human rights supercede national sovereignty? Who has the authority to enforce human rights that a government is violating? The United Nations? Regional bodies like the Organization of American States and the European Union? A single country (as the United States would claim to be doing in the Iraq War that began in 2003)? The Covenant of the League of Nations—the predecessor of the United Nations created after World War I—had contained a clause allowing the League to intervene when a government violated the rights of its own citizens.

One reason for the lack of an enforcement mechanism in the Universal Declaration of Human Rights was that both the United States and the Soviet Union refused to accept outside interference in their internal affairs or restraints on their ability to conduct foreign policy as they desired. John Foster Dulles, an American delegate to the conference that created the UN, opposed any statement affirming human rights out of fear that it

VISIONS OF FREEDOM

Human Rights. *This cartoon from 1947 depicts delegates to a meeting of the UN Human Rights Commission as unruly schoolchildren. Eleanor Roosevelt lectures delegates from various countries about human rights. "Now children," she says, "all together: 'The rights of the individual are above the rights of the state.'" At the lower left, John Foster Dulles, an American delegate, aims a slingshot at the Soviet ambassador to the UN, Andrei Y. Vishinsky, who stands in the lower right corner wearing a dunce cap. Charles Malik of Lebanon offers the teacher an apple. Several delegates seem bored; others are attentive.*

QUESTIONS

1. What does the cartoon suggest about the degree of commitment to human rights in the postwar world?

2. What definition of freedom do the words of Eleanor Roosevelt illustrate?

would lead to an international investigation of "the Negro question in this country." In 1947, the NAACP did file a petition with the United Nations asking it to investigate racism in the United States as a violation of human rights. Conditions in states like Mississippi should be of concern to all mankind, it argued, because if democracy failed to function in "the leading democracy in the world," the prospects for democracy were weakened everywhere. But the UN decided that it lacked jurisdiction. Nonetheless, since the end of World War II, the enjoyment of human rights has increasingly taken its place in definitions of freedom across the globe, especially, perhaps, where such rights are flagrantly violated.

After the Cold War ended, the idea of human rights would play an increasingly prominent role in world affairs. But during the 1950s, Cold War imperatives shaped the concept. Neither the United States nor the Soviet Union could resist emphasizing certain provisions of the Universal Declaration while ignoring others. The Soviets claimed to provide all citizens with social and economic rights, but violated democratic rights and civil liberties. Many Americans condemned the nonpolitical rights as a step toward socialism. In 1950, Freedom House began yearly assessments of the status of freedom in the world's nations. It adopted purely political criteria, emphasizing citizens' rights to participate in open elections and to speak out on public issues. Considering access to employment, housing, education, medical care, and the like as part of the definition of freedom, the reports argued, would be a serious mistake.

Eleanor Roosevelt saw the Universal Declaration of Human Rights as an integrated body of principles, a combination of traditional civil and political liberties with the social conditions of freedom outlined in her husband's Economic Bill of Rights of 1944. But to make it easier for member states to ratify the document, the UN divided it into two "covenants"—Civil and Political Rights, and Economic, Social, and Cultural Rights. It took until 1992 for the U.S. Congress to ratify the first. It has never approved the second.

THE TRUMAN PRESIDENCY

THE FAIR DEAL

With the end of World War II, President Truman's first domestic task was to preside over the transition from a wartime to a peacetime economy. More than 12 million men remained in uniform in August 1945. They wanted nothing more than to return home to their families. Demobilization proceeded at a rapid pace. Within a year, the armed forces had been reduced to 3 million. Some returning soldiers found the adjustment to civilian life difficult. The divorce rate in 1945 rose to double its prewar level. Others took advantage of the GI Bill of Rights (discussed in the previous chapter) to obtain home mortgages, set up small businesses, and embark on college educations. The majority of returning soldiers entered the labor force—one reason why more than 2 million women workers lost their jobs. The government abolished wartime agencies that regulated industrial production and labor relations, and it dismantled wartime price controls, leading to a sharp rise in prices.

In the immediate aftermath of World War II, President Truman, backed by party liberals and organized labor, moved to revive the stalled momentum of the New Deal. Truman's program, which he announced in

September 1945 and would later call the Fair Deal, focused on improving the social safety net and raising the standard of living of ordinary Americans. He called on Congress to increase the minimum wage, enact a program of national health insurance, and expand public housing, Social Security, and aid to education. Truman, complained one Republican leader, was "out–New Dealing the New Deal."

THE POSTWAR STRIKE WAVE

In 1946, a new wave of labor militancy swept the country. The AFL and CIO launched Operation Dixie, a campaign to bring unionization to the South and, by so doing, shatter the hold of anti-labor conservatives on the region's politics. More than 200 labor organizers entered the region, seeking support especially in the southern textile industry, the steel industry in the Birmingham region, and agriculture. With war production at an end, overtime work diminished even as inflation soared following the removal of price controls. The resulting drop in workers' real income sparked the largest strike wave in American history. Nearly 5 million workers—including those in the steel, auto, coal, and other key industries—walked off their jobs, demanding wage increases. The strike of 750,000 steelworkers represented the largest single walkout in American history to that date. Even Hollywood studios shut down because of a strike of actors and other employees of the movie industry that lasted for the better part of a year. One historian calls this period "the closest thing to a national general strike in industry in the twentieth century."

President Truman feared the strikes would seriously disrupt the economy. When railroad workers stopped work and set up picket lines, the infuriated president prepared a speech in which he threatened to draft them all into the army and "hang a few traitors"—language toned down by his advisers. The walkout soon ended, as did a coal strike after the Truman administration secured a court order requiring the miners to return to work. To resolve other strikes, Truman appointed federal "fact-finding boards," which generally recommended wage increases, although not enough to restore workers' purchasing power to wartime levels.

THE REPUBLICAN RESURGENCE

In the congressional elections of 1946, large numbers of middle-class voters, alarmed by the labor turmoil, voted Republican. Many workers, disappointed by Truman's policies, stayed at home. This was a lethal combination for the Democratic Party. For the first time since the 1920s, Republicans swept to control of both houses of Congress. Meanwhile, in the face of vigorous opposition from southern employers and public officials and the reluctance of many white workers to join interracial labor unions, Operation Dixie had failed to unionize the South or dent the political control of conservative Democrats in the region. The election of 1946 ensured that a conservative coalition of Republicans and southern Democrats would continue to dominate Congress.

A few of the numerous World War II veterans who attended college after the war, thanks to the GI Bill.

Congress turned aside Truman's Fair Deal program. It enacted tax cuts for wealthy Americans and, over the president's veto, in 1947 passed the Taft-Hartley Act, which sought to reverse some of the gains made by organized labor in the past decade. The measure authorized the president to suspend strikes by ordering an eighty-day "cooling-off period," and it banned sympathy strikes and secondary boycotts (labor actions directed not at an employer but at those who did business with him). It outlawed the closed shop, which required a worker to be a union member when taking up a job, and authorized states to pass "right-to-work" laws, prohibiting other forms of compulsory union membership. It also forced union officials to swear that they were not communists. While hardly a "slave-labor bill," as the AFL and CIO called it, the Taft-Hartley Act made it considerably more difficult to bring unorganized workers into unions. Over time, as population and capital investment shifted to states with "right-to-work" laws like Texas, Florida, and North Carolina, Taft-Hartley contributed to the decline of organized labor's share of the nation's workforce.

POSTWAR CIVIL RIGHTS

During his first term, Truman reached out in unprecedented ways to the nation's black community. The war, as noted in the previous chapter, had inspired a new black militancy and led many whites to reject American racial practices as reminiscent of Hitler's theory of a master race. In the years immediately following World War II, the status of black Americans enjoyed a prominence in national affairs unmatched since Reconstruction.

Between 1945 and 1951, eleven states from New York to New Mexico established fair employment practices commissions, and numerous cities passed laws against discrimination in access to jobs and public accommodations. (Some of these measures addressed other racial groups besides blacks: for example, California in 1947 repealed its laws permitting local school districts to provide segregated education for children of Chinese descent and those barring aliens from owning land.) A broad civil rights coalition involving labor, religious groups, and black organizations supported these measures. The NAACP, its ranks swollen during the war, launched a voter registration campaign in the South. By 1952, 20 percent of black southerners were registered to vote, nearly a seven-fold increase since 1940. (Most of the gains took place in the Upper South—in Alabama and Mississippi, the heartland of white supremacy, the numbers barely budged.) Law enforcement agencies finally took the crime of lynching seriously. In 1952, for the first time since record keeping began seventy years earlier, no lynchings took place in the United States.

In another indication that race relations were in flux, the Brooklyn Dodgers in 1947 challenged the long-standing exclusion of black players from major league baseball by adding Jackie Robinson to their team. Robinson, who possessed both remarkable athletic ability and a passion for

Racial segregation and exclusion were not confined to the South in the post–World War II period. Here, in 1947, picketers stand outside a Seattle grocery store that refused to serve non-whites. A campaign by black activists supported by a coalition of unions, church groups, Jewish organizations, and communists forced most of the city's stores and restaurants to treat customers on an equal basis.

equality, had been tried and acquitted for insubordination in 1944 when he refused to move to the back of a bus at Fort Hood, Texas, while serving in the army. But he promised Dodger owner Branch Rickey that he would not retaliate when subjected to racist taunts by opposing fans and players. His dignity in the face of constant verbal abuse won Robinson nationwide respect, and his baseball prowess earned him the Rookie of the Year award. His success opened the door to the integration of baseball and led to the demise of the Negro Leagues, to which black players had previously been confined.

TO SECURE THESE RIGHTS

In October 1947, a Commission on Civil Rights appointed by the president issued *To Secure These Rights*, one of the most devastating indictments ever published of racial inequality in America. It called on the federal government to assume the responsibility for abolishing segregation and ensuring equal treatment in housing, employment, education, and the criminal justice system. Truman hailed the report as "an American charter of human freedom." The impact of America's race system on the nation's ability to conduct the Cold War was not far from his mind. Truman noted that if the United States were to offer the "peoples of the world" a "choice of freedom or enslavement," it must "correct the remaining imperfections in our practice of democracy."

In February 1948, Truman presented an ambitious civil rights program to Congress, calling for a permanent federal civil rights commission, national laws against lynching and the poll tax, and action to ensure equal access to jobs and education. Congress, as Truman anticipated, approved none of his proposals. But in July 1948, just as the presidential campaign was getting under way, Truman issued an executive order desegregating the armed forces. The armed services became the first large institution in American life to promote racial integration actively and to attempt to root out long-standing racist practices. The Korean War would be the first American conflict fought by an integrated army since the War of Independence.

Truman genuinely despised racial discrimination. But his focus on civil rights also formed part of a strategy to win reelection by reinvigorating and expanding the political coalition Roosevelt had created. With calls for federal health insurance, the repeal of the Taft-Hartley Act, and aid to public education, the Democratic platform of 1948 was the most progressive in the party's history. Led by Hubert Humphrey, the young mayor of Minneapolis, party liberals overcame southern resistance and added a strong civil rights plank to the platform.

Jackie Robinson sliding into third base, 1949.

A scene from Brotherhood of Man, *a 1946 animation used in connection with an organizing campaign by the United Automobile Workers. It suggests the common interests of workers of diverse races.*

Blacks, led by A. Philip Randolph (left), picketing at the 1948 Democratic national convention. The delegates' adoption of a strong civil rights plank led representatives of several southern states to withdraw and nominate their own candidate for president, Strom Thurmond.

THE DIXIECRAT AND WALLACE REVOLTS

"I say the time has come," Humphrey told the Democratic national convention, "to walk out of the shadow of states' rights and into the sunlight of human rights." Whereupon numerous southern delegates—dubbed Dixiecrats by the press—walked out of the gathering. They soon formed the States' Rights Democratic Party and nominated for president Governor Strom Thurmond of South Carolina. Although his platform called for the "complete segregation of the races" and his campaign drew most of its support from those alarmed by Truman's civil rights initiatives, Thurmond denied charges of racism. The real issue of the election, Thurmond insisted, was freedom—the States' Rights Democratic Party, he declared, stood for "individual liberty and freedom, the right of people to govern themselves." Truman's plans for extending federal power into the South to enforce civil rights, Thurmond charged, would "convert America into a Hitler state."

Also in 1948, a group of left-wing critics of Truman's foreign policy formed the Progressive Party and nominated former vice president Henry A. Wallace for president. Wallace advocated an expansion of social welfare programs at home and denounced racial segregation even more vigorously than Truman. When he campaigned in the South, angry white crowds attacked him. But his real difference with the president concerned the Cold War. Wallace called for international control of nuclear weapons and a renewed effort to develop a relationship with the Soviet Union based on economic cooperation rather than military confrontation. He announced his willingness to accept support from all Americans who agreed with him, including socialists and communists. The influence of the now much-reduced Communist Party in Wallace's campaign led to an exodus of New Deal liberals and severe attacks on his candidacy. A vote for Wallace, Truman declared, was in effect a vote for Stalin.

THE 1948 CAMPAIGN

Wallace threatened to draw votes from Truman on the left, and Thurmond to undermine the president's support in the South, where whites had voted solidly for the Democrats throughout the twentieth century. But Truman's main opponent, fortunately for the president, was the colorless Republican Thomas A. Dewey. Certain of victory and an ineffective speaker and campaigner, Dewey seemed unwilling to commit himself on controversial issues. His speeches, wrote one hostile newspaper, amounted to nothing more than clichés: "Agriculture is important. Our rivers are full of fish. You cannot have freedom without liberty. Our future lies ahead." Truman, by contrast, ran an aggressive campaign. He crisscrossed the country by train, delivering fiery attacks on the Republican-controlled "do-nothing Congress." Truman revived New Deal rhetoric denouncing Wall Street and charged his opponent with threatening to undermine Social Security and other New Deal benefits. "Don't let them take it away," he repeated over and over.

The four-way 1948 campaign was the last before television put a premium on brief political advertisements and entertaining slogans rather than substantive debate, and the last in which a full spectrum of ideologies was presented to the American public. Virtually every public-opinion poll and newspaper report predicted a Dewey victory. Truman's success—by 303 to 189 electoral votes—represented one of the greatest upsets in American political history. For the first time since 1868, blacks (in the North, where they enjoyed the right to vote) played a decisive role in the outcome. Thurmond carried four Deep South states, demonstrating that the race issue, couched in terms of individual freedom, had the potential of leading traditionally Democratic white voters to desert their party. In retrospect, the States' Rights campaign offered a preview of the political transformation that by the end of the twentieth century would leave every southern state in the Republican column. As for Wallace, he suffered the humiliation of polling fewer popular votes (1.16 million) than Thurmond (1.17 million). His crushing defeat inaugurated an era in which public criticism of the foundations of American foreign policy became all but impossible.

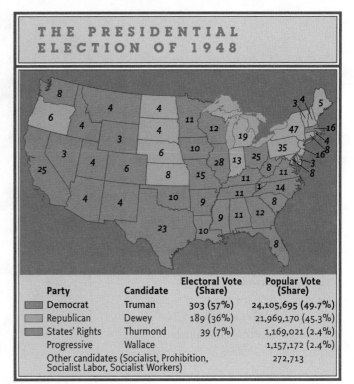

THE PRESIDENTIAL ELECTION OF 1948

Party	Candidate	Electoral Vote (Share)	Popular Vote (Share)
Democrat	Truman	303 (57%)	24,105,695 (49.7%)
Republican	Dewey	189 (36%)	21,969,170 (45.3%)
States' Rights	Thurmond	39 (7%)	1,169,021 (2.4%)
Progressive	Wallace		1,157,172 (2.4%)
Other candidates (Socialist, Prohibition, Socialist Labor, Socialist Workers)			272,713

THE ANTICOMMUNIST CRUSADE

For nearly half a century, the Cold War profoundly affected American life. There would be no return to "normalcy" as after World War I. The military-industrial establishment created during World War II would be permanent, not temporary. The United States retained a large and active federal government and poured money into weapons development and overseas bases. National security became the stated reason for a host of government projects, including aid to higher education and the building of a new national highway system (justified by the need to speed the evacuation of major cities in the event of nuclear war). The Cold War encouraged a culture of secrecy and dishonesty. Not until decades later was it revealed that during the 1950s and 1960s both the Soviet and American governments conducted experiments in which unwitting soldiers were exposed to chemical, biological, and nuclear weapons. American nuclear tests, conducted on Pacific islands and in Nevada, exposed thousands of civilians to radiation that caused cancer and birth defects.

Cold War military spending helped to fuel economic growth and support scientific research that not only perfected weaponry but also led to improved aircraft, computers, medicines, and other products with a large impact on civilian life. Since much of this research took place at universities, the Cold War promoted the rapid expansion of American higher

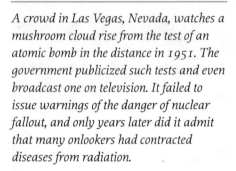

A crowd in Las Vegas, Nevada, watches a mushroom cloud rise from the test of an atomic bomb in the distance in 1951. The government publicized such tests and even broadcast one on television. It failed to issue warnings of the danger of nuclear fallout, and only years later did it admit that many onlookers had contracted diseases from radiation.

education. The Cold War reshaped immigration policy, with refugees from communism being allowed to enter the United States regardless of national-origin quotas. The international embarrassment caused by American racial policies contributed to the dismantling of segregation. And like other wars, the Cold War encouraged the drawing of a sharp line between patriotic Americans and those accused of being disloyal. Containment—not only of communism but of unorthodox opinions of all kinds—took place at home as well as abroad. At precisely the moment when the United States celebrated freedom as the foundation of American life, the right to dissent came under attack.

LOYALTY AND DISLOYALTY

Dividing the world between liberty and slavery automatically made those who could be linked to communism enemies of freedom. Although the assault on civil liberties came to be known as McCarthyism, it began before Senator Joseph R. McCarthy of Wisconsin burst onto the national scene in 1950. In 1947, less than two weeks after announcing the Truman Doctrine, the president established a loyalty review system in which government employees were required to demonstrate their patriotism without being allowed to confront accusers or, in some cases, knowing the charges against them. The loyalty program failed to uncover any cases of espionage. But the federal government dismissed several hundred persons from their jobs, and thousands resigned rather than submit to investigation.

Also in 1947, the House Un-American Activities Committee (HUAC) launched a series of hearings about communist influence in Hollywood. Calling well-known screenwriters, directors, and actors to appear before the committee ensured it a wave of national publicity, which its members relished. Celebrities like producer Walt Disney and actors Gary Cooper

Movie stars, led by actors Humphrey Bogart and Lauren Bacall, on their way to attend the 1947 hearings of the House Un-American Activities Committee, in a demonstration of support for those called to testify about alleged communist influence in Hollywood.

and Ronald Reagan testified that the movie industry harbored numerous communists. But ten "unfriendly witnesses" refused to answer the committee's questions about their political beliefs or to "name names" (identify individual communists) on the grounds that the hearings violated the First Amendment's guarantees of freedom of speech and political association. The committee charged the Hollywood Ten, who included the prominent screenwriters Ring Lardner Jr. and Dalton Trumbo, with contempt of Congress, and they served jail terms of six months to a year. Hollywood studios blacklisted them (denied them employment), along with more than 200 others who were accused of communist sympathies or who refused to name names.

THE SPY TRIALS

A series of highly publicized legal cases followed, which fueled the growing anticommunist hysteria. Whittaker Chambers, an editor at *Time* magazine, testified before HUAC that during the 1930s, Alger Hiss, a high-ranking State Department official, had given him secret government documents to pass to agents of the Soviet Union. Hiss vehemently denied the charge, but a jury convicted him of perjury and he served five years in prison. A young congressman from California and a member of HUAC, Richard Nixon achieved national prominence because of his dogged pursuit of Hiss. In another celebrated case, the Truman administration put the leaders of the Communist Party on trial for advocating the overthrow of the government. In 1951, eleven of them were sentenced to five years in prison.

The most sensational trial involved Julius and Ethel Rosenberg, a working-class Jewish communist couple from New York City (quite different from Hiss, a member of the eastern Protestant "establishment"). In 1951, a jury convicted the Rosenbergs of conspiracy to pass secrets

Demonstrators at a 1953 rally in Washington, D.C., demanding the execution of Julius and Ethel Rosenberg.

concerning the atomic bomb to Soviet agents during World War II (when the Soviets were American allies). Their chief accuser was David Greenglass, Ethel Rosenberg's brother, who had worked at the Los Alamos nuclear research center.

The case against Julius Rosenberg rested on highly secret documents that could not be revealed in court. (When they were released many years later, the scientific information they contained seemed too crude to justify the government's charge that Julius had passed along the "secret of the atomic bomb," although he may have helped the Soviets speed up their atomic program.) The government had almost no evidence against Ethel Rosenberg, and Greenglass later admitted that he had lied in some of his testimony about her. Indeed, prosecutors seem to have indicted her in the hope of pressuring Julius to confess and implicate others. But in the atmosphere of hysteria, their conviction was certain. Even though they had been convicted of conspiracy, a far weaker charge than spying or treason, Judge Irving Kaufman called their crime "worse than murder." They had helped, he declared, to "cause" the Korean War. Despite an international outcry, the death sentence was carried out in 1953. Controversy still surrounds the degree of guilt of both Hiss and the Rosenbergs, although almost no one today defends the Rosenbergs' execution. But these trials powerfully reinforced the idea that an army of Soviet spies was at work in the United States.

MCCARTHY AND MCCARTHYISM

In this atmosphere, a little-known senator from Wisconsin suddenly emerged as the chief national pursuer of subversives and gave a new name to the anticommunist crusade. Joseph R. McCarthy had won election to the Senate in 1946, partly on the basis of a fictional war record (he falsely claimed to have flown combat missions in the Pacific). In a speech at Wheeling, West Virginia, in February 1950, McCarthy announced that he had a list of 205 communists working for the State Department. The charge was preposterous, the numbers constantly changed, and McCarthy never identified a single person guilty of genuine disloyalty. But with a genius for self-promotion, McCarthy used the Senate subcommittee he chaired to hold hearings and level wild charges against numerous individuals as well as the Defense Department, the Voice of America, and other government agencies. Although many Republicans initially supported his rampage as a weapon against the Truman administration, McCarthy became an embarrassment to the party after the election of Republican Dwight D. Eisenhower as president in 1952. But McCarthy did not halt his campaign. He even questioned Eisenhower's anticommunism.

McCarthy's downfall came in 1954, when a Senate committee investigated his charges that the army had harbored

Senator Joseph R. McCarthy at the Army-McCarthy hearings of 1954. McCarthy points to a map detailing charges about the alleged extent of the communist menace, while the army's lawyer, Joseph Welch, listens in disgust.

and "coddled" communists. The nationally televised Army-McCarthy hearings revealed McCarthy as a bully who browbeat witnesses and made sweeping accusations with no basis in fact. The dramatic high point came when McCarthy attacked the loyalty of a young lawyer in the firm of Joseph Welch, the army's chief lawyer. "Let us not assassinate this lad further," Welch pleaded. "You have done enough. Have you no sense of decency, sir?" After the hearings ended, the Republican-controlled Senate voted to "condemn" McCarthy for his behavior. He died three years later. But the word "McCarthyism" had entered the political vocabulary, a shorthand for character assassination, guilt by association, and abuse of power in the name of anticommunism.

AN ATMOSPHERE OF FEAR

By the early 1950s, the anticommunist crusade had created a pervasive atmosphere of fear. One commentator described Washington, D.C., as a city rife with "spying, suspicion, [and] defamation by rumor," with "democratic freedoms" at risk as power slipped into the hands of those "whose values are the values of dictatorship and whose methods are the methods of the police state." But anticommunism was as much a local as a national phenomenon. States created their own committees, modeled on HUAC, that investigated suspected communists and other dissenters. States and localities required loyalty oaths of teachers, pharmacists, and members of other professions, and they banned communists from fishing, holding a driver's license, and, in Indiana, working as a professional wrestler.

Private organizations like the American Legion, National Association of Manufacturers, and Daughters of the American Revolution also persecuted individuals for their beliefs. The Better America League of southern California gathered the names of nearly 2 million alleged subversives in the region. Previous membership in organizations with communist influence or even participation in campaigns in which communists had taken part, such as the defense of the government of Spain during the Spanish Civil War of the 1930s, suddenly took on sinister implications. Throughout the country in the late 1940s and 1950s, those who failed to testify about their past and present political beliefs and to inform on possible communists frequently lost their jobs.

Local anticommunist groups forced public libraries to remove from their shelves "un-American" books like the tales of Robin Hood, who took from the rich to give to the poor. Universities refused to allow left-wing speakers to appear on campus and fired teachers who refused to sign loyalty oaths or to testify against others.

As during World War I, the courts did nothing to halt the political repression, demonstrating once again James Madison's warning that popular hysteria could override "parchment barriers" like the Bill of Rights that sought to prevent infringements on freedom. In 1951, in *Dennis v. United States*, the Supreme Court upheld the jailing of Communist Party leaders even though the charges concerned their beliefs, not any actions they had taken. Even many liberals retreated from the idea that freedom of expression was a birthright of all Americans. The American Civil Liberties Union condemned McCarthy's tactics but refused to defend the indicted Communist Party leaders.

"Fire!" *Cartoonist Herbert Block, known as "Herblock," offered this comment in 1949 on the danger to American freedom posed by the anticommunist crusade.*

THE USES OF ANTICOMMUNISM

There undoubtedly were Soviet spies in the United States. Yet the tiny Communist Party hardly posed a threat to American security. And the vast majority of those jailed or deprived of their livelihoods during the McCarthy era were guilty of nothing more than holding unpopular beliefs and engaging in lawful political activities.

Anticommunism had many faces and purposes. A popular mass movement, it grew especially strong among ethnic groups like Polish-Americans, with roots in eastern European countries now dominated by the Soviet Union, and among American Catholics in general, who resented and feared communists' hostility to religion. Government agencies like the Federal Bureau of Investigation (FBI) used anticommunism to expand their power. Under director J. Edgar Hoover, the FBI developed files on thousands of American citizens, including political dissenters, homosexuals, and others, most of whom had no connection to communism.

Anticommunism also served as a weapon wielded by individuals and groups in battles unrelated to defending the United States against subversion. McCarthy and his Republican followers often seemed to target not so much Stalin as the legacy of Roosevelt and the New Deal. For many Democrats, aggressive anticommunism became a form of self-defense against Republican charges of disloyalty and a weapon in a struggle for the party's future. The campaign against subversion redrew the boundaries of acceptable Democratic liberalism to exclude both communists and those willing to cooperate with them as in the days of the Popular Front. Indeed, "sympathetic association" with communists—past or present—became grounds for dismissal from one's job under the government's loyalty program.

As the historian Henry Steele Commager argued in a 1947 magazine article, the anticommunist crusade promoted a new definition of loyalty—conformity. Anything other than "uncritical and unquestioning acceptance of America as it is," wrote Commager, could now be labeled unpatriotic. For business, anticommunism became part of a campaign to identify government intervention in the economy with socialism. White supremacists employed anticommunism against black civil rights, business used it against unions, and upholders of sexual morality and traditional gender roles raised the cry of subversion against feminism and homosexuality, both supposedly responsible for eroding the country's fighting spirit. (Those barred from government service now included homosexuals and members of nudist colonies.)

ANTICOMMUNIST POLITICS

At its height, from the late 1940s to around 1960, the anticommunist crusade powerfully structured American politics and culture. Especially after their unexpected defeat in 1948, Republicans in Congress used a drumbeat of charges of subversion to block Truman's political program. The most important actions of Congress were ones the president opposed. After launching the government's loyalty program in 1947, Truman had become increasingly alarmed at the excesses of the anticommunist crusade. He vetoed the McCarran Internal Security Bill of 1950, which required "subversive" groups to register with the government, allowed the denial of passports to their members, and authorized their deportation or detention on presidential order. But Congress quickly gave the measure the two-thirds majority necessary for it to become law.

The McCarran-Walter Act of 1952, the first major piece of immigration legislation since 1924, also passed over the president's veto. Truman had appointed a Commission on Immigration, whose report, *Whom Shall We Welcome?*, called for replacing the quotas based on national origins with a more flexible system taking into account family reunion, labor needs, and political asylum. But the McCarran-Walter Act kept the quotas in place. It also authorized the deportation of immigrants identified as communists, even if they had become citizens. But the renewed fear of aliens sparked by the anticommunist crusade went far beyond communists. In 1954, the federal government launched Operation Wetback, which employed the military to invade Mexican-American neighborhoods and round up and deport illegal aliens. Within a year, some 1 million Mexicans had been deported.

Truman did secure passage of a 1950 law that added previously excluded self-employed and domestic workers to Social Security. Otherwise, however, the idea of expanding the New Deal welfare state faded. In its place, private welfare arrangements proliferated. The labor contracts of unionized workers established health insurance plans, automatic cost of living wage increases, paid vacations, and pension plans that supplemented Social Security. Western European governments provided these benefits to all citizens. In the United States, union members in major industries enjoyed them, but not the nonunionized majority of the population, a situation that created increasing inequality among laboring Americans.

THE COLD WAR AND ORGANIZED LABOR

Every political and social organization had to cooperate with the anticommunist crusade or face destruction, a wrenching experience for movements like labor and civil rights, in which communists had been some of the most militant organizers. After the passage of the Taft-Hartley Act of 1947, which withdrew bargaining rights and legal protection from unions whose leaders failed to swear that they were not communists, the CIO expelled numerous left-wing officials and eleven communist-led unions, representing nearly 1 million workers. Organized labor emerged as a major supporter of the foreign policy of the Cold War. Internal battles over the role of communists and their allies led to the purging of some of the most militant union leaders, often the ones most committed to advancing equal rights to women and racial minorities in the workplace. This left organized labor less able to respond to the economy's shift to an emphasis on service rather than manufacturing, and to the rise of the civil rights movement.

COLD WAR CIVIL RIGHTS

The civil rights movement also underwent a transformation. At first, mainstream black organizations like the NAACP and Urban League protested the Truman administration's loyalty program. They wondered aloud why the program and congressional committees defined communism as "un-American," but not racism. Anticommunist investigators often cited attendance at interracial gatherings as evidence of disloyalty. But while a few prominent black leaders, notably the singer and actor Paul Robeson and the veteran crusader for equality W. E. B. Du Bois, became outspoken critics of

VOICES OF FREEDOM

FROM National Security Council, NSC-68 (1950)

A critical document of early Cold War thinking, NSC-68 called for the United States to pursue a global crusade against communism in the name of freedom. Although not made public until years later, the manifesto had a strong impact in government circles and helped to spur a sharp increase in military spending.

The Soviet Union, unlike previous aspirants to hegemony, is animated by a new fanatic faith, antithetical to our own, and seeks to impose its absolute authority over the rest of the world.... The Kremlin regards the United States as the only major threat to the achievement of its fundamental design. There is a basic conflict between the idea of freedom under a government of laws, and the idea of slavery under the grim oligarchy of the Kremlin, which has come to a crisis with the polarization of power ... and the exclusive possession of atomic weapons by the two protagonists.... The implacable purpose of the slave state to eliminate the challenge of freedom has placed the two great powers at opposite poles. It is this fact which gives the present polarization of power the quality of crisis.

The free society values the individual as an end in himself, requiring of him only that measure of self-discipline and self-restraint which make the rights of each individual compatible with the rights of every other individual. The freedom of the individual has as its counterpart, therefore, the negative responsibility of the individual not to exercise his freedom in ways inconsistent with the freedom of other individuals and the positive responsibility to make constructive use of his freedom in the building of a just society.

From this idea of freedom with responsibility derives the marvelous diversity, the deep tolerance, the lawfulness of the free society. This is the explanation of the strength of free men. It constitutes the integrity and the vitality of a free and democratic system. The free society attempts to create and maintain an environment in which every individual has the opportunity to realize his creative powers. It also explains why the free society tolerates those within it who would use their freedom to destroy it. By the same token, in relations between nations, the prime reliance of the free society is on the strength and appeal of its idea, and it feels no compulsion sooner or later to bring all societies into conformity with it.

For the free society does not fear, it welcomes, diversity. It derives its strength from its hospitality even to antipathetic [hostile] ideas. It is a market for free trade in ideas, secure in its faith that free men will take the best wares....

The idea of freedom is the most contagious idea in history, more contagious than the idea of submission to authority.

FROM HENRY STEELE COMMAGER, "Who Is Loyal to America?" *Harper's* (September 1947)

In a sharply worded essay written in 1947, the prominent historian Henry Steele Commager commented on how the anticommunist crusade was stifling the expression of dissent and promoting an idea of patriotism that equated loyalty to the nation with the uncritical acceptance of American society and institutions.

Increasingly, Congress is concerned with the eradication of disloyalty and the defense of Americanism, and scarcely a day passes . . . that the outlines of the new loyalty and the new Americanism are not etched more sharply in public policy. . . . In the making is a revival of the red hysteria of the early 1920s, one of the shabbiest chapters in the history of American democracy, and more than a revival, for the new crusade is designed not merely to frustrate Communism but to formulate a positive definition of Americanism, and a positive concept of loyalty.

What is this new loyalty? It is, above all, conformity. It is the uncritical and unquestioning acceptance of America as it is—the political institutions, the social relationships, the economic practices. It rejects inquiry into the race question or socialized medicine, or public housing, or into the wisdom or validity of our foreign policy. It regards as particularly heinous any challenge to what is called "the system of private enterprise," identifying that system with Americanism. It abandons . . . the once popular concept of progress, and regards America as a finished product, perfect and complete.

It is, it must be added, easily satisfied. For it wants not intellectual conviction nor spiritual conquest, but mere outward conformity. In matters of loyalty, it takes the word for the deed, the gesture for the principle. It is content with the flag salute. . . . It is satisfied with membership in respectable organizations and, as it assumes that every member of a liberal organization is a Communist, concludes that every member of a conservative one is a true American. It has not yet learned that not everyone who saith Lord, Lord, shall enter into the kingdom of Heaven. It is designed neither to discover real disloyalty nor to foster true loyalty.

The concept of loyalty as conformity is a false one. It is narrow and restrictive, denies freedom of thought and of conscience. . . . What do men know of loyalty who make a mockery of the Declaration of Independence and the Bill of Rights?

QUESTIONS

1. What does NSC-68 see as the essential elements of the "free society"?

2. Why does Commager feel that the new patriotism makes "a mockery" of the Bill of Rights?

3. Is there any connection between the idea of a global battle over the future of freedom outlined in NSC-68 and the infringements on civil liberties at home deplored by Commager?

the Cold War, most felt they had no choice but to go along. The NAACP purged communists from local branches. When the government deprived Robeson of his passport and indicted Du Bois for failing to register as an agent of the Soviet Union, few prominent Americans, white or black, protested. (The charge against Du Bois was so absurd that even at the height of McCarthyism, the judge dismissed it.)

The Cold War caused a shift in thinking and tactics among civil rights groups. Organizations like the Southern Conference for Human Welfare, in which communists and noncommunists had cooperated in linking racial equality with labor organizing and economic reform, had been crucial to the struggles of the 1930s and war years. Their demise left a gaping hole that the NAACP, with its narrowly legalistic strategy, could not fill. Black organizations embraced the language of the Cold War and used it for their own purposes. They insisted that by damaging the American image abroad, racial inequality played into the Russians' hands. Thus, they helped to cement Cold War ideology as the foundation of the political culture, while complicating the idea of American freedom.

President Truman, as noted above, had called for greater attention to civil rights in part to improve the American image abroad. All in all, however, the height of the Cold War was an unfavorable time to raise questions about the imperfections of American society. In 1947, two months after the Truman Doctrine speech, Undersecretary of State Dean Acheson delivered a major address defending the president's pledge to aid "free peoples" seeking to preserve their "democratic institutions." Acheson chose as his audience the Delta Council, an organization of Mississippi planters, bankers, and merchants. He seemed unaware that to make the case for the Cold War, he had ventured into what one historian has called the "American Siberia," a place of grinding poverty whose black population (70 percent of the total) enjoyed neither genuine freedom nor democracy. Most of the Delta's citizens were denied the very liberties supposedly endangered by communism.

After 1948, little came of the Truman administration's civil rights flurry. State and local laws banning discrimination in employment and housing remained largely unenforced. In 1952, the Democrats showed how quickly the issue had faded by nominating for president Adlai Stevenson of Illinois, a candidate with little interest in civil rights, with southern segregationist John Sparkman as his running mate. The following year, Hortense Gabel, director of the eminently respectable New York State Committee Against Discrimination in Housing, reported that the shadow of fear hung over the civil rights movement. Given the persecution of dissent and the widespread sentiment that equated any criticism of American society with disloyalty, "a great many people are shying away from all activity in the civil liberties and civil rights fronts."

Time would reveal that the waning of the civil rights impulse was only temporary. But it came at a crucial moment, the late 1940s and early 1950s, when the United States experienced the greatest economic boom in its history. The rise of an "affluent society" transformed American life, opening new opportunities for tens of millions of white Americans in rapidly expanding suburbs. But it left blacks trapped in the declining rural areas of the South and urban ghettos of the North. The contrast between new opportunities and widespread prosperity for whites and continued discrimination for blacks would soon inspire a civil rights revolution and, with it, yet another redefinition of American freedom.

SUGGESTED READING

BOOKS

Biondi, Martha. *To Stand and Fight: The Struggle for Civil Rights in Postwar New York City* (2003). A comprehensive account of the broad coalition that battled for racial justice in New York City, in areas such as jobs, education, and housing.

Donovan, Robert. *Conflict and Crisis: The Presidency of Harry S. Truman, 1945–1948* (1977). A careful account of Truman's first administration and his surprising election victory in 1948.

Dudziak, Mary L. *Cold War Civil Rights: Race and the Image of American Democracy* (2000). Analyzes how the Cold War influenced and in some ways encouraged the civil rights movement at home.

Gaddis, John. *Strategies of Containment: A Critical Analysis of Postwar American National Security* (1982). An influential analysis of the development of the containment policy central to American foreign policy during the Cold War.

Gleason, Abbott. *Totalitarianism: The Inner History of the Cold War* (1995). Traces the development and uses of a key idea in Cold War America.

Glendon, Mary Ann. *A World Made New: Eleanor Roosevelt and the Universal Declaration of Human Rights* (2001). Relates the drafting of the Universal Declaration of Human Rights and the response of governments around the world, including the United States.

Hogan, Michael. *The Marhsall Plan* (1987). A detailed look at a pillar of early Cold War policy.

Hunt, Michael. *Ideology and U.S. Foreign Policy* (1987). Discusses how ideas, including the idea of freedom, have shaped America's interactions with the rest of the world.

Leffler, Melvyn P. *A Preponderance of Power: National Security, the Truman Administration, and the Cold War* (1992). An influential account of the origins of the Cold War.

Lipsitz, George. *Rainbow at Midnight: Labor and Culture in the 1940s* (1994). Examines the labor movement and its role in American life in the decade of perhaps its greatest influence.

Saunders, Frances S. *The Cultural Cold War: The CIA and the World of Arts and Letters* (2000). Describes how the CIA and other government agencies secretly funded artists and writers as part of the larger Cold War.

Schrecker, Ellen. *Many Are the Crimes: McCarthyism in America* (1998). A full account of the anticommunist crusade at home and its impact on American intellectual and social life.

Stueck, William. *The Korean War: An International History* (1995). Studies the Korean War in its full global context.

Sugrue, Thomas. *Origins of the Urban Crisis: Race and Inequality in Postwar Detroit* (1996). Explores race relations in a key industrial city after World War II and how they set the stage for the upheavals of the 1960s.

Williams, William A. *The Tragedy of American Diplomacy* (1959). An influential critique of America's Cold War foreign policy.

WEBSITES

Cold War International History Project: www.wilsoncenter.org/index.cfm?fuseaction=topics.home&topic_id=1409

Korea + 50: No Longer Forgotten: www.trumanlibrary.org/korea/

REVIEW QUESTIONS

1. What major ideological conflicts, security interests, and events brought about the Cold War?

2. What major changes in traditional U.S. foreign policy enabled America to fight the Cold War?

3. How did framing the Cold War in absolute terms as a battle between freedom and slavery influence Americans' ability to understand many world events?

4. Why did the United States not support movements for colonial independence around the world?

5. How did the government attempt to shape public opinion during the Cold War?

6. Explain the differences between the United States' and the Soviet Union's application of the UN Universal Declaration of Human Rights.

7. How did the anticommunist crusade affect organized labor in the postwar period?

8. What long-term significance did the 1948 presidential election have for the politics of postwar America?

9. What were the major components of Truman's Fair Deal?

10. How did the Cold War affect civil liberties in the United States?

FREEDOM QUESTIONS

1. In their ideological war, the Cold War superpowers promoted two very different social systems. Describe them and explain why each superpower felt its social system promoted freedom and social justice.

2. Identify the major ways in which the government used the anticommunist crusade to deprive some Americans of their freedoms.

3. How did Strom Thurmond and the Dixiecrats use ideas of freedom to justify their positions on civil rights and race?

4. Starting with the Truman Doctrine, explain how the United States promoted its Cold War actions as a global defense of freedom. How accurate was this claim?

KEY TERMS

containment (p. 952)

Truman Doctrine (p. 954)

Marshall Plan (p. 953)

National Security Council (p. 954)

General Agreement on Tariffs and Trade (p. 955)

Soviet atomic bomb (p. 956)

North Atlantic Treaty Organization (p. 956)

NSC-68 (p. 958)

"hearts and minds" (p. 961)

"Militant Liberty" (p. 962)

totalitarianism (p. 963)

the Fair Deal (p. 966)

Taft-Hartley Act (p. 968)

To Secure These Rights (p. 969)

Dixiecrats (p. 970)

loyalty review system (p. 972)

Hollywood Ten (p. 973)

Army-McCarthy hearings (p. 974)

conformity (p. 976)

McCarran-Walter Act (p. 977)

REVIEW TABLE

Landmark Events in the Early Cold War

Event	Date	Significance
Truman Doctrine	1947	Commited the United States to a policy of containment
Marshall Plan	1947	Provided economic aid to Europe for reconstruction
National Security Council established	1947	Assembled intelligence gathering and economic and military advisors to help the president fight the Cold War
Berlin blockade and airlift	1948–1949	Demonstrated an American commitment to containment
Creation of NATO	1949	First formal long-term peacetime military alliance, created to protect western Europe from Soviet expansion
Korean War	1950–1953	First hot war of the Cold War

Part 6

WHAT KIND OF NATION?
1953–2010

In the last half of the twentieth century, the United States experienced profound changes both at home and in its role in the larger world. The Cold War produced increasing American involvement in the affairs of other nations across the globe. Sometimes indirectly, sometimes through direct military intervention, the United States sought to prevent the further spread of communism and to ensure the existence of governments friendly to American strategic and economic interests. The sudden and unexpected collapse of communism in the Soviet Union and eastern Europe between 1989 and 1991 left the United States by far the world's foremost military power. At home, these years witnessed far-reaching changes in the nature of American society and a dramatic expansion in the rights of American citizens and their understandings of freedom.

On the surface, the decade of the 1950s seemed uneventful. It was a time of widespread affluence in the United States, the beginning of an unprecedented economic expansion that lasted until the early 1970s. Millions of Americans moved to the suburbs, where they enjoyed access to an astonishing array of consumer goods that poured out of American factories, including cars, television sets, and household appliances. The postwar "baby boom" dramatically increased the population. American understandings of freedom centered on the enjoyment of economic affluence and consumer choice within the context of traditional family life, with women finding fulfillment within their suburban homes.

Even during this time of "consensus," when sharp political divisions and economic strife seemed to have vanished from American life, seeds of discontent sprouted. A few artists and social commentators began to criticize the stifling atmosphere of

conformity. The Supreme Court's decision in 1954 outlawing racial segregation in public schools, justified, in part, by the damage Jim Crow inflicted on the world standing of the United States in the Cold War, helped to inspire the revival of the struggle for racial justice. The Montgomery bus boycott of 1955 launched the southern phase of the civil rights movement, which forced the entire country to rethink whether the United States could genuinely call itself "the land of the free" if it confined millions of Americans to second-class citizenship.

These seeds of protest flowered in the 1960s, a decade of social conflict and of dramatic expansion of the boundaries of American freedom. The civil rights revolution reached its climax with demonstrations throughout the South and the passage in 1964 and 1965 of national laws protecting blacks' civil rights and restoring to them the right to vote in the South. Although the movement splintered thereafter and the nation failed to address adequately the economic plight of non-whites trapped in decaying urban ghettos, the 1960s ended with the structure of legal segregation having been dismantled. The black movement inspired other aggrieved groups—Latinos, Indians, homosexuals, and women—to press their own grievances and claim their own "liberation." Their efforts further enlarged freedom's boundaries and helped to propel the idea of freedom into the most intimate areas of life. Under the leadership of Chief Justice Earl Warren, the Supreme Court gave constitutional recognition to the "rights revolution." By the end of the decade, both the meaning and the boundaries of freedom had expanded enormously.

At the same time, the country became more and more deeply involved in the Vietnam War. In this Cold War conflict, American policymakers

viewed the nationalist movement in Vietnam, led by homegrown communists, as part of a worldwide conspiracy directed from Moscow. As the United States committed hundreds of thousands of soldiers to Vietnam in the mid-1960s, the foreign policy consensus disintegrated. For the first time in American history, college students took the lead in radical protest, organizing massive protests against the war. Political disaffection helped to spawn the counterculture, a youth rebellion against prevailing middle-class mores. Having brought twentieth-century liberalism to its high point with his Great Society programs that sought to uplift the poor, encourage the arts, and provide medical care to the aged and needy, President Lyndon B. Johnson saw his party split over the war and his public support disintegrate.

Known as a time of radical protest, the 1960s also spawned a conservative backlash against the civil rights movement, the sexual revolution, public disorder, and the expansion of federal power. During the 1970s and 1980s, businessmen, antigovernment activists, a Christian Right that sought to restore what it considered to be traditional moral values, and Cold Warriors who desired a reinvigorated anticommunist crusade came together in an increasingly powerful conservative coalition. Their rise to power was hastened by the end of the postwar economic boom in 1973 and the inability of President Jimmy Carter to address the slump effectively. In 1980, conservative Ronald Reagan was elected president, ushering in the Reagan Revolution.

Reagan drastically increased military spending, cut funding for some social programs, reduced taxes, and attacked labor unions. Like Franklin D. Roosevelt, he consciously sought to redefine the meaning of freedom, associating it with anticommunism, free enterprise, and reduced government intervention in the economy. Although he put into effect conservative economic policies, Reagan failed to halt the rights revolution that had begun in the 1960s. Throughout the 1980s and 1990s, many conservatives lamented the fact that fewer and fewer women were embracing the traditional role of homemaker and that gays were gaining more and more recognition of their rights. Although conservatives launched a furious campaign to overturn the Supreme Court's 1973 decision legalizing abortion, they failed to achieve

success. Moreover, thanks to a 1965 law that ended the national-origins quotas for immigrants, newcomers from Asia and Latin America poured into the United States, setting off political battles over the country's increasingly visible racial and ethnic diversity.

The abrupt end of the Cold War between 1989 and 1991 left the United States as the world's lone superpower. This reinforced prevailing American understandings of freedom, emphasizing political democracy, free markets, and unrestrained individual choice in personal matters. During the 1990s, Americans became increasingly aware of the process of "globalization"—the international flow of people, investment, goods, and information across national boundaries. Some welcomed it as an expansion of economic freedom. Others worried that manufacturing jobs were leaving the United States for low-wage areas abroad and that crucial decisions affecting people's day-to-day lives were being made by institutions like the World Bank and World Trade Organization, over which no democratic control existed.

Events at the dawn of the twenty-first century revealed the extent and limitations of American power. The attacks of September 11, 2001, which killed some 3,000 persons, highlighted the nation's vulnerability at a time when terrorists, like goods and money, seemed able to cross national boundaries with ease. In response, President George W. Bush committed the United States to a "war on terrorism," a war without easily definable enemies, a predictable timetable, or a clear definition of victory. The federal government claimed the power to arrest persons suspected of involvement with terrorism, primarily individuals of Middle Eastern origin, without charge and to hold them indefinitely. The 2003 Iraq War, launched by the United States and Great Britain over the opposition of most members of the United Nations, suggested that in the post–Cold War world, America no longer needed to build alliances or concern itself with world opinion. Although the invasion successfully overthrew the Iraqi dictator Sadaam Hussein, an anti-American insurgency soon developed, along with strife between Iraq's Shiite and Sunni Muslims. By the end of 2006, the United States was bogged down in a seemingly interminable war, which was soon becoming increasingly unpopular at home.

These events raised anew vital questions already debated many times in the country's history. What is the balance between civil liberties and security in times of crisis? What are the economic conditions of freedom? Should the country consider itself a democracy or an empire? Should certain groups have their rights diminished because of their racial or ethnic origins? The answers to these questions would go a long way toward defining the meaning and boundaries of American freedom in the twenty-first century.

Chapter 24

An Affluent Society, 1953–1960

A portrait of affluence: In this photograph by Alex Henderson, Steve Czekalinski, an employee of the DuPont Corporation, poses with his family and the food they consumed in a single year, 1951. The family spent $1,300 (around $11,000 in today's money) on food, including 699 bottles of milk, 578 pounds of meat, and 131 dozen eggs. Nowhere else in the world in 1951 was food so available and inexpensive.

FOCUS QUESTIONS

- What were the main characteristics of the affluent society of the 1950s?

- How were the 1950s a period of consensus in both domestic policies and foreign affairs?

- What were the major thrusts of the civil rights movement in this period?

- What was the significance of the presidential election of 1960?

I n 1958, during a "thaw" in the Cold War, the United States and the Soviet Union agreed to exchange national exhibitions in order to allow citizens of each "superpower" to become acquainted with life in the other. The Soviet Exhibition, unveiled in New York City in June 1959, featured factory machinery, scientific advances, and other illustrations of how communism had modernized a backward country. The following month, the American National Exhibition opened in Moscow. A showcase of consumer goods and leisure equipment, complete with stereo sets, a movie theater, home appliances, and twenty-two different cars, the exhibit, *Newsweek* observed, hoped to demonstrate the superiority of "modern capitalism with its ideology of political and economic freedom." Yet the exhibit's real message was not freedom but consumption—or, to be more precise, the equating of the two.

When Vice President Richard Nixon prepared for his trip to Moscow to launch the exhibition, a former ambassador to Russia urged him to emphasize American values: "We are idealists; they are materialists." But the events of the opening day seemed to reverse these roles. Nixon devoted his address, entitled "What Freedom Means to Us," not to freedom of expression or differing forms of government, but to the "extraordinarily high standard of living" in the United States, with its 56 million cars and 50 million television sets. The United States, he declared, had achieved what Soviets could only dream of—"prosperity for all in a classless society."

The Moscow exhibition became the site of a classic Cold War confrontation over the meaning of freedom—the "kitchen debate" between

Vice President Richard Nixon and Soviet premier Nikita Khrushchev during the "kitchen debate," a discussion, among other things, of the meaning of freedom, which took place at the 1959 American National Exposition in Moscow.

Nixon and Soviet premier Nikita Khrushchev. Twice during the first day Nixon and Khrushchev engaged in unscripted debate about the merits of capitalism and communism. The first took place in the kitchen of a model suburban ranch house, the second in a futuristic "miracle kitchen" complete with a mobile robot that swept the floors. Supposedly the home of an average steelworker, the ranch house was the exhibition's centerpiece. It represented, Nixon declared, the mass enjoyment of American freedom within a suburban setting—freedom of choice among products, colors, styles, and prices. It also implied a particular role for women. Throughout his exchanges with Khrushchev, Nixon used the words "women" and "housewives" interchangeably. Pointing to the automatic floor sweeper, the vice president remarked that in the United States "you don't need a wife."

Nixon's decision to make a stand for American values in the setting of a suburban kitchen was a brilliant stroke. Nixon recognized that "soft power"—the penetration across the globe of American goods and popular culture—was an even more potent form of influence than military might. Indeed, his stance reflected the triumph during the 1950s of a conception of freedom centered on economic abundance and consumer choice within the context of traditional family life—a vision that seemed to offer far more opportunities for the "pursuit of happiness" to men than women. In reply, Khrushchev ridiculed consumer culture and the American obsession with household gadgets. "Don't you have a machine," he quipped, "that puts food in the mouth and pushes it down?" Many of the items on display, he continued, served "no useful purpose." Yet, in a sense, the Soviet leader conceded the debate when he predicted—quite incorrectly—that within seven years his country would surpass the United States in the production of consumer goods. For if material abundance was a battleground in the Cold War, American victory was certain.

THE GOLDEN AGE

The end of World War II was followed by what one scholar has called the "golden age" of capitalism, a period of economic expansion, stable prices, low unemployment, and rising standards of living that continued until 1973. Between 1946 and 1960, the American gross national product more than doubled and much of the benefit flowed to ordinary citizens in rising wages. In every measurable way—diet, housing, income, education, recreation—most Americans lived better than their parents and grandparents had. By 1960, an estimated 60 percent of Americans enjoyed what the government defined as a middle-class standard of living. The official poverty rate, 30 percent of all families in 1950, had declined to 22 percent a decade later (still, to be sure, representing more than one in five Americans).

Numerous innovations came into widespread use in these years, transforming Americans' daily lives. They included television, home air-conditioning, automatic dishwashers, inexpensive long-distance telephone calls, and jet air travel. Services like electricity, central heating, and indoor plumbing that within living memory had been enjoyed only by the rich and solidly middle class now became features of common life.

A CHANGING ECONOMY

Despite the economic recovery of western Europe and Japan after World War II, the United States remained the world's predominant industrial power. Major industries like steel, automobiles, and aircraft dominated the domestic and world markets for their products. Like other wars, the Cold War fueled industrial production and promoted a redistribution of the nation's population and economic resources. The West, especially the Seattle area, southern California, and the Rocky Mountain states, benefited enormously from government contracts for aircraft, guided missiles, and radar systems. The South became the home of numerous military bases and government-funded shipyards. Growth in the construction of aircraft engines and submarines counterbalanced the decline of New England's old textile and machinery industries, many of which relocated in the South to take advantage of low-cost nonunion labor.

In retrospect, the 1950s appear as the last decade of the industrial age in the United States. Since then, the American economy has shifted rapidly toward services, education, information, finance, and entertainment, while employment in manufacturing has declined. Even during the 1950s, the number of factory laborers fell slightly while clerical workers grew by nearly 25 percent and salaried employees in large corporate enterprises rose by 60 percent. Unions' very success in raising wages inspired employers to mechanize more and more elements of manufacturing in order to reduce labor costs. In 1956, for the first time in American history, white-collar workers outnumbered blue-collar factory and manual laborers.

The long-term trend toward fewer and larger farms continued. During the 1950s, the farm population fell from 23 million to 15 million, yet agricultural production rose by 50 percent, thanks to more efficient machinery, the application of chemical fertilizers and insecticides, increased use of irrigation to open land to cultivation in the West, and the development of new crop strains. The decade witnessed an acceleration of the transformation of southern life that had begun during World War II. New tractors and harvesting machinery and a continuing shift from cotton production to less labor-intensive soybean and poultry raising reduced the need for farm workers. More than 3 million black and white hired hands and sharecroppers migrated out of the region. The center of gravity of American farming shifted decisively to Texas, Arizona, and especially California. The large corporate farms of California, worked by Latino and Filipino migrant laborers, poured forth an endless supply of fruits and vegetables for the domestic and world markets. Items like oranges and orange juice, once luxuries, became an essential part of the American diet.

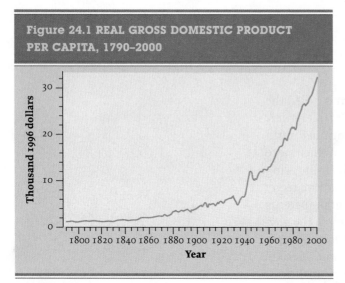

Figure 24.1 REAL GROSS DOMESTIC PRODUCT PER CAPITA, 1790–2000

Levittown, New York, perhaps the nation's most famous suburban community, photographed in 1954. Eventually, home owners would make individualized changes to their houses, so today Levittown looks far less uniform than when it was built.

A SUBURBAN NATION

The main engines of economic growth during the 1950s, however, were residential construction and spending on consumer goods. The postwar baby boom (discussed later) and the shift of population from cities to suburbs created an enormous demand for housing, television sets, home appliances, and cars. By 1960, suburban residents of single-family homes outnumbered urban dwellers and those living in rural areas. (Today, they outnumber both combined.)

During the 1950s, the number of houses in the United States doubled, nearly all of them built in the suburbs that sprang up across the landscape. The dream of home ownership, the physical embodiment of hopes for a better life, came within reach of the majority of Americans. William and Alfred Levitt, who shortly after the war built the first Levittown on 1,200 acres of potato fields on Long Island near New York City, became the most famous suburban developers. Levittown's more than 10,000 houses were assembled quickly from prefabricated parts and priced well within the reach of most Americans. Levittown was soon home to 40,000 people. At the same time, suburbs required a new form of shopping center—the mall—to which people drove in their cars. In contrast to traditional mixed-use city centers crowded with pedestrians, malls existed solely for shopping and had virtually no public space.

THE GROWTH OF THE WEST

But it was California that became the most prominent symbol of the postwar suburban boom. Between World War II and 1975, more than 30 million Americans moved west of the Mississippi River. One-fifth of the population growth of the 1950s occurred in California

This aerial view of Westchester, a community in Los Angeles, California, in 1949, illustrates how suburban "sprawl" spread over the landscape in the postwar era.

Ernst Haas's 1969 photograph of Albuquerque, New Mexico, could have been taken in any one of scores of American communities. As cities spread out, "strips," consisting of motels, gas stations, and nationally franchised businesses, became common. Meanwhile, older downtown business sections stagnated.

alone. In 1963, it surpassed New York to become the nation's most populous state.

Most western growth took place in metropolitan areas, not on farms. But "centerless" western cities like Houston, Phoenix, and Los Angeles differed greatly from traditional urban centers in the East. Rather than consisting of downtown business districts linked to residential neighborhoods by public transportation, western cities were decentralized clusters of single-family homes and businesses united by a web of highways. The Los Angeles basin, the largest western suburban region, had once had an extensive system of trains, trolleys, and buses. But local governments dismantled these lines after World War II, and the state and federal governments replaced them with freeways for cars and trucks. Suburban growth spilled into farm regions like the San Fernando and San Bernardino Valleys. By one estimate, one-third of southern California's land area (presumably not including mountains and deserts) was paved over with roads and parking lots. Life centered around the car; people drove to and from work and did their shopping at malls reachable only by driving. In other sections of the country as well, shopping shifted to suburban centers, and old downtown business districts stagnated. The spread of suburban homes created millions of new lawns. Today, more land is cultivated in grass than any agricultural crop in the United States.

A CONSUMER CULTURE

"The consumer is the key to our economy," declared Jack Straus, chairman of the board of Macy's, New York City's leading department store. "Our ability to consume is endless. The luxuries of today are the necessities of tomorrow." The roots of the consumer culture of the 1950s date back to the 1920s and even earlier. But never before had affluence, or consumerism, been so widespread. In a consumer culture, the measure of freedom became the ability to gratify market desires. Modern society, wrote Clark

In this 1950 photograph, television sets move through an assembly line.

Kerr, president of the University of California, may well have reduced freedom "in the workplace" by subjecting workers to stringent discipline on the job, but it offered a far greater range of "goods and services," and therefore "a greater scope of freedom" in Americans' "personal lives."

In a sense, the 1950s represented the culmination of the long-term trend in which consumerism replaced economic independence and democratic participation as central definitions of American freedom. Attitudes toward debt changed as well. Low interest rates and the spread of credit cards encouraged Americans to borrow money to purchase consumer goods. Americans became comfortable living in never-ending debt, once seen as a loss of economic freedom.

Consumer culture demonstrated the superiority of the American way of life to communism and virtually redefined the nation's historic mission to extend freedom to other countries. From Coca-Cola to Levi's jeans, American consumer goods, once a status symbol for the rich in other countries, were now marketed to customers around the globe. The country's most powerful weapon in the Cold War, insisted a reporter for *House Beautiful* magazine, was "the freedom offered by washing machines and dishwashers, vacuum cleaners, automobiles, and refrigerators."

THE TV WORLD

Thanks to television, images of middle-class life and advertisements for consumer goods blanketed the country. By the end of the 1950s, nearly nine of ten American families owned a TV set. Television replaced newspapers as the most common source of information about public events, and TV watching became the nation's leading leisure activity. Television changed Americans' eating habits (the frozen TV dinner, heated and eaten while watching a program, went on sale in 1954), and it provided Americans of all regions and backgrounds with a common cultural experience.

Introduced in 1954, the frozen TV dinner was marketed in a package designed to look like a TV set. Within a year, Swanson had sold 25 million dinners.

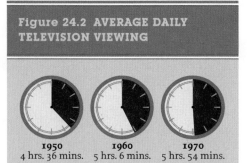

Figure 24.2 AVERAGE DAILY TELEVISION VIEWING

| 1950 | 1960 | 1970 |
| 4 hrs. 36 mins. | 5 hrs. 6 mins. | 5 hrs. 54 mins. |

With a few exceptions, like the Army-McCarthy hearings mentioned in the previous chapter, TV avoided controversy and projected a bland image of middle-class life. Popular shows of the early 1950s, such as *The Goldbergs* (with Jewish immigrants as the central characters) and *The Honeymooners* (in which Jackie Gleason played a bus driver), featured working-class families living in urban apartments. By the end of the decade, they had been replaced as the dominant programs by quiz shows, westerns, and comedies set in suburban homes like *Leave It to Beaver* and *The Adventures of Ozzie and Harriet*. Television also became the most effective advertising medium ever invented. To polish their image, large corporations sponsored popular programs—*The General Electric Theater* (hosted for several years by Ronald Reagan), *Alcoa Presents*, and others. TV ads, aimed primarily at middle-class suburban viewers, conveyed images of the good life based on endless consumption.

A NEW FORD

"The concept of freedom," wrote one commentator in 1959, "has become as familiar to us as an old hat or a new Ford." And a new Ford—or Chrysler or Chevrolet—now seemed essential to the enjoyment of freedom's benefits. Along with a home and television set, the car became part of what sociologists called "the standard consumer package" of the 1950s. By 1960, 80 percent of American families owned at least one car, and 14 percent had two or more, nearly all manufactured in the United States. Most were designed to go out of style within a year or two, promoting further purchases.

Auto manufacturers and oil companies vaulted to the top ranks of corporate America. Detroit and its environs were home to immense auto factories. The River Rouge complex had 62,000 employees, Willow Run 42,000. Since the military increasingly needed high-technology goods rather than the trucks and tanks that had rolled off assembly lines in World War II, the region around the Great Lakes lagged in defense contracts. In the long term, the continued funneling of federal dollars from the North and Midwest to the Sunbelt would prove devastating to the old industrial heartland. But during the 1950s, the booming automobile industry, with its demand for steel, rubber, and other products, assured the region's continued prosperity.

A 1959 Cadillac Eldorado Biarritz, an example of the design excesses of 1950s car makers. Behemoths like this, which got less than fifteen miles to a gallon of gasoline, depended on the availability of cheap fuel. When gas prices rose in later decades, consumers turned to smaller, more fuel-efficient foreign cars, helping to bring about the decline and fall of the American automobile industry.

THE INTERSTATE HIGHWAY SYSTEM

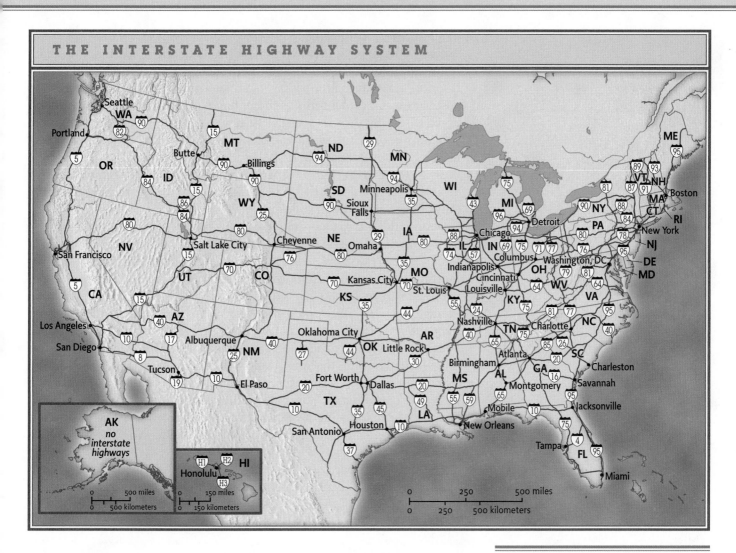

The automobile, the pivot on which suburban life turned, transformed the nation's daily life, just as the interstate highway system (discussed later) transformed Americans' travel habits, making possible long-distance vacationing by car and commuting to work from ever-increasing distances. The result was an altered American landscape, leading to the construction of motels, drive-in movie theaters, and roadside eating establishments. The first McDonald's fast food restaurant opened in Illinois in 1954. Within ten years, having been franchised by California businessman Ray Kroc, approximately 700 McDonald's stands had been built, which had sold over 400 million hamburgers. The car symbolized the identification of freedom with individual mobility and private choice. On the road, Americans were constantly reminded in advertising, television shows, and popular songs, they truly enjoyed freedom. They could imagine themselves as modern versions of western pioneers, able to leave behind urban crowds and workplace pressures for the "open road."

Begun in 1956 and completed in 1993, the interstate highway system dramatically altered the American landscape and Americans' daily lives. It made possible more rapid travel by car and stimulated the growth of suburbs along its many routes.

WOMEN AT WORK AND AT HOME

The emergence of suburbia as a chief site of what was increasingly called the "American way of life" placed pressure on the family—and especially women—to live up to freedom's promise. After 1945, women lost most of

Figure 24.3 THE BABY BOOM AND ITS DECLINE

Birthrate, 1940–1970*

*Based on estimated total live births per 1,000 population.

the industrial jobs they had performed during the war. As during most of American history, women who worked outside the home remained concentrated in low-salary, nonunion jobs, such as clerical, sales, and service labor, rather than better-paying manufacturing positions. After a sharp postwar drop in female employment, the number of women at work soon began to rise. By 1955, it exceeded the level of World War II. But the nature and aims of women's work had changed. The modern woman, said *Look* magazine, worked part-time, to help support the family's middle-class lifestyle, not to help pull it out of poverty or to pursue personal fulfillment or an independent career. Working women in 1960 earned, on average, only 60 percent of the income of men.

Despite the increasing numbers of wage-earning women, the suburban family's breadwinner was assumed to be male, while the wife remained at home. Films, TV shows, and advertisements portrayed marriage as the most important goal of American women. And during the 1950s, men and women reaffirmed the virtues of family life. They married younger (at an average age of twenty-two for men and twenty for women), divorced less frequently than in the past, and had more children (3.2 per family). A "baby boom" that lasted into the mid-1960s followed the end of the war. At a time of low immigration, the American population rose by nearly 30 million (almost 20 percent) during the 1950s. The increase arose mostly from the large number of births, but it also reflected the fact that Americans now lived longer than in the past, thanks to the wide availability of "miracle drugs" like penicillin that had been developed during World War II to combat bacterial infections.

The family also became a weapon in the Cold War. The ability of women to remain at home, declared a government official, "separates us from the Communist world," where a high percentage of women worked. To be sure,

Jack Gould's 1946 photograph of a hospital maternity ward captures the first year of the postwar baby boom.

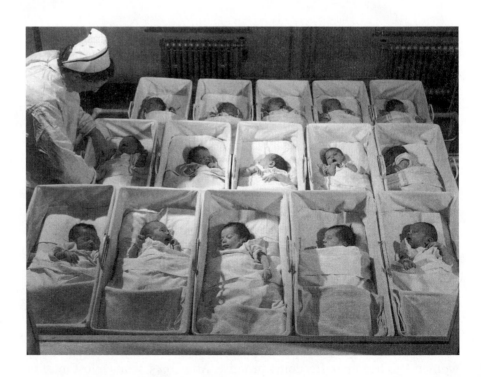

the family life exalted during the 1950s differed from the patriarchal household of old. It was a modernized relationship, in which both partners reconciled family obligations with personal fulfillment through shared consumption, leisure activities, and sexual pleasure. Thanks to modern conveniences, the personal freedom once associated with work could now be found at home. Frozen and prepared meals, exulted one writer in 1953, offered housewives "freedom from tedium, space, work, and their own inexperience"—quite a change from the Four Freedoms of World War II.

Like other forms of dissent, feminism seemed to have disappeared from American life or was widely dismissed as evidence of mental disorder. Prominent psychologists insisted that the unhappiness of individual women or even the desire to work for wages stemmed from a failure to accept the "maternal instinct." "The independent woman," declared the book *Modern Woman: The Lost Sex* (1947) "is a contradiction in terms." The idea of domestic life as a refuge and of full-time motherhood as a woman's "sphere" had a long history in the United States. But in the postwar suburbs, where family life was physically separated from work, relatives, and the web of social organizations typical of cities, it came close to realization.

Advertisers during the 1950s sought to convey the idea that women would enjoy their roles as suburban homemakers, as in this ad for a vacuum cleaner, which equates housework with a game of golf.

A SEGREGATED LANDSCAPE

For millions of city dwellers, the suburban utopia fulfilled the dream, postponed by depression and war, of home ownership and middle-class incomes. For beneficiaries of postwar prosperity, in the words of a Boston worker who made heroic sacrifices to move his family to the suburbs, the home became "the center of freedom." The move to the suburbs also promoted Americanization, cutting residents off from urban ethnic communities and bringing them fully into the world of mass consumption. But if the suburbs offered a new site for the enjoyment of American freedom, they retained at least one familiar characteristic—rigid racial boundaries.

Suburbia has never been as uniform as either its celebrants or its critics claimed. There are upper-class suburbs, working-class suburbs, industrial suburbs, and "suburban" neighborhoods within city limits. But if the class uniformity of suburbia has been exaggerated, its racial uniformity was all too real. As late as the 1990s, nearly 90 percent of suburban whites lived in communities with non-white populations of less than 1 percent—the legacy of decisions by government, real-estate developers, banks, and residents.

During the postwar suburban boom, federal agencies continued to insure mortgages that barred resale of houses to non-whites, thereby financing housing segregation. Even after the Supreme Court in 1948 declared such provisions legally unenforceable, banks and private developers barred non-whites from the suburbs and the government refused to subsidize their mortgages except in segregated enclaves. In 1960, blacks represented less than 3 percent of the population of Chicago's suburbs. The vast new communities built by William Levitt refused to allow blacks,

Elliott Erwitt's photograph of a young mother in New Rochelle, a suburb of New York City, suggests that life for the suburban woman could be less idyllic than many advertisements implied.

Suburban builders sometimes openly advertised the fact that their communities excluded minorities. This photograph was taken in southern California in 1948.

including army veterans, to rent or purchase homes. "If we sell one house to a Negro family," Levitt explained, "then 90 or 95 percent of our white customers will not buy into the community." After a lawsuit, Levitt finally agreed during the 1960s to sell homes to non-whites, but at a pace that can only be described as glacial. In 1990, his Long Island community, with a population of 53,000, included 127 black residents.

PUBLIC HOUSING AND URBAN RENEWAL

A Housing Act passed by Congress in 1949 authorized the construction of more than 800,000 units of public housing in order to provide a "decent home for every American family." But the law set an extremely low ceiling on the income of residents—a rule demanded by private contractors seeking to avoid competition from the government in building homes for the middle class. This regulation limited housing projects to the very poor. Since white urban and suburban neighborhoods successfully opposed the construction of public housing, it was increasingly confined to segregated neighborhoods in inner cities, reinforcing the concentration of poverty in urban non-white neighborhoods. At the same time, under programs of "urban renewal," cities demolished poor neighborhoods in city centers that occupied potentially valuable real estate. In their place, developers constructed

An aerial photograph of Boulevard Houses, a low-income housing project in Brooklyn, illustrates how public housing concentrated poor Americans in structures separated from surrounding neighborhoods.

retail centers and all-white middle-income housing complexes, and states built urban public universities like Wayne State in Detroit and the University of Illinois at Chicago. Los Angeles displaced a neighborhood of mixed ethnic groups in Chavez Ravine in order to build a stadium for the Dodgers, whose move in 1958 after sixty-eight years in Brooklyn seemed to symbolize the growing importance of California on the national scene. White residents displaced by urban renewal often moved to the suburbs. Non-whites, unable to do so, found housing in run-down city neighborhoods.

THE DIVIDED SOCIETY

Suburbanization hardened the racial lines of division in American life. Between 1950 and 1970, about 7 million white Americans left cities for the suburbs. Meanwhile, nearly 3 million blacks moved from the South to the North, greatly increasing the size of existing urban ghettos and creating entirely new ones. And half a million Puerto Ricans, mostly small coffee and tobacco farmers and agricultural laborers forced off the land when American sugar companies expanded their landholdings on the island, moved to the mainland. Most ended up in New York City's East Harlem, until then an Italian-American community. Although set in a different part of New York, the popular Broadway musical *West Side Story* dramatized the tensions between Puerto Rican newcomers and longtime urban residents. By the late 1960s, more Puerto Ricans lived in New York City than San Juan, the island's capital.

The process of racial exclusion became self-reinforcing. Non-whites remained concentrated in manual and unskilled jobs, the result of employment discrimination and their virtual exclusion from educational opportunities at public and private universities, including those outside the South. In 1950, only 12 percent of employed blacks held white-collar positions, compared with 45 percent of whites. As the white population and industrial jobs fled the old city centers for the suburbs, poorer blacks and Latinos remained trapped in urban ghettos, seen by many whites as places of crime, poverty, and welfare.

Suburbanites, for whom the home represented not only an emblem of freedom but the family's major investment, became increasingly fearful that any non-white presence would lower the quality of life and destroy property values. *Life* magazine quoted a white suburbanite discussing a prospective black neighbor: "He's probably a nice guy, but every time I see him, I see $2,000 drop off the value of my house." Residential segregation was reinforced by "blockbusting"—a tactic of real-estate brokers who circulated exaggerated warnings of an impending influx of non-whites, to persuade alarmed white residents to sell their homes hastily. Because of this practice, some all-white neighborhoods quickly became all-minority enclaves rather than places where members of different races lived side by side.

"Freedom is equal housing too" became a slogan in the campaign for residential integration. But suburban home ownership long remained a white entitlement, with the freedom of non-whites to rent or purchase a home where they desired overridden by the claims of private property and "freedom of association." Even as the old divisions between white ethnic Americans faded in the suburban melting pot, racial barriers in housing, and therefore in public education and jobs, were reinforced.

Students at an East Harlem elementary school in 1947. Most have recently migrated from Puerto Rico to the mainland with their families, although some are probably children of the area's older Italian-American community.

THE END OF IDEOLOGY

Cold War affluence coexisted with urban decay and racism, the seeds from which protest would soon flower. Yet to many observers in the 1950s it seemed that the ills of American society had been solved. In contrast to the turmoil of the 1930s and the immediate postwar years, the 1950s was a placid time, because of both widespread affluence and the narrowing of the boundaries of permissible political debate. The boom and bust cycles, mass unemployment, and economic insecurity of the past seemed largely to have disappeared. Scholars celebrated the "end of ideology" and the triumph of a democratic, capitalist "consensus" in which all Americans except the maladjusted and fanatics shared the same liberal values of individualism, respect for private property, and belief in equal opportunity. If problems remained, their solutions required technical adjustments, not structural change or aggressive political intervention.

As for religious differences, the source of persistent tension in American history, these were absorbed within a common "Judeo-Christian" heritage, a notion that became central to the cultural and political dialogue of the 1950s. This newly invented tradition sought to demonstrate that Catholics, Protestants, and Jews shared the same history and values and had all contributed to the evolution of American society. In the era of McCarthyism, ideological differences may have been un-American, but group pluralism reigned supreme, with the free exercise of religion yet another way of differentiating the American way of life from life under communism.

The idea of a unified Judeo-Christian tradition overlooked the long history of hostility among religious denominations. But it reflected the decline of anti-Semitism and anti-Catholicism in the wake of World War II, as well as the ongoing secularization of American life. During the 1950s, a majority of Americans—the highest proportion in the nation's history— were affiliated with a church or synagogue. Evangelists like Billy Graham used radio and television to spread the message of Christianity and anticommunism to millions. But as Will Herberg argued in his influential book

This postage stamp depicts four chaplains who perished during the sinking of an American ship during World War II. Its original design listed their denominations: Catholic, Protestant, and Jewish. When the stamp was issued in 1948, these words were omitted, in keeping with the emphasis on the newly invented idea of a Judeo-Christian tradition shared by all Americans.

Protestant-Catholic-Jew (1955), religion now had less to do with spiritual activities or sacred values than with personal identity, group assimilation, and the promotion of traditional morality. In an affluent suburban society, Herberg argued, the "common religion" was the American way of life, a marriage of democratic values and economic prosperity—in a phrase, "free enterprise."

SELLING FREE ENTERPRISE

The economic content of Cold War freedom increasingly came to focus on consumer capitalism, or, as it was now universally known, "free enterprise." More than political democracy or freedom of speech, which many allies of the United States outside western Europe lacked, an economic system resting on private ownership united the nations of the Free World. A week before his Truman Doctrine speech, in a major address on economic policy, the president reduced Roosevelt's Four Freedoms to three. Freedom of speech and worship remained, but freedom from want and fear had been replaced by freedom of enterprise, "part and parcel," said Truman, of the American way of life.

Even more than during World War II, what one historian calls the "selling of free enterprise" became a major industry, involving corporate advertising, school programs, newspaper editorials, and civic activities. Convinced that ads represented "a new weapon in the world-wide fight for freedom," the Advertising Council invoked cherished symbols like the Statue of Liberty and the Liberty Bell in the service of "competitive free enterprise." To be sure, the free enterprise campaigners did not agree on every issue. Some businessmen believed that defending free enterprise required rolling back much of the power that labor unions had gained in the past decade, dismantling New Deal regulations, and restricting the economic role of government. Representing what might be called business's more liberal wing, the Advertising Council, in its "American Economic System" ad campaign of 1949, reaffirmed labor's right to collective bargaining and the importance of government–business cooperation. Indeed, despite talk of the glories of the free market, government policies played a crucial role in the postwar boom. The rapid expansion of the suburban middle class owed much to federal tax subsidies, mortgage guarantees for home purchases, dam and highway construction, military contracts, and benefits under the GI Bill.

PEOPLE'S CAPITALISM

Free enterprise seemed an odd way of describing an economy in which a few large corporations dominated key sectors. Until well into the twentieth century, most ordinary Americans had been deeply suspicious of big business, associating it with images of robber barons who manipulated politics, suppressed economic competition, and treated their workers unfairly. Americans, wrote David Lilienthal, chairman of the Atomic Energy Commission, must abandon their traditional fear that concentrated economic power endangered "our very liberties." Large-scale production was not only necessary to fighting the Cold War, but it enhanced freedom by multiplying consumer goods. "By freedom," wrote Lilienthal, "I mean

TV became the most effective advertising medium in history. Here, an advertisement for Ford, one of the largest American corporations, is being filmed. The background evokes the idea of driving on the open road as a form of individual freedom.

essentially *freedom to choose.* . . . It means a maximum range of choice for the consumer when he spends his dollar." By the end of the 1950s, public-opinion surveys revealed that more than 80 percent of Americans believed that "our freedom depends on the free enterprise system."

The United States, declared *Fortune* magazine, anticipating Vice President Nixon's remark in the 1959 kitchen debate, had achieved the Marxist goal of a classless society. A sharp jump in the number of individuals investing in Wall Street inspired talk of a new "people's capitalism." In 1953, 4.5 million Americans—only slightly more than in 1928—owned shares of stock. By the mid-1960s, the number had grown to 25 million. In the face of widespread abundance, who could deny that the capitalist marketplace embodied individual freedom or that poverty would soon be a thing of the past? "It was American Freedom," proclaimed *Life* magazine, "by which and through which this amazing achievement of wealth and power was fashioned."

THE LIBERTARIAN CONSERVATIVES

During the 1950s, a group of thinkers began the task of reviving conservatism and reclaiming the idea of freedom from liberals. Although largely ignored outside their own immediate circle, they developed ideas that would define conservative thought for the next half-century. One was opposition to a strong national government, an outlook that had been given new political life in conservatives' bitter reaction against the New Deal. To these "libertarian" conservatives, freedom meant individual autonomy, limited government, and unregulated capitalism.

These ideas had great appeal to conservative entrepreneurs, especially in the rapidly growing South and West. Many businessmen who desired to pursue their economic fortunes free of government regulation, high taxes, and labor unions found intellectual reinforcement in the writings of the young economist Milton Friedman. In 1962, Friedman published *Capitalism and Freedom*, which identified the free market as the necessary foundation for individual liberty. This was not an uncommon idea during the Cold War, but Friedman pushed it to extreme conclusions. He called for turning over to the private sector virtually all government functions and the repeal of minimum wage laws, the graduated income tax, and the Social Security system. Friedman extended the idea of unrestricted free choice into virtually every realm of life. Government, he insisted, should seek to regulate neither the economy nor individual conduct.

THE NEW CONSERVATISM

Friedman was indirectly criticizing not only liberalism but also the "new conservatism," a second strand of thought that became increasingly prominent in the 1950s. Convinced that the Free World needed to arm itself morally and intellectually, not just militarily, for the battle against communism, "new conservatives" like writers Russell Kirk and Richard Weaver insisted that toleration of difference—a central belief of modern liberalism—offered no substitute for the search for absolute truth. Weaver's book, *Ideas Have Consequences* (1948), a rambling philosophical treatise that surprisingly became the most influential statement of this new traditionalism, warned that the West was suffering from moral decay and called for a return to a civilization based on values grounded in the Christian tradition and in timeless notions of good and evil.

The "new conservatives" understood freedom as first and foremost a moral condition. It required a decision by independent men and women to lead virtuous lives, or governmental action to force them to do so. Although they wanted government expelled from the economy, new conservatives trusted it to regulate personal behavior, to restore a Christian morality they saw as growing weaker and weaker in American society.

Here lay the origins of a division in conservative ranks that would persist into the twenty-first century. Unrestrained individual choice and moral virtue are radically different starting points from which to discuss freedom. Was the purpose of conservatism, one writer wondered, to create the "free man" or the "good man"? Libertarian conservatives spoke the language of progress and personal autonomy; the "new conservatives" emphasized tradition, community, and moral commitment. The former believed that too many barriers existed to the pursuit of individual liberty. The latter condemned an excess of individualism and a breakdown of common values.

Fortunately for conservatives, political unity often depends less on intellectual coherence than on the existence of a common foe. And two powerful enemies became focal points for the conservative revival—the Soviet Union abroad and the federal government at home. Anticommunism, however, did not clearly distinguish conservatives from liberals, who also supported the Cold War. What made conservatism distinct was its antagonism to "big government" in America, at least so long as it was controlled by liberals who, conservatives believed, tolerated or encouraged immorality. Republican control of the presidency did not lessen conservatives' hostility to the federal government, partly because they did not consider President Eisenhower one of their own.

THE EISENHOWER ERA

IKE AND NIXON

Dwight D. Eisenhower, or "Ike," as he was affectionately called, emerged from World War II as the military leader with the greatest political appeal, partly because his public image of fatherly warmth set him apart from other successful generals like the arrogant Douglas MacArthur. Eisenhower's party affiliation was unknown. In 1948, he voted for Truman, and he accepted Truman's invitation to return to Europe as Supreme Commander of NATO forces. Both parties wanted him as their candidate in 1952. But Eisenhower became convinced that Senator Robert A. Taft of Ohio, a leading contender for the Republican nomination, would lead the United States back toward isolationism. Eisenhower entered the contest and won the Republican nomination.

As his running mate, Eisenhower chose Richard Nixon of California, a World War II veteran who had made a name for himself by vigorous anti-communism. In his first campaign for Congress, in 1946, Nixon attacked his opponent as an advocate of "state socialism." He gained greater fame by his pursuit of Alger Hiss while a member of the House Un-American Activities Committee. Nixon won election to the U.S. Senate in 1950 in a campaign in which he suggested that the Democratic candidate, Congresswoman Helen Gahagan Douglas, had communist sympathies.

These tactics gave Nixon a lifelong reputation for opportunism and dishonesty. But Nixon was also a shrewd politician, who pioneered efforts to transform the Republican Party's image from defender of business to champion of the "forgotten man"—the hardworking citizen burdened by heavy taxation and unresponsive government bureaucracies. "Freedom for the individual, for private enterprise," he insisted, had made America great. In using populist language to promote free market economics, Nixon helped to lay the foundation for the triumph of conservatism a generation later.

Dwight D. Eisenhower's popularity was evident at this appearance in Baltimore during the 1952 presidential campaign.

THE 1952 CAMPAIGN

Almost as soon as he won the vice-presidential nomination, Nixon ran into trouble over press reports that wealthy Californians had created a private fund for his family. Eisenhower considered dropping him from the ticket. But in an emotional nationally televised thirty-minute address in which he drew attention to his ordinary upbringing, war service, and close-knit family, Nixon denied the accusations. The "Checkers speech," named after the family dog—the one gift Nixon acknowledged receiving, but insisted he would not return—rescued his political career. It illustrated how television was beginning to transform politics by allowing candidates to bring a carefully crafted image directly into Americans' living rooms. The 1952 campaign became the first to make extensive use of TV ads. Parties, one observer complained, were "selling the president like toothpaste."

More important to the election's outcome, however, was Eisenhower's popularity (invoked in the Republican campaign slogan "I Like Ike") and the public's weariness with the Korean War. Ike's pledge to "go to Korea" in search of peace signaled his intention to bring the conflict to an end. He won a resounding victory over the Democratic candidate, Adlai Stevenson. Four years later, Eisenhower again defeated Stevenson, by an even wider margin. His popularity, however, did not extend to his party. Republicans won a razor-thin majority in Congress in 1952, but Democrats regained control in 1954 and retained it for the rest of the decade. In 1956, Eisenhower became the first president to be elected without his party controlling either house of Congress.

During the 1950s, voters at home and abroad seemed to find reassurance in selecting familiar, elderly leaders to govern them. At age sixty-two, Eisenhower was one of the oldest men ever elected president. But he seemed positively youthful compared with Winston Churchill, who returned to office as prime minister of Great Britain at age seventy-seven, Charles DeGaulle, who assumed the presidency of France at sixty-eight, and Konrad Adenauer, who served as chancellor of West Germany from age seventy-three until well into his eighties. In retrospect, Eisenhower's presidency seems almost uneventful, at least in domestic affairs—an interlude between the bitter party battles of the Truman administration and the social upheavals of the 1960s.

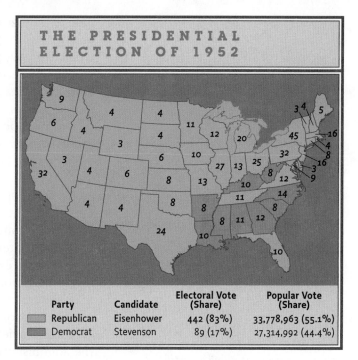

THE PRESIDENTIAL ELECTION OF 1952

Party	Candidate	Electoral Vote (Share)	Popular Vote (Share)
Republican	Eisenhower	442 (83%)	33,778,963 (55.1%)
Democrat	Stevenson	89 (17%)	27,314,992 (44.4%)

MODERN REPUBLICANISM

With a Republican serving as president for the first time in twenty years, the tone in Washington changed. Wealthy businessmen dominated Eisenhower's cabinet. Defense Secretary Charles Wilson, the former president of General Motors, made the widely publicized statement: "What is good for the country is good for General Motors, and vice versa." A champion of the business community and a fiscal conservative, Ike worked to scale back government spending, including the military budget. But while right-wing Republicans saw his victory as an invitation to roll back the New Deal, Eisenhower realized that such a course would be disastrous. "Should any political party attempt to abolish Social Security, unemployment insurance, and eliminate labor laws and farm programs," he declared, "you would not hear of that party again in our political history."

Eisenhower called his domestic agenda Modern Republicanism. It aimed to sever his party's identification in the minds of many Americans with Herbert Hoover, the Great Depression, and indifference to the economic conditions of ordinary citizens. The core New Deal programs not only remained in place, but expanded. In 1955, millions of agricultural workers became eligible for the first time for Social Security. Nor did Ike

"Do you call C-minus catching up with Russia?" Alan Dunn's cartoon for the New Yorker *magazine comments on how Soviet success in launching an artificial earth satellite spurred a focus on improving scientific education in the United States.*

reduce the size and scope of government. Despite the use of "free enterprise" as a weapon in the Cold War, the idea of a "mixed economy" in which the government played a major role in planning economic activity was widely accepted throughout the Western world. America's European allies like Britain and France expanded their welfare states and nationalized key industries like steel, shipbuilding, and transportation (that is, the government bought them from private owners and operated and subsidized them).

The United States had a more limited welfare state than western Europe and left the main pillars of the economy in private hands. But it too used government spending to promote productivity and boost employment. Eisenhower presided over the largest public-works enterprise in American history, the building of the 41,000-mile interstate highway system. As noted in the previous chapter, Cold War arguments—especially the need to provide rapid exit routes from cities in the event of nuclear war—justified this multibillion-dollar project. But automobile manufacturers, oil companies, suburban builders, and construction unions had very practical reasons for supporting highway construction regardless of any Soviet threat. When the Soviets launched *Sputnik*, the first artificial earth satellite, in 1957, the administration responded with the National Defense Education Act, which for the first time offered direct federal funding to higher education.

All in all, rather than dismantling the New Deal, Eisenhower's modern Republicanism consolidated and legitimized it. By accepting its basic premises, he ensured that its continuation no longer depended on Democratic control of the presidency.

THE SOCIAL CONTRACT

The 1950s also witnessed an easing of the labor conflict of the two previous decades. The passage of the Taft-Hartley Act in 1947 (discussed in the previous chapter) had reduced labor militancy. In 1955, the AFL and CIO merged to form a single organization representing 35 percent of all nonagricultural workers. In leading industries, labor and management hammered out what has been called a new "social contract." Unions signed long-term agreements that left decisions regarding capital investment, plant location, and output in management's hands, and they agreed to try to prevent unauthorized "wildcat" strikes. Employers stopped trying to eliminate existing unions and granted wage increases and fringe benefits such as private pension plans, health insurance, and automatic adjustments to pay to reflect rises in the cost of living.

Unionized workers shared fully in 1950s prosperity. Although the social contract did not apply to the majority of workers, who did not belong to unions, it did bring benefits to those who labored in nonunion jobs. For example, trade unions in the 1950s and 1960s were able to use their political power to win a steady increase in the minimum wage, which was earned mostly by nonunion workers at the bottom of the employment pyramid. But these "spillover effects" were limited. The majority of workers did not enjoy anything close to the wages, benefits, and job security of unionized workers in such industries as automobiles and steel.

Indeed, nonunion employers continued to fight vehemently against labor organization, and groups like the National Association of Manufacturers still viewed unions as an unacceptable infringement on the power of employers. Some firms continued to shift jobs to the less-unionized suburbs and South. By the end of the 1950s, the social contract was weakening. In 1959, the steel industry sought to tighten work rules and limit wage increases in an attempt to boost profits battered by a recession that hit two years earlier. The plan sparked a strike of 500,000 steelworkers, which successfully beat back the proposed changes.

MASSIVE RETALIATION

Soon after he entered office, Eisenhower approved an armistice that ended fighting in Korea. But this failed to ease international tensions. Ike took office at a time when the Cold War had entered an extremely dangerous phase. In 1952, the United States exploded the first hydrogen bomb—a weapon far more powerful than those that had devastated Hiroshima and Nagasaki. The following year, the Soviets matched this achievement. Both sides feverishly developed long-range bombers capable of delivering weapons of mass destruction around the world.

A professional soldier, Ike hated war, which he viewed as a tragic waste. "Every gun that is made," he said in 1953, "every warship launched . . . signifies a theft from those who hunger and are not fed." But his secretary of state, John Foster Dulles, was a grim Cold Warrior. In 1954, Dulles announced an updated version of the doctrine of containment. "Massive retaliation," as it was called, declared that any Soviet attack on an American ally would be countered by a nuclear assault on the Soviet Union itself. In some ways, this reliance on the nuclear threat was a way to enable the budget-conscious Eisenhower to reduce spending on conventional military forces. During his presidency, the size of the armed services fell by nearly half. But the number of American nuclear warheads rose from 1,000 in 1953 to 18,000 in 1960.

Massive retaliation ran the risk that any small conflict, or even a miscalculation, could escalate into a war that would destroy both the United States and the Soviet Union. Critics called the doctrine "brinksmanship," warning of the danger of Dulles's apparent willingness to bring the world to the brink of nuclear war. The reality that all-out war would result in "mutual assured destruction" (or MAD, in military shorthand) did succeed in making both great powers cautious in their direct dealings with one another. But it also inspired widespread fear of impending nuclear war. Government programs encouraging Americans to build bomb shelters in their backyards, and school drills that trained children to hide under their desks in the event of an atomic attack, aimed to convince Americans that nuclear war was survivable. But these measures only increased the atmosphere of fear.

IKE AND THE RUSSIANS

In his inaugural address, Eisenhower repeated the familiar Cold War formula: "Freedom is pitted against slavery; lightness against dark." But the

An advertisement for a government film explaining to children how to survive a nuclear attack by hiding under their desks. Thousands of schools instituted these "duck and cover" drills. They were meant to reduce Americans' fear of nuclear war.

Louis Severance and his son in their underground fallout shelter near Akron, Michigan. Manufacturers of such shelters assured purchasers that occupants could survive for five days after a nuclear war.

end of the Korean War and the death of Stalin, both of which occurred in 1953, convinced him that rather than being blind zealots, the Soviets were reasonable and could be dealt with in conventional diplomatic terms. In 1955, Ike met in Geneva, Switzerland, with Nikita Khrushchev, the new Soviet leader, at the first "summit" conference since Potsdam a decade earlier. The following year, Khrushchev delivered a speech to the Communist Party Congress in Moscow that detailed Stalin's crimes, including purges of political opponents numbering in the millions. The revelations created a crisis of belief among communists throughout the world. In the United States, three-quarters of the remaining Communist Party members abandoned the organization, realizing that they had been blind to the nature of Stalin's rule.

Khrushchev's call in the same 1956 speech for "peaceful coexistence" with the United States raised the possibility of an easing of the Cold War. The "thaw" was abruptly shaken that fall, however, when Soviet troops put down an anticommunist uprising in Hungary. Many conservative Republicans had urged eastern Europeans to resist communist rule, and Secretary of State Dulles himself had declared "liberation," rather than containment, to be the goal of American policy. But Eisenhower refused to extend aid to the Hungarian rebels, an indication that he believed it impossible to "roll back" Soviet domination of eastern Europe.

In 1958, the two superpowers agreed to a voluntary halt to the testing of nuclear weapons. The pause lasted until 1961. It had been demanded by the National Committee for a Sane Nuclear Policy, which publicized the danger to public health posed by radioactive fallout from nuclear tests. In 1959, Khrushchev toured the United States and had a friendly meeting with Eisenhower at Camp David. But the spirit of cooperation ended abruptly in 1960, when the Soviets shot down an American U-2 spy plane over their territory. Eisenhower first denied that the plane had been involved in espionage and refused to apologize even after the Russians produced the captured pilot. The incident torpedoed another planned summit meeting.

THE EMERGENCE OF THE THIRD WORLD

Even as Europe, where the Cold War began, settled into what appeared to be a permanent division between a communist East and a capitalist West, an intense rivalry, which sometimes took a military form, persisted in what came to be called the Third World. The term was invented to describe developing countries aligned with neither of the two Cold War powers and desirous of finding their own model of development between Soviet centralized economic planning and free market capitalism. The Bandung Conference, which brought leaders of twenty-nine Asian and African nations together in Indonesia in 1955, seemed to announce the emergence of a new force in global affairs, representing a majority of the world's population. But none of these countries could avoid being strongly affected by the political, military, and economic contest of the Cold War.

The post–World War II era witnessed the crumbling of European empires. The "winds of change," said British prime minister Harold Macmillan, were sweeping Africa and Asia. Decolonization began when India and Pakistan (the latter carved out of India to give Muslims their own nation) achieved independence in 1947. Ten years later, Britain's Gold Coast colony in West Africa emerged as the independent nation of Ghana. Other new nations—including Indonesia, Malaysia, Nigeria, Kenya, and Tanzania—soon followed. In 1975, Portugal, which five centuries earlier had created the first modern overseas empire, granted independence to its African colonies of Mozambique and Angola.

Mohammed Mossadegh, prime minister of Iran, views the Liberty Bell during his visit to the United States in 1951. The U.S.-sponsored coup that overthrew Mossadegh in 1953 created resentments that helped lead to Iran's Islamic Revolution twenty-five years later.

Decolonization presented the United States with a complex set of choices. It created power vacuums in the former colonies into which, Americans feared, communists would move. The Soviet Union strongly supported the dissolution of Europe's overseas empires, and communists participated in movements for colonial independence. Many noncommunist leaders, like Jawaharlal Nehru of India and Kwame Nkrumah of Ghana, saw socialism of one sort or another as the best route to achieving economic independence and narrowing the social inequalities fostered by imperialism. Most of the new Third World nations resisted alignment with either major power bloc, hoping to remain neutral in the Cold War. On the other hand, many nationalists sincerely admired the United States and, indeed, saw the American struggle for independence as a model for their own struggles. Ho Chi Minh, the communist leader of the Vietnamese movement against rule by France, modeled his 1945 proclamation of nationhood on the American Declaration of Independence. He even requested that President Truman establish a protectorate over Vietnam to guarantee its independence.

THE COLD WAR IN THE THIRD WORLD

By the end of the 1950s, the division of Europe appeared to be set in stone. Much of the focus of the Cold War shifted to the Third World. The policy of containment easily slid over into opposition to any government, whether communist or not, that seemed to threaten American strategic or economic interests. Jacobo Arbenz Guzmán in Guatemala and Mohammed Mossadegh in Iran were elected, homegrown nationalists, not agents of Moscow. But they were determined to reduce foreign corporations' control over their countries' economies. Arbenz embarked on a sweeping land-reform policy that threatened the domination of Guatemala's economy by the American-owned United Fruit Company. Mossadegh nationalized the Anglo-Iranian Oil Company, whose refinery in Iran was Britain's largest remaining overseas asset. Their foes quickly branded both as communists. In 1953 and 1954, the Central Intelligence Agency organized the ouster of both governments—a clear violation of the UN Charter, which barred a member state from taking military action against another except in self-defense.

In 1956, Israel, France, and Britain—without prior consultation with the United States—invaded Egypt after the country's nationalist leader, Gamal Abdel Nasser, nationalized the Suez Canal, jointly owned by Britain and France. A furious Eisenhower forced them to abandon the invasion. After the Suez fiasco, the United States moved to replace Britain as the dominant Western

The military junta installed in Guatemala by the CIA in 1954 enters Guatemala City in a Jeep driven by CIA agent Carlos Castillo Armas. Although hailed by the Eisenhower administration as a triumph for freedom, the new government suppressed democracy in Guatemala and embarked on a murderous campaign to stamp out opposition.

power in the Middle East, and American companies increasingly dominated the region's oil fields. In 1957, Eisenhower extended the principle of containment to the region, issuing the Eisenhower Doctrine, which pledged the United States to defend Middle Eastern governments threatened by communism or Arab nationalism. A year later, Ike dispatched 5,000 American troops to Lebanon to protect a government dominated by pro-Western Christians against Nasser's effort to bring all Arab states into a single regime under his rule.

ORIGINS OF THE VIETNAM WAR

In Vietnam, the expulsion of the Japanese in 1945 led not to independence but to a French military effort to preserve their Asian empire, which dated to the late nineteenth century, against Ho Chi Minh's nationalist forces. Anticommunism led the United States into deeper and deeper involvement. Following a policy initiated by Truman, the Eisenhower administration funneled billions of dollars in aid to bolster French efforts. By the early 1950s, the United States was paying four-fifths of the cost of the war. Wary of becoming bogged down in another land war in Asia immediately after Korea, however, Ike declined to send in American troops when France requested them to avert defeat in 1954. He also rejected the National Security Council's advice to use nuclear weapons, leaving France no alternative but to agree to Vietnamese independence.

A peace conference in Geneva divided Vietnam temporarily into northern and southern districts, with elections scheduled for 1956 to unify the country. But the staunchly anticommunist southern leader Ngo Dinh Diem, urged on by the United States, refused to hold elections, which would almost certainly have resulted in a victory for Ho Chi Minh's communists. Diem's close ties to wealthy Catholic families—in predominantly Buddhist South Vietnam—and to landlords in a society dominated by small farmers who had been promised land by Ho alienated an increasing number of his subjects. American aid poured into South Vietnam in order to bolster the Diem regime. By the time Eisenhower left office, Diem nevertheless faced a full-scale guerrilla revolt by the communist-led National Liberation Front.

Events in Guatemala, Iran, and Vietnam, considered great successes at the time by American policymakers, cast a long shadow over American foreign relations. Little by little, the United States was becoming accustomed to intervention, both open and secret, in far-flung corners of the world. Despite the Cold War rhetoric of freedom, American leaders seemed more comfortable dealing with reliable military regimes than democratic governments. A series of military governments succeeded Arbenz. They reversed his social reforms and inaugurated three decades of repression in which some 200,000 Guatemalans perished. The shah of Iran replaced Mossadegh and agreed to give British and American oil companies 40 percent of his nation's oil revenues. He remained in office until 1979 as one of the world's most tyrannical rulers, until his overthrow in a revolution led by the fiercely anti-American radical Islamist Ayatollah Khomeini. In Vietnam, the American decision to prop up Diem's regime laid the groundwork for what would soon become the most disastrous military involvement in American history.

Save the Holy Places, *a 1948 cartoon by Herbert Block, suggests that American diplomacy in the Middle East was primarily concerned with access to oil.*

Commuters returning from work in downtown Chicago, leaving the railroad station at suburban Park Forest, Illinois, in 1953. Social critics of the 1950s claimed that Americans had become "organization men," too conformist to lead independent lives.

MASS SOCIETY AND ITS CRITICS

The fatherly Eisenhower seemed the perfect leader for the placid society of the 1950s. Consensus was the dominant ideal in an era in which McCarthyism had defined criticism of the social and economic order as disloyalty and most Americans located the enjoyment of freedom in private pleasures rather than the public sphere. With the mainstreams of both parties embracing the Cold War, political debate took place within extremely narrow limits. Even *Life* magazine commented that American freedom might be in greater danger from "disuse" than from communist subversion.

Dissenting voices could be heard. Some intellectuals wondered whether the celebration of affluence and the either-or mentality of the Cold War obscured the extent to which the United States itself fell short of the ideal of freedom. In 1957, political scientist Hans J. Morgenthau noted that free enterprise had created "new accumulations" of power, "as dangerous to the freedom of the individual as the power of the government had ever been." More radical in pointing to the problem of unequal power in American society, the sociologist C. Wright Mills challenged the self-satisfied vision of democratic pluralism that dominated mainstream social science in the 1950s. Mills wrote of a "power elite"—an interlocking directorate of corporate leaders, politicians, and military men whose domination of government and society had made political democracy obsolete. Freedom, Mills insisted, meant more than "the chance to do as one pleases." It rested on the ability "to formulate the available choices," and this most Americans were effectively denied.

Even as the government and media portrayed the United States as a beacon of liberty locked in a titanic struggle with its opposite, one strand of social analysis in the 1950s contended that Americans did not enjoy genuine freedom. These critics identified as the culprit not the unequal structure of power criticized by Mills, but the modern age itself, with its psychological and cultural discontents. Modern mass society, some writers worried, inevitably produced loneliness and anxiety, causing mankind to yearn for stability and authority, not freedom. In *The Lonely Crowd* (1950), the decade's most influential work of social analysis, the sociologist David Riesman described Americans as "other-directed" conformists who lacked the inner resources to lead truly independent lives. Other social critics charged that corporate bureaucracies had transformed employees into "organization men" incapable of independent thought.

Some commentators feared that the Russians had demonstrated a greater ability to sacrifice for common public goals than Americans. What kind of nation, the economist John Kenneth Galbraith asked in *The Affluent Society* (1958), neglected investment in schools, parks, and public services, while producing ever more goods to fulfill desires created by advertising? Was the spectacle of millions of educated middle-class women seeking happiness in suburban dream houses a reason for celebration or a waste of precious "woman power" at a time when the Soviets trumpeted the accomplishments of their female scientists, physicians, and engineers? Books like Galbraith's, along with William Whyte's *The Organization Man* (1956) and Vance Packard's *The Hidden Persuaders* (1957), which criticized the monotony of modern work, the emptiness of suburban life, and the pervasive influence of advertising, created the vocabulary for an assault on the nation's social values that lay just over the horizon. In the 1950s, however, while criticism of mass society became a minor industry among intellectuals, it failed to dent widespread complacency about the American way.

REBELS WITHOUT A CAUSE

The social critics did not offer a political alternative or have any real impact on the parties or government. Nor did other stirrings of dissent. With teenagers a growing part of the population thanks to the baby boom, the emergence of a popular culture geared to the emerging youth market suggested that significant generational tensions lay beneath the bland surface of 1950s life. J. D. Salinger's 1951 novel *Catcher in the Rye* and the 1955 films *Blackboard Jungle* and *Rebel without a Cause* (the latter starring James Dean as an aimlessly rebellious youth) highlighted the alienation of at least some young people from the world of adult respectability. These works helped to spur a mid-1950s panic about "juvenile delinquency." *Time* magazine devoted a cover story to "Teenagers on the Rampage," and a Senate committee held hearings in 1954 on whether violent comic books caused criminal behavior among young people. (One witness even criticized Superman comics for arousing violent emotions among its readers.) To head off federal regulation, publishers—like movie producers in the 1920s—adopted a code of conduct for their industry that strictly limited the portrayal of crime and violence in comic books.

Elvis Presley's gyrating hips appealed to teenagers but alarmed many adults during the 1950s.

Cultural life during the 1950s seemed far more daring than politics. Indeed, many adults found the emergence of a mass-marketed teenage culture that rejected middle-class norms more alarming than the actual increase in juvenile arrests. Teenagers wore leather jackets and danced to rock-and-roll music that brought the hard-driving rhythms and sexually provocative movements of black musicians and dancers to enthusiastic young white audiences. They made Elvis Presley, a rock-and-roll singer with an openly sexual performance style, an immensely popular entertainment celebrity.

Challenges of various kinds also arose to the family-centered image of personal fulfillment. *Playboy* magazine, which began publication in 1953, reached a circulation of more than 1 million copies per month by 1960. It extended the consumer culture into the most intimate realms of life, offering men a fantasy world of sexual gratification outside the family's confines. Although considered sick or deviant by the larger society and subject to constant police harassment, gay men and lesbians created their own subcultures in major cities.

Rebels without a cause. Teenage members of a youth gang, photographed at Coney Island, Brooklyn, in the late 1950s.

THE BEATS

In New York City and San Francisco, as well as college towns like Madison, Wisconsin, and Ann Arbor, Michigan, the Beats, a small group of poets and writers, railed against mainstream culture. The novelist Jack Kerouac coined the term "beat"—a play on

FROM The Southern Manifesto (1956)

Drawn up early in 1956 and signed by 101 southern members of the Senate and House of Representatives, the Southern Manifesto repudiated the Supreme Court decision in *Brown v. Board of Education* and offered support to the campaign of resistance in the South.

The unwarranted decision of the Supreme Court in the public school cases is now bearing the fruit always produced when men substitute naked power for established law. . . .

We regard the decisions of the Supreme Court in the school cases as a clear abuse of judicial power. It climaxes a trend in the Federal Judiciary undertaking to legislate, in derogation [violation] of the authority of Congress, and to encroach upon the reserved rights of the States and the people.

The original Constitution does not mention education. Neither does the 14th Amendment nor any other amendment. The debates preceding the submission of the 14th Amendment clearly show that there was no intent that it should affect the system of education maintained by the States.

In the case of *Plessy v. Ferguson* in 1896 the Supreme Court expressly declared that under the 14th Amendment no person was denied any of his rights if the States provided separate but equal facilities. This decision . . . restated time and again, became a part of the life of the people of many of the States and confirmed their habits, traditions, and way of life. It is founded on elemental humanity and commonsense, for parents should not be deprived by Government of the right to direct the lives and education of their own children.

Though there has been no constitutional amendment or act of Congress changing this established legal principle almost a century old, the Supreme Court of the United States, with no legal basis for such action, undertook to exercise their naked judicial power and substituted their personal political and social ideas for the established law of the land.

This unwarranted exercise of power by the Court, contrary to the Constitution, is creating chaos and confusion in the States principally affected. It is destroying the amicable relations between the white and Negro races that have been created through 90 years of patient effort by the good people of both races. It has planted hatred and suspicion where there has been heretofore friendship and understanding.

With the gravest concern for the explosive and dangerous condition created by this decision and inflamed by outside meddlers: . . . we commend the motives of those States which have declared the intention to resist forced integration by any lawful means. . . .

FROM MARTIN LUTHER KING JR.,
Speech at Montgomery, Alabama (December 5, 1955)

On the evening of Rosa Parks's arrest for refusing to give up her seat on a Montgomery bus to a white passenger, a mass rally of local African-Americans decided to boycott city buses in protest. In his speech to the gathering, the young Baptist minister Martin Luther King Jr. invoked Christian and American ideals of justice and democracy—themes he would strike again and again during his career as the leading national symbol of the civil rights struggle.

We are here this evening . . . because first and foremost we are American citizens, and we are determined to apply our citizenship to the fullness of its means. We are here also because of our love for democracy. . . . Just the other day . . . one of the finest citizens in Montgomery—not one of the finest Negro citizens but one of the finest citizens in Montgomery—was taken from a bus and carried to jail and arrested because she refused to give her seat to a white person. . . .

Mrs. Rosa Parks is a fine person. And since it had to happen I'm happy that it happened to a person like Mrs. Parks, for nobody can doubt the boundless outreach of her integrity! Nobody can doubt the height of her character, nobody can doubt that depth of her Christian commitment and devotion to the teachings of Jesus. And I'm happy since it had to happen, it happened to a person that nobody can call a disturbing factor in the community. Mrs. Parks is a fine Christian person, unassuming, and yet there is integrity and character there. And just because she refused to get up, she was arrested.

I want to say, that we are not here advocating violence. We have never done that. . . . We believe in the teachings of Jesus. The only weapon that we have in our hands this evening is the weapon of protest. . . . There will be no white persons pulled out of their homes and taken out to some distant road and lynched. . . .

We are not wrong in what we are doing. If we are wrong, then the Supreme Court of this nation is wrong. If we are wrong, the Constitution of the United States is wrong. If we are wrong, God Almighty is wrong. . . . If we are wrong, justice is a lie. . . .

We, the disinherited of this land, we who have been oppressed so long, are tired of going through the long night of captivity. And now we are reaching out for the daybreak of freedom and justice and equality. . . . Right here in Montgomery when the history books are written in the future, somebody will have to say, "There lived a race of people, a *black* people, . . . a people who had the moral courage to stand up for their rights. And thereby they injected a new meaning into the veins of history and of civilization."

QUESTIONS

1. Why does the Southern Manifesto claim that the Supreme Court decision is a threat to constitutional government?

2. How do religious convictions shape King's definition of freedom?

3. How do these documents illustrate contrasting understandings of freedom in the wake of the civil rights movement?

A Beat coffeehouse in San Francisco, photographed in 1958, where poets, artists, and others who rejected 1950s mainstream culture gathered.

"beaten down" and "beatified" (or saintlike). His *On the Road*, written in the early 1950s but not published until 1957, recounted in a seemingly spontaneous rush of sights, sounds, and images its main character's aimless wanderings across the American landscape. The book became a bible for a generation of young people who rejected the era's middle-class culture but had little to put in its place.

"I saw the best minds of my generation destroyed by madness, starving hysterical naked," wrote the Beat poet Allen Ginsberg in *Howl* (1955), a brilliant protest against materialism and conformism written while the author was under the influence of hallucinogenic drugs. Ginsberg became nationally known when San Francisco police in 1956 confiscated his book and arrested bookstore owners for selling an obscene work. (A judge later overturned the ban on the grounds that *Howl* possessed redeeming social value.) Rejecting the work ethic, the "desperate materialism" of the suburban middle class, and the militarization of American life by the Cold War, the Beats celebrated impulsive action, immediate pleasure (often enhanced by drugs), and sexual experimentation. Despite Cold War slogans, they insisted, personal and political repression, not freedom, were the hallmarks of American society.

THE FREEDOM MOVEMENT

Not until the 1960s would young white rebels find their cause, as the seeds of dissent planted by the social critics and Beats flowered in an outpouring of political activism, new attitudes toward sexuality, and a full-fledged generational rebellion. A more immediate challenge to the complacency of the 1950s arose from the twentieth century's greatest citizens' movement—the black struggle for equality.

ORIGINS OF THE MOVEMENT

Today, with the birthday of Martin Luther King Jr. a national holiday and the struggles of Montgomery, Little Rock, Birmingham, and Selma celebrated as heroic episodes in the history of freedom, it is easy to forget that at the time, the civil rights revolution came as a great surprise. Looking back, its causes seem clear: the destabilization of the racial system during World War II; the mass migration out of the segregated South that made black voters an increasingly important part of the Democratic Party coalition; and the Cold War and rise of independent states in the Third World, both of which made the gap between America's rhetoric and its racial reality an international embarrassment. Yet few predicted the emergence of the southern mass movement for civil rights.

In *An American Dilemma* (1944), Gunnar Myrdal had suggested that the challenge to racial inequality would arise in the North, where blacks had far greater opportunities for political organization than in the South. With blacks' traditional allies on the left decimated by McCarthyism, most union leaders unwilling to challenge racial inequalities within their own ranks, and the NAACP concentrating on court battles, new constituencies and new tactics were sorely needed. The movement found in the southern black church the organizing power for a militant, nonviolent assault on segregation.

The United States in the 1950s was still a segregated, unequal society. Half of the nation's black families lived in poverty. Because of labor contracts that linked promotions and firings to seniority, non-white workers, who had joined the industrial labor force later than whites, lost their jobs first in times of economic downturn. In the South, evidence of Jim Crow abounded—in separate public institutions and the signs "white" and "colored" at entrances to buildings, train carriages, drinking fountains, restrooms, and the like. In the North and West, the law did not require segregation, but custom barred blacks from many colleges, hotels, and restaurants, and from most suburban housing. Las Vegas, Nevada, for example, was as strictly segregated as any southern city. Hotels and casinos did not admit blacks except in the most menial jobs. Lena Horne, Sammy Davis Jr., Louis Armstrong, and other black entertainers played the hotel-casinos on the "strip" but could not stay as guests where they performed.

In 1950, seventeen southern and border states and Washington, D.C., had laws requiring the racial segregation of public schools, and several others permitted local districts to impose it. Around 40 percent of the nation's 28 million schoolchildren studied in legally segregated schools, and millions more attended classes in northern communities where housing patterns and school district lines created de facto segregation—separation in fact if not in law. Few white Americans felt any urgency about confronting racial inequality. "Segregation," the white writer John Egerton later recalled, "didn't restrict me in any way, so it was easy to accept things the way they were, to take my freedom for granted and not worry about anyone else's."

THE LEGAL ASSAULT ON SEGREGATION

With Truman's civil rights initiative having faded and the Eisenhower administration being reluctant to address the issue, it fell to the courts to confront the problem of racial segregation. In the Southwest, the League of United

A segregated school in West Memphis, Arkansas, photographed for Life *magazine in 1949. Education in the South was separate but hardly equal.*

Latin American Citizens (LULAC), the equivalent of the NAACP, challenged restrictive housing, employment discrimination, and the segregation of Latino students. They won an important victory in 1946 in the case of *Mendez v. Westminster*, when the California Supreme Court ordered the schools of Orange County desegregated. In response, the state legislature repealed all school laws requiring racial segregation. The governor who signed the measure, Earl Warren, had presided over the internment of Japanese-Americans during World War II as the state's attorney general. After the war, he became convinced that racial inequality had no place in American life. When Chief Justice Fred Vinson died in 1953, Eisenhower appointed Earl Warren to replace him. Warren would play the key role in deciding *Brown v. Board of Education*, the momentous case that outlawed school segregation.

For years, the NAACP, under the leadership of attorney Thurgood Marshall, had pressed legal challenges to the "separate but equal" doctrine laid down by the Court in 1896 in *Plessy v. Ferguson* (see Chapter 17). At first, the NAACP sought to gain admission to white institutions of higher learning for which no black equivalent existed. In 1938, the Supreme Court ordered the University of Missouri Law School to admit Lloyd Gaines, a black student, because the state had no such school for blacks. Missouri responded by setting up a segregated law school, satisfying the courts. But in 1950, the Supreme Court unanimously ordered Heman Sweatt admitted to the University of Texas Law School even though the state had established a "school" for him in a basement containing three classrooms and no library. There was no way, the Court declared, that this hastily constructed law school could be "equal" to the prestigious all-white institution.

THE *BROWN* CASE

Marshall now launched a frontal assault on segregation itself. He brought the NAACP's support to local cases that had arisen when black parents challenged unfair school policies. To do so required remarkable courage. In Clarendon County, South Carolina, Levi Pearson, a black farmer who brought a lawsuit on behalf of his children, saw his house burned to the ground. The Clarendon case attacked not segregation itself but the unequal funding of schools. The local school board spent $179 per white child and $43 per black, and unlike white pupils, black children attended class in buildings with no running water or indoor toilets and were not provided with buses to transport them to classes. Five such cases from four states and the District of Columbia were combined in a single appeal that reached the Supreme Court late in 1952.

When cases are united, they are listed alphabetically and the first case gives the entire decision its name. In this instance, the first case arose from a state outside the old Confederacy. Oliver Brown went to court because his daughter, a third grader, was forced to walk across dangerous railroad tracks each morning rather than being allowed to attend a nearby school restricted to whites. His lawsuit became *Brown v. Board of Education of Topeka, Kansas.*

Thurgood Marshall decided that the time had come to attack not the unfair applications of the "separate but equal" principle but the doctrine itself. Even with the same funding and facilities, he insisted, segregation was inherently unequal since it stigmatized one group of citizens as unfit to associate with others. Drawing on studies by New York psychologists Kenneth and Mamie Clark, Marshall argued that segregation did lifelong damage to black children, undermining their self-esteem. In its legal brief, the Eisenhower administration did not directly support Marshall's position, but it urged the justices to consider "the problem of racial discrimination . . . in the context of the present world struggle between freedom and tyranny." Other peoples, it noted, "cannot understand how such a practice can exist in a country which professes to be a staunch supporter of freedom, justice, and democracy."

The new chief justice, Earl Warren, managed to create unanimity on a divided Court, some of whose members disliked segregation but feared that a decision to outlaw it would spark widespread violence. On May 17, 1954, Warren himself read aloud the decision, only eleven pages long. Segregation in public education, he concluded, violated the equal protection of the laws guaranteed by the Fourteenth Amendment. "In the field of education, the doctrine of 'separate but equal' has no place. Separate educational facilities are inherently unequal."

The black press hailed the *Brown* decision as a "second Emancipation Proclamation." And like its predecessor it was in many ways a limited document. The decision did not address segregation in institutions other than public schools or ban all racial classifications in the law, such as statutes prohibiting interracial marriage. It did not address the de facto school segregation of the North, which rested on housing patterns rather than state law. It did not order immediate implementation but instead called for hearings as to how segregated schooling should be dismantled. But *Brown* marked the emergence of the "Warren Court" as an active agent of social change. And it inspired a wave of optimism that discrimination would soon disappear. "What a wonderful world of possibilities are unfolded for the children," wrote the black novelist Ralph Ellison.

THE MONTGOMERY BUS BOYCOTT

Brown did not cause the modern civil rights movement, which, as noted in the previous two chapters, began during World War II and continued in

The mug shot of Rosa Parks, taken in December 1955 at a Montgomery, Alabama, police station after she was arrested for refusing to give up her seat on a city bus to a white passenger.

cities like New York after the war. But the decision did ensure that when the movement resumed after waning in the early 1950s, it would have the backing of the federal courts. Mass action against Jim Crow soon reappeared. On December 1, 1955, Rosa Parks, a black tailor's assistant who had just completed her day's work in a Montgomery, Alabama, department store, refused to surrender her seat on a city bus to a white rider, as required by local law. Parks's arrest sparked a year-long bus boycott, the beginning of the mass phase of the civil rights movement in the South. Within a decade, the civil rights revolution had overturned the structure of legal segregation and regained the right to vote for black southerners. In 2000, *Time* magazine named Rosa Parks one of the 100 most significant persons of the twentieth century.

Parks is widely remembered today as a "seamstress with tired feet," a symbol of ordinary blacks' determination to resist the daily injustices and indignities of the Jim Crow South. In fact, her life makes clear that the civil rights revolution built on earlier struggles. Parks was a veteran of black politics. During the 1930s, she took part in meetings protesting the conviction of the Scottsboro Boys. She served for many years as secretary to E. D. Nixon, the local leader of the NAACP. In 1943, she tried to register to vote, only to be turned away because she supposedly failed a literacy test. After two more attempts, Parks succeeded in becoming one of the few blacks in Montgomery able to cast a ballot. In 1954, she attended a training session for political activists at the Highlander School in Tennessee, a meeting ground for labor and civil rights radicals.

No one knows exactly why Parks decided not to give up her seat that day. Perhaps it was because an all-white jury in Mississippi had just acquitted the murderers of Emmett Till, a black teenager who had allegedly whistled at a white woman. Jo Ann Robinson, a professor at the all-black Alabama State University, had been calling for a boycott of public transportation since 1954. When news of Parks's arrest spread, hundreds of blacks gathered in a local church and vowed to refuse to ride the buses until accorded equal treatment. For 381 days, despite legal harassment and occasional violence, black maids, janitors, teachers, and students walked to their destinations or rode an informal network of taxis. Finally, in November 1956, the Supreme Court ruled segregation in public transportation unconstitutional. The boycott ended in triumph.

THE DAYBREAK OF FREEDOM

The Montgomery bus boycott marked a turning point in postwar American history. It launched the movement for racial justice as a nonviolent crusade based in the black churches of the South. It gained the support of northern liberals and focused unprecedented and unwelcome international attention on the country's racial policies. And it marked the emergence of twenty-six-year-old Martin Luther King Jr., who had recently arrived in Montgomery to become pastor of a Baptist church, as the movement's national symbol. On the night of the first protest meeting, King's call to action electrified the audience: "We, the disinherited of this land, we who have been oppressed so long, are tired of going through the long night of captivity. And now we are reaching out for the daybreak of freedom and justice and equality."

From the beginning, the language of freedom pervaded the black movement. It resonated in the speeches of civil rights leaders and in the hand-lettered placards of the struggle's foot soldiers. On the day of Rosa Parks's court appearance in December 1955, even before the bus boycott had officially been announced, a torn piece of cardboard appeared on a bus shelter in Montgomery's Court Square, advising passengers: "Don't ride the buses today. Don't ride it for freedom." During the summer of 1964, when civil rights activists established "freedom schools" for black children across Mississippi, lessons began with students being asked to define the word. Some gave specific answers ("going to public libraries"), some more abstract ("standing up for your rights"). Some insisted that freedom meant legal equality, others saw it as liberation from years of deference to and fear of whites. "Freedom of the mind," wrote one, was the greatest freedom of all.

For adults as well, freedom had many meanings. It meant enjoying the political rights and economic opportunities taken for granted by whites. It required eradicating historic wrongs such as segregation, disenfranchisement, confinement to low-wage jobs, and the ever-present threat of violence. It meant the right to be served at lunch counters and downtown department stores, central locations in the consumer culture, and to be addressed as "Mr.," "Miss," and "Mrs.," rather than "boy" and "auntie."

THE LEADERSHIP OF KING

In King's soaring oratory, the protesters' understandings of freedom fused into a coherent whole. For the title of his first book, relating the boycott's history, King chose the title *Stride Toward Freedom.* His most celebrated oration, the "I Have a Dream" speech of 1963, began by invoking the unfulfilled promise of emancipation ("one hundred years later, the Negro still is not free") and closed with a cry borrowed from a black spiritual: "Free at last! Free at last! Thank God Almighty, we are free at last!"

A master at appealing to the deep sense of injustice among blacks and to the conscience of white America, King presented the case for black rights in a vocabulary that merged the black experience with that of the nation. Having studied the writings on peaceful civil disobedience of Henry David Thoreau and Mohandas (Mahatma) Gandhi, as well as the nonviolent protests the Congress of Racial Equality had organized in the 1940s, King outlined a philosophy of struggle in which evil must be met with good, hate with Christian love, and violence with peaceful demands for change. "There will be no white persons pulled out of their homes and taken out to some distant road and lynched," he declared in his speech at the launching of the Montgomery bus boycott.

Echoing Christian themes derived from his training in the black church, King's speeches resonated deeply in both black communities and the broader culture. He repeatedly invoked the Bible to preach justice and forgiveness, even toward those "who desire to deprive you of freedom." Like Frederick Douglass before him, King appealed to white America by stressing the protesters' love of country and devotion to national values. The "daybreak of freedom," King made clear, meant a new dawn for the whole of American society. And like W. E. B. Du Bois, he linked the American "color line" with the degradation of non-white peoples overseas. "The great

Black residents of Montgomery, Alabama, walking to work during the bus boycott of 1955–1956.

struggle of the Twentieth Century," he declared in a 1956 sermon, "has been between the exploited masses questing for freedom and the colonial powers seeking to maintain their domination." If Africa was gaining its freedom, he asked, why must black America lag behind?

MASSIVE RESISTANCE

Buoyed by success in Montgomery, King in 1956 took the lead in forming the Southern Christian Leadership Conference, a coalition of black ministers and civil rights activists, to press for desegregation. But despite the movement's success in popular mobilization, the fact that Montgomery's city fathers agreed to the boycott's demands only after a Supreme Court ruling indicated that without national backing, local action might not be enough to overturn Jim Crow. The white South's refusal to accept the *Brown* decision reinforced the conviction that black citizens could not gain their constitutional rights without Washington's intervention. This was not immediately forthcoming. When the Supreme Court finally issued its implementation ruling in 1955, the justices declared that desegregation should proceed "with all deliberate speed." This vague formulation unintentionally encouraged a campaign of "massive resistance" that paralyzed civil rights progress in much of the South.

In 1956, 82 of 106 southern congressmen—and every southern senator except Lyndon B. Johnson of Texas and Albert Gore and Estes Kefauver of Tennessee—signed a Southern Manifesto, denouncing the *Brown* decision as a "clear abuse of judicial power," and calling for resistance to "forced integration" by "any lawful means." State after state passed laws to block desegregation. Some made it illegal for the NAACP to operate within their borders. Virginia pioneered the strategy of closing any public schools

If the civil rights movement borrowed the language of freedom, Cold War opponents of racial integration seized on the language of anticommunism to discredit the movement. This photograph is from a 1959 rally in Little Rock, Arkansas.

VISIONS OF FREEDOM

The Problem We All Live With. *This 1964 painting by Norman Rockwell, which accompanied an article in* Look *magazine, depicts federal marshals escorting six-year-old Ruby Bridges to kindergarten in New Orleans in 1960 in accordance with a court order to integrate the city's schools. "There was a large crowd of people outside the school," she later recalled. "They were throwing things and shouting." But Rockwell, intent on focusing on the child, presents the mob only through their graffiti and tomatoes thrown against the wall, and does not show the faces of the marshals. Because of the decision to send her to the formerly white school, Bridges's father lost his job, and her grandparents, who worked as sharecroppers in Mississippi, were evicted from their land. In 2001, President Bill Clinton presented her with the Presidential Citizens Medal.*

QUESTION

1. What does the painting suggest about the relationship of federal power and individual freedom?

2. Do you think that Rockwell's decision to show the mob only indirectly makes the painting more or less powerful?

ordered to desegregate and offering funds to enable white pupils, but not black, to attend private institutions. Prince Edward County, Virginia, shut its schools entirely in 1959; not until 1964 did the Supreme Court order them reopened. Many states adopted "freedom of choice" plans that allowed white students to opt out of integrated schools. As a symbol of defiance, Georgia's legislature incorporated the Confederate battle flag into its state flag in 1956, and Alabama and South Carolina soon began flying the battle flag over their state capitol buildings.

EISENHOWER AND CIVIL RIGHTS

The federal government tried to remain aloof from the black struggle. Thanks to the efforts of Senate majority leader Lyndon B. Johnson, who hoped to win liberal support for a run for president in 1960, Congress in 1957 passed the first national civil rights law since Reconstruction. It targeted the denial of black voting rights in the South, but with weak enforcement provisions it added few voters to the rolls. President Eisenhower failed to provide moral leadership. He called for Americans to abide by the law, but he made it clear that he found the whole civil rights issue distasteful. He privately told aides that he disagreed with the Supreme Court's reasoning. Ike failed to act in 1956 when a federal court ordered that Autherine Lucy be admitted to the University of Alabama; a mob prevented her from registering and the board of trustees expelled her. The university remained all-white into the 1960s.

In 1957, however, after Governor Orval Faubus of Arkansas used the National Guard to prevent the court-ordered integration of Little Rock's Central High School, Eisenhower dispatched federal troops to the city. In the face of a howling mob, soldiers of the 101st Airborne Division escorted

Federal troops at Little Rock's Central High School, enforcing a court order for integration in 1957.

nine black children into the school. Events in Little Rock showed that in the last instance, the federal government would not allow the flagrant violation of court orders. But because of massive resistance, the pace of the movement slowed in the final years of the 1950s. When Eisenhower left office, fewer than 2 percent of black students attended desegregated schools in the states of the old Confederacy.

THE WORLD VIEWS THE UNITED STATES

Ever since the beginning of the Cold War, American leaders had worried about the impact of segregation on the country's international reputation. President Truman had promoted his civil rights initiative, in part, by reminding Americans that they could not afford to "ignore what the world thinks of our record." The State Department filed a brief in the *Brown* case noting the damage segregation was doing to the country's image overseas.

Foreign nations and colonies paid close attention to the unfolding of the American civil rights movement. The global reaction to the *Brown* decision was overwhelmingly positive. "At Last! Whites and Blacks in the United States on the same school benches!" proclaimed a newspaper in Senegal, West Africa. But the slow pace of change led to criticism that embarrassed American diplomats seeking to win the loyalty of people in the non-white world. In a public forum in India, the American ambassador was peppered with questions about American race relations. Was it true that the Haitian ambassador to the United States had to live in a black ghetto in Washington? Why did no black person hold a high public office? Of course, the Soviet Union played up American race relations as part of the global "battle for hearts and minds of men" that was a key part of the Cold War.

THE ELECTION OF 1960

KENNEDY AND NIXON

The presidential campaign of 1960 turned out to be one of the closest in American history. Republicans chose Vice President Richard Nixon as their candidate to succeed Eisenhower. Democrats nominated John F. Kennedy, a senator from Massachusetts and a Roman Catholic, whose father, a millionaire Irish-American businessman, had served as ambassador to Great Britain during the 1930s. Kennedy's chief rivals for the nomination were Hubert Humphrey, leader of the party's liberal wing, and Lyndon B. Johnson of Texas, the Senate majority leader, who accepted Kennedy's offer to run for vice president.

The atmosphere of tolerance promoted by World War II had weakened traditional anti-Catholicism. But as recently as 1949, Paul Blanshard's *American Freedom and Catholic Power*, which accused the Church of being antidemocratic, morally repressive, and essentially un-American, had become a national best-seller. Many Protestants remained reluctant to vote for a Catholic, fearing that Kennedy would be required to support Church doctrine on controversial public issues or, in a more extreme version, take orders from the pope. Kennedy addressed the question directly. "I do not speak for my church on public matters," he insisted, and "the church does

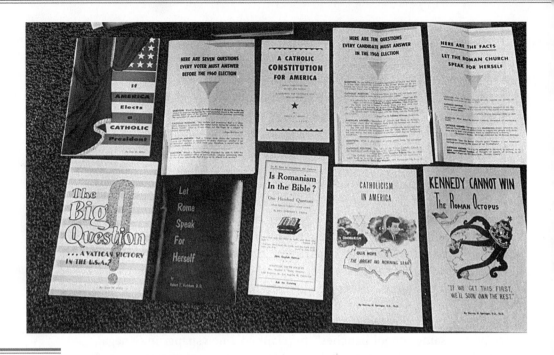

The 1960 presidential campaign produced a flood of anti-Catholic propaganda. Kennedy's victory, the first for an American Catholic, was a major step in the decline of this long-standing prejudice.

not speak for me." His defeat of Humphrey in the Democratic primary in overwhelmingly Protestant West Virginia put the issue of his religion to rest. At age forty-three, Kennedy became the youngest major-party nominee for president in the nation's history.

Both Kennedy and Nixon were ardent Cold Warriors. But Kennedy pointed to Soviet success in putting *Sputnik,* the first earth satellite, into orbit and subsequently testing the first intercontinental ballistic missile (ICBM) as evidence that the United States had lost the sense of national purpose necessary to fight the Cold War. He warned that Republicans had allowed a "missile gap" to develop in which the Soviets had achieved technological and military superiority over the United States. In fact, as both Kennedy and Nixon well knew, American economic and military capacity far exceeded that of the Soviets. But the charge persuaded many Americans that the time had come for new leadership. The stylishness of Kennedy's wife, Jacqueline, which stood in sharp contrast to the more dowdy public appearance of Mamie Eisenhower and Pat Nixon, reinforced the impression that Kennedy would conduct a more youthful, vigorous presidency.

In the first televised debate between presidential candidates, judging by viewer response, the handsome Kennedy bested Nixon, who was suffering from a cold and appeared tired and nervous. Those who heard the encounter on the radio thought Nixon had won, but, on TV, image counted for more than substance. In November, Kennedy eked out a narrow victory, winning the popular vote by only 120,000 out of 69 million votes cast (and, Republicans charged, benefiting from a fraudulent vote count by the notoriously corrupt Chicago Democratic machine).

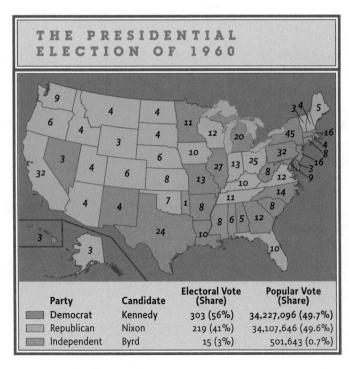

THE PRESIDENTIAL ELECTION OF 1960

Party	Candidate	Electoral Vote (Share)	Popular Vote (Share)
Democrat	Kennedy	303 (56%)	34,227,096 (49.7%)
Republican	Nixon	219 (41%)	34,107,646 (49.6%)
Independent	Byrd	15 (3%)	501,643 (0.7%)

THE END OF THE 1950S

In January 1961, shortly before leaving office, Eisenhower delivered a televised Farewell Address, modeled to some extent on George Washington's address of 1796. Knowing that the missile gap was a myth, Ike warned against the drumbeat of calls for a new military buildup. He urged Americans to think about the dangerous power of what he called the "military-industrial complex"—the conjunction of "an immense military establishment" with a "permanent arms industry"—with an influence felt in "every office" in the land. "We must never let the weight of this combination," he advised his countrymen, "endanger our liberties or democratic processes." Few Americans shared Ike's concern—far more saw the alliance of the Defense Department and private industry as a source of jobs and national security rather than a threat to democracy. A few years later, however, with the United States locked in an increasingly unpopular war, Eisenhower's warning would come to seem prophetic.

By then, other underpinnings of 1950s life were also in disarray. The tens of millions of cars that made suburban life possible were spewing toxic lead, an additive to make gasoline more efficient, into the atmosphere. Penned in to the east by mountains that kept automobile emissions from being dispersed by the wind, Los Angeles had become synonymous with smog, a type of air pollution produced by cars. Chlorofluorocarbons, used in air conditioners, deodorants, and aerosol hair sprays, were releasing chemicals into the atmosphere that damaged the ozone layer, producing global warming and an increase in skin cancer. (Both leaded gasoline and chlorofluorocarbons had been invented by General Motors research scientist Thomas Midgley. He "had more impact on the atmosphere," writes one historian, "than any other single organism" in the history of the world.) The chemical insecticides that enabled agricultural conglomerates to produce the country's remarkable abundance of food were poisoning farm workers,

A photograph of John F. Kennedy and his wife, Jacqueline, strolling along the pier at Hyannisport, Massachusetts, illustrates their youthful appeal.

Residents of Los Angeles don gas masks at a 1954 luncheon to protest the government's failure to combat the air pollution, or "smog," that hung over the city.

Andy Warhol's 1962 painting Green Coca-Color Bottles *uses one of the most famous international symbols of American consumerism both to celebrate abundance and to question the sterile uniformity of 1950s consumer culture. Asked why he painted Coke bottles, he replied that artists paint what they see. Previous artists painted landscapes and city buildings; he painted things present in American life wherever one looked.*

consumers, and the water supply. Housewives were rebelling against a life centered in suburban dream houses. Blacks were increasingly impatient with the slow progress of racial change. The United States, in other words, had entered that most turbulent of decades, the 1960s.

SUGGESTED READING

BOOKS

Belgrad, Daniel. *The Culture of Spontaneity: Improvisation and the Arts in Postwar America* (1998). Explores how developments in the arts reflected and encouraged the idea of the free individual.

Branch, Taylor. *Parting the Waters: America in the King Years, 1954–1963* (1988). A comprehensive account of the civil rights movement from the *Brown* decision to the early 1960s.

Cohen, Lizabeth. *A Consumer's Republic: The Politics of Mass Consumption in Postwar America* (2003). Considers how the glorification of consumer freedom shaped American public policy and the physical landscape.

De Grazia, Victoria. *Irresistible Empire: America's Advance through Twentieth-Century Europe* (2005). An examination of American "soft power" and its triumphant penetration of twentieth-century Europe.

Fones-Wolf, Elizabeth A. *Selling Free Enterprise: The Business Assault on Labor and Liberalism, 1945–1960* (1994). Examines the carefully developed campaign whereby business leaders associated capitalism and a union-free workplace with freedom.

Freeman, Joshua B. *Working-Class New York: Life and Labor since World War II* (2000). An account of the lives of laborers in the nation's largest city, tracing the rise and decline of the labor movement.

Hirsch, Arnold R. *Making the Second Ghetto: Race and Housing in Chicago, 1940–1960* (1983). Describes how the migration of African-Americans from the South to Chicago during the 1940s and 1950s reshaped the city.

Jackson, Kenneth T. *Crabgrass Frontier: The Suburbanization of America* (1985). The standard account of the development of American suburbia.

Jacobs, Meg. *Pocketbook Politics: Economic Citizenship in Twentieth-Century America* (2005). Discusses how consumer freedom became central to Americans' national identity after World War II.

Klarman, Michael J. *From Jim Crow to Civil Rights: The Supreme Court and the Struggle for Racial Equality* (2004). A full study of Supreme Court cases dealing with civil rights, and how they both reflected and helped to stimulate social change.

May, Elaine T. *Homeward Bound: American Families in the Cold War Era* (1988). Studies the nuclear family as a bastion of American freedom during the Cold War, at least according to official propaganda.

Nicolaides, Becky M. *My Blue Heaven: Life and Politics in the Working-Class Suburbs of Los Angeles, 1920–1965* (2002). Traces the transformation of Southgate, an industrial neighborhood of Los Angeles, into an all-white suburb, and the political results.

Patterson, James T. *Grand Expectations: The United States, 1945–1974* (1996). A comprehensive account of American history over the three decades following World War II.

Pells, Richard. *The Liberal Mind in a Conservative Age: American Intellectuals in the 1940s and 1950s* (1984). Examines how American writers and artists responded to the Cold War.

Phillips-Fein, Kim. *Invisible Hands: The Making of the Conservative Movement from the New Deal to Reagan* (2009). Relates how a group of economic thinkers and businessmen worked to fashion a conservative movement in an attempt to reverse many of the policies of the New Deal.

Wall, Wendy L. *Inventing the "American Way": The Politics of Consensus from the New Deal to the Civil Rights Movement* (2008). A careful examination of the political and ideological world of the Cold War era.

Westad, Odd Arne. *The Global Cold War* (2005). A wide-ranging analysis of how the Cold War played out in the Third World.

WEBSITES

Brown v. Board of Education: www.lib.umich.edu/exhibits/brownarchive/

Herblock's History: Political Cartoons from the Crash to the Millennium: www.loc.gov/rr/print/swann/herblock/

Levittown: Documents of an Ideal American Suburb: http://tigger.uic.edu/~pbhales/Levittown.html

REVIEW QUESTIONS

1. Explain the meaning of the "American standard of living" during the 1950s.

2. Describe how the automobile transformed American communities and culture in the 1950s.

3. Identify the prescribed roles and aspirations for women during the social conformity of the 1950s.

4. How did the growth of suburbs affect the racial lines of division in American society?

5. Explain the ideological rifts between conservatives in the 1950s. Why did many view President Eisenhower as "not one of them"?

6. What was the new "social contract" between labor and management, and how did it benefit both sides as well as the nation as a whole?

7. How did the United States and Soviet Union shift the focus of the Cold War to the Third World?

8. What were the most significant factors that contributed to the growing momentum of the civil rights movement in the 1960s?

9. How did many southern whites, led by their elected officials, resist desegregation and civil rights in the name of "freedom"?

10. Explain the significance of American race relations for U.S. relations overseas.

FREEDOM QUESTIONS

1. What was the role of consumerism in ideas of American freedom in the 1950s?

2. To what extent was the Cold War a struggle to promote freedom in the world, and how did it affect the freedoms of Americans at home?

3. What were the arguments posed by social critics of Cold War society and culture?

4. What basic freedoms did African-Americans seek through the civil rights movement of this period?

5. According to President Eisenhower, what dangers were posed by a military-industrial complex?

KEY TERMS

Levittown (p. 993)

"standard consumer package" (p. 996)

women at work (p. 998)

housing discrimination (p. 999)

"end of ideology" (p. 1002)

Capitalism and Freedom (p. 1005)

"Checkers speech" (p. 1006)

Sputnik (p. 1008)

"social contract" (p. 1008)

National Defense Education Act (p. 1008)

massive retaliation (p. 1009)

Iranian coup (p. 1011)

juvenile delinquency (p. 1015)

rock-and-roll music (p. 1015)

the Beats (p. 1015)

school segregation (p. 1019)

League of United Latin American Citizens (p. 1019)

Brown v. Board of Education (p. 1020)

Montgomery bus boycott (p. 1021)

"missile gap" (p. 1028)

military-industrial complex (p. 1029)

REVIEW TABLE

Landmark Events in the Civil Rights Movement in the 1950s

Event	Date	Significance
Brown v. Board of Education	1954	Ended segregation in public education, reversing the 1896 *Plessy v. Ferguson* decision
Montgomery bus boycott	1955–1956	Mobilized a community to successfully fight Jim Crow, ending segregation on public buses and launching the leadership career of Martin Luther King, Jr.
Integration of Little Rock's Central High School	1957	Led the federal government to uphold the law of the nation and enforce the *Brown* decision

CHAPTER 25

The Sixties, 1960–1968

Signs, a 1970 painting by Robert Rauschenberg, presents a collage of images from the turbulent 1960s, including (clockwise from the upper left corner) troops putting down urban rioting, Robert F. Kennedy, singer Janis Joplin, peace demonstrators, John F. Kennedy, Martin Luther King Jr. after his assassination, and an astronaut on the moon.

- What were the major events in the civil rights movement of the early 1960s?

- What were the major crises and policy initiatives of the Kennedy presidency?

- What were the purposes and strategies of Johnson's Great Society programs?

- How did the civil rights movement change in the mid-1960s?

- How did the Vietnam War transform American politics and culture?

- What were the sources and significance of the rights revolution of the late 1960s?

- In what ways was 1968 a climactic year for the Sixties?

On the afternoon of February 1, 1960, four students from North Carolina Agricultural and Technical State University, a black college in Greensboro, North Carolina, entered the local Woolworth's department store. After making a few purchases, they sat down at the lunch counter, an area reserved for whites. Told that they could not be served, they remained in their seats until the store closed. They returned the next morning and the next. As the protest continued, other students, including a few local whites, joined in. Demonstrations spread across the country. After resisting for five months, Woolworth's in July agreed to serve black customers at its lunch counters.

The sit-in reflected mounting frustration at the slow pace of racial change. White Greensboro prided itself on being free of prejudice. In 1954, the city had been the first in the South to declare its intention of complying with the *Brown* decision. But by 1960 only a handful of black students had been admitted to all-white schools, the economic gap between blacks and whites had not narrowed, and Greensboro was still segregated.

More than any other event, the Greensboro sit-in launched the 1960s: a decade of political activism and social change. Sit-ins had occurred before, but never had they sparked so massive a response. Similar demonstrations soon took place throughout the South, demanding the integration not only of lunch counters but of parks, pools, restaurants, bowling alleys, libraries, and other facilities as well. By the end of 1960, some 70,000 demonstrators had taken part in sit-ins. Angry whites often assaulted them. But having been trained in nonviolent resistance, the protesters did not strike back.

Even more than elevating blacks to full citizenship, declared the writer James Baldwin, the civil rights movement challenged the United States to rethink "what it really means by freedom"—including whether freedom applied to all Americans or only to part of the population. With their freedom rides, freedom schools, freedom marches, and the insistent cry "freedom now," black Americans and their white allies made freedom once again the rallying cry of the dispossessed. Thousands of ordinary men and women—maids and laborers alongside students, teachers, businessmen, and ministers—risked physical and economic retribution to lay claim to freedom. Their courage inspired a host of other challenges to the status quo, including a student movement known as the New Left, the "second wave" of feminism, and activism among other minorities.

By the time the decade ended, these movements had challenged the 1950s' understanding of freedom linked to the Cold War abroad and consumer choice at home. They exposed the limitations of traditional New Deal liberalism. They forced a reconsideration of the nation's foreign policy and extended claims to freedom into the most intimate areas of life. They made American society confront the fact that certain groups,

Participants in a sit-in in Raleigh, North Carolina, in 1960. The protesters, probably students from a local college, brought books and newspapers to emphasize the seriousness of their intentions and their commitment to nonviolence.

including students, women, members of racial minorities, and homosexuals, felt themselves excluded from full enjoyment of American freedom.

Reflecting back years later on the struggles of the 1960s, one black organizer in Memphis remarked, "All I wanted to do was to live in a free country." Of the movement's accomplishments, he added, "You had to fight for every inch of it. Nobody gave you anything. Nothing."

THE FREEDOM MOVEMENT

THE RISING TIDE OF PROTEST

With the sit-ins, college students for the first time stepped onto the stage of American history as the leading force for social change. In April 1960, Ella Baker, a longtime civil rights organizer, called a meeting of young activists in Raleigh, North Carolina. About 200 black students and a few whites attended. Out of the gathering came the Student Non-Violent Coordinating Committee (SNCC), dedicated to replacing the culture of segregation with a "beloved community" of racial justice and to empowering ordinary blacks to take control of the decisions that affected their lives. "We can't count on adults," declared SNCC organizer Robert Moses. "Very few . . . are not afraid of the tremendous pressure they will face. This leaves the young people to be the organizers, the agents of social and political change."

Other forms of direct action soon followed the sit-ins. Blacks in Biloxi and Gulfport, Mississippi, engaged in "wade-ins," demanding access to segregated public beaches. Scores were arrested and two black teenagers

Civil rights demonstrators in Orangeburg, South Carolina, in 1960.

were killed. In 1961, the Congress of Racial Equality (CORE) launched the Freedom Rides. Integrated groups traveled by bus into the Deep South to test compliance with court orders banning segregation on interstate buses and trains and in terminal facilities. Violent mobs assaulted them. Near Anniston, Alabama, a firebomb was thrown into the vehicle and the passengers beaten as they escaped. In Birmingham, Klansmen attacked riders with bats and chains, while police refused to intervene. Many of the Freedom Riders were arrested. But their actions led the Interstate Commerce Commission to order buses and terminals desegregated.

As protests escalated, so did the resistance of local authorities. Late in 1961, SNCC and other groups launched a campaign of nonviolent protests against racial discrimination in Albany, Georgia. The protests lasted a year, but despite filling the jails with demonstrators—a tactic adopted by the movement to gain national sympathy—they failed to achieve their goals. In September 1962, a court ordered the University of Mississippi to admit James Meredith, a black student. The state police stood aside as a mob, encouraged by Governor Ross Barnett, rampaged through the streets of Oxford, where the university is located. Two bystanders lost their lives in the riot. President Kennedy was forced to dispatch the army to restore order.

BIRMINGHAM

The high point of protest came in the spring of 1963, when demonstrations took place in towns and cities across the South, dramatizing black discontent over inequality in education, employment, and housing. In one week in June, there were more than 15,000 arrests in 186 cities. The dramatic culmination came in Birmingham, Alabama, a citadel of segregation. Even for

Demonstrators in downtown Birmingham, Alabama, during the civil rights campaign of 1963.

the Deep South, Birmingham was a violent city—there had been over fifty bombings of black homes and institutions since World War II. Local blacks had been demonstrating, with no result, for greater economic opportunities and an end to segregation by local businesses.

With the movement flagging, some of its leaders invited Martin Luther King Jr. to come to Birmingham. While serving a nine-day prison term in April 1963 for violating a ban on demonstrations, King composed one of his most eloquent pleas for racial justice, the "Letter from Birmingham Jail." Responding to local clergymen who counseled patience, King related the litany of abuses faced by black southerners, from police brutality to the daily humiliation of having to explain to their children why they could not enter amusement parks or public swimming pools. The "white moderate," King declared, must put aside fear of disorder and commit himself to racial justice.

A fireman assaulting young African-American demonstrators with a high-pressure hose during the climactic demonstrations in Birmingham. Broadcast on television, such pictures proved a serious problem for the United States in its battle for the "hearts and minds" of people around the world and forced the Kennedy administration to confront the contradiction between the rhetoric of freedom and the reality of racism.

In May, King made the bold decision to send black schoolchildren into the streets of Birmingham. Police chief Eugene "Bull" Connor unleashed his forces against the thousands of young marchers. The images, broadcast on television, of children being assaulted with nightsticks, high-pressure fire hoses, and attack dogs produced a wave of revulsion throughout the world and turned the Birmingham campaign into a triumph for the civil rights movement. It led President Kennedy, as will be related later, to endorse the movement's goals. Leading businessmen, fearing that the city was becoming an international symbol of brutality, brokered an end to the demonstrations that desegregated downtown stores and restaurants and promised that black salespeople would be hired.

But more than these modest gains, the events in Birmingham forced white Americans to decide whether they had more in common with fellow citizens demanding their basic rights or with violent segregationists. The question became more insistent in the following weeks. In June 1963, a sniper killed Medgar Evers, field secretary of the NAACP in Mississippi. In September, a bomb exploded at a black Baptist church in Birmingham, killing four young girls. (Not until the year 2002 was the last of those who committed this act of domestic terrorism tried and convicted.)

THE MARCH ON WASHINGTON

On August 28, 1963, two weeks before the Birmingham church bombing, 250,000 black and white Americans converged on the nation's capital for the March on Washington, often considered the high point of the nonviolent civil rights movement. Organized by a coalition of civil rights, labor, and church organizations led by A. Philip Randolph, the black unionist who had threatened a similar march in 1941, it was the largest public demonstration in the nation's history to that time. Calls for the passage of a civil rights bill pending before Congress took center stage. But the march's goals also included a public-works program to reduce unemployment, an increase in

Part of the crowd that gathered at the Lincoln Memorial for the 1963 March on Washington to demand "Jobs and Freedom."

the minimum wage, and a law barring discrimination in employment. These demands, and the marchers' slogan, "Jobs and Freedom," revealed how the black movement had, for the moment, forged an alliance with white liberal groups. On the steps of the Lincoln Memorial, King delivered his most famous speech, including the words, "I have a dream that one day this nation will rise up and live out the true meaning of its creed: 'We hold these truths to be self-evident, that all men are created equal.'" (See the Appendix for the full text.)

The March on Washington reflected an unprecedented degree of black-white cooperation in support of racial and economic justice. But it also revealed some of the movement's limitations, and the tensions within it. Even though female activists like Jo Ann Robinson and Ella Baker had played crucial roles in civil rights organizing, every speaker at the Lincoln Memorial was male. The organizers ordered SNCC leader John Lewis (later a congressman from Georgia) to tone down his speech, the original text of which called on blacks to "free ourselves of the chains of political and economic slavery" and march "through the heart of Dixie the way Sherman did . . . and burn Jim Crow to the ground." Lewis's rhetoric forecast the more militant turn many in the movement would soon be taking.

"Seek the freedom in 1963 promised in 1863," read one banner at the March on Washington. And civil rights activists resurrected the Civil War–era vision of national authority as the custodian of American freedom. Despite the fact that the federal government had for many decades promoted segregation, blacks' historical experience suggested that they had more hope for justice from national power than from local governments or civic institutions—home owners' associations, businesses, private clubs—still riddled with racism. It remained unclear whether the federal government would take up this responsibility.

THE KENNEDY YEARS

John F. Kennedy served as president for less than three years and, in domestic affairs, had few tangible accomplishments. But his administration is widely viewed today as a moment of youthful glamour, soaring hopes, and dynamic leadership at home and abroad. Later revelations of the sexual liaisons Kennedy obsessively pursued while in the White House have not significantly damaged his reputation among the general public.

Kennedy's inaugural address of January 1961 announced a watershed in American politics: "The torch has been passed," he declared, "to a new generation of Americans" who would "pay any price, bear any burden," to "assure the survival and success of liberty." The speech seemed to urge

Americans to move beyond the self-centered consumer culture of the 1950s: "Ask not what your country can do for you; ask what you can do for your country." But while the sit-ins were by now a year old, the speech said nothing about segregation or race. At the outset of his presidency, Kennedy regarded civil rights as a distraction from his main concern—vigorous conduct of the Cold War.

KENNEDY AND THE WORLD

Kennedy's agenda envisioned new initiatives aimed at countering communist influence in the world. One of his administration's first acts was to establish the Peace Corps, which sent young Americans abroad to aid in the economic and educational progress of developing countries and to improve the image of the United States there. By 1966, more than 15,000 young men and women were serving as Peace Corps volunteers. When the Soviets in April 1961 launched a satellite carrying the first man into orbit around the earth, Kennedy announced that the United States would mobilize its resources to land a man on the moon by the end of the decade. The goal seemed almost impossible when announced, but it was stunningly accomplished in 1969.

Kennedy also formulated a new policy toward Latin America, the Alliance for Progress. A kind of Marshall Plan for the Western Hemisphere, although involving far smaller sums of money, it aimed, Kennedy said, to promote both "political" and "material freedom." Begun in 1961 with much fanfare about alleviating poverty and counteracting the appeal of communism, the Alliance for Progress failed. Unlike the Marshall Plan, military regimes and local elites controlled Alliance for Progress aid. They enriched themselves while the poor saw little benefit.

Like his predecessors, Kennedy viewed the entire world through the lens of the Cold War. This outlook shaped his dealings with Fidel Castro, who had led a revolution that in 1959 ousted Cuban dictator Fulgencio Batista. Until Castro took power, Cuba was an economic dependency of the United States. When his government began nationalizing American landholdings and other investments and signed an agreement to sell sugar to the Soviet Union, the Eisenhower administration suspended trade with the island. The CIA began training anti-Castro exiles for an invasion of Cuba.

In April 1961, Kennedy allowed the CIA to launch its invasion, at a site known as the Bay of Pigs. Military advisers predicted a popular uprising that would quickly topple the Castro government. But the assault proved to be a total failure. Of 1,400 invaders, more than 100 were killed and 1,100 captured. Cuba became ever more closely tied to the Soviet Union. The Kennedy administration tried other methods, including assassination attempts, to get rid of Castro's government.

THE MISSILE CRISIS

Meanwhile, relations between the two "superpowers" deteriorated. In August 1961, in order to stem a growing tide of emigrants fleeing from East to West Berlin, the Soviets constructed a wall separating the two parts of the city. Until its demolition in 1989, the Berlin Wall would stand as a tangible symbol of the Cold War and the division of Europe.

The most dangerous crisis of the Kennedy administration, and in many ways of the entire Cold War, came in October 1962, when American spy planes discovered that the Soviet Union was installing missiles in Cuba capable of reaching the United States with nuclear weapons. The Russians' motive—whether they hoped to alter the world balance of power or simply stave off another American invasion of Cuba—may never be known. But the Kennedy administration considered the missiles' presence intolerable. Rejecting advice from military leaders that he authorize an attack on Cuba, which would almost certainly have triggered a Soviet response in Berlin and perhaps a nuclear war, Kennedy imposed a blockade, or "quarantine," of the island and demanded the missiles' removal. After tense behind-the-scenes negotiations, Soviet premier Nikita Khrushchev agreed to withdraw the missiles; Kennedy pledged that the United States would not invade Cuba and secretly agreed to remove American Jupiter missiles from Turkey, from which they could reach the Soviet Union.

For thirteen days, the world teetered on the brink of all-out nuclear war. The crisis seems to have lessened Kennedy's passion for the Cold War. Indeed, he appears to have been shocked by the casual way military leaders spoke of "winning" a nuclear exchange in which tens of millions of Americans and Russians were certain to die. In 1963, Kennedy moved to reduce Cold War tensions. In a speech at American University, he called for greater cooperation with the Soviets. He warned against viewing the Cold War simply as a battle between the forces of light and those of darkness: "No government or social system is so evil that its people must be considered as lacking in virtue." That summer, the two countries agreed to a treaty banning the testing of nuclear weapons in the atmosphere and in space. In announcing the agreement, Kennedy paid tribute to the small movement against nuclear weapons that had been urging such a ban for several years. He even sent word to Castro through a journalist that he desired a more constructive relationship with Cuba.

New York City train passengers reading the news of President Kennedy's assassination, November 22, 1963.

KENNEDY AND CIVIL RIGHTS

In his first two years in office, Kennedy was preoccupied with foreign policy. But in 1963, the crisis over civil rights eclipsed other concerns. Until then, Kennedy had been reluctant to take a forceful stand on black demands. He seemed to share FBI director J. Edgar Hoover's fear that the movement was inspired by communism. Attorney General Robert F. Kennedy, the president's brother, approved FBI wiretaps on King. Despite promising during the 1960 campaign to ban discrimination in federally assisted housing, Kennedy waited until the end of 1962 to issue the order. He used federal force when obstruction of the law became acute, as at the University of Mississippi. But he failed to protect civil rights workers from violence, insisting that law enforcement was a local matter.

Events in Birmingham in May 1963 forced Kennedy's hand. Kennedy realized that the United States simply could not declare itself the champion of freedom throughout the world while maintaining a system of racial inequality at home. In June, he went on national television to call for the passage of a law banning discrimination in all places of public accommodation, a major goal of the civil rights movement. The nation, he asserted, faced a moral crisis: "We preach freedom around the world . . . , but are we to say to the world, and much more importantly, to each other, that this is a land of the free except for Negroes?"

Kennedy did not live to see his civil rights bill enacted. On November 22, 1963, while riding in a motorcade through Dallas, Texas, he was shot and killed. Most likely, the assassin was Lee Harvey Oswald, a troubled former marine. Partly because Oswald was murdered two days later by a local nightclub owner while in police custody, speculation about a possible conspiracy continues to this day. In any event, Kennedy's death brought an abrupt and utterly unexpected end to his presidency. As with Pearl Harbor or September 11, 2001, an entire generation would always recall the moment when they first heard the news of Kennedy's death. It fell to his successor, Lyndon B. Johnson, to secure passage of the civil rights bill and to launch a program of domestic liberalism far more ambitious than anything Kennedy had envisioned.

Lyndon B. Johnson being sworn in as president on the plane taking him to Washington from Dallas. On the left is Lady Bird Johnson, and on the right, Jacqueline Kennedy.

LYNDON JOHNSON'S PRESIDENCY

Unlike John F. Kennedy, raised in a wealthy and powerful family, Lyndon Johnson grew up in one of the poorest parts of the United States, the central Texas hill country. Kennedy seemed to view success as his birthright; Johnson had to struggle ferociously to achieve wealth and power. By the 1950s, he had risen to become majority leader of the U.S. Senate. But Johnson never forgot the poor Mexican and white children he had taught in a Texas school in the early 1930s. Far more interested than Kennedy in domestic reform, he continued to hold the New Deal view that government had an obligation to assist less-fortunate members of society.

THE CIVIL RIGHTS ACT OF 1964

When he became president, nobody expected that Johnson would make the passage of civil rights legislation his first order of business or that he would come to identify himself with the black movement more passionately than any previous president. Just five days after Kennedy's assassination, however, Johnson called on Congress to enact the civil rights bill as the most fitting memorial to his slain predecessor. "We have talked long enough about equal rights in this country," he declared. "It is now time to write the next chapter and write it in the books of law."

In 1964, Congress passed the Civil Rights Act, which prohibited racial discrimination in employment, institutions like hospitals and schools, and privately owned public accommodations such as restaurants, hotels, and

Fannie Lou Hamer testifying at the Democratic national convention of 1964 on behalf of the Mississippi Freedom Democratic Party.

theaters. It also banned discrimination on the grounds of sex—a provision added by opponents of civil rights in an effort to derail the entire bill and embraced by liberal and female members of Congress as a way to broaden its scope. Johnson knew that many whites opposed the new law. After signing it, he turned to an aide and remarked, "I think we delivered the South to the Republican Party."

FREEDOM SUMMER

The 1964 law did not address a major concern of the civil rights movement—the right to vote in the South. That summer, a coalition of civil rights groups, including SNCC, CORE, and the NAACP, launched a voter registration drive in Mississippi. Hundreds of white college students from the North traveled to the state to take part in Freedom Summer. An outpouring of violence greeted the campaign, including thirty-five bombings and numerous beatings of civil rights workers. In June, three young activists—Michael Schwerner and Andrew Goodman, white students from the North, and James Chaney, a local black youth, were kidnapped by a group headed by a deputy sheriff and murdered near Philadelphia, Mississippi. Between 1961 and 1965, an estimated twenty-five black civil rights workers paid with their lives. But the deaths of the two white students focused unprecedented attention on Mississippi and on the apparent inability of the federal government to protect citizens seeking to enjoy their constitutional rights. (In June 2005, forty-one years after Freedom Summer, a Mississippi jury convicted a member of the Ku Klux Klan of manslaughter in the deaths of the three civil rights workers.)

Freedom Summer led directly to one of the most dramatic confrontations of the civil rights era—the campaign by the Mississippi Freedom Democratic Party (MFDP) to take the seats of the state's all-white official party at the 1964 Democratic national convention in Atlantic City, New Jersey. With blacks unable to participate in the activities of the Democratic Party or register to vote, the civil rights movement in Mississippi had created the MFDP, open to all residents of the state. At televised hearings before the credentials committee, Fannie Lou Hamer of the MFDP held a national audience spellbound with her account of growing up in poverty in the Yazoo-Mississippi Delta and of the savage beatings she had endured at the hands of police. Like many other black activists, Hamer was a deeply religious person who believed that Christianity rested on the idea of freedom and that the movement had been divinely inspired. "Is this America," she asked, "the land of the free and home of the brave, where . . . we [are] threatened daily because we want to live as decent human beings?" Johnson feared a southern walkout, as had happened at the 1948 party convention, if the MFDP were seated. Party liberals, including Johnson's running mate, Hubert Humphrey, pressed for a compromise in which two black delegates would be granted seats. But the MFDP rejected the proposal.

THE 1964 ELECTION

The events at Atlantic City severely weakened black activists' faith in the responsiveness of the political system and forecast the impending breakup of the coalition between the civil rights movement and the liberal wing of the Democratic Party. For the moment, however, the movement rallied behind Johnson's campaign for reelection. Johnson's opponent, Senator Barry Goldwater of Arizona, had published *The Conscience of a Conservative* (1960), which sold more than 3 million copies. The book demanded a more aggressive conduct of the Cold War (he even suggested that nuclear war might be "the price of freedom"). But Goldwater directed most of his critique against "internal" dangers to freedom, especially the New Deal welfare state, which he believed stifled individual initiative and independence. He called for the substitution of private charity for public welfare programs and Social Security, and the abolition of the graduated income tax. Goldwater had voted against the Civil Rights Act of 1964. His acceptance speech at the Republican national convention contained the explosive statement, "Extremism in the defense of liberty is no vice."

Stigmatized by the Democrats as an extremist who would repeal Social Security and risk nuclear war, Goldwater went down to a disastrous defeat. Johnson received almost 43 million votes to Goldwater's 27 million. Democrats swept to two-to-one majorities in both houses of Congress. Although few realized it, the 1964 campaign marked a milestone in the resurgence of American conservatism. Goldwater's success in the Deep South, where he carried five states, coupled with the surprisingly strong showing of segregationist governor George Wallace of Alabama in Democratic primaries in Wisconsin, Indiana, and Maryland, suggested that politicians could strike electoral gold by appealing to white opposition to the civil rights movement.

One indication of problems for the Democrats came in California, with the passage by popular referendum of Proposition 14, which repealed a 1963 law banning racial discrimination in the sale of real estate. Backed by the state's realtors and developers, California conservatives made the "freedom" of home owners to control their

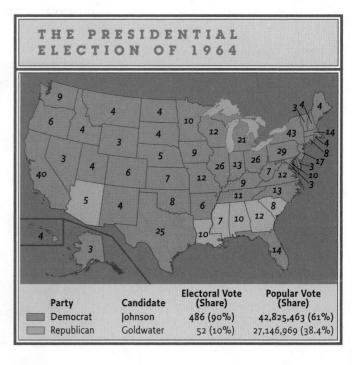

THE PRESIDENTIAL ELECTION OF 1964

Party	Candidate	Electoral Vote (Share)	Popular Vote (Share)
Democrat	Johnson	486 (90%)	42,825,463 (61%)
Republican	Goldwater	52 (10%)	27,146,969 (38.4%)

property the rallying cry of the campaign against the fair housing law. Although Johnson carried California by more than 1 million votes, Proposition 14 received a considerable majority, winning three-fourths of the votes cast by whites.

THE CONSERVATIVE SIXTIES

The 1960s, today recalled as a decade of radicalism, clearly had a conservative side as well. With the founding in 1960 of Young Americans for Freedom (YAF), conservative students emerged as a force in politics. There were striking parallels between the Sharon Statement, issued by ninety young people who gathered at the estate of conservative intellectual William F. Buckley in Sharon, Connecticut, to establish YAF, and the Port Huron Statement of SDS of 1962 (discussed later in this chapter). Both manifestos portrayed youth as the cutting edge of a new radicalism, and both claimed to offer a route to greater freedom. The Sharon Statement summarized beliefs that had circulated among conservatives during the past decade—the free market underpinned "personal freedom," government must be strictly limited, and "international communism," the gravest threat to liberty, must be destroyed.

YAF aimed initially to take control of the Republican Party from leaders who had made their peace with the New Deal and seemed willing to coexist with communism. YAF members became Barry Goldwater's shock troops in 1964. Despite his landslide defeat in the general election, Goldwater's nomination was a remarkable triumph for a movement widely viewed as composed of fanatics out to "repeal the twentieth century."

Goldwater also brought new constituencies to the conservative cause. His campaign aroused enthusiasm in the rapidly expanding suburbs of southern California and the Southwest. Orange County, California, many of whose residents had recently arrived from the East and Midwest and worked in defense-related industries, became a nationally known center of grassroots conservative activism. The funds that poured into the Goldwater campaign

A 1967 rally by members of Young Americans for Freedom, a conservative group that flourished in the 1960s.

from the Sunbelt's oilmen and aerospace entrepreneurs established a new financial base for conservatism. And by carrying five states of the Deep South, Goldwater showed that the civil rights revolution had redrawn the nation's political map, opening the door to a "southern strategy" that would eventually lead the entire region into the Republican Party.

Well before the rise of Black Power, a reaction against civil rights gains offered conservatives new opportunities and threatened the stability of the Democratic coalition. During the 1950s, many conservatives had responded favorably to southern whites' condemnation of the *Brown v. Board of Education* desegregation decision as an invasion of states' rights. The *National Review*, an influential conservative magazine, referred to whites as "the advanced race" and defended black disenfranchisement on the grounds that "the claims of civilization supersede those of universal suffrage." In 1962, YAF bestowed its Freedom Award on Senator Strom Thurmond of South Carolina, one of the country's most prominent segregationists. During the 1960s, most conservatives abandoned talk of racial superiority and inferiority. But conservative appeals to law and order, "freedom of association," and the evils of welfare often had strong racial overtones. Racial divisions would prove to be a political gold mine for conservatives.

A white resident of Selma offers her support to civil rights demonstrators.

THE VOTING RIGHTS ACT

One last legislative triumph, however, lay ahead for the civil rights movement. In January 1965, King launched a voting rights campaign in Selma, Alabama, a city where only 355 of 15,000 black residents had been allowed to register to vote. In March, defying a ban by Governor Wallace, King attempted to lead a march from Selma to the state capital, Montgomery. When the marchers reached the bridge leading out of the city, state police assaulted them with cattle prods, whips, and tear gas.

Once again, violence against nonviolent demonstrators flashed across television screens throughout the world, compelling the federal government to take action. Calling Selma a milestone in "man's unending search for freedom," Johnson asked Congress to enact a law securing the right to vote. He closed his speech by quoting the demonstrators' song, "We Shall Overcome." Never before had the movement received so powerful an endorsement from the federal government. Congress quickly passed the Voting Rights Act of 1965, which allowed federal officials to register voters. Black southerners finally regained the suffrage that had been stripped from them at the turn of the twentieth century. In addition, the Twenty-fourth Amendment to the Constitution outlawed the poll tax, which had long prevented poor blacks (and some whites) from voting in the South.

IMMIGRATION REFORM

By 1965, with court orders and new federal laws prohibiting discrimination in public accommodations, employment, and voting, the civil rights movement had succeeded in eradicating the legal bases of second-class citizenship. The belief that racism should no longer serve as a basis of public policy spilled over into other realms. In 1965, the Hart-Celler Act abandoned the national-origins quota system of immigration, which had excluded Asians and severely restricted southern and eastern Europeans. The law established new, racially neutral criteria for immigration, notably family reunification and possession of skills in demand in the United States. On the other hand, because of growing hostility in the Southwest to Mexican immigration, the law established the first limit, 120,000, on newcomers from the Western Hemisphere. This created, for the first time, the category of "illegal aliens" from the Americas. The Act set the quota for the rest of the world at 170,000. The total annual number of immigrants, 290,000, represented a lower percentage of the American population than had been admitted when the nationality quotas were established in 1924. However, because of special provisions for refugees from communist countries, immigration soon exceeded these caps.

The new law had many unexpected results. At the time, immigrants represented only 5 percent of the American population—the lowest proportion since the 1830s. No one anticipated that the new quotas not only would lead to an explosive rise in immigration but also would spark a dramatic shift in which newcomers from Latin America, the Caribbean, and Asia came to outnumber those from Europe. Taken together, the civil rights revolution and immigration reform marked the triumph of a pluralist conception of Americanism. By 1976, 85 percent of respondents to a public-opinion survey agreed with the statement, "The United States was meant to be . . . a country made up of many races, religions, and nationalities."

THE GREAT SOCIETY

After his landslide victory of 1964, Johnson outlined the most sweeping proposal for governmental action to promote the general welfare since the New Deal. Johnson's initiatives of 1965–1967, known collectively as the Great Society, provided health services to the poor and elderly in the new Medicaid and Medicare programs and poured federal funds into education and urban development. New cabinet offices—the Departments of Transportation and of Housing and Urban Development—and new agencies, such as the Equal Employment Opportunity Commission, the National Endowments for the Humanities and for the Arts, and a national public broadcasting network, were created. These measures greatly expanded the powers of the federal government, and they completed and extended the social agenda (with the exception of national health insurance) that had been stalled in Congress since 1938.

Unlike the New Deal, however, the Great Society was a response to prosperity, not depression. The mid-1960s were a time of rapid economic expansion, fueled by increased government spending and a tax cut on individuals and businesses initially proposed by Kennedy and enacted in 1964. Johnson and Democratic liberals believed that economic growth made it possible to fund ambitious new government programs and to improve the quality of life.

As part of his War on Poverty, President Lyndon Johnson visited Appalachia, one of the poorest places in the United States.

THE WAR ON POVERTY

The centerpiece of the Great Society, however, was the crusade to eradicate poverty, launched by Johnson early in 1964. After the talk of universal affluence during the 1950s, economic deprivation had been rediscovered by political leaders, thanks in part to Michael Harrington's 1962 book *The Other America*. Harrington revealed that 40 to 50 million Americans lived in poverty, often in isolated rural areas or urban slums "invisible" to the middle class. He showed that technological improvements like the mechanization of agriculture and the automation of industry, which produced a higher standard of living overall, eliminated the jobs of farm laborers and unskilled workers, locking them in poverty. The civil rights movement heightened the urgency of the issue, even though, as Harrington made clear, whites made up a majority of the nation's poor.

During the 1930s, Democrats had attributed poverty to an imbalance of economic power and flawed economic institutions. In the 1960s, the administration attributed it to an absence of skills and a lack of proper attitudes and work habits. Thus, the War on Poverty did not consider the most direct ways of eliminating poverty—guaranteeing an annual income for all Americans, creating jobs for the unemployed, promoting the spread of unionization, or making it more difficult for businesses to shift production to the low-wage South or overseas. Nor did it address the economic changes that were reducing the number of well-paid manufacturing jobs and leaving poor families in rural areas like Appalachia and decaying urban ghettos with little hope of economic advancement.

One of the Great Society's most popular and successful components, food stamps, offered direct aid to the poor. But, in general, the War on Poverty concentrated not on direct economic aid but on equipping the poor with skills and rebuilding their spirit and motivation. The new Office of Economic Opportunity oversaw a series of initiatives designed to lift the poor into the social and economic mainstream. It provided Head Start (an early childhood education program), job training, legal services, and scholarships for poor college students. It also created VISTA, a domestic version of the Peace Corps for the inner cities. In an echo of SNCC's philosophy of empowering ordinary individuals to take control of their lives, the War on Poverty required that poor people play a leading part in the design and implementation of local policies, a recipe for continuing conflict with local political leaders accustomed to controlling the flow of federal dollars.

FREEDOM AND EQUALITY

Johnson defended the Great Society in a vocabulary of freedom derived from the New Deal, when his own political career began, and reinforced by the civil rights movement. Soon after assuming office in 1963, he resurrected the phrase "freedom from want," all but forgotten during the 1950s. Echoing FDR, Johnson told the 1964 Democratic convention, "The man who is hungry, who cannot find work or educate his children, who is bowed by want, that man is not fully free." Recognizing that black poverty was fundamentally different from white, since its roots lay in "past injustice and present prejudice," Johnson sought to redefine the relationship between freedom and equality. Economic liberty, he insisted, meant more than equal opportunity: "You do not wipe away the scars of centuries by saying: Now you are free to go where you want, do as you desire, and choose

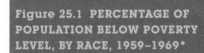

Figure 25.1 **PERCENTAGE OF POPULATION BELOW POVERTY LEVEL, BY RACE, 1959–1969***

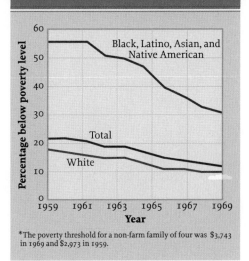

*The poverty threshold for a non-farm family of four was $3,743 in 1969 and $2,973 in 1959.

During the 1960s, an expanding economy and government programs assisting the poor produced a steady decrease in the percentage of Americans living in poverty.

the leaders you please. . . . We seek . . . not just equality as a right and a theory, but equality as a fact and as a result."

Johnson's Great Society may not have achieved equality "as a fact," but it represented a remarkable reaffirmation of the idea of social citizenship. It was the most expansive effort in the nation's history to mobilize the powers of the national government to address the needs of the least-advantaged Americans, especially those, like blacks, largely excluded from the original New Deal entitlements such as Social Security.

Coupled with the decade's high rate of economic growth, the War on Poverty succeeded in reducing the incidence of poverty from 22 percent to 13 percent of American families during the 1960s. It has fluctuated around the latter figure ever since. The sum spent, however, was too low to end poverty altogether or to transform conditions of life in poor urban neighborhoods. By the 1990s, thanks to the civil rights movement and the Great Society, the historic gap between whites and blacks in education, income, and access to skilled employment narrowed considerably. But with deindustrialization and urban decay affecting numerous families and most suburbs still being off-limits to non-whites, the median wealth of white households remained ten times greater than that of blacks, and nearly a quarter of all black children still lived in poverty.

THE CHANGING BLACK MOVEMENT

Even at its moment of triumph, the civil rights movement confronted a crisis as it sought to move from access to schools, public accommodations, and the voting booth to the economic divide separating blacks from other Americans. In the mid-1960s, economic issues rose to the forefront of the civil rights agenda. Violent outbreaks in black ghettos outside the South

A burned store mannequin lies on the street and smoke rises in the background as a policeman patrols Los Angeles during the Watts riot of 1965.

drew attention to the national scope of racial injustice and to inequalities in jobs, education, and housing that the dismantling of legal segregation left intact. Much of the animosity that came to characterize race relations arose from the belief of many whites that the legislation of 1964 and 1965 had fulfilled the nation's obligation to assure blacks equality before the law, while blacks, aware of the discrimination they still faced in jobs, education, housing, and the criminal justice system, pushed for more government action, sparking fears of "reverse discrimination."

THE GHETTO UPRISINGS

The first riots—really, battles between angry blacks and the predominantly white police (widely seen by many ghetto residents as an occupying army)—erupted in Harlem in 1964. Far larger was the Watts uprising of 1965, which took place in the black ghetto of Los Angeles only days after Johnson signed the Voting Rights Act. An estimated 50,000 persons took part in this "rebellion," attacking police and firemen, looting white-owned businesses, and burning buildings. It required 15,000 police and National Guardsmen to restore order, by which time thirty-five people lay dead, 900 were injured, and $30 million worth of property had been destroyed.

By the summer of 1967, violence had become so widespread that some feared racial civil war. Urban uprisings in that year left twenty-three dead in Newark and forty-three in Detroit, where entire blocks went up in flames and property damage ran into the hundreds of millions of dollars. The violence led Johnson to appoint a commission headed by Illinois governor Otto Kerner to study the causes of urban rioting. Released in 1968, the Kerner Report blamed the violence on "segregation and poverty" and offered a powerful indictment of "white racism." It depicted a country in danger of being torn apart by racial antagonism: "Our nation is moving toward two societies, one black, one white—separate and unequal." But the report failed to offer any clear proposals for change.

With black unemployment twice that of whites and the average black family income little more than half the white norm, the movement looked for ways to "make freedom real" for black Americans. In 1964, King called for a "Bill of Rights for the Disadvantaged" to mobilize the nation's resources to abolish economic deprivation. His proposal was directed against poverty in general, but King also insisted that after "doing something special *against* the Negro for hundreds of years," the United States had an obligation to "do something special *for* him now"—an early call for what would come to be known as "affirmative action." A. Philip Randolph and civil rights veteran Bayard Rustin proposed a Freedom Budget, which envisioned spending $100 billion over ten years on a federal program of job creation and urban redevelopment.

In 1966, King launched the Chicago Freedom Movement, with demands quite different from its predecessors in the South—an end to discrimination by employers and unions, equal access to mortgages, the integration of public housing, and the construction of low-income housing scattered throughout the region. Confronting the entrenched power of Mayor Richard J. Daley's political machine and the ferocious opposition of white home owners, the movement failed. King's tactics—marches, sit-ins, mass arrests—proved ineffective in the face of the North's less pervasive but

In 1965, Martin Luther King Jr. and the black labor leader A. Philip Randolph called for a Freedom Budget, which they claimed would eliminate poverty by 1975. The proposal illustrated how the focus of the civil rights movement was shifting from desegregation to economic inequality.

still powerful system of racial inequality. As he came to realize the difficulty of combating the economic plight of black America, King's language became more and more radical. He called for nothing less than a "revolution in values" that would create a "better distribution of wealth" for "all God's children."

MALCOLM X

The civil rights movement's first phase had produced a clear set of objectives, far-reaching accomplishments, and a series of coherent if sometimes competitive organizations. The second witnessed political fragmentation and few significant victories. Even during the heyday of the integration struggle, the fiery orator Malcolm X had insisted that blacks must control the political and economic resources of their communities and rely on their own efforts rather than working with whites. Having committed a string of crimes as a youth, Malcolm Little was converted in jail to the teachings of the Nation of Islam, or Black Muslims, who preached a message of white evil and black self-discipline. Malcolm dropped his "slave surname" in favor of "X," symbolizing blacks' separation from their African ancestry. On his release from prison he became a spokesman for the Muslims and a sharp critic of the ideas of integration and nonviolence, and of King's practice of appealing to American values. "I don't see any American dream," he proclaimed. "I see an American nightmare."

Female students on the campus of Howard University in Washington, D.C., sport the Afro, a hairstyle representative of the "black is beautiful" campaign of the 1960s.

On a 1964 trip to Mecca, Saudi Arabia, Islam's spiritual home, Malcolm X witnessed harmony among Muslims of all races. He now began to speak of the possibility of interracial cooperation for radical change in the United States. But when members of the Nation of Islam assassinated him in February 1965 after he had formed his own Organization of Afro-American Unity, Malcolm X left neither a consistent ideology nor a coherent movement. Most whites considered him an apostle of racial violence. However, his call for blacks to rely on their own resources struck a chord among the urban poor and younger civil rights activists. His *Autobiography*, published in 1966, became a great bestseller. Today, streets, parks, and schools are named after him.

THE RISE OF BLACK POWER

Malcolm X was the intellectual father of "Black Power," a slogan that came to national attention in 1966 when SNCC leader Stokely Carmichael used it during a civil rights march in Mississippi. Black Power immediately became a rallying cry for those bitter over the federal government's failure to stop violence against civil rights workers, white attempts to determine movement strategy (as at the Democratic convention of 1964), and the civil rights movement's failure to have any impact on the economic problems of black ghettos.

One who embraced the idea proclaimed, "Black Power means Black Freedom"—freedom, especially, from whites who tried to dictate the movement's goals. A highly imprecise idea, Black Power suggested everything from the election of more black officials (hardly a radical notion) to the belief that black Americans were a colonized people whose freedom could only be won through a revolutionary struggle for self-determination. But however employed, the idea reflected the radicalization of young civil rights activists and sparked an explosion of racial self-assertion, reflected in the slogan "black is beautiful." The abandonment of the word "Negro" in favor of "Afro-American," as well as the popularity of black beauty pageants, African styles of dress, and the "natural," or "Afro," hairdo among both men and women, signified much more than a change in language and fashion. They reflected a new sense of racial pride and a rejection of white norms.

Inspired by the idea of black self-determination, SNCC and CORE repudiated their previous interracialism, and new militant groups sprang into existence. Many of these groups proved short-lived. But both traditional civil rights organizations and black politicians adopted some of their ideas. Most prominent of the new groups, in terms of publicity, if not numbers, was the Black Panther Party. Founded in Oakland, California, in 1966, it became notorious for advocating armed self-defense in response to police brutality. It demanded the release of black prisoners because of racism in the criminal justice system. The party's youthful members alarmed whites by wearing military garb, although they also ran health clinics, schools, and children's breakfast programs. But internal disputes and a campaign against the Black Panthers by police and the FBI, which left several leaders dead in shootouts, destroyed the organization.

Black unemployment declined throughout the second half of the 1960s. But by 1967, with the escalation of U.S. military involvement in Vietnam, the War on Poverty had ground to a halt. By then, with ghetto uprisings punctuating the urban landscape, the antiwar movement assuming massive proportions, and millions of young people ostentatiously rejecting mainstream values, American society faced its greatest crisis since the Depression.

VIETNAM AND THE NEW LEFT

OLD AND NEW LEFTS

To most Americans, the rise of a protest movement among white youth came as a complete surprise. For most of the century, colleges had been conservative institutions that drew their students from a privileged segment of the population. During the 1950s, young people had been called a "silent generation." If blacks' grievances appeared self-evident, those of white college students were difficult to understand. What persuaded large numbers of children of affluence to reject the values and institutions of their society? In part, the answer lay in a redefinition of the meaning of freedom by what came to be called the New Left.

What made the New Left new was its rejection of the intellectual and political categories that had shaped radicalism and liberalism for most of the twentieth century. It challenged not only mainstream America

Betye Saar's 1972 installation, The Liberation of Aunt Jemima, *illustrates modes of thought associated with Black Power. Quaker Oats Company has long used an image of a black woman reminiscent of the stereotypical slave "mammy" as a symbol for its brand of pancake mix. Saar gives Aunt Jemima a rifle to go along with her broom. In front of her is another Aunt Jemima, holding a light-skinned baby, a symbol, according to the artist, of the sexual exploitation of black women by white men. Images in the background reveal how Quaker Oats had already modified its advertising image, giving her a smaller kerchief and an Afro hairdo. By the end of the twentieth century, the kerchief had disappeared entirely, and Aunt Jemima had become slimmer and younger and was not smiling quite so broadly.*

but also what it dismissively called the Old Left. Unlike the Communist Party, it did not take the Soviet Union as a model or see the working class as the main agent of social change. Instead of economic equality and social citizenship, the language of New Deal liberals, the New Left spoke of loneliness, isolation, and alienation, of powerlessness in the face of bureaucratic institutions and a hunger for authenticity that affluence could not provide. These discontents galvanized a mass movement among what was rapidly becoming a major sector of the American population. By 1968, thanks to the coming of age of the baby-boom generation and the growing number of jobs that required post–high school skills, more than 7 million students attended college, more than the number of farmers or steelworkers.

The New Left was not as new as it claimed. Its call for a democracy of citizen participation harked back to the American Revolution, and its critique of the contrast between American values and American reality, to the abolitionists. Its emphasis on authenticity in the face of conformity recalled the bohemians of the years before World War I, and its critique of consumer culture drew inspiration from 1950s writers on mass society. But the New Left's greatest inspiration was the black freedom movement. More than any other event, the sit-ins catalyzed white student activism.

Here was the unlikely combination that created the upheaval known as The Sixties—the convergence of society's most excluded members demanding full access to all its benefits, with the children of the middle class rejecting the social mainstream. The black movement and white New Left shared basic assumptions—that the evils to be corrected were deeply embedded in social institutions and that only direct confrontation could persuade Americans of the urgency of far-reaching change.

THE FADING CONSENSUS

The years 1962 and 1963 witnessed the appearance of several path-breaking books that challenged one or another aspect of the 1950s consensus. James Baldwin's *The Fire Next Time* gave angry voice to the black revolution. Rachel Carson's *Silent Spring* exposed the environmental costs of economic growth. Michael Harrington's *The Other America* revealed the persistence of poverty amid plenty. *The Death and Life of Great American Cities*, by Jane Jacobs, criticized urban renewal, the removal of the poor from city centers, and the destruction of neighborhoods to build highways, accommodating cities to the needs of drivers rather than pedestrians. What made cities alive, she insisted, was density and diversity, the social interaction of people of different backgrounds encountering each other on urban streets.

Yet in some ways the most influential critique of all arose in 1962 from Students for a Democratic Society (SDS), an offshoot of the socialist League for Industrial Democracy. Meeting at Port Huron, Michigan, some sixty college students adopted a document that captured the mood and summarized the beliefs of this generation of student protesters.

The Port Huron Statement devoted four-fifths of its text to criticism of institutions ranging from political parties to corporations, unions, and the

military-industrial complex. But what made the document the guiding spirit of a new radicalism was the remainder, which offered a new vision of social change. "We seek the establishment," it proclaimed, of "a democracy of individual participation, [in which] the individual shares in those social decisions determining the quality and direction of his life." Freedom, for the New Left, meant "participatory democracy." Although rarely defined with precision, this became a standard by which students judged existing social arrangements—workplaces, schools, government—and found them wanting. The idea suggested a rejection of the elitist strain that had marked liberal thinkers from the Progressives to postwar advocates of economic planning, in which government experts would establish national priorities in the name of the people.

THE RISE OF SDS

By the end of 1962, SDS had grown to 8,000 members. Then, in 1964, events at the University of California at Berkeley revealed the possibility for a far broader mobilization of students in the name of participatory democracy. A Cold War "multiversity," Berkeley was an immense, impersonal institution where enrollments in many classes approached 1,000 students. The spark that set student protests alight was a new rule prohibiting political groups from using a central area of the campus to spread their ideas. Students—including conservatives outraged at being barred from distributing their own literature—responded by creating the Free Speech movement. Freedom of expression, declared Mario Savio, a student leader, "represents the very dignity of what a human being is.... That's what

Police arresting Mario Savio, a leader of the Free Speech movement, as he addresses a crowd on the campus of the University of California at Berkeley in 1966.

marks us off from the stones and the stars. You can speak freely." Likening the university to a factory, Savio called on students to "throw our body against the machines."

Thousands of Berkeley students became involved in the protests in the months that followed. Their program moved from demanding a repeal of the new rule to a critique of the entire structure of the university and of an education geared toward preparing graduates for corporate jobs. When the university gave in on the speech ban early in 1965, one activist exulted that the students had succeeded in reversing "the worldwide drift from freedom."

AMERICA AND VIETNAM

By 1965 the black movement and the emergence of the New Left had shattered the climate of consensus of the 1950s. But what transformed protest into a full-fledged generational rebellion was the war in Vietnam. What one historian has called "the greatest miscalculation in the history of American foreign relations" was a logical extension of Cold War policies and assumptions. The war tragically revealed the danger that Walter Lippmann had warned of at the outset of the Cold War—viewing the entire world and every local situation within it through the either-or lens of an anticommunist crusade. A Vietnam specialist in the State Department who attended a policy meeting in August 1963 later recalled "the abysmal ignorance around the table of the particular facts of Vietnam. . . . They made absolutely no distinctions between countries with completely different historical experiences. . . . They [believed] that we could manipulate other states and build nations; that we knew all the answers."

Few Americans had any knowledge of Vietnam's history and culture. Successive administrations reduced a complex struggle for national independence, led by homegrown communists who enjoyed widespread support throughout their country in addition to Soviet backing, to a test of "containment." As noted in the previous chapter, the Truman and Eisenhower administrations had cast their lot with French colonialism in the region. After the French defeat, they financed the creation of a pro-American South Vietnamese government, in violation of the Geneva Accords of 1954 that had promised elections to unify Vietnam. By the 1960s, the United States was committed to the survival of this corrupt regime.

Fear that the public would not forgive them for "losing" Vietnam made it impossible for Presidents Kennedy and Johnson to remove the United States from an increasingly untenable situation. Kennedy's foreign policy advisers saw Vietnam as a test of whether the United States could, through "counterinsurgency"—intervention to counter internal uprisings in noncommunist countries—halt the spread of Third World revolutions. Despite the dispatch of increased American aid and numerous military advisers,

South Vietnamese leader Ngo Dinh Diem lost control of the countryside to the communist-led Viet Cong. Diem resisted American advice to broaden his government's base of support. In October 1963, after large Buddhist demonstrations against his regime, the United States approved a military coup that led to Diem's death. When Kennedy was assassinated the following month, there were 17,000 American military advisers in South Vietnam. Shortly before his death, according to the notes of a White House meeting, Kennedy questioned "the wisdom of involvement in Vietnam." But he took no action to end the American presence.

Secretary of Defense Robert McNamara, on the left, and his deputy, Cyrus Vance, at a May 1965 meeting at the White House where the war in Vietnam was discussed. A bust of President Kennedy stands in the background. McNamara later wrote in his memoirs that his misgivings only grew as the war progressed.

LYNDON JOHNSON'S WAR

Lyndon B. Johnson came to the presidency with little experience in foreign relations. Johnson had misgivings about sending American troops to Vietnam. "I don't see that we can ever hope to get out of there once we are committed," he remarked to one senator in 1964. But he knew that Republicans had used the "loss" of China as a weapon against Truman. "I am not going to be the president," he vowed, "who saw Southeast Asia go the way China went."

In August 1964, North Vietnamese vessels encountered an American ship on a spy mission off its coast. When North Vietnamese patrol boats fired on the American vessel, Johnson proclaimed that the United States was a victim of "aggression." In response, Congress passed the Gulf of Tonkin resolution, authorizing the president to take "all necessary measures to repel armed attack" in Vietnam. Only two members—Senators Ernest Gruening of Alaska and Wayne Morse of Oregon—voted against giving Johnson this blank check. The nearest the United States ever came to a formal declaration of war, the resolution passed without any discussion of American goals and strategy in Vietnam. (Over forty years later, in December 2005, the National Security Agency finally released hundreds of pages of secret documents that made it clear that no North Vietnamese attack had actually taken place.)

During the 1964 campaign, Johnson insisted that he had no intention of sending American troops to Vietnam. But immediately after Johnson's reelection, the National Security Council recommended that the United States begin air strikes against North Vietnam and introduce American ground troops in the south. When the Viet Cong in February 1965 attacked an American air base in South Vietnam, Johnson put the plan into effect. At almost the same time, he intervened in the Dominican Republic. Here, military leaders in 1963 had overthrown the left-wing but noncommunist Juan Bosch, the country's first elected president since 1924. In April 1965, another group of military men attempted to restore Bosch to power but were defeated by the ruling junta. Fearing the unrest would lead to "another Cuba," Johnson dispatched 22,000 American troops. The intervention

FROM YOUNG AMERICANS FOR FREEDOM, The Sharon Statement (September 1960)

Although the 1960s is usually thought of as a decade of youthful radicalism, it also witnessed the growth of conservative movements. The Sharon Statement marked the emergence of Young Americans for Freedom as a force for conservatism in American politics.

In this time of moral and political crisis, it is the responsibility of the youth of America to affirm certain eternal truths. We, as young conservatives, believe:

That foremost among the transcendent values is the individual's use of his God-given free will, whence derives his right to be free from the restrictions of arbitrary force;

That liberty is indivisible, and that political freedom cannot long exist without economic freedom;

That the purposes of government are to protect those freedoms through the preservation of internal order, the provision of national defense, and the administration of justice;

That when government ventures beyond these lawful functions, it accumulates power which tends to diminish order and liberty; . . .

That the market economy, allocating resources by the free play of supply and demand, is the single economic system compatible with the requirements of personal freedom and constitutional government, and that it is at the same time the most productive supplier of human needs; . . .

That the forces of international Communism are, at present, the greatest single threat to these liberties;

That the United States should stress victory over, rather than coexistence with, this menace.

FROM TOM HAYDEN AND OTHERS,
The Port Huron Statement (June 1962)

One of the most influential documents of the 1960s emerged in 1962 from a meeting sponsored by the Students for a Democratic Society in Port Huron, Michigan. Its call for a "democracy of individual participation" inspired many of the social movements of the decade and offered a critique of institutions ranging from the government to universities that failed to live up to this standard.

We are the people of this generation, bred in at least modest comfort, housed now in universities, looking uncomfortably to the world we inherit. . . . Freedom and equality for each individual, government of, by, and for the people—these American values we found good principles by which we could live as men.

As we grew, however, our comfort was penetrated by events too troubling to dismiss. First, the . . . Southern struggle against racial bigotry compelled most of us from silence to activism. Second, . . . the proclaimed peaceful intentions of the United States contradicted its economic and military investments in the Cold War. . . . The conventional moral terms of the age, the politician moralities—"free world," "people's democracies"—reflect realities poorly if at all, and seem to function more as ruling myths than as descriptive principles. But neither has our experience in the universities brought us moral enlightenment. Our professors and administrators sacrifice controversy to public relations; . . . their skills and silence are purchased by investors in the arms race. . . .

We regard *men* as infinitely precious and possessed of unfulfilled capacities for reason, freedom, and love. In affirming these principles we are aware of countering perhaps the dominant conceptions of man in the twentieth century: that he is a thing to be manipulated, and that he is inherently incapable of directing his own affairs. We oppose the depersonalization that reduces human beings to the status of things—if anything, the brutalities of the twentieth century teach that means and ends are intimately related, that vague appeals to "posterity" cannot justify the mutilations of the present. . . . We see little reason why men cannot meet with increasing skill the complexities and responsibilities of their situation, if society is organized not for minority, but for majority, participation in decision-making.

We would replace power rooted in possession, privilege, or circumstance by power and uniqueness rooted in love, reflectiveness, reason, and creativity. As a social system we seek the establishment of a democracy of individual participation [so] that the individual [can] share in those social decisions determining the quality and direction of his life. . . . A new left must consist of younger people. . . . [It] must start controversy throughout the land, if national policies and national apathy are to be reversed.

QUESTIONS

1. How do the young conservatives who wrote the Sharon Statement understand freedom?

2. What do the authors of the Port Huron Statement appear to mean by participatory democracy?

3. What are the main differences, and are there any similarities, between the outlooks of the young conservatives and the young radicals?

THE VIETNAM WAR, 1964–1975

CHINA

NORTH VIETNAM

BURMA (MYANMAR)

Dien Bien Phu

Hanoi ⊗
Haiphong

U.S. air raids 1966–1968, 1972

Gulf of Tonkin

LAOS

Thanh Hoa

⊗ Gulf of Tonkin incident August 1964

Hainan

Vinh

Mekong R.

Vientiane

17th Parallel demarcation line
Geneva accords, July 1954

Dong Hoi

Demilitarized zone

Invasion of Laos
February–March 1971

Hue ⊗

Tet offensive
January–February 1968

Da Nang

THAILAND

⊗ My Lai massacre
March 1968

Ho Chi Minh Trail

Pleiku

Qui Nhon

CAMBODIA

SOUTH VIETNAM

South China Sea

Invasion of Cambodia
April–June 1970

Na Trang

Phnom Penh

Gulf of Thailand

Saigon ⊗

Mekong Delta

Tet offensive
January–February 1968
Surrender of South Vietnam
April 30, 1975

⊗	Major battles or actions
—	U.S. and South Vietnamese offensives
—	North Vietnamese offensives
- - -	North Vietnamese supply routes

0   100   200 miles
0   100   200 kilometers

A war of aerial bombing and small guerilla skirmishes rather than fixed land battles, Vietnam was the longest war in American history and the only one the United States has lost.

outraged many Latin Americans. But the operation's success seemed to bolster Johnson's determination in Vietnam.

By 1968, the number of American troops in Vietnam exceeded half a million, and the conduct of the war had become more and more brutal. The North Vietnamese mistreated American prisoners of war held in a camp known sardonically by the inmates as the Hanoi Hilton. (One prisoner of war, John McCain, who spent six years there, courageously refused to be exchanged unless his companions were freed with him. McCain later became a senator from Arizona and the Republican candidate for president in 2008.) American planes dropped more tons of bombs on the small countries of North and South Vietnam than both sides used in all of World War II. They spread chemicals that destroyed forests to deprive the Viet Cong of hiding places and dropped bombs filled with napalm, a gelatinous form of gasoline that burns the skin of anyone exposed to it. The army pursued Viet Cong and North Vietnamese forces in "search and destroy" missions that often did not dis-

American soldiers in South Vietnam carrying wounded men to safety after a 1966 battle.

tinguish between combatants and civilians. Weekly reports of enemy losses or "body counts" became a fixation of the administration. But the United States could not break its opponents' ability to fight or make the South Vietnamese government any more able to survive on its own.

THE ANTIWAR MOVEMENT

As casualties mounted and American bombs poured down on North and South Vietnam, the Cold War foreign policy consensus began to unravel. By 1968, the war had sidetracked much of the Great Society and had torn families, universities, and the Democratic Party apart. With the entire political leadership, liberal no less than conservative, committed to the war for most of the 1960s, young activists lost all confidence in "the system."

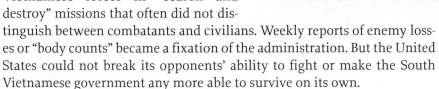

A massive 1969 antiwar demonstration on the Mall in Washington.

Opposition to the war became the organizing theme that united people with all kinds of doubts and discontents. "We recoil with horror," said a SNCC position paper, "at the inconsistency of a supposedly 'free' society where responsibility to freedom is equated with the responsibility to lend oneself to military aggression." With college students exempted from the draft, the burden of fighting fell on the working class and the poor. In 1967, Martin Luther King Jr. condemned the administration's Vietnam policy as an unconscionable use of violence and for draining resources from needs at home. At this point, King was the most prominent American to speak out against the war.

As for SDS, the war seemed the opposite of participatory democracy, since American involvement had come through secret commitments and decisions made by political elites, with no real public debate. In April 1965, SDS invited opponents of American policy in Vietnam to assemble in Washington, D.C. The turnout of 25,000 amazed the organizers, offering the first hint that the antiwar movement would soon enjoy a mass constituency. At the next antiwar rally, in November 1965, SDS leader Carl Ogelsby openly challenged the foundations of Cold War thinking. He linked Vietnam to a critique of American interventions in Guatemala and Iran, support for South African apartheid, and Johnson's dispatch of troops to the Dominican Republic, all rooted in obsessive anticommunism. Some might feel, Ogelsby concluded, "that I sound mighty anti-American. To these, I say: 'Don't blame *me* for *that!* Blame those who mouthed my liberal values and broke my American heart.'" The speech, observed one reporter, marked a "declaration of independence" for the New Left.

By 1967, young men were burning their draft cards or fleeing to Canada to avoid fighting in what they considered an unjust war. In October of that year, 100,000 antiwar protestors assembled at the Lincoln Memorial in Washington, D.C. Many marched across the Potomac River to the Pentagon, where photographers captured them placing flowers in the rifle barrels of soldiers guarding the nerve center of the American military.

THE COUNTERCULTURE

The New Left's definition of freedom initially centered on participatory democracy, a political concept. But as the 1960s progressed, young Americans' understanding of freedom increasingly expanded to include cultural freedom as well. Although many streams flowed into the generational rebellion known as the "counterculture," the youth revolt was inconceivable without the war's destruction of young Americans' belief in authority. By the late 1960s, millions of young people openly rejected the values and behavior of their elders. Their ranks included not only college students but also numerous young workers, even though most unions strongly opposed antiwar demonstrations and countercultural displays (a reaction that further separated young radicals from former allies on the traditional left). For the first time in American history, the flamboyant rejection of respectable norms in clothing, language, sexual behavior, and drug use, previously confined to artists and bohemians, became the basis of a mass movement. Its rallying cry was "liberation."

Here was John Winthrop's nightmare of three centuries earlier come to pass—a massive redefinition of freedom as a rejection of all authority.

Two young members of the counterculture at their wedding in New Mexico.

VISIONS OF FREEDOM

Antiwar Protest. *The First Amendment guarantees Americans the right of free speech, and to assemble to protest government policies. Rarely in American history have these rights been used on so massive a scale as during the 1960s. This photograph of an antiwar demonstrator placing flowers in the rifles of U.S. soldiers outside the Pentagon (the headquarters of the American military, in the nation's capital) at a 1967 rally against the Vietnam War was reproduced around the world. Some 100,000 protesters took part in this demonstration.*

QUESTIONS

1. Do you think that the photographer intended to suggest that peaceful protest is an effective way of spreading the antiwar message?

2. What elements of life in the 1960s seem to clash in this image?

Timothy Leary, promoter of the hallucinogenic drug LSD, listening to the band Quicksilver Messenger Service at the Human Be-In in San Francisco in 1967.

"Your sons and your daughters are beyond your command," Bob Dylan's song "The Times They Are A-Changin'" bluntly informed mainstream America. To be sure, the counterculture in some ways represented not rebellion but the fulfillment of the consumer marketplace. It extended into every realm of life the definition of freedom as the right to individual choice. Given the purchasing power of students and young adults, countercultural emblems—colorful clothing, rock music, images of sexual freedom, even symbols of black revolution and Native American resistance—were soon being mass-marketed as fashions of the day. Self-indulgence and self-destructive behavior were built into the counterculture. To followers of Timothy Leary, the Harvard scientist turned prophet of mind-expansion, the psychedelic drug LSD embodied a new freedom—"the freedom to expand your own consciousness." In 1967, Leary organized a Human Be-In in San Francisco, where he urged a crowd of 20,000 to "turn on, tune in, drop out."

PERSONAL LIBERATION AND THE FREE INDIVIDUAL

But there was far more to the counterculture than new consumer styles or the famed trio of sex, drugs, and rock and roll. To young dissenters, personal liberation represented a spirit of creative experimentation, a search for a way of life in which friendship and pleasure eclipsed the single-minded pursuit of wealth. It meant a release from bureaucratized education and work, repressive rules of personal behavior, and, above all, a militarized state that, in the name of freedom, rained destruction on a faraway people. It also encouraged new forms of radical action. "Underground" newspapers pioneered a personal and politically committed style of journalism. The Youth International Party, or "yippies," introduced humor and theatricality as elements of protest. From the visitor's gallery of the New York Stock Exchange, yippie founder Abbie Hoffman showered dollar bills onto the floor, bringing trading to a halt as brokers scrambled to retrieve the money.

The counterculture emphasized the ideal of community, establishing quasi-independent neighborhoods in New York City's East Village and San Francisco's Haight-Ashbury district and, in an echo of nineteenth-century utopian communities like New Harmony, some 2,000 communes nationwide. Rock festivals, like Woodstock in upstate New York in 1969, brought together hundreds of thousands of young people to celebrate their alternative lifestyle and independence from adult authority. The opening song at Woodstock, performed by Richie Havens, began with eight repetitions of the single word "freedom."

The counterculture's notion of liberation centered on the free individual. Nowhere was this more evident than in the place occupied by sexual freedom in the generational rebellion. Starting in 1960, the mass marketing of birth-control pills made possible what "free lovers" had long demanded—the separation of sex from procreation. By the late 1960s, sexual freedom had become as much an element of the youth rebellion as long hair and drugs. Rock music celebrated the free expression of sexuality. The musical *Hair*, which gave voice to the youth rebellion, flaunted nudity on Broadway. The sexual revolution was central to another mass movement that emerged in the 1960s—the "second wave" of feminism.

THE NEW MOVEMENTS AND THE RIGHTS REVOLUTION

The civil rights revolution, soon followed by the rise of the New Left, inspired other Americans to voice their grievances and claim their rights. Many borrowed the confrontational tactics of the black movement and activist students, adopting their language of "power" and "liberation" and their rejection of traditional organizations and approaches. By the late 1960s, new social movements dotted the political landscape.

THE FEMININE MYSTIQUE

The achievement of the vote had not seemed to affect women's lack of power and opportunity. When the 1960s began, only a handful of women held political office, newspapers divided job ads into "male" and "female" sections, with the latter limited to low-wage clerical positions, and major universities limited the number of female students they accepted. In many states, husbands still controlled their wives' earnings. As late as 1970, the Ohio Supreme Court held that a wife was "at most a superior servant to her husband," without "legally recognized feelings or rights."

During the 1950s, some commentators had worried that the country was wasting its "woman power," a potential weapon in the Cold War. But the public reawakening of feminist consciousness did not get its start until the publication in 1963 of Betty Friedan's *The Feminine Mystique*. Friedan had written pioneering articles during the 1940s on pay discrimination against women workers and racism in the workplace for the newspaper of the United Electrical Workers' union. But, like other social critics of the 1950s, she now took as her themes the emptiness of consumer culture and the discontents of the middle class. Her opening chapter, "The Problem That Has No Name," painted a devastating picture of talented, educated women trapped in a world that viewed marriage and motherhood as their primary goals. Somehow, after more than a century of agitation for access to the public sphere, women's lives still centered on the home. In Moscow in 1959, Richard Nixon had made the suburban home an emblem of American freedom. For Friedan, invoking the era's most powerful symbol of evil, it was a "comfortable concentration camp."

Few books have had the impact of *The Feminine Mystique*. Friedan was deluged by desperate letters from female readers relating how the suburban dream had become a nightmare. "Freedom," wrote an Atlanta woman, "was a word I had always taken for granted. [I now realized that] I had voluntarily enslaved myself." To be sure, a few of Friedan's correspondents insisted

A poster listing some of the performers who took part in the Woodstock festival in 1969. A dove of peace sits on the guitar, symbolizing the overlap between the antiwar movement and counterculture.

In 1967, in a celebrated incident arising from the new feminism, a race official tried to eject Kathrine Switzer from the Boston Marathon, only to be pushed aside by other runners. Considered too fragile for the marathon (whose course covers more than twenty-six miles), women were prohibited from running. Switzer completed the race and today hundreds of thousands of women around the world compete in marathons each year.

that for a woman to create "a comfortable, happy home for her family" was "what God intended." But the immediate result of *The Feminine Mystique* was to focus attention on yet another gap between American rhetoric and American reality.

The law slowly began to address feminist concerns. In 1963, Congress passed the Equal Pay Act, barring sex discrimination among holders of the same jobs. The Civil Rights Act of 1964, as noted earlier, prohibited inequalities based on sex as well as race. Deluged with complaints of discrimination by working women, the Equal Employment Opportunity Commission established by the law became a major force in breaking down barriers to female employment. The year 1966 saw the formation of the National Organization for Women (NOW), with Friedan as president. Modeled on civil rights organizations, it demanded equal opportunity in jobs, education, and political participation and attacked the "false image of women" spread by the mass media.

WOMEN'S LIBERATION

If NOW grew out of a resurgence of middle-class feminism, a different female revolt was brewing within the civil rights and student movements. As in the days of abolitionism, young women who had embraced an ideology of social equality and personal freedom and learned methods of political organizing encountered inequality and sexual exploitation. Women like Ella Baker and Fannie Lou Hamer had played major roles in grassroots civil rights organizing. But many women in the movement found themselves relegated to typing, cooking, and cleaning for male coworkers. Some were pressured to engage in sexual liaisons. Echoing the words of Abby Kelley a century earlier, a group of female SNCC activists concluded in a

1965 memorandum that "there seem to be many parallels that can be drawn between the treatment of Negroes and the treatment of women in our society as a whole." What bothered them most was the status of women within the movement, where assumptions of male supremacy seemed as deeply rooted as in society at large.

The same complaints arose in SDS. "The Movement is supposed to be for human liberation," wrote one student leader. "How come the condition of women inside it is no better than outside?" The rapidly growing number of women in college provided a ready-made constituency for the new feminism. By 1967, women throughout the country were establishing "consciousness-raising" groups to discuss the sources of their discontent. The time, many concluded, had come to establish a movement of their own, more radical than NOW. The new feminism burst onto the national scene at the Miss America beauty pageant of 1968, when protesters filled a "freedom trash can" with objects of "oppression"—girdles, brassieres, high-heeled shoes, and copies of *Playboy* and *Cosmopolitan*. (Contrary to legend, they did not set the contents on fire, which would have been highly dangerous on the wooden boardwalk. But the media quickly invented a new label for radical women—"bra burners.") Inside the hall, demonstrators unfurled banners carrying the slogans "Freedom for Women" and "Women's Liberation."

A 1970 women's liberation demonstration at the Statue of Liberty.

PERSONAL FREEDOM

The women's liberation movement inspired a major expansion of the idea of freedom by insisting that it should be applied to the most intimate realms of life. Introducing the terms "sexism" and "sexual politics" and the phrase "the personal is political" into public debate, they insisted that sexual relations, conditions of marriage, and standards of beauty were as much "political" questions as the war, civil rights, and the class tensions that had traditionally inspired the Left to action. The idea that family life is not off-limits to considerations of power and justice repudiated the family-oriented public culture of the 1950s, and it permanently changed Americans' definition of freedom.

Radical feminists' first public campaign demanded the repeal of state laws that underscored women's lack of self-determination by banning abortions or leaving it up to physicians to decide whether a pregnancy could be terminated. Without the right to control her own reproduction, wrote one activist, "woman's other 'freedoms' are tantalizing mockeries that cannot be exercised." In 1969, a group of feminists disrupted legislative hearings on New York's law banning abortions, where the experts scheduled to testify consisted of fourteen men and a Roman Catholic nun.

The call for legalized abortions merged the nineteenth-century demand that a woman control her own body with the Sixties emphasis on sexual freedom. But the concerns of women's liberation went far beyond sexuality. *Sisterhood Is Powerful*, an influential collection of essays, manifestos, and personal accounts published in 1970, touched on a remarkable array of issues, from violence against women to inequalities in the law, churches, workplaces, and family life. By this time, feminist ideas had entered the mainstream. In 1962, a poll showed that two-thirds of American women did not feel themselves to be victims of discrimination. By 1974, two-thirds did.

*Part of the Gay Liberation Day
demonstration in New York City
in June 1970.*

*César Chavez speaking at a 1965 rally to
support the national grape boycott.*
Huelga, *on the banner behind him, means*
"strike" in Spanish. On the front of the
platform is an image of Our Lady of
Guadalupe, the patron saint of Mexico.
Like the civil rights movement, the United
Farm Workers merged religious and
political language and imagery.

GAY LIBERATION

In a decade full of surprises, perhaps the greatest of all was the emergence of the movement for gay liberation. Efforts of one kind or another for greater rights for racial minorities and women had a long history. Homosexuals, wrote Harry Hay, who in 1951 founded the Mattachine Society, the first gay rights organization, were "the one group of disadvantaged people who didn't even think of themselves as a group." Gay men and lesbians had long been stigmatized as sinful or mentally disordered. Most states made homosexual acts illegal, and police regularly harassed the gay subcultures that existed in major cities like San Francisco and New York. McCarthyism, which viewed homosexuality as a source of national weakness, made the discrimination to which gays were subjected even worse. Although homosexuals had achieved considerable success in the arts and fashion, most kept their sexual orientation secret, or "in the closet."

The Mattachine Society had worked to persuade the public that apart from their sexual orientation, gays were average Americans who ought not to be persecuted. But as with other groups, the Sixties transformed the gay movement. If one moment marked the advent of "gay liberation," it was a 1969 police raid on the Stonewall Bar in New York's Greenwich Village, a gathering place for homosexuals. Rather than bowing to police harassment, as in the past, gays fought back. Five days of rioting followed, and a militant movement was born. Gay men and lesbians stepped out of the "closet" to insist that sexual orientation is a matter of rights, power, and identity. Prejudice against homosexuals persisted. But within a few years, "gay pride" marches were being held in numerous cities.

LATINO ACTIVISM

As in the case of blacks, a movement for legal rights had long flourished among Mexican-Americans. But the mid-1960s saw the flowering of a new militancy challenging the group's second-class economic status. Like Black Power advocates, the movement emphasized pride in both the Mexican past and the new Chicano culture that had arisen in the United States. Unlike the Black Power movement and SDS, it was closely linked to labor struggles. Beginning in 1965, César Chavez, the son of migrant farm workers and a disciple of King, led a series of nonviolent protests, including marches, fasts, and a national boycott of California grapes, to pressure growers to agree to labor contracts with the United Farm Workers union (UFW). The UFW was as much a mass movement for civil rights as a campaign for economic betterment. The boycott mobilized Latino communities throughout the Southwest and drew national attention to the pitifully low wages and oppressive working conditions of migrant laborers. In 1970, the major growers agreed to contracts with the UFW.

In New York City, the Young Lords Organization, modeled on the Black Panthers, staged street demonstrations to protest the high unemployment rate among the city's Puerto Ricans and the lack of city services in Latino neighborhoods. (In one protest, they dumped garbage on city streets to draw attention to the city's failure to collect refuse in poor areas.) Like SNCC and SDS, the Latino movement gave rise to feminist dissent. Many Chicano and Puerto Rican men regarded feminist demands as incompatible with the Latino heritage of *machismo* (an exaggerated sense of manliness, including the right to dominate women). Young female activists, however, viewed the sexual double standard and the inequality of women as incompatible with freedom for all members of *la raza* (the race, or people).

RED POWER

The 1960s also witnessed an upsurge of Indian militancy. The Truman and Eisenhower administrations had sought to dismantle the reservation system and integrate Indians into the American mainstream—a policy known as "termination," since it meant ending recognition of the remaining elements of Indian sovereignty. Many Indian leaders protested vigorously against this policy, and it was abandoned by President Kennedy. Johnson's War on Poverty channeled increased federal funds to reservations. But like other minority groups, Indian activists compared their own status to that of underdeveloped countries overseas. They demanded not simply economic aid but self-determination, like the emerging nations of the Third World. Using language typical of the late 1960s, Clyde Warrior, president of the National Indian Youth Council, declared, "We are not free in the most basic sense of the word. We are not allowed to make those basic human choices about our personal life and the destiny of our communities."

Founded in 1968, the American Indian Movement staged protests demanding greater tribal self-government and the restoration of economic resources guaranteed in treaties. In 1969, a group calling itself "Indians of All Nations" occupied (or from their point of view, re-occupied) Alcatraz Island in San Francisco Bay, claiming that it had been illegally seized from its original inhabitants. The protest, which lasted into 1971, launched the Red Power movement. In the years that followed, many Indian tribes would win greater control over education and economic development on the reservations. Indian activists would bring land claims suits, demanding and receiving monetary settlements for past dispossession. As a result of a rising sense of self-respect, the number of Americans identifying themselves as Indians doubled between 1970 and 1990.

The occupation of Alcatraz Island in San Francisco Bay in 1969 by "Indians of All Tribes" symbolized the emergence of a new militancy among Native Americans.

SILENT SPRING

Liberation movements among racial minorities, women, and gays challenged long-standing social inequalities. Another movement, environmentalism, called into question different pillars of American life—the equation of progress with endless increases in consumption and the faith that science, technology, and economic growth would advance the social welfare.

Concern for preserving the natural environment dated back to the creation of national parks and other conservation efforts during the Progressive era. But in keeping with the spirit of the Sixties, the new environmentalism was more activist and youth-oriented, and it spoke the language of empowering citizens to participate in decisions that affected their lives. Its emergence reflected the very affluence celebrated by proponents of the American Way. As the "quality of life"—including physical fitness, health, and opportunities to enjoy leisure activities—occupied a greater role in the lives of middle-class Americans, the environmental consequences of economic growth received increased attention. When the 1960s began, complaints were already being heard about the bulldozing of forests for suburban development and the contamination produced by laundry detergents and chemical lawn fertilizers seeping into drinking supplies.

The publication in 1962 of *Silent Spring* by the marine biologist Rachel Carson brought home to millions of readers the effects of DDT, an insecticide widely used by home owners and farmers against mosquitoes, gypsy moths, and other insects. In chilling detail, Carson related how DDT killed birds and animals and caused sickness among humans. Chemical and pesticide companies launched a campaign to discredit her—some critics called the book part of a communist plot. *Time* magazine even condemned Carson as "hysterical" and "emotional"—words typically used by men to discredit women.

THE NEW ENVIRONMENTALISM

Carson's work launched the modern environmental movement. The Sierra Club, founded in the 1890s to preserve forests, saw its membership more than triple, and other groups sprang into existence to alert the country to the dangers of water contamination, air pollution, lead in paint, and the extinction of animal species. Nearly every state quickly banned the use of DDT. In 1969, television brought home to a national audience the death of birds and fish and the despoiling of beaches caused by a major oil spill off the coast of California, exposing the environmental dangers of oil transportation and ocean drilling for oil.

Despite vigorous opposition from business groups that considered its proposals a violation of property rights, environmentalism attracted the broadest bipartisan support of any of the new social movements. Under Republican president Richard Nixon, Congress during the late 1960s and early 1970s passed a series of measures to protect the environment, including the Clean Air and Clean Water Acts and the Endangered Species Act. On April 22, 1970, the first Earth Day, some 20 million people, most of them under the age of thirty, participated in rallies, concerts, and teach-ins.

Closely related to environmentalism was the consumer movement, spearheaded by the lawyer Ralph Nader. His book *Unsafe at Any Speed* (1965) exposed how auto manufacturers produced highly dangerous vehicles. General Motors, whose Chevrolet Corvair Nader singled out for its tendency to roll over in certain driving situations, hired private investigators to discredit him. When their campaign was exposed, General Motors paid Nader a handsome settlement, which he used to fund investigations of other dangerous products and of misleading advertising.

Nader's campaigns laid the groundwork for the numerous new consumer protection laws and regulations of the 1970s. Unlike 1960s movements that emphasized personal liberation, environmentalism and the consumer movement called for limiting some kinds of freedom—especially the right to use private property in any way the owner desired—in the name of a greater common good.

THE RIGHTS REVOLUTION

It is one of the more striking ironies of the 1960s that although the "rights revolution" began in the streets, it achieved constitutional legitimacy through the Supreme Court, historically the most conservative branch of government. Under the guidance of Chief Justice Earl Warren, the Court vastly expanded the rights enjoyed by all Americans and placed them beyond the reach of legislative and local majorities.

As noted in Chapter 21, the Court's emergence as a vigorous guardian of civil liberties had been foreshadowed in 1937, when it abandoned its commitment to freedom of contract while declaring that the right of free expression deserved added protection. The McCarthy era halted progress toward a broader conception of civil liberties. It resumed on June 17, 1957, known as "Red Monday" by conservatives, when the Court moved to rein in the anticommunist crusade. The justices overturned convictions of individuals for advocating the overthrow of the government, failing to answer questions before the House Un-American Activities Committee, and refusing to disclose their political beliefs to state officials. The government, Warren declared, could prosecute illegal actions, but not "unorthodoxy or dissent." By the time Warren retired in 1969, the Court had reaffirmed the right of even the most unpopular viewpoints to First Amendment protection and had dismantled the Cold War loyalty security system.

Civil liberties had gained strength in the 1930s because of association with the rights of labor; in the 1950s and 1960s, they became intertwined with civil rights. Beginning with *NAACP v. Alabama* in 1958, the Court struck down southern laws that sought to destroy civil rights organizations by forcing them to make public their membership lists. In addition, in the landmark ruling in *New York Times v. Sullivan* (1964), it overturned a libel judgment by an Alabama jury against the nation's leading newspaper for carrying an advertisement critical of how local officials treated civil rights demonstrators. The "central meaning of the First Amendment," the justices declared, lay in the right of citizens to criticize their government. For good measure, they declared the Sedition Act of 1798 unconstitutional over a century and a half after it had expired. Before the 1960s, few Supreme Court cases had dealt with newspaper publishing. *Sullivan* created the modern constitutional law of freedom of the press.

The Court in the 1960s continued the push toward racial equality, overturning numerous local Jim Crow laws. In *Loving v. Virginia* (1967), it declared unconstitutional the laws still on the books in sixteen states that prohibited interracial marriage. This aptly named case arose from the interracial marriage of Richard and Mildred Loving. Barred by Virginia law from marrying, they did so in Washington, D.C., and later returned to their home state. Two weeks after their arrival, the local sheriff entered their home in the middle of the night, roused the couple from bed, and arrested them. The Lovings were sentenced to five years in prison, although the judge gave them the option of leaving Virginia instead. They departed for Washington, but five years later, wishing to return, they sued

Karl Hubenthal's December 8, 1976, cartoon for the Los Angeles Herald-Examiner *celebrates the rights revolution as an expansion of American liberty.*

in federal court, claiming that their rights had been violated. In 1968, in *Jones v. Alfred H. Mayer Co.*, the Court forbade discrimination in the rental or sale of housing. Eliminating "badges of slavery," such as unequal access to housing, the ruling suggested, was essential to fulfilling at long last the promise of emancipation.

POLICING THE STATES

The Court simultaneously pushed forward the process of imposing upon the states the obligation to respect the liberties outlined in the Bill of Rights. It required states to abide by protections against illegal search and seizure, the right of a defendant to a speedy trial, the prohibition against cruel and unusual punishment, and the right of poor persons accused of a crime to receive counsel from publicly supplied attorneys. Among the most important of these decisions was the 5-4 ruling in *Miranda v. Arizona* (1966). This held that an individual in police custody must be informed of the rights to remain silent and to confer with a lawyer before answering questions and must be told that any statements might be used in court. The decision made "Miranda warnings" standard police practice.

The Court also assumed the power to oversee the fairness of democratic procedures at the state and local levels. *Baker v. Carr* (1962) established the principle that districts electing members of state legislatures must be equal in population. This "one-man, one-vote" principle overturned apportionment systems in numerous states that had allowed individuals in sparsely inhabited rural areas to enjoy the same representation as residents of populous city districts.

The justices also moved to reinforce the "wall of separation" between church and state. In 1961, they unanimously declared unconstitutional a clause in Maryland's constitution requiring that public officials declare their belief "in the existence of God." In the following two years, they decreed that prayers and Bible readings in public schools also violated the First Amendment. President Kennedy pointed out that Americans remained perfectly free to pray at home or in church, but these rulings proved to be the most unpopular of all the Warren Court's decisions. Polls showed that 80 percent of Americans favored allowing prayer in public schools.

THE RIGHT TO PRIVACY

The Warren Court not only expanded existing liberties but also outlined entirely new rights in response to the rapidly changing contours of American society. Most dramatic was its assertion of a constitutional right to privacy in *Griswold v. Connecticut* (1965), which overturned a state law prohibiting the use of contraceptives. Justice William O. Douglas, who wrote the decision, had once declared, "The right to be let alone is the beginning of all freedom." Apart from decisions of the 1920s that affirmed the right to marry and raise children without government interference, however, few legal precedents existed regarding privacy. The Constitution does not mention the word. Nonetheless, Douglas argued that a constitutionally protected "zone of privacy" within marriage could be inferred from the "penumbras" (shadows) of the Bill of Rights.

Griswold linked privacy to the sanctity of marriage. But the Court soon transformed it into a right of individuals. It extended access to birth control to unmarried adults and ultimately to minors—an admission by the Court that law could not reverse the sexual revolution. These decisions led directly to the most controversial decision that built on the rulings of the Warren Court (even though it occurred in 1973, four years after Warren's retirement). This was *Roe v. Wade*, which created a constitutional right to terminate a pregnancy. The Court declared access to abortion a fundamental freedom protected by the Constitution, a fulfillment of radical feminists' earliest demand. *Roe* provoked vigorous opposition, which has continued to this day. Only two states banned contraception when *Griswold* was decided; *Roe* invalidated the laws of no fewer than forty-six.

Griswold and *Roe* unleashed a flood of rulings and laws that seemed to accept the feminist view of the family as a collection of sovereign individuals rather than a unit with a single head. The legal rights of women within the domestic sphere expanded dramatically. Law enforcement authorities for the first time began to prosecute crimes like rape and assault by husbands against their wives. Today, some notion of privacy is central to most Americans' conception of freedom.

The rights revolution completed the transformation of American freedom from a set of entitlements enjoyed mainly by white men into an open-ended claim to equality, recognition, and self-determination. For the rest of the century, the government and legal system would be inundated by demands by aggrieved groups of all kinds, and the Supreme Court would devote much of its time to defining the rights of Americans.

1968

A YEAR OF TURMOIL

The Sixties reached their climax in 1968, a year when momentous events succeeded each other so rapidly that the foundations of society seemed to be dissolving. Late January 1968 saw the Tet offensive, in which Viet Cong and North Vietnamese troops launched well-organized uprisings in cities throughout South Vietnam, completely surprising American military leaders. The United States drove back the offensive and inflicted heavy losses. But the intensity of the fighting, brought into America's homes on television, shattered public confidence in the Johnson administration, which had repeatedly proclaimed victory to be "just around the corner." Leading members of the press and political establishment joined the chorus criticizing American involvement. Eugene McCarthy, an antiwar senator from Minnesota, announced that he would seek the Democratic nomination. In March, aided by a small army

Television brought the Vietnam War into Americans' living rooms, helping to spur antiwar sentiment. The woman seems to have taken a break from washing dishes to watch the news.

Striking sanitation workers in Memphis, Tennessee. As their signs suggest, they demanded respect as well as higher wages. Having traveled to Memphis to support the strikers, Martin Luther King Jr. was assassinated on April 4, 1968.

of student volunteers, McCarthy received more than 40 percent of the vote in the New Hampshire primary. With public support dissolving, Johnson rejected the military's request to send 200,000 more troops to Vietnam. In March, he stunned the nation by announcing that he had decided not to seek reelection. Peace talks soon opened in Paris.

Meanwhile, Martin Luther King Jr. was organizing a Poor People's March, hoping to bring thousands of demonstrators to Washington to demand increased anti-poverty efforts. On April 4, having traveled to Memphis to support a strike of the city's grossly underpaid black garbage collectors, King was killed by a white assassin. The greatest outbreak of urban violence in the nation's history followed in ghettos across the country. Washington, D.C., had to be occupied by soldiers before order was restored. As a gesture to King's memory, Congress passed its last major civil rights law, the Open Housing Act, which prohibited discrimination in the sale and rental of homes and apartments, although with weak enforcement mechanisms.

At the end of April, students protesting Columbia University's involvement in defense research and its plan to build a gymnasium in a public park occupied seven campus buildings. New York police removed them in an assault that left hundreds of protesters and bystanders injured and led to a strike that closed the campus. In June, a young Palestinian nationalist assassinated Robert F. Kennedy, who was seeking the Democratic nomination as an opponent of the war. In August, tens of thousands of antiwar activists descended on Chicago for protests at the Democratic national convention, where the delegates nominated Vice President Hubert Humphrey as their presidential candidate. The city's police, never known for restraint, assaulted the marchers with nightsticks, producing hundreds of injuries outside the convention hall and pandemonium inside it.

A later investigation called the event a "police riot." Nonetheless, the government indicted eight political radicals for conspiring to incite the violence. They included Tom Hayden of SDS, yippie leader Abbie Hoffman, and Bobby Seale of the Black Panthers. Five were found guilty after a tumultuous trial. But an appeals court overturned the convictions because Judge Julius Hoffman (no relation to Abbie Hoffman) had been flagrantly biased against the defendants.

THE GLOBAL 1968

Like 1848 and 1919, 1968 was a year of worldwide upheaval. In many countries, young radicals challenged existing power structures, often borrowing language and strategies from the decade's social movements in the United States and adapting them to their own circumstances. Television carried events in one country instantaneously across the globe.

Massive antiwar demonstrations took place in London, Rome, Paris, Munich, and Tokyo, leading to clashes with police and scores of injuries. In

Italy, students occupied university buildings, bringing education to a halt. In Paris, a nationwide student uprising began in May 1968 that echoed American demands for educational reform and personal liberation. Unlike in the United States, millions of French workers soon joined the protest, adding their own demands for higher wages and greater democracy in the workplace. The result was a general strike that paralyzed the country and nearly led to the collapse of the government before it ended. In communist Czechoslovakia, leaders bent on reform came to power by promising to institute "socialism with a human face," only to be ousted by a Soviet invasion. Soldiers fired on students demonstrating for greater democracy on the eve of the opening of the Olympic Games in Mexico City, leading to more than 500 deaths. In Northern Ireland, which remained part of Great Britain after the rest of Ireland achieved independence, the police attacked a peaceful march of Catholics demanding an end to religious discrimination who were inspired by the American civil rights movement. This event marked the beginning of The Troubles, a period of both peaceful protest and violent conflict in the region that did not end until the turn of the twenty-first century.

A mural in Belfast, Northern Ireland, depicts the black American abolitionist Frederick Douglass, illustrating how the movement for Catholic civil rights associated itself with the struggle for racial justice in the United States. The text points out that Douglass lectured in Ireland in the 1840s on abolitionism, women's rights, and Irish independence.

And throughout the world, the second wave of American feminism found echoes among women who resented being relegated to unequal citizenship. American women influenced, and were influenced by, movements in other countries, particularly in Europe, which demanded equal rights and challenged demeaning representations of women in advertising and the mass media. As in the United States, personal liberation, including a woman's right to control her own body, became a rallying cry. In Catholic European countries like France and Italy, women's movements won significant legal changes, making it easier to obtain divorces and decriminalizing abortion. *Our Bodies, Ourselves*, a book originally published in 1973 by a group of Boston women, dealt frankly with widely misunderstood aspects of women's health, including pregnancy and childbirth, menopause, birth control, and sexually transmitted diseases. It was quickly translated into twenty languages.

NIXON'S COMEBACK

In the United States, instead of radical change, the year's events opened the door for a conservative reaction. Turmoil in the streets produced a demand for public order. Black militancy produced white "backlash," which played an increasing role in politics. The fact that the unelected Supreme Court was inventing and protecting "rights" fed the argument that faraway bureaucrats rode roughshod over local traditions.

In August, Richard Nixon capped a remarkable political comeback by winning the Republican nomination. He campaigned as the champion of the "silent majority"—ordinary

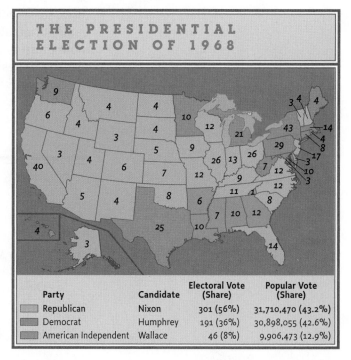

THE PRESIDENTIAL ELECTION OF 1968

Party	Candidate	Electoral Vote (Share)	Popular Vote (Share)
Republican	Nixon	301 (56%)	31,710,470 (43.2%)
Democrat	Humphrey	191 (36%)	30,898,055 (42.6%)
American Independent	Wallace	46 (8%)	9,906,473 (12.9%)

Americans who believed that change had gone too far—and called for a renewed commitment to "law and order." Humphrey could not overcome the deep divide in his party. With 43 percent of the vote, Nixon had only a razor-thin margin over his Democratic rival. But George Wallace, running as an independent and appealing to resentments against blacks' gains, Great Society programs, and the Warren Court, received an additional 13 percent. Taken together, the Nixon and Wallace totals, which included a considerable number of former Democratic voters, indicated that four years after Johnson's landslide election ushered in the Great Society, liberalism was on the defensive.

The year 1968 did not mark the end of the 1960s. The Great Society would achieve an unlikely culmination during the Nixon administration. The second wave of feminism achieved its largest following during the 1970s. Nixon's election did, however, inaugurate a period of growing conservatism in American politics. The conservative ascendancy would usher in yet another chapter in the story of American freedom.

THE LEGACY OF THE SIXTIES

The 1960s transformed American life in ways unimaginable when the decade began. It produced new rights and new understandings of freedom. It made possible the entrance of numerous members of racial minorities into the mainstream of American life, while leaving unsolved the problem of urban poverty. It set in motion a transformation of the status of women. It changed what Americans expected from government—from clean air and water to medical coverage in old age. At the same time, it undermined public confidence in national leaders. Relations between young and old, men and women, and white and non-white, along with every institution in society, changed as a result.

Just as the Civil War and New Deal established the framework for future political debates, so, it seemed, Americans were condemned to refight the battles of the 1960s long after the decade had ended. Race relations, feminism, social policy, the nation's proper role in world affairs—these issues hardly originated in the 1960s. But the events of those years made them more pressing and more divisive. As the country became more conservative, the Sixties would be blamed for every imaginable social ill, from crime and drug abuse to a decline of respect for authority. Yet during the 1960s, the United States had become a more open, more tolerant—in a word, a freer—country.

SUGGESTED READING

BOOKS

Anderson, John A., III. *The Other Side of the Sixties: Young Americans for Freedom and the Rise of Conservative Politics* (1997). Considers conservative students of the 1960s and how they laid the groundwork for the later growth of their movement.

Anderson, Terry H. *The Movement and the Sixties: Protest in America from Greensboro to Wounded Knee* (1995). Offers an account of the numerous social protests that took place in the 1960s.

Brick, Howard. *Age of Contradiction: American Thought and Culture in the 1960s* (1998). A careful examination of the complex currents of thought that circulated during the decade.

Carson, Clayborne. *In Struggle: SNCC and the Black Awakening of the 1960s* (1981). A study of the Student Non-Violent Coordinating Committee and its impact on the 1960s.

D'Emilio, John. *Sexual Politics, Sexual Communities: The Making of a Homosexual Minority in the United States, 1940–1970* (1983). Explores the status of gay men and lesbians in mid-twentieth-century America and the rise of the gay movement.

Dittmer, John. *Local People: The Struggle for Civil Rights in Mississippi* (1994). Traces the civil rights movement in one state, looked at from the experience of grassroots activists.

Herring, George C. *America's Longest War: The United States and Vietnam, 1950–1975* (2002 ed.). The fullest study of how the United States became involved in the war in Vietnam, and the course of the conflict.

Horwitz, Morton J. *The Warren Court and the Pursuit of Justice* (1998). Analyzes how the Supreme Court redefined the rights of Americans under Chief Justice Earl Warren.

Isserman, Maurice, and Michael Kazin. *America Divided: The Civil War of the 1960s* (2000). A comprehensive account of the social movements and political debates of the 1960s.

Matusow, Allen J. *The Unraveling of America: A History of Liberalism in the 1960s* (1984). Examines how liberalism triumphed and then dissolved during the 1960s.

Porter, Gareth. *Perils of Dominance: Imbalance of Power and the Road to Vietnam* (2005). Discusses the assumptions of policymakers and their effect on foreign policy, especially the idea that American power could not be resisted.

Rosen, Ruth. *The World Split Open: How the Modern Women's Movement Changed America* (2000). Considers how the "second wave" of feminism transformed the lives of American women and men.

Rossinow, Douglas C. *The Politics of Authenticity: Liberalism, Christianity, and the New Left in America* (1998). A careful look at some of the intellectual roots of New Left radicalism.

Sale, Kirkpatrick. *The Green Revolution: The American Environmental Movement, 1962–1992* (1993). A brief history of one of the most significant movements to emerge from the 1960s.

Skretny, John. *The Minority Rights Revolution* (2002). An account of the rights revolution and how it affected American society and its understanding of the rights of citizens.

WEBSITES

A Visual Journey: Photographs by Lisa Law, 1965–1971: http://americanhistory.si.edu/lisalaw/1.htm

Free Speech Movement Digital Archive: http://bancroft.berkeley.edu/FSM/

Freedom Now!: www.stg.brown.edu/projects/FreedomNow/

The Wars for Vietnam, 1945–1975: http://vietnam.vassar.edu/index.html

REVIEW QUESTIONS

1. What was the significance of the 1963 March on Washington?

2. In what ways were President Kennedy's foreign policy decisions shaped by Cold War ideology?

3. Explain the significance of the Civil Rights Act of 1964 and the Voting Rights Act of 1965.

4. Explain why many blacks, especially in the North, did not believe that the civil rights legislation went far enough in promoting black freedom.

5. What were the effects of President Johnson's Great Society and War on Poverty programs?

6. In what ways was the New Left not as new as it claimed?

7. What were the goals of U.S. involvement in Vietnam?

8. How did the civil rights movement influence the broader rights revolution of the 1960s?

9. Identify the origins, goals, and composition of the feminist, or women's liberation, movement.

10. Describe how the social movements of the 1960s in the United States became part of a global movement for change by 1968.

FREEDOM QUESTIONS

1. How was the Great Society rooted in New Deal ideas of freedom?

2. Explain the concepts of freedom held by the conservative Young Americans for Freedom and the liberal Students for a Democratic Society. Why did conservatives object to the goal of "participatory democracy"?

3. What were the cultural freedoms embraced by the counterculture?

4. How did the women's liberation movement expand the idea of freedom?

KEY TERMS

Student Non-Violent Coordinating Committee (p. 1037)

Freedom Rides (p. 1038)

March on Washington (p. 1039)

Bay of Pigs (p. 1041)

Cuban missile crisis (p. 1041)

Civil Rights Act (p. 1043)

Sharon Statement (p. 1046)

Voting Rights Act (p. 1047)

Hart-Celler Act (p. 1047)

Great Society (p. 1048)

War on Poverty (p. 1048)

Kerner Report (p. 1051)

Black Power (p. 1052)

Port Huron Statement (p. 1054)

Gulf of Tonkin resolution (p. 1057)

The Feminine Mystique (p. 1065)

Mattachine Society (p. 1068)

Red Power movement (p. 1069)

Silent Spring (p. 1070)

Baker v. Carr (p. 1072)

Tet offensive (p. 1073)

REVIEW TABLE

The Rights Revolution

Group	Leading Figure	Major Organization	Platform
Feminists	Betty Friedan	National Organization for Women	To increase opportunities for women in the workplace and in education
Environmentalists	Rachel Carson	Sierra Club	To reduce harmful chemicals in the environment and bring awareness through the celebration of Earth Day
Latinos	César Chavez	United Farm Workers Union	To improve work conditions and obtain civil rights for migrant farm workers
Gays	Harry Hay	Mattachine Society	To persuade the public that sexual preferences ought not to be persecuted
Indians	Clyde Warrior	American Indian Movement	To demand greater tribal self-government and the restoration of economic resources

CHAPTER 26

The Triumph of Conservatism, 1969–1988

Ronald Reagan addressing the Republican national convention of 1980, which nominated him for president. His election that fall brought modern conservatism to the White House and launched the Reagan Revolution.

FOCUS QUESTIONS

• What were the major policies of the Nixon administration on social and economic issues?

• How did Vietnam and the Watergate scandal affect popular trust in the government?

• In what ways did the opportunities of most Americans diminish in the 1970s?

• What were the roots of the rise of conservatism in the 1970s?

• How did the Reagan presidency affect Americans both at home and abroad?

Beginning with the dramatic 1960 contest between John F. Kennedy and Richard M. Nixon, the journalist Theodore White published best-selling accounts of four successive races for the presidency. Covering the 1964 election, White attended civil rights demonstrations and rallies for Barry Goldwater, the Republican nominee. White noticed something that struck him as odd: "The dominant word of these two groups, which loathe each other, is 'freedom.' Both demand either Freedom Now or Freedom for All. The word has such emotive power behind it that . . . a reporter is instantly denounced for questioning what they mean by the word 'freedom.'" The United States, White concluded, sorely needed "a commonly agreed-on concept of freedom."

White had observed firsthand the struggle over the meaning of freedom set in motion by the 1960s, as well as the revival of conservatism in the midst of an era known for radicalism. Goldwater's campaign helped to crystalize and popularize ideas that would remain the bedrock of conservatism for years to come. To intense anticommunism, Goldwater added a critique of the welfare state for destroying "the dignity of the individual." He demanded a reduction in taxes and governmental regulations. Goldwater showed that with liberals in control in Washington, conservatives could claim for themselves the tradition of antigovernment populism, thus broadening their electoral base and countering their image as upper-crust elitists.

The second half of the 1960s and the 1970s would witness pivotal developments that reshaped American politics—the breakup of the political coalition forged by Franklin D. Roosevelt; an economic crisis that traditional liberal remedies seemed unable to solve; a shift of population and economic resources to conservative strongholds in the Sunbelt of the South and West; the growth of an activist, conservative Christianity increasingly aligned with the Republican Party; and a series of setbacks for the United States overseas. Together, they led to growing popularity for conservatives' ideas, including their understanding of freedom.

PRESIDENT NIXON

From the vantage point of the early twenty-first century, it is difficult to recall how marginal conservatism seemed at the end of World War II. Associated in many minds with conspiracy theories, anti-Semitism, and preference for social hierarchy over democracy and equality, conservatism seemed a relic of a discredited past. "In the United States at this time," wrote the social critic Lionel Trilling in 1949, "liberalism is not only the dominant but even the sole intellectual tradition. For it is the plain fact that nowadays

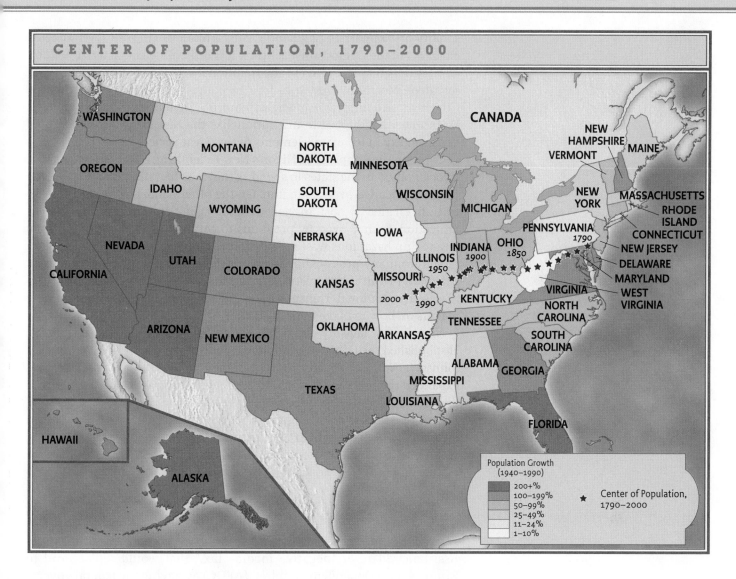

CENTER OF POPULATION, 1790–2000

Population Growth
(1940–1990)

200+%
100–199%
50–99%
25–49%
11–24%
1–10%

★ Center of Population, 1790–2000

there are no conservative or reactionary ideas in general circulation." When conservative ideas did begin to spread, liberals like Trilling explained them as a rejection of the modern world by the alienated or psychologically disturbed.

Nonetheless, as noted in the previous two chapters, the 1950s and 1960s witnessed a conservative rebirth. And in 1968, a "backlash" among formerly Democratic voters against both black assertiveness and antiwar demonstrations helped to propel Richard Nixon into the White House. But conservatives found Nixon no more to their liking than his predecessors. Nixon echoed conservative language, especially in his condemnation of student protesters and his calls for law and order, but in office he expanded the welfare state and moved to improve American relations with the Soviet Union and China. During his presidency, the social changes set in motion by the 1960s—seen by conservatives as forces of moral decay—continued apace.

NIXON'S DOMESTIC POLICIES

Having won the presidency by a very narrow margin, Nixon moved toward the political center on many issues. A shrewd politician, he worked to solidify his support among Republicans while reaching out to disaffected elements of the Democratic coalition. It is difficult to characterize Nixon's domestic agenda according to the traditional categories of liberal and conservative. Mostly interested in foreign policy, he had no desire to battle Congress, still under Democratic control, on domestic issues. Just as Eisenhower had helped to institutionalize the New Deal, Nixon accepted and even expanded many elements of the Great Society.

Conservatives applauded Nixon's New Federalism, which offered federal "block grants" to the states to spend as they saw fit, rather than for specific purposes dictated by Washington. On the other hand, the Nixon administration created a host of new federal agencies. The Environmental Protection Agency oversaw programs to combat water and air pollution, cleaned up hazardous wastes, and required "environmental impact" statements from any project that received federal funding. The Occupational Safety and Health Administration sent inspectors into the nation's workplaces. The National Transportation Safety Board instructed automobile makers on how to make their cars safer.

Nixon spent lavishly on social services and environmental initiatives. He abolished the Office of Economic Opportunity, which had coordinated Johnson's War on Poverty. But he signed congressional measures that expanded the food stamp program and indexed Social Security benefits to inflation—meaning that they would rise automatically as the cost of living increased. The Endangered Species Act prohibited spending federal funds on any project that might extinguish an animal species. The Clean Air Act set air quality standards for carbon monoxide and other chemicals released by cars and factories and led to a dramatic decline in air pollution.

NIXON AND WELFARE

Perhaps Nixon's most startling initiative was his proposal for a Family Assistance Plan, or "negative income tax," that would replace Aid to Families with Dependent Children (AFDC) by having the federal government guarantee a minimum income for all Americans. Universally known as "welfare," AFDC provided assistance, often quite limited, to poor families who met local eligibility requirements. Originally a New Deal program that mainly served the white poor, welfare had come to be associated with blacks, who by 1970 accounted for nearly half the recipients. The AFDC rolls expanded rapidly during the 1960s, partly because the federal government relaxed eligibility standards. This arose from an increase in births to unmarried women, which produced a sharp rise in the number of poor female-headed households, and from an aggressive campaign by welfare rights groups to encourage people to apply for benefits. Conservative politicians now attacked recipients of welfare as people who preferred to live at the expense of honest taxpayers rather than by working.

A striking example of Nixon's willingness to break the political mold, his plan to replace welfare with a guaranteed annual income failed to win approval by Congress. It proved too radical for conservatives, who saw it as a reward for laziness, while liberals denounced the proposed level of $1,600 per year for a needy family of four as inadequate.

NIXON AND RACE

Nixon's racial policies offer a similarly mixed picture. To consolidate support in the white South, he nominated to the Supreme Court Clement Haynsworth and G. Harold Carswell, conservative southern jurists with records of support for segregation. Both were rejected by the Senate. On the other hand, because the courts finally lost patience with southern delaying tactics, extensive racial integration at last came to public schools in the South. In Nixon's first three years in office, the proportion of southern black students attending integrated schools rose from 32 percent to 77 percent.

For a time, the Nixon administration also pursued "affirmative action" programs to upgrade minority employment. Under Johnson, the Department of Labor had required contractors receiving federal money to establish "specific goals and timetables"—that is, to establish what number of minorities should be hired, and by when—to implement equal employment opportunity. Soon after taking office, the Nixon administration expanded this initiative with the Philadelphia Plan, which required that construction contractors on federal projects hire specific numbers of minority workers. Secretary of Labor George Shultz, who initiated the idea, sincerely hoped to open more jobs for black workers. Nixon seems to have viewed the plan mainly as a way of fighting inflation by weakening the power of the building trades unions. Their control over the labor market, he believed, pushed wages to unreasonably high levels, raising the cost of construction. And, he calculated, if the plan caused dissension between blacks and labor unions—two pillars of the Democratic coalition—Republicans could only benefit.

Trade unions of skilled workers like plumbers and electrical workers, which had virtually no black members, strongly opposed the Philadelphia Plan. After a widely publicized incident in May 1970, when a group of construction workers assaulted antiwar demonstrators in New York City, Nixon suddenly decided that he might be able to woo blue-collar workers in preparation for his 1972 reelection campaign. He soon attacked the very affirmative action goals his administration had initiated. He abandoned the Philadelphia Plan in favor of an ineffective one that stressed voluntary local efforts toward minority hiring instead of federal requirements.

Richard Nixon (on the right) and former Alabama governor George Wallace at an "Honor America" celebration in February 1974. Nixon's "southern strategy" sought to woo Wallace's supporters into the Republican Party.

THE BURGER COURT

When Earl Warren retired as chief justice in 1969, Nixon appointed Warren Burger, a federal court-of-appeals judge, to succeed him. An outspoken critic of the "judicial activism" of the Warren Court—its willingness to expand old rights and create new ones by overturning acts of Congress and the states—Burger was expected to lead the justices in a conservative direction. But like Nixon, he surprised many of his supporters. While the pace of change slowed, the Burger Court, at least initially, consolidated and expanded many of the judicial innovations of the 1960s.

In 1971, in *Swann v. Charlotte-Mecklenburg Board of Education*, which arose from North Carolina, the justices unanimously approved a lower court's plan that required the extensive transportation of students to achieve school integration. The decision led to hundreds of cases in which judges throughout the country ordered the use of busing as a tool to achieve integration. With many white parents determined to keep their children in neighborhood schools and others willing to move to the suburbs or enroll them in private academies to avoid integration, busing became a lightning rod for protests. One of the most bitter fights took place in Boston in the mid-1970s. Residents of the tightly knit Irish-American community of South Boston demonstrated vociferously and sometimes violently against a busing plan decreed by a local judge.

The Supreme Court soon abandoned the idea of overturning local control of schools, or moving students great distances to achieve integration. In 1973, it rebuffed a group of Texas Latinos who sued to overturn the use of property taxes to finance public education. Because of the great disparity in wealth between districts, spending on predominantly Mexican-American schools stood far below that for white ones. But in *San Antonio Independent School District v. Rodriguez*, a 5-4 Court majority ruled that the Constitution did not require equality of school funding. In the following year, in *Milliken v. Bradley* (1974), the justices overturned a lower court order that required Detroit's predominantly white suburbs to enter into a regional desegregation plan with the city's heavily minority school system. By absolving suburban districts of responsibility for assisting in integrating urban schools, the decision guaranteed that housing segregation would be mirrored in public education. Indeed, by the 1990s, public schools in the North were considerably more segregated than those in the South.

THE COURT AND AFFIRMATIVE ACTION

Efforts to promote greater employment opportunities for minorities also spawned politically divisive legal issues. Many whites came to view affirmative action programs as a form of "reverse discrimination," claiming that, in violation of the Fourteenth Amendment's equal protection clause, they granted minorities special advantages over whites. Even as affirmative action programs quickly spread from blacks to encompass women, Latinos, Asian-Americans, and Native Americans, conservatives demanded that the Supreme Court invalidate all such policies. The justices refused, but they found it difficult to devise a consistent approach to this politically charged issue.

In *Griggs v. Duke Power Company* (1971), the Court ruled that even racially neutral job requirements such as a written examination were illegal if they operated to exclude a disproportionate number of non-white applicants and were not directly related to job performance. Later in the decade, in *United Steelworkers of America v. Weber* (1979), it upheld a program devised by the Kaiser Aluminum & Chemical Corporation and its union that set quotas for training and hiring non-white workers in skilled jobs. Since this private, voluntary agreement did not involve government action, the Court ruled, it did not violate the Fourteenth Amendment's ban on state policies that discriminated among citizens.

The justices, however, proved increasingly hostile to governmental affirmative action policies. In *Regents of the University of California v. Bakke* (1978), the Court overturned an admissions program of the University of California at Davis, a public university, which set aside 16 of 100 places in the entering medical school class for minority students. Justice Lewis F. Powell, a Nixon appointee who cast the deciding vote in the 5-4 decision, rejected the idea of fixed affirmative action quotas. He added, however, that race could be used as one factor among many in admissions decisions, so affirmative action continued at most colleges and universities. During the 1990s, as courts in different parts of the country interpreted *Bakke* in different ways, the legal status of affirmative action would remain ambiguous. In 2003, a 5-4 majority reaffirmed the *Bakke* principle that institutions of higher learning may use race as a consideration in admissions decisions.

THE CONTINUING SEXUAL REVOLUTION

To the alarm of conservatives, during the 1970s the sexual revolution passed from the counterculture into the social mainstream. The number of Americans who told public-opinion polls that premarital sex was wrong plummeted. The number of divorces soared, reaching more than 1 million in 1975, double the number ten years earlier. The age at which both men and women married rose dramatically. The figure for divorces in 1975 exceeded the number of first-time marriages. A popular 1978 film, *An Unmarried Woman*, portrayed the dissolution of a marriage as a triumph for the wife, who discovered her potential for individual growth only after being abandoned by her husband. As a result of women's changing aspirations and the availability of birth control and legal abortions, the American birthrate declined dramatically. By 1976, the average woman was bearing 1.7 children during her lifetime, less than half the figure of 1957 and below the level at which a population reproduces itself. Like all averages, these figures conceal significant variations. Poorer Americans, especially in the South and rural heartland, had more children than educated urbanites. A 1971 survey of the last five graduating classes at Bryn Mawr, an elite women's college, reported the birth of more than seventy children. A similar survey covering the classes of 1971 through 1975 found that only three had been born.

During the Nixon years, women made inroads into areas from which they had long been excluded. In 1972, Congress approved Title IX, which banned gender discrimination in higher education, and the Equal Credit Opportunity Act, which required that married women be given access to credit in their own name. The giant corporation American Telephone and Telegraph (AT&T) entered into a landmark agreement in which it agreed to pay millions of dollars to workers who had suffered gender discrimination and to upgrade employment opportunities for women. The number of women at work continued its upward climb. In 1960, only 20 percent of women with young children had been in the workforce. The figure reached 40 percent in 1980, and 55 percent in 1990. Working women were motivated by varied aims. Some sought careers in professions and skilled jobs previously open only to men. Others, spurred by the need to bolster family income as the economy faltered, flooded into the

Year	Divorces
1950	385
1955	377
1960	393
1965	479
1970	708
1975	1,036
1980	1,189

Table 26.1 RATE OF DIVORCE: DIVORCES OF EXISTING MARRIAGES PER 1,000 NEW MARRIAGES, 1950–1980

One result of the sexual revolution was a sharp rise in the age at which Americans chose to marry, and an increase in the number of divorces.

Daryl Koehn, of Kansas, celebrates in 1977 on learning that she has been chosen as one of the first group of women allowed to study at Oxford University as a Rhodes Scholar. Since their establishment in 1903, the scholarships had been limited to men.

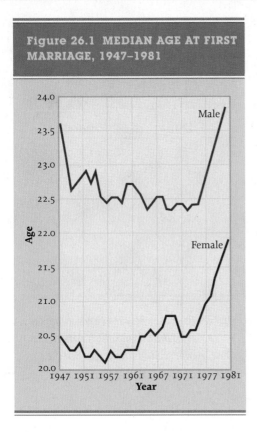

Figure 26.1 MEDIAN AGE AT FIRST MARRIAGE, 1947–1981

traditional, low-wage, "pink-collar" sector, working as cashiers, secretaries, and telephone operators.

In addition, the gay and lesbian movement, born at the end of the 1960s, expanded greatly during the 1970s and became a major concern of the right. In 1969, there had been about fifty local gay rights groups in the United States; ten years later, their numbers reached into the thousands. They began to elect local officials, persuaded many states to decriminalize homosexual relations, and succeeded in convincing cities with large gay populations to pass antidiscrimination laws. They actively encouraged gay men and lesbians to "come out of the closet"—that is, to reveal their sexual orientation. During the 1970s, the American Psychiatric Association removed homosexuality from its list of mental diseases.

As pre–World War I bohemians saw many of their ideas absorbed into the mass culture of the 1920s, values and styles of the 1960s became part of 1970s America, dubbed by the writer Tom Wolfe the "Me Decade." When asked in a Gallup poll to rate a series of ideas, respondents gave the highest ranking not to "following God's will," "high income," or "a sense of accomplishment," but to "freedom to choose." The demand of student protesters that individuals be empowered to determine their own "lifestyle" emerged in depoliticized form in Americans' obsession with self-improvement through fitness programs, health food diets, and new forms of psychological therapy.

NIXON AND DÉTENTE

Just as domestic policies and social trends under Nixon disappointed conservatives, they viewed his foreign policy as dangerously "soft" on communism. To be sure, in the Third World, Nixon and Henry Kissinger, his national security adviser and secretary of state, continued their predecessors' policy of attempting to undermine governments deemed dangerous to American strategic or economic interests. Nixon funneled arms to dictatorial pro-American regimes in Iran, the Philippines, and South Africa. After Chile in 1970 elected socialist Salvador Allende as president, the CIA worked with his domestic opponents to destabilize the regime. On September 11, 1973, Allende was overthrown and killed in a military coup, which installed a bloody dictatorship under General Augusto Pinochet. Thousands of Allende backers, including a few Americans then in Chile, were tortured and murdered, and many others fled the country. The Nixon administration knew of the coup plans in advance but failed to warn Allende, and it continued to back Pinochet despite his brutal policies. Democracy did not return to Chile until the end of the 1980s.

In his relations with the major communist powers, however, Nixon fundamentally altered Cold War policies. Nixon had launched his political career as a fierce and, critics charged, unscrupulous anticommunist. But in the language of foreign relations, he and Kissinger were "realists." They had more interest in power than ideology and preferred international stability to relentless conflict. Nixon also hoped that if relations with the Soviet Union improved, the Russians would influence North Vietnam to agree to an end to the Vietnam War on terms acceptable to the United States.

Nixon realized that far from being part of a unified communist bloc, China had its own interests, different from those of the Soviet Union, and was destined to play a major role on the world stage. The policy of refusing to recognize China's communist government had reached a dead end. In 1971, Kissinger flew secretly to China, paving the way for Nixon's own astonishing public visit of February 1972. The trip led to the Beijing government's taking up China's seat at the United Nations, previously occupied by the exiled regime on Taiwan. Full diplomatic relations between the United States and the People's Republic of China were not established until 1979. But Nixon's visit sparked a dramatic increase in trade between the two countries.

Richard Nixon at a banquet celebrating his visit to China in February 1972. To his right is Premier Chou En-lai.

Three months after his trip to Beijing, Nixon became the first American president to visit the Soviet Union, where he engaged in intense negotiations with his Soviet counterpart, Leonid Brezhnev. Out of this "summit" meeting came agreements for increased trade and two landmark arms-control treaties. SALT (named for the Strategic Arms Limitation Talks under way since 1969) froze each country's arsenal of intercontinental missiles capable of carrying nuclear warheads. The Anti–Ballistic Missile Treaty banned the development of systems designed to intercept incoming missiles, so that neither side would be tempted to attack the other without fearing devastating retaliation. Nixon and Brezhnev proclaimed a new era of "peaceful coexistence," in which "détente" (cooperation) would replace the hostility of the Cold War.

VIETNAM AND WATERGATE

NIXON AND VIETNAM

Despite Nixon's foreign policy triumphs, one issue would not go away—Vietnam. Nixon ran for president in 1968 declaring that he had a "secret plan" to end the war. On taking office, he announced a new policy, Vietnamization. Under this plan, American troops would gradually be withdrawn while South Vietnamese soldiers, backed by continued American bombing, did more and more of the fighting. But Vietnamization neither limited the war nor ended the antiwar movement. Hoping to cut North Vietnamese supply lines, Nixon in 1970 ordered American troops into neutral Cambodia. The invasion did not achieve its military goals, but it destabilized the Cambodian government and set in motion a chain of events that eventually brought to power the Khmer Rouge. Before being ousted by a Vietnamese invasion in 1979, this local communist movement attempted to force virtually all Cambodians into rural communes and committed widespread massacres in that unfortunate country.

As the war escalated, protests again spread on college campuses. In the wake of the killing of four antiwar protesters at Kent State University by the Ohio National Guard and two by police at Jackson State University in

Mississippi, the student movement reached its high-water mark. In the spring of 1970, more than 350 colleges and universities experienced strikes, and troops occupied 21 campuses. The protests at Kent State, a public university with a largely working-class student body, and Jackson State, a black institution, demonstrated how antiwar sentiment had spread far beyond elite campuses like Berkeley and Columbia.

At the same time, troop morale in Vietnam plummeted. Although all young men were subject to the draft, for most of the war college students received exemptions. As a result, the army was predominantly composed of working-class whites and members of racial minorities. Unlike in previous wars, blacks complained not about exclusion from the army but about the high number of black soldiers among the casualties.

In 1965 and 1966, blacks accounted for more than 20 percent of American casualties, double their proportion in the army as a whole. After protests from black leaders, President Johnson ordered the number of black soldiers in combat units reduced. For the war as a whole, blacks made up 14 percent of deaths among enlisted men.

The same social changes sweeping the home front were evident among troops in Vietnam. Soldiers experimented with drugs, openly wore peace and black power symbols, refused orders, and even assaulted unpopular officers. In 1971, thousands deserted the army, while at home Vietnam veterans held antiwar demonstrations. The decline of discipline within the army convinced increasing numbers of high-ranking officers that the United States must extricate itself from Vietnam.

Public support for the war was rapidly waning. In 1969, the *New York Times* published details of the My Lai massacre of 1968, in which a company

A distraught young woman kneels beside one of the four Kent State University students killed by members of the Ohio National Guard at an antiwar demonstration in 1970.

In 1971, in one of the most dramatic demonstrations of the entire era, hundreds of veterans deposited on the steps of the Capitol medals they had received while fighting in Vietnam.

of American troops had killed some 350 South Vietnamese civilians. After a military investigation, one soldier, Lieutenant William Calley, was found guilty of directing the atrocity. (The courts released him from prison in 1974.) In 1971, the *Times* began publishing the Pentagon Papers, a classified report prepared by the Defense Department that traced American involvement in Vietnam back to World War II and revealed how successive presidents had misled the American people about it. In a landmark freedom-of-the-press decision, the Supreme Court rejected Nixon's request for an injunction to halt publication. In 1973, Congress passed the War Powers Act. The most vigorous assertion of congressional control over foreign policy in the nation's history, it required the president to seek congressional approval for the commitment of American troops overseas.

THE END OF THE VIETNAM WAR

Early in 1973, Nixon achieved what had eluded his predecessors—a negotiated settlement in Vietnam. The Paris peace agreement, the result of five years of talks, made possible the final withdrawal of American troops. The compromise left in place the government of South Vietnam, but it also left North Vietnamese and Viet Cong soldiers in control of parts of the South. American bombing ceased, and the military draft came to an end. Henceforth, volunteers would make up the armed forces. But the agreement did not solve the basic issue of the war—whether Vietnam would be one country or two. That question was answered in the spring of 1975, when the North Vietnamese launched a final military offensive. The government of South Vietnam collapsed; the United States did not intervene except to evacuate the American embassy, and Vietnam was reunified under communist rule.

The only war the United States has ever lost, Vietnam was a military, political, and social disaster. By the time it ended, 58,000 Americans had been killed, along with 3 million to 4 million Vietnamese. The war cost the United States an estimated $100 billion. But the nonmonetary price was far higher. Vietnam undermined Americans' confidence in their own institutions and challenged long-standing beliefs about the country and its purposes.

Two decades after the war ended, former secretary of defense Robert McNamara published a memoir in which he admitted that the policy he had helped to shape had been "terribly wrong." Ignorance of the history and culture of Vietnam and a misguided belief that every communist movement in the world was a puppet of Moscow, he wrote, had led the country into a war that he now profoundly regretted. The *New York Times* rejected McNamara's apology. The "ghosts of those unlived lives," the young men sent to their death "for no purpose," it declared, could not so easily be wished away. But the *Times* itself, like the rest of the political establishment, had supported the war for most of its duration. For far too long, they had accepted its basic premise—that the United States had the right to decide the fate of a faraway people about whom it knew almost nothing.

Buttons and flags for sale at a rally in the early 1970s illustrate the linkage of support for the Vietnam War and strong feelings of patriotism, building blocks of the new conservatism.

WATERGATE

By the time the war ended, Richard Nixon was no longer president. His domestic policies and foreign policy successes had contributed greatly to his reelection in 1972. He won a landslide victory over liberal Democrat George McGovern, receiving 60 percent of the popular vote. Nixon made deep inroads into former Democratic strongholds in the South and among working-class white northerners. He carried every state but Massachusetts. But his triumph soon turned into disaster.

Nixon was obsessed with secrecy and could not accept honest difference of opinion. He viewed every critic as a threat to national security and developed an "enemies list" that included reporters, politicians, and celebrities unfriendly to the administration. When the Pentagon Papers were published, Nixon created a special investigative unit known as the "plumbers" to gather information about Daniel Ellsberg, the former government official who had leaked them to the press. The plumbers raided the office of Ellsberg's psychiatrist in search of incriminating records. In June 1972, five former employees of Nixon's reelection committee took part in a break-in at Democratic Party headquarters in the Watergate apartment complex in Washington, D.C. A security guard called police, who arrested the intruders.

No one knows precisely what the Watergate burglars were looking for (perhaps they intended to install listening devices), and the botched robbery played little role in the 1972 presidential campaign. But in 1973, Judge John J. Sirica, before whom the burglars were tried, determined to find out who had sponsored the break-in. A pair of *Washington Post* journalists began publishing investigative stories that made it clear that persons close to the president had ordered the burglary and then tried to "cover up" White House involvement. Congressional hearings followed that revealed a wider pattern of wiretapping, break-ins, and attempts to sabotage political opposition. When it became known that Nixon had made tape recordings of conversations in his office, a special prosecutor the president had reluctantly appointed to investigate the Watergate affair demanded copies. The Supreme Court unanimously ordered Nixon to provide them—a decision that reaffirmed the principle that the president is not above the law.

NIXON'S FALL

Week after week, revelations about the scandal unfolded. By mid-1974, it had become clear that whether or not Nixon knew in advance of the Watergate break-in, he had become involved immediately afterward in authorizing payments to the burglars to remain silent or commit perjury, and he had ordered the FBI to halt its investigation of the crime. In August 1974, the House Judiciary Committee voted to recommend that Nixon be impeached for conspiracy to obstruct justice. His political support having evaporated, Nixon became the only president in history to resign.

Nixon's presidency remains a classic example of the abuse of political power. In 1973, his vice president, Spiro T. Agnew, resigned after revelations that he had accepted bribes from construction firms while serving as governor of Maryland. Nixon's attorney general, John Mitchell, and White House aides H. R. Haldeman and John Ehrlichman were convicted of obstruction of justice in the Watergate affair and went to jail. As for the

Herbert Block's 1973 cartoon depicts Americans' disbelief as revelations related to the Watergate scandal unfolded in Washington.

president, he insisted that he had done nothing wrong—or at any rate, that previous presidents had also been guilty of lying and illegality.

Although it hardly excused his behavior, Nixon had a point. His departure from office was followed by Senate hearings headed by Frank Church of Idaho that laid bare a history of abusive actions that involved every administration since the beginning of the Cold War. In violation of the law, the FBI had spied on millions of Americans and had tried to disrupt the civil rights movement. The CIA had conducted secret operations to overthrow foreign governments and had tried to assassinate foreign leaders. It had even recruited a secret army to fight in Laos, a neighbor of Vietnam. Abuses of power, in other words, went far beyond the misdeeds of a single president.

Along with Watergate, the Pentagon Papers, and the Vietnam War itself, the Church Committee revelations seriously undermined Americans' confidence in their own government. They led Congress to enact new restrictions on the power of the FBI and CIA to spy on American citizens or conduct operations abroad without the knowledge of lawmakers. Congress also strengthened the Freedom of Information Act (FOIA), initially enacted in 1966. Since 1974, the FOIA has allowed scholars, journalists, and ordinary citizens to gain access to millions of pages of records of federal agencies.

Liberals, who had despised Nixon throughout his career, celebrated his downfall. They did not realize that the revulsion against Watergate undermined the foundations of liberalism itself, already weakened by the divisions of the 1960s. For liberalism rests, in part, on belief in the ability of government, especially the federal government, to solve social problems and promote both the public good and individual freedom. Nixon's fall and the revelations of years of governmental misconduct helped to convince many Americans that conservatives were correct when they argued that to protect liberty it was necessary to limit Washington's power over Americans' lives. The Watergate crisis also distracted attention from the economic crisis that began in the fall of 1973. Its inability to fashion a response to this crisis, which gripped the United States for much of the 1970s, dealt liberalism yet another blow.

THE END OF THE GOLDEN AGE

THE DECLINE OF MANUFACTURING

During the 1970s, the long period of postwar economic expansion and consumer prosperity came to an end, succeeded by slow growth and high inflation. There were many reasons for the end of capitalism's "golden age." With American prosperity seemingly unassailable and the military-industrial complex thriving, successive administrations had devoted little attention to the less positive economic consequences of the Cold War. To strengthen its anticommunist allies, the United States promoted the industrial reconstruction of Japan and Germany and the emergence of new centers of manufacturing in places like South Korea and Taiwan. It encouraged American companies to invest in overseas plants and did not complain when allies protected their own industries while seeking unrestricted access to the American market. Imports of foreign steel, for example, led to growing problems for this key industry at home. The strong dollar, linked to gold by the Bretton Woods agreement of 1944, made it harder to sell American goods overseas (discussed in Chapter 22).

In 1971, for the first time in the twentieth century, the United States experienced a merchandise trade deficit—that is, it imported more goods than it exported. By 1980, nearly three-quarters of goods produced in the United States were competing with foreign-made products and the number of manufacturing workers, 38 percent of the American workforce in 1960, had fallen to 28 percent. Moreover, the war in Vietnam produced ever-higher federal deficits and rising inflation.

In 1971, Nixon announced the most radical change in economic policy since the Great Depression. He took the United States off the gold standard, ending the Bretton Woods agreement that fixed the value of the dollar and other currencies in terms of gold. Henceforth, the world's currencies would "float" in relation to one another, their worth determined not by treaty but by international currency markets. Nixon hoped that lowering the dollar's value in terms of the German mark and Japanese yen would promote exports by making American goods cheaper overseas and reduce imports since foreign products would be more expensive in the United States. But the end of fixed currency rates injected a new element of instability into the world economy. Nixon also ordered wages and prices frozen for ninety days.

STAGFLATION

These policies temporarily curtailed inflation and reduced imports. But in 1973, a brief war broke out between Israel and its neighbors Egypt and Syria. Middle Eastern Arab states retaliated for Western support of Israel by quadrupling the price of oil and suspending the export of oil to the United States for several months. Long lines of cars appeared at American gas stations, which either ran out of fuel or limited how much a customer could buy. A second "oil shock" occurred in 1979 as a result of the revolution that overthrew the shah of Iran, discussed later.

Because the rapidly growing demand for fuel by cars and factories outstripped domestic supplies, by 1973 the United States imported one-third of its oil. Europe and Japan depended even more heavily on oil imports. To promote energy conservation, Congress lowered the speed limit on interstate highways to fifty-five miles per hour, and many public buildings reduced heat and lighting.

The energy crisis of the 1970s drew increased attention to domestic energy resources like oil, coal, and natural gas. While the rest of the economy stagnated, western energy production grew apace. Oil was discovered in Alaska in 1968, and in 1977 a pipeline opened to facilitate its shipment to the rest of the country. Coal production in Wyoming boomed. Western energy companies benefited from the high oil prices set by OPEC—the Organization of Petroleum Exporting Countries.

During the oil crisis of 1973, Americans confronted rising gasoline prices and widespread shortages. Some gas stations closed and were turned to other uses, like this one in Potlatch, Washington, which became a religious meeting hall, the pumps now offering salvation rather than gasoline.

But rising oil prices rippled through the world economy, contributing to the combination of stagnant economic growth and high inflation known as "stagflation." Between 1973 and 1981, the rate of inflation in developed countries was 10 percent per year, and the rate of economic growth only 2.4 percent, a sharp deterioration from the economic conditions of the 1960s. The so-called misery index—the sum of the unemployment and inflation rates—stood at 10.8 when the decade began. By 1980, it had almost doubled. As oil prices rose, many Americans shifted from large domestically produced cars, known for high gasoline consumption, to smaller, more fuel-efficient imports. By the end of the decade, Japan had become the world's leading automobile producer, and imports accounted for nearly 25 percent of car sales in the United States.

THE BELEAGUERED SOCIAL COMPACT

The economic crisis contributed to a breakdown of the postwar social compact. Faced with declining profits and rising overseas competition, corporations stepped up the trend, already under way before 1970, toward eliminating well-paid manufacturing jobs through automation and shifting production to low-wage areas of the United States and overseas. The effects on older industrial cities were devastating. By 1980, Detroit and Chicago had lost more than half the manufacturing jobs that had existed three decades earlier.

Smaller industrial cities suffered even sharper declines. As their tax bases shriveled, many found themselves unable to maintain public services. In Paterson, New Jersey, where great silk factories had arisen in the early twentieth century, deindustrialization left a landscape of abandoned manufacturing plants. The poverty rate reached 20 percent, the city sold off public library buildings to raise cash, and the schools became so run down and overcrowded that the state government took control. The accelerating flow of jobs, investment, and population to the nonunion, low-wage states of the Sunbelt increased the political influence of this conservative region.

Table 26.2 THE MISERY INDEX, 1970–1980			
Year	*Rate of Inflation (%)*	*Rate of Unemployment (%)*	*Misery Index (%)*
1970	5.9	4.9	10.8
1971	4.3	5.9	10.2
1972	3.3	5.6	8.9
1973	6.2	4.9	11.1
1974	11.0	5.6	16.6
1975	9.1	8.5	17.6
1976	5.8	7.7	13.5
1977	6.5	7.1	13.6
1978	7.7	6.1	13.8
1979	11.3	5.8	17.1
1980	13.5	7.1	20.6

The World Trade Center under construction in New York City in the 1970s.

Figure 26.2 REAL AVERAGE WEEKLY WAGES, 1955–1990

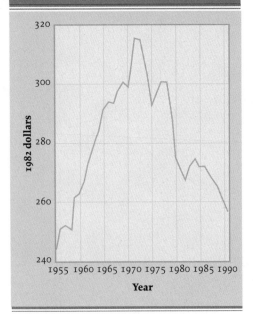

Because of economic dislocations and deindustrialization, Americans' real wages (wages adjusted to take account of inflation) peaked in the early 1970s and then began a sharp, prolonged decline.

Of population growth in metropolitan areas, during the 1970s, 96 percent occurred in the South and West. San Jose and Phoenix, with populations around 100,000 in 1950, neared 1 million by 1990.

In some manufacturing centers, political and economic leaders welcomed the opportunity to remake their cities as finance, information, and entertainment hubs. In New York, the construction of the World Trade Center, completed in 1977, symbolized this shift in the economy. Until destroyed by terrorists twenty-four years later, the 110-story "twin towers" stood as a symbol of New York's grandeur. But to make way for the World Trade Center, the city displaced hundreds of small electronics, printing, and other firms, causing the loss of thousands of manufacturing jobs.

LABOR ON THE DEFENSIVE

Always a junior partner in the Democratic coalition, the labor movement found itself forced onto the defensive. It has remained there ever since. One example of the weakening of unions' power came in 1975 with the New York City fiscal crisis. Deeply in debt and unable to market its bonds, the city faced the prospect of bankruptcy. The solution to the crisis required a reduction of the city's workforce, severe cuts in the budgets of schools, parks, and the subway system, and an end to the century-old policy of free tuition at the City University. Even in this center of unionism, working-class New Yorkers had no choice but to absorb job losses and a drastic decline in public services.

The weakening of unions and the continuation of the economy's long-term shift from manufacturing to service employment had an adverse impact on ordinary Americans. Between 1953 and 1973, median family income had doubled. But beginning in 1973, real wages essentially did not rise for twenty years. The 1970s was one of only two decades in the twentieth century (the other being the 1930s) that ended with Americans on average poorer than when it began. The popular song "The River," by Bruce Springsteen, captured the woes of blue-collar workers: "Is a dream a lie if it don't come true / Or is it something worse?"

FORD AS PRESIDENT

Economic problems dogged the presidencies of Nixon's successors. Gerald Ford, who had been appointed to replace Vice President Agnew, succeeded to the White House when Nixon resigned. Ford named Nelson Rockefeller of New York as his own vice president. Thus, for the only time in American history, both offices were occupied by persons for whom no one had actually voted. Among his first acts as president, Ford pardoned Nixon, shielding him from prosecution for obstruction of justice. Ford claimed that he wanted the country to put the Watergate scandal behind it. But the pardon proved to be widely unpopular.

In domestic policy, Ford's presidency lacked significant accomplishment. Ford and his chief economic adviser, Alan Greenspan, believed that Americans spent too much on consumption and saved too little, leaving business with insufficient money for investment. They called for cutting taxes on business and lessening government regulation of the economy. But the Democratic majority in Congress was in no mood to accept these traditional Republican policies. To combat inflation, Ford urged Americans to shop wisely, reduce expenditures, and wear WIN buttons (for "Whip Inflation Now"). Although inflation fell, joblessness continued to rise. During the steep recession of 1974–1975 unemployment exceeded 9 percent, the highest level since the Depression.

In the international arena, 1975 witnessed the major achievement of Ford's presidency. In a continuation of Nixon's policy of détente, the United States and Soviet Union signed an agreement at Helsinki, Finland, that recognized the permanence of Europe's post–World War II boundaries (including the division of Germany). In addition, both superpowers agreed to respect the basic liberties of their citizens. Secretary of State Kissinger and his Soviet counterpart, Andrey Gromyko, assumed that this latter pledge would have little practical effect. But over time, the Helsinki Accords inspired movements for greater freedom within the communist countries of eastern Europe.

THE CARTER ADMINISTRATION

In the presidential election of 1976, Jimmy Carter, a former governor of Georgia, narrowly defeated Ford. A graduate of the U.S. Naval Academy who later became a peanut farmer, Carter was virtually unknown outside his state when he launched his campaign for the Democratic nomination. But realizing that Watergate and Vietnam had produced a crisis in confidence in the federal government, he turned his obscurity into an advantage. Carter ran for president as an "outsider," making a virtue of the fact that he had never held federal office. A devout "born-again" Baptist, he spoke openly of his religious convictions. His promise, "I'll never lie to you," resonated with an electorate tired of official dishonesty.

Carter had much in common with Progressives of the early twentieth century. His passions were making government more efficient, protecting the environment, and raising the moral tone of politics. Unlike the Progressives, however, he embraced the aspirations of black Americans. His inaugural address as governor of Georgia in 1971 had apologized for past mistreatment of the state's black population. As president, Carter appointed an unprecedented number of blacks to important positions, including Andrew Young, a former lieutenant of Martin Luther King Jr., as ambassador to the United Nations.

CARTER AND THE ECONOMIC CRISIS

Although his party controlled both houses, Carter often found himself at odds with Congress. He viewed inflation, not unemployment, as the country's main economic problem, and to combat it he promoted cuts in spending on domestic programs. In the hope that increased competition would reduce prices, his administration deregulated the trucking and airline industries. Carter supported the Federal Reserve Bank's decision to raise interest rates to curtail economic activity until both wages and prices fell, traditionally a Republican policy. But oil prices kept rising,

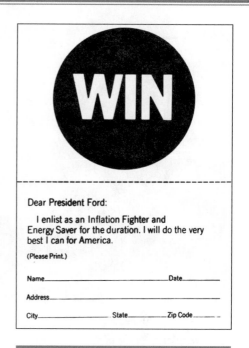

President Gerald Ford tried to enlist Americans in his "Whip Inflation Now" program. It did not succeed.

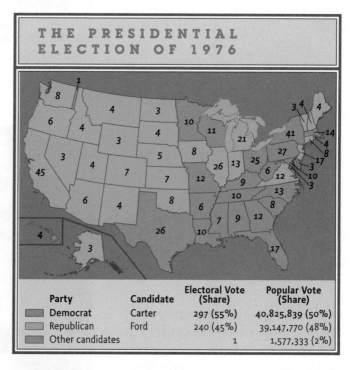

THE PRESIDENTIAL ELECTION OF 1976

Party	Candidate	Electoral Vote (Share)	Popular Vote (Share)
Democrat	Carter	297 (55%)	40,825,839 (50%)
Republican	Ford	240 (45%)	39,147,770 (48%)
Other candidates		1	1,577,333 (2%)

The deregulation of the airline industry produced lower fares, but also a drastic decline in service. Before deregulation, with prices fixed, airlines sought to attract customers by providing good service. Today, fares are low, but passengers are jammed in like sardines and have to pay for checked baggage, onboard meals, and other amenities.

thanks to the overthrow of the shah of Iran, discussed later, and inflation did not decline.

Carter also believed that expanded use of nuclear energy could help reduce dependence on imported oil. For years, proponents of nuclear power had hailed it as an inexpensive way of meeting the country's energy needs. By the time Carter took office, more than 200 nuclear plants were operating or on order. But in 1979 the industry suffered a near-fatal blow when an accident at the Three Mile Island plant in Pennsylvania released a large amount of radioactive steam into the atmosphere. The rise of the environmental movement had promoted public skepticism about scientific experts who touted the miraculous promise of technological innovations without concern for their social consequences. The Three Mile Island mishap reinforced fears about the environmental hazards associated with nuclear energy and put a halt to the industry's expansion.

Since the New Deal, Democrats had presented themselves as the party of affluence and economic growth. But Carter seemed to be presiding over a period of national decline. It did not help his popularity when, in a speech in 1979, he spoke of a national "crisis of confidence" and seemed to blame it on the American people themselves and their "mistaken idea of freedom" as "self-indulgence and consumption."

THE EMERGENCE OF HUMAN RIGHTS POLITICS

Under Carter, a commitment to promoting human rights became a centerpiece of American foreign policy for the first time. He was influenced by the proliferation of information about global denials of human rights spread by nongovernmental agencies like Amnesty International and the International League for Human Rights. The American membership of Amnesty International, a London-based organization, grew from 6,000 to

The 1979 accident at the Three Mile Island nuclear plant in Pennsylvania brought a halt to the industry's expansion.

35,000 between 1970 and 1976. Its reports marked a significant break with dominant ideas about international affairs since World War II, which had viewed the basic division in the world as between communist and noncommunist countries. Such reports, along with congressional hearings, fact-finding missions, and academic studies of human rights, exposed misdeeds not only by communist countries, but also by American allies, especially the death squads of Latin American dictatorships. "Information is the core work of the movement," Amnesty International declared. Its findings aroused widespread indignation and pressured elected officials in the United States to try to do something to promote human rights abroad.

In 1978, Carter cut off aid to the brutal military dictatorship governing Argentina, which in the name of anticommunism had launched a "dirty war" against its own citizens, kidnapping off the streets and secretly murdering an estimated 10,000 to 30,000 persons. Carter's action was a dramatic gesture, as Argentina was one of the most important powers in Latin America and previous American administrations had turned a blind eye to human rights abuses by Cold War allies. By the end of his presidency, the phrase "human rights," had acquired political potency. Its very vagueness was both a weakness and a strength. It was difficult to define exactly what rights should and should not be considered universally applicable, but various groups could and did unite under the umbrella of global human rights.

Carter believed that in the post-Vietnam era, American foreign policy should de-emphasize Cold War thinking. Combating poverty in the Third World, preventing the spread of nuclear weapons, and promoting human rights should take priority over what he called "the inordinate fear of communism that once led us to embrace any dictator who joined us in that fear." In one of his first acts as president, he offered an unconditional pardon to Vietnam-era draft resisters. In a 1977 address, he insisted that foreign policy could not be separated from "questions of justice, equity, and human rights."

Carter's emphasis on pursuing peaceful solutions to international problems and his willingness to think outside the Cold War framework yielded important results. In 1979, he brought the leaders of Egypt and Israel to the presidential retreat at Camp David and brokered a historic peace agreement between the two countries. He improved American relations with Latin America by agreeing to a treaty, ratified by the Senate in 1978, that provided for the transfer of the Panama Canal to local control by the year 2000. In 1979, he resisted calls for intervention when a popular revolution led by the left-wing Sandinista movement overthrew Nicaraguan dictator Anastasio Somoza, a longtime ally of the United States. Carter attempted to curb the murderous violence of death squads allied to the right-wing government of El Salvador, and in 1980 he suspended military aid after the murder of four American nuns by members of the country's army. He signed the SALT II agreement with the

President Jimmy Carter (center), *Egyptian president Anwar Sadat* (left), *and Israeli prime minister Menachem Begin* (right) *celebrating the signing of the 1979 peace treaty between Israel and Egypt.*

Soviets, which reduced the number of missiles, bombers, and nuclear warheads.

Both conservative Cold Warriors and foreign policy "realists" severely criticized Carter's emphasis on human rights. He himself found it impossible to translate rhetoric into action. He criticized American arms sales to the rest of the world. But with thousands of jobs and billions of dollars in corporate profits at stake, he did nothing to curtail them. The United States continued its support of allies with records of serious human rights violations such as the governments of Guatemala, the Philippines, South Korea, and Iran. Indeed, the American connection with the shah of Iran, whose secret police regularly jailed and tortured political opponents, proved to be Carter's undoing.

THE IRAN CRISIS AND AFGHANISTAN

Occupying a strategic location on the southern border of the Soviet Union, Iran was a major supplier of oil and an importer of American military equipment. At the end of 1977, Carter traveled there to help celebrate the shah's rule, causing the internal opposition to become more and more anti-American. Early in 1979, a popular revolution inspired by the exiled Muslim cleric Ayatollah Khomeini overthrew the shah and declared Iran an Islamic republic.

The Iranian revolution marked an ideological shift in opposition movements in the Middle East from socialism and Arab nationalism to religious fundamentalism. This would have important long-term consequences for the United States. More immediately, when Carter in November 1979 allowed the deposed shah to seek medical treatment in the United States, Khomeini's followers invaded the American embassy in Tehran and seized fifty-three hostages. They did not regain their freedom until January 1981, on the day Carter's term as president ended. Events in Iran made Carter seem helpless and inept and led to a rapid fall in his popularity.

Another crisis that began in 1979 undermined American relations with Moscow. At the end of that year, the Soviet Union sent thousands of troops into Afghanistan to support a friendly government threatened by an Islamic rebellion. In the long run, Afghanistan became the Soviet Vietnam, an unwinnable conflict whose mounting casualties seriously weakened the government at home. Initially, however, it seemed another example of declining American power.

Declaring the invasion the greatest crisis since World War II (a considerable exaggeration), the president announced the Carter Doctrine, declaring that the United States would use military force, if necessary, to protect its interests in the Persian Gulf. He placed an embargo on grain exports to the Soviet Union and organized a Western boycott of the 1980 Olympics, which took place in Moscow. He withdrew the SALT II treaty from consideration by the Senate and dramatically increased American military spending. In a reversion to the Cold War principle that any opponent of the Soviet Union deserved American support, the United States funneled aid to fundamentalist Muslims in Afghanistan who fought a decade-long guerrilla war against the Soviets. The alliance had unforeseen consequences. A faction of Islamic fundamentalists known as the Taliban eventually came to power in Afghanistan. Tragically, they would prove as hostile to the United States as to Moscow.

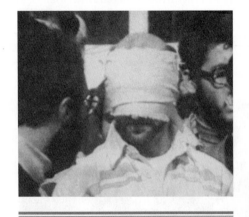

Television gave extensive coverage to the plight of American hostages in Iran in 1979–1980, leading many Americans to view the Carter administration as weak and inept.

In an unsuccessful attempt to bring down inflation, Carter had abandoned the Keynesian economic policy of increased government spending to combat recession in favor of high interest rates. He had cut back on social spending and the federal government's economic regulations, while projecting a major increase in the military budget. By 1980, détente had been eclipsed and the Cold War reinvigorated. Thus, many of the conservative policies associated with his successor, Ronald Reagan, were already in place when Carter's presidency ended.

THE RISING TIDE OF CONSERVATISM

The combination of domestic and international dislocations during the 1970s created a widespread sense of anxiety among Americans and offered conservatives new political opportunities. Economic problems heightened the appeal of lower taxes, reduced government regulation, and cuts in social spending to spur business investment. Fears about a decline of American power in the world led to calls for a renewal of the Cold War. The civil rights and sexual revolutions produced resentments that undermined the Democratic coalition. Rising urban crime rates reinforced demands for law and order and attacks on courts considered too lenient toward criminals. These issues brought new converts to the conservative cause.

As the 1970s went on, conservatives abandoned overt opposition to the black struggle for racial justice. The fiery rhetoric and direct confrontation tactics of Bull Connor, George Wallace, and other proponents of massive resistance were succeeded by appeals to freedom of association, local control, and resistance to the power of the federal government. This language of individual freedom resonated throughout the country, appealing especially to the growing, predominantly white, suburban population that was fleeing the cities and their urban problems. The suburbs would become one of the bastions of modern conservatism.

But it was not just a reaction to the 1960s and the spread of conservative ideas that nourished the movement. Like predecessors as diverse as the civil rights and labor movements, conservatives organized at the grass roots. In order to spread conservative doctrines, they ran candidates for office even when they had little chance of winning, and worked to change the policies of local institutions like school boards, town councils, and planning commissions.

One set of recruits was the "neoconservatives," a group of intellectuals who charged that the 1960s had produced a decline in moral standards and respect for authority. Once supporters of liberalism, they had come to believe that even well-intentioned government social programs did more harm than good. Welfare, for example, not only failed to alleviate poverty but also encouraged single motherhood and undermined the work ethic. High taxes and expensive government regulations drained resources from productive enterprises, stifling economic growth. Neoconservatives repudiated the attempts by Nixon, Ford, and Carter to reorient foreign policy away from the Cold War. Carter's focus on human rights and alleged blindness to the Soviet threat, they argued, endangered the "survival of freedom." Conservative "think tanks" created during the 1970s, like the Heritage Foundation and the American Enterprise Institute, refined and spread these ideas.

The Reverend Jerry Falwell, leader of the Moral Majority, with some of his followers.

THE RELIGIOUS RIGHT

The rise of religious fundamentalism during the 1970s expanded conservatism's popular base. Challenged by the secular and material concerns of American society, some denominations tried to bring religion into harmony with these interests; others reasserted more traditional religious values. The latter approach seemed to appeal to growing numbers of Americans. Even as membership in mainstream denominations like Episcopalianism and Presbyterianism declined, evangelical Protestantism flourished. Some observers spoke of a Third Great Awakening (like those of the 1740s and early nineteenth century). The election of Carter, the first "born-again" Christian to become president, highlighted the growing influence of evangelical religion. But unlike Carter, most fundamentalists who entered politics did so as conservatives.

Evangelical Christians had become more and more alienated from a culture that seemed to them to trivialize religion and promote immorality. They demanded the reversal of Supreme Court decisions banning prayer in public schools, protecting pornography as free speech, and legalizing abortion. Although it spoke of restoring traditional values, the Religious Right proved remarkably adept at using modern technology, including mass mailings and televised religious programming, to raise funds for their crusade and spread their message. In 1979, Jerry Falwell, a Virginia minister, created the self-styled Moral Majority, devoted to waging a "war against sin" and electing "pro-life, pro-family, pro-America" candidates to office. Falwell identified supporters of abortion rights, easy divorce, and "military unpreparedness" as the forces of Satan, who sought to undermine God's "special plans for this great, free country of ours."

Christian conservatives seemed most agitated by the ongoing sexual revolution, which they saw as undermining the traditional family and promoting immorality. As a result of the 1960s, they believed, American freedom was out of control. The growing assertiveness of the new gay movement spurred an especially fierce reaction. In 1977, after a campaign led by the popular singer Anita Bryant, a familiar fixture in televised orange juice commercials, Dade County, Florida, passed an anti-gay ordinance under the banner "Save Our Children."

THE BATTLE OVER THE EQUAL RIGHTS AMENDMENT

During the 1970s, "family values" moved to the center of conservative politics, nowhere more so than in the battle over the Equal Rights Amendment (ERA). Originally proposed during the 1920s by Alice Paul and the Women's Party, the ERA had been revived by second-wave feminists. In the wake of the rights revolution, the amendment's affirmation that

Doug Marlette's cartoon comments on the continuing gap in pay between men and women, the kind of inequality that inspired support for the proposed Equal Rights Amendment.

"equality of rights under the law" could not be abridged "on account of sex" hardly seemed controversial. In 1972, with little opposition, Congress approved the ERA and sent it to the states for ratification. Designed to eliminate obstacles to the full participation of women in public life, it aroused unexpected protest from those who claimed it would discredit the role of wife and homemaker.

The ERA debate reflected a division among women as much as a battle of the sexes. To its supporters, the amendment offered a guarantee of women's freedom in the public sphere. To its foes, freedom for women still resided in the divinely appointed roles of wife and mother. Phyllis Schlafly, who helped to organize opposition to the ERA, insisted that the "free enterprise system" was the "real liberator of women," since labor-saving home appliances offered more genuine freedom than "whining about past injustices" or seeking fulfillment outside the home. Opponents claimed that the ERA would let men "off the hook" by denying their responsibility to provide for their wives and children. Polls consistently showed that a majority of Americans, male and female, favored the ERA. But thanks to the mobilization of conservative women, the amendment failed to achieve ratification by the required thirty-eight states.

THE ABORTION CONTROVERSY

An even more bitter battle emerged in the 1970s over abortion rights, another example, to conservatives, of how liberals in office promoted sexual immorality at the expense of moral values. The movement to reverse the 1973 *Roe v. Wade* decision began among Roman Catholics, whose church condemned abortion under any circumstances. But it soon enlisted evangelical Protestants and social conservatives more generally. Life, the movement insisted, begins at conception, and abortion is nothing less than murder. Between this position and the feminist insistence that a woman's right to control her body includes the right to a safe, legal abortion, compromise was impossible. Ironically, both sides showed how the rights revolution had reshaped the language of politics. Defenders of abortion exalted "the right to

A 1979 anti-abortion rally in Washington, D.C., on the sixth anniversary of the Supreme Court's decision in Roe v. Wade, *which barred states from limiting a woman's right to terminate a pregnancy.*

choose" as the essence of freedom. Opponents called themselves the "right to life" movement and claimed to represent the rights of the "unborn child."

The abortion issue drew a bitter, sometimes violent line through American politics. It affected battles over nominees to judicial positions and led to demonstrations at family-planning and abortion clinics. The anti-abortion movement won its first victory in 1976 when Congress, over President Ford's veto, ended federal funding for abortions for poor women through the Medicaid program. By the 1990s, a few fringe anti-abortion activists were placing bombs at medical clinics and murdering doctors who terminated pregnancies. To the end of the century, most women would continue to have the legal right of access to abortion. But in many areas the procedure became more and more difficult to obtain as hospitals and doctors stopped providing it.

THE TAX REVOLT

With liberals unable to devise an effective policy to counteract deindustrialization and declining real wages, economic anxieties also created a growing constituency for conservative economics. Unlike during the Great Depression, economic distress inspired a critique of government rather than of business. New environmental regulations led to calls for less government intervention in the economy. These were most strident in the West, where measures to protect the environment threatened irrigation projects and private access to public lands. But everywhere, the economy's descent from affluence to "stagflation" increased the appeal of the conservative argument that government regulation raised business costs and eliminated jobs.

Economic decline also broadened the constituency receptive to demands for lower taxes. To conservatives, tax reductions served the dual purpose of enhancing business profits and reducing the resources available to

Women demonstrating in support for abortion rights.

VISIONS OF FREEDOM

Phyllis Schlafly Campaigning against the Equal Rights Amendment. *The activist Phyllis Schlafly, pictured here leading a rally at the Illinois State Capitol in 1978, was instrumental in grassroots organization of conservative men and women in opposition to the proposed Equal Rights Amendment to the Constitution, which would have barred all legal inequalities based on sex. She claimed that the amendment would take away "the right to be a housewife." The amendment's defeat was a major victory for the conservative movement.*

QUESTIONS

1. What does the image suggest about conflicting ideas of the role of women in American society in the wake of the social and political divisions created by the feminist movement of the 1960s and 1970s?

2. Why do opponents claim that the proposed amendment was a "blow" against American families?

government, thus making new social programs financially impossible. Many Americans found taxes increasingly burdensome. On paper, their incomes were rising, although the gains were nullified by inflation. Rising wages pushed families into higher tax brackets, increasing the percentage of their income they had to pay the government.

In 1978, conservatives sponsored and California voters approved Proposition 13, a ban on further increases in property taxes. The vote demonstrated that the level of taxation could be a powerful political issue. Proposition 13 proved to be a windfall for businesses and home owners, while reducing funds available for schools, libraries, and other public services. Many voters, however, proved willing to accept this result of lower taxes. As anti-tax sentiment flourished throughout the country, many states followed California's lead.

A parallel upsurge of grassroots conservatism was reflected in the Sagebrush Rebellion (the name given to a bill passed by the Nevada legislature in 1979). Using the language of freedom from government tyranny, leaders in western states denounced control of large areas of land by the Bureau of Land Management in Washington, D.C., and insisted that the states themselves be given decision-making power over issues like grazing rights, mining development, and whether public lands should be closed to fishing and hunting. With the federal government reluctant to give up control over public lands in the West, the Sagebrush Rebellion had few concrete accomplishments, but it underscored the rising tide of antigovernment sentiment.

THE ELECTION OF 1980

By 1980, Carter's approval rating had fallen to 21 percent—lower than Nixon's at the time of his resignation. A conservative tide seemed to be rising throughout the Western world. In 1979, Margaret Thatcher became prime minister of Great Britain. She promised to restore economic competitiveness by curtailing the power of unions, reducing taxes, selling state-owned industries to private owners, and cutting back the welfare state. In the United States, Ronald Reagan's 1980 campaign for the presidency brought together the many strands of 1970s conservatism. He pledged to end stagflation and restore the country's dominant role in the world and its confidence in itself. "Let's make America great again," he proclaimed. "The era of self-doubt is over."

Reagan also appealed skillfully to "white backlash." He kicked off his campaign in Philadelphia, Mississippi, where three civil rights workers had been murdered in 1964, with a speech emphasizing his belief in states' rights. Many white southerners understood this doctrine as including opposition to federal intervention on behalf of civil rights. During the campaign, Reagan repeatedly condemned welfare "cheats," school busing, and affirmative action. The Republican platform reversed the party's long-standing support for the Equal Rights Amendment and condemned moral permissiveness. Although not personally religious and the first divorced man to run for president,

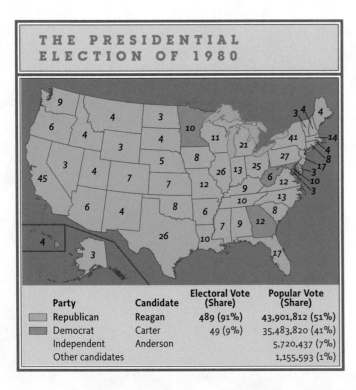

THE PRESIDENTIAL ELECTION OF 1980

Party	Candidate	Electoral Vote (Share)	Popular Vote (Share)
Republican	Reagan	489 (91%)	43,901,812 (51%)
Democrat	Carter	49 (9%)	35,483,820 (41%)
Independent	Anderson		5,720,437 (7%)
Other candidates			1,155,593 (1%)

Reagan won the support of the Religious Right and conservative upholders of "family values."

Riding a wave of dissatisfaction with the country's condition, Reagan swept into the White House. He carried such Democratic strongholds as Illinois, Texas, and New York. Because moderate Republican John Anderson, running for president as an independent, received about 7 percent of the popular vote, Reagan won only a bare majority, although he commanded a substantial margin in the electoral college. Carter received 41 percent, a humiliating defeat for a sitting president.

Jimmy Carter's reputation improved after he left the White House. He went to work for Habitat for Humanity, an organization that constructs homes for poor families. In the 1990s, he negotiated a cease-fire between warring Muslim and Serb forces in Bosnia and arranged a peaceful transfer of power from the military to an elected government in Haiti. In 2002, Carter was awarded the Nobel Peace Prize. His presidency, however, is almost universally considered a failure. And his defeat in 1980 launched the Reagan Revolution, which completed the transformation of freedom from the rallying cry of the left to a possession of the right.

THE REAGAN REVOLUTION

Ronald Reagan followed a most unusual path to the presidency. Originally a New Deal Democrat and head of the Screen Actors Guild (the only union leader ever to reach the White House), he emerged in the 1950s as a spokesman for the General Electric Corporation, preaching the virtues of unregulated capitalism. His nominating speech for Barry Goldwater at the 1964 Republican convention brought Reagan to national attention. Two years later, California voters elected Reagan as governor, establishing him as conservatives' best hope of capturing the presidency. In 1976, he challenged President Ford for the Republican nomination and came close to winning it. His victory in 1980 brought to power a diverse coalition of old and new conservatives: Sunbelt suburbanites and urban working-class ethnics; antigovernment crusaders and advocates of a more aggressive foreign policy; libertarians who believed in freeing the individual from restraint and the Christian Right, which sought to restore what they considered traditional moral values to American life.

REAGAN AND AMERICAN FREEDOM

Reagan's opponents often underestimated him. By the time he left office at the age of seventy-seven, he had become the oldest man ever to serve as president. He "rose at the crack of noon," as one reporter put it, and relied on his wife to arrange his official schedule. Unlike most modern presidents, he was content to outline broad policy themes and leave their implementation to others.

Reagan, however, was hardly a political novice, having governed California during the turbulent 1960s. An excellent public speaker, his optimism and affability appealed to large numbers of Americans. Reagan made conservatism seem progressive, rather than an attempt to turn back the tide of progress. He frequently quoted Thomas Paine: "We have it in our

VOICES OF FREEDOM

From Redstockings Manifesto (1969)

Redstockings was one of the radical feminist movements that arose in the late 1960s. Based in New York, it issued this manifesto, which, in language typical of the era, illustrates how at its most radical edge, feminism had evolved from demands for equal treatment for women to a total critique of male power and a call for women's "liberation."

After centuries of individual and preliminary political struggle, women are uniting to achieve their final liberation from male supremacy. Redstockings is dedicated to building this unity and winning our freedom.

Women are an oppressed class. Our oppression is total, affecting every facet of our lives. We are exploited as sex objects, breeders, domestic servants, and cheap labor. We are considered inferior beings, whose only purpose is to enhance men's lives. Our humanity is denied. Our prescribed behavior is enforced by the threat of physical violence.

Because we have lived so intimately with our oppressors, in isolation from each other, we have been kept from seeing our personal suffering as a political condition. . . .

We identify the agents of our oppression as men. Male supremacy is the oldest, most basic form of domination. . . . Men have controlled all political, economic, and cultural institutions and backed up this control with physical force. . . .

Our chief task at present is to develop female class consciousness through sharing experience and publicly exposing the sexist foundation of all our institutions. Consciousness-raising is not "therapy," which implies the existence of individual solutions and falsely assumes that the male-female relationship is purely personal, but the only method by which we can ensure that our program for liberation is based on the concrete realities of our lives. . . . The first requirement for raising class consciousness is honesty, in private and in public, with ourselves and other women.

We identify with all women. We define our best interest as that of the poorest, most brutally exploited women. . . .

We call on all our sisters to unite with us in struggle.

We call on all men to give up their male privileges and support women's liberation in the interest of our humanity and their own.

July 7, 1969, New York City

FROM JERRY FALWELL,
Listen, America! (1980)

The Reverend Jerry Falwell, a Virginia minister who in 1979 founded the self-proclaimed Moral Majority, was one of the leading conservative activists of the 1970s and 1980s. In language reminiscent of Puritan jeremiads about the decline of moral values, Falwell helped to mobilize evangelical Christians to ally with the Republican Party.

We must reverse the trend America finds herself in today. Young people between the ages of twenty-five and forty have been born and reared in a different world than Americans of years past. The television set has been their primary baby-sitter. From the television set they have learned situation ethics and immorality—they have learned a loss of respect for human life. They have learned to disrespect the family as God has established it. They have been educated in a public-school system that is permeated with secular humanism. They have been taught that the Bible is just another book of literature. They have been taught that there are no absolutes in our world today. They have been introduced to the drug culture. They have been reared by the family and the public school in a society that is greatly void of discipline and character-building....

Every American who looks at the facts must share a deep concern and burden for our country.... If Americans will face the truth, our nation can be turned around and can be saved from the evils and the destruction that have fallen upon every other nation that has turned its back on God....

I personally feel that the home and the family are still held in reverence by the vast majority of the American public. I believe there is still a vast number of Americans who love their country, are patriotic, and are willing to sacrifice for her.... I believe that Americans want to see this country come back to basics, back to values, back to biblical morality, back to sensibility, and back to patriotism....

It is now time to take a stand on certain moral issues, and we can only stand if we have leaders. We must stand against the Equal Rights Amendment, the feminist revolution, and the homosexual revolution.... The hope of reversing the trends of decay in our republic now lies with the Christian public in America. We cannot expect help from the liberals. They certainly are not going to call our nation back to righteousness and neither are the pornographers, the smut peddlers, and those who are corrupting our youth. Moral Americans must be willing to put their reputations, their fortunes, and their very lives on the line for this great nation of ours. Would that we had the courage of our forefathers who knew the great responsibility that freedom carries with it.

QUESTIONS

1. How do the authors of the Redstockings Manifesto seem to define women's freedom?

2. What does Falwell see as the main threats to moral values?

3. How do the two documents differ in their views about the role of women in American society?

A delegate to the Republican national convention of 1980 wears a hat festooned with the flags of the United States and Texas, and a button with a picture of her hero, Ronald Reagan.

power to begin the world over again." Reagan repeatedly invoked the idea that America has a divinely appointed mission as a "beacon of liberty and freedom." Freedom, indeed, became the watchword of the Reagan Revolution. In his public appearances and state papers, Reagan used the word more often than any president before him.

Reagan reshaped the nation's agenda and political language more effectively than any president since Franklin D. Roosevelt. Like FDR, he seized on the vocabulary of his opponents and gave it new meaning. Reagan promised to free government from control by "special interests," but these were racial minorities, unionists, and others hoping to use Washington's power to attack social inequalities, not businessmen seeking political favors, the traditional target of liberals. His Justice Department made the principle that the Constitution must be "color-blind"—a remark hurled at the Supreme Court majority by Justice John Marshall Harlan in 1896 to challenge a system of legal segregation—a justification for gutting civil-rights enforcement.

Overall, Reagan proved remarkably successful at seizing control of the terms of public debate. On issues ranging from taxes to government spending, national security, crime, welfare, and "traditional values," he put Democrats on the defensive. But he also proved to be a pragmatist, recognizing when to compromise so as not to fragment his diverse coalition of supporters.

REAGANOMICS

Like Roosevelt and Johnson before him, Reagan spoke of "economic freedom" and proposed an "economic Bill of Rights." But in contrast to his predecessors, who used these phrases to support combating poverty and strengthening economic security, economic freedom for Reagan meant curtailing the power of unions, dismantling regulations, and radically reducing taxes. Taxation, he declared, violated the principle that "the right to earn your own keep and keep what you earn" was "what it means to be free."

In 1981, Reagan persuaded Congress to reduce the top tax rate from 70 percent to 50 percent and to index tax brackets to take inflation into account. Five years later, the Tax Reform Act reduced the rate on the wealthiest Americans to 28 percent. These measures marked a sharp retreat from the principle of progressivity (the idea that the wealthy should pay a higher percentage of their income in taxes than other citizens), one of the ways twentieth-century societies tried to address the unequal distribution of wealth. Reagan also appointed conservative heads of regulatory agencies, who cut back on environmental protection and workplace safety rules about which business had complained for years.

Since the New Deal, liberals had tried to promote economic growth by using the power of the government to bolster ordinary Americans' purchasing power. Reagan's economic program, known as "supply-side economics" by proponents and "trickle-down economics" by critics, relied on high interest rates to curb inflation and lower tax rates, especially for businesses and high-income Americans, to stimulate private investment. The policy assumed that cutting taxes would inspire Americans at all income levels to work harder, since they would keep more of the money they earned. Everyone would benefit from increased business profits, and because of a growing economy, government receipts would rise despite lower tax rates.

REAGAN AND LABOR

Reagan inaugurated an era of hostility between the federal government and organized labor. In August 1981, when 13,000 members of PATCO, the union of air traffic controllers, began a strike in violation of federal law, Reagan fired them all. He used the military to oversee the nation's air traffic system until new controllers could be trained. Reagan's action inspired many private employers to launch anti-union offensives. The hiring of workers to replace permanently those who had gone on strike, a rare occurrence before 1980, became widespread. Manufacturing employment, where union membership was concentrated, meanwhile continued its long-term decline. By the mid-1990s, the steel industry employed only 170,000 persons—down from 600,000 in 1973. When Reagan left office, both the service and retail sectors employed more Americans than manufacturing, and only 11 percent of workers with non-government jobs were union members.

This photograph of the remains of the Sprague Electric Company in North Adams, Massachusetts, which closed in 1985, depicts the aftermath of deindustrialization. Today, the building is the site of the Massachusetts Museum of Contemporary Art.

"Reaganomics," as critics dubbed the administration's policies, initially produced the most severe recession since the 1930s. A long period of economic expansion, however, followed the downturn of 1981–1982. As companies "downsized" their workforces, shifted production overseas, and took advantage of new technologies such as satellite communications, they became more profitable. At the same time, the rate of inflation, 13.5 percent at the beginning of 1981, declined to 3.5 percent in 1988, partly because a period of expanded oil production that drove down prices succeeded the shortages of the 1970s. The stock market rose substantially. In October 1987, the market suffered its sharpest drop since 1929, but stocks soon resumed their upward climb.

THE PROBLEM OF INEQUALITY

Together, Reagan's policies, rising stock prices, and deindustrialization resulted in a considerable rise in economic inequality. By the mid-1990s, the richest 1 percent of Americans owned 40 percent of the nation's wealth, twice their share twenty years earlier. Most spent their income not on productive investments and charity as supply-side economists had promised, but on luxury goods, real-estate speculation, and corporate buyouts that often led to plant closings as operations were consolidated. The income of middle-class families, especially those with a wife who did not work outside the home, stagnated while that of the poorest one-fifth of the population declined. Because of falling investment in public housing, the release of mental patients from state hospitals, and cuts in welfare, homeless persons became a visible fixture on the streets of cities from New York to Los Angeles.

Deindustrialization and the decline of the labor movement had a particularly devastating impact on minority workers, who had only recently

A homeless Los Angeles family, forced to live in their car, photographed in 1983.

gained a foothold in better-paying manufacturing jobs. Thanks to the opening of colleges and professional schools to minority students as a result of the civil rights movement and affirmative action programs, the black middle class expanded considerably. But black workers, traditionally the last hired and first fired, were hard hit by economic changes.

During the 1970s, Jim Crow had finally ended in many workplaces and unions. But just as decades of painful efforts to obtain better jobs bore fruit, hundreds of thousands of black workers lost their jobs when factories closed their doors. In South Gate, a working-class suburb of Los Angeles, for example, the giant Firestone tire factory shut down in 1980, only a few years after black and Latino workers had made their first breakthroughs in employment. When the national unemployment rate reached 8.9 percent at the end of 1981, the figure for blacks exceeded 20 percent. Nor did black workers share fully in the recovery that followed. Few had the education to take advantage of job openings in growing "knowledge-based" industries like technology and information services. Overall, during the 1980s black males fell farther than any other group in the population in terms of wages and jobs.

THE SECOND GILDED AGE

In retrospect, the 1980s, like the 1890s, would be widely remembered as a decade of misplaced values. Buying out companies generated more profits than running them; making deals, not making products, became the way to get rich. The merger of Nabisco and R.J. Reynolds Tobacco Company in 1988 produced close to $1 billion in fees for lawyers, economic advisers, and stockbrokers. "Greed is healthy," declared Wall Street financier Ivan Boesky (who ended up in prison for insider stock trading). "Yuppie"—the young

A family of affluent "yuppies"—young urban professionals—posing in their New York City apartment with their child-care worker and baby.

urban professional who earned a high income working in a bank or stock brokerage firm and spent lavishly on designer clothing and other trappings of the good life—became a household word. Television shows like *Dallas* and *Dynasty* chronicled the activities of the very rich for a mass audience.

Taxpayers footed the bill for some of the consequences. The deregulation of savings and loan associations—banks that had generally confined themselves to financing home mortgages—allowed these institutions to invest in unsound real-estate ventures and corporate mergers. Losses piled up, and the Federal Savings and Loan Insurance Corporation, which insured depositors' accounts, faced bankruptcy. After Reagan left office, the federal government bailed out the savings and loan institutions, at a cost to taxpayers estimated at $250 billion.

Supply-side advocates insisted that lowering taxes would enlarge government revenue by stimulating economic activity. But spurred by large increases in funds for the military, federal spending far outstripped income, producing large budget deficits, despite assurances by supply-siders that this would not happen. During Reagan's presidency, the national debt tripled to $2.7 trillion. Nonetheless, Reagan remained immensely popular. He took credit for economic expansion while blaming congressional leaders for the ballooning federal deficit. He won a triumphant reelection in 1984. His opponent, Walter Mondale (best remembered for choosing Congresswoman Geraldine Ferraro of New York as his running mate, the first woman candidate on a major-party presidential ticket), carried only his home state of Minnesota and the District of Columbia.

CONSERVATIVES AND REAGAN

While he implemented their economic policies, Reagan in some ways disappointed ardent conservatives. The administration sharply reduced funding for Great Society antipoverty programs such as food stamps, school lunches, and federal financing of low-income housing. But it left intact core elements of the welfare state, such as Social Security, Medicare, and Medicaid, which many conservatives wished to curtail significantly or repeal. The Reagan era did little to advance the social agenda of the Christian Right. Abortion remained legal, women continued to enter the labor force in unprecedented numbers, and Reagan even appointed the first female member of the Supreme Court, Sandra Day O'Connor. In 1986, in *Bowers v. Hardwick*, in a rare victory for cultural conservatives, the Supreme Court did uphold the constitutionality of state laws outlawing homosexual acts. (In 2003, the justices would reverse the *Bowers* decision, declaring laws that criminalized homosexuality unconstitutional.)

Reagan gave verbal support to a proposed constitutional amendment restoring prayer in public schools but did little to promote its passage. The administration launched a "Just Say No" campaign against illegal drug use. But this failed to halt the spread in urban areas of crack, a potent, inexpensive form of cocaine that produced an upsurge of street crime and family breakdown. Reagan's Justice Department cut back on civil rights enforcement and worked to curtail affirmative action programs. But to the end of Reagan's presidency, the Supreme Court continued to approve plans by private employers and city and state governments to upgrade minority employment.

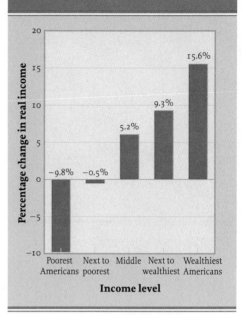

Figure 26.3 CHANGES IN FAMILIES' REAL INCOME, 1980–1990

The wealthiest American families benefited the most from economic expansion during the 1980s, while the poorest 40 percent of the population saw their real incomes decline. (Real income indicates income adjusted to take account of inflation.)

The drug crack being openly sold on the streets of New York City in 1986.

REAGAN AND THE COLD WAR

In foreign policy, Reagan breathed new life into the rhetorical division of the world into a free West and unfree East. He resumed vigorous denunciation of the Soviet Union—calling it an "evil empire"—and sponsored the largest military buildup in American history, including new long-range bombers and missiles. In 1983, he proposed an entirely new strategy, the Strategic Defense Initiative, based on developing a space-based system to intercept and destroy enemy missiles. The idea was not remotely feasible technologically, and, if deployed, it would violate the Anti-Ballistic Missile Treaty of 1972. But it appealed to Reagan's desire to reassert America's worldwide power. He persuaded NATO, over much opposition, to introduce short-range nuclear weapons into Europe to counter Soviet forces. But the renewed arms race and Reagan's casual talk of winning a nuclear war caused widespread alarm at home and abroad. In the early 1980s, a movement for a nuclear freeze—a halt to the development of nuclear weapons—attracted millions of supporters in the United States and Europe. In 1983, half of the American population watched *The Day After*, a television program that unflinchingly depicted the devastation that would be caused by a nuclear war.

Reagan came into office determined to overturn the "Vietnam syndrome"—as widespread public reluctance to commit American forces overseas was called. He sent American troops to the Caribbean island of Grenada to oust a pro-Cuban government, and he ordered the bombing of Libya in retaliation for the country's alleged involvement in a terrorist attack on a West Berlin nightclub in which an American died. In 1982, Reagan dispatched marines as a peacekeeping force to Lebanon, where a civil war raged between the Christian government, supported by Israeli forces, and Muslim insurgents. But he quickly withdrew them after a bomb exploded at their barracks, killing 241 Americans. The public, Reagan realized, would support minor operations like Grenada but remained unwilling to sustain heavy casualties abroad.

Hollywood joined enthusiastically in the revived Cold War. The 1984 film Red Dawn *depicted a Soviet invasion of the United States.*

Reagan generally relied on military aid rather than American troops to pursue his foreign policy objectives. Abandoning the Carter administration's emphasis on human rights, Reagan embraced the idea, advanced in 1979 by neoconservative writer Jeane Kirkpatrick, that the United States should oppose "totalitarian" communists but assist "authoritarian" non-communist regimes. Kirkpatrick became the American ambassador to the United Nations, and the United States stepped up its alliances with Third World anticommunist dictatorships like the governments of Chile and South Africa. The administration poured in funds to combat insurgencies against the governments of El Salvador and Guatemala, whose armies and associated death squads committed flagrant abuses against their own citizens. When El Salvador's army massacred hundreds of civilians in the town of El Mozote in 1981, the State Department denied that the event, widely reported in the press, had taken place.

THE IRAN-CONTRA AFFAIR

American involvement in Central America produced the greatest scandal of Reagan's presidency, the Iran-Contra affair. In 1984, Congress banned military aid to the Contras (derived from the Spanish word for "against") fighting the Sandinista government of Nicaragua, which, as noted earlier, had ousted the American-backed dictator Anastasio Somoza in 1979. In 1985, Reagan secretly authorized the sale of arms to Iran—now involved in a war with its neighbor, Iraq—in order to secure the release of a number of American hostages held by Islamic groups in the Middle East. CIA director William Casey and Lieutenant Colonel Oliver North of the National Security Council set up a system that diverted some of the proceeds to buy military supplies for the Contras in defiance of the congressional ban. The scheme continued for nearly two years.

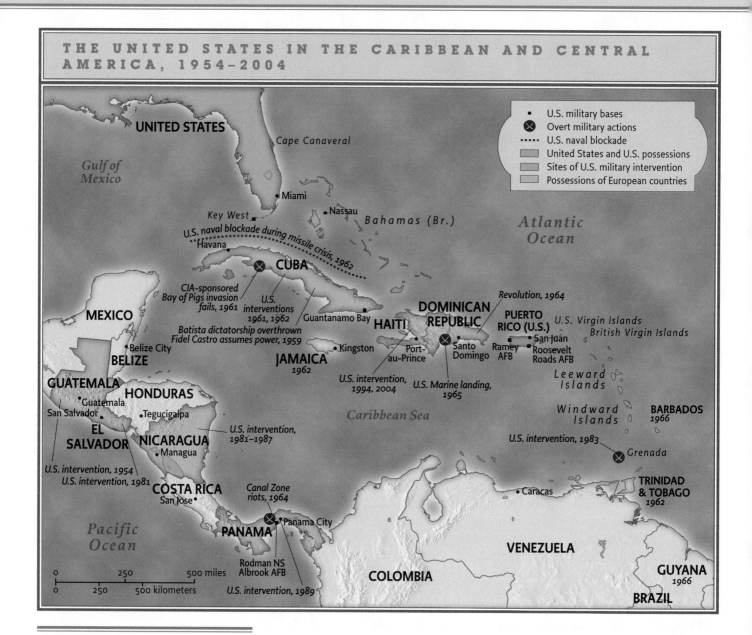

THE UNITED STATES IN THE CARIBBEAN AND CENTRAL AMERICA, 1954–2004

- U.S. military bases
- Overt military actions
- U.S. naval blockade
- United States and U.S. possessions
- Sites of U.S. military intervention
- Possessions of European countries

As in the first part of the twentieth century, the United States intervened frequently in Caribbean and Central American countries during and immediately after the Cold War.

In 1987, after a Middle Eastern newspaper leaked the story, Congress held televised hearings that revealed a pattern of official duplicity and violation of the law reminiscent of the Nixon era. Eleven members of the administration eventually were convicted of perjury or destroying documents, or pleaded guilty before being tried. Reagan denied knowledge of the illegal proceedings, but the Iran-Contra affair undermined confidence that he controlled his own administration.

REAGAN AND GORBACHEV

In his second term, to the surprise of both his foes and supporters, Reagan softened his anticommunist rhetoric and established good relations with Soviet premier Mikhail Gorbachev. Gorbachev had come to power in 1985, bent on reforming the Soviet Union's repressive political system and reinvigorating its economy. The country had fallen farther and farther behind the United States in the production and distribution of consumer goods, and it relied increasingly on agricultural imports to feed itself. Gorbachev inaugurated policies known as *glasnost* (political openness) and *perestroika* (economic reform).

Gorbachev realized that significant change would be impossible without reducing his country's military budget. Reagan was ready to negotiate. A series of talks between 1985 and 1987 yielded more progress on arms control than in the entire postwar period to that point, including an agreement to eliminate intermediate- and short-range nuclear missiles in Europe. In 1988, Gorbachev began pulling Soviet troops out of Afghanistan. Having entered office as an ardent Cold Warrior, Reagan left with hostilities between the superpowers much diminished. He even repudiated his earlier comment that the Soviet Union was an "evil empire," saying that it referred to "another era."

REAGAN'S LEGACY

Reagan's presidency revealed the contradictions at the heart of modern conservatism. Rhetorically, he sought to address the concerns of the Religious Right, advocating a "return to spiritual values" as a way to strengthen traditional families and local communities. But in some ways, the Reagan Revolution undermined the very values and institutions conservatives held dear. Intended to discourage reliance on government handouts by rewarding honest work and business initiative, Reagan's policies inspired a speculative frenzy that enriched architects of corporate takeovers and investors in the stock market while leaving in their wake plant closings, job losses, and devastated communities. Nothing proved more threatening to local traditions or family stability than deindustrialization, insecurity about employment, and the relentless downward pressure on wages. Nothing did more to undermine a sense of common national purpose than the widening gap between rich and poor.

Because of the Iran-Contra scandal and the enormous deficits the government had accumulated, Reagan left the presidency with his reputation somewhat tarnished. Nonetheless, few figures have so successfully changed the landscape and language of politics. Reagan's vice president, George H. W. Bush, defeated Michael Dukakis, the governor of Massachusetts, in the 1988 election partly because Dukakis could not respond effectively to the charge that he was a "liberal"—now a term of political abuse. Conservative assumptions about the virtues of the free market and the evils of "big government" dominated the mass media and political debates. Those receiving public assistance had come to be seen not as citizens entitled to help in coping with economic misfortune, but as a drain on taxes. During the 1990s, these and other conservative ideas would be embraced almost as fully by President Bill Clinton, a Democrat, as by Reagan and the Republicans.

THE ELECTION OF 1988

The 1988 election seemed to show politics sinking to new lows. Television advertisements and media exposés now dominated political campaigns. The race for the Democratic nomination had hardly begun before the

President Reagan visited Moscow in 1988, cementing his close relationship with Soviet leader Mikhail Gorbachev. They were photographed in Red Square.

Conservatives celebrate the inauguration of George H. W. Bush, January 1989.

front-runner, Senator Gary Hart of Colorado, withdrew after a newspaper reported that he had spent the night at his Washington town house with a woman other than his wife. Both parties ran negative campaigns. Democrats ridiculed the Republican vice-presidential nominee, Senator Dan Quayle of Indiana, for factual and linguistic mistakes. Republicans spread unfounded rumors that Michael Dukakis's wife had burned an American flag during the 1960s. The low point of the campaign came in a Republican television ad depicting the threatening image of Willie Horton, a black murderer and rapist who had been furloughed from prison during Dukakis's term as governor of Massachusetts. Rarely in the modern era had a major party appealed so blatantly to racial fears. Before his death in 1991, Lee Atwater, who masterminded Bush's campaign, apologized for the Horton ad.

Although he did not match Reagan's landslide victory of 1984, Bush achieved a substantial majority, winning 54 percent of the popular vote. Democratic success in retaining control of Congress suggested that an electoral base existed for a comeback. But this would only occur if the party fashioned a new appeal to replace traditional liberalism, which had been eclipsed by the triumph of conservatism.

SUGGESTED READING

BOOKS

Adler, William M. *Mollie's Job: A Story of Life and Work on the Global Assembly Line* (2000). Tracks how a manufacturing job moved from the North to the South and eventually out of the country, and what happened to the workers who held it.

Allitt, Patrick. *Religion in America since 1945* (2003). A survey of the main trends of religious development since World War II.

Anderson, Terry H. *The Pursuit of Fairness: A History of Affirmative Action* (2004). A careful study of the origins and development of affirmative action policies.

Busch, Andrew E. *Ronald Reagan and the Politics of Freedom* (2001). Discusses how Ronald Reagan interpreted the idea of freedom and how it influenced his presidency.

Dallek, Matthew. *The Right Moment: Ronald Reagan's First Victory and the Decisive Turning Point in American Politics* (2000). An examination of the causes of Reagan's election in 1980 and its impact on American politics.

Fitzgerald, Frances. *Way Out There in the Blue: Reagan, Star Wars and the End of the Cold War* (2000). A critical appraisal of one of the key military initiatives of Reagan's presidency.

Greenberg, David. *Nixon's Shadow: The History of an Image* (2003). Explores how Nixon's supporters and enemies thought about him during his long political career.

Himmelstein, Jerome L. *To the Right: The Transformation of American Conservatism* (1990). Studies the development of conservative ideas since World War II.

Kruse, Kevin. *White Flight: Atlanta and the Making of Modern Conservatism* (2005). Explores how conservative politics took root in the predominantly white suburbs of Atlanta, with implications for similar communities across the country.

Kutler, Stanley I. *The Wars of Watergate: The Last Crisis of Richard Nixon* (1990). The most thorough analysis of the Watergate scandal that brought down President Nixon.

Luker, Kristin. *Abortion and the Politics of Motherhood* (1984). Describes how the abortion issue affected American politics and the ideas about gender relations that lay behind the debate.

Martin, William. *With God on Our Side: The Rise of the Religious Right in America* (1996). Traces the development of religious conservatism and its impact on American society.

Mathews, Donald G., and Jane S. De Hart. *Sex, Gender, and the Politics of ERA* (1990). An in-depth examination of the debate over the Equal Rights Amendment and why its opponents were successful.

McGirr, Lisa. *Suburban Warriors: The Origins of the New American Right* (2001). An influential study of the rise of conservatism in Orange County, California, once one of its more powerful centers.

Schulman, Bruce J. *The Seventies: The Great Shift in American Culture, Society, and Politics* (2001). A survey of the numerous political, social, and economic changes that took place during the 1970s.

Stein, Judith. *Running Steel, Running America: Race, Economic Policy, and the Decline of Liberalism* (1998). Examines the decline of the American steel industry and how the Cold War and presidential policies from Eisenhower to Carter contributed to it.

Wilentz, Sean. *The Age of Reagan: A History, 1974–2008* (2008). Explores how Ronald Reagan set the terms of public debate during and after his presidency.

WEBSITES

China and the United States: From Hostility to Engagement: www.gwu.edu/~nsarchiv/NSAEBB/NSAEBB19/

National Security Archive: www.gwu.edu/~nsarchiv/

REVIEW QUESTIONS

1. Which of Nixon's domestic policies did other conservatives oppose, and why?

2. How did the Burger Court modify but not overturn the rights revolution of the 1960s?

3. What were the main features of Nixon's policy of "realism" in dealing with China and the Soviet Union?

4. Describe the basic events and the larger significance of the Watergate scandal.

5. What were the major causes for the decline of the U.S. economy in the 1970s?

6. Compare Carter's and Reagan's explanations for the severe recession of the late 1970s.

7. Identify the groups and their agendas that combined to create the new conservative base in the 1970s and 1980s.

8. What impact did Ronald Reagan have on the American political scene?

9. Why was there growth in economic inequality in the 1980s?

FREEDOM QUESTIONS

1. How did conservatives introduce competing definitions of freedom into the fights for women's rights, especially into the struggle over the Equal Rights Amendment and abortion?

2. What impact did the Reagan Revolution have on the meanings of American freedom?

3. Explain how its supporters defended Reaganomics as a promotion of human liberty.

4. Assess the decisions of the Burger Court on the issue of affirmative action.

KEY TERMS

REVIEW TABLE

Triumph of Conservatism

Event	Dates	Background	Significance
Sharon Statement	1960	Platform of the Young Americans for Freedom	Conservative students emerged as a force in politics
Goldwater campaign	1964	Barry Goldwater (R) lost presidential election to Lyndon Johnson (D)	His victory in the southern states identified a growing conservative electorate frustrated with civil rights and big government
Equal Rights Amendment battle	1972–1982	Ten-year battle over ratification of the ERA by the states	Conservatives who saw the ERA as anti-family succeeded in its defeat
Moral Majority	1979	Organized by Jerry Falwell to wage a war against sin	It was used as a vehicle for political influence, helping elect Ronald Reagan
Sagebrush Rebellion	1979	Bill passed by Nevada legislature denouncing federal control over land	Grassroots initiative that argued the states, not D.C., ought to determine grazing rights, mining development, and land use
Reagan election	1980	Ronald Reagan (R) defeated Jimmy Carter (D)	His overwhelming victory marked the high tide of conservatism
Air traffic controllers' strike	1981	ATC strikers' demands go unmet and all are fired who did not return to work	Ronald Reagan's actions inspired other employers to take anti-union offensives
Bowers v. Hardwick	1986	Held that state laws outlawing homosexual acts were constitutional	Victory for cultural conservatives

CHAPTER 27

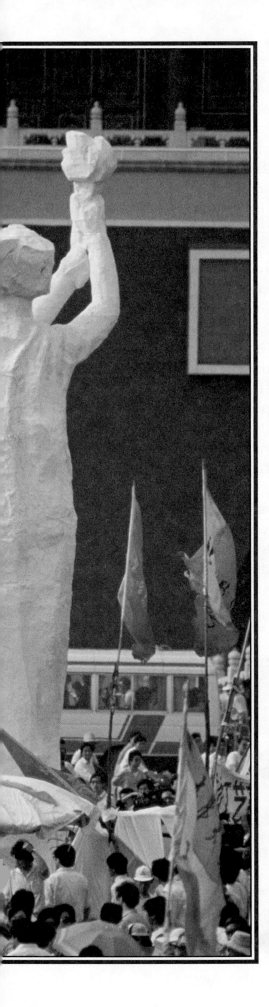

Globalization and Its Discontents, 1989–2000

The Goddess of Democracy and Freedom, a statue reminiscent of the Statue of Liberty, was displayed by pro-democracy advocates during the 1989 demonstrations in Beijing's Tiananmen Square. After allowing it to continue for two months, the Chinese government sent troops to crush the peaceful occupation of the square. To this day, it is difficult in China to discuss openly the events of 1989.

FOCUS QUESTIONS

• What were the major international initiatives of the Clinton administration in the aftermath of the Cold War?

• What forces drove the economic resurgence of the 1990s?

• What cultural conflicts emerged in the 1990s?

• How did a divisive political partisanship affect the election of 2000?

• What were the prevailing ideas of American freedom at the end of the century?

In December 1999, delegates from around the world gathered in Seattle for a meeting of the World Trade Organization (WTO), a 135-nation group created five years earlier to reduce barriers to international commerce and settle trade disputes. To the astonishment of residents of the city, more than 30,000 persons gathered to protest the meeting. Their marches and rallies brought together factory workers, who claimed that global free trade encouraged corporations to shift production to low-wage centers overseas, and "tree-huggers," as some reporters called environmentalists, who complained about the impact on the earth's ecology of unregulated economic development.

Some of the latter dressed in costumes representing endangered species—monarch butterflies whose habitats were disappearing because of the widespread destruction of forests by lumber companies, and sea turtles threatened by unrestricted ocean fishing. Protesters drew attention to the depletion of ozone in the atmosphere, which shields the earth from harmful solar radiation. The heightened use of aerosol sprays and refrigerants containing damaging chemicals had caused a large hole in the ozone layer. A handful of self-proclaimed anarchists embarked on a window-breaking spree at local stores. The police sealed off the downtown and made hundreds of arrests, and the WTO gathering disbanded.

Once a center of labor radicalism, the Seattle area in 1999 was best known as the home of Microsoft, developer of the Windows operating system used in most of the world's computers. The company's worldwide reach symbolized "globalization," the process by which people, investment, goods, information, and culture increasingly flowed across national

Protesters dressed as sea turtles, an endangered species, at the demonstrations against the World Trade Organization in Seattle, December 1999.

boundaries. Globalization has been called "*the* concept of the 1990s." During that decade, the media resounded with announcements that a new era in human history had opened, with a borderless economy and a "global civilization" that would soon replace traditional cultures. Some commentators claimed that the nation-state itself had become obsolete in the globalized world.

Globalization, of course, was hardly a new phenomenon. The internationalization of commerce and culture and the reshuffling of the world's peoples had been going on since the explorations of the fifteenth century. But the scale and scope of late-twentieth-century globalization was unprecedented. Thanks to satellites and the Internet, information and popular culture flowed instantaneously to every corner of the world. Manufacturers and financial institutions scoured the world for profitable investment opportunities.

Perhaps most important, the collapse of communism between 1989 and 1991 opened the entire world to the spread of market capitalism and to the idea that government should interfere as little as possible with economic activity. The Free World triumphed over its communist rival, the free market over the idea of a planned economy, and the free individual over ideas of shared community and social citizenship. American politicians and social commentators increasingly criticized the regulation of wages and working conditions, assistance to the less fortunate, and environmental protections as burdens on international competitiveness. During the 1990s, presidents George H. W. Bush, a Republican, and Bill Clinton, a Democrat, both spoke of an American mission to create a single global free market as the path to rising living standards, the spread of democracy, and greater worldwide freedom.

Similar demonstrations at economic summits overseas followed the Seattle protests. The media called the loose coalition of groups who organized the protests the "antiglobalization" movement. In fact, they challenged not globalization itself but its social consequences. Globalization, the demonstrators claimed, accelerated the worldwide creation of wealth but widened gaps between rich and poor countries and between haves and have-nots within societies. Decisions affecting the day-to-day lives of millions of people were made by institutions—the World Trade Organization, International Monetary Fund, World Bank, and multinational corporations—that operated without any democratic input. These international organizations required developing countries seeking financial aid to open their economies to penetration from abroad while reducing spending on domestic social concerns. Demonstrators demanded not an end to global trade and capital flows, but the establishment of international standards for wages, labor conditions, and the environment, and greater investment in health and education in poor countries.

Douglas Harp's 1993 lithograph drew attention to the development of a hole in the atmosphere's ozone layer, exposing human beings to increased solar radiation.

Even President Clinton, a staunch advocate of free trade, told the Seattle delegates that the protesters were "telling us in the streets" that "we've been silent" about the effects of globalization. The Battle of Seattle placed on the national and international agendas a question that promises to be among the most pressing concerns of the twenty-first century—the relationship between globalization, economic justice, and freedom.

THE POST-COLD WAR WORLD

THE CRISIS OF COMMUNISM

The year 1989 was one of the most momentous of the twentieth century. In April, tens of thousands of student demonstrators occupied Tiananmen Square in the heart of Beijing, demanding greater democracy in China. Workers, teachers, and even some government officials joined them, until their numbers swelled to nearly 1 million. Both the reforms Mikhail Gorbachev had introduced in the Soviet Union and the example of American institutions inspired the protesters. The students erected a figure reminiscent of the Statue of Liberty, calling it "The Goddess of Democracy and Freedom." In June, Chinese troops crushed the protest, killing an unknown number of people, possibly thousands.

In the fall of 1989, pro-democracy demonstrations spread across eastern Europe. Gorbachev made it clear that unlike in the past, the Soviet Union would not intervene. The climactic event took place on November 9 when

Demonstrators dancing atop the Berlin Wall on November 10, 1989. The next day, crowds began dismantling it, in the most dramatic moment of the collapse of communist rule in eastern Europe.

crowds breached the Berlin Wall, which since 1961 had stood as the Cold War's most prominent symbol. One by one, the region's communist governments agreed to give up power. In 1990, a reunified German nation absorbed East Germany. The remarkably swift and almost entirely peaceful collapse of communism in eastern Europe became known as the "velvet revolution."

Meanwhile, the Soviet Union itself slipped deeper and deeper into crisis. Gorbachev's attempts at economic reform produced only chaos, and his policy of political openness allowed long-suppressed national and ethnic tensions to rise to the surface. In 1990, the Baltic republics of Estonia, Latvia, and Lithuania, which had been absorbed into the Soviet Union in 1940, declared their independence. In August 1991, a group of military leaders attempted to seize power to overturn the government's plan to give greater autonomy to the various parts of the Soviet Union. Russian president Boris Yeltsin mobilized crowds in Moscow that restored Gorbachev to office. Gorbachev then resigned from the Communist Party, ending its eighty-four-year rule. One after another, the republics of the Soviet Union declared themselves sovereign states. At the end of 1991, the Soviet Union ceased to exist; in its place were fifteen new independent nations.

The sudden and unexpected collapse of communism marked the end of the Cold War and a stunning victory for the United States and its allies. For the first time since 1917, there existed a truly worldwide capitalist system. Even China, while remaining under Communist Party rule, had already embarked on market reforms and rushed to attract foreign investment. Other events suggested that the 1990s would also be a "decade of democracy." In 1990, South Africa released Nelson Mandela, head of the African National Congress, from prison. Four years later, as a result of the first democratic elections in the country's history, Mandela became president, ending the system of state-sponsored racial inequality, known as "apartheid," and white minority government. Peace came to Central America, with negotiated ends to the civil war in El Salvador and an election in Nicaragua won by opponents of the Sandinistas in 1990. Throughout Latin America and Africa, civilian governments replaced military rule.

President Bill Clinton with Nelson Mandela, during Clinton's visit to South Africa in 1998. Mandela's election as president of South Africa in 1994, ending decades of white minority rule, was one of the most significant triumphs of democracy in the 1990s.

A NEW WORLD ORDER?

The sudden shift from a bipolar world to one of unquestioned American predominance promised to redefine the country's global role. President George H. W. Bush spoke of the coming of a "new world order." But no one knew what its characteristics would be.

Bush's first major foreign policy action was a throwback to the days of American interventionism in the Western Hemisphere. At the end of 1989, he dispatched troops to Panama to overthrow the government of General Manuel Antonio Noriega, a former ally of the United States who had become involved in the international drug trade. Although the invasion cost the lives of over 3,000 Panamanians and was condemned by the United Nations General Assembly as a violation of international law, the administration deemed it a great success. The United States installed a new government and flew Noriega to Florida, where he was tried and convicted on drug charges.

EASTERN EUROPE AFTER THE COLD WAR

The end of the Cold War and breakup of the Soviet Union, Czechoslovakia, and Yugoslavia redrew the map of eastern Europe (compare this map with the map of Cold War Europe in Chapter 23). Two additional nations that emerged from the Soviet Union lie to the east and are not indicated here: Kyrgyzstan and Tajikistan.

THE GULF WAR

A far more serious crisis arose in 1990 when Iraq invaded and annexed Kuwait, an oil-rich sheikdom on the Persian Gulf. Fearing that Iraqi dictator Saddam Hussein might next attack Saudi Arabia, a longtime ally that supplied more oil to the United States than any other country, Bush rushed troops to defend the kingdom and warned Iraq to withdraw from Kuwait or face war. His policy aroused intense debate in the United States. Critics insisted that diplomacy be given a chance to resolve the crisis. Bush spoke of defending the freedom of Saudi Arabia and restoring that of Kuwait. Antiwar activists pointed out that neither qualified as a free country—both, for example, denied women the right to vote. But the Iraqi invasion so flagrantly violated international law that Bush succeeded in building a forty-nation coalition committed to restoring Kuwait's independence, secured the support of the United Nations, and sent half a million American troops along with a naval armada to the region.

In February 1991, the United States launched Operation Desert Storm, which quickly drove the Iraqi army from Kuwait. Tens of thousands of Iraqis and 184 Americans died in the conflict. The United Nations ordered Iraq to disarm and imposed economic sanctions that produced widespread civilian suffering for the rest of the decade. But Hussein remained in place. So did a large American military establishment in Saudi Arabia, to the outrage of Islamic fundamentalists who deemed its presence an affront to their faith.

VISIONS OF FREEDOM

Workers trying to deal with crowds of customers at the opening of the first McDonald's restaurant in Beijing in 1992. By the end of the century, there were 200 McDonald's in China and the company was serving hamburgers in more than 100 countries, one example of the globalization of the world economy during the 1990s. The company's spread also provoked protests from those who claimed its food was unhealthy or fattening.

QUESTIONS

1. What does the image tell us about economic and cultural globalization in the 1990s?

2. Compare this image to the one on pp. 1122–1123 as a measure of American influence in China and the world.

President Bush, with Defense Secretary Dick Cheney (left) *and General Colin Powell* (right), *chair of the Joint Chiefs of Staff, at a meeting in January 1991, shortly before the beginning of the Gulf War. Cheney and Powell would play major roles in the administration of Bush's son, President George W. Bush.*

The Gulf War was the first post–Cold War international crisis. Despite assembling a broad coalition, the United States did nearly all of the fighting itself. Relying on high-tech weaponry like cruise missiles that reached Iraq from bases and aircraft carriers hundreds of miles away, the United States was able to prevail quickly and avoid the prolonged involvement and high casualties of Vietnam. The Soviet Union, in the process of disintegration, remained on the sidelines. In the war's immediate aftermath, Bush's public approval rating rose to an unprecedented 89 percent.

VISIONS OF AMERICA'S ROLE

In a speech to Congress, President Bush identified the Gulf War as the first step in the struggle to create a world rooted in democracy and global free trade. But it remained unclear how this broad vision would be translated into policy. Soon after the end of the war, General Colin Powell, chairman of the Joint Chiefs of Staff, and Dick Cheney, the secretary of defense, outlined different visions of the future. Powell predicted that the post–Cold War world would be a dangerous environment with conflicts popping up in unexpected places. To avoid being drawn into an unending role as global policeman, he insisted, the United States should not commit its troops abroad without clear objectives and a timetable for withdrawal. Cheney argued that with the demise of the Soviet Union, the United States possessed the power to reshape the world and prevent hostile states from achieving regional power. It must be willing to use force, independently if necessary, to maintain its strategic dominance. For the rest of the 1990s, it was not certain which definition of the American role in the post–Cold War world would predominate.

THE ELECTION OF CLINTON

Had a presidential election been held in 1991, Bush would undoubtedly have been victorious. But in that year the economy slipped into recession. In a kind of hangover from the speculative excesses of the Reagan years, unemployment rose and family income stagnated. Despite victory in the

Cold War and the Gulf, public-opinion polls showed that more and more Americans believed the country was on the wrong track. No one seized more effectively on the widespread sense of unease than Bill Clinton, a former governor of Arkansas. In 1992, Clinton won the Democratic nomination by combining social liberalism (he supported abortion rights, gay rights, and affirmative action for racial minorities) with elements of conservatism (he pledged to reduce government bureaucracy and, borrowing a page from Republicans, promised to "end welfare as we know it").

A charismatic campaigner, Clinton conveyed sincere concern for voters' economic anxieties. To counter Republican rhetoric urging voters to blame their woes on "welfare queens" and others who cheated honest taxpayers, Clinton argued that deindustrialization caused rising inequality and the loss of good jobs. In his speech accepting the nomination, he spoke of people "working harder than ever, spending less time with their children, working nights and weekends," while "those who cut corners and cut deals have been rewarded."

Bush, by contrast, seemed out of touch with the day-to-day lives of ordinary Americans. On the wall of Democratic headquarters, Clinton's campaign director posted the slogan, "It's the Economy, Stupid"—a reminder that the economic downturn was the Democrats' strongest card. Bush was further weakened when conservative leader Pat Buchanan delivered a fiery televised speech at the Republican national convention that declared cultural war against gays, feminists, and supporters of abortion rights. This seemed to confirm the Democratic portrait of Republicans as intolerant and divisive. From a peak of 89 percent in 1991, Bush's popularity slumped to 29 percent during the 1992 campaign.

A third candidate, the eccentric Texas billionaire Ross Perot, also entered the fray. He attacked Bush and Clinton as lacking the economic know-how to deal with the recession and the ever-increasing national debt. That millions of Americans considered Perot a credible candidate—at one point, polls showed him leading both Clinton and Bush—testified to widespread dissatisfaction with the major parties. Perot's support faded as election day approached, but he still received 19 percent of the popular vote, the best result for a third-party candidate since Theodore Roosevelt in 1912. Clinton won by a substantial margin, a humiliating outcome for Bush, given his earlier popularity.

CLINTON IN OFFICE

In his first two years in office, Clinton turned away from some of the social and economic policies of the Reagan and Bush years. He appointed several blacks and women to his cabinet, including Janet Reno, the first female attorney general, and named two supporters of abortion rights, Ruth Bader Ginsburg and Stephen Breyer, to the Supreme Court. He modified the military's strict ban on gay soldiers, instituting a "don't ask, don't tell" policy by which officers would not seek out gays for dismissal from the armed

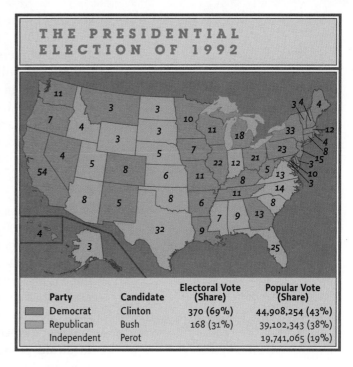

THE PRESIDENTIAL ELECTION OF 1992

Party	Candidate	Electoral Vote (Share)	Popular Vote (Share)
Democrat	Clinton	370 (69%)	44,908,254 (43%)
Republican	Bush	168 (31%)	39,102,343 (38%)
Independent	Perot		19,741,065 (19%)

Edward Sorel's illustration for the cover of the New Yorker *depicts Bill Clinton at his 1993 inauguration, flanked by some of his predecessors as president.*

forces. His first budget raised taxes on the wealthy and significantly expanded the Earned Income Tax Credit (EITC)—a cash payment for low-income workers begun during the Ford administration. The most effective antipoverty policy since the Great Society, the EITC raised more than 4 million Americans, half of them children, above the poverty line during Clinton's presidency.

Clinton shared his predecessor's passion for free trade. Despite strong opposition from unions and environmentalists, he obtained congressional approval in 1993 of the North American Free Trade Agreement (NAFTA), a treaty negotiated by Bush that created a free-trade zone consisting of Canada, Mexico, and the United States.

The major policy initiative of Clinton's first term was a plan devised by a panel headed by his wife, Hillary, a lawyer who had pursued an independent career after their marriage, to address the rising cost of health care and the increasing number of Americans who lacked health insurance. In Canada and western Europe, governments provided universal medical coverage. The United States had the world's most advanced medical technology and a woefully incomplete system of health insurance. The Great Society had provided coverage for the elderly and poor through the Medicare and Medicaid programs. Many employers offered health insurance to their workers. But tens of millions of Americans lacked any coverage at all. Beginning in the 1980s, moreover, businesses shifted their employees from individual doctors to health maintenance organizations (HMOs), which reduced costs by limiting physicians' fees and, critics charged, denying patients needed medical procedures.

Announced with great fanfare by Hillary Rodham Clinton at congressional hearings in 1993, Clinton's plan would have provided universal coverage through large groupings of organizations like the HMOs. Doctors and health insurance and drug companies attacked it vehemently, fearing government regulations that would limit reimbursement for medical procedures, insurance rates, and the price of drugs. Too complex to be easily understood by most voters, and vulnerable to criticism for further expanding the unpopular federal bureaucracy, the plan died in 1994. Nothing took its place. By 2008, some 50 million Americans, most of them persons who held full-time jobs, still lacked health insurance, meaning that illness could quickly become a financial disaster.

THE "FREEDOM REVOLUTION"

With the economy recovering slowly from the recession and Clinton's first two years in office seemingly lacking in significant accomplishments, voters in 1994 turned against the administration. For the first time since the 1950s, Republicans won control of both houses of Congress. They proclaimed their triumph the "Freedom Revolution." Newt Gingrich, a conservative congressman from Georgia who became the new Speaker of the House, masterminded their campaign. Gingrich had devised a platform called the "Contract with America," which promised to curtail the scope of government, cut back on taxes and economic and environmental regulations, overhaul the welfare system, and end affirmative action.

Viewing their electoral triumph as an endorsement of the Contract, Republicans moved swiftly to implement its provisions. The House

Congressman Newt Gingrich of Georgia at a rally in September 1994 announcing the "Contract with America," the Republican program for the congressional elections that fall. The Republican sweep resulted in Gingrich's election as Speaker of the House.

approved deep cuts in social, educational, and environmental programs, including the popular Medicare system. With the president and Congress unable to reach agreement on a budget, the government in December 1995 shut down all nonessential operations, including Washington, D.C., museums and national parks.

Gingrich had assumed that the public shared his intense ideological convictions. He discovered that in 1994 they had voted against Clinton, not for the full implementation of the Contract with America. Most Americans blamed Congress for the impasse, and Gingrich's popularity plummeted.

CLINTON'S POLITICAL STRATEGY

Like Truman after the Republican sweep of 1946, Clinton rebuilt his popularity by campaigning against a radical Congress. He opposed the most extreme parts of his opponents' program, while adopting others. In his state of the union address of January 1996, he announced that "the era of big government is over," in effect turning his back on the tradition of Democratic Party liberalism and embracing the antigovernment outlook associated with Republicans since the days of Barry Goldwater. He also approved the Telecommunications Act of 1996, which deregulated broadcasting and telephone companies and gave billions of dollars worth of digital frequencies to existing broadcasters without charge.

Also in 1996, ignoring the protests of most Democrats, Clinton signed into law a Republican bill that abolished the program of Aid to Families with Dependent Children (AFDC), commonly known as "welfare." Grants of money to the states, with strict limits on how long recipients could receive payments, replaced it. At the time of its abolition, AFDC assisted 14 million individuals, 9 million of them children. Thanks to stringent new eligibility requirements imposed by the states and the economic boom of the late 1990s, welfare rolls plummeted. But the number of children living in poverty remained essentially unchanged. Nonetheless, Clinton had succeeded in one of his primary goals: by the late 1990s, welfare, a hotly contested issue for twenty years or more, had disappeared from political debate.

Commentators called Clinton's political strategy "triangulation." This meant embracing the most popular Republican policies, like welfare reform, while leaving his opponents with extreme positions unpopular among suburban middle-class voters, such as hostility to abortion rights and environmental protection. Clinton's strategy enabled him to neutralize Republican claims that Democrats were the party of high taxes and lavish spending on persons who preferred dependency to honest labor. Clinton's passion for free trade alienated many working-class Democrats but convinced middle-class voters that the party was not beholden to the unions.

Clinton easily defeated Republican Bob Dole in the presidential contest of 1996, becoming the first Democrat elected to two terms since FDR. Clinton had accomplished for Reaganism what Eisenhower had done for the New Deal, and Nixon for the Great Society—consolidating a basic shift in American politics by accepting many of the premises of his opponents.

CLINTON AND WORLD AFFAIRS

Like Jimmy Carter before him, Clinton's primary political interests concerned domestic, not international, affairs. But with the United States now indisputably the world's dominant power, Clinton, like Carter, took steps to encourage the settlement of long-standing international conflicts and tried to elevate support for human rights to a central place in international relations. He met only mixed success.

Clinton strongly supported a 1993 agreement, negotiated at Oslo, Norway, in which Israel for the first time recognized the legitimacy of the Palestine Liberation Organization. The Oslo Accords seemed to outline a road to Mideast peace. But neither side proved willing to implement them fully. Israeli governments continued to build Jewish settlements on Palestinian land in the West Bank—a part of Jordan that Israel had occupied during the 1967 Six-Day War. The new Palestinian Authority, which shared in governing parts of the West Bank as a stepping stone to full statehood, proved to be corrupt, powerless, and unable to curb the growth of groups bent on violence against Israel. At the end of his presidency, Clinton brought Israeli and Palestinian leaders to Camp David to try to work out a final peace treaty. But the meeting failed, and violence soon resumed.

Like Carter, Clinton found it difficult to balance concern for human rights with strategic and economic interests and to formulate clear guidelines for humanitarian interventions overseas. For example, the United States did nothing in 1994 when tribal massacres racked Rwanda, in central Africa. More than 800,000 people were slaughtered, and 2 million refugees fled the country.

THE BALKAN CRISIS

The most complex foreign policy crisis of the Clinton years arose from the disintegration of Yugoslavia, a multi-ethnic state in southeastern Europe that had been carved from the old Austro-Hungarian empire after World War I. As in the rest of eastern Europe, the communist government that had ruled Yugoslavia since the 1940s collapsed in 1989. Within a few years, the country's six provinces dissolved into five new states. Ethnic conflict plagued several of these new nations. In 1992, Serbs in Bosnia, which

A 1992 photograph of refugees in war-torn Bosnia illustrates the humanitarian crisis in the Balkans during the 1990s.

straddled the historic boundary between Christianity and Islam in south-eastern Europe, launched a war aimed at driving out Muslims and Croats. They conducted the war with unprecedented ferocity, using mass murder and rape as military strategies. "Ethnic cleansing"—a terrible new term meaning the forcible expulsion from an area of a particular ethnic group—now entered the international vocabulary. By the end of 1993, more than 100,000 Bosnians, nearly all of them civilians, had perished.

With the Cold War over, protection of human rights in the Balkans gave NATO a new purpose. After considerable indecision, NATO launched air strikes against Bosnian Serb forces, with American planes contributing. UN troops, including 20,000 Americans, arrived as peacekeepers. In 1998, ethnic cleansing again surfaced, this time by Yugoslavian troops and local Serbs against the Albanian population of Kosovo, a province of Serbia. More than 800,000 Albanians fled the region. To halt the bloodshed, NATO launched a two-month war in 1999 against Yugoslavia that led to the deployment of American and UN forces in Kosovo.

HUMAN RIGHTS

During Clinton's presidency, human rights played an increasingly important role in international affairs. Hundreds of nongovernmental agencies throughout the world defined themselves as protectors of human rights. During the 1990s, the agenda of international human rights organizations expanded to include access to health care, women's rights, and the rights of indigenous peoples like the Aborigines of Australia and the descendants of the original inhabitants of the Americas. Human rights emerged as a justification for interventions in matters once considered to be the internal affairs of sovereign nations. The United States dispatched the military to distant parts of the world to assist in international missions to protect civilians.

New institutions emerged that sought to punish violations of human rights. The Rwandan genocide produced a UN-sponsored war crimes court that sentenced the country's former prime minister to life in prison. An international tribunal put Yugoslav president Slobodan Milošević on trial for sponsoring the massacre of civilians. The European Court of Human Rights overruled legal decisions by national courts that violated individual rights. Spanish and British courts considered charging former Chilean dictator Augusto Pinochet with murder, although he proved to be too ill to stand trial. It remained to be seen whether these initiatives would grow into an effective international system of protecting human rights across national boundaries. Despite adopting human rights as a slogan, many governments continued to violate them in practice.

A NEW ECONOMY?

Clinton's popularity rested in part on the American economy's remarkable performance in the mid- and late 1990s. After recovery from the recession of 1990–1991, economic expansion continued for the rest of the decade. By 2000, unemployment stood below 4 percent, a figure not seen since the 1960s. Many economists had insisted that if unemployment fell that low, inflation would inevitably increase. Yet prices barely rose during the boom, because rising worldwide oil production kept the cost of energy low and weak unions and increased global competition made it difficult for workers to achieve significant wage increases and for corporations to raise prices. The boom became the longest uninterrupted period of economic expansion in the nation's history. Because Reagan and Bush had left behind massive budget deficits, Clinton worked hard to balance the federal budget—a goal traditionally associated with fiscal conservatives. Since economic growth produced rising tax revenues, Clinton during his second term not only balanced the budget but actually produced budget surpluses.

The first Starbucks store, which opened in Seattle in 1971. By the early twenty-first century, Starbucks had more than 7,000 such establishments in countries around the globe.

Two architects of the computer revolution, Steve Jobs (standing), the head of Apple Computer, and Bill Gates (via the Internet), founder of Microsoft, at a 1997 convention.

THE COMPUTER REVOLUTION

Many commentators spoke of the 1990s as the dawn of a "new economy," in which computers and the Internet would produce vast new efficiencies and the production and sale of information would occupy the central place once held by the manufacture of goods. Computers had first been developed during and after World War II to solve scientific problems and do calculations involving enormous amounts of data. The early ones were extremely large, expensive, and, by modern standards, slow. Research for the space program of the 1960s spurred the development of improved computer technology, notably the miniaturization of parts thanks to the development of the microchip on which circuits could be imprinted.

Microchips made possible the development of entirely new consumer products. Video cassette recorders, handheld video games, cellular phones, and digital cameras were mass-produced at affordable prices during the 1990s, mostly in Asia and Latin America rather than the United States. But it was the computer that transformed American life. Beginning in the 1980s, companies like Apple and IBM marketed computers for business and home use. As computers became smaller, faster, and less expensive, they found a place in businesses of every kind. In occupations as diverse as clerical work, banking, architectural design, medical diagnosis, and even factory production, they transformed the American workplace. They also changed private life. By the year 2000, nearly half of all American households owned a personal computer, used for entertainment, shopping, and sending and receiving electronic mail. Centers of computer technology, such as Silicon Valley south of San Francisco, the Seattle and Austin metropolitan areas, and lower Manhattan, boomed during the 1990s.

Hollywood, as always, reflected changes in popular consciousness, in this case the impact of the computer revolution. In *War of the Worlds*, a 1953 movie based on a novel by H. G. Wells, technologically superior aliens invade earth

Young people seemed to adapt to the computer revolution more readily than their elders. Here nine-year-old Anna Walter teaches several adults how to use the Internet in Wichita, Kansas.

only to succumb to disease viruses to which they have no resistance. In *Independence Day*, one of the most successful movies of the 1990s, a similar invasion is thwarted in part by the introduction of a different kind of virus—a program that disables computers—into the control mechanism of the alien spaceship.

The Internet, first developed as a high-speed military communications network, was simplified and opened to commercial and individual use through personal computers. The Internet expanded the flow of information and communications more radically than any invention since the printing press. At a time when the ownership of newspapers, television stations, and publishing houses was becoming concentrated in the hands of a few giant media conglomerates, the fact that anyone with a computer could post his or her ideas for worldwide circulation led "netizens" ("citizens" of the Internet) to hail the advent of a new, democratic public sphere in cyberspace.

GLOBAL ECONOMIC PROBLEMS

American economic expansion in the 1990s seemed all the more remarkable since other advanced countries found themselves bogged down in difficulty. In western Europe, unemployment remained far higher than in the United States. Japan, which some commentators of the 1980s had expected to surpass the United States as the world's leading economic power, was locked in a long-term recession. Despite an influx of Western loans and investment, Russia moved from one economic crisis to another. Relying strongly on advice from American free-market economists and the Clinton administration, Russian president Boris Yeltsin presided over a policy of "shock therapy" that privatized state-owned enterprises and imposed severe cuts in wages and in the guaranteed jobs, health care, and housing Russians had become used to under communism. Foreign investors and a new Russian business class (many of them Yeltsin's relatives and cronies, and former party officials) reaped a windfall, while most of the population plunged into poverty.

Many Third World countries faced large trade deficits and problems repaying loans from foreign banks and other institutions. A sharp decline in the value of the Thai currency in 1997 sparked a fiscal crisis throughout Asia, only resolved by massive loans from the International Monetary Fund. These bailouts inspired criticisms, echoed at the Seattle protests of 1999, that globalization increased social inequality. Foreign investors had their loans repaid, but receiving nations were required to balance their budgets by stringent cutbacks in public spending, so that the burden fell disproportionately on the poor.

THE STOCK MARKET BOOM AND BUST

In the United States, economic growth and talk of a new economy sparked a frenzied boom in the stock market that was reminiscent of the 1920s. Investors, large and small, poured funds into stocks, spurred by the rise of

Technicians at the offices of FHP Wireless in Belmont, California, one of numerous technology companies launched with great fanfare in the late 1990s. Unlike many, FHP survived. In 2002, Fortune magazine listed it as one of the country's "cool companies." It is now called Tropos Networks.

discount and online firms that advertised aggressively and charged lower fees than traditional brokers. By 2000, a majority of American households owned stocks directly or through investment in mutual funds and pension and retirement accounts.

Investors were especially attracted to the new "dot coms"—companies that conducted business via the Internet and seemed to symbolize the promise of the new economy. Standard & Poor's index of 500 stocks (S&P 500) increased 20 percent or more each year from 1996 to 1999, a remarkable performance. But the NASDAQ, a stock exchange dominated by new technology companies, rose more than 500 percent from 1998 to 1999. Many of these "high-tech" companies never turned a profit. But economic journalists and stock brokers explained that the new economy had so revolutionized business that traditional methods of assessing a company's value no longer applied

Inevitably, the bubble burst. On April 14, 2000, stocks suffered their largest one-day point drop in history. For the first time since the Depression, stock prices declined for three successive years (2000–2002), wiping out billions of dollars in Americans' net worth and pension funds. The value of NASDAQ stocks fell by nearly 80 percent between 2000 and 2002. Not until 2006 would the general stock index again reach the level of early 2000, while the NASDAQ still remains far below its record high. By 2001, the American economy had fallen into a recession. Talk of a new economy, it appeared, had been premature.

THE ENRON SYNDROME

Only after the market dropped did it become apparent that the stock boom of the 1990s had been fueled in part by fraud. For a time in 2001 and 2002, Americans were treated almost daily to revelations of incredible greed and corruption on the part of respected brokerage firms, accountants, and

"Let's say I was Enron, how would you do my taxes?"

Cartoonist David Jacobson's comment on the Enron scandal.

company executives. During the late 1990s, accounting firms like Arthur Andersen, giant banks like J.P. Morgan Chase and Citigroup, and corporate lawyers pocketed extravagant fees for devising complex schemes to help push up companies' stock prices by hiding their true financial condition. Enron, a Houston-based energy company that epitomized the new economy—it bought and sold electricity rather than actually producing it—reported as profits billions of dollars in operating losses. Brokers at respected Wall Street firms advised favored clients to sell risky stocks while foisting them on ordinary customers. When stock prices began to fall, insiders jumped ship while brokers urged hapless individual investors to hold on to their shares, many of which ended up being worthless.

In the early twenty-first century, the bill came due for many corporate criminals. The founder of Adelphia Communications was convicted of misuse of company funds. A jury found the chairman of Tyco International guilty of looting the company of millions of dollars. A number of former chief executives faced long prison terms. Kenneth Lay and Jeffrey Skilling, chief officers of Enron, were convicted by a Texas jury of multiple counts of fraud. (Lay died before sentencing.) Even reputable firms like J.P. Morgan, Chase, and Citigroup agreed to pay billions of dollars to compensate investors on whom they had pushed worthless stocks.

FRUITS OF DEREGULATION

At the height of the 1990s boom, with globalization in full swing, stocks rising, and the economy expanding, the economic model of free trade and deregulation appeared unassailable. But the retreat from government economic regulation, a policy embraced by both the Republican Congress and President Clinton, left no one to represent the public interest.

The sectors of the economy most affected by the scandals—energy, telecommunications, and stock trading—had all been subjects of deregulation.

Enron could manipulate energy prices because Congress had granted it an exemption from laws regulating the price of natural gas and electricity. WorldCom, a communications giant that, like Enron, issued fraudulent earnings statements, had benefited from the Telecommunications Act of 1996, mentioned earlier, that privatized the airwaves.

Many stock frauds stemmed from the repeal in 1999 of the Glass-Steagall Act, a New Deal measure that had separated commercial banks, which accept deposits and make loans, from investment banks, which invest in stocks and real estate and take larger risks. The repeal made possible the emergence of "superbanks" that combined these two functions. Phil Gramm, the Texas congressman who wrote the repeal bill, which Clinton signed, explained his thinking in this way: "Glass-Steagall came at a time when the thinking was that government was the answer. In this era of economic prosperity, we have decided that freedom is the answer."

But banks took their new freedom as an invitation to engage in all sorts of misdeeds, knowing that they had become so big that if anything happened, the federal government would have no choice but to rescue them. Conflicts of interest proliferated. Banks financed risky new stock offerings by fledgling Internet companies while their investment arms peddled the shares to an unsuspecting public. Worse, these banks poured money into risky mortgages. When the housing bubble collapsed in 2007–2008, the banks suffered losses that threatened to bring down the entire financial system. The Bush and Obama administrations felt they had no choice but to expend hundreds of billions of dollars of taxpayer money to save the banks from their own misconduct.

RISING INEQUALITY

The boom that began in 1995 benefited nearly all Americans. For the first time since the early 1970s, average real wages and family incomes began to grow significantly. Economic expansion at a time of low unemployment brought rapid increases in wages for families at all income levels. It aided low-skilled workers, especially non-whites, who had been left out of previous periods of growth. By 2000, the number of long-term unemployed, 2 million in 1993, had declined to around 700,000. Yet, despite these gains, average wages for nonsupervisory workers, adjusted for inflation, remained below the level of the 1970s. Overall, in the last two decades of the twentieth century, the poor and the middle class became worse off while the rich became significantly richer.

Between 1977 and 1999, the average after-tax income of the poorest one-fifth of Americans fell 12 percent, and that of the middle one-fifth decreased by 3 percent. In contrast, thanks to the soaring stock market and increasingly generous pay for top executives, the income of the top one-fifth rose 38 percent. The wealth of the richest Americans exploded during the 1990s. Sales of luxury goods like yachts and mansions boomed. Bill Gates, head of Microsoft and the country's richest person, owned as much wealth as the bottom 40 percent of the American population put together. In 1965, the salary of the typical corporate chief executive officer (CEO) had been 26 times the annual income of the typical worker. In 2000, the ratio had increased to 310 to 1.

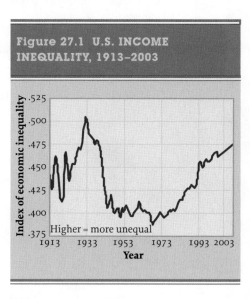

Figure 27.1 U.S. INCOME INEQUALITY, 1913–2003

The "Gini index" measures economic inequality; the higher the number, the more unequally income is distributed. As the graph shows, inequality peaked just before the Great Depression, fell dramatically during the New Deal, World War II, and the postwar economic boom, and then began a steady upward climb in the early 1970s.

From Bill Clinton,
Speech on Signing of NAFTA (1993)

The North American Free Trade Agreement was signed by President Bill Clinton early in his first term. It created a free-trade zone (an area where goods can travel freely without paying import duties) composed of Canada, the United States, and Mexico. Clinton asked Americans to accept economic globalization as an inevitable form of progress and the path to future prosperity. "There will be no job loss," he promised. Things did not entirely work out that way.

As President, it is my duty to speak frankly to the American people about the world in which we now live. Fifty years ago, at the end of World War II, an unchallenged America was protected by the oceans and by our technological superiority and, very frankly, by the economic devastation of the people who could otherwise have been our competitors. We chose then to try to help rebuild our former enemies and to create a world of free trade supported by institutions which would facilitate it. . . . As a result, jobs were created, and opportunity thrived all across the world. . . .

For the last 20 years, in all the wealthy countries of the world—because of changes in the global environment, because of the growth of technology, because of increasing competition—the middle class that was created and enlarged by the wise policies of expanding trade at the end of World War II has been under severe stress. Most Americans are working harder for less. They are vulnerable to the fear tactics and the averseness to change that are behind much of the opposition to NAFTA. But I want to say to my fellow Americans: When you live in a time of change, the only way to recover your security and to broaden your horizons is to adapt to the change—to embrace, to move forward. . . . The only way we can recover the fortunes of the middle class in this country so that people who work harder and smarter can, at least, prosper more, the only way we can pass on the American dream of the last 40 years to our children and their children for the next 40, is to adapt to the changes which are occurring.

In a fundamental sense, this debate about NAFTA is a debate about whether we will embrace these changes and create the jobs of tomorrow or try to resist these changes, hoping we can preserve the economic structures of yesterday. . . . I believe that NAFTA will create 1 million jobs in the first 5 years of its impact. . . . NAFTA will generate these jobs by fostering an export boom to Mexico by tearing down tariff walls. . . . There will be no job loss.

FROM GLOBAL EXCHANGE, SEATTLE,
Declaration for Global Democracy (December 1999)

The demonstrations that disrupted the December 1999 meeting of the World Trade Organization in Seattle brought to public attention a widespread dissatisfaction with the effects of economic "globalization." In this declaration, organizers of the protest offered their critique.

As citizens of global society, recognizing that the World Trade Organization is unjustly dominated by corporate interests and run for the enrichment of the few at the expense of all others, we demand:

Representatives from all sectors of society must be included in all levels of trade policy formulations. All global citizens must be democratically represented in the formulation, implementation, and evaluation of all global social and economic policies.

Global trade and investment must not be ends in themselves, but rather the instruments for achieving equitable and sustainable development including protection for workers and the environment.

Global trade agreements must not undermine the ability of each nation-state or local community to meet its citizens' social, environmental, cultural or economic needs.

The World Trade Organization must be replaced by a democratic and transparent body accountable to citizens—not to corporations.

No globalization without representation!

QUESTIONS

1. Why does Clinton feel that free trade is necessary to American prosperity?

2. Why do the Seattle protesters feel that the World Trade Organization is a threat to democracy?

3. How do these documents reflect contradictory arguments about the impact of globalization in the United States?

A cartoonist offered this view in 1993 of the results of the North American Free Trade Agreement, suggesting that the United States was exporting manufacturing factories and jobs, and receiving immigrant workers in exchange.

Barbie's Liberty, *a satirical work by the artist Hans Haacke, recasts the Barbie doll, one of America's most successful toys, in the image of the Statue of Liberty to comment on the loss of manufacturing jobs to low-wage areas overseas.*

Dot-com millionaires and well-paid computer designers and programmers received much publicity. But companies continued to shift manufacturing jobs overseas. Thanks to NAFTA, which eliminated barriers to imports from Mexico, a thriving industrial zone emerged just across the southern border of the United States, where American manufacturers built plants to take advantage of cheap labor and weak environmental and safety regulations. Despite low unemployment, companies' threats to shut down and move exerted downward pressure on American wages. In 2000, the United States no longer led the world in the hourly wages of manufacturing workers, lagging behind several countries in Europe. In terms of the distribution of income and wealth, the United States was the most unequal society in the developed world.

High-tech firms did not create enough high-paying jobs to compensate. Microsoft, symbol of the new economy, employed only 30,000 people. In 1970, General Motors had been the country's largest corporate employer. In the early-twenty-first century, it had been replaced by Wal-Mart, a giant discount retail chain that paid most of its 1.6 million workers slightly more than the minimum wage. Wal-Mart aggressively opposed efforts at collective bargaining. Not a single one of its employees belonged to a union.

In 2000, well over half the labor force worked for less than fourteen dollars per hour, a wage on which families found it very difficult to make ends meet. Because of the decline in union membership and the spread of part-time employment, fewer and fewer workers enjoyed fringe benefits common in union contracts, such as employer-provided health insurance. In "dual cities" like Los Angeles and New York, high-tech computer companies and firms engaging in international finance coexisted with sweatshops reminiscent of the Progressive era, where workers toiled in overcrowded conditions for the minimum wage or less. Poverty was not limited to urban areas. The highest rates of poverty could be found in isolated rural regions that experienced the continuation of the long-term decline in family farming.

Of the twenty-five poorest counties in the United States in 2000, nine were located in Nebraska and South Dakota.

At the end of the twentieth century, the United States, more than ever before, was a suburban nation. Two-thirds of new jobs were created in the suburbs. Suburbs were no longer places from which people commuted to jobs in central cities—their office parks, industrial plants, and huge shopping malls employed many local residents. Nor were suburbs as racially segregated as in the past. In 2000, one-quarter of the suburban population was black, and Hispanics represented a majority of the population in the suburbs of Los Angeles and Miami. But suburbs remained divided by income—there were rich suburbs, middle-class suburbs, and poor suburbs, with little connection between them.

CULTURE WARS

The end of the Cold War ushered in hopes for a new era of global harmony. Instead, what one observer called a "rebellion of particularisms"—renewed emphasis on group identity and insistent demands for group recognition and power—racked the international arena during the 1990s. In the nineteenth and twentieth centuries, socialism and nationalism had united people of different backgrounds in pursuit of common goals. Now, in Africa, Asia, the Middle East, and parts of Europe, the waning of movements based on socialism and the declining power of nation-states arising from globalization seemed to unleash long-simmering ethnic and religious antagonisms. Partly in reaction to the global spread of a secular culture based on consumption and mass entertainment, intense religious movements attracted increasing numbers of followers—Hindu nationalism in India, orthodox Judaism in Israel, Islamic fundamentalism in much of the Muslim world, and evangelical Christianity in the United States. Like other nations, although in a far less extreme way and with little accompanying violence, the United States experienced divisions arising from the intensification of ethnic and racial identities and religious fundamentalism.

THE NEWEST IMMIGRANTS

Because of shifts in immigration, cultural and racial diversity became increasingly visible in the United States. Until the immigration law of 1965, the vast majority of twentieth-century newcomers had hailed from

Table 27.1 IMMIGRATION TO THE UNITED STATES, 1960–2000

Decade	Total	Europe	Asia	Western Hemisphere	Africa	Oceania
1961–1970	3,321,584	1,123,492	427,642	1,716,374	28,954	25,122
1971–1980	4,493,302	800,368	1,588,178	1,982,735	80,779	41,242
1981–1990	7,337,030	761,550	2,738,157	3,615,225	176,893	45,205
1991–2000	9,052,999	1,359,737	2,795,672	4,486,806	354,939	55,845

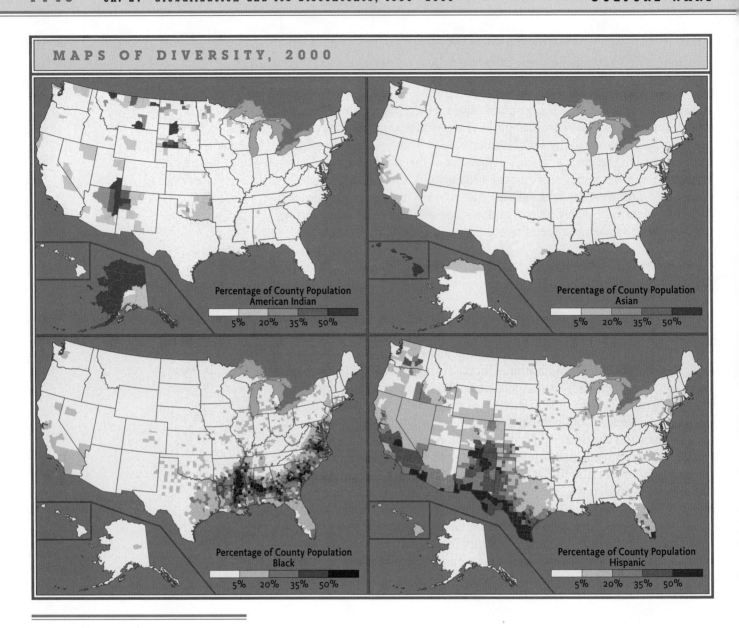

MAPS OF DIVERSITY, 2000

Percentage of County Population
American Indian
5%   20%   35%   50%

Percentage of County Population
Asian
5%   20%   35%   50%

Percentage of County Population
Black
5%   20%   35%   50%

Percentage of County Population
Hispanic
5%   20%   35%   50%

Based on the 2000 Census, these maps show that nearly every state has a significant non-white population.

Europe. That measure, as noted in Chapter 25, sparked a wholesale shift in immigrants' origins. Between 1965 and 2000, nearly 24 million immigrants entered the United States, a number only slightly lower than the 27 million during the peak period of immigration between 1880 and 1924. About 50 percent came from Latin America and the Caribbean, 35 percent from Asia, and smaller numbers from the Middle East and Africa. Only 10 percent arrived from Europe, mostly from the war-torn Balkans and the former Soviet Union.

In 2000, the number of foreign-born persons living in the United States stood at more than 31 million, or 11 percent of the population. Although less than the peak proportion of 14 percent in 1910, in absolute numbers this represented the largest immigrant total in the nation's history. The immigrant influx changed the country's religious and racial map. By 2000, more than 3 million Muslims resided in the United States, and the combined population of Buddhists and Hindus exceeded 1 million.

As in the past, most immigrants became urban residents, with New York City, Los Angeles, Chicago, and Miami the most common destinations. New ethnic communities emerged, with homes, shops, restaurants, foreign-language newspapers, radio and television stations, and ethnic professionals like businessmen and lawyers. Unlike in the past, rather than being concentrated in one or two parts of city centers, immigrants quickly moved into outlying neighborhoods and older suburbs. The immigrant influx revitalized neighborhoods like New York City's Washington Heights (a Dominican enclave) and Flushing (a center for Asian newcomers). By the turn of the century, more than half of all Latinos lived in suburbs. Orange County, California, which had been a stronghold of suburban conservatism between 1960 and 1990, elected a Latina Democrat to Congress in the late 1990s. While most immigrants settled on the East and West Coasts, some moved to other parts of the country. They brought cultural and racial diversity to once-homogeneous communities in the American heartland.

Post-1965 immigration formed part of the worldwide uprooting of labor arising from globalization. In 2000, the global immigrant population was estimated at 100 million. Those who migrated to the United States came from a wide variety of backgrounds. They included poor, illiterate refugees from places of economic and political crisis—Central Americans escaping the region's civil wars and poverty, Haitians and Cambodians fleeing repressive governments. But many immigrants were well-educated professionals from countries like India and South Korea, where the availability of skilled jobs had not kept pace with the spread of higher education. In the year 2000, more than 40 percent of all immigrants to the United States had a college education.

For the first time in American history, women made up the majority of newcomers, reflecting the decline of manufacturing jobs that had previously absorbed immigrant men, as well as the spread of employment opportunities in traditionally female fields like care of children and the elderly and retail sales. (Many were paid by their employers "off the books," without withholding taxes. This practice became a focus of public discussion in 1993 when President Clinton was forced to withdraw two female cabinet nominees when it came to light that they had hired undocumented immigrants as housekeepers and paid them in this manner.) Thanks to cheap global communications and jet travel, modern-day immigrants retained strong ties with their countries of origin, frequently phoning and visiting home.

Recent immigrants reciting the Pledge of Allegiance during a naturalization ceremony.

THE NEW DIVERSITY

Latinos formed the largest single immigrant group. This term was invented in the United States and included people from quite different origins—Mexicans, Central and South Americans, and migrants from Spanish-speaking Caribbean islands like Cuba, the Dominican Republic, and Puerto Rico (although the last group, of course, were American citizens, not immigrants). With 95 million people, Mexico in 2000 had become the world's largest Spanish-speaking nation. Its poverty, high birthrate, and proximity to the United States made it a source of massive legal and illegal immigration. In 2000, Mexican-Americans made up a majority of the Hispanic population of the United States and nearly half the residents of Los Angeles.

Latina nannies pushing baby carriages in Beverly Hills, California. In the 1990s, for the first time in American history, female immigrants outnumbered male immigrants.

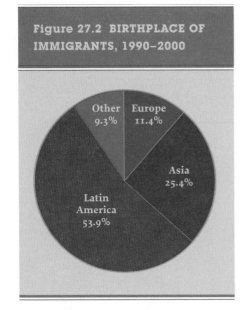

Figure 27.2 BIRTHPLACE OF IMMIGRANTS, 1990–2000

Other 9.3%
Europe 11.4%
Asia 25.4%
Latin America 53.9%

During the 1990s, immigration from Latin America and Asia eclipsed immigration from Europe, traditionally the main source of newcomers to the United States.

Numbering more than 45 million in 2007, Latinos had become the largest minority group in the United States. Latinos were highly visible in entertainment, sports, and politics. Indeed, the Hispanic presence transformed American life. José was now the most common name for baby boys in Texas and the third most popular in California. Smith remained the most common American surname, but Garcia, Rodriguez, Gonzales, and other Hispanic names were all in the top fifty.

Latino communities remained far poorer than the rest of the country. A flourishing middle class developed in Los Angeles, Miami, and other cities with large Spanish-speaking populations. But most immigrants from Mexico and Central America competed at the lowest levels of the job market. The influx of legal and illegal immigrants swelled the ranks of low-wage urban workers and agricultural laborers. Latinos lagged far behind other Americans in education. In 2007, their poverty rate stood at nearly double the national figure of 12.5 percent. Living and working conditions among predominantly Latino farm workers in the West fell back to levels as dire as when César Chavez established the United Farm Workers union in the 1960s.

Asian-Americans also became increasingly visible in the 1990s. There had long been a small population of Asian ancestry in California and New York City, but only after 1965 did immigration from Asia assume large proportions. By 2000, the number of Asian-Americans stood at 11.9 million, eight times the figure of 1970. Like Latinos, Asian-Americans were a highly diverse population, including well-educated Koreans, Indians, and Japanese, as well as poor refugees from Cambodia, Vietnam, and China. Growing up in tight-knit communities that placed great emphasis on education, young Asian-Americans poured into American colleges and universities. Once subjected to harsh discrimination, Asian-Americans now achieved remarkable success. White Americans hailed them as a

The U.S. Border Patrol apprehending Mexicans who had entered the country in violation of immigration laws, near San Diego, California. In 1990, more than 1 million immigrants were arrested and deported after crossing the border illegally.

"model minority." By 2007, the median family income of Asian-Americans, $66,000, surpassed that of whites. But more than any other group, Asian-Americans clustered at opposite ends of the income spectrum. Large numbers earned either more than $75,000 per year (doctors, engineers, and entrepreneurs) or under $5,000 (unskilled laborers in sweatshops and restaurants).

The United States, of course, had long been a multiracial society. But for centuries race relations had been shaped by the black-white divide and the experience of slavery and segregation. The growing visibility of Latinos and Asians suggested that a two-race system no longer adequately described American life. Multiracial imagery filled television, films, and advertising. Interracial marriage, at one time banned in forty-two states, became more common and acceptable. Among Asian-Americans at the turn of the century, half of all marriages involved a non-Asian partner. The

Korean youngsters rehearsing a dance at the Veterans' Administration Medical Center in Columbia, South Carolina, an illustration of the growing diversity of American society.

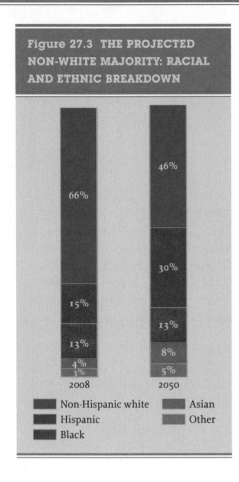

Figure 27.3 THE PROJECTED NON-WHITE MAJORITY: RACIAL AND ETHNIC BREAKDOWN

2008: 66%, 15%, 13%, 4%, 3%
2050: 46%, 30%, 13%, 8%, 5%

- Non-Hispanic white
- Hispanic
- Black
- Asian
- Other

Despite the ups and downs of unemployment, the rate for non-whites remains persistently higher than that for whites.

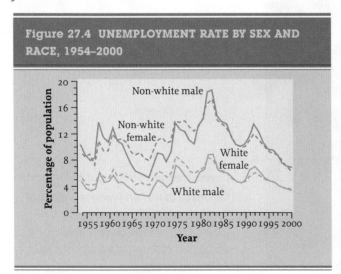

Figure 27.4 UNEMPLOYMENT RATE BY SEX AND RACE, 1954–2000

figure for Latinos was 30 percent. Some commentators spoke of the "end of racism" and the emergence of a truly color-blind society. Others argued that while Asians and some Latinos were being absorbed into an expanded category of "white" Americans, the black-white divide remained almost as impenetrable as ever.

One thing, however, seemed clear at the dawn of the twenty-first century: diversity was here to stay. In 2000, whites made up around 70 percent of the population, blacks and Hispanics around 13 percent each, and Asians 6 percent. Because the birthrate of racial minorities is higher than that of whites, the Census Bureau projected that by 2050, only 50 percent of the American population would be white, a little less than 25 percent would be Hispanic, and blacks and Asians would account for around 13 percent each.

AFRICAN-AMERICANS IN THE 1990S

Compared with the situation in 1900 or 1950, the most dramatic change in American life at the turn of the century was the absence of legal segregation and the presence of blacks in areas of American life from which they had once been almost entirely excluded. Thanks to the decline in overt discrimination and the effectiveness of many affirmative action programs, blacks now worked in unprecedented numbers alongside whites in corporate board rooms, offices, and factories. The number of black policemen, for example, rose from 24,000 to 65,000 between 1970 and 2000, and in the latter year, 37 percent of the black population reported having attended college. The economic boom of the late 1990s aided black Americans enormously; the average income of black families rose more rapidly than that of whites.

One major change in black life was the growing visibility of Africans among the nation's immigrants. Between 1970 and 2000, twice as many Africans immigrated to the United States as had entered during the entire period of the Atlantic slave trade. For the first time, all the elements of the African diaspora—natives of Africa, Caribbeans, Central and South Americans of African descent, Europeans with African roots—could be found in the United States alongside the descendants of American slaves. Nigeria, Ghana, and Ethiopia provided the largest number of African immigrants, and they settled overwhelmingly in urban areas, primarily in New York, California, Texas, and the District of Columbia. Some were impoverished refugees fleeing civil wars in Somalia, Sudan, and Ethiopia, but many more were professionals—more than half the African newcomers had college educations, the highest percentage for any immigrant group. Indeed, some African countries complained of a "brain drain" as physicians, teachers, and other highly skilled persons sought opportunities in the United States that did not exist in their own underdeveloped countries. While some prospered, others found it difficult to transfer their credentials to the United States and found jobs driving taxis and selling African crafts at street fairs.

Most African-Americans, nonetheless, remained in a more precarious situation than whites or many recent immigrants. The black unemployment rate remained double that

Table 27.2 HOME OWNERSHIP RATES BY GROUP, 1970–2000				
	1970	*1980*	*1990*	*2000*
Whites	65.0%	67.8%	68.2%	73.8%
Blacks	41.6	44.4	43.4	47.2
Latinos	43.7	43.4	42.4	46.3
All families	62.9	64.4	64.2	67.4

of whites, and in 2007 their median family income of $34,000 and poverty rate of 25 percent put them behind whites, Asians, and Latinos. Half of all black children lived in poverty, two-thirds were born out of wedlock, and in every index of social well-being from health to quality of housing, blacks continued to lag. Despite the continued expansion of the black middle class, a far lower percentage of blacks than whites owned their homes or held professional and managerial jobs. Housing segregation remained pervasive. In 2000, more than one-third of the black population lived in suburbs, but mostly in predominantly black communities. The gap in wealth between blacks and whites remained enormous. In 2007, the total assets of the median white family (bank accounts, stocks, the value of a home, etc.) stood at $87,000. For black families, the figure was $5,400.

THE ROLE OF THE COURTS

As in the late nineteenth century, the Supreme Court in the last years of the twentieth century little by little retreated from the civil rights revolution. The justices made it increasingly difficult for victims of discrimination to win lawsuits and proved increasingly sympathetic to the pleas of whites that affirmative action plans discriminated against them. In *Patterson v. McLean Credit Union* (1989), the Court barred a black employee who suffered racial harassment while working from suing for damages under the Civil Rights Act of 1866. That law, the justices maintained, only prohibited discrimination at the moment of signing a contract, not on the job.

In the same year, the Court overturned a Richmond law reserving 30 percent of city construction contracts for minority businesses. Less than 1 percent of such contracts had gone to black-owned companies in the five years before the city council enacted the new law. But Justice Sandra Day O'Connor, who wrote the opinion, insisted that in the absence of clear statements of racism by government officials (hardly a likely occurrence), one could not prove the existence of discrimination. Blacks, she speculated, may have been "attracted to other industries than construction," as if their distribution among the occupations had historically been a matter of free choice.

Despite the nation's growing racial diversity, school segregation—now resulting from housing patterns and the divide between urban and suburban school districts rather than laws requiring racial separation—was on the rise. Most city public school systems consisted overwhelmingly of minority students, large numbers of whom failed to receive an adequate education. The courts released more and more districts from desegregation orders. By 2000, the nation's black and Latino students were more isolated

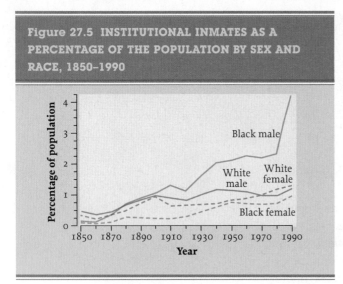

Figure 27.5 INSTITUTIONAL INMATES AS A PERCENTAGE OF THE POPULATION BY SEX AND RACE, 1850–1990

from white pupils than in 1970. Nearly 80 percent of white students attended schools where they encountered few if any pupils of another race. Since school funding rested on property taxes, poor communities continued to have less to spend on education than wealthy ones.

THE SPREAD OF IMPRISONMENT

During the 1960s, the nation's prison population had declined. But in the 1970s, with urban crime rates rising, politicians of both parties sought to convey the image of being "tough on crime." They insisted that the judicial system should focus on locking up criminals for long periods rather than rehabilitating them. They treated drug addiction as a violation of the law rather than as a disease. State governments greatly increased the penalties for crime and reduced the possibility of parole. Successive presidents launched "wars" on the use of illegal drugs. As a result, the number of Americans in prison rose dramatically, most of them incarcerated for non-violent drug offenses.

During the 1990s, thanks to the waning of the "crack" epidemic and more effective urban police tactics, crime rates dropped dramatically across the country. But because of the sentencing laws of the previous two decades, this did nothing to stem the increase of the prison population. In 2008, it reached 2.3 million, ten times the figure of 1970. Several million more individuals were on parole, probation, or under some other kind of criminal supervision. These figures dwarfed those of every other Western society.

As the prison population grew, a "prison-industrial complex" emerged. Struggling communities battered by deindustrialization saw prisons as a source of jobs and income. Between 1990 and 1995, the federal government and the states constructed more than 200 new prisons. In 2008, five states spent more money on their prison systems than on higher education. Convict labor, a practice the labor movement had managed to curtail in the late nineteenth century, revived in the late twentieth. Private companies in Oregon "leased" prisoners for three dollars per day. A call to Trans World Airlines for a flight reservation was likely to be answered by a California inmate.

THE BURDEN OF IMPRISONMENT

Members of racial minorities experienced most strongly the paradox of growing islands of unfreedom in a nation that prided itself on liberty. In 1950, whites accounted for 70 percent of the nation's prison population and non-whites 30 percent. By 2000, these figures had been reversed. One reason was that severe penalties faced those convicted of using or selling crack, a particularly potent form of cocaine concentrated among the urban poor, while the use of powder cocaine, the drug of choice in suburban America, led to far lighter sentences.

The percentage of the black population in prison stood eight times higher than the proportion for white Americans. More than one-quarter of all black men could expect to serve time in prison at some time during their lives. A criminal record made it very difficult for ex-prisoners to find

KEY TERMS

"new world order" (p. 1127)

Gulf War (p. 1130)

the Perot candidacy (p. 1131)

Contract with America (p. 1132)

North American Free Trade
    Agreement (p. 1132)

welfare reform (p. 1134)

Oslo Accords (p. 1134)

Balkan crisis (p. 1134)

"ethnic cleansing" (p. 1135)

Patterson v. McLean Credit Union
    (p. 1151)

"tough on crime" movement
    (p. 1152)

Americans with Disabilities Act
    (p. 1154)

multiculturalism (p. 1155)

Defense of Marriage Act (p. 1157)

Clinton impeachment (p. 1159)

REVIEW TABLE

The New Diversity of America

Group	Origins	Population in 2000	Demographics
Latinos	Mexico, Caribbean, Central and South America	35 million	Largest minority group in the United States as of 2001
Asian-Americans	Korea, China, Southeast Asia, Japan	11.9 million	Fastest-growing immigrant group in America
African-Americans	Africa, Caribbean	36.4 million	Majority still live in the South and three-fifths of all blacks live in only ten states
Indians	North America	4 million	Growth from natural births as well as a renewed sense of pride identifying oneself as Indian

CHAPTER 28

September 11 and the Next American Century

Barack Obama and his family greet enthusiastic supporters at an outdoor celebration in Chicago on the night of his election as president on November 4, 2008.

FOCUS QUESTIONS

• What were the major policy elements of the war on terror in the wake of September 11, 2001?

• How did the war in Iraq unfold in the wake of 9/11?

• How did the war on terror affect the economy and American liberties?

• What events eroded support for President Bush's policies during his second term?

• What kinds of change did voters hope for when they elected Barack Obama?

No member of the present generation will ever forget when he or she first learned of the events of September 11, 2001. That beautiful late-summer morning began with the sun rising over the East Coast of the United States in a crystal-clear sky. But September 11 soon became one of the most tragic dates in American history.

Around 8 A.M., hijackers seized control of four jet airliners filled with passengers. They crashed two into the World Trade Center in New York City, igniting infernos that soon caused these buildings, which dominated the lower Manhattan skyline, to collapse. A third plane hit a wing of the Pentagon, the country's military headquarters, in Washington, D.C. On the fourth aircraft, passengers who had learned of these events via their cell phones overpowered the hijackers. The plane crashed in a field near Pittsburgh, killing all aboard. Counting the nineteen hijackers, the more than 200 passengers, pilots, and flight attendants, and the victims on the ground, around 3,000 people died on September 11. The victims included nearly 400 police and firefighters who had rushed to the World Trade Center in a rescue effort and perished when the "twin towers" collapsed. Most of the dead were Americans, but citizens of more than eighty other countries also lost their lives. Relatives and friends desperately seeking information about the fate of those lost in the attacks printed thousands of "missing" posters. These remained in public places in New York and Washington for weeks, grim reminders of the lives extinguished on September 11.

The attack dealt New York City and the country as a whole a severe blow. Immediate damage and recovery costs ran into the billions of dollars. An estimated 80,000 persons lost their jobs in the New York area. They included employees of financial firms housed in the World Trade Center, as well as waiters, retail sales clerks, and cleaning workers dismissed when business in lower Manhattan ground to a halt and tourism to the city plummeted. The loss of tax revenue plunged the city into a deep fiscal crisis. Major airlines also faced bankruptcy as Americans became afraid to fly.

The Bush administration quickly blamed Al Qaeda, a shadowy terrorist organization headed by Osama bin Laden, for the attacks. A wealthy Islamic fundamentalist from Saudi Arabia, bin Laden had joined the fight against the Soviet occupation of Afghanistan in the 1980s. He had developed a relationship with the Central Intelligence Agency and received American funds to help build his mountain bases. But after the Gulf War of 1991, his anger increasingly turned against the United States. Bin Laden was especially outraged by the presence of American military bases in Saudi Arabia and by American support for Israel in its ongoing conflict with the Palestinians. More generally, bin Laden and his followers saw the United States, with its religious pluralism, consumer culture, and open sexual mores, as the antithesis of the rigid values in which they believed. He feared that American influence was corrupting Saudi Arabia, Islam's spiritual home, and helping to keep the Saudi royal family, which failed to oppose this development, in power. But if Al Qaeda believed in traditional Islamic values, it also acted much like a modern transnational organization, taking full advantage of globalization. The terrorists moved freely across national borders, financed themselves through international capital flows, and communicated via e-mail and the Internet.

Terrorism—the targeting of civilian populations by violent organizations who hope to spread fear for a political purpose—has a long history, including in the United States. During the Reconstruction era after the Civil War, the Ku Klux Klan and similar groups launched a reign of terror that led to the deaths of thousands of American citizens, most of them newly emancipated slaves. Between the assassination of President William McKinley in 1901 and the Wall Street bombing of 1920, anarchists committed numerous acts of violence. Antigovernment extremist Timothy McVeigh killed 168 persons when he exploded a bomb at a federal office building in Oklahoma City in 1995.

In the last three decades of the twentieth century, terrorist groups who held the United States and other Western countries responsible for the plight of the Palestinians had engaged in hijackings and murders. In October 1985, a group of Palestinians seized control of the *Achille Lauro*, an Italian cruise ship, and killed an American Jewish passenger. In 1988, a bomb planted by operatives based in Libya destroyed a Pan American flight over Scotland, killing all 259 persons on board. After the Gulf War, Osama bin Laden declared "war" on the United States. Terrorists associated with Al Qaeda exploded a truck-bomb at the World Trade Center in 1993, killing six persons, and set off blasts in 1998 at American

The twin towers of the World Trade Center after being struck by hijacked airplanes on September 11, 2001. Shortly after this photograph was taken, the towers collapsed.

A bystander gazes at some of the missing posters with photographs of those who died on September 11.

In the years following September 11, 2001, fear remained a prominent feature of American life. Authorities urged Americans to monitor each other's activities. This sign, widely displayed on subway and railroad cars, advised New Yorkers, "If you see something, say something." As the sign notes, 1,944 reports of suspicious behavior were made to the police in 2007. These reports included Muslims seen counting in the subway (they turned out to be men counting prayers with the equivalent of rosary beads) and individuals taking pictures of railroad tracks. The 1,944 reports resulted in eighteen arrests. None involved a terrorist plot, though they did include persons selling false driver's licenses and dealing illegally in fireworks.

embassies in Kenya and Tanzania, in which more than 200 persons, mostly African embassy workers, died. Thus, a rising terrorist threat was visible before September 11. Nonetheless, the attack came as a complete surprise. With the end of the Cold War in 1991, most Americans felt more secure, especially within their own borders, than they had for decades.

September 11 enveloped the country in a cloud of fear. The sense of being under assault was heightened in the following weeks, when unknown persons sent letters to prominent politicians and television journalists, containing spores that cause the deadly disease anthrax. Five individuals—postal workers and others who handled the letters—died. In the months that followed, as the government periodically issued "alerts" concerning possible new attacks, national security remained at the forefront of Americans' consciousness, and fear of terrorism powerfully affected their daily lives.

In the immediate aftermath of September 11, the Bush administration announced a "war on terrorism." Over the next two years, the United States embarked on wars in Afghanistan and Iraq, the second with very limited international support. It created a new Department of Homeland Security to coordinate efforts to improve security at home, and it imposed severe limits on the civil liberties of those suspected of a connection with terrorism and, more generally, on immigrants from the Middle East.

The attacks of September 11, 2001, gave new prominence to ideas deeply embedded in the American past—that freedom was the central quality of American life, and that the United States had a mission to spread freedom throughout the world and to fight those it saw as freedom's enemies. The attacks and events that followed also lent new urgency to questions that had recurred many times in American history: Should the United States act in the world as a republic or an empire? What is the proper balance between liberty and security? Who deserves the full enjoyment of American freedom? None had an easy answer.

THE WAR ON TERRORISM

BUSH BEFORE SEPTEMBER 11

Before becoming president, George W. Bush had been an executive in the oil industry and had served as governor of Texas. He had worked to dissociate the Republican Party from the harsh anti-immigrant rhetoric of the mid-1990s and had proven himself an effective proponent of what he called "compassionate conservatism." Because of his narrow margin of victory in the election of 2000, he came into office without a broad popular mandate. He had received fewer votes than his opponent, Al Gore, and his party commanded only tiny majorities in the House of Representatives and Senate. Nonetheless, from the outset Bush pursued a strongly conservative agenda. In 2001, he persuaded Congress to enact the largest tax cut in American history. With the economy slowing, he promoted the plan as a way of stimulating renewed growth. In keeping with the "supply-side" economic outlook embraced twenty years earlier by Ronald Reagan, most of the tax cuts were directed toward the wealthiest Americans, on the assumption that they would invest the money they saved in taxes in economically productive activities.

Bush also proposed changes in environmental policies, including opening Alaska's Arctic National Wildlife Refuge to drilling for oil and allowing timber companies to operate in national forests, claiming that this would reduce forest fires. But soon after the passage of the tax bill, Senator Jim Jeffords of Vermont, a moderate Republican, abandoned the party and declared himself an independent. His action gave Democrats a one-vote margin in the Senate and made it difficult for Bush to achieve further legislative victories.

BUSH AND THE WORLD

In foreign policy, Bush emphasized American freedom of action, unrestrained by international treaties and institutions. During the 2000 campaign, he had criticized the Clinton administration's penchant for "nation-building"— American assistance in creating stable governments in chaotic parts of the world. Once in office, Bush announced plans to push ahead with a national missile defense system (another inheritance from the Reagan era) even though this required American withdrawal from the Anti–Ballistic Missile Treaty of 1972, which barred the deployment of such systems. He repudiated a treaty establishing an International Criminal Court to try violators of human rights, fearing that it would assert its jurisdiction over Americans. Critics charged that Bush was resuming the tradition of American isolationism, which had been abandoned after World War II.

To great controversy, the Bush administration announced that it would not abide by the Kyoto Protocol of 1997, which sought to combat global warming—a slow rise in the earth's temperature that scientists warned could have disastrous effects on the world's climate. Global warming is caused when gases released by burning fossil fuels such as coal and oil remain in the upper atmosphere, trapping heat reflected from the earth. Evidence of this development first surfaced in the 1990s, when scientists studying layers of ice in Greenland concluded that the earth's temperature had risen significantly during the past century. Further investigations revealed that areas of the Antarctic once under ice had become covered by grass, and that glaciers across the globe are retreating.

Today, most scientists consider global warming a serious situation. Climate change threatens to disrupt long-established patterns of agriculture, and the melting of glaciers and the polar ice caps because of rising temperatures may raise ocean levels and flood coastal cities.

By the time Bush took office, some 180 nations, including the United States, had agreed to accept the goals set in the Kyoto Protocol for reducing the output of greenhouse gases from fossil fuels. Since the United States burns far more fossil fuel than any other nation, Bush's repudiation of the treaty, on the grounds that it would weaken the American economy, infuriated much of the world, as well as environmentalists at home.

"THEY HATE FREEDOM"

September 11 transformed the international situation, the domestic political environment, and the Bush presidency. An outpouring of popular patriotism followed the attacks, all the more impressive because it was spontaneous, not orchestrated by the government or private organizations. Throughout the country, people demonstrated their sense of resolve and their sympathy for the victims by displaying the American flag. Public trust in government rose dramatically, and public servants like firemen and policemen became national heroes. After two decades in which the dominant language of American politics centered on deregulation and individualism, the country experienced a renewed feeling of common social purpose. Americans of all backgrounds shared the sense of having lived through a traumatic experience.

The Bush administration benefited from this patriotism and identification with government. The president's popularity soared. As in other crises, Americans looked to the federal government, and especially the president, for reassurance, leadership, and decisive action. Bush seized the opportunity to give his administration a new direction and purpose. Like presidents before him, he made freedom the rallying cry for a nation at war.

On September 20, 2001, Bush addressed a joint session of Congress and a national television audience. His speech echoed the words of FDR, Truman, and Reagan: "Freedom and fear are at war. The advance of human freedom . . . now depends on us." The country's antagonists, Bush went on, "hate our freedoms, our freedom of religion, our freedom of speech, our

This photograph of three emergency-response workers at the World Trade Center site suggests that the composition of the construction industry labor force had become more diverse as a result of the civil rights movement.

A homemade float in a July 4, 2002, parade in Amherst, Massachusetts, illustrates how the "twin towers" had become a symbol of American patriotism.

freedom to assemble and disagree with each other." In later speeches, he repeated this theme. Why did terrorists attack the United States, the president repeatedly asked. His answer: "Because we love freedom, that's why. And they hate freedom."

THE BUSH DOCTRINE

Bush's speech announced a new foreign policy principle, which quickly became known as the Bush Doctrine. The United States would launch a war on terrorism. Unlike previous wars, this one had a vaguely defined enemy—terrorist groups around the world that might threaten the United States or its allies—and no predictable timetable for victory. The American administration would make no distinction between terrorists and the governments that harbored them, and it would recognize no middle ground in the new war: "Either you are with us, or you are with the terrorists." Bush demanded that Afghanistan, ruled by a group of Islamic fundamentalists called the Taliban, surrender Osama bin Laden, who had established a base in the country. When the Taliban refused, the United States on October 7, 2001, launched air strikes against its strongholds.

Bush gave the war in Afghanistan the name "Enduring Freedom." By the end of the year, the combination of American bombing and ground combat by the Northern Alliance (Afghans who had been fighting the Taliban for years) had driven the regime from power. A new government, friendly to and dependent on the United States, took its place. It repealed Taliban laws denying women the right to attend school and banning movies, music, and other expressions of Western culture but found it difficult to establish full control over the country. Fewer than 100 Americans died in the war, while Afghan military and civilian casualties numbered in the thousands. But bin Laden had not been found, and many Taliban supporters continued to pose a threat to the new government's stability. Indeed, by early 2007, the Taliban had reasserted their power in some parts of Afghanistan, and no end was in sight to the deployment of American troops there.

Supporters of the Bush administration who turned out in Washington, D.C., late in 2001 to confront demonstrators opposed to the war in Afghanistan.

Like the surprise attack on Pearl Harbor in 1941, September 11 not only plunged the United States into war but also transformed American foreign policy, inspiring a determination to reshape the world in terms of American ideals and interests. Remarkable changes quickly followed the assault on Afghanistan. To facilitate further military action in the Middle East, the United States established military bases in Central Asia, including former republics of the Soviet Union like Kyrgyzstan, Uzbekistan, and Tajikistan. Such an action would have been inconceivable before the end of the Cold War. The administration sent troops to the Philippines to assist that government in combating an Islamic insurgency, and it announced plans to establish a greater military presence in Africa. It solidified its ties with the governments of Pakistan and Indonesia, which confronted opposition from Islamic fundamentalists.

The toppling of the Taliban, Bush repeatedly insisted, marked only the beginning of the war on terrorism. In his State of the Union address of January 2002, the president accused Iraq, Iran, and North Korea of harboring terrorists and developing "weapons of mass destruction"—nuclear, chemical, and biological—that posed a potential threat to the United States. He called the three countries an "axis of evil," even though no evidence connected them with the attacks of September 11 and they had never cooperated with one another (Iraq and Iran, in fact, had fought a long and bloody war in the 1980s).

THE NATIONAL SECURITY STRATEGY

In September 2002, one year after the September 11 attacks, the Bush administration released a document called the National Security Strategy. Like NSC-68 of 1950 (discussed in Chapter 23), the National Security Strategy outlined a fundamental shift in American foreign policy. And like NSC-68, it began with a discussion not of weaponry or military strategy, but of freedom.

The document defined freedom as consisting of political democracy, freedom of expression, religious toleration, free trade, and free markets. These, it proclaimed, were universal ideals, "right and true for every person, in every society." It went on to promise that the United States would "extend the benefits of freedom" by fighting not only "terrorists" but also "tyrants" around the world. Since nothing less than freedom was at stake, the document insisted that the United States must maintain an overwhelming preponderance of military power, not allowing any other country to challenge either its overall strength or its dominance in any region of the world. And to replace the Cold War doctrine of deterrence, which assumed that the certainty of retaliation would prevent attacks on the

United States and its allies, the National Security Strategy announced a new foreign policy principle—"preemptive" war. If the United States believed that a nation posed a possible future threat to its security, it had the right to attack before such a threat materialized.

AN AMERICAN EMPIRE?

The "axis of evil" speech and National Security Strategy sent shock waves around the world. In the immediate aftermath of September 11, a wave of sympathy for the United States had swept across the globe. Most of the world supported the war in Afghanistan as a legitimate response to the terrorist attacks. By late 2002, however, many persons overseas feared that the United States was claiming the right to act as a world policeman in violation of international law.

Relations between the United States and Europe, warned Ivo Daalder, a Dutch-born former official of the Clinton administration, were on a "collision course," because Washington had become "dismissive of the perspectives of others." Critics, including leaders of close American allies, wondered whether dividing the world into friends and enemies of freedom ran the danger of repeating some of the mistakes of the Cold War. Anti-Americanism in the Middle East, they argued, reached far beyond bin Laden's organization and stemmed not simply from dislike of American freedom but, rightly or wrongly, from opposition to specific American policies—toward Israel, the Palestinians, and the region's corrupt and undemocratic regimes. And like the battle against communism, the war on terrorism seemed to be leading the United States to forge closer and closer ties with repressive governments like Pakistan and the republics of Central Asia that consistently violated human rights.

Charges quickly arose that the United States was bent on establishing itself as a new global empire. Indeed, September 11 and its aftermath highlighted not only the vulnerability of the United States but also its overwhelming strength. In every index of power—military, economic, cultural—the United States far outpaced the rest of the world. It accounted for just under one-third of global economic output and more than one-third of global military spending. Its defense budget exceeded that of the next twenty powers combined. The United States maintained military bases throughout the world and deployed its navy on every ocean. It was not surprising that in such circumstances many American policymakers felt that the country had a responsibility to impose order in a dangerous world, even if this meant establishing its own rules of international conduct.

In public discussion in the United States after September 11, the word "empire," once a term of abuse, came back into widespread use. The need to "shoulder the burdens of empire" emerged as a common theme in discussions among foreign policy analysts and political commentators who embraced the new foreign policy. As we have seen, the idea of the United States as an empire has a long history, dating back to Jefferson's "empire of liberty" (see Chapter 7) and McKinley's "benevolent imperialism" (see Chapter 17). But talk of a new American empire alarmed people at home and abroad who did not desire to have the United States reconstruct the world in its own image.

VOICES OF FREEDOM

FROM
The National Security Strategy of the United States
(September 2002)

The National Security Strategy, issued in 2002 by the Bush administration, outlined a new foreign and military policy for the United States in response to the terrorist attacks of September 11, 2001. It announced the doctrine of preemptive war—that the United States retained the right to use its military power against countries that might pose a threat in the future. But the document began with a statement of the administration's definition of freedom and its commitment to spreading freedom to the entire world.

The great struggles of the twentieth century between liberty and totalitarianism ended with a decisive victory for the forces of freedom—and a single sustainable model for national success: freedom, democracy, and free enterprise.... These values of freedom are right and true for every person, in every society....

Today, the international community has the best chance since the rise of the nation-state in the seventeenth century to build a world where great powers compete in peace instead of continually prepare for war.... The United States will use this moment of opportunity to extend the benefits of freedom across the globe. We will actively work to bring the hope of democracy, development, free markets, and free trade to every corner of the world....

In building a balance of power that favors freedom, the United States is guided by the conviction that all nations have important responsibilities. Nations that enjoy freedom must actively fight terror. Nations that depend on international stability must help prevent the spread of weapons of mass destruction.... Throughout history, freedom has been threatened by war and terror; it has been challenged by the clashing wills of powerful states and the evil designs of tyrants; and it has been tested by widespread poverty and disease. Today, humanity holds in its hands the opportunity to further freedom's triumph over all these foes. The United States welcomes our opportunity to lead in this great mission.

Speech to the Islamic World (2009)

In June 2009, President Obama traveled to Egypt to deliver a speech aimed at repairing American relations with the Islamic world, severely damaged by the war in Iraq and the sense that many Americans identified all Muslims with the actions of a few terrorists. Entitled "A New Beginning," it acknowledged past American misdeeds and promised to respect Islamic traditions and values rather than trying to impose American ideas on the world's more than 1 billion Muslims.

I have come here to seek a new beginning between the United States and Muslims around the world; one based upon mutual interest and mutual respect. . . . I consider it part of my responsibility as President of the United States to fight against negative stereotypes of Islam wherever they appear. But that same principle must apply to Muslim perceptions of America. Just as Muslims do not fit a crude stereotype, America is not the crude stereotype of a self-interested empire. The United States has been one of the greatest sources of progress that the world has ever known. . . . We were founded upon the ideal that all are created equal, and we have shed blood and struggled for centuries to give meaning to those words—within our borders, and around the world. . . . Moreover, freedom in America is indivisible from the freedom to practice one's religion. That is why there is a mosque in every state of our union, and over 1,200 mosques within our borders. . . . America is not—and never will be—at war with Islam.

Let me also address the issue of Iraq. Unlike Afghanistan, Iraq was a war of choice that provoked strong differences in my country and around the world. Although I believe that the Iraqi people are ultimately better off without the tyranny of Saddam Hussein, I also believe that events in Iraq have reminded America of the need to use diplomacy and build international consensus to resolve our problems whenever possible. . . . And finally, just as America can never tolerate violence by extremists, we must never alter our principles. 9/11 was an enormous trauma to our country. The fear and anger that it provoked was understandable, but in some cases, it led us to act contrary to our ideals. We are taking concrete actions to change course. I have unequivocally prohibited the use of torture by the United States, and I have ordered the prison at Guantanamo Bay closed by early next year. . . .

Let me be clear: no system of government can or should be imposed upon one nation by any other. That does not lessen my commitment, however, to governments that reflect the will of the people. Each nation gives life to this principle in its own way, grounded in the traditions of its own people. America does not presume to know what is best for everyone.

QUESTIONS:

1. How does the National Security Strategy define the global mission of the United States?

2. How does Obama hope to change relations between the United States and Islamic countries?

3. In what ways is Obama's speech a repudiation of the assumptions of the National Security Strategy?

CONFRONTING IRAQ

These tensions became starkly evident in the Bush administration's next initiative. The Iraqi dictatorship of Saddam Hussein had survived its defeat in the Gulf War of 1991. Hussein's opponents charged that he had flouted United Nations resolutions barring the regime from developing new weapons. During the Clinton administration, the United States had occasionally bombed Iraqi military sites in retaliation for Hussein's lack of cooperation with UN weapons inspectors.

From the outset of the Bush administration, a group of conservative policymakers including Vice President Dick Cheney, Secretary of Defense Donald Rumsfeld, and Deputy Defense Secretary Paul D. Wolfowitz were determined to oust Hussein from power. They developed a military strategy to accomplish this—massive initial air strikes followed by invasion by a relatively small number of troops. They insisted that the oppressed Iraqi people would welcome an American army as liberators and quickly establish a democratic government, allowing for the early departure of American soldiers. This group seized on the opportunity presented by the attacks of September 11 to press their case, and President Bush adopted their outlook. Secretary of State Colin Powell, who believed the conquest and stabilization of Iraq would require hundreds of thousands of American soldiers and should not be undertaken without the support of America's allies, found himself marginalized in the administration.

Even though Hussein was not an Islamic fundamentalist, and no known evidence linked him to the terrorist attacks of September 11, the Bush administration in 2002 announced a goal of "regime change" in Iraq. Hussein, administration spokesmen insisted, must be ousted from power because he had developed an arsenal of chemical and bacterial "weapons of mass destruction" and was seeking to acquire nuclear arms. American newspaper and television journalists repeated these claims with almost no independent investigation. The UN Security Council agreed to step up weapons inspections, but the Bush administration soon declared that inspectors could never uncover Hussein's military capabilities. Early in 2003, despite his original misgivings, Secretary of State Powell delivered a speech before the UN outlining the administration's case. He claimed that Hussein possessed a mobile chemical weapons laboratory, had hidden weapons of mass destruction in his many palaces, and was seeking to acquire uranium in Africa to build nuclear weapons. (Every one of these assertions later turned out to be false.) Shortly after Powell's address, the president announced his intention to go to war with or without the approval of the United Nations. Congress passed a resolution authorizing the president to use force if he deemed it necessary.

THE IRAQ WAR

The decision to go to war split the Western alliance and inspired a massive antiwar movement throughout the

Steve Benson's 2003 cartoon, which alters a renowned World War II photograph of soldiers raising an American flag, illustrates widespread skepticism about American motivations in the Iraq War.

IRAQ WAR MEMORIAL

world. In February 2003, between 10 million and 15 million people across the globe demonstrated against the impending war. There were large-scale protests in the United States, which brought together veterans of the antiwar movement during the Vietnam era and a diverse group of young activists united in the belief that launching a war against a nation because it might pose a security threat in the future violated international law and the UN Charter.

Foreign policy "realists," including members of previous Republican administrations like Brent Scowcroft, the national security adviser under the first President Bush, warned that the administration's preoccupation with Iraq deflected attention from its real foe, Al Qaeda, which remained capable of launching terrorist attacks. They insisted that the United States could not unilaterally transform the Middle East into a bastion of democracy, as the administration claimed was its long-term aim.

Both traditional foes of the United States like Russia and China, and traditional allies like Germany and France, refused to support a "preemptive" strike against Iraq. Many Americans resented international criticism. Some restaurants stopped selling French wines, and the Senate dining room renamed french fries as "freedom fries," recalling the rechristening of items with German names during World War I.

Unable to obtain approval from the United Nations for attacking Iraq, the United States went to war anyway in March 2003, with Great Britain as its sole significant ally. President Bush called the war "Operation Iraqi Freedom." Its purpose, he declared, was to "defend our freedom" and "bring freedom to others." The Hussein regime proved no match for the American armed forces, with their precision bombing, satellite-guided missiles, and well-trained soldiers. Within a month, American troops occupied Baghdad. After hiding out for several months, Hussein was captured by American forces and subsequently put on trial before an Iraqi court. Late in 2006, he was found guilty of ordering the killing of many Iraqis during his reign, and was sentenced to death and executed.

Part of the massive crowd that gathered in New York City on February 15, 2003, a day of worldwide demonstrations against the impending war against Iraq.

ANOTHER VIETNAM?

Soon after the fall of Baghdad, a triumphant President Bush appeared in an air force flight suit on the deck of an aircraft carrier beneath a banner reading "Mission Accomplished." But after the fall of Hussein, everything seemed to go wrong. Rather than parades welcoming American liberators, looting and chaos followed the fall of the Iraqi regime. With too few American troops to establish order, mobs promptly sacked libraries, museums, government offices, and businesses, and seized caches of weapons. An insurgency quickly developed that targeted American soldiers and Iraqis cooperating with them. Sectarian violence soon swept throughout Iraq, with militias of Shiite and Sunni Muslims fighting each other. (Under Hussein, Sunnis, a minority of Iraq's population, had dominated the government and army; now, the Shiite majority sought to exercise power and

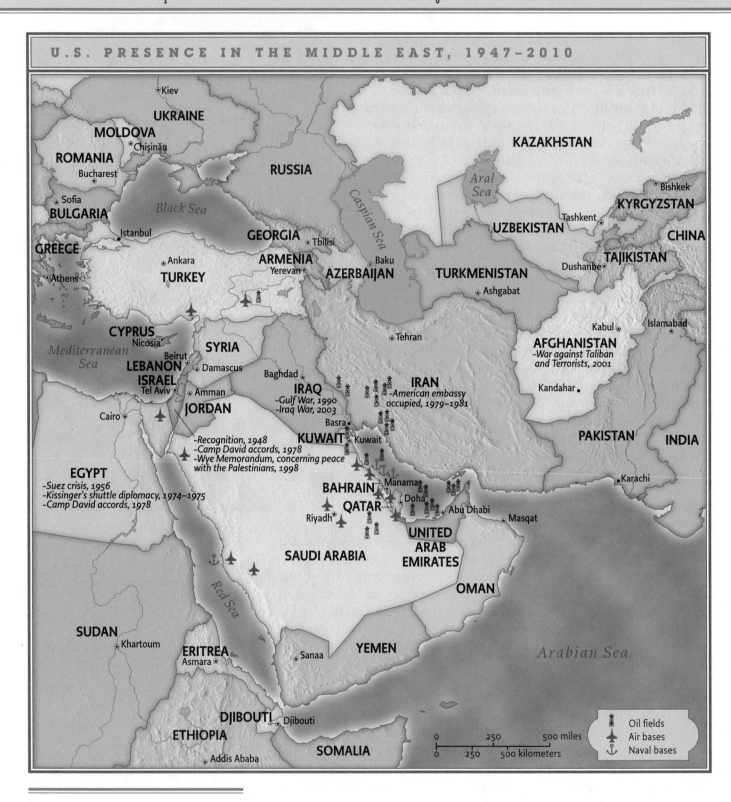

U.S. PRESENCE IN THE MIDDLE EAST, 1947–2010

IRAN
-American embassy
occupied, 1979–1981

AFGHANISTAN
-War against Taliban
and Terrorists, 2001

IRAQ
-Gulf War, 1990
-Iraq War, 2003

-Recognition, 1948
-Camp David accords, 1978
-Wye Memorandum, concerning peace
with the Palestinians, 1998

EGYPT
-Suez crisis, 1956
-Kissinger's shuttle diplomacy, 1974–1975
-Camp David accords, 1978

🛢️	Oil fields
✈️	Air bases
⚓	Naval bases

Since World War II, the United States has become more and more deeply involved in the affairs of the Middle East, whose countries are together the world's largest exporter of oil.

exact revenge.) Despite holding a number of elections in Iraq, the United States found it impossible to create an Iraqi government strong enough to impose order on the country. By 2006, American intelligence agencies concluded, Iraq had become what it had not been before—a haven for terrorists bent on attacking Americans.

Fewer than 200 American soldiers died in the initial phase of the Iraq War. But by the end of 2006, Iraq stood at the brink of civil war. American deaths had reached nearly 3,000, with 20,000 or more wounded. According to the estimates of U.S. and Iraqi scientists, hundreds of thousands of Iraqis, most of them civilians, had also died, and tens of thousands more had fled to neighboring countries seeking safety. Initially, the Bush administration had estimated that the war would cost $60 billion, to be paid for largely by Iraq's own oil revenues. By early 2006, expenditures had reached $200 billion and were climbing fast, and the insurgency prevented Iraq from resuming significant oil production. Some economists estimated that the Iraq War would end up costing the United States nearly $2 trillion, an almost unimaginable sum.

With no end in sight to the conflict, comparisons with the American experience in Vietnam became commonplace. Iraq and Vietnam, of course, have very different histories, cultures, and geographies. But in both wars, American policy was made by officials who had little or no knowledge of the countries to which they were sending troops and distrusted State Department experts on these regions, who tended be skeptical about the possibility of achieving quick military and long-term political success. The war's architects preferred to get their knowledge of Iraq from Saddam Hussein's exiled opponents, who exaggerated their own popularity and the degree of popular support for an American invasion. Administration officials gave little thought to postwar planning.

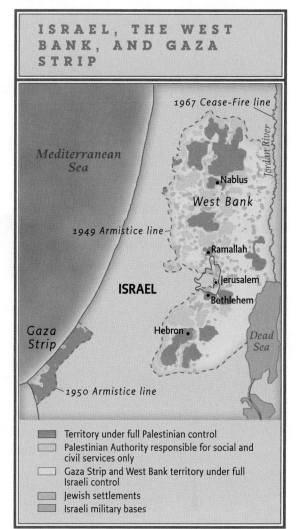

ISRAEL, THE WEST BANK, AND GAZA STRIP

- ■ Territory under full Palestinian control
- □ Palestinian Authority responsible for social and civil services only
- □ Gaza Strip and West Bank territory under full Israeli control
- ▨ Jewish settlements
- ▧ Israeli military bases

THE WORLD AND THE WAR

The war marked a new departure in American foreign policy. The United States had frequently intervened unilaterally in the affairs of Latin American countries. But outside the Western Hemisphere it had previously been reluctant to use force except as part of an international coalition. And while the United States had exerted enormous influence in the Middle East since World War II, never before had it occupied a nation in the center of the world's most volatile region.

Rarely in its history had the United States found itself so isolated from world public opinion. Initially, the war in Iraq proved to be popular in the United States. After all, unlike earlier wars, this one brought no calls for public sacrifice from the administration. There were no tax increases, and no reintroduction of the draft to augment the hard-pressed all-volunteer army. Many Americans believed the administration's claims that Saddam Hussein had something to do with September 11 and had stockpiled weapons of mass destruction. The realization that in fact Hussein had no such weapons discredited the administration's rationale for the war. Subsequent investigations revealed that intelligence reports at variance with administration claims had been sidetracked or ignored. With the weapons argument discredited, the Bush administration increasingly defended the war as an effort to bring freedom to the people of Iraq. This argument resonated with deeply rooted American values. But by early 2007, polls showed that a large majority of Americans considered the invasion of Iraq a mistake, and the war a lost cause.

President Bush standing on the deck of the aircraft carrier Abraham Lincoln *on May 10, 2003, announcing the end of combat operations in Iraq. A banner proclaims, "Mission Accomplished." Unfortunately, the war was not in fact over.*

Much of the outside world now viewed the United States as a superpower unwilling to abide by the rules of international law. They believed that a nation whose Declaration of Independence had proclaimed its signers' "decent respect to the opinions of mankind" had become indifferent or hostile to the views of others. As early as 2003, a survey of global opinion had found that even in western Europe, large numbers of people viewed the United States as a threat to world peace. The fact that Iraq possessed the world's second-largest reserves of oil reinforced suspicions that American motives had less to do with freedom than self-interest.

The Iraq War severely strained the United Nations and the Western alliance created in the aftermath of World War II. But whatever the outcome, for the third time in less than a century, the United States had embarked on a crusade to create a new world order.

THE AFTERMATH OF SEPTEMBER 11 AT HOME

SECURITY AND LIBERTY

Like earlier wars, the war on terrorism raised anew the problem of balancing security and liberty. In the immediate aftermath of the attacks, Congress rushed to passage the USA Patriot Act, a mammoth bill (it ran to more than 300 pages) that few members of the House or Senate had actually read. It conferred unprecedented powers on law-enforcement agencies charged with preventing the new, vaguely defined crime of "domestic terrorism," including the power to wiretap, spy on citizens, open letters, read e-mail, and obtain personal records from third parties like universities and libraries without the knowledge of a suspect. Unlike during World Wars I and II, with their campaigns of hatred against German-Americans and Japanese-Americans, the Bush administration made a point of discouraging anti-Arab and anti-Muslim sentiment. Nonetheless, at least 5,000 foreigners with Middle Eastern connections were rounded up, and more than 1,200 arrested. Many with no link to terrorism were held for months, without either a formal charge or a public notice of their fate. The administration also set up a detention camp at the U.S. naval base at Guantànamo Bay, Cuba, for persons captured in Afghanistan or otherwise accused of terrorism. More than 700 persons, the nationals of many foreign countries, were detained there.

In November 2001, the Bush administration issued an executive order authorizing the holding of secret military tribunals for noncitizens deemed to have assisted terrorism. In such trials, traditional constitutional protections, such as the right of the accused to choose a lawyer and see all the evidence, would not apply. A few months later, the Justice Department declared that American citizens could be held indefinitely without charge and not allowed to see a lawyer, if the government declared them to be "enemy combatants." The president's press secretary, Ari Fleischer, warned Americans to "watch what they say," and Attorney General John Ashcroft declared that criticism of administration policies aided the country's terrorist enemies.

THE POWER OF THE PRESIDENT

In the new atmosphere of heightened security, numerous court orders and regulations of the 1970s, inspired by abuses of the CIA, FBI, and local police forces, were rescinded, allowing these agencies to resume surveillance of Americans without evidence that a crime had been committed. Some of these measures were authorized by Congress, but the president implemented many of them unilaterally, claiming the authority to ignore laws that restricted his power as commander-in-chief in wartime. Thus, soon after September 11, President Bush authorized the National Security Agency (NSA) to eavesdrop on Americans' telephone conversations without a court warrant, a clear violation of a law limiting the NSA to foreign intelligence gathering.

Two centuries earlier, in the 1790s, James Madison had predicted that for many years to come, the danger to individual liberty would lie in abuse of power by Congress. This is why the Bill of Rights barred Congress, not the president or the states, from abridging civil liberties. But, Madison continued, in the long run, the president might pose the greatest danger, especially in time of war. "In war," he wrote, the discretionary power of the Executive is extended." No nation, Madison believed, could preserve its freedom "in the midst of continual warfare." Madison's remarkable warning about how presidents might seize the power afforded them in war to limit freedom has been borne out at many points in American history–from Lincoln's suspension of the writ of habeas corpus to Wilson's suppression of free speech and Franklin D. Roosevelt's internment of Japanese-Americans. The administration of George W. Bush was no exception. But no other president had ever made so sweeping an assertion of the power to violate both longstanding constitutional principles, such as the right to trial by jury, and any law he chooses during wartime.

The majority of Americans seemed willing to accept the administration's contention that restraints on time-honored liberties were necessary to fight terrorism, especially since these restraints applied primarily to Muslims and immigrants from the Middle East. Others recalled previous times when wars produced limitations on civil liberties and public officials equated political dissent with lack of patriotism: the Alien and Sedition Acts during the "quasi-war" with France in 1798, the suspension of the writ of habeas corpus during the Civil War, the severe repression of free speech and persecution of German-Americans during World War I, Japanese-American internment in World War II, and McCarthyism during the Cold War. These episodes underscored the fragility of principles most Americans have learned to take for granted—civil liberties and the ideal of equality before the law, regardless of race and ethnicity. The debate over liberty and security seemed certain to last as long as the war on terrorism itself.

THE TORTURE CONTROVERSY

Officials of the Bush administration also insisted in the aftermath of September 11 that the United States need not be bound by international law in pursuing the war on terrorism. They were especially eager to sidestep the Geneva Conventions and the International Convention Against Torture, which regulate the treatment of prisoners of war and prohibit torture and other forms of physical and mental coercion. In January 2002, the Justice Department produced a memorandum stating that these rules did not apply to captured members of Al Qaeda as they were "unlawful combatants," not members of regularly constituted armies. White House counsel Alberto Gonzales, who later became attorney general, advised the president that the Geneva Accords were "quaint" and "obsolete" in this "new kind of war." In February 2003, President Bush issued a directive that denied Al Qaeda and Taliban prisoners the Geneva protections.

Amid strong protests from Secretary of State Powell and senior military officers who feared that the new policy would encourage the retaliatory mistreatment of American prisoners of war, in April 2003 the president prohibited the use of torture except where special permission had been granted. Nonetheless, the Defense Department approved methods of interrogation that most observers considered torture. In addition, the CIA set up a series of jails in foreign countries outside the traditional chain of military command and took part in the "rendition" of suspects—that is, kidnapping them and spiriting them to prisons in Egypt, Yemen, Syria, and former communist states of eastern Europe, where torture is practiced.

In this atmosphere and lacking clear rules of behavior, some military personnel—in Afghanistan, at Abu Ghraib prison in Iraq, and at Guantànamo—beat prisoners who were being held for interrogation, subjected them to electric shocks, let them be attacked by dogs, and forced them to strip naked and lie atop other prisoners. Some prisoners in U.S. custody died from their maltreatment. As it turned out, the military guards and interrogators who committed these acts had not been adequately trained for their missions. Indeed, some took photographs of the maltreatment of prisoners and circulated them by e-mail. Inevitably, the photos became public. Their exposure around the world in newspapers, on television, and on the Internet undermined the reputation of the United States as a country that adheres to standards of civilized behavior and the rule of law.

The military investigated prisoner abuse but punished only a few low-level

Based on an infamous photograph, circulated around the world, of an Iraqi prisoner abused while in American custody, this 2004 cartoon suggests how such mistreatment damaged the image of the United States.

VISIONS OF FREEDOM

Disclaimer: Certain restrictions apply. Subject to change without notice. The right of *Freedom* is made available "as is" and without warranty of any kind. The right of *Freedom* may be exercised on the strict understanding that neither the Government nor its ministers, employees, or agents shall be liable for losses of any kind.

Freedom: Certain Restrictions Apply. *This work by the artist George Mill includes language that parodies the small print in advertisements and consumer warranties. The disclaimer reads: "Certain restrictions apply. Subject to change without notice. The right of freedom is made available 'as is' and without warranty of any kind." This was part of a 2008 exhibit in which artists produced works on the theme "Thoughts on Freedom." Many of the works suggested that the policies of the Bush administration had made Americans' freedom more precarious.*

QUESTIONS

1. What "restrictions" on freedom do you think the artist has in mind?

2. What is the purpose of juxtaposing the large word "FREEDOM" with the small print?

soldiers, not the commanders who were supposed to be in charge of these prisons and had tolerated or failed to halt the abuse. After much debate, Congress in 2005 inserted in the Defense Appropriations Act a measure sponsored by Senator John McCain of Arizona (a former prisoner of war in Vietnam) banning the use of torture. President Bush signed the bill but issued a "signing statement" reaffirming his right as commander-in-chief to set rules for the military by himself.

Late in 2008 and early the following year, previously secret government documents were released demonstrating that torture was the result not of missteps by a few "bad apples," as the administration had claimed, but decisions at the highest levels of government. Secretary of Defense Donald Rumsfeld, Attorney General Alberto Gonzales, and other officials had authorized the torture of persons captured in the war on terrorism, over the objections of many in the military. Ironically, some of the techniques used, especially water-boarding (simulated drowning), had been employed by the government during the Korean War to train soldiers how to withstand torture if captured by the enemy. No one in the administration seemed concerned about what these practices might do to the reputation of the United States as a law-abiding nation. The revelations left a difficult question for the administration of Barack Obama—whether or not to prosecute officials and interrogators who had violated international treaties and American laws.

THE ECONOMY UNDER BUSH

In the congressional elections of 2002, Bush took full advantage of his post–September 11 popularity, campaigning actively for Republican candidates. His intervention was credited with helping his party increase its small majorities in the House and Senate, in defiance of the traditional pattern in which the president's party loses seats in midterm elections. Continuing chaos in Iraq began to undermine support for Bush's foreign policy. But the main threat to the president's reelection appeared to be the condition of the American economy. During 2001, the economy slipped into a recession—that is, it contracted rather than grew. Growth resumed at the end of the year, but, with businesses reluctant to make new investments after the overexpansion of the 1990s, it failed to generate new jobs.

THE "JOBLESS" RECOVERY

Talk of "economic pain" reappeared in public discussions. The sectors that had expanded the most in the previous decade contracted rapidly. The computer industry slashed more than 40 percent of its jobs during the first two years of the Bush presidency. Thanks to the Internet, jobs as computer programmers and other highly skilled technology positions could be shifted to India, which had a large number of well-educated persons willing to work for far less than their American counterparts. Employment in the media, advertising, and telecommunications industries also fell.

The difficulties of these sectors received much publicity. But in fact, 90 percent of the jobs lost during the recession of 2001–2002 were in manufacturing. Despite the renewed spirit of patriotism, deindustrialization continued. Textile firms closed southern plants and shifted production to cheap-labor factories in China and India. Maytag, a manufacturer of washing machines, refrigerators, and other home appliances, announced plans to close its factory in Galesburg, Illinois, where wages averaged fifteen dollars per hour, to open a new one in Mexico, where workers earned less than one-seventh that amount.

Even after economic recovery began, the problems of traditional industries continued. Employment in steel—520,000 in 1970—had dropped to 120,000 by 2004. Late in 2005, facing declining profits and sales, General Motors, which once had 600,000 employees, announced plans to reduce its American workforce to 86,000. Major companies also moved to eliminate the remnants of the post–World War II "social contract," in which industries provided manufacturing workers with both high-paying jobs and the promise that they would be provided for in old age. Many eliminated or sharply reduced pensions and health benefits for retired workers. Between 1988 and 2004, the number of private businesses with pension plans fell by two-thirds.

Rapid job creation during the 1990s had benefited those at the bottom of the economic scale, and especially racial minorities. Now, they suffered the most from the economy's continued shedding of jobs in the early 2000s. For example, the black and Latino unemployment rates stood at double that for whites. Indeed, Bush became the first president since Herbert Hoover to see the economy lose jobs over the course of a four-year term.

The Bush administration responded to economic difficulties by supporting the Federal Reserve Board's policy of reducing interest rates and by proposing another round of tax cuts. In 2003, the president signed into law a $320-billion tax reduction, one of the largest in American history. In accordance with supply-side theory, the cuts were again geared to reducing the tax burden on wealthy individuals and corporations. Left to future generations were the questions of how to deal with a rapidly mounting federal deficit (which exceeded $400 billion, a record, in 2004) and how to pay for the obligations of the federal government and the needs of American society.

The economy grew at the healthy rate of 4.2 percent in 2004. But job creation proceeded more slowly than during previous recoveries. Because of the continuing decline in union membership (which fell to 8 percent of private sector employees in 2006), the failure of Congress to raise the minimum wage (which between 1997 and 2006 remained at $5.15 per hour, thereby steadily falling in real value), the continuing shift of higher-paying manufacturing jobs overseas, and the skewing of the tax cuts toward the most wealthy Americans, economic inequality continued to increase. The real income of average American families fell slightly despite the economic recovery. The number of Americans without health insurance continued its upward climb, reaching 16 percent of the population by 2005. Nearly all the benefits of growth went to the top 5 percent of the population.

THE WINDS OF CHANGE

THE 2004 ELECTION

With Bush's popularity sliding because of the war in Iraq and a widespread sense that many Americans were not benefiting from economic growth, Democrats in 2004 sensed a golden opportunity to retake the White House. They nominated as their candidate John Kerry, a senator

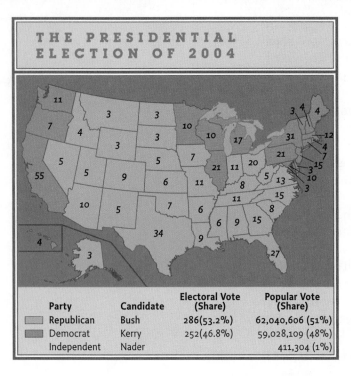

THE PRESIDENTIAL ELECTION OF 2004

Party	Candidate	Electoral Vote (Share)	Popular Vote (Share)
Republican	Bush	286 (53.2%)	62,040,606 (51%)
Democrat	Kerry	252 (46.8%)	59,028,109 (48%)
Independent	Nader		411,304 (1%)

from Massachusetts and the first Catholic to run for president since John F. Kennedy in 1960. A decorated combat veteran in Vietnam, Kerry had joined the antiwar movement after leaving the army. The party hoped that Kerry's military experience would insulate him from Republican charges that Democrats were too weak-willed to be trusted to protect the United States from further terrorist attacks, while his antiwar credentials in Vietnam would appeal to voters opposed to the invasion of Iraq.

Kerry proved a surprisingly ineffective candidate. An aloof man who lacked the common touch, he failed to generate the same degree of enthusiasm among his supporters as Bush did among his. Kerry's inability to explain why he voted in favor of the Iraq War in the Senate only to denounce it later as a major mistake enabled Republicans to portray him as lacking the kind of resolution necessary in dangerous times. Meanwhile, Karl Rove, Bush's chief political adviser, worked assiduously to mobilize the Republican Party's conservative base by having Republicans stress the president's stance on cultural issues—opposition to the extension of the right to marry to homosexuals (which the Supreme Court of Massachusetts had ruled must receive legal recognition in that state), opposition to abortion rights, and so on.

Throughout the campaign, polls predicted a very close election. Bush won a narrow victory, with a margin of 2 percent of the popular vote and thirty-four electoral votes. The results revealed a remarkable electoral stability. Both sides had spent tens of millions of dollars in advertising and had mobilized new voters—nearly 20 million since 2000. But in the end, only three states voted differently than four years earlier—New Hampshire, which Kerry carried, and Iowa and New Mexico, which swung to Bush.

Post-election polls initially suggested that "moral values" held the key to the election outcome, leading some commentators to urge Democrats to make peace with the Religious Right. Most evangelical Christians, indeed, voted for Bush. But the "moral values" category was a grab-bag indicating everything from hostility to abortion rights to the desire for a leader who says what he means and apparently means what he says. More important to the outcome were the attacks of September 11 and the sense of being engaged in a worldwide war on terror. No American president who has sought reelection during wartime has ever been defeated (although Harry S. Truman and Lyndon Johnson declined to run again during unpopular wars). The Bush campaign consistently and successfully appealed to fear, with continuous reminders of September 11 and warnings of future attacks.

Republicans also slightly increased their majorities in the House of Representatives and the Senate. But the most striking feature of the congressional races was that by the careful drawing of district lines in state legislatures, both parties had managed to make a majority of the seats "safe" ones. Only three incumbents were defeated for reelection, and nearly all the House seats were won by a margin of 10 percent or more. In the old days, one commentator quipped, voters chose their political leaders. Today, politicians choose their voters.

BUSH'S SECOND TERM

In his second inaugural address, in January 2005, Bush outlined a new American goal—"ending tyranny in the world." Striking a more conciliatory tone than during his first administration, he promised that the United States would not try to impose "our style of government" on others and that it would in the future seek the advice of allies. He said nothing specific about Iraq but tried to shore up falling support for the war by invoking the ideal of freedom: "The survival of liberty in our land increasingly depends on the success of liberty in other lands." In his first inaugural, in January 2001, Bush had used the words "freedom," "free," or "liberty" seven times. In his second, they appeared forty-nine times. Again and again, Bush insisted that the United States stands for the worldwide triumph of freedom.

Republicans were overjoyed by Bush's electoral triumph. "Now comes the revolution," declared one conservative leader. But the ongoing chaos in Iraq, coupled with a spate of corruption scandals surrounding Republicans in Congress and the White House, eroded Bush's standing. Vice President Cheney's chief of staff was convicted of perjury in connection with an investigation of the illegal "leak" to the press of the name of a CIA operative whose husband had criticized the manipulation of intelligence before the invasion of Iraq. He was the first White House official to be indicted while holding office since Orville Babcock, Grant's chief of staff, in 1875. A Texas grand jury indicted Tom DeLay, the House majority leader, for violating campaign finance laws, and Jack Abramoff, a Republican activist and lobbyist, pleaded guilty to defrauding his clients and bribing public officials. A "culture of corruption," Democrats charged, had overtaken the nation's capital.

Bush's popularity continued to decline. At one point in 2006, his approval rating fell to 31 percent. Bush did get Congress in 2005 to extend the life of the Patriot Act, with a few additional safeguards for civil liberties. But otherwise, the first two years of his second term were devoid of significant legislative achievement. Bush launched a highly publicized campaign to "reform" the Social Security system, the most enduring and popular legacy of the New Deal, by allowing workers to set up private retirement accounts—a step toward eliminating the entire system, Democrats charged—but it got nowhere. Congress rejected the president's proposal to open the Arctic National Wildlife Refuge to oil drilling, and it refused to eliminate the estate tax, a tax on property owned at a person's death, which affected only the richest 1 percent of Americans.

HURRICANE KATRINA

A further blow to the Bush administration's standing came in August 2005, when Hurricane Katrina slammed ashore near New Orleans. Situated below sea level between the Mississippi River and Lake Pontchartrain, New Orleans has always been vulnerable to flooding. For years, scientists had predicted a catastrophe if a hurricane hit the city. But requests to strengthen its levee system had been ignored by the federal government. When the storm hit on August 29 the levees broke, and nearly the entire city, with a population of half a million, was inundated. Nearby areas of the Louisiana and Mississippi Gulf Coast were also hard hit.

A satellite photograph superimposed on a map of the Gulf Coast shows the immensity of Hurricane Katrina as its eye moved over New Orleans.

The natural disaster quickly became a man-made one, with ineptitude evident from local government to the White House. The mayor of New Orleans had been slow to order an evacuation, fearing this would damage the city's tourist trade. When he finally instructed residents to leave, a day before the storm's arrival, he neglected to provide for the thousands who did not own automobiles and were too poor to find other means of transportation. In November 2002, a new Department of Homeland Security had been created, absorbing many existing intelligence agencies, including the Federal Emergency Management Agency (FEMA), which is responsible for disaster planning and relief within the United States. FEMA was headed by Michael Brown, who lacked experience in disaster management and had apparently been appointed because he was a college friend of his predecessor in the office. Although warned of impending disaster by the National Weather Service, FEMA had done almost no preparation. Vacationing in Texas, the president announced that New Orleans had "dodged the bullet" when the storm veered away from a direct hit. When he finally visited the city, he seemed unaware of the scope of devastation. If the Bush administration had prided itself on anything, it was competence in dealing with disaster. Katrina shattered that image.

THE NEW ORLEANS DISASTER

For days, vast numbers of people, most of them poor African-Americans, remained abandoned amid the floodwaters. The government was not even aware that thousands had gathered at the New Orleans Convention Center, without food, water, or shelter, until television reporters asked federal officials about their status. For days, bodies floated in the streets and people died in city hospitals and nursing homes. By the time aid began to arrive, damage stood at $80 billion, the death toll was around 1,500, and two-thirds of the city's population had been displaced. The televised images of misery in the streets of New Orleans shocked the world and shamed the country. To leave the poorest behind and unhelped, one editorial writer commented, was like abandoning wounded soldiers on a battlefield.

Hurricane Katrina shone a bright light on both the heroic and the less praiseworthy sides of American life. Where government failed, individual citizens stepped into the breach. People with boats rescued countless survivors from rooftops and attics, private donations flowed in to aid the victims, and neighboring states like Texas opened their doors to thousands of refugees. Like the publication of Jacob Riis's *How the Other Half Lives* (1890) and Michael Harrington's *The Other America* (1962), the hurricane's aftermath alerted Americans to the extent of poverty in the world's richest country. Generations of state and local policies pursuing economic growth via low-wage, nonunion employment and low investment in education, health, and social welfare had produced a large impoverished population in the South. Once a racially mixed city, New Orleans was now essentially segregated, with a population two-thirds black, surrounded by mostly white suburbs. Nearly 30 percent of New Orleans's population lived in poverty, and of these, seven-eighths were black.

For a moment, people previously invisible to upper- and middle-class America appeared on television screens and magazine covers. Stung by criticism of his response to the hurricane, President Bush spoke of the need to take aggressive action against "deep, persistent poverty" whose roots lay in "a history of racial discrimination." But unwilling to raise taxes, the Republican Congress instead cut billions of dollars from Medicaid, food stamps, and other social programs to help pay for rebuilding efforts along the Gulf Coast. A year after the hurricane hit, the population of New Orleans stood at half the pre-storm total, and reconstruction had barely begun in many neighborhoods.

Hurricane Katrina had another result as well. The shutting down of oil refining capacity on the Gulf Coast led to an immediate rise in the price of oil, and thus of gasoline for American drivers. With the rapidly growing economies of China and India needing more and more oil, and with instability in the Middle East threatening to affect oil production, prices remained at historic highs throughout 2006. Despite decades of talk about the need to develop alternative energy supplies, the United States remained as dependent as ever on imported oil and extremely vulnerable to potential disruptions of oil imports. Rising prices threatened to derail the economic recovery by dampening consumer spending on other goods. They also dealt yet another blow to American automobile manufacturers, who had staked their futures on sales of light trucks and sport utility vehicles (SUVs). These vehicles generated high profits for the car companies but achieved very low gas mileage. When gas prices rose, consumers shifted their purchasing to smaller cars with better fuel efficiency, most of which were produced by Japanese and other foreign automakers.

Residents of New Orleans, stranded on a rooftop days after flood waters engulfed the city, frantically attempt to attract the attention of rescue helicopters.

THE IMMIGRATION DEBATE

In the spring of 2006, an issue as old as the American nation suddenly burst again onto the center stage of politics—immigration. As we have seen, the Hart-Celler Act of 1965 led to a radical shift in the origins of those entering the United States, and especially the rapid growth of the Hispanic population. The influx of immigrants proceeded apace during the first five years of the twenty-first century. By 2005, immigrants represented 12.4 percent of the nation's population, up from 11.2 percent in 2000. Many of these newcomers were bypassing traditional immigrant destinations and heading for areas in the Midwest, small-town New England, and the Upper South. The city with the highest rate of growth of its immigrant population from 1990 to 2005 was Nashville, Tennessee. Racial and ethnic diversity was now a fact of life in the American heartland.

Alongside legal immigrants, undocumented newcomers made their way to the United States, mostly from Mexico. At the end of 2005, it was estimated, there were 11 million illegal aliens in the United States, 7 million of them members of the workforce. Economists disagree about their impact. It seems clear that the presence of large numbers of uneducated, low-skilled workers pushes down wages at the bottom of the economic ladder, especially affecting African-Americans. On the other hand, immigrants both legal and illegal receive regular paychecks, spend money, and pay taxes. They fill jobs for which American workers seem to be unavailable because the wages are so low. It is estimated that more than one-fifth of construction workers, domestic workers, and agricultural workers are in the United States illegally.

As noted in previous chapters, Mexican immigration has long been a controversial subject, especially in the Southwest. Before 1924, there were no limits on immigration from the Western Hemisphere. During the 1930s, hundreds of thousands of Mexican-Americans were repatriated. The *bracero* program of the 1940s and 1950s brought thousands of Mexicans into the United States under labor contracts as migrant agricultural workers. Operation Wetback in 1954 sent 1 million Mexicans home. Since the rise of the Chicano movement of the late 1960s and 1970s, the Mexican-American community has generally defended the rights of undocumented workers, although some advocates have feared that the presence of illegal aliens lowers the standing—in the eyes of other Americans—of everyone of Mexican descent. Unions generally fear that such workers lower wages for all low-skilled workers and make labor organizing more difficult.

In 1986, the Reagan administration had granted amnesty—that is, the right to remain in the United States and become citizens—to 3 million illegal immigrants. During the 1990s, conservatives in states with significant populations of illegal immigrants, especially California, had called for a tough crackdown on their entry and rights within the United States. As governor of Texas, by contrast, George W. Bush had strived to win Hispanic support and downplayed the immigration issue. But in 2006, with many Americans convinced that the United States had lost control of its borders and that immigration was in part responsible for the stagnation of real wages, the House of Representatives approved a bill making it a felony to be in the country illegally and a crime to offer aid to illegal immigrants.

THE IMMIGRANT RIGHTS MOVEMENT

The response was utterly unexpected: a series of massive demonstrations in the spring of 2006 by immigrants—legal and illegal—and their supporters, demanding the right to remain in the country as citizens. In cities from New York to Chicago, Los Angeles, Phoenix, and Dallas, hundreds of thousands of protesters took to the streets. Nashville experienced the largest public demonstration in its history, a march of more than 10,000 mostly Hispanic immigrants. People living at the margins of American society suddenly found their voice. "All that we want is to have a shot at the American dream," said one. Another, an Iraq War veteran who marched with his parents, who had come to the country illegally, said, "I've fought for freedom overseas. Now I'm fighting for freedom here."

At the same time, church groups used to sheltering and feeding the destitute denounced the proposed bill as akin to the Fugitive Slave Law of 1850 for making it a crime to help a suffering human being and vowed to resist it. On the other hand, many conservatives condemned the marches as "ominous" and their display of the flags of the marchers' homelands as "repellant." When the Senate passed a different immigrant bill, tightening patrols of the border but offering a route to citizenship for illegal aliens, the House refused to approve it. All Congress could agree on was a measure to build a 700-mile wall along part of the U.S.-Mexico border. In early 2007, the immigration issue was at a stalemate and its ultimate resolution impossible to predict.

THE CONSTITUTION AND LIBERTY

As in the 1980s and 1990s, conservatives proved far more successful in implementing their views in economic and foreign policy than in the ongoing culture wars. Two significant Supreme Court decisions in June

In April 2006, millions of people demonstrated for immigrant rights. This photograph shows part of the immense crowd in Chicago, bearing the flags of many nations.

2003 revealed how the largely conservative justices had come to accept that the social revolution that began during the 1960s could not be undone.

In two cases arising from challenges to the admissions policies of the University of Michigan, the Supreme Court issued its most important rulings on affirmative action since the *Bakke* case twenty-five years earlier. A 5-4 majority upheld the right of colleges and universities to take race into account in admissions decisions. Writing for the majority, Justice Sandra Day O'Connor argued that such institutions have a legitimate interest in creating a "diverse" student body to enhance education. The Bush administration had urged the Court to reject affirmative action. But O'Connor was strongly influenced by briefs on its behalf filed by corporate executives and retired military officers. In today's world, they argued, the United States cannot compete in the global economy or maintain effective armed services without drawing its college-trained business and military leaders from a wide variety of racial and ethnic backgrounds.

In the second decision, in *Lawrence v. Texas*, a 6-3 majority declared unconstitutional a Texas law making homosexual acts a crime. Written by Justice Anthony Kennedy, the majority opinion overturned the Court's 1986 ruling in *Bowers v. Hardwick*, which had upheld a similar Georgia law. Today, Kennedy insisted, the idea of liberty includes not only "freedom of thought, belief, [and] expression" but "intimate conduct" as well. The decision was a triumph for the feminist and gay movements, which had long campaigned to extend the idea of freedom into the most personal realms of life. And it repudiated the conservative view that constitutional interpretation must rest either on the "original intent" of the founding fathers or on a narrow reading of the document's text. Instead, Kennedy reaffirmed the liberal view of the Constitution as a living document whose protections expand as society changes. "Times can blind us to certain truths," he wrote, "and later generations can see that laws once thought necessary and proper in fact serve only to oppress. As the Constitution endures, persons in every generation can invoke its principles in their own search for greater freedom."

THE COURT AND THE PRESIDENT

Nor did the Supreme Court prove receptive to President Bush's claim of authority to disregard laws and treaties and to suspend constitutional protections of individual liberties. In a series of decisions, the Court reaffirmed the rule of law both for American citizens and for foreigners held prisoner by the United States.

The first cases were decided in 2004. In *Rasul v. Bush*, the Court allowed a British citizen held at Guantànamo Bay, Cuba, to challenge his incarceration in federal court. In *Hamdi v. Rumsfeld*, it considered the lawsuit of Yasir Hamdi, an American citizen who had moved to Saudi Arabia and been captured in Afghanistan. Hamdi was imprisoned in a military jail in South Carolina without charge or the right to see a lawyer. The Court ruled that he had a right to a judicial hearing. "A state of war," wrote Sandra Day O'Connor for the 8-1 majority, "is not a blank check for the president when it comes to the rights of the nation's citizens." Even Justice Antonin Scalia, the Court's most prominent conservative, rejected the president's claim of authority to imprison a citizen at will as antithetical to "the very core of liberty." After claiming in court that Hamdi was so dangerous that he could not even be allowed a hearing, the administration allowed him to return to Saudi Arabia on condition that he relinquish his American citizenship.

By the time the next significant case, *Hamdan v. Rumsfeld*, came before the Court in 2006, President Bush had appointed two new justices—Chief Justice John Roberts, to replace William Rehnquist, who died in 2005, and Samuel Alito Jr., who succeeded the retiring Sandra Day O'Connor. The Court was clearly becoming more conservative. But in June 2006, by a 5-3 margin (with Roberts not participating because he had ruled on the case while serving on an appeals court), the justices offered a stinging rebuke to the key presumptions of the Bush administration—that the Geneva Conventions do not apply to prisoners captured in the war on terrorism, that the president can unilaterally set up secret military tribunals in which defendants have very few if any rights, and that the Constitution does not apply at Guantànamo. Congress, the majority noted, had never authorized such tribunals, and they clearly violated the protections afforded to prisoners of war by the Geneva Conventions, which, the Court declared, was the law of the land.

Like the Nixon tapes case of 1974, the decision was a striking illustration of the separation of powers envisioned by the Constitution's framers, an affirmation that the courts have the right and responsibility to oversee actions by the president. However, it was unusual that the decision came in wartime. The Court had upheld jailings under the Sedition Act in World War I, and Japanese internment in World War II. Previously, the Court had only exerted its oversight authority once peace arrived. But Bush's claims of presidential authority had been so sweeping that a judicial reaction was all but inevitable.

As the "war on terror" entered its sixth year later in 2006, the scope of the president's power to detain and punish suspects outside of normal legal procedures remained unresolved. In September 2006, in response to the *Hamdan* decision, Congress enacted a bill authorizing the establishment of special military tribunals to try accused terrorists and giving the president the authority to jail without charge anyone he declared to be an "illegal enemy combatant." The measure authorized certain kinds of harsh treatment of prisoners, with evidence obtained during coercive interrogations usable in these new courts, and stripped detainees in military prisons of the right to challenge their detention in federal courts. Many military lawyers objected strongly to these provisions, as did other army officials, fearing that captured U.S. soldiers might be subjected to the same treatment. It remained to be seen whether the Supreme Court would allow Congress to override the Geneva Conventions and eliminate judicial oversight of the treatment of prisoners.

In June 2008, for the third time in four years, the Supreme Court rebuffed the Bush administration's strategy of denying detainees at Guantánamo Bay the normal protections guaranteed by the Constitution. Written by Justice Anthony Kennedy, the 5-4 decision in *Boumediene v. Bush* affirmed the detainees' right to challenge their detention in U.S. courts. "The laws and Constitution are designed," Kennedy wrote, "to survive, and remain in force, in extraordinary times." Security, he added, consists not simply in military might, but "in fidelity to freedom's first principles," including freedom from arbitrary arrest and the right of a person to go to court to challenge his or her imprisonment.

THE MIDTERM ELECTIONS OF 2006

With President Bush's popularity having plummeted because of the war in Iraq and the Hurricane Katrina disaster, Congress beset by scandal after scandal, and public opinion polls revealing that a majority of Americans believed the country to be "on the wrong track," Democrats expected to reap major gains in the congressional elections of 2006. They were not disappointed. Interest in the election ran high. Voter turnout in 2006 exceeded 40 percent of those eligible, the highest figure for a midterm election since 1990. In a sweeping repudiation of the administration, voters gave Democrats control of both houses of Congress for the first time since the Republican sweep of 1994. In January 2007, Democrat Nancy Pelosi of California became the first female Speaker of the House in American history. No sooner had the votes been counted than political observers began to speculate about the presidential election of 2008—the first time since 1952 that the major party candidates for the highest office in the land would not include a sitting president or vice president.

As the end of his second term approached, Bush's popularity sank to historic lows. This occurred even though, in November 2008, the United States and Iraq approved an agreement providing for the withdrawal of all American troops by 2011—thus ensuring that one of the longest and most unpopular wars in American history would come to an end. By sending more troops to Iraq in 2007 (a step that Bush, mindful of memories of Vietnam, called a "surge" rather than an escalation) and by forging alliances with local tribal leaders anxious to end the bloodshed, the administration had achieved a significant decline in violence in Iraq, making American withdrawal seem possible. By the time Bush left office, more than 4,000 American soldiers had died in Iraq. But no one could predict what a postwar Iraq would look like.

In January 2009, as Bush's presidency came to an end, only 22 percent of Americans approved of his performance in office—the lowest figure since such polls began in the mid-twentieth century. Indeed, it was difficult to think of many substantive achievements during Bush's eight years in office. His foreign policy alienated most of the world, leaving the United States militarily weakened and diplomatically isolated. Because of the tax cuts for the wealthy that he pushed through Congress during his first term, as well as the cost of the wars in Iraq and Afghanistan, the large budget surplus he had inherited was transformed into an immense deficit. His initiatives on immigration and Social Security reform went nowhere. The percentage of Americans living in poverty and those without health insurance rose substantially during Bush's presidency.

THE HOUSING BUBBLE

At one point in his administration, Bush might have pointed to the economic recovery that began in 2001 as a major success. But late in 2007, the economy entered a recession. And in 2008, the American banking system suddenly found itself on the brink of collapse, threatening to drag the national and world economies into a repeat of the Great Depression.

The roots of the crisis of 2008 lay in a combination of public and private policies that favored economic speculation, free-wheeling spending, and

A stalled residential project in Merced, California, symbolizes the collapse of the housing bubble in 2008. Merced, like many communities in California, was the site of numerous housing developments planned to be built when prices were at their peak. When prices fell, developers declared bankruptcy. In 2008, the half-finished project sat vacant.

get-rich-quick schemes over more traditional avenues to economic growth and personal advancement. For years, the Federal Reserve Bank kept interest rates at unprecedented low levels, first to help the economy recover from the bursting of the technology bubble in 2000 and then to enable more Americans to borrow money to purchase homes. The result was a new bubble, as housing prices rose rapidly. Consumer indebtedness also rose dramatically as people who owned houses took out second mortgages, or simply spent to the limits on their credit cards. In mid-2008, when the median family income was around $50,000, the average American family owed an $84,000 home mortgage, $14,000 in auto and student loans, $8,500 to credit card companies, and $10,000 in home equity loans.

All this borrowing fueled increased spending. The yearly savings of the average family amounted to less than $400. An immense influx of cheap goods from China accelerated the loss of manufacturing jobs in the United States (which continued their decline despite the overall economic recovery) but also enabled Americans to keep buying, even though for most, household income stagnated during the Bush years. Indeed, China helped to finance the American spending spree by buying up hundreds of billions of dollars worth of federal bonds—in effect loaning money to the United States so that it could purchase Chinese-made goods. Banks and other lending institutions issued more and more "subprime" mortgages—risky loans to people who lacked the income to meet their monthly payments. The initially low interest rates on these loans were set to rise dramatically after a year or two. Banks assumed that home prices would keep rising, and if they had to foreclose, they could easily resell the property at a profit.

Wall Street bankers developed complex new ways of repackaging and selling these mortgages to investors. Insurance companies, including the world's largest, American International Group (AIG), insured these new financial products against future default. Credit rating agencies gave these

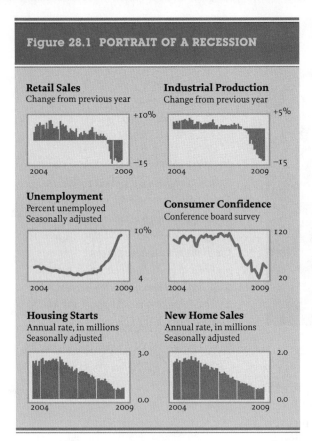

Figure 28.1 PORTRAIT OF A RECESSION

Retail Sales
Change from previous year

+10%
−15
2004   2009

Industrial Production
Change from previous year

+5%
−15
2004   2009

Unemployment
Percent unemployed
Seasonally adjusted

10%
4
2004   2009

Consumer Confidence
Conference board survey

120
20
2004   2009

Housing Starts
Annual rate, in millions
Seasonally adjusted

3.0
0.0
2004   2009

New Home Sales
Annual rate, in millions
Seasonally adjusted

2.0
0.0
2004   2009

These graphs offer a vivid visual illustration of the steep decline in the American economy in 2008 and the first part of 2009.

securities their highest ratings, even though they were based on loans that clearly would never be repaid. Believing that the market must be left to regulate itself, the Federal Reserve Bank and other regulatory agencies did nothing to slow the speculative frenzy. Banks and investment firms reported billions of dollars in profits, and rewarded their executives with unheard-of bonuses.

THE GREAT RECESSION

In 2006 and 2007, overbuilding had reached the point where home prices began to fall. More and more home owners found themselves owing more money than their homes were worth. As mortgage rates reset, increasing numbers of borrowers defaulted— that is, they could no longer meet their monthly mortgage payments. The value of the new mortgage-based securities fell precipitously. Banks suddenly found themselves with billions of dollars of worthless investments on their books. In 2008, the situation became a full-fledged crisis, as banks stopped making loans, business dried up, and the stock market collapsed. Once above 14,000, the Dow Jones Industrial Average plunged to around 8,000—the worst percentage decline since 1931. Some $7 trillion in shareholder wealth was wiped out. Lehman Brothers, a venerable investment house, recorded a $2.3 billion loss and went out of existence, in history's biggest bankruptcy. Leading banks seemed to be on the verge of failure.

With the value of their homes and stock market accounts in free fall, Americans cut back on spending, leading to business failures and a rapid rise in unemployment. By the end of 2008, 2.5 million jobs had been lost — the most in any year since the end of World War II. Unemployment was concentrated in manufacturing and construction, sectors dominated by men. As a result, by mid-2009, for the first time in American history, more women than men in the United States held paying jobs.

In the last three months of 2008, and again in the first three of 2009, the gross domestic product of the United States decreased by 6 percent—a remarkably swift contraction. Even worse than the economic meltdown was the meltdown of confidence as millions of Americans lost their jobs and/or their homes and saw their retirement savings and pensions, if invested in the stock market, disappear. In April 2009, the recession that began in December 2007 became the longest since the Great Depression. In an era of globalization, economic crises inevitably spread worldwide. The decline in spending in the United States led to unemployment in China, and plunging car sales led to a sharp decline in oil prices and economic problems in oil-producing countries like Russia, Nigeria, and Saudi Arabia. Housing bubbles collapsed around the world, from Ireland to Dubai.

The mortgage crisis affected minorities the most. Many had been steered by banks into subprime mortgages even when they had the assets and income to qualify for more traditional, lower-cost loans. As a result, foreclosures were highest in minority areas, and the gains blacks, Asians, and Hispanics had made in home ownership between 1995 and 2004 now eroded.

"A CONSPIRACY AGAINST THE PUBLIC"

In *The Wealth of Nations* (1776), Adam Smith wrote: "People of the same trade seldom meet together, even for merriment and diversion, but the conversation ends in a conspiracy against the public." This certainly seemed an apt description of the behavior of leading bankers and investment houses whose greed helped to bring down the American economy. Like the scandals of the 1920s and 1990s, those of the Bush era damaged confidence in the ethics of corporate leaders. Indeed, striking parallels existed between these three decades — the get-rich-quick ethos, the close connection between business and government, the passion for deregulation, and widespread corruption.

Fueled by revelations of corporate misdeeds, the reputation of stock brokers and bankers fell to lows last seen during the Great Depression. One poll showed that of various social groups, bankers ranked third from the bottom in public esteem—just above prostitutes and convicted felons. Resentment was fueled by the fact that Wall Street had long since abandoned the idea that pay should be linked to results. By the end of 2008, the worst year for the stock market since the Depression, Wall Street firms had fired 240,000 employees. But they also paid out $20 billion in bonuses to top executives. Even the executives of Lehman Brothers, a company that went bankrupt (and, it later turned out, had shortchanged New York City by hundreds of millions of dollars in corporate and other taxes), received $5.7 billion in bonuses in 2007 and 2008.

It was also revealed that Bernard Madoff, a Wall Street investor who claimed to have made enormous profits for his clients, had in fact run a Ponzi scheme in which investors who wanted to retrieve their money were paid with funds from new participants. Madoff sent fictitious monthly financial statements to his clients but he never actually made stock purchases for them. When the scheme collapsed, Madoff's investors suffered losses amounting to around $50 billion. In 2009, Madoff pleaded guilty to

This cartoon suggests that the near-collapse of the financial system in 2008 indicates the need for "a little more regulation."

fraud and was sentenced to 150 years in prison. In some ways, Madoff's scheme was a metaphor for the American economy at large over the previous decade. Its growth had been based on borrowing from others and spending money people did not have. The popular musical group Coldplay related what had happened:

> I used to rule the world. . . .
>
> I discovered that my castles stand
>
> On pillars of salt and pillars of sand.

THE COLLAPSE OF MARKET FUNDAMENTALISM

The crisis exposed the dark side of market fundamentalism—the ethos of deregulation that had dominated world affairs for the preceding thirty years. Alan Greenspan, the head of the Federal Reserve Bank from 1987 to 2006, had steered the American economy through crises ranging from the stock market collapse of 1987 to the terrorist attacks of 2001. Greenspan had presided over much of the era of deregulation, artificially low interest rates, and excessive borrowing and spending. He and his successors had promoted the housing bubble and saw all sorts of speculative behavior flourish with no governmental intervention. In effect, they allowed securities firms to regulate themselves.

In 2008, Greenspan admitted to Congress that there had been a "flaw" in his long-held conviction that free markets would automatically produce the best results for all and that regulation would damage banks, Wall Street, and the mortgage market. He himself, he said, was in a state of "shocked disbelief," as the crisis turned out to be "much broader than anything I could have imagined." Greenspan's testimony seemed to mark the end of an era. Every president from Ronald Reagan onward had lectured the rest of the world on the need to adopt the American model of unregulated economic competition, and berated countries like Japan and Germany for assisting failing businesses. Now, the American model lay in ruins and a new role for government in regulating economic activity seemed inevitable.

BUSH AND THE CRISIS

In the fall of 2008, with the presidential election campaign in full swing, the Bush administration seemed unable to come up with a response to the crisis. In keeping with the free market ethos, it allowed Lehman Brothers to fail. But this immediately created a domino effect, with the stock prices of other banks and investment houses collapsing, and the administration quickly reversed course. It persuaded a reluctant Congress to appropriate $700 billion dollars to bail out other floundering firms. Insurance companies like AIG, banks like Citigroup and Bank of America, and giant financial companies like the Federal Home Loan Mortgage Corporation (popularly known as Freddie Mac) and the Federal National Mortgage Association (Fannie Mae), which insured most mortgages in the country, were deemed "too big to fail"—that is, they were so interconnected with other institutions that their collapse would drive the economy into a full-fledged depression. Through the federal bailout, taxpayers in effect took temporary ownership of these companies, absorbing the massive losses created by their previous malfeasance. Most of this money was distributed with no requirements as to its use. Few of the rescued firms used the public funds to assist home owners threatened with foreclosure; indeed, since they pocketed lucrative fees from those who could not pay their mortgages, they had no incentive to help them keep their homes or sell them. Giant banks and investment houses that received public money redirected some of it to enormous bonuses to top employees. But despite the bailout, the health of the banking system remained fragile. Firms still had balance sheets weighed down with "toxic assets"—billions and billions of dollars in worthless loans.

The crisis also revealed the limits of the American "safety net" compared with other industrialized countries. In western Europe, workers who lose their jobs typically receive many months of unemployment insurance amounting to a significant percentage of their lost wages. In the United States, only one-third of out-of-work persons even qualify for unemployment insurance, and it runs out after a few months. The abolition of "welfare" (the national obligation to assist the neediest Americans) during the Clinton administration left the American safety net a patchwork of a few national programs like food stamps, supplemented by locally administered aid. The poor were dependent on aid from the states, which found their budgets collapsing as revenues from property and sales taxes dried up. California, which in 2009 faced a budget gap of $26 billion, was forced to slash spending for education, health care, and services for the poor. In the United States as a whole, only one-fifth of poor children and their parents received any public relief at all.

THE RISE OF OBAMA

With the economy in crisis and President Bush's popularity at low ebb, the time was ripe for a Democratic victory in the election of 2008. To the surprise of nearly all political pundits, the long series of winter and spring caucuses and primary elections resulted in the nomination not of Hilary Rodham Clinton, the initial favorite, but Barack Obama, a relatively little-known forty-seven-year-old senator from Illinois when the campaign began. Obama was the first black candidate to win the nomination of a major party. His triumph was a tribute both to his own exceptional skills as a speaker and campaigner, and to how American politics had changed.

Obama's life story exemplified the enormous changes American society had undergone since 1960. Without the civil rights movement, his election would have been inconceivable. He was the product of an interracial marriage, which ended in divorce when he was two years old, between a Kenyan immigrant and a white American woman. When Obama was born in 1961, their marriage was still illegal in many states. He attended Columbia College and Harvard Law School, and worked in Chicago as a community organizer before going into politics. He also wrote two best-selling books about his upbringing in Indonesia (where his

A cartoon in the Boston Globe *suggests the progress that has been made since Rosa Parks refused to give up her seat on a bus to a white passenger.*

mother worked as an anthropologist) and Hawaii (where his maternal grandparents helped to raise him) and his search for a sense of identity given his complex background. Obama was elected to the U.S. Senate in 2004 and first gained national attention with an eloquent speech at the Democratic national convention that year.

Clinton sought the Democratic nomination by emphasizing her political experience, both as First Lady and as a senator from New York. Obama realized that in 2008 people were hungry for change, not experience. Indeed, while Clinton's nomination would also have been path-breaking—no woman has ever been the presidential candidate of a major party—Obama succeeded in making her seem a representative of the status quo. His early opposition to the Iraq War, for which Clinton had voted in the Senate, won the support of the party's large antiwar element; his race galvanized the support of black voters; and his youth and promise of change appealed to the young.

Obama recognized how the Internet had changed politics. He established an e-mail list containing the names of millions of voters with whom he could communicate instantaneously, and used web-based networks to raise enormous sums of money in small donations. His campaign put out videos on popular Internet sites. With its widespread use of modern technology and massive mobilization of new voters, Obama's was the first political campaign of the twenty-first century.

THE 2008 CAMPAIGN

Having won the nomination, Obama faced Senator John McCain, the Republican nominee, in the general election. At age sevety-two, McCain was the oldest man ever to run for president, and he seemed even more a representative of the old politics than Clinton. Citing his willingness to break with his party on issues like campaign finance reform, McCain tried to portray himself not as part of the establishment but as a "maverick," or rebel. He surprised virtually everyone by choosing as his running mate Sarah Palin, the little-known governor of Alaska, in part as an attempt to woo Democratic women disappointed at their party's rejection of Hilary Clinton. Palin quickly went on the attack, accusing Democrats of being unpatriotic, lacking traditional values, and not representing the "real America." This proved extremely popular with the Republican party's conservative base. But her performances in speeches and interviews soon made it clear that she lacked familiarity with many of the domestic and foreign issues a new administration would confront. Her selection raised questions among many Americans about McCain's judgment.

But the main obstacles for the McCain campaign were President Bush's low popularity and the financial crisis that reached bottom in September and October. Obama's promise of change seemed more appealing than ever. On election day, he swept to victory with 53 percent of the popular vote and a large majority in the electoral college. His election redrew the nation's political map. Obama

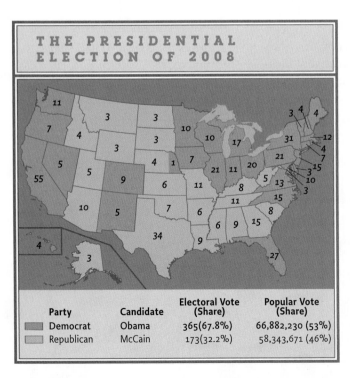

THE PRESIDENTIAL ELECTION OF 2008

Party	Candidate	Electoral Vote (Share)	Popular Vote (Share)
Democrat	Obama	365 (67.8%)	66,882,230 (53%)
Republican	McCain	173 (32.2%)	58,343,671 (46%)

carried not only Democratic strongholds in New England, the mid-Atlantic states, the industrial Midwest, and the West Coast, but also states that had been reliably Republican for years. He cracked the solid South, winning Virginia, North Carolina, and Florida. He did extremely well in suburbs throughout the country. He even carried Indiana, where Bush had garnered 60 percent of the vote in 2004, but which now was hard hit by unemployment. Obama put together a real "rainbow" coalition, winning nearly the entire black vote and a large majority of Hispanics (who helped him to carry Colorado, Nevada, and Florida). He did exceptionally well among young voters. Obama carried every age group except persons over 65. Thus, he was elected even though he received only 43 percent of the nation's white vote.

THE AGE OF OBAMA?

Obama's victory seemed to mark the end of a political era that began with Richard Nixon and his "southern strategy." Instead of using control of the South as the base to build a national majority, Republicans now ran the danger of becoming a regional and marginalized southern party. In the wake of the Iraq War, the economic meltdown, and the enthusiasm aroused by Obama's candidacy, Republican appeals to patriotism, low taxes, and resentment against the social changes sparked by the 1960s seemed oddly out of date. Democrats not only regained the presidency but ended up with 60 of the 100 seats in the Senate and a large majority in the House. The groups carried by Obama—young voters, Hispanics, suburbanites—represented the growing parts of the population, auguring well for future Democratic success. In an increasingly multi-ethnic,multiracial nation, winning a majority of the white vote no longer translated into national victory. Republicans would have to find a way to appeal to the voters of the new America.

The election of the nation's first African-American president represented a historic watershed. Whether it constituted what political scientists call a "critical election"—one that changes the basic assumptions governing national policy—remained to be seen. Critical elections have been few and far between in American history. The election of Jefferson in 1800 dealt a death blow to the Federalist Party. Jackson's in 1828 ushered in the politics of popular democracy. Lincoln's in 1860 ended southern control of the national government. William McKinley in 1896 and Franklin D. Roosevelt in 1932 created new political alignments and enduring national majorities for their parties. Ronald Reagan's election in 1980 established a new set of governing principles. Most presidential elections, however, have left the policies of the federal government largely unchanged, even when a new party was victorious. Only time would tell whether Obama's election announced the end of the Age of Reagan, the era of economic deregulation, the demonization of the federal government, and an aggressive foreign policy abroad, and the beginning of something fundamentally different.

OBAMA'S INAUGURATION

Few presidents have come into office facing as serious a set of problems as Barack Obama. The economy was in crisis and the country involved in two wars. But Americans, including many who had not voted for him, viewed Obama's election as a cause for optimism. Two days after his victory, a poll found two-thirds of Americans describing themselves as proud of the result, and 60 percent excited at the prospect of an Obama administration.

On January 20, 2009, a day after the Martin Luther King Jr. holiday and more than forty-five years after King's "I Have a Dream" speech, Obama was inaugurated as president. More than 1 million people traveled to Washington to view the historic event. In his inaugural address (see the full text in the Appendix), Obama offered a stark rebuke to eight years of Bush policies and, more broadly, to the premises that had shaped government policy since the election of Reagan. He promised a foreign policy based on diplomacy rather than unilateral force, pledged to protect the environment, spoke of the need to combat income inequality and lack of access to health care, and blamed a culture of "greed and irresponsibility" for helping to bring on the economic crisis. He promised to renew respect for the Constitution. Unlike Bush, Obama said little about freedom in his speech, other than to note that the country could enjoy liberty and security at the same time rather than having to choose between them. Instead of freedom, he spoke of community and responsibility. His address harked back to the revolutionary-era ideal of putting the common good before individual self-interest.

OBAMA'S FIRST MONTHS

In many ways, Obama's first policy initiatives lived up to the promise of change. In his first three months, he announced plans to close the prison at Guantánamo Bay in Cuba, barred the use of torture, launched a diplomatic initiative to repair relations with the Muslim world, reversed the previous administration's executive orders limiting women's reproductive rights, and abandoned Bush's rhetoric about a God-given American mission to spread freedom throughout the world. When Supreme Court justice David Souter announced his retirement, Obama named Sonia Sotomayor, the first Hispanic and third woman in the Court's history, to replace him. The Senate confirmed her in August 2009.

Obama's first budget recalled the New Deal and Great Society. Breaking with the Reagan-era motto, "Government is the problem, not the solution," it anticipated active government support for health care reform, clean energy, and public education, paid for in part by allowing Bush's tax cuts for the wealthy to expire in 2010. He pushed through Congress a "stimulus" package amounting to nearly $800 billion in new government spending— for construction projects, the extension of unemployment benefits, and aid to the states to enable them to balance their budgets.

In the spring of 2009, Republicans and independents opposed to President Obama's "stimulus" plan held "tea parties" around the country, seeking to invoke the tradition of the Boston Tea Party and its opposition to taxation. In this demonstration in Austin, Texas, some participants wore hats reminiscent of the revolutionary era. One participant carries a sign urging the state to secede from the Union.

The largest single spending appropriation in American history, the bill was meant to pump money into the economy in order to save and create jobs and to ignite a resumption of economic activity.

For most of Obama's first year in office, congressional debate revolved around a plan to restructure the nation's health care system so as to provide insurance coverage to the millions of Americans who lacked it, and to end abusive practices by insurance companies, such as their refusal to cover patients with existing illnesses. After months of increasingly bitter debate, in March 2010, Congress passed a sweeping health-care bill that required all Americans to purchase health insurance and most businesses to provide it to their employees. It also offered subsidies to persons of modest incomes so they could afford insurance, and required insurance companies to accept all applicants. This was the most far-reaching piece of domestic social legislation since the Great Society of the 1960s, and it aroused strong partisan opposition. Claiming that it amounted to a "government takeover" of the health-care industry (even though plans for a government-run insurance program had been dropped from the bill), every Republican in Congress voted against the bill.

Like many of his predecessors, Obama found that criticizing presidential power from outside is one thing, dismantling it from inside another. He reversed his previous promise to abolish the military tribunals Bush had established. He pledged to complete the planned withdrawal from Iraq, but dispatched 17,000 more American troops to Afghanistan, and in December 2009 announced plans to send another 30,000, creating the danger that his administration would become bogged down in another military quagmire. His stimulus package marked a new departure, but he chose his economic advisers from Wall Street and continued the Bush administration policy of pouring taxpayer money into the banks and assuming responsibility for many of their debts. In the meantime, the economy continued to hemorrhage jobs (the unemployment rate reached 10.2 percent in November). As 2010 neared its midpoint it remained unclear how long it would take for the financial system to resume normal operations and for the country to emerge from the Great Recession.

The design for a series of office buildings that will replace the World Trade Center illustrate the juxtaposition of optimism and fear in the aftermath of September 11, 2001. The soaring towers underscore Americans' capacity for recovery and regeneration. But at the insistence of the New York City police, the base of the Freedom Tower, at the left, consists of reinforced concrete, giving the building, at ground level, the appearance of a fortress.

LEARNING FROM HISTORY

"The owl of Minerva takes flight at dusk." Minerva was the Roman goddess of wisdom, and this saying suggests that the meaning of events only becomes clear once they are over. It is still far too soon to assess the full impact of September 11 on American life and the long-term consequences of the changes at home and abroad it inspired.

As of the end of 2009, the world seemed far more unstable than anyone could have predicted when the Cold War ended nearly twenty years

...UNTIL JUSTICE ROLLS DOWN LIKE WATERS AND RIGHTEOUSNESS LIKE A MIGHTY STREAM

MARTIN LUTHER KING JR

Seeking the lessons of history: a young visitor at the Civil Rights Memorial in Montgomery, Alabama.

earlier. An end to the war on terror seemed as remote as ever. The future of Iraq and Afghanistan remained uncertain, and Pakistan, traditionally the closest ally of the United States in that volatile region, experienced serious political instability. No settlement of the long-standing conflict between Israel and its Arab neighbors seemed in sight. Iran, its power in the region enhanced by the American removal of its chief rival, Saddam Hussein's regime in Iraq, appeared to be bent on acquiring nuclear weapons, which the United States vowed to prevent, raising the prospect of future conflict. Other regions of the world also presented daunting problems for American policymakers. North Korea had acquired nuclear weapons and refused international pressure to give them up. China's rapidly growing economic power posed a challenge to American predominance. A series of Latin American countries elected presidents who rejected the doctrines of globalization and global free trade pressed so insistently by the United States.

No one could predict how any of these crises, or others yet unimagined, would be resolved. And taking a longer view, a study by American intelligence agencies predicted that by 2025 the United States would remain the world's most powerful nation, but that its economic and military predominance will have declined significantly. A "multipolar world," with countries like China and India emerging as major powers, would succeed the era of unquestioned American dominance. How the continuing global financial crisis would affect these developments remained to be seen.

What *is* clear is that September 11 and its aftermath drew new attention to essential elements of the history of American freedom. As in the past, freedom is central to Americans' sense of themselves as individuals and as a nation. Americans continue to debate contemporary issues in a political landscape shaped by ideas of freedom. Indeed, freedom remains, as it has always been, an evolving concept, its definition open to disagreement, its boundaries never fixed or final. Freedom is neither self-enforcing nor self-correcting. It cannot be taken for granted, and its preservation requires eternal vigilance, especially in times of crisis.

More than half a century ago, the African-American poet Langston Hughes urged Americans both to celebrate the freedoms they enjoy and to remember that freedom has always been incomplete:

> There are words like *Freedom*
> Sweet and wonderful to say.
> On my heartstrings freedom sings
> All day everyday.
>
> There are words like *Liberty*
> That almost make me cry.
> If you had known what I know
> You would know why.

SUGGESTED READING

BOOKS

Bacevich, Andrew. *American Empire: The Realities and Consequences of U.S. Diplomacy* (2003). Examines how the idea of an American empire reemerged after September 11, and some of the results.

Brinkley, Douglas. *The Great Deluge: Hurricane Katrina, New Orleans, and the Mississippi Gulf Coast* (2006). A scathing account of how government at all levels failed the people of New Orleans.

Cole, David. *Terrorism and the Constitution* (rev. ed., 2006). Explores the constitutional issues raised by the war on terrorism.

Krugman, Paul, *The Return of Depression Economics and the Crisis of 2008* (2009). A leading economist explains the origins of the Great Recession.

Lakoff, George. *Whose Freedom? The Battle over America's Most Important Idea* (2006). Describes how conservatives and liberals continue to interpret freedom in very different ways.

Levitas, Mitchell, ed. *A Nation Challenged: A Visual History of 9/11 and Its Aftermath* (2002). Presents striking photographs of the terrorist attacks and the days that followed.

Little, Douglas. *American Orientalism: The United States and the Middle East since 1945* (2003). A careful study of American relations with a volatile region since World War II.

Nye, Joseph S., Jr. *The Paradox of American Power* (2002). An argument that despite its overwhelming power, the United States cannot do as it pleases in international affairs.

Packer, George. *The Assassin's Gate: America in Iraq* (2005). An early supporter of the war in Iraq explains what went wrong.

Zakaria, Fareed. *The Future of Freedom: Illiberal Democracy at Home and Abroad* (2003). A foreign policy analyst discusses how the United States should respond to threats to freedom in the world.

WEBSITES

September 11 Digital Archive: http://911digitalarchive.org

The White House: www.whitehouse.gov

REVIEW QUESTIONS

1. Describe how President Bush's foreign policy initiatives departed from the traditional policies practiced by every president since World War II.

2. How did September 11 transform America's stance toward the world?

3. What were the roots of the Bush administration's policy in Iraq?

4. Was Iraq another Vietnam for the United States? Explain.

5. What impact did the war on terror have on liberties at home?

6. What were the major thrusts of the Bush administration's economic policies?

7. How did Supreme Court decisions since 2001 indicate that the rights revolution was here to stay?

8. What were the political effects of Hurricane Katrina?

9. How were the business scandals of the Bush era similar to those of the 1920s and 1990s?

10. What factors led to the rapid rise and political success of Barack Obama?

FREEDOM QUESTIONS

1. Do you think President Bush was correct in saying that the country's antagonists "hate our freedom" Explain.

2. Did the war on terror strike the proper balance between freedom and security?

3. How did the war on terror expand the powers of the president?

4. In what ways did the Obama campaign connect with the history of American freedom?

5. Given what you now know about American history, what is your definition of American freedom, and how is it best attained?

KEY TERMS

Kyoto Protocol (p. 1173)

the Bush Doctrine (p. 1175)

war in Afghanistan (p. 1175)

"axis of evil" (p. 1176)

preemptive war (p. 1177)

signing statements (p. 1188)

"jobless" recovery (p. 1188)

culture of corruption (p. 1191)

Hurricane Katrina (p. 1191)

Lawrence v. Texas (p. 1196)

Hamdi v. Rumsfeld (p. 1196)

Boumediene v. Bush (p. 1197)

"housing bubble" (p. 1199)

Great Recession (p. 1200)

Sonia Sotomayor (p. 1206)

REVIEW TABLE

Significant Changes in American Policy since September 11

Policy	Explanation
Bush Doctrine	America commits itself to a war against terrorism
USA PATRIOT Act	Confers unprecedented powers on law-enforcement agencies
National Security Strategy	Advocates preemptive war for the first time in American history
New Beginning	Obama pledges to emphasize diplomacy, not war

Appendix

DOCUMENTS

TABLES AND FIGURES

THE DECLARATION OF INDEPENDENCE (1776)

When in the course of human events, it becomes necessary for one people to dissolve the political bands which have connected them with another, and to assume among the Powers of the earth, the separate and equal station to which the Laws of Nature and of Nature's God entitle them, a decent respect to the opinions of mankind requires that they should declare the causes which impel them to the separation.

We hold these truths to be self-evident, that all men are created equal, that they are endowed by their Creator with certain unalienable rights, that among these are Life, Liberty, and the pursuit of Happiness. That to secure these rights, Governments are instituted among Men, deriving their just powers from the consent of the governed. That whenever any Form of Government becomes destructive of these ends, it is the Right of the People to alter or to abolish it, and to institute new Government, laying its foundation on such principles and organizing its powers in such form, as to them shall seem most likely to effect their Safety and Happiness. Prudence, indeed, will dictate that Governments long established should not be changed for light and transient causes; and accordingly all experience hath shown, that mankind are more disposed to suffer, while evils are sufferable, than to right themselves by abolishing the forms to which they are accustomed. But when a long train of abuses and usurpations, pursuing invariably the same Object evinces a design to reduce them under absolute Despotism, it is their right, it is their duty, to throw off such Government, and to provide new Guards for their future security.—Such has been the patient sufferance of these Colonies; and such is now the necessity which constrains them to alter their former Systems of Government. The history of the present King of Great Britain is a history of repeated injuries and usurpations, all having in direct object the establishment of an absolute Tyranny over these States. To prove this, let Facts be submitted to a candid world.

He has refused his Assent to Laws, the most wholesome and necessary for the public good.

He has forbidden his Governors to pass Laws of immediate and pressing importance, unless suspended in their operation till his Assent should be obtained; and when so suspended, he has utterly neglected to attend to them.

He has refused to pass other Laws for the accommodation of large districts of people, unless those people would relinquish the right of Representation in the Legislature, a right inestimable to them and formidable to tyrants only.

He has called together legislative bodies at places unusual, uncomfortable, and distant from the depository of their public Records, for the sole purpose of fatiguing them into compliance with his measures.

He has dissolved Representative Houses repeatedly, for opposing with manly firmness his invasions on the rights of the people.

He has refused for a long time, after such dissolutions, to cause others to be elected; whereby the Legislative powers, incapable of Annihilation, have returned to the People at large for their exercise; the State remaining in the mean time exposed to all dangers of invasion from without, and convulsions within.

He has endeavoured to prevent the population of these States; for that purpose obstructing the Laws of Naturalization of Foreigners; refusing to pass others to encourage their migrations hither, and raising the conditions of new Appropriations of Lands.

He has obstructed the Administration of Justice, by refusing his Assent to Laws for establishing Judiciary powers.

He has made Judges dependent on his Will alone, for the tenure of their offices, and the amount and payment of their salaries.

He has erected a multitude of New Offices, and sent hither swarms of Officers to harass our People, and eat out their substance.

He has kept among us, in times of peace, Standing Armies without the Consent of our legislatures.

He has affected to render the Military independent of and superior to the Civil Power.

He has combined with others to subject us to a jurisdiction foreign to our constitution, and unacknowledged by our laws; giving his Assent to their Acts of pretended Legislation:

For quartering large bodies of armed troops among us:

For protecting them, by a mock Trial, from Punishment for any Murders which they should commit on the Inhabitants of these States:

For cutting off our Trade with all parts of the world:

For imposing taxes on us without our Consent:

For depriving us of many cases, of the benefits of Trial by jury:

For transporting us beyond Seas to be tried for pretended offences:

For abolishing the free System of English Laws in a neighbouring Province, establishing therein an Arbitrary government, and enlarging its Boundaries so as to render it at once an example and fit instrument for introducing the same absolute rule into these Colonies:

For taking away our Charters, abolishing our most valuable Laws, and altering fundamentally the Forms of our Governments:

For suspending our own Legislatures, and declaring themselves invested with Power to legislate for us in all cases whatsoever.

He has abdicated Government here, by declaring us out of his Protection and waging War against us.

He has plundered our seas, ravaged our Coasts, burnt our towns, and destroyed the lives of our people.

He is at this time transporting large armies of foreign mercenaries to compleat the works of death, desolation, and tyranny, already begun with circumstances of Cruelty & perfidy scarcely paralleled in the most barbarous ages, and totally unworthy the Head of a civilized nation.

He has constrained our fellow Citizens taken Captive on the high Seas to bear Arms against their Country, to become the executioners of their friends and Brethren, or to fall themselves by their Hands.

He has excited domestic insurrections amongst us, and has endeavoured to bring on the inhabitants of our frontiers, the merciless Indian Savages, whose known rule of warfare, is an undistinguished destruction of all ages, sexes, and conditions.

In every stage of these Oppressions We have Petitioned for Redress in the most humble terms: Our repeated Petitions have been answered only by repeated injury. A Prince, whose character is thus marked by every act which may define a Tyrant, is unfit to be the ruler of a free people.

Nor have We been wanting in attention to our British brethren. We have warned them from time to time of attempts by their legislature to extend an unwarrantable jurisdiction over us. We have reminded them of the circumstances of our emigration and settlement here. We have appealed to their native justice and magnanimity, and we have conjured them by the ties of our common kindred to disavow these usurpations, which, would inevitably interrupt our connections and correspondence. They too must have been deaf to the voice of justice and of consanguinity. We must, therefore, acquiesce in the necessity, which denounces our Separation, and hold them, as we hold the rest of mankind, Enemies in War, in Peace Friends.

WE, THEREFORE, the Representatives of the UNITED STATES OF AMERICA, in General Congress, Assembled, appealing to the Supreme Judge of the world for the rectitude of our intentions, do, in the Name, and by Authority of the good People of these Colonies, solemnly publish and declare, That these United Colonies are, and of Right ought to be FREE AND INDEPENDENT STATES; that they are Absolved from all Allegiance to the British Crown, and that all political connection between them and the State of Great Britain, is and ought to be totally dissolved; and that as Free and Independent States, they have full Power to levy War, conclude Peace, contract Alliances, establish Commerce, and to do all other Acts and Things which Independent States may of right do. And for the support of this Declaration, with a firm reliance on the Protection of Divine Providence, we mutually pledge to each other our Lives, our Fortunes, and our sacred Honor.

The foregoing Declaration was, by order of Congress, engrossed, and signed by the following members:

John Hancock

NEW HAMPSHIRE
Josiah Bartlett
William Whipple
Matthew Thornton

MASSACHUSETTS BAY
Samuel Adams
John Adams
Robert Treat Paine
Elbridge Gerry

RHODE ISLAND
Stephen Hopkins
William Ellery

CONNECTICUT
Roger Sherman
Samuel Huntington
William Williams
Oliver Wolcott

NEW YORK
William Floyd
Philip Livingston
Francis Lewis
Lewis Morris

NEW JERSEY
Richard Stockton
John Witherspoon
Francis Hopkinson
John Hart
Abraham Clark

PENNSYLVANIA
Robert Morris
Benjamin Rush
Benjamin Franklin
John Morton
George Clymer
James Smith
George Taylor
James Wilson
George Ross

DELAWARE
Caesar Rodney
George Read
Thomas M'Kean

MARYLAND
Samuel Chase
William Paca
Thomas Stone
Charles Carroll, of Carrollton

VIRGINIA
George Wythe
Richard Henry Lee
Thomas Jefferson
Benjamin Harrison
Thomas Nelson, Jr.
Francis Lightfoot Lee
Carter Braxton

NORTH CAROLINA
William Hooper
Joseph Hewes
John Penn

SOUTH CAROLINA
Edward Rutledge
Thomas Heyward, Jr.
Thomas Lynch, Jr.
Arthur Middleton

GEORGIA
Button Gwinnett
Lyman Hall
George Walton

Resolved, That copies of the Declaration be sent to the several assemblies, conventions, and committees, or councils of safety, and to the several commanding officers of the continental troops; that it be proclaimed in each of the United States, at the head of the army.

We the People of the United States, in order to form a more perfect Union, establish Justice, insure domestic Tranquility, provide for the common defence, promote the general Welfare, and secure the Blessings of Liberty to ourselves and our Posterity, do ordain and establish this Constitution for the United States of America.

ARTICLE. I.

Section. 1. All legislative Powers herein granted shall be vested in a Congress of the United States, which shall consist of a Senate and House of Representatives.

Section. 2. The House of Representatives shall be composed of Members chosen every second Year by the People of the several States, and the Electors in each State shall have the Qualifications requisite for Electors of the most numerous Branch of the State Legislature.

No Person shall be a Representative who shall not have attained to the Age of twenty five Years, and been seven Years a Citizen of the United States, and who shall not, when elected, be an Inhabitant of that State in which he shall be chosen.

Representatives and direct Taxes shall be apportioned among the several States which may be included within this Union, according to their respective Numbers, which shall be determined by adding to the whole Number of free Persons, including those bound to Service for a Term of Years, and excluding Indians not taxed, three fifths of all other Persons. The actual Enumeration shall be made within three Years after the first Meeting of the Congress of the United States, and within every subsequent Term of ten Years, in such Manner as they shall by Law direct. The Number of Representatives shall not exceed one for every thirty Thousand, but each State shall have at Least one Representative; and until such enumeration shall be made, the State of New Hampshire shall be entitled to chuse three, Massachusetts eight, Rhode-Island and Providence Plantations one, Connecticut five, New York six, New Jersey four, Pennsylvania eight, Delaware one, Maryland six, Virginia ten, North Carolina five, South Carolina five, and Georgia three.

When vacancies happen in the Representation from any state, the Executive Authority thereof shall issue Writs of Election to fill such Vacancies.

The House of Representatives shall chuse their Speaker and other Officers; and shall have the sole Power of Impeachment.

Section. 3. The Senate of the United States shall be composed of two Senators from each State, chosen by the legislature thereof, for six Years; and each Senator shall have one Vote.

Immediately after they shall be assembled in Consequence of the first Election, they shall be divided as equally as may be into three Classes. The Seats of the Senators of the first Class shall be vacated at the Expiration of the second Year, of the second Class at the Expiration of the fourth Year, and of the third Class at the Expiration of the sixth Year, so that one third may be chosen every second Year; and if Vacancies happen by Resignation, or otherwise, during the Recess of the Legislature of any State, the Executive thereof may make temporary Appointments until the next Meeting of the Legislature, which shall then fill such Vacancies.

No Person shall be a Senator who shall not have attained to the Age of thirty Years, and been nine Years a Citizen of the United States, and who shall not, when elected, be an Inhabitant of that State for which he shall be chosen.

The Vice President of the United States shall be President of the Senate, but shall have no Vote, unless they be equally divided.

The Senate shall chuse their other Officers, and also a President pro tempore, in the Absence of the Vice President, or when he shall exercise the Office of President of the United States.

The Senate shall have the sole Power to try all Impeachments. When sitting for that Purpose, they shall be on Oath or Affirmation. When the President of the United States is tried, the Chief Justice shall preside: And no Person shall be convicted without the Concurrence of two thirds of the Members present.

Judgment in Cases of Impeachment shall not extend further than to removal from Office, and disqualification to hold and enjoy any Office of honor, Trust or Profit under the United States: but the Party convicted shall nevertheless be liable and subject to Indictment, Trial, Judgment and Punishment, according to Law.

Section. 4. The Times, Places and Manner of holding Elections for Senators and Representatives, shall be prescribed in each State by the Legislature thereof; but the Congress may at any time by Law make or alter such Regulations, except as to the Places of chusing Senators.

The Congress shall assemble at least once in every Year, and such Meeting shall be on the first Monday in December, unless they shall by Law appoint a different Day.

Section. 5. Each House shall be the Judge of the Elections, Returns and Qualifications of its own Members, and a Majority of each shall constitute a Quorum to do Business; but a smaller Number may adjourn from day to day, and may be authorized to compel the Attendance of absent Members, in such Manner, and under such Penalties as each House may provide.

Each House may determine the Rules of its Proceedings, punish its Members for disorderly Behaviour, and, with the Concurrence of two thirds, expel a Member.

Each House shall keep a Journal of its Proceedings, and from time to time publish the same, excepting such Parts as may in their Judgment require Secrecy; and the Yeas and Nays of the Members of either House on any question shall, at the Desire of one fifth of those Present, be entered on the Journal.

Neither House, during the Session of Congress, shall, without the Consent of the other, adjourn for more than three days, not to any other Place than that in which the two Houses shall be sitting.

Section. 6. The Senators and Representatives shall receive a Compensation for their Services, to be ascertained by Law, and paid out of the Treasury of the United States. They shall in all Cases, except Treason, Felony and Breach of the Peace, be privileged from Arrest during their Attendance at the Session of their respective Houses, and in going to and returning from the same; and for any Speech or Debate in either House, they shall not be questioned in any other Place.

No Senator or Representative shall, during the Time for which he was elected, be appointed to any civil Office under the Authority of the United States, which shall have been created, or the Emoluments whereof shall have been encreased during such time; and no Person holding any Office under the United States, shall be a Member of either House during his Continuance in Office.

Section. 7. All Bills for raising Revenue shall originate in the House of Representatives; but the Senate may propose or concur with Amendments as on other Bills.

Every Bill which shall have passed the House of Representatives and the Senate shall, before it become a Law, be presented to the President of the United States; If he approve he shall sign it, but if not he shall return it, with his Objections to that House in which it shall have originated, who shall enter the Objections at large on their Journal, and proceed to reconsider it. If after such Reconsideration two thirds of that House shall agree to pass the Bill, it shall be sent, together with the Objections, to the other House, by which it shall likewise be reconsidered, and if approved by two thirds of that House, it shall become a Law. But in all such Cases the Votes of both Houses shall be determined by Yeas and Nays, and the Names of the Persons voting for and against the Bill shall be entered on the Journal of each House respectively. If any Bill shall not be returned by the President within ten Days (Sundays excepted) after it shall have been presented to him, the Same shall be a Law, in like Manner as if he had signed it, unless the Congress by their Adjournment prevent its Return, in which Case it shall not be a Law.

Every Order, Resolution, or Vote to which the Concurrence of the Senate and House of Representatives may be necessary (except on a question of Adjournment) shall be presented to the President of the United States; and before the Same shall take Effect, shall be approved by him, or being disapproved by him, shall be repassed by two thirds of the Senate and House of Representatives, according to the Rules and Limitations prescribed in the Case of a Bill.

Section. 8. The Congress shall have Power To lay and collect Taxes, Duties, Imposts and Excises, to pay the Debts and provide for the common Defence and general Welfare of the United States; but all Duties, Imposts and Excises shall be uniform throughout the United States;

To borrow Money on the credit of the United States;

To regulate Commerce with foreign Nations, and among the several States, and with the Indian Tribes;

To establish an uniform Rule of Naturalization, and uniform Laws on the subject of Bankruptcies throughout the United States;

To coin Money, regulate the Value thereof, and of foreign Coin, and fix the Standard of Weights and Measures;

To provide for the Punishment of counterfeiting the Securities and current Coin of the United States;

To establish Post Offices and Post Roads;

To promote the Progress of Science and useful Arts, by securing for limited Times to Authors and Inventors the exclusive Right to their respective Writings and Discoveries;

To constitute Tribunals inferior to the supreme Court;

To define and punish Piracies and Felonies committed on the high Seas, and Offences against the Law of Nations;

To declare War, grant Letters of Marque and Reprisal, and make Rules concerning Captures on Land and Water;

To raise and support Armies, but no Appropriation of Money to that Use shall be for a longer Term than two Years;

To provide and maintain a Navy;

To make Rules for the Government and Regulation of the land and naval Forces;

To provide for calling forth the Militia to execute the Laws of the Union, suppress Insurrections and repel Invasions;

To provide for organizing, arming, and disciplining, the Militia, and for governing such Part of them as may be employed in the Service of the United States, reserving to the States respectively, the Appointment of the Officers, and the Authority of training the Militia according to the discipline prescribed by Congress;

To exercise exclusive Legislation in all Cases whatsoever, over such District (not exceeding ten Miles square) as may, by Cession of Particular States, and the Acceptance of Congress, become the Seat of the Government of the United States, and to exercise like Authority over all Places purchased by the Consent of the Legislature of the State in which the Same shall be, for the Erection of Forts, Magazines, Arsenals, dock-Yards, and other needful Buildings;—And

To make all Laws which shall be necessary and proper for carrying into Execution the foregoing Powers, and all other Powers vested by this Constitution in the Government of the United States, or in any Department or Officer thereof.

Section. 9. The Migration or Importation of such Persons as any of the States now existing shall think proper to admit, shall not be prohibited by the Congress prior to the Year one thousand eight hundred and eight, but a Tax or duty may be imposed on such Importation, not exceeding ten dollars for each Person.

The Privilege of the Writ of Habeas Corpus shall not be suspended, unless when in Cases of Rebellion or Invasion the public Safety may require it.

No Bill of Attainder or ex post facto Law shall be passed.

No Capitation, or other direct, Tax shall be laid, unless in Proportion to the Census or Enumeration herein before directed to be taken.

No Tax or Duty shall be laid on Articles exported from any State.

No Preference shall be given by any Regulation of Commerce or Revenue to the Ports of one State over those of another: nor shall Vessels bound to, or from, one State, be obliged to enter, clear, or pay Duties in another.

No Money shall be drawn from the Treasury, but in Consequence of Appropriations made by Law; and a regular Statement and Account of the Receipts and Expenditures of all public Money shall be published from time to time.

No Title of Nobility shall be granted by the United States: And no Person holding any Office of Profit or Trust under them, shall, without the Consent of the Congress, accept of any present, Emolument, Office, or Title, of any kind whatever, from any King, Prince, or foreign State.

Section. 10. No State shall enter into any Treaty, Alliance, or Confederation; grant Letters of Marque and Reprisal; coin Money; emit Bills of Credit; make any Thing but gold and silver Coin a Tender in Payment of Debts; pass any Bill of Attainder, ex post facto Law, or Law impairing the Obligation of Contracts, or grant any Title of Nobility.

No State shall, without the Consent of the Congress, lay any Imposts or Duties on Imports or Exports, except what may be absolutely necessary for executing its inspection Laws: and the net Produce of all Duties and Imposts, laid by any State on Imports or Exports, shall be for the Use of the Treasury of the United States; and all such Laws shall be subject to the Revision and Controul of the Congress.

No State shall, without the Consent of Congress, lay any Duty of Tonnage, keep Troops, or Ships of War in time of Peace, enter into any Agreement or Compact with another State, or with a foreign Power, or engage in War, unless actually invaded, or in such imminent Danger as will not admit of delay.

ARTICLE. II.

Section. 1. The executive Power shall be vested in a President of the United States of America. He shall hold his Office during the term of four Years, and, together with the Vice President, chosen for the same Term, be elected, as follows:

Each State shall appoint, in such Manner as the Legislature thereof may direct, a Number of Electors, equal to the whole Number of Senators and Representatives to which the State may be entitled in the Congress: but no Senator or Representative, or Person holding an Office of Trust or Profit under the United States, shall be appointed an Elector.

The Electors shall meet in their respective States, and vote by Ballot for two Persons, of whom one at least shall not be an Inhabitant of the same State with themselves. And they shall make a List of all the Persons voted for, and of the Number of Votes for each; which List they shall sign and certify, and transmit sealed to the Seat of the Government of the United States, directed to the President of the Senate. The President of the Senate shall, in the Presence of the Senate and House of Representatives, open all the Certificates, and the Votes shall then be counted. The Person having the greatest Number of Votes shall be the President, if such Number be a Majority of the whole Number of Electors appointed; and if there be more than one who have such Majority, and have an equal Number of Votes, then the House of Representatives shall immediately chuse by Ballot one of them for President; and if no Person have a Majority, then from the five highest on the List the said House shall in like Manner chuse the President. But in chusing the President, the Votes shall be taken by States, the Representation from each State having one Vote; A quorum for this Purpose shall consist of a Member or Members from two thirds of the States, and a Majority of all the States shall be necessary to a Choice. In every Case, after the Choice of the President, the Person having the greatest Number of Votes of the Electors shall be the Vice President. But if there should remain two or more who have equal Votes, the Senate shall chuse from them by Ballot the Vice President.

The Congress may determine the Time of chusing the Electors, and the Day on which they shall give their Votes; which Day shall be the same throughout the United States.

No Person except a natural born Citizen, or a Citizen of the United States, at the time of the Adoption of this Constitution, shall be eligible to the Office of President; neither shall any Person be eligible to that Office who shall not have attained to the Age of thirty five Years, and been fourteen Years a Resident within the United States.

In Case of the Removal of the President from Office, or of his Death, Resignation, or Inability to discharge the Powers and Duties of the said Office, the Same shall devolve on the Vice President, and the Congress may by Law provide for the Case of Removal, Death, Resignation or Inability, both of the President and Vice President, declaring what Officer shall then act as President, and such Officer shall act accordingly, until the Disability be removed, or a President shall be elected.

The President shall, at stated Times, receive for his Services, a Compensation, which shall neither be encreased or diminished during the Period for which he shall have been elected, and he shall not receive within that Period any other Emolument from the United States, or any of them.

Before he enters on the Execution of his Office, he shall take the following Oath or Affirmation:—"I do solemnly swear (or affirm) that I will faithfully execute the Office of President of the United States, and will to the best of my Ability, preserve, protect and defend the Constitution of the United States."

Section. 2. The President shall be Commander in Chief of the Army and Navy of the United States, and of the Militia of the several States, when called into the actual Service of the United States; he may require the Opinion, in writing, of the principal Officer in each of the executive Departments, upon any Subject relating to the Duties of their respective Offices, and he shall have Power to grant Reprieves and Pardons for Offences against the United States, except in Cases of Impeachment.

He shall have Power, by and with the Advice and Consent of the Senate, to make Treaties, provided two thirds of the Senators present concur; and he shall nominate, and by and with the Advice and Consent of the Senate, shall appoint Ambassadors, other public Ministers and Consuls, Judges of the supreme Court, and all other Officers of the United States, whose Appointments are not herein otherwise provided for, and which shall be established by Law; but the Congress may by Law vest the Appointment of such inferior Officers, as they think proper, in the President alone, in the Courts of Law, or in the Heads of Departments.

The President shall have Power to fill up all Vacancies that may happen during the Recess of the Senate, by granting Commissions which shall expire at the End of their next Session.

Section. 3. He shall from time to time give to the Congress Information of the State of the Union, and recommend to their Consideration such Measures as he shall judge necessary and expedient; he may, on extraordinary Occasions, convene both Houses, or either of them, and in Case of Disagreement between them, with Respect to the Time of Adjournment, he may adjourn them to such Time as he shall think proper; he shall receive Ambassadors and other public Ministers; he shall take Care that the Laws be faithfully executed, and shall Commission all the Officers of the United States.

Section. 4. The President, Vice President and all civil Officers of the United States, shall be removed from Office on Impeachment for, and Conviction of, Treason, Bribery, or other high Crimes and Misdemeanors.

Article. III.

Section. 1. The judicial Power of the United States, shall be vested in one supreme Court, and in such inferior Courts as the Congress may from time to time ordain and establish. The Judges, both of the supreme and inferior Courts, shall hold their Offices during good Behavior, and shall, at stated Times, receive for their Services, a Compensation, which shall not be diminished during their Continuance in Office.

Section. 2. The judicial Power shall extend to all Cases, in Law and Equity, arising under this Constitution, the Laws of the United States, and Treaties made, or which shall be made, under their Authority;—to all Cases affecting Ambassadors, other public Ministers and Consuls;—to all Cases of admiralty and maritime Jurisdiction;—the Controversies to which the United States shall be a Party;—to Controversies between two or more States;—between a State and Citizens of another State;—between Citizens of different States;—between Citizens of the same State claiming Lands under Grants of different States, and between a State, or the Citizens thereof, and foreign States, Citizens or Subjects.

In all cases affecting Ambassadors, other public Ministers and Consuls, and those in which a State shall be Party, the supreme Court shall have original Jurisdiction. In all the other Cases before mentioned, the supreme Court shall have appellate Jurisdiction, both as to Law and Fact, with such Exceptions, and under such Regulations as the Congress shall make.

The Trial of all Crimes, except in Cases of Impeachment, shall be by Jury; and such Trial shall be held in the State where the said Crimes shall have been committed; but when not committed within any State, the Trial shall be at such Place or Places as the Congress may by Law have directed.

Section. 3. Treason against the United States, shall consist only in levying War against them, or in adhering to their Enemies, giving them Aid and Comfort. No Person shall be convicted of Treason unless on the Testimony of two Witnesses to the same overt Act, or on Confession in open Court.

The Congress shall have Power to declare the Punishment of Treason, but no Attainder of Treason shall work Corruption of Blood, or Forfeiture except during the Life of the Person attainted.

Article. IV.

Section. 1. Full Faith and Credit shall be given in each State to the public Acts, Records, and judicial Proceedings of every other State. And the Congress may by general Laws prescribe the Manner in which such Acts, Records and Proceedings shall be proved, and the Effect thereof.

Section. 2. The Citizens of each State shall be entitled to all Privileges and Immunities of Citizens in the several States.

A Person charged in any State with Treason, Felony, or other Crime, who shall flee from Justice, and be found in another State, shall on Demand of the executive Authority of the State from which he fled, be delivered up, to be removed to the State having Jurisdiction of the Crime.

No Person held to Service or Labour in one State, under the Laws thereof, escaping into another, shall, in Consequence of any Law or Regulation therein, be discharged from such Service or Labour, but shall be delivered up on Claim of the Party to whom such Service or Labour may be due.

Section. 3. New States may be admitted by the Congress into this Union; but no new State shall be formed or erected within the Jurisdiction of any other State; nor any State be formed by the Junction of two or more States, or Parts of States, without the consent of the Legislatures of the States concerned as well as of the Congress.

The Congress shall have Power to dispose of and make all needful Rules and Regulations respecting the Territory or other Property belonging to the United States; and nothing in this Constitution shall be so construed as to Prejudice any Claims of the United States, or of any particular States.

Section. 4. The United States shall guarantee to every State in this Union a Republican Form of Government, and shall protect each of them against Invasion; and on Application of the Legislature, or of the Executive (when the Legislature cannot be convened) against domestic Violence.

ARTICLE. V.

The Congress, whenever two thirds of both Houses shall deem it necessary, shall propose Amendments to this Constitution, or, on the Application of the Legislatures of two thirds of the several States, shall call a Convention for proposing Amendments, which, in either Case, shall be valid to all Intents and Purposes, as Part of this Constitution, when ratified by the Legislatures of three fourths of the several States, or by Conventions in three fourths thereof, as the one or the other Mode of Ratification may be proposed by the Congress; Provided that no Amendment which may be made prior to the Year One thousand eight hundred and eight shall in any Manner affect the first and fourth Clauses in the Ninth Section of the first Article; and that no State, without its Consent, shall be deprived of its equal Suffrage in the Senate.

ARTICLE. VI.

All Debts contracted and Engagements entered into, before the Adoption of this Constitution, shall be as valid against the United States under this Constitution, as under the Confederation.

This Constitution, and the Laws of the United States which shall be made in Pursuance thereof; and all Treaties made, or which shall be made, under the Authority of the United States, shall be the supreme Law of the Land; and the Judges in every State shall be bound thereby, any Thing in the Constitution or Laws of any State to the Contrary notwithstanding.

The Senators and Representatives before mentioned, and the Members of the several State Legislatures, and all executive and judicial Officers, both of the United States and of the several States, shall be bound by Oath or Affirmation, to support this Constitution; but no religious Test shall ever be required as a Qualification to any Office or public Trust under the United States.

ARTICLE. VII.

The Ratification of the Conventions of nine States, shall be sufficient for the Establishment of this Constitution between the States so ratifying the Same.

Done in Convention by the Unanimous Consent of the States present the Seventeenth Day of September in the Year of our Lord one thousand seven hundred and Eighty seven and of the Independence of the United States of America the Twelfth. In witness thereof We have hereunto subscribed our Names,

G^o. *WASHINGTON*—Presd^t.
and deputy from Virginia

NEW HAMPSHIRE
John Langdon
Nicholas Gilman

MASSACHUSETTS
Nathaniel Gorham
Rufus King

CONNECTICUT
Wm Saml Johnson
Roger Sherman

NEW YORK
Alexander Hamilton

NEW JERSEY
Wil: Livingston
David A. Brearley
Wm Paterson
Jona: Dayton

PENNSYLVANIA
B Franklin
Thomas Mifflin
Robt Morris
Geo. Clymer
Thos FitzSimons
Jared Ingersoll
James Wilson
Gouv Morris

DELAWARE
Geo: Read
Gunning Bedford jun
John Dickinson
Richard Bassett
Jaco: Broom

MARYLAND
James McHenry
Dan of St Thos Jenifer
Danl Carroll

VIRGINIA
John Blair—
James Madison Jr.

NORTH CAROLINA
Wm Blount
Richd Dobbs Spaight
Hu Williamson

SOUTH CAROLINA
J. Rutledge
Charles Cotesworth Pinckney
Charles Pinckney
Pierce Butler

GEORGIA
William Few
Abr Baldwin

AMENDMENTS TO THE CONSTITUTION

Articles in addition to, and Amendment of the Constitution of the United States of America, proposed by Congress, and ratified by the Legislatures of the several States, pursuant to the fifth Article of the original Constitution.

AMENDMENT I.*

Congress shall make no law respecting an establishment of religion, or prohibiting the free exercise thereof; or abridging the freedom of speech, or of the press; or the right of the people peaceably to assemble, and to petition the Government for a redress of grievances.

AMENDMENT II.

A well regulated Militia, being necessary to the security of a free State, the right of the people to keep and bear Arms, shall not be infringed.

AMENDMENT III.

No Soldier shall, in time of peace be quartered in any house, without the consent of the Owner, nor in time of war, but in a manner to be prescribed by law.

AMENDMENT IV.

The right of the people to be secure in their persons, houses, papers, and effects, against unreasonable searches and seizures, shall not be violated, and no Warrants shall issue, but upon probable cause, supported by Oath or affirmation, and particularly describing the place to be searched, and the persons or things to be seized.

AMENDMENT V.

No person shall be held to answer for a capital, or otherwise infamous crime, unless on a presentment or indictment of a Grand Jury, except in cases arising in the land or naval forces, or in the Militia, when in actual service in time of War or public danger; nor shall any person be subject for the same offence to be twice put in jeopardy of life or limb; nor shall be compelled in any criminal case to be a witness against himself, nor be deprived of life, liberty, or property, without due process of law; nor shall private property be taken for public use, without just compensation.

AMENDMENT VI.

In all criminal prosecutions, the accused shall enjoy the right to a speedy and public trial, by an impartial jury of the State and district wherein the crime shall have been committed, which district shall have been previously ascertained by law, and to be informed of the nature and cause of the accusation; to be confronted with the witnesses against him; to have compulsory process for obtaining witnesses in his favor, and to have the Assistance of Counsel for his defence.

AMENDMENT VII.

In Suits at common law, where the value in controversy shall exceed twenty dollars, the right of trial by jury shall be preserved, and no fact tried by a jury, shall be otherwise re-examined in any Court of the United States, than according to the rules of the common law.

AMENDMENT VIII.

Excessive bail shall not be required, nor excessive fines imposed, nor cruel and unusual punishments inflicted.

AMENDMENT IX.

The enumeration in the Constitution, of certain rights, shall not be construed to deny or disparage others retained by the people.

AMENDMENT X.

The powers not delegated to the United States by the Constitution, nor prohibited by it to the States, are reserved to the States respectively, or to the people.

AMENDMENT XI.

The Judicial power of the United States shall not be construed to extend to any suit in law or equity, commenced or prosecuted against one of the United States by Citizens of another State, or by Citizens or Subjects of any Foreign State. [January 8, 1798]

AMENDMENT XII.

The Electors shall meet in their respective states, and vote by ballot for President and Vice-President, one of whom, at least, shall not be an inhabitant of the same state with themselves; they shall name in their ballots the person voted for as President, and in distinct ballots the person voted for as Vice-President, and they shall make distinct lists of all persons voted for as President, and of all persons voted for as Vice President, and of the number of votes for each, which lists they shall sign and certify, and transmit sealed to the seat of the government of the United States, directed to the President of the Senate;—The President of the Senate shall, in the presence of the Senate and

*The first ten Amendments (the Bill of Rights) were ratified in 1791.

House of Representatives, open all the certificates and the votes shall then be counted;—The person having the greatest number of votes for President, shall be the President, if such number be a majority of the whole number of Electors appointed; and if no person have such majority, then from the persons having the highest numbers not exceeding three on the list of those voted for as President, the House of Representatives shall choose immediately, by ballot, the President. But in choosing the President, the votes shall be taken by states, the representation from each state having one vote; a quorum for this purpose shall consist of a member or members from two-thirds of the states, and a majority of all the states shall be necessary to a choice. And if the House of Representatives shall not choose a President whenever the right of choice shall devolve upon them, before the fourth day of March next following, then the Vice-President shall act as President, as in the case of the death or other constitutional disability of the President.—The person having the greatest number of votes as Vice-President, shall be the Vice-President, if such number be a majority of the whole number of Electors appointed, and if no person have a majority, then from the two highest numbers on the list, the Senate shall choose the Vice-President; a quorum for the purpose shall consist of two-thirds of the whole number of Senators, and a majority of the whole number shall be necessary to a choice. But no person constitutionally ineligible to the office of President shall be eligible to that of Vice-President of the United States. [September 25, 1804]

AMENDMENT XIII.

Section 1. Neither slavery nor involuntary servitude, except as a punishment for crime whereof the party shall have been duly convicted, shall exist within the United States, or any place subject to their jurisdiction.

Section 2. Congress shall have power to enforce this article by appropriate legislation. [December 18, 1865]

AMENDMENT XIV.

Section 1. All persons born or naturalized in the United States, and subject to the jurisdiction thereof, are citizens of the United States and of the State wherein they reside. No State shall make or enforce any law which shall abridge the privileges or immunities of citizens of the United States; nor shall any State deprive any person of life, liberty, or property, without due process of law; nor deny to any person within its jurisdiction the equal protection of the laws.

Section 2. Representatives shall be apportioned among the several States according to their respective numbers, counting the whole number of persons in each State, excluding Indians not taxed. But when the right to vote at any election for the choice of electors for President and Vice President of the United States, Representatives in Congress, the Executive and Judicial officers of a State, or the members of the Legislature thereof, is denied to any of the male inhabitants of such State, being twenty-one years of age, and citizens of the United States, or in any way abridged, except for participation in rebellion, or other crime, the basis of representation therein shall be reduced in the proportion which the number of such male citizens shall bear to the whole number of male citizens twenty-one years of age in such State.

Section 3. No person shall be a Senator or Representative in Congress, or elector of President and Vice President, or hold any office, civil or military, under the United States, or under any State, who, having previously taken an oath, as a member of Congress, or as an officer of the United States, or as a member of any State legislature, or as an executive or judicial officer of any State, to support the Constitution of the United States, shall have engaged in insurrection or rebellion against the same, or given aid or comfort to the enemies thereof. But Congress may by a vote of two-thirds of each House, remove such disability.

Section 4. The validity of the public debt of the United States, authorized by law, including debts incurred for payment of pensions and bounties for services in suppressing insurrection or rebellion, shall not be questioned. But neither the United States nor any State shall assume or pay any debt or obligation incurred in aid of insurrection or rebellion against the United States, or any claim for the loss or emancipation of any slave; but all such debts, obligations and claims shall be held illegal and void.

Section 5. The Congress shall have power to enforce, by appropriate legislation, the provisions of this article. [July 28, 1868]

AMENDMENT XV.

Section 1. The right of citizens of the United States to vote shall not be denied or abridged by the United States or by any State on account of race, color, or previous condition of servitude—

Section 2. The Congress shall have power to enforce this article by appropriate legislation. [March 30, 1870]

AMENDMENT XVI.

The Congress shall have power to lay and collect taxes on incomes, from whatever source derived, without apportionment among the several States, and without regard to any census or enumeration. [February 25, 1913]

AMENDMENT XVII.

The Senate of the United States shall be composed of two senators from each State, elected by the people thereof, for six years; and each Senator shall have one vote. The electors in each State shall have the qualifications requisite for electors of the most numerous branch of the State legislatures.

When vacancies happen in the representation of any State in the Senate, the executive authority of such State shall issue writs of election to fill such vacancies: *Provided,* That the legislature of any State may empower the executive thereof to make temporary appointments until the people fill the vacancies by election as the legislature may direct.

This amendment shall not be so construed as to affect the election or term of any senator chosen before it becomes valid as part of the Constitution. [May 31, 1913]

AMENDMENT XVIII.

After one year from the ratification of this article, the manufacture, sale, or transportation of intoxicating liquors within, the importation thereof into, or the exportation thereof from the United States and all territory subject to the jurisdiction thereof for beverage purposes is hereby prohibited.

The Congress and the several States shall have concurrent power to enforce this article by appropriate legislation.

This article shall be inoperative unless it shall have been ratified as an amendment to the Constitution by the legislatures of the several States, as provided in the Constitution, within seven years from the date of the submission thereof to the States by Congress. [January 29, 1919]

AMENDMENT XIX.

The right of citizens of the United States to vote shall not be denied or abridged by the United States or by any State on account of sex.

The Congress shall have power by appropriate legislation to enforce the provisions of this article. [August 26, 1920]

AMENDMENT XX.

Section 1. The terms of the President and Vice-President shall end at noon on the twentieth day of January, and the terms of Senators and Representatives at noon on the third day of January, of the years in which such terms would have ended if this article had not been ratified; and the terms of their successors shall then begin.

Section 2. The Congress shall assemble at least once in every year, and such meeting shall begin at noon on the third day of January, unless they shall by law appoint a different day.

Section 3. If, at the time fixed for the beginning of the term of the President, the President-elect shall have died, the Vice-President-elect shall become President. If a President shall not have been chosen before the time fixed for the beginning of his term, or if the President-elect shall have failed to qualify,

then the Vice-President-elect shall act as President until a President shall have qualified; and the Congress may by law provide for the case wherein neither a President-elect nor a Vice-President-elect shall have qualified, declaring who shall then act as President, or the manner in which one who is to act shall be selected, and such person shall act accordingly until a President or Vice-President shall have qualified.

Section 4. The Congress may by law provide for the case of the death of any of the persons from whom the House of Representatives may choose a President whenever the right of choice shall have devolved upon them, and for the case of the death of any of the persons from whom the Senate may choose a Vice-President whenever the right of choice shall have devolved upon them.

Section 5. Sections 1 and 2 shall take effect on the 15th day of October following the ratification of this article.

Section 6. This article shall be inoperative unless it shall have been ratified as an amendment to the Constitution by the legislatures of three-fourths of the several States within seven years from the date of its submission. [February 6, 1933]

AMENDMENT XXI.

Section 1. The eighteenth article of amendment to the Constitution of the United States is hereby repealed.

Section 2. The transportation or importation into any State, Territory or possession of the United States for delivery or use therein of intoxicating liquors, in violation of the laws thereof, is hereby prohibited.

Section 3. This article shall be inoperative unless it shall have been ratified as an amendment to the Constitution by convention in the several States, as provided in the Constitution, within seven years from the date of the submission thereof to the States by the Congress. [December 5, 1933]

AMENDMENT XXII.

Section 1. No person shall be elected to the office of the President more than twice, and no person who has held the office of President, or acted as President, for more than two years of a term to which some other person was elected President shall be elected to the office of the President more than once. But this Article shall not apply to any person holding the office of President when this Article was proposed by the Congress, and shall not prevent any person who may be holding the office of President, or acting as President, during the term within which this Article becomes operative from holding the office of President or acting as President during the remainder of such term.

Section 2. This article shall be inoperative unless it shall have been ratified as an amendment to the Constitution by the legislatures of three-fourths of the several States within seven years from the date of its submission to the States by the Congress. [February 27, 1951]

AMENDMENT XXIII.

Section 1. The District constituting the seat of government of the United States shall appoint in such manner as the Congress may direct:

A number of electors of President and Vice-President equal to the whole number of Senators and Representatives in Congress to which the District would be entitled if it were a State, but in no event more than the least populous State; they shall be in addition to those appointed by the States, but they shall be considered, for the purposes of the election of President and Vice-President, to be electors appointed by a State; and they shall meet in the District and perform such duties as provided by the twelfth article of amendment.

Section 2. The Congress shall have the power to enforce this article by appropriate legislation. [March 29, 1961]

AMENDMENT XXIV.

Section 1. The right of citizens of the United States to vote in any primary or other election for President or Vice President, for electors for President or Vice President, or for Senator or Representative in Congress, shall not be denied or abridged by the United States or any State by reason of failure to pay any poll tax or other tax.

Section 2. The Congress shall have power to enforce this article by appropriate legislation. [January 23, 1964]

AMENDMENT XXV.

Section 1. In case of the removal of the President from office or of his death or resignation, the Vice President shall become President.

Section 2. Whenever there is a vacancy in the office of Vice President, the President shall nominate a Vice President who shall take office upon confirmation by a majority vote of both Houses of Congress.

Section 3. Whenever the President transmits to the President pro tempore of the Senate and the Speaker of the House of Representatives his written declaration that he is unable to discharge the powers and duties of his office, and until he

transmits to them a written declaration to the contrary, such powers and duties shall be discharged by the Vice President as Acting President.

Section 4. Whenever the Vice President and a majority of either the principal officers of the executive departments or of such other body as Congress may by law provide, transmit to the President pro tempore of the Senate and the Speaker of the House of Representatives their written declaration that the President is unable to discharge the powers and duties of his office, the Vice President shall immediately assume the powers and duties of the office as Acting President.

Thereafter, when the President transmits to the President pro tempore of the Senate and the Speaker of the House of Representatives his written declaration that no inability exists, he shall resume the powers and duties of his office unless the Vice President and a majority of either the principal officers of the executive departments or of such other body as Congress may by law provide, transmit within four days to the President pro tempore of the Senate and the Speaker of the House of Representatives their written declaration that the President is unable to discharge the powers and duties of his office. Thereupon Congress shall decide the issue, assembling within forty-eight hours for that purpose if not in session. If the Congress, within twenty-one days after receipt of the latter written declaration, or, if Congress is not in session, within twenty-one days after Congress is required to assemble, determines by two-thirds vote of both Houses that the President is unable to discharge the powers and duties of his office, the Vice President shall continue to discharge the same as Acting President; otherwise, the President shall resume the powers and duties of his office. [February 10, 1967]

AMENDMENT XXVI.

Section 1. The right of citizens of the United States, who are eighteen years of age or older, to vote shall not be denied or abridged by the United States or by any State on account of age.

Section 2. The Congress shall have power to enforce this article by appropriate legislation. [June 30, 1971]

AMENDMENT XXVII.

No law, varying the compensation for the services of the Senators and Representatives shall take effect, until an election of Representatives shall have intervened. [May 8, 1992]

FROM GEORGE WASHINGTON'S FAREWELL ADDRESS (1796)

Friends and Citizens:

The period for a new election of a citizen to administer the executive government of the United States being not far distant, and the time actually arrived when your thoughts must be employed in designating the person who is to be clothed with that important trust, it appears to me proper, especially as it may conduce to a more distinct expression of the public voice, that I should now apprise you of the resolution I have formed, to decline being considered among the number of those out of whom a choice is to be made.

* * *

In looking forward to the moment which is intended to terminate the career of my public life, my feelings do not permit me to suspend the deep acknowledgment of that debt of gratitude which I owe to my beloved country for the many honors it has conferred upon me; still more for the steadfast confidence with which it has supported me; and for the opportunities I have thence enjoyed of manifesting my inviolable attachment, by services faithful and persevering, though in usefulness unequal to my zeal. If benefits have resulted to our country from these services, let it always be remembered to your praise, and as an instructive example in our annals, that under circumstances in which the passions, agitated in every direction, were liable to mislead, amidst appearances sometimes dubious, vicissitudes of fortune often discouraging, in situations in which not unfrequently want of success has countenanced the spirit of criticism, the constancy of your support was the essential prop of the efforts, and a guarantee of the plans by which they were effected. Profoundly penetrated with this idea, I shall carry it with me to my grave, as a strong incitement to unceasing vows that heaven may continue to you the choicest tokens of its beneficence; that your union and brotherly affection may be perpetual; that the free Constitution, which is the work of your hands, may be sacredly maintained; that its administration in every department may be stamped with wisdom and virtue; that, in fine, the happiness of the people of these States, under the auspices of liberty, may be made complete by so careful a preservation and so prudent a use of this blessing as will acquire to them the glory of recommending it to the applause, the affection, and adoption of every nation which is yet a stranger to it.

Here, perhaps, I ought to stop. But a solicitude for your welfare, which cannot end but with my life, and the apprehension of danger, natural to that solicitude, urge me, on an occasion like the present, to offer to your solemn contemplation, and to recommend to your frequent review, some sentiments which are the result of much reflection, of no inconsiderable observation, and which appear to me all-important to the permanency of your felicity as a people. These will be offered to you with the more freedom, as you can only see in them the disinterested warnings of a parting friend, who can possibly have no personal motive to bias his counsel. Nor can I forget, as an encouragement to it, your indulgent reception of my sentiments on a former and not dissimilar occasion.

Interwoven as is the love of liberty with every ligament of your hearts, no recommendation of mine is necessary to fortify or confirm the attachment.

The unity of government which constitutes you one people is also now dear to you. It is justly so, for it is a main pillar in the edifice of your real independence, the support of your tranquility at home, your peace abroad; of your safety; of your prosperity; of that very liberty which you so highly prize. But as it is easy to foresee that, from different causes and from different quarters, much pains will be taken, many artifices employed to weaken in your minds the conviction of this truth; as this is the point in your political fortress against which the batteries of internal and external enemies will be most constantly and actively (though often covertly and insidiously) directed, it is of infinite moment that you should properly estimate the immense value of your national union to your collective and individual happiness; that you should cherish a cordial, habitual, and immovable attachment to it; accustoming yourselves to think and speak of it as of the palladium of your political safety and prosperity; watching for its preservation with jealous anxiety; discountenancing whatever may suggest even a suspicion that it can in any event be abandoned; and indignantly frowning upon the first dawning of every attempt to alienate any portion of our country from the rest, or to enfeeble the sacred ties which now link together the various parts.

For this you have every inducement of sympathy and interest. Citizens, by birth or choice, of a common country, that country has a right to concentrate your affections. The name of American, which belongs to you in your national capacity, must always exalt the just pride of patriotism more than any appellation derived from local discriminations. With slight shades of difference, you have the same religion, manners, habits, and political principles. You have in a common cause fought and triumphed together; the independence and liberty you possess are the work of joint counsels, and joint efforts of common dangers, sufferings, and successes.

But these considerations, however powerfully they address themselves to your sensibility, are greatly outweighed by those which apply more immediately to your interest. Here every portion of our country finds the most commanding motives for carefully guarding and preserving the union of the whole.

The North, in an unrestrained intercourse with the South, protected by the equal laws of a common government, finds in the productions of the latter great additional resources of maritime and commercial enterprise and precious materials of manufacturing industry. The South, in the same intercourse, benefiting by the agency of the North, sees its agriculture grow and its commerce expand. Turning partly into its own channels the seamen of the North, it finds its particular navigation invigorated; and, while it contributes, in different ways, to nourish and increase the general mass of the national navigation, it looks forward to the protection of a maritime strength, to which itself is unequally adapted. The East, in a like intercourse with the West, already finds, and in the progressive improvement of interior communications by land and water, will more and more find a valuable vent for the commodities which it brings from abroad, or manufactures at home. The West derives from the East supplies requisite to its growth and comfort, and, what is perhaps of still greater consequence, it must of necessity owe the secure enjoyment of indispensable outlets for its own productions to the weight, influence, and the future maritime strength of the Atlantic side of the Union, directed by an indissoluble community of interest as one nation. Any other tenure by which the West can hold this essential advantage, whether derived from its own separate strength, or from an apostate and unnatural connection with any foreign power, must be intrinsically precarious.

While, then, every part of our country thus feels an immediate and particular interest in union, all the parts combined cannot fail to find in the united mass of means and efforts greater strength, greater resource, proportionably greater security from external danger, a less frequent interruption of their peace by foreign nations; and, what is of inestimable value, they must derive from union an exemption from those broils and wars between themselves, which so frequently afflict neighboring countries not tied together by the same governments, which their own rival ships alone would be sufficient to produce, but which opposite foreign alliances, attachments, and intrigues would stimulate and embitter. Hence, likewise, they will avoid the necessity of those overgrown military establishments which, under any form of government, are inauspicious to liberty, and which are to be regarded as particularly hostile to republican liberty. In this sense it is that your union ought to be considered as a main prop of your liberty, and that the love of the one ought to endear to you the preservation of the other.

These considerations speak a persuasive language to every reflecting and virtuous mind, and exhibit the continuance of the Union as a primary object of patriotic desire. Is there a doubt whether a common government can embrace so large a sphere? Let experience solve it. To listen to mere speculation in such a case were criminal. We are authorized to hope that a proper organization of the whole with the auxiliary agency of governments for the respective subdivisions, will afford a happy issue to the experiment. It is well worth a fair and full experiment. With such powerful and obvious motives to union, affecting all parts of our country, while experience

shall not have demonstrated its impracticability, there will always be reason to distrust the patriotism of those who in any quarter may endeavor to weaken its bands.

* * *

To the efficacy and permanency of your Union, a government for the whole is indispensable. No alliance, however strict, between the parts can be an adequate substitute; they must inevitably experience the infractions and interruptions which all alliances in all times have experienced. Sensible of this momentous truth, you have improved upon your first essay, by the adoption of a constitution of government better calculated than your former for an intimate union, and for the efficacious management of your common concerns. This government, the offspring of our own choice, uninfluenced and unawed, adopted upon full investigation and mature deliberation, completely free in its principles, in the distribution of its powers, uniting security with energy, and containing within itself a provision for its own amendment, has a just claim to your confidence and your support. Respect for its authority, compliance with its laws, acquiescence in its measures, are duties enjoined by the fundamental maxims of true liberty. The basis of our political systems is the right of the people to make and to alter their constitutions of government. But the Constitution which at any time exists, till changed by an explicit and authentic act of the whole people, is sacredly obligatory upon all. The very idea of the power and the right of the people to establish government presupposes the duty of every individual to obey the established government.

* * *

I have already intimated to you the danger of parties in the State, with particular reference to the founding of them on geographical discriminations. Let me now take a more comprehensive view, and warn you in the most solemn manner against the baneful effects of the spirit of party generally.

This spirit, unfortunately, is inseparable from our nature, having its root in the strongest passions of the human mind. It exists under different shapes in all governments, more or less stifled, controlled, or repressed; but, in those of the popular form, it is seen in its greatest rankness, and is truly their worst enemy.

The alternate domination of one faction over another, sharpened by the spirit of revenge, natural to party dissension, which in different ages and countries has perpetrated the most horrid enormities, is itself a frightful despotism. But this leads at length to a more formal and permanent despotism. The disorders and miseries which result gradually incline the minds of men to seek security and repose in the absolute power of an individual; and sooner or later the chief of some prevailing faction, more able or more fortunate than his competitors, turns this disposition to the purposes of his own elevation, on the ruins of public liberty.

Without looking forward to an extremity of this kind (which nevertheless ought not to be entirely out of sight), the common and continual mischiefs of the spirit of party are sufficient to make it the interest and duty of a wise people to discourage and restrain it.

It serves always to distract the public councils and enfeeble the public administration. It agitates the community with ill-founded jealousies and false alarms, kindles the animosity of one part against another, foments occasionally riot and insurrection. It opens the door to foreign influence and corruption, which finds a facilitated access to the government itself through the channels of party passions. Thus the policy and the will of one country are subjected to the policy and will of another.

There is an opinion that parties in free countries are useful checks upon the administration of the government and serve to keep alive the spirit of liberty. This within certain limits is probably true; and in governments of a monarchical cast, patriotism may look with indulgence, if not with favor, upon the spirit of party. But in those of the popular character, in governments purely elective, it is a spirit not to be encouraged. From their natural tendency, it is certain there will always be enough of that spirit for every salutary purpose. And there being constant danger of excess, the effort ought to be by force of public opinion, to mitigate and assuage it. A fire not to be quenched, it demands a uniform vigilance to prevent its bursting into a flame, lest, instead of warming, it should consume.

It is important, likewise, that the habits of thinking in a free country should inspire caution in those entrusted with its administration, to confine themselves within their respective constitutional spheres, avoiding in the exercise of the powers of one department to encroach upon another. The spirit of encroachment tends to consolidate the powers of all the departments in one, and thus to create, whatever the form of government, a real despotism. A just estimate of that love of power, and proneness to abuse it, which predominates in the human heart, is sufficient to satisfy us of the truth of this position. The necessity of reciprocal checks in the exercise of political power, by dividing and distributing it into different depositaries, and constituting each the guardian of the public weal against invasions by the others, has been evinced by experiments ancient and modern; some of them in our country and under our own eyes. To preserve them must be as necessary as to institute them. If, in the opinion of the people, the distribution or modification of the constitutional powers be in any particular wrong, let it be corrected by an amendment in the way which the Constitution designates. But let there be no change by usurpation; for though this, in one instance, may be the instrument of good, it is the customary weapon by which free governments are destroyed. The precedent must always greatly overbalance in permanent evil any partial or transient benefit, which the use can at any time yield.

* * *

Observe good faith and justice towards all nations; cultivate peace and harmony with all. Religion and morality enjoin this conduct; and can it be, that good policy does not equally enjoin it? It will be worthy of a free, enlightened, and at no distant period, a great nation, to give to mankind the magnanimous and too novel example of a people always guided by an exalted justice and benevolence. Who can doubt that, in the course of time and things, the fruits of such a plan would richly repay any temporary advantages which might be lost by a steady adherence to it? Can it be that Providence has not connected the permanent felicity of a nation with its virtue? The experiment, at least, is recommended by every sentiment which ennobles human nature. Alas! is it rendered impossible by its vices?

In the execution of such a plan, nothing is more essential than that permanent, inveterate antipathies against particular nations, and passionate attachments for others, should be excluded; and that, in place of them, just and amicable feelings towards all should be cultivated. The nation which indulges towards another a habitual hatred or a habitual fondness is in some degree a slave. It is a slave to its animosity or to its affection, either of which is sufficient to lead it astray from its duty and its interest. Antipathy in one nation against another disposes each more readily to offer insult and injury, to lay hold of slight causes of umbrage, and to be haughty and intractable, when accidental or trifling occasions of dispute occur. Hence, frequent collisions, obstinate, envenomed, and bloody contests. The nation, prompted by ill-will and resentment, sometimes impels to war the government, contrary to the best calculations of policy. The government sometimes participates in the national propensity, and adopts through passion what reason would reject; at other times it makes the animosity of the nation subservient to projects of hostility instigated by pride, ambition, and other sinister and pernicious motives. The peace often, sometimes perhaps the liberty, of nations, has been the victim.

* * *

The great rule of conduct for us in regard to foreign nations is in extending our commercial relations, to have with them as little political connection as possible. So far as we have already formed engagements, let them be fulfilled with perfect good faith. Here let us stop. Europe has a set of primary interests which to us have none; or a very remote relation. Hence she must be engaged in frequent controversies, the causes of which are essentially foreign to our concerns. Hence, therefore, it must be unwise in us to implicate ourselves by artificial ties in the ordinary vicissitudes of her politics, or the ordinary combinations and collisions of her friendships or enmities.

Our detached and distant situation invites and enables us to pursue a different course. If we remain one people under an efficient government, the period is not far off when we may defy material injury from external annoyance; when we may take such an attitude as will cause the neutrality we may at any time resolve upon to be scrupulously respected; when belligerent nations, under the impossibility of making acquisitions upon us, will not lightly hazard the giving us provocation; when we may choose peace or war, as our interest, guided by justice, shall counsel.

Why forego the advantages of so peculiar a situation? Why quit our own to stand upon foreign ground? Why, by interweaving our destiny with that of any part of Europe, entangle our peace and prosperity in the toils of European ambition, rivalship, interest, humor or caprice?

It is our true policy to steer clear of permanent alliances with any portion of the foreign world; so far, I mean, as we are now at liberty to do it; for let me not be understood as capable of patronizing infidelity to existing engagements. I hold the maxim no less applicable to public than to private affairs, that honesty is always the best policy. I repeat it, therefore, let those engagements be observed in their genuine sense. But, in my opinion, it is unnecessary and would be unwise to extend them.

Taking care always to keep ourselves by suitable establishments on a respectable defensive posture, we may safely trust to temporary alliances for extraordinary emergencies.

Harmony, liberal intercourse with all nations, are recommended by policy, humanity, and interest. But even our commercial policy should hold an equal and impartial hand; neither seeking nor granting exclusive favors or preferences; consulting the natural course of things; diffusing and diversifying by gentle means the streams of commerce, but forcing nothing; establishing (with powers so disposed, in order to give trade a stable course, to define the rights of our merchants, and to enable the government to support them) conventional rules of intercourse, the best that present circumstances and mutual opinion will permit, but temporary, and liable to be from time to time abandoned or varied, as experience and circumstances shall dictate; constantly keeping in view that it is folly in one nation to look for disinterested favors from another; that it must pay with a portion of its independence for whatever it may accept under that character; that, by such acceptance, it may place itself in the condition of having given equivalents for nominal favors, and yet of being reproached with ingratitude for not giving more.

* * *

Relying on its kindness in this as in other things, and actuated by that fervent love towards it, which is so natural to a man who views in it the native soil of himself and his progenitors for several generations, I anticipate with pleasing expectation that retreat in which I promise myself to realize, without alloy, the sweet enjoyment of partaking, in the midst of my fellow-citizens, the benign influence of good laws under a free government, the ever-favorite object of my heart, and the happy reward, as I trust, of our mutual cares, labors, and dangers.

Geo. Washington

The Seneca Falls Declaration of Sentiments and Resolutions (1848)

1. Declaration of Sentiments

When, in the course of human events, it becomes necessary for one portion of the family of man to assume among the people of the earth a position different from that which they have hitherto occupied, but one to which the laws of nature and of nature's God entitle them, a decent respect to the opinions of mankind requires that they should declare the causes that impel them to such a course.

We hold these truths to be self-evident: that all men and women are created equal; that they are endowed by their Creator with certain inalienable rights; that among these are life, liberty, and the pursuit of happiness; that to secure these rights governments are instituted, deriving their just powers from the consent of the governed. Whenever any form of government becomes destructive of these ends, it is the right of those who suffer from it to refuse allegiance to it, and to insist upon the institution of a new government, laying its foundation on such principles, and organizing its powers in such form, as to them shall seem most likely to effect their safety and happiness. Prudence, indeed, will dictate that governments long established should not be changed for light and transient causes; and accordingly all experience hath shown that mankind are more disposed to suffer, while evils are sufferable, than to right themselves by abolishing the forms to which they are accustomed. But when a long train of abuses and usurpations, pursuing invariably the same object, evinces a design to reduce them under absolute despotism, it is their duty to throw off such government, and to provide new guards for their future security. Such has been the patient sufferance of the women under this government, and such is now the necessity which constrains them to demand the equal station to which they are entitled. The history of mankind is a history of repeated injuries and usurpations on the part of man toward woman, having in direct object the establishment of an absolute tyranny over her. To prove this, let facts be submitted to a candid world.

He has never permitted her to exercise her inalienable right to the elective franchise.

He has compelled her to submit to laws, in the formation of which she had no voice.

He has withheld from her rights which are given to the most ignorant and degraded men—both natives and foreigners.

Having deprived her of this first right of a citizen, the elective franchise, thereby leaving her without representation in the halls of legislation, he has oppressed her on all sides.

He has made her, if married, in the eye of the law, civilly dead. He has taken from her all right in property, even to the wages she earns.

He has made her, morally, an irresponsible being, as she can commit many crimes with impunity, provided they be done in the presence of her husband.

In the covenant of marriage, she is compelled to promise obedience to her husband, he becoming, to all intents and purposes, her master—the law giving him power to deprive her of her liberty, and to administer chastisement.

He has so framed the laws of divorce, as to what shall be the proper causes, and in case of separation, to whom the guardianship of the children shall be given, as to be wholly regardless of the happiness of women—the law, in all cases, going upon a false supposition of the supremacy of man, and giving all power into his hands.

After depriving her of all rights as a married woman, if single, and the owner of property, he has taxed her to support a government which recognizes her only when her property can be made profitable to it.

He has monopolized nearly all the profitable employments, and from those she is permitted to follow, she receives but a scanty remuneration. He closes against her all the avenues to wealth and distinction which he considers most honorable to himself. As a teacher of theology, medicine, or law, she is not known.

He has denied her the facilities for obtaining a thorough education, all colleges being closed against her.

He allows her in Church, as well as State, but a subordinate position, claiming Apostolic authority for her exclusion from the ministry, and, with some exceptions, from any public participation in the affairs of the Church.

He has created a false public sentiment by giving to the world a different code of morals for men and women, by which moral delinquencies which exclude women from society, are not only tolerated, but deemed of little account in man.

He has usurped the prerogative of Jehovah himself, claiming it as his right to assign for her a sphere of action, when that belongs to her conscience and to her God.

He has endeavored, in every way that he could, to destroy her confidence in her own powers, to lessen her self-respect and to make her willing to lead a dependent and abject life.

Now, in view of this entire disfranchisement of one-half the people of this country, their social and religious degradation—in view of the unjust laws above mentioned, and because women do feel themselves aggrieved, oppressed, and fraudulently deprived of their most sacred rights, we insist that they have immediate admission to all the rights and privileges which belong to them as citizens of the United States.

In entering upon the great work before us, we anticipate no small amount of misconception, misrepresentation, and ridicule; but we shall use every instrumentality within our power to effect our object. We shall employ agents, circulate tracts, petition the State and National legislatures, and endeavor to enlist the pulpit and the press in our behalf. We hope this Convention will be followed by a series of Conventions embracing every part of the country.

2. Resolutions

WHEREAS, The great precept of nature is conceded to be, that "man shall pursue his own true and substantial happiness." Blackstone in his Commentaries remarks, that this law of Nature being coeval with mankind, and dictated by God himself, is of course superior in obligation to any other. It is binding over all the globe, in all countries and at all times; no human laws are of any validity if contrary to this, and such of them as are valid, derive all their force, and all their validity, and all their authority, mediately and immediately, from this original; therefore,

Resolved, That such laws as conflict, in any way, with the true and substantial happiness of woman, are contrary to the great precept of nature and of no validity, for this is "superior in obligation to any other."

Resolved, That all laws which prevent woman from occupying such a station in society as her conscience shall dictate, or which place her in a position inferior to that of man, are contrary to the great precept of nature, and therefore of no force or authority.

Resolved, That woman is man's equal—was intended to be so by the Creator, and the highest good of the race demands that she should be recognized as such.

Resolved, That the women of this country ought to be enlightened in regard to the laws under which they live, that they may no longer publish their degradation by declaring themselves satisfied with their present position, nor their ignorance, by asserting that they have all the rights they want.

Resolved, That inasmuch as man, while claiming for himself intellectual superiority, does accord to woman moral superiority, it is pre-eminently his duty to encourage her to speak and teach, as she has an opportunity, in all religious assemblies.

Resolved, That the same amount of virtue, delicacy, and refinement of behavior that is required of woman in the social state, should also be required of man, and the same transgressions should be visited with equal severity on both man and woman.

Resolved, That the objection of indelicacy and impropriety, which is so often brought against woman when she addresses a public audience, comes with a very ill-grace from those who encourage, by their attendance, her appearance on the stage, in the concert. Or in feats of the circus.

Resolved, That woman has too long rested satisfied in the circumscribed limits which corrupt customs and a perverted application of the Scriptures have marked out for her, and that it is time she should move in the enlarged sphere which her great Creator has assigned her.

Resolved, That it is the duty of the women of this country to secure to themselves their sacred right to the elective franchise.

Resolved, That the equality of human rights results necessarily from the fact of the identity of the race in capabilities and responsibilities.

Resolved, therefore, That, being invested by the Creator with the same capabilities, and the same consciousness of responsibility for their exercise, it is demonstrably the right and duty of woman, equally with man, to promote every righteous cause by every righteous means; and especially in regard to the great subjects of morals and religion, it is self-evidently her right to participate with her brother in teaching them, both in private and in public, by writing and by speaking, by any instrumentalities proper to be used, and in any assemblies proper to be held; and this being a self-evident truth growing out of the divinely implanted principles of human nature, any custom or authority adverse to it, whether modern or wearing the hoary sanction of antiquity, is to be regarded as a self-evident falsehood, and at war with mankind.

Resolved, That the speedy success of our cause depends upon the zealous and untiring efforts of both men and women, for the overthrow of the monopoly of the pulpit, and for the securing to women an equal participation with men in the various trades, professions, and commerce.

FROM FREDERICK DOUGLASS'S "WHAT, TO THE SLAVE, IS THE FOURTH OF JULY?" SPEECH (1852)

* * *

This, for the purpose of this celebration, is the Fourth of July. It is the birthday of your National Independence, and of your political freedom. This, to you, is what the Passover was to the emancipated people of God. It carries your minds back to the day, and to the act of your great deliverance; and to the signs and to the wonders associated with that act and that day. This celebration also marks the beginning of another year of your national life; and reminds you that the Republic of America is now seventy-six years old. I am glad, fellow citizens, that your nation is so young. Seventy-six years, though a good old age for a man, is but a mere speck in the life of a nation. Three score years and ten is the allotted time for individual men; but nations number their years by thousands. According to this fact, you are, even now, only in the beginning of your national career, still lingering in the period of childhood. I repeat, I am glad this is so. There is hope in the thought, and hope is much needed, under the dark clouds which lower above the horizon. The eye of the reformer is met with angry flashes, portending disastrous times; but his heart may well beat lighter at the thought that America is young, and that she is still in the impressible stage of her existence. May he not hope that high lessons of wisdom, of justice and of truth, will yet give direction to her destiny? Were the nation older, the patriot's heart might be sadder and the reformer's brow heavier. Its future might be shrouded in gloom and the hope of its prophets go out in sorrow. There is consolation in the thought that America is young. Great streams are not easily turned from channels worn deep in the course of ages. They may sometimes rise in quiet and stately majesty, and inundate the land, refreshing and fertilizing the earth with their mysterious properties. They may also rise in wrath and fury, and bear away on their angry waves the accumulated wealth of years of toil and hardship. They, however, gradually flow back to the same old channel and flow on as serenely as ever. But, while the river may not be turned aside, it may dry up and leave nothing behind but the withered branch and the unsightly rock, to howl in the abyss-sweeping wind, the sad tale of departed glory. As with rivers, so with nations.

Fellow citizens, I shall not presume to dwell at length on the associations that cluster about this day. The simple story of it is, that seventy-six years ago the people of this country were British subjects. The style and title of your "sovereign people" (in which you now glory) was not then born. You were under the British Crown. Your fathers esteemed the English government as the home government, and England as the fatherland. This home government, you know, although a considerable distance from your home, did, in the exercise of its parental prerogatives, impose upon its colonial children such restraints, burdens and limitations as, in its mature judgment, it deemed wise, right and proper.

* * *

Feeling themselves harshly and unjustly treated by the home government, your fathers, like men of honesty and men of spirit, earnestly sought redress. They petitioned and remonstrated, they did so in a decorous, respectful and loyal manner. Their conduct was wholly unexceptionable. This, however, did not answer the purpose. They saw themselves treated with sovereign indifference, coldness and scorn. Yet they persevered. They were not the men to look back.

* * *

Citizens, your fathers . . . succeeded; and today you reap the fruits of their success. The freedom gained is yours; and you, therefore, may properly celebrate this anniversary. The Fourth of July is the first great fact in your nation's history—the very ringbolt in the chain of your yet undeveloped destiny.

Pride and patriotism, not less than gratitude, prompt you to celebrate and to hold it in perpetual remembrance. I have said that the Declaration of Independence is the ringbolt to the chain of your nation's destiny; so, indeed, I regard it. The principles contained in that instrument are saving principles. Stand by those principles, be true to them on all occasions, in all places, against all foes, and at whatever cost.

* * *

[The fathers of this republic] were peace men, but they preferred revolution to peaceful submission to bondage. They were quiet men; but they did not shrink from agitating against oppression. They showed forbearance, but that they knew its limits. They believed in order, but not in the order of tyranny. With them, nothing was "settled" that was not right. With them, justice, liberty and humanity were "final," not slavery and oppression. You may well cherish the memory of such men. They were great in their day and generation. Their solid manhood stands out the more as we contrast it with these degenerate times.

* * *

Fellow citizens, pardon me, allow me to ask, why am I called upon to speak here today? What have I, or those I represent, to do with your national independence? Are the great principles of political freedom and of natural justice, embodied in that Declaration of Independence, extended to us? and am I, therefore, called upon to bring our humble offering to the national altar and to confess the benefits and express devout gratitude for the blessings resulting from your independence to us?

* * *

But such is not the state of the case. I say it with a sad sense of the disparity between us. I am not included within the pale of this glorious anniversary! Your high independence only reveals the immeasurable distance between us. The blessings in which you, this day, rejoice, are not enjoyed in common. The rich inheritance of justice, liberty, prosperity and independence, bequeathed by your fathers, is shared by you, not by me. The sunlight that brought light and healing to you, has brought stripes and death to me. This Fourth of July is *yours*, not *mine*. *You* may rejoice, *I* must mourn.

* * *

Fellow citizens, above your national, tumultuous joy I hear the mournful wail of millions! whose chains, heavy and grievous yesterday, are today rendered more intolerable by the jubilee shouts that reach them. If I do forget, if I do not faithfully remember those bleeding children of sorrow this day, "may my right hand forget her cunning, and may my tongue cleave to the roof of my mouth!" To forget them, to pass lightly over their wrongs and to chime in with the popular theme would be treason most scandalous and shocking and would make me a reproach before God and the world. My subject, then, fellow citizens, is American slavery. I shall see this day and its popular characteristics from the slave's point of view. Standing there identified with the American bondman, making his wrongs mine, I do not hesitate to declare, with all my soul, that the character and conduct of this nation never looked blacker to me than on this Fourth of July. Whether we turn to the declarations of the past or to the professions of the present, the conduct of the nation seems equally hideous and revolting. America is false to the past, false to the present, and solemnly binds herself to be false to the future.

* * *

For the present, it is enough to affirm the equal manhood of the Negro race. It is not astonishing that, while we are plowing, planting and reaping, using all kinds of mechanical tools, erecting houses, constructing bridges, building ships, working in metals of brass, iron, copper, silver and gold; that, while we are reading, writing and ciphering, acting as clerks, merchants and secretaries, having among us lawyers, doctors, ministers, poets, authors, editors, orators and teachers; that, while we are engaged in all manner of enterprises common to other men, digging gold in California, capturing the whale in the Pacific, feeding sheep and cattle on the hillside, living, moving, acting, thinking, planning, living in families as husbands, wives and children, and, above all, confessing and worshiping the Christian's God and looking hopefully for life and immortality beyond the grave, we are called upon to prove that we are men!

Would you have me argue that man is entitled to liberty? that he is the rightful owner of his own body? You have already declared it. Must I argue the wrongfulness of slavery?

Is that a question for republicans? Is it to be settled by the rules of logic and argumentation, as a matter beset with great difficulty, involving a doubtful application of the principle of justice, hard to be understood? How should I look today, in the presence of Americans, dividing and subdividing a discourse, to show that men have a natural right to freedom, speaking of it relatively and positively, negatively and affirmatively? To do so would be to make myself ridiculous and to offer an insult to your understanding. There is not a man beneath the canopy of heaven that does not know that slavery is wrong *for him*.

* * *

What, to the American slave, is your Fourth of July? I answer: a day that reveals to him, more than all other days in the year, the gross injustice and cruelty to which he is the constant victim. To him, your celebration is a sham; your boasted liberty an unholy license; your national greatness swelling vanity; your sounds of rejoicing are empty and heartless; your denunciation of tyrants brass-fronted impudence; your shouts of liberty and equality hollow mockery; your prayers and hymns, your sermons and thanksgivings, with all your religious parade and solemnity, are to Him mere bombast, fraud, deception, impiety and hypocrisy—a thin veil to cover up crimes which would disgrace a nation of savages. There is not a nation on the earth guilty of practices more shocking and bloody than are the people of the United States at this very hour.

Go where you may, search where you will, roam through all the monarchies and despotisms of the Old World, travel through South America, search out every abuse, and when you have found the last, lay your facts by the side of the everyday practices of this nation, and you will say with me, that, for revolting barbarity and shameless hypocrisy, America reigns without a rival.

* * *

Americans! your republican politics, not less than your republican religion, are flagrantly inconsistent. You boast of your love of liberty, your superior civilization and your pure Christianity, while the whole political power of the nation (as embodied in the two great political parties) is solemnly pledged to support and perpetuate the enslavement of three millions of your countrymen. You hurl your anathemas at the crowned-headed tyrants of Russia and Austria and pride yourselves on your democratic institutions, while you yourselves consent to be the mere *tools* and *bodyguards* of the tyrants of Virginia and Carolina. You invite to your shores fugitives of oppression from abroad, honor them with banquets, greet them with ovations, cheer them, toast them, salute them, protect them, and pour out your money to them like water; but the fugitives from your own land you advertise, hunt, arrest, shoot and kill. You glory in your refinement and your universal education; yet you maintain a system as barbarous and dreadful as ever stained the character of a nation—a system begun in avarice, supported in pride, and perpetuated in cruelty. You shed tears over fallen Hungary, and make the sad story of her wrongs the theme of your poets, statesmen and orators, till your gallant sons are ready to fly to arms to vindicate her cause against the oppressor;* but, in regard to the ten thousand wrongs of the American slave, you would enforce the strictest silence and would hail him as an enemy of the nation who dares to make those wrongs the subject of public discourse! You are all on fire at the mention of liberty for France or for Ireland, but are as cold as an iceberg at the thought of liberty for the enslaved of America. You discourse eloquently on the dignity of labor; yet, you sustain a system which, in its very essence, casts a stigma upon labor. You can bare your bosom to the storm of British artillery to throw off a three-penny tax on tea, and yet wring the last hard-earned farthing from the grasp of the black laborers of your country. You profess to believe "that of one blood God made all nations of men to dwell on the face of all the earth"† and hath commanded all men, everywhere, to love one another; yet you notoriously hate (and glory in your hatred) all men whose skins are not colored like your own. You declare before the world, and are understood by the world to declare, that you *"hold these truths to be self-evident, that all men are created equal;*

*The fledgling Hungarian republic was invaded by Austria and Russia in 1849.
†Acts 17:26.

and are endowed by their Creator with certain unalienable rights; and that among these are, life, liberty and the pursuit of happiness"; and yet, you hold securely, in a bondage which, according to your own Thomas Jefferson, *"is worse than ages of that which your fathers rose in rebellion to oppose," a seventh part* of the inhabitants of your country.

Fellow citizens, I will not enlarge further on your national inconsistencies. The existence of slavery in this country brands your republicanism as a sham, your humanity as a base pretense, and your Christianity as a lie. It destroys your moral power abroad; it corrupts your politicians at home. It saps the foundation of religion; it makes your name a hissing and a byword to a mocking earth. It is the antagonistic force in your government, the only thing that seriously disturbs and endangers your union. It fetters your progress; it is the enemy of improvement; the deadly foe of education; it fosters pride; it breeds insolence; it promotes vice; it shelters crime; it is a curse to the earth that supports it; and yet you cling to it as if it were the sheet anchor of all your hopes.

* * *

Allow me to say, in conclusion, notwithstanding the dark picture I have this day presented, of the state of the nation, I do not despair of this country. There are forces in operation which must inevitably work the downfall of slavery.

* * *

The Gettysburg Address (1863)

Four score and seven years ago our fathers brought forth on this continent, a new nation, conceived in Liberty, and dedicated to the proposition that all men are created equal.

Now we are engaged in a great civil war, testing whether that nation, or any nation so conceived and so dedicated, can long endure. We are met on a great battle field of that war. We have come to dedicate a portion of that field, as a final resting place for those who here gave their lives that that nation might live. It is altogether fitting and proper that we should do this.

But, in a larger sense, we can not dedicate—we can not consecrate—we can not hallow—this ground. The brave men, living and dead, who struggled here, have consecrated it, far above our poor power to add or detract. The world will little note, nor long remember what we say here, but it can never forget what they did here. It is for us the living, rather, to be dedicated here to the unfinished work which they who fought here have thus far so nobly advanced. It is rather for us to be here dedicated to the great task remaining before us—that from these honored dead we take increased devotion to that cause for which they gave the last full measure of devotion—that we here highly resolve that these dead shall not have died in vain—that this nation, under God, shall have a new birth of freedom—and that government of the people, by the people, for the people, shall not perish from the earth.

Abraham Lincoln
November 19, 1863

Abraham Lincoln's Second Inaugural Address (1865)

Fellow Countrymen:

At this second appearing to take the oath of the presidential office, there is less occasion for an extended address than there was at the first. Then a statement, somewhat in detail, of a course to be pursued, seemed fitting and proper. Now, at the expiration of four years, during which public declarations have been constantly called forth on every point and phase of the great contest which still absorbs the attention, and engrosses the energies of the nation, little that is new could be presented. The progress of our arms, upon which all else chiefly depends, is as well known to the public as to myself; and it is, I trust, reasonably satisfactory and encouraging to all. With high hope for the future, no prediction in regard to it is ventured.

On the occasion corresponding to this four years ago, all thoughts were anxiously directed to an impending civil war. All dreaded it—all sought to avert it. While the inaugural address was being delivered from this place, devoted altogether to *saving* the Union without war, insurgent agents were in the city seeking to *destroy* it without war—seeking to dissolve the Union, and divide effects, by negotiation. Both parties deprecated war; but one of them would *make* war rather than let the nation survive; and the other would *accept* war rather than let it perish. And the war came.

One eighth of the whole population were colored slaves, not distributed generally over the Union, but localized in the southern part of it. These slaves constituted a peculiar and powerful interest. All knew that this interest was, somehow, the cause of the war. To strengthen, perpetuate, and extend this interest was the object for which the insurgents would rend the Union, even by war; while the government claimed no right to do more than to restrict the territorial enlargement of it. Neither party expected for the war, the magnitude, or the duration, which it has already attained. Neither anticipated that the *cause* of the conflict might cease with, or even before, the conflict itself should cease. Each looked for an easier triumph, and a result less fundamental and astounding. Both read the same Bible, and pray to the same God; and each invokes His aid against the other. It may seem strange that any men should dare to ask a just God's assistance in wringing their bread from the sweat of other men's faces; but let us judge not that we be not judged. The prayers of both could not be answered; that of neither has been answered fully. The Almighty has His own purposes. "Woe unto the world because of offences! for it must needs be that offences come; but woe to that man by whom the offence cometh." If we shall suppose that American slavery is one of those offences which, in the providence of God, must needs come, but which, having continued through His appointed time, He now wills to remove, and that He gives to both North and South, this terrible war, as the woe due to those by whom the offence came, shall we discern therein any departure from those divine attributes which the believers in a living God always ascribe to Him? Fondly do we hope, fervently do we pray—that this mighty scourge of war may speedily pass away. Yet, if God wills that it continue until all the wealth piled by the bondsman's two hundred and fifty years of unrequited toil shall be sunk, and until every drop of blood drawn with the lash shall be paid by another drawn with the sword, as was said three thousand years ago, so still it must be said "the judgments of the Lord are true and righteous altogether."

With malice toward none; with charity for all; with firmness in the right as God gives us to see the right, let us strive on to finish the work we are in; to bind up the nation's wounds; to care for him who shall have borne the battle and for his widow and his orphan, to do all which may achieve and cherish a just and a lasting peace, among ourselves and with all nations.

THE POPULIST PLATFORM OF 1892

Assembled upon the 116th anniversary of the Declaration of Independence, the People's Party of America, in their first national convention, invoking upon their action the blessing of Almighty God, puts forth in the name and on behalf of the people of this country, the following preamble and declaration of principles:

PREAMBLE

The conditions which surround us best justify our co-operation; we meet in the midst of a nation brought to the verge of moral, political, and material ruin. Corruption dominates the ballot-box, the Legislatures, the Congress, and touches even the ermine of the bench. The people are demoralized; most of the States have been compelled to isolate the voters at the polling places to prevent universal intimidation and bribery. The newspapers are largely subsidized or muzzled, public opinion silenced, business prostrated, homes covered with mortgages, labor impoverished, and the land concentrating in the hands of the capitalists. The urban workmen are denied the right to organize for self-protection, imported pauperized labor beats down their wages, a hireling standing army, unrecognized by our laws, is established to shoot them down, and they are rapidly degenerating into European conditions. The fruits of the toil of millions are boldly stolen to build up the fortunes for a few, unprecedented in the history of mankind; and the possessors of these, in turn, despise the Republic and endanger liberty. From the same prolific womb of governmental injustice we breed the two great classes—tramps and millionaires.

The national power to create money is appropriated to enrich bondholders; a vast public debt, payable in legal tender currency, has been funded into gold-bearing bonds, thereby adding millions to the burdens of the people. Silver, which has been accepted as coin since the dawn of history, has been demonetized to add to the purchasing power of gold by decreasing the value of all forms of property as well as human labor, and the supply of currency is purposely abridged to fatten usurers, bankrupt enterprise, and enslave industry. A vast conspiracy against mankind has been organized on two continents, and it is rapidly taking possession of the world. If not met and overthrown at once it forebodes terrible social convulsions, the destruction of civilization, or the establishment of an absolute despotism.

We have witnessed for more than a quarter of a century the struggles of the two great political parties for power and plunder, while grievous wrongs have been inflicted upon the suffering people. We charge that the controlling influences dominating both these parties have permitted the existing dreadful conditions to develop without serious effort to prevent or restrain them. Neither do they now promise us any substantial reform. They have agreed together to ignore in the coming campaign every issue but one. They propose to drown the outcries of a plundered people with the uproar of a sham battle over the tariff, so that capitalists, corporations, national banks, rings, trusts, watered stock, the demonetization of silver, and the oppressions of the usurers may all be lost sight of. They propose to sacrifice our homes, lives, and children on the altar of mammon; to destroy the multitude in order to secure corruption funds from the millionaires.

Assembled on the anniversary of the birthday of the nation, and filled with the spirit of the grand general and chief who established our independence, we seek to restore the government of the Republic to the hands of "the plain people," with which class it originated. We assert our purpose to be identical with the purposes of the National Constitution, "to form a more perfect union and establish justice, insure domestic tranquility, provide for the common defense, promote the general welfare, and secure the blessings of liberty for ourselves and our posterity." We declare that this Republic can only endure as a free government while built upon the love of the whole people for each other and for the nation; that it cannot be pinned together by bayonets; that the civil war is over, and that every passion and resentment which grew out of it must die with it; and that we must be in fact, as we are in name, one united brotherhood of free men.

Our country finds itself confronted by conditions for which there is no precedent in the history of the world; our annual agricultural productions amount to billions of dollars in value, which must, within a few weeks or months, be exchanged for billions of dollars of commodities consumed in their production; the existing currency supply is wholly inadequate to make this exchange; the results are falling prices, the formation of combines and rings, the impoverishment of the producing class. We pledge ourselves, if given power, we will labor to correct these evils by wise and reasonable legislation, in accordance with the terms of our platform. We believe that the power of government—in other words, of the people—should be expanded (as in the case of the postal service) as rapidly and as far as the good sense of an intelligent people and the teaching of experience shall justify, to the end that oppression, injustice, and poverty shall eventually cease in the land.

While our sympathies as a party of reform are naturally upon the side of every proposition which will tend to make men intelligent, virtuous, and temperate, we nevertheless regard these questions—important as they are—as secondary to the great issues now pressing for solution, and upon which not only our individual prosperity but the very existence of free institutions depend; and we ask all men to first help us to determine whether we are to have a republic to administer before we differ as to the conditions upon which it is to be administered, believing that the forces of reform this day organized will never cease to move forward until every wrong is remedied, and equal rights and equal privileges securely established for all the men and women of this country.

PLATFORM

We declare, therefore—

First.—That the union of the labor forces of the United States this day consummated shall be permanent and perpetual; may its spirit enter into all hearts for the salvation of the Republic and the uplifting of mankind!

Second.—Wealth belongs to him who creates it, and every dollar taken from industry without an equivalent is robbery. "If any will not work, neither shall he eat." The interests of rural and civic labor are the same; their enemies are identical.

Third.—We believe that the time has come when the railroad corporations will either own the people or the people must own the railroads; and, should the government enter upon the work of owning and managing all railroads, we should favor an amendment to the Constitution by which all persons engaged in the government service shall be placed under a civil-service regulation of the most rigid character, so as to prevent the increase of the power of the national administration by the use of such additional government employees.

FINANCE.—We demand a national currency, safe, sound, and flexible, issued by the general government only, a full legal tender for all debts, public and private, and that without the use of banking corporations, a just, equitable, and efficient means of distribution direct to the people, at a tax not to exceed two per cent per annum, to be provided as set forth in the sub-treasury plan of the Farmers' Alliance, or a better system; also by payments in discharge of its obligations for public improvements.

1. We demand free and unlimited coinage of silver and gold at the present legal ratio of 16 to 1.

2. We demand that the amount of circulating medium be speedily increased to not less than $50 per capita.

3. We demand a graduated income tax.

4. We believe that the money of the country should be kept as much as possible in the hands of the people, and hence we demand that all State and national revenues shall be limited to the necessary expenses of the government, economically and honestly administered.

5. We demand that postal savings banks be established by the government for the safe deposit of the earnings of the people and to facilitate exchange.

TRANSPORTATION.—Transportation being a means of exchange and a public necessity, the government should own and operate the railroads in the interest of the people. The telegraph and telephone, like the post-office system, being a necessity for the transmission of news, should be owned and operated by the government in the interest of the people.

LAND.—The land, including all the natural sources of wealth, is the heritage of the people, and should not be monopolized for speculative purposes, and alien ownership of land should be prohibited. All land now held by railroads and other corporations in excess of their actual needs, and all lands now owned by aliens should be reclaimed by the government and held for actual settlers only.

EXPRESSION OF SENTIMENTS

Your committee on Platform and Resolutions beg leave unanimously to report the following:

Whereas, Other questions have been presented for our consideration, we hereby submit the following, not as a part of the Platform of the People's Party, but as resolutions expressive of the sentiment of this Convention:

1. *Resolved*, That we demand a free ballot and a fair count in all elections, and pledge ourselves to secure it to every legal voter without federal intervention, through the adoption by the States of the unperverted Australian or secret ballot system.

2. *Resolved*, That the revenue derived from a graduated income tax should be applied to the reduction of the burden of taxation now levied upon the domestic industries of this country.

3. *Resolved*, That we pledge our support to fair and liberal pensions to ex-Union soldiers and sailors.

4. *Resolved*, That we condemn the fallacy of protecting American labor under the present system, which opens our ports to the pauper and criminal classes of the world, and crowds out our wage-earners; and we denounce the present ineffective laws against contract labor, and demand the further restriction of undesirable emigration.

5. *Resolved*, that we cordially sympathize with the efforts of organized workingmen to shorten the hours of labor, and demand a rigid enforcement of the existing eight-hour law on Government work, and ask that a penalty clause be added to the said law.

6. *Resolved*, That we regard the maintenance of a large standing army of mercenaries, known as the Pinkerton system, as a menace to our liberties, and we demand its abolition; and we condemn the recent invasion of the Territory of Wyoming by the hired assassins of plutocracy, assisted by federal officers.

7. *Resolved*, That we commend to the favorable consideration of the people and the reform press the legislative system known as the initiative and referendum.

8. *Resolved*, That we favor a constitutional provision limiting the office of President and Vice-President to one term, and providing for the election of Senators of the United States by a direct vote of the people.

9. *Resolved*, That we oppose any subsidy or national aid to any private corporation for any purpose.

10. *Resolved*, That this convention sympathizes with the Knights of Labor and their righteous contest with the tyrannical combine of clothing manufacturers of Rochester, and declare it to be the duty of all who hate tyranny and oppression to refuse to purchase the goods made by the said manufacturers, or to patronize any merchants who sell such goods.

FRANKLIN D. ROOSEVELT'S FIRST INAUGURAL ADDRESS (1933)

I am certain that my fellow Americans expect that on my induction into the Presidency I will address them with a candor and a decision which the present situation of our Nation impels. This is preeminently the time to speak the truth, the whole truth, frankly and boldly. Nor need we shrink from honestly facing conditions in our country today. This great Nation will endure as it has endured, will revive and will prosper. So, first of all, let me assert my firm belief that the only thing we have to fear is fear itself—nameless, unreasoning, unjustified terror which paralyzes needed efforts to convert retreat into advance. In every dark hour of our national life a leadership of frankness and vigor has met with that understanding and support of the people themselves which is essential to victory. I am convinced that you will again give that support to leadership in these critical days.

In such a spirit on my part and on yours we face our common difficulties. They concern, thank God, only material things. Values have shrunken to fantastic levels; taxes have risen; our ability to pay has fallen; government of all kinds is faced by serious curtailment of income; the means of exchange are frozen in the currents of trade; the withered leaves of industrial enterprise lie on every side; farmers find no markets for their produce; the savings of many years in thousands of families are gone.

More important, a host of unemployed citizens face the grim problem of existence, and an equally great number toil with little return. Only a foolish optimist can deny the dark realities of the moment.

Yet our distress comes from no failure of substance. We are stricken by no plague of locusts. Compared with the perils which our forefathers conquered because they believed and were not afraid, we have still much to be thankful for. Nature still offers her bounty and human efforts have multiplied it. Plenty is at our doorstep, but a generous use of it languishes in the very sight of the supply. Primarily this is because the rulers of the exchange of mankind's goods have failed, through their own stubbornness and their own incompetence, have admitted their failure, and abdicated. Practices of the unscrupulous money changers stand indicted in the court of public opinion, rejected by the hearts and minds of men.

True they have tried, but their efforts have been cast in the pattern of an outworn tradition. Faced by failure of credit they have proposed only the lending of more money. Stripped of the lure of profit by which to induce our people to follow their false leadership, they have resorted to exhortations, pleading tearfully for restored confidence. They know only the rules of a generation of self-seekers. They have no vision, and when there is no vision the people perish.

The money changers have fled from their high seats in the temple of our civilization. We may now restore that temple to the ancient truths. The measure of the restoration lies in the extent to which we apply social values more noble than mere monetary profit.

Happiness lies not in the mere possession of money; it lies in the joy of achievement, in the thrill of creative effort. The joy and moral stimulation of work no longer must be forgotten in the mad chase of evanescent profits. These dark days will be worth all they cost us if they teach us that our true destiny is not to be ministered unto but to minister to ourselves and to our fellow men.

Recognition of the falsity of material wealth as the standard of success goes hand in hand with the abandonment of the false belief that public office and high political position are to be valued only by the standards of pride of place and personal profit; and there must be an end to a conduct in banking and in business which too often has given to a sacred trust the likeness of callous and selfish wrongdoing. Small wonder that confidence languishes, for it thrives only on honesty, on honor, on the sacredness of obligations, on faithful protection, on unselfish performance; without them it cannot live.

Restoration calls, however, not for changes in ethics alone. This Nation asks for action, and action now.

Our greatest primary task is to put people to work. This is no unsolvable problem if we face it wisely and courageously. It can be accomplished in part by direct recruiting by the Government itself, treating the task as we would treat the emergency of a war, but at the same time, through this employment, accomplishing greatly needed projects to stimulate and reorganize the use of our natural resources.

Hand in hand with this we must frankly recognize the overbalance of population in our industrial centers and, by engaging on a national scale in a redistribution, endeavor to provide a better use of the land for those best fitted for the land. The task can be helped by definite efforts to raise the values of agricultural products and with this the power to purchase the output of our cities. It can be helped by preventing realistically the tragedy of the growing loss through foreclosure of our small homes and our farms. It can be helped by insistence that the Federal, State, and local governments act forthwith on the demand that their cost be drastically reduced. It can be helped by the unifying of relief activities which today are often scattered, uneconomical, and unequal. It can be helped by national planning for and supervision of all forms of transportation and of communications and other utilities which have a definitely public character. There are many ways in which it can be helped, but it can never be helped merely by talking about it. We must act and act quickly.

Finally, in our progress toward a resumption of work we require two safeguards against a return of the evils of the old order; there must be a strict supervision of all banking and credits and investments; there must be an end to speculation with other people's money, and there must be provision for an adequate but sound currency.

There are the lines of attack. I shall presently urge upon a new Congress, in special session, detailed measures for their fulfillment, and I shall seek the immediate assistance of the several States.

Through this program of action we address ourselves to putting our own national house in order and making income balance outgo. Our international trade relations, though vastly important, are in point of time and necessity secondary to the establishment of a sound national economy. I favor as a practical policy the putting of first things first. I shall spare no effort to restore world trade by international economic readjustment, but the emergency at home cannot wait on that accomplishment.

The basic thought that guides these specific means of national recovery is not narrowly nationalistic. It is the insistence, as a first consideration, upon the interdependence of the various elements in all parts of the United States—a recognition of the old and permanently important manifestation of the American spirit of the pioneer. It is the way to recovery. It is the immediate way. It is the strongest assurance that the recovery will endure.

In the field of world policy I would dedicate this Nation to the policy of the good neighbor—the neighbor who resolutely respects himself and, because he does so, respects the rights of others—the neighbor who respects his obligations and respects the sanctity of his agreements in and with a world of neighbors.

If I read the temper of our people correctly, we now realize as we have never realized before our interdependence on each other; that we cannot merely take but we must give as well; that if we are to go forward, we must move as a trained and loyal army willing to sacrifice for the good of a common discipline, because without such discipline no progress is made, no leadership becomes effective. We are, I know, ready and willing to submit our lives and property to such discipline, because it makes possible a leadership which aims at a larger good. This I propose to offer, pledging that the larger purposes will bind upon us all as a sacred obligation with a unity of duty hitherto evoked only in time of armed strife.

With this pledge taken, I assume unhesitatingly the leadership of this great army of our people dedicated to a disciplined attack upon our common problems.

Action in this image and to this end is feasible under the form of government which we have inherited from our ancestors. Our Constitution is so simple and practical that it is possible always to meet extraordinary needs by changes in emphasis and arrangement without loss of essential form. That is why our constitutional system has proved itself the most superbly enduring political mechanism the modern world has produced. It has met every stress of vast expansion of territory, of foreign wars, of bitter internal strife, of world relations.

It is to be hoped that the normal balance of executive and legislative authority may be wholly adequate to meet the unprecedented task before us. But it may be that an unprecedented demand and need for undelayed action may call for temporary departure from that normal balance of public procedure.

I am prepared under my constitutional duty to recommend the measures that a stricken nation in the midst of a stricken world may require. These measures, or such other measures as the Congress may build out of its experience and wisdom, I shall seek, within my constitutional authority, to bring to speedy adoption.

But in the event that the Congress shall fail to take one of these two courses, and in the event that the national emergency is still critical, I shall not evade the clear course of duty that will then confront me. I shall ask the Congress for the one remaining instrument to meet the crisis—broad Executive power to wage a war against the emergency, as great as the power that would be given to me if we were in fact invaded by a foreign foe.

For the trust reposed in me I will return the courage and the devotion that befit the time. I can do no less.

We face the arduous days that lie before us in the warm courage of national unity; with the clear consciousness of seeking old and precious moral values; with the clean satisfaction that comes from the stern performance of duty by old and young alike. We aim at the assurance of a rounded and permanent national life.

We do not distrust the future of essential democracy. The people of the United States have not failed. In their need they have registered a mandate that they want direct, vigorous action. They have asked for discipline and direction under leadership. They have made me the present instrument of their wishes. In the spirit of the gift I take it.

In this dedication of a Nation we humbly ask the blessing of God. May He protect each and every one of us. May He guide me in the days to come.

Martin Luther King Jr.'s, "I Have a Dream" Speech (1963)

I am happy to join with you today in what will go down in history as the greatest demonstration for freedom in the history of our nation.

Five score years ago, a great American, in whose symbolic shadow we stand today, signed the Emancipation Proclamation. This momentous decree came as a great beacon light of hope to millions of Negro slaves who had been seared in the flames of withering injustice. It came as a joyous daybreak to end the long night of captivity.

But one hundred years later, the Negro still is not free. One hundred years later, the life of the Negro is still sadly crippled by the manacles of segregation and the chains of discrimination. One hundred years later, the Negro is still languishing in the corners of American society and finds himself an exile in his own land. And so we've come here today to dramatize a shameful condition.

In a sense we have come to our nation's capital to cash a check. When the architects of our republic wrote the magnificent words of the Constitution and the Declaration of Independence, they were signing a promissory note to which every American was to fall heir. This note was a promise that all men, yes black men as well as white men, would be guaranteed the "unalienable Rights of Life, Liberty, and the pursuit of Happiness." It is obvious today that America has defaulted on this promissory note insofar as her citizens of color are concerned. Instead of honoring this sacred obligation, America has given the Negro people a bad check,—a check which has come back marked "insufficient funds."

But we refuse to believe that the bank of justice is bankrupt. We refuse to believe that there are insufficient funds in the great vaults of opportunity of this nation. And so we've come to cash this check,—a check that will give us upon demand the riches of freedom and the security of justice.

We have also come to this hallowed spot to remind America of the fierce urgency of now. This is no time to engage in the luxury of cooling off or to take the tranquilizing drug of gradualism. Now is the time to make real the promises of democracy. Now is the time to rise from the dark and desolate valley of segregation to the sunlit path of racial justice. Now is the time to lift our nation from the quicksands of racial injustice to the solid rock of brotherhood. Now is the time to make justice a reality for all of God's children.

It would be fatal for the nation to overlook the urgency of the moment. This sweltering summer of the Negro's legitimate discontent will not pass until there is an invigorating autumn of freedom and equality. Nineteen sixty-three is not an end, but a beginning. And those who hope that the Negro needed to blow off steam and will now be content will have a rude awakening if the nation returns to business as usual. There will be neither rest nor tranquility in America until the Negro is granted his citizenship rights. The whirlwinds of revolt will continue to shake the foundation of our nation until the bright day of justice emerges.

But there is something that I must say to my people, who stand on the warm threshold which leads into the palace of justice: In the process of gaining our rightful place, we must not be guilty of wrongful deeds. Let us not seek to satisfy our thirst for freedom by drinking from the cup of bitterness and hatred. We must forever conduct our struggle on the high plane of dignity and discipline. We must not allow our creative protest to degenerate into physical violence. Again and again, we must rise to the majestic heights of meeting physical force with soul force. The marvelous new militancy which has engulfed the Negro community must not lead us to a distrust of all white people, for many of our white brothers, as evidenced by their presence here today, have come to realize that their destiny is tied up with our destiny. And they have come to realize that their freedom is inextricably bound to our freedom. We cannot walk alone.

And as we walk, we must make the pledge that we shall march ahead. We cannot turn back. There are those who are asking the devotees of civil rights, "When will you be satisfied?"

We can never be satisfied as long as the Negro is the victim of unspeakable horrors of police brutality. We can never be satisfied as long as our bodies, heavy with the fatigue of travel, cannot gain lodging in the motels of the highways and the hotels of the cities. We cannot be satisfied as long as the Negro's basic mobility is from a smaller ghetto to a larger one. We can never be satisfied as long as our children are stripped of their selfhood and robbed of their dignity by signs stating "for whites only." We cannot be satisfied as long as a Negro in Mississippi cannot vote and a Negro in New York believes he has nothing for which to vote. No, no, we are not satisfied, and we will not be satisfied until, "justice rolls down like waters and righteousness like a mighty stream."

I am not unmindful that some of you have come here out of great trials and tribulations. Some of you have come fresh from narrow jail cells. Some of you have come from areas where your quest for freedom left you battered by the storms of persecution and staggered by the winds of police brutality. You have been the veterans of creative suffering. Continue to work with the faith that unearned suffering is redemptive.

Go back to Mississippi, go back to Alabama, go back to South Carolina, go back to Georgia, go back to Louisiana, go back to the slums and ghettos of our northern cities, knowing that somehow this situation can and will be changed. Let us not wallow in the valley of despair.

I say to you today, my friends, so even though we face the difficulties of today and tomorrow, I still have a dream. It is a dream deeply rooted in the American dream.

I have a dream that one day this nation will rise up and live out the true meaning of its creed: "We hold these truths to be self-evident, that all men are created equal."

I have a dream that one day on the red hills of Georgia, the sons of former slaves and the sons of former slave owners will be able to sit down together at the table of brotherhood.

I have a dream that one day even the state of Mississippi, a state sweltering with the heat of injustice, sweltering with the heat of oppression, will be transformed into an oasis of freedom and justice.

I have a dream that my four little children will one day live in a nation where they will not be judged by the color of their skin but by the content of their character. I have a dream today.

I have a dream that one day down in Alabama, with its vicious racists, with its governor having his lips dripping with the words of "interposition" and "nullification," one day right there in Alabama little black boys and black girls will be able to join hands with little white boys and white girls as sisters and brothers. I have a dream today.

I have a dream that one day "every valley shall be exalted, and every hill and mountain shall be made low; the rough places will be made plain, and the crooked places will be made straight; and the glory of the Lord shall be revealed, and all flesh shall see it together."

This is our hope. This is the faith that I go back to the South with. With this faith we will be able to hew out of the mountain of despair a stone of hope. With this faith will be able to transform the jangling discords of our nation into a beautiful symphony of brotherhood. With this faith we will be able to work together, to pray together, to struggle together, to go to jail together, to stand up for freedom together, knowing that we will be free one day. This will be the day, this will be the day when all of God's children will be able to sing with a new meaning:

My country, 'tis of thee, sweet land of liberty, of thee I sing.
Land where my fathers died, land of the pilgrim's pride,
From every mountainside, let freedom ring.

And if America is to be a great nation this must become true. And so let freedom ring from the prodigious hilltops of New Hampshire.

Let freedom ring from the mighty mountains of New York.

Let freedom ring from the heightening Alleghenies of Pennsylvania.

Let freedom ring from the snowcapped Rockies of Colorado.

Let freedom ring from the curvaceous peaks of California.

But not only that: let freedom ring from Stone Mountain of Georgia.

Let freedom ring from Lookout Mountain of Tennessee.

Let freedom ring from every hill and molehill of Mississippi. From every mountainside, let freedom ring.

And when this happens, when we allow freedom to ring, when we let it ring from every village and every hamlet, from every state and every city, we will be able to speed up that day when all of God's children, black men and white men, Jews and Gentiles, Protestants and Catholics, will be able to join hands and sing in the words of the old Negro spiritual:

Free at last! Free at last!
Thank God Almighty, we are free at last!

Ronald Reagan's First Inaugural Address (1981)

WEST FRONT OF THE U.S. CAPITOL
JANUARY 20, 1981

Senator Hatfield, Mr. Chief Justice, Mr. President, Vice President Bush, Vice President Mondale, Senator Baker, Speaker O'Neill, Reverend Moomaw, and my fellow citizens.

To a few of us here today this is a solemn and most momentous occasion, and yet in the history of our nation it is a commonplace occurrence. The orderly transfer of authority as called for in the Constitution routinely takes place, as it has for almost two centuries, and few of us stop to think how unique we really are. In the eyes of many in the world, this every-four-year ceremony we accept as normal is nothing less than a miracle.

Mr. President, I want our fellow citizens to know how much you did to carry on this tradition. By your gracious cooperation in the transition process, you have shown a watching world that we are a united people pledged to maintaining a political system which guarantees individual liberty to a greater degree than any other, and I thank you and your people for all your help in maintaining the continuity which is the bulwark of our republic. The business of our nation goes forward. These United States are confronted with an economic affliction of great proportions. We suffer from the longest and one of the worst sustained inflations in our national history. It distorts our economic decisions, penalizes thrift, and crushes the struggling young and the fixed-income elderly alike. It threatens to shatter the lives of millions of our people.

Idle industries have cast workers into unemployment, human misery, and personal indignity. Those who do work are denied a fair return for their labor by a tax system which penalizes successful achievement and keeps us from maintaining full productivity. But great as our tax burden is, it has not kept pace with public spending. For decades we have piled deficit upon deficit, mortgaging our future and our children's future for the temporary convenience of the present. To continue this long trend is to guarantee tremendous social, cultural, political, and economic upheavals.

You and I, as individuals, can, by borrowing, live beyond our means, but for only a limited period of time. Why, then, should we think that collectively, as a nation, we're not bound by that same limitation? We must act today in order to preserve tomorrow. And let there be no misunderstanding: We are going to begin to act, beginning today. The economic ills we suffer have come upon us over several decades. They will not go away in days, weeks, or months, but they will go away. They will go away because we as Americans have the capacity now, as we've had in the past, to do whatever needs to be done to preserve this last and greatest bastion of freedom.

In this present crisis, government is not the solution to our problem; government is the problem. From time to time we've been tempted to believe that society has become too complex to be managed by self-rule, that government by an elite group is superior to government for, by, and of the people. Well, if no one among us is capable of governing himself, then who among us has the capacity to govern someone else? All of us together, in and out of government, must bear the burden. The solutions we seek must be equitable, with no one group singled out to pay a higher price.

We hear much of special interest groups. Well, our concern must be for a special interest group that has been too long neglected. It knows no sectional boundaries or ethnic and racial divisions, and it crosses political party lines. It is made up of men and women who raise our food, patrol our streets, man our mines and factories, teach our children, keep our homes, and heal us when we're sick—professionals, industrialists, shopkeepers, clerks, cabbies, and truck drivers. They are, in short, "we the people," this breed called Americans.

Well, this administration's objective will be a healthy, vigorous, growing economy that provides equal opportunities for all Americans, with no barriers born of bigotry or discrimination. Putting America back to work means putting all Americans back to work. Ending inflation means freeing all Americans from the terror of runaway living costs. All must share in the productive work of this "new beginning," and all must share in the bounty of a revived economy. With the idealism and fair play which are the core of our system and our strength, we can have a strong and prosperous America, at peace with itself and the world.

So, as we begin, let us take inventory. We are a nation that has a government—not the other way around. And this makes us special among the nations of the Earth. Our government has no power except that granted it by the people. It is time to check and reverse the growth of government, which shows signs of having grown beyond the consent of the governed.

It is my intention to curb the size and influence of the federal establishment and to demand recognition of the distinction between the powers granted to the federal government and those reserved to the states or to the people. All of us need to be reminded that the federal government did not create the states; the states created the federal government.

Now, so there will be no misunderstanding, it's not my intention to do away with government. It is rather to make it work—work with us, not over us; to stand by our side, not ride on our back. Government can and must provide opportunity, not smother it; foster productivity, not stifle it.

If we look to the answer as to why for so many years we achieved so much, prospered as no other people on earth, it was because here in this land we unleashed the energy and individual genius of man to a greater extent than has ever been done before. Freedom and the dignity of the individual have been more available and assured here than in any other place on earth. The price for this freedom at times has been high, but we have never been unwilling to pay the price.

It is no coincidence that our present troubles parallel and are proportionate to the intervention and intrusion in our lives that result from unnecessary and excessive growth of government. It is time for us to realize that we're too great a nation to limit ourselves to small dreams. We're not, as some would have us believe, doomed to an inevitable decline. I do not believe in a fate that will fall on us no matter what we do. I do believe in a fate that will fall on us if we do nothing. So, with all the creative energy at our command, let us begin an era of national renewal. Let us renew our determination, our courage, and our strength. And let us renew our faith and our hope.

We have every right to dream heroic dreams. Those who say that we're in a time when there are no heroes, they just don't know where to look. You can see heroes every day going in and out of factory gates. Others, a handful in number, produce enough food to feed all of us and then the world beyond. You meet heroes across a counter, and they're on both sides of that counter. There are entrepreneurs with faith in themselves and faith in an idea who create new jobs, new wealth and opportunity. They're individuals and families whose taxes support the government and whose voluntary gifts support church, charity, culture, art, and education. Their patri-

otism is quiet, but deep. Their values sustain our national life.

Now, I have used the words "they" and "their" in speaking of these heroes. I could say "you" and "your," because I'm addressing the heroes of whom I speak—you, the citizens of this blessed land. Your dreams, your hopes, your goals are going to be the dreams, the hopes, and the goals of this administration, so help me God.

We shall reflect the compassion that is so much a part of your makeup. How can we love our country and not love our countrymen; and loving them, reach out a hand when they fall, heal them when they're sick, and provide opportunity to make them self-sufficient so they will be equal in fact and not just in theory?

Can we solve the problems confronting us? Well, the answer is an unequivocal and emphatic "yes." To paraphrase Winston Churchill, I did not take the oath I've just taken with the intention of presiding over the dissolution of the world's strongest economy.

In the days ahead I will propose removing the roadblocks that have slowed our economy and reduced productivity. Steps will be taken aimed at restoring the balance between the various levels of government. Progress may be slow, measured in inches and feet, not miles, but we will progress. It is time to reawaken this industrial giant, to get government back within its means, and to lighten our punitive tax burden. And these will be our first priorities, and on these principles there will be no compromise.

On the eve of our struggle for independence a man who might have been one of the greatest among the Founding Fathers, Dr. Joseph Warren, president of the Massachusetts Congress, said to his fellow Americans, "Our country is in danger, but not to be despaired of . . . On you depend the fortunes of America. You are to decide the important questions upon which rests the happiness and the liberty of millions yet unborn. Act worthy of yourselves." Well, I believe we, the Americans of today, are ready to act worthy of ourselves, ready to do what must be done to ensure happiness and liberty for ourselves, our children, and our children's children. And as we renew ourselves here in our own land, we will be seen as having greater strength throughout the world. We will again be the exemplar of freedom and a beacon of hope for those who do not now have freedom.

To those neighbors and allies who share our freedom, we will strengthen our historic ties and assure them of our support and firm commitment. We will match loyalty with loyalty. We will strive for mutually beneficial relations. We will not use our friendship to impose on their sovereignty, for our own sovereignty is not for sale. As for the enemies of freedom, those who are potential adversaries, they will be reminded that peace is the highest aspiration of the American people. We will negotiate for it, sacrifice for it; we will not surrender for it, now or ever.

Our forbearance should never be misunderstood. Our reluctance for conflict should not be misjudged as a failure of will. When action is required to preserve our national security, we will act. We will maintain sufficient strength to prevail if need be, knowing that if we do so we have the best chance of never having to use that strength. Above all, we must realize that no arsenal or no weapon in the arsenals of the world is so formidable as the will and moral courage of free men and women. It is a weapon our adversaries in today's world do not have. It is a weapon that we as Americans do have. Let that be understood by those who practice terrorism and prey upon their neighbors. I'm told that tens of thousands of prayer meetings are being held on this day, and for that I'm deeply grateful. We are a nation under God, and I believe God intended for us to be free. It would be fitting and good, I think, if on each Inaugural Day in future years it should be declared a day of prayer.

This is the first time in our history that this ceremony has been held, as you've been told, on the West Front of the Capitol. Standing here, one faces a magnificent vista, opening up on the city's special beauty and history. At the end of this open mall are those shrines to the giants on whose shoulders we stand.

Directly in front of me, the monument to a monumental man, George Washington, father of our country. A man of humility who came to greatness reluctantly. He led Americans out of revolutionary victory into infant nationhood. Off to one side, the stately memorial to Thomas Jefferson. The Declaration of Independence flames with his eloquence. And then, beyond the Reflecting Pool, the dignified columns of the Lincoln Memorial. Whoever would understand in his heart the meaning of America will find it in the life of Abraham Lincoln.

Beyond those monuments to heroism is the Potomac River, and on the far shore the sloping hills of Arlington National Cemetery, with its row upon row of simple white markers bearing crosses and Stars of David. They add up to only a tiny fraction of the price that has been paid for our freedom. Each one of those markers is a monument to the kind of hero I spoke of earlier. Their lives ended in places called Belleau Wood, the Argonne, Omaha Beach, Salerno, and halfway around the world on Guadalcanal, Tarawa, Pork Chop Hill, the Chosin Reservoir, and in a hundred rice paddies and jungles of a place called Vietnam.

Under one such marker lies a young man, Martin Treptow, who left his job in a small town barbershop in 1917 to go to France with the famed Rainbow Division. There, on the western front, he was killed trying to carry a message between battalions under heavy artillery fire.

We're told that on his body was found a diary. On the flyleaf under the heading "My Pledge," he had written these words: "America must win this war. Therefore I will work, I will save, I will sacrifice, I will endure, I will fight cheerfully and do my utmost, as if the issue of the whole struggle depended on me alone."

The crisis we are facing today does not require of us the kind of sacrifice that Martin Treptow and so many thousands of others were called upon to make. It does require, however, our best effort and our willingness to believe in ourselves and to believe in our capacity to perform great deeds, to believe that together with God's help we can and will resolve the problems which now confront us.

And after all, why shouldn't we believe that? We are Americans.

God bless you, and thank you.

Barack Obama's Inaugural Address (2009)

My fellow citizens: I stand here today humbled by the task before us, grateful for the trust you've bestowed, mindful of the sacrifices borne by our ancestors.

I thank President Bush for his service to our nation—(*applause*)—as well as the generosity and cooperation he has shown throughout this transition.

Forty-four Americans have now taken the presidential oath. The words have been spoken during rising tides of prosperity and the still waters of peace. Yet, every so often, the oath is taken amidst gathering clouds and raging storms. At these moments, America has carried on not simply because of the skill or vision of those in high office, but because we, the people, have remained faithful to the ideals of our forebears and true to our founding documents.

So it has been: so it must be with this generation of Americans.

That we are in the midst of crisis is now well understood. Our nation is at war against a far-reaching network of violence and hatred. Our economy is badly weakened, a consequence of greed and irresponsibility on the part of some, but also our collective failure to make hard choices and prepare the nation for a new age. Homes have been lost, jobs shed, businesses shuttered. Our health care is too costly, our schools fail too many—and each day brings further evidence that the ways we use energy strengthen our adversaries and threaten our planet.

These are the indicators of crisis, subject to data and statistics. Less measurable, but no less profound, is a sapping of confidence across our land; a nagging fear that America's decline is inevilable, that the next generation must lower its sights.

Today I say to you that the challenges we face are real. They are serious and they are many. They will not be met easily or in a short span of time. But know this America: They will be met. (*Applause*)

On this day, we gather because we have chosen hope over fear, unity of purpose over conflict and discord. On this day, we come to proclaim an end to the petty grievances and false promises, the recriminations and worn-out dogmas that for far too long have strangled our politics. We remain a young nation. But in the words of Scripture, the time has come to set aside childish things. The time has come to reaffirm our enduring spirit; to choose our better history; to carry forward that precious gift, that noble idea passed on from generation to generation; the God-given promise that all are equal, all are free, and all deserve a chance to pursue their full measure of happiness. (*Applause*)

In reaffirming the greatness of our nation we understand that greatness is never a given. It must be earned. Our journey has never been one of short-cuts or settling for less. It has not been the path for the faint-hearted, for those that prefer leisure over work, or seek only the pleasures of riches and fame. Rather, it has been the risk-takers, the doers, the makers of things—some celebrated, but more often men and women obscure in their labor—who have carried us up the long rugged path towards prosperity and freedom.

For us, they packed up their few worldly possessions and traveled across oceans in search of a new life. For us, they toiled in sweatshops, and settled the West, endured the lash of the whip, and plowed the hard earth. For us, they fought and died in places like Concord and Gettysburg, Normandy and Khe Sahn.

Time and again these men and women struggled and sacrificed and worked till their hands were raw so that we might live a better life. They saw America as bigger than the sum of our individual ambitions, greater than all the differences of birth or wealth or faction.

This is the journey we continue today. We remain the most prosperous, powerful nation on Earth. Our workers are no less productive than when this crisis began. Our minds are no less inventive, our goods and services no less needed than they were last week, or last month, or last year. Our capacity remains undiminished. But our time of standing pat, of protecting narrow interests and putting off unpleasant decisions—that time has surely passed. Starting today, we must pick ourselves up, dust ourselves off, and begin again the work of remaking America. (*Applause*)

For everywhere we look, there is work to be done. The state of our economy calls for action, bold and swift. And we will act, not only to create new jobs, but to lay a new foundation for growth. We will build the roads and bridges, the electric grids and digital lines that feed our commerce and bind us together. We'll restore science to its rightful place, and wield technology's wonders to raise health care's quality and lower its cost. We will harness the sun and the winds and the soil to fuel our cars and run our factories. And we will transform our schools and colleges and universities to meet the demands of a new age. All this we can do. All this we will do.

Now, there are some who question the scale of our ambitions, who suggest that our system cannot tolerate too many big plans. Their memories are short, for they have forgotten what this country has already done, what free men and women can achieve when imagination is joined to common purpose, and necessity to courage. What the cynics fail to understand is that the ground has shifted beneath them, that the stale political arguments that have consumed us for so long no longer apply.

The question we ask today is not whether our government is too big or too small, but whether it works—whether it helps families find jobs at a decent wage, care they can afford, a retirement that is dignified. Where the answer is yes, we intend to move forward. Where the answer is no, programs will end. And those of us who manage the public's dollars will be held to account, to spend wisely, reform bad habits, and do our business in the light of day, because only then can we restore the vital trust between a people and their government.

Nor is the question before us whether the market is a force for good or ill. Its power to generate wealth and expand freedom is unmatched. But this crisis has reminded us that without a watchful eye, the market can spin out of control. The nation cannot prosper long when it favors only the prosperous. The success of our economy has always depended not just on the size of our gross domestic product, but on the reach of our prosperity, on the ability to extend opportunity to every willing heart—not out of charity, but because it is the surest route to our common good. (*Applause*)

As for our common defense, we reject as false the choice between our safety and our ideals. Our Founding Fathers— (*applause*)—our Founding Fathers, faced with perils that we can scarcely imagine, drafted a charter to assure the rule of law and the rights of man—a charter expanded by the blood of generations. Those ideals still light the world, and we will not give them up for expedience sake. (*Applause*)

And so, to all the other peoples and governments who are watching today, from the grandest capitals to the small village where my father was born, know that America is a friend of each nation, and every man, woman and child who seeks a future of peace and dignity. And we are ready to lead once more. (*Applause*)

Recall that earlier generations faced down fascism and communism not just with missiles and tanks, but with the sturdy alliances and enduring convictions. They understood that our power alone cannot protect us, nor does it entitle us to do as we please. Instead they knew that our power grows through its prudent use; our security emanates from the justness of our cause, the force of our example, the tempering qualities of humility and restraint.

We are the keepers of this legacy. Guided by these principles once more we can meet those new threats that demand even greater effort, even greater cooperation and understanding between nations. We will begin to responsibly leave Iraq to its people and forge a hard-earned peace in Afghanistan. With old friends and former foes, we'll work tirelessly to lessen the nuclear threat, and roll back the specter of a warming planet.

We will not apologize for our way of life, nor will we waver in its defense. And for those who seek to advance their aims by inducing terror and slaughtering innocents, we say to you now that our spirit is stronger and cannot be broken—you cannot outlast us, and we will defeat you. (*Applause*)

For we know that our patchwork heritage is a strength, not a weakness. We are a nation of Christians and Muslims, Jews and Hindus, and non-believers. We are shaped by every language and culture, drawn from every end of this Earth: and because we have tasted the bitter swill of civil war and segregation, and emerged from that dark chapter stronger and more united, we cannot help but believe that the old hatreds shall someday pass; that the lines of tribe shall soon dissolve; that as the world grows smaller, our common humanity shall reveal itself; and that America must play its role in ushering in a new era of peace.

To the Muslim world, we seek a new way forward, based on mutual interest and mutual respect. To those leaders around the globe who seek to sow conflict, or blame their society's ills on the West, know that your people will judge you on what you can build, not what you destroy. (*Applause*)

To those who cling to power through corruption and deceit and the silencing of dissent, know that you are on the wrong side of history, but that we will extend a hand if you are willing to unclench your fist. (*Applause*)

To the people of poor nations, we pledge to work alongside you to make your farms flourish and let clean waters flow; to nourish starved bodies and feed hungry minds. And to those nations like ours that enjoy relative plenty, we say we can no longer afford indifference to the suffering outside our borders, nor can we consume the world's resources without regard to effect. For the world has changed, and we must change with it.

As we consider the role that unfolds before us, we remember with humble gratitude those brave Americans who at this very hour patrol far-off deserts and distant mountains. They have something to tell us, just as the fallen heroes who lie in Arlington whisper through the ages.

We honor them not only because they are the guardians of our liberty, but because they embody the spirit of service—a willingness to find meaning in something greater than themselves.

And yet at this moment, a moment that will define a generation, it is precisely this spirit that must inhabit us all. For as much as government can do, and must do, it is ultimately the faith and determination of the American people upon which this nation relies. It is the kindness to take in a stranger when the levees break, the selflessness of workers who would rather cut their hours than see a friend lose their job which sees us through our darkest hours. It is the firefighter's courage to storm a stairway filled with smoke, but also a parent's willingness to nurture a child that finally decides our fate.

Our challenges may be new. The instruments with which we meet them may be new. But those values upon which our success depends—honesty and hard work, courage and fair play, tolerance and curiosity, loyalty and patriotism—these things are old. These things are true. They have been the quiet force of progress throughout our history.

What is demanded, then, is a return to these truths. What is required of us now is a new era of responsibility—a recognition on the part of every American that we have duties to ourselves, our nation and the world; duties that we do not grudgingly accept, but rather seize gladly, firm in the knowledge that there is nothing so satisfying to the spirit, so defining of our character than giving our all to a difficult task.

This is the price and the promise of citizenship. This is the source of our confidence—the knowledge that God calls on us to shape an uncertain destiny. This is the meaning of our liberty and our creed, why men and women and children of every race and every faith can join in celebration across this magnificent mall; and why a man whose father less than 60 years ago might not have been served in a local restaurant can now stand before you to take a most sacred oath. (*Applause*)

So let us mark this day with remembrance of who we are and how far we have traveled. In the year of America's birth, in the coldest of months, a small band of patriots huddled by dying campfires on the shores of an icy river. The capital was abandoned. The enemy was advancing. The snow was stained with blood. At the moment when the outcome of our revolution was most in doubt, the father of our nation ordered these words to be read to the people:

"Let it be told to the future world . . . that in the depth of winter, when nothing but hope and virtue could survive . . . that the city and the country, alarmed at one common danger, came forth to meet [it]."

America: In the face of our common dangers, in this winter of our hardship, let us remember these timeless words. With hope and virtue, let us brave once more the icy currents, and endure what storms may come. Let it be said by our children's children that when we were tested we refused to let this journey end, that we did not turn back nor did we falter; and with eyes fixed on the horizon and God's grace upon us, we carried forth that great gift of freedom and delivered it safely to future generations.

Thank you. God bless you. And God bless the United States of America. (*Applause*)

Year	Number of States	Candidates	Parties	Popular Vote	% of Popular Vote	Electoral Vote	% Voter Participation
1789	11	**GEORGE WASHINGTON** John Adams Other candidates	NO PARTY DESIGNATIONS			69 34 35	
1792	15	**GEORGE WASHINGTON** John Adams George Clinton Other candidates	NO PARTY DESIGNATIONS			132 77 50 5	
1796	16	**JOHN ADAMS** Thomas Jefferson Thomas Pinckney Aaron Burr Other candidates	FEDERALIST Republican Federalist Republican			71 68 59 30 48	
1800	16	**THOMAS JEFFERSON** Aaron Burr John Adams Charles C. Pinckney John Jay	REPUBLICAN Republican Federalist Federalist Federalist			73 73 65 64 1	
1804	17	**THOMAS JEFFERSON** Charles C. Pinckney	REPUBLICAN Federalist			162 14	
1808	17	**JAMES MADISON** Charles C. Pinckney George Clinton	REPUBLICAN Federalist Republican			122 47 6	
1812	18	**JAMES MADISON** DeWitt Clinton	REPUBLICAN Federalist			128 89	

Year	Number of States	Candidates	Parties	Popular Vote	% of Popular Vote	Electoral Vote	% Voter Participation
1816	19	**JAMES MONROE** Rufus King	REPUBLICAN Federalist			183 34	
1820	24	**JAMES MONROE** John Quincy Adams	REPUBLICAN Independent			231 1	
1824	24	**JOHN QUINCY ADAMS** Andrew Jackson William H. Crawford Henry Clay	NO PARTY DESIGNATIONS	108,740 153,544 46,618 47,136	31.0 43.0 13.0 13.0	84 99 41 37	26.9
1828	24	**ANDREW JACKSON** John Quincy Adams	DEMOCRAT National Republican	647,286 508,064	56.0 44.0	178 83	57.6
1832	24	**ANDREW JACKSON** Henry Clay William Wirt John Floyd	DEMOCRAT National Republican Anti-Masonic Democrat	687,502 530,189 101,051	54.5 37.5 8.0	219 49 7 11	55.4
1836	26	**MARTIN VAN BUREN** William H. Harrison Hugh L. White Daniel Webster William P. Mangum	DEMOCRAT Whig Whig Whig Whig	765,483 739,795	51.0 49.0	170 73 26 14 11	57.8
1840	26	**WILLIAM H. HARRISON** Martin Van Buren	WHIG Democrat	1,274,624 1,127,781	53.0 47.0	234 60	80.2

Year	Number of States	Candidates	Parties	Popular Vote	% of Popular Vote	Electoral Vote	% Voter Participation
1844	26	**JAMES K. POLK**	DEMOCRAT	1,338,464	50.0	170	78.9
		Henry Clay	Whig	1,300,097	48.0	105	
		James G. Birney	Liberty	62,300	2.0		
1848	30	**ZACHARY TAYLOR**	WHIG	1,360,967	47.5	163	72.7
		Lewis Cass	Democrat	1,222,342	42.5	127	
		Martin Van Buren	Free Soil	291,263	10.0		
1852	31	**FRANKLIN PIERCE**	DEMOCRAT	1,601,117	51.0	254	69.6
		Winfield Scott	Whig	1,385,453	44.0	42	
		John P. Hale	Free Soil	155,825	5.0		
1856	31	**JAMES BUCHANAN**	DEMOCRAT	1,832,955	45.0	174	78.9
		John C. Frémont	Republican	1,339,932	33.0	114	
		Millard Fillmore	American	871,731	22.0	8	
1860	33	**ABRAHAM LINCOLN**	REPUBLICAN	1,865,593	40.0	180	81.2
		Stephen A. Douglas	Northern Democrat	1,382,713	29.0	12	
		John C. Breckinridge	Southern Democrat	848,356	18.0	72	
		John Bell	Constitutional Union	592,906	13.0	39	
1864	36	**ABRAHAM LINCOLN**	REPUBLICAN	2,206,938	55.0	212	73.8
		George B. McClellan	Democrat	1,803,787	45.0	21	
1868	37	**ULYSSES S. GRANT**	REPUBLICAN	3,013,421	53.0	214	78.1
		Horatio Seymour	Democrat	2,706,829	47.0	80	

Year	Number of States	Candidates	Parties	Popular Vote	% of Popular Vote	Electoral Vote	% Voter Participation
1872	37	**ULYSSES S. GRANT** Horace Greeley	REPUBLICAN Democrat	3,596,745 2,843,446	55.6 43.9	286 66	71.3
1876	38	**RUTHERFORD B. HAYES** Samuel J. Tilden	REPUBLICAN Democrat	4,036,572 4,284,020	48.0 51.0	185 184	81.8
1880	38	**JAMES A. GARFIELD** Winfield S. Hancock James B. Weaver	REPUBLICAN Democrat Greenback-Labor	4,453,295 4,414,082 308,578	48.4 48.3 3.5	214 155	79.4
1884	38	**GROVER CLEVELAND** James G. Blaine Benjamin F. Butler John P. St. John	DEMOCRAT Republican Greenback-Labor Prohibition	4,879,507 4,850,293 175,370 150,369	48.5 48.2 1.8 1.5	219 182	77.5
1888	38	**BENJAMIN HARRISON** Grover Cleveland Clinton B. Fisk Anson J. Streeter	REPUBLICAN Democrat Prohibition Union Labor	5,447,129 5,537,857 249,506 146,935	47.9 48.6 2.2 1.3	233 168	79.3
1892	44	**GROVER CLEVELAND** Benjamin Harrison James B. Weaver John Bidwell	DEMOCRAT Republican People's Prohibition	5,555,426 5,182,690 1,029,846 264,133	46.1 43.0 8.5 2.2	277 145 22	74.7
1896	45	**WILLIAM McKINLEY** William J. Bryan	REPUBLICAN Democrat	7,102,246 6,492,559	51.0 47.0	271 176	79.3

Year	Number of States	Candidates	Parties	Popular Vote	% of Popular Vote	Electoral Vote	% Voter Participation
1900	45	**WILLIAM McKINLEY**	REPUBLICAN	7,218,491	52.0	292	73.2
		William J. Bryan	Democrat; Populist	6,356,734	46.0	155	
		John C. Wooley	Prohibition	208,914	1.5		
1904	45	**THEODORE ROOSEVELT**	REPUBLICAN	7,628,461	56.4	336	65.2
		Alton B. Parker	Democrat	5,084,223	37.6	140	
		Eugene V. Debs	Socialist	402,283	3.0		
		Silas C. Swallow	Prohibition	258,536	1.9		
1908	46	**WILLIAM H. TAFT**	REPUBLICAN	7,675,320	52.0	321	65.4
		William J. Bryan	Democrat	6,412,294	43.4	162	
		Eugene V. Debs	Socialist	420,793	2.8		
		Eugene W. Chafin	Prohibition	253,840	1.7		
1912	48	**WOODROW WILSON**	DEMOCRAT	6,296,547	41.9	435	58.8
		Theodore Roosevelt	Progressive	4,118,571	27.4	88	
		William H. Taft	Republican	3,486,720	23.2	8	
		Eugene V. Debs	Socialist	900,672	6.0		
		Eugene W. Chafin	Prohibition	206,275	1.4		
1916	48	**WOODROW WILSON**	DEMOCRAT	9,127,695	49.4	277	61.6
		Charles E. Hughes	Republican	8,533,507	46.2	254	
		A. L. Benson	Socialist	585,113	3.2		
		J. Frank Hanly	Prohibition	220,506	1.2		
1920	48	**WARREN G. HARDING**	REPUBLICAN	16,153,115	60.6	404	49.2
		James M. Cox	Democrat	9,133,092	34.3	127	
		Eugene V. Debs	Socialist	915,490	3.4		
		P. P. Christensen	Farmer-Labor	265,229	1.0		
1924	48	**CALVIN COOLIDGE**	REPUBLICAN	15,719,921	54.0	382	48.9
		John W. Davis	Democrat	8,386,704	29.0	136	
		Robert M. La Follette	Progressive	4,832,532	16.5	13	

Year	Number of States	Candidates	Parties	Popular Vote	% of Popular Vote	Electoral Vote	% Voter Participation
1928	48	**HERBERT C. HOOVER**	REPUBLICAN	21,437,277	58.2	444	56.9
		Alfred E. Smith	Democrat	15,007,698	40.9	87	
1932	48	**FRANKLIN D. ROOSEVELT**	DEMOCRAT	22,829,501	57.7	472	56.9
		Herbert C. Hoover	Republican	15,760,684	39.8	59	
		Norman Thomas	Socialist	884,649	2.2		
1936	48	**FRANKLIN D. ROOSEVELT**	DEMOCRAT	27,757,333	60.8	523	61.0
		Alfred M. Landon	Republican	16,684,231	36.6	8	
		William Lemke	Union	892,267	2.0		
1940	48	**FRANKLIN D. ROOSEVELT**	DEMOCRAT	27,313,041	54.9	449	62.5
		Wendell L. Willkie	Republican	22,348,480	44.9	82	
1944	48	**FRANKLIN D. ROOSEVELT**	DEMOCRAT	25,612,610	53.5	432	55.9
		Thomas E. Dewey	Republican	22,017,617	46.0	99	
1948	48	**HARRY S. TRUMAN**	DEMOCRAT	24,179,345	49.7	303	53.0
		Thomas E. Dewey	Republican	21,991,291	45.3	189	
		J. Strom Thurmond	States' Rights	1,176,125	2.4	39	
		Henry A. Wallace	Progressive	1,157,326	2.4		
1952	48	**DWIGHT D. EISENHOWER**	REPUBLICAN	33,936,234	55.1	442	63.3
		Adlai E. Stevenson	Democrat	27,314,992	44.4	89	

Year	Number of States	Candidates	Parties	Popular Vote	% of Popular Vote	Electoral Vote	% Voter Participation
1956	48	**DWIGHT D. EISENHOWER**	REPUBLICAN	35,590,472	57.6	457	60.6
		Adlai E. Stevenson	Democrat	26,022,752	42.1	73	
1960	50	**JOHN F. KENNEDY**	DEMOCRAT	34,226,731	49.7	303	62.8
		Richard M. Nixon	Republican	34,108,157	49.6	219	
1964	50	**LYNDON B. JOHNSON**	DEMOCRAT	43,129,566	61.0	486	61.9
		Barry M. Goldwater	Republican	27,178,188	38.4	52	
1968	50	**RICHARD M. NIXON**	REPUBLICAN	31,785,480	43.2	301	60.9
		Hubert H. Humphrey	Democrat	31,275,166	42.6	191	
		George C. Wallace	American Independent	9,906,473	12.9	46	
1972	50	**RICHARD M. NIXON**	REPUBLICAN	47,169,911	60.7	520	55.2
		George S. McGovern	Democrat	29,170,383	37.5	17	
		John G. Schmitz	American	1,099,482	1.4		
1976	50	**JIMMY CARTER**	DEMOCRAT	40,830,763	50.0	297	53.5
		Gerald R. Ford	Republican	39,147,793	48.0	240	
1980	50	**RONALD REAGAN**	REPUBLICAN	43,904,153	50.9	489	52.6
		Jimmy Carter	Democrat	35,483,883	41.1	49	
		John B. Anderson	Independent	5,720,060	6.6		
		Ed Clark	Libertarian	921,299	1.1		

Year	Number of States	Candidates	Parties	Popular Vote	% of Popular Vote	Electoral Vote	% Voter Participation
1984	50	**RONALD REAGAN** Walter F. Mondale	REPUBLICAN Democrat	54,455,075 37,577,185	58.8 40.5	525 13	53.1
1988	50	**GEORGE H. BUSH** Michael Dukakis	REPUBLICAN Democrat	48,886,097 41,809,074	53.4 45.6	426 111	50.1
1992	50	**BILL CLINTON** George H. Bush H. Ross Perot	DEMOCRAT Republican Independent	44,909,326 39,103,882 19,741,657	42.9 37.4 18.9	370 168	55.0
1996	50	**BILL CLINTON** Bob Dole H. Ross Perot	DEMOCRAT Republican Reform Party	47,402,357 39,198,755 8,085,402	49.2 40.7 8.4	379 159	49.0
2000	50	**GEORGE W. BUSH** Albert Gore Ralph Nader	REPUBLICAN Democrat Green Party	50,455,156 50,992,335 2,882,738	47.9 48.4 2.7	271 266	50.4
2004	50	**GEORGE W. BUSH** John F. Kerry	REPUBLICAN Democrat	62,040,610 59,028,111	50.7 48.3	286 251	56.2
2008	50	**BARACK H. OBAMA** John S. McCain	DEMOCRAT Republican	66,882,230 58,343,671	53% 46%	365 173	56.8

Candidates receiving less than 1 percent of the popular vote have been omitted. Thus, the percentage of popular vote given for any election year may not total 100 percent. Before the passage of the Twelfth Amendment in 1804, the electoral college voted for two presidential candidates; the runner-up became vice president.

ADMISSION OF STATES

Order of Admission	State	Date of Admission	Order of Admission	State	Date of Admission
1	Delaware	December 7, 1787	26	Michigan	January 26, 1837
2	Pennsylvania	December 12, 1787	27	Florida	March 3, 1845
3	New Jersey	December 18, 1787	28	Texas	December 29, 1845
4	Georgia	January 2, 1788	29	Iowa	December 28, 1846
5	Connecticut	January 9, 1788	30	Wisconsin	May 29, 1848
6	Massachusetts	February 7, 1788	31	California	September 9, 1850
7	Maryland	April 28, 1788	32	Minnesota	May 11, 1858
8	South Carolina	May 23, 1788	33	Oregon	February 14, 1859
9	New Hampshire	June 21, 1788	34	Kansas	January 29, 1861
10	Virginia	June 25, 1788	35	West Virginia	June 30, 1863
11	New York	July 26, 1788	36	Nevada	October 31, 1864
12	North Carolina	November 21, 1789	37	Nebraska	March 1, 1867
13	Rhode Island	May 29, 1790	38	Colorado	August 1, 1876
14	Vermont	March 4, 1791	39	North Dakota	November 2, 1889
15	Kentucky	June 1, 1792	40	South Dakota	November 2, 1889
16	Tennessee	June 1, 1796	41	Montana	November 8, 1889
17	Ohio	March 1, 1803	42	Washington	November 11, 1889
18	Louisiana	April 30, 1812	43	Idaho	July 3, 1890
19	Indiana	December 11, 1816	44	Wyoming	July 10, 1890
20	Mississippi	December 10, 1817	45	Utah	January 4, 1896
21	Illinois	December 3, 1818	46	Oklahoma	November 16, 1907
22	Alabama	December 14, 1819	47	New Mexico	January 6, 1912
23	Maine	March 15, 1820	48	Arizona	February 14, 1912
24	Missouri	August 10, 1821	49	Alaska	January 3, 1959
25	Arkansas	June 15, 1836	50	Hawaii	August 21, 1959

Population of the United States

Year	Number of States	Population	% Increase	Population per Square Mile
1790	13	3,929,214		4.5
1800	16	5,308,483	35.1	6.1
1810	17	7,239,881	36.4	4.3
1820	23	9,638,453	33.1	5.5
1830	24	12,866,020	33.5	7.4
1840	26	17,069,453	32.7	9.8
1850	31	23,191,876	35.9	7.9
1860	33	31,443,321	35.6	10.6
1870	37	39,818,449	26.6	13.4
1880	38	50,155,783	26.0	16.9
1890	44	62,947,714	25.5	21.1
1900	45	75,994,575	20.7	25.6
1910	46	91,972,266	21.0	31.0
1920	48	105,710,620	14.9	35.6
1930	48	122,775,046	16.1	41.2
1940	48	131,669,275	7.2	44.2
1950	48	150,697,361	14.5	50.7
1960	50	179,323,175	19.0	50.6
1970	50	203,235,298	13.3	57.5
1980	50	226,504,825	11.4	64.0
1985	50	237,839,000	5.0	67.2
1990	50	250,122,000	5.2	70.6
1995	50	263,411,707	5.3	74.4
2000	50	281,421,906	6.8	77.0
2005	50	296,410,404	5.3	81.7

HISTORICAL STATISTICS OF THE UNITED STATES

LABOR FORCE—SELECTED CHARACTERISTICS EXPRESSED AS A PERCENTAGE OF THE LABOR FORCE: 1800–2000

Year	Agriculture	Manufacturing	Domestic service	Clerical, sales, and service	Professions	Slave	Nonwhite	Foreign-born	Female
1800	74.4	—	2.4	—	—	30.2	32.6	—	21.4
1860	55.8	13.8	5.4	4.8[1]	3.0[1]	21.7	23.6	24.5[1]	19.6
1910	30.7	20.8	5.5	14.1	4.7	—	13.4	22.0	20.8
1950	12.0	26.4	2.5	27.3	8.9	—	10.0	8.7	27.9
2000	2.4	14.7	0.6	38.0[2]	15.6	—	16.5	10.3[2]	46.6

[1]Values for 1870 are presented here because the available data for 1860 exclude slaves.
[2]1990.
Note: "Clerical, sales, and service" excludes domestic service.

IMMIGRATION, BY ORIGIN (in thousands)

Period	Europe	Americas	Asia
1820–30	106	12	—
1831–40	496	33	—
1841–50	1,597	62	—
1851–60	2,453	75	42
1861–70	2,065	167	65
1871–80	2,272	404	70
1881–90	4,735	427	70
1891–1900	3,555	39	75
1901–10	8,065	362	324
1911–20	4,322	1,144	247
1921–30	2,463	1,517	112
1931–40	348	160	16
1941–50	621	355	32
1951–60	1,326	997	150
1961–70	1,123	1,716	590
1971–80	800	1,983	1,588
1981–90	762	3,616	2,738
1991–2000	1,100	3,800	2,200

UNEMPLOYMENT RATE, 1890–2010

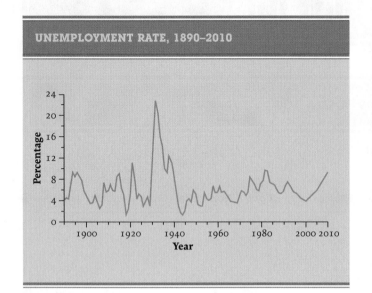

VOTER PARTICIPATION IN PRESIDENTIAL ELECTIONS, 1824–2008

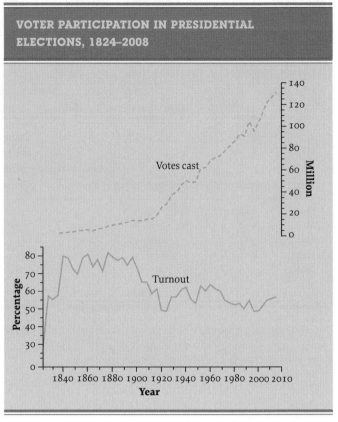

UNION MEMBERSHIP AS A PERCENTAGE OF NONAGRICULTURAL EMPLOYMENT, 1880–2009

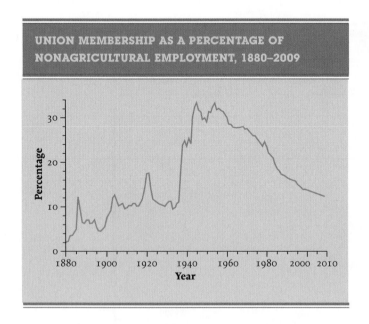

BIRTHRATE, 1820–2009

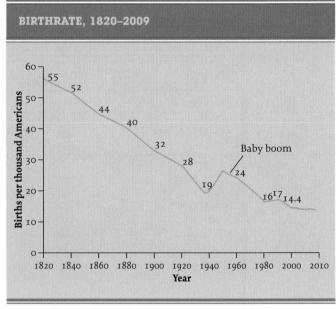

Abolitionism Social movement of the pre–Civil War era that advocated the immediate emancipation of the slaves and their incorporation into American society as equal citizens.

Agricultural Adjustment Act (1933) New Deal legislation that established the Agricultural Adjustment Administration (AAA) to improve agricultural prices by limiting market supplies; declared unconstitutional in *United States v. Butler* (1936).

Aid to Families with Dependent Children Federal program, also known as "welfare," of financial assistance to needy American families; created in 1935 as part of the Social Security Act; abolished in 1996.

Alamo, Battle of the Siege in the Texas War for Independence, 1836, in which the San Antonio mission fell to the Mexicans.

Alien and Sedition Acts (1798) Four measures passed during the undeclared war with France that limited the freedoms of speech and press and restricted the liberty of noncitizens.

America First Committee Largely midwestern isolationist organization supported by many prominent citizens, 1940–1941.

American Civil Liberties Union Organization founded during World War I to protest the suppression of freedom of expression in wartime; played a major role in court cases that achieved judicial recognition of Americans' civil liberties.

American Colonization Society Organized in 1816 to encourage colonization of free blacks to Africa; West African nation of Liberia founded in 1822 to serve as a homeland for them.

American Federation of Labor Founded in 1881 as a federation of trade unions composed mostly of skilled, white, native-born workers; its long-term president was Samuel Gompers.

American System Program of internal improvements and protective tariffs promoted by Speaker of the House Henry Clay in his presidential campaign of 1824; his proposals formed the core of Whig ideology in the 1830s and 1840s.

Amistad Ship that transported slaves from one port in Cuba to another, seized by the slaves in 1839. They made their way northward to the United States, where the status of the slaves became the subject of a celebrated court case; eventually most were able to return to Africa.

Anarchism Belief that all institutions that exercise power over individuals, especially government, are illegitimate; it flourished among certain native-born individualists in the nineteenth century and radical immigrants in the early twentieth century.

Antietam, Battle of One of the bloodiest battles of the Civil War, fought to a standoff on September 17, 1862, in western Maryland.

Antifederalists Opponents of the Constitution who saw it as a limitation on individual and states' rights; their demands led to the addition of a Bill of Rights to the document.

Appomattox Courthouse, Virginia Site of the surrender of Confederate general Robert E. Lee to Union general Ulysses S. Grant on April 9, 1865, marking the end of the Civil War.

Army-McCarthy hearings Televised U.S. Senate hearings in 1954 on Senator Joseph McCarthy's charges of disloyalty in the army; his tactics contributed to his censure by the Senate.

Articles of Confederation First frame of government for the United States; in effect from 1781 to 1788, it provided for a weak central authority and was soon replaced by the Constitution.

Atlanta Compromise Speech to the Cotton States and International Exposition in 1895 by educator Booker T. Washington, the leading black spokesman of the day; black scholar W. E. B. Du Bois gave the speech its derisive name and criticized Washington for encouraging blacks to accommodate segregation and disenfranchisement.

Atlantic Charter Issued August 12, 1941, following meetings in Newfoundland between President Franklin D. Roosevelt and British prime minister Winston Churchill, the charter signaled the Allies' cooperation and stated their war aims.

Atomic Energy Commission Created in 1946 to supervise peacetime uses of atomic energy.

Axis powers In World War II, the nations of Germany, Italy, and Japan.

Aztec Mesoamerican people who were conquered by the Spanish under Hernán Cortés, 1519–1528.

Baby boom Markedly higher birthrate in the years following World War II; led to the biggest demographic "bubble" in American history.

Bacon's Rebellion Unsuccessful 1676 revolt led by planter Nathaniel Bacon against Virginia governor William Berkeley's administration because of governmental corruption and because Berkeley had failed to protect settlers from Indian raids and did not allow them to occupy Indian lands.

Baker v. Carr **(1962)** U.S. Supreme Court decision that established the principle of "one man, one vote," that is, that legislative districts must be equal in population.

Bakke v. Regents of the University of California **(1978)** Case in which the U.S. Supreme Court ruled against the California university system's use of racial quotas in admissions but allowed the use of race as one factor in admissions decisions.

Balance of trade Ratio of imports to exports.

Bank of the United States Proposed by the first secretary of the treasury, Alexander Hamilton, the bank opened in 1791 and operated until 1811 to issue a uniform currency, make business loans, and collect tax monies. The Second Bank of the United States was chartered in 1816 but President Andrew Jackson vetoed the recharter bill in 1832.

Barbary pirates Plundering pirates off the Mediterranean coast of Africa; President Thomas Jefferson's refusal to pay them tribute to protect American ships sparked an undeclared naval war with North African nations, 1801–1805.

Barbed wire First practical fencing material for the Great Plains was invented in 1873 and rapidly spelled the end of the open range.

Bay of Pigs invasion Hoping to inspire a revolt against Fidel Castro, the CIA sent 1,500 Cuban exiles to invade their homeland on April 17, 1961, but the mission was a spectacular failure.

Bill of Rights First ten amendments to the U.S. Constitution, adopted in 1791 to guarantee individual rights against infringement by the federal government.

Black Codes (1865–1866) Laws passed in southern states to restrict the rights of former slaves; to nullify the codes, Congress passed the Civil Rights Act of 1866 and the Fourteenth Amendment.

Black Legend Idea that the Spanish New World empire was more oppressive toward the Indians than other European empires; was used as a justification for English imperial expansion.

Black Power Post-1966 rallying cry of a more militant civil rights movement.

Bland-Allison Act (1878) Passed over President Rutherford B. Hayes's veto, the inflationary measure authorized the purchase each month of 2 to 4 million dollars' worth of silver for coinage.

"Bleeding Kansas" Violence between pro- and antislavery settlers in the Kansas Territory, 1856.

Boston Massacre Clash between British soldiers and a Boston mob, March 5, 1770, in which five colonists were killed.

Boston Tea Party On December 16, 1773, the Sons of Liberty, dressed as Indians, dumped hundreds of chests of tea into Boston Harbor to protest the Tea Act of 1773, under which the British exported to the colonies millions of pounds of cheap—but still taxed—tea, thereby undercutting the price of smuggled tea and forcing payment of the tea duty.

Boxer Rebellion Chinese nationalist protest against Western commercial domination and cultural influence, 1900; a coalition of American, European, and Japanese forces put down the rebellion and reclaimed captured embassies in Peking (Beijing) within the year.

Bracero **program** System agreed to by Mexican and American governments in 1942 under which tens of thousands of Mexicans entered the United States to work temporarily in agricultural jobs in the Southwest; lasted until 1964 and inhibited labor organization among farm workers since *braceros* could be deported at any time.

Brains trust Group of advisers—many of them academics—assembled by Franklin D. Roosevelt to recommend New Deal policies during the early months of his presidency.

Bretton Woods Town in New Hampshire and site of international agreement in 1944 by which the American dollar replaced the British pound as the most important international currency, and the World Bank and International Monetary Fund were created to promote rebuilding after World War II and to ensure that countries did not devalue their currencies.

Brook Farm Transcendentalist commune in West Roxbury, Massachusetts, populated from 1841 to 1847 principally by writers (Nathaniel Hawthorne, for one) and other intellectuals.

Brown v. Board of Education of Topeka (1954) U.S. Supreme Court decision that struck down racial segregation in public education and declared "separate but equal" unconstitutional.

Bull Run, Battles of (First and Second Manassas) First land engagement of the Civil War took place on July 21, 1861, at Manassas Junction, Virginia, at which Union troops quickly retreated; one year later, on August 29–30, Confederates captured the federal supply depot and forced Union troops back to Washington.

Bunker Hill, Battle of First major battle of the Revolutionary War; it actually took place at nearby Breed's Hill, Massachusetts, on June 17, 1775.

"Burned-over district" Area of western New York strongly influenced by the revivalist fervor of the Second Great Awakening; Disciples of Christ and Mormons are among the many sects that trace their roots to the phenomenon.

Bush v. Gore (2000) U.S. Supreme Court case that determined the winner of the disputed 2000 presidential election.

Calvinism Doctrine of predestination expounded by Swiss theologian John Calvin in 1536; influenced the Puritan, Presbyterian, German and Dutch Reformed, and Huguenot churches in the colonies.

Camp David accords Peace agreement between the leaders of Israel and Egypt, brokered by President Jimmy Carter in 1978.

Carpetbaggers Derisive term for northern emigrants who participated in the Republican governments of the Reconstruction South.

Chancellorsville, Battle of Confederate general Robert E. Lee won his last major victory and General "Stonewall" Jackson died in this Civil War battle in northern Virginia on May 1–4, 1863.

Chinese Exclusion Act (1882) Halted Chinese immigration to the United States.

Civil Rights Act of 1866 Along with the Fourteenth Amendment, guaranteed the rights of citizenship to former slaves.

Civil Rights Act of 1957 First federal civil rights law since Reconstruction; established the Civil Rights Commission and the Civil Rights Division of the Department of Justice.

Civil Rights Act of 1964 Outlawed discrimination in public accommodations and employment.

Closed shop Hiring requirement that all workers in a business must be union members.

Coercive Acts/Intolerable Acts (1774) Four parliamentary measures in reaction to the Boston Tea Party that forced payment for the tea, disallowed colonial trials of British soldiers, forced their quartering in private homes, and reduced the number of elected officials in Massachusetts.

Cold War Term for tensions, 1945–1989, between the Soviet Union and the United States, the two major world powers after World War II.

Commonwealth v. Hunt (1842) Landmark ruling of the Massachusetts Supreme Court establishing the legality of labor unions.

Communitarianism Social reform movement of the nineteenth century driven by the belief that by establishing small communities based on common ownership of property, a less competitive and individualistic society could be developed.

Compromise of 1850 Complex compromise devised by Senator Henry Clay that admitted California as a free state, included a stronger fugitive slave law, and delayed determination of the slave status of the New Mexico and Utah territories.

Compromise of 1877 Deal made by a Republican and Democratic special congressional commission to resolve the disputed presidential election of 1876; Republican Rutherford B. Hayes, who had lost the popular vote, was declared the winner in exchange for the withdrawal of federal troops from involvement in politics in the South, marking the end of Reconstruction.

Congress of Industrial Organizations (CIO) Umbrella organization of semiskilled industrial unions, formed in 1935 as the Committee for Industrial Organization and renamed in 1938.

Congress of Racial Equality (CORE) Civil rights organization started in 1942 and best known for its Freedom Rides, bus journeys challenging racial segregation in the South in 1961.

Conspicuous consumption Phrase referring to extravagant spending to raise social standing, coined by Thorstein Veblen in *The Theory of the Leisure Class* (1899).

Constitutional Convention Meeting in Philadelphia, May 25–September 17, 1787, of representatives from twelve colonies—excepting Rhode Island—to revise the existing Articles of Confederation; convention soon resolved to produce an entirely new constitution.

Containment General U.S. strategy in the Cold War that called for containing Soviet expansion; originally devised by U.S. diplomat George F. Kennan.

Continental army Army authorized by the Continental Congress in 1775 to fight the British; commanded by General George Washington.

Continental Congress Representatives of the colonies met first in Philadelphia in 1774 to formulate actions against British policies; the Second Continental Congress (1775–1789) conducted the war and adopted the Declaration of Independence and the Articles of Confederation.

Convict leasing System developed in the post–Civil War South that generated income for the states and satisfied planters' need for cheap labor by renting prisoners out; the convicts were often treated poorly.

Copperheads Republican term for northerners opposed to the Civil War; it derived from the name of a poisonous snake.

Coral Sea, Battle of the Fought on May 7–8, 1942, near the eastern coast of Australia, it was the first U.S. naval victory over Japan in World War II.

Cotton gin Invented by Eli Whitney in 1793, the machine separated cotton seed from cotton fiber, speeding cotton processing and making profitable the cultivation of the more hardy, but difficult to clean, short-staple cotton; led directly to the dramatic nineteenth-century expansion of slavery in the South.

Counterculture "Hippie" youth culture of the 1960s, which rejected the values of the dominant culture in favor of illicit drugs, communes, free sex, and rock music.

Court-packing plan President Franklin D. Roosevelt's failed 1937 attempt to increase the number of U.S. Supreme Court justices from nine to fifteen in order to save his Second New Deal programs from constitutional challenges.

Coverture Principle in English and American law that a married woman lost her legal identity, which became "covered" by that of her husband, who therefore controlled her person and the family's economic resources.

Crédit Mobilier scandal Millions of dollars in overcharges for building the Union Pacific Railroad were exposed; high officials of the Ulysses S. Grant administration were implicated but never charged.

Creoles (*Criollos* in Spanish) Persons born in the New World of European ancestry.

Cuban missile crisis Caused when the United States discovered Soviet offensive missile sites in Cuba in October 1962; the U.S.-Soviet confrontation was the Cold War's closest brush with nuclear war.

Crop-lien system Merchants extended credit to tenants based on their future crops, but high interest rates and the uncertainties of farming often led to inescapable debts.

D-Day June 6, 1944, when an Allied amphibious assault landed on the Normandy coast and established a foothold in Europe, leading to the liberation of France from German occupation.

***Dartmouth College v. Woodward* (1819)** U.S. Supreme Court upheld the original charter of the college against New Hampshire's attempt to alter the board of trustees; set precedent of support of contracts against state interference.

Dawes Act Law passed in 1887 meant to encourage adoption of white norms among Indians; broke up tribal holdings into small farms for Indian families, with the remainder sold to white purchasers.

Declaration of Independence Document adopted on July 4, 1776, that made the break with Britain official; drafted by a committee of the Second Continental Congress, including principal writer Thomas Jefferson.

Deindustrialization Term describing decline of manufacturing in old industrial areas in the late twentieth century as companies shifted production to low-wage centers in the South and West or in other countries.

Deism Enlightenment thought applied to religion; emphasized reason, morality, and natural law.

Democratic-Republican Societies Organizations created in the mid-1790s by opponents of the policies of the Washington administration and supporters of the French Revolution.

Department of Homeland Security Created to coordinate federal antiterrorist activity following the 2001 terrorist attacks on the World Trade Center and Pentagon.

Depression Period in which economic output declines sharply and unemployment rises; it applied especially to the Great Depression of the 1930s.

Depression of 1893 Worst depression of the nineteenth century, set off by a railroad failure, too much speculation on Wall Street, and low agricultural prices.

Disenfranchise To deprive of the right to vote; in the United States, exclusionary policies were used to deny groups, especially African-Americans and women, their voting rights.

Division of Powers The division of political power between the state and federal governments under the U.S. Constitution (also known as federalism).

Dixiecrats Deep South delegates who walked out of the 1948 Democratic National Convention in protest of the party's support for civil rights legislation and later formed the States' Rights Democratic (Dixiecrat) Party, which nominated Strom Thurmond of South Carolina for president.

Dominion of New England Consolidation into a single colony of the New England colonies—and later New York and New Jersey—by royal governor Edmund Andros in 1686; dominion reverted to individual colonial governments three years later.

Dred Scott v. Sandford **(1857)** U.S. Supreme Court decision in which Chief Justice Roger B. Taney ruled that Congress could not prohibit slavery in the territories, on the grounds that such a prohibition would violate the Fifth Amendment rights of slaveholders, and that no black person could be a citizen of the United States.

Due-process clause Clause in the Fifth and the Fourteenth Amendments to the U.S. Constitution guaranteeing that states could not "deprive any person of life, liberty, or property, without due process of law."

Dust Bowl Great Plains counties where millions of tons of topsoil were blown away from parched farmland in the 1930s; massive migration of farm families followed.

Eighteenth Amendment (1919) Prohibition amendment that made illegal the manufacture, sale, or transportation of alcoholic beverages; repealed in 1933.

Ellis Island Reception center in New York Harbor through which most European immigrants to America were processed from 1892 to 1954.

Emancipation Proclamation (1863) President Abraham Lincoln issued a preliminary proclamation on September 22, 1862, freeing the slaves in areas under Confederate control as of January 1, 1863, the date of the final proclamation, which also authorized the enrollment of black soldiers into the Union army.

Embargo Act of 1807 Attempt to exert economic pressure by prohibiting all exports from the United States, instead of waging war in reaction to continued British impressment of American sailors; smugglers easily circumvented the embargo, and it was repealed two years later.

Emergency Banking Relief Act (1933) First New Deal measure that provided for reopening the banks under strict conditions and took the United States off the gold standard.

Emergency Immigration Act of 1921 Limited U.S. immigration to 3 percent of each foreign-born nationality in the 1910 census; three years later, Congress restricted immigration even further.

Encomienda System under which officers of the Spanish conquistadores gained ownership of Indian land.

Enlightenment Revolution in thought in the eighteenth century that emphasized reason and science over the authority of traditional religion.

Environmental Protection Agency (EPA) Created in 1970 during the first administration of President Richard M. Nixon to oversee federal pollution control efforts.

Equal Rights Amendment Amendment to guarantee equal rights for women, introduced in 1923 but not passed by Congress until 1972; it failed to be ratified by the states.

Era of Good Feelings Contemporary characterization of the administration of popular Republican president James Monroe, 1817–1825.

Erie Canal Most important and profitable of the canals of the 1820s and 1830s; stretched from Buffalo to Albany, New York, connecting the Great Lakes to the East Coast and making New York City the nation's largest port.

Espionage and Sedition Acts (1917–1918) Limited criticism of government leaders and policies by imposing fines and prison terms on those who opposed American participation in the First World War.

Eugenics "Science" of improving the human race by regulating who can bear children; flourished in early twentieth century and led to laws for involuntary sterilization of the "feeble-minded."

Fair Deal Domestic reform proposals of the Truman administration; included civil rights legislation, national health insurance, and repeal of the Taft-Hartley Act, but only extensions of some New Deal programs were enacted.

Fair Employment Practices Commission Created in 1941 by executive order, the FEPC sought to eliminate racial discrimination in jobs; it possessed little power but represented a step toward civil rights for African-Americans.

Family wage Idea that male workers should earn a wage sufficient to enable them to support their entire family without their wives having to work outside the home.

Federal Trade Commission Act (1914) Established the Federal Trade Commission to enforce existing antitrust laws that prohibited business combinations in restraint of trade.

The Federalist Collection of eighty-five essays that appeared in the New York press in 1787–1788 in support of the Constitution; written by Alexander Hamilton, James Madison, and John Jay and published under the pseudonym "Publius."

Federalist Party One of the two first national political parties; led by George Washington, John Adams, and Alexander Hamilton, it favored a strong central government.

Feminism Term that entered the lexicon in the early twentieth century to describe the movement for full equality for women, in political, social, and personal life.

Fifteenth Amendment Constitutional Amendment ratified in 1870, which prohibited states from discriminating in voting privileges on the basis of race.

"Fifty-four forty or fight" Democratic campaign slogan in the presidential election of 1844, urging that the northern border of Oregon be fixed at 54°40′ north latitude.

Filibuster In the nineteenth century, invasions of Central American countries launched privately by groups of Americans seeking to establish personal rule and spread slavery; in the twentieth century, term for the practice of members of the U.S. Senate delivering interminable speeches in order to prevent voting on legislation.

***Fletcher v. Peck* (1810)** U.S. Supreme Court decision in which Chief Justice John Marshall upheld the initial fraudulent sale contracts in the Yazoo Fraud cases; it upheld the principle of sanctity of a contract.

Fordism Early twentieth-century term describing the economic system pioneered by Ford Motor Company based on high wages and mass consumption.

Fort McHenry Fort in Baltimore Harbor unsuccessfully bombarded by the British in September 1814; Francis Scott Key, a witness to the battle, was moved to write the words to "The Star-Spangled Banner."

Fort Sumter First battle of the Civil War, in which the federal fort in Charleston (South Carolina) Harbor was captured by the Confederates on April 14, 1861, after two days of shelling.

Fourteen Points President Woodrow Wilson's 1918 plan for peace after World War I; at the Versailles peace conference, however, he failed to incorporate all of the points into the treaty.

Fourteenth Amendment (1868) Guaranteed rights of citizenship to former slaves, in words similar to those of the Civil Rights Act of 1866.

Franchise The right to vote.

"Free person of color" Negro or mulatto person not held in slavery; immediately before the Civil War, there were nearly a half million in the United States, split almost evenly between North and South.

Free Soil Party Formed in 1848 to oppose slavery in the territory acquired in the Mexican War; nominated Martin Van Buren for president in 1848. By 1854 most of the party's members had joined the Republican Party.

Free Speech Movement Founded in 1964 at the University of California at Berkeley by student radicals protesting restrictions on their right to distribute political publications.

Freedmen's Bureau Reconstruction agency established in 1865 to protect the legal rights of former slaves and to assist with their education, jobs, health care, and landowning.

French and Indian War Known in Europe as the Seven Years' War, the last (1755–1763) of four colonial wars fought between England and France for control of North America east of the Mississippi River.

Fugitive Slave Act of 1850 Gave federal government authority in cases involving runaway slaves; aroused considerable opposition in the North.

Fundamentalism Anti-modernist Protestant movement started in the early twentieth century that proclaimed the literal truth of the Bible; the name came from *The Fundamentals*, published by conservative leaders.

Gadsden Purchase (1853) Thirty thousand square miles in present-day Arizona and New Mexico bought by Congress from Mexico primarily for the Southern Pacific Railroad's transcontinental route.

Gag Rule Rule adopted by House of Representatives in 1836 prohibiting consideration of abolitionist petitions; opposition, led by former president John Quincy Adams, succeeded in having it repealed in 1844.

Gentlemen's Agreement (1907) The United States would not exclude Japanese immigrants if Japan would voluntarily limit the number of immigrants coming to the United States.

Gettysburg, Battle of Fought in southern Pennsylvania, July 1–3, 1863; the Confederate defeat and the simultaneous loss at Vicksburg marked the military turning point of the Civil War.

***Gibbons v. Ogden* (1824)** U.S. Supreme Court decision reinforcing the "commerce clause" (the federal government's right to regulate interstate commerce) of the Constitution; Chief Justice John Marshall ruled against the State of New York's granting of steamboat monopolies.

Gideon v. Wainwright (1963) U.S. Supreme Court decision guaranteeing legal counsel for indigent felony defendants.

The Gilded Age Mark Twain and Charles Dudley Warner's 1873 novel, the title of which became the popular name for the period from the end of the Civil War to the turn of the century.

Glass-Steagall Act (Banking Act of 1933) Established the Federal Deposit Insurance Corporation and included banking reforms, some designed to control speculation. Repealed in 1999, opening the door to scandals involving banks and stock investment companies.

Globalization Term that became prominent in the 1990s to describe the rapid acceleration of international flows of commerce, financial resources, labor, and cultural products.

Gold standard Policy at various points in American history by which the value of a dollar is set at a fixed price in terms of gold (in the post–World War II era, for example, $35 per ounce of gold).

Good Neighbor Policy Proclaimed by President Franklin D. Roosevelt in his first inaugural address in 1933, it sought improved diplomatic relations between the United States and its Latin American neighbors.

Grandfather clause Loophole created by southern disfranchising legislatures of the 1890s for illiterate white males whose grandfathers had been eligible to vote in 1867.

Granger movement Political movement that grew out of the Patrons of Husbandry, an educational and social organization for farmers founded in 1867; the Grange had its greatest success in the Midwest of the 1870s, lobbying for government control of railroad and grain elevator rates and establishing farmers' cooperatives.

Great Awakening Fervent religious revival movement in the 1720s through the 1740s that was spread throughout the colonies by ministers like New England Congregationalist Jonathan Edwards and English revivalist George Whitefield.

Great Compromise (Connecticut Compromise) Settled the differences between the New Jersey and Virginia delegations to the Constitutional Convention by providing for a bicameral legislature, the upper house of which would have equal representation for each state and the lower house of which would be apportioned by population.

Great Depression Worst economic depression in American history; it was spurred by the stock market crash of 1929 and lasted until World War II.

Great Migration Large-scale migration of southern blacks during and after World War I to the North, where jobs had become available during the labor shortage of the war years.

Great Society Term coined by President Lyndon B. Johnson in his 1965 State of the Union address, in which he proposed legislation to address problems of voting rights, poverty, diseases, education, immigration, and the environment.

Greenback-Labor Party Formed in 1876 in reaction to economic depression, the party favored issuance of unsecured paper money to help farmers repay debts; the movement for free coinage of silver took the place of the greenback movement by the 1880s.

Griswold v. Connecticut (1965) Supreme Court decision that, in overturning Connecticut law prohibiting the use of contraceptives, established a constitutional right to privacy.

Gulf War Military action in 1991 in which an international coalition led by the United States drove Iraq from Kuwait, which it had occupied the previous year.

Habeas corpus, Writ of An essential component of English common law and of the U.S. Constitution that guarantees that citizens may not be imprisoned without due process of law; literally means, "you may have the body"; suspended by President Lincoln during the Civil War and limited by President Bush after the attacks of September 11, 2001.

Hacienda Large-scale farm in the Spanish New World empire worked by Indian laborers.

Harlem Renaissance African-American literary and artistic movement of the 1920s centered in New York City's Harlem neighborhood; writers Langston Hughes, Jean Toomer, Zora Neale Hurston, and Countee Cullen were among those active in the movement.

Harpers Ferry, Virginia Site of abolitionist John Brown's failed raid on the federal arsenal, October 16–17, 1859; Brown became a martyr to his cause after his capture and execution.

Hart-Celler Act (1965) Eliminated the national origins quota system for immigration established by laws in 1921 and 1924; led to radical change in the origins of immigrants to the United States, with Asians and Latin Americans outnumbering Europeans.

Hartford Convention Meeting of New England Federalists on December 15, 1814, to protest the War of 1812; proposed seven constitutional amendments (limiting embargoes and changing requirements for officeholding, declaration of war, and admission of new states), but the war ended before Congress could respond.

Hawley-Smoot Tariff Act (1930) Raised tariffs to an unprecedented level and worsened the Great Depression by raising prices and discouraging foreign trade.

Haymarket affair Violence during an anarchist protest at Haymarket Square in Chicago on May 4, 1886; the deaths of eight, including seven policemen, led to the trial of eight anarchist leaders for conspiracy to commit murder.

Hessians German soldiers, most from Hesse-Cassel principality (hence, the name), paid to fight for the British in the Revolutionary War.

Holding company Investment company that holds controlling interest in the securities of other companies.

Homestead Act (1862) Authorized Congress to grant 160 acres of public land to a western settler, who had to live on the land for five years to establish title.

Homestead Strike Violent strike at the Carnegie Steel Company near Pittsburgh in 1892 that culminated in the defeat of the Amalgamated Association of Iron and Steel Workers, the first steelworkers' union.

House Un-American Activities Committee (HUAC) Formed in 1938 to investigate subversives in the government and holders of radical ideas more generally; best-known investigations were of Hollywood notables and of former State Department official Alger Hiss, who was accused in 1948 of espionage and Communist Party membership. Abolished in 1975.

Hundred Days Extraordinarily productive first three months of President Franklin D. Roosevelt's administration in which a special session of Congress enacted fifteen of his New Deal proposals.

Impeachment Bringing charges against a public official; for example, the House of Representatives can impeach a president for "treason, bribery, or other high crimes and misdemeanors" by majority vote, and after the trial the Senate can remove the president by a vote of two-thirds. Two presidents, Andrew Johnson and Bill Clinton, have been impeached and tried before the Senate; neither was convicted.

Implied powers Federal powers beyond those specifically enumerated in the U.S. Constitution; based on the "elastic clause" of Article I, Section 8, of the Constitution that allows Congress to enact laws that promote the "general welfare."

"In God We Trust" Phrase placed on all new U.S. currency as of 1954.

Indentured servant Settler who signed on for a temporary period of servitude to a master in exchange for passage to the New World; Virginia and Pennsylvania were largely peopled in the seventeenth and eighteenth centuries by English and German indentured servants.

Indian Removal Act (1830) Signed by President Andrew Jackson, the law permitted the negotiation of treaties to obtain the Indians' lands in exchange for their relocation to what would become Oklahoma.

Individualism Term that entered the language in the 1820s to describe the increasing emphasis on the pursuit of personal advancement and private fulfillment free of outside interference.

Industrial Workers of the World Radical union organized in Chicago in 1905 and nicknamed the Wobblies; its opposition to World War I led to its destruction by the federal government under the Espionage Act.

Inflation An economic condition in which prices rise continuously.

Insular Cases Series of cases between 1901 and 1904 in which the Supreme Court ruled that constitutional protection of individual rights did not fully apply to residents of "insular" territories acquired by the United States in the Spanish-American War, such as Puerto Rico and the Philippines.

Interstate Commerce Commission Reacting to the U.S. Supreme Court's ruling in *Wabash Railroad v. Illinois* (1886), Congress established the ICC to curb abuses in the railroad industry by regulating rates.

Iran-Contra affair Scandal of the second Reagan administration involving sales of arms to Iran in partial exchange for release of hostages in Lebanon and use of the arms money to aid the Contras in Nicaragua, which had been expressly forbidden by Congress.

Iraq War Military campaign in 2003 in which the United States, unable to gain approval by the United Nations, unilaterally occupied Iraq and removed dictator Saddam Hussein from power.

Iron Curtain Term coined by Winston Churchill to describe the Cold War divide between western Europe and the Soviet Union's eastern European satellites.

Jamestown, Virginia Site in 1607 of the first permanent English settlement in the New World.

Japanese-American internment Policy adopted by the Roosevelt administration in 1942 under which 110,000 persons of Japanese descent, most of them American citizens, were removed from the West Coast and forced to spend most of World War II in internment camps; it was the largest violation of American civil liberties in the twentieth century.

Jay's Treaty Treaty with Britain negotiated in 1794 by Chief Justice John Jay; Britain agreed to vacate forts in the Northwest Territories, and festering disagreements (border with Canada, prewar debts, shipping claims) would be settled by commission.

Jim Crow Minstrel show character whose name became synonymous with racial segregation.

Kansas-Nebraska Act (1854) Law sponsored by Illinois senator Stephen A. Douglas to allow settlers in newly organized territories north of the Missouri border to decide the slavery issue for themselves; fury over the resulting repeal of the Missouri Compromise of 1820 led to violence in Kansas and to the formation of the Republican Party.

Kellogg-Briand Pact Representatives of sixty-two nations in 1928 signed the pact (also called the Pact of Paris) to outlaw war.

Keynesianism Economic theory derived from the writings of British economist John Maynard Keynes, which rejected the laissez-faire approach in favor of public spending to stimulate economic growth, even at the cost of federal deficits; dominated economic policies of administrations from the 1940s to the mid-1970s.

Knights of Labor Founded in 1869, the first national union lasted, under the leadership of Terence V. Powderly, only into the 1890s; supplanted by the American Federation of Labor.

Know-Nothing (American) Party Nativist, anti-Catholic third party organized in 1854 in reaction to large-scale German and Irish immigration; the party's only presidential candidate was Millard Fillmore in 1856.

Korean War Conflict touched off in 1950 when Communist North Korea invaded South Korea; fighting, largely by U.S. forces, continued until 1953.

Ku Klux Klan Organized in Pulaski, Tennessee, in 1866 to terrorize former slaves who voted and held political offices during Reconstruction; a revived organization in the 1910s and 1920s stressed white, Anglo-Saxon, fundamentalist Protestant supremacy; the Klan revived a third time to fight the civil rights movement of the 1950s and 1960s in the South.

Laissez-faire Term adopted from French, meaning "let people do as they choose," describing opposition to government action to regulate economic or personal behavior.

Land Ordinance of 1785 Directed surveying of the Northwest Territory into townships of thirty-six sections (square miles) each, the sale of the sixteenth section of which was to be used to finance public education.

League of Nations Organization of nations to mediate disputes and avoid war established after World War I as part of the Treaty of Versailles; President Woodrow Wilson's "Fourteen Points" speech to Congress in 1918 proposed the formation of the league, which the United States never joined.

Lend-Lease Act (1941) Permitted the United States to lend or lease arms and other supplies to the Allies, signifying increasing likelihood of American involvement in World War II.

Levittown Low-cost, mass-produced developments of suburban tract housing built by William Levitt after World War II on Long Island and elsewhere.

Lexington and Concord, Battle of The first shots fired in the Revolutionary War, on April 19, 1775, near Boston; approximately 100 minutemen and 250 British soldiers were killed.

Leyte Gulf, Battle of Largest sea battle in history, fought on October 25, 1944, and won by the United States off the Philippine island of Leyte; Japanese losses were so great that they could not rebound.

Liberalism Originally, political philosophy that emphasized the protection of liberty by limiting the power of government to interfere with the natural rights of citizens; in the twentieth century, belief in an activist government promoting greater social and economic equality.

Liberty Party Abolitionist political party that nominated James G. Birney for president in 1840 and 1844; merged with the Free Soil Party in 1848.

Lincoln-Douglas debates Series of senatorial campaign debates in 1858 focusing on the issue of slavery in the territories; held in Illinois between Republican Abraham Lincoln, who made a national reputation for himself, and incumbent Democratic senator Stephen A. Douglas, who managed to hold onto his seat.

Little Bighorn, Battle of Most famous battle of the Great Sioux War took place in 1876 in the Montana Territory; combined Sioux and Cheyenne warriors massacred a vastly outnumbered U.S. Cavalry commanded by Lieutenant Colonel George Armstrong Custer.

Lochner v. New York **(1905)** Decision by Supreme Court overturning a New York law establishing a limit on the number of hours per week bakers could be compelled to work; "Lochnerism" became a way of describing the liberty of contract jurisprudence, which opposed all governmental intervention in the economy.

Louisiana Purchase President Thomas Jefferson's 1803 purchase from France of the important port of New Orleans and 828,000 square miles west of the Mississippi River to the Rocky Mountains; it more than doubled the territory of the United States at a cost of only $15 million.

Loyalists Colonists who remained loyal to Great Britain during the War of Independence.

Lusitania British passenger liner sunk by a German U-boat, May 7, 1915, creating a diplomatic crisis and public outrage at the loss of 128 Americans (roughly 10 percent of the total aboard); Germany agreed to pay reparations, and the United States waited two more years to enter World War I.

Lyceum movement Founded in 1826, the movement promoted adult public education through lectures and performances.

Lynching Practice, particularly widespread in the South between 1890 and 1940, in which persons (usually black) accused of a crime were murdered by mobs before standing trial. Lynchings often took place before large crowds, with law enforcement authorities not intervening.

Manhattan Project Secret American program during World War II to develop an atomic bomb; J. Robert Oppenheimer led the team of physicists at Los Alamos, New Mexico.

Manifest Destiny Phrase first used in 1845 to urge annexation of Texas; used thereafter to encourage American settlement of European colonial and Indian lands in the Great Plains and the West and, more generally, as a justification for American empire.

Marbury v. Madison **(1803)** First U.S. Supreme Court decision to declare a federal law—the Judiciary Act of 1801—unconstitutional.

March on Washington Civil rights demonstration on August 28, 1963, where the Reverend Martin Luther King Jr., gave his "I Have a Dream" speech on the steps of the Lincoln Memorial.

Marshall Plan U.S. program for the reconstruction of post–World War II Europe through massive aid to former enemy nations as well as allies; proposed by General George C. Marshall in 1947.

Massive resistance In reaction to the *Brown* decision of 1954, effort by southern states to defy federally mandated school integration.

Maya Pre-Columbian society in Mesoamerica before about A.D. 900.

Mayflower Compact Signed in 1620 aboard the *Mayflower* before the Pilgrims landed at Plymouth, the document committed the group to majority-rule government.

McCarran Internal Security Act (1950) Passed over President Harry S. Truman's veto, the law required registration of American Communist Party members, denied them passports, and allowed them to be detained as suspected subversives.

McCarthyism Post–World War II Red Scare focused on the fear of Communists in U.S. government positions; peaked during the Korean War; most closely associated with Joseph McCarthy, a major instigator of the hysteria.

McCulloch v. Maryland **(1819)** U.S. Supreme Court decision in which Chief Justice John Marshall, holding that Maryland could not tax the Second Bank of the United States, supported the authority of the federal government versus the states.

McNary-Haugen bill Vetoed by President Calvin Coolidge in 1927 and 1928, the bill to aid farmers would have artificially raised agricultural prices by selling surpluses overseas for low prices and selling the reduced supply in the United States for higher prices.

Meat Inspection Act (1906) Passed largely in reaction to Upton Sinclair's *The Jungle*, the law set strict standards of cleanliness in the meatpacking industry.

Medicaid Great Society program established in 1965 that provided free medical care to the poor.

Medicare Key component of Great Society of Lyndon B. Johnson; government program created in 1965 to pay medical costs of elderly and disabled Americans.

Mercantilism Policy of Great Britain and other imperial powers of regulating the economies of colonies to benefit the mother country.

Mestizo Spanish word for person of mixed Native American and European ancestry.

Mexican War Controversial war with Mexico for control of California and New Mexico, 1846–1848; the Treaty of Guadalupe Hidalgo fixed the border at the Rio Grande and extended the United States to the Pacific coast, annexing more than a half-million square miles of Mexican territory.

Midway, Battle of Decisive American victory near Midway Island in the South Pacific on June 4, 1942; the Japanese navy never recovered its superiority over the U.S. navy.

Minstrel show Blackface vaudeville entertainment popular in the decades surrounding the Civil War.

***Miranda v. Arizona* (1966)** U.S. Supreme Court decision required police to advise persons in custody of their rights to legal counsel and against self-incrimination.

Missouri Compromise Deal proposed by Kentucky senator Henry Clay in 1820 to resolve the slave/free imbalance in Congress that would result from Missouri's admission as a slave state; Maine's admission as a free state offset Missouri, and slavery was prohibited in the remainder of the Louisiana Territory north of the southern border of Missouri.

Molly Maguires Secret organization of Irish coal miners that used violence to intimidate mine officials in the 1870s.

***Monitor* and *Merrimac*, Battle of the** First engagement between ironclad ships; fought at Hampton Roads, Virginia, on March 9, 1862.

Monroe Doctrine President James Monroe's declaration to Congress on December 2, 1823, that the American continents would be thenceforth closed to European colonization, and that the United States would not interfere in European affairs.

Montgomery bus boycott Sparked by Rosa Parks's arrest on December 1, 1955, for refusing to surrender her seat to a white passenger, a successful year-long boycott protesting segregation on city buses; led by the Reverend Martin Luther King Jr.

Moral Majority Televangelist Jerry Falwell's political lobbying organization, the name of which became synonymous with the Religious Right—conservative evangelical Protestants who helped ensure President Ronald Reagan's 1980 victory.

Mormons Founded in 1830 by Joseph Smith, the sect (officially, the Church of Jesus Christ of Latter-day Saints) was a product of the intense revivalism of the "burned-over district" of New York; Smith's successor Brigham Young led 15,000 followers to Utah in 1847 to escape persecution.

Muckrakers Writers who exposed corruption and abuses in politics, business, meatpacking, child labor, and more, primarily in the first decade of the twentieth century; their popular books and magazine articles spurred public interest in reform.

Mugwumps Reform wing of the Republican Party that supported Democrat Grover Cleveland for president in 1884 over Republican James G. Blaine, whose influence peddling had been revealed in the Mulligan letters of 1876.

Multiculturalism Term that became prominent in the 1990s to describe a growing emphasis on group racial and ethnic identity and demands that jobs, education, and politics reflect the increasingly diverse nature of American society.

***Munn v. Illinois* (1877)** U.S. Supreme Court ruling that upheld a Granger law allowing the state to regulate grain elevators.

NAFTA Approved in 1993, the North American Free Trade Agreement with Canada and Mexico allowed goods to travel across their borders free of tariffs; critics argued that American workers would lose their jobs to cheaper Mexican labor.

Nat Turner Rebellion Most important slave uprising in nineteenth-century America, led by a slave preacher who, with his followers, killed about sixty white persons in Southampton County, Virginia, in 1831.

National Association for the Advancement of Colored People (NAACP) Founded in 1910, this civil rights organization brought lawsuits against discriminatory practices and published *The Crisis*, a journal edited by African-American scholar W. E. B. Du Bois.

National Defense Education Act (1958) Passed in reaction to America's perceived inferiority in the space race; encouraged education in science and modern languages through student loans, university research grants, and aid to public schools.

National Industrial Recovery Act (1933) Passed on the last of the Hundred Days, it created public-works jobs through the Federal Emergency Relief Administration and established a system of self-regulation for industry through the National Recovery Administration, which was ruled unconstitutional in 1935.

National Organization for Women Founded in 1966 by writer Betty Friedan and other feminists, NOW pushed for abortion rights, nondiscrimination in the workplace, and other forms of equality for women.

National Road First federal interstate road, built between 1811 and 1838 and stretching from Cumberland, Maryland, to Vandalia, Illinois.

National Security Act (1947) Authorized the reorganization of government to coordinate military branches and security agencies; created the National Security Council, the Central Intelligence Agency, and the National Military Establishment (later renamed the Department of Defense).

National Youth Administration Created in 1935 as part of the Works Progress Administration, it employed millions of youths who had left school.

Nativism Anti-immigrant and anti-Catholic feeling especially prominent in the 1830s through the 1850s; the largest group was New York's Order of the Star-Spangled Banner, which expanded into the American (Know-Nothing) Party in 1854.

Naval stores Tar, pitch, and turpentine made from pine resin and used in shipbuilding; an important industry in the southern colonies, especially North Carolina.

Navigation Acts Passed by the English Parliament to control colonial trade and bolster the mercantile system, 1650–1775; enforcement of the acts led to growing resentment by colonists.

Neutrality Acts Series of laws passed between 1935 and 1939 to keep the United States from becoming involved in war by prohibiting American trade and travel to warring nations.

New Deal Franklin D. Roosevelt's campaign promise, in his speech to the Democratic National Convention of 1932, to combat the Great Depression with a "new deal for the American people"; the phrase became a catchword for his ambitious plan of economic programs.

New Freedom Democrat Woodrow Wilson's political slogan in the presidential campaign of 1912; Wilson wanted to improve the banking system, lower tariffs, and, by breaking up monopolies, give small businesses freedom to compete.

New Frontier John F. Kennedy's program, stymied by a Republican Congress and his abbreviated term; his successor Lyndon B. Johnson had greater success with many of the same concepts.

New Harmony Founded in Indiana by British industrialist Robert Owen in 1825, the short-lived New Harmony Community of Equality was one of the few nineteenth-century communal experiments not based on religious ideology.

New Left Radical youth protest movement of the 1960s, named by leader Tom Hayden to distinguish it from the Old (Marxist-Leninist) Left of the 1930s.

New Nationalism Platform of the Progressive Party and slogan of former president Theodore Roosevelt in the presidential campaign of 1912; stressed government activism, including regulation of trusts, conservation, and recall of state court decisions that had nullified progressive programs.

New Orleans, Battle of Last battle of the War of 1812, fought on January 8, 1815, weeks after the peace treaty was signed but prior to the news reaching America; General Andrew Jackson led the victorious American troops.

New South *Atlanta Constitution* editor Henry W. Grady's 1886 term for the prosperous post–Civil War South he envisioned: democratic, industrial, urban, and free of nostalgia for the defeated plantation South.

Nineteenth Amendment (1920) Granted women the right to vote.

Nisei Japanese-Americans; literally, "second generation."

Normalcy Word coined by future president Warren G. Harding as part of a 1920 campaign speech—"not nostrums, but normalcy"—signifying public weariness with Woodrow Wilson's internationalism and domestic reforms.

North Atlantic Treaty Organization (NATO) Alliance founded in 1949 by ten western European nations, the United States, and Canada to deter Soviet expansion in Europe.

Northwest Ordinance of 1787 Created the Northwest Territory (area north of the Ohio River and west of Pennsylvania), established conditions for self-government and statehood, included a Bill of Rights, and permanently prohibited slavery.

Nullification Concept of invalidation of a federal law within the borders of a state; first expounded in Thomas Jefferson's draft of Kentucky resolution against Alien and Sedition Acts (1798); cited by South Carolina in its Ordinance of Nullification (1832) of the Tariff of Abominations, used by southern states to explain their secession from the Union (1861), and cited again by southern states to oppose the *Brown v. Board of Education* decision (1954).

Office of Price Administration Created in 1941 to control wartime inflation and price fixing resulting from shortages of many consumer goods, the OPA imposed wage and price freezes and administered a rationing system.

Okies Displaced farm families from the Oklahoma dust bowl who migrated to California during the 1930s in search of jobs.

Oneida Community Utopian community founded in 1848; the Perfectionist religious group practiced "complex marriage" under leader John Humphrey Noyes.

OPEC Organization of Petroleum Exporting Countries.

Open Door Policy In hopes of protecting the Chinese market for U.S. exports, Secretary of State John Hay demanded in 1899 that Chinese trade be open to all nations.

Open shop Situation in which union membership is not a condition of employment in a factory or other business.

Operation Dixie CIO's largely ineffective post–World War II campaign to unionize southern workers.

Oregon Trail Route of wagon trains bearing settlers from Independence, Missouri, to the Oregon Country in the 1840s through the 1860s.

Ostend Manifesto Memorandum written in 1854 from Ostend, Belgium, by the U.S. ministers to England, France, and Spain recommending purchase or seizure of Cuba in order to increase the United States' slaveholding territory.

Panic of 1819 Financial collapse brought on by sharply falling cotton prices, declining demand for American exports, and reckless western land speculation.

Panic of 1837 Beginning of major economic depression lasting about six years; touched off by a British financial crisis and made worse by falling cotton prices, credit and currency problems, and speculation in land, canals, and railroads.

Panic of 1857 Beginning of economic depression lasting about two years and brought on by falling grain prices and a weak financial system; the South was largely protected by international demand for its cotton.

Panic of 1873 Onset of severe six-year depression marked by bank failures and railroad and insurance bankruptcies.

Peace of Paris Signed on September 3, 1783, the treaty ending the Revolutionary War and recognizing American independence from Britain also established the border between Canada and the United States, fixed the western border at the Mississippi River, and ceded Florida to Spain.

Pendleton Civil Service Act (1883) Established the Civil Service Commission and marked the end of the spoils system.

Pentagon Papers Informal name for the Defense Department's secret history of the Vietnam conflict; leaked to the press by former official Daniel Ellsberg and published in the *New York Times* in 1971.

Philippine War American military campaign that suppressed the movement for Philippine independence after the Spanish-American War; America's death toll was over 4,000 and the Philippines' was far higher.

Pilgrims Puritan Separatists who broke completely with the Church of England and sailed to the New World aboard the *Mayflower*, founding Plymouth Colony on Cape Cod in 1620.

Pinckney's Treaty Treaty with Spain negotiated by Thomas Pinckney in 1795; established United States boundaries at the Mississippi River and the thirty-first parallel and allowed open transportation on the Mississippi.

Plantation An early word for a colony, a settlement "planted" from abroad among an alien population in Ireland or the New World. Later, a large agricultural enterprise that used unfree labor to produce a crop for the world market.

Planter In the antebellum South, the owner of a large farm worked by twenty or more slaves.

Platt Amendment (1901) Amendment to Cuban constitution that reserved the United States' right to intervene in Cuban affairs and forced newly independent Cuba to host American naval bases on the island.

Plessy v. Ferguson (1896) U.S. Supreme Court decision supporting the legality of Jim Crow laws that permitted or required "separate but equal" facilities for blacks and whites.

Poll tax Tax that must be paid in order to be eligible to vote; used as an effective means of disenfranchising black citizens after Reconstruction, since they often could not afford even a modest fee.

Popular sovereignty Allowed settlers in a disputed territory to decide the slavery issue for themselves; program most closely associated with Senator Stephen A. Douglas of Illinois.

Populist Party Founded in 1892, it advocated a variety of reform issues, including free coinage of silver, income tax, postal savings, regulation of railroads, and direct election of U.S. senators.

Potsdam Conference Last meeting of the major Allied powers, the conference took place outside Berlin from July 17 to August 2, 1945; United States president Harry Truman, Soviet dictator Joseph Stalin, and British prime minister Clement Attlee finalized plans begun at Yalta.

Proclamation of Amnesty and Reconstruction President Lincoln's proposal for reconstruction, issued in 1863, allowed southern states to rejoin the Union if 10 percent of the 1860 electorate signed loyalty pledges, accepted emancipation, and had received presidential pardons.

Proclamation of 1763 Royal directive issued after the French and Indian War prohibiting settlement, surveys, and land grants west of the Appalachian Mountains; caused considerable resentment among colonists hoping to move west.

Progressive Party Created when former president Theodore Roosevelt broke away from the Republican Party to run for president again in 1912; the party supported progressive reforms similar to the Democrats but stopped short of seeking to eliminate trusts. Also the name of party backing Robert La Follette for president in 1924.

Progressivism Broad-based reform movement, 1900–1917, that sought governmental action in solving problems in many areas of American life, including education, public health, the economy, the environment, labor, transportation, and politics.

Proposition 13 Measure approved by California voters in 1978 prohibiting future increases in property taxes; marked beginning of "tax revolt" as major political impulse.

Public sphere The world of political organization and debate in private associations and publications outside the control of government.

Pueblo Revolt Uprising in 1680 in which Pueblo Indians temporarily drove Spanish colonists out of modern-day New Mexico.

Pullman Strike Strike against the Pullman Palace Car Company in the company town of Pullman, Illinois, on May 11, 1894, by the American Railway Union under Eugene V. Debs; the strike was crushed by court injunctions and federal troops two months later.

Pure Food and Drug Act (1906) First law to regulate manufacturing of food and medicines; prohibited dangerous additives and inaccurate labeling.

Puritans English religious group that sought to purify the Church of England; founded the Massachusetts Bay Colony under John Winthrop in 1630.

Quakers (Society of Friends) Religious group in England and America whose members believed all persons possessed the "inner light" or spirit of God; they were early proponents of abolition of slavery and equal rights for women.

Radical Republicans Group within the Republican Party in the 1850s and 1860s that advocated strong resistance to the expansion of slavery, opposition to compromise with the South in the secession crisis of 1860–1861, emancipation and arming of black soldiers during the Civil War, and equal civil and political rights for blacks during Reconstruction.

Railroad Strike of 1877 Interstate strike, crushed by federal troops, which resulted in extensive property damage and many deaths.

Reaganomics Popular name for President Ronald Reagan's philosophy of "supply side" economics, which combined tax cuts with an unregulated marketplace.

Reconstruction Act (1867) Established temporary military governments in ten Confederate states—excepting Tennessee—and required that the states ratify the Fourteenth Amendment and permit freedmen to vote.

Reconstruction Finance Corporation Federal program established in 1932 under President Herbert Hoover to loan money to banks and other institutions to help them avert bankruptcy.

Red Scare Fear among many Americans after World War I of Communists in particular and noncitizens in general, a reaction to the Russian Revolution, mail bombs, strikes, and riots.

Redeemers Conservative white Democrats, many of them planters or businessmen, who reclaimed control of the South following the end of Reconstruction.

Regulators Groups of backcountry Carolina settlers who protested colonial policies.

Republican Party Organized in 1854 by antislavery Whigs, Democrats, and Free Soilers in response to the passage of the Kansas-Nebraska Act; nominated John C. Frémont for president in 1856 and Abraham Lincoln in 1860; also the name of the party formed by Thomas Jefferson and James Madison in the 1790s.

Republicanism Political theory in eighteenth-century England and America that celebrated active participation in public life by economically independent citizens as central to freedom.

Revolution of 1800 First time that an American political party surrendered power to the opposition party; Jefferson, a Republican, had defeated incumbent Adams, a Federalist, for president.

Right-to-work State laws enacted to prevent imposition of the closed shop; any worker, whether or not a union member, could be hired.

Roe v. Wade (1973) U.S. Supreme Court decision requiring states to permit first-trimester abortions.

Roosevelt Corollary (1904) President Theodore Roosevelt announced in what was essentially a corollary to the Monroe

Doctrine that the United States could intervene militarily to prevent interference from European powers in the Western Hemisphere.

Rough Riders The first U.S. Volunteer Cavalry, led in battle in the Spanish-American War by Theodore Roosevelt; they were victorious in their only battle near Santiago, Cuba, and Roosevelt used the notoriety to aid his political career.

Santa Fe Trail Beginning in the 1820s, a major trade route from St. Louis, Missouri, to Santa Fe, New Mexico Territory.

Saratoga, Battle of Major defeat of British general John Burgoyne and more than 5,000 British troops at Saratoga, New York, on October 17, 1777.

Scalawags Southern white Republicans—some former Unionists—who supported Reconstruction governments.

Schenck v. U.S. (1919) U.S. Supreme Court decision upholding the wartime Espionage and Sedition Acts; in the opinion he wrote for the case, Justice Oliver Wendell Holmes set the now-familiar "clear and present danger" standard.

Scientific management Management campaign to improve worker efficiency using measurements like "time and motion" studies to achieve greater productivity; introduced by Frederick Winslow Taylor in 1911.

Scopes trial (1925) Trial of John Scopes, Tennessee teacher accused of violating state law prohibiting teaching of the theory of evolution; it became a nationally celebrated confrontation between religious fundamentalism and civil liberties.

Scottsboro case (1931) In overturning verdicts against nine black youths accused of raping two white women, the U.S. Supreme Court established precedents in *Powell v. Alabama* (1932), that adequate counsel must be appointed in capital cases, and in *Norris v. Alabama* (1935), that African-Americans cannot be excluded from juries.

Second Great Awakening Religious revival movement of the early decades of the nineteenth century, in reaction to the growth of secularism and rationalist religion; began the predominance of the Baptist and Methodist churches.

Segregation Policy of separating persons on the basis of race in schools, transportation, and other public facilities; *de facto* segregation refers to social customs that accomplish this, *de jure* segregation to laws requiring it.

Seneca Falls Convention First women's rights meeting and the genesis of the women's suffrage movement; held in July 1848 in a church in Seneca Falls, New York, organized by Elizabeth Cady Stanton and Lucretia Coffin Mott.

"Separate but equal" Principle underlying legal racial segregation, upheld in *Plessy v. Ferguson* (1896) and struck down in *Brown v. Board of Education* (1954).

Separation of Powers Feature of the U.S. Constitution, sometimes called "checks and balances," in which power is divided between executive, legislative, and judicial branches of the national government so that no one can dominate the other two and endanger citizens' liberties.

Servicemen's Readjustment Act (1944) The "GI Bill of Rights" provided money for education and other benefits to military personnel returning from World War II.

Settlement houses Late-nineteenth-century movement to offer a broad array of social services in urban immigrant neighborhoods; Chicago's Hull House was one of hundreds of settlement houses that operated by the early twentieth century.

Seventeenth Amendment (1913) Progressive reform that required U.S. senators to be elected directly by voters; previously, senators were chosen by state legislatures.

Shakers Founded by Mother Ann Lee in England, the United Society of Believers in Christ's Second Appearing settled in Watervliet, New York, in 1774 and subsequently established eighteen additional communes in the Northeast, Indiana, and Kentucky.

Sharecropping Type of farm tenancy that developed after the Civil War in which landless workers—often former slaves—farmed land in exchange for farm supplies and a share of the crop.

Shays's Rebellion (1787) Massachusetts farmer Daniel Shays and 1,200 compatriots, seeking debt relief through issuance of paper currency and lower taxes, attempted to prevent courts from seizing property from indebted farmers.

Sherman Antitrust Act (1890) First law to restrict monopolistic trusts and business combinations; extended by the Clayton Antitrust Act of 1914.

Sherman Silver Purchase Act (1890) In replacing and extending the provisions of the Bland-Allison Act of 1878, it increased the amount of silver periodically bought for coinage.

Single tax Concept of taxing only landowners as a remedy for poverty, promulgated by Henry George in *Progress and Poverty* (1879).

Sit-down strikes Tactic adopted by labor unions in the mid- and late 1930s, whereby striking workers refused to leave factories, making production impossible; proved highly effective in the organizing drive of the Congress of Industrial Organizations.

Sit-ins Tactic adopted by young civil rights activists, beginning in 1960, of demanding service at lunch counters or public accommodations and refusing to leave if denied access; marked the beginning of the most militant phase of the civil rights struggle.

Sixteenth Amendment (1913) Legalized the federal income tax.

Smith v. Allwright (1944) U.S. Supreme Court decision that outlawed all-white Democratic Party primaries in Texas.

Social Darwinism Application of Charles Darwin's theory of natural selection to society; used the concept of the "survival of the fittest" to justify class distinctions and to explain poverty.

Social Gospel Preached by liberal Protestant clergymen in the late nineteenth and early twentieth centuries; advocated the application of Christian principles to social problems generated by industrialization.

Social Security Act (1935) Created the Social Security system with provisions for a retirement pension, unemployment insurance, disability insurance, and public assistance (welfare).

Socialist Party Political party demanding public ownership of major economic enterprises in the United States as well as reforms like recognition of labor unions and women's suffrage; reached peak of influence in 1912 when presidential candidate Eugene V. Debs received over 900,000 votes.

Sons of Liberty Organizations formed by Samuel Adams, John Hancock, and other radicals in response to the Stamp Act.

South Carolina Exposition and Protest Written in 1828 by Vice-President John C. Calhoun of South Carolina to protest the so-called Tariff of Abominations, which seemed to favor northern industry; introduced the concept of state interposition and became the basis for South Carolina's Nullification Doctrine of 1833.

Southeast Asia Treaty Organization (SEATO) Pact among mostly Western nations signed in 1954; designed to deter Communist expansion and cited as a justification for U.S. involvement in Vietnam.

Southern Christian Leadership Conference (SCLC) Civil rights organization founded in 1957 by the Reverend Martin Luther King Jr., and other civil rights leaders.

Spoils system The term—meaning the filling of federal government jobs with persons loyal to the party of the president—originated in Andrew Jackson's first term.

Sputnik First artificial satellite to orbit the earth; launched October 4, 1957, by the Soviet Union.

Stalwarts Conservative Republican Party faction during the presidency of Rutherford B. Hayes, 1877–1881; led by Senator Roscoe B. Conkling of New York, Stalwarts opposed civil service reform and favored a third term for President Ulysses S. Grant.

Stamp Act (1765) Parliament required that revenue stamps be affixed to all colonial printed matter, documents, and playing cards; the Stamp Act Congress met to formulate a response, and the act was repealed the following year.

Standard Oil Company Founded in 1870 by John D. Rockefeller in Cleveland, Ohio, it soon grew into the nation's first industry-dominating trust; the Sherman Antitrust Act (1890) was enacted in part to combat abuses by Standard Oil.

Staple crop Important cash crop, for example, cotton or tobacco.

Steamboats Paddlewheelers that could travel both up- and down-river in deep or shallow waters; they became commercially viable early in the nineteenth century and soon developed into America's first inland freight and passenger service network.

Strategic Defense Initiative ("Star Wars") Defense Department's plan during the Reagan administration to build a system to destroy incoming missiles in space.

Student Nonviolent Coordinating Committee (SNCC) Founded in 1960 to coordinate civil rights sit-ins and other forms of grassroots protest.

Students for a Democratic Society (SDS) Major organization of the New Left, founded at the University of Michigan in 1960 by Tom Hayden and Al Haber.

Sugar Act (Revenue Act of 1764) Parliament's tax on refined sugar and many other colonial products.

Taft-Hartley Act (1947) Passed over President Harry Truman's veto, the law contained a number of provisions to weaken labor unions, including the banning of closed shops.

Tariff Federal tax on imported goods.

Tariff of Abominations (Tariff of 1828) Taxed imported goods at a very high rate; aroused strong opposition in the South.

Tariff of 1816 First true protective tariff, intended to protect certain American goods against foreign competition.

Tax Reform Act (1986) Lowered federal income tax rates to 1920s levels and eliminated many loopholes.

Teapot Dome Harding administration scandal in which Secretary of the Interior Albert B. Fall profited from secret leasing to private oil companies of government oil reserves at Teapot Dome, Wyoming, and Elk Hills, California.

Tennessee Valley Authority Created in 1933 to control flooding in the Tennessee River valley, provide work for the region's unemployed, and produce inexpensive electric power for the region.

Tenure of Office Act (1867) Required the president to obtain Senate approval to remove any official whose appointment had also required Senate approval; President Andrew Johnson's violation of the law by firing Secretary of War Edwin Stanton led to Johnson's impeachment.

Tet Offensive Surprise attack by the Viet Cong and North Vietnamese during the Vietnamese New Year of 1968; turned American public opinion strongly against the war in Vietnam.

Thirteenth Amendment Constitutional amendment adopted in 1865 that irrevocably abolished slavery throughout the United States.

Three Mile Island Nuclear power plant near Harrisburg, Pennsylvania, site of 1979 accident that released radioactive steam into the air; public reaction ended the nuclear power industry's expansion.

Title IX Part of the Educational Amendments Act of 1972 that banned gender discrimination in higher education.

Tonkin Gulf Resolution (1964) Passed by Congress in reaction to supposedly unprovoked attacks on American warships off the coast of North Vietnam; it gave the president unlimited authority to defend U.S. forces and members of SEATO.

Townshend Acts (1767) Parliamentary measures (named for the chancellor of the Exchequer) that taxed tea and other commodities, and established a Board of Customs Commissioners and colonial vice-admiralty courts.

Trail of Tears Cherokees' own term for their forced removal, 1838–1839, from the Southeast to Indian lands (later Oklahoma); of 15,000 forced to march, 4,000 died on the way.

Transcendentalism Philosophy of a small group of mid-nineteenth-century New England writers and thinkers, including Ralph Waldo Emerson, Henry David Thoreau, and Margaret Fuller; they stressed personal and intellectual self-reliance.

Transcontinental railroad First line across the continent from Omaha, Nebraska, to Sacramento, California, established in 1869 with the linkage of the Union Pacific and Central Pacific railroads at Promontory, Utah.

Truman Doctrine President Harry S. Truman's program announced in 1947 of aid to European countries—particularly Greece and Turkey—threatened by communism.

Trust Companies combined to limit competition.

Twenty-first Amendment (1933) Repealed the prohibition of the manufacture, sale, and transportation of alcoholic beverages, effectively nullifying the Eighteenth Amendment.

Twenty-second Amendment (1951) Limited presidents to two full terms of office or two terms plus two years of an assumed term; passed in reaction to President Franklin D. Roosevelt's unprecedented four elected terms.

Twenty-sixth Amendment (1971) Lowered the voting age from twenty-one to eighteen.

U.S.S. *Maine* Battleship that exploded in Havana Harbor on February 15, 1898, resulting in 266 deaths; the American public, assuming that the Spanish had mined the ship, clamored for war, and the Spanish-American War was declared two months later.

Uncle Tom's Cabin Harriet Beecher Stowe's 1852 antislavery novel popularized the abolitionist position.

Underground Railroad Operating in the decades before the Civil War, the "railroad" was a clandestine system of routes and safehouses through which slaves were led to freedom in the North.

Understanding clause Added to southern state constitutions in the late nineteenth century, it allowed illiterate whites to circumvent literacy tests for voting by demonstrating that they understood a passage in the Constitution; black citizens would be judged by white registrars to have failed.

Unitarianism Late-eighteenth-century liberal offshoot of the New England Congregationalist Church; rejecting the Trinity, Unitarianism professed the oneness of God and the goodness of rational man.

United Farm Workers Union for the predominantly Mexican-American migrant laborers of the Southwest, organized by César Chavez in 1962.

United Nations Organization of nations to maintain world peace, established in 1945 and headquartered in New York.

Universal Negro Improvement Association Black nationalist movement active in the United States from 1916 to 1923, led by Marcus Garvey.

V-E Day May 8, 1945, the day World War II officially ended in Europe.

Vertical integration Company's avoidance of middlemen by producing its own supplies and providing for distribution of its product.

Veto President's constitutional power to reject legislation passed by Congress; a two-thirds vote in both houses of Congress can override a veto.

Vicksburg, Battle of The fall of Vicksburg, Mississippi, to General Ulysses S. Grant's army on July 4, 1863, after two months of siege was a turning point in the war because it gave the Union control of the Mississippi River.

Vietnam War Longest war in which the United States has been involved; began with giving American financial assistance to France, who sought to maintain control over Vietnam colony; moved to dispatching advisers to bolster the government of South Vietnam; and finally sent over 500,000 American soldiers by the mid-1960s; resulted in massive antiwar movement, eventual American withdrawal, and communist victory in 1975; only war the United States has lost.

Virginia and Kentucky Resolutions (1798–1799) Passed by the Virginia and the Kentucky legislatures; written by James Madison and Thomas Jefferson in response to the Alien and Sedition Acts, the resolutions advanced the state-compact theory of the Constitution. Virginia's resolution called on the federal courts to protect free speech. Jefferson's draft for Kentucky stated that a state could nullify federal law, but this was deleted.

Virginia and New Jersey Plans Differing opinions of delegations to the Constitutional Convention: New Jersey wanted one legislative body with equal representation for each state; Virginia's plan called for a strong central government and a two-house legislature apportioned by population.

Volstead Act (1919) Enforced the Prohibition amendment, beginning January 1920.

Voting Rights Act of 1965 Passed in the wake of Martin Luther King Jr.'s, Selma to Montgomery March, it authorized federal protection of the right to vote and permitted federal enforcement of minority voting rights in individual counties, mostly in the South.

Wabash Railroad v. Illinois (1886) Reversing the U.S. Supreme Court's ruling in *Munn v. Illinois*, the decision disallowed state regulation of interstate commerce.

Wade-Davis bill (1864) Radical Republicans' plan for reconstruction that required loyalty oaths, abolition of slavery, repudiation of war debts, and denial of political rights to high-ranking Confederate officials; President Lincoln refused to sign the bill.

Wagner Act (National Labor Relations Act of 1935) Established the National Labor Relations Board and facilitated unionization by regulating employment and bargaining practices.

War Industries Board Run by financier Bernard Baruch, the board planned production and allocation of war materiel, supervised purchasing, and fixed prices, 1917–1919.

War of 1812 Fought with Britain, 1812–1814, over issues that included impressment of American sailors, interference with shipping, and collusion with Northwest Territory Indians; settled by the Treaty of Ghent in 1814.

War on Poverty Announced by President Lyndon B. Johnson in his 1964 State of the Union address; under the Economic Opportunity Bill signed later that year, Head Start, VISTA, and the Jobs Corps were created, and programs were created for students, farmers, and businesses in efforts to eliminate poverty.

War Powers Act Law passed in 1973, reflecting growing opposition to American involvement in Vietnam War; required congressional approval before president sent troops abroad.

War Production Board Created in 1942 to coordinate industrial efforts in World War II; similar to the War Industries Board in World War I.

Warren Court The U.S. Supreme Court under Chief Justice Earl Warren, 1953–1969, decided such landmark cases as *Brown v. Board of Education* (school desegregation), *Baker v. Carr* (legislative redistricting), and *Gideon v. Wainwright* and *Miranda v. Arizona* (rights of criminal defendants).

Washington Armaments Conference Leaders of nine world powers met in 1921–1922 to discuss the naval race; resulting treaties limited to a specific ratio the carrier and battleship tonnage of each nation (Five-Power Naval Treaty), formally ratified the Open Door to China (Nine-Power Treaty), and agreed to respect each other's Pacific territories (Four-Power Treaty).

Watergate Washington office and apartment complex that lent its name to the 1972–1974 scandal of the Nixon administration; when his knowledge of the break-in at the Watergate and subsequent coverup was revealed, Nixon resigned the presidency under threat of impeachment.

Webster-Hayne debate U.S. Senate debate of January 1830 between Daniel Webster of Massachusetts and Robert Hayne of South Carolina over nullification and states' rights.

Whig Party Founded in 1834 to unite factions opposed to President Andrew Jackson, the party favored federal responsibility for internal improvements; the party ceased to exist by the late 1850s, when party members divided over the slavery issue.

Whiskey Rebellion Violent protest by western Pennsylvania farmers against the federal excise tax on whiskey, 1794.

Wilmot Proviso Proposal to prohibit slavery in any land acquired in the Mexican War, but southern senators, led by John C. Calhoun of South Carolina, defeated the measure in 1846 and 1847.

Women's Christian Temperance Union Largest female reform society of the late nineteenth century; it moved from opposing sale of liquor to demanding the right to vote for women.

Works Progress Administration (WPA) Part of the Second New Deal, it provided jobs for millions of the unemployed on construction and arts projects.

Wounded Knee, Battle of Last incident of the Indian Wars took place in 1890 in the Dakota Territory, where the U.S. Cavalry killed over 200 Sioux men, women, and children.

Writs of assistance One of the colonies' main complaints against Britain, the writs allowed unlimited search warrants without cause to look for evidence of smuggling.

XYZ affair French foreign minister Tallyrand's three anonymous agents demanded payments to stop French plundering of American ships in 1797; refusal to pay the bribe was followed by two years of undeclared sea war with France (1798–1800).

Yalta conference Meeting of Franklin D. Roosevelt, Winston Churchill, and Joseph Stalin at a Crimean resort to discuss the postwar world on February 4–11, 1945; Joseph Stalin claimed large areas in eastern Europe for Soviet domination.

Yellow journalism Sensationalism in newspaper publishing that reached a peak in the circulation war between Joseph Pulitzer's *New York World* and William Randolph Hearst's *New York Journal* in the 1890s; the papers' accounts of events in Havana Harbor in 1898 led directly to the Spanish-American War.

Yeoman farmers Small landowners (the majority of white families in the Old South) who farmed their own land and usually did not own slaves.

Yick Wo v. Hopkins Supreme Court decision in 1886 overturning San Francisco law that, as enforced, discriminated against Chinese-owned laundries; established principle that equal protection of the law embodied in Fourteenth Amendment applied to all Americans, not just former slaves.

Yorktown, Battle of Last battle of the Revolutionary War; General Lord Charles Cornwallis along with over 7,000 British troops surrendered at Yorktown, Virginia, on October 17, 1781.

Young Americans for Freedom Organization of conservative students founded in 1960; played major role in 1964 presidential campaign of Barry Goldwater and in rebirth of conservatism in the 1960s.

Zimmermann Telegram From the German foreign secretary to the German minister in Mexico, February 1917, instructing him to offer to recover Texas, New Mexico, and Arizona for Mexico if it would fight the United States to divert attention from Germany in the event that the United States joined the war.

PHOTOS

Author Photo: © Flynn Larsen
2 (left) The John Carter Library at Brown University; **2 (right)** Library of Congress; **3 (top)** Corbis; **3 (bottom right)** Unidentified artist, British, 18th century or first quarter 19th century; *Quaker Meeting*; Oil on canvas; 64.1 × 76.2cm (25 1/4 × 30in.); Museum of Fine Arts, Boston; Bequest of Maxim Karolik; 64.456; **4–5** Bridgeman Art Library; **7** Cliché Bibliothèque nationale de France, Paris; **10** Photo Courtesy of Edward E. Ayer Collection, The Newberry Library, Chicago; **11 (top)** National Park Service, Chaco Culture National Historic Park, Chaco Archive neg. no. 25462; **11 (bottom)** Timothy O'Sullivan, *Ancient Ruins in the Canon de Chelle, N. M. in a Niche 50 Feet above Present Canon Bed*, albumen silver print, 1873; Amon Carter Museum, Fort Worth, Texas P1982.27.38; **12** The London Art Archive/Alamy; **15** British National Archives; **16** Bridgeman Art Library; **17 (top)** Library of Congress; **17 (bottom)** Courtesy Lilly Library, Indiana University, Bloomington, IN; **22** The Mariners' Museum, Newport News, VA; **23** Biblioteca Estense Universitaria, Modena; **24** By permission of the British Library; **26** Florence, Library Medicea Laurenziana, ms. Med. Palat. 220. By permission of the Ministero per I Beni e le Attivita' Culturali; **27** Granger Collection; **28** William L. Clements Library, University of Michigan; **29** Courtesy of the Library of Congress, *Huexotzinco Codex*, Painting V, Manuscript 1531; **30** Museo de America, Madrid, 1980.03.01, .02, .09; **31** Instituto Nacional de Antropologia e Historia, Chapultepec Castle, Mexico City; **32** Rare Books Division, The New York Public Library, Astor, Lenox, and Tilden Foundations; **33** Library of Congress; **34** Museo Naval, Madrid; **37** Library of Congress, Prints & Photographs Division, Edward S. Curtis Collection; **40** National Museum of American History, Smithsonian Institute, Behring Center; **41** History Collection, Nova Scotia Library; **43** Collection du monastère des Ursulines de Québec, Museé des Ursulines de Québec (1997.1017); **44** Bettmann/Corbis; **46** Alamy; **47** Museum of the City of New York/Bridgeman Art Library; **48** The Colonial Williamsburg Foundation; **52–53** Woburn Abbey, Bedfordshire, UK/The Bridgeman Art Library; **55** The London Art Archive/Alamy; **57** The John Carter Brown Library at Brown University; **58** The Library Company of Philadelphia; **59** Henry E. Huntington Library #3373; **60** GLC 4110. Document signed: contracts relating to the indenture of James Mahony, 31 March 1773. (The Gilder Lehrman Collection, courtesy of the Gilder Lehrman Institute of American History, New York.); **61** Bridgeman Art Library; **62** Museum of Art, Rhode Island School of Design. Gift of Robert Winthrop. Photography by Erik Gould; **64 (top)** Corbis; **64 (bottom)** National Portrait Gallery, Smithsonian Institution/Art Resource, NY; **65** Library of Congress; **66** Library of Congress; **66** George Arents Collection, New York Public Library; **67** Corbis; **69** Library of Congress; **70** Courtesy, American Antiquarian Society; **71** Courtesy of the John Carter Brown Library at Brown University; **72** Granger Collection; **73** Courtesy of the Massachusetts Archives; **74** Worcester Art Museum, Worcester, Massachusetts, Gift of William A. Savage; **75** Massachussetts Historical Society; **81** Annenberg Rare Book and Manuscript Library, Van Pelt-Dietrich Library Center, U Penn; **82** Library of Congress; **83** *Self-Portrait*, by Thomas Smith, 1948.19, Worcester Art Museum, Worcester, Massachusetts; **84** *Mrs. Elizabeth Freake and Baby Mary*, unknown artist, 1963.134, Worcester Art Museum, Worcester, Massachusetts; **85** Historical Picture Archive/Corbis; **86 (top)** Private Collection/Bridgeman Art Library; **86 (bottom)** © National Portrait Gallery, London; **87** By permission of the British Library; **88** The Cromwell Museum, Huntingdon; **92–93** The Colonial Williamsburg Foundation; **94** The John Carter Brown Library at Brown University; **98** Library of Congress; **100** Germantown Historical Society, Philadelphia, PA; **101** Unidentified artist, British, 18th century or first quarter 19th century; *Quaker Meeting*; Oil on canvas; 64.1 × 76.2cm (25 1/4 × 30in.); Museum of Fine Arts, Boston; Bequest of Maxim Karolik; 64.456; **103** British Library 1786.c.9; **104** Courtesy of the John Carter Brown Library at Brown University; **105** Colonial Williamsburg Foundation; **107** National Maritime Museum, London; **109** Springhill, County Londonderry, Northern Ireland, National Trust Photographic Library/Derrick E. Witty/Bridgeman Art Library; **112** Courtesy of the Peabody Essex Museum; **116** National Archives; **117** The Historical Society of Pennsylvania; **121** Benjamin West, Pennsylvania Academy of the Fine Arts; Joseph and Sarah Harrison Collection; **122** The Library Company of Philadelphia; **123 (top)** Winterthur Museum; **123 (bottom)** Courtesy of the Maryland Historical Society 1900.5.1; **124** Photograph © 2010 Museum of Fine Arts, Boston; **125** Geoffrey Clements/Corbis; **126** Colonial Williamsburg Foundation; **129** Fenimore Art Museum, Cooperstown, New York; **130** Gift of Edgar William and Bernice Chrysler Garbisch, Image © 2006 Board of Trustees, National Gallery of Art, Washington; **134–35** Abby Aldrich Rockefeller Folk Art Museum, Colonial Williamsburg Foundation, Williamsburg, VA; **137** Library of Congress; **138** The John Carter Library at Brown University; **141** Library of Congress; **142 (top)** Courtesy of the Maryland Historical Society; **142 (bottom)** Colonial Williamsburg Foundation; **143** Courtesy of the Maryland Historical Society, **145** Granger Collection; **146** Newport Historical Society (53.3); **149** Charleston Library Society; **151** By Courtesy of the National Portrait Gallery, London; **152** Chicago Historical Society; **153** By courtesy of the Trustees of Sir John Soane's Museum; **154 (top)** Library of Congress; **154 (bottom)** © National Portrait Gallery, London; **155** Library of Congress; **158** This item is reproduced by permission of The Huntington Library, San Marino, California; **159** Bettmann/Corbis; **161** Wikimedia; **162** National Portrait Gallery, London; **163** Library of Congress; **165** Courtesy of the Bancroft Library, University of California, Berkeley; **166** Courtesy of Tulane University; **167** Granger Collection; **168** Library of Congress; **174** Library of Congress; **179 (top)** Corbis; **179 (bottom)** MPI/Getty Images; **180 (top)** Courtesy of the Beineke Rare Book and Manuscript Library, Yale University; **180 (bottom)** © New Bedford Whaling Museum; **181 (top)** Print Collection, Miriam and Ira D. Wallach Division of Art, Prints, and Photographs, The New York Public Library; Astor, Lenox, and Tilden Foundations; **181 (bottom)** The Saint Louis Art Museum; **182–83** The Colonial Williamsburg Foundation; **185** By permission of the Houghton Library, Harvard University; **186** © copyright the Trustees of The British Museum; **187 (top)** Corbis; **187 (bottom)** The Colonial Williamsburg Foundation; **188** Granger Collection; **189** Kunhardt/Picture History; **193** Library of Congress; **194 (top)** Michael Nicholson/Corbis; **194 (bottom)** Library of Congress; **195** Library of Congress; **197** Miriam and Ira D. Wallach Division of Art, Prints and Photographs, New York Public Library; **198** Chicago Historical Society; **199 (top)** National Portrait Gallery, London; **199 (bottom)** American Philosophical Society; **203** Library of Congress; **204** American Antiquarian Society; **205** Sid Lapidus Collection. Rare Books Division. Department of Rare Books and Special Collections. Princeton University Library; **206** Library of Congress; **207** Anne S. K. Brown Military Collection, Brown University; **208** Morristown National Historic Park; **212** Library of Congress; **214** Library of Congress Prints and Photographs Division; **218–19** York County Historical Society/The Bridgeman Art Library; **221** National Gallery of Art, Washington, Gift of Mrs. Robert Homans; **222** Cliché Bibliothèque nationale de France, Paris; **224** Historical Society of Pennsylvania; **226** Courtesy of the New-York Historical Society; **228** Granger Collection; **229** Courtesy of the Beineke Rare Book and Manuscript Library, Yale University; **230** American Antiquarian Society; **231** Bettmann/Corbis; **232** The Library

Company of Philadelphia; **234** Library of Congress; **237** Courtesy of the Bostonian Society; **239** Corbis; **240** American Antiquarian Society; **242** Library of Congress; **243** National Archives, London; **246** Courtesy of The New-York Historical Society; **247** Library Company of Philadelphia. Gift of the artist, 1792; **248** Museum of Art, Rhode Island School of Design. Gift of Miss Lucy Truman Aldrich; **249 (top)** Courtesy the Rhode Island Historical Society; **249 (bottom)** Southern Historical Collection, Wilson Library, The University of North Carolina at Chapel Hill; **250** Courtesy, Winterthur Museum, gift of Henry Francis du Pont. **251 (top)** Charles Wilson Peale, Portrait of John and Elizabeth Lloyd Cadwalader, and their daughter Anne, Philadelphia Museum of Art: Purchased from the Cadwalader Collection with funds contributed by the Myrin Trust and the gift of an anonymous donor; **251 (bottom)** Chicago Historical Society; **252** American Antiquarian Society; **256–57** Granger Collection; **262** American Antiquarian Society; **265** Print Collection, Miriam and Ira D. Wallach Division of Art, Prints, and Photographs, The New York Public Library; Astor, Lenox, and Tilden Foundations; **266 (top)** Library of Congress; **266 (bottom)** Independence National Historical Park; **267** New York Public Library; **268** Library of Congress; **270** The Library of Virginia; **271** MPI/Getty Images; **272** From the collection of the National Constitution Center, Philadelphia, gift of Robert L. McNeil, Jr. **273** Library of Congress; **275** Courtesy of the New-York Historical Society; **279** Courtesy of the New-York Historical Society; **280** Library of Congress; **282** The Buffalo and Erie County Historical Society; **283** Chicago Historical Society; **287** Granger Collection; **292–93** Library of Congress; **294** Chicago Historical Society; **295** Fenimore Art Museum, Cooperstown, New York. Photo by Richard Walker; **296** Courtesy of the Maryland Historical Society; **297** Library of Congress; **298** I. N. Stokes Collection, Miriam and Ira D. Wallach Division of Art, Prints, and Photographs, The New York Public Library; Astor, Lenox, and Tilden Foundations; **299** Library of Congress; **300** Courtesy, Winterthur Museum, Bequest of Hery F. DuPont; **301** Print Collection, Miriam and Ira D. Wallach Division of Art, Prints, and Photographs, The New York Public Library; Astor, Lenox, and Tilden Foundations; **304 (top)** Chicago Historical Society; **304 (bottom)** © National Portrait Gallery, London; **305** Museum of Early Southern Decorative Arts, Winston-Salem, NC; **307** Library of Congress; **308** National Museum of American History, Smithsonian Institution, Behring Center; **309** The Library Company of Philadelphia; **311** Corbis; **312** Library of Congress; **313** In Private Collection; **315** Missouri Historical Society, St. Louis; **316** Chicago Historical Society, "A View of New Orleans taken from the Plantation of Marigny," Nov 1803, by Boqueto de Woieseri; **318** Courtesy of the New-York Historical Society; **320** Unidentified artist, circa 1805, Benjamin Hawkins and the Creek Indian, circa 1805, oil on canvas, 35 7/8 × 49 7/8 inches, Greenville County Museum of

Art, Greenville, SC; **321** Photo by Mark Sexton. © Peabody Essex Museum, 2003, all rights reserved; **323** Granger Collection **324** I. N. Stokes Collection, Miriam and Ira D. Wallach Division of Art, Prints, and Photographs, The New York Public Library; Astor, Lenox, and Tilden Foundations; **328–29** Library of Congress; **331** I. N. Stokes Collection, Miriam and Ira D. Wallach Division of Art, Prints, and Photographs, The New York Public Library; Astor, Lenox, and Tilden Foundations; **332** Courtesy of the Maryland Historical Society; **333** Chicago Historical Society; **334** I. N. Phelps Stokes Collection, Miriam and Ira D. Wallach Division of Art, Prints and Photographs, The New York Public Library, Astor, Lenox and Tilden Foundations; **336** Courtesy of the Maryland Historical Society; **337** Edwin Whitefield, Minnesota Historical Society; **340** Abby Aldrich Rockefeller Folk Art Museum, Colonial Williamsburg Foundation, Williamsburg, VA; **342** Library of Congress; **343** Cincinnati Museum Center/Getty Images; **345 (both)** Library of Congress; **347 (top)** American Textile History Museum, Lowell, Mass; **347 (bottom)** Barfoot, American, Progress of Cotton, Reeding or Drawing In, No. 9, Mabel Brady Garvan Collection, Yale University Art Gallery; **348** Courtesy of Alice Friedman; **349** Bishop Hill State Historic Site/Illinois Historic Preservation Agency; **353** Corbis; **356** Abby Aldrich Rockefeller Folk Musuem, The Colonial Williamsburg Foundation; **357** © New Bedford Whaling Museum; **358** Library of Congress; **359 (left)** J. Franklin Reigart, the United States Album (Lancaster, 1844); **359 (right)** Çorbis; **360** John Neagle, American, 1796–1865; *Pat Lyon at the Forge*, 1826–27; Oil on canvas; 238.12 × 172.72 cm (93 3/4 × 68 in.); Museum of Fine Arts, Boston; Henry H. and Zoe Oliver Sherman Fund; 1975.806; **361** Library of Congress; **362** *The Crowning of Flora by Jacob Marling*, 1816. Chrysler Museum of Art, Norfolk, VA. Gift of Edgar William and Bernice Chrysler Garbisch, 80.181.20; **363 (top)** Library of Congress; **364 (bottom)** Gift of Edgar William and Bernice Chrysler Garbisch, Image © 2006 Board of Trustees, National Gallery of Art, Washington; **364** Kilroe Collection, Butler Library, Columbia University; **365** Library of Congress; **373** Library of Congress; **370–71** Granger Collection; **374** Courtesy the Rhode Island Historical Society, Dorr Liberation Society, Rhode Island, 1844, engraving, Rhi X3 6692; **375** General Research Division, The New York Public Library, Astor, Lenox and Tilden Foundation; **377** Library of Congress; **378** Library of Congress; **379** The Corcoran Gallery of Art/Corbis; **389** Bettmann/Corbis; **390** Library of Congress; **392** *Stump Speaking* (oil on canvas), Bingham, George Caleb (1811–79)/Private Collection/The Bridgeman Art Library; **393** Joseph Yeager, *The Procession of Victuallers*, 1821, Philadelphia Museum of Art: Gift of the Estate of Charles M. B. Cadwalader; **394** The Saint Louis Art Museum; **396** Library of Congress; **397** Library of Congress; **398 (top)** *John Wesley Jarvis, Black Hawk and His Son, Whirling Thunder*, from the collection

of Gilcrease Museum, Tulsa, Oklahoma; **398 (bottom)** Library of Congress; **400** Charles Deas, *The Trapper and His Family*, © Museum of Fine Arts, Boston; **401** Smithsonian American Art Museum, Washington, DC/Art Resource, NY; **402** Library of Congress; **404** Library of Congress; **405** Library of Congress; **414–15** Bettmann/Corbis; **411 (top)** Merseyside Maritime Museum, Liverpool; **411 (bottom)** Collection of Dr. and Mrs. John Livingston and Mrs. Elizabeth Livingston Jaeger, Photo: Hearts and Hands Media Arts. Photography courtesy of Hearts & Hands Media Arts, from the book and film *Hearts and Hands: A Social History of 19th Century Women and their Quilts* (New Day Films); **412** Courtesy of the State Preservation Board, Austin, Texas, photographer F. Thomson, Post 1990, CHA 1989.68, post conservation; **413 (top)** Chicago Historical Society; **413 (bottom)** Library of Congress; **416** Samuel J. Miller, Frederick Douglass, 1847–52, cased half-plate daguerreotype, plate: 14 × 10.6 cm, Major Acquisitions Centennial Endowment, The Art Institute of Chicago; **417** Library of Congress; **419 (both)** Library of Congress; **420** Hulton Archive/Getty Images; **421** Library of Congress; **422** Louisiana State Museum; **423** Library of Congress; **425** LSU Museum of Art 87.23 Gift of the Friends of LSU Museum of Art and Mrs. Ben Hamilton in memory of her mother, Mrs. Tela Meir © David Humphreys 2004.11; **426** Library of Congress; **427** Merseyside Maritime Museum, Liverpool; **429** Chicago Historical Society; **434** Courtesy of the Maryland Historical Society; **437 (top)** New Hampshire Historical Society; **437 (bottom)** American Social History Project; **438** Library of Congress; **439** North Carolina Museum of Art, Raleigh, Purchased with funds from the State of North Carolina; **440 (top)** Chicago Historical Society; **440 (bottom)** Abby Aldrich Rockefeller Folk Art Museum, Colonial Williamsburg Foundation, Williamsburg, VA; **441** provided courtesy © HarpWeek., LLC; **442** Historic New Orleans Collection 1960.46; **445** Chicago Historical Society; **446** Chicago Historical Society; **448** Library of Congress; **452–53** Courtesy of the Massachusetts Historical Society. Banner, William Lloyd Garrison (1805–79) "Proclaim Liberty Throughout all the Land unto all the inhabitants thereof." MHS image #332; **455** Madison County Historical Society, Oneida, NY; **457** Library of Congress; **459** New York Public Library; **460** Library of Congress; **461** Library of Congress; **462** Corbis; **463** Courtesy of the New-York Historical Society; **464** Granger Collection; **465** Library of Congress; **466** Bettmann/Coris; **467** Library of Congress; **468** The Boston Athenaeum, TBMR VEP .An 847. *The Anti-Slavery Alphabet*, a children's book (1847); **469** Library of Congress; **470** Chicago Historical Society; **471** Chicago Historical Society; **472 (both)** Library of Congress; **473** Library of Congress; **474** Corbis; **475** *Destruction by Fire of Pennsylvania Hall, on the Night of the 17th May*, 1838 by J. C. Wild, printed by J. T. Bowen. The Library Company of Philadelphia; **477** Collection of Dr. and Mrs. John Livingston and Mrs. Elizabeth Livingston Jaeger, Photo: Hearts and Hands Media Arts.

Berstein/*LOOK* Magazine; **1020** Photo by Ed Clark/Time Life Pictures/Getty Images; **1022** AP Photo; **1023** Don Cravens/Time & Life Pictures/Getty Images; **1024** Library of Congress; **1025** Collection of the Norman Rockwell Museum, Stockbridge, Massachusetts; **1026** Bettmann/Corbis; **1028** Time & Life Pictures/Getty Images; 1029 **(both)** Bettmann/Corbis; **1030** Andy Warhol (1928–87), *Green Coca-Cola Bottles*, 1962, Synthetic polymer, silkscreen ink and graphite on canvas, overall (canvas): 82 3/8 × 57 in (209.2 × 144.8 cm). Framed: 83 3/4 × 58 5/8 × 2 in (212.7 × 148.9 × 5.1 cm). Whitney Museum of American Art, NY; purchase, with funds from the Friends of the Whitney Museum of American Art 68.25. Photography by Sandak. © 2004 Andy Warhol Foundation for the Visual Arts/ARS, New York; **1035–36** © Robert Rauschenberg/Licensed by VAGA, New York, NY; **1037** Image courtesy of the Raleigh City Museum; **1038 (top)** Library of Congress; **1038 (bottom)** AP Photo; **1039** Bettmann/Corbis; **1040** Bettmann/Corbis; **1042** Photo by Carl Mydans/Time Life Pictures/Getty Images; **1043** Cecil Stoughton, White House/John Fitzgerald Kennedy Library, Boston; **1044** AP Photo; **1046** Bettmann/Corbis; **1047** Bruce Davidson/Magnum Photos; **1048** LBJ Library photo by Cecil Stoughton; **1050** Black Gallery of California, Los Angeles; **1051** George Meany Memorial Archives; **1052** Scurlock Studio Records, Archives Center, National Museum of American History, Smithsonian Institution; **1053** University of California, Berkeley Art Museum; purchased with the aid of funds from the National Endowment for the Arts (selected by the Committee for the Acquisition of Afro-American Art); **1055** Photo by C. Clark Kissinger; 1056 Time Life/Getty Images; **1057** Photograph by Yoichi Okamoto, courtesy of the Lyndon Baines Johnson Library; **1061 (top)** Larry Burrows/Time Life Pictures/Getty Images; **1061 (bottom)** JP Laffont/Sygma/Corbis; **1062** © Lisa Law; **1063** Courtesy of Bernie Boston; **1064** Courtesy of Gene Anthony; **1065** Getty Images; **1066** Boston Globe/Paul J. Connell/Landov; **1067** Bettmann/Corbis; **1068 (top)** JP Laffont/Sygma/Corbis; **1068 (bottom)** George Meany Memorial Archives/Eisenberg photo; **1069** AP Photo; **1071** Karl Hubenthal Cartoon/L. A. Herald-Examiner; **1073** uncredited photo in American Decades 1970–79, Victor Bondi, ed. Gale Research Inc, 1995; **1074** Copyrighted photo by Richard Copley; **1075** Wikipedia; **1080–81** Courtesy Ronald Reagan Library; **1085** National Archives; **1087** © Co Rentmeester; **1089** Photo by Ollie Atkins/White House/Time Life Pictures/Getty Images; **1090 (top)** John Filo/Getty Images; **1090 (bottom)** Leonard Freed/Magnum; **1091** David Fenton/Getty Images; **1092** from *Herblock Special Report* (W. W. Norton, 1974); **1094** National Archives; **1095** AP Photo; **1097** Courtesy Gerald R. Ford Library; **1098 (top)** Fox Photos/Getty Images; **1098 (bottom)** J. L. Atlas/Corbis/Sygma; **1099** AP Photo; **1100** AP Photo; **1102** William E. Savro/The New York Times/Redux; **1103** Boston Globe; **1104 (top)** Bettmann/Corbis; **1104 (bottom)** Mark Meyer/Time & Life Pictures/Getty Images; **1105** Bettmann/Corbis; **1110** Time Life Pictures/Getty Images; **1111** Remains of the Sprague Electric Company (closed in 1985) on the site of the Massachusetts Museum of Contemporary Art, North Adams, MA, 1995, photo by Michael Jacobson-Hardy; **1112 (top)** Mary Ellen Mark; **1112 (bottom)** Diego Goldberg/Corbis/Sygma; **1114** Angel Franco/Woodfin Camp and Associates; **1115** Photofest; **1117** AP Photo; **1118** © 2001 Susanna Raab, all rights reserved; **1122–23** Corbis; **1124** Patrick Hagerty/Corbis Sygma; **1125** Courtesy of the designer, Douglas G. Harp, www.harpandcompany.com; **1126** AP Photo; **1127** Ira Wyman/Sygma/Corbis; **1129** James Zeng-Huang/Corbis Sygma; **1130** AP Photo; **1131** Courtesy of Edward Sorel, published as the cover of *The New Yorker*; **1133** AP Photo; **1135** Antoine Gyori/Corbis Sygma; **1136** Michael Regoli; **1137** AP Photo; **1138** AP Photo; **1139** © 2004 Bob Sacha; **1140** Reprinted with permission of David Jacobson; **1144 (top)** Copyright 1993 Robert Ariail/The State; **1144 (bottom)** © 2004 Artists Rights Society [ARS], New York/VG Bild-Kunst, Bonn; **1147** Gilles Mingasson/Getty Images; **1148** Catherine Karnow/Corbis; **1149 (top)** Stephanie Maze/Corbis; **1149 (bottom)** McClatchy-Tribune Information Services. All Rights Reserved. Reprinted with Permission; **1153** AP Photo; **1154** Reuters/Corbis; **1155** The Aldrich Contemporary Art Museum; **1156** AP Photo; **1158** Jetta Fraser; **1159** Associated Press, *The Daily Oklahoman*, photo by Jim Argo; **1160 (top)** "Balance" from *Herblock: A Cartoonist's Life* (Times Books, 1998); **1160 (bottom)** Reuters/Corbis; 1161 "It's Still a Representative Form of Government—They Represent Us" copyright 2000 by Herblock in *The Washington Post*; **1163** A. Ramey/Woodfin Camp and Associates; **1168–69** Ralf-Finn Hestoft/Corbis; **1171 (top)** Steve Ludlum/The New York Times/ Redux; **1171 (bottom)** Bettmann/Corbis; **1172** Aaron McElroy "Saw Something, and Said Something"; **1174** Earl Dotter, earldotter.com; **1175** *Daily Hampshire Gazette*; **1176** Serge J-F. Levy; **1178** Steve Benson/Creators Syndicate; **1179** Mario Tama/Getty Images; **1182** AP Photo; **1184** Michael Ramirez/ Copley News Service; **1185** Author: George Mill, Title: Freedom: Certain Restrictions Apply; **1190** NOAA; **1191** AP Photo; **1193** AP Photo; **1197** Jim Wilson/The New York Times/Redux; **1199** AUTH ©2009 *The Philadelphia Inquirer*. Reprinted with permission of UNIVERSAL UCLICK. All rights reserved; **1201** © Tribune Media Services, Inc. All Rights Reserved. Reprinted with permission; **1204** AP Photo; **1205** © Handout-Lower Manhattan Development Corporation/Reuters/Corbis; **1206** Copyright: Eli Reed/Magnum Photos.

Text, Tables, and Figures

38 Bartolomé de las Casas: *History of the Indies*, translated and edited by Andrée Collard (New York: Harper & Row, 1971), pp. 82, 112–115. Copyright © 1971 by Andrée M. Collard, renewed © 1999 by Joyce J. Contrucci. Reprinted by permission of Joyce J. Contrucci; **114** (Table 3.1) Aaron S. Fogleman, "From Slaves, Convicts, and Servants to Free Passengers: The Transformation of Immigration in the Era of the American Revolution," *Journal of American History* 85 (June 1998), 43–76; **118** Elizabeth Sprigs: Elizabeth Sprigs Letter to John Spyer, September 22, 1756, *Colonial Captivities, Marches, and Journeys*, Isabel M. Calder (Macmillan, 1935), pp. 151–152. We have made diligent efforts to contact the copyright holder to obtain permission to reprint this selection. If you have information that would help us, please write to Permissions Department, W. W. Norton & Company, Inc., 500 Fifth Avenue, New York, NY 10110; **119** Johannes Hänner: Letter by an Immigrant to Pennsylvania, 1769, *Unpublished Documents on Emigration from the Archives of Switzerland*, Albert B. Faust, *Deutsch-Amerikanische Geschichtsblätter*, Vol 18–19, pp. 37–39. Translation by Volker Berghahn. Reprinted by permission of Volker Berghahn; **147** (Table 4.1) Ira Berlin, *Many Thousands Gone: The First Two Centuries of Slavery in North America* (Cambridge, Mass.: Harvard University Press, 1998), 369–70; **244** Abigail Adams: "Abigail Adams to John Adams, 31 March 1776." Reprinted by permission of the publisher from *The Adams Papers: Adams Family Correspondence*, *Volume I: December 1761–May 1776*, edited by L.H. Butterfield, Cambridge, Mass.: The Belknap Press of Harvard University Press, Copyright © 1963 by the Massachusetts Historical Society; **286** (Table 7.1) U.S. Bureau of the Census, *A Century of Population Growth* (Washington, D.C., 1900), 47, 57; **302** Democratic-Republican Society of Pennsylvania: Excerpt from minutes of The Democratic Society of Pennsylvania, December 18, 1794. The Historical Society of Pennsylvania (HSP), Collection # Am. 315/3150. Reprinted with permission; **315**; **339** (Table 9.1) U.S. Bureau of the Census, *Historical Statistics of the United States* (Washington, D.C., 1975), 24–36; **417** (Table 11.1) U.S. Bureau of the Census, *A Century of Population Growth* (Washington, D.C., 1900) 133; **423** (Table 11.2) Census of 1850; **430** Joseph Taper: Excerpts from "Letter from Joseph Taper to Joseph Long, November 11, 1840" in the Joseph Long Papers located in the Rare Book, Manuscript, and Special Collections Library, Duke University. Reprinted by permission; **433** Table 11.3) Census of 1860; **635** (Table 16.1) U.S. Bureau of the Census, *Historical Statistics of the United States* (Washington D.C., 1975), 134; **696** (Table 17.1) Arwin D. Smallwood, *The Atlas of African-American History and Politics* (New York, 1998), 106; **726** (Table 18.1) U.S. Bureau of the Census, *Historical Statistics of the United States* (Washington, D.C., 1975), 11–12; **731** (Table 18.2) Census of 1920; **734** (Table 18.3) U.S. Bureau of the Census, *Historical Statistics of the United States* (Washington, D.C., 1975) 131; **735** (Table 18.4) U.S. Bureau of the Census, *Historical Statistics of the United States* (Washington, D.C., 1975) 139; **736**

Page numbers in *italics* refer to illustrations.

AP* Skills Handbooks

INTRODUCTION TO THE HISTORICAL SKILLS HANDBOOKS

The introduction of this book explained the importance of reading, analyzing, and using documents and visual sources in AP* U.S. History. These materials play a vital role for success, both in this course and on the national examination given in May.

The following handbooks present and then test strategies for working with documents and visuals. Each skill handbook outlines a process for unlocking data from a source, then models it with an example from your textbook. Finally, you can use the technique with ten sources from your book. These worksheets are available for download by your instructor. These steps allow you to see how primary sources can be analyzed and effectively used in your AP* U.S. History class.

PRIMARY DOCUMENT SKILLS HANDBOOK

Primary documents are the principal conduit for historical inquiry in AP* U.S. History. Your teacher will employ them extensively in your class throughout the year. You will be expected to summarize documents, analyze their content, and determine their meaning. Therefore, it is critical that you develop a systematic way to examine primary documents. Your examination should include sourcing and contextualizing the material. When you source a document, you identify its author, determine the date it was written, establish its purpose, and recognize its intended audience. In addition, you must place the item in the context of the time when it was written. By establishing the background of the material, you expand your understanding of the document and its milieu.

DECIPHERING TEXTUAL DOCUMENTS WITH THE 5 Ws STRATEGY

In the chapters of your textbook, sections called Voices of Freedom present myriad sources that add depth to various topics and events. These selections also are designed to advance the overarching theme that throughout American history, freedom has been an ever-changing idea without a fixed or immutable definition. The Voices of Freedom highlight clashing views on the nature of liberty throughout American history. The documents are accompanied by two or three questions that help to frame the accounts in their time and promote critical thinking. Although these questions are excellent, you need to delve more deeply into the meaning of the documents and systematically explore their substance. To do this, you should apply the **5 Ws** of analysis.

Ask yourself:

> **When** was the document written? Contextualize it as much as possible by providing the background events that led to its creation.
>
> **Who** wrote it? Try to identify the author, his or her background, and possible bias.
>
> **What** did it say? Limit yourself to three or four main ideas. This will allow you to summarize the salient points of the document.
>
> **Where** was it directed? Look for both the specific audience and a possible larger audience.
>
> **Why** was it written? Make inferences about reasons behind the document.

Beyond applying the 5 Ws to the sources, you will also be asked to consider ways that the selections can be linked to aspects of AP* U.S. History. Specifically, you will examine how document analysis can strengthen your skills in writing answers to Document-Based Questions. You may be asked to write paragraphs or short answers about different pairs of Voices of Freedom documents and how they demonstrate the opposing views of liberty within a specific era of United States history. In other cases, you may investigate the changing boundaries of freedom over multiple eras. You will always, however, be asked to use the selections as evidence in written exercises that enhance and build DBQ skills and proficiencies.

HOW TO USE THE 5 Ws

Below is an example of how you can use the 5 Ws to analyze a text and how these documents might be applied to your AP* U.S. History instruction. Review the two documents in the Voices of Freedom on pages 78–79.

JOHN WINTHROP

When was it written?

July 3, 1645 (end of the Great Migration period, yet the colony was well established)

Who wrote it?

Governor of Massachusetts; enforcer of rules; had expelled Roger Williams in 1635.

What did it say? (3–4 main ideas)

There were two types of liberty—natural and civil/federal. Men must reject natural liberty because it led to evil as well as good. It was inconsistent with authority. Accept civil liberty because it is moral, calling for subjection to the church under Christ.

Where was it directed?

Directed to settlers of Massachusetts to justify rule and to rein in those who are disobeying church rules.

Why was it written?

Settlers may have been restless, perhaps rejecting church rules and laws of colony.

VOICES OF FREEDOM

FROM JOHN WINTHROP, Speech to the Massachusetts General Court (July 3, 1645)

John Winthrop, governor of the Massachusetts Bay Colony, describes two very different definitions of liberty in this speech.

The great questions that have troubled the country, are about the authority of the magistrates and the liberty of the people.... Concerning liberty, I observe a great mistake in the country about that. There is a twofold liberty, natural (I mean as our nature is now corrupt) and civil or federal. The first is common to man with beasts and other creatures. By this, man, as he stands in relation to man simply, hath liberty to do what he lists; it is a liberty to do evil as well as to [do] good. This liberty is incompatible and inconsistent with authority, and cannot endure the least restraint of the most just authority. The exercise and maintaining of this liberty makes men grow more evil, and in time to be worse than brute beasts.... This is that great enemy of truth and peace, that wild beast, which all the ordinances of God are bent against, to restrain and subdue it.

The other kind of liberty I call civil or federal, it may also be termed moral.... This liberty is the proper end and object of authority, and cannot subsist without it; and it is a liberty to that only which is good, just, and honest.... This liberty is maintained and exercised in a way of subjection to authority; it is of the same kind of liberty wherewith Christ hath made us free. The woman's own choice makes...a man her husband; yet being so chosen, he is her lord, and she is to be subject to him, yet in a way of liberty, not of bondage; and a true wife accounts her subjection her honor and freedom, and would not think her condition safe and free, but in her subjection to her husband's authority. Such is the liberty of the church under the authority of Christ.

78

AP* Application

Write a paragraph that describes how Massachusetts Bay and Rhode Island defined liberty and its limits during the first half of the seventeenth century. Cite at least one sentence from each document to support your answer. (This is the beginning of the DBQ process of using documents to answer questions.)

ROGER WILLIAMS

From Roger Williams,
Letter to the Town of
Providence (1655)

A pioneer of the idea of religious toleration in the colonies, Roger Williams left Massachusetts to found Rhode Island, where, unlike in Puritan Massachusetts, he established separation of church and state. Believing his views had been misunderstood by some of the settlers of Providence, he wrote this letter to explain his understanding of liberty and its extent and limits.

That ever I should speak or write a tittle, that tends to . . . an infinite liberty of conscience, is a mistake, and which I have ever disclaimed and abhorred. To prevent such mistakes, I shall at present only propose this case: There goes many a ship to sea, with many hundred souls in one ship, whose weal or woe is common, and is a true picture of a commonwealth, or a human combination or society. It hath fallen out sometimes, that both papists and protestants, Jews and Turks [Muslims], may be embarked in one ship; upon which supposal I affirm, that all the liberty of conscience, that ever I pleaded for, turns upon these two hinges—that none of the papists, protestants, Jews, or Turks, be forced to come to the ship's prayers or worship, nor compelled from their own particular prayers or worship, if they practice any. I further add, that I never denied, that notwithstanding this liberty, the commander of this ship ought to command the ship's course, yea, and also command that justice, peace and sobriety, be kept and practiced, both among the seamen and all the passengers. If any of the seamen refuse to perform their services, or passengers to pay their freight; if any refuse to help, in person or purse, towards the common charges or defense; if any refuse to obey the common laws and orders of the ship, concerning their common peace or preservation; if any shall mutiny and rise up against their commanders and officers, because all are not equal in Christ, therefore no masters nor officers, no laws nor orders, nor corrections nor punishments;—I say, I never denied, but in such cases, whatever is pretended, the commander or commanders may judge, resist, compel and punish such transgressors.

QUESTIONS

1. Why does Winthrop consider "natural" liberty dangerous?

2. In what ways does Williams place limits on liberty?

3. How do the views of Winthrop and Williams differ, and in what ways are they similar?

79

When was it written?

1655 (He established Rhode Island in the mid-1630s, after his banishment.)

Who wrote it?

Founder of Rhode Island, banished from Massachusetts Bay Colony when he challenged church and state being linked together.

What did it say? (3–4 main ideas)

All should be free to worship as they please, yet Williams saw limits to liberty. No one could mutiny or rise up against laws of colony, and no one could infringe on the rights of others.

Where was it directed?

Directed to the settlers of Rhode Island and to settlers in other colonies who believed Rhode Island had gone too far in granting religious freedom.

Why was it written?

To justify separation of church and state, but also to establish limits of religious liberty.

Suggested Answer:

Your answer should recognize that the leaders of Massachusetts Bay and Rhode Island realized that liberty in the first half of the seventeenth century was not unlimited. For the Puritans, liberty was of a "civil or federal" nature and "maintained and exercised in a way of subjection to authority. . . ." John Winthrop believed freedom was "under the authority of Christ." In Rhode Island, the concept of liberty was more expansive, yet Roger Williams also realized "an infinite liberty of conscience, is a mistake. . . ." and that people must abide by "the common laws and orders" of the colony in order for "justice, peace, and sobriety [to] be kept and practiced. . . ."

Visual Document Skills Handbook

Earlier in this textbook, we discussed the value of photographs and other pictures as sources in AP* U.S. History. This category of visuals introduces the highest level of reality into a history classroom. Your textbook recognizes the utility of these types of materials and is filled with interesting and provocative images that can grab your attention and expand your understanding of America's past.

In the Visions of Freedom features found throughout this text, you will find questions to guide you as you extract meaning from photographs and other images. These Visions help you realize how Americans perceived freedom during various eras and suggest that the concept of liberty changed over the course of history. In most cases, these images reflect contemporary insights into events, issues, and persons at moments in time.

ANALYZING AND EXTRACTING INFORMATION FROM PHOTOGRAPHS AND ILLUSTRATIONS

For your AP* curriculum, photographs and other images offer another possible source to use in supporting a historical argument. They are useful in developing a point of view about the changing contours of American development. These images, however, like maps and cartoons, play an ancillary role in answering questions and problems. You must always use them in conjunction with your textbook, your class lectures and discussions, and other primary and/or visual sources in order to address the complexity of an issue or topic. In an AP* course, it is also critical that you do more than "read" an image such as a photograph; you must use the image to advance a written position and/or argument.

Like other visual or textual primary sources, photographs and other pictures must be analyzed in a consistent and systematic manner. To do this, you should SCOPE the photograph/picture.

When you SCOPE an image, you determine its:

Setting: When was it created? What else was happening at the time? This is called contextualizing the image.

Caption: What does the label or title of the image say? (Dr. Foner does much of this for you in his text.)

Objects: What do you see in the photograph or image? What types of people are depicted? What are they doing? What buildings or things do you see?

Point of view: What was the creator trying to say with the image? Infer its meaning.

Expanded meaning: What larger point can you infer or deduce from the image?

HOW TO USE SCOPE

On these pages is an example of how you can use SCOPE with an illustration in your textbook. In addition to the analysis, a suggested application of the image to your AP* curriculum is offered.

In order to understand how you can use the SCOPE strategy, read the textbook description of the Boston Massacre on page 192 and then SCOPE the Visions of Freedom on page 193.

VISIONS OF FREEDOM

The Boston Massacre. *Less than a month after the Boston Massacre of 1770, in which five colonists died, Paul Revere produced this engraving of the event. Although it inaccurately depicts what was actually a disorganized brawl between residents of Boston and British soldiers, this image became one of the most influential pieces of political propaganda of the revolutionary era.*

QUESTIONS

1. How does Revere depict the British and colonists in this encounter, and who does he blame for the five colonists' deaths?

2. What attitude toward British authorities is Revere attempting to promote through this engraving?

SCOPE Assignment:

Read page 192 in your textbook and SCOPE the picture on page 193.

Engrav'd Printed & Sold by PAUL REVERE BOSTON

Setting:

April 1770, the height of the tension in Boston between British soldiers and colonials as the Redcoats patrolled the streets and enforced unpopular policies.

Caption:

The inaccurate depiction of the "Boston Massacre," which became a useful piece of political propaganda for the colonials.

Objects:

British soldiers in firing-squad position; unarmed colonials dead and dying; other colonials aiding the wounded; buildings in the center of Boston.

Point of View:

The shootings were a premeditated, well-coordinated execution of Patriots.

Expanded meaning:

The British soldiers were vicious, violent men who trampled on the lives and rights of the Bostonians.

AP* Application

Using the information on page 192 of your textbook, the Visions of Freedom on page 193, and Thomas Paine's essay "Common Sense" in the Voices of Freedom on page 200, construct a short answer that explains how the colonists used propaganda to promote their cause before the American Revolution.

Suggested Answer:

Among other points, your answer should define propaganda as a one-sided argument to convince someone or some group to support a specific point of view. And you should note that both the Revere engraving and Paine's "Common Sense" told only the colonial side of the dispute over independence and were designed to sway opinions in favor of action against the British.

Map Skills Handbook

An earlier section of this textbook noted the importance of maps in expanding and reinforcing your understanding of U.S. history. These images also play an important role in the AP* curriculum, because they often appear as sources on the annual exam, both in the multiple-choice section and for the DBQ essay.

UNDERSTANDING THE FULL VALUE OF MAPS

Your textbook contains many useful maps that can help you develop your AP* skills. Along with the written text and other visuals, maps can address various issues and questions presented in your textbook. Maps are part of the historical record that you can use in conjunction with other sources to answer historical problems and prepare for the AP* exam.

In every case, however, you should not consider maps in isolation. Study them in conjunction with the materials that precede and follow them. You must always read the text sections that accompany a map before attempting to analyze it. This will contextualize the image and help you understand its meaning.

When you analyze a map, begin by focusing on the most obvious information it contains. Students often look at a map briefly and assume they understand it. Try to slow down your reading of a map by noting its title and the areas that are presented in it. Once you know what areas the map outlines, begin to expand your thinking. Where possible, make inferences about the historical period the map is describing. Use the TARGET strategy described below to unlock the information a map contains.

When you TARGET a map, you determine its:

Title: Try to connect the title to the Focus Question addressed in the chapter opener.

Area(s): Which specific geographic areas does the map show? Don't forget to examine the key.

Regions: Which region(s) seem to be undergoing changes or developments? Infer the meaning of these changes.

Groups: Which group(s) might be affected by changes or developments? Infer the meaning of these developments for the groups involved.

Economic: Issues raised by development. (Note that military or political maps might not have this information.)

Theme: What is the central theme of the map? What is its message or overall point? Recall the title of the map.

Below is an example of how you can use TARGET to analyze a map in this textbook. In addition to the analysis, a suggested application of the map to the AP* course is presented. Study this example and discuss it with your classmates.

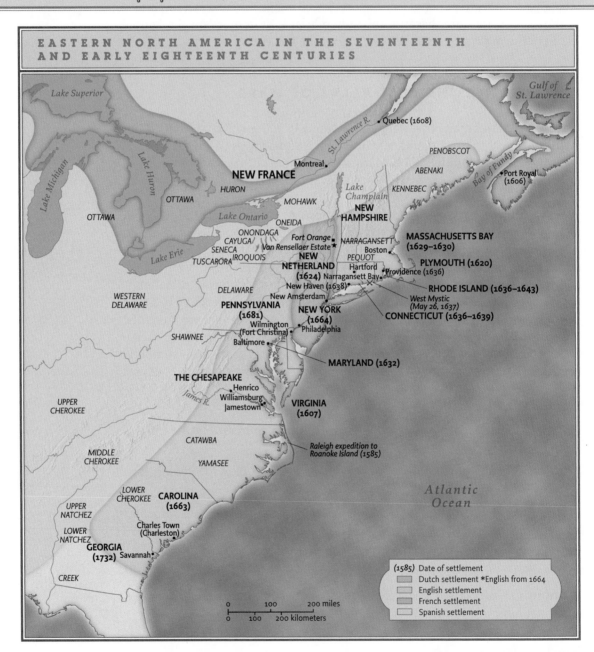

EASTERN NORTH AMERICA IN THE SEVENTEENTH AND EARLY EIGHTEENTH CENTURIES

By the early eighteenth century, numerous English colonies populated eastern North America, while the French had established their own presence to the north and west.

the first Navigation Act, which aimed to wrest control of world trade from the Dutch, whose merchants profited from free trade with all parts of the world and all existing empires. Additional measures followed in 1660 and 1663. England's new economic policy, mercantilism, rested on the idea that England should enjoy the profits arising from the English empire.

According to the Navigation laws, certain "enumerated" goods—essentially

TARGET Assignment:

After reading pages 95–101 in the textbook, examine the map on page 96. Below is a sample of how you can use TARGET to analyze the map and how you can apply it to a question from the review section of the chapter (p. 132).

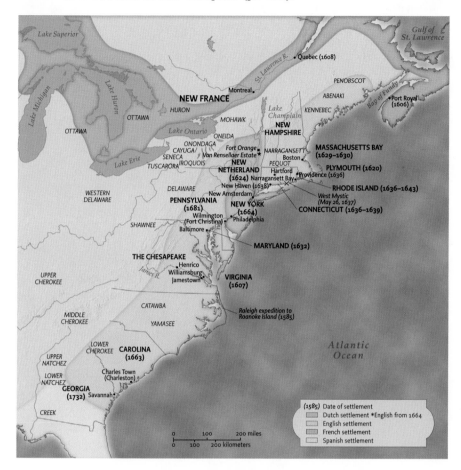

Title:

"Eastern North America in the seventeenth and early eighteenth centuries." This map shows how the British colonies were positioned to expand westward.

Areas:

New France, the New England colonies, New Netherlands, Pennsylvania, the Chesapeake area, Georgia, Carolina, and the Spanish territories.

Regions:

The English colonies dominated the Atlantic coast and were expanding westward, encroaching on Indian, Spanish, and Dutch territories.

Groups:

English, Dutch, French, and Spanish colonists; Indian tribes.

Economic:

English expansion brought economic change to eastern North America. The expansion raised the question, Who would trade with the Native Americans? This expansion also affected coastal trade in the Atlantic world.

AP* Application

Apply the map analysis to help answer question 6 on page 132. ("By the end of the seventeenth century, commerce was the foundation of empire and the leading cause of competition between European empires. Explain how the North American colonies were directly linked to Atlantic commerce by laws and trade.")

Suggested Answer:

The map shows how diverse populations and distribution of land claims promoted English coastal development and trade. It also indicates potential conflicts with New Netherlands and the Spanish in the south and west.

Theme:

The diversity of European settlements set the stage for English expansion and conflict between Europeans and Indians for control of eastern North America.

Cartoon Skills Handbook

Cartoons are arguably the most prevalent nontext source found in the AP* U.S. History curriculum and on the exam. They appear regularly as sources for DBQ essays and also are very numerous in the multiple-choice section of the test. Your textbook recognizes the importance of these representations. Many interesting and useful cartoons are sprinkled throughout the chapters to enhance your study of U.S. history. A close scrutiny of these images can be a useful tool when you prepare for the annual AP* examination in May.

CONTEXTUALIZING AND FINDING MEANING IN CARTOONS WITH THE TACKLE STRATEGY

As with the other kinds of sources that you have examined, unlocking the meaning of a cartoon requires careful study. Contextualization plays a critical role in this process. In fact, placing cartoons in their historical context may be the most important factor in understanding their meaning. You must be able to recognize the time and circumstances that make up a cartoon's background in order to determine the artist's point of view and purpose in creating the image. Moreover, you must approach cartoon analysis in a consistent and systematic fashion. You must do more than just look at a cartoon; you must dissect it for its content and try to connect it to a specific event or issue. In order to master a cartoon, you should TACKLE it.

Use TACKLE to determine:

Time: When was the cartoon drawn? This is how you will begin the process of contextualization.

Audience: Toward what person or persons was the cartoon directed?

Context: What else was happening at the time? What is the background of the image?

Key action: What is taking place within the cartoon?

Label of cartoon: What does the label or caption mean? Does it match the action inside the drawing? This comparison will provide insights into the author's point of view.

Expanded purpose: Why do you think the artist created the cartoon? What larger issue might have been involved? An inference may be in order here.

HOW TO USE TACKLE

Below is an example of how you can use TACKLE to analyze the cartoon on page 307 in your textbook. You will see how you might use the cartoon to address an AP* U.S. history problem.

tion of virtually any public assembly or publication critical of the government. While more lenient than many such measures in Europe (it did not authorize legal action before publication and allowed for trials by jury), the new law meant that opposition editors could be prosecuted for almost any political comment they printed. The main target was the Republican press, seen by Federalists as a group of upstart workingmen (most editors had started out as printers) whose persistent criticism of the administration fomented popular rebelliousness and endangered "genuine liberty."

The passage of these measures launched what Jefferson—recalling events in Salem, Massachusetts, a century earlier—termed a "reign of witches." Eighteen individuals, including several Republican newspaper editors, were charged under the Sedition Act. Ten were convicted for spreading "false, scandalous, and malicious" information about the government. Matthew Lyon, a member of Congress from Vermont and editor of a Republican newspaper, *The Scourge of Aristocracy*, received a sentence of four months in prison and a fine of $1,000. (Lyon had been the first former printer and most likely the first former indentured servant elected to Congress.) The government also imprisoned Thomas Cooper, a lawyer and physician in Pennsylvania who had emigrated from England in 1794, for writings accusing the Adams administration of pro-British bias. In Massachusetts, authorities indicted several men for erecting a liberty pole bearing the inscription, "No Stamp Act, no Sedition, no Alien Bill, no Land Tax; Downfall to the Tyrants of America."

Congressional Pugilists, *a 1798 cartoon depicting a fight on the floor of Congress between Connecticut Federalist Roger Griswold and Matthew Lyon, a Republican from Vermont. Lyon would soon be jailed under the Sedition Act for criticizing the Adams administration in his newspaper.*

THE VIRGINIA AND KENTUCKY RESOLUTIONS

The Alien and Sedition Acts failed to silence the Republican press. Some newspapers ceased publication, but new ones, with names like *Sun of Liberty* and *Tree of Liberty*, entered the field. The Sedition Act thrust freedom of expression to the center of discussions of American liberty. Madison and Jefferson mobilized opposition, drafting resolutions adopted by the Virginia and Kentucky legislatures. Both resolutions attacked the Sedition Act as an unconstitutional violation of the First Amendment. Virginia's, written by Madison, called on the federal courts to protect free speech. The original version of Jefferson's Kentucky resolution went further, asserting that states could nullify laws of Congress that violated the Constitution—that is, states could unilaterally prevent the enforcement of such laws within their borders. The legislature prudently deleted this passage. The resolutions were directed against assaults on freedom of expression by the federal government, not the states. Jefferson took care to insist that the states "fully possessed" the authority to punish "seditious" speech, even if the national government did not. Indeed, state-level prosecutions of newspapers for seditious libel did not end when the Sedition Act expired in 1801.

TACKLE Assignment:

Read pages 305–308 in your textbook, then use the TACKLE strategy to analyze the cartoon on page 307. After you have completed the reading and analysis, discuss the suggested AP* application with your classmates.

AP* Application

After reading the textbook for context and analyzing the cartoon, write an answer to the following question: "In what ways does the cartoon 'CONGRESSIONAL PUGLILISTS' depict early partisanship in the American Republic?"

Suggested Answer:

This cartoon was a satirical statement about the actions of the Congress of 1798 concerning the Alien and Sedition Acts and the tension with France. It attempted to show that violence and outrageous behavior had replaced rational debate and deliberation. Although the cartoon condemned such partisan actions, it recognized the growing differences between the two parties.

Time:

1798

Audience:

Members of the Congress (to shame them); American voters

Context:

(from textbook) "The undeclared war with France [and] passage of the Alien and Sedition Acts had heightened tensions and exposed partisan nerves, also gave rise to violence on the floor of the Congress."

Key actions:

Exaggerated fighting between Roger Griswold and Matthew Lyon. Other members of Congress look on—some gleefully, others upset.

Label:

"CONGRESSIONAL PUGILISTS," a satire on the fighting between two members. The cartoon depicts them with their hair wild. They are trying to kick one another and strike one another with tongs and a cane.

Expanded purpose:

To ridicule the partisanship and division that various acts and policies had created.

Practicing Document-Based Questions (DBQs)

In this section you will have an opportunity to work on six Document-Based Questions (DBQs): one from each of the six units in *Give Me Liberty!*. Before attempting any of the historical problems posed, you should consult your notes, class discussions, and textbook on each topic. You should also remind yourself of the process for writing a DBQ, which was outlined on pages xliv–xlv in the front of your book. These tips will help you to plan and organize your answer.

In addition, make sure that you review each of the four strategies for primary source interpretation that are explained and modeled in the AP* skills handbooks (see the 5 Ws for primary source documents, TACKLE for cartoons, TARGET for maps, and SCOPE for photographs and pictures). These procedures and activities offer important tools for extracting data from various sources and using this information to make a historical argument, which is essential in answering a DBQ. These four approaches to source analysis will help you answer each of the six practice DBQs and improve your overall performance in your AP* United States History class.

UNITED STATES HISTORY
SECTION II
Part A
(Suggested writing time—45 minutes)
Percent of Section II score—45

Directions: The following question requires you to construct a coherent essay that integrates your interpretation of Documents A–H <u>and</u> your knowledge of the period referred to in the question. High scores will be earned only by essays that both cite key pieces of evidence and draw on outside knowledge of the period.

1. How was liberty defined in the American colonies from 1700–1763? In what ways did restrictive definitions of liberty contribute to persistent discontent within the colonies?

Document A

Source: Samuel Sewall, *The Selling of Joseph: A Memorial*, Boston, 1700.

Forasmuch as Liberty is in real value unto Life: None aught to part with it themselves, or deprive others of it, but upon most mature Consideration.

The numerousness of slaves at this day in the province, and the uneasiness of them under their slavery, hath put many upon thinking whether the foundation of it be firmly and well laid, so as to sustain the vast weight that is built upon it. It is most certain that all men, as they are the Sons of Adam, . . . have equal right unto liberty, and all other outward comforts of life.

Document B

Source: William Penn, *Pennsylvania Charter of Privileges and Liberties*, 1701.

I the said William Penn do declare . . . that all persons who also profess to believe in Jesus Christ, . . . shall be capable . . . to serve this Government in any capacity, both legislatively and executively. . . .

For the well governing of this Province and Territories, there shall be an Assembly yearly chosen, by the freemen thereof, to consist of four persons out of each county, . . . which Assembly shall have power to choose a Speaker and other officers, . . . prepare Bills in order to pass into Laws, impeach criminals, and redress grievances and shall have all other powers and privileges of an Assembly, according to the rights of the free-born subjects of England.

Document C

Source: 1732 Portrait of Daniel, Peter, and Andrew Oliver, sons of a wealthy Boston merchant.

Document D

Source: *The Trial of John Peter Zenger*, London, 1735, pp. 19–46.

The question before the court and you, gentlemen of the jury, is not of small or private concern. It is not the cause of a poor printer. . . . No! It may, in its consequence, affect every freeman . . . It is the cause of liberty. And . . . every man who prefers freedom to a life of slavery will bless and honor you, . . . by an impartial and uncorrupt verdict . . . that to which nature and the laws of our country have given us a right—the liberty both of exposing and opposing arbitrary power . . . by speaking and writing truth.

Document E

Source: Advertisement in the *South Carolina Gazette*, June 11, 1747.

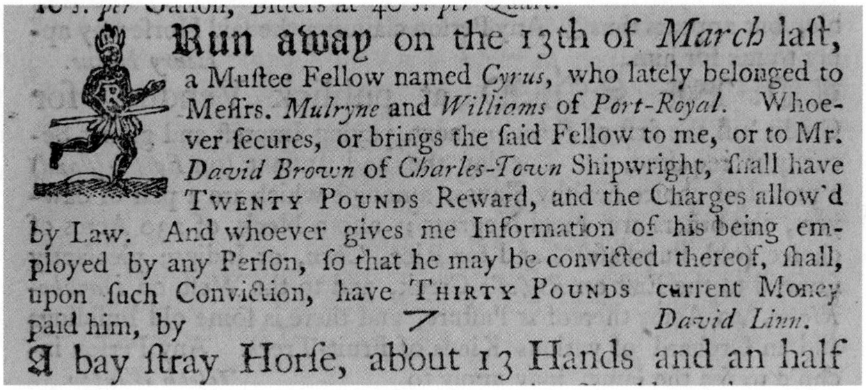

Run away on the 13th of *March* laſt, a Muſtee Fellow named *Cyrus*, who lately belonged to Meſſrs. *Mulryne* and *Williams* of *Port-Royal*. Whoever ſecures, or brings the ſaid Fellow to me, or to Mr. *David Brown* of *Charles-Town* Shipwright, ſhall have TWENTY POUNDS Reward, and the Charges allow'd by Law. And whoever gives me Information of his being employed by any Perſon, ſo that he may be convicted thereof, ſhall, upon ſuch Conviction, have THIRTY POUNDS current Money paid him, by   *David Linn.*

A bay ſtray Horſe, about 13 Hands and an half

Document F

Source: Gottlieb Mittelberger, *Gottlieb Mittelberger's Journey to Pennsylvania in the Year 1750 and Return to Germany in the Year 1754*, trans. Carl Theo Eben, Philadelphia, 1898, pp. 28–38.

When the ships have landed at Philadelphia after their long voyage, no one is permitted to leave them except those who pay for the passage or can give good security; the others, who cannot pay, must remain on board the ships till they are purchased and are released from the ships by their purchasers . . . When a husband or wife has died at sea, when the ship has made more than half of her trip, the survivor must pay or serve not only for himself or herself, but also for the deceased. When both parents have died over halfway at sea, their children, especially when they are young and have nothing to pawn or pay, must stand for their own and their parents passage, and serve till they are twenty-one years old.

Document G

Source: Elizabeth Sprigs, Letter by a Female Indentured Servant, September 22, 1756.

O Dear Father, . . . What we unfortunate English people suffer here is beyond the probability of you in England to conceive. Let it suffice that I am one of the unhappy number, am toiling almost day and night, . . . and then tied up and whipped to that degree that you now serve any animal. Scarce any think but Indian corn and salt to eat and the even begrudged nay many Negroes are better used, almost naked no shoes nor stockings to wear, . . .

Document H

Source: Pontiac, Speeches, 1762 and 1763.

Englishmen, although you have conquered the French, you have not conquered us! We are not your slaves. These lakes, these woods, and mountains were left to us by our ancestors. They are our inheritance; and we will part with them to none. Your nation supposes that we, like the white people, cannot live without bread and pork and beef! But you ought to know that He, the Great Spirit and Master of Life, has provided for us in these spacious lakes, and on these woody mountains.

UNITED STATES HISTORY
SECTION II
Part A
(Suggested writing time—45 minutes)
Percent of Section II score—45

Directions: The following question requires you to construct a coherent essay that integrates your interpretation of Documents A–I <u>and</u> your knowledge of the period referred to in the question. High scores will be earned only by essays that both cite key pieces of evidence and draw on outside knowledge of the period.

2. How did ideas of freedom help Americans construct a sense of themselves as a nation in the period 1776–1800? Who was included in this emerging national identity, and who was left out?

Document A

Source: Thomas Paine, *Common Sense*, January 1776.

I challenge the warmest advocate for reconciliation to show a single advantage that this continent can reap by being connected with Great Britain. . . . Ye that dare oppose, not only the tyranny, but the tyrant, stand forth! Every spot of the old world is overrun with oppression. Freedom hath been hunted around the globe. . . . Europe regards her like a stranger, and England hath given her warning to depart. O! Receive the fugitive, and prepare in time an asylum for mankind.

Document B

Source: Abigail Adams, letter to John Adams, March 1776.

I have sometimes been ready to think that the passion for Liberty cannot be equally strong in the breasts of those who have been accustomed to deprive their fellow creatures of theirs. . . . I desire that you would Remember the Ladies, and be more generous and favorable to them than your ancestors. . . . Remember that all men would be tyrants if they could. If particular care and attention is not paid to the Ladies we are determined to foment a Revolution, and will not hold ourselves bound by any such laws in which we have no voice or representation.

Document C

Source: J. Hector St. de Crèvecoeur, "What Then, Is the American?" 1782.

Urged by a variety of motives, here they came. Everything has tended to regenerate them; new laws, a new mode of living, a new social system; here they are becoming men: in Europe they were as so many useless plants, . . .

What then is the American, this new man? He is either an European, or the descendant of an European, hence a strange mixture of blood, which you will find in no other country. . . . He is an American, who leaving behind him all his ancient prejudices and manners, receives new ones from the new mode of life he has embraced, the new government he obeys, and the new rank he holds.

Document D

Source: Noah Webster, "An Examination into the Leading Principles of the Federal Constitution," September 1787.

A general and tolerable equal distribution of landed property is the whole basis of national freedom. . . . The liberty of press, trial by jury, the Habeas Corpus writ, even Magna Carta itself, although justly deemed the palladia of freedom, are all inferior considerations, when compared with a general distribution of real property among every class of people. . . . Let the people have property, and they *will* have power—a power that will forever be exerted to prevent a restriction of the press, and abolition of trial by jury, or the abridgement of any other privilege. . . .

Document E

Source: Advertisement in Richmond newspaper, December 1787.

Document F

Source: George Washington's letter to the Jewish Congregation of Newport, Rhode Island, 1790.

The Citizens of the United States of America. . . . All possess alike liberty of conscience and immunities of citizenship. . . . For happily the Government of the United States, which gives to bigotry no sanction, [and asks] only that they who live under the protection should demean themselves as good citizens, in giving it on all occasions their effectual support . . . May the Children of the Stock of Abraham, who dwell in this land, . . . continue to merit and enjoy the good will of the other Inhabitants; . . .

Document G

Source: A medal presented to a Seneca chief by George Washington, 1792.

GEORGE WASHINGTON
PRESIDENT.
1792.

Document H

Source: Address of the Democratic-Republican Society of Pennsylvania, December 1794.

Freedom of thought, and a free communication of opinions by speech through the medium of the press, are the safeguards of our Liberties. . . . This liberty is an imprescriptible [unlimited] right, independent of any Constitution or social impact: it is as complete a right as that which any man has to the enjoyment of his life. . . .

Document I

Source: *American Mercury*, Hartford, Connecticut, July 1800.

What is liberty? Is it a something that men may keep without care and lose without injury? No citizens. Liberty is a tender plant, which wants the constant vigilance of its owner. . . . It is not enough that we have a republican form of government, we must acquire a *republican mind*. We must be frugal, sober, industrious, self-dependent, privately and publicly hospitable. . . . We must eradicate national prejudices. . . . We must always remember that *men*, and not soil, constitute the state.

UNITED STATES HISTORY
SECTION II
Part A
(Suggested writing time—45 minutes)
Percent of Section II score—45

Directions: The following question requires you to construct a coherent essay that integrates your interpretation of Documents A–I <u>and</u> your knowledge of the period referred to in the question. High scores will be earned only by essays that both cite key pieces of evidence from the documents and draw on outside information of the period.

3. The upheavals between the North and South from 1855–1865 revolved around ideas of freedom and who deserved access to its benefits. Evaluate this statement using the documents and your knowledge of the period 1855–1865.

Document A

Source: A contemporary print about the attack on Senator Charles Sumner, May 1856.

Document B

Source: The Irrepressible Conflict, a speech by William Seward, October, 25, 1858.

One of the chief elements of the value of human life is freedom in the pursuit of happiness. The slave system is . . . intolerant, unjust, and inhuman, toward the laborer. . . . The free-labor system conforms to the divine law of equality, which is written in the hearts and consciences of men, . . . The slave system is one of constant danger, distrust, suspicion, and watchfulness. . . . The two systems are at once perceived to be incongruous. But they are more than incongruous—they are incompatible. . . . Shall I tell you what this collision means? . . . It is an irrepressible conflict between opposing and enduring forces.

Document C

Source: South Carolina Ordinance of Secession, 1860.

The State of South Carolina having resumed her separate and equal place among nation deems . . . that she should declare the immediate causes which have led to this act . . . the Constitution of the United States was established by compact between the States, . . . We affirm that the ends for which this Government was instituted have been defeated, and the Government itself has been made destructive of them by the action of the non-slaveholding States. . . . Those States . . . have denied the right of property established in the fifteen States . . . they have denounced as sinful the institution of Slavery; . . . We . . . have solemnly declared that the Union between this State and other States of North America dissolved. . . .

Document D

Source: Map of Southern States 1860–1861.

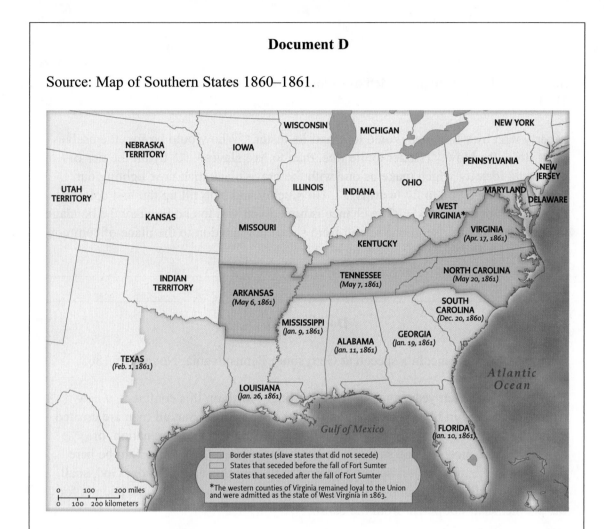

Document E

Source: Speech of Alexander H. Stephens, March 21, 1861.

The [Confederate] Constitution has put at rest forever all the agitating questions relating to our peculiar institutions. . . . most of the leading statesman at the formation of the old Constitution [believed] that the enslavement of the African was in violation of the laws of nature. . . . Our new Government is founded upon exactly the opposite idea; . . . its cornerstone rests, upon the great truth that the negro is not equal to the white man; that slavery, subordination to the superior race, is his natural and moral condition. . . .

Document F

Source: Frederick Douglass, Men of Color, to Arms, Broadside, Rochester, March 21, 1863.

Liberty won by white men would lose half its luster. "Who would be free themselves must strike the blow." "Better to die free, than to live slaves. . . ." by all the ties of blood and identity which make us one with the brave black men now fighting our battles . . . I urge you to fly to arms. . . . Go quickly and help fill up the first colored regiment from the North . . . The chance is now given you to end in a day the bondage of centuries, and to rise in one bound from social degradation to the plane of common equality with all other varieties of men . . .

Document G

Source: Abraham Lincoln's speech at Gettysburg Pennsylvania, November 1863.

Four score and seven years ago our fathers brought forth on this continent, a new nation, conceived in liberty, and dedicated to the proposition that all men are created equal. Now we are engaged in a great civil war, testing whether that nation, or any nation so conceived and so dedicated can long endure. . . . [and] . . . to be here dedicated to the great task remaining before us . . . that this nation, under God, shall have a new birth of freedom—and that government of the people, by the people, for the people, shall not perish from the earth.

Document H

Source: Letter, Marcus M. Spiegel, January 1864.

I am [in] favor of doing away with the institution of Slavery. I am willing for the Planters to hire them and in favor of making the negro work at all events; inasmuch as he is naturally lazy and indolent, but never hereafter will I either speak or vote in favor of Slavery; this is no hasty conclusion but a deep conviction. Yet I never mean hereafter to be a politician, but quietly as a good citizen doing duty to God, my family, my Country and myself.

Document I

Source: Eliza Frances Andrews, *The Wartime Journal of a Georgia Girl 1864–1865*, June 27, 1865 (in Bidwell Spencer King Jr. Macon Ga. 1960).

The next war . . . I think will be against the negroes, who are already becoming discontented with freedom, so different from what they were taught to expect. Instead of wealth and idleness it has brought them idleness, indeed, but starvation and misery with it . . . A race war is sure to come, sooner or later, and we shall have only the Yankees to thank for it. . . . No power on earth can raise an inferior, savage race above their civilized masters and keep them there. . . .

UNITED STATES HISTORY
SECTION II
Part A
(Suggested writing time—45 minutes)
Percent of Section II score—45

Directions: The following question requires you to construct a coherent essay that integrates your interpretation of Documents A–I <u>and</u> your knowledge of the period referred to in the question. High scores will be earned only by essays that both cite key pieces of evidence from the documents and draw on outside knowledge of the period.

4. How successful were African Americans in achieving their visions of freedom from 1865 to 1900? What challenges to this vision did they face? How did they attempt to meet these challenges?

Document A

Source: Sharecropping Contract, 1866.

Thomas J. Ross agrees to employ the Freedmen to plant and raise a crop. . . . The said Ross agrees to furnish the land to cultivate, and sufficient numbers of mules & horses and feed them to make and house said crop . . . and to give unto said Freedmen whose names appear below one half of all cotton, corn and wheat that is raised. . . . Should the said Ross furnish us any of the above supplies or any other kind of expenses, during the said year, are to settle and pay him out of the net proceeds of our part of the crop. . . . The said Ross shall keep a regular book account, . . .

Document B

Source: The First Vote, engraving, *Harper's Weekly*, November 1867.

Document C

Source: Ku Klux Klan Members in Their Disguises, *Harper's Weekly*, December 1868.

Document D

Source: Speech of Honorable Robert B. Elliott about the Civil Rights bill, January 1874.

Sir, equality before the law is now the broad, universal, glorious rule and mandate of the Republic. No State can violate that . . . but, if Congress shall do it duty, if Congress shall enforce the great guarantees which the Supreme Court has declared to be the one pervading purpose of all the recent amendments, then their [southern states] unwise and unenlightened conduct will fail . . . No language could convey a more complete assertion of power of Congress over the subject embraced in this present bill than is expressed [in the Fourteenth Amendment]. . . .

Document E

Source: U. S. Supreme Court, *Civil Rights Cases, 109 U.S. 3*, October 1883.

The 1st and 2nd sections of the Civil Rights Act passed March 1st 1876 are unconstitutional enactments as applied to the several States, not being authorized by the XIIIth or XIVth Amendments of the Constitution. . . . The XIVth Amendment is prohibitory upon the States only, and the legislation authorized to be adopted by Congress for enforcing it is not direct legislation on the matters respecting which the States are prohibited from making or enforcing certain laws. . . .

Document F

Source: Tennessee Law, 1891.

All railroad carrying passengers in the state (other than street railroads) shall provide equal but separate accommodations for the white and colored races, by providing two or more passenger cars for each passenger train, or by dividing the cars by partition, so as to secure separate accommodations.

Document G

Source: Ida B. Welles, *The Crusade for Justice*, 1892.

But Thomas Moss, Calvin McDowell and Henry Stewart had been lynched in Memphis, . . . and they had committed no crime against white women. This is what opened my eyes to what lynching really was. An excuse to get rid of Negroes who were acquiring wealth and property. . . . The more I studied the situation, the more I was convinced that the Southerner had never gotten over his resentment that the Negro was no longer his play thing, . . . The federal laws for Negro protection passed during Reconstruction had been made a mockery by the South. . . .

Document H

Source: Booker T. Washington, Atlanta Exposition Speech, 1895.

To those of my race who . . . don't realize the importance of developing friendly relations with southern whites . . . I would say: "Cast down your bucket where you are. Cast it down in making friends of the people of all races by whom we are surrounded. . . .

In all things that are purely social we can be as separate as the fingers, yet one as the hand in all things essential to mutual progress. . . . The wisest among my race understand that demonstrating on questions of social equality is foolish. . . . The opportunity to earn a dollar in a factory just now is worth much more than the opportunity to spend a dollar in an opera house.

Document I

Source: John Marshall Harlan, Dissent in *Plessy v. Ferguson*, October 1896.

But in view of the Constitution, . . . there is in this country no superior, dominant, ruling class of citizens. There is no caste here. Our Constitution is color-blind, and neither knows nor tolerates classes among citizens. . . . The humblest is the peer of the most powerful. . . . It is therefore, to be regretted that this high tribunal, the final expositor of the fundamental law of the land, has reached the conclusion that it is competent for a State to regulate the enjoyment by citizens of their civil rights solely upon the basis of race.

UNITED STATES HISTORY
SECTION II
Part A
(Suggested writing time—45 minutes)
Percent of Section II score—45

Directions: The following question requires you to construct a coherent essay that integrates your interpretation of Documents A–J <u>and</u> your knowledge of the period referred to in the question. High scores will be earned only by essays that both cite key pieces of evidence and draw on outside knowledge of the period.

5. How did World War II and the early Cold War both expand and contract the boundaries of freedom for many Americans? In your response, consider both domestic and international factors in the period 1940–1950.

Document A

Source: Franklin Roosevelt, Annual Message to Congress, January 6, 1941.

. . . [W]e look forward to a world founded upon four essential human freedoms. The first is freedom of speech and expression—everywhere in the world. The second is freedom of every person to worship God in his own way—everywhere in the world. The third is freedom from want— . . . everywhere in the world. The fourth is freedom from fear—which, translated into world terms, means a world-wide reduction of armaments . . . and in such a thorough fashion that no nation will be in a position to commit an act of physical aggression against any neighbor—anywhere in the world.

Document B

Source: "My Children!" *Detroit Free Press*, June 19, 1941.

Document C

Source: Franklin Roosevelt, Executive Order 8802, June 25, 1941.

Whereas it is the policy of the United States to encourage full participation in the national defense program by all citizens of the United States, regardless of race, creed, color, or national origin, in the firm belief that the democratic way of life within the Nation can be defended successfully only with the help and support of all groups within its borders; . . .

I do hereby reaffirm the policy of the United States that there shall be no discrimination in the employment of workers in defense industries or government because of race, creed, color, or national origin, . . . [and] to provide for the full and equitable participation of all workers in defense industries, . . .

Document D

Source: "Evacuation to Manzanar," An Eyewitness Account by Yuri Tateishi, April 26, 1942.

When we got to Manzanar, it was getting dark and we were given numbers first. We went to the mess hall, and I remember the first meal we were given in those tin plates and tin cups. . . . We were used to a regular home atmosphere, and seeing those hay mattresses—so makeshift, with hay sticking out—a barren room with nothing but those hay mattresses. . . .

You felt like a prisoner. . . . [And] you're kept inside a barbed-wire fence, and you know you can't go out.

Document E

Source: Henry A. Wallace, Speech at the Free World Association, May 8, 1942.

We who live in the United States may think there is nothing very revolutionary about freedom of religion, freedom of expression, and freedom from the fear of secret police. But when we begin to think about the significance of freedom from want for the average man, then we know that the revolution of the past 150 years has not been completed, either here in the United States or in any other nation in the world. We know that this revolution cannot stop until freedom from want has actually been attained.

Document F

Source: *McCall's Magazine*, September, 1942.

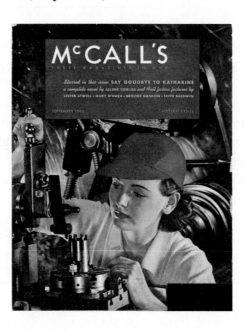

Document G

Source: The Truman Doctrine, March 12, 1947.

At the present moment in world history nearly every nation must choose between
alternative ways of life. . . . One way of life is based upon the will of the majority,
and is distinguished by free institutions, representative government, free elections, . . .
The second way of life is based upon the will of a minority forcibly imposed upon the
majority. It relies upon terror and oppression, . . . I believe that it must be the policy
of the United States to support free people who are resisting attempted subjugation by
armed minorities or by outside pressures.

Document H

Source: Picketing at the 1948 Democratic National Convention, 1948.

Document I

Source: Platform of the States' Rights Democratic Party, 1948.

We stand for social and economic justice, which we believe can be guaranteed to all citizens only by a strict adherence to our Constitution and the avoidance of any invasion or destruction of the constitutional rights of the states and individuals. . . .

We stand for the segregation of the races and the racial integrity of each race; the constitutional right to choose one's associates; to accept private employment without governmental interference, and to earn one's living in any lawful way. . . . We favor home rule, local self-government, and a limited interference with individual rights.

Document J

Source: Joe McCarthy, Congressional Record, 1950.

Today we are engaged in a final, all-out battle between communistic atheism and Christianity . . . The reason why we find ourselves in a position of impotency is not because our only powerful enemy has sent men to invade our shores, but rather because of the traitorous actions of those who have been treated so well by this Nation . . . I have in my hand 57 cases of individuals who appear to be either card carrying members or certainly loyal to the Communist Party, but who nevertheless are still helping to shape our foreign policy.

UNITED STATES HISTORY
SECTION II
Part A
(Suggested writing time—45 minutes)
Percent of Section II score—45

Directions: The following question requires you to construct a coherent essay that integrates your interpretation of Documents A–J <u>and</u> your knowledge of the period referred to in the question. High scores will be earned only by essays that both cite key pieces of evidence and draw on outside knowledge of the period.

6. How did cultural struggles reveal conflicting definitions of liberty among Americans during the 1960s and the early 1970s? In what ways did this unrest expose inequities and lead to social and political change?

Document A

Source: Raleigh, North Carolina sit-in, 1960.

Document B

Source: James Baldwin, "They Can't Turn Back," *Mademoiselle*, August 1960.

Many Americans may have forgotten . . . the reign of terror in the 1920's that drove Negroes out of the South. . . . This was forty years ago, and not enough has happened—not enough freedom has happened. . . . It seems to me that [students] are the only people in this country now who really believe in freedom. Insofar as they can make it real for themselves, they will make it real for all of us. The question with which they present the nation is whether or not we really want to be free. . . .

Document C

Source: Young Americans for Freedom, the Sharon Statement, September, 1960.

That liberty is indivisible, and that political freedom cannot long exist without economic freedom; . . . That the purposes of government are to protect those freedoms through the preservation of internal order, the provision of national defense, and the administration of justice; . . . That when government ventures beyond these lawful functions, it accumulates power which tends to diminish order and liberty; . . . [And] That the market economy, . . . is the single economic system compatible with the requirements of personal freedom and constitutional government, . . .

Document D

Source: Tom Hayden and Others, the Port Huron Statement, 1962.

Freedom and equality for each individual, government of, by, and for the people—these American values we found good, principles by which we could live as men. We would replace power rooted in possession, privilege, or circumstance by power and uniqueness rooted in love, reflectiveness, reason, and creativity. As a social system we seek the establishment of a democracy of individual participation. . . . [Younger people] must start controversy throughout the land, if national policies and national apathy are to be reversed.

Document E

Source: Barry Goldwater, "Extremism in the Defense of Liberty," speech given at the 28th Republican National Convention, 1964.

Those who seek power, even though they seek it to do what they regard as good, are simply demanding the right to enforce their own version of heaven on earth. And let me remind you, they are the very ones who always create the most hellish tyrannies. Absolute power does corrupt, and those who seek it must be suspect and most be opposed. Their mistaken course stems from false notions of equality, . . . Equality, rightly understood, as our founding fathers understood it, leads to liberty and to the emancipation of creative differences. I would remind you that extremism in the defense of liberty is no vice. And let me remind you also that moderation in the pursuit of justice is no virtue.

Document F

Source: Paul Potter, Speech at Washington Anti-War Demonstration, April 17, 1965.

If the people in this country are to end the war in Vietnam, and to change the institutions which created it; then the people of this country must create a massive social movement. . . . By social movement I mean more than petitions or letters of protest, or tacit support of dissident Congressmen; I mean people who are willing to change their lives, who are willing to challenge the system, to take the problem of change seriously . . . What we must do is begin to build a democratic and humane society in which Vietnams are unthinkable, . . .

Document G

Source: Lyndon B. Johnson, Commencement Address at Howard University, June 4, 1965.

Freedom is the right to share, share fully and equally, in American society—to vote, to hold a job, to enter a public place, to go to school. It is the right to be treated in every part of our national life as a person equal in dignity and promise to all others. . . . Thus it is not enough just to open the gates of opportunity. All our citizens must have the ability to walk through those gates. . . . We seek not just freedom but opportunity. We seek not just legal equity but human ability, not just equality as a right and a theory but equality as a fact and equality as a result.

Document H

Source: Antiwar Protest, 1967.

Document I

Source: César Chavez, "Letter from Delano," 1969.

We advocate militant nonviolence as our means for social revolution and to achieve justice for our people, but we are not blind or deaf to the desperate and moody winds of human frustration, impatience and rage that blow among us . . . Participation and self-determination remain the best experience of freedom. . . . Only the enslaved in despair have the need of violent overthrow. . . . we hate the agribusiness system that seeks to keep us enslaved, and we shall overcome and change it not by retaliation or bloodshed but by a determined nonviolent struggle. . . .

Document J

Source: Phyllis Schlafly, "The Fraud of the Equal Rights Amendment," 1972.

The claim that American women are downtrodden and unfairly treated is the fraud of the century. The truth is that American women never had it so good. Why should we lower ourselves to "equal rights" when we already have the status of special privilege? . . . Many women are under the mistaken impression that "women's lib" means more job employment opportunities for women, equal pay for equal work, . . . But all this is . . . the deadly poison masquerading as "women's lib." The women's libbers are radicals who are waging a total assault on the family, on marriage, and on children.

PRACTICING FREE-RESPONSE QUESTIONS (FRQS)

In this section you will find a series of free-response questions (FRQs), two from each of the six parts of *Give Me Liberty!*. These questions are similar to the types of questions you will encounter in Parts B and C of the essay section of the AP* United States History exam. Remember: in both Part B and Part C, you must choose one essay prompt from among two options. The questions in Part B typically ask about an aspect of American history leading up to the nineteenth century; those in Part C tend to deal with the twentieth century.

To prepare for the AP* test, choose an FRQ from among the options below and write your response in a separate booklet. To best simulate the conditions of the examination, try answering two essay questions in one sitting: one question from Parts 1–3 and one question from Parts 4–6. Be sure to limit yourself to 35 minutes per question.

Before you begin, you should review pages xlv–xlvi to remind you of valuable tips and strategies to use when you write a free-response essay. This section will also emphasize the critical elements of an effective essay answer. Remember, you must always plan your essay *before* you begin to write.

Part 1: American Colonies to 1763

1. How and why did democratic ideals develop in the British colonies from 1607–1765?

2. What impact did political and religious dissent have in shaping colonial developments and identity from 1619–1750?

Part 2: A New Nation, 1763–1840

1. To what extent was the creation of the Constitution both a reflection and a repudiation of the ideals of the American Revolution?

2. How was American foreign policy a response to perceived and real threats to United States interest and security from 1790–1825?

Part 3: Slavery, Freedom, and the Crisis of the Union, 1840–1877

1. Analyze the political developments that account for the rise of nativism in the 1840s and 1850s, and the 1920s.

2. To what extent was the Mexican War and its aftermath a "dose of poison" for the United States?

Part 4: Toward a Global Presence, 1870–1920

1. Evaluate the strategies that the following African Americans proposed in dealing with the Jim Crow system from 1895–1925.

   – Booker T. Washington   – W.E.B. DuBois   – Marcus Garvey

2. The two main political parties failed the American people in the last three decades of the nineteenth century: the Republicans abandoned earlier principles and gave into expediency; the Democrats refused to change with the times.

   Assess the validity of this statement.

Part 5: Depression and Wars, 1920–1953

1. In what ways did the New Deal alter the social and economic lives of many Americans?

2. Given the goals and strategies of the Allied powers following World War II, how might the Cold War be considered "inevitable"?

Part 6: What Kind of Nation? 1953–2010

1. The reform movements of the 1960s expanded democratic ideals and strengthened the social fabric of the nation.

    Evaluate this statement with reference to the civil rights, anti-war, and women's movements.

2. What impact did the end of the Cold War have on America's domestic and foreign agendas in the 1990s?